Simula[illegible]ng and Analysis

FIFTH EDITION

Averill M. Law

President
Averill M. Law & Associates, Inc.
Tucson, Arizona, USA
www.averill-law.com

Mc Graw Hill Education

SIMULATION MODELING AND ANALYSIS, FIFTH EDITION
International Edition 2015

Published by McGraw-Hill Education, 2 Penn Plaza, New York, NY 10121.

10 09 08 07 06 05 04 03 02 01
20 15 14
CTP MPM

When ordering this title, use ISBN 978-1-259-25438-3 or MHID 1-259-25438-0

Printed in Singapore

www.mhhe.com

ABOUT THE AUTHOR

Averill M. Law is President of Averill M. Law & Associates, Inc. (Tucson, Arizona), a company specializing in simulation training, consulting, and software. He was previously Professor of Decision Sciences at the University of Arizona and Associate Professor of Industrial Engineering at the University of Wisconsin–Madison. He has a Ph.D. and an M.S. in industrial engineering and operations research from the University of California at Berkeley, an M.A. in mathematics from California State University at Long Beach, and a B.S. in mathematics from Pennsylvania State University.

Dr. Law has presented more than 525 simulation and statistics short courses in 19 countries, including onsite seminars for ALCOA, AT&T, Boeing, Caterpillar, Coca-Cola, CSX, Defence Research and Development Canada, GE, GM, IBM, Intel, Lockheed Martin, Los Alamos National Lab, Missile Defense Agency, Motorola, NASA, National Security Agency, NATO (Netherlands), Northrop Grumman, Norwegian Defence Research Establishment, Sasol Technology (South Africa), 3M, Time Warner, UPS, U.S. Air Force, U.S. Army, U.S. Forces Korea, U.S. Navy, Verizon, Whirlpool, and Xerox. He has been a simulation consultant to organizations such as Accenture, Boeing, Booz Allen & Hamilton, ConocoPhillips, Defense Modeling and Simulation Office, Hewlett-Packard, Kaiser Aluminum, Kimberly-Clark, M&M/Mars, SAIC, Sandia National Labs, Swedish Defence Materiel Administration, 3M, Tropicana, U.S. Air Force, U.S. Army, U.S. Marine Corps, U.S. Navy, Veteran's Administration, and Xerox.

He is the developer of the ExpertFit distribution-fitting software, which automates the selection of simulation input probability distributions. ExpertFit is used by more than 2000 organizations worldwide. He also developed the videotapes *Simulation of Manufacturing Systems* and *How to Conduct a Successful Simulation Study*.

Dr. Law was awarded the INFORMS Simulation Society Lifetime Professional Achievement Award in 2009. He is the author (or coauthor) of three books and numerous papers on simulation, operations research, statistics, manufacturing, and communications networks. His article "Statistical Analysis of Simulation Output Data" was the first invited feature paper on simulation to appear in a major research journal, namely, *Operations Research*. His series of papers on the simulation of manufacturing systems won the 1988 Institute of Industrial Engineers' best publication award. During his academic career, the Office of Naval Research supported his simulation research for eight consecutive years. He was President of the INFORMS College on Simulation. He wrote a regular column on simulation for *Industrial Engineering* during 1990 and 1991. He has been the keynote speaker at simulation conferences worldwide.

For Steffi, Heather, Adam, and Brian, and in memory of Sallie and David.

CONTENTS

LIST OF SYMBOLS

Notation or abbreviation	Page number of definition	Notation or abbreviation	Page number of definition
γ	285, 504	$\Phi(z)$	233
$\Gamma(\alpha)$	288	$\chi^2_{k-1,1-\alpha}$	347
ζ	274, 560	$\Psi(\hat{\alpha})$	289
λ	74, 381	ω	74
$\lambda(t)$	382	$\hat{}$	13
$\Lambda(t)$	382	$\approx$	233
μ	222	$\in$	17
$\boldsymbol{\mu}, \hat{\boldsymbol{\mu}}$	370	$\sim$	286
ν	237, 495	$\xrightarrow{\mathcal{D}}$	332
ρ	75	$\binom{t}{x}$	308
ρ_{ij}	225	$\lfloor x \rfloor$	307
ρ_j	227	$\lceil x \rceil$	424
σ	224	$\{\}$	215
σ^2	222		
Σ	370		
$\hat{\Sigma}$	370		

PREFACE

The goal of this fifth edition of *Simulation Modeling and Analysis* remains the same as that for the first four editions: to give a comprehensive and state-of-the-art treatment of all the important aspects of a simulation study, including modeling, simulation software, model verification and validation, input modeling, random-number generators, generating random variates and processes, statistical design and analysis of simulation experiments, and to highlight major application areas such as manufacturing. The book strives to motivate intuition about simulation and modeling, as well as to present them in a technically correct yet clear manner. There are many examples and problems throughout, as well as extensive references to the simulation and related literature for further study.

The book can serve as the primary text for a variety of courses, for example

- A first course in simulation at the junior, senior, or beginning-graduate-student level in engineering, manufacturing, business, or computer science (Chaps. 1 through 4 and parts of Chaps. 5 through 9 and 13). At the end of such a course, the student will be prepared to carry out complete and effective simulation studies, and to take advanced simulation courses.
- A second course in simulation for graduate students in any of the above disciplines (most of Chaps. 5 through 12). After completing this course, the student should be familiar with the more advanced methodological issues involved in a simulation study, and should be prepared to understand and conduct simulation research.
- An introduction to simulation as part of a general course in operations research or management science (parts of Chaps. 1, 3, 5, 6, 9, and 13).

For instructors who have adopted the book for use in a course, I have made available for download from the website www.mhhe.com/law a number of teaching support materials. These include a comprehensive set of solutions to the Problems and all the computer code for the simulation models and random-number generators in Chaps. 1, 2, and 7. Adopting instructors should contact their local McGraw-Hill representative for login identification and a password to gain access to the material on this site; local representatives can be identified by calling 1-800-338-3987 or by using the representative locator at www.mhhe.com.

The book can also serve as a definitive reference for simulation practitioners and researchers. To this end I have included a detailed discussion of many practical examples gleaned in part from my own experiences and consulting projects. I have also made major efforts to link subjects to the relevant research literature, both in print and on the web, and to keep this material up to date. Prerequisites for understanding the book are knowledge of basic calculus-based probability and statistics (although I give a review of these topics in Chap. 4) and some experience with computing. For Chaps. 1 and 2 the reader should also be familiar with a general-purpose programming language such as C. Occasionally I will also make use of a small amount of linear algebra or matrix theory. More advanced or technically difficult material is located in starred sections or in appendixes to chapters. At the beginning of each chapter, I suggest sections for a first reading of that chapter.

I have made numerous changes and additions to the fourth edition of the book to arrive at this fifth edition, but the organization has remained mostly the same. I have moved the material on other types of simulation from Chap. 1 to a new Chap. 13, which is discussed below. Chapter 2 on modeling complex systems has been updated to reflect the latest research on efficient event-list management. Chapter 3 has been rewritten and expanded to reflect the current state of the art in simulation software. A common example is now given in three of the leading general-purpose simulation packages. The discussion of confidence intervals and hypothesis tests in Chap. 4 has been greatly enhanced, making the chapter a much more self-contained treatment of the basic probability and statistics needed for the remainder of the book. Chapter 5 makes clearer the distinction between validating and calibrating a model, which is often misunderstood. For Chap. 6 on input modeling, the latest developments in accounting for input-model uncertainty and in modeling arrival processes are discussed. Chapter 7 provides recommendations on the best-available random-number generators. Chapter 8 on generating random variates and processes has only had minor updates. Many of the statistical design-and-analysis methods of Chaps. 9 through 12 have been expanded and updated extensively to reflect current practice and recent research. In particular, Chap. 9 contains a comprehensive discussion of the latest fixed-sample-size and sequential methods for estimating the steady-state mean of a simulated system. The discussion of ranking-and-selection procedures in Chap. 10 has been expanded to include newer and more efficient methods that are not based on the classical indifference-zone approach. Chapter 11 on variance-reduction techniques has only had minor changes. In Chap. 12, I give a much more comprehensive and self-contained discussion of design of experiments and metamodeling, with a particular emphasis on what designs and metamodels to use specifically for simulation modeling. The discussion of simulating manufacturing systems is now in a new Chap. 14, which is available on the book's website www.mhhe.com/law, rather than in the book itself. It has been brought up to date in terms of the latest simulation-software packages and uses of simulation for manufacturing applications. There is a *new* Chap. 13 that discusses agent-based simulation and system dynamics, as well as other types of simulation that were previously discussed in Chap. 1 of the fourth edition. A student version of the ExpertFit distribution-fitting software is now available on the book's website; it can be used to analyze the data sets corresponding to the examples and problems in Chap. 6. The references for all the chapters are collected together at the end of the book, to make this material more compact and convenient to the reader. A large and thorough subject index enhances the book's value as a reference.

CourseSmart
Learn Smart. Choose Smart.

This text is available as an eBook at www.CourseSmart.com. At CourseSmart you can take advantage of significant savings off the cost of a print textbook, reduce their impact on the environment, and gain access to powerful web tools for learning. CourseSmart eBooks can be viewed online or downloaded to a computer. The eBooks allow readers to do full text searches, add highlighting and notes, and share notes with others. CourseSmart has the largest selection of eBooks available anywhere. Visit www.CourseSmart.com to learn more and to try a sample chapter.

I would first like to thank my former coauthor David Kelton for his numerous contributions to the first three editions of the book. The formal reviewers for the fifth edition were Christos Alexopoulos (Georgia Institute of Technology), Russell Barton (Pennsylvania State University), Chun-Hung Chen (George Mason University), Shane Henderson (Cornell University), Jack Kleijnen (Tilberg University), Pierre L'Ecuyer (Université de Montréal), Charles Macal (Argonne National Lab), Michael North (Argonne National Lab), and Douglas Samuelson (InfoLogix). They each read one new or significantly changed chapter in great detail and made many valuable suggestions. Knowing that I will certainly inadvertently commit grievous errors of omission, I would nonetheless like to thank the following individuals for their help in various ways: Wayne Adams, Mark Anderson, Sigrun Andradóttir, Jay April, Robert Axtell, Emmett Beeker, Marco Better, Edmund Bitinas, A. J. Bobo, Andrei Borshchev, Nathanael Brown, John Carson, Loren Cobb, Eric Frisco, David Galligan, Nigel Gilbert, Fred Glover, David Goldsman, Daniel Green, Charles Harrell, Thomas Hayson, James Henriksen, Raymond Hill, Kathryn Hoad, Terril Hurst, Andrew Ilachinski, Jeffrey Joines, Harry King, David Krahl, Emily Lada, Michael Lauren, Steffi Law, Thomas Lucas, Gregory McIntosh, Janet McLeavey, Anup Mokashi, Daniel Muller, Rodney Myers, William Nordgren, Ernie Page, Dennis Pegden, David Peterson, Stuart Robinson, Paul Sanchez, Susan Sanchez, Lee Schruben, David Siebert, Jeffrey Smith, David Sturrock, Ali Tafazzoli, Andrew Waller, Hong Wan, Robert Weber, Preston White, and James Wilson.

Averill M. Law
Tucson, AZ

CHAPTER 1

Basic Simulation Modeling

Recommended sections for a first reading: 1.1 through 1.4 (except 1.4.7), 1.7, 1.8

1.1 THE NATURE OF SIMULATION

This is a book about techniques for using computers to imitate, or *simulate*, the operations of various kinds of real-world facilities or processes. The facility or process of interest is usually called a *system*, and in order to study it scientifically we often have to make a set of assumptions about how it works. These assumptions, which usually take the form of mathematical or logical relationships, constitute a *model* that is used to try to gain some understanding of how the corresponding system behaves.

If the relationships that compose the model are simple enough, it may be possible to use mathematical methods (such as algebra, calculus, or probability theory) to obtain *exact* information on questions of interest; this is called an *analytic* solution. However, most real-world systems are too complex to allow realistic models to be evaluated analytically, and these models must be studied by means of simulation. In a *simulation* we use a computer to evaluate a model *numerically*, and data are gathered in order to *estimate* the desired true characteristics of the model.

As an example of the use of simulation, consider a manufacturing company that is contemplating building a large extension on to one of its plants but is not sure if the potential gain in productivity would justify the construction cost. It certainly would not be cost-effective to build the extension and then remove it later if it does not work out. However, a careful simulation study could shed some light on the question by simulating the operation of the plant as it currently exists and as it *would* be *if* the plant were expanded.

Application areas for simulation are numerous and diverse. Below is a list of some particular kinds of problems for which simulation has been found to be a useful and powerful tool:

- Designing and analyzing manufacturing systems
- Evaluating military weapons systems or their logistics requirements
- Determining hardware requirements or protocols for communications networks
- Determining hardware and software requirements for a computer system
- Designing and operating transportation systems such as airports, freeways, ports, and subways
- Evaluating designs for service organizations such as call centers, fast-food restaurants, hospitals, and post offices
- Reengineering of business processes
- Analyzing supply chains
- Determining ordering policies for an inventory system
- Analyzing mining operations

Simulation is one of the most widely used operations-research and management-science techniques, if not *the* most widely used. One indication of this is the Winter Simulation Conference, which attracts 600 to 800 people every year. In addition, there are several other simulation conferences that often have more than 100 participants per year.

There are also several surveys related to the use of operations-research techniques. For example, Lane, Mansour, and Harpell (1993) reported from a longitudinal study, spanning 1973 through 1988, that simulation was consistently ranked as one of the three most important "operations-research techniques." The other two were "math programming" (a catch-all term that includes many individual techniques such as linear programming, nonlinear programming, etc.) and "statistics" (which is not an operations-research technique per se). Gupta (1997) analyzed 1294 papers from the journal *Interfaces* (one of the leading journals dealing with applications of operations research) from 1970 through 1992, and found that simulation was second only to "math programming" among 13 techniques considered.

There have been, however, several impediments to even wider acceptance and usefulness of simulation. First, models used to study large-scale systems tend to be very complex, and writing computer programs to execute them can be an arduous task indeed. This task has been made much easier in recent years by the development of excellent software products that automatically provide many of the features needed to "program" a simulation model. A second problem with simulation of complex systems is that a large amount of computer time is sometimes required. However, this difficulty has become much less severe as computers become faster and cheaper. Finally, there appears to be an unfortunate impression that simulation is just an exercise in computer programming, albeit a complicated one. Consequently, many simulation "studies" have been composed of heuristic model building, programming, and a single run of the program to obtain "the answer." We fear that this attitude, which neglects the important issue of how a properly coded model should be used to make inferences about the system of interest, has doubtless led to erroneous conclusions being drawn from many simulation studies. These questions of simulation *methodology*, which are largely independent of the software and hardware used, form an integral part of the latter chapters of this book.

Perspectives on the historical evolution of simulation modeling may be found in Nance and Sargent (2002).

In the remainder of this chapter (as well as in Chap. 2) we discuss systems and models in considerably greater detail and then show how to write computer programs in a general-purpose language to simulate systems of varying degrees of complexity. All of the computer code shown in this chapter can be downloaded from www.mhhe.com/law.

1.2
SYSTEMS, MODELS, AND SIMULATION

A *system* is defined to be a collection of entities, e.g., people or machines, that act and interact together toward the accomplishment of some logical end. [This definition was proposed by Schmidt and Taylor (1970).] In practice, what is meant by "the system" depends on the objectives of a particular study. The collection of entities that comprise a system for one study might be only a subset of the overall system for another. For example, if one wants to study a bank to determine the number of tellers needed to provide adequate service for customers who want just to cash a check or make a savings deposit, the system can be defined to be that portion of the bank consisting of the tellers and the customers waiting in line or being served. If, on the other hand, the loan officer and the safe-deposit boxes are to be included, the definition of the system must be expanded in an obvious way. [See also Fishman (1978, p. 3).] We define the *state* of a system to be that collection of variables necessary to describe a system at a particular time, relative to the objectives of a study. In a study of a bank, examples of possible state variables are the number of busy tellers, the number of customers in the bank, and the time of arrival of each customer in the bank.

We categorize systems to be of two types, discrete and continuous. A *discrete* system is one for which the state variables change instantaneously at separated points in time. A bank is an example of a discrete system, since state variables—e.g., the number of customers in the bank—change only when a customer arrives or when a customer finishes being served and departs. A *continuous* system is one for which the state variables change continuously with respect to time. An airplane moving through the air is an example of a continuous system, since state variables such as position and velocity can change continuously with respect to time. Few systems in practice are wholly discrete or wholly continuous; but since one type of change predominates for most systems, it will usually be possible to classify a system as being either discrete or continuous.

At some point in the lives of most systems, there is a need to study them to try to gain some insight into the relationships among various components, or to predict performance under some new conditions being considered. Figure 1.1 maps out different ways in which a system might be studied.

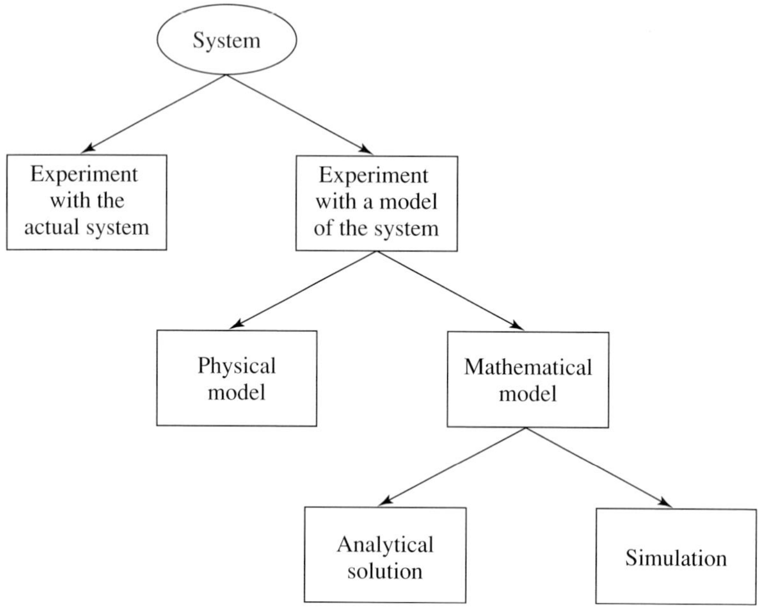

FIGURE 1.1
Ways to study a system.

- *Experiment with the Actual System vs. Experiment with a Model of the System.* If it is possible (and cost-effective) to alter the system physically and then let it operate under the new conditions, it is probably desirable to do so, for in this case there is no question about whether what we study is valid. However, it is rarely feasible to do this, because such an experiment would often be too costly or too disruptive to the system. For example, a bank may be contemplating reducing the number of tellers to decrease costs, but actually trying this could lead to long customer delays and alienation. More graphically, the "system" might not even exist, but we nevertheless want to study it in its various proposed alternative configurations to see how it should be built in the first place; examples of this situation might be a proposed communications network, or a strategic nuclear weapons system. For these reasons, it is usually necessary to build a *model* as a representation of the system and study it as a surrogate for the actual system. When using a model, there is always the question of whether it accurately reflects the system for the purposes of the decisions to be made; this question of model *validity* is taken up in detail in Chap. 5.
- *Physical Model vs. Mathematical Model.* To most people, the word "model" evokes images of clay cars in wind tunnels, cockpits disconnected from their airplanes to be used in pilot training, or miniature supertankers scurrying about in a swimming pool. These are examples of *physical* models (also called *iconic* models), and are not typical of the kinds of models that are usually of interest in operations research and systems analysis. Occasionally, however, it has been found useful to build physical models to study engineering or management

systems; examples include tabletop scale models of material-handling systems, and in at least one case a full-scale physical model of a fast-food restaurant inside a warehouse, complete with full-scale, real (and presumably hungry) humans [see Swart and Donno (1981)]. But the vast majority of models built for such purposes are *mathematical*, representing a system in terms of logical and quantitative relationships that are then manipulated and changed to see how the model reacts, and thus how the system *would* react—*if* the mathematical model is a valid one. Perhaps the simplest example of a mathematical model is the familiar relation $d = rt$, where r is the rate of travel, t is the time spent traveling, and d is the distance traveled. This might provide a valid model in one instance (e.g., a space probe to another planet after it has attained its flight velocity) but a very poor model for other purposes (e.g., rush-hour commuting on congested urban freeways).

- *Analytical Solution vs. Simulation.* Once we have built a mathematical model, it must then be examined to see how it can be used to answer the questions of interest about the system it is supposed to represent. If the model is simple enough, it may be possible to work with its relationships and quantities to get an exact, *analytical* solution. In the $d = rt$ example, if we know the distance to be traveled and the velocity, then we can work with the model to get $t = d/r$ as the time that will be required. This is a very simple, closed-form solution obtainable with just paper and pencil, but some analytical solutions can become extraordinarily complex, requiring vast computing resources; inverting a large nonsparse matrix is a well-known example of a situation in which there is an analytical formula known in principle, but obtaining it numerically in a given instance is far from trivial. If an analytical solution to a mathematical model is available and is computationally efficient, it is usually desirable to study the model in this way rather than via a simulation. However, many systems are highly complex, so that valid mathematical models of them are themselves complex, precluding any possibility of an analytical solution. In this case, the model must be studied by means of *simulation*, i.e., numerically exercising the model for the inputs in question to see how they affect the output measures of performance.

While there may be a small element of truth to pejorative old saws such as "method of last resort" sometimes used to describe simulation, the fact is that we are very quickly led to simulation in most situations, due to the sheer complexity of the systems of interest and of the models necessary to represent them in a valid way.

Given, then, that we have a mathematical model to be studied by means of simulation (henceforth referred to as a *simulation model*), we must then look for particular tools to do this. It is useful for this purpose to classify simulation models along three different dimensions:

- *Static vs. Dynamic Simulation Models.* A *static* simulation model is a representation of a system at a particular time, or one that may be used to represent a system in which time simply plays no role; examples of static simulations are certain Monte Carlo models, discussed in Sec. 13.5. On the other hand, a *dynamic* simulation model represents a system as it evolves over time, such as a conveyor system in a factory.

- *Deterministic vs. Stochastic Simulation Models.* If a simulation model does not contain any probabilistic (i.e., random) components, it is called *deterministic*; a complicated (and analytically intractable) system of differential equations describing a chemical reaction might be such a model. In deterministic models, the output is "determined" once the set of input quantities and relationships in the model have been specified, even though it might take a lot of computer time to evaluate what it is. Many systems, however, must be modeled as having at least some random input components, and these give rise to *stochastic* simulation models. (For an example of the danger of ignoring randomness in modeling a system, see Sec. 4.7.) Most queueing and inventory systems are modeled stochastically. Stochastic simulation models produce output that is itself random, and must therefore be treated as only an estimate of the true characteristics of the model; this is one of the main disadvantages of simulation (see Sec. 1.8) and is dealt with in Chaps. 9 through 12 of this book.
- *Continuous vs. Discrete Simulation Models.* Loosely speaking, we define *discrete* and *continuous* simulation models analogously to the way discrete and continuous systems were defined above. More precise definitions of discrete (event) simulation and continuous simulation are given in Secs. 1.3 and 13.3, respectively. It should be mentioned that a discrete model is not always used to model a discrete system, and vice versa. The decision whether to use a discrete or a continuous model for a particular system depends on the specific objectives of the study. For example, a model of traffic flow on a freeway would be discrete if the characteristics and movement of individual cars are important. Alternatively, if the cars can be treated "in the aggregate," the flow of traffic can be described by differential equations in a continuous model. More discussion on this issue can be found in Sec. 5.2, and in particular in Example 5.2.

The simulation models we consider in the remainder of this book, except for those in Chap. 13, will be discrete, dynamic, and stochastic and will henceforth be called *discrete-event simulation models*. (Since deterministic models are a special case of stochastic models, the restriction to stochastic models involves no loss of generality.)

1.3 DISCRETE-EVENT SIMULATION

Discrete-event simulation concerns the modeling of a system as it evolves over time by a representation in which the state variables change instantaneously at separate points in time. (In more mathematical terms, we might say that the system can change at only a *countable* number of points in time.) These points in time are the ones at which an event occurs, where an *event* is defined as an instantaneous occurrence that may change the state of the system. Although discrete-event simulation could conceptually be done by hand calculations, the amount of data that must be stored and manipulated for most real-world systems dictates that discrete-event simulations be done on a digital computer. (In Sec. 1.4.2 we carry out a small hand simulation, merely to illustrate the logic involved.)

EXAMPLE 1.1. Consider a service facility with a single server—e.g., a one-operator barbershop or an information desk at an airport—for which we would like to estimate the (expected) average delay in queue (line) of arriving customers, where the delay in queue of a customer is the length of the time interval from the instant of his arrival at the facility to the instant he begins being served. For the objective of estimating the average delay of a customer, the state variables for a discrete-event simulation model of the facility would be the status of the server, i.e., either idle or busy, the number of customers waiting in queue to be served (if any), and the time of arrival of each person waiting in queue. The status of the server is needed to determine, upon a customer's arrival, whether the customer can be served immediately or must join the end of the queue. When the server completes serving a customer, the number of customers in the queue is used to determine whether the server will become idle or begin serving the first customer in the queue. The time of arrival of a customer is needed to compute his delay in queue, which is the time he begins being served (which will be known) minus his time of arrival. There are two types of events for this system: the arrival of a customer and the completion of service for a customer, which results in the customer's departure. An arrival is an event since it causes the (state variable) server status to change from idle to busy or the (state variable) number of customers in the queue to increase by 1. Correspondingly, a departure is an event because it causes the server status to change from busy to idle or the number of customers in the queue to decrease by 1. We show in detail how to build a discrete-event simulation model of this single-server queueing system in Sec. 1.4.

In the above example both types of events actually changed the state of the system, but in some discrete-event simulation models events are used for purposes that do not actually effect such a change. For example, an event might be used to schedule the end of a simulation run at a particular time (see Sec. 1.4.6) or to schedule a decision about a system's operation at a particular time (see Sec. 1.5) and might not actually result in a change in the state of the system. This is why we originally said that an event *may* change the state of a system.

1.3.1 Time-Advance Mechanisms

Because of the dynamic nature of discrete-event simulation models, we must keep track of the current value of simulated time as the simulation proceeds, and we also need a mechanism to advance simulated time from one value to another. We call the variable in a simulation model that gives the current value of simulated time the *simulation clock*. The unit of time for the simulation clock is never stated explicitly when a model is written in a general-purpose language such as C, and it is assumed to be in the same units as the input parameters. Also, there is generally no relationship between simulated time and the time needed to run a simulation on the computer.

Historically, two principal approaches have been suggested for advancing the simulation clock: *next-event time advance* and *fixed-increment time advance*. Since the first approach is used by all major simulation software and by most people programming their model in a general-purpose language, and since the second is a special case of the first, we shall use the next-event time-advance approach for all discrete-event simulation models discussed in this book. A brief discussion of fixed-increment time advance is given in App. 1A (at the end of this chapter).

With the next-event time-advance approach, the simulation clock is initialized to zero and the times of occurrence of future events are determined. The simulation clock is then advanced to the time of occurrence of the *most imminent* (first) of these future events, at which point the state of the system is updated to account for the fact that an event has occurred, and our knowledge of the times of occurrence of future events is also updated. Then the simulation clock is advanced to the time of the (new) most imminent event, the state of the system is updated, and future event times are determined, etc. This process of advancing the simulation clock from one event time to another is continued until eventually some prespecified stopping condition is satisfied. Since all state changes occur only at event times for a discrete-event simulation model, periods of inactivity are skipped over by jumping the clock from event time to event time. (Fixed-increment time advance does not skip over these inactive periods, which can eat up a lot of computer time; see App. 1A.) It should be noted that the successive jumps of the simulation clock are generally variable (or unequal) in size.

EXAMPLE 1.2. We now illustrate in detail the next-event time-advance approach for the single-server queueing system of Example 1.1. We need the following notation:

t_i = time of arrival of the ith customer ($t_0 = 0$)
$A_i = t_i - t_{i-1}$ = interarrival time between $(i-1)$st and ith arrivals of customers
S_i = time that server actually spends serving ith customer (exclusive of customer's delay in queue)
D_i = delay in queue of ith customer
$c_i = t_i + D_i + S_i$ = time that ith customer completes service and departs
e_i = time of occurrence of ith event of any type (ith value the simulation clock takes on, excluding the value $e_0 = 0$)

Each of these defined quantities will generally be a random variable. Assume that the probability distributions of the interarrival times $A_1, A_2, \ldots$ and the service times $S_1, S_2, \ldots$ are known and have cumulative distribution functions (see Sec. 4.2) denoted by F_A and F_S, respectively. (In general, F_A and F_S would be determined by collecting data from the system of interest and then specifying distributions consistent with these data using the techniques of Chap. 6.) At time $e_0 = 0$ the status of the server is idle, and the time t_1 of the first arrival is determined by generating A_1 from F_A (techniques for generating random observations from a specified distribution are discussed in Chap. 8) and adding it to 0. The simulation clock is then advanced from e_0 to the time of the next (first) event, $e_1 = t_1$. (See Fig. 1.2, where the curved arrows represent advancing the simulation clock.) Since the customer arriving at time t_1 finds the server idle, she immediately enters service and has a delay in queue of $D_1 = 0$ and the status of the server is changed from idle to busy. The time, c_1, when the arriving customer will complete service is computed by generating S_1 from F_S and adding it to t_1. Finally, the time of the second arrival, t_2, is computed as $t_2 = t_1 + A_2$, where A_2 is generated from F_A. If $t_2 < c_1$, as depicted in Fig. 1.2, the simulation clock is advanced from e_1 to the time of the next event, $e_2 = t_2$. (If c_1 were less than t_2, the clock would be advanced from e_1 to c_1.) Since the customer arriving at time t_2 finds the server already busy, the number of customers in the queue is increased from 0 to 1 and the time of arrival of this customer is recorded; however, his service time S_2 is not generated at this time. Also, the time of the third arrival, t_3, is computed as $t_3 = t_2 + A_3$. If $c_1 < t_3$, as depicted in the figure, the simulation clock is advanced from e_2 to the time of the next event, $e_3 = c_1$, where the customer

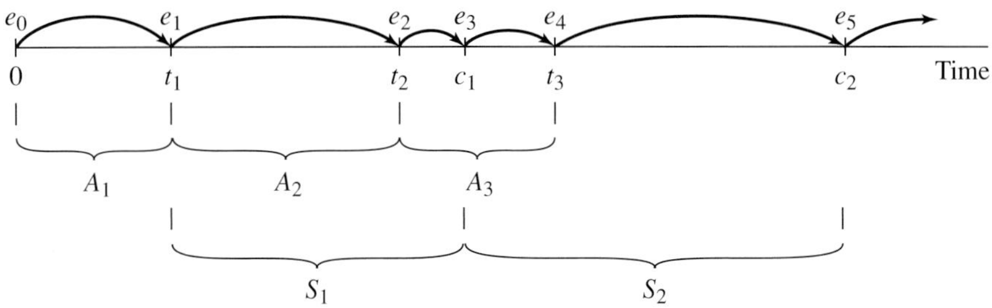

FIGURE 1.2
The next-event time-advance approach illustrated for the single-server queueing system.

completing service departs, the customer in the queue (i.e., the one who arrived at time t_2) begins service and his delay in queue and service-completion time are computed as $D_2 = c_1 - t_2$ and $c_2 = c_1 + S_2$ (S_2 is now generated from F_S), and the number of customers in the queue is decreased from 1 to 0. If $t_3 < c_2$, the simulation clock is advanced from e_3 to the time of the next event, $e_4 = t_3$, etc. The simulation might eventually be terminated when, say, the number of customers whose delays have been observed reaches some specified value.

1.3.2 Components and Organization of a Discrete-Event Simulation Model

Although simulation has been applied to a great diversity of real-world systems, discrete-event simulation models all share a number of common components and there is a logical organization for these components that promotes the programming, debugging, and future changing of a simulation model's computer program. In particular, the following components will be found in most discrete-event simulation models using the next-event time-advance approach programmed in a general-purpose language:

System state: The collection of state variables necessary to describe the system at a particular time

Simulation clock: A variable giving the current value of simulated time

Event list: A list containing the next time when each type of event will occur

Statistical counters: Variables used for storing statistical information about system performance

Initialization routine: A subprogram to initialize the simulation model at time 0

Timing routine: A subprogram that determines the next event from the event list and then advances the simulation clock to the time when that event is to occur

Event routine: A subprogram that updates the system state when a particular type of event occurs (there is one event routine for each event type)

Library routines: A set of subprograms used to generate random observations from probability distributions that were determined as part of the simulation model

Report generator: A subprogram that computes estimates (from the statistical counters) of the desired measures of performance and produces a report when the simulation ends

Main program: A subprogram that invokes the timing routine to determine the next event and then transfers control to the corresponding event routine to update the system state appropriately. The main program may also check for termination and invoke the report generator when the simulation is over.

The logical relationships (flow of control) among these components are shown in Fig. 1.3. The simulation begins at time 0 with the main program invoking the initialization routine, where the simulation clock is set to zero, the system state and the statistical counters are initialized, and the event list is initialized. After control has been returned to the main program, it invokes the timing routine to determine which type of event is most imminent. If an event of type i is the next to occur, the simulation clock is advanced to the time that event type i will occur

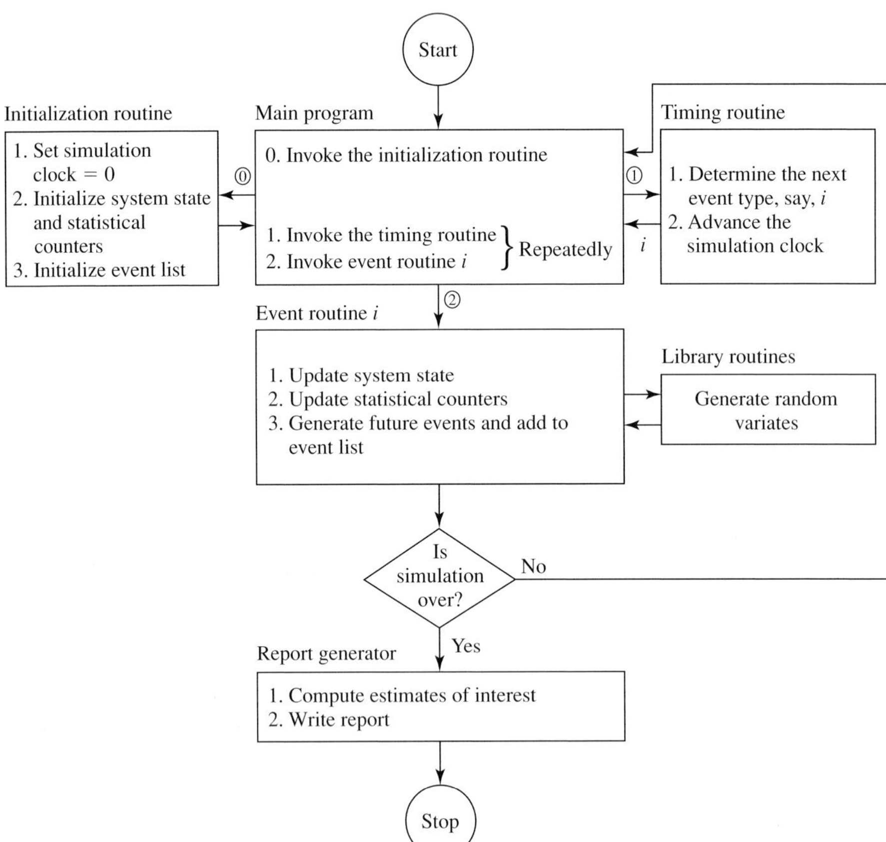

FIGURE 1.3
Flow of control for the next-event time-advance approach.

and control is returned to the main program. Then the main program invokes event routine i, where typically three types of activities occur: (1) The system state is updated to account for the fact that an event of type i has occurred; (2) information about system performance is gathered by updating the statistical counters; and (3) the times of occurrence of future events are generated, and this information is added to the event list. Often it is necessary to generate random observations from probability distributions in order to determine these future event times; we will refer to such a generated observation as a *random variate*. After all processing has been completed, either in event routine i or in the main program, a check is typically made to determine (relative to some stopping condition) if the simulation should now be terminated. If it is time to terminate the simulation, the report generator is invoked from the main program to compute estimates (from the statistical counters) of the desired measures of performance and to produce a report. If it is not time for termination, control is passed back to the main program and the main program–timing routine–main program–event routine–termination check cycle is repeated until the stopping condition is eventually satisfied.

Before concluding this section, a few additional words about the system state may be in order. As mentioned in Sec. 1.2, a system is a well-defined collection of *entities*. Entities are characterized by data values called *attributes*, and these attributes are part of the system state for a discrete-event simulation model. Furthermore, entities with some common property are often grouped together in *lists* (or *files* or *sets*). For each entity there is a *record* in the list consisting of the entity's attributes, and the order in which the records are placed in the list depends on some specified rule. (See Chap. 2 for a discussion of efficient approaches for storing lists of records.) For the single-server queueing facility of Examples 1.1 and 1.2, the entities are the server and the customers in the facility. The server has the attribute "server status" (busy or idle), and the customers waiting in queue have the attribute "time of arrival." (The number of customers in the queue might also be considered an attribute of the server.) Furthermore, as we shall see in Sec. 1.4, these customers in queue will be grouped together in a list.

The organization and action of a discrete-event simulation program using the next-event time-advance mechanism as depicted above are fairly typical when programming such simulations in a general-purpose programming language such as C; it is called the *event-scheduling approach* to simulation modeling, since the times of future events are explicitly coded into the model and are scheduled to occur in the simulated future. It should be mentioned here that there is an alternative approach to simulation modeling, called the *process approach*, that instead views the simulation in terms of the individual entities involved, and the code written describes the "experience" of a "typical" entity as it "flows" through the system; programming simulations modeled from the process point of view usually requires the use of special-purpose simulation software, as discussed in Chap. 3. Even when taking the process approach, however, the simulation is actually executed behind the scenes in the event-scheduling logic as described above.

1.4 SIMULATION OF A SINGLE-SERVER QUEUEING SYSTEM

This section shows in detail how to simulate a single-server queueing system such as a one-operator barbershop. Although this system seems very simple compared with those usually of real interest, how it is simulated is actually quite representative of the operation of simulations of great complexity.

In Sec. 1.4.1 we describe the system of interest and state our objectives more precisely. We explain intuitively how to simulate this system in Sec. 1.4.2 by showing a "snapshot" of the simulated system just after each event occurs. Section 1.4.3 describes the language-independent organization and logic of the C code given in Sec. 1.4.4. The simulation's results are discussed in Sec. 1.4.5, and Sec. 1.4.6 alters the stopping rule to another common way to end simulations. Finally, Sec. 1.4.7 briefly describes a technique for identifying and simplifying the event and variable structure of a simulation.

1.4.1 Problem Statement

Consider a single-server queueing system (see Fig. 1.4) for which the interarrival times $A_1, A_2, \ldots$ are *independent and identically distributed* (IID) random variables.

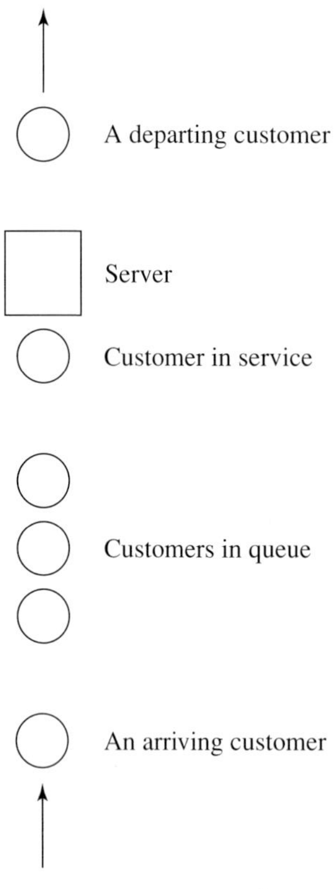

FIGURE 1.4
A single-server queueing system.

("Identically distributed" means that the interarrival times have the same probability distribution.) A customer who arrives and finds the server idle enters service immediately, and the service times $S_1, S_2, \ldots$ of the successive customers are IID random variables that are independent of the interarrival times. A customer who arrives and finds the server busy joins the end of a single queue. Upon completing service for a customer, the server chooses a customer from the queue (if any) in a first-in, first-out (FIFO) manner. (For a discussion of other queue disciplines and queueing systems in general, see App. 1B.)

The simulation will begin in the "empty-and-idle" state; i.e., no customers are present and the server is idle. At time 0, we will begin waiting for the arrival of the first customer, which will occur after the first interarrival time, A_1, rather than at time 0 (which would be a possibly valid, but different, modeling assumption). We wish to simulate this system until a fixed number (n) of customers have completed their delays in queue; i.e., the simulation will stop when the nth customer enters service. Note that the *time* the simulation ends is thus a random variable, depending on the observed values for the interarrival and service-time random variables.

To measure the performance of this system, we will look at estimates of three quantities. First, we will estimate the expected average delay in queue of the n customers completing their delays during the simulation; we denote this quantity by $d(n)$. The word "expected" in the definition of $d(n)$ means this: On a given run of the simulation (or, for that matter, on a given run of the actual system the simulation model represents), the actual average delay observed of the n customers depends on the interarrival and service-time random variable observations that happen to have been obtained. On another run of the simulation (or on a different day for the real system) there would probably be arrivals at different times, and the service times required would also be different; this would give rise to a different value for the average of the n delays. Thus, the average delay on a given run of the simulation is properly regarded as a random variable itself. What we want to estimate, $d(n)$, is the *expected value* of this random variable. One interpretation of this is that $d(n)$ is the average of a large (actually, infinite) number of n-customer average delays. From a single run of the simulation resulting in customer delays $D_1, D_2, \ldots, D_n$, an obvious estimator of $d(n)$ is

$$\hat{d}(n) = \frac{\sum_{i=1}^{n} D_i}{n}$$

which is just the average of the n D_i's that were observed in the simulation [so that $\hat{d}(n)$ could also be denoted by $\overline{D}(n)$]. [Throughout this book, a hat (ˆ) above a symbol denotes an estimator.] It is important to note that by "delay" we do not exclude the possibility that a customer could have a delay of zero in the case of an arrival finding the system empty and idle (with this model, we know for sure that $D_1 = 0$); delays with a value of 0 *are* counted in the average, since if many delays were zero this would represent a system providing very good service, and our output measure should reflect this. One reason for taking the average of the D_i's, as opposed to just looking at them individually, is that they will not have the same distribution (e.g., $D_1 = 0$, but D_2 could be positive), and the average gives us a single composite measure of all the customers' delays; in this sense, this is not the usual "average" taken in basic statistics, as the individual terms are not independent random observations from the same distribution. Note also that by itself, $\hat{d}(n)$ is an estimator based on a sample of size *1*, since we are making only one complete simulation run. From elementary statistics, we know that a sample of size 1 is not worth much; we return to this issue in Chaps. 9 through 12.

While an estimate of $d(n)$ gives information about system performance from the customers' point of view, the management of such a system may want different information; indeed, since most real simulations are quite complex and may be time-consuming to run, we usually collect many output measures of performance, describing different aspects of system behavior. One such measure for our simple model here is the expected average number of customers in the queue (but not being served), denoted by $q(n)$, where the n is necessary in the notation to indicate that this average is taken over the time period needed to observe the n delays defining our stopping rule. This is a different kind of "average" than the average delay in queue, because it is taken over (continuous) time, rather than over customers (being discrete). Thus, we need to define what is meant by this *time*-average number of customers in queue. To do this, let $Q(t)$ denote the number of customers in queue at time t, for any real number $t \geq 0$, and let $T(n)$ be the time required to observe our n delays in queue. Then for any time t between 0 and $T(n)$, $Q(t)$ is a nonnegative integer. Further, if we let p_i be the expected *proportion* (which will be between 0 and 1) of the time that $Q(t)$ is equal to i, then a reasonable definition of $q(n)$ would be

$$q(n) = \sum_{i=0}^{\infty} i p_i$$

Thus, $q(n)$ is a weighted average of the possible values i for the queue length $Q(t)$, with the weights being the expected proportion of time the queue spends at each of its possible lengths. To estimate $q(n)$ from a simulation, we simply replace the p_i's with estimates of them, and get

$$\hat{q}(n) = \sum_{i=0}^{\infty} i \hat{p}_i \tag{1.1}$$

where $\hat{p}_i$ is the *observed* (rather than expected) proportion of the time *during the simulation* that there were i customers in the queue. Computationally, however, it is easier to rewrite $\hat{q}(n)$ using some geometric considerations. If we let T_i be the *total* time during the simulation that the queue is of length i, then $T(n) = T_0 + T_1 + T_2 + \cdots$ and $\hat{p}_i = T_i/T(n)$, so that we can rewrite Eq. (1.1) above as

$$\hat{q}(n) = \frac{\sum_{i=0}^{\infty} i T_i}{T(n)} \tag{1.2}$$

Figure 1.5 illustrates a possible time path, or *realization*, of $Q(t)$ for this system in the case of $n = 6$; ignore the shading for now. Arrivals occur at times 0.4, 1.6, 2.1, 3.8, 4.0, 5.6, 5.8, and 7.2. Departures (service completions) occur at times 2.4, 3.1, 3.3, 4.9, and 8.6, and the simulation ends at time $T(6) = 8.6$. Remember in looking

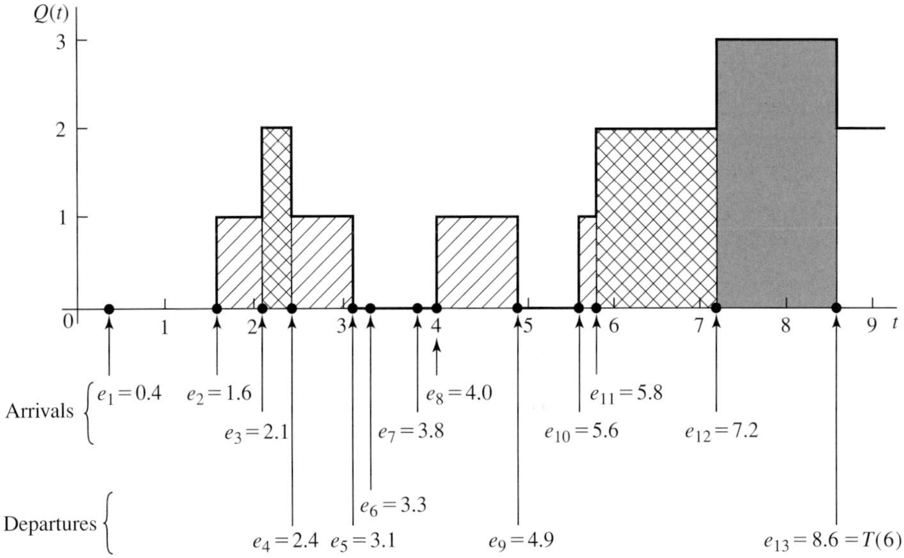

FIGURE 1.5
$Q(t)$, arrival times, and departure times for a realization of a single-server queueing system.

at Fig. 1.5 that $Q(t)$ does not count the customer in service (if any), so between times 0.4 and 1.6 there is one customer in the system being served, even though the queue is empty [$Q(t) = 0$]; the same is true between times 3.1 and 3.3, between times 3.8 and 4.0, and between times 4.9 and 5.6. Between times 3.3 and 3.8, however, the system is empty of customers and the server is idle, as is obviously the case between times 0 and 0.4. To compute $\hat{q}(n)$, we must first compute the T_i's, which can be read off Fig. 1.5 as the (sometimes separated) intervals over which $Q(t)$ is equal to 0, 1, 2, and so on:

$$T_0 = (1.6 - 0.0) + (4.0 - 3.1) + (5.6 - 4.9) = 3.2$$
$$T_1 = (2.1 - 1.6) + (3.1 - 2.4) + (4.9 - 4.0) + (5.8 - 5.6) = 2.3$$
$$T_2 = (2.4 - 2.1) + (7.2 - 5.8) = 1.7$$
$$T_3 = (8.6 - 7.2) = 1.4$$

($T_i = 0$ for $i \geq 4$, since the queue never grew to those lengths in this realization.) The numerator in Eq. (1.2) is thus

$$\sum_{i=0}^{\infty} iT_i = (0 \times 3.2) + (1 \times 2.3) + (2 \times 1.7) + (3 \times 1.4) = 9.9 \qquad (1.3)$$

and so our estimate of the time-average number in queue from this particular simulation run is $\hat{q}(6) = 9.9/8.6 = 1.15$. Now, note that each of the nonzero terms on the right-hand side of Eq. (1.3) corresponds to one of the shaded areas in Fig. 1.5: 1×2.3 is the diagonally shaded area (in four pieces), 2×1.7 is the cross-hatched area (in two pieces), and 3×1.4 is the screened area (in a single piece). In other words, the summation in the numerator of Eq. (1.2) is just the *area under the $Q(t)$ curve between the beginning and the end of the simulation*. Remembering that "area under a curve" is an integral, we can thus write

$$\sum_{i=0}^{\infty} iT_i = \int_0^{T(n)} Q(t)\, dt$$

and the estimator of $q(n)$ can then be expressed as

$$\hat{q}(n) = \frac{\int_0^{T(n)} Q(t)\, dt}{T(n)} \tag{1.4}$$

While Eqs. (1.4) and (1.2) are equivalent expressions for $\hat{q}(n)$, Eq. (1.4) is preferable since the integral in this equation can be accumulated as simple areas of rectangles as the simulation progresses through time. It is less convenient to carry out the computations to get the summation in Eq. (1.2) explicitly. Moreover, the appearance of Eq. (1.4) suggests a continuous average of $Q(t)$, since in a rough sense, an integral can be regarded as a continuous summation.

The third and final output measure of performance for this system is a measure of how busy the server is. The expected *utilization* of the server is the expected proportion of time during the simulation [from time 0 to time $T(n)$] that the server is busy (i.e., not idle), and is thus a number between 0 and 1; denote it by $u(n)$. From a single simulation, then, our estimate of $u(n)$ is $\hat{u}(n)$ = the *observed* proportion of time during the simulation that the server is busy. Now $\hat{u}(n)$ could be computed directly from the simulation by noting the times at which the server changes status (idle to busy or vice versa) and then doing the appropriate subtractions and division. However, it is easier to look at this quantity as a continuous-time average, similar to the average queue length, by defining the "busy function"

$$B(t) = \begin{cases} 1 & \text{if the server is busy at time } t \\ 0 & \text{if the server is idle at time } t \end{cases}$$

and so $\hat{u}(n)$ could be expressed as the proportion of time that $B(t)$ is equal to 1. Figure 1.6 plots $B(t)$ for the same simulation realization as used in Fig. 1.5 for $Q(t)$. In this case, we get

$$\hat{u}(n) = \frac{(3.3 - 0.4) + (8.6 - 3.8)}{8.6} = \frac{7.7}{8.6} = 0.90 \tag{1.5}$$

indicating that the server was busy about 90 percent of the time during this simulation. Again, however, the numerator in Eq. (1.5) can be viewed as the area under the $B(t)$ function over the course of the simulation, since the height of $B(t)$ is always either 0 or 1. Thus,

$$\hat{u}(n) = \frac{\int_0^{T(n)} B(t)\, dt}{T(n)} \tag{1.6}$$

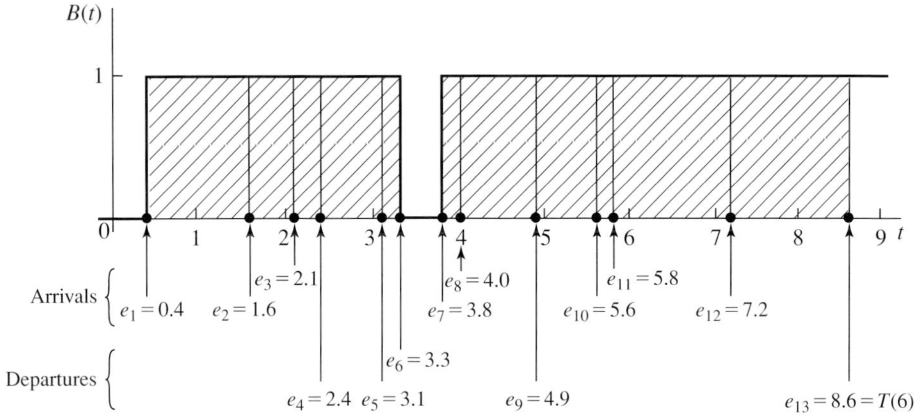

FIGURE 1.6
$B(t)$, arrival times, and departure times for a realization of a single-server queueing system (same realization as in Fig. 1.5).

and we see again that $\hat{u}(n)$ is the continuous average of the $B(t)$ function, corresponding to our notion of utilization. As was the case for $\hat{q}(n)$, the reason for writing $\hat{u}(n)$ in the integral form of Eq. (1.6) is that computationally, as the simulation progresses, the integral of $B(t)$ can easily be accumulated by adding up areas of rectangles. For many simulations involving "servers" of some sort, utilization statistics are quite informative in identifying bottlenecks (utilizations near 100 percent, coupled with heavy congestion measures for the queue leading in) or excess capacity (low utilizations); this is particularly true if the "servers" are expensive items such as robots in a manufacturing system or large mainframe computers in a data-processing operation.

To recap, the three measures of performance are the average delay in queue $\hat{d}(n)$, the time-average number of customers in queue $\hat{q}(n)$, and the proportion of time the server is busy $\hat{u}(n)$. The average delay in queue is an example of a *discrete-time statistic*, since it is defined relative to the collection of random variables $\{D_i\}$ that have a discrete "time" index, $i = 1, 2, \ldots$. The time-average number in queue and the proportion of time the server is busy are examples of *continuous-time statistics*, since they are defined on the collection of random variables $\{Q(t)\}$ and $\{B(t)\}$, respectively, each of which is indexed on the continuous time parameter $t \in [0, \infty)$. (The symbol $\in$ means "contained in." Thus, in this case, t can be any nonnegative real number.) Both discrete-time and continuous-time statistics are common in simulation, and they furthermore can be other than averages. For example, we might be interested in the *maximum* of all the delays in queue observed (a discrete-time statistic), or the *proportion* of time during the simulation that the queue contained at least five customers (a continuous-time statistic).

The events for this system are the arrival of a customer and the departure of a customer (after a service completion); the state variables necessary to estimate $d(n)$, $q(n)$, and $u(n)$ are the status of the server (0 for idle and 1 for busy), the number of customers in the queue, the time of arrival of each customer currently in the queue (represented as a list), and the time of the last (i.e., most recent) event. The time of the last event, defined to be e_{i-1} if $e_{i-1} \le t < e_i$ (where t is the current time in the simulation), is needed to compute the width of the rectangles for the area accumulations in the estimates of $q(n)$ and $u(n)$.

1.4.2 Intuitive Explanation

We begin our explanation of how to simulate a single-server queueing system by showing how its simulation model would be represented inside the computer at time $e_0 = 0$ and the times $e_1, e_2, \ldots, e_{13}$ at which the 13 successive events occur that are needed to observe the desired number, $n = 6$, of delays in queue. For expository convenience, we assume that the interarrival and service times of customers are

$$A_1 = 0.4, A_2 = 1.2, A_3 = 0.5, A_4 = 1.7, A_5 = 0.2,$$
$$A_6 = 1.6, A_7 = 0.2, A_8 = 1.4, A_9 = 1.9, \ldots$$

$$S_1 = 2.0, S_2 = 0.7, S_3 = 0.2, S_4 = 1.1, S_5 = 3.7, S_6 = 0.6, \ldots$$

Thus, between time 0 and the time of the first arrival there is 0.4 time unit, between the arrivals of the first and second customers there are 1.2 time units, etc., and the service time required for the first customer is 2.0 time units, etc. Note that it is not necessary to declare what the time units are (minutes, hours, etc.), but only to be sure that all time quantities are expressed in the *same* units. In an actual simulation (see Sec. 1.4.4), the A_i's and the S_i's would be generated from their corresponding probability distributions, as needed, during the course of the simulation. The numerical values for the A_i's and the S_i's given above have been artificially chosen so as to generate the same simulation realization as depicted in Figs. 1.5 and 1.6 illustrating the $Q(t)$ and $B(t)$ processes.

Figure 1.7 gives a snapshot of the system itself and of a computer representation of the system at each of the times $e_0 = 0$, $e_1 = 0.4, \ldots, e_{13} = 8.6$. In the "system" pictures, the square represents the server, and circles represent customers; the numbers inside the customer circles are the times of their arrivals. In the "computer representation" pictures, the values of the variables shown are *after* all processing has been completed at that event. Our discussion will focus on how the computer representation changes at the event times.

$t = 0$: *Initialization.* The simulation begins with the main program invoking the initialization routine. Our modeling assumption was that initially the system is empty of customers and the server is idle, as depicted in the "system" picture of Fig. 1.7*a*. The model state variables are initialized to represent this: Server status is 0 [we use 0 to represent an idle server and 1 to represent a busy server, similar to the definition of the $B(t)$ function], and the number of customers in the queue is 0. There is a one-dimensional array to store the times of arrival of customers *currently in the queue*; this array is initially empty, and as the simulation progresses, its length will grow and shrink. The time of the last (most recent) event is initialized to 0, so that at the time of the first event (when it is used), it will have its correct value. The simulation

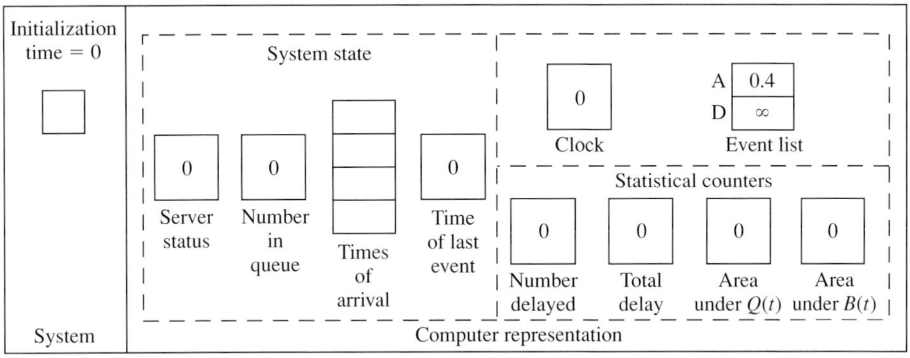

(a)

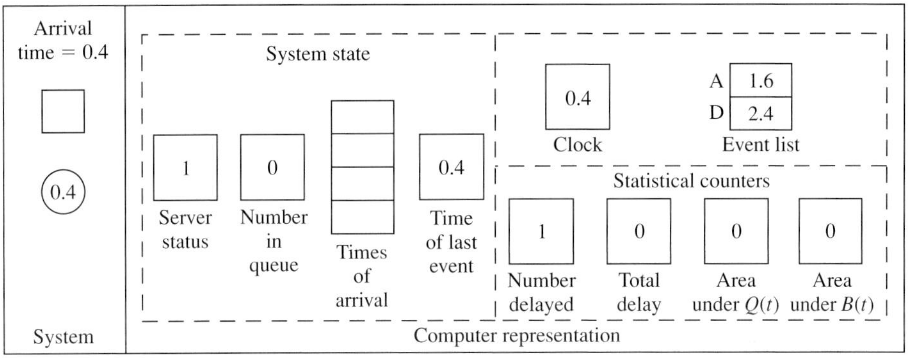

(b)

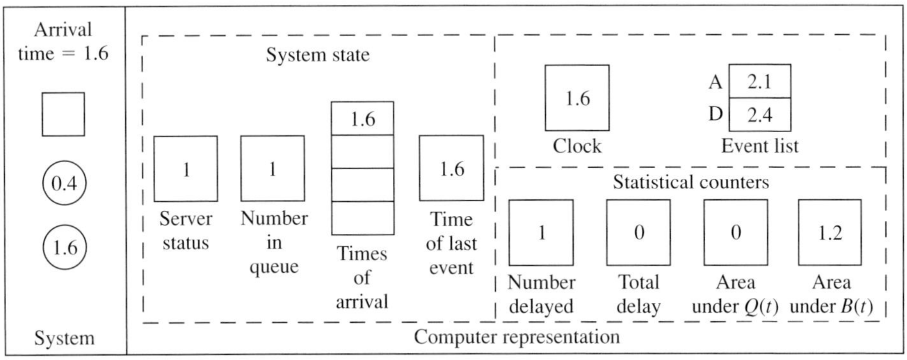

(c)

FIGURE 1.7
Snapshots of the system and of its computer representation at time 0 and at each of the 13 succeeding event times.

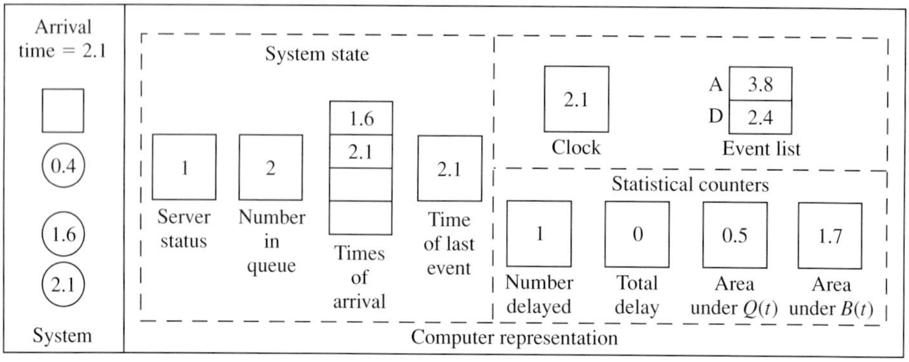

(*d*)

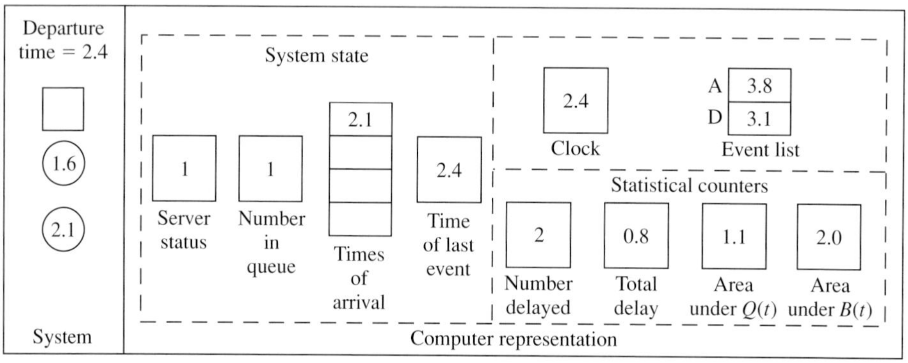

(*e*)

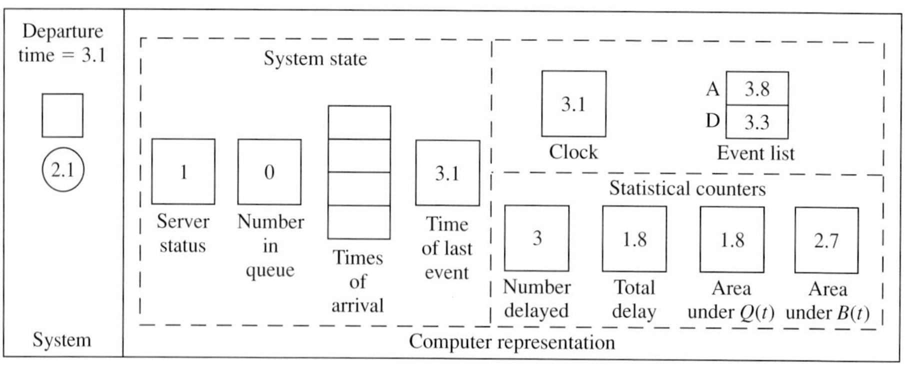

(*f*)

FIGURE 1.7
(*continued*)

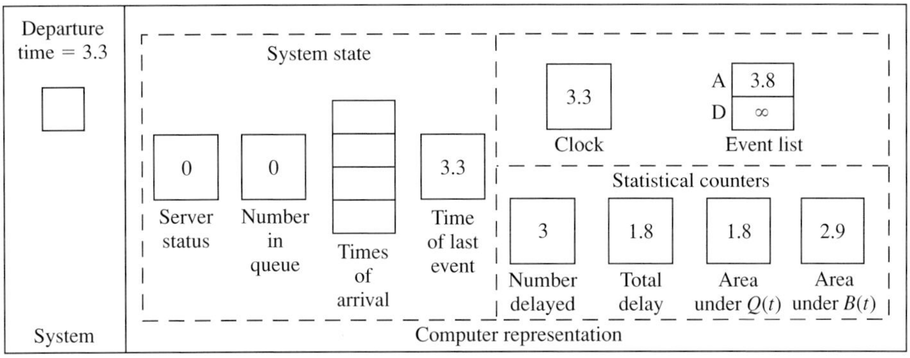

(*g*)

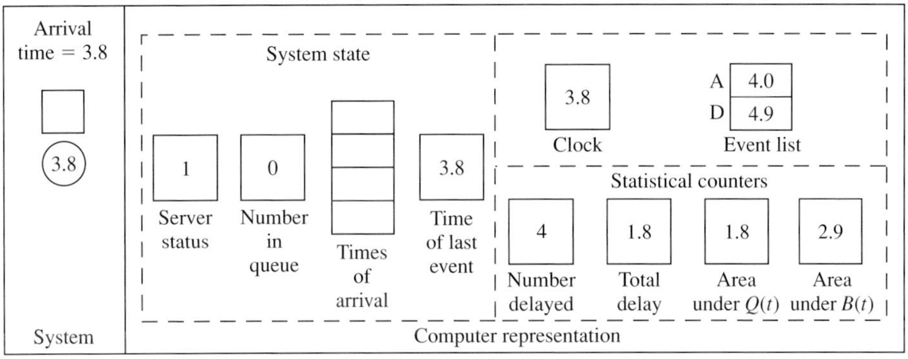

(*h*)

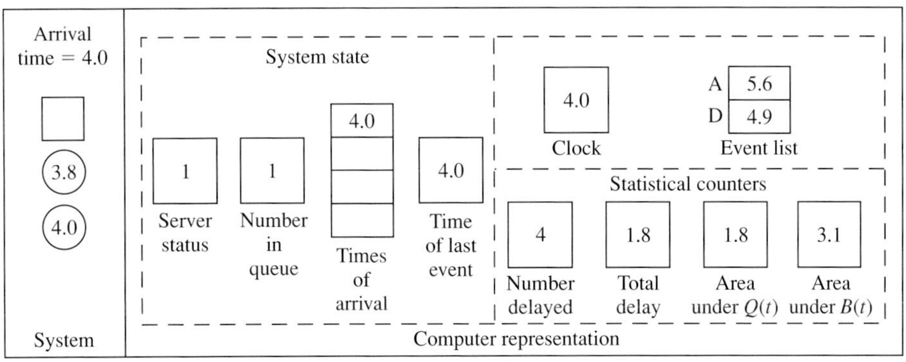

(*i*)

FIGURE 1.7
(*continued*)

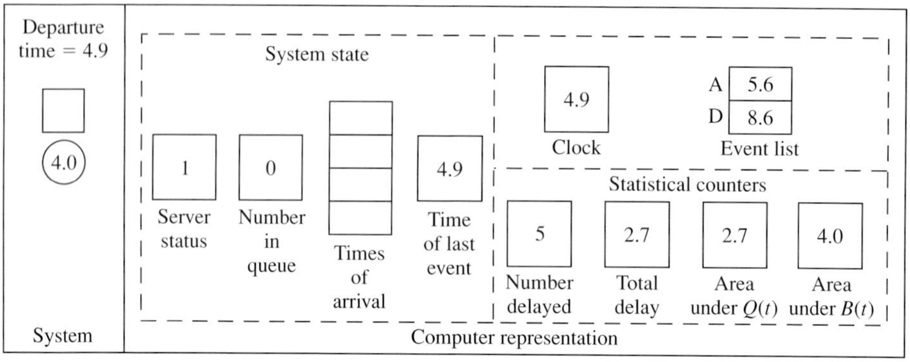

(*j*)

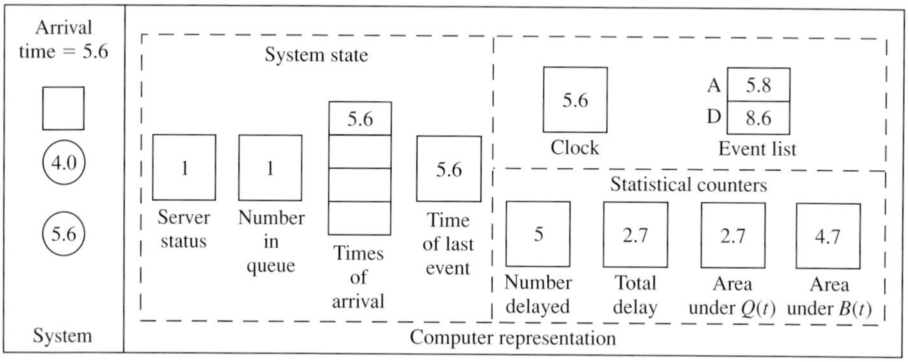

(*k*)

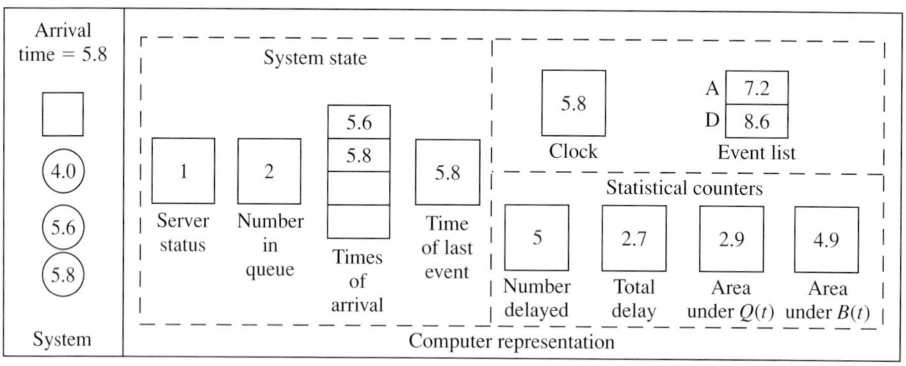

(*l*)

FIGURE 1.7
(*continued*)

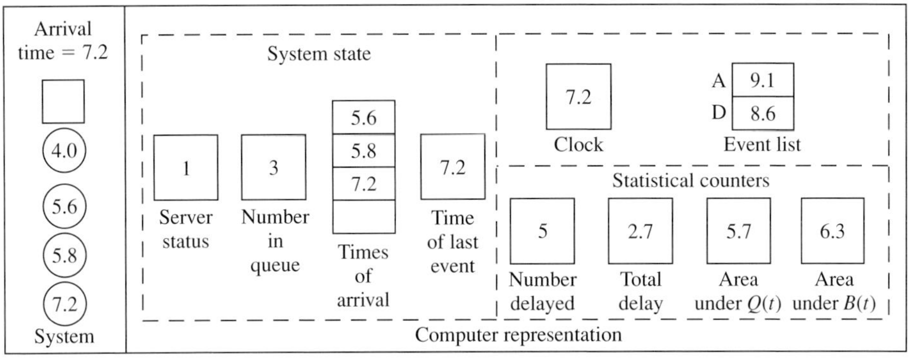

(*m*)

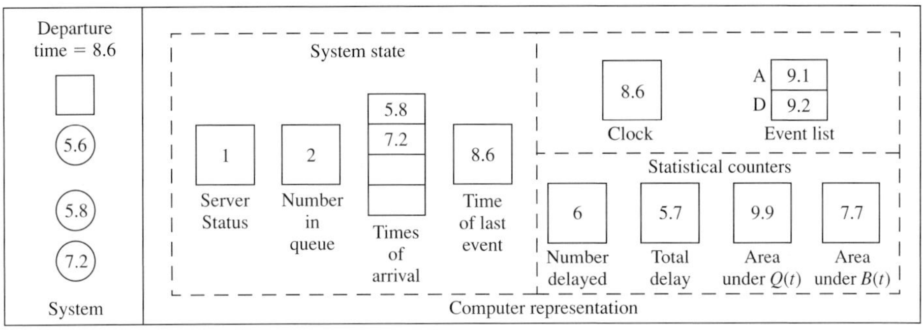

(*n*)

FIGURE 1.7
(*continued*)

clock is set to 0, and the *event list*, giving the times of the next occurrence of each of the event types, is initialized as follows. The time of the first arrival is $0 + A_1 = 0.4$, and is denoted by "A" next to the event list. Since there is no customer in service, it does not even make sense to talk about the time of the next departure ("D" by the event list), and we know that the first event will be the initial customer arrival at time 0.4. However, the simulation progresses in general by looking at the event list and picking the smallest value from it to determine what the next event will be, so by scheduling the next departure to occur at time ∞ (or a very large number in a computer program), we effectively eliminate the departure event from consideration and force the next event to be an arrival. Finally, the four statistical counters are initialized to 0. When all initialization is done, control is returned to the main program, which then calls the timing routine to determine the next event. Since $0.4 < \infty$, the next event will be an arrival at time 0.4, and the timing routine advances the clock to this time, then passes control back to the main program with the information that the next event is to be an arrival.

$t = 0.4$: *Arrival of customer 1.* At time 0.4, the main program passes control to the arrival routine to process the arrival of the first customer. Figure 1.7*b* shows the system and its computer representation *after* all changes have been made to process this arrival. Since this customer arrived to find the server idle (status equal to 0), he begins service immediately and has a delay in queue of $D_1 = 0$ (which *does* count as a delay). The server status is set to 1 to represent that the server is now busy, but the queue itself is still empty. The clock has been advanced to the current time, 0.4, and the event list is updated to reflect this customer's arrival: The next arrival will be $A_2 = 1.2$ time units from now, at time $0.4 + 1.2 = 1.6$, and the next departure (the service completion of the customer now arriving) will be $S_1 = 2.0$ time units from now, at time $0.4 + 2.0 = 2.4$. The number delayed is incremented to 1 (when this reaches $n = 6$, the simulation will end), and $D_1 = 0$ is added into the total delay (still at zero). The area under $Q(t)$ is updated by adding in the product of the *previous* value (i.e., the level it had between the last event and now) of $Q(t)$ (0 in this case) times the width of the interval of time from the last event to now, $t -$ (time of last event) $= 0.4 - 0$ in this case. Note that the time of the last event used here is its *old* value (0), before it is updated to its new value (0.4) in this event routine. Similarly, the area under $B(t)$ is updated by adding in the product of its previous value (0) times the width of the interval of time since the last event. [Look back at Figs. 1.5 and 1.6 to trace the accumulation of the areas under $Q(t)$ and $B(t)$.] Finally, the time of the last event is brought up to the current time, 0.4, and control is passed back to the main program. It invokes the timing routine, which scans the event list for the smallest value, and determines that the next event will be another arrival at time 1.6; it updates the clock to this value and passes control back to the main program with the information that the next event is an arrival.

$t = 1.6$: *Arrival of customer 2.* At this time we again enter the arrival routine, and Fig. 1.7*c* shows the system and its computer representation after all changes have been made to process this event. Since this customer arrives to find the server busy (status equal to 1 upon her arrival), she must queue up in the first location in the queue, her time of arrival is stored in the first location in the array, and the number-in-queue variable rises to 1. The time of the next arrival in the event list is updated to $A_3 = 0.5$ time unit from now, $1.6 + 0.5 = 2.1$; the time of the next departure is not changed, since its value of 2.4 is the departure time of customer 1, who is still in service at this time. Since we are not observing the end of anyone's delay in queue, the number-delayed and total-delay variables are unchanged. The area under $Q(t)$ is increased by 0 [the previous value of $Q(t)$] times the time since the last event, $1.6 - 0.4 = 1.2$. The area under $B(t)$ is increased by 1 [the previous value of $B(t)$] times this same interval of time, 1.2. After updating the time of the last event to now, control is passed back to the main program and then to the timing routine, which determines that the next event will be an arrival at time 2.1.

$t = 2.1$: *Arrival of customer 3.* Once again the arrival routine is invoked, as depicted in Fig. 1.7*d*. The server stays busy, and the queue grows by one customer, whose time of arrival is stored in the queue array's second location. The next arrival is updated to $t + A_4 = 2.1 + 1.7 = 3.8$, and the next departure is still the same, as we are still waiting for the service completion of customer 1. The delay counters are unchanged, since this is not the end of anyone's delay in queue, and the two area accumulators are updated by adding in 1 [the previous values of both $Q(t)$ and $B(t)$] times the time since the last event, $2.1 - 1.6 = 0.5$. After bringing the time of the last event up to the present, we go back to the main program and invoke the timing routine, which looks at the event list to determine that the next event will be a departure at time 2.4, and updates the clock to that time.

$t = 2.4$: *Departure of customer 1.* Now the main program invokes the departure routine, and Fig. 1.7*e* shows the system and its representation after this occurs. The server will maintain its busy status, since customer 2 moves out of the first place in queue and into service. The queue shrinks by 1, and the time-of-arrival array is moved up one place, to represent that customer 3 is now first in line. Customer 2, now entering service, will require $S_2 = 0.7$ time unit, so the time of the next departure (that of customer 2) in the event list is updated to S_2 time units from now, or to time $2.4 + 0.7 = 3.1$; the time of the next arrival (that of customer 4) is unchanged, since this was scheduled earlier at the time of customer 3's arrival, and we are still waiting at this time for customer 4 to arrive. The delay statistics are updated, since at this time customer 2 is entering service and is completing her delay in queue. Here we make use of the time-of-arrival array, and compute the second delay as the current time minus the second customer's time of arrival, or $D_2 = 2.4 - 1.6 = 0.8$. (Note that the value of 1.6 was stored in the first location in the time-of-arrival array *before* it was changed, so this delay computation would have to be done before advancing the times of arrival in the array.) The area statistics are updated by adding in $2 \times (2.4 - 2.1)$ for $Q(t)$ [note that the previous value of $Q(t)$ was used], and $1 \times (2.4 - 2.1)$ for $B(t)$. The time of the last event is updated, we return to the main program, and the timing routine determines that the next event is a departure at time 3.1.

$t = 3.1$: *Departure of customer 2.* The changes at this departure are similar to those at the departure of customer 1 at time 2.4 just discussed. Note that we observe another delay in queue, and that after this event is processed the queue is again empty, but the server is still busy.

$t = 3.3$: *Departure of customer 3.* Again, the changes are similar to those in the above two departure events, with one important exception: Since the queue is now empty, the server becomes idle and we must set the next departure time in the event list to ∞, since the system now looks the same as it did at time 0 and we want to force the next event to be the arrival of customer 4.

$t = 3.8$: *Arrival of customer 4.* Since this customer arrives to find the server idle, he has a delay of 0 (i.e., $D_4 = 0$) and goes right into service. Thus, the changes here are very similar to those at the arrival of the first customer at time $t = 0.4$.

The remaining six event times are depicted in Fig. 1.7i through 1.7n, and readers should work through these to be sure they understand why the variables and arrays are as they appear; it may be helpful to follow along in the plots of $Q(t)$ and $B(t)$ in Figs. 1.5 and 1.6. With the departure of customer 5 at time $t = 8.6$, customer 6 leaves the queue and enters service, at which time the number delayed reaches 6 (the specified value of n) and the simulation ends. At this point, the main program invokes the report generator to compute the final output measures [$\hat{d}(6) = 5.7/6 = 0.95$, $\hat{q}(6) = 9.9/8.6 = 1.15$, and $\hat{u}(6) = 7.7/8.6 = 0.90$] and write them out.

A few specific comments about the above example illustrating the logic of a simulation should be made:

- Perhaps the key element in the dynamics of a simulation is the interaction between the simulation clock and the event list. The event list is maintained, and the clock jumps to the next event, as determined by scanning the event list at the end of each event's processing for the smallest (i.e., next) event time. This is how the simulation progresses through time.
- While processing an event, no "simulated" time passes. However, even though time is standing still for the model, care must be taken to process updates of the state variables and statistical counters in the appropriate order. For example, it would be incorrect to update the number in queue before updating the area-under-$Q(t)$ counter, since the height of the rectangle to be used is the *previous* value of $Q(t)$ [before the effect of the current event on $Q(t)$ has been implemented]. Similarly, it would be incorrect to update the time of the last event before updating the area accumulators. Yet another type of error would result if the queue list were changed at a departure before the delay of the first customer in queue were computed, since his time of arrival to the system would be lost.
- It is sometimes easy to overlook contingencies that seem out of the ordinary but that nevertheless must be accommodated. For example, it would be easy to forget that a departing customer could leave behind an empty queue, necessitating that the server be idled and the departure event again be eliminated from consideration. Also, termination conditions are often more involved than they might seem at first sight; in the above example, the simulation stopped in what seems to be the "usual" way, after a departure of one customer, allowing another to enter service and contribute the last delay needed, but the simulation *could* actually have ended instead with an arrival event—how?
- In some simulations it can happen that two (or more) entries in the event list are tied for smallest, and a decision rule must be incorporated to break such *time ties* (this happens with the inventory simulation considered later in Sec. 1.5). The tie-breaking rule can affect the results of the simulation, so must be chosen in accordance with

how the system is to be modeled. In many simulations, however, we can ignore the possibility of ties, since the use of continuous random variables may make their occurrence an event with probability 0. In the above model, for example, if the interarrival-time or service-time distribution is continuous, then a time tie in the event list is a probability-zero event (though it could still happen during the computer simulation due to finite accuracy in representation of real numbers).

The above exercise is intended to illustrate the changes and data structures involved in carrying out a discrete-event simulation from the event-scheduling point of view, and contains most of the important ideas needed for more complex simulations of this type. The interarrival and service times used could have been drawn from a random-number table of some sort, constructed to reflect the desired probability distributions; this would result in what might be called a *hand simulation*, which in principle could be carried out to any length. The tedium of doing this should now be clear, so we will next turn to the use of computers (which are not easily bored) to carry out the arithmetic and bookkeeping involved in longer or more complex simulations.

1.4.3 Program Organization and Logic

In this section we set up the necessary ingredients for the C program to simulate the single-server queueing system, which is given in Sec. 1.4.4.

There are several reasons for choosing a general-purpose language such as C, rather than more powerful high-level simulation software, for introducing computer simulation at this point:

- By learning to simulate in a general-purpose language, in which one must pay attention to every detail, there will be a greater understanding of how simulations actually operate, and thus less chance of conceptual errors if a switch is later made to high-level simulation software.
- Despite the fact that there is now very good and powerful simulation software available (see Chap. 3), it is sometimes necessary to write at least parts of complex simulations in a general-purpose language if the specific, detailed logic of complex systems is to be represented faithfully.
- General-purpose languages are widely available, and entire simulations are sometimes still written in this way.

It is not our purpose in this book to teach any particular simulation software in detail, although we survey several packages in Chap. 3. With the understanding promoted by our more general approach and by going through our simulations in this and the next chapter, the reader should find it easier to learn a specialized simulation-software product.

The single-server queueing model that we will simulate in the following section differs in two respects from the model used in the previous section:

- The simulation will end when $n = 1000$ delays in queue have been completed, rather than $n = 6$, in order to collect more data (and maybe to impress the reader with the patience of computers, since we have just slugged it out by hand in the $n = 6$ case in the preceding section). It is important to note that this change in the stopping rule changes the model itself, in that the output measures are defined relative to the stopping rule; hence the presence of the "n" in the notation for the quantities $d(n)$, $q(n)$, and $u(n)$ being estimated.

- The interarrival and service times will now be modeled as independent random variables from exponential distributions with mean 1 minute for the interarrival times and mean 0.5 minute for the service times. The exponential distribution with mean β (any positive real number) is continuous, with probability density function

$$f(x) = \frac{1}{\beta} e^{-x/\beta} \qquad \text{for } x \geq 0$$

(See Chaps. 4 and 6 for more information on density functions in general, and on the exponential distribution in particular.) We make this change here since it is much more common to generate input quantities (which drive the simulation) such as interarrival and service times from specified distributions than to assume that they are "known" as we did in the preceding section. The choice of the exponential distribution with the above particular values of β is essentially arbitrary, and is made primarily because it is easy to generate exponential random variates on a computer. (Actually, the assumption of exponential interarrival times is often quite realistic; assuming exponential service times, however, is less plausible.) Chapter 6 addresses in detail the important issue of how one chooses distribution forms and parameters for modeling simulation input random variables.

The single-server queue with exponential interarrival and service times is commonly called the *M/M/1 queue*, as discussed in App. 1B.

To simulate this model, we need a way to generate random variates from an exponential distribution. First, a *random-number generator* (discussed in detail in Chap. 7) is invoked to generate a variate U that is distributed (continuously) uniformly between 0 and 1; this distribution will henceforth be referred to as U(0, 1) and has probability density function

$$f(x) = \begin{cases} 1 & \text{if } 0 \leq x \leq 1 \\ 0 & \text{otherwise} \end{cases}$$

It is easy to show that the probability that a U(0, 1) random variable falls in any subinterval $[x, x + \Delta x]$ contained in the interval [0, 1] is (uniformly) Δx (see Sec. 6.2.2). The U(0, 1) distribution is fundamental to simulation modeling because, as we shall see in Chap. 8, a random variate from any distribution can be generated by first generating one or more U(0, 1) random variates and then performing some kind of transformation. After obtaining U, we shall take the natural logarithm of it, multiply the result by β, and finally change the sign to return what we will show to be an exponential random variate with mean β, that is, $-\beta \ln U$.

To see why this algorithm works, recall that the *(cumulative) distribution function* of a random variable X is defined, for any real x, to be $F(x) = P(X \leq x)$

(Chap. 4 contains a review of basic probability theory). If X is exponential with mean β, then

$$\begin{aligned} F(x) &= \int_0^x \frac{1}{\beta} e^{-t/\beta}\, dt \\ &= 1 - e^{-x/\beta} \end{aligned}$$

for any real $x \geq 0$, since the probability density function of the exponential distribution at the argument $t \geq 0$ is $(1/\beta)e^{-t/\beta}$. To show that our method is correct, we can try to verify that the value it returns will be less than or equal to x (any nonnegative real number), with probability $F(x)$ given above:

$$\begin{aligned} P(-\beta \ln U \leq x) &= P\left(\ln U \geq -\frac{x}{\beta}\right) \\ &= P(U \geq e^{-x/\beta}) \\ &= P(e^{-x/\beta} \leq U \leq 1) \\ &= 1 - e^{-x/\beta} \end{aligned}$$

The first line in the above is obtained by dividing through by $-\beta$ (recall that $\beta > 0$, so $-\beta < 0$ and the inequality reverses), the second line is obtained by exponentiating both sides (the exponential function is monotone increasing, so the inequality is preserved), the third line is just rewriting, together with knowing that U is in [0, 1] anyway, and the last line follows since U is U(0, 1), and the interval $[e^{-x/\beta}, 1]$ is contained within the interval [0, 1]. Since the last line is $F(x)$ for the exponential distribution, we have verified that our algorithm is correct. Chapter 8 discusses how to generate random variates and processes in general.

In our program, we will use a particular method for random-number generation to obtain the variate U described above, as expressed in the C code of Figs. 7.5 and 7.6 in App. 7A of Chap. 7. While most compilers do have some kind of built-in random-number generator, many of these are of extremely poor quality and should not be used; this issue is discussed fully in Chap. 7.

It is convenient (if not the most computationally efficient) to modularize the programs into several subprograms to clarify the logic and interactions, as discussed in general in Sec. 1.3.2. In addition to a main program, the simulation program includes routines for initialization, timing, report generation, and generating exponential random variates, as in Fig. 1.3. It also simplifies matters if we write a separate routine to update the continuous-time statistics, being the accumulated areas under the $Q(t)$ and $B(t)$ curves. The most important action, however, takes place in the routines for the events, which we number as follows:

Event description	**Event type**
Arrival of a customer to the system	1
Departure of a customer from the system after completing service	2

Figure 1.8 contains a flowchart for the arrival event. First, the time of the next arrival in the future is generated and placed in the event list. Then a check is made

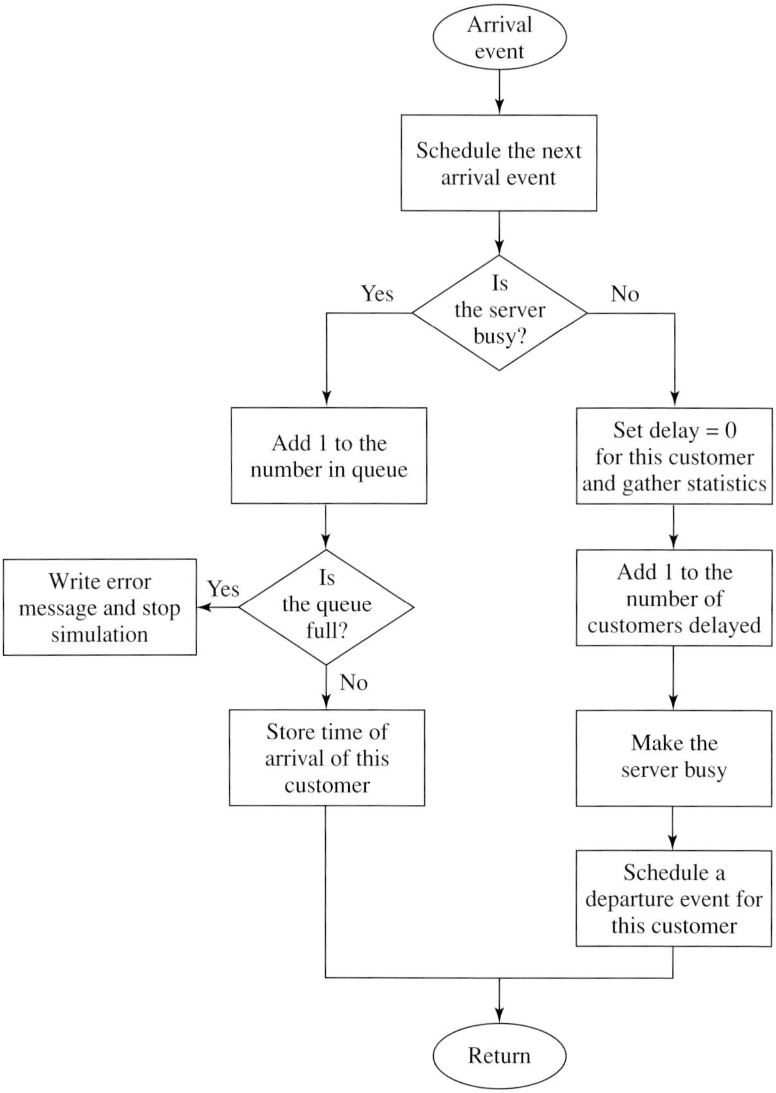

FIGURE 1.8
Flowchart for arrival routine, queueing model.

to determine whether the server is busy. If so, the number of customers in the queue is incremented by 1, and we ask whether the storage space allocated to hold the queue is already full (see the code in Sec. 1.4.4). If the queue is already full, an error message is produced and the simulation is stopped; if there is still room in the queue, the arriving customer's time of arrival is put at the (new) end of the queue. (This queue-full check could be eliminated if using dynamic storage allocation in a programming language that supports this.) On the other hand, if the arriving customer finds the server idle, then this customer has a delay of 0, which *is* counted as a delay, and the number of customer delays completed is incremented by 1. The

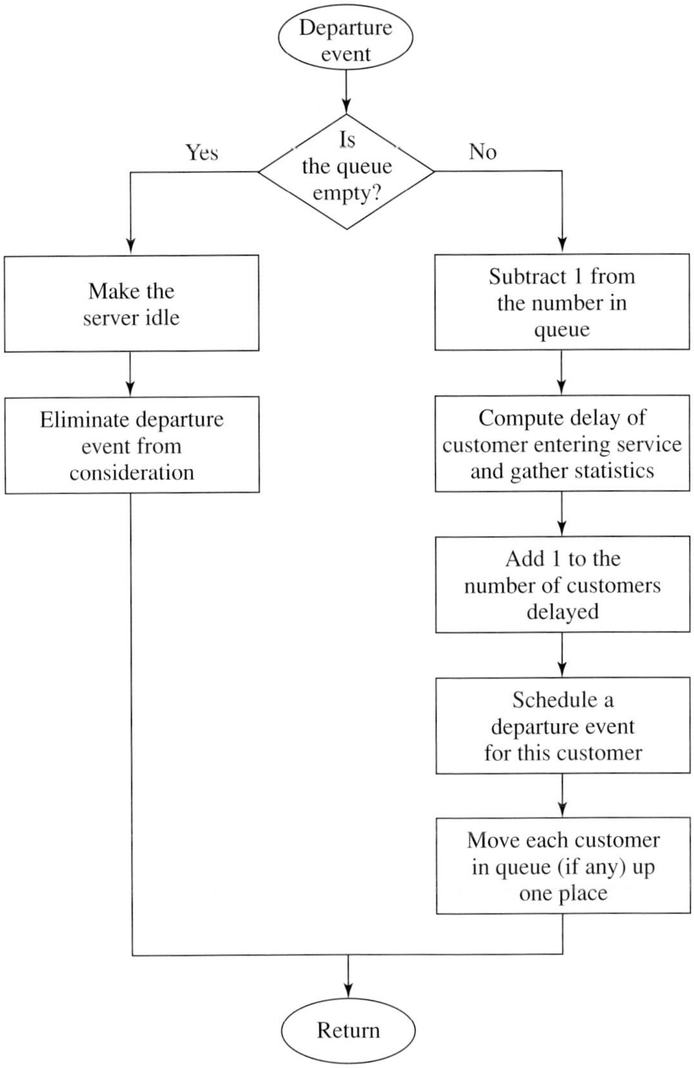

FIGURE 1.9
Flowchart for departure routine, queueing model.

server must be made busy, and the time of departure from service of the arriving customer is scheduled into the event list.

The departure event's logic is depicted in the flowchart of Fig. 1.9. Recall that this routine is invoked when a service completion (and subsequent departure) occurs. If the departing customer leaves no other customers behind in queue, the server is idled and the departure event is eliminated from consideration, since the next event must be an arrival. On the other hand, if one or more customers are left behind by the departing customer, the first customer in queue will leave the queue and enter service, so the queue length is reduced by 1, and the delay in queue of this customer is computed and registered in the appropriate statistical counter. The number delayed is increased by 1, and a departure event for the customer now entering service is scheduled. Finally, the rest of the queue (if any) is advanced one place. Our implementation of the list for the queue will be very simple in this chapter, and is certainly not the most efficient; Chap. 2 discusses better ways of handling lists to model such things as queues.

In the next section we give an example of how the above setup can be used to write a program in C. The results are discussed in Sec. 1.4.5. This program is neither the simplest nor the most efficient possible, but was instead designed to illustrate how one might organize a program for more complex simulations.

1.4.4 C Program

This section presents a C program for the *M*/*M*/1 queue simulation. We use the ANSI-standard version of the language, as defined by Kernighan and Ritchie (1988), and in particular use function prototyping. We have also taken advantage of C's facility to give variables and functions fairly long names, which thus should be self-explanatory. (For instance, the current value of simulated time is in a variable called sim_time.) We have run our C program on several different computers and compilers. The numerical results differed in some cases due to inaccuracies in floating-point operations. This can matter if, e.g., at some point in the simulation two events are scheduled very close together in time, and roundoff error results in a different sequencing of the event's occurrences. The C math library must be linked, which might require setting an option depending on the compiler. All code is available at www.mhhe.com/law.

The external definitions are given in Fig. 1.10. The header file lcgrand.h (listed in Fig. 7.6) is included to declare the functions for the random-number generator.

```
/* External definitions for single-server queueing system. */

#include <stdio.h>
#include <math.h>
#include "lcgrand.h"  /* Header file for random-number generator. */

#define Q_LIMIT 100  /* Limit on queue length. */
#define BUSY      1  /* Mnemonics for server's being busy */
#define IDLE      0  /* and idle. */

int   next_event_type, num_custs_delayed, num_delays_required, num_events,
      num_in_q, server_status;
float area_num_in_q, area_server_status, mean_interarrival, mean_service,
      sim_time, time_arrival[Q_LIMIT + 1], time_last_event, time_next_event[3],
      total_of_delays;
FILE  *infile, *outfile;

void  initialize(void);
void  timing(void);
void  arrive(void);
void  depart(void);
void  report(void);
void  update_time_avg_stats(void);
float expon(float mean);
```

FIGURE 1.10
C code for the external definitions, queueing model.

The symbolic constant Q_LIMIT is set to 100, our guess (which might have to be adjusted by trial and error) as to the longest the queue will ever get. (As mentioned earlier, this guess could be eliminated if we were using dynamic storage allocation; while C supports this, we have not used it in our examples.) The symbolic constants BUSY and IDLE are defined to be used with the server_status variable, for code readability. File pointers *infile and *outfile are defined to allow us to open the input and output files from within the code, rather than at the operating-system level. Note also that the event list, as we have discussed it so far, will be implemented in an array called time_next_event, whose 0th entry will be ignored in order to make the index agree with the event type.

The code for the main function is shown in Fig. 1.11. The input and output files are opened, and the number of event types for the simulation is initialized to 2 for this model. The input parameters then are read in from the file mm1.in, which contains a single line with the numbers 1.0, 0.5, and 1000, separated by blanks. After writing a report heading and echoing the input parameters (as a check that they were read correctly), the initialization function is invoked. The "while" loop then executes the simulation as long as more customer delays are needed to fulfill the 1000-delay stopping rule. Inside the "while" loop, the timing function is first invoked to determine the type of the next event to occur and to advance the simulation clock to its time. Before processing this event, the function to update the areas under the $Q(t)$ and $B(t)$ curves is invoked; by doing this at this time we automatically update these areas before processing each event. Then a switch statement, based on next_event_type (=1 for an arrival and 2 for a departure), passes control to the appropriate event function. After the "while" loop is done, the report function is invoked, the input and output files are closed, and the simulation ends.

Code for the initialization function is given in Fig. 1.12. Each statement here corresponds to an element of the computer representation in Fig. 1.7*a*. Note that the time of the first arrival, time_next_event[1], is determined by adding an exponential random variate with mean mean_interarrival, namely, expon(mean_interarrival), to the simulation clock, sim_time = 0. (We explicitly used "sim_time" in this statement, although it has a value of 0, to show the general form of a statement to determine the time of a future event.) Since no customers are present at time sim_time = 0, the time of the next departure, time_next_event[2], is set to 1.0e + 30 (C notation for 10^{30}), guaranteeing that the first event will be an arrival.

The timing function, which is given in Fig. 1.13, is used to compare time_next_event[1], time_next_event[2], . . . , time_next_event[num_events] (recall that num_events was set in the main function) and to set next_event_type equal to the event type whose time of occurrence is the smallest. In case of ties, the lowest-numbered event type is chosen. Then the simulation clock is advanced to the time of occurrence of the chosen event type, min_time_next_event. The program is complicated slightly by an error check for the event list's being empty, which we define to mean that all events are scheduled to occur at time $= 10^{30}$. If this is ever the case (as indicated by next_event_type = 0), an error message is produced along with the current clock time (as a possible debugging aid), and the simulation is terminated.

```
main()  /* Main function. */
{
    /* Open input and output files. */

    infile  = fopen("mm1.in",  "r");
    outfile = fopen("mm1.out", "w");

    /* Specify the number of events for the timing function. */

    num_events = 2;

    /* Read input parameters. */

    fscanf(infile, "%f %f %d", &mean_interarrival, &mean_service,
           &num_delays_required);

    /* Write report heading and input parameters. */

    fprintf(outfile, "Single-server queueing system\n\n");
    fprintf(outfile, "Mean interarrival time%11.3f minutes\n\n",
            mean_interarrival);
    fprintf(outfile, "Mean service time%16.3f minutes\n\n", mean_service);
    fprintf(outfile, "Number of customers%14d\n\n", num_delays_required);

    /* Initialize the simulation. */

    initialize();

    /* Run the simulation while more delays are still needed. */

    while (num_custs_delayed < num_delays_required) {

        /* Determine the next event. */

        timing();

        /* Update time-average statistical accumulators. */

        update_time_avg_stats();

        /* Invoke the appropriate event function. */

        switch (next_event_type) {
            case 1:
                arrive();
                break;
            case 2:
                depart();
                break;
        }
    }

    /* Invoke the report generator and end the simulation. */

    report();

    fclose(infile);
    fclose(outfile);

    return 0;
}
```

FIGURE 1.11
C code for the main function, queueing model.

```
void initialize(void)  /* Initialization function. */
{
    /* Initialize the simulation clock. */

    sim_time = 0.0;

    /* Initialize the state variables. */

    server_status   = IDLE;
    num_in_q        = 0;
    time_last_event = 0.0;

    /* Initialize the statistical counters. */

    num_custs_delayed  = 0;
    total_of_delays    = 0.0;
    area_num_in_q      = 0.0;
    area_server_status = 0.0;

    /* Initialize event list.  Since no customers are present, the departure
       (service completion) event is eliminated from consideration. */

    time_next_event[1] = sim_time + expon(mean_interarrival);
    time_next_event[2] = 1.0e+30;
}
```

FIGURE 1.12
C code for function initialize, queueing model.

```
void timing(void)  /* Timing function. */
{
    int   i;
    float min_time_next_event = 1.0e+29;

    next_event_type = 0;

    /* Determine the event type of the next event to occur. */

    for (i = 1; i <= num_events; ++i)
        if (time_next_event[i] < min_time_next_event) {
            min_time_next_event = time_next_event[i];
            next_event_type     = i;
        }

    /* Check to see whether the event list is empty. */

    if (next_event_type == 0) {

        /* The event list is empty, so stop the simulation. */

        fprintf(outfile, "\nEvent list empty at time %f", sim_time);
        exit(1);
    }

    /* The event list is not empty, so advance the simulation clock. */

    sim_time = min_time_next_event;
}
```

FIGURE 1.13
C code for function timing, queueing model.

```
void arrive(void)  /* Arrival event function. */
{
    float delay;

    /* Schedule next arrival. */

    time_next_event[1] = sim_time + expon(mean_interarrival);

    /* Check to see whether server is busy. */

    if (server_status == BUSY) {

        /* Server is busy, so increment number of customers in queue. */

        ++num_in_q;

        /* Check to see whether an overflow condition exists. */

        if (num_in_q > Q_LIMIT) {

            /* The queue has overflowed, so stop the simulation. */

            fprintf(outfile, "\nOverflow of the array time_arrival at");
            fprintf(outfile, " time %f", sim_time);
            exit(2);
        }

        /* There is still room in the queue, so store the time of arrival of the
           arriving customer at the (new) end of time_arrival. */

        time_arrival[num_in_q] = sim_time;
    }

    else {

        /* Server is idle, so arriving customer has a delay of zero.  (The
           following two statements are for program clarity and do not affect
           the results of the simulation.) */

        delay            = 0.0;
        total_of_delays += delay;

        /* Increment the number of customers delayed, and make server busy. */

        ++num_custs_delayed;
        server_status = BUSY;

        /* Schedule a departure (service completion). */

        time_next_event[2] = sim_time + expon(mean_service);
    }
}
```

FIGURE 1.14
C code for function arrive, queueing model.

The code for event function arrive is in Fig. 1.14, and follows the discussion as given in Sec. 1.4.3 and in the flowchart of Fig. 1.8. Note that "sim_time" is the time of arrival of the customer who is just now arriving, and that the queue-overflow check is made by asking whether num_in_q is now greater than Q_LIMIT, the length for which the array time_arrival was dimensioned.

Event function depart, whose code is shown in Fig. 1.15, is invoked from the main program when a service completion (and subsequent departure) occurs; the

```
void depart(void)  /* Departure event function. */
{
    int   i;
    float delay;

    /* Check to see whether the queue is empty. */

    if (num_in_q == 0) {

        /* The queue is empty so make the server idle and eliminate the
           departure (service completion) event from consideration. */

        server_status      = IDLE;
        time_next_event[2] = 1.0e+30;
    }

    else {

        /* The queue is nonempty, so decrement the number of customers in
           queue. */

        --num_in_q;

        /* Compute the delay of the customer who is beginning service and update
           the total delay accumulator. */

        delay            = sim_time - time_arrival[1];
        total_of_delays += delay;

        /* Increment the number of customers delayed, and schedule departure. */

        ++num_custs_delayed;
        time_next_event[2] = sim_time + expon(mean_service);

        /* Move each customer in queue (if any) up one place. */

        for (i = 1; i <= num_in_q; ++i)
            time_arrival[i] = time_arrival[i + 1];
    }
}
```

FIGURE 1.15
C code for function depart, queueing model.

logic for it was discussed in Sec. 1.4.3, with the flowchart in Fig. 1.9. Note that if the statement "time_next_event[2] = 1.0e + 30;" just before the "else" were omitted, the program would get into an infinite loop. (Why?) Advancing the rest of the queue (if any) one place by the "for" loop near the end of the function ensures that the arrival time of the next customer entering service (after being delayed in queue) will always be stored in time_arrival[1]. Note that if the queue were now empty (i.e., the customer who just left the queue and entered service had been the only one in queue), then num_in_q would be equal to 0, and this loop would not be executed at all since the beginning value of the loop index, i, starts out at a value (1) that would already exceed its final value (num_in_q = 0). (Managing the queue in this simple way is certainly inefficient, and could be improved by using pointers; we return to this issue in Chap. 2.) A final comment about depart concerns the subtraction of time_arrival[1] from the clock value, sim_time, to obtain the delay in queue. If the simulation is to run for a long period of (simulated) time, both sim_time and time_arrival[1] would become very large numbers in comparison with the

```
void report(void)  /* Report generator function. */
{
    /* Compute and write estimates of desired measures of performance. */

    fprintf(outfile, "\n\nAverage delay in queue%11.3f minutes\n\n",
            total_of_delays / num_custs_delayed);
    fprintf(outfile, "Average number in queue%10.3f\n\n",
            area_num_in_q / sim_time);
    fprintf(outfile, "Server utilization%15.3f\n\n",
            area_server_status / sim_time);
    fprintf(outfile, "Time simulation ended%12.3f minutes", sim_time);
}
```

FIGURE 1.16
C code for function report, queueing model.

difference between them; thus, since they are both stored as floating-point (float) numbers with finite accuracy, there is potentially a serious loss of precision when doing this subtraction. For this reason, it may be necessary to make both sim_time and the time_arrival array of type double if we are to run this simulation out for a long period of time.

The code for the report function, invoked when the "while" loop in the main program is over, is given in Fig. 1.16. The average delay is computed by dividing the total of the delays by the number of customers whose delays were observed, and the time-average number in queue is obtained by dividing the area under $Q(t)$, now updated to the end of the simulation (since the function to update the areas is called from the main program before processing either an arrival or departure, one of which will end the simulation), by the clock value at termination. The server utilization is computed by dividing the area under $B(t)$ by the final clock time, and all three measures are written out directly. We also write out the final clock value itself, to see how long it took to observe the 1000 delays.

Function update_time_avg_stats is shown in Fig. 1.17. This function is invoked just before processing each event (of any type) and updates the areas under the two functions needed for the continuous-time statistics; this routine is separate for

```
void update_time_avg_stats(void)  /* Update area accumulators for time-average
                                      statistics. */
{
    float time_since_last_event;

    /* Compute time since last event, and update last-event-time marker. */

    time_since_last_event = sim_time - time_last_event;
    time_last_event       = sim_time;

    /* Update area under number-in-queue function. */

    area_num_in_q      += num_in_q * time_since_last_event;

    /* Update area under server-busy indicator function. */

    area_server_status += server_status * time_since_last_event;
}
```

FIGURE 1.17
C code for function update_time_avg_stats, queueing model.

```
float expon(float mean)  /* Exponential variate generation function. */
{
    /* Return an exponential random variate with mean "mean". */

    return -mean * log(lcgrand(1));
}
```

FIGURE 1.18
C code for function expon.

coding convenience only, and is *not* an event routine. The time since the last event is first computed, and then the time of the last event is brought up to the current time in order to be ready for the next entry into this function. Then the area under the number-in-queue function is augmented by the area of the rectangle under $Q(t)$ during the interval since the previous event, which is of width time_since_last_event and of height num_in_q; remember, this function is invoked *before* processing an event, and state variables such as num_in_q still have their previous values. The area under $B(t)$ is then augmented by the area of a rectangle of width time_since_last_event and height server_status; this is why it is convenient to define server_status to be either 0 or 1. Note that this function, like depart, contains a subtraction of two floating-point numbers (sim_time − time_last_event), both of which could become quite large relative to their difference if we were to run the simulation for a long time; in this case it might be necessary to declare both sim_time and time_last_event to be of type double.

The function expon, which generates an exponential random variate with mean β = mean (passed into expon), is shown in Fig. 1.18, and follows the algorithm discussed in Sec. 1.4.3. The random-number generator lcgrand, used here with an int argument of 1, is discussed fully in Chap. 7, and is shown specifically in Fig. 7.5. The C predefined function log returns the natural logarithm of its argument.

The program described here must be combined with the random-number-generator code from Fig. 7.5. This could be done by separate compilations, followed by linking the object codes together in an installation-dependent way.

1.4.5 Simulation Output and Discussion

The output (in a file named mm1.out) is shown in Fig. 1.19. In this run, the average delay in queue was 0.430 minute, there was an average of 0.418 customer in the queue, and the server was busy 46 percent of the time. It took 1027.915 simulated minutes to run the simulation to the completion of 1000 delays, which seems reasonable since the expected time between customer arrivals was 1 minute. (It is not a coincidence that the average delay, average number in queue, and utilization are all so close together for this model; see App. 1B.)

Note that these particular numbers in the output were determined, at root, by the numbers the random-number generator happened to come up with this time. If a different random-number generator were used, or if this one were used in another way (with another "seed" or "stream," as discussed in Chap. 7), then different numbers would have been produced in the output. Thus, these numbers are not to be regarded

```
Single-server queueing system

Mean interarrival time         1.000 minutes

Mean service time              0.500 minutes

Number of customers             1000


Average delay in queue         0.430 minutes

Average number in queue        0.418

Server utilization             0.460

Time simulation ended       1027.915 minutes
```

FIGURE 1.19
Output report, queueing model.

as "The Answers," but rather as estimates (and perhaps poor ones) of the expected quantities we want to know about, $d(n)$, $q(n)$, and $u(n)$; the statistical analysis of simulation output data is discussed in Chaps. 9 through 12. Also, the results are functions of the input parameters, in this case the mean interarrival and service times, and the $n = 1000$ stopping rule; they are also affected by the way we initialized the simulation (empty and idle).

In some simulation studies, we might want to estimate *steady-state* characteristics of the model (see Chap. 9), i.e., characteristics of a model after the simulation has been running a very long (in theory, an infinite amount of) time. For the simple *M/M/*1 queue we have been considering, it is possible to compute *analytically* the steady-state average delay in queue, the steady-state time-average number in queue, and the steady-state server utilization, all of these measures of performance being 0.5 [see, e.g., Ross (2003, pp. 480–487)]. Thus, if we wanted to determine these steady-state measures, our estimates based on the stopping rule $n = 1000$ delays were not too far off, at least in absolute terms. However, we were somewhat lucky, since $n = 1000$ was chosen arbitrarily! In practice, the choice of a stopping rule that will give good estimates of steady-state measures is quite difficult. To illustrate this point, suppose for the *M/M/*1 queue that the arrival rate of customers were increased from 1 per minute to 1.98 per minute (the mean interarrival time is now 0.505 minute), that the mean service time is unchanged, and that we wish to estimate the steady-state measures from a run of length $n = 1000$ delays, as before. We performed this simulation run and got values for the average delay, average number in queue, and server utilization of 17.404 minutes, 34.831, and 0.997, respectively. Since the true steady-state values of these measures are 49.5 minutes, 98.01, and 0.99 (respectively), it is clear that the stopping rule cannot be chosen arbitrarily. We discuss how to specify the run length for a steady-state simulation in Chap. 9.

The reader may have wondered why we did not estimate the expected average waiting time in the system of a customer, $w(n)$, rather than the expected average delay in queue, $d(n)$, where the waiting time of a customer is defined as the time interval from the instant the customer arrives to the instant the customer completes service and departs. There were two reasons. First, for many queueing systems we believe that the customer's delay in queue while waiting for other customers to be served is the most troublesome part of the customer's wait in the system. Moreover, if the queue represents part of a manufacturing system where the "customers" are actually parts waiting for service at a machine (the "server"), then the delay in queue represents a loss, whereas the time spent in service is "necessary." Our second reason for focusing on the delay in queue is one of statistical efficiency. The usual estimator of $w(n)$ would be

$$\hat{w}(n) = \frac{\sum_{i=1}^{n} W_i}{n} = \frac{\sum_{i=1}^{n} D_i}{n} + \frac{\sum_{i=1}^{n} S_i}{n} = \hat{d}(n) + \overline{S}(n) \tag{1.7}$$

where $W_i = D_i + S_i$ is the waiting time in the system of the ith customer and $\overline{S}(n)$ is the average of the n customers' service times. Since the service-time distribution would have to be known to perform a simulation in the first place, the expected or mean service time, $E(S)$, would also be known and an alternative estimator of $w(n)$ is

$$\tilde{w}(n) = \hat{d}(n) + E(S)$$

[Note that $\overline{S}(n)$ is an unbiased estimator of $E(S)$ in Eq. (1.7).] In almost all queueing simulations, $\tilde{w}(n)$ will be a more efficient (less variable) estimator of $w(n)$ than $\hat{w}(n)$ and is thus preferable (both estimators are unbiased). Therefore, if one wants an estimate of $w(n)$, estimate $d(n)$ and add the known expected service time, $E(S)$. In general, the moral is to replace estimators by their expected values whenever possible (see the discussion of indirect estimators in Sec. 11.5).

1.4.6 Alternative Stopping Rules

In the above queueing example, the simulation was terminated when the number of customers delayed became equal to 1000; the final value of the simulation clock was thus a random variable. However, for many real-world models, the simulation is to stop after some fixed amount of time, say 8 hours. Since the interarrival and service times for our example are continuous random variables, the probability of the simulation's terminating after exactly 480 minutes is 0 (neglecting the finite accuracy of a computer). Therefore, to stop the simulation at a specified time, we introduce a dummy "end-simulation" event (call it an event of type 3), which is scheduled to occur at time 480. When the time of occurrence of this event (being held in the third spot of the event list) is less than all other entries in the event list, the report generator is called and the simulation is terminated. The number of customers delayed is now a random variable.

These ideas can be implemented in the program by making changes in the external definitions, the main function, and the initialize and report functions, as shown in Figs. 1.20 through 1.23; the rest of the program is unaltered. In Figs. 1.20 and 1.21, note that we now have three events; that the desired simulation run length, time_end, is now an input parameter (num_delays_required has been removed); and

```
/* External definitions for single-server queueing system, fixed run length. */

#include <stdio.h>
#include <math.h>
#include "lcgrand.h"  /* Header file for random-number generator. */

#define Q_LIMIT 100  /* Limit on queue length. */
#define BUSY      1  /* Mnemonics for server's being busy */
#define IDLE      0  /* and idle. */

int   next_event_type, num_custs_delayed, num_events, num_in_q, server_status;
float area_num_in_q, area_server_status, mean_interarrival, mean_service,
      sim_time, time_arrival[Q_LIMIT + 1], time_end, time_last_event,
      time_next_event[4], total_of_delays;
FILE  *infile, *outfile;

void  initialize(void);
void  timing(void);
void  arrive(void);
void  depart(void);
void  report(void);
void  update_time_avg_stats(void);
float expon(float mean);
```

FIGURE 1.20
C code for the external definitions, queueing model with fixed run length.

that the "switch" statement has been changed. To stop the simulation, the original "while" loop has been replaced by a "do while" loop in Fig. 1.21, where the loop keeps repeating itself as long as the type of event just executed is not 3 (end simulation); after a type 3 event is chosen for execution, the loop ends and the simulation stops. In the main program (as before), we invoke update_time_avg_stats before entering an event function, so that in particular the areas will be updated to the end of the simulation here when the type 3 event (end simulation) is next. The only change to the initialization function in Fig. 1.22 is the addition of the statement time_next_event[3] = time_end, which schedules the end of the simulation. The only change to the report function in Fig. 1.23 is to write the number of customers delayed instead of the time the simulation ends, since in this case we know that the ending time will be 480 minutes but will not know how many customer delays will have been completed during that time.

The output file (named mm1alt.out) is shown in Fig. 1.24. The number of customer delays completed was 475 in this run, which seems reasonable in a 480-minute run where customers are arriving at an average rate of 1 per minute. The same three measures of performance are again numerically close to each other, but the first two are somewhat less than their earlier values in the 1000-delay simulation. A possible reason for this is that the current run is roughly only half as long as the earlier one, and since the initial conditions for the simulation are empty and idle (an uncongested state), the model in this shorter run has less chance to become congested. Again, however, this is just a single run and is thus subject to perhaps considerable uncertainty; there is no easy way to assess the degree of uncertainty from only a single run.

If the queueing system being considered had actually been a one-operator barbershop open from 9 A.M. to 5 P.M., stopping the simulation after exactly 8 hours

```
main()  /* Main function. */
{
    /* Open input and output files. */

    infile  = fopen("mm1alt.in",  "r");
    outfile = fopen("mm1alt.out", "w");

    /* Specify the number of events for the timing function. */

    num_events = 3;

    /* Read input parameters. */

    fscanf(infile, "%f %f %f", &mean_interarrival, &mean_service, &time_end);

    /* Write report heading and input parameters. */

    fprintf(outfile, "Single-server queueing system with fixed run");
    fprintf(outfile, " length\n\n");
    fprintf(outfile, "Mean interarrival time%11.3f minutes\n\n",
            mean_interarrival);
    fprintf(outfile, "Mean service time%16.3f minutes\n\n", mean_service);
    fprintf(outfile, "Length of the simulation%9.3f minutes\n\n", time_end);

    /* Initialize the simulation. */

    initialize();

    /* Run the simulation until it terminates after an end-simulation event
       (type 3) occurs. */

    do {

        /* Determine the next event. */

        timing();

        /* Update time-average statistical accumulators. */

        update_time_avg_stats();

        /* Invoke the appropriate event function. */

        switch (next_event_type) {
            case 1:
                arrive();
                break;
            case 2:
                depart();
                break;
            case 3:
                report();
                break;
        }

    /* If the event just executed was not the end-simulation event (type 3),
       continue simulating.  Otherwise, end the simulation. */

    } while (next_event_type != 3);

    fclose(infile);
    fclose(outfile);

    return 0;
}
```

FIGURE 1.21
C code for the main function, queueing model with fixed run length.

```
void initialize(void)  /* Initialization function. */
{
    /* Initialize the simulation clock. */

    sim_time = 0.0;

    /* Initialize the state variables. */

    server_status   = IDLE;
    num_in_q        = 0;
    time_last_event = 0.0;

    /* Initialize the statistical counters. */

    num_custs_delayed  = 0;
    total_of_delays    = 0.0;
    area_num_in_q      = 0.0;
    area_server_status = 0.0;

    /* Initialize event list.  Since no customers are present, the departure
       (service completion) event is eliminated from consideration.  The end-
       simulation event (type 3) is scheduled for time time_end. */

    time_next_event[1] = sim_time + expon(mean_interarrival);
    time_next_event[2] = 1.0e+30;
    time_next_event[3] = time_end;
}
```

FIGURE 1.22
C code for function initialize, queueing model with fixed run length.

```
void report(void)  /* Report generator function. */
{
    /* Compute and write estimates of desired measures of performance. */

    fprintf(outfile, "\n\nAverage delay in queue%11.3f minutes\n\n",
            total_of_delays / num_custs_delayed);
    fprintf(outfile, "Average number in queue%10.3f\n\n",
            area_num_in_q / sim_time);
    fprintf(outfile, "Server utilization%15.3f\n\n",
            area_server_status / sim_time);
    fprintf(outfile, "Number of delays completed%7d",
            num_custs_delayed);
}
```

FIGURE 1.23
C code for function report, queueing model with fixed run length.

```
Single-server queueing system with fixed run length

Mean interarrival time      1.000 minutes

Mean service time           0.500 minutes

Length of the simulation  480.000 minutes


Average delay in queue      0.399 minutes

Average number in queue     0.394

Server utilization          0.464

Number of delays completed    475
```

FIGURE 1.24
Output report, queueing model with fixed run length.

might leave a customer with hair partially cut. In such a case, we might want to close the door of the barbershop after 8 hours but continue to run the simulation until all customers present when the door closes (if any) have been served. The reader is asked in Prob. 1.10 to supply the program changes necessary to implement this stopping rule (see also Sec. 2.6).

1.4.7 Determining the Events and Variables

We defined an event in Sec. 1.3 as an instantaneous occurrence that may change the system state, and in the simple single-server queue of Sec. 1.4.1 it was not too hard to identify the events. However, the question sometimes arises, especially for complex systems, of how one determines the number and definition of events in general for a model. It may also be difficult to specify the state variables needed to keep the simulation running in the correct event sequence and to obtain the desired output measures. There is no completely general way to answer these questions, and different people may come up with different ways of representing a model in terms of events and variables, all of which may be correct. But there are some principles and techniques to help simplify the model's structure and to avoid logical errors.

Schruben (1983b) presented an *event-graph* method, which was subsequently refined and extended by Sargent (1988) and Som and Sargent (1989). In this approach proposed events, each represented by a *node*, are connected by *directed arcs* (arrows) depicting how events may be scheduled from other events and from themselves. For example, in the queueing simulation of Sec. 1.4.3, the arrival event schedules another future occurrence of itself and (possibly) a departure event, and the departure event may schedule another future occurrence of itself; in addition, the arrival event must be initially scheduled in order to get the simulation going. Event graphs connect the proposed set of events (nodes) by arcs indicating the type of event scheduling that can occur. In Fig. 1.25 we show the event graph for our single-server queueing system, where the heavy, smooth arrows indicate that an event at the end of the arrow *may* be scheduled from the event at the beginning of the arrow in a (possibly) *nonzero* amount of time, and the thin jagged arrow indicates that the event at its end is scheduled initially. Thus, the arrival event reschedules itself and may schedule a departure (in the case of an arrival who finds the server idle), and the departure event may reschedule itself (if a departure leaves behind someone else in queue).

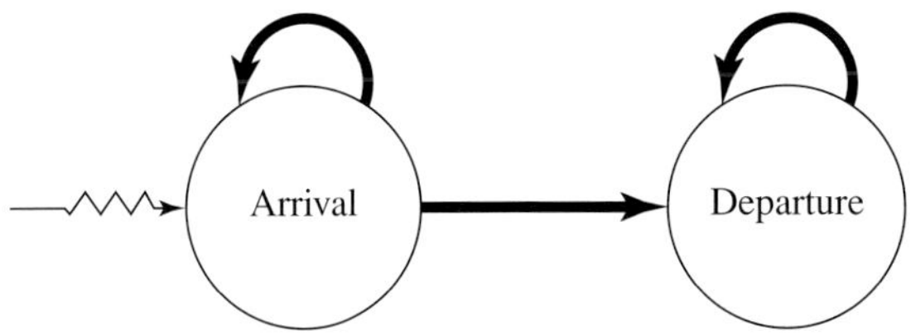

FIGURE 1.25
Event graph, queueing model.

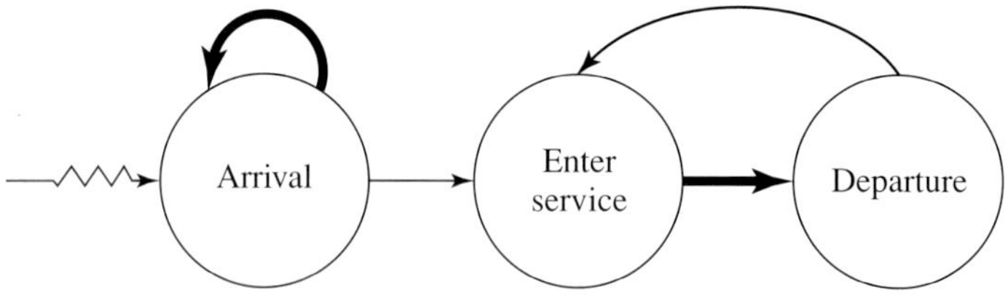

FIGURE 1.26
Event graph, queueing model with separate "enter-service" event.

For this model, it could be asked why we did not explicitly account for the act of a customer's entering service (either from the queue or upon arrival) as a separate event. This certainly can happen, and it could cause the state to change (i.e., the queue length to fall by 1). In fact, this could have been put in as a separate event without making the simulation incorrect, and would give rise to the event diagram in Fig. 1.26. The two thin smooth arrows each represent an event at the beginning of an arrow potentially scheduling an event at the end of the arrow without any intervening time, i.e., immediately; in this case the straight thin smooth arrow refers to a customer who arrives to an empty system and whose "enter-service" event is thus scheduled to occur immediately, and the curved thin smooth arrow represents a customer departing with a queue left behind, and so the first customer in the queue would be scheduled to enter service immediately. The number of events has now increased by 1, and so we have a somewhat more complicated representation of our model. One of the uses of event graphs is to simplify a simulation's event structure by eliminating unnecessary events. There are several "rules" that allow for simplification, and one of them is that if an event node has incoming arcs that are all thin and smooth (i.e., the only way this event is scheduled is by other events and without any intervening time), then this event can be eliminated from the model and its action built into the events that schedule it in zero time. Here, the "enter-service" event could be eliminated, and its action put partly into the arrival event (when a customer arrives to an idle server and begins service immediately) and partly into the departure event (when a customer finishes service and there is a queue from which the next customer is taken to enter service); this takes us back to the simpler event graph in Fig. 1.25. Basically, "events" that can happen only in conjunction with other events do not need to be in the model. Reducing the number of events not only simplifies model conceptualization, but may also speed its execution. Care must be taken, however, when "collapsing" events in this way to handle priorities and time ties appropriately.

Another rule has to do with initialization. The event graph is decomposed into *strongly connected* components, within each of which it is possible to "travel" from every node to every other node by following the arcs in their indicated directions. The graph in Fig. 1.25 decomposes into two strongly connected components (with a single node in each), and that in Fig. 1.26 has two strongly connected components (one of which is the arrival node by itself, and the other of which consists of the enter-service and departure nodes). The initialization rule states that in any strongly

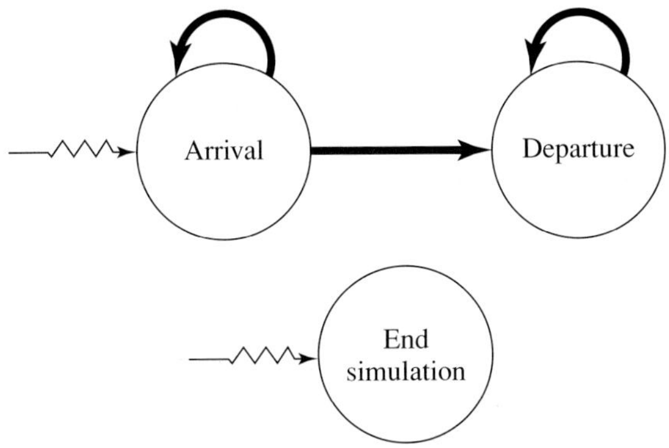

FIGURE 1.27
Event graph, queueing model with fixed run length.

connected component of nodes that has no incoming arcs from other event nodes outside the component, there must be at least one node that is initially scheduled; if this rule were violated, it would never be possible to execute any of the events in the component. In Figs. 1.25 and 1.26, the arrival node is such a strongly connected component since it has no incoming arcs from other nodes, and so it must be initialized. Figure 1.27 shows the event graph for the queueing model of Sec. 1.4.6 with the fixed run length, for which we introduced the dummy "end-simulation" event. Note that this event is itself a strongly connected component without any arcs coming in, and so it must be initialized; i.e., the end of the simulation is scheduled as part of the initialization. Failure to do so would result in erroneous termination of the simulation.

We have presented only a partial and simplified account of the event-graph technique. There are several other features, including event-canceling relations, ways to combine similar events into one, refining the event-scheduling arcs to include conditional scheduling, and incorporating the state variables needed; see the original paper by Schruben (1983b). Sargent (1988) and Som and Sargent (1989) extend and refine the technique, giving comprehensive illustrations involving a flexible manufacturing system and computer network models. Event graphs can also be used to test whether two apparently different models might in fact be equivalent [Yücesan and Schruben (1992)], as well as to forecast how computationally intensive a model will be when it is executed [Yücesan and Schruben (1998)]. Schruben and Schruben (www.sigmawiki.com) developed a software package, SIGMA, for interactive event-graph modeling that runs a model and generates source code. A general event-graph review and tutorial are given by Buss (1996), and advanced applications of event graphs are described in Schruben et al. (2003).

In modeling a system, the event-graph technique can be used to simplify the structure and to detect certain kinds of errors, and is especially useful in complex models involving a large number of interrelated events. Other considerations should also be kept in mind, such as continually asking why a particular state variable is needed; see Prob. 1.4.

1.5 SIMULATION OF AN INVENTORY SYSTEM

We shall now see how simulation can be used to compare alternative ordering policies for an inventory system. Many of the elements of our model are representative of those found in actual inventory systems.

1.5.1 Problem Statement

A company that sells a single product would like to decide how many items it should have in inventory for each of the next n months (n is a fixed input parameter). The times between demands are IID exponential random variables with a mean of 0.1 month. The sizes of the demands, D, are IID random variables (independent of when the demands occur), with

$$D = \begin{cases} 1 & \text{w.p. } \frac{1}{6} \\ 2 & \text{w.p. } \frac{1}{3} \\ 3 & \text{w.p. } \frac{1}{3} \\ 4 & \text{w.p. } \frac{1}{6} \end{cases}$$

where w.p. is read "with probability."

At the beginning of each month, the company reviews the inventory level and decides how many items to order from its supplier. If the company orders Z items, it incurs a cost of $K + iZ$, where $K = \$32$ is the *setup cost* and $i = \$3$ is the *incremental cost* per item ordered. (If $Z = 0$, no cost is incurred.) When an order is placed, the time required for it to arrive (called the *delivery lag* or *lead time*) is a random variable that is distributed uniformly between 0.5 and 1 month.

The company uses a stationary (s, S) policy to decide how much to order, i.e.,

$$Z = \begin{cases} S - I & \text{if } I < s \\ 0 & \text{if } I \geq s \end{cases}$$

where I is the inventory level at the beginning of the month.

When a demand occurs, it is satisfied immediately if the inventory level is at least as large as the demand. If the demand exceeds the inventory level, the excess of demand over supply is backlogged and satisfied by future deliveries. (In this case, the new inventory level is equal to the old inventory level minus the demand size, resulting in a negative inventory level.) When an order arrives, it is first used to eliminate as much of the backlog (if any) as possible; the remainder of the order (if any) is added to the inventory.

So far, we have discussed only one type of cost incurred by the inventory system, the ordering cost. However, most real inventory systems also have two additional types of costs, *holding* and *shortage* costs, which we discuss after introducing some additional notation. Let $I(t)$ be the inventory level at time t [note that $I(t)$ could be positive, negative, or zero]; let $I^+(t) = \max\{I(t), 0\}$ be the number of items physically on hand in the inventory at time t [note that $I^+(t) \geq 0$]; and

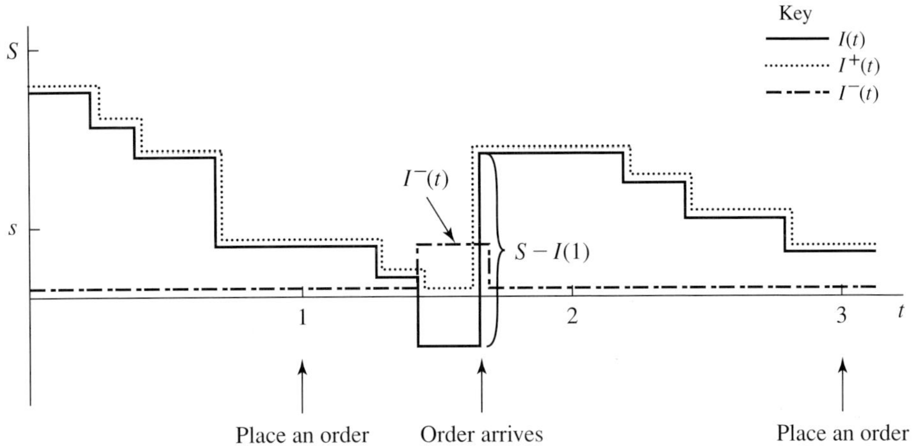

FIGURE 1.28
A realization of $I(t)$, $I^+(t)$, and $I^-(t)$ over time.

let $I^-(t) = \max\{-I(t), 0\}$ be the backlog at time t [$I^-(t) \geq 0$ as well]. A possible realization of $I(t)$, $I^+(t)$, and $I^-(t)$ is shown in Fig. 1.28. The time points at which $I(t)$ decreases are the ones at which demands occur.

For our model, we shall assume that the company incurs a holding cost of $h = \$1$ per item per month held in (positive) inventory. The holding cost includes such costs as warehouse rental, insurance, taxes, and maintenance, as well as the opportunity cost of having capital tied up in inventory rather than invested elsewhere. We have ignored in our formulation the fact that some holding costs are still incurred when $I^+(t) = 0$. However, since our goal is to *compare* ordering policies, ignoring this factor, which after all is independent of the policy used, will not affect our assessment of which policy is best. Now, since $I^+(t)$ is the number of items held in inventory at time t, the time-average (per month) number of items held in inventory for the n-month period is

$$\bar{I}^+ = \frac{\int_0^n I^+(t)\, dt}{n}$$

which is akin to the definition of the time-average number of customers in queue given in Sec. 1.4.1. Thus, the average holding cost per month is $h\bar{I}^+$.

Similarly, suppose that the company incurs a backlog cost of $\pi = \$5$ per item per month in backlog; this accounts for the cost of extra record keeping when a backlog exists, as well as loss of customers' goodwill. The time-average number of items in backlog is

$$\bar{I}^- = \frac{\int_0^n I^-(t)\, dt}{n}$$

so the average backlog cost per month is $\pi\bar{I}^-$.

Assume that the initial inventory level is $I(0) = 60$ and that no order is outstanding. We simulate the inventory system for $n = 120$ months and use the average total cost per month (which is the sum of the average ordering cost per month, the average holding cost per month, and the average shortage cost per month) to compare the following nine inventory policies:

s	20	20	20	20	40	40	40	60	60
S	40	60	80	100	60	80	100	80	100

We do not address here the issue of how these particular policies were chosen for consideration; statistical techniques for making such a determination are discussed in Chap. 12.

Note that the state variables for a simulation model of this inventory system are the inventory level $I(t)$, the amount of an outstanding order from the company to the supplier, and the time of the last event [which is needed to compute the areas under the $I^+(t)$ and $I^-(t)$ functions].

1.5.2 Program Organization and Logic

Our model of the inventory system uses the following types of events:

Event description	Event type
Arrival of an order to the company from the supplier	1
Demand for the product from a customer	2
End of the simulation after n months	3
Inventory evaluation (and possible ordering) at the beginning of a month	4

We have chosen to make the end of the simulation event type 3 rather than type 4, since at time 120 both "end-simulation" and "inventory-evaluation" events will eventually be scheduled and we would like to execute the former event first at this time. (Since the simulation is over at time 120, there is no sense in evaluating the inventory and possibly ordering, incurring an ordering cost for an order that will never arrive.) The execution of event type 3 before event type 4 is guaranteed because the timing routine gives preference to the lowest-numbered event if two or more events are scheduled to occur at the same time. In general, a simulation model should be designed to process events in an appropriate order when time ties occur. An event graph (see Sec. 1.4.7) appears in Fig. 1.29.

There are three types of random variates needed to simulate this system. The interdemand times are distributed exponentially, so the same algorithm (and code) as developed in Sec. 1.4 can be used here. The demand-size random variate D must be discrete, as described above, and can be generated as follows. First divide the unit interval into the contiguous subintervals $C_1 = [0, \frac{1}{6})$, $C_2 = [\frac{1}{6}, \frac{1}{2})$, $C_3 = [\frac{1}{2}, \frac{5}{6})$, and $C_4 = [\frac{5}{6}, 1]$, and obtain a U(0, 1) random variate U from the random-number

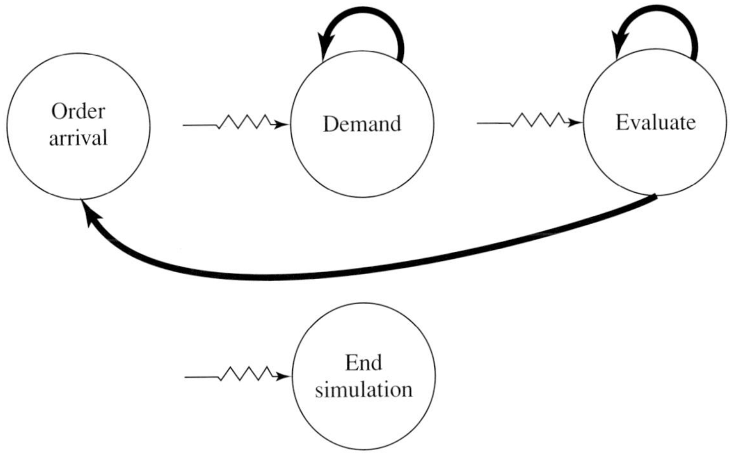

FIGURE 1.29
Event graph, inventory model.

generator. If U falls in C_1, return $D = 1$; if U falls in C_2, return $D = 2$; and so on. Since the width of C_1 is $\frac{1}{6} - 0 = \frac{1}{6}$, and since U is uniformly distributed over [0, 1], the probability that U falls in C_1 (and thus that we return $D = 1$) is $\frac{1}{6}$; this agrees with the desired probability that $D = 1$. Similarly, we return $D = 2$ if U falls in C_2, having probability equal to the width of C_2, $\frac{1}{2} - \frac{1}{6} = \frac{1}{3}$, as desired; and so on for the other intervals. The subprogram to generate the demand sizes uses this principle and takes as input the cutoff points defining the above subintervals, which are the *cumulative* probabilities of the distribution of D.

The delivery lags are uniformly distributed, but not over the unit interval [0,1]. In general, we can generate a random variate distributed uniformly over any interval $[a,b]$ by generating a U(0, 1) random number U, and then returning $a + U(b - a)$. That this method is correct seems intuitively clear, but will be formally justified in Sec. 8.3.1.

We now describe the logic for event types 1, 2, and 4, which actually involve state changes.

The order-arrival event is flowcharted in Fig. 1.30, and must make the changes necessary when an order (which was previously placed) arrives from the supplier. The inventory level is increased by the amount of the order, and the order-arrival event must be eliminated from consideration. (See Prob. 1.12 for consideration of the issue of whether there could be more than one order outstanding at a time for this model with these parameters.)

A flowchart for the demand event is given in Fig. 1.31, and processes the changes necessary to represent a demand's occurrence. First, the demand size is generated, and the inventory is decremented by this amount. Finally, the time of the next demand is scheduled into the event list. Note that this is the place where the inventory level might become negative.

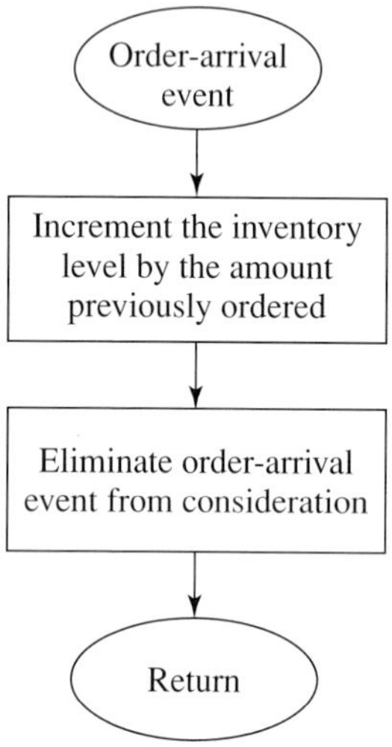

FIGURE 1.30
Flowchart for order-arrival routine, inventory model.

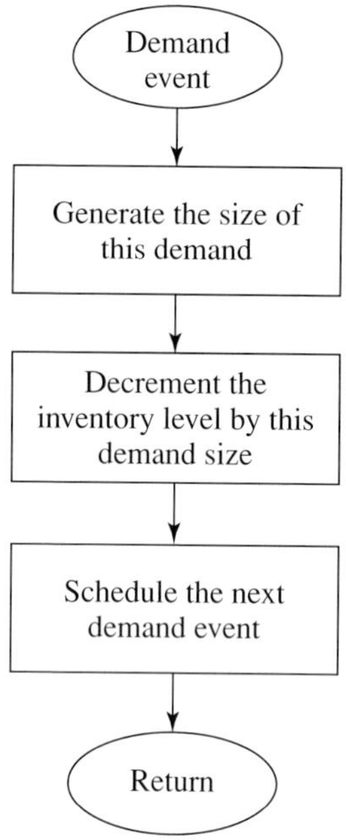

FIGURE 1.31
Flowchart for demand routine, inventory model.

The inventory-evaluation event, which takes place at the beginning of each month, is flowcharted in Fig. 1.32. If the inventory level $I(t)$ at the time of the evaluation is at least s, then no order is placed, and nothing is done except to schedule the next evaluation into the event list. On the other hand, if $I(t) < s$, we want to place an order for $S - I(t)$ items. This is done by storing the amount of the order $[S - I(t)]$ until the order arrives, and scheduling its arrival time. In this case as well, we want to schedule the next inventory-evaluation event.

As in the single-server queueing model, it is convenient to write a separate nonevent routine to update the continuous-time statistical accumulators. For this model, however, doing so is slightly more complicated, so we give a flowchart for this activity in Fig. 1.33. The principal issue is whether we need to update the area under $I^-(t)$ or $I^+(t)$ (or neither). If the inventory level since the last event has been negative, then we have been in backlog, so the area under $I^-(t)$ only should be updated. On the other hand, if the inventory level has been positive, we need only update the area under $I^+(t)$. If the inventory level has been zero (a possibility), then neither update is needed. The code for this routine also brings the variable for the time of the last event up to the present time. This routine will be invoked from the main program just after returning from the timing routine, regardless of the event type or whether the inventory level is actually changing at this point. This provides a simple (if not the most computationally efficient) way of updating integrals for continuous-time statistics.

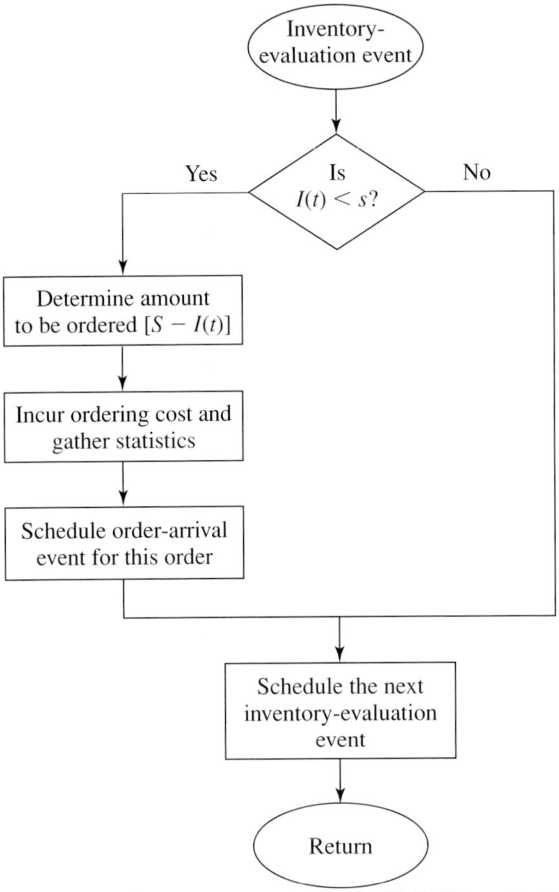

FIGURE 1.32
Flowchart for inventory-evaluation routine, inventory model.

Section 1.5.3 contains a program to simulate this model in C. Neither the timing nor exponential-variate-generation subprograms will be shown, as they are the same as for the single-server queueing model in Sec. 1.4. The reader should also note the considerable similarity between the main programs of the queueing and inventory models.

1.5.3 C Program

The external definitions are shown in Fig. 1.34. The array prob_distrib_demand will be used to hold the cumulative probabilities for the demand sizes, and is passed into the random-integer-generation function random_integer. As for the queueing model, we must include the header file lcgrand.h (in Fig. 7.6) for the random-number generator of Fig. 7.5. All code is available at www.mhhe.com/law.

The code for the main function is given in Fig. 1.35. After opening the input and output files, the number of events is set to 4. The input parameters (except s and S) are then read in and written out, and a report heading is produced; for each (s, S)

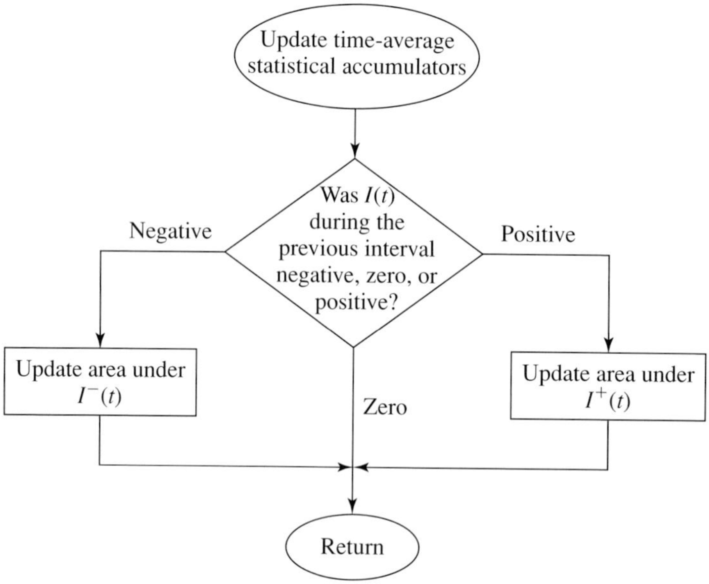

FIGURE 1.33
Flowchart for routine to update the continuous-time statistical accumulators, inventory model.

```
/* External definitions for inventory system. */

#include <stdio.h>
#include <math.h>
#include "lcgrand.h"  /* Header file for random-number generator. */

int   amount, bigs, initial_inv_level, inv_level, next_event_type, num_events,
      num_months, num_values_demand, smalls;
float area_holding, area_shortage, holding_cost, incremental_cost, maxlag,
      mean_interdemand, minlag, prob_distrib_demand[26], setup_cost,
      shortage_cost, sim_time, time_last_event, time_next_event[5],
      total_ordering_cost;
FILE  *infile, *outfile;

void  initialize(void);
void  timing(void);
void  order_arrival(void);
void  demand(void);
void  evaluate(void);
void  report(void);
void  update_time_avg_stats(void);
float expon(float mean);
int   random_integer(float prob_distrib []);
float uniform(float a, float b);
```

FIGURE 1.34
C code for the external definitions, inventory model.

```
main()  /* Main function. */
{
    int i, num_policies;

    /* Open input and output files. */

    infile  = fopen("inv.in",  "r");
    outfile = fopen("inv.out", "w");

    /* Specify the number of events for the timing function. */

    num_events = 4;

    /* Read input parameters. */

    fscanf(infile, "%d %d %d %d %f %f %f %f %f %f %f",
           &initial_inv_level, &num_months, &num_policies, &num_values_demand,
           &mean_interdemand, &setup_cost, &incremental_cost, &holding_cost,
           &shortage_cost, &minlag, &maxlag);
    for (i = 1; i <= num_values_demand; ++i)
        fscanf(infile, "%f", &prob_distrib_demand[i]);

    /* Write report heading and input parameters. */

    fprintf(outfile, "Single-product inventory system\n\n");
    fprintf(outfile, "Initial inventory level%24d items\n\n",
            initial_inv_level);
    fprintf(outfile, "Number of demand sizes%25d\n\n", num_values_demand);
    fprintf(outfile, "Distribution function of demand sizes  ");
    for (i = 1; i <= num_values_demand; ++i)
        fprintf(outfile, "%8.3f", prob_distrib_demand[i]);
    fprintf(outfile, "\n\nMean interdemand time%26.2f\n\n", mean_interdemand);
    fprintf(outfile, "Delivery lag range%29.2f to%10.2f months\n\n", minlag,
            maxlag);
    fprintf(outfile, "Length of the simulation%23d months\n\n", num_months);
    fprintf(outfile, "K =%6.1f   i =%6.1f   h =%6.1f   pi =%6.1f\n\n",
            setup_cost, incremental_cost, holding_cost, shortage_cost);
    fprintf(outfile, "Number of policies%29d\n\n", num_policies);
    fprintf(outfile, "                 Average        Average");
    fprintf(outfile, "          Average        Average\n");
    fprintf(outfile, " Policy       total cost    ordering cost");
    fprintf(outfile, " holding cost   shortage cost");

    /* Run the simulation varying the inventory policy. */

    for (i = 1; i <= num_policies; ++i) {

        /* Read the inventory policy, and initialize the simulation. */

        fscanf(infile, "%d %d", &smalls, &bigs);
        initialize();

        /* Run the simulation until it terminates after an end-simulation event
           (type 3) occurs. */

        do {

            /* Determine the next event. */

            timing();

            /* Update time-average statistical accumulators. */

            update_time_avg_stats();

            /* Invoke the appropriate event function. */
```

FIGURE 1.35
C code for the main function, inventory model.

```
            switch (next_event_type) {
                case 1:
                    order_arrival();
                    break;
                case 2:
                    demand();
                    break;
                case 4:
                    evaluate();
                    break;
                case 3:
                    report();
                    break;
            }

        /* If the event just executed was not the end-simulation event (type 3),
           continue simulating.  Otherwise, end the simulation for the current
           (s,S) pair and go on to the next pair (if any). */

        } while (next_event_type != 3);
    }

    /* End the simulations. */

    fclose(infile);
    fclose(outfile);

    return 0;
}
```

FIGURE 1.35
(continued)

pair the simulation will then produce in the report function a single line of output corresponding to this heading. Then a "for" loop is begun, each iteration of which performs an entire simulation for a given (s, S) pair; the first thing done in the loop is to read the next (s, S) pair. The model is initialized, and a "do while" loop is used to keep simulating as long as the type 3 (end-simulation) event does not occur, as in Sec. 1.4.6. Inside this loop, the timing function is used to determine the next event type and to update the simulation clock. After returning from timing with the next event type, the continuous-time statistics are updated before executing the event routine itself. A "switch" statement is then used as before to transfer control to the appropriate event routine. Unlike the fixed-time stopping rule of Sec. 1.4.6, when the "do while" loop ends here, we do not stop the program, but go to the next step of the enclosing "for" loop to read in the next (s, S) pair and do a separate simulation; the entire program stops only when the "for" loop is over and there are no more (s, S) pairs to consider.

The initialization function appears in Fig. 1.36. Observe that the first inventory evaluation is scheduled at time 0 since, in general, the initial inventory level could be less than s. Note also that event type 1 (order arrival) is eliminated from consideration, since our modeling assumption was that there are no outstanding orders initially.

The event functions order_arrival, demand, and evaluate are shown in Figs. 1.37 through 1.39, and correspond to the general discussion given in Sec. 1.5.2, and

```
void initialize(void)  /* Initialization function. */
{
    /* Initialize the simulation clock. */

    sim_time = 0.0;

    /* Initialize the state variables. */

    inv_level       = initial_inv_level;
    time_last_event = 0.0;

    /* Initialize the statistical counters. */

    total_ordering_cost = 0.0;
    area_holding        = 0.0;
    area_shortage       = 0.0;

    /* Initialize the event list.  Since no order is outstanding, the order-
       arrival event is eliminated from consideration. */

    time_next_event[1] = 1.0e+30;
    time_next_event[2] = sim_time + expon(mean_interdemand);
    time_next_event[3] = num_months;
    time_next_event[4] = 0.0;
}
```

FIGURE 1.36
C code for function initialize, inventory model.

```
void order_arrival(void)  /* Order arrival event function. */
{
    /* Increment the inventory level by the amount ordered. */

    inv_level += amount;

    /* Since no order is now outstanding, eliminate the order-arrival event from
       consideration. */

    time_next_event[1] = 1.0e+30;
}
```

FIGURE 1.37
C code for function order_arrival, inventory model.

```
void demand(void)  /* Demand event function. */
{
    /* Decrement the inventory level by a generated demand size. */

    inv_level -= random_integer(prob_distrib_demand);

    /* Schedule the time of the next demand. */

    time_next_event[2] = sim_time + expon(mean_interdemand);
}
```

FIGURE 1.38
C code for function demand, inventory model.

```
void evaluate(void)  /* Inventory-evaluation event function. */
{
    /* Check whether the inventory level is less than smalls. */

    if (inv_level < smalls) {

        /* The inventory level is less than smalls, so place an order for the
           appropriate amount. */

        amount              = bigs - inv_level;
        total_ordering_cost += setup_cost + incremental_cost * amount;

        /* Schedule the arrival of the order. */

        time_next_event[1] = sim_time + uniform(minlag, maxlag);
    }

    /* Regardless of the place-order decision, schedule the next inventory
       evaluation. */

    time_next_event[4] = sim_time + 1.0;
}
```

FIGURE 1.39
C code for function evaluate, inventory model.

```
void report(void)  /* Report generator function. */
{
    /* Compute and write estimates of desired measures of performance. */

    float avg_holding_cost, avg_ordering_cost, avg_shortage_cost;

    avg_ordering_cost = total_ordering_cost / num_months;
    avg_holding_cost  = holding_cost * area_holding / num_months;
    avg_shortage_cost = shortage_cost * area_shortage / num_months;
    fprintf(outfile, "\n\n(%3d,%3d)%15.2f%15.2f%15.2f%15.2f",
            smalls, bigs,
            avg_ordering_cost + avg_holding_cost + avg_shortage_cost,
            avg_ordering_cost, avg_holding_cost, avg_shortage_cost);
}
```

FIGURE 1.40
C code for function report, inventory model.

to the flowcharts in Figs. 1.30 through 1.32. In evaluate, note that the variable total_ordering_cost is increased by the ordering cost for any order that might be placed here.

The report generator is listed in Fig. 1.40, and computes the three components of the total cost separately, adding them together to get the average total cost per month. The current values of s and S are written out for identification purposes, along with the average total cost and its three components (ordering, holding, and shortage costs).

Function update_time_avg_stats, which was discussed in general in Sec. 1.5.2 and flowcharted in Fig. 1.33, is shown in Fig. 1.41. Note that if the inventory level inv_level is zero, neither the "if" nor the "else if" condition is satisfied, resulting in no update at all, as desired. As in the single-server queueing model of Sec. 1.4, it

```
void update_time_avg_stats(void)  /* Update area accumulators for time-average
                                     statistics. */
{
    float time_since_last_event;

    /* Compute time since last event, and update last-event-time marker. */

    time_since_last_event = sim_time - time_last_event;
    time_last_event       = sim_time;

    /* Determine the status of the inventory level during the previous interval.
       If the inventory level during the previous interval was negative, update
       area_shortage.  If it was positive, update area_holding.  If it was zero,
       no update is needed. */

    if (inv_level < 0)
        area_shortage -= inv_level * time_since_last_event;
    else if (inv_level > 0)
        area_holding  += inv_level * time_since_last_event;
}
```

FIGURE 1.41
C code for function update_time_avg_stats, inventory model.

```
int random_integer(float prob_distrib[])  /* Random integer generation
                                             function. */
{
    int   i;
    float u;

    /* Generate a U(0,1) random variate. */

    u = lcgrand(1);

    /* Return a random integer in accordance with the (cumulative) distribution
       function prob_distrib. */

    for (i = 1; u >= prob_distrib[i]; ++i)
        ;
    return i;
}
```

FIGURE 1.42
C code for function random_integer.

might be necessary to make both the sim_time and time_last_event variables be of type double to avoid severe roundoff error in their subtraction at the top of the routine if the simulation is to be run for a long period of simulated time.

The code for function random_integer is given in Fig. 1.42, and is general in that it will generate an integer according to distribution function prob_distrib[I], provided that the values of prob_distrib[I] are specified. (In our case, prob_distrib[1] $= \frac{1}{6}$, prob_distrib[2] $= \frac{1}{2}$, prob_distrib[3] $= \frac{5}{6}$, and prob_distrib[4] $= 1$, all specified to three-decimal accuracy on input.) The logic agrees with the discussion in Sec. 1.5.2; note that the input array prob_distrib must contain the *cumulative* distribution function rather than the probabilities that the variate takes on its possible values.

The function uniform is given in Fig. 1.43, and is as described in Sec. 1.5.2.

```
float uniform(float a, float b)  /* Uniform variate generation function. */
{
    /* Return a U(a,b) random variate. */

    return a + lcgrand(1) * (b - a);
}
```

FIGURE 1.43
C code for function uniform.

1.5.4 Simulation Output and Discussion

The simulation report (in file inv.out) is given in Fig. 1.44. For this model, there were some differences in the results across different compilers and computers, even though the same random-number-generator algorithm was being used; see the discussion at the beginning of Sec. 1.4.4 for an explanation of this discrepancy.

```
Single-product inventory system

Initial inventory level                     60 items

Number of demand sizes                       4

Distribution function of demand sizes     0.167    0.500    0.833    1.000

Mean interdemand time                      0.10 months

Delivery lag range                         0.50 to      1.00 months

Length of the simulation                   120 months

K =   32.0    i =    3.0    h =    1.0    pi =    5.0

Number of policies                           9
```

Policy	Average total cost	Average ordering cost	Average holding cost	Average shortage cost
(20, 40)	126.61	99.26	9.25	18.10
(20, 60)	122.74	90.52	17.39	14.83
(20, 80)	123.86	87.36	26.24	10.26
(20,100)	125.32	81.37	36.00	7.95
(40, 60)	126.37	98.43	25.99	1.95
(40, 80)	125.46	88.40	35.92	1.14
(40,100)	132.34	84.62	46.42	1.30
(60, 80)	150.02	105.69	44.02	0.31
(60,100)	143.20	89.05	53.91	0.24

FIGURE 1.44
Output report, inventory model.

The three separate components of the average total cost per month were reported to see how they respond individually to changes in s and S, as a possible check on the model and the code. For example, fixing $s = 20$ and increasing S from 40 to 100 increases the holding cost steadily from \$9.25 per month to \$36.00 per month, while reducing shortage cost at the same time; the effect of this increase in S on the ordering cost is to reduce it, evidently since ordering up to larger values of S implies that these larger orders will be placed less frequently, thereby avoiding the fixed ordering cost more often. Similarly, fixing S at, say, 100, and increasing s from 20 to 60 leads to a decrease in shortage cost (\$7.95, \$1.30, \$0.24) but an increase in holding cost (\$36.00, \$46.42, \$53.91), since increases in s translate into less willingness to let the inventory level fall to low values. While we could probably have predicted the *direction* of movement of these components of cost without doing the simulation, it would not have been possible to say much about their *magnitude* without the aid of the simulation output.

Since the overall criterion of *total* cost per month is the sum of three components that move in sometimes different directions in reaction to changes in s and S, we cannot predict even the direction of movement of this criterion without the simulation. Thus, we simply look at the values of this criterion, and it would *appear* that the (20, 60) policy is the best, having an average total cost of \$122.74 per month. However, in the present context where the length of the simulation is fixed (the company wants a planning horizon of 10 years), what we *really* want to estimate for each policy is the *expected* average total cost per month for the first 120 months. The numbers in Fig. 1.44 are *estimates* of these expected values, each estimate based on a sample of size *1* (simulation run or replication). Since these estimates may have large variances, the ordering of them may differ considerably from the ordering of the expected values, which is the desired information. In fact, if we reran the nine simulations using different U(0, 1) random variates, the estimates obtained might differ greatly from those in Fig. 1.44. Furthermore, the ordering of the new estimates might also be different.

We conclude from the above discussion that when the simulation run length is fixed by the problem context, it will generally not be sufficient to make a single simulation run of each policy or system of interest. In Chap. 9 we address the issue of just how many runs are required to get a good estimate of a desired expected value. Chapters 10 and 12 consider related problems when we are concerned with several different expected values arising from alternative system designs.

1.6 PARALLEL/DISTRIBUTED SIMULATION AND THE HIGH LEVEL ARCHITECTURE

The simulations in Secs. 1.4 and 1.5 (as well as those to be considered in Chap. 2) all operate in basically the same way. A simulation clock and an event list interact to determine which event will be processed next, the simulation clock is advanced to the time of this event, and the computer executes the event logic, which may include updating state variables, updating the event list, and collecting statistics. This logic is executed in order of the events' simulated time of occurrence; i.e., the simulation is *sequential*. Furthermore, all work is done on a single computer.

In recent years computer technology has enabled individual processors or computers to be linked together into *parallel* or *distributed* computing environments. This allows the possibility of executing different parts of a *single* simulation model on multiple processors operating at the same time, or in "parallel," and thus reducing the overall time to complete the simulation. Alternatively, two or more *different* simulation models operating on separate computers might be tied together over a network to produce one overall simulation model, where the individual models interact with each other over time. In this section we introduce these alternative approaches to executing a simulation model.

1.6.1 Parallel Simulation

Parallel discrete-event simulation [see Fujimoto (1998, 2000, 2003)] is concerned with the execution of a simulation model on a tightly coupled computer system (e.g., a supercomputer or a shared-memory multiprocessor). By spreading the execution of a simulation over several different processors, it is hoped that the model execution time can be reduced considerably (up to a factor equal to the number of processors). For example, if one is simulating a communications network with thousands of nodes or a large military model, then the execution time could be excessive and parallel simulation might be considered. Another possible use for parallel simulation is in real-time decision making. For example, in an air-traffic control system, it might be of interest to simulate several hours of air traffic to decide "now" how best to reroute traffic [see Wieland (1998)].

To develop a parallel simulation, a model is decomposed into several *logical processes* (LPs) (or submodels). The individual LPs (or groups of them) are assigned to different processors, each of which goes to work simulating its piece of the model. The LPs communicate with each other by sending time-stamped messages or events to each other. For example, a manufacturing system is typically modeled as an interconnected network of queueing systems, each representing a different workstation. When a job leaves one workstation, an "arrival" event must be sent to the next station on the job's routing (unless the job is leaving the system).

A crucial issue in parallel simulation is to ensure that events in the *overall* simulation model, regardless of their LP, are processed in their proper time sequence. For example, if the arrival of a particular job to one station is supposed to take place before the departure of another job from a different station, then there must be a synchronization mechanism to make sure that this takes place. If each LP processes all its events (generated either by itself or by another LP) in increasing order of event time, a requirement called the *local causality constraint*, then it can be shown that the parallel simulation will produce exactly the same results as if the overall simulation model were run sequentially on a single computer.

Each LP can be viewed as a sequential discrete-event simulation model, having its own local state variables, event list, and simulation clock. The overall parallel simulation model, however, does *not* have global counterparts, as would be the case in a sequential simulation model.

Historically, two different types of synchronization mechanisms have been used: conservative and optimistic. In *conservative synchronization* [see Bryant (1977) and Chandy and Misra (1979)], the goal is to absolutely avoid violating the local causality constraint. For example, suppose that a particular LP is currently at simulation time 25 and is ready to process its next event that has an event time of 30. Then the synchronization mechanism must make sure that this LP won't later receive an event from another LP with an event time of less than 30. Thus, the goal is to determine when it is actually "safe" to process a particular event, i.e., when can it be guaranteed that no event will later be received by this LP with a smaller event time.

Conservative synchronization mechanisms have two disadvantages [see Fujimoto (1998, pp. 444–446)]:

1. They cannot fully exploit the parallelism that is available in a simulation application. If event A could possibly affect event B in any way, then A and B must be executed sequentially. If the simulation model is such that A seldom affects B, then A and B could have been processed concurrently most of the time.
2. They are not very robust—a seemingly small change in the model can result in serious degradation in performance.

In *optimistic synchronization*, violations of the local causality constraint are allowed to occur, but the synchronization mechanism detects violations and recovers from them. As above, each LP simulates its own piece of the model forward in time, but does *not* wait to receive messages from other processors that may be moving along at different rates—this waiting is necessary for conservative synchronization.

The *time-warp* mechanism [see Jefferson (1985)] is the best-known optimistic approach. If an LP receives a message that should have been received in its past (and, thus, possibly affecting its actions from that point on), then a *rollback* occurs for the receiving LP, whereby its simulation clock reverts to the (earlier) time of the incoming message. For example, if LP A has been simulated up to time 50 and a message from LP B comes in that should have been received at time 40, then the clock for A is rolled back to 40, and the simulation of A between times 40 and 50 is canceled since it might have been done incorrectly without knowing the contents of the time-40 message. Part of the canceled work may have been sending messages to other LPs, each of which is nullified by sending a corresponding *antimessage*—the antimessages may themselves generate secondary rollbacks at their destination LPs, etc.

Optimistic synchronization mechanisms can exploit the parallelism in a simulation application better than a conservative approach, since they are not limited by the worst-case scenario (see disadvantage 1 for conservative synchronization). However, they do have these disadvantages [see Fujimoto (1998, pp. 449–451)]:

1. They incur the overhead computations associated with executing rollbacks.
2. They require more computer memory since the state of each LP must be saved periodically to recover from a rollback.

The air-traffic-control application described above used an optimistic synchronization mechanism and ran on a four-processor, shared-memory Sun workstation. Another example of optimistic synchronization is the Global-Scale Agent Model (GSAM) of disease propagation [see Parker and Epstein (2011)]. It has been used to simulate a disease outbreak in a population of *6.5 billion* people.

Since computer-processor speeds doubled every 18 months for many years, an increasingly smaller number of simulation models require the use of parallel simulation to execute in a reasonable amount of time. On the other hand, parallel simulation can enable certain models to be run that do not fit into the memory provided by a single machine. For example, Fujimoto et al. (2003) have shown that parallel-simulation methodology allows one to dramatically increase the *size* of communications networks that can be simulated.

1.6.2 Distributed Simulation and the High Level Architecture

Distributed simulation is primarily used to create an overall simulation model, which is a composition of two or more individual simulation models that are located on networked computers. Interest in this form of distributed simulation began with the desire to create real-time, man-in-the-loop simulations that could be used for training military personnel. The SIMNET (SIMulator NETworking) project, which ran from 1983 to 1990, demonstrated the viability of this concept. This led to the creation of a set of protocols for interconnecting simulations, which was known as the Distributed Interactive Simulation (DIS) standard. DIS has given way to the High Level Architecture (HLA) [see Dahmann et al. (1998), Kuhl et al. (2000), and the website www.msco.mil], which was developed by the U.S. Department of Defense (DoD) under the leadership of the Defense Modeling and Simulation Office (DMSO), which has been redesignated as the Modeling & Simulation Coordination Office (MSCO).

The HLA (IEEE Standard 1516-2010) is a software architecture designed to promote the reuse and interoperation of simulations. It was based on the premise that no one simulation could satisfy all uses and applications in the defense industry, and it will ultimately reduce the time and cost required to create a synthetic environment for a new purpose. The HLA can combine the following DoD-defined types of simulations:

- Live—real people operating real systems (e.g., a field test)
- Virtual—real people operating simulated systems (e.g., people in a tank-cockpit simulator fighting simulation-generated enemy forces)
- Constructive—simulated people operating simulated systems (e.g., a discrete-event simulation)

All DoD simulations are supposed to be HLA-compliant beginning January 1, 2001 unless a waiver is obtained.

An HLA *federation* consists of a collection of interacting individual simulations, called *federates*, a Runtime Infrastructure (RTI), and an interface, as shown in Fig. 1.45. The RTI provides a set of general-purpose services that support the

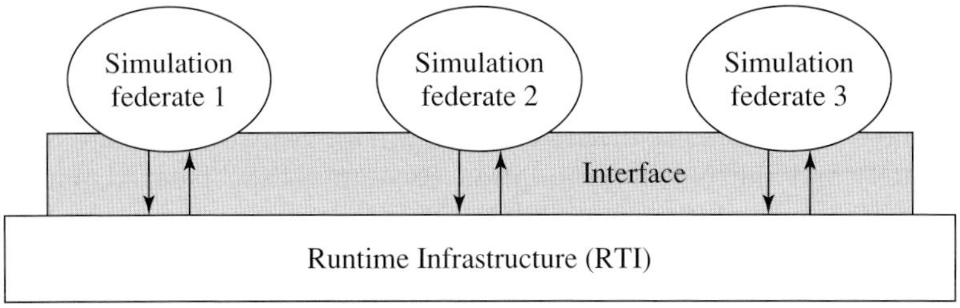

FIGURE 1.45
Functional view of an HLA federation.

simulations in carrying out federate-to-federate interactions, and it also provides functions for federation management. All interactions among the federates go through the RTI, whose software and algorithms are not defined by the HLA. (RTI software can be purchased from third-party vendors.) The HLA runtime interface specification provides a standard mechanism for federates to interact with the RTI, to invoke the RTI services to support interactions among the federates, and to respond to requests from the RTI. The interface is implementation-independent and doesn't depend on the "object" models (e.g., for an entity) and data-exchange requirements of any federate. [HLA objects do not have methods as in classical object-oriented simulation (see Sec. 3.6).]

The HLA is formally defined by three components: the interface specification, the object model template, and the rules. The HLA interface specification describes the runtime services provided to the federates by the RTI and to the RTI by the federates. There are six classes of services that provide capabilities for creation and operation of a federation, for time management (i.e., synchronization), for efficient routing of data among the federates during the execution of the federation, etc.

The HLA object models are descriptions of the essential sharable elements of the federation in object terms. Since the HLA is oriented toward interoperability, object models describe the critical aspects of federates and federations that are shared across the overall simulation model. The HLA puts no constraints on the content of the object models, but does require that these models be documented in a standard format called the Object Model Template (OMT). There are two types of object models: the Federation Object Model (FOM) and the Simulation Object Model (SOM). The HLA FOM describes the set of objects, attributes, and interactions (e.g., an event) that are shared across a federation. The HLA SOM describes a simulation (federate) in terms of the objects, attributes, and interactions that it can offer to future federations, which facilitates the assessment of whether the simulation is appropriate for participation in a new federation.

The HLA rules summarize the key principles underlying the HLA and are divided into two groups: federation and federate rules. Federation rules specify that every federation must have a FOM, that all object representations in a federation reside in the federates rather than in the RTI, etc. Federate rules state that the public information for a simulation is documented in a SOM, that local time management is done using the time-management services provided by the RTI, etc. [See Fujimoto (2003) for a discussion of time management in the HLA.]

HLA federations within the DoD have been used for training military personnel, for test and evaluation of military equipment, and for the analysis of new military systems and tactics. An example of the latter type of application is provided by the U.S. Navy's use of HLA to federate the Network Warfare Simulation (NETWARS) and the Naval Simulation System (NSS) [see Alspaugh et al. (2004) and Murphy and Flournoy (2002)]. This federation uses conservative time management.

There is also interest in distributed simulation and the HLA outside of the defense community. For example, the National Institute of Standards and Technology (NIST) MISSION Project applied HLA to distributed simulations of supply chains involving multiple organizations (e.g., a supplier and a transportation company) [see McLean and Riddick (2000)]. A distributed simulation might be necessary because an organization wants to hide the details of its operations from the other supply-chain organizations.

Although HLA was originally designed to federate two or more individual simulations, it is now also being used to self-federate multiple copies of the *same* simulation model. For example, Fujimoto et al. (2003) and Bodoh and Wieland (2003) use this approach to parallelize simulation models of large-scale communications networks and commercial air-traffic control, respectively.

A totally different use of distributed simulation is to make independent replications of a stand-alone simulation model on networked computers. This will allow an analyst to make more replications of a particular system configuration in a given amount of "wall-clock" time, which will result in more statistically precise estimates of the performance measures of interest. This will also allow an analyst to simulate a larger number of different system configurations in a given amount of wall-clock time when trying to "optimize" the performance of a system of interest (see Sec. 12.5). The simulation packages AutoMod and Simio (see Chap. 3) explicitly support this use of distributed simulation.

Additional information on parallel and distributed simulation can be found in the journal *ACM Transactions on Modeling and Computer Simulation* (TOMACS), as well as in the annual *Proceedings of the Winter Simulation Conference* and the *Proceedings of the Workshop on Principles of Advanced and Distributed Simulation*.

1.7 STEPS IN A SOUND SIMULATION STUDY

Now that we have looked in some detail at the inner workings of a discrete-event simulation, we need to step back and realize that model programming is just part of the overall effort to design or analyze a complex system by simulation. Attention must be paid to a variety of other concerns such as modeling system randomness, validation, statistical analysis of simulation output data, and project management. Figure 1.46 shows the steps that will compose a typical, sound simulation study [see also Banks et al. (2010, pp. 16–21) and Law (2003)]. The number beside the symbol representing each step refers to the more detailed description of that step below. Note that a simulation study is not a simple

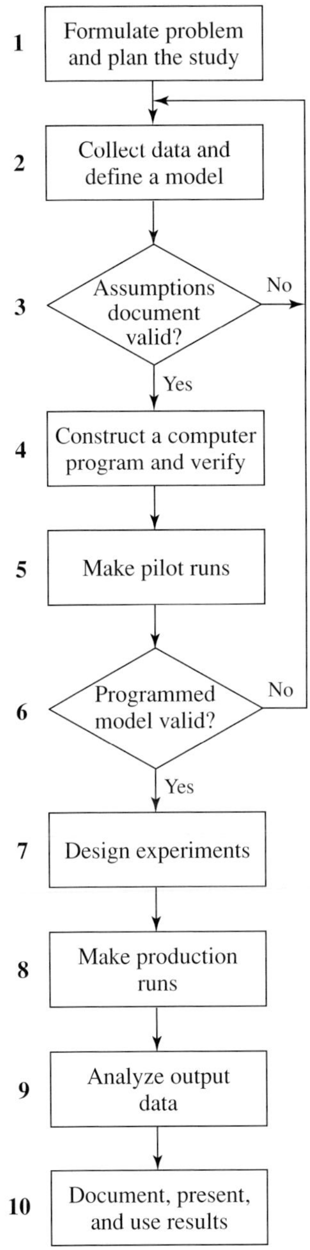

FIGURE 1.46
Steps in a simulation study.

sequential process. As one proceeds with the study, it may be necessary to go back to a previous step.

1. *Formulate the problem and plan the study.*

a. Problem of interest is stated by manager.
- Problem may not be stated correctly or in quantitative terms.
- An iterative process is often necessary.

b. One or more kickoff meetings for the study are conducted, with the project manager, the simulation analysts, and subject-matter experts (SMEs) in attendance. The following things are discussed:
   - Overall objectives of the study
   - *Specific* questions to be answered by the study (required to decide level of model detail)
   - Performance measures that will be used to evaluate the efficacy of different system configurations
   - Scope of the model
   - System configurations to be modeled (required to decide generality of simulation program)
   - Time frame for the study and the required resources

c. Select the software for the model (see Chap. 3)

2. *Collect data and define a model.*

a. Collect information on the system structure and operating procedures.
   - No single person or document is sufficient.
   - Some people may have inaccurate information—make sure that true SMEs are identified.
   - Operating procedures may not be formalized.

b. Collect data (if possible) to specify model parameters and input probability distributions (see Chap. 6).

c. Delineate above information and data in a *written* assumptions document (see Sec. 5.4.3).

d. Collect data (if possible) on the performance of the existing system (for validation purposes in step 6).

e. Choosing the level of model detail (see Sec. 5.2), which is an art, should depend on the following:
   - Project objectives
   - Performance measures
   - Data availability
   - Credibility concerns
   - Computer constraints
   - Opinions of SMEs
   - Time and money constraints

f. There should *not* be a one-to-one correspondence between each element of the model and the corresponding element of the system.

g. Start with a "simple" model and embellish it as needed. Modeling each aspect of the system will seldom be required to make effective decisions, and might result in excessive model execution time, in missed deadlines, or in obscuring important system factors.

h. Interact with the manager (and other key project personnel) on a regular basis (see Sec. 5.4.2).

3. *Is the assumptions document valid?*

   a. Perform a structured walk-through of the assumptions document before an audience of managers, analysts, and SMEs (see Sec. 5.4.3). This will
   - Help ensure that the model's assumptions are correct and complete
   - Promote interaction among the project members
   - Promote ownership of the model
   - Take place *before* programming begins, to avoid significant reprogramming later

4. *Construct a computer program and verify.*

   a. Program the model in a programming language (e.g., C, C++, or Java) or in simulation software (e.g., Arena, ExtendSim, Flexsim, and ProModel). Benefits of using a programming language are that one is often known, they offer greater program control, they have a low *purchase* cost, and they may result in a smaller model-execution time. The use of simulation software (see Chap. 3), on the other hand, reduces programming time and results in a lower *project* cost.

   b. Verify (debug) the simulation computer program (see Sec. 5.3).

5. *Make pilot runs.*

   a. Make pilot runs for validation purposes in step 6.

6. *Is the programmed model valid?*

   a. If there is an existing system, then compare model and system (from step 2) performance measures for the existing system (see Sec. 5.4.5).

   b. Regardless of whether there is an existing system, the simulation analysts and SMEs should review the model results for correctness.

   c. Use sensitivity analyses (see Sec. 5.4.4) to determine what model factors have a significant impact on performance measures and, thus, have to be modeled carefully.

7. *Design experiments.*

   a. Specify the following for each system configuration of interest:
   - Length of each simulation run
   - Length of the warmup period, if one is appropriate
   - Number of independent simulation runs using different random numbers (see Chap. 7)—facilitates construction of confidence intervals

8. *Make production runs.*

   a. Production runs are made for use in step 9.

9. *Analyze output data.*

a. Two major objectives in analyzing output data are to
- Determine the absolute performance of certain system configurations (see Chap. 9)
- Compare alternative system configurations in a relative sense (see Chap. 10 and Sec. 11.2)

10. *Document, present, and use results.*

a. Document assumptions (see step 2), computer program, and study's results for use in the current and future projects.

b. Present study's results.
- Use animation (see Sec. 3.4.3) to communicate model to managers and other people who are not familiar with all the model details.
- Discuss model building and validation process to promote credibility.
- Results are used in decision-making process if they are *both* valid and credible.

1.8 ADVANTAGES, DISADVANTAGES, AND PITFALLS OF SIMULATION

We conclude this introductory chapter by listing some good and bad characteristics of simulation (as opposed to other methods of studying systems), and by noting some common mistakes made in simulation studies that can impair or even ruin a simulation project. This subject was also discussed to some extent in Sec. 1.2, but now that we have worked through some simulation examples, it is possible to be more specific.

As mentioned in Sec. 1.2, simulation is a widely used and increasingly popular method for studying complex systems. Some possible advantages of simulation that may account for its widespread appeal are the following.

- Most complex, real-world systems with stochastic elements cannot be accurately described by a mathematical model that can be evaluated *analytically*. Thus, a simulation is often the only type of investigation possible.
- Simulation allows one to estimate the performance of an existing system under some projected set of operating conditions.
- Alternative proposed system designs (or alternative operating policies for a single system) can be compared via simulation to see which best meets a specified requirement.
- In a simulation we can maintain much better control over experimental conditions than would generally be possible when experimenting with the system itself (see Chap. 11).
- Simulation allows us to study a system with a long time frame—e.g., an economic system—in compressed time, or alternatively to study the detailed workings of a system in expanded time.

Simulation is not without its drawbacks. Some disadvantages are as follows.

- Each run of a *stochastic* simulation model produces only *estimates* of a model's true characteristics for a particular set of input parameters. Thus, several independent runs of the model will probably be required for each set of input parameters to be studied (see Chap. 9). For this reason, simulation models are generally not as good at optimization as they are at comparing a fixed number of specified alternative system designs. On the other hand, an analytic model, *if appropriate*, can often easily produce the *exact* true characteristics of that model for a variety of sets of input parameters. Thus, if a "valid" analytic model is available or can easily be developed, it will generally be preferable to a simulation model.
- Simulation models are often expensive and time-consuming to develop.
- The large volume of numbers produced by a simulation study or the persuasive impact of a realistic animation (see Sec. 3.4.3) often creates a tendency to place greater confidence in a study's results than is justified. If a model is not a "valid" representation of a system under study, the simulation results, no matter how impressive they appear, will provide little useful information about the actual system.

When deciding whether or not a simulation study is appropriate in a given situation, we can only advise that these advantages and drawbacks be kept in mind and that all other relevant facets of one's particular situation be brought to bear as well. Finally, note that in some studies both simulation and analytic models might be useful. In particular, simulation can be used to check the validity of assumptions needed in an analytic model. On the other hand, an analytic model can suggest reasonable alternatives to investigate in a simulation study.

Assuming that a decision has been made to use simulation, we have found the following pitfalls to the successful completion of a simulation study [see also Law and McComas (1989)]:

- Failure to have a well-defined set of objectives at the beginning of the simulation study
- Failure to have the entire project team involved at the beginning of the study
- Inappropriate level of model detail
- Failure to communicate with management throughout the course of the simulation study
- Misunderstanding of simulation by management
- Treating a simulation study as if it were primarily an exercise in computer programming
- Failure to have people with a knowledge of simulation methodology (Chaps. 5, 6, 9, etc.) and statistics on the modeling team
- Failure to collect good system data
- Inappropriate simulation software
- Obliviously using simulation-software products whose complex macro statements may not be well documented and may not implement the desired modeling logic

- Belief that easy-to-use simulation packages, which require little or no programming, require a significantly lower level of technical competence
- Misuse of animation
- Failure to account correctly for sources of randomness in the actual system
- Using arbitrary distributions (e.g., normal, uniform, or triangular) as input to the simulation
- Analyzing the output data from one simulation run (replication) using formulas that assume independence
- Making a single replication of a particular system design and treating the output statistics as the "true answers"
- Failure to have a warmup period, if the steady-state behavior of a system is of interest
- Comparing alternative system designs on the basis of one replication for each design
- Using the wrong performance measures

We will have more to say about what *to* do (rather than what *not* to do) in the remaining chapters of this book.

APPENDIX 1A FIXED-INCREMENT TIME ADVANCE

As mentioned in Sec. 1.3.1, the second principal approach for advancing the simulation clock in a discrete-event simulation model is called *fixed-increment time advance*. With this approach, the simulation clock is advanced in increments of exactly Δt time units for some appropriate choice of Δt. After each update of the clock, a check is made to determine if any events should have occurred during the previous interval of length Δt. If one or more events were scheduled to have occurred during this interval, these events are considered to occur at the *end* of the interval and the system state (and statistical counters) are updated accordingly. The fixed-increment time-advance approach is illustrated in Fig. 1.47, where the curved arrows represent the advancing of the simulation clock and e_i ($i = 1, 2, \ldots$) is the *actual* time of occurrence of the ith event of any type (*not* the ith value of the simulation clock). In the time interval $[0, \Delta t)$, an event occurs at time e_1 but is considered to occur at time Δt by the model. No events occur in the interval $[\Delta t, 2\Delta t)$, but the model checks to determine that this is the case. Events occur at the times

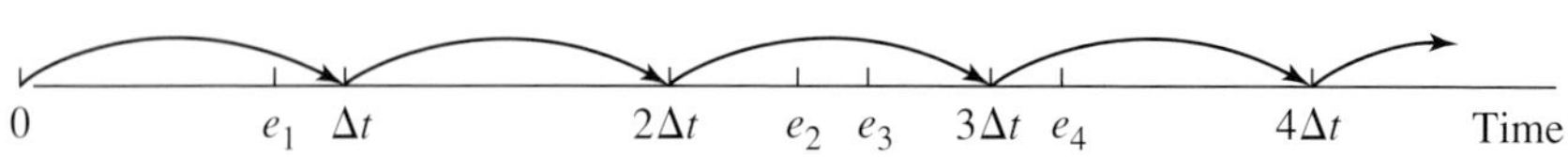

FIGURE 1.47
Illustration of fixed-increment time advance.

e_2 and e_3 in the interval $[2\Delta t, 3\Delta t)$, but both events are considered to occur at time $3\Delta t$, etc. A set of rules must be built into the model to decide in what order to process events when two or more events are considered to occur at the same time by the model. Two disadvantages of fixed-increment time advance are the errors introduced by processing events at the end of the interval in which they occur and the necessity of deciding which event to process first when events that are not simultaneous in reality are treated as such by the model. These problems can be made less severe by making Δt smaller, but this increases the amount of checking for event occurrences that must be done and results in an increase in execution time. Because of these considerations, fixed-increment time advance is generally not used for discrete-event simulation models when the times between successive events can vary greatly.

The primary uses of this approach appear to be for systems where it can reasonably be assumed that all events *actually* occur at one of the times $n\,\Delta t$ ($n = 0, 1, 2, \ldots$) for an appropriately chosen Δt and, unfortunately, for agent-based simulation (see Sec. 13.2). For example, data in economic systems are often available only on an annual basis, and it is natural in a simulation model to advance the simulation clock in increments of 1 year. [See Naylor (1971) for a discussion of simulation of economic systems. See also Sec. 13.6 for discussion of an inventory system that can be simulated, without loss of accuracy, by fixed-increment time advance.]

Note that fixed-increment time advance can be realized when using the next-event time-advance approach by artificially scheduling "events" to occur every Δt time units.

APPENDIX 1B
A PRIMER ON QUEUEING SYSTEMS

A *queueing system* consists of one or more servers that provide service of some kind to arriving customers. Customers who arrive to find all servers busy (generally) join one or more *queues* (or lines) in front of the servers, hence the name "queueing" system.

Historically, a large proportion of all discrete-event simulation studies have involved the modeling of a real-world queueing system, or at least some component of the system being simulated was a queueing system. Thus, we believe that it is important for the student of simulation to have at least a basic understanding of the components of a queueing system, standard notation for queueing systems, and measures of performance that are often used to indicate the quality of service being provided by a queueing system. Some examples of real-world queueing systems that have often been simulated are given in Table 1.1. For additional information on queueing systems in general, see Gross et al. (2009). Bertsekas and Gallager (1992) is recommended for those interested in queueing models of communications networks. Finally, Shanthikumar and Buzacott (1993) discuss stochastic models of manufacturing systems.

TABLE 1.1
Examples of queueing systems

System	Servers	Customers
Bank	Tellers	Customers
Hospital	Doctors, nurses, beds	Patients
Computer system	Central processing unit, input/output devices	Jobs
Manufacturing system	Machines, workers	Parts
Airport	Runways, gates, security check-in stations	Airplanes, travelers
Communications network	Nodes, links	Messages, packets

1B.1 COMPONENTS OF A QUEUEING SYSTEM

A queueing system is characterized by three components: arrival process, service mechanism, and queue discipline. Specifying the *arrival process* for a queueing system consists of describing how customers arrive to the system. Let A_i be the interarrival time between the arrivals of the $(i-1)$st and ith customers (see Sec. 1.3). If $A_1, A_2, \ldots$ are assumed to be IID random variables, we shall denote the *mean* (or expected) *interarrival time* by $E(A)$ and call $\lambda = 1/E(A)$ the *arrival rate* of customers.

The *service mechanism* for a queueing system is articulated by specifying the number of servers (denoted by s), whether each server has its own queue or there is one queue feeding all servers, and the probability distribution of customers' service times. Let S_i be the service time of the ith arriving customer. If $S_1, S_2, \ldots$ are IID random variables, we shall denote the *mean service time* of a customer by $E(S)$ and call $\omega = 1/E(S)$ the *service rate* of a server.

The *queue discipline* of a queueing system refers to the rule that a server uses to choose the next customer from the queue (if any) when the server completes the service of the current customer. Commonly used queue disciplines include

FIFO: Customers are served in a first-in, first-out manner.
LIFO: Customers are served in a last-in, first-out manner (see Prob. 2.17).
Priority: Customers are served in order of their importance (see Prob. 2.22) or on the basis of their service requirements (see Probs. 1.24, 2.20, and 2.21).

1B.2 NOTATION FOR QUEUEING SYSTEMS

Certain queueing systems occur so often in practice that standard notations have been developed for them. In particular, consider the queueing system shown in Fig. 1.48, which has the following characteristics:

1. s servers in parallel and one FIFO queue feeding all servers
2. $A_1, A_2, \ldots$ are IID random variables.
3. $S_1, S_2, \ldots$ are IID random variables.
4. The A_i's and S_i's are independent.

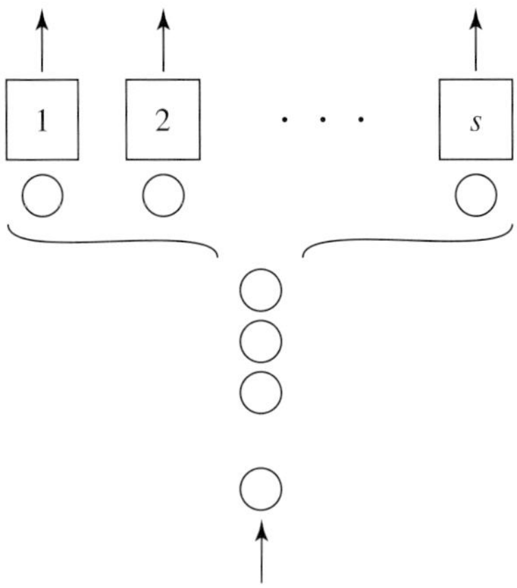

FIGURE 1.48
A *GI*/*G*/*s* queue.

We call such a system a *GI*/*G*/*s* queue, where *GI* (general independent) refers to the distribution of the A_i's and *G* (general) refers to the distribution of the S_i's. If specific distributions are given for the A_i's and the S_i's (as is always the case for simulation), symbols denoting these distributions are used in place of *GI* and *G*. The symbol *M* is used for the exponential distribution because of the Markovian, i.e., memoryless, property of the exponential distribution (see Prob. 4.30), the symbol E_k for a *k*-Erlang distribution (if *X* is a *k*-Erlang random variable, then $X = \sum_{i=1}^{k} Y_i$, where the Y_i's are IID exponential random variables), and *D* for deterministic (or constant) times. Thus, a single-server queueing system with exponential interarrival times and service times and a FIFO queue discipline is called an *M*/*M*/1 queue.

For any *GI*/*G*/*s* queue, we shall call the quantity $\rho = \lambda/(s\omega)$ the *utilization factor* of the queueing system ($s\omega$ is the service rate of the system when all servers are busy). It is a measure of how heavily the resources of a queueing system are utilized.

1B.3 MEASURES OF PERFORMANCE FOR QUEUEING SYSTEMS

There are many possible measures of performance for queueing systems. We now describe four such measures that are usually used in the mathematical study of queueing systems. The reader should not infer from our choices that these measures are necessarily the most relevant or important in practice (see Chap. 9 for further discussion). As a matter of fact, for some real-world systems these measures may not even be well defined; i.e., they may not exist.

Let

D_i = delay in queue of *i*th customer

$W_i = D_i + S_i$ = waiting time in system of *i*th customer

$Q(t)$ = number of customers in queue at time t

$L(t)$ = number of customers in system at time t [$Q(t)$ plus number of customers being served at time t]

Then the measures

$$d = \lim_{n\to\infty} \frac{\sum_{i=1}^{n} D_i}{n} \qquad \text{w.p. 1}$$

and

$$w = \lim_{n\to\infty} \frac{\sum_{i=1}^{n} W_i}{n} \qquad \text{w.p. 1}$$

(if they exist) are called the *steady-state average delay* and the *steady-state average waiting time*. Similarly, the measures

$$Q = \lim_{T\to\infty} \frac{\int_0^T Q(t)\, dt}{T} \qquad \text{w.p. 1}$$

and

$$L = \lim_{T\to\infty} \frac{\int_0^T L(t)\, dt}{T} \qquad \text{w.p. 1}$$

(if they exist) are called the *steady-state time-average number in queue* and the *steady-state time-average number in system*. Here and throughout this book, the qualifier "w.p. 1" (with probability 1) is given for mathematical correctness and has little practical significance. For example, suppose that $\Sigma_{i=1}^{n} D_i/n \to d$ as $n \to \infty$ (w.p. 1) for some queueing system. This means that if one performs a very large (an infinite) number of experiments, then in virtually every experiment $\Sigma_{i=1}^{n} D_i/n$ converges to the finite quantity d. Note that $\rho < 1$ is a necessary condition for d, w, Q, and L to exist for a $GI/G/s$ queue.

Among the most general and useful results for queueing systems are the *conservation equations*

$$Q = \lambda d \qquad \text{and} \qquad L = \lambda w$$

These equations hold for every queueing system for which d and w exist [see Stidham (1974)]. (Section 11.5 gives a simulation application of these relationships.) Another equation of considerable practical value is given by

$$w = d + E(S)$$

(see Sec. 1.4.5 and also Sec. 11.5 for further discussion).

It should be mentioned that the measures of performance discussed above can be analytically computed for $M/M/s$ queues ($s \ge 1$), $M/G/1$ queues for any distribution G, and for certain other queueing systems. In general, the interarrival-time distribution, the service-time distribution, or both must be exponential (or a variant of exponential, such as k-Erlang) for analytic solutions to be possible [see Gross et al. (2009)].

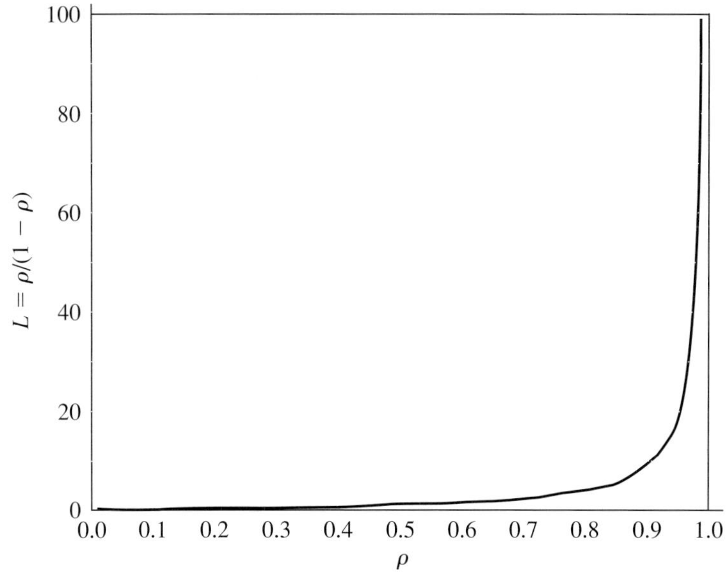

FIGURE 1.49
Plot of $L = \rho/(1 - \rho)$ for the *M/M/*1 queue.

For example, in the case of an *M/M/*1 queue, it can be shown analytically that the steady-state average number in system is given by

$$L = \rho/(1 - \rho)$$

which we plot as a function of ρ in Fig. 1.49. Note that L is clearly not a linear function of ρ, and for $\rho > 0.8$ the plot of L increases exponentially. Although the formula for L is specifically for the *M/M/*1 queue, the nonlinear behavior seen in Fig. 1.49 is indicative of queueing systems in general.

Another interesting (and instructive) example of an analytical solution is the steady-state average delay in queue for an *M/G/*1 queue, given by

$$d = \frac{\lambda\{\text{Var}(S) + [E(S)]^2\}}{2[1 - \lambda E(S)]}$$

where Var(S) denotes the variance of the service-time distribution [see, for example, Ross (2003, p. 508) for a derivation of this formula]. Thus, we can see that if $E(S)$ is large, then congestion (here measured by d) will be larger; this is certainly to be expected. The formula also brings out the perhaps less obvious fact that congestion also increases if the *variability* of the service-time distribution is large, even if the mean service time stays the same. Intuitively, this is because a highly variable service-time random variable will have a greater chance of taking on a large value (since it must be positive), which means that the (single) server will be tied up for a long time, causing the queue to build up.

PROBLEMS

1.1. Describe what you think would be the most effective way to study each of the following systems, in terms of the possibilities in Fig. 1.1, and discuss why.
(*a*) A small section of an existing factory
(*b*) A freeway interchange that has experienced severe congestion
(*c*) An emergency room in an existing hospital
(*d*) A pizza-delivery operation
(*e*) The shuttle-bus operation for a rental-car agency at an airport
(*f*) A battlefield communications network

1.2. For each of the systems in Prob. 1.1, suppose that it has been decided to make a study via a simulation model. Discuss whether the simulation should be static or dynamic, deterministic or stochastic, and continuous or discrete.

1.3. For the single-server queueing system in Sec. 1.4, define $L(t)$ to be the *total* number of customers in the system at time t (including the queue and the customer in service at time t, if any).
(*a*) Is it true that $L(t) = Q(t) + 1$? Why or why not?
(*b*) For the same realization considered for the hand simulation in Sec. 1.4.2, make a plot of $L(t)$ vs. t (similar to Figs. 1.5 and 1.6) between times 0 and $T(6)$.
(*c*) From your plot in part (*b*), compute $\hat{\ell}(6)$ = the time-average number of customers in the system during the time interval $[0, T(6)]$. What is $\hat{\ell}(6)$ estimating?
(*d*) Augment Fig. 1.7 to indicate how $\hat{\ell}(6)$ is computed during the course of the simulation.

1.4. For the single-server queue of Sec. 1.4, suppose that we did not want to estimate the expected average delay in queue; the model's structure and parameters remain the same. Does this change the state variables? If so, how?

1.5. For the single-server queue of Sec. 1.4, let W_i = the *total* time in the system of the ith customer to finish service, which includes the time in queue plus the time in service of this customer. For the same realization considered for the hand simulation in Sec. 1.4.2, compute $\hat{w}(m)$ = the average time in system of the first m customers to exit the system, for $m = 5$; do this by augmenting Fig. 1.7 appropriately. How does this change the state variables, if at all?

1.6. From Fig. 1.5, it is clear that the maximum length of the queue was 3. Write a general expression for this quantity (for the n-delay stopping rule), and augment Fig. 1.7 so that it can be computed systematically during the simulation.

1.7. Modify the code for the single-server queue in Sec. 1.4.4 to compute and write in addition the following measures of performance:
(*a*) The time-average number in the system (see Prob. 1.3)
(*b*) The average total time in the system (see Prob. 1.5)
(*c*) The maximum queue length (see Prob. 1.6)
(*d*) The maximum delay in queue
(*e*) The maximum time in the system
(*f*) The proportion of customers having a delay in queue in excess of 1 minute
Run this program, using the random-number generator given in App. 7A.

1.8. The algorithm in Sec. 1.4.3 for generating an exponential random variate with mean β was to return $-\beta \ln U$, where U is a $U(0, 1)$ random variate. This algorithm could validly be changed to return $-\beta \ln(1 - U)$. Why?

1.9. Run the single-server queueing simulation of Sec. 1.4.4 ten times by placing a loop around most of the main program, beginning just before the initialization and ending just after invoking the report generator. Discuss the results. (This is called *replicating* the simulation 10 times independently.)

1.10. For the single-server queueing simulation of Sec. 1.4, suppose that the facility opens its doors at 9 A.M. (call this time 0) and closes its doors at 5 P.M., but operates until all customers present (in service or in queue) at 5 P.M. have been served. Change the code to reflect this stopping rule, and estimate the same performance measures as before.

1.11. For the single-server queueing system of Sec. 1.4, suppose that there is room in the queue for only two customers, and that a customer arriving to find that the queue is full just goes away (this is called *balking*). Simulate this system for a stopping rule of exactly 480 minutes, and estimate the same quantities as in Sec. 1.4, as well as the expected number of customers who balk.

1.12. Consider the inventory simulation of Sec. 1.5.

(*a*) For this model with these parameters, there can never be more than one order outstanding (i.e., previously ordered but not yet delivered) at a time. Why?

(*b*) Describe specifically what changes would have to be made if the delivery lag were uniformly distributed between 0.5 and 6.0 months (rather than between 0.5 and 1.0 month); no other changes to the model are being considered. Should ordering decisions be based only on the inventory level $I(t)$?

1.13. Modify the inventory simulation of Sec. 1.5 so that it makes five replications of each (s, S) policy; see Prob. 1.9. Discuss the results. Which inventory policy is best? Are you sure?

1.14. A service facility consists of two servers in series (tandem), each with its own FIFO queue (see Fig. 1.50). A customer completing service at server 1 proceeds to server 2, while a customer completing service at server 2 leaves the facility. Assume that the interarrival times of customers to server 1 are IID exponential random variables with mean 1 minute. Service times of customers at server 1 are IID exponential random variables with mean 0.7 minute, and at server 2 are IID exponential random variables with mean 0.9 minute. Run the simulation for exactly 1000 minutes and estimate for each server the expected average delay in queue of a customer, the expected time-average number of customers in queue, and the expected utilization.

1.15. In Prob. 1.14, suppose that there is a travel time from the exit from server 1 to the arrival to queue 2 (or to server 2). Assume that this travel time is distributed uniformly

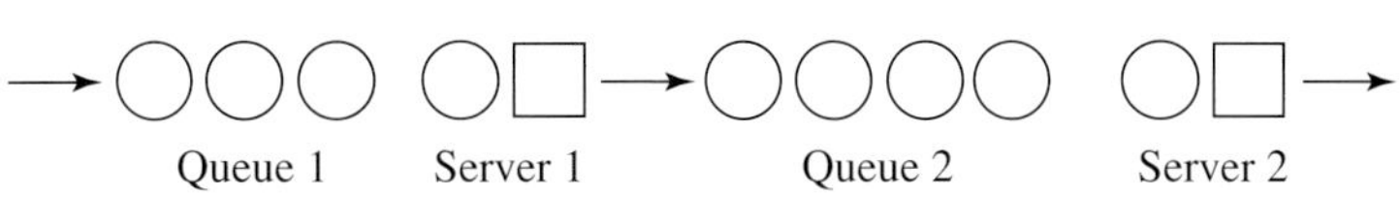

FIGURE 1.50
A tandem queueing system.

between 0 and 2 minutes. Modify the simulation and rerun it under the same conditions to obtain the same performance measures. What is the required dimension (i.e., length) of the event list?

1.16. In Prob. 1.14, suppose that no queueing is allowed for server 2. That is, if a customer completing service at server 1 sees that server 2 is idle, she proceeds directly to server 2, as before. However, a customer completing service at server 1 when server 2 is busy with another customer must stay at server 1 until server 2 gets done; this is called *blocking*. While a customer is blocked from entering server 2, she receives no additional service from server 1, but prevents server 1 from taking the first customer, if any, from queue 1. Furthermore, "fresh" customers continue to arrive to queue 1 during a period of blocking. Compute the same six performance measures as in Prob. 1.14.

1.17. For the inventory system of Sec. 1.5, suppose that if the inventory level $I(t)$ at the beginning of a month is less than zero, the company places an *express order* to its supplier. [If $0 \leq I(t) < s$, the company still places a normal order.] An express order for Z items costs the company $48 + 4Z$ dollars, but the delivery lag is now uniformly distributed on [0.25, 0.50] month. Run the simulation for all nine policies and estimate the expected average total cost per month, the expected proportion of time that there is a backlog, that is, $I(t) < 0$, and the expected number of express orders placed. Is express ordering worth it?

1.18. For the inventory simulation of Sec. 1.5, suppose that the inventory is *perishable*, having a shelf life distributed uniformly between 1.5 and 2.5 months. That is, if an item has a shelf life of l months, then l months after it is placed in inventory it spoils and is of no value to the company. (Note that different items in an order from the supplier will have different shelf lives.) The company discovers that an item is spoiled only upon examination before a sale. If an item is determined to be spoiled, it is discarded and the next item in the inventory is examined. Assume that items in the inventory are processed in a FIFO manner. Repeat the nine simulation runs and assume the same costs as before. Also compute the proportion of items taken out of the inventory that are discarded due to being spoiled.

1.19. Consider a service facility with s (where $s \geq 1$) parallel servers. Assume that interarrival times of customers are IID exponential random variables with mean $E(A)$ and that service times of customers (regardless of the server) are IID exponential random variables with mean $E(S)$. If a customer arrives and finds an idle server, the customer begins service immediately, choosing the leftmost (lowest-numbered) idle server if there are several available. Otherwise, the customer joins the tail of a *single* FIFO queue that supplies customers to all the servers. (This is called an $M/M/s$ queue; see App. 1B.) Write a general program to simulate this system that will estimate the expected average delay in queue, the expected time-average number in queue, and the expected utilization of each of the servers, based on a stopping rule of n delays having been completed. The quantities s, $E(A)$, $E(S)$, and n should be input parameters. Run the model for $s = 5$, $E(A) = 1$, $E(S) = 4$, and $n = 1000$.

1.20. Repeat Prob. 1.19, but now assume that an arriving customer finding more than one idle server chooses among them with equal probability. For example, if $s = 5$ and a customer arrives to find servers 1, 3, 4, and 5 idle, he chooses each of these servers with probability 0.25.

1.21. Customers arrive to a bank consisting of three tellers in parallel.

(*a*) If there is a single FIFO queue feeding all tellers, what is the required dimension (i.e., length) of the event list for a simulation model of this system?

(*b*) If each teller has his own FIFO queue and if a customer can *jockey* (i.e., jump) from one queue to another (see Sec. 2.6 for the jockeying rules), what is the required dimension of the event list? Assume that jockeying takes no time.

(*c*) Repeat part (*b*) if jockeying takes 3 seconds.

Assume in all three parts that no events are required to terminate the simulation.

1.22. A manufacturing system contains m machines, each subject to randomly occurring breakdowns. A machine runs for an amount of time that is an exponential random variable with mean 8 hours before breaking down. There are s (where s is a fixed, positive integer) repairmen to fix broken machines, and it takes one repairman an exponential amount of time with mean 2 hours to complete the repair of one machine; no more than one repairman can be assigned to work on a broken machine even if there are other idle repairmen. If more than s machines are broken down at a given time, they form a FIFO "repair" queue and wait for the first available repairman. Further, a repairman works on a broken machine until it is fixed, regardless of what else is happening in the system. Assume that it costs the system \$50 for each hour that each machine is broken down and \$10 an hour to employ each repairman. (The repairmen are paid an hourly wage regardless of whether they are actually working.) Assume that $m = 5$, but write general code to accommodate a value of m as high as 20 by changing an input parameter. Simulate the system for exactly 800 hours for each of the employment policies $s = 1, 2, \ldots, 5$ to determine which policy results in the smallest expected average cost per hour. Assume that at time 0 all machines have just been "freshly" repaired.

1.23. For the facility of Prob. 1.10, suppose that the server normally takes a 30-minute lunch break at the first time after 12 noon that the facility is empty. If, however, the server has not gone to lunch by 1 P.M., the server will go after completing the customer in service at 1 P.M. (Assume in this case that all customers in the queue at 1 P.M. will wait until the server returns.) If a customer arrives while the server is at lunch, the customer *may* leave immediately without being served; this is called *balking*. Assume that whether such a customer balks depends on the amount of time remaining before the server's return. (The server posts his time of return from lunch.) In particular, a customer who arrives during lunch will balk with the following probabilities:

Time remaining before server's return (minutes)	**Probability of a customer's balking**
[20, 30)	0.75
[10, 20)	0.50
[0, 10)	0.25

(The random-integer-generation method discussed in Sec. 1.5.2 can be used to determine whether a customer balks. For a simpler approach, see Sec. 8.4.1.) Run the simulation and estimate the same measures of performance as before. (Note that the server is not busy when at lunch and that the time-average number in queue is computed including data from the lunch break.) In addition, estimate the expected number of customers who balk.

1.24. For the single-server queueing facility of Sec. 1.4, suppose that a customer's service time is known at the instant of arrival. Upon completing service for a customer, the server chooses from the queue (if any) the customer with the smallest service time. Run the simulation until 1000 customers have completed their delays and estimate the expected average delay in queue, the expected time-average number in queue, and the expected proportion of customers whose delay in queue is greater than 1 minute. (This priority queue discipline is called *shortest job first.*)

1.25. For the tandem queue of Prob. 1.14, suppose that with probability 0.2, a customer completing service at server 2 is *dissatisfied* with her overall service and must be completely served over again (at least once) by both servers. Define the delay in queue of a customer (in a particular queue) to be the total delay in that queue for all of that customer's passes through the facility. Simulate the facility for each of the following cases (estimate the same measures as before):
(*a*) Dissatisfied customers join the tail of queue 1.
(*b*) Dissatisfied customers join the head of queue 1.

1.26. A service facility consists of two type A servers and one type B server (not necessarily in the psychological sense). Assume that customers arrive at the facility with interarrival times that are IID exponential random variables with a mean of 1 minute. Upon arrival, a customer is determined to be either a type 1 customer or a type 2 customer, with respective probabilities of 0.75 and 0.25. A type 1 customer can be served by any server but will choose a type A server if one is available. Service times for type 1 customers are IID exponential random variables with a mean of 0.8 minute, regardless of the type of server. Type 1 customers who find all servers busy join a single FIFO queue *for type 1 customers*. A type 2 customer requires service from *both* a type A server *and* the type B server *simultaneously*. Service times for type 2 customers are uniformly distributed between 0.5 and 0.7 minute. Type 2 customers who arrive to find both type A servers busy *or* the type B server busy join a single FIFO queue *for type 2 customers*. Upon completion of service of *any* customer, preference is given to a type 2 customer if one is present and if both a type A and the type B server are then idle. Otherwise, preference is given to a type 1 customer. Simulate the facility for exactly 1000 minutes and estimate the expected average delay in queue and the expected time-average number in queue for each type of customer. Also estimate the expected proportion of time that each server spends on each type of customer.

1.27. A supermarket has two checkout stations, regular and express, with a single checker per station; see Fig. 1.51. Regular customers have exponential interarrival times with mean 2.1 minutes and have exponential service times with mean 2.0 minutes. Express

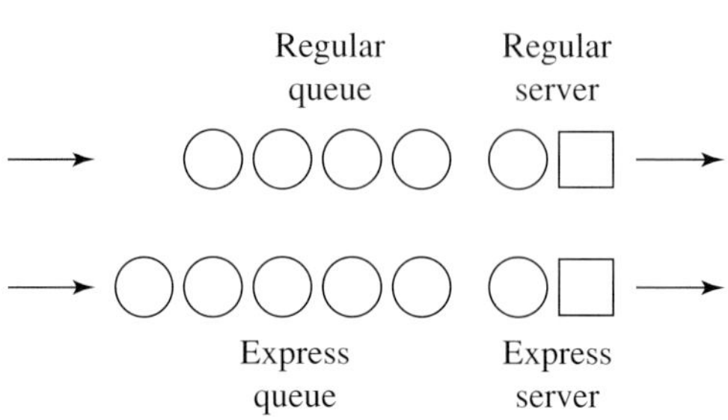

FIGURE 1.51
A supermarket checkout operation.

customers have exponential interarrival times with mean 1.1 minutes and exponential service times with mean 0.9 minute. The arrival processes of the two types of customers are independent of each other. A regular customer arriving to find at least one checker idle begins service immediately, choosing the regular checker if both are idle; regular customers arriving to find both checkers busy join the end of the regular queue. Similarly, an express customer arriving to find an idle checker goes right into service, choosing the express checker if both are idle; express customers arriving to find both checkers busy join the end of the express queue, even if it is longer than the regular queue. When either checker finishes serving a customer, he takes the next customer from his queue, if any, and if his queue is empty but the other one is not, he takes the first customer from the other queue. If both queues are empty, the checker becomes idle. Note that the mean service time of a customer is determined by the customer type, and not by whether the checker is the regular or express one. Initially, the system is empty and idle, and the simulation is to run for exactly 8 hours. Compute the average delay in each queue, the time-average number in each queue, and the utilization of each checker. What recommendations would you have for further study or improvement of this system? (On June 21, 1983, the Cleveland *Plain Dealer*, in a story entitled "Fast Checkout Wins over Low Food Prices," reported that "Supermarket shoppers think fast checkout counters are more important than attractive prices, according to a survey [by] the Food Marketing Institute. . . . The biggest group of shoppers, 39 percent, replied 'fast checkouts,' . . . and 28 percent said good or low prices . . . [reflecting] growing irritation at having to stand in line to pay the cashier.")

1.28. A one-pump gas station is always open and has two types of customers. A police car arrives every 30 minutes (exactly), with the first police car arriving at time 15 minutes. Regular (nonpolice) cars have exponential interarrival times with mean 5.6 minutes, with the first regular car arriving at time 0. Service times at the pump for all cars are exponential with mean 4.8 minutes. A car arriving to find the pump idle goes right into service, and regular cars arriving to find the pump busy join the end of a single queue. A police car arriving to find the pump busy, however, goes to the front of the line, ahead of any regular cars in line. [If there are already other police cars at the front of the line, assume that an arriving police car gets in line ahead of them as well. (How could this happen?)] Initially the system is empty and idle, and the simulation is to run until exactly 500 cars (of any type) have completed their delays in queue. Estimate the expected average delay in queue for each type of car separately, the expected time-average number of cars (of either type) in queue, and the expected utilization of the pump.

1.29. Of interest in telephony are models of the following type. Between two large cities, A and B, are a fixed number, n, of long-distance lines or circuits. Each line can operate in either direction (i.e., can carry calls originating in A or B) but can carry only one call at a time; see Fig. 1.52. If a person in A or B wants to place a call to the other city

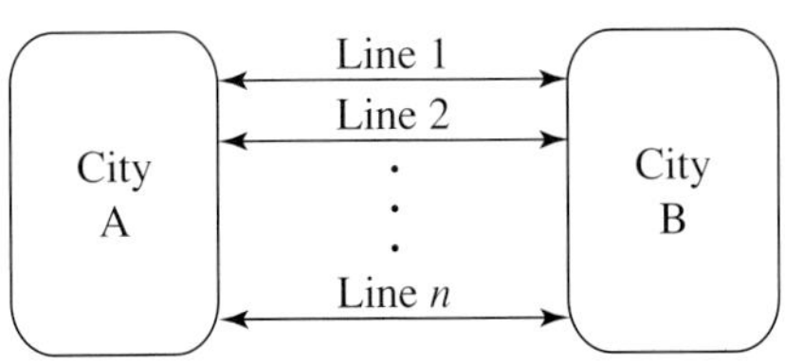

FIGURE 1.52
A long-distance telephone system.

and a line is open (i.e., idle), the call goes through immediately on one of the open lines. If all n lines are busy, the person gets a recording saying that she must hang up and try later; there are no facilities for queueing for the next open line, so these *blocked* callers just go away. The times between attempted calls from A to B are exponential with mean 10 seconds, and the times between attempted calls from B to A are exponential with mean 12 seconds. The length of a conversation is exponential with mean 4 minutes, regardless of the city of origin. Initially all lines are open, and the simulation is to run for 12 hours; compute the time-average number of lines that are busy, the time-average proportion of lines that are busy, the total number of attempted calls (from either city), the number of calls that are blocked, and the proportion of calls that are blocked. Determine approximately how many lines would be needed so that no more than 5 percent of the attempted calls will be blocked.

1.30. City buses arrive to the maintenance facility with exponential interarrival times with mean 2 hours. The facility consists of a single inspection station and two identical repair stations; see Fig. 1.53. Every bus is inspected, and inspection times are distributed uniformly between 15 minutes and 1.05 hours; the inspection station is fed by a single FIFO queue. Historically, 30 percent of the buses have been found during inspection to need some repair. The two parallel repair stations are fed by a single FIFO queue, and repairs are distributed uniformly between 2.1 hours and 4.5 hours. Run the simulation for 160 hours and compute the average delay in each queue, the average length of each queue, the utilization of the inspection station, and the utilization of the repair station (defined to be half of the time-average number of busy repair stations, since there are two stations). Replicate the simulation 5 times. Suppose that the arrival rate of buses quadrupled, i.e., the mean interarrival time decreased to 30 minutes. Would the facility be able to handle it? Can you answer this question without simulation?

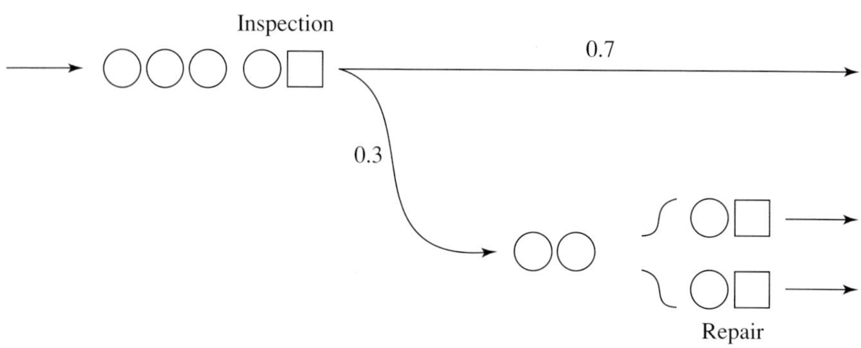

FIGURE 1.53
A bus maintenance depot.

CHAPTER 2

Modeling Complex Systems

Recommended sections for a first reading: 2.1 through 2.5

2.1 INTRODUCTION

In Chap. 1 we looked at simulation modeling in general, and then modeled and coded two specific systems. Those systems were very simple, and it was possible to program them directly in a general-purpose language, without using any special simulation software or support programs (other than a random-number generator). Most real-world systems, however, are quite complex, and coding them without supporting software can be a difficult and time-consuming task.

In this chapter we first discuss an activity that takes place in most simulations: list processing. A group of ANSI-standard C support functions, simlib, is then introduced, which takes care of some standard list-processing tasks as well as several other common simulation activities, such as processing the event list, accumulating statistics, generating random numbers and observations from a few distributions, as well as calculating and writing out results. We then use simlib in four example simulations, the first of which is just the single-server queueing system from Sec. 1.4 (included to illustrate the use of simlib on a familiar model); the last three examples are somewhat more complex.

Our purpose in this chapter is to illustrate how more complex systems can be modeled, and to show how list processing and the simlib utility functions can aid in their programming. Our intention in using a package such as simlib is purely pedagogical; it allows the reader to move quickly into modeling more complex systems and to appreciate how real simulation-software packages handle lists and other data. We do not mean to imply that simlib is as comprehensive or efficient as, or in any other way comparable to, the modern commercial simulation software discussed in

Chaps. 3 and 14; in fact, the complete source code for simlib is given in App. 2A and Fig. 7.5, and can be downloaded from www.mhhe.com/law (along with the code for all the examples in this chapter). A FORTRAN 77 version of simlib, along with some documentation specific to it and code for the four example models discussed in this chapter, can also be downloaded from this website.

2.2 LIST PROCESSING IN SIMULATION

The simulation models considered in Chap. 1 were really quite simple in that they contained either one or no *lists* of *records* other than the event list. Furthermore, the records in these lists consisted of a single *attribute* and were always processed in a first-in, first-out (FIFO) manner. In the queueing example, there was a FIFO list containing the records of all customers waiting in queue, and each customer record consisted of a single attribute, the time of arrival. In the inventory example there were no lists other than the event list. However, most complex simulations require many lists, each of which may contain a large number of records, consisting in turn of possibly many attributes each. Furthermore, it is often necessary to process these lists in a manner other than FIFO. For example, in some models one must be able to remove that record in a list with the smallest value for a specified attribute (other than the time the record was placed in the list). If this large amount of information is not stored and manipulated efficiently, the model may require so much execution time or so many storage locations that the simulation study would not be feasible.

In Sec. 2.2.1 we discuss two approaches to storing lists of records in a computer—sequential and linked allocation—and then explain why the latter approach is preferable for complex simulations. In Sec. 2.2.2 we present a treatment of linked storage allocation that is sufficient for the development of a simple C-based simulation "language," simlib, in Sec. 2.3. This language, which can be completely mastered in just a few hours of study, provides considerable insight into the nature of the special-purpose simulation software discussed in Chaps. 3 and 14, which requires much more time to learn. More important, simlib provides a vehicle for explaining how to simulate systems that are considerably more complicated than those discussed in Chap. 1.

2.2.1 Approaches to Storing Lists in a Computer

There are two principal approaches to storing lists of records in a computer. In the *sequential-allocation* approach, used in Chap. 1, the records in a list are put into physically adjacent storage locations, one record after another. This was the approach taken in Sec. 1.4 with the list of arrival times for customers in the queue.

In the *linked-allocation* approach, each record in a list contains its usual attributes and, in addition, *pointers* (or *links*) giving the *logical* relationship of the record to other records in the list. Records in a list that follow each other logically need not be stored in physically adjacent locations. A detailed discussion of linked allocation is given in Sec. 2.2.2. Linked allocation of lists has several advantages for simulation modeling:

- The time required to process certain kinds of lists can be significantly reduced. For the queueing example of Sec. 1.4, every time a customer completed service (and left a nonempty queue behind) we had to move each entry in the arrival-time array up one storage location; this would be quite inefficient if the queue were long, in which case the array would contain a large number of records. As we shall see in Example 2.1, linked allocation expedites processing of such arrays.
- For simulation models where the event list contains a large number of event records simultaneously, we can speed up event-list processing considerably; see Example 2.2 and Sec. 2.8 for further discussion.
- For some simulation models, the amount of computer memory required for storage can be reduced; see the discussion at the end of Sec. 2.2.2.
- Linked allocation provides a general framework that allows one to store and manipulate many lists simultaneously with ease, whereby records in different lists may be processed in different ways. This generality is one of the reasons for the use of the linked-allocation approach by all major simulation software.

2.2.2 Linked Storage Allocation

In this section we present a discussion of linked storage allocation sufficient for development of the simple C-based simulation "language" simlib, described in the next section. For a more complete and general discussion of list-processing principles, see, for example, Knuth (1997, chap. 2).

Suppose that a list of records is to be stored in an array, that the rows of the array correspond to the records, and that the columns of the array correspond to the attributes (or data fields) that make up the records. For the queueing simulation of Sec. 1.4, each customer waiting in the queue had a record in the arrival-time list, and each record consisted of a single attribute, the corresponding customer's time of arrival. In general, a customer's record might have additional attributes such as age, a priority number, service requirement, etc.

A list of records is called *doubly linked* if each record has associated with it a predecessor link and a successor link. The *successor link* (or *forward pointer*) for a particular record gives the *physical* row number in the array of the record that *logically* succeeds the specified record. If no record succeeds the specified record, the successor link is set to zero. The *predecessor link* (or *backward pointer*) for a particular record gives the physical row number in the array of the record that logically precedes the specified record. If no record precedes the specified record, the predecessor link is set to zero. The number of the physical row in the array that contains the record that is logically first in the list is identified by a *head pointer*, which is set to zero when the list contains no records. The physical row number of the record that is logically last in the list is identified by a *tail pointer*, which is set to zero when the list is empty.

At any given time a list will probably occupy only a subset of the rows of the array in which it is physically stored. The "empty" rows of the array that are available for future use are linked together in a *list of available space* (LAS). The LAS is usually processed in a LIFO (last-in, first-out) manner: This means that when a row is needed to store an additional record, the row is taken from the head of the LAS; and when a row is no longer needed to store a record, the row is returned to the head of the LAS. Since all operations are done at the head of the LAS, it requires neither a tail pointer nor predecessor links. (We call such a list *singly linked.*) At time 0 in a simulation, all rows in the array are members of the LAS, the successor link of row i is set to $i + 1$ (except for that of the last row, which is set to 0), all predecessor links are set to 0, and the head of the LAS is set to 1. (The predecessor link for a particular row is set to a positive integer only when that row is occupied by a record.) In languages that support dynamic storage allocation (like C), the LAS can be thought of as all memory available for dynamic allocation.

EXAMPLE 2.1. For the queueing simulation of Sec. 1.4, consider the list containing the customers waiting in *queue* to be served. Each record in this list has the single attribute, "time of arrival." Suppose that at time 25 in the simulation there are three customers in queue, with times of arrival 10, 15, and 25, and that these records are stored in (physical) rows 2, 3, and 1 of an array with 5 rows and 1 column. (To make the figures below manageable, we assume that there will never be more than five customers in queue at any time.) Rows 4 and 5 are members of the LAS. The situation is depicted in Fig. 2.1. Note that the head pointer of the list is equal to 2, the successor link for the record in row 2 is equal to 3, the predecessor link for the record in row 3 is equal to 2, etc.

Suppose that the next event in the simulation (after time 25) is the arrival of a customer at time 40 and that we would like to add an appropriate record to the list, which is to be processed in a FIFO manner. Since the head pointer for the LAS is equal to 4,

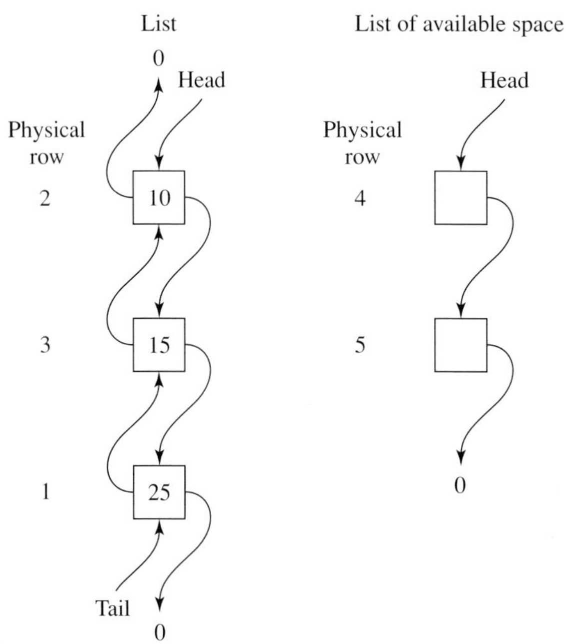

FIGURE 2.1
State of the lists for the queueing simulation at time 25.

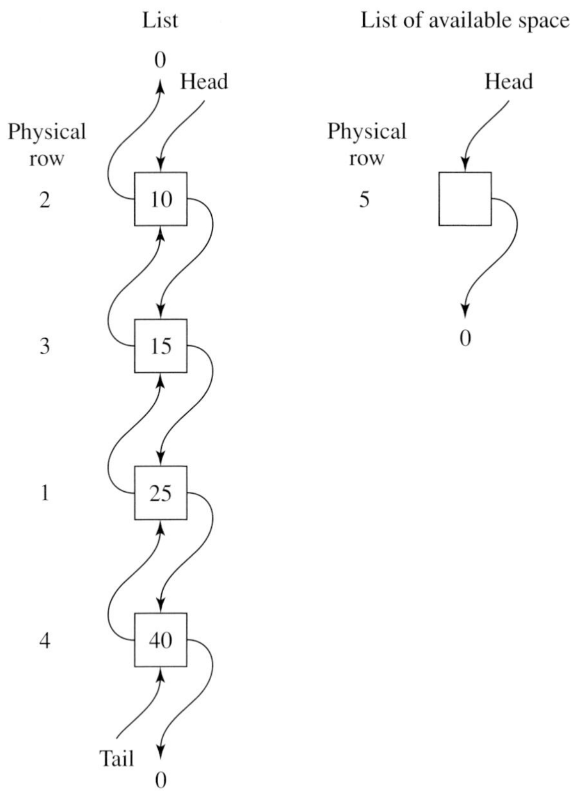

FIGURE 2.2
State of the lists for the queueing simulation at time 40.

the record for the arriving customer will be placed in physical row 4 of the array and the head pointer of the LAS is now set to 5, which is the value of the successor link for row 4. Since the new record will be added to the tail of the list and the tail pointer for the list is now equal to 1, the successor link for the record in row 1 is set to 4, the predecessor link for the new record, i.e., the one in (physical) row 4, is set to 1, the successor link for the new record is set to 0, and the tail pointer for the list is set to 4. The state of both lists after these changes have been made is shown in Fig. 2.2.

Suppose that the next event in the simulation (after time 40) is the service completion at time 50 of the customer who was being served (at least since time 25) and that we want to remove the record of the customer at the head of the list so that this customer can begin service. Since the head pointer for the list is equal to 2 and the successor link for the record in (physical) row 2 is equal to 3, the time of arrival of the record in row 2 is used to compute the delay of the customer who will enter service (this delay is $50 - 10$), the head pointer for the list is set to 3, the predecessor link for the record in row 3 is set to 0, and row 2 (which is no longer needed) is placed at the head of the LAS by setting its head pointer to 2 and the successor link for row 2 to 5 (the previous head of the LAS). The state of both lists after these changes have been made is shown in Fig. 2.3.

Thus, removing a record from the head of the list always requires setting only four links or pointers. Contrast this with the brute-force approach of Chap. 1, which requires moving each record in the (sequential) list up by one location. If the list contained, say,

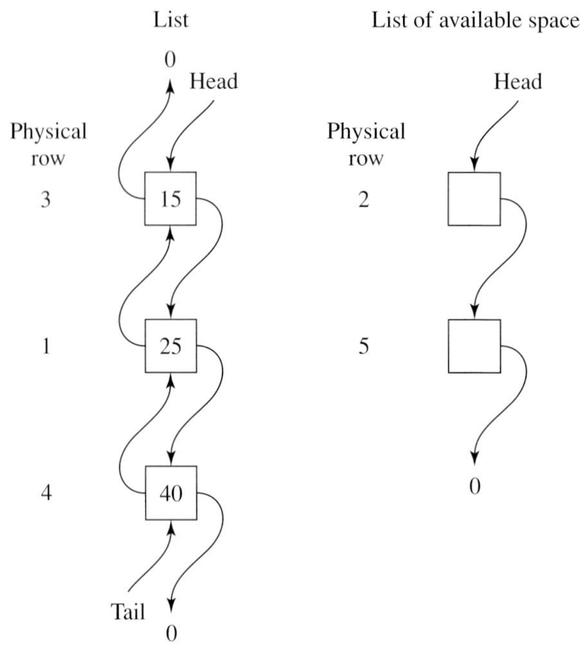

FIGURE 2.3
State of the lists for the queueing simulation at time 50.

100 records, this would be a much more time-consuming task than with the linked-list approach.

While storing a queue as a linked list as in the above example seems fairly natural, the next example illustrates how the event list can also be processed as a linked list.

EXAMPLE 2.2. For the inventory simulation of Sec. 1.5, the event list was stored in an array with each of the four event types having a dedicated physical location. If an event was not currently scheduled to occur, its entry in the list was set to ∞ (represented as 10^{30} in the computer). However, for many complex simulations written in a general-purpose language and for simulations using the special-purpose simulation software described in Chaps. 3 and 14, the event list is stored as a linked list ranked in increasing order on event time. Now, events having an event time of ∞ are simply not included in the event list. Moreover, since the event list is kept ranked in increasing order on the event times (attribute 1), the next event to occur will always be at the head of the list, so we need only remove this record to determine the next event time (attribute 1) and its type (attribute 2). For instance, suppose that the event list for the inventory simulation is to be stored in an array of 4 rows and 2 columns, column 1 being for the attribute "event time" and column 2 being for the attribute "event type," i.e., 1, 2, 3, or 4. Suppose that at time 0 we know that the first demand for the product (event type 2) will occur at time 0.25, the first inventory evaluation (event type 4) will occur immediately at time 0, the simulation will end (event type 3) at time 120, and there is no outstanding order scheduled to arrive (event type 1). The state of the event list and the LAS just after initialization at time 0 is shown in Fig. 2.4. Note that event type 1 is not included in the event list, and that event type 2 is in (physical) row 1 of the array since it was the first event record to be placed in the event list.

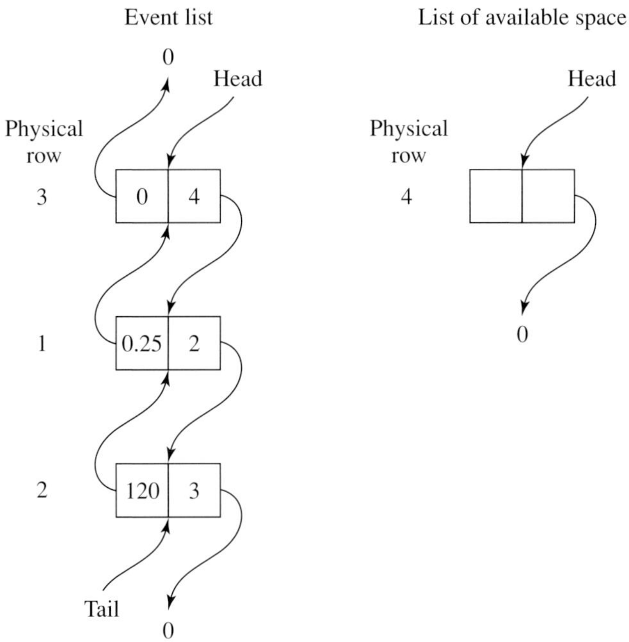

FIGURE 2.4
State of the lists for the inventory simulation just after initialization at time 0.

To determine the next (first) event to occur at time 0, the first record is removed from the event list, the simulation clock is updated to the first attribute of this record, i.e., the clock is set to 0, the event type of the next event to occur is set to the second attribute of this record, i.e., is set to 4, and row 3, which contained this record, is placed at the head of the LAS. Since the next event type is 4, an inventory-evaluation event will occur next (at time 0). Suppose that an order is placed at time 0 and that it will arrive from the supplier at time 0.6. To place this order-arrival event in the event list, first 0.6 and 1 are placed in columns 1 and 2, respectively, of row 3 (the head of the LAS), and then this new record is added to the event list by logically proceeding down the event list (using the successor links) until the correct location is found. In particular, attribute 1 of the new record (0.6) is first compared with attribute 1 of the record in row 1 (0.25). Since $0.6 > 0.25$, the new record should be farther down the event list. Next, 0.6 is compared with attribute 1 of the record in row 2 (120). (Note that the successor link of the record in row 1 is equal to 2.) Since $0.6 < 120$, the new record is logically placed between the records in physical rows 1 and 2 by adjusting the successor and predecessor links for the three records. After this has been done, another inventory-evaluation event is scheduled at time 1 and placed in the event list in a manner similar to that for the order-arrival event. The state of both lists after all processing has been done at time 0 is shown in Fig. 2.5.

In the above discussion, a single list was stored in an array where the empty rows were members of the LAS, but we could just as well store many different lists simultaneously in the same physical array. There is a single LAS, and the beginning

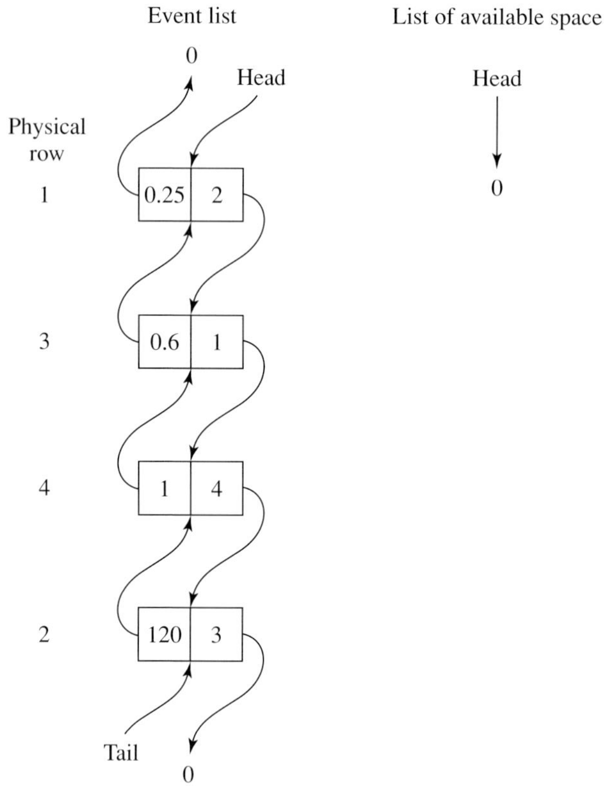

FIGURE 2.5
State of the lists for the inventory simulation after all processing has been done at time 0.

and end of each list are identified by separate head and tail pointers. This approach can lead to significant savings in storage space for some applications. For example, suppose that a simulation requires 20 lists, each containing up to 100 records of 10 attributes each. Using the sequential storage method (as in Chap. 1), 20 arrays with 100 rows and 10 columns each would be required, for a total storage requirement of 20,000 locations. Suppose, however, that at any given time an average of only 25 percent of all available rows are actually being used. Then an alternative approach might be to store all 20 lists in one array consisting of 1000 rows and 10 columns. This approach would require 10,000 locations for the array plus an additional 2040 locations for the links and pointers, for a total of 12,040 storage locations. Furthermore, at a particular point in a simulation, some lists may be occupying more than their "fair" share of the available rows without causing a memory overflow condition.

The simple simulation language simlib, developed in the next section, stores all lists (including the event list) in dynamic memory, which is allocated when needed to store a new record in a list, and is freed for other uses after a record is removed from a list.

2.3 A SIMPLE SIMULATION LANGUAGE: simlib

In this section we describe an easy-to-understand C-based simulation "language," simlib, which implements the concept of linked storage allocation presented in Sec. 2.2.2. The language makes it easy to file a record in a list (the record may be filed first in the list, last in the list, or so that the list is kept ranked in increasing or decreasing order on a specified attribute), to remove a record from a list (either the first record or the last record in the list may be removed), to process the event list, to compute discrete-time statistics on variables of interest (e.g., the average delay in queue in a queueing system), to compute continuous-time statistics on variables of interest (e.g., the time-average number of items in an inventory system), to generate the random variates used in the examples in this chapter and in Chap. 1, and to provide output in a "standard" format if desired. Although simlib provides many of the important features found in special-purpose simulation software (see Chaps. 3 and 14), it is designed for neither completeness nor computational efficiency. Our reasons for presenting it here are to provide some insight into the operation of simulation software and to provide a vehicle for understanding how to simulate systems that are much more complicated than those in Chap. 1.

The heart of simlib is a collection of doubly linked lists, all residing together in dynamic memory, with space allocated as new records are filed into the lists, and space freed as records are removed from the lists. There is a maximum of 25 lists, and the records in each list can have up to 10 attributes, with all data stored as type float. Since simlib uses dynamic storage allocation, the total number of records in all the lists is limited only by the amount of memory available on the computer.

List 25 is always reserved for the event list, with attribute 1 being the event time and attribute 2 being the event type. This list is furthermore kept sorted in increasing order on attribute 1 (event time) so that the top (first) record always refers to the next event.

To use simlib, the file simlib.h must be #included by the user. This file in turn #includes the file simlibdefs.h. These files are shown in Figs. 2.47 and 2.48 in App. 2A, and they contain (among other things) declarations and definitions of the following variables and constants germane to the user:

sim_time	The simulation clock, a float variable, updated by simlib function timing (see the discussion of function timing below)
next_event_type	The type of the next event, an int variable, determined by simlib function timing (see the discussion of function timing below)
transfer[i]	A float array with indices i = 1, 2, . . . , 10 (index i = 0 is not used) for transferring into and out of the lists used in the simulation, where transfer[i] refers to attribute i of a record. The transfer array is also used by simlib as a place to transfer to the user the values of certain summary statistics.
maxatr	The maximum number of attributes for any record in any list in the simulation model, an int variable. If maxatr is not set in the main function by the user, a default value of 10 is used; maxatr cannot be greater than 10.

	Setting maxatr to a value less than 10, if possible, will result in faster program execution. Because of the way simlib is written, the user must specify maxatr to be at least 4.
list_size[list]	The current number of records in list "list", an int array, which is automatically updated by simlib. The user should not need to alter the value of list_size[list], but only query its value if appropriate. For example, if list 3 has been set up to represent a queue, then list_size[3] will always be the number in this queue, so that we can tell if it is empty by asking if list_size[3] is equal to 0.
list_rank[list]	The attribute number, if any, according to which the records in list "list" are to be ranked (in increasing or decreasing order) by simlib function list_file; this is an int array. For example, if list 4 is to be kept so that the records are ranked on attribute 2, then the user would need to set list_rank[4] to be equal to 2 before using list_file to file a record in list 4; one of the arguments in function list_file controls whether the ranking is increasing or decreasing. Typically, list_rank[list] is set by the user in the main function. If list "list" is not ranked (i.e., records are inserted only at the end or the beginning), then list_rank[list] need not be set at all. Note that list_rank[25] is set to 1 in the simlib initialization routine init_simlib, since attribute 1 of the event list (list number 25) is always the event time, and we wish to keep the event list ranked in increasing order of the event times.
FIRST	A symbolic constant for the option of filing or removing a record at the beginning of a list, automatically set to 1 in simlibdefs.h
LAST	A symbolic constant for the option of filing or removing a record at the end of a list, automatically set to 2 in simlibdefs.h
INCREASING	A symbolic constant for the option of keeping a list ranked in increasing order according to the attribute specified in the list_rank array, automatically set to 3 in simlibdefs.h
DECREASING	A symbolic constant for the option of keeping a list ranked in decreasing order according to the attribute specified in the list_rank array, automatically set to 4 in simlibdefs.h
LIST_EVENT	A symbolic constant for the number of the event list, 25, automatically set to 25 in simlibdefs.h
EVENT_TIME	A symbolic constant for the attribute number of the event time in the event list, automatically set to 1 in simlibdefs.h
EVENT_TYPE	A symbolic constant for the attribute number of the event type in the event list, automatically set to 2 in simlibdefs.h

These variables and arrays are used or set by the user during the simulation, as appropriate, and must have the names and types given above, as declared in simlib.h.

There are some 19 functions composing simlib, each designed to perform a frequently occurring simulation activity:

- **init_simlib.** This function, to be invoked from the user-written main function at the beginning of each simulation run, allocates storage for the lists, initializes the successor and predecessor links as well as the head and tail pointers for each list, initializes the simulation clock to 0, sets list_rank[LIST_EVENT] to EVENT_TIME to keep the event list ranked on event times, and sets maxatr to a default value of 10. Also, the statistical accumulators for functions sampst and timest (see their discussion below) are set to 0.

- **list_file(option, list).** This function places the attributes of a record that the user has placed in the transfer array into list "list" ("list" is an int) in a location controlled by the int argument "option". That is, when list_file is invoked, transfer[i] is placed in list "list" as attribute i of the new record, for i = 1, 2, . . . , maxatr. The following options are available:

option	Action
1 (or FIRST)	File the record in transfer before the first record currently in list "list".
2 (or LAST)	File the record in transfer after the last record currently in list "list".
3 (or INCREASING)	File the record in transfer into list "list" so that the list is kept ranked in increasing order on attribute list_rank[list], which must have been given a value previously. (If two records have the same value of attribute list_rank[list], the rule is FIFO.)
4 (or DECREASING)	File the record in transfer into list "list" so that the list is kept ranked in decreasing order on attribute list_rank[list], which must have been given a value previously. (If two records have the same value of attribute list_rank[list], the rule is FIFO.)

Thus, list_file(1, 3) would file transfer[1], . . . , transfer[maxatr] into list 3, with this becoming the first record in the list; list_file(FIRST, 3) would do the same thing. If we want list 2 to be kept ranked in decreasing order according to attribute 4 of the records in that list, then we could execute list_file(DECREASING, 2), making sure that we had set list_rank[2] to 4 previously, probably in the main function. Finally, we could schedule an event into the event list by executing list_file(INCREASING, LIST_EVENT) after setting (at least) transfer[1] to the time of occurrence of this event, and transfer[2] to the type of this event (see the description of simlib function event_schedule below, however, for an easier way to schedule events into the event list). Storage is dynamically allocated by list_file for the new record in list "list".

- **list_remove(option, list).** Invoking this function removes a record from list "list" (an int), and copies it (i.e., its attributes) into the transfer array. The int argument "option" determines which record is removed:

option	Action
1 (or FIRST)	Remove the first record from list "list" and place it into the transfer array.
2 (or LAST)	Remove the last record from list "list" and place it into the transfer array.

After invoking list_remove, the elements in transfer, now being equal to those in the record just removed, are typically used for some purpose in the simulation. For example, list_remove(2, 1) removes the last record in list 1 and places it in the transfer array; list_remove(LAST, 1) does the same thing. Storage is dynamically freed by list_remove since space in list "list" for the record just removed is no longer needed.

- **timing.** This function, invoked by the user from the main function, accomplishes what the timing functions of Chap. 1 did, except now timing is an internal simlib function, and it uses the list structure of the event list exactly as described in Example 2.2. The type of the next event, next_event_type (a simlib int variable declared in simlib.h), is determined, and the clock, sim_time, is updated to the time of this next event. Actually, timing simply invokes list_remove(FIRST, LIST_EVENT) to remove the first record from list 25, the event list; since the event list is kept in increasing order on the event time, we know that this will be the next event to occur. Thus, attributes 1 through maxatr of the first event record are placed in transfer, and can be used if desired. In particular, it is sometimes advantageous to make use of attributes *other* than 1 and 2 in event records; see Secs. 2.6 and 2.7 as well as Prob. 2.3.
- **event_schedule(time_of_event, type_of_event).** The user can invoke this function to schedule an event to occur at time time_of_event (a float) of type type_of_event (an int) into the event list. Normally, event_schedule will be invoked to schedule an event in the simulated future, so time_of_event would be of the form sim_time + time_interval, where time_interval is an interval of time from now until the event is to happen. If attributes other than 1 (event time) and 2 (event type) of event records are being used in the event list, it is the user's responsibility to place their values in the appropriate locations in the transfer array before invoking event_schedule.
- **event_cancel(event_type).** This function cancels (removes) the first event in the event list with event type event_type (an int), if there is such an event, and places the attributes of the canceled event record in the transfer array. If the event list does not have an event of type event_type, no action is taken by event_cancel. If event_cancel finds an event of type event_type and cancels it, the function returns an int value of 1; if no such event is found, the function returns an int value of 0.
- **sampst(value, variable).** This function accumulates and summarizes discrete-time data, such as customer delays in a queue. There is provision for up to 20 "sampst variables," maintained and summarized separately, and indexed by the int argument "variable". For example, a model could involve three separate queues, and sampst variables 1, 2, and 3 could be used to accumulate and summarize customer delays in each of these queues, separately. There are three different typical uses of sampst:

  During the simulation. Each time a new value of sampst variable "variable" is observed (e.g., the end of a delay in queue), its value is placed in the float argument "value", and sampst is invoked. For instance, if we have defined sampst variable 2 to be the delays in queue 2 of a model, we could execute sampst(delay2, 2) after having placed the desired delay in the float variable delay2. The function sampst internally maintains separate registers for each variable, in which statistics are accumulated to produce the output described below.

At the end of the simulation. The user can invoke sampst with the *negative* of the variable "variable" desired, to produce summary statistics that are placed into the transfer array as follows:

i	transfer[i]
1	Mean (average) of the values of variable "variable" observed
2	Number of values of variable "variable" observed
3	Maximum value of variable "variable" observed
4	Minimum value of variable "variable" observed

In addition, sampst returns as a float the mean (in its name), the same thing that is placed into transfer[1], as a convenience since means are often desired. For example, executing sampst(0.0, −2) would place the summary statistics on sampst variable 2 in the transfer array, as described above, and return the mean; the desired summary statistics would then typically be written out by the user, or perhaps used in some other way. Note that in this use of sampst, the value of "value" is ignored. (A technicality: If no values for variable "variable" were observed, the mean, maximum, and minimum are undefined. In this case, sampst returns the mean as 0, the maximum as -10^{30}, and the minimum as 10^{30}.)

To reset all sampst variable accumulators. The accumulators for all sampst variables are reinitialized, as at the start of the simulation, by executing sampst(0.0, 0); note that this is done in init_simlib at time 0. This capability would be useful *during* a simulation if we wanted to start observing data only after the simulation had "warmed up" for some time, as described in Sec. 9.5.1; see also Prob. 2.7.

- **timest(value, variable).** This function is similar to sampst, but operates instead on continuous-time data such as the number-in-queue function; see Sec. 1.4.1. Again, the int argument "variable" refers to one of up to 20 "timest variables" on which data are accumulated and summarized when desired. For example, timest variables 1, 2, and 3 could refer to the number of customers in queues 1, 2, and 3, respectively. As with sampst, there are three "typical" uses:

  During the simulation. Each time timest variable "variable" attains a new value, we must execute timest(value, variable), where the float argument "value" contains the *new* (i.e., *after* the change) value of the variable. For example, if the length of queue 2 changes as a result of an arrival or departure to the float variable q2, we would execute timest(q2, 2) to do the proper accumulation. The accumulators for timest are initialized in init_simlib under the assumption that all continuous-time functions being tracked by timest are initially zero; this can be overridden by executing timest(value, variable) just after invoking init_simlib, where value contains the desired (nonzero) initial value of timest variable "variable". (This would be done for each desired timest variable.)

At the end of the simulation. The user can invoke timest with the *negative* of the variable "variable" desired, to produce summary statistics that are placed into the transfer array as follows:

i	transfer[i]
1	Time average of the values of variable "variable" observed, *updated to the time of this invocation*
2	Maximum value of variable "variable" observed up to the time of this invocation
3	Minimum value of variable "variable" observed up to the time of this invocation

In addition, timest returns as a float the time average (in its name), the same thing that is placed into transfer[1], as a convenience since means are often desired. For example, executing timest(0.0, −2) would place the summary statistics on timest variable 2 in the transfer array, as described above, and return the time average; the desired summary statistics would then typically be written out by the user, or perhaps used in some other way.

To reset all timest variable accumulators. The accumulators for all timest variables are reinitialized to zero, as at the start of the simulation, by executing timest(0.0, 0); this is done in init_simlib at time 0. Note that this assumes that all timest variables should have the value 0, which can be overridden by immediately executing timest(value, variable) to reset timest variable "variable" to the value "value".

- **filest(list).** This function, typically invoked only at the end of a simulation run, provides summary data on the number of records in list "list", placing them into the transfer array in a manner similar to timest, as follows:

i	transfer[i]
1	Time-average number of records in list "list", *updated to the time of this invocation*
2	Maximum number of records in list "list", up to the time of this invocation
3	Minimum number of records in list "list", up to the time of this invocation

In addition, filest returns as a float the time average (in its name), the same thing that is placed into transfer[1], as a convenience since means are often desired. Internally, simlib treats the number of records in a list as a continuous-time function whose value may rise or fall only at the times of events, so that it is sensible to speak of the time-average number of records in a list, etc. In addition, simlib automatically tracks each list in this way, and can produce these statistics when filest is invoked. Who cares about the history of list lengths? This capability turns out to be quite convenient, since the number of records in a list often has some physical meaning. For example, a queue will usually be represented in a simulation by a list, and the number of records in that list is thus identical to the number of customers in the queue; hence the time-average and maximum number of customers in the queue are simply the time average and maximum of the number of records in the list. Another example is a list being used to represent a server, where the list will have one record in it if the server is busy and will be empty if the server is idle; the server utilization is thus the time-average number of records in this list, since the only possibilities for its length are 0 and 1. In this way, we can often (but not always) avoid explicitly tracking a continuous-time function via timest. However, timest should probably be used instead of filest if the corresponding list is set up merely for convenience in statistics collection, especially when the function being tracked rises or falls by increments other than 1 (e.g., the inventory level in the model of Sec. 1.5), due to the overhead in filing and removing many dummy records. Moreover, timest would have to be used instead of filest if the function being tracked can take on noninteger values. [Internally, simlib treats the number of records in list "list" as timest variable 20 + list, so that there are actually 45 timest variables, but only the first 20 are accessible to the user. Then filest simply invokes timest with variable = −(20 + list) to get statistics on list "list".]

- **out_sampst(unit, lowvar, highvar).** If desired, this function may be invoked to produce the summary statistics on sampst variables lowvar through highvar (inclusively) and write them to file "unit"; lowvar and highvar are both int arguments.This produces "standard" output format (which fits within an 80-character line), and obviates the need for the *final* invocation of sampst (but *not* the invocations during the course of the simulation) and also eliminates the need for fprintf statements, formatting, etc. The disadvantage of using out_sampst is that the annotation and layout of the output cannot be controlled or customized. For example, out_sampst(outfile, 1, 3) would write summary statistics to file outfile on sampst variables 1, 2, and 3; sampst(outfile, 4, 4) would write summary statistics on sampst variable 4. In the simlib simulations later in this chapter, we show examples of using (and ignoring) this standard-format output option.
- **out_timest(unit, lowvar, highvar).** Similar to out_sampst, this optional function may be used to produce standard-format output on file "unit" for timest variables lowvar through highvar.
- **out_filest(unit, lowfile, highfile).** This function uses filest to produce summary statistics on the number of records in files lowfile through highfile, written to file "unit"; lowfile and highfile are both int arguments.
- **expon(mean, stream).** This function returns a float with an observation from an exponential distribution with mean "mean" (a float argument). The int argument stream is the user-specified random-number stream number, discussed more fully in Sec. 7.1 and App. 7A. For now, we can think of the stream number as a separate, independent random-number generator (or list of random numbers) to be used for the purpose of generating the desired observations from the exponential distribution. It is generally a good idea to "dedicate" a random-number stream to a particular source of randomness in a simulation, such as stream 1 for interarrivals and stream 2 for service times, etc., to facilitate the use of *variance-reduction techniques* (see Chap. 11). These techniques can often provide a great improvement in the statistical precision of simulations. Furthermore, using dedicated streams can facilitate program verification (debugging). Except for the

stream specification, this is the same function used in Sec. 1.4.4 for generating observations from an exponential distribution. There are 100 separate streams available in simlib; i.e., "stream" must be an int between 1 and 100 inclusively, and the length of each stream is 100,000 random numbers.

- **random_integer(prob_distrib[], stream).** This function returns an int with an observation from a discrete probability distribution with *cumulative* distribution-function values specified by the user in the float array prob_distrib. For i a positive integer between 1 and 25, prob_distrib[i] should be specified by the user, before invoking random_integer, to be the desired probability of generating a value *less than or equal to* i. If the range of random integers desired is 1, 2, . . . , k, where k < 25, then prob_distrib[k] should be set to 1.0, and it is then not necessary to specify prob_distrib[j] for j > k. The int argument stream, between 1 and 100, gives the random-number stream to be used. Except for the random-number stream specification, this is the same function used for the inventory model in Sec. 1.5.3.
- **uniform(a, b, stream).** This function returns a float with an observation from a (continuous) uniform distribution between a and b (both float arguments). As before, stream is an int between 1 and 100 giving the random-number stream to be used.
- **erlang(m, mean, stream).** This function returns a float with an observation from an m-Erlang distribution with mean "mean" using random-number stream "stream"; m is an int, mean is a float, and stream is an int. This distribution will be discussed in Sec. 2.7.
- **lcgrand(stream).** This is the random-number generator used by simlib, a function returning a float with an observation from a (continuous) uniform distribution between 0 and 1, using stream "stream" (an int argument). Its code is given in Fig. 7.5 in App. 7A, instead of in App. 2A. When using simlib, and in particular #including the file simlib.h, it is not necessary to #include lcgrand.h from Fig. 7.6 in App. 7A, since simlib.h contains the required declarations.
- **lcgrandst(zset, stream).** This function "sets" the random-number *seed* for stream "stream" to the long argument zset. It is shown in Fig. 7.5 in App. 7A.
- **lcgrandgt(stream).** This function returns a long with the current underlying integer for the random-number generator for stream "stream"; it is shown in Fig. 7.5 in App. 7A, and discussed more fully in Chap. 7. It could be used to restart a subsequent simulation (using lcgrandst) from where the current one left off, as far as random-number usage is concerned.

This completes the description of simlib, but before proceeding with concrete examples of its use, we conclude this section with an overview of how simlib's components are typically used together in a simulation. It is still up to the user to write a C main function and event functions, but the simlib functions will make the coding much easier. First, we must determine the events and decide what lists will be used for what purpose; the numbering of lists and their attributes is in large measure arbitrary, but it is essential to be consistent. Also, any sampst and timest variables to be used must be defined, as should the usage of random-number streams. In addition to the global variables defined by simlib (via the header file simlib.h), the user will generally need to declare some global and perhaps local variables through the model. In the main function, the following activities take place, roughly in the order listed:

1. Read and write (for confirmation) the input parameters.
2. Invoke init_simlib to initialize the simlib variables.
3. (If necessary) Set list_rank[list] to the attribute number on which list "list" is to be ranked, for lists that need to be kept in some sort of order according to the value of a particular attribute. (If no lists other than the event list are to be ranked, then this step is skipped.)
4. Set maxatr to the maximum number of attributes used in any list. Note that maxatr must be at least 4 for proper operation of simlib. If this is skipped, maxatr defaults to 10 and the simulation will run correctly, but setting maxatr to a smaller value will make the simulation faster, since it avoids repeated copying of unused attributes into and out of the lists.
5. (If necessary) Invoke timest to initialize any timest variables that are not to be zero initially.
6. Initialize the event list by invoking event_schedule for each event to be scheduled at time 0. If event attributes beyond the first (event time) and second (event type) are used in the data structure, it is the user's responsibility to set transfer[3], transfer[4], etc., before invoking event_schedule for that event. Events that cannot occur are simply not placed into the event list.
7. Invoke timing to determine next_event_type and update sim_time to the time of that event.
8. Invoke the appropriate event function (user-written, but using simlib variables and functions where possible), as determined by next_event_type. This is typically done with a case statement, routing control to one of several event-function-invocation statements, as was done in the C programs of Chap. 1.
9. When the simulation ends, invoke a report-generator function (user-written), which in turn will invoke sampst, timest, or filest and then write out the desired summary statistics. Alternatively, the report generator could invoke out_sampst, out_timest, or out_filest to write out the summary statistics in standard format.

While the simulation is running, lists are maintained by using list_file and list_remove, together with the transfer array to transfer the data in the attributes of records into and out of lists. When needed, sampst and timest are used to gather statistics on variables of interest.

A final note on simlib's capabilities concerns error checking. While no software package can detect all errors and suggest how to fix them, there are special opportunities to do some of this in simulation programs, as discussed in Chap. 1. Accordingly, simlib contains several such error checks, and will write out a message (to standard output) indicating the nature of the error and the clock value when it occurred. For example, simlib function timing checks for a "time reversal," i.e., an attempt to schedule an event at a time earlier than the present. Also, there are checks for illegal list numbers, illegal variable numbers, etc., and for attempting to remove a record from a list that is empty.

In Secs. 2.4 through 2.7 we show how to use simlib to simulate systems of varying complexity.

2.4 SINGLE-SERVER QUEUEING SIMULATION WITH simlib

2.4.1 Problem Statement

In this section we show how to simulate the single-server queueing system from Sec. 1.4, using simlib. The model is exactly the same, so that we can concentrate on the use of simlib without having to worry about the structure of a new model. We will use the 1000-delay stopping rule, as originally described in Sec. 1.4.3.

2.4.2 simlib Program

The first step is to identify the events; they are the same as before—an arrival is a type 1 event, and a departure (service completion) is a type 2 event.

Next, we must define the simlib lists and the attributes in their records. It is important to write this down, as it will be referenced while the program is developed:

List	Attribute 1	Attribute 2
1, queue	Time of arrival to queue	—
2, server	—	—
25, event list	Event time	Event type

Note that list 1 (representing the queue) is quite similar to the array time_arrival used in Sec. 1.4.4, except that now we are taking advantage of simlib's list-processing capabilities; list 1 has only a single attribute. List 2 represents the server and either will be empty (if the server is idle) or will contain a single record (if the server is busy); a record in list 2 when the server is busy is a "dummy" record, in that it has no actual attributes. The purpose for defining such a list is to allow the use of filest at the end of the simulation to get the server utilization. Also, we can tell whether the server is busy by asking whether list_size[2] is equal to 1. This use of a dummy list is convenient in that the server_status variable is eliminated, and we need not use timest during or at the end of the simulation to get the utilization. However, it is not the most computationally efficient approach, since all the machinery of the linked lists is invoked whenever the server changes status, rather than simply altering the value of a server_status variable. (This is a good example of the tradeoff between computation time and analyst's time in coding a model.) Finally, list 25 is the event list, with attribute 1 being event time and attribute 2 being event type; this is required in all simlib programs, but for some models we will use additional attributes for the event record in list 25.

Next, we should identify all sampst and timest variables used. Our only sampst variable is as follows:

sampst variable number	Meaning
1	Delays in queue

```
/* External definitions for single-server queueing system using simlib. */

#include "simlib.h"              /* Required for use of simlib.c. */

#define EVENT_ARRIVAL          1  /* Event type for arrival. */
#define EVENT_DEPARTURE        2  /* Event type for departure. */
#define LIST_QUEUE             1  /* List number for queue. */
#define LIST_SERVER            2  /* List number for server. */
#define SAMPST_DELAYS          1  /* sampst variable for delays in queue. */
#define STREAM_INTERARRIVAL    1  /* Random-number stream for interarrivals. */
#define STREAM_SERVICE         2  /* Random-number stream for service times. */

/* Declare non-simlib global variables. */

int   num_custs_delayed, num_delays_required;
float mean_interarrival, mean_service;
FILE  *infile, *outfile;

/* Declare non-simlib functions. */

void init_model(void);
void arrive(void);
void depart(void);
void report(void);
```

FIGURE 2.6
C code for the external definitions, queueing model with simlib.

Since we can obtain both the number-in-queue and utilization statistics using filest (or out_filest if standard output format is acceptable), we do not need any timest variables for this model.

Finally, we allocate separate random-number streams for generating the interarrival and service times, as follows:

Stream	Purpose
1	Interarrival times
2	Service times

Figure 2.6 shows the external declarations, which are at the top of the file mm1smlb.c. The first thing we do is #include the header file simlib.h, which is required for all programs using simlib. To make the code more readable and more general, we define symbolic constants for the event types, list numbers, the sampst variable, and the random-number streams. We must still declare some non-simlib variables for the model, though far fewer than in Sec. 1.4.4 since much of the information is held internally by simlib. And we must still have our own functions, init_model to initialize this particular model, arrive and depart for the events, and a report generator, but we no longer need a timing function or the expon function since they are provided by simlib.

Figure 2.7 shows the main function, which must still be written by the user. After opening the input and output files, we read the input parameters and then immediately write them out for confirmation that they were read properly (and to document our output). Invoking init_simlib initializes simlib, after which we set maxatr to 4; while we have no records with more than two attributes, maxatr must be at least 4 for simlib to operate properly. We are not using any ranked lists (other

```
main()  /* Main function. */
{
    /* Open input and output files. */

    infile  = fopen("mm1smlb.in",  "r");
    outfile = fopen("mm1smlb.out", "w");

    /* Read input parameters. */

    fscanf(infile, "%f %f %d", &mean_interarrival, &mean_service,
           &num_delays_required);

    /* Write report heading and input parameters. */

    fprintf(outfile, "Single-server queueing system using simlib\n\n");
    fprintf(outfile, "Mean interarrival time%11.3f minutes\n\n",
            mean_interarrival);
    fprintf(outfile, "Mean service time%16.3f minutes\n\n", mean_service);
    fprintf(outfile, "Number of customers%14d\n\n\n", num_delays_required);

    /* Initialize simlib */

    init_simlib();

    /* Set maxatr = max(maximum number of attributes per record, 4) */

    maxatr = 4;  /* NEVER SET maxatr TO BE SMALLER THAN 4. */

    /* Initialize the model. */

    init_model();

    /* Run the simulation while more delays are still needed. */

    while (num_custs_delayed < num_delays_required) {

        /* Determine the next event. */

        timing();

        /* Invoke the appropriate event function. */

        switch (next_event_type) {
            case EVENT_ARRIVAL:
                arrive();
                break;
            case EVENT_DEPARTURE:
                depart();
                break;
        }
    }

    /* Invoke the report generator and end the simulation. */

    report();

    fclose(infile);
    fclose(outfile);

    return 0;
}
```

FIGURE 2.7
C code for the main function, queueing model with simlib.

```
void init_model(void)  /* Initialization function. */
{
    num_custs_delayed = 0;

    event_schedule(sim_time + expon(mean_interarrival, STREAM_INTERARRIVAL),
                   EVENT_ARRIVAL);
}
```

FIGURE 2.8
C code for function init_model, queueing model with simlib.

than the event list), so we do not need to set anything in the list_rank array; also, both of the continuous-time functions (queue length and server status) are initially zero, so we need not override their default values. The user-written function init_model is then invoked to set up our own, non-simlib modeling variables. The rest of the main function is similar to Fig. 1.11 for the non-simlib version of this model, except that we need not update the continuous-time statistical accumulators since simlib takes care of that internally.

Figure 2.8 shows init_model, which begins by setting the num_custs_delayed counter to 0 for the number of delays observed. The first arrival event is then scheduled by invoking event_schedule with the desired event time (a float) as the first argument and the event type (an int) as the second argument; note that adding sim_time to the generated exponential interarrival time in the first argument is not strictly necessary here since sim_time is now zero, but we write it this way to show the general form and to emphasize that the first argument of event_schedule is the (absolute) time in the simulated future when the event is to occur, not the interval of time from now until then. In Chap. 1 we had to set the time of impossible events to ∞ (actually, 10^{30}), but now we simply leave them out of the event list, ensuring that they cannot be chosen to happen next. Thus, we just do not schedule a departure event at all here.

In Fig. 2.9 is the code for event function arrive, which begins by using event_schedule to schedule the next arrival event, in a manner similar to that in init_model (here, adding sim_time to the generated exponential interarrival time *is* necessary since sim_time will be positive). We then check to see whether the server is busy, by asking whether the server list contains a (dummy) record; this is done by checking whether list_size[LIST_SERVER] is equal to 1. If so, the arriving customer must join the end of the queue, which is done by placing the time of arrival (the current clock value, sim_time) into the first location of the transfer array, and by filing this record at the end (option = LAST = 2) of the queue list (list = LIST_QUEUE = 1). Note that we do not have to check for overflow of the queue here since simlib is automatically allocating storage dynamically for the lists as it is needed. On the other hand, if the server is idle, the customer experiences a delay of 0, which is noted by invoking sampst; this *is* necessary even though the delay is 0, since sampst will also increment the number of observations by 1. We increment num_custs_delayed since a delay is being observed, and a departure event is scheduled into the event list; note that we are dedicating stream EVENT_DEPARTURE (=2) to generating service times.

Event function depart, in Fig. 2.10, checks whether the queue is empty, by looking at the length of the queue list, held by simlib in list_size[LIST_QUEUE]. If so,

```
void arrive(void)  /* Arrival event function. */
{
    /* Schedule next arrival. */

    event_schedule(sim_time + expon(mean_interarrival, STREAM_INTERARRIVAL),
                   EVENT_ARRIVAL);

    /* Check to see whether server is busy (i.e., list SERVER contains a
       record). */

    if (list_size[LIST_SERVER] == 1) {

        /* Server is busy, so store time of arrival of arriving customer at end
           of list LIST_QUEUE. */

        transfer[1] = sim_time;
        list_file(LAST, LIST_QUEUE);
    }

    else {

        /* Server is idle, so start service on arriving customer, who has a
           delay of zero.  (The following statement IS necessary here.) */

        sampst(0.0, SAMPST_DELAYS);

        /* Increment the number of customers delayed. */

        ++num_custs_delayed;

        /* Make server busy by filing a dummy record in list LIST_SERVER. */

        list_file(FIRST, LIST_SERVER);

        /* Schedule a departure (service completion). */

        event_schedule(sim_time + expon(mean_service, STREAM_SERVICE),
                       EVENT_DEPARTURE);
    }
}
```

FIGURE 2.9
C code for function arrive, queueing model with simlib.

the server is made idle by removing the (dummy) record from list LIST_SERVER, the only action needed; note that we are removing the first record in the list, but we could also have removed the last one since there is only one record there. On the other hand, if there is a queue, the first customer is removed from it, and that customer's time of arrival is placed in transfer[1] by list_remove. The delay in queue of that customer is thus sim_time − transfer[1], which is computed and tallied in sampst, and the number of delays observed is incremented; as in the examples of Chap. 1, if the simulation were to be run for a long period of simulated time, it might be necessary to make both sim_time and transfer of type double to avoid loss of precision in the subtraction to compute the delay in queue. Finally, the service completion of this customer is scheduled by invoking event_schedule. Note that we need no longer move the queue up, since this is done internally by simlib, using linked lists as discussed in Example 2.1.

The report-generation function is shown in Fig. 2.11, and uses the standard output formatting in out_sampst for the delay-in-queue measure and out_filest for the

```
void depart(void)  /* Departure event function. */
{
    /* Check to see whether queue is empty. */

    if (list_size[LIST_QUEUE] == 0)

        /* The queue is empty, so make the server idle and leave the departure
           (service completion) event out of the event list. (It is currently
           not in the event list, having just been removed by timing before
           coming here.) */

        list_remove(FIRST, LIST_SERVER);

    else {

        /* The queue is nonempty, so remove the first customer from the queue,
           register delay, increment the number of customers delayed, and
           schedule departure. */

        list_remove(FIRST, LIST_QUEUE);
        sampst(sim_time - transfer[1], SAMPST_DELAYS);
        ++num_custs_delayed;
        event_schedule(sim_time + expon(mean_service, STREAM_SERVICE),
                       EVENT_DEPARTURE);
    }
}
```

FIGURE 2.10
C code for function depart, queueing model with simlib.

```
void report(void)  /* Report generator function. */
{
    /* Get and write out estimates of desired measures of performance. */

    fprintf(outfile, "\nDelays in queue, in minutes:\n");
    out_sampst(outfile, SAMPST_DELAYS, SAMPST_DELAYS);
    fprintf(outfile, "\nQueue length (1) and server utilization (2):\n");
    out_filest(outfile, LIST_QUEUE, LIST_SERVER);
    fprintf(outfile, "\nTime simulation ended:%12.3f minutes\n", sim_time);
}
```

FIGURE 2.11
C code for function report, queueing model with simlib.

number-in-queue and utilization measures. Note that we write out brief headers before invoking out_sampst and out_filest to make the report a little more readable.

2.4.3 Simulation Output and Discussion

The output file mm1smlb.out is given in Fig. 2.12, and illustrates the standard format produced by out_sampst and out_filest. We use general formatting of the numerical results to avoid the possibility of overflowing the field widths. We get all characteristics of the output measures, i.e., average, maximum, and minimum, as well as the number of observations for the discrete-time variables used by sampst. We also write out the final clock value, as a check.

An important point is that these numerical results are *not* the same as those in Fig. 1.19 for the non-simlib version of this same model; in fact, they are quite a bit different, with the average delay in queue changing from 0.430 in Chap. 1 to 0.525

```
Single-server queueing system using simlib

Mean interarrival time        1.000 minutes

Mean service time             0.500 minutes

Number of customers            1000


Delays in queue, in minutes:
```

SAMPST variable number	Average	Number of values	Maximum	Minimum
1	0.5248728E+00	0.1000000E+04	0.5633087E+01	0.0000000E+00

```
Queue length (1) and server utilization (2):
```

File number	Time average	Maximum	Minimum
1	0.5400774E+00	0.8000000E+01	0.0000000E+00
2	0.5106925E+00	0.1000000E+01	0.0000000E+00

```
Time simulation ended:     971.847 minutes
```

FIGURE 2.12
Output report, queueing model with simlib.

here, a difference of some 22 percent. The reason for this is that we are now using the concept of "dedicating" a random-number stream to a particular source of randomness, while in Chap. 1 we used the same stream (number 1) for everything. Both programs are correct, and this illustrates the need for careful statistical analysis of simulation output data, as discussed in Chaps. 9 through 12.

While using simlib did simplify the coding of this model considerably, the value of such a package becomes more apparent in complex models with richer list structures. Such models are considered next, in Secs. 2.5 through 2.7.

2.5 TIME-SHARED COMPUTER MODEL

In this section we use simlib to simulate a model of a time-shared computer facility considered by Adiri and Avi-Itzhak (1969).

2.5.1 Problem Statement

A company has a computer system consisting of a single central processing unit (CPU) and n terminals, as shown in Fig. 2.13. The operator of each terminal "thinks"

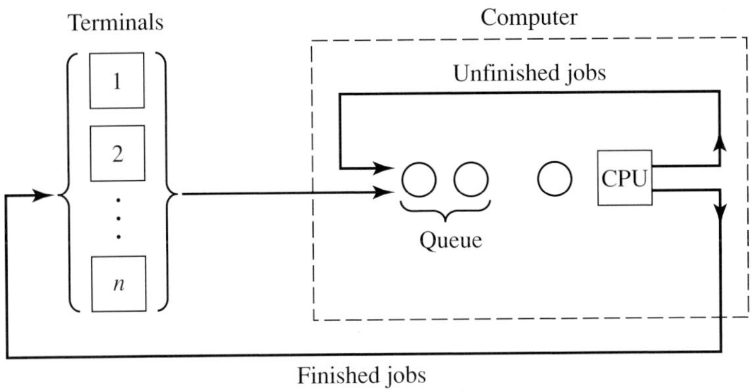

FIGURE 2.13
Time-shared computer model.

for an amount of time that is an exponential random variable with mean 25 seconds, and then sends to the CPU a job having service time distributed exponentially with mean 0.8 second. Arriving jobs join a single queue for the CPU but are served in a *round-robin* rather than FIFO manner. That is, the CPU allocates to each job a maximum service *quantum* of length $q = 0.1$ second. If the (remaining) service time of a job, s seconds, is no more than q, the CPU spends s seconds, plus a fixed swap time of $\tau = 0.015$ second, processing the job, which then returns to its terminal. However, if $s > q$, the CPU spends $q + \tau$ seconds processing the job, which then joins the end of the queue, and its remaining service time is decremented by q seconds. This process is repeated until the job's service is eventually completed, at which point it returns to its terminal, whose operator begins another think time.

Let R_i be the response time of the ith job to finish service, which is defined as the time elapsing between the instant the job leaves its terminal and the instant it is finished being processed at the CPU. For each of the cases $n = 10, 20, \ldots, 80$, we use simlib to simulate the computer system for 1000 job completions (response times) and estimate the expected average response time of these jobs, the expected time-average number of jobs waiting in the queue, and the expected utilization of the CPU. Assume that all terminals are in the think state at time 0. The company would like to know how many terminals it can have on its system and still provide users with an average response time of no more than 30 seconds.

2.5.2 simlib Program

The events for this model are:

Event description	Event type
Arrival of a job to the CPU from a terminal, at the end of a think time	1
End of a CPU run, when a job either completes its service requirement or has received the maximum processing quantum q	2
End of the simulation	3

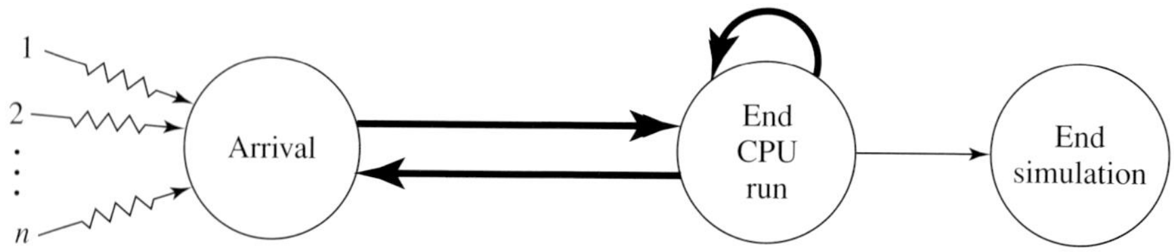

FIGURE 2.14
Event graph, computer model.

Note that we have defined an end-simulation event, even though the stopping rule for this model is not a fixed point in simulated time. The end-simulation event is scheduled at the time the 1000th response time is observed, and is scheduled to occur immediately, i.e., at that time. Clearly, there are other ways in which this stopping rule could be implemented, as discussed below.

An event graph (see Sec. 1.4.7) for this model is shown in Fig. 2.14. The n separate initializations of the arrival (i.e., end-think-time) event refer to the fact that each of the n terminals will be initially scheduled to have such an event. Note also that the arrival and end-CPU-run events can potentially schedule each other; an arrival can schedule the end of a CPU run if the arriving job finds the CPU idle, and an end-CPU-run event can schedule an arrival if the job exiting the CPU is finished and returns to its terminal. Also, an end-CPU-run event can schedule itself in the case of a job's leaving the CPU before its total processing is finished, and looping back to the queue only to find that the queue is empty and the CPU is idle since all other jobs are at their terminals. Finally, note that the end-simulation event can be scheduled only from the end-CPU-run event and in zero time, in the case that a finished job leaves the CPU and supplies the last (1000th) response time required; as discussed in Sec. 1.4.7, an event having incoming arcs that are all thin and smooth (representing a scheduling of the event in zero time from the event from which the smooth arrow emanates) can be eliminated from the model and its action incorporated elsewhere. Problem 2.2 deals with this issue for this model.

Three lists of records will be used, one corresponding to the jobs in queue (list 1), one for the job being served by the CPU (list 2), and one for the event list (list 25, as usual). These lists have the following attributes:

List	Attribute 1	Attribute 2
1, queue	Time of arrival of job to computer	Remaining service time
2, CPU	Time of arrival of job to computer	Remaining service time after the present CPU pass (negative if the present CPU pass is the last one needed for this job)
25, event list	Event time	Event type

As in Sec. 2.4, we are using a list to represent a server (list 2 for the CPU), thereby facilitating estimation of the CPU utilization via filest at the end of the simulation. Here, however, this "server" list's attributes are *not* dummies; they carry necessary information about the job in service, since it may have to revisit the CPU several times, and its time of arrival and remaining service time must be carried along for it to be processed correctly. Note also that we have matched up the attributes in lists 1 and 2, so that transferring a record between these lists can be done simply by invoking list_remove and then list_file without having to rearrange the attributes in the transfer array. Finally, we are not explicitly keeping track of the terminal of origin for a job, so that when its processing is complete in the computer we do not know what terminal to send it back to in order for its next think time to begin. This would certainly not do in reality, since the terminal operators would be getting each others' output back, but in the *simulation* we need not represent the ownership of each job by a particular terminal since we want only overall (i.e., over all the terminals) performance measures for the response times. Furthermore, all the terminals are probabilistically identical, as the think-time and CPU-time distributions are the same. Problem 2.3 asks that the model be enriched by collecting separate response-time statistics for each terminal, and allowing the terminal characteristics to vary; any of these changes would require that the terminal of origin of a job be carried along with it while it is inside the computer.

Since there is only a single discrete-time statistic of interest (the response times), we need only a single sampst variable:

sampst variable number	Meaning
1	Response times

For each of the continuous-time statistics desired (number in queue and CPU utilization), there is a corresponding list whose length represents the desired quantity, so we can again obtain the output via filest, and we do not need any of our own timest variables.

There are two types of random variables for this model, and we use the following stream assignments:

Stream	Purpose
1	Think times
2	Service times

Figure 2.15 shows the global external definitions for this model, which are at the top of the file tscomp.c. After #including the header file simlib.h, we define symbolic constants for the event types, list numbers, sampst variable number, and random-number streams. The non-simlib variables are declared, including ints for the minimum and maximum number of terminals across the simulations (min_terms = 10 and max_terms = 80), the increment in the number of terminals across the simulations (incr_terms = 10), the number of terminals for a particular simulation (num_terms), the number of response times observed in the current simulation (num_responses), and the number of responses required (num_responses_required = 1000); floats are required only for the input parameters for mean think and service times, the quantum q, and the swap time τ. The user-written, non-simlib functions are declared, including event functions for arrival and end-CPU-run events; we have written a non-event function, start_CPU_run, to process a particular activity that

```
/* External definitions for time-shared computer model. */

#include "simlib.h"              /* Required for use of simlib.c. */

#define EVENT_ARRIVAL          1  /* Event type for arrival of job to CPU. */
#define EVENT_END_CPU_RUN      2  /* Event type for end of a CPU run. */
#define EVENT_END_SIMULATION   3  /* Event type for end of the simulation. */
#define LIST_QUEUE             1  /* List number for CPU queue. */
#define LIST_CPU               2  /* List number for CPU. */
#define SAMPST_RESPONSE_TIMES  1  /* sampst variable for response times. */
#define STREAM_THINK           1  /* Random-number stream for think times. */
#define STREAM_SERVICE         2  /* Random-number stream for service times. */

/* Declare non-simlib global variables. */

int   min_terms, max_terms, incr_terms, num_terms, num_responses,
      num_responses_required, term;
float mean_think, mean_service, quantum, swap;
FILE  *infile, *outfile;

/* Declare non-simlib functions. */

void arrive(void);
void start_CPU_run(void);
void end_CPU_run(void);
void report(void);
```

FIGURE 2.15
C code for the external definitions, computer model.

may occur when either an arrival or an end-CPU-run event occurs, avoiding having to repeat this same block of code in each of those event functions. There is not a separate model-initialization function since there is little required to initialize this model (beyond what simlib does in init_simlib), so this activity was simply put into the main function. For this model we chose not to use the standard output formatting option, since we are really doing eight separate simulations and would like to arrange the output data in a customized table, with one line per simulation; also, we wish to get only the mean of the output performance measures rather than all of their characteristics (maximum, etc.).

The main function is shown in Fig. 2.16. As usual, we open the input and output files, read the input parameters, and then write them out in a report heading. Since we will be doing eight simulations, with one output line per simulation, we also write out column headings for the output at this time. A "for" loop setting num_terms in turn to 10, 20, . . . , 80 then begins, and encompasses the rest of the main function except for closing the files at the very end; a separate simulation is run, including initialization and results writing, within this "for" loop for each value of num_terms. Each simulation begins with a fresh initialization of simlib by invoking init_simlib, then sets maxatr to 4, initializes num_responses to 0, and schedules the first arrival to the CPU from each terminal by invoking event_schedule for each of the num_terms terminals. Note that we will then have num_terms events scheduled in the event list, all of type 1, each one representing the end of the initial think time for a particular terminal. A "do while" loop then starts, invoking the timing function and the appropriate event function as long as the event type is not the end-simulation event; when the event just executed is the end-simulation event (and report has been invoked), the "do while" loop ends and we go back to the enclosing

```
main()  /* Main function. */
{
    /* Open input and output files. */

    infile  = fopen("tscomp.in",  "r");
    outfile = fopen("tscomp.out", "w");

    /* Read input parameters. */

    fscanf(infile, "%d %d %d %d %f %f %f %f",
           &min_terms, &max_terms, &incr_terms, &num_responses_required,
           &mean_think, &mean_service, &quantum, &swap);

    /* Write report heading and input parameters. */

    fprintf(outfile, "Time-shared computer model\n\n");
    fprintf(outfile, "Number of terminals%9d to%4d by %4d\n\n",
            min_terms, max_terms, incr_terms);
    fprintf(outfile, "Mean think time  %11.3f seconds\n\n", mean_think);
    fprintf(outfile, "Mean service time%11.3f seconds\n\n", mean_service);
    fprintf(outfile, "Quantum          %11.3f seconds\n\n", quantum);
    fprintf(outfile, "Swap time        %11.3f seconds\n\n", swap);
    fprintf(outfile, "Number of jobs processed%12d\n\n\n",
            num_responses_required);
    fprintf(outfile, "Number of      Average         Average");
    fprintf(outfile, "       Utilization\n");
    fprintf(outfile, "terminals   response time  number in queue     of CPU");

    /* Run the simulation varying the number of terminals. */

    for (num_terms = min_terms; num_terms <= max_terms;
         num_terms += incr_terms) {

        /* Initialize simlib */

        init_simlib();

        /* Set maxatr = max(maximum number of attributes per record, 4) */

        maxatr = 4;  /* NEVER SET maxatr TO BE SMALLER THAN 4. */

        /* Initialize the non-simlib statistical counter. */

        num_responses = 0;

        /* Schedule the first arrival to the CPU from each terminal. */

        for (term = 1; term <= num_terms; ++term)
            event_schedule(expon(mean_think, STREAM_THINK), EVENT_ARRIVAL);

        /* Run the simulation until it terminates after an end-simulation event
           (type EVENT_END_SIMULATION) occurs. */

        do {

            /* Determine the next event. */

            timing();

            /* Invoke the appropriate event function. */

            switch (next_event_type) {
                case EVENT_ARRIVAL:
                    arrive();
                    break;
```

FIGURE 2.16
C code for the main function, computer model.

```
                case EVENT_END_CPU_RUN:
                    end_CPU_run();
                    break;
                case EVENT_END_SIMULATION:
                    report();
                    break;
            }

        /* If the event just executed was not the end-simulation event (type
           EVENT_END_SIMULATION), continue simulating.  Otherwise, end the
           simulation. */

        } while (next_event_type != EVENT_END_SIMULATION);
    }

    fclose(infile);
    fclose(outfile);

    return 0;
}
```

FIGURE 2.16
(*continued*)

"for" loop on the number of terminals. The end-simulation event is not scheduled initially, but will be scheduled in the function end_CPU_run at the time of the 1000th response-time completion, to occur at that time, whereupon the main function will invoke function report and end the current simulation. When the outer "for" loop ends, we have run all the simulations we want, including producing the output for each, and so the entire program ends by closing the files.

The arrival event is flowcharted in Fig. 2.17 and the code is in Fig. 2.18. While in the computer (i.e., in the queue or in the CPU), each job has its own record with

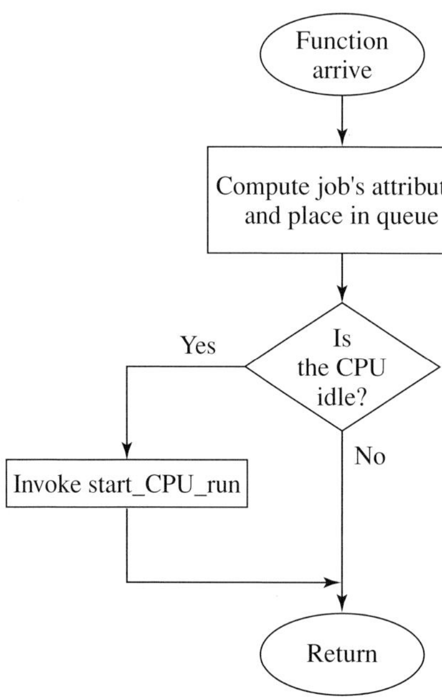

FIGURE 2.17
Flowchart for arrival function, computer model.

```
void arrive(void)  /* Event function for arrival of job at CPU after think
                      time. */
{

    /* Place the arriving job at the end of the CPU queue.
       Note that the following attributes are stored for each job record:
            1. Time of arrival to the computer.
            2. The (remaining) CPU service time required (here equal to the
               total service time since the job is just arriving). */

    transfer[1] = sim_time;
    transfer[2] = expon(mean_service, STREAM_SERVICE);
    list_file(LAST, LIST_QUEUE);

    /* If the CPU is idle, start a CPU run. */

    if (list_size[LIST_CPU] == 0)
        start_CPU_run();
}
```

FIGURE 2.18
C code for function arrive, computer model.

attributes as described earlier. Since this event represents a job's arrival to the computer at the end of a think time, its attributes must be defined now, so the time of arrival is stored in the first attribute and the total service requirement is generated and stored in the second attribute. The record for this newly arrived job is then placed at the end of the queue. It could be, however, that the CPU is actually idle (i.e., the number of records in list LIST_CPU, list_size[LIST_CPU], is equal to 0), in which case the function start_CPU_run is invoked to take this job out of the queue (it would be the only one there) and place it in the CPU to begin its processing. Implicit in the logic of this function is that a job arriving to the computer and finding the CPU idle cannot just go right in, but must first enter the queue and then be removed immediately; this is really a physical assumption that does matter, since there is a swap time incurred whenever a job leaves the queue and enters the CPU, as executed by function start_CPU_run, to be discussed next.

The non-event function start_CPU_run is flowcharted in Fig. 2.19, and its code is in Fig. 2.20. This function is designed to be invoked from the event function arrive, as just discussed, or from the event function end_CPU_run; thus it must be general enough to handle either case. The purpose of the function is to take the first job out of the queue, place it in the CPU, and schedule the time when it will leave the CPU, by virtue of either being completely done or having used up an entire quantum. The first thing to do is to remove the job from the front of the queue, which is done by invoking list_remove. Next, the time that the job will occupy the CPU is computed, being the smaller of a quantum and the remaining service time (held in the job's second attribute, having just been placed in transfer[2] by list_remove), plus a swap time. Before filing the job's record in the CPU list, its remaining service time (in transfer[2]) is decremented by a full quantum, even if it needs only a partial quantum to get done; in this case the second attribute of the job becomes negative, and we use this condition as a flag that the job, when leaving the CPU after the pass just beginning, is done and is to be sent back to its terminal. On the other hand, if the job will not be done after this pass through the CPU, it will be getting a full

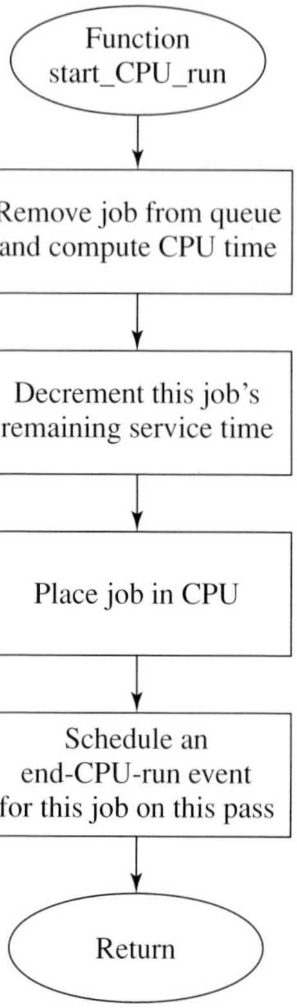

FIGURE 2.19
Flowchart for function start_CPU_run, computer model.

```
void start_CPU_run(void)  /* Non-event function to start a CPU run of a job. */
{
    float run_time;

    /* Remove the first job from the queue. */

    list_remove(FIRST, LIST_QUEUE);

    /* Determine the CPU time for this pass, including the swap time. */

    if (quantum < transfer[2])
        run_time = quantum + swap;
    else
        run_time = transfer[2] + swap;

    /* Decrement remaining CPU time by a full quantum.  (If less than a full
       quantum is needed, this attribute becomes negative.  This indicates that
       the job, after exiting the CPU for the current pass, will be done and is
       to be sent back to its terminal.) */

    transfer[2] -= quantum;

    /* Place the job into the CPU. */

    list_file(FIRST, LIST_CPU);

    /* Schedule the end of the CPU run. */

    event_schedule(sim_time + run_time, EVENT_END_CPU_RUN);
}
```

FIGURE 2.20
C code for function start_CPU_run, computer model.

quantum of service this time, and its second attribute should be decremented by a full quantum, correctly representing the (nonnegative) remaining service time needed after this CPU pass. Finally, the job is placed in the CPU list by invoking list_file (note that transfer[1], the time of this job's arrival to the computer, is already correctly set since it is from the record that was just removed from the queue list, where the first attribute has the same definition), and the end of this CPU run is scheduled into the event list.

Event function end_CPU_run is invoked from the main function when a job completes a pass through the CPU; it is flowcharted in Fig. 2.21, and its code is listed in Fig. 2.22. The job is first removed from the CPU, after which a check is made to see if it still needs more CPU time, i.e., if its second attribute is positive. If so, it is simply put back at the end of the queue (note that the attributes for the queue and CPU lists match up, so that the contents of transfer are correct), and start_CPU_run is invoked to remove the first job from the queue and begin its processing. On the other hand, if the job coming out of the CPU is finished, its response time, sim_time − transfer[1], is registered with sampst; as before for long simulations, both sim_time and transfer might have to be of type double to avoid loss of precision in this subtraction. The end of its next think time is scheduled, and the number of response times observed is incremented. Then a check is made to see whether this response time was the last one required; if so, an end-simulation event is scheduled to occur immediately (the first argument passed to event_schedule is sim_time, the current simulation time), and the timing function will pick off this end-simulation event immediately (i.e., without the passage of any simulated time), and the main function will invoke the report function to end this simulation. If, however, the simulation is not over, start_CPU_run is invoked provided that the queue is not empty; if the queue is empty, no action is taken and the simulation simply continues.

The report generator is listed in Fig. 2.23, and it simply writes to the output file a single line with the number of terminals for the simulation just completed, the average returned by sampst for the response times, and the time averages returned by filest for the queue length and server utilization (recall that sampst, timest, and filest return in their names the averages they compute, in addition to placing the average into transfer[1]).

2.5.3 Simulation Output and Discussion

The output file, tscomp.out, is shown in Fig. 2.24. As expected, congestion in the computer gets worse as the number of terminals rises, as measured by the average response time, average queue length, and CPU utilization. In particular, it appears that this system could handle about 60 terminals before the average response time degrades to a value much worse than 30 seconds. At this level, we see that the average queue length would be around 30 jobs, which could be useful for determining the amount of space needed to hold these jobs (the maximum queue length might have been a better piece of information for this purpose); further, the CPU would be busy nearly all the time with such a system. However, our usual caveat applies to

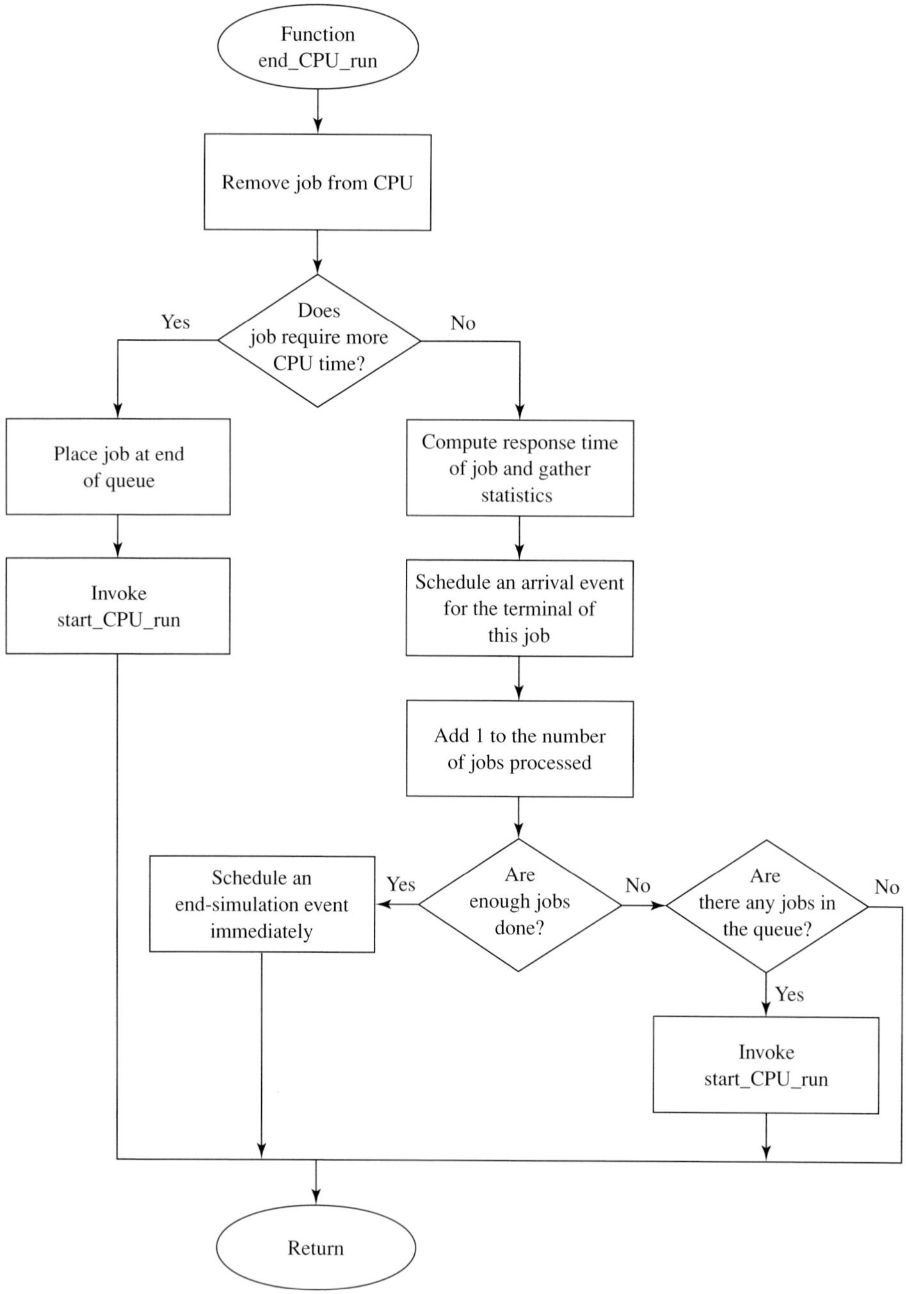

FIGURE 2.21
Flowchart for function end_CPU_run, computer model.

```
void end_CPU_run(void)  /* Event function to end a CPU run of a job. */
{
    /* Remove the job from the CPU. */

    list_remove(FIRST, LIST_CPU);

    /* Check to see whether this job requires more CPU time. */

    if (transfer[2] > 0.0) {

        /* This job requires more CPU time, so place it at the end of the queue
           and start the first job in the queue. */

        list_file(LAST, LIST_QUEUE);
        start_CPU_run();
    }

    else {

        /* This job is finished, so collect response-time statistics and send it
           back to its terminal, i.e., schedule another arrival from the same
           terminal. */

        sampst(sim_time - transfer[1], SAMPST_RESPONSE_TIMES);

        event_schedule(sim_time + expon(mean_think, STREAM_THINK),
                       EVENT_ARRIVAL);

        /* Increment the number of completed jobs. */

        ++num_responses;

        /* Check to see whether enough jobs are done. */

        if (num_responses >= num_responses_required)

            /* Enough jobs are done, so schedule the end of the simulation
               immediately (forcing it to the head of the event list). */

            event_schedule(sim_time, EVENT_END_SIMULATION);

        else

            /* Not enough jobs are done; if the queue is not empty, start
               another job. */

            if (list_size[LIST_QUEUE] > 0)
                start_CPU_run();
    }
}
```

FIGURE 2.22
C code for function end_CPU_run, computer model.

```
void report(void)  /* Report generator function. */
{
    /* Get and write out estimates of desired measures of performance. */

    fprintf(outfile, "\n\n%5d%16.3f%16.3f%16.3f", num_terms,
            sampst(0.0, -SAMPST_RESPONSE_TIMES), filest(LIST_QUEUE),
            filest(LIST_CPU));
}
```

FIGURE 2.23
C code for function report, computer model.

```
Time-shared computer model

Number of terminals        10 to  80 by   10

Mean think time         25.000 seconds

Mean service time        0.800 seconds

Quantum                  0.100 seconds

Swap time                0.015 seconds

Number of jobs processed          1000
```

Number of terminals	Average response time	Average number in queue	Utilization of CPU
10	1.324	0.156	0.358
20	2.165	0.929	0.658
30	5.505	4.453	0.914
40	12.698	12.904	0.998
50	24.593	23.871	0.998
60	31.712	32.958	1.000
70	42.310	42.666	0.999
80	47.547	51.158	1.000

FIGURE 2.24
Output report, computer model.

these conclusions: The output data on which they are based resulted from just a single run of the system (of somewhat arbitrary length) and are thus of unknown precision.

2.6 MULTITELLER BANK WITH JOCKEYING

We now use simlib to simulate a multiteller bank where the customers are allowed to jockey (move) from one queue to another if it seems to be to their advantage. This model also illustrates how to deal with another common stopping rule for a simulation.

2.6.1 Problem Statement

A bank with five tellers opens its doors at 9 A.M. and closes its doors at 5 P.M., but operates until all customers in the bank by 5 P.M. have been served. Assume that the interarrival times of customers are IID exponential random variables with mean 1 minute and that service times of customers are IID exponential random variables with mean 4.5 minutes.

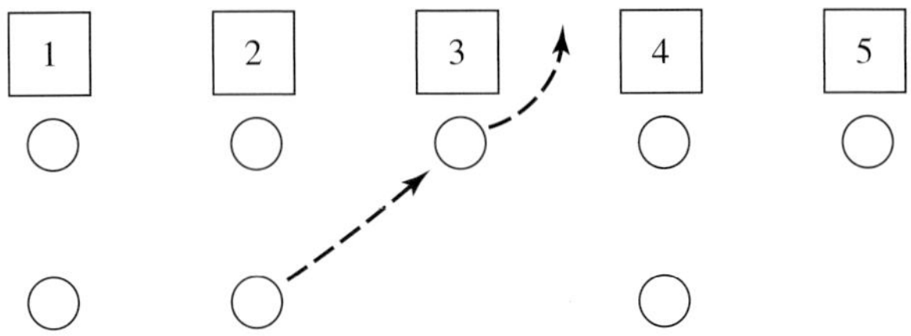

FIGURE 2.25
The customer being served by teller $i = 3$ completes service, causing the customer from the tail of queue $j = 2$ to jockey.

Each teller has a separate queue. An arriving customer joins the shortest queue, choosing the leftmost shortest queue in case of ties. Let n_i be the total number of customers in front of teller i (including customers in queue as well as the customer in service, if any) at a particular instant. If the completion of a customer's service at teller i causes $n_j > n_i + 1$ for some other teller j, then the customer from the tail of queue j jockeys to the tail of queue i. (If there are two or more such customers, the one from the closest, leftmost queue jockeys.) If teller i is idle, the jockeying customer begins service at teller i; see Fig. 2.25.

The bank's management is concerned with operating costs as well as the quality of service currently being provided to customers, and is thinking of changing the number of tellers. For each of the cases $n = 4, 5, 6$, and 7 tellers, we use simlib to simulate the bank and estimate the expected time-average total number of customers in queue, the expected average delay in queue, and the expected maximum delay in queue. In all cases we assume that no customers are present when the bank opens.

2.6.2 simlib Program

The events for this model are:

Event description	Event type
Arrival of a customer to the bank	1
Departure of a customer upon completion of his or her service	2
Bank closes its doors at 5 P.M.	3

An event graph for this model is given in Fig. 2.26. It is identical to that for the single-server queue with fixed run length (see Fig. 1.27), except that the end-simulation event has been replaced by the close-doors event. Even though these two events fit into the event diagram in the same way, the action they must take is quite different.

This model requires $2n + 1$ lists of records, where n is the number of tellers for a particular simulation run. Lists 1 through n contain the records of the customers waiting in the respective queues. Lists $n + 1$ through $2n$ are used to indicate

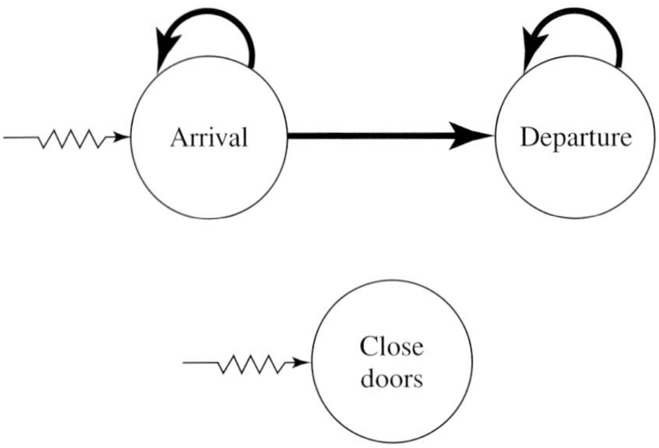

FIGURE 2.26
Event graph, bank model.

whether the tellers are busy. If list $n + i$ (where $i = 1, 2, \ldots, n$) contains one record, teller i is busy; if it contains no records, teller i is idle. Finally, list 25 is the event list, as usual. The attributes for all these lists are as follows:

List	Attribute 1	Attribute 2	Attribute 3
1 through n, queues	Time of arrival to queue	—	—
$n + 1$ through $2n$, tellers	—	—	—
25, event list	Event time	Event type	Teller number if event type = 2

Here again we are using separate lists for the servers in the model; in this case the only reason for doing so is to represent the busy/idle status of the servers, since no meaningful information is stored in the attributes of the records in these lists, and we are not asking for server utilization statistics. Note also that we are taking advantage of the opportunity to store more than just the event time and type in the records in the event list. The reason for this is that in the case of a departure event (type 2), we need to know the teller number from which the departure will occur in order to manage the queues and the jockeying rules correctly. A programming implication of this is that we must remember to define a value for transfer[3] before invoking the simlib function event_schedule for type 2 events, since event_schedule copies the attributes into only transfer[1] and transfer[2] before filing the event record into the event list.

The statistics collection in this model is somewhat different. Since there are several different queues, a customer may experience his or her delay (the time elapsing between arrival to the system and commencement of service at *some* server) in several different queues, due to the possibility of jockeying. The customer carries along the time of his or her arrival (in attribute 1 of the queue lists) regardless of what queue he or she may be in, so that the delay can be computed when service begins. Thus, we simply lump all the customer delays together into a single sampst variable:

sampst variable number	Meaning
1	Delay in queue (or queues)

By using sampst, we will automatically get the maximum delay in queue (or queues) as well.

We also want to get the time-average total number of customers in queue, which is computed as follows. If we let $Q_i(t)$ be the number of customers in queue i at time t, for $i = 1, 2, \ldots, n$, then

$$Q(t) = \sum_{i=1}^{n} Q_i(t) \tag{2.1}$$

is the total number of customers in all the queues at time t. Thus, what we want to compute is

$$\hat{q} = \frac{\int_0^T Q(t)\,dt}{T} \tag{2.2}$$

where T is the time the simulation ends (as determined by the stopping rule described above). However, if we substitute Eq. (2.1) into Eq. (2.2) and use linearity of integrals, we get

$$\hat{q} = \hat{q}_1 + \hat{q}_2 + \cdots + \hat{q}_n$$

where

$$\hat{q}_i = \frac{\int_0^T Q_i(t)\,dt}{T}$$

is simply the time-average number of customers in queue i. All this really says is that the average of the sum of the individual queue lengths is the sum of their average lengths. Thus, we can use filest (applied to the lists for the individual queues) at the end of the simulation to obtain the $\hat{q}_i$'s, and then just add them together to get $\hat{q}$. To be sure, $\hat{q}$ could be obtained directly by defining a timest variable corresponding to $Q(t)$, incrementing it upon each arrival, and decrementing it with the commencement of each service; but we have to keep the queue lists anyway, so the above approach is preferred. (Problem 2.4 considers an extension of this model where we want to know the maximum total number of customers in the queues as well as the above statistics; the question addressed there concerns whether the maximum of the total is equal to the total of the maxima.)

There are two types of random variables in this model: interarrival times and service times. We use the following stream assignments:

Stream	Purpose
1	Interarrival times
2	Service times

```
/* External definitions for multiteller bank. */

#include "simlib.h"               /* Required for use of simlib.c. */

#define EVENT_ARRIVAL         1   /* Event type for arrival of a customer. */
#define EVENT_DEPARTURE       2   /* Event type for departure of a customer. */
#define EVENT_CLOSE_DOORS     3   /* Event type for closing doors at 5 P.M. */
#define SAMPST_DELAYS         1   /* sampst variable for delays in queue(s). */
#define STREAM_INTERARRIVAL   1   /* Random-number stream for interarrivals. */
#define STREAM_SERVICE        2   /* Random-number stream for service times. */

/* Declare non-simlib global variables. */

int   min_tellers, max_tellers, num_tellers, shortest_length, shortest_queue;
float mean_interarrival, mean_service, length_doors_open;
FILE  *infile, *outfile;

/* Declare non-simlib functions. */

void arrive(void);
void depart(int teller);
void jockey(int teller);
void report(void);
```

FIGURE 2.27
C code for the external definitions, bank model.

Figure 2.27 shows the external definitions and global variables for the model. As usual, we #include the simlib header file simlib.h and then define symbolic constants for the event types, sampst variable, and random-number stream numbers. Next, ints are declared for the minimum and maximum number of tellers (4 and 7, respectively) for the different simulations we will carry out, and for the number of tellers for a given simulation; the "short" ints pertain to queue-selection decisions of arriving customers. The input parameters are declared as floats; length_doors_open is assumed to be read in units of hours, while the time units used elsewhere in the simulation are minutes, so an adjustment must be made in the code for this. The functions are prototyped, with arrive being for type 1 events, depart for type 2 events (with an int argument giving the teller number from which the departure is to occur), jockey being a non-event function with int argument being the teller number where a service is being completed (so is the possible destination for a jockeying customer), and report writing the results when the simulation ends at *or after* 5 P.M.

The main function is shown in Fig. 2.28, and it begins by opening the input and output files, reading the input parameters, writing them back out, and producing a report heading. As in the computer model, there is a for loop around most of the main function, with the index num_tellers representing the number of tellers n for the current model variant. Invoking init_simlib initializes simlib (note that this must be done for each model variant, so is inside the for loop), and maxatr is set to 4 (we have no more than 3 attributes in any of our records, but maxatr can be no less than 4 for simlib to work properly). The first arrival is scheduled, and the close-doors event is also scheduled, taking care to change the time units to minutes. A while loop then begins, continuing to run the current simulation so long as the event list is not empty, after which the current simulation is terminated; some explanation is required to argue why this is a valid way to implement the termination rule for

```
main()  /* Main function. */
{
    /* Open input and output files. */

    infile  = fopen("mtbank.in",  "r");
    outfile = fopen("mtbank.out", "w");

    /* Read input parameters. */

    fscanf(infile, "%d %d %f %f %f", &min_tellers, &max_tellers,
           &mean_interarrival, &mean_service, &length_doors_open);

    /* Write report heading and input parameters. */

    fprintf(outfile, "Multiteller bank with separate queues & jockeying\n\n");
    fprintf(outfile, "Number of tellers%16d to%3d\n\n",
            min_tellers, max_tellers);
    fprintf(outfile, "Mean interarrival time%11.3f minutes\n\n",
            mean_interarrival);
    fprintf(outfile, "Mean service time%16.3f minutes\n\n", mean_service);
    fprintf(outfile,
            "Bank closes after%16.3f hours\n\n\n\n", length_doors_open);

    /* Run the simulation varying the number of tellers. */

    for (num_tellers = min_tellers; num_tellers <= max_tellers; ++num_tellers) {

        /* Initialize simlib */

        init_simlib();

        /* Set maxatr = max(maximum number of attributes per record, 4) */

        maxatr = 4;  /* NEVER SET maxatr TO BE SMALLER THAN 4. */

        /* Schedule the first arrival. */

        event_schedule(expon(mean_interarrival, STREAM_INTERARRIVAL),
                       EVENT_ARRIVAL);

        /* Schedule the bank closing.  (Note need for consistency of units.) */

        event_schedule(60 * length_doors_open, EVENT_CLOSE_DOORS);

        /* Run the simulation while the event list is not empty. */

        while (list_size[LIST_EVENT] != 0) {

            /* Determine the next event. */

            timing();

            /* Invoke the appropriate event function. */

            switch (next_event_type) {

                case EVENT_ARRIVAL:
                    arrive();
                    break;
                case EVENT_DEPARTURE:
                    depart((int) transfer[3]);  /* transfer[3] is teller
                                                   number. */
                    break;
                case EVENT_CLOSE_DOORS:
                    event_cancel(EVENT_ARRIVAL);
                    break;
            }
        }
```

FIGURE 2.28
C code for the main function, bank model.

```
        /* Report results for the simulation with num_tellers tellers. */

        report();
    }

    fclose(infile);
    fclose(outfile);

    return 0;
}
```

FIGURE 2.28
(continued)

the model. So long as it is before 5 P.M. the close-doors event will be in the event list, and there will always be the next arrival scheduled, so the list will not be empty. At 5 P.M. the close-doors event will occur, removing this event record from the list, and the action of this event will be to remove (using simlib function event_cancel) the next-arrival event, thus "choking off" the arrival stream and removing this event from the event list from then on (since an arrival is scheduled only upon initialization and by the preceding arrival). The only other types of events are the departure events; and if there are any customers left in the bank at 5 P.M., some of them will be in service and their departure events will be in the event list. Eventually (or perhaps immediately at 5 P.M. if there happen to be no customers in the bank at that time), all the customers in the bank will receive service and depart, at which point the event list will become empty and the simulation will end. As long as the while loop is executing, we have the usual activities of invoking the timing function, passing control to arrive or depart for an arrival or departure event (note the int cast on the argument passed to depart, being the teller number in the third attribute of a departure event record), and executing the close-doors event, as described above, when it becomes time to do so. When the while loop ends, the current simulation is over and report is invoked to produce the output. After the for loop ends, all the simulations are over, so we close the input and output files and terminate the program.

A flowchart and the code for the arrival event are given in Figs. 2.29 and 2.30. The function begins by scheduling the next arrival event. Then a for loop begins, with index variable "teller" running over the teller numbers, and each teller is looked at in turn (list numbers $n + 1, n + 2, \ldots, 2n$) to see whether they are idle (i.e., whether list_size[num_tellers + teller] is equal to 0). As soon as an idle teller is found, the customer's delay of 0 is registered in sampst, the teller is made busy by filing a dummy record in that teller's list, and this customer's service-completion event is scheduled. Then the return statement transfers control back to the main function, and neither the rest of the arrive function nor the rest of this for loop (if any) is executed. The remainder of the function refers to the case when all tellers are busy, and the rest of this for loop refers to other, higher-numbered tellers at whom we don't want to look in any case due to the preference for the lowest-numbered idle teller. If this for loop is completed, then all tellers are busy, and the next for loop searches across the queues to find the shortest one, choosing the lowest-numbered one if there is a tie. This tie-breaking rule is implemented by the

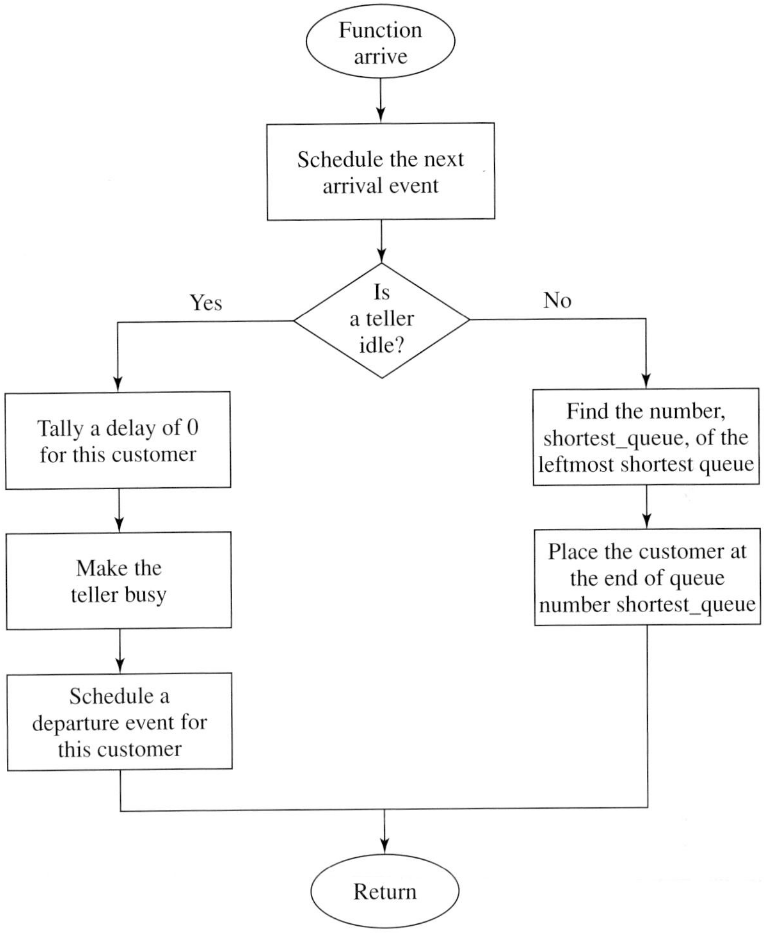

FIGURE 2.29
Flowchart for arrival function, bank model.

strict inequality (<) in the if statement in the for loop, meaning that in the left-to-right search a new choice of the queue would be taken only if the new queue is strictly shorter than the earlier choice. After finishing this for loop, the int shortest_queue will contain the queue number chosen, and the arriving customer is put at the end of that queue, with the time of arrival being the only attribute needed.

Event function depart, with the flowchart and code given in Figs. 2.31 and 2.32, is invoked from the main program when a customer completes service; the int argument "teller" is the number of the teller who is completing a service. If the queue for this teller is empty (list_size[teller] is 0), the teller is made idle by removing the dummy record from the corresponding list, and function jockey is invoked to determine whether a customer from another queue can jockey into service at teller number "teller", who just became idle. On the other hand, if the queue for this teller is not empty, the first customer is removed, his or her delay in queue

```
void arrive(void)  /* Event function for arrival of a customer to the bank. */
{
    int teller;

    /* Schedule next arrival. */

    event_schedule(sim_time + expon(mean_interarrival, STREAM_INTERARRIVAL),
                   EVENT_ARRIVAL);

    /* If a teller is idle, start service on the arriving customer. */

    for (teller = 1; teller <= num_tellers; ++teller) {

        if (list_size[num_tellers + teller] == 0) {

            /* This teller is idle, so customer has delay of zero. */

            sampst(0.0, SAMPST_DELAYS);

            /* Make this teller busy (attributes are irrelevant). */

            list_file(FIRST, num_tellers + teller);

            /* Schedule a service completion. */

            transfer[3] = teller;  /* Define third attribute of type-two event-
                                      list record before event_schedule. */

            event_schedule(sim_time + expon(mean_service, STREAM_SERVICE),
                           EVENT_DEPARTURE);

            /* Return control to the main function. */

            return;
        }
    }

    /* All tellers are busy, so find the shortest queue (leftmost shortest in
       case of ties). */

    shortest_length = list_size[1];
    shortest_queue  = 1;
    for (teller = 2; teller <= num_tellers; ++teller)
        if (list_size[teller] < shortest_length) {
            shortest_length = list_size[teller];
            shortest_queue  = teller;
        }

    /* Place the customer at the end of the leftmost shortest queue. */

    transfer[1] = sim_time;
    list_file(LAST, shortest_queue);
}
```

FIGURE 2.30
C code for function arrive, bank model.

(sim_time − transfer[1]) is registered in sampst, and the service-completion event is scheduled; for long simulations, sim_time and transfer might have to be made type double to avoid loss of precision in the subtraction to calculate the delay in queue. Note that it is our responsibility to define transfer[3] to be the teller number before invoking event_schedule, since this function only copies the time and type of event (attributes 1 and 2) into the transfer array before filing it into the event list. In any case, we must invoke jockey to see if any customers from *other* queues want to

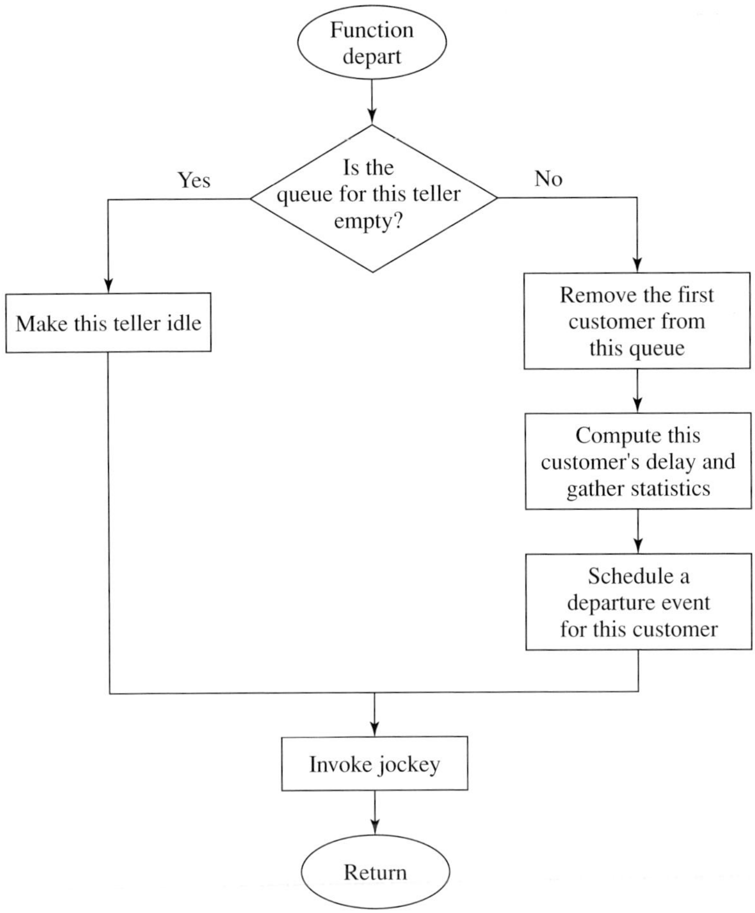

FIGURE 2.31
Flowchart for departure function, bank model.

jockey into this queue. (No customers should jockey after an arrival occurs, since this would not decrease their expected time to departure.)

The non-event function jockey is invoked with an int argument "teller" to see if a customer can jockey to the queue for teller "teller" from another (longer) queue, or possibly right into service at teller "teller" if he just became idle; its flowchart and code are shown in Figs. 2.33 and 2.34. The int variable jumper will hold the queue number of the jockeying customer, if any; it is set to zero initially and is made positive only if such a customer is found. The int variable min_distance is the (absolute) distance (in number of queues) of a potential jockeyer to the destination queue, and it is set to a large number initially, since we want to scan for the minimum such distance. The number of customers facing teller "teller" is the int variable ni, that is, ni $= n_i$ for $i =$ "teller". The for loop examines the queues (other_teller) to see if any of them satisfy the jockeying requirements, represented

```
void depart(int teller)  /* Departure event function. */
{
    /* Check to see whether the queue for teller "teller" is empty. */

    if (list_size[teller] == 0)

        /* The queue is empty, so make the teller idle. */

        list_remove(FIRST, num_tellers + teller);

    else {

        /* The queue is not empty, so start service on a customer. */

        list_remove(FIRST, teller);
        sampst(sim_time - transfer[1], SAMPST_DELAYS);
        transfer[3] = teller;  /* Define before event_schedule. */
        event_schedule(sim_time + expon(mean_service, STREAM_SERVICE),
                       EVENT_DEPARTURE);
    }

    /* Let a customer from the end of another queue jockey to the end of this
       queue, if possible. */

    jockey(teller);
}
```

FIGURE 2.32
C code for function depart, bank model.

here by the condition other_teller $\neq$ teller (since a customer would not jockey to his or her own queue) and nj $>$ ni $+$ 1, where nj is the number of customers facing teller other_teller, that is, nj $= n_j$ for $j =$ other_teller. If both of these conditions are satisfied, then the customer at the end of queue number other_teller would like to jockey, and this customer will (temporarily, perhaps) be issued a jockeying pass if she is strictly closer to the target queue than earlier customers who would also like to jockey (i.e., if the variable "distance", the number of queues this would-be jockeyer is away, is strictly less than the distance of the earlier closest would-be jockeyer). Note that in the case of two closest would-be jockeyers (one on the left and one on the right), we would jockey the one from the left since the one on the right would have to have been *strictly* closer. When this for loop ends, jumper will be zero if the other queue lengths were such that nobody wants to jockey, in which case control is passed back to the main function and no action is taken. If, however, jumper is positive, then it is equal to the queue number from which a customer will jockey, and that customer is removed from the end of his queue. A check is then made to see whether the teller who just finished service is busy (with the customer who was first in this teller's queue), in which case the jockeying customer just joins the end of his new queue. If this teller is idle, however, the jockeying customer jockeys right into service, so his delay is computed and registered, the server is made busy again, and the jockeying customer's service completion is scheduled.

The code for the report generator is in Fig. 2.35, and starts with a loop to add up the average numbers in the separate queues to get the average total number in queue, as explained earlier; this is then written out together with the number of

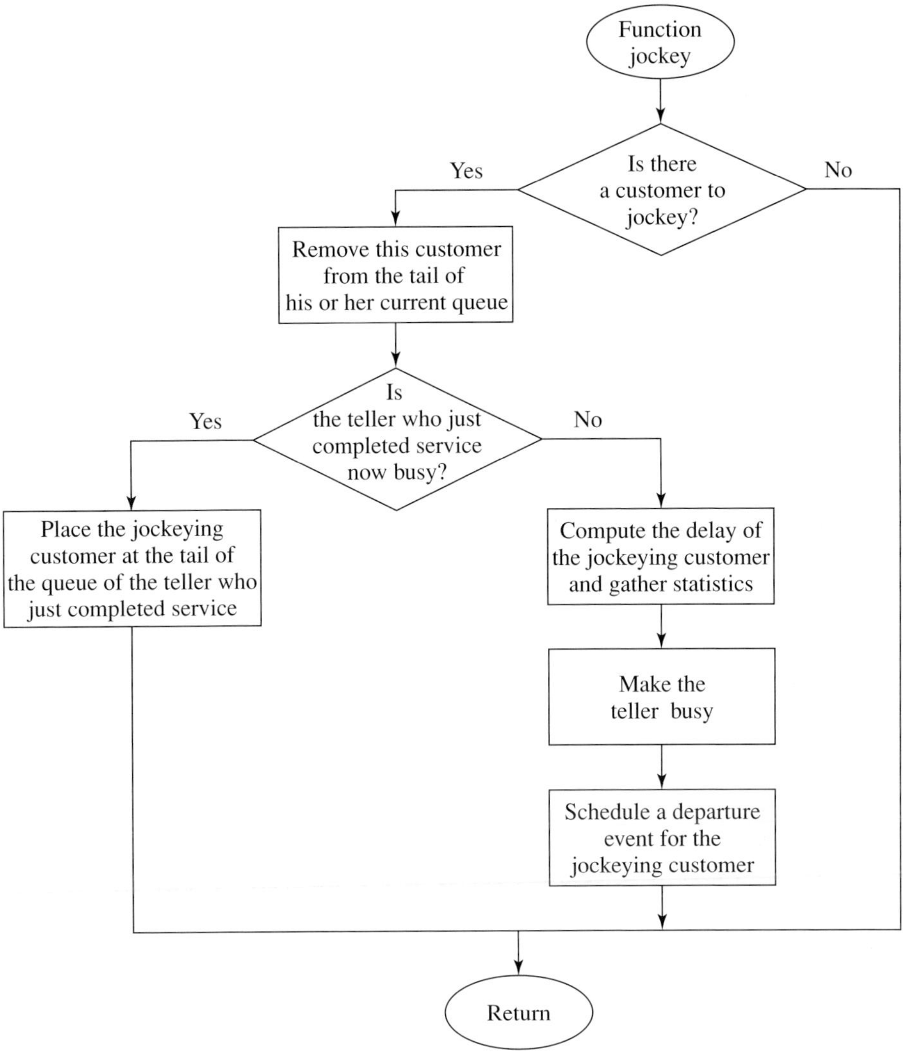

FIGURE 2.33
Flowchart for function jockey, bank model.

tellers in this model variant. Finally, the standard-format output function is invoked for the sole sampst variable to write out the average and maximum of the customer delays in queue(s).

2.6.3 Simulation Output and Discussion

Figure 2.36 contains the results (in the file mtbank.out) of the simulations. Compared to the current policy of five tellers, a reduction to four tellers would seem to penalize customer service quality heavily in terms of both delays in queue and the

```
void jockey(int teller) /* Jockey a customer to the end of queue "teller" from
                           the end of another queue, if possible. */
{
    int jumper, min_distance, ni, nj, other_teller, distance;

    /* Find the number, jumper, of the queue whose last customer will jockey to
       queue or teller "teller", if there is such a customer. */

    jumper       = 0;
    min_distance = 1000;
    ni           = list_size[teller] + list_size[num_tellers + teller];

    /* Scan all the queues from left to right. */

    for (other_teller = 1; other_teller <= num_tellers; ++other_teller) {

        nj = list_size[other_teller] + list_size[num_tellers + other_teller];
        distance = abs(teller - other_teller);

        /* Check whether the customer at the end of queue other_teller qualifies
           for being the jockeying choice so far. */

        if (other_teller != teller && nj > ni + 1 && distance < min_distance) {

            /* The customer at the end of queue other_teller is our choice so
               far for the jockeying customer, so remember his queue number and
               its distance from the destination queue. */

            jumper       = other_teller;
            min_distance = distance;
        }
    }

    /* Check to see whether a jockeying customer was found. */

    if (jumper > 0) {

        /* A jockeying customer was found, so remove him from his queue. */

        list_remove(LAST, jumper);

        /* Check to see whether the teller of his new queue is busy. */

        if (list_size[num_tellers + teller] > 0)

            /* The teller of his new queue is busy, so place the customer at the
               end of this queue. */

            list_file(LAST, teller);

        else {

            /* The teller of his new queue is idle, so tally the jockeying
               customer's delay, make the teller busy, and start service. */

            sampst(sim_time - transfer[1], SAMPST_DELAYS);
            list_file(FIRST, num_tellers + teller);
            transfer[3] = teller;  /* Define before event_schedule. */
            event_schedule(sim_time + expon(mean_service, STREAM_SERVICE),
                           EVENT_DEPARTURE);
        }
    }
}
```

FIGURE 2.34
C code for function jockey, bank model.

```
void report(void)  /* Report generator function. */
{
    int   teller;
    float avg_num_in_queue;

    /* Compute and write out estimates of desired measures of performance. */

    avg_num_in_queue = 0.0;
    for (teller = 1; teller <= num_tellers; ++teller)
        avg_num_in_queue += filest(teller);
    fprintf(outfile, "\n\nWith%2d tellers, average number in queue = %10.3f",
            num_tellers, avg_num_in_queue);
    fprintf(outfile, "\n\nDelays in queue, in minutes:\n");
    out_sampst(outfile, SAMPST_DELAYS, SAMPST_DELAYS);
}
```

FIGURE 2.35
C code for function report, bank model.

```
Multiteller bank with separate queues & jockeying

Number of tellers               4 to  7

Mean interarrival time      1.000 minutes

Mean service time           4.500 minutes

Bank closes after           8.000 hours


With 4 tellers, average number in queue =      51.319

Delays in queue, in minutes:

 sampst                          Number
variable                           of
 number       Average            values          Maximum          Minimum
____________________________________________________________________________

    1         63.2229           501.000          156.363          0.000000
____________________________________________________________________________


With 5 tellers, average number in queue =       2.441

Delays in queue, in minutes:

 sampst                          Number
variable                           of
 number       Average            values          Maximum          Minimum
____________________________________________________________________________

    1         2.48149           483.000          21.8873          0.000000
____________________________________________________________________________


With 6 tellers, average number in queue =       0.718

Delays in queue, in minutes:

 sampst                          Number
variable                           of
 number       Average            values          Maximum          Minimum
____________________________________________________________________________

    1        0.763755           467.000          16.5103          0.000000
____________________________________________________________________________
```

FIGURE 2.36
Output report, bank model.

```
With 7 tellers, average number in queue =       0.179

Delays in queue, in minutes:
```

sampst variable number	Average	Number of values	Maximum	Minimum
1	0.176180	493.000	6.97122	0.000000

FIGURE 2.36
(*continued*)

queue lengths. In the other direction, adding a sixth teller would bring a substantial improvement in customer service and average queue lengths; whether this is economically advisable would depend on how management values this improvement in customer service with respect to the cost of the extra teller. It seems unlikely in this example that adding a seventh teller could be justified, since the service improvement does not appear great relative to the six-teller system. Note also that we know how many customers were served during the day in each system variant, being the number of delays observed. There is little variation in this quantity across the system variants, since the arrival rate is the same and the lobby has unlimited space.

Problem 2.4(*b*) and (*c*) embellishes this model by adding new output measures (a measure of server utilization and the maximum total number of customers in the queues), and Prob. 2.4(*d*) further enhances the model by considering the realistic possibility of a limit on the size of the bank's lobby to hold the customers in the queues.

2.7 JOB-SHOP MODEL

In this section, we use simlib to simulate a model of a manufacturing system. This example, the most complex one we have considered, illustrates how simulation can be used to identify bottlenecks in a production process.

2.7.1 Problem Statement

A manufacturing system consists of five workstations, and at present stations 1, 2, . . . , 5 consist of 3, 2, 4, 3, and 1 identical machine(s), respectively, as shown in Fig. 2.37. In effect, the system is a network of five multiserver queues. Assume that jobs arrive at the system with interarrival times that are IID exponential random variables with mean 0.25 hour. There are three types of jobs, and arriving jobs are of type 1, 2, and 3 with respective probabilities 0.3, 0.5, and 0.2. Job types 1, 2, and 3 require 4, 3, and 5 tasks to be done, respectively, and each task must be

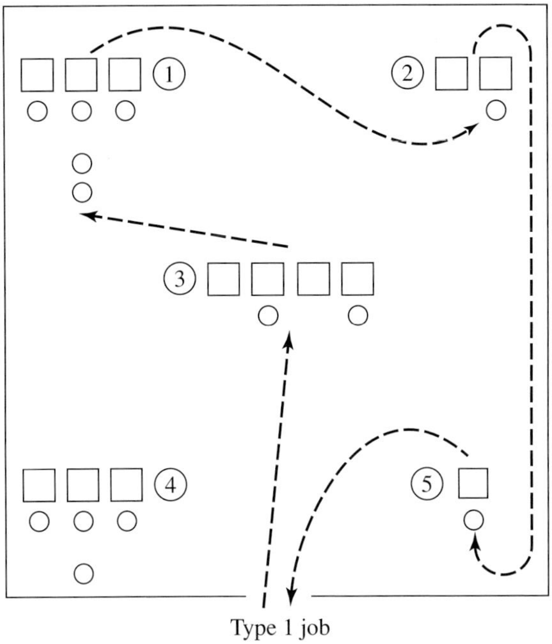

FIGURE 2.37
Manufacturing system with five workstations, showing the route of type 1 jobs.

done at a specified station and in a prescribed order. The routings for the different job types are:

Job type	Workstations in routing
1	3, 1, 2, 5
2	4, 1, 3
3	2, 5, 1, 4, 3

Thus, type 2 jobs first have a task done at station 4, then have a task done at station 1, and finally have a task done at station 3.

If a job arrives at a particular station and finds all machines in that station already busy, the job joins a single FIFO queue at that station. The time to perform a task at a particular machine is an independent 2-Erlang random variable whose mean depends on the job type and the station to which the machine belongs. (If X is a 2-Erlang random variable with mean r, then $X = Y_1 + Y_2$, where Y_1 and Y_2 are independent exponential random variables each with mean $r/2$. Alternatively X is known as a gamma random variable with shape parameter 2 and scale parameter $r/2$. See Sec. 6.2.2 for further details.) We chose the 2-Erlang distribution to represent service times because experience has shown that if one collects data on the time to perform some task, the histogram of these data will often have a shape similar to that of the density function for an Erlang distribution. The mean service times for each job type and each task are:

Job type	Mean service times for successive tasks, hours
1	0.50, 0.60, 0.85, 0.50
2	1.10, 0.80, 0.75
3	1.20, 0.25, 0.70, 0.90, 1.00

Thus, a type 2 job requires a mean service time of 1.10 hours at station 4 (where its first task will be done).

Assuming no loss of continuity between successive days' operations of the system, we simulate the system for 365 eight-hour days and estimate the expected average total delay in queue (exclusive of service times) for each job type and the expected overall average job total delay. We use the true job-type probabilities 0.3, 0.5, and 0.2 as weights in computing the latter quantity. In addition, we estimate the expected average number in queue, the expected utilization (using simlib function timest), and the expected average delay in queue for each station.

Suppose that all machines cost approximately the same and that the system has the opportunity to purchase one new machine with an eye toward efficiency improvement. We will use the results of the above simulation to decide what additional simulation runs should be made. (Each of these new runs will involve a total of 14 machines, being 1 more than the original number.) From these additional runs, we will use the overall average job total delay to help decide what type of machine the system should purchase.

2.7.2 simlib Program

The events for this model are quite straightforward:

Event description	Event type
Arrival of a job to the system	1
Departure of a job from a particular station	2
End of the simulation	3

Note that for this model, the departure event refers to a job's departing from *any* station on its route, so does not represent the job's leaving the system unless the departure is from the final station on its route. An event graph for this model is given in Fig. 2.38.

We will use the following list structure:

List	Attribute 1	Attribute 2	Attribute 3	Attribute 4
1 through 5, queues	Time of arrival to station	Job type	Task number	—
25, event list	Event time	Event type	Job type	Task number

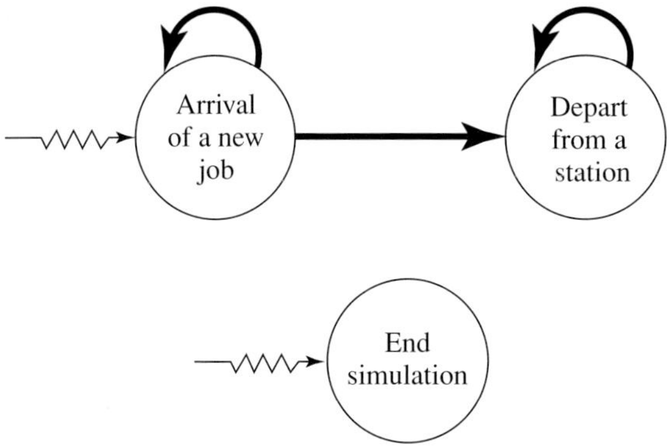

FIGURE 2.38
Event graph, job-shop model.

The "time of arrival" in attribute 1 of a queue list refers to the arrival time of the job to the station for *that* list, rather than the original arrival time to the system. The "task number" of a job represents how far along it is on its route, and will be equal to 1 for the first task, 2 for the second task, and so on; for example, task number 2 for a job of type 3 refers to its processing at station 5. Thus, the station for a job can be determined by knowing the job type and task number.

The delays of the jobs in the queues are used in different ways in this model, so the sampst variable structure is richer than in our previous models. We want the average delay in queue for each station (regardless of job type), and sampst variables 1 through 5 will be used for this. Also, we want to find the average delay in all the queues visited by each job type (regardless of station), for which sampst variables 6 through 8 will be used:

sampst variable number	Meaning
1	Delay in queue at station 1
2	Delay in queue at station 2
3	Delay in queue at station 3
4	Delay in queue at station 4
5	Delay in queue at station 5
6	Delay in queues for job type 1
7	Delay in queues for job type 2
8	Delay in queues for job type 3

Thus, each delay in each queue will be registered into two different sampst variables, one for the station and another for the job type.

For the continuous-time statistics, we will use filest as before and will now use timest as well. Since we have a list for each queue, we can easily get the time-average number in each of the queues by using filest. We also want to observe the utilization of each station; since there may be more than one machine in a station, this is defined as the time-average number of machines that are busy in the station, divided by the total number of machines in the station. To find the average number of busy machines in a station, we will keep our own (i.e., non-simlib) array num_machines_busy[j], which we will maintain as the number of machines currently busy in station j, and timest will be invoked whenever this changes value for any station. Thus, we have the following timest variables:

timest variable number	Meaning
1	Number of machines busy in station 1
2	Number of machines busy in station 2
3	Number of machines busy in station 3
4	Number of machines busy in station 4
5	Number of machines busy in station 5

For this model, there are three types of random variables needed, to which we assign the following streams:

Stream	Purpose
1	Interarrival times
2	Job types
3	Service times

Stream 3 is used to generate the service times of all jobs, regardless of type; in some simulations we might want to dedicate a separate stream to generate the service time of each job type or at each station in order to control the exact characteristics of each job type or each station.

The external definitions for the program are in Fig. 2.39. After the required #include of simlib.h, we define symbolic constants for the event types, random-number stream numbers, as well as maximum values for the number of stations and job types; these maxima will be used to allocate space in arrays, and using them instead of putting the numbers directly in the array declarations makes the program more general. We next declare several ints and int arrays with names that are mostly self-explanatory; we will use i as a job-type index and j as a station or task-number index. The number of machines that exist in station j is num_machines[j], the total number of tasks (i.e., station visits) for a job of type i is num_tasks[i], and route[i][j] is the station for task j for a type i job. Several floats and float arrays are declared: mean_interarrival is in units of hours (being the time unit for the model), but length_simulation is the length of the simulation in 8-hour days (= 365) so a time-unit adjustment will have to be made; prob_distrib_job_type[i] is the probability that a job will be of type *less than or equal to* i; and mean_service[i][j] is the mean service time (in hours) of task j for a job of type i. The functions are then declared; note that an int argument new_job is passed into arrive, with a value of 1 if this is a new arrival to the system (in which case arrive will serve as an event function) and with a value of 2 if this is the non-event of a job's leaving one station and "arriving" at the next station along its route (in which case arrive will serve as a non-event "utility" function).

The main function, which is somewhat lengthy but of the usual form, is in Fig. 2.40. Note the correction done in the invocation of event_schedule for the end-simulation event to maintain consistency of time units.

```
/* External definitions for job-shop model. */

#include "simlib.h"              /* Required for use of simlib.c. */

#define EVENT_ARRIVAL          1 /* Event type for arrival of a job to the
                                    system. */
#define EVENT_DEPARTURE        2 /* Event type for departure of a job from a
                                    particular station. */
#define EVENT_END_SIMULATION   3 /* Event type for end of the simulation. */
#define STREAM_INTERARRIVAL    1 /* Random-number stream for interarrivals. */
#define STREAM_JOB_TYPE        2 /* Random-number stream for job types. */
#define STREAM_SERVICE         3 /* Random-number stream for service times. */
#define MAX_NUM_STATIONS       5 /* Maximum number of stations. */
#define MAX_NUM_JOB_TYPES      3 /* Maximum number of job types. */

/* Declare non-simlib global variables. */

int   num_stations, num_job_types, i, j, num_machines[MAX_NUM_STATIONS + 1],
      num_tasks[MAX_NUM_JOB_TYPES +1],
      route[MAX_NUM_JOB_TYPES +1][MAX_NUM_STATIONS + 1],
      num_machines_busy[MAX_NUM_STATIONS + 1], job_type, task;
float mean_interarrival, length_simulation, prob_distrib_job_type[26],
      mean_service[MAX_NUM_JOB_TYPES +1][ MAX_NUM_STATIONS + 1];
FILE  *infile, *outfile;

/* Declare non-simlib functions. */

void  arrive(int new_job);
void  depart(void);
void  report(void);
```

FIGURE 2.39
C code for the external definitions, job-shop model.

The function arrive, flowcharted in Fig. 2.41 and listed in Fig. 2.42, begins by checking new_job to determine whether it is being used as an event function to process a new arrival to the system (new_job = 1), or whether it is being used as the last part of a station-departure event to process an existing job's arrival at the next station along its route (new_job = 2). If this is a new arrival, the next arrival is scheduled and the job type of this new arrival is generated as a random integer between 1 and 3, using simlib function random_integer and the cumulative probabilities in prob_distrib_job_type; finally, the task number for this new job is initialized to 1. As we will see in the discussion of depart below, if this is not a new arrival, its job type and task number will already have the correct values in the global variables job_type and task. Regardless of whether the job is new, the function continues by determining the station of the arrival from its job type and task number, by a lookup in the route array. Then a check is made to see whether all the machines in the station are busy. If so, the job is just put at the end of the station's queue. If not, the job has a zero delay here (registered in sampst for both the station and the job type), a machine in this station is made busy, and this is noted in the appropriate timest variable. Note the use of the float cast on the int array num_machines_busy to transform its value into a float, as required by timest. Finally, this job's exit from the station is scheduled, being careful to define event-record attributes beyond the first two before invoking event_schedule.

```
main()  /* Main function. */
{
    /* Open input and output files. */

    infile  = fopen("jobshop.in",  "r");
    outfile = fopen("jobshop.out", "w");

    /* Read input parameters. */

    fscanf(infile, "%d %d %f %f", &num_stations, &num_job_types,
           &mean_interarrival, &length_simulation);
    for (j = 1; j <= num_stations; ++j)
        fscanf(infile, "%d", &num_machines[j]);
    for (i = 1; i <= num_job_types; ++i)
        fscanf(infile, "%d", &num_tasks[i]);
    for (i = 1; i <= num_job_types; ++i) {
        for (j = 1; j <= num_tasks[i]; ++j)
            fscanf(infile, "%d", &route[i][j]);
        for (j = 1; j <= num_tasks[i]; ++j)
            fscanf(infile, "%f", &mean_service[i][j]);
    }
    for (i = 1; i <= num_job_types; ++i)
        fscanf(infile, "%f", &prob_distrib_job_type[i]);

    /* Write report heading and input parameters. */

    fprintf(outfile, "Job-shop model\n\n");
    fprintf(outfile, "Number of workstations%21d\n\n", num_stations);
    fprintf(outfile, "Number of machines in each station     ");
    for (j = 1; j <= num_stations; ++j)
        fprintf(outfile, "%5d", num_machines[j]);
    fprintf(outfile, "\n\nNumber of job types%25d\n\n", num_job_types);
    fprintf(outfile, "Number of tasks for each job type      ");
    for (i = 1; i <= num_job_types; ++i)
        fprintf(outfile, "%5d", num_tasks[i]);
    fprintf(outfile, "\n\nDistribution function of job types  ");
    for (i = 1; i <= num_job_types; ++i)
        fprintf(outfile, "%8.3f", prob_distrib_job_type[i]);
    fprintf(outfile, "\n\nMean interarrival time of jobs%14.2f hours\n\n",
            mean_interarrival);
    fprintf(outfile, "Length of the simulation%20.1f eight-hour days\n\n\n",
            length_simulation);
    fprintf(outfile, "Job type     Workstations on route");
    for (i = 1; i <= num_job_types; ++i) {
        fprintf(outfile, "\n\n%4d        ", i);
        for (j = 1; j <= num_tasks[i]; ++j)
            fprintf(outfile, "%5d", route[i][j]);
    }
    fprintf(outfile, "\n\n\nJob type     ");
    fprintf(outfile, "Mean service time (in hours) for successive tasks");
    for (i = 1; i <= num_job_types; ++i) {
        fprintf(outfile, "\n\n%4d    ", i);
        for (j = 1; j <= num_tasks[i]; ++j)
            fprintf(outfile, "%9.2f", mean_service[i][j]);
    }

    /* Initialize all machines in all stations to the idle state. */

    for (j = 1; j <= num_stations; ++j)
        num_machines_busy[j] = 0;

    /* Initialize simlib */

    init_simlib();
```

FIGURE 2.40

C code for the main function, job-shop model.

```
    /* Set maxatr = max(maximum number of attributes per record, 4) */

    maxatr = 4;   /* NEVER SET maxatr TO BE SMALLER THAN 4. */

    /* Schedule the arrival of the first job. */

    event_schedule(expon(mean_interarrival, STREAM_INTERARRIVAL),
                   EVENT_ARRIVAL);

    /* Schedule the end of the simulation.  (This is needed for consistency of
       units.) */

    event_schedule(8 * length_simulation, EVENT_END_SIMULATION);

    /* Run the simulation until it terminates after an end-simulation event
       (type EVENT_END_SIMULATION) occurs. */

    do {

        /* Determine the next event. */

        timing();

        /* Invoke the appropriate event function. */

        switch (next_event_type) {
            case EVENT_ARRIVAL:
                arrive(1);
                break;
            case EVENT_DEPARTURE:
                depart();
                break;
            case EVENT_END_SIMULATION:
                report();
                break;
        }

    /* If the event just executed was not the end-simulation event (type
       EVENT_END_SIMULATION), continue simulating.  Otherwise, end the
       simulation. */

    } while (next_event_type != EVENT_END_SIMULATION);

    fclose(infile);
    fclose(outfile);

    return 0;
}
```

FIGURE 2.40
(continued)

A flowchart and listing for event function depart are given in Figs. 2.43 and 2.44. The values of job_type and task for the departing job are obtained from the departure event record, which was just placed in the transfer array by timing, and the station "station" from which this job is leaving is then looked up in the route array. If the queue for this station is empty, a machine in this station is made idle, and timest is notified of this. If there is a queue, the first job is removed from it (having job type job_type_queue and task number task_queue, to maintain its distinction from the earlier job that is leaving this station), its delay is registered in the two appropriate sampst variables, and its departure from this station is scheduled; again, for long simulations both sim_time and transfer might have to be of

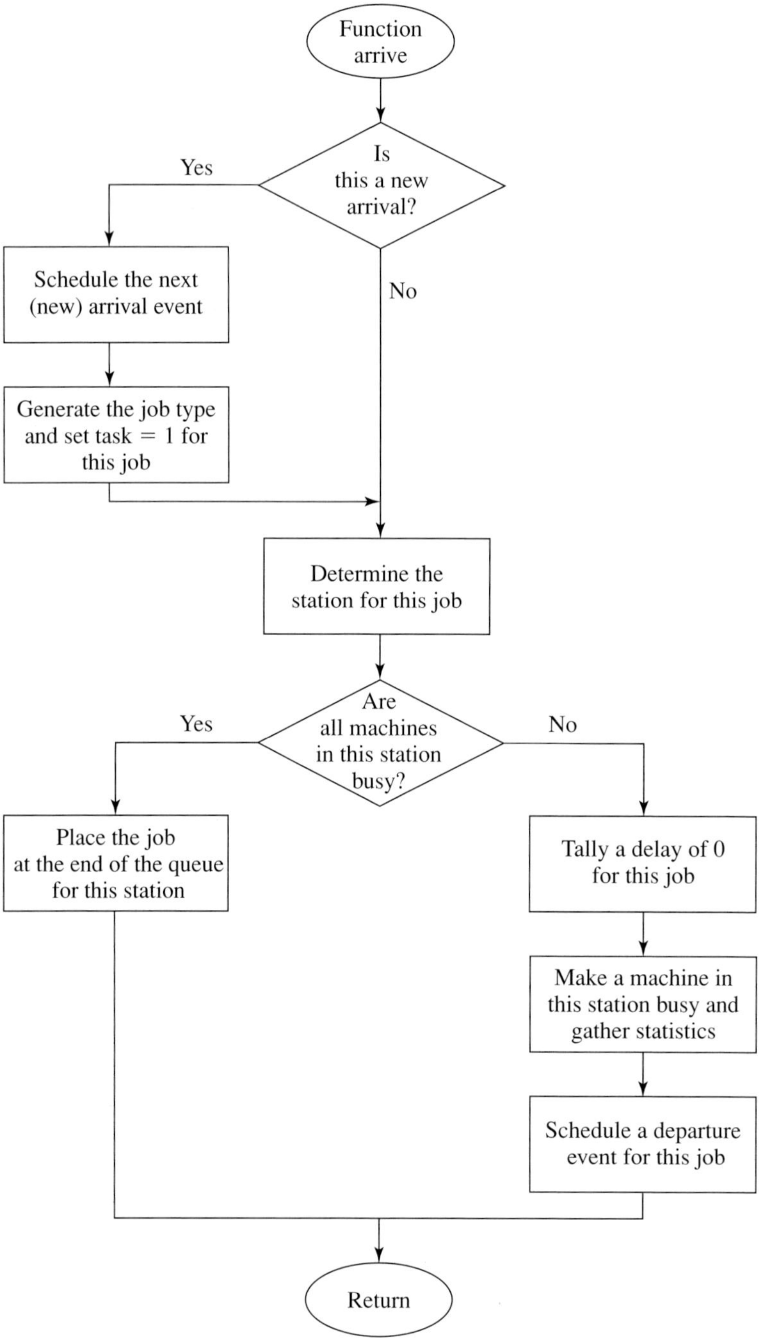

FIGURE 2.41
Flowchart for arrival function, job-shop model.

```
void arrive(int new_job)  /* Function to serve as both an arrival event of a job
                             to the system, as well as the non-event of a job's
                             arriving to a subsequent station along its
                             route. */
{
    int station;

    /* If this is a new arrival to the system, generate the time of the next
       arrival and determine the job type and task number of the arriving
       job. */


    if (new_job == 1) {

        event_schedule(sim_time + expon(mean_interarrival, STREAM_INTERARRIVAL),
                       EVENT_ARRIVAL);
        job_type = random_integer(prob_distrib_job_type, STREAM_JOB_TYPE);
        task     = 1;
    }

    /* Determine the station from the route matrix. */

    station = route[job_type][task];

    /* Check to see whether all machines in this station are busy. */

    if (num_machines_busy[station] == num_machines[station]) {

        /* All machines in this station are busy, so place the arriving job at
           the end of the appropriate queue. Note that the following data are
           stored in the record for each job:
             1. Time of arrival to this station.
             2. Job type.
             3. Current task number. */

        transfer[1] = sim_time;
        transfer[2] = job_type;
        transfer[3] = task;
        list_file(LAST, station);
    }

    else {

        /* A machine in this station is idle, so start service on the arriving
           job (which has a delay of zero). */

        sampst(0.0, station);                           /* For station. */
        sampst(0.0, num_stations + job_type);           /* For job type. */
        ++num_machines_busy[station];
        timest((float) num_machines_busy[station], station);

        /* Schedule a service completion.  Note defining attributes beyond the
           first two for the event record before invoking event_schedule. */

        transfer[3] = job_type;
        transfer[4] = task;
        event_schedule(sim_time
                       + erlang(2, mean_service[job_type][task],
                                STREAM_SERVICE),
                       EVENT_DEPARTURE);
    }
}
```

FIGURE 2.42
C code for the function arrive, job-shop model.

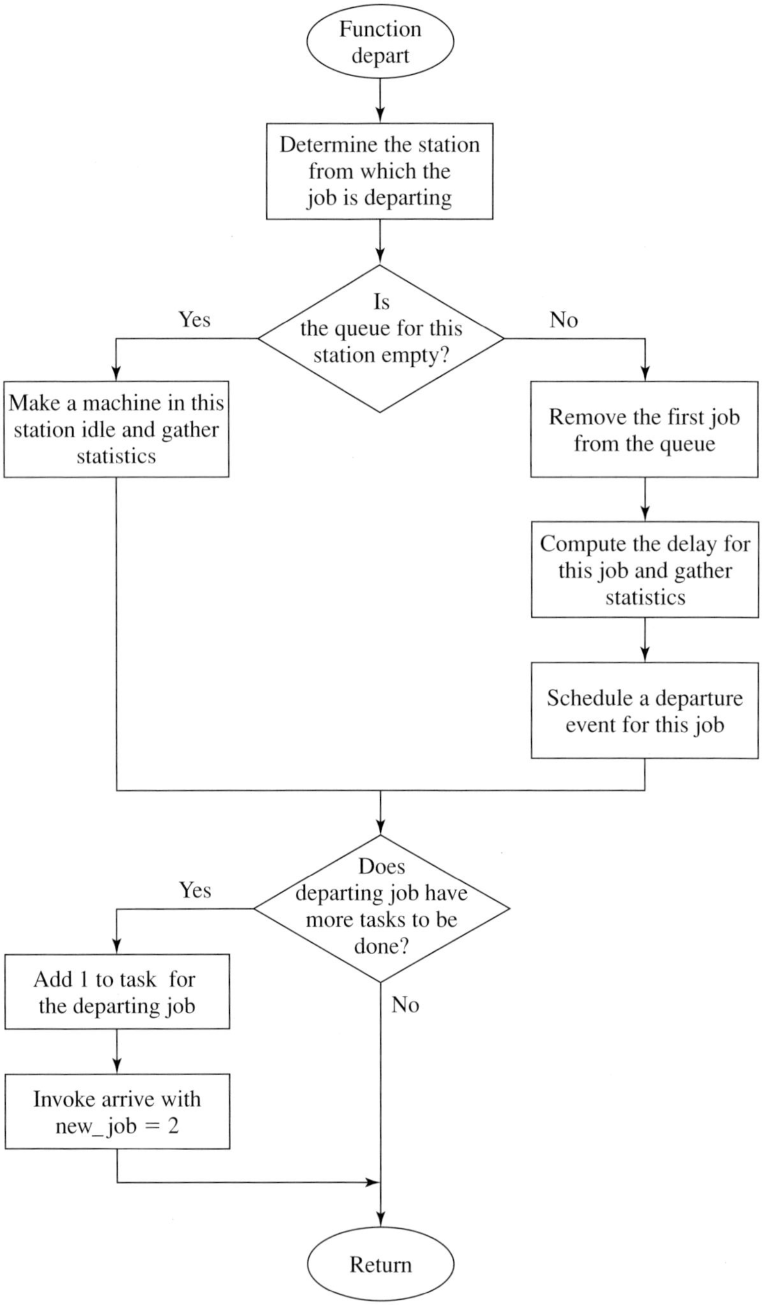

FIGURE 2.43
Flowchart for departure function, job-shop model.

```
void depart(void)  /* Event function for departure of a job from a particular
                      station. */
{
    int station, job_type_queue, task_queue;

    /* Determine the station from which the job is departing. */

    job_type = transfer[3];
    task     = transfer[4];
    station  = route[job_type][task];

    /* Check to see whether the queue for this station is empty. */

    if (list_size[station] == 0) {

        /* The queue for this station is empty, so make a machine in this
           station idle. */

        --num_machines_busy[station];
        timest((float) num_machines_busy[station], station);
    }

    else {

        /* The queue is nonempty, so start service on first job in queue. */

        list_remove(FIRST, station);

        /* Tally this delay for this station. */

        sampst(sim_time - transfer[1], station);

        /* Tally this same delay for this job type. */

        job_type_queue = transfer[2];
        task_queue     = transfer[3];
        sampst(sim_time - transfer[1], num_stations + job_type_queue);

        /* Schedule end of service for this job at this station.  Note defining
           attributes beyond the first two for the event record before invoking
           event_schedule. */

        transfer[3] = job_type_queue;
        transfer[4] = task_queue;
        event_schedule(sim_time
                       + erlang(2, mean_service[job_type_queue][task_queue],
                                STREAM_SERVICE),
                       EVENT_DEPARTURE);
}

    /* If the current departing job has one or more tasks yet to be done, send
       the job to the next station on its route. */

    if (task < num_tasks[job_type]) {
        ++task;
        arrive(2);
    }
}
```

FIGURE 2.44
C code for the function depart, job-shop model.

```
void report(void)  /* Report generator function. */
{
    int   i;
    float overall_avg_job_tot_delay, avg_job_tot_delay, sum_probs;

    /* Compute the average total delay in queue for each job type and the
       overall average job total delay. */

    fprintf(outfile, "\n\n\n\nJob type      Average total delay in queue");
    overall_avg_job_tot_delay = 0.0;
    sum_probs                 = 0.0;
    for (i = 1; i <= num_job_types; ++i) {
        avg_job_tot_delay = sampst(0.0, -(num_stations + i)) * num_tasks[i];
        fprintf(outfile, "\n\n%4d%27.3f", i, avg_job_tot_delay);
        overall_avg_job_tot_delay += (prob_distrib_job_type[i] - sum_probs)
                                     * avg_job_tot_delay;
        sum_probs = prob_distrib_job_type[i];
    }
    fprintf(outfile, "\n\nOverall average job total delay =%10.3f\n",
            overall_avg_job_tot_delay);

    /* Compute the average number in queue, the average utilization, and the
       average delay in queue for each station. */

    fprintf(outfile,
           "\n\n\n Work      Average number      Average       Average delay");
    fprintf(outfile,
             "\nstation       in queue       utilization        in queue");
    for (j = 1; j <= num_stations; ++j)
        fprintf(outfile, "\n\n%4d%17.3f%17.3f%17.3f", j, filest(j),
                timest(0.0, -j) / num_machines[j], sampst(0.0, -j));
}
```

FIGURE 2.45
C code for the function report, job-shop model.

type double to avoid excessive roundoff error in the subtraction for the delay calculation. Finally, if the job leaving this station still has more tasks to be done, its task number is incremented and it is sent on its way to the next station on its route by invoking arrive, now with new_job set to 2 to indicate that this is not a newly arriving job.

The code for the report-generator function is in Fig. 2.45. The first for loop computes the average total delay in all the queues for each job type i; the word "total" is used here to indicate that this is to be the average delay summed for *all* the queues along the route for each job type. We must multiply the average returned in sampst by the number of tasks for this job type, num_tasks[i], since sampst was invoked for each job of this type that left the system num_tasks[i] times rather than once, so that the denominator used by sampst to compute the average is num_tasks[i] times too large. We then weight these average total delays by the probabilities for the job types and add them up to get the overall average job total delay; we use these true (exact) probabilities of job types to obtain a more precise (less variable) estimate than if we simply averaged all the job total delays regardless of job type. Also, we must take successive differences in the prob_distrib_ job_type array to recover the probabilities of the job types' occurring, since this array contains the *cumulative* probabilities. (A technicality: The above multiplication of the sampst average by num_tasks[i] is slightly incorrect. Since there will generally be some jobs left in the system at the end of the simulation that have not experienced their delays in all the queues, they should not have had *any* of their delays registered in sampst. However, since this simulation is $365 \times 8 = 2920$ hours long and since there are 4 job arrivals expected each hour, there will be an expected 11,680 job arrivals, so this error is likely to be minor. See Prob. 2.5 for an alternative way of collecting the total delays in queue by job type, which avoids this difficulty.) The function closes with a for loop to write out, for each station j, the time-average number in queue, the utilization (computed as the time-average number of machines busy divided by the number of machines in the station), and the average delay in queue.

The function to generate an m-Erlang random variable is in Fig. 2.66 in App. 2A (it is part of simlib, not this model), and follows the physical model for the Erlang distribution described earlier. Note that we must divide the desired expectation of the final Erlang random variable by m to determine the expectation of the component exponential random variables. Also, the user-specified stream number, "stream", is taken as input here and simply passed through to the exponential generator (Fig. 2.63 in App. 2A) and then on to the random-number generator lcgrand.

2.7.3 Simulation Output and Discussion

Figure 2.46 shows the output file (jobshop.out) for this simulation. Weighted by job type, the average time spent by jobs waiting in the queues was almost 11 hours; this

```
Job-shop model

Number of workstations                      5

Number of machines in each station          3    2    4    3    1

Number of job types                         3

Number of tasks for each job type           4    3    5

Distribution function of job types       0.300    0.800    1.000

Mean interarrival time of jobs            0.25 hours

Length of the simulation                 365.0 eight-hour days


Job type      Workstations on route

   1             3    1    2    5

   2             4    1    3

   3             2    5    1    4    3
```

FIGURE 2.46
Output report, job-shop model.

Job type	Mean service time (in hours) for successive tasks				
1	0.50	0.60	0.85	0.50	
2	1.10	0.80	0.75		
3	1.20	0.25	0.70	0.90	1.00

Job type	Average total delay in queue
1	10.022
2	9.403
3	15.808

Overall average job total delay = 10.870

Work station	Average number in queue	Average utilization	Average delay in queue
1	12.310	0.969	3.055
2	11.404	0.978	5.677
3	0.711	0.719	0.177
4	17.098	0.961	6.110
5	2.095	0.797	1.043

FIGURE 2.46
(*continued*)

is not the average time in the system, since it does not include processing times at the stations (see Prob. 2.6). We might add that this model produced different numerical results on different computer systems due to its length and complexity, affording greater opportunity for roundoff error and change in order of use of the random-number stream.

Looking at the statistics by station, it appears that the bottlenecks are at stations 1, 2, and 4, although the order of their apparent severity depends on whether we look at average number in queue, utilization, or average delay in queue. Thus, we made three additional runs, adding a machine to each of these stations (stations 3 and 5 appear to be comparatively uncongested, so we did not consider them for a new machine) to see which type of new machine would have the greatest impact on the system's efficiency. Using the overall average job total delay as a single measure of performance, the results from these additional simulations are given in Table 2.1. From simply looking at these numbers, we see that a machine should apparently be added to station 4 to achieve the greatest reduction in overall average job total delay. As usual, however, this conclusion is rather tentative, since we have only a single simulation run of each model variant; this is especially true in this case, since the results for the three new machine configurations are really much too close to call.

TABLE 2.1
Estimated expected overall average job total delays for current and proposed machine configurations

Number of machines in stations	Overall average job total delay, in hours
3, 2, 4, 3, 1 (current configuration)	10.9
4, 2, 4, 3, 1 (add a machine to station 1)	8.1
3, 3, 4, 3, 1 (add a machine to station 2)	7.6
3, 2, 4, 4, 1 (add a machine to station 4)	7.5

2.8
EFFICIENT EVENT-LIST MANAGEMENT

Common to all dynamic simulations we have considered in this and the preceding chapter is the need to schedule events in some way, as well as to determine which of the events scheduled should occur next. We have looked at two different ways to handle the event list. In Chap. 1 it was stored sequentially, with the storage index number being the event type, and the next-event determination was made by searching the event list from top to bottom for the smallest event time. Then in this chapter, armed with simlib's ability to handle linked lists, we stored the event list as a doubly linked list ranked in increasing order on the event-time attribute while using another attribute for the event type; it was easy to determine the next event since it was always on top of the event list. Placing an event record on the list, however, was more work, since it involved searching for the correct location. In either case, a search of the event list is required, either when taking the event off the list or when putting it on.

The need for some sort of event-list processing in dynamic simulations has led a number of researchers to investigate whether other methods might be faster, at least for some types of simulations. For complex simulations involving a large number of events, much of the computer time required to perform the simulation can be expended on even-list processing. Comfort (1981) reported that for one example class of models, the number of instructions required to process the event list can comprise as much as 40 percent of the total number of instructions for the whole simulation. McCormack and Sargent (1981) provide additional evidence that the choice of event-processing algorithm can have a great impact on the simulation execution time. Henriksen (1983) used the term "spectacular failure" to describe the performance (in the case of one example model) of the simple top-to-bottom search to insert event records into the event list.

One way to improve the simlib method of determining the correct location of a new event record would be to use a more efficient data structure and search technique. One well-known approach uses a *median-pointer linked list*, which introduces a pointer to the median record in the event list (with respect to the number of records), in addition to the head and tail pointers. When a new record is to be placed on the list, the record corresponding to the median pointer is first examined to determine whether the new record should be placed in the first half or the second half of the event list. The appropriate half of the event list is then searched sequentially to determine the new record's location, with McCormack and Sargent's empirical results suggesting that the first (second) half of the event list should be searched from the front (back). For simulations in which the event list can become very long (such as the time-shared computer model of Sec. 2.5 with a very large number of terminals), such a method could make a real difference in overall computation time (see Prob. 2.34).

Many other algorithms have been proposed for event-list management, including various types of heaps and trees [see Knuth (1998b)], calendar queues [Brown (1988)], ladder queues [Tang et al. (2005)], and Henriksen's algorithm (1977). Papers that give empirical evaluations of various event-list algorithms include Chung et al. (1993), Jones (1986), and Rönngren and Ayani (1997).

The choice of the best event-list-processing algorithm may depend on the type of simulation, the parameters and probability distributions used, and other factors that influence how the events are distributed in the event list. For example, in a simulation for which the time elapsing between when an event is scheduled (i.e., put on the event list) and when it occurs (i.e., taken off the event list) is more or less the same for all events, the events will tend to be inserted toward the end of the list in a linked-list data structure; in this case, it could be advantageous to search the event list from bottom to top, since in most cases the search would end quickly. Most modern simulation-software packages (see Chaps. 3 and 14) use efficient event-list-processing algorithms.

APPENDIX 2A
C CODE FOR simlib

The C code for the simlib functions is given in Figs. 2.47 through 2.66. The header file simlib.h, which the user must #include, is in Fig. 2.47; this file in turn #includes simlibdefs.h in Fig. 2.48. Figures 2.49 through 2.66, along with the random-number generator lcgrand in Fig. 7.5 in App. 7A, compose the file simlib.c. All this code can be downloaded from www.mhhe.com/law.

In timest in Fig. 2.57, a subtraction occurs at two points involving the simulation clock sim_time and the time of the last event involving this variable, tlvc[ ]. For long simulations, both could become very large relative to their difference, so might have to be made of type double to avoid loss of precision in this subtraction.

```
/* This is simlib.h. */

/* Include files. */

#include <stdio.h>
#include <stdlib.h>
#include <math.h>
#include "simlibdefs.h"

/* Declare simlib global variables. */

extern int    *list_rank, *list_size, next_event_type, maxatr, maxlist;
extern float  *transfer, sim_time, prob_distrib[26];
```

FIGURE 2.47
Header file simlib.h.

```
extern struct master {
    float  *value;
    struct master *pr;
    struct master *sr;
} **head, **tail;

/* Declare simlib functions. */

extern void  init_simlib(void);
extern void  list_file(int option, int list);
extern void  list_remove(int option, int list);
extern void  timing(void);
extern void  event_schedule(float time_of_event, int type_of_event);
extern int   event_cancel(int event_type);
extern float sampst(float value, int varibl);
extern float timest(float value, int varibl);
extern float filest(int list);
extern void  out_sampst(FILE *unit, int lowvar, int highvar);
extern void  out_timest(FILE *unit, int lowvar, int highvar);
extern void  out_filest(FILE *unit, int lowlist, int highlist);
extern float expon(float mean, int stream);
extern int   random_integer(float prob_distrib[], int stream);
extern float uniform(float a, float b, int stream);
extern float erlang(int m, float mean, int stream);
extern float lcgrand(int stream);
extern void  lcgrandst(long zset, int stream);
extern long  lcgrandgt(int stream);
```

FIGURE 2.47
(continued)

```
/* This is simlibdefs.h. */

/* Define limits. */

#define MAX_LIST    25      /* Max number of lists. */
#define MAX_ATTR    10      /* Max number of attributes. */
#define MAX_SVAR    25      /* Max number of sampst variables. */
#define TIM_VAR     25      /* Max number of timest variables. */
#define MAX_TVAR    50      /* Max number of timest variables + lists. */
#define EPSILON      0.001  /* Used in event_cancel. */

/* Define array sizes. */

#define LIST_SIZE   26      /* MAX_LIST + 1. */
#define ATTR_SIZE   11      /* MAX_ATTR + 1. */
#define SVAR_SIZE   26      /* MAX_SVAR + 1. */
#define TVAR_SIZE   51      /* MAX_TVAR + 1. */

/* Define options for list_file and list_remove. */

#define FIRST        1      /* Insert at (remove from) head of list. */
#define LAST         2      /* Insert at (remove from) end of list. */
#define INCREASING   3      /* Insert in increasing order. */
#define DECREASING   4      /* Insert in decreasing order. */

/* Define some other values. */

#define LIST_EVENT  25      /* Event list number. */
#define INFINITY     1.E30  /* Not really infinity, but a very large number. */

/* Pre-define attribute numbers of transfer for event list. */

#define EVENT_TIME   1      /* Attribute 1 in event list is event time. */
#define EVENT_TYPE   2      /* Attribute 2 in event list is event type. */
```

FIGURE 2.48
Included file simlibdefs.h.

```
/* This is simlib.c (adapted from SUPERSIMLIB, written by Gregory Glockner). */

/* Include files. */

#include <stdio.h>
#include <stdlib.h>
#include <math.h>
#include "simlibdefs.h"

/* Declare simlib global variables. */

int    *list_rank, *list_size, next_event_type, maxatr = 0, maxlist = 0;
float  *transfer, sim_time, prob_distrib[26];
struct master {
    float  *value;
    struct master *pr;
    struct master *sr;
} **head, **tail;

/* Declare simlib functions. */

void  init_simlib(void);
void  list_file(int option, int list);
void  list_remove(int option, int list);
void  timing(void);
void  event_schedule(float time_of_event, int type_of_event);
int   event_cancel(int event_type);
float sampst(float value, int variable);
float timest(float value, int variable);
float filest(int list);
void  out_sampst(FILE *unit, int lowvar, int highvar);
void  out_timest(FILE *unit, int lowvar, int highvar);
void  out_filest(FILE *unit, int lowlist, int highlist);
void  pprint_out(FILE *unit, int i);
float expon(float mean, int stream);
int   random_integer(float prob_distrib[], int stream);
float uniform(float a, float b, int stream);
float erlang(int m, float mean, int stream);
float lcgrand(int stream);
void  lcgrandst(long zset, int stream);
long  lcgrandgt(int stream);
```

FIGURE 2.49
External simlib definitions.

```
void init_simlib()
{

/* Initialize simlib.c.  List LIST_EVENT is reserved for event list, ordered by
   event time.  init_simlib must be called from main by user. */

    int list, listsize;

    if (maxlist < 1) maxlist = MAX_LIST;
    listsize = maxlist + 1;

    /* Initialize system attributes. */

    sim_time = 0.0;
    if (maxatr < 4) maxatr = MAX_ATTR;

    /* Allocate space for the lists. */
```

FIGURE 2.50
simlib function init_simlb.

```
    list_rank = (int *)            calloc(listsize,   sizeof(int));
    list_size = (int *)            calloc(listsize,   sizeof(int));
    head      = (struct master **) calloc(listsize,   sizeof(struct master *));
    tail      = (struct master **) calloc(listsize,   sizeof(struct master *));
    transfer  = (float *)          calloc(maxatr + 1, sizeof(float));

    /* Initialize list attributes. */

    for(list = 1; list <= maxlist; ++list) {
        head [list]     = NULL;
        tail [list]     = NULL;
        list_size[list] = 0;
        list_rank[list] = 0;
    }

    /* Set event list to be ordered by event time. */

    list_rank[LIST_EVENT] = EVENT_TIME;

    /* Initialize statistical routines. */

    sampst(0.0, 0);
    timest(0.0, 0);
}
```

FIGURE 2.50
(*continued*)

```
void list_file(int option, int list)
{

/* Place transfr into list "list".
   Update timest statistics for the list.
   option = FIRST place at start of list
            LAST  place at end of list
            INCREASING  place in increasing order on attribute list_rank(list)
            DECREASING  place in decreasing order on attribute list_rank(list)
            (ties resolved by FIFO) */

    struct master *row, *ahead, *behind, *ihead, *itail;
    int    item, postest;

    /* If the list value is improper, stop the simulation. */

    if(!((list >= 0) && (list <= MAX_LIST))) {
        printf("\nInvalid list %d for list_file at time %f\n", list, sim_time);
        exit(1);
    }

    /* Increment the list size. */

    list_size[list]++;

    /* If the option value is improper, stop the simulation. */

    if(!((option >= 1) && (option <= DECREASING))) {
        printf(
            "\n%d is an invalid option for list_file on list %d at time %f\n",
            option, list, sim_time);
        exit(1);
    }
```

FIGURE 2.51
simlib function list_file.

```
/* If this is the first record in this list, just make space for it. */

if(list_size[list] == 1) {

    row        = (struct master *) malloc(sizeof(struct master));
    head[list] = row ;
    tail[list] = row ;
    (*row).pr  = NULL;
    (*row).sr  = NULL;
}

else { /* There are other records in the list. */

    /* Check the value of option. */

    if ((option == INCREASING) || (option == DECREASING)) {
        item = list_rank[list];
        if(!((item >= 1) && (item <= maxatr))) {
            printf(
                "%d is an improper value for rank of list %d at time %f\n",
                item, list, sim_time) ;
            exit(1);
        }

        row    = head[list];
        behind = NULL; /* Dummy value for the first iteration. */

        /* Search for the correct location. */

        if (option == INCREASING) {
            postest = (transfer[item] >= (*row).value[item]);
            while (postest) {
                behind  = row;
                row     = (*row).sr;
                postest = (behind != tail[list]);
                if (postest)
                    postest = (transfer[item] >= (*row).value[item]);
            }
        }

        else {

            postest = (transfer[item] <= (*row).value[item]);
            while (postest) {
                behind  = row;
                row     = (*row).sr;
                postest = (behind != tail[list]);
                if (postest)
                    postest = (transfer[item] <= (*row).value[item]);
            }
        }

        /* Check to see if position is first or last.  If so, take care of
           it below. */

        if (row == head[list])

            option = FIRST;

        else

            if (behind == tail[list])

                option = LAST;
```

FIGURE 2.51
(continued)

```
            else { /* Insert between preceding and succeeding records. */

                ahead         = (*behind).sr;
                row           = (struct master *)
                                    malloc(sizeof(struct master));
                (*row).pr     = behind;
                (*behind).sr = row;
                (*ahead).pr   = row;
                (*row).sr     = ahead;
            }
        } /* End if inserting in increasing or decreasing order. */

        if (option == FIRST) {
            row          = (struct master *) malloc(sizeof(struct master));
            ihead        = head[list];
            (*ihead).pr = row;
            (*row).sr    = ihead;
            (*row).pr    = NULL;
            head[list]   = row;
        }
        if (option == LAST) {
            row          = (struct master *) malloc(sizeof(struct master));
            itail        = tail[list];
            (*row).pr    = itail;
            (*itail).sr = row;
            (*row).sr    = NULL;
            tail[list]   = row;
        }
    }

    /* Copy the row values from the transfer array. */

    (*row).value = (float *) calloc(maxatr + 1, sizeof(float));
    for (item = 0; item <= maxatr; ++item)
        (*row).value[item] = transfer[item];


    /* Update the area under the number-in-list curve. */

    timest((float)list_size[list], TIM_VAR + list);
}
```

FIGURE 2.51
(continued)

```
void list_remove(int option, int list)
{

/* Remove a record from list "list" and copy attributes into transfer.
   Update timest statistics for the list.
   option = FIRST remove first record in the list
            LAST  remove last record in the list */

    struct master *row, *ihead, *itail;

    /* If the list value is improper, stop the simulation. */

    if(!((list >= 0) && (list <= MAX_LIST))) {
        printf("\nInvalid list %d for list_remove at time %f\n",
               list, sim_time);
        exit(1);
    }
```

FIGURE 2.52
simlib function list_remove.

```
    /* If the list is empty, stop the simulation. */

    if(list_size[list] <= 0) {
        printf("\nUnderflow of list %d at time %f\n", list, sim_time);
        exit(1);
    }

    /* Decrement the list size. */

    list_size[list]--;

    /* If the option value is improper, stop the simulation. */

    if(!(option == FIRST || option == LAST)) {
        printf(
            "\n%d is an invalid option for list_remove on list %d at time %f\n",
            option, list, sim_time);
        exit(1);
    }

    if(list_size[list] == 0) {

        /* There is only 1 record, so remove it. */

        row        = head[list];
        head[list] = NULL;
        tail[list] = NULL;
    }

    else {

        /* There is more than 1 record, so remove according to the desired
           option. */

        switch(option) {

            /* Remove the first record in the list. */

            case FIRST:
                row           = head[list];
                ihead         = (*row).sr;
                (*ihead).pr = NULL;
                head[list]    = ihead;
                break;

            /* Remove the last record in the list. */

            case LAST:
                row           = tail[list];
                itail         = (*row).pr;
                (*itail).sr = NULL;
                tail[list]    = itail;
                break;
        }
    }

    /* Copy the data and free memory. */

    free((char *)transfer);
    transfer = (*row).value;
    free((char *)row);

    /* Update the area under the number-in-list curve. */

    timest((float)list_size[list], TIM_VAR + list);
}
```

FIGURE 2.52
(continued)

```
void timing()
{

/* Remove next event from event list, placing its attributes in transfer.
   Set sim_time (simulation time) to event time, transfer[1].
   Set next_event_type to this event type, transfer[2]. */

    /* Remove the first event from the event list and put it in transfer[]. */

    list_remove(FIRST, LIST_EVENT);

    /* Check for a time reversal. */

    if(transfer[EVENT_TIME] < sim_time) {
        printf(
            "\nAttempt to schedule event type %f for time %f at time %f\n",
            transfer[EVENT_TYPE], transfer[EVENT_TIME], sim_time);
        exit(1);
    }

    /* Advance the simulation clock and set the next event type. */

    sim_time        = transfer[EVENT_TIME];
    next_event_type = transfer[EVENT_TYPE];
}
```

FIGURE 2.53
simlib function timing.

```
void event_schedule(float time_of_event, int type_of_event)
{

/* Schedule an event at time event_time of type event_type.  If attributes
   beyond the first two (reserved for the event time and the event type) are
   being used in the event list, it is the user's responsibility to place their
   values into the transfer array before invoking event_schedule. */

    transfer[EVENT_TIME] = time_of_event;
    transfer[EVENT_TYPE] = type_of_event;
    list_file(INCREASING, LIST_EVENT);
}
```

FIGURE 2.54
simlib function event_schedule.

```
int event_cancel(int event_type)
{

/* Remove the first event of type event_type from the event list, leaving its
   attributes in transfer.  If something is cancelled, event_cancel returns 1;
   if no match is found, event_cancel returns 0. */

    struct       master *row, *ahead, *behind;
    static float high, low, value;

    /* If the event list is empty, do nothing and return 0. */

    if(list_size[LIST_EVENT] == 0) return 0;
```

FIGURE 2.55
simlib function event_cancel.

```
    /* Search the event list. */

    row   = head[LIST_EVENT];
    low   = event_type - EPSILON;
    high  = event_type + EPSILON;
    value = (*row).value[EVENT_TYPE] ;

    while (((value <= low) || (value >= high)) && (row != tail[LIST_EVENT])) {
        row   = (*row).sr;
        value = (*row).value[EVENT_TYPE];
    }

    /* Check to see if this is the end of the event list. */

    if (row == tail[LIST_EVENT]) {

        /* Double check to see that this is a match. */

        if ((value > low) && (value < high)) {
            list_remove(LAST, LIST_EVENT);
            return 1;
        }

        else /* no match */
            return 0;
    }

    /* Check to see if this is the head of the list.  If it is at the head, then
       it MUST be a match. */

    if (row == head[LIST_EVENT]) {
        list_remove(FIRST, LIST_EVENT);
        return 1;
    }

    /* Else remove this event somewhere in the middle of the event list. */

    /* Update pointers. */

    ahead         = (*row).sr;
    behind        = (*row).pr;
    (*behind).sr = ahead;
    (*ahead).pr  = behind;

    /* Decrement the size of the event list. */

    list_size[LIST_EVENT]--;

    /* Copy and free memory. */

    free((char *)transfer);       /* Free the old transfer. */
    transfer = (*row).value;      /* Transfer the data. */
    free((char *)row);            /* Free the space vacated by row. */

    /* Update the area under the number-in-event-list curve. */

    timest((float)list_size[LIST_EVENT], TIM_VAR + LIST_EVENT);
    return 1;
}
```

FIGURE 2.55

(continued)

```
float sampst(float value, int variable)
{

/* Initialize, update, or report statistics on discrete-time processes:
   sum/average, max (default -1E30), min (default 1E30), number of observations
   for sampst variable "variable", where "variable":
       = 0 initializes accumulators
       > 0 updates sum, count, min, and max accumulators with new observation
       < 0 reports stats on variable "variable" and returns them in transfer:
           [1] = average of observations
           [2] = number of observations
           [3] = maximum of observations
           [4] = minimum of observations */

    static int   ivar, num_observations[SVAR_SIZE];
    static float max[SVAR_SIZE], min[SVAR_SIZE], sum[SVAR_SIZE];

    /* If the variable value is improper, stop the simulation. */

    if(!(variable >= -MAX_SVAR) && (variable <= MAX_SVAR)) {
        printf("\n%d is an improper value for a sampst variable at time %f\n",
            variable, sim_time);
        exit(1);
    }

    /* Execute the desired option. */

    if(variable > 0) { /* Update. */
        sum[variable] += value;
        if(value > max[variable]) max[variable] = value;
        if(value < min[variable]) min[variable] = value;
        num_observations[variable]++;
        return 0.0;
    }

    if(variable < 0) { /* Report summary statistics in transfer. */
        ivar        = -variable;
        transfer[2] = (float) num_observations[ivar];
        transfer[3] = max[ivar];
        transfer[4] = min[ivar];
        if(num_observations[ivar] == 0)
            transfer[1] = 0.0;
        else
            transfer[1] = sum[ivar] / transfer[2];
        return transfer[1];
    }

    /* Initialize the accumulators. */

    for(ivar=1; ivar <= MAX_SVAR; ++ivar) {
        sum[ivar]              = 0.0;
        max[ivar]              = -INFINITY;
        min[ivar]              =  INFINITY;
        num_observations[ivar] = 0;
    }
}
```

FIGURE 2.56
simlib function sampst.

```
float timest(float value, int variable)
{

/* Initialize, update, or report statistics on continuous-time processes:
   integral/average, max (default -1E30), min (default 1E30)
   for timest variable "variable", where "variable":
       = 0 initializes counters
       > 0 updates area, min, and max accumulators with new level of variable
       < 0 reports stats on variable "variable" and returns them in transfer:
           [1] = time-average of variable updated to the time of this call
           [2] = maximum value variable has attained
           [3] = minimum value variable has attained
   Note that variables TIM_VAR + 1 through TVAR_SIZE are used for automatic
   record keeping on the length of lists 1 through MAX_LIST. */

    int          ivar;
    static float area[TVAR_SIZE], max[TVAR_SIZE], min[TVAR_SIZE],
                 preval[TVAR_SIZE], tlvc[TVAR_SIZE], treset;

    /* If the variable value is improper, stop the simulation. */

    if(!(variable >= -MAX_TVAR) && (variable <= MAX_TVAR)) {
        printf("\n%d is an improper value for a timest variable at time %f\n",
            variable, sim_time);
        exit(1);
    }

    /* Execute the desired option. */

    if(variable > 0) { /* Update. */
        area[variable] += (sim_time - tlvc[variable]) * preval[variable];
        if(value > max[variable]) max[variable] = value;
        if(value < min[variable]) min[variable] = value;
        preval[variable] = value;
        tlvc[variable]   = sim_time;
        return 0.0;
    }

    if(variable < 0) { /* Report summary statistics in transfer. */
        ivar         = -variable;
        area[ivar]   += (sim_time - tlvc[ivar]) * preval[ivar];
        tlvc[ivar]   = sim_time;
        transfer[1]  = area[ivar] / (sim_time - treset);
        transfer[2]  = max[ivar];
        transfer[3]  = min[ivar];
        return transfer[1];
    }

    /* Initialize the accumulators. */

    for(ivar = 1; ivar <= MAX_TVAR; ++ivar) {
        area[ivar]   = 0.0;
        max[ivar]    = -INFINITY;
        min[ivar]    =  INFINITY;
        preval[ivar] = 0.0;
        tlvc[ivar]   = sim_time;
    }
    treset = sim_time;
}
```

FIGURE 2.57
simlib function timest.

```
float filest(int list)
{

/* Report statistics on the length of list "list" in transfer:
       [1] = time-average of list length updated to the time of this call
       [2] = maximum length list has attained
       [3] = minimum length list has attained
   This uses timest variable TIM_VAR + list. */

    return timest(0.0, -(TIM_VAR + list));
}
```

FIGURE 2.58
simlib function filest.

```
void out_sampst(FILE *unit, int lowvar, int highvar)
{

/* Write sampst statistics for variables lowvar through highvar on file
   "unit". */

    int ivar, iatrr;

    if(lowvar>highvar || lowvar > MAX_SVAR || highvar > MAX_SVAR) return;

    fprintf(unit, "\n sampst                         Number");
    fprintf(unit, "\nvariable                          of");
    fprintf(unit, "\n number       Average           values          Maximum");
    fprintf(unit, "          Minimum");
    fprintf(unit, "\n___________________________________");
    fprintf(unit, "_____________________________________");
    for(ivar = lowvar; ivar <= highvar; ++ivar) {
        fprintf(unit, "\n\n%5d", ivar);
        sampst(0.00, -ivar);
        for(iatrr = 1; iatrr <= 4; ++iatrr) pprint_out(unit, iatrr);
    }
    fprintf(unit, "\n___________________________________");
    fprintf(unit, "___________________________________\n\n\n");
}
```

FIGURE 2.59
simlib function out_sampst.

```
void out_timest(FILE *unit, int lowvar, int highvar)
{

/* Write timest statistics for variables lowvar through highvar on file
   "unit". */

    int ivar, iatrr;

    if(lowvar > highvar || lowvar > TIM_VAR || highvar > TIM_VAR ) return;


    fprintf(unit, "\n  timest");
    fprintf(unit, "\n variable       Time");
    fprintf(unit, "\n  number       average           Maximum          Minimum");
    fprintf(unit, "\n___________________________________________________________");
    for(ivar = lowvar; ivar <= highvar; ++ivar) {
        fprintf(unit, "\n\n%5d", ivar);
        timest(0.00, -ivar);
        for(iatrr = 1; iatrr <= 3; ++iatrr) pprint_out(unit, iatrr);
    }
    fprintf(unit, "\n___________________________________________________________");
    fprintf(unit, "\n\n\n");
}
```

FIGURE 2.60
simlib function out_timest.

```
void out_filest(FILE *unit, int lowlist, int highlist)
{

/* Write timest list-length statistics for lists lowlist through highlist on
   file "unit". */

    int list, iatrr;

    if(lowlist > highlist || lowlist > MAX_LIST || highlist > MAX_LIST) return;

    fprintf(unit, "\n  File          Time");
    fprintf(unit, "\n number       average            Maximum            Minimum");
    fprintf(unit, "\n_____________________________________________________________________");
    for(list = lowlist; list <= highlist; ++list) {
        fprintf(unit, "\n\n%5d", list);
        filest(list);
        for(iatrr = 1; iatrr <= 3; ++iatrr) pprint_out(unit, iatrr);
    }
    fprintf(unit, "\n_____________________________________________________________________");
    fprintf(unit, "\n\n\n");
}
```

FIGURE 2.61
simlib function out_filest.

```
void pprint_out(FILE *unit, int i) /* Write ith entry in transfer to file
                                      "unit". */
{
    if(transfer[i] == -1e30 || transfer[i] == 1e30)
        fprintf(unit," %#15.6G ", 0.00);
    else
        fprintf(unit," %#15.6G ", transfer[i]);
}
```

FIGURE 2.62
simlib function pprint_out.

```
float expon(float mean, int stream) /* Exponential variate generation
                                       function. */
{
    return -mean * log(lcgrand(stream));

}
```

FIGURE 2.63
simlib function expon.

```
int random_integer(float prob_distrib[], int stream) /* Discrete-variate
                                                        generation function. */
{
    int   i;
    float u;

    u = lcgrand(stream);

    for (i = 1; u >= prob_distrib[i]; ++i)
        ;
    return i;
}
```

FIGURE 2.64
simlib function random_integer.

```
float uniform(float a, float b, int stream) /* Uniform variate generation
                                               function. */
{
    return a + lcgrand(stream) * (b - a);
}
```

FIGURE 2.65
simlib function uniform.

```
float erlang(int m, float mean, int stream)  /* Erlang variate generation
                                                function. */
{
    int   i;
    float mean_exponential, sum;

    mean_exponential = mean / m;
    sum = 0.0;
    for (i = 1; i <= m; ++i)
        sum += expon(mean_exponential, stream);
    return sum;
}
```

FIGURE 2.66
simlib function erlang.

PROBLEMS

The following problems are to be done using simlib wherever possible.

2.1. For the single-server queue with simlib in Sec. 2.4, replace the dummy list for the server with a variable of your own representing the server status (busy or idle), and use timest instead of filest to get the server utilization.

2.2. For the time-shared computer model of Sec. 2.5, combine the end-simulation event with the end-run event. Redraw the event diagram, and alter and run the program with this simplified event structure.

2.3. For the time-shared computer model of Sec. 2.5, suppose that we want to collect the average response time for each terminal individually, as well as overall. Alter the simulation to do this, and run for the case of $n = 10$ terminals only. (*Hint*: You will have to add another attribute to represent a job's terminal of origin, and you will need to define additional sampst variables as well.)

2.4. For the multiteller bank model of Sec. 2.6, suppose that we want to know the maximum number of customers who are ever waiting in the queues. Do the following parts in order, i.e., with each part building on the previous ones.

(*a*) Explain why this cannot be obtained by adding up the maxima of the individual queues.

(*b*) Modify the program to collect this statistic, and write it out. Run for each of the cases of $n = 4$, 5, 6, and 7 tellers.

(*c*) Add to this an additional output measure, being the utilization of the servers. Since there are multiple servers, the utilization is defined here as the time-average number of servers busy, divided by the number of servers. Note that this will be a number between 0 and 1.

(*d*) Now suppose that the bank's lobby is large enough to hold only 25 customers in the queues (total). If a customer arrives to find that there are already a total of 25 customers in the queues, he or she just goes away and the business is lost; this is called *balking* and is clearly unfortunate. Change the program to reflect balking, where the capacity of 25 should be read in as an input parameter. In addition to all the other output measures, observe the number of customers who balk during the course of the simulation.

2.5. In the manufacturing-system model of Sec. 2.7, correct the minor error described in the report generator regarding the collection of the total job delay in queue by job type. To do this, add an attribute to each job representing the cumulative delay in queue so far. When the job leaves the system, tally this value in sampst. Rerun the simulation for this alternative approach using the "current configuration" of the number of machines at each station.

2.6. For the manufacturing-system model of Sec. 2.7, estimate the expected overall average job time in system, being the weighted average of the expected times in system (delays in queue plus processing times) for the three job types, using the probabilities of occurrence of the job types as the weights. (*Hint*: You won't need a computer to do this.)

2.7. For the original configuration of the manufacturing system of Sec. 2.7, run the model for 100 eight-hour days, but use only the data from the last 90 days to estimate the quantities of interest. In effect, the state of the system at time 10 days represents the initial conditions for the simulation. The idea of "warming up" the model before beginning data collection is a common simulation practice, discussed in Sec. 9.5.1. (You may want to look at the code for simlib routine timest in Fig. 2.57, paying special attention to the variable treset, to understand how the continuous-time statistics will be computed.)

2.8. For the manufacturing-system model of Sec. 2.7, suggest a different definition of the attributes that would simplify the model's coding.

2.9. Do Prob. 1.15, except use simlib. Use stream 1 for interarrival times, stream 2 for service times at server 1, stream 3 for service times at server 2, and stream 4 for the travel times.

2.10. Do Prob. 1.22, except use simlib. Use stream 1 for the machine-up times and stream 2 for the repair times.

2.11. Do Prob. 1.24, except use simlib. Use stream 1 for interarrival times and stream 2 for service times. Note how much easier this model is to simulate with the list-processing tools.

2.12. Do Prob. 1.26, except use simlib. Use stream 1 for interarrival times, stream 2 for determining the customer type, stream 3 for service times of type 1 customers, and stream 4 for service times of type 2 customers.

2.13. Do Prob. 1.27, except use simlib. Use streams 1 and 2 for interarrival times and service times, respectively, for regular customers, and streams 3 and 4 for interarrival times and service times, respectively, of express customers.

2.14. Do Prob. 1.28, except use simlib. Use stream 1 for interarrival times for regular cars and stream 2 for service times for all cars.

2.15. Do Prob. 1.30, except use simlib. Use stream 1 for interarrival times, stream 2 for inspection times, stream 3 to decide whether a bus needs repair, and stream 4 for repair times.

2.16. For the inventory example of Sec. 1.5, suppose that the delivery lag is distributed uniformly between 1 and 3 months, so there could be between 0 and 3 outstanding orders at a time. Thus, the company bases its ordering decision at the beginning of each month on the sum of the (net) inventory level [denoted by $I(t)$ in Sec. 1.5] and the inventory on order; this sum could be positive, zero, or negative. For each of the nine inventory policies, run the model for 120 months and estimate the expected average total cost per month and the expected proportion of time there is a backlog. Note that holding and shortage costs are still based on the net inventory level. Use stream 1 for interdemand times, stream 2 for demand sizes, and stream 3 for delivery lags.

2.17. Problem 1.18 described a modification of the inventory system of Sec. 1.5 in which the items were perishable. Do this problem, using simlib, and in addition consider the case of LIFO (as well as FIFO) processing of the items in inventory. Use the same stream assignments as in Prob. 2.16, and in addition use stream 4 for the shelf lives.

2.18. For the time-shared computer model of Sec. 2.5, suppose that instead of processing jobs in the queue in a round-robin manner, the CPU chooses the job from the queue that has made the fewest number of previous passes through the CPU. In case of ties, the rule is FIFO. (This is equivalent to using the time of arrival to the queue to break ties.) Run the model with $n = 60$ terminals for 1000 job completions.

2.19. Ships arrive at a harbor with interarrival times that are IID exponential random variables with a mean of 1.25 days. The harbor has a dock with two berths and two cranes for unloading the ships; ships arriving when both berths are occupied join a FIFO queue. The time for one crane to unload a ship is distributed uniformly between 0.5 and 1.5 days. If only one ship is in the harbor, both cranes unload the ship and the (remaining) unloading time is cut in half. When two ships are in the harbor, one crane works on each ship. If both cranes are unloading one ship when a second ship arrives, one of the cranes immediately begins serving the second ship and the remaining service time of the first ship is doubled. Assuming that no ships are in the harbor at time 0, run the simulation for 90 days and compute the minimum, maximum, and average time that ships are in the harbor (which includes their time in berth). Also estimate the expected utilization of each berth and of the cranes. Use stream 1 for the interarrival times and stream 2 for the unloading times. [This problem is a paraphrasing of an example in Russell (1976, p. 134).]

2.20. Jobs arrive at a single-CPU computer facility with interarrival times that are IID exponential random variables with mean 1 minute. Each job specifies upon its arrival the maximum amount of processing time it requires, and the maximum times for successive jobs are IID exponential random variables with mean 1.1 minutes. However, if m is the specified maximum processing time for a particular job, the actual processing time is distributed uniformly between $0.55m$ and $1.05m$. The CPU will never process a job for more than its specified maximum; a job whose required processing time exceeds its specified maximum leaves the facility without completing service.

Simulate the computer facility until 1000 jobs have left the CPU if (*a*) jobs in the queue are processed in a FIFO manner, and (*b*) jobs in the queue are ranked in increasing order of their specified maximum processing time. For each case, compute the average and maximum delay in queue of jobs, the proportion of jobs that are delayed in queue more than 5 minutes, and the maximum number of jobs ever in queue. Use stream 1 for the interarrival times, stream 2 for the maximum processing times, and stream 3 for the actual processing times. Which operating policy would you recommend?

2.21. In a quarry, trucks deliver ore from three shovels to a single crusher. Trucks are assigned to specific shovels, so that a truck will always return to its assigned shovel after dumping a load at the crusher. Two different truck sizes are in use, 20 and 50 tons. The size of the truck affects its loading time at the shovel, travel time to the crusher, dumping time at the crusher, and return-trip time from the crusher back to its shovel, as follows (all times are in minutes):

	20-ton truck	50-ton truck
Load	Exponentially distributed with mean 5	Exponentially distributed with mean 10
Travel	Constant 2.5	Constant 3
Dump	Exponentially distributed with mean 2	Exponentially distributed with mean 4
Return	Constant 1.5	Constant 2

To each shovel are assigned two 20-ton trucks and one 50-ton truck. The shovel queues are all FIFO, and the crusher queue is ranked in decreasing order of truck size, the rule's being FIFO in case of ties. Assume that at time 0 all trucks are at their respective shovels, with the 50-ton trucks just beginning to be loaded. Run the simulation model for 8 hours and estimate the expected time-average number in queue for each shovel and for the crusher. Also estimate the expected utilizations of all four pieces of equipment. Use streams 1 and 2 for the loading times of the 20-ton and 50-ton trucks, respectively, and streams 3 and 4 for the dumping times of the 20-ton and 50-ton trucks, respectively. [This problem is taken from Pritsker (1995, pp. 153–158).]

2.22. A batch-job computer facility with a single CPU opens its doors at 7 A.M. and closes its doors at midnight, but operates until all jobs present at midnight have been processed. Assume that jobs arrive at the facility with interarrival times that are exponentially distributed with mean 1.91 minutes. Jobs request either express (class 4), normal (class 3), deferred (class 2), or convenience (class 1) service; and the classes occur with respective probabilities 0.05, 0.50, 0.30, and 0.15. When the CPU is idle, it will process the highest-class (priority) job present, the rule's being FIFO within a class. The times required for the CPU to process class 4, 3, 2, and 1 jobs are 3-Erlang random variables (see Sec. 2.7) with respective means 0.25, 1.00, 1.50, and 3.00 minutes. Simulate the computer facility for each of the following cases:

(*a*) A job being processed by the CPU is not preempted by an arriving job of a higher class.

(*b*) If a job of class i is being processed and a job of class j (where $j > i$) arrives, the arriving job preempts the job being processed. The preempted job joins the queue and takes the highest priority in its class, and only its remaining service time needs to be completed at some future time.

Estimate for each class the expected time-average number of jobs in queue and the expected average delay in queue. Also estimate the expected proportion of time that the CPU is busy and the expected proportion of CPU busy time spent on each class. Note that it is convenient to have one list for each class's queue and also an input parameter that is set to 0 for case (*a*) and 1 for case (*b*). Use stream 1 for the interarrival times, stream 2 for the job-class determination, and streams 3, 4, 5, and 6 for the processing times for classes 4, 3, 2, and 1, respectively.

2.23. A port in Africa loads tankers with crude oil for overwater shipment, and the port has facilities for loading as many as three tankers simultaneously. The tankers, which arrive at the port every 11 ± 7 hours, are of three different types. (All times given as a "$\pm$" range in this problem are distributed uniformly over the range.) The relative frequency of the various types and their loading-time requirements are:

Type	Relative frequency	Loading time, hours
1	0.25	18 ± 2
2	0.25	24 ± 4
3	0.50	36 ± 4

There is one tug at the port. Tankers of all types require the services of a tug to move from the harbor into a berth and later to move out of a berth into the harbor. When the tug is available, any berthing or deberthing activity takes about an hour. It takes the tug 0.25 hour to travel from the harbor to the berths, or vice versa, when not pulling a tanker. When the tug finishes a berthing activity, it will deberth the first tanker in the deberthing queue if this queue is not empty. If the deberthing queue is empty but the harbor queue is not, the tug will travel to the harbor and begin berthing the first tanker in the harbor queue. (If both queues are empty, the tug will remain idle at the berths.) When the tug finishes a deberthing activity, it will berth the first tanker in the harbor queue if this queue is not empty and a berth is available. Otherwise, the tug will travel to the berths, and if the deberthing queue is not empty, will begin deberthing the first tanker in the queue. If the deberthing queue is empty, the tug will remain idle at the berths.

The situation is further complicated by the fact that the area experiences frequent storms that last 4 ± 2 hours. The time between the end of one storm and the onset of the next is an exponential random variable with mean 48 hours. The tug will not start a new activity when a storm is in progress but will always finish an activity already in progress. (The berths will operate during a storm.) If the tug is traveling from the berths to the harbor without a tanker when a storm begins, it will turn around and head for the berths.

Run the simulation model for a 1-year period (8760 hours) and estimate:

(*a*) The expected proportion of time the tug is idle, is traveling without a tanker, and is engaged in either a berthing or deberthing activity

(*b*) The expected proportion of time each berth is unoccupied, is occupied but not loading, and is loading

(*c*) The expected time-average number of tankers in the deberthing queue and in the harbor queue

(*d*) The expected average in-port residence time of each type of tanker

Use stream 1 for interarrivals, stream 2 to determine the type of a tanker, stream 3 for loading times, stream 4 for the duration of a storm, and stream 5 for the time between the end of one storm and the start of the next.

A shipper considering bidding on a contract to transport oil from the port to the United Kingdom has determined that five tankers of a particular type would have to be committed to this task to meet contract specifications. These tankers would require 21 ± 3 hours to load oil at the port. After loading and deberthing, they would travel to the United Kingdom, offload the oil, return to the port for reloading, etc. The round-trip travel time, including offloading, is estimated to be 240 ± 24 hours. Rerun the simulation and estimate, in addition, the expected average in-port residence time of the proposed additional tankers. Assume that at time 0 the five additional tankers are in the harbor queue. Use the same stream assignments as before, and in addition use stream 6 for the oil-loading times at the port and stream 7 for the round-trip travel times for these new tankers. [This problem is an embellishment of one in Schriber (1974, p. 329).]

2.24. In Prob. 2.23, suppose that the tug has a two-way radio giving it the position and status of each tanker in the port. As a result, the tug changes its operating policies, as follows. If the tug is traveling from the harbor to the berths without a tanker and is less than halfway there when a new tanker arrives, it will turn around and go pick up the new tanker. If the tug is traveling from the berths to the harbor without a tanker and is less than halfway there when a tanker completes its loading, it will turn around and go pick up the loaded tanker. Run the simulation with the same parameters and stream assignments as before, under this new operating policy.

2.25. In Prob. 2.24, suppose in addition that if the tug is traveling from the harbor to the berths without a tanker and the deberthing queue is empty when a new tanker arrives, it will turn around and go pick up the new tanker, regardless of its position. Run the simulation with the same parameters and stream assignments as before, under this operating policy.

2.26. Two-piece suits are processed by a dry cleaner as follows. Suits arrive with exponential interarrival times having mean 10 minutes, and are all initially served by server 1, perhaps after a wait in a FIFO queue; see Fig. 2.67. Upon completion of service at server 1, one piece of the suit (the jacket) goes to server 2, and the other part (the pants) to server 3. During service at server 2, the jacket has a probability of 0.05 of being damaged, and while at server 3 the probability of a pair of pants being damaged is 0.10. Upon leaving server 2, the jackets go into a queue for server 4; upon leaving server 3, the pants go into a different queue for server 4. Server 4 matches and reassembles suit parts, initiating this when he is idle and two parts from the same suit are available. If both parts of the reassembled suit are undamaged, the suit is returned to the customer. If either (or both) of the parts is (are) damaged, the suit goes to customer relations (server 5). Assume that all service times are exponential, with the following means (in minutes) and use the indicated stream assignments:

Server number	Mean service time, in minutes	Stream
1	6	1
2	4	2
3	5	3
4	5 (undamaged)	4
4	8 (damaged)	5
5	12	6

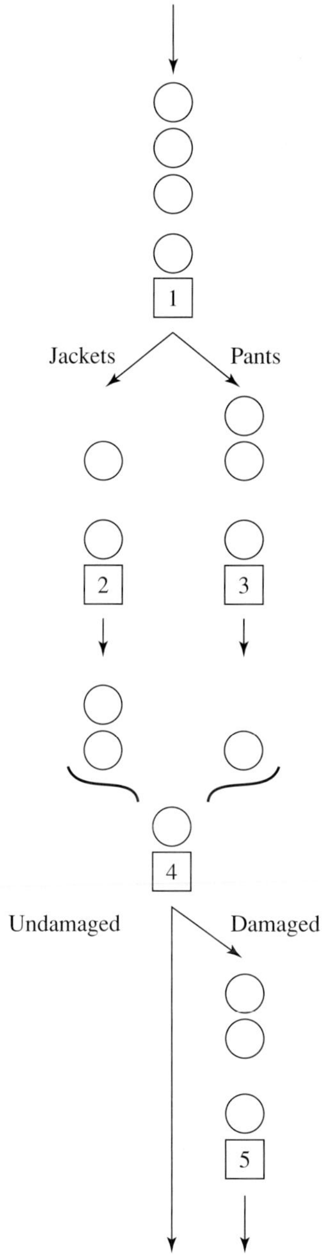

FIGURE 2.67
A dry-cleaning operation.

In addition, use stream 7 for interarrival times, and streams 8 and 9 for determining whether the pieces are damaged at servers 2 and 3, respectively. The system is initially empty and idle, and runs for exactly 12 hours. Observe the average and maximum time in the system for each type of outcome (damaged or not), separately, the average and maximum length of each queue, and the utilization of each server. What would happen if the arrival rate were to double (i.e., the interarrival-time mean were 5 minutes instead of 10 minutes)? In this case, if you could place another person anywhere in the system to help out with one of the 5 tasks, where should it be?

2.27. A queueing system has two servers (A and B) in series, and two types of customers (1 and 2). Customers arriving to the system have their types determined immediately upon their arrival. An arriving customer is classified as type 1 with probability 0.6. However, an arriving customer may balk, i.e., may not actually join the system, if the queue for server A is too long. Specifically, assume that if an arriving customer finds m ($m \geq 0$) other customers already in the queue for A, he will join the system with probability $1/(m + 1)$, regardless of the type (1 or 2) of customer he may be. Thus, for example, an arrival finding nobody else in the queue for A (i.e., $m = 0$) will join the system for sure [probability $= 1/(0 + 1) = 1$], whereas an arrival finding 5 others in the queue for A will join the system with probability $\frac{1}{6}$. All customers are served by A. (If A is busy when a customer arrives, the customer joins a FIFO queue.) Upon completing service at A, type 1 customers leave the system, while type 2 customers are served by B. (If B is busy, type 2 customers wait in a FIFO queue.) Compute the average *total* time each type of customer spends in the *system*, as well as the number of balks. Also compute the time-average and maximum length of each queue, and both server utilizations. Assume that all interarrival and service times are exponentially distributed, with the following parameters:

- Mean interarrival time (for any customer type) = 1 minute
- Mean service time at server A (regardless of customer type) = 0.8 minute
- Mean service time at server B = 1.2 minutes

Initially the system is empty and idle, and is to run until 1000 customers (of either type) have left the system. Use stream 1 for determining the customer type, stream 2 for deciding whether a customer balks, stream 3 for interarrivals, stream 4 for service times at A (of both customer types), and stream 5 for service times at B.

2.28. An antiquated computer operates in a batch multiprocessing mode, meaning that it starts many (up to a fixed maximum of $k = 4$) jobs at a time, runs them simultaneously, but cannot start any new jobs until all the jobs in a batch are done. Within a batch, each job has its own completion time, and leaves the CPU when it finishes. There are three priority classes, with jobs of class 1 being the highest priority and class 3 jobs being the lowest priority. When the CPU finishes the last job in a batch, it first looks for jobs in the class 1 queue and takes as many as possible from it, up to a maximum of k. If there were fewer than k jobs in the class 1 queue, as many jobs as possible from the class 2 queue are taken to bring the total of class 1 and class 2 jobs to no more than the maximum batch size, k. If still more room is left in the batch, the CPU moves on to the class 3 queue. If the total number of jobs waiting in all the queues is less than k, the CPU takes them all and begins running this partially full batch; it cannot begin any jobs that subsequently arrive until it finishes all of its current batch. If no jobs at all are waiting in the queues, the CPU becomes idle, and the next arriving job will start the CPU running with a batch of size 1. Note that when a batch begins running, there may be jobs of several different classes running together in the same batch.

Within a class queue, the order of jobs taken is to be *either* FIFO or shortest job first (SJF); the simulation is to be written to handle either queue discipline by changing only an input parameter. (Thus, a job's service requirement should be generated when it arrives, and stored alongside its time of arrival in the queue. For FIFO, this would not really be necessary, but it simplifies the general programming.) The service requirement of a class i job is distributed uniformly between constants $a(i)$ and $b(i)$ minutes. Each class has its own separate arrival process, i.e., the interarrival time between two successive class i jobs is exponentially distributed with mean $r(i)$ minutes. Thus, at any given point in the simulation, there should be three separate arrivals scheduled, one for each class. If a job arrives to find the CPU busy, it joins the queue for its class in the appropriate place, depending on whether the FIFO or SJF option is in force. A job arriving to find the CPU idle begins service immediately; this would be a batch of size 1. The parameters are as follows:

i	$r(i)$	$a(i)$	$b(i)$
1	0.2	0.05	0.11
2	1.6	0.94	1.83
3	5.4	4.00	8.00

Initially the system is empty and idle, and the simulation is to run for exactly 720 minutes. For each queue, compute the average, minimum, and maximum delay, as well as the time-average and maximum length. Also, compute the utilization of the CPU, defined here as the proportion of time it is busy regardless of the number of jobs running. Finally, compute the time-average number of jobs running in the CPU (where 0 jobs are considered running when the CPU is idle). Use streams 1, 2, and 3 for the interarrival times of jobs of class 1, 2, and 3, respectively, and streams 4, 5, and 6 for their respective service requirements. Suppose that a hardware upgrade could increase k to 6. Would this be worth it?

2.29. Consider a queueing system with a fixed number $n = 5$ of parallel servers fed by a single queue. Customers arrive with interarrival times that are exponentially distributed with mean 5 (all times are in minutes). An arriving customer finding an idle server will go directly into service, choosing the leftmost idle server if there are several, while an arrival finding all servers busy joins the end of the queue. When a customer (initially) enters service, her service requirement is distributed uniformly between $a = 2$ and $b = 2.8$, but upon completion of her initial service, she may be "dissatisfied" with her service, which occurs with probability $p = 0.2$. If the service was satisfactory, the customer simply leaves the system, but if her service was not satisfactory, she will require further service. The determination as to whether a service was satisfactory is to be made when the service is completed. If an unsatisfactory service is completed and there are no other customers waiting in the queue, the dissatisfied customer immediately begins another service time at her same server. On the other hand, if there is a queue when an unsatisfactory service is completed, the dissatisfied customer must join the queue (according to one of two options, described below), and the server takes the first person from the queue to serve next. Each time a customer *re*enters service, her service time and probability of being dissatisfied are lower; specifically, a customer who has *already* had i (unsatisfactory) services has a next service time that is distributed uniformly between $a/(i + 1)$ and $b/(i + 1)$, and her probability of being dissatisfied with this next service is $p/(i + 1)$. Theoretically, there is no upper limit on the number of times a given customer will have to be served to be finally satisfied.

There are two possible rules concerning what to do with a dissatisfied customer when other people are waiting in queue; the program is to be written so that respecifying a single input parameter will change the rule from (i) to (ii):

(i) A customer who has just finished an unsatisfactory service joins the end of the queue.

(ii) A customer who has just finished an unsatisfactory service rejoins the queue so that the next person taken from the (front of the) queue will be the customer who has already had the largest number of services; the rule is FIFO in case of ties. This rule is in the interest of both equity and efficiency, since customers with a long history of unsatisfactory service tend to require shorter service and also tend to be more likely to be satisfied with their next service.

Initially the system is empty and idle, and the simulation is to run for exactly 480 minutes. Compute the average and maximum total time in system [including all the delay(s) in queue and service time(s) of a customer], and the number of satisfied customers who leave the system during the simulation. Also compute the average and maximum length of the queue, and the time-average and maximum number of servers that were busy. Use stream 1 for interarrivals, stream 2 for all service times, and stream 3 to determine whether each service was satisfactory.

2.30. The student-center cafeteria at Big State University is trying to improve its service during the lunch rush from 11:30 A.M. to 1:00 P.M. Customers arrive together in groups of size 1, 2, 3, and 4, with respective probabilities 0.5, 0.3, 0.1, and 0.1. Interarrival times between groups are exponentially distributed with mean 30 seconds. Initially, the system is empty and idle, and is to run for the 90-minute period. Each arriving customer, whether alone or part of a group, takes one of three routes through the cafeteria (groups in general split up after they arrive):

- Hot-food service, then drinks, then cashier
- Specialty-sandwich bar, then drinks, then cashier
- Drinks (only), then cashier

The probabilities of these routes are respectively 0.80, 0.15, and 0.05; see Fig 2.68. At the hot-food counter and the specialty-sandwich bar, customers are served one at a time (although there might actually be one or two workers present, as discussed below). The drinks stand is self-service, and assume that nobody ever has to queue up here; this is equivalent to thinking of the drinks stand as having infinitely many servers. There are either two or three cashiers (see below), each having his own queue, and there is no jockeying; customers arriving to the cashiers simply choose the shortest queue. All queues in the model are FIFO.

In Fig. 2.68, ST stands for service time at a station, and ACT stands for the accumulated (future) cashier time due to having visited a station; the notation ~U(a, b) means that the corresponding quantity is distributed uniformly between a and b seconds. For example, a route 1 customer goes first to the hot-food station, joins the queue there if necessary, receives service there that is uniformly distributed between 50 and 120 seconds, "stores away" part of a (future) cashier time that is uniformly distributed between 20 and 40 seconds, then spends an amount of time uniformly distributed between 5 seconds and 20 seconds getting a drink, and accumulates an additional amount of (future) cashier time distributed uniformly between 5 seconds and 10 seconds. Thus, his service requirement at a cashier will be the sum of the U(20, 40) and U(5, 10) random variates he "picked up" at the hot-food and drinks stations.

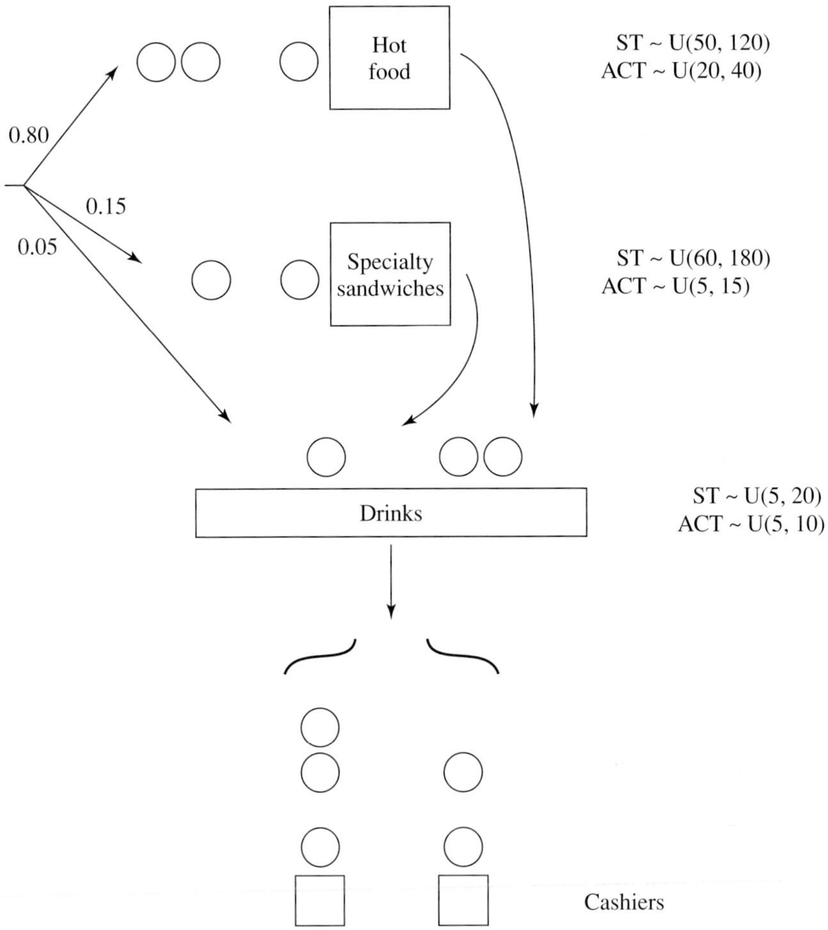

FIGURE 2.68
The BSU cafeteria.

Report the following measures of system performance:

- The average and maximum delays in queue for hot food, specialty sandwiches, and cashiers (regardless of which cashier)
- The time-average and maximum number in queue for hot food and specialty sandwiches (separately), and the time-average and maximum total number in all cashier queues
- The average and maximum total delay in all the queues for each of the three types of customers (separately)
- The overall average total delay for all customers, found by weighting their individual average total delays by their respective probabilities of occurrence
- The time-average and maximum total number of customers in the entire system (for reporting to the fire marshall)

There are several questions about the system's operation. For security reasons, there must be at least 2 cashiers, and the maximum number of cashiers is 3. Also, there must be at least one person working at each of the hot-food and specialty-sandwich stations.

Thus, the minimum number of employees is 4; run this as the "base-case" model. Then, consider adding employees, in several ways:

(*a*) Five employees, with the additional person used in one of the following ways:
   (i) As a third cashier
   (ii) To help at the hot-food station. In this case, customers are still served one at a time, but their service time is cut in half, being distributed uniformly between 25 seconds and 60 seconds.
   (iii) To help at the specialty-sandwich bar, meaning that service is still one at a time, but distributed uniformly between 30 seconds and 90 seconds

(*b*) Six employees, in one of the following configurations:
   (i) Two cashiers, and two each at the hot-food and specialty-sandwich stations
   (ii) Three cashiers, two at hot food, and one at specialty sandwiches
   (iii) Three cashiers, one at hot food, and two at specialty sandwiches

(*c*) Seven employees, with three cashiers, and two each at the hot-food and specialty-sandwich stations

Run the simulation for all seven expansion possibilities, and make a recommendation as to the best employee deployment at each level of the number of employees. In all cases, use stream 1 for the interarrival times between groups, stream 2 for the group sizes, stream 3 for an individual's route choice, streams 4, 5, and 6 for the STs at the hot-food, specialty-sandwich, and drinks stations, respectively, and streams 7, 8, and 9 for the ACTs at these respective stations.

2.31. Consolidated Corkscrews (CC) is a multinational manufacturer of precision carbon-steel corkscrews for heavy-duty, high-speed use. Each corkscrew is made on a metal lathe, and in order to meet rising consumer demand for their product, CC is planning a new plant with six lathes. They are not sure, however, how this new plant should be constructed, or how the maintenance department should be equipped. Each lathe has its own operator, who is also in charge of repairing the lathe when it breaks down. Reliability data on lathe operation indicate that the "up" time of a lathe is exponentially distributed with mean 75 minutes. When a lathe goes down, its operator immediately calls the tool crib to request a tool kit for repairs. The plant has a fixed number, m, of tool kits, so there may or may not be a kit in the crib when an operator calls for one. If a tool kit is not available, the operator requesting one is placed in a FIFO queue and must wait his or her turn for a kit; when one later becomes available, it is then placed on a conveyor belt and arrives t_i minutes later to lathe i, where t_i might depend on the lathe number, i, requesting the kit. If a kit is available, it is immediately placed on a conveyor belt and arrives at the broken lathe t_i minutes later; in this case the operator's queue delay is counted as 0. When an operator of a broken lathe receives a tool kit, he or she begins repair, which takes an amount of time distributed as a 3-Erlang random variable with mean 15 minutes. When the repair is complete, the lathe is brought back up and the tool kit is sent back to the tool crib, where it arrives t_i minutes later, if it is sent back from lathe i. Initially, assume that all lathes are up and have just been "freshly repaired," and that all m tool kits are in the crib. CC wants to know about the projected operation of the plant over a continuous 24-hour day by looking at:

- The proportion of time that each of the six lathes is down
- The time-average number of lathes that are down
- The time-average number of tool kits sitting idle in the crib
- The average delay in queue of operators requesting a tool kit

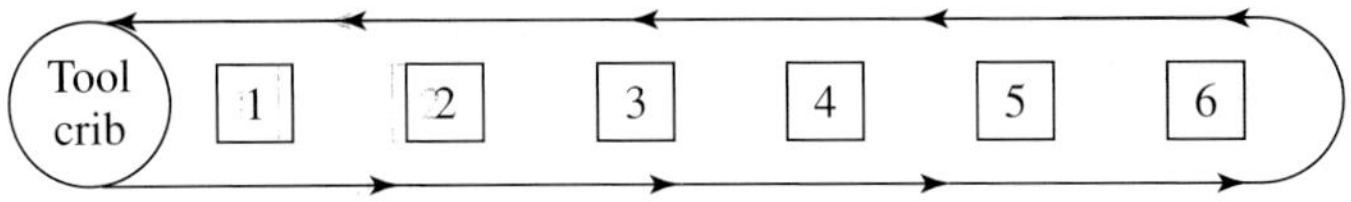

FIGURE 2.69
The linear design.

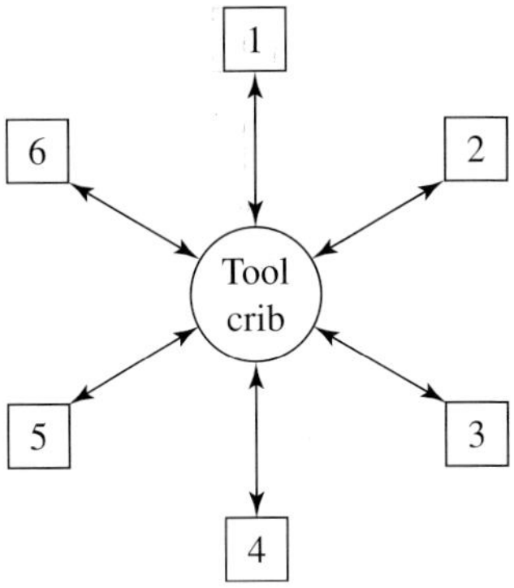

FIGURE 2.70
The circular design.

There are two major questions to be addressed:

(*a*) How should the plant be laid out? Two layouts are under consideration:

(i) In the linear design (see Fig. 2.69), the lathes are placed in a straight line with the tool crib at the left end, and a single conveyor belt for the tool kits can reach all lathes. In this case, $t_i = 2i$ minutes, for $i = 1, 2, \ldots, 6$.

(ii) In the circular design, the lathes are placed around the tool crib (see Fig. 2.70), and each lathe has its own conveyor belt to the crib; here, $t_i = 3$ for all lathe numbers i. This is a more expensive design, but results in shorter travel times for the kits.

(*b*) How many tool kits should there be? As tool kits are quite expensive, CC does not want to purchase more than necessary.

Carry out the necessary simulations and advise CC on questions (*a*) and (*b*). In all cases, use stream 1 for the lathe-up times, and stream 2 for repair times.

2.32. The engines on jet aircraft must be periodically inspected and, if necessary, repaired. An inspection/repair facility at a large airport handles seven different types of jets, as described in the table below. The times between successive arrivals of planes of type i (where $i = 1, 2, \ldots, 7$) are exponentially distributed with mean $a(i)$, as given in the table; all times are in days. There are n parallel service stations, each of which sequentially handles the inspection and repair of all the engines on a plane, but can deal with only one engine at a time. For example, a type 2 plane has three engines, so when it enters service, each engine must undergo a complete inspection and repair process (as described below) before the next engine on this plane can begin service, and all three engines must be inspected and (if necessary) repaired before the plane leaves the service station. Each service station is capable of dealing with any type of plane. As usual, a plane arriving to find an idle service station goes directly into service, while an arriving plane finding all service stations occupied must join a single queue.

Plane type (i)	Number of engines	$a(i)$	$A(i)$	$B(i)$	$p(i)$	$r(i)$	$c(i)$
1	4	8.1	0.7	2.1	0.30	2.1	2.1
2	3	2.9	0.9	1.8	0.26	1.8	1.7
3	2	3.6	0.8	1.6	0.18	1.6	1.0
4*	4	8.4	1.9	2.8	0.12	3.1	3.9
5	4	10.9	0.7	2.2	0.36	2.2	1.4
6	2	6.7	0.9	1.7	0.14	1.7	1.1
7*	3	3.0	1.6	2.0	0.21	2.8	3.7

Two of the seven types of planes are classified as widebody (denoted by an asterisk * in the above table), while the other five are classified as regular. Two disciplines for the queue are of interest:

(i) Simple FIFO with all plane types mixed together in the same queue

(ii) Nonpreemptive priority given to widebody jets, with the rule being FIFO within the widebody and regular classifications

For each engine on a plane (independently), the following process takes place (i denotes the plane type):

- The engine is initially inspected, taking an amount of time distributed uniformly between $A(i)$ and $B(i)$.
- A decision is made as to whether repair is needed; the probability that repair is needed is $p(i)$. If no repair is needed, inspection of the jet's next engine begins; or if this was the last engine, the jet leaves the facility.
- If repair is needed, it is carried out, taking an amount of time distributed as a 2-Erlang random variable with mean $r(i)$.
- After repair, another inspection is done, taking an amount of time distributed uniformly between $A(i)/2$ and $B(i)/2$ (i.e., half as long as the initial inspection, since tear-down is already done). The probability that the engine needs further repair is $p(i)/2$.
- If the initial repair was successful, the engine is done. If the engine still fails inspection, it requires further repair, taking an amount of time distributed as 2-Erlang with mean $r(i)/2$, after which it is inspected again, taking an amount of time distributed uniformly between $A(i)/2$ and $B(i)/2$; it fails this inspection with probability $p(i)/2$, and would need yet more repair, which would take a 2-Erlang amount of time with mean $r(i)/2$. This procedure continues until the engine finally passes inspection. The mean repair time stays at $r(i)/2$, the probability of failure stays at $p(i)/2$, and the inspection times stay between $A(i)/2$ and $B(i)/2$.

A cost of $c(i)$ (measured in tens of thousands of dollars) is incurred for every (full) day a type i plane is down, i.e., is in queue or in service. The general idea is to study how the total (summed across all plane types) average daily downtime cost depends on the number of service stations, n. Initially the system is empty and idle, and the simulation is to run for 365 round-the-clock days. Observe the average delay in queue for each plane type and the overall average delay in queue for all plane types, the time-average number of planes in queue, the time-average number of planes down for each plane type separately, and the total average daily downtime cost for all planes added together. Try various values of n to get a feel for the system's behavior. Recommend a choice for n, as well as which of the queue disciplines (i) or (ii) above appears to lead to the most cost-effective operation. Use streams 1 through 7 for the interarrival times of plane types $i = 1$ through $i = 7$, respectively, streams 8 through 14 for their

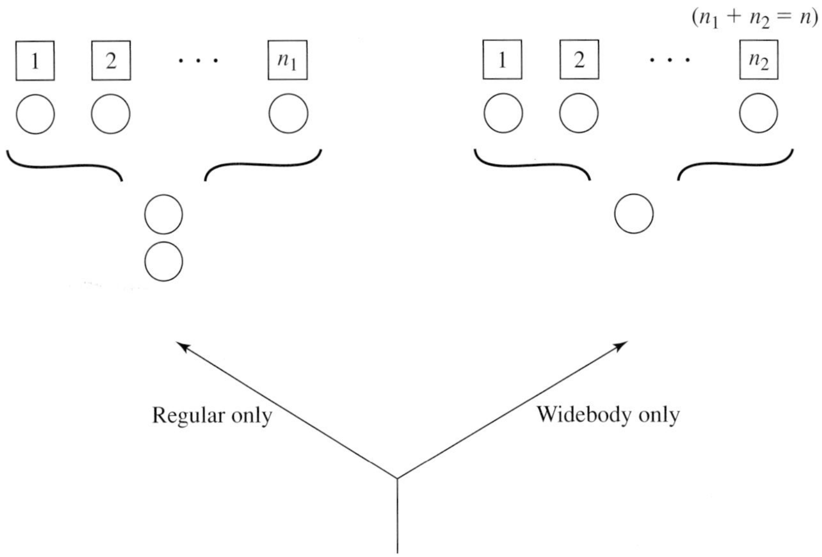

FIGURE 2.71
Alternative layout for the aircraft-repair facility.

respective inspection times (first or subsequent), streams 15 through 21 to determine whether they need (additional) repair, and streams 22 through 28 for their repair times (first or subsequent).

As an alternative to the above layout, consider separating entirely the service of the widebody and regular jets. That is, take n_2 of the n stations and send all the widebody jets there (with a single queue of widebodies feeding all n_2 stations), and the remaining $n_1 = n - n_2$ stations are for regular jets only; see Fig. 2.71. Do you think that this alternative layout would be better? Why? Use the same parameters and stream assignments as above.

2.33. Write a C function "delete" to delete the (logically) first record from list "list" with a value "value" (a float-valued representation of an integer, for example, 5.0 to represent 5) for attribute "attribute". Place the attributes of the deleted record in the transfer array. To delete a desired record, a statement of the form "delete(list, value, attribute)" should be executed. If there is an error condition (e.g., there is no matching record in the list), return a value of 0; otherwise return a value of 1. Also, update the statistics for list "list" by invoking timest (see the code for function remove in App. 2A).

2.34. Write a C function "insert" to insert a new event record into the event list, using the median-pointer algorithm discussed in Sec. 2.8. If two event records have the same event time, give preference to the event with the lowest-numbered event type.

2.35. For the bank model in Sec. 2.6, suppose that after a customer has waited in queue a certain amount of time, the customer *may* leave without being served; this is called *reneging*. Assume that the amount of time a customer will wait in queue before considering reneging is distributed uniformly between 5 and 10 minutes; if this amount of time does elapse while the customer is in queue, the customer will actually leave with the following probabilities:

Position in queue when time elapses	1	2	3	≥ 4
Probability of reneging	0.00	0.25	0.50	1.00

Using the function "delete" from Prob. 2.33, run the simulation model with five tellers and estimate (in addition to what was estimated before) the expected proportion of customers who renege and the expected average delay in queue of the reneging customers. Use the same stream assignments as in Sec. 2.6, and in addition use stream 3 for the time a customer will wait in queue before considering reneging, and stream 4 for determining if he or she actually reneges if this time elapses.

2.36 A five-story office building is served by a single elevator. People arrive to the ground floor (floor 1) with independent exponential interarrival times having mean 1 minute. A person will go to each of the upper floors with probability 0.25. It takes the elevator 15 seconds to travel one floor. Assume, however, that there is no loading or unloading time for the elevator at a particular floor. A person will stay on a particular floor for an amount of time that is distributed uniformly between 15 and 120 minutes. When a person leaves floor i (where $i = 2, 3, 4, 5$), he or she will go to floor 1 with probability 0.7, and will go to each of the other three floors with probability 0.1. The elevator can carry six people, and starts on floor 1. If there is not room to get all people waiting at a particular floor on the arriving elevator, the excess remain in queue. A person coming down to floor 1 departs from the building immediately. The following control logic also applies to the elevator:

- When the elevator is going up, it will continue in that direction if a current passenger wants to go to a higher floor or if a person on a higher floor wants to get on the elevator.
- When the elevator is going down, it will continue in that direction if it has at least one passenger or if there is a waiting passenger at a lower floor.
- If the elevator is at floor i (where $i = 2, 3, 4$) and going up (down), then it will not immediately pick up a person who wants to go down (up) at that floor.
- When the elevator is idle, its home base is floor 1.
- The elevator decides at each floor what floor it will go to next. It will not change directions between floors.

Use the following random-number stream assignments:

1, interarrival times of people to the building
2, next-floor determination (generate upon arrival at origin floor)
3, length of stay on a particular floor (generate upon arrival at floor)

Run a simulation for 20 hours and gather statistics on:

(*a*) Average delay in queue in each direction (if appropriate), for each floor
(*b*) Average of individual delays in queue over all floors and all people
(*c*) Proportion of time that the elevator is moving with people, is moving empty, and is idle (on floor 1)
(*d*) Average and maximum number in the elevator
(*e*) Proportion of people who cannot get on the elevator since it is full, for each floor

Rerun the simulation if the home base for the elevator is floor 3. Which home base gives the smallest average delay [output statistic (*b*)]?

2.37. Coal trains arrive to an unloading facility with independent exponential interarrival times with mean 10 hours. If a train arrives and finds the system idle, the train is unloaded immediately. Unloading times for the train are independent and distributed uniformly between 3.5 and 4.5 hours. If a train arrives to a busy system, it joins a FIFO queue.

The situation is complicated by what the railroad calls "hogging out." In particular, a train crew can work for only 12 hours, and a train cannot be unloaded without a crew present. When a train arrives, the remaining crew time (out of 12 hours) is independent and distributed uniformly between 6 and 11 hours. When a crew's 12 hours expire, it leaves immediately and a replacement crew is called. The amount of time between when a replacement crew is called and when it actually arrives is independent and distributed uniformly between 2.5 and 3.5 hours.

If a train is being unloaded when its crew hogs out, unloading is suspended until a replacement crew arrives. If a train is in queue when its crew hogs out, the train cannot leave the queue until its replacement crew arrives. Thus, the unloading equipment can be idle with one or more trains in queue.

Run the simulation for 720 hours (30 days) and gather statistics on:

(*a*) Average and maximum time a train spends in the system
(*b*) Proportion of time unloading equipment is busy, idle, and hogged out
(*c*) Average and maximum number of trains in queue
(*d*) Proportion of trains that hog out 0, 1, and 2 times

Note that if a train is in queue when its crew hogs out, the record for this train must be accessed. (This train may be anywhere in the queue.) Use the C function "delete" from Prob. 2.33.

2.38. Consider a car-rental system shown in Fig. 2.72, with all distances given in miles. People arrive at location i (where $i = 1, 2, 3$) with independent exponential interarrival times at respective rates of 14, 10, and 24 per hour. Each location has a FIFO queue with unlimited capacity. There is one bus with a capacity of 20 people and a speed of 30 miles per hour. The bus is initially at location 3 (car rental), and leaves immediately in a counterclockwise direction. All people arriving at a terminal want to go to the car rental. All people arriving at the car rental want to go to terminals 1 and 2 with

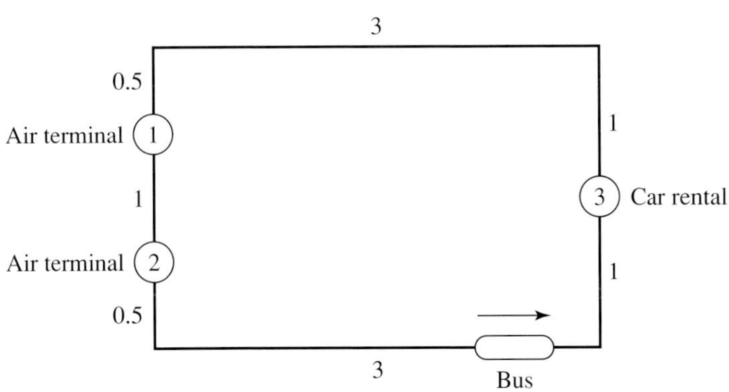

FIGURE 2.72
A car rental system.

respective probabilities 0.583 and 0.417. When a bus arrives at a location, the following rules apply:

- People are first unloaded in a FIFO manner. The time to unload one person is distributed uniformly between 16 and 24 seconds.
- People are then loaded on the bus up to its capacity, with a loading time per person that is distributed uniformly between 15 and 25 seconds.
- The bus always spends at least 5 minutes at each location. If no loading or unloading is in process after 5 minutes, the bus will leave immediately.

Run a simulation for 80 hours and gather statistics on:
(*a*) Average and maximum number in each queue
(*b*) Average and maximum delay in each queue
(*c*) Average and maximum number on the bus
(*d*) Average, maximum, and minimum time the bus is stopped at each location
(*e*) Average, maximum, and minimum time for the bus to make a loop (departure from the car rental to the next such departure)
(*f*) Average, maximum, and minimum time a person is in the system by arrival location

Use the following random-number stream assignments:
i, interarrival times at location i (where $i = 1, 2, 3$)
4, unloading times
5, loading times
6, determining destination of an arrival at the car rental

CHAPTER 3

Simulation Software

Recommended sections for a first reading: 3.1 through 3.4

3.1 INTRODUCTION

In studying the simulation examples in Chaps. 1 and 2, the reader probably noticed several features needed in programming most discrete-event simulation models, including:

- Generating random numbers, that is, observations from a U(0,1) probability distribution
- Generating random variates from a specified probability distribution (e.g., exponential)
- Advancing simulated time
- Determining the next event from the event list and passing control to the appropriate block of code
- Adding records to, or deleting records from, a list
- Collecting output statistics and reporting the results
- Detecting error conditions

As a matter of fact, it is the commonality of these and other features to most simulation programs that led to the development of special-purpose simulation packages. Furthermore, we believe that the improvement and greater ease of use of these packages have been major factors in the increased popularity of simulation in recent years.

We discuss in Sec. 3.2 the relative merits of using a simulation package rather than a programming language such as C, C++, or Java for building simulation models. In Sec. 3.3 we present a classification of simulation software, including a discussion of general-purpose and application-oriented simulation packages. Desirable features for simulation packages, including animation, are described in Sec. 3.4. Section 3.5 gives brief descriptions of Arena, ExtendSim, and Simio, which are popular general-purpose simulation packages. A simulation model of a small factory is also given for each package. In Sec. 3.6 we describe object-oriented simulation software. Finally, in Sec. 3.7 we delineate a number of different application-oriented simulation packages.

The publication *OR/MS Today* has a survey of simulation software on a fairly regular basis.

3.2 COMPARISON OF SIMULATION PACKAGES WITH PROGRAMMING LANGUAGES

One of the most important decisions a modeler or analyst must make in performing a simulation study concerns the choice of software. If the selected software is not flexible enough or is too difficult to use, then the simulation project may produce erroneous results or may not even be completed. The following are some advantages of using a simulation package rather than a general-purpose programming language:

- Simulation packages automatically provide most of the features needed to build a simulation model (see Secs. 3.1 and 3.4), resulting in a significant decrease in "programming" time and a reduction in overall project cost.
- They provide a natural framework for simulation modeling. Their basic modeling constructs are more closely akin to simulation than are those in a general-purpose programming language like C.
- Simulation models are generally easier to modify and maintain when written in a simulation package.
- They provide better error detection because many potential types of errors are checked for automatically. Since fewer modeling constructs need to be included in a model, the chance of making an error will probably be smaller. (Conversely, errors in a new version of a simulation package itself may be difficult for a user to find, and the software may be used incorrectly because documentation is sometimes lacking.)

On the other hand, some simulation models (particularly for defense-related applications) are still written in a general-purpose programming language. Some advantages of such a choice are as follows:

- Most modelers already know a programming language, but this is often not the case with a simulation package.
- A simulation model efficiently written in C, C++, or Java may require less execution time than a model developed in a simulation package. This is so because a simulation package is designed to address a wide variety of systems with one set of modeling constructs, whereas a C program can be more closely tailored to a particular application. This consideration has, however, become less important with the availability of inexpensive, high-speed PCs.

- Programming languages may allow greater programming flexibility than certain simulation packages.
- The programming languages C++ and Java are object-oriented (see Sec. 3.6), which is of considerable importance to many analysts and programmers, such as those in the defense industry. On the other hand, most simulation packages are not truly object-oriented.
- Software cost is generally lower, but total project cost may not be.

Although there are advantages to using both types of software, we believe, in general, that a modeler would be prudent to give serious consideration to using a simulation package. If such a decision has indeed been made, we feel that the criteria discussed in Sec. 3.4 will be useful in deciding which particular simulation package to choose.

3.3 CLASSIFICATION OF SIMULATION SOFTWARE

In this section we discuss various aspects of simulation packages.

3.3.1 General-Purpose vs. Application-Oriented Simulation Packages

There are two main types of simulation packages for discrete-event simulation, namely, general-purpose simulation software and application-oriented simulation software. A *general-purpose simulation package* can be used for any application, but might have special features for certain ones (e.g., for manufacturing or process reengineering). On the other hand, an *application-oriented simulation package* is designed to be used for a certain class of applications such as manufacturing, health care, or communications networks. A list of application-oriented simulation packages is given in Sec. 3.7.

3.3.2 Modeling Approaches

In the programs in Chaps. 1 and 2, we used the *event-scheduling approach* to discrete-event simulation modeling. A system is modeled by identifying its characteristic events and then writing a set of event routines that give a detailed description of the state changes taking place at the time of each event. The simulation evolves over time by executing the events in increasing order of their time of occurrence. Here a basic property of an event routine is that no simulated time passes during its execution.

On the other hand, most contemporary simulation packages use the process approach to simulation modeling. A *process* is a time-ordered sequence of interrelated events separated by intervals of time, which describes the entire experience of an "entity" as it flows through a "system." The process corresponding to an entity arriving to and being served at a single server is shown in Fig. 3.1. A system or simulation model may have several different types of processes. Corresponding to each

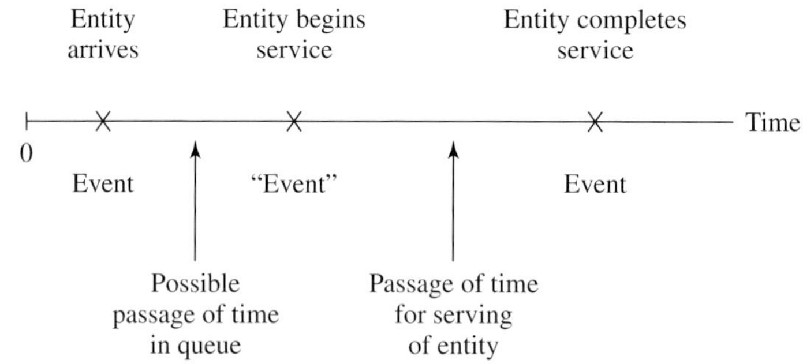

FIGURE 3.1
Process describing the flow of an entity through a system.

process in the model, there is a process "routine" that describes the entire history of its "process entity" as it moves through the corresponding process. A process routine explicitly contains the passage of simulated time and generally has multiple entry points.

To illustrate the nature of the *process approach* more succinctly, Fig. 3.2 gives a flowchart for a prototype customer-process routine in the case of a single-server queueing system. (This process routine describes the entire experience of a customer progressing through the system.) Unlike an event routine, this process routine has multiple entry points at blocks 1, 5, and 9. Entry into this routine at block 1 corresponds to the arrival event for a customer entity that is the most imminent event in the event list. At block 1 an arrival event record is placed in the event list for the *next* customer entity to arrive. (This next customer entity will arrive at a time equal to the time the *current* customer entity arrives plus an interarrival time.) To determine whether the customer entity currently arriving can begin service, a check is made (at block 2) to see whether the server is idle. If the server is busy, this customer entity is placed at the end of the queue (block 3) and is made to wait (at block 4) until selected for service at some undetermined time in the future. (This is called a *conditional wait.*) Control is then returned to the "timing routine" to determine what customer entity's event is the most imminent *now*. (If we think of a flowchart like the one in Fig. 3.2 as existing for each customer entity in the system, control will next be passed to the appropriate entry point for the flowchart corresponding to the most imminent event for some other customer.) When this customer entity (the one made to wait at block 4) is activated at some point in the future (when it is first in queue and another customer completes service and makes the server idle), it is removed from the queue *at block 5* and begins service immediately, thereby making the server busy (block 6). A customer entity arriving to find the server idle also begins service immediately (at block 6); in either case, we are now at block 7. There the departure time for the customer beginning service is determined, and a corresponding event record is placed in the event list. This customer entity is then made to wait (at block 8) until its service has been completed. (This is an *unconditional wait*, since its activation

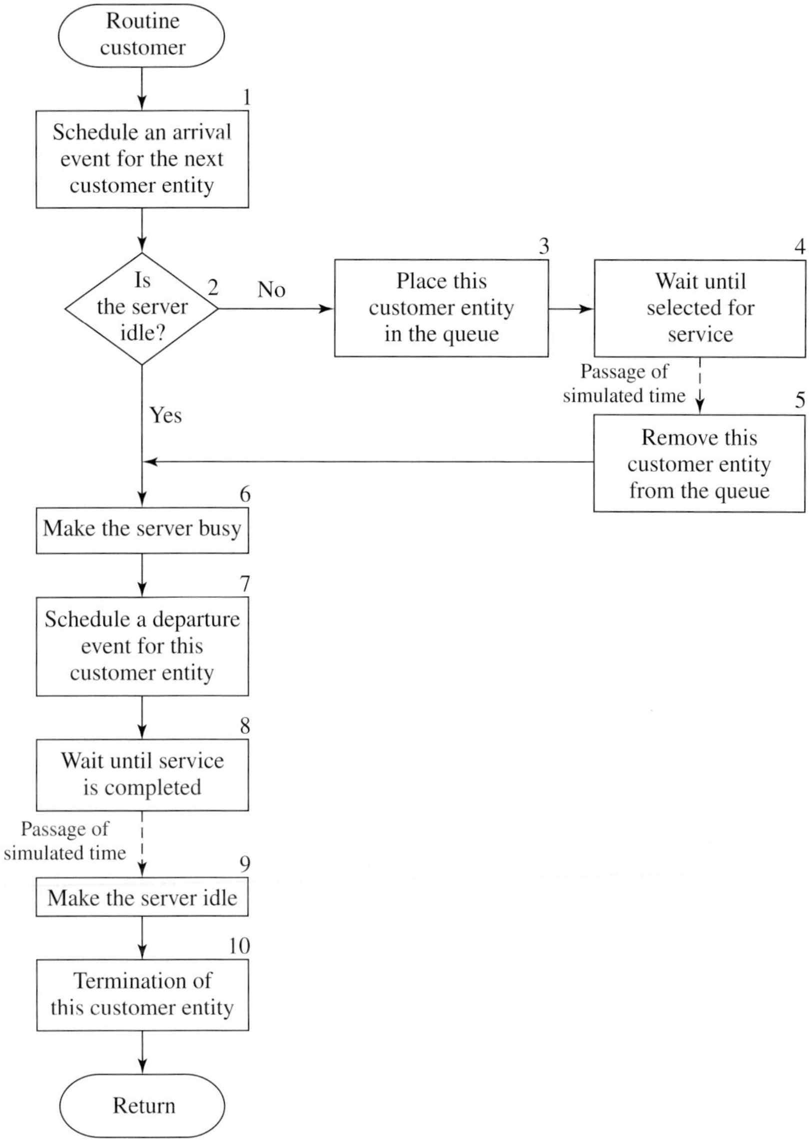

FIGURE 3.2
Prototype customer-process routine for a single-server queueing system.

time is known.) Control is returned to the timing routine to determine what customer entity will be processed next. When the customer made to wait at block 8 is activated at the end of its service, this makes the server idle *at block 9* (allowing the first customer in the queue to become active immediately), and then this customer is removed from the system at block 10.

TABLE 3.1
Entities, attributes, resources, and queues for some common simulation applications

Type of system	Entities	Attributes	Resources	Queues
Manufacturing	Part	Part number, due date	Machines, workers	Queues or buffers
Communications	Message	Destination, message length	Nodes, links	Buffers
Airport	Airplane	Flight number, weight	Runways, gates	Queues
Insurance agency	Application, claim	Name, policy number, amount	Agents, clerks	Queues

A simulation using the process approach also evolves over time by executing the events in order of their time of occurrence. Internally, the process and event-scheduling approaches to simulation are very similar (e.g., both approaches use a simulation clock, an event list, a timing routine, etc.). However, the process approach is more natural in some sense, since one process routine describes the entire experience of the corresponding process entity.

3.3.3 Common Modeling Elements

Simulation packages typically include entities, attributes, resources, and queues as part of their modeling framework. An *entity* (see Table 3.1 for examples) is created, travels through some part of the simulated system, and then is usually destroyed. Entities are distinguished from each other by their *attributes*, which are pieces of information stored with the entity. As an entity moves through the simulated system, it requests the use of *resources*. If a requested resource is not available, then the entity joins a *queue*. The entities in a particular queue may be served in a FIFO (first-in, first-out) manner, served in a LIFO (last-in, first-out) manner, or ranked on some attribute in increasing or decreasing order.

3.4 DESIRABLE SOFTWARE FEATURES

There are numerous features to consider when selecting simulation software. We categorize these features as being in one of the following groups:

- General capabilities (including modeling flexibility and ease of use)
- Hardware and software requirements
- Animation and dynamic graphics
- Statistical capabilities
- Customer support and documentation
- Output reports and graphics

We now discuss each group of features in turn.

3.4.1 General Capabilities

In our opinion, the most important feature for a simulation-software product to have is *modeling flexibility* or, in other words, the ability to model a system whose operating procedures can have any amount of complexity. Note that no two systems are exactly alike. Thus, a simulation package that relies on a *fixed* number of modeling constructs with no capability to do some kind of programming in any manner is bound to be inadequate for certain systems encountered in practice. Ideally, it should be possible to model any system using only the constructs provided in the software—it should not be necessary to use routines written in a programming language such as C. The following are some specific capabilities that make a simulation product flexible:

- Ability to define and change attributes for entities and also global variables, and to use both in decision logic (e.g., if-then-else constructs)
- Ability to use mathematical expressions and mathematical functions (logarithms, exponentiation, etc.)
- Ability to create new modeling constructs and to modify existing ones, and to store them in libraries for use in current and future models

The second most important feature for a simulation product is *ease of use* (and ease of learning), and many contemporary simulation packages have a graphical user interface to facilitate this. The software product should have modeling constructs (e.g., icons or blocks) that are neither too "primitive" nor too "macro." In the former case, a large number of constructs will be required to model even a relatively simple situation; in the latter case, each construct's dialog box will contain an excessive number of options if it is to allow for adequate flexibility. In general, the use of tabs in dialog boxes can help manage a large number of options.

Hierarchical modeling is useful in modeling complex systems. *Hierarchy* allows a user to combine several basic modeling constructs into a new higher-level construct. These new constructs might then be combined into an even higher-level construct, etc. This latter construct can be added to the library of available constructs and can then be reused in this model or future models (see Sec. 3.5.2 for an example). This ability to reuse pieces of model logic increases one's modeling efficiency. Hierarchy is an important concept in a number of simulation packages. It is also a useful way to manage "screen clutter" for a graphically oriented model that consists of many icons or blocks.

The software should have good *debugging aids* such as an interactive debugger. A powerful debugger allows the user to do things such as:

- Follow a single entity through the model to see if it is processed correctly
- See the state of the model every time a particular event occurs (e.g., a machine breakdown)
- Set the value of certain attributes or variables to "force" an entity down a logical path that occurs with small probability

Fast model execution speed is important for certain applications such as large military models and models in which a large number of entities must be processed (e.g., for a high-speed communications network). We programmed a simple manufacturing system in six simulation products and found that, for this model, one product was as much as 11 times faster than another.

It is desirable to be able to develop *user-friendly model "front ends"* when the simulation model is to be used by someone other than the model developer. This capability allows the developer to create an interface by which the nonexpert user can easily enter model parameters such as the mean service time or how long to run the simulation.

Most simulation software vendors offer a *run-time version* of their software, which, roughly speaking, allows the user to change model data but not logic by employing a user-friendly "front end." Applications of a run-time version include:

- Allowing a person in one division of an organization to run a model that was developed by a person in another division who owns a developmental version of the simulation software
- Sales tool for equipment suppliers or system integrators
- Training

Note that a run-time license generally has a considerably lower cost than a normal developmental license or is free.

A feature that is of considerable interest is the ability to *import data from* (and *export data to*) *other applications* (e.g., an Excel spreadsheet or a database).

Traditionally, simulation products have provided performance measures (throughput, mean time in system, etc.) for the system of interest. Now some products also include a *cost module*, which allows costs to be assigned to such things as equipment, labor, raw materials, work in process, finished goods, etc.

In some discrete-event simulations (e.g., steelmaking), it may be necessary to have certain capabilities available from continuous simulation. We call such a simulation a *combined discrete-continuous simulation* (see Sec. 13.4).

Occasionally, one might have a complex set of logic written in a programming language that needs to be integrated into a simulation model. Thus, it is desirable for a simulation package to be able to invoke *external routines*.

It is useful for the simulation package to be easily *initialized in a nonempty and idle state*. For example, in a simulation of a manufacturing system, it might be desirable to initialize the model with all machines busy and all buffers half full, in order to reduce the time required for the model to reach "steady state."

Another useful feature is that *the state of a simulation can be saved at the end of a run* and used to restart easily the simulation at a later time.

Finally, *cost* is usually an important consideration in the purchase of simulation software. Currently, the cost of simulation software for a PC ranges from \$1000 to \$100,000 or even more. However, there are other costs that must be considered, such as maintenance fees, upgrade fees, and the cost for any additional hardware and software that might be required (see Sec. 3.4.2).

3.4.2 Hardware and Software Requirements

In selecting simulation software, one must consider what *computer platforms* the software is available for. Almost all software is available for Windows-based PCs, and some products are also available for Apple computers. If a software package is available for several platforms, then it should be *compatible across platforms*. The amount of *RAM required* to run the software should be considered as well as *what operating systems are supported*. It is highly desirable if independent replications of a simulation model can be made simultaneously on multiple processor cores or on networked computers.

3.4.3 Animation and Dynamic Graphics

The availability of built-in animation is one of the reasons for the increased use of simulation modeling. In an *animation*, key elements of the system are represented on the screen by icons that dynamically change position, color, and shape as the simulation model evolves through time. (See the Color Plates at the back of the book.) For example, in a manufacturing system, an icon representing a forklift truck will change position when there is a corresponding change in the model, and an icon representing a machine might change color when the machine changes state (e.g., idle to busy) in the model.

The following are some of the uses of animation:

- Communicating the essence of a simulation model (or simulation itself) to a manager or to other people who may not be aware of (or care about) the technical details of the model
- Debugging the simulation computer program
- Showing that a simulation model is *not* valid
- Suggesting improved operational procedures for a system (some things may not be apparent from looking at just the simulation's numerical results)
- Training operational personnel
- Promoting communication among the project team

There are two fundamental types of animation: concurrent and post-processed (also called *playback*). In *concurrent animation* the animation is being displayed at the same time that the simulation is running. Note, however, that the animation is normally turned off when making production runs, because the animation slows down the execution of the simulation. In *post-processed animation*, state changes in the simulation are saved to a disk file and used to drive the graphics *after* the simulation is over. Some simulation software products have both types of animation.

We now discuss desirable features for animation. First, the simulation software should provide *default animation* as part of the model-building process. Since animation is primarily a communications device, it should be possible to *create high-resolution icons* and to save them for later reuse. The software should come with a *library of standard icons*, or it should be possible to *import icons* from an external source (e.g., Google Warehouse). The software should provide *smooth movement of icons*; icons should not "flash" or "jump." There should be a control to *speed up or slow down the animation*. It should be possible to *zoom* in or out and to *pan* to see different parts of a system too large to fit on one screen. Some software products have *named animation views*, so that one can construct a menu of views corresponding to different parts of the simulated system. It is desirable if the animation uses *vector-based graphics* (pictures are drawn with lines, arcs, and fills) rather than *pixel-based graphics* (pictures are drawn by turning individual pixels on or off). The former type of graphics allows rotation of an object (e.g., a helicopter rotor) as well as a vehicle to maintain its proper orientation as it goes around a corner.

Some simulation products with concurrent animation allow the user to stop the simulation "on the fly" while observing the animation, make changes to certain model parameters (e.g., the number of machines in a workstation), and then instantly restart the simulation. However, this can be *statistically dangerous* if the state of the system and the statistical counters are not reset.

Many simulation packages provide *three-dimensional animation* (the vantage point from which to view the animation can be rotated around all three axes), which might be important for management presentations and for situations in which vertical clearances are important. In these products it may also be possible to provide the viewer of the animation with a perspective of "riding through the system on the back of an entity."

It should be possible to *import CAD drawings and clip art* into an animation.

It is often desirable to display *dynamic graphics and statistics* on the screen as the simulation executes. Examples of dynamic graphics are clocks, dials, level meters (perhaps representing a queue), and dynamically updated histograms and time plots (see Sec. 3.4.6). An example of the latter would be to update a plot of the number in some queue as the simulation moves through time.

3.4.4 Statistical Capabilities

If a simulation product does not have good statistical-analysis features, then it is impossible to obtain correct results from a simulation study. First, the software must have a good *random-number generator* (see Chap. 7), that is, a mechanism for generating independent observations from a uniform distribution on the interval [0, 1]. Note that not all random-number generators found on computers or in software products have acceptable statistical properties. The generator should have at least 100 different streams (preferably far more) that can be assigned to different sources of randomness (e.g., interarrival times or service times) in a simulation model—this will allow different system designs to be compared in a more statistically efficient manner (see Sec. 11.2). The simulation software should produce the same results on different executions if the default seeds are used for the various streams—the seeds should not depend on the internal clock of the computer. On the other hand, the user should be able to set the seed for each stream, if desired.

In general, each source of randomness in the system of interest should be represented in the simulation model by a *probability distribution* (see Chap. 6), not just the perceived mean value. If it is possible to find a standard *theoretical distribution* that is a good model for a particular source of randomness, then this distribution should be used in the model. At a minimum, the following *continuous* distributions should be available: exponential, gamma, Weibull, lognormal, normal, uniform, beta, and triangular. The last distribution is typically used as a model for a source of randomness when no system data are available. Note also that *very few* input random variables in real simulations have a normal distribution. The following *discrete* distributions should also be available: binomial, geometric, negative binomial, Poisson, and discrete uniform.

If a theoretical distribution cannot be found that is a good representation for a source of randomness, then an *empirical* (or *user-defined*) *distribution* based on the data should be used (see Sec. 6.2.4). In this case, random numbers are used to sample from a distribution function constructed from the observed system data.

There should be (a single) command available for making *independent replications* (or *runs*) of the simulation model. This means:

- Each run uses separate sets of different random numbers.
- Each run uses the same initial conditions.
- Each run resets the statistical counters.

Note that simulation results from different runs are independent and also probabilistic copies of each other. This allows (simple) classical statistical procedures to be applied to the results from different runs (see Chap. 9).

There should be a statistically sound method available for constructing a *confidence interval* for a mean (e.g., the mean time in system for a part in a factory). The method should be easy to understand and should provide good statistical results. In this regard, we feel that the *method of replication* (see Secs. 9.4.1 and 9.5.2) is definitely the superior approach.

If one is trying to determine the long-run or "steady-state" behavior of a system, then it is generally desirable to specify a warmup period for the simulation, that is, a point in simulated time when the statistical counters (but not the state of the system) are reset. Ideally, the simulation software should also be able to *determine a value for the warmup period* based on making pilot runs. There is currently at least one simulation product that uses Welch's graphical approach (see Sec. 9.5.1) to specify a warmup period.

It should be possible to construct a *confidence interval for the difference between the means of two simulated systems* (e.g., the current system and a proposed system) by using the method of replication (see Sec. 10.2).

The simulation software should allow the user to specify *what performance measures to collect output data on*, rather than produce reams of default output data that are of no interest to the user.

At least one simulation product allows the user to perform *statistical experimental designs* (see Chap. 12) with the software, such as full factorial designs or fractional factorial designs. When we perform a simulation study, we would like to know what input factors (decision variables) have the greatest impact on the performance measures of interest. Experimental designs tell us what simulation experiments (runs) to make so that the effect of each factor can be determined. Some designs also allow us to determine interactions among the factors.

A topic that is of interest to some people planning to buy simulation software is "*optimization*" (see Sec. 12.5). Suppose that there are a number of decision variables (input factors) of interest, each with its own range of acceptable values. (There may also be linear constraints on the decision variables.) In addition, there is an objective function to be maximized (or minimized) that is a function of one or more simulation output random variables (e.g., throughput in a manufacturing system) and of certain decision variables. Then the goal of an "optimizer" is to make runs of the simulation model (each run uses certain settings of the decision variables) in an intelligent manner and to determine eventually a combination of the decision variables that produces an optimal or near-optimal solution. These optimization modules use heuristics such as genetic algorithms, simulated annealing, neural networks, scatter search, and tabu search.

3.4.5 Customer Support and Documentation

The simulation software vendor should provide *public training* on the software on a regular basis, and it should also be possible to have *customized training* presented at the client's site. Good *technical support* is extremely important for questions on how to use the software and in case a bug in the software is discovered. Technical support, which is usually in the form of telephone help, should be such that a response is received in at most one day.

Good documentation is a crucial requirement for using any software product. *It should be possible, in our opinion, to learn a simulation package without taking a formal training course.* Generally, there will be a user's guide or reference manual. There should be *numerous detailed examples* available. Most products now have *context-dependent online help*, which we consider very important. (It is not sufficient merely to have a copy of the documentation available in the software.) Several products have a library of "mini examples" to illustrate the various modeling constructs.

There should be a *detailed description of how each modeling construct works*, particularly if its operating procedures are complex. For example, if a simulation-software product for communications networks offers a module for a particular type of local-area network, then its logic should be carefully delineated and any simplifying assumptions made relative to the standard stated.

It is highly desirable to have a *university-quality textbook* available for the simulation package.

Most simulation products offer a *free demo* and, in some cases, a working version of the software can be downloaded from the vendor's website, which will allow small models to be developed and run.

It is useful if the vendor publishes an *electronic newsletter* and has a yearly *users' conference*. The vendor should have *regular updates of the software* (perhaps, once a year).

3.4.6 Output Reports and Graphics

Standard reports should be provided for the estimated performance measures. It should also be possible to *customize reports*, perhaps for management presentations. Since a simulation product should be flexible enough so that it can compute estimates of user-defined performance measures, it should also be possible to write these estimates into a custom report. For each performance measure (e.g., time in system for a factory), the average observed value, the minimum observed value, and the maximum observed value are usually given. If a standard deviation is also given (based on one simulation run), then the user should be sure that it is based on a statistically acceptable method (such as batch means with appropriate batch sizes, as discussed in Sec. 9.5.3), or else it should be viewed as *highly suspect*. [Variance and standard-deviation estimates require independent data, which are rarely produced by one run of a simulation model (see Sec. 4.4).] It should be possible to obtain reports at intermediate points during a simulation run as well as at the end.

The simulation product should provide a variety of (static) graphics. First, it should be possible to make a *histogram* (see Fig. 14.29) for a set of observed data. For continuous (discrete) data, a histogram is a graphical estimate of the underlying probability density (mass) function that produced the data. Time plots are also very important. In a *time plot* (see, for example, Fig. 14.27) one or more key system variables (e.g., the numbers in certain queues) are plotted over the length of the simulation, providing a long-term indication of the dynamic behavior of the simulated system. (An animation provides a short-term indication of the dynamic behavior of a system.) Some simulation products allow the simulation results to be presented in *bar charts* or *pie charts*. Finally, a *correlation plot* (see Fig. 6.29) is a useful way to measure the dependence in the output data produced from one simulation run.

It should be possible to *export individual model output observations* (e.g., times in system) to other software packages such as spreadsheets, databases, statistics packages, and graphical packages for further analysis and display.

3.5 GENERAL-PURPOSE SIMULATION PACKAGES

In Secs. 3.5.1 through 3.5.3 we give brief descriptions of Arena, ExtendSim, and Simio, respectively, which are (at this writing) popular general-purpose simulation packages. In each case we also show how to build a model of a small factory. Section 3.5.4 lists some additional general-purpose simulation packages.

3.5.1 Arena

Arena [see Rockwell (2013) and Kelton et al. (2010)] is a general-purpose simulation package marketed by Rockwell Automation (Wexford, Pennsylvania) that is commonly used for applications such as manufacturing, supply chains, defense, health care, and contact centers. There are two different versions of Arena, namely, the Standard Edition and the Professional Edition.

Modeling constructs, which are called "modules" in Arena, are functionally arranged into a number of "templates." (A module contains logic, a user interface, and, in some cases, options for animation.) The "Basic Process" template contains modules that are used in virtually every model for modeling arrivals, departures, services, and decision logic of entities. The "Advanced Process" template contains modules that are used to perform more advanced process logic and to access external data files in Excel, Access, and SQL databases. The "Advanced Transfer" template contains modules for modeling various types of conveyors, forklift trucks, automated guided vehicles, and other material-handling equipment. The "Flow Process" template is used for modeling tanks, pipes, valves, and batch-processing operations. Also the lower-level "Blocks" and "Elements" templates are used in modeling some complex real-world systems; these two templates constitute what was previously called the SIMAN simulation language.

A model is constructed in Arena by dragging modules into the model window, connecting them to indicate the flow of entities through the simulated system, and then detailing the modules by using dialog boxes or Arena's built-in spreadsheet. A model can have an unlimited number of levels of hierarchy.

"Visual Designer" is used to create concurrent three-dimensional (3-D) animations and "live-data dashboards," which display dynamic graphics (e.g., histograms, pie charts, and time plots). (Two-dimensional animation is also available.) It also allows one to "watch the logic execute" and to perform sophisticated graphical model debugging. AVI files can be generated directly from Arena for sharing animations with other people, and each Arena license includes one additional runtime-only license (see Sec. 3.4.1).

There are an unlimited number of random-number streams (see Chap. 7) available in Arena. Furthermore, the user has access to 12 standard theoretical probability distributions and also to empirical distributions. Arena has a built-in capability for modeling nonstationary Poisson processes (see Sec. 6.12.2), which is a model for entity arrivals with a time-varying rate.

There is an easy mechanism for making independent replications of a particular simulated system and for obtaining point estimates and confidence intervals for performance measures of interest. It is also possible to construct a confidence interval for the difference between the means of two systems. A number of plots are available, such as histograms, time plots, bar charts, and correlation plots. The "OptQuest for Arena" (see Sec. 12.5.2) optimization module is available as an option.

Activity-based costing is incorporated into Arena, providing value-added and non-value-added cost and time reports. Simulation results are stored in a database and are presented using Crystal Reports, which is embedded in Arena.

Microsoft Visual Basic for Applications (VBA) and a complete ActiveX object model are available in Arena. This capability allows more sophisticated control and logic including the creation of user-friendly "front ends" for entering model parameters, the production of customized reports, etc. This technology is also used for Arena's interfaces with many external applications including the Visio drawing package.

Arena Professional Edition includes the ability to create customized modules and to store them in a new template. Arena also has an option that permits a model to run in real time (or any multiple thereof) and to dynamically interact with other

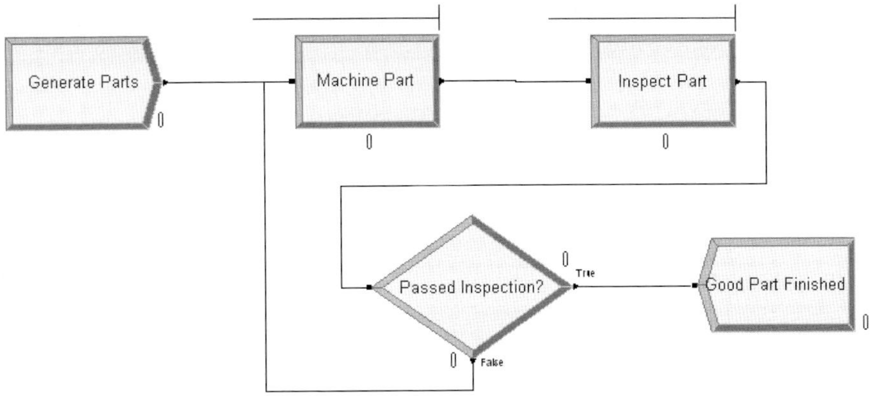

FIGURE 3.3
Arena model for the manufacturing system.

processes; this supports applications such as the High Level Architecture (see Sec. 1.6.2) and testing of hardware/software control systems.

We now develop an Arena model for the simple manufacturing system of Example 9.25, which consists of a machine and an inspector. However, we assume here that the machine never breaks down. Figure 3.3 shows the five required logic modules and the necessary connections to define the entity flow.

The "Create" module, whose dialog box is shown in Fig. 3.4, is used to generate arrivals of parts. We label the module "Generate Parts" and specify that interarrival times are exponentially distributed [denoted "Random (Expo)"] with a mean of 1 minute. The Create module is connected to the "Process" module (see Fig. 3.5), which is

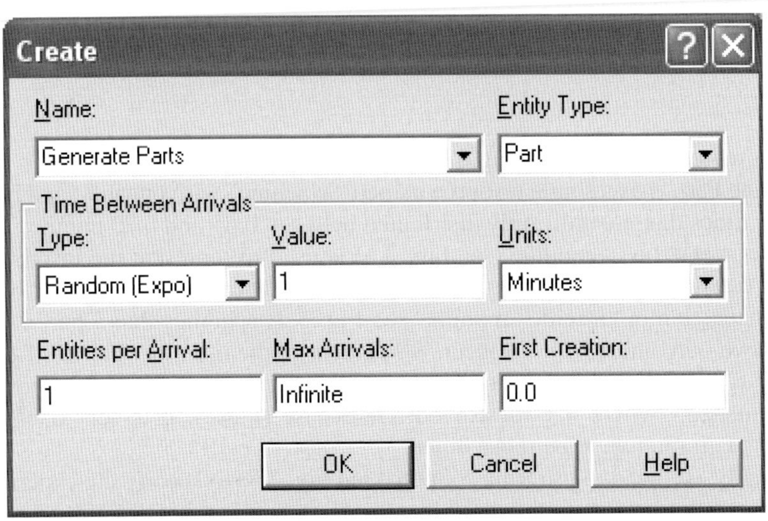

FIGURE 3.4
Dialog box for the Arena Create module "Generate Parts."

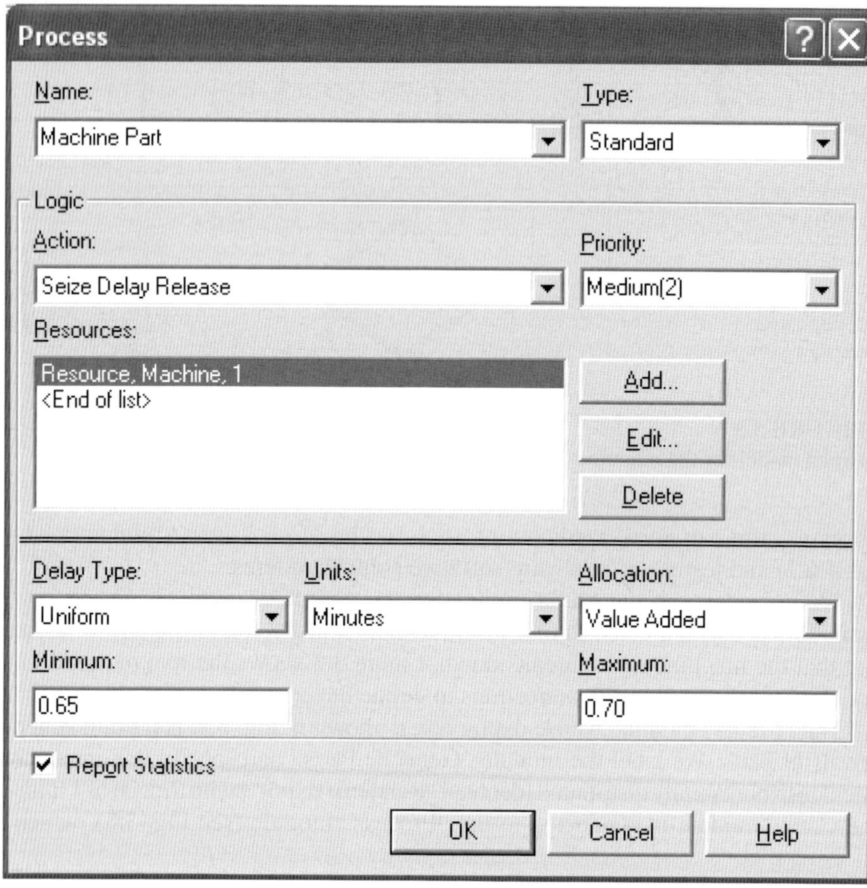

FIGURE 3.5
Dialog box for the Arena Process module "Machine Part."

used to represent the processing of a part at the machine. This module is labeled "Machine Part," has a single resource named "Machine" with one unit, and has processing times that are uniformly distributed between 0.65 and 0.70 minute.

The next Process module (see Fig. 3.6) is used to represent the inspector. We specify that inspection times are uniformly distributed between 0.75 and 0.80 minute. After inspection, a "Decide" module (see Fig. 3.7) specifies that a part can have one of two outcomes: "True" (occurs 90 percent of the time) or "False." If the part is good (True), then it is sent to the "Depart" module (not shown) labeled "Good Part Finished," where it is destroyed. Otherwise (False), it is sent back to the Machine Part module to be remachined.

Finally, we need to use Run > Setup (see Fig. 3.8) to specify the experimental parameters. We state that one run of length 100,000 minutes is desired.

The results from running the simulation are given in Fig. 3.9, from which we see that the average time in system of a part is 4.64 minutes. Additional output statistics can be obtained from the options on the left-hand side of the screen.

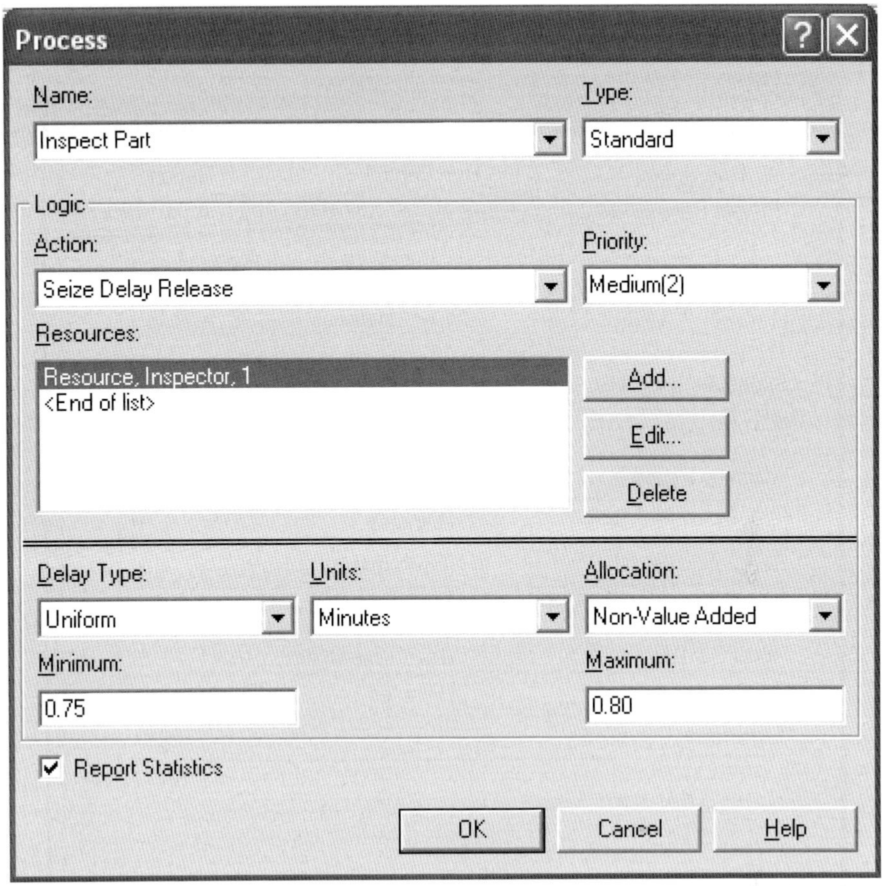

FIGURE 3.6
Dialog box for the Arena Process module "Inspect Part."

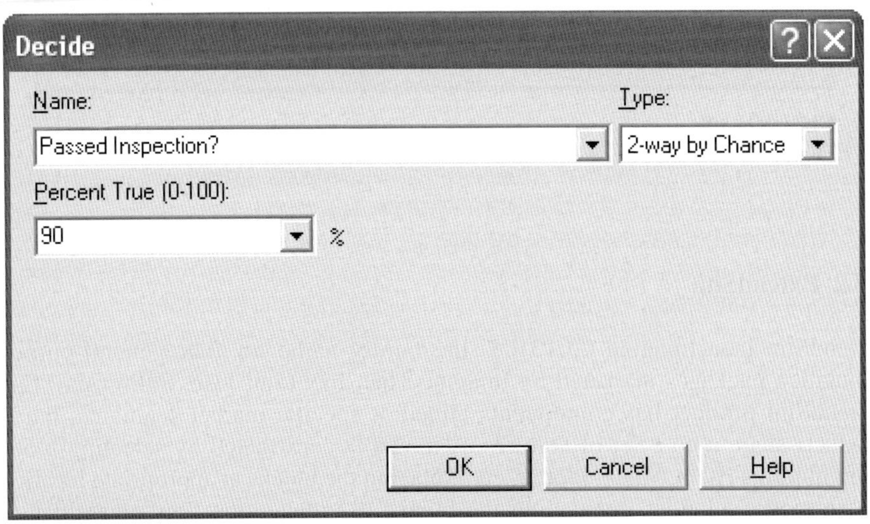

FIGURE 3.7
Dialog box for the Arena Decide module "Passed Inspection?"

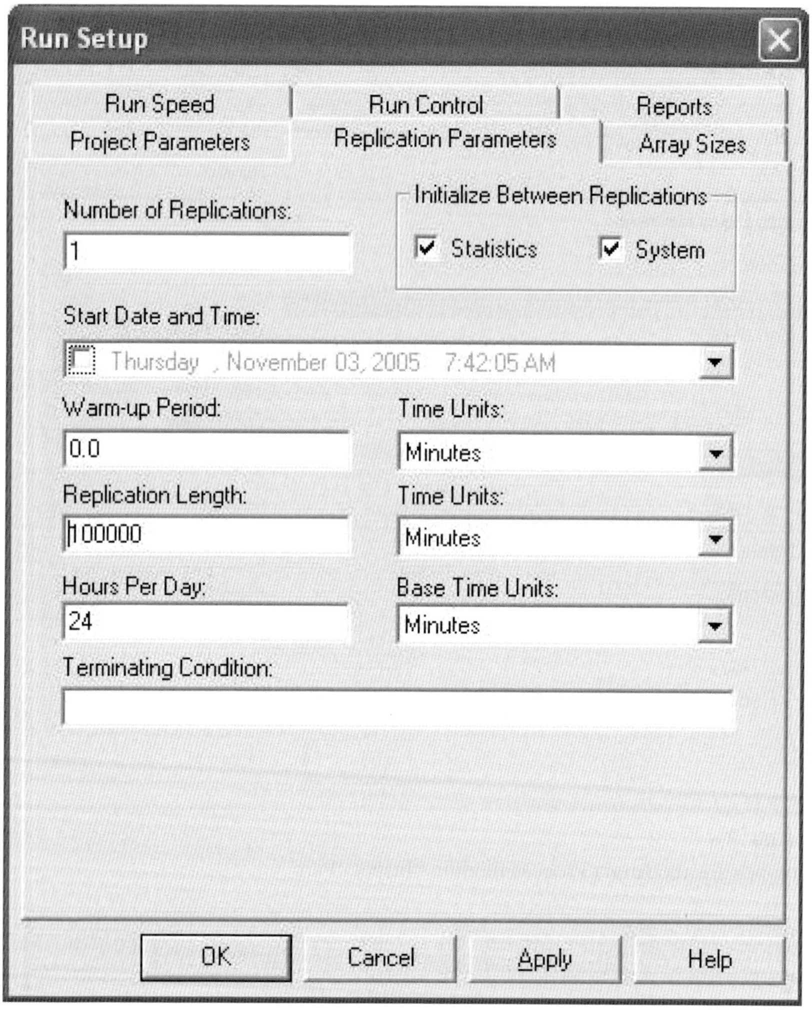

FIGURE 3.8
Dialog box for the Arena Run Setup configuration options.

3.5.2 ExtendSim

ExtendSim [see Imagine (2013)] is the family name for four general-purpose simulation packages marketed by Imagine That, Inc. (San Jose, California). Each ExtendSim product has components aimed at specific market segments, but all products share a core set of features. A model is constructed by selecting blocks from libraries (Item, Value, Plotter, etc.), placing the blocks at appropriate locations in the model window, connecting the blocks to indicate the flow of entities (or values) through the system, and then detailing the blocks using dialog boxes.

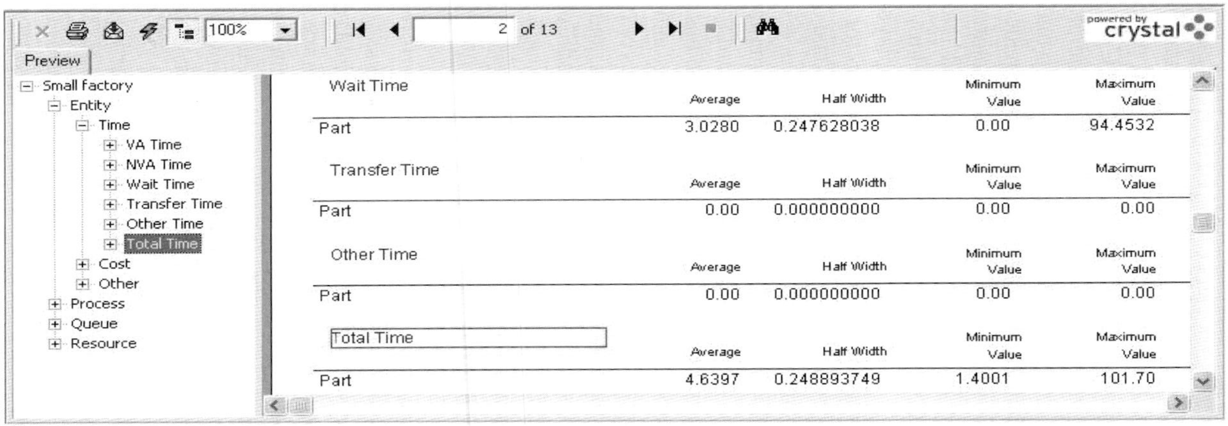

FIGURE 3.9
Simulation results for the Arena model of the manufacturing system.

ExtendSim can model a wide variety of system configurations using the blocks supplied with the product. If needed, the internal ModL language can be used to customize existing blocks and to create entirely new blocks. These "new" blocks can be placed in a new library for reuse in the current model or future models. The code corresponding to a particular block can be viewed by right-clicking on the block and selecting "Open Structure"; this feature is useful for understanding the actual operation of the block. ModL can also access applications and procedures created with external programming languages such as Visual Basic and C++.

A model can have an unlimited number of levels of hierarchy (see below) and also use inheritance (see Sec. 3.6). A "Navigator" allows one to move from one hierarchical level to another. All ExtendSim products provide a basic 2-D animation, and the ExtendSim Suite product also provides 3-D animation.

Each simulation model in ExtendSim has an associated "Notebook," which can contain pictures, text, dialog items, and model results. Thus, a Notebook can be used as a "front end" for a model or as a vehicle for displaying important model results as the simulation is actually running. The parameters for each model can also be stored in, and accessed from, the model's internal relational database; this is useful for data consolidation and management.

There are an essentially unlimited number of random-number streams available in ExtendSim. Furthermore, the user has access to 34 standard theoretical probability distributions and also to empirical distributions. ExtendSim has an easy mechanism for making independent replications of a simulation model and for obtaining point estimates and confidence intervals for performance measures of interest. A number of plots are available such as histograms, time plots, bar charts, and Gantt charts.

There is an activity-based costing capability in ExtendSim that allows one to assign fixed and variable costs to an entity as it moves through a simulated system. For example, in a manufacturing system a part might be assigned a fixed cost for the required raw materials and a variable cost that depends on how long the part spends waiting in queue.

ExtendSim's "Item" library contains blocks for performing discrete-event simulation (entity arrival, service, departure, etc.), as well as for material handling (see Sec. 14.3 for further discussion of material handling) and routing. (An entity is called an "Item" in ExtendSim.) The optional "Rate" library provides blocks for modeling high-speed, high-volume manufacturing systems (e.g., canning lines) within a discrete-event environment. The blocks in the "Value" library are used to perform continuous simulation (see Sec. 13.3) and to provide modeling support (mathematical calculations, simulation-based optimization, data sharing with other applications, etc.) for discrete-event simulation.

ExtendSim's "Scenario Manager" allows the modeler to investigate how the simulation model's responses change from one scenario (a set of values for the model's input parameters or factors) to another. The scenarios of interest can either be entered manually or are specified automatically by the Scenario Manager in the case of a factorial design (see Sec. 12.2). Additionally, the modeler specifies the number of independent replications (each using different random numbers) of each scenario that is desired. The Scenario Manager runs the scenarios iteratively, records the responses for each replication, and the responses are then summarized across the replications for each scenario. The model factors and their corresponding

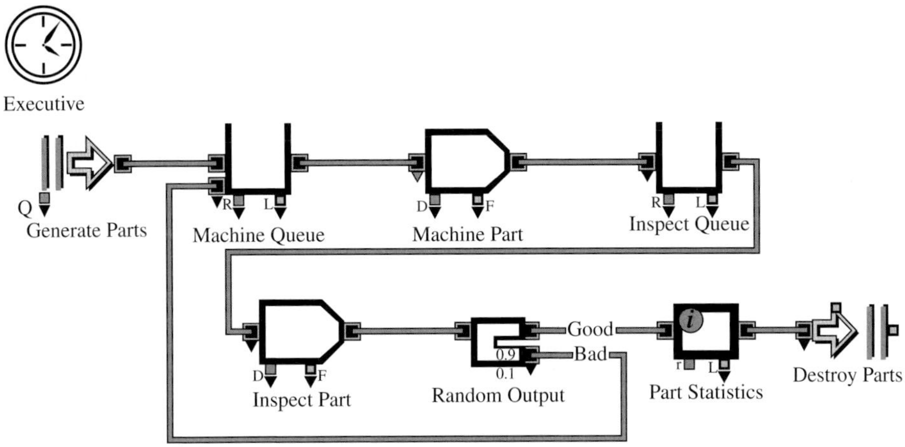

FIGURE 3.10
ExtendSim model for the manufacturing system.

responses can be exported to ExtendSim's database, the JMP and Minitab statistical packages, or Excel for further analysis. ExtendSim also has a built-in optimization module (see Sec. 12.5.2).

We now show how to build an ExtendSim model for the manufacturing system discussed in Sec. 3.5.1. In particular, Fig. 3.10 shows the required blocks and connections for the model; the connections correspond to the flow of entities (parts for this model). All the blocks in this model are from the ExtendSim Item library. We have placed a descriptive label below each block, which we will refer to in the discussion of the model below.

The "Executive" block, which is not graphically connected to any other block, manages the event list for an ExtendSim model. The first block actually in the model is a "Create" block labeled "Generate Parts" (see its dialog box in Fig. 3.11), which is used to generate parts having exponential interarrival times with a mean of 1 minute. This is followed by a "Queue" block labeled "Machine Queue" (Fig. 3.12), which stores the parts while they are waiting for processing. This queue has infinite capacity by default and merges the parts from the Create block with those parts that need to be reworked after inspection.

Following the Machine Queue block is an "Activity" block labeled "Machine Part." In the dialog box for this latter block (Fig. 3.13), we specify that one part can be processed at a time. We also select "Uniform, Real" as the processing-time distribution and then set its minimum and maximum values to 0.65 and 0.70 minute, respectively. This Activity block is connected to a second Queue block labeled "Inspect Queue," where parts wait for the inspection process. The output of this Queue block is connected to a second Activity block labeled "Inspect Part," where inspection times are uniformly distributed between 0.75 and 0.80 minute.

The Activity block corresponding to the inspector is connected to the "Select Item Out" block labeled "Random Output," which is used to determine whether a part is good or bad. In its dialog box (Fig. 3.14), we specify that parts will leave randomly through the block's outputs. In the table we enter the probabilities

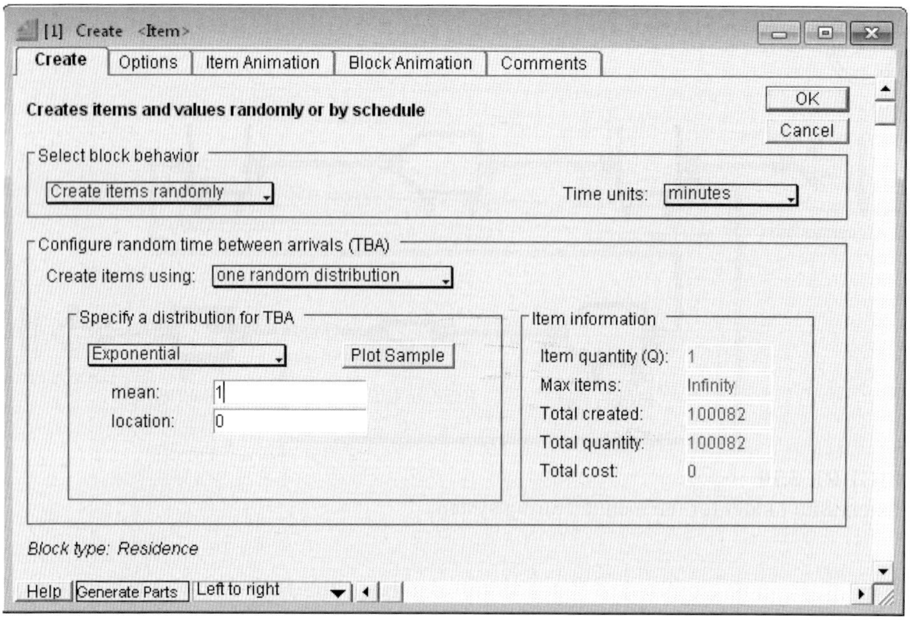

FIGURE 3.11
Dialog box for the ExtendSim Create block “Generate Parts.”

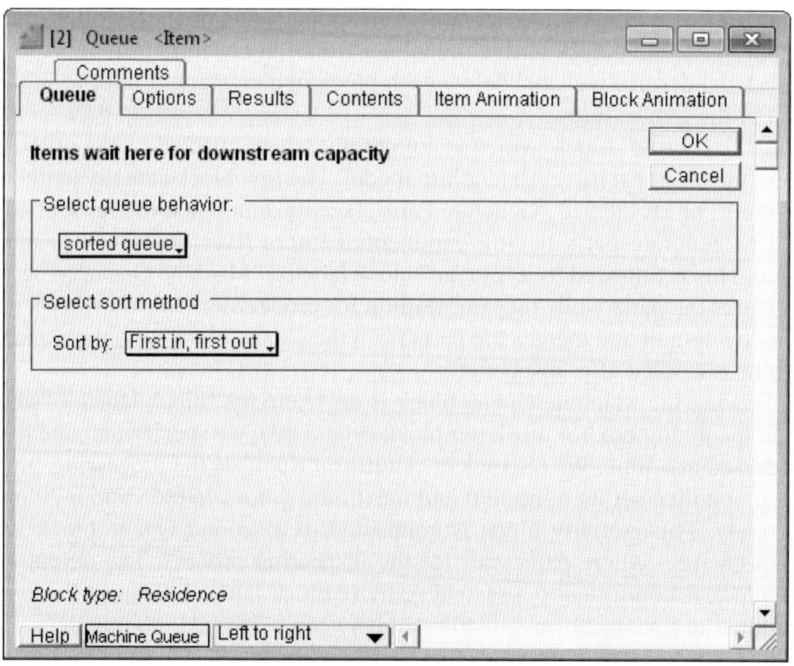

FIGURE 3.12
Dialog box for the ExtendSim Queue block “Machine Queue.”

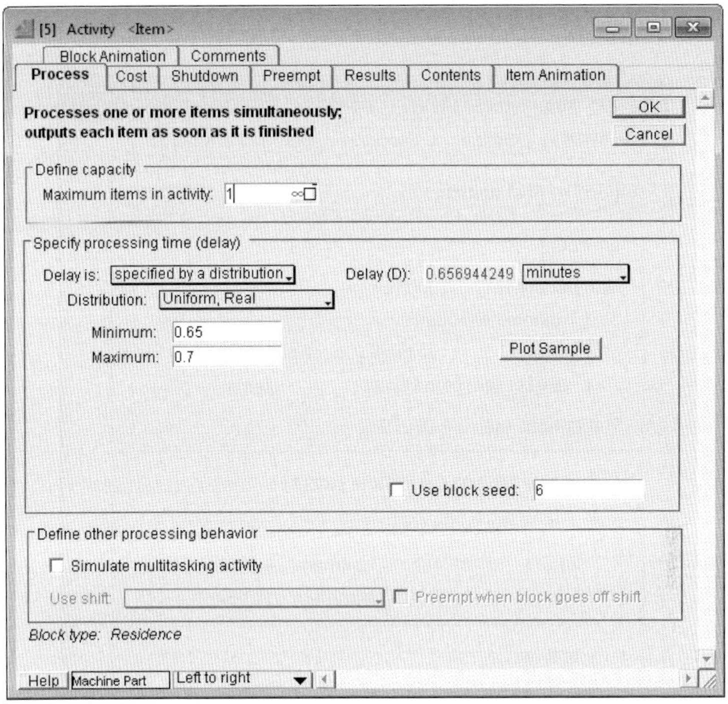

FIGURE 3.13
Dialog box for the ExtendSim Activity block "Machine Part."

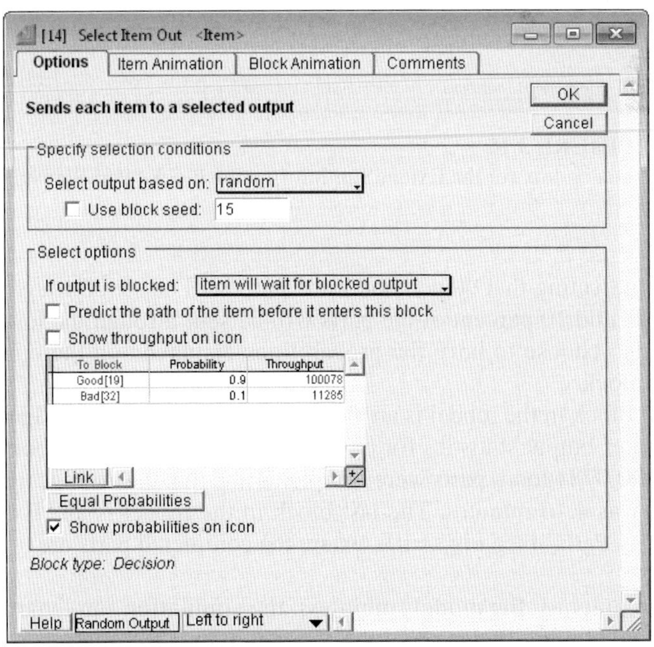

FIGURE 3.14
Dialog box for the ExtendSim Select Item Out block "Random Output."

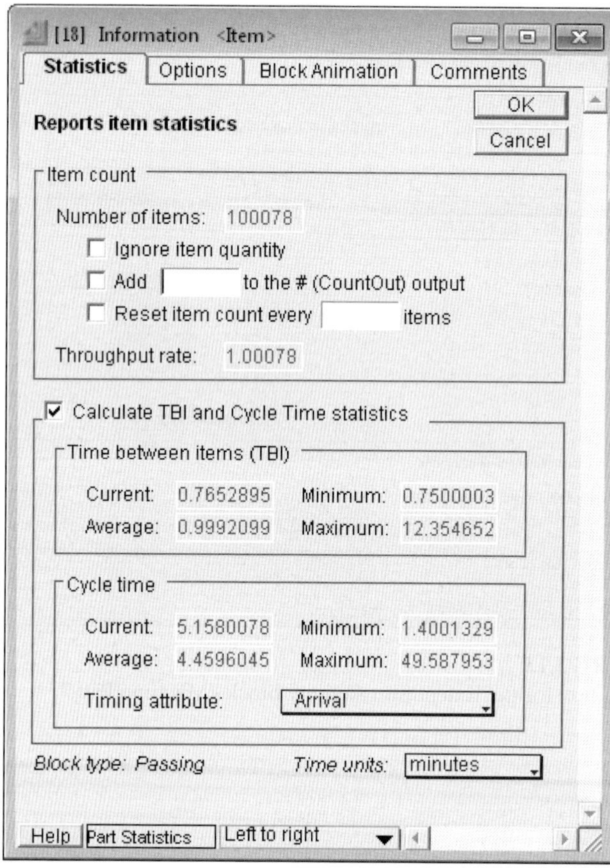

FIGURE 3.15
Dialog box for the ExtendSim Information block "Part Statistics."

0.9 and 0.1, indicating that 90 percent of the parts will be sent through the top output as "Good" and 10 percent of the parts will be sent through the lower output as "Bad." We also choose to have the probabilities displayed on the output connections of this block.

The next block in the model is an "Information" block labeled "Part Statistics," which computes output statistics for completed parts. In its dialog box (Fig. 3.15), we see that 100,078 (good) parts were completed and that the average time in system (cycle time) was 4.46 minutes. The last block in the model is an "Exit" block labeled "Destroy Parts" (see Fig. 3.10), where the completed parts are removed from the model.

The time units for the model (minutes), the simulation run length (100,000), and the desired number of runs (1) are specified in the "Simulation Setup" option that is accessed from the "Run" pull-down menu (not shown) at the top of the screen. The Notebook for the model (Fig. 3.16), which is accessed from the

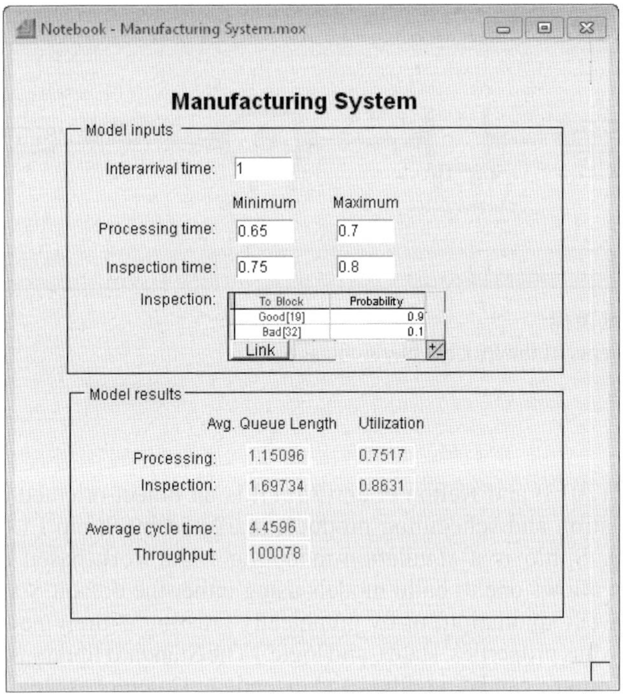

FIGURE 3.16
ExtendSim Notebook for the manufacturing system.

"Window" pull-down menu, brings together important input parameters and results for the model.

In Fig. 3.17 we give a version of the ExtendSim model that uses hierarchy (see Sec. 3.4.1). If we double-click on the hierarchical block named "Process" (at the first level of hierarchy), then we go down to the second level of hierarchy where we see the original Machine Queue and Machine Part blocks, as shown in Fig. 3.18.

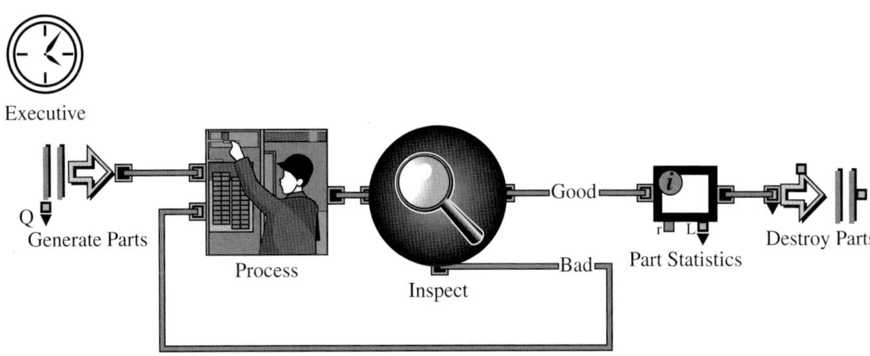

FIGURE 3.17
Hierarchical ExtendSim model for the manufacturing system.

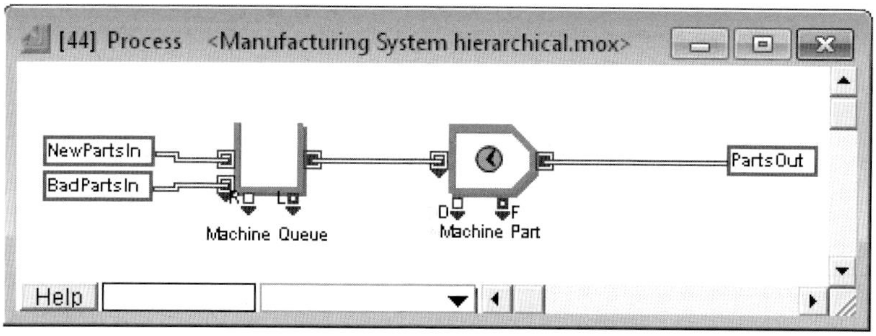

FIGURE 3.18
Components of the Process hierarchical block.

3.5.3 Simio

Simio [Simio (2013) and Kelton et al. (2011)] is an object-oriented (see Sec. 3.6) suite of simulation and scheduling products marketed by Simio LLC (Sewickley, Pennsylvania). Simio is a *sim*ulation-modeling framework based on *i*ntelligent *o*bjects, which allows one to build models using either the default Standard Library (for discrete-event simulation) or by graphically creating entirely new objects. (An object in Simio has properties, states, and logic.) The Standard library, which contains 15 object definitions, can be modified and extended using process logic (see below), and new objects can be stored in libraries for use in other simulation projects.

An object in a library might be a customer, machine, doctor, or anything else that you might find in a system. A model is constructed in Simio by dragging objects into the "Facility" window, connecting them by links to indicate the flow of entities through the simulated system, and then detailing the objects by using a property editor. The model logic and animation are built in a single step, typically in a two-dimensional view for ease of modeling. However, one can switch to a three-dimensional (3-D) perspective view with just a single keystroke.

Building an object in Simio is identical to building a model, since there is no difference between the two constructs. Whenever you build a model, it is by definition an object that can be used in another model. For example, if you combine two machines and a robot into a model of a workstation, then the workstation model is itself an object that can then be used in other models. Every model that is built in Simio is automatically a building block that can be used in constructing hierarchical models.

When you instantiate an object into a model, you may specify "properties" (static input parameters) of the object that govern the behavior of this specific instance of the object. For example, a property of a machine might be its processing time. The developer of an object decides on the number of properties and their meanings. Properties in Simio can be numerical values, Boolean variables, text strings, etc.

In addition to properties, objects have "states" that change values as a result of the execution of the object's logic. A state for a machine might be its status (e.g., idle or busy). Properties and states together constitute the attributes of an object.

An object in Simio may be defined from one of five base classes, which provides the underlying behavior for the object. The first class is the "fixed object," which has a fixed location in the model and is used to represent something in a system that does not move from one location to another, such as a machine in a factory or an operating room in a hospital.

An "entity" is an object that can move through 3-D space over a network of links and nodes. Examples of entities are parts in a manufacturing system, and patients, nurses, and doctors in a hospital. Note that in traditional simulation packages entities are passive and are acted upon by the model processes (see Sec. 3.3.2). However, in Simio the entities are intelligent objects that can control their own behavior.

"Link" and "node" objects are used to build networks over which entities may flow. A link defines a pathway for entities to move from one object to another, whereas a node defines the beginning or ending point of a link. Links and nodes can be combined together into complex networks. A link could be an escalator with a fixed travel time or it could represent a conveyor.

The final class of objects is a "transporter," which is a subclass of the entity class. A transporter is an entity that has the added capabilities to pick up, carry, and drop off one or more other entities. A transporter could be used to model a bus, a forklift truck, or any other object that has the ability to carry other entities from one location to another.

A key feature of Simio is the ability to create a wide range of object behaviors from the base classes. The Simio modeling framework is application-domain neutral, i.e., these base classes are not specific to a particular application area such as manufacturing or health care. However, it is easy to build application-oriented libraries composed of intelligent objects from the base classes. Simio's design philosophy dictates that domain-specific logic belongs in the objects built by users, and it is not programmed into the core system.

The process approach (see Sec. 3.3.2) is commonly used for extending an object's logic or for building new objects. A process is defined in Simio using a flowchart, where each step in the flowchart defines some action to perform. There are over 50 different process steps available in Simio to perform specific actions such as delay by time, wait to seize a resource, etc. Process logic can be inserted into a specific instance of an object to modify or extend its behaviors. For example, an object representing a machine might use process logic to seize and hold a repairman during a breakdown.

There are an essentially unlimited number of random-number streams available in Simio. Furthermore, the user has access to 19 standard theoretical probability distributions and to empirical distributions. There is an easy mechanism for making independent replications of a simulation model and for obtaining point estimates and confidence intervals for performance measures of interest. A number of plots are available such as time plots, histograms, bar charts, and pie charts.

Simio provides a 3-D interactive environment for building and running simulation models, which is useful for accurately modeling spatial relationships and for communicating model behavior to the simulation project's stakeholders. However, Simio also provides a set of sophisticated features for performing and analyzing simulation experiments. In particular, a model may have an associated "experiment" that specifies a set of scenarios to execute. Each scenario *may* have one or more input controls and will have one or more output responses. The input controls are factors that are changed from one scenario to the next (e.g., the number of machines in a workstation), and the output responses are the measures of performance (e.g., average time in system of a part) that are used to evaluate the efficacy of the different scenarios. Furthermore, each scenario can be replicated a specified number of times and these replications can be simultaneously executed across multiple processor cores or across different computers on a network, which will greatly reduce the time required for experimentation. Simio's built-in analysis tools include a procedure for automatically selecting the best scenario from a set of candidate scenarios [see Sec. 10.4.3 and Kim and Nelson (2001)] and SMORE plots [see Nelson (2008)]. A SMORE plot simultaneously displays a point estimate and confidence interval for the expected value of a response, as well as a superimposed box plot (see Sec. 6.4.3). The "OptQuest for Simio" (see Sec. 12.5.2) optimization module is available as an option.

Although Simio is primarily oriented toward performing discrete-event simulation using an object-oriented approach, Simio also supports modeling continuous-flow systems, performing agent-based simulation (because of its object orientation), and performing discrete-event simulation using the process approach. Moreover, Simio can also be used in an operational setting as a risk-based planning and scheduling tool to improve the day-to-day functioning of an organization.

We now develop a Simio model of the simple manufacturing system discussed in Sec. 3.5.1. The Simio model for this system is shown in Figure 3.19 and is composed of a "Source" object named "Part_Arrivals" that creates the jobs arriving to the system, a "Server" object named "Machine_Part" that models the machining operation, a Server object named "Inspect_Part" that models the inspection process, and a "Sink" object named "Part_Departures," where entities leave the system. In this example, we use a zero-time link called a "Connector" to define the travel paths between the Source, Servers, and Sink objects.

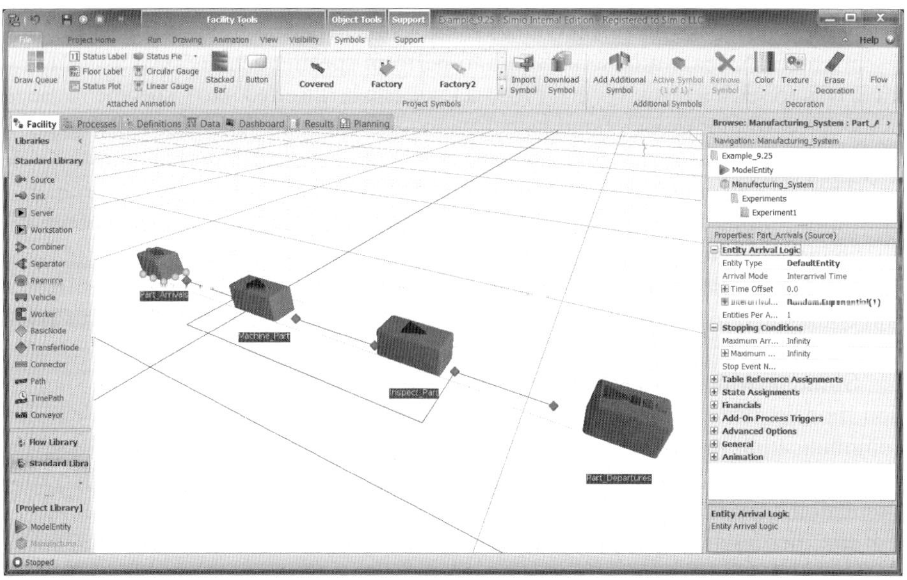

FIGURE 3.19
Simio model for the manufacturing system.

The small circular "selection handles" surrounding the Part_Arrivals object indicate that the object was selected for editing (by clicking on it with the mouse). The properties of a selected object are edited using the "Property Editor," which is on the lower-right side of the screen. The Part_Arrivals object is used to generate arrivals to the system based on an "Arrival Mode." The default "Interarrival Time" mode used in this example specifies that the distribution of interarrival times is exponential with a mean of 1 minute. [Alternatively, the "Time Varying Arrival Rate" mode generates arrivals in accordance with a nonstationary Poisson process (see Sec. 6.12.2) and the "Arrival Table" mode schedules arrivals using data stored in a table or an external source such as a spreadsheet.]

Figure 3.20 displays the properties for the Machine_Part object. The properties are organized into categories that can be expanded and collapsed with the +/− signs to the left of the category name. These properties specify that "Processing Time" is uniformly distributed on the interval [0.65, 0.70] minute. Note that this expression can be typed in directly or specified using an "Expression Editor," which can be accessed using a pull-down arrow on the right side of the field (not shown). If failures of Machine_Part

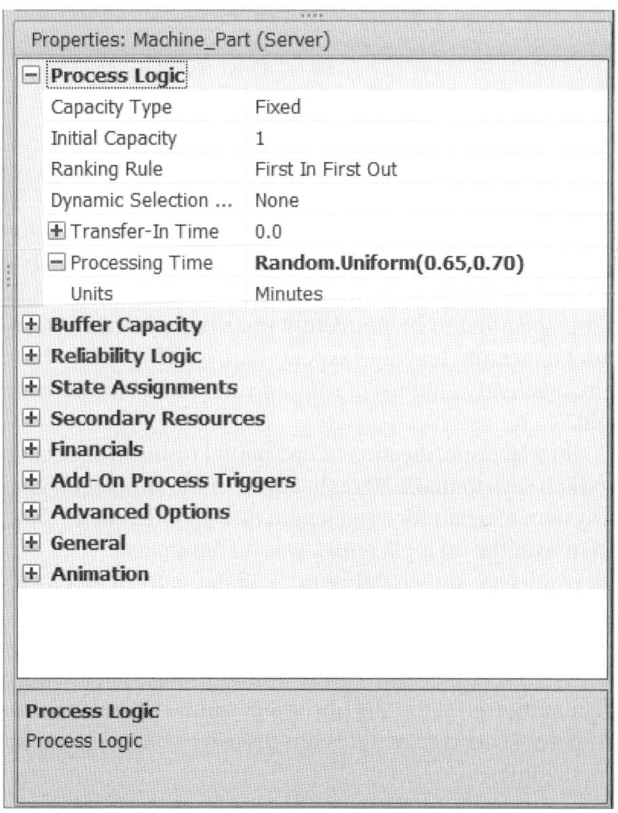

FIGURE 3.20
Properties of the Machine_Part object.

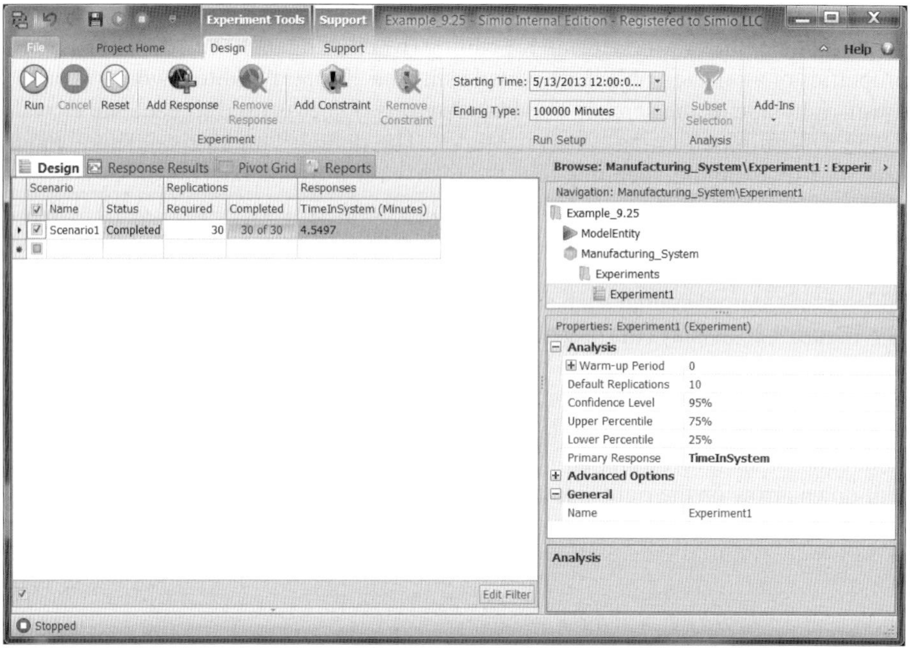

FIGURE 3.21
Design view for specifying an experiment.

were desired, then they would be specified under the "Reliability Logic" category. The "Financials" category can be used to specify usage rates for activity-based costing.

We do not show the Property Editor for the Inspect_Part object, where the inspection times are specified to be uniformly distributed on the interval [0.75, 0.80] minute. The two connectors leaving Inspect_Part (see Fig. 3.19) have link weights of 0.9 and 0.1, respectively, and use a routing rule on its exit node that is based on "By Link Weight."

Figure 3.21 shows the specification of and partial results from a simple experiment for our model, which says to make 30 replications of the simulation and to observe the average time in system of a part for a run length of 100,000 minutes. Note that the average time in system over the 30 replications was 4.55 minutes.

These same results are shown in Figure 3.22 in the form of a SMORE plot. This plot shows a point estimate ("dot") and a 95 percent confidence interval ("small" shaded rectangle over the dot) for the expected average time in system. Superimposed over this is a box plot showing the minimum, 25th percentile, median, 75th percentile, and maximum of the 30 observed values of average time in system. Finally, the two outer shaded rectangles are 95 percent confidence intervals for the 25th and 75th percentiles.

A standard report that is automatically produced by a simulation model can potentially contain a large amount of output statistics, which can make it difficult to find the information that is really of interest. To help alleviate this problem, Simio presents the simulation results in the form of a "Pivot Grid" (similar to a pivot table

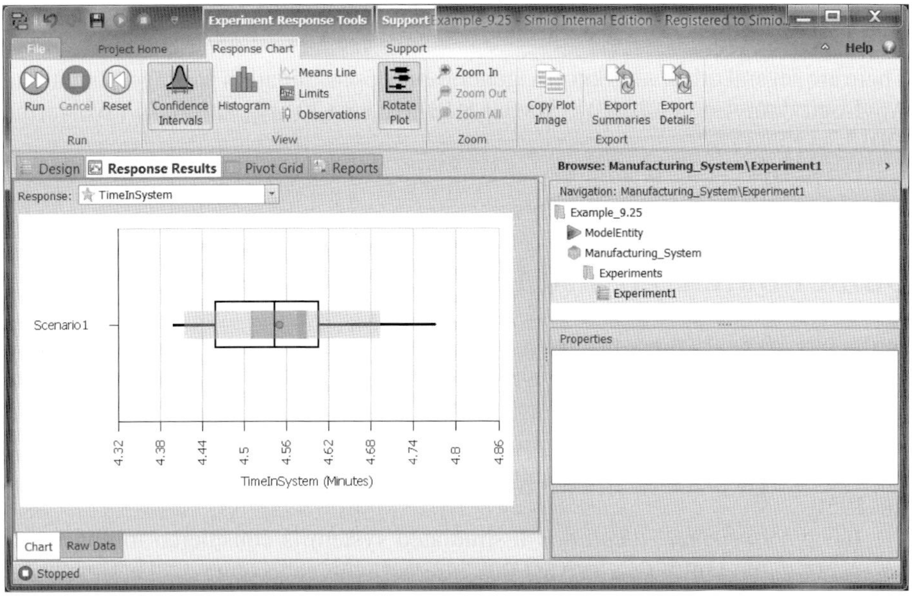

FIGURE 3.22
SMORE plot for average time in system.

in Excel), which can easily be customized to display the statistics of interest in an appropriate format. A Pivot Grid for the simulation results produced by the 30 replications is shown in Figure 3.23. Note that the machine and inspector had a utilization of 0.75 and 0.86, respectfully.

Object Type	Object Name	Data Source	Category	Data Item	Statistic	Scenario1 Average	Scenario1 Minimum	Scenario1 Maximum	Scenario1 Half Width
ModelEntity	DefaultEntity	[Population]	Content	NumberInSystem	Average	4.5548	4.3925	4.7878	0.0436
					Maximum	33.5000	27.0000	43.0000	1.6370
			FlowTime	TimeInSystem	Average (Minutes)	4.5497	4.3988	4.7710	0.0393
					Maximum (Minutes)	69.2576	45.7114	90.1023	3.5776
					Minimum (Minutes)	1.4005	1.4001	1.4012	0.0001
Server	Machine_Part	[Resource]	Capacity	UnitsUtilized	Average	0.7508	0.7465	0.7574	0.0009
					Maximum	1.0000	1.0000	1.0000	0.0000
		InputBuffer	Content	NumberInStation	Average	1.1666	1.1284	1.2200	0.0098
					Maximum	19.1333	15.0000	26.0000	0.8589
			HoldingTime	TimeInStation	Average (Minutes)	1.0487	1.0204	1.0922	0.0078
					Maximum (Minutes)	12.5002	9.8503	17.3396	0.5746
					Minimum (Minutes)	0.0000	0.0000	0.0000	0.0000
	Inspect_Part	[Resource]	Capacity	UnitsUtilized	Average	0.8620	0.8571	0.8697	0.0011
					Maximum	1.0000	1.0000	1.0000	0.0000
		InputBuffer	Content	NumberInStation	Average	1.7754	1.6449	1.9691	0.0338
					Maximum	26.2667	20.0000	35.0000	1.4308
			HoldingTime	TimeInStation	Average (Minutes)	1.5959	1.4820	1.7654	0.0290
					Maximum (Minutes)	19.9031	14.6897	26.8397	1.1073
					Minimum (Minutes)	0.0000	0.0000	0.0000	0.0000
Sink	Part_Departures	[DestroyedObjects]	FlowTime	TimeInSystem	Average (Minutes)	4.5497	4.3988	4.7710	0.0393
					Maximum (Minutes)	69.2576	45.7114	90.1023	3.5776
					Minimum (Minutes)	1.4005	1.4001	1.4012	0.0001
					Observations	100,102.6333	99,482.0000	100,878.0000	118.1014

FIGURE 3.23
Simulation results displayed in a Pivot Grid.

3.5.4 Other General-Purpose Simulation Packages

There are several other well-known, general-purpose simulation packages, including AnyLogic [AnyLogic (2013)], SIMUL8 [SIMUL8 (2013)], and SLX [Wolverine (2013)].

3.6 OBJECT-ORIENTED SIMULATION

In the last 20 years there has been a lot of interest in object-oriented simulation [see, e.g., Joines and Roberts (1998) and Levasseur (1996)]. This is probably an outgrowth of the strong interest in object-oriented programming in general. Actually, both object-oriented simulation and programming originated from the object-oriented simulation language SIMULA, which was introduced in the 1960s.

In *object-oriented simulation* a simulated system is considered to consist of *objects* (e.g., an entity or a server) that interact with each other as the simulation evolves through time. There may be several instances of certain object types (e.g., entities) present concurrently during the execution of a simulation. Objects contain *data* and have *methods* (see Example 3.1). Data describe the state of an object at a particular point in time, while methods describe the actions that the object is capable of performing. The data for a particular object instance can only be *changed* by its own methods. Other object instances (of the same or of different types) can only *view* its data. This is called *encapsulation*.

Examples of true object-oriented simulation packages are AnyLogic, FlexSim, and Simio. Three major features of such a simulation package are inheritance, polymorphism, and encapsulation (defined above). *Inheritance* means that if one defines a new object type (sometimes called a *child*) in terms of an existing object type (the *parent*), then the child type "inherits" all the characteristics of the parent type. Optionally, certain characteristics of the child can be changed or new ones added. *Polymorphism* is when different object types with the same ancestry can have methods with the same name, but when invoked may cause different behavior in the various objects. [See Levasseur (1996) for examples of inheritance and polymorphism.]

EXAMPLE 3.1. In a manufacturing system, the fabrication area and the assembly area might be considered as objects (first level of hierarchy). In turn, the fabrication area might consist of machine, worker, and forklift-truck objects (second level of hierarchy). Data for a forklift might include its speed and the maximum weight that it can lift. A method for a forklift might be the dispatching rule that it uses to choose the next job.

Some vendors claim that their simulation software is object-oriented, but in some cases the software may not include inheritance, polymorphism, or encapsulation. Furthermore, certain of the above three features are sometimes assigned different meanings.

The following are possible advantages of object-oriented simulation:

- It promotes code reusability because existing objects can be reused or easily modified.
- It helps manage complexity by breaking the system into different objects.
- It makes model changes easier when a parent object can be modified and its children objects realize the modifications.
- It facilitates large projects with several programmers.

Possible disadvantages of the object-oriented approach are:

- Some object-oriented simulation packages may have a steep learning curve.
- One must do many projects and reuse objects to achieve its full benefits.

3.7 EXAMPLES OF APPLICATION-ORIENTED SIMULATION PACKAGES

In this section we list some of the application-oriented simulation packages that are currently available.

Manufacturing. AutoMod [Applied Materials (2013)], Enterprise Dynamics [INCONTROL (2013)], FlexSim [FlexSim (2013)], Plant Simulation [Siemens (2013)], ProModel [ProModel (2013)], and WITNESS [Lanner (2013)] (see Sec. 14.3 for further discussion).

Communications networks. OPNET Modeler [Riverbed (2013)] and QualNet [SCALABLE (2013)].

Health care. FlexSim Healthcare [FlexSim (2013)] and MedModel [ProModel (2013)].

Process reengineering and services. Process Simulator [ProModel (2013)], ProcessModel [ProcessModel (2013)], and ServiceModel [ProModel (2013)].

Animation (stand-alone). Proof Animation [Wolverine (2013)].

CHAPTER 4

Review of Basic Probability and Statistics

Recommended sections for a first reading: 4.1 through 4.7

4.1 INTRODUCTION

The completion of a successful simulation study involves much more than constructing a flowchart of the system under study, translating the flowchart into a computer "program," and then making one or a few replications of each proposed system configuration. The use of probability and statistics is such an integral part of a simulation study that every simulation modeling team should include at least one person who is thoroughly trained in such techniques. In particular, probability and statistics are needed to understand how to model a probabilistic system (see Sec. 4.7), validate the simulation model (Chap. 5), choose the input probability distributions (Chap. 6), generate random samples from these distributions (Chaps. 7 and 8), perform statistical analyses of the simulation output data (Chaps. 9 and 10), and design the simulation experiments (Chaps. 11 and 12).

In this chapter we establish statistical notation used throughout the book and review some basic probability and statistics particularly relevant to simulation. We also point out the potential dangers of applying classical statistical techniques based on independent observations to simulation output data, which are rarely, if ever, independent.

4.2 RANDOM VARIABLES AND THEIR PROPERTIES

An *experiment* is a process whose outcome is not known with certainty. The set of all possible outcomes of an experiment is called the *sample space* and is denoted by S. The outcomes themselves are called the *sample points* in the sample space.

EXAMPLE 4.1. If the experiment consists of flipping a coin, then

$$S = \{H, T\}$$

where the symbol { } means the "set consisting of," and "H" and "T" mean that the outcome is a head and a tail, respectively.

EXAMPLE 4.2. If the experiment consists of tossing a die, then

$$S = \{1, 2, \ldots, 6\}$$

where the outcome i means that i appeared on the die, $i = 1, 2, \ldots, 6$.

A *random variable* is a function (or rule) that assigns a real number (any number greater than $-\infty$ and less than ∞) to each point in the sample space S.

EXAMPLE 4.3. Consider the experiment of rolling a pair of dice. Then

$$S = \{(1, 1), (1, 2), \ldots, (6, 6)\}$$

where (i, j) means that i and j appeared on the first and second die, respectively. If X is the random variable corresponding to the sum of the two dice, then X assigns the value 7 to the outcome (4, 3).

EXAMPLE 4.4. Consider the experiment of flipping two coins. If X is the random variable corresponding to the number of heads that occur, then X assigns the value 1 to either the outcome (H, T) or the outcome (T, H).

In general, we denote random variables by capital letters such as X, Y, Z and the values that random variables take on by lowercase letters such as x, y, z.

The *distribution function* (sometimes called the *cumulative* distribution function) $F(x)$ of the random variable X is defined for each real number x as follows:

$$F(x) = P(X \leq x) \qquad \text{for } -\infty < x < \infty$$

where $P(X \leq x)$ means the probability associated with the event $\{X \leq x\}$. [See Ross (2003, chap. 1) for a discussion of events and probabilities.] Thus, $F(x)$ is the probability that, when the experiment is done, the random variable X will have taken on a value no larger than the number x.

A distribution function $F(x)$ has the following properties:

1. $0 \leq F(x) \leq 1$ for all x.
2. $F(x)$ is nondecreasing [i.e., if $x_1 < x_2$, then $F(x_1) \leq F(x_2)$].
3. $\lim_{x\to\infty} F(x) = 1$ and $\lim_{x\to-\infty} F(x) = 0$ (since X takes on only finite values).

A random variable X is said to be *discrete* if it can take on at most a countable number of values, say, $x_1, x_2, \ldots$. ("Countable" means that the set of possible values can be put in a one-to-one correspondence with the set of positive integers. An example of an uncountable set is all real numbers between 0 and 1.) Thus, a random variable that takes on only a finite number of values $x_1, x_2, \ldots, x_n$ is discrete. The probability that the discrete random variable X takes on the value x_i is given by

$$p(x_i) = P(X = x_i) \qquad \text{for } i = 1, 2, \ldots$$

and we must have

$$\sum_{i=1}^{\infty} p(x_i) = 1$$

where the summation means add together $p(x_1)$, $p(x_2)$, ... All probability statements about X can be computed (at least in principle) from $p(x)$, which is called the *probability mass function* for the discrete random variable X. If $I = [a, b]$, where a and b are real numbers such that $a \leq b$, then

$$P(X \in I) = \sum_{a \leq x_i \leq b} p(x_i)$$

where the symbol $\in$ means "contained in" and the summation means add together $p(x_i)$ for all x_i such that $a \leq x_i \leq b$. The distribution function $F(x)$ for the discrete random variable X is given by

$$F(x) = \sum_{x_i \leq x} p(x_i) \qquad \text{for all } -\infty < x < \infty$$

EXAMPLE 4.5. For the inventory example of Sec. 1.5, the size of the demand for the product is a discrete random variable X that takes on the values 1, 2, 3, 4 with respective probabilities $\frac{1}{6}, \frac{1}{3}, \frac{1}{3}, \frac{1}{6}$. The probability mass function and the distribution function for X are given in Figs. 4.1 and 4.2. Furthermore,

$$P(2 \leq X \leq 3) = p(2) + p(3) = \tfrac{1}{3} + \tfrac{1}{3} = \tfrac{2}{3}$$

EXAMPLE 4.6. A manufacturing system produces parts that then must be inspected for quality. Suppose that 90 percent of the inspected parts are good (denoted by 1) and 10 percent are bad and must be scrapped (denoted by 0). If X denotes the outcome of inspecting a part, then X is a discrete random variable with $p(0) = 0.1$ and $p(1) = 0.9$. (See the discussion of the Bernoulli random variable in Sec. 6.2.3.)

We now consider random variables that can take on an uncountably infinite number of different values (e.g., all nonnegative real numbers). A random variable X is said to be *continuous* if there exists a nonnegative function $f(x)$ such that for

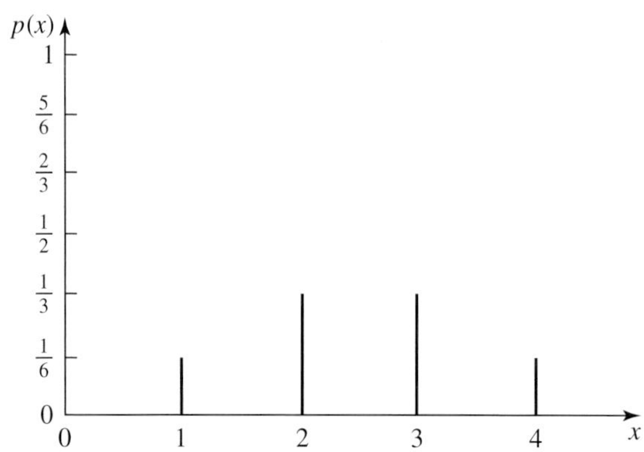

FIGURE 4.1
$p(x)$ for the demand-size random variable X.

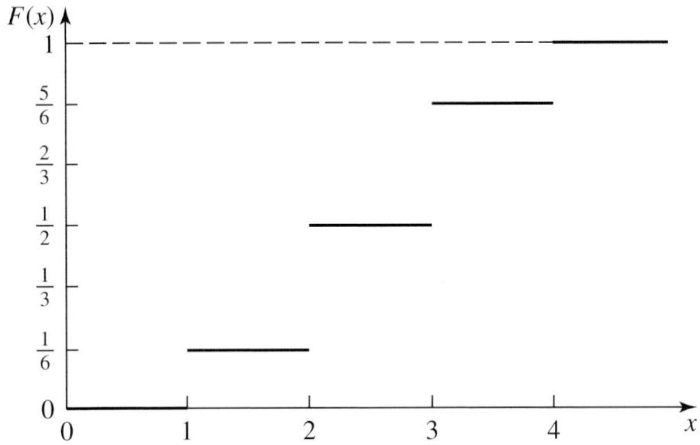

FIGURE 4.2
$F(x)$ for the demand-size random variable X.

any set of real numbers B (e.g., B could be all real numbers between 1 and 2),

$$P(X \in B) = \int_B f(x)\,dx \qquad \text{and} \qquad \int_{-\infty}^{\infty} f(x)\,dx = 1$$

[Thus, the total area under $f(x)$ is 1. Also, if X is a nonnegative random variable, as is often the case in simulation applications, the second range of integration is from 0 to ∞.] All probability statements about X can (in principle) be computed from $f(x)$, which is called the *probability density function* for the continuous random variable X.

For a discrete random variable X, $p(x)$ is the actual probability associated with the value x. However, $f(x)$ is *not* the probability that a continuous random variable X equals x. For any real number x,

$$P(X = x) = P(X \in [x, x]) = \int_x^x f(y)\,dy = 0$$

Since the probability associated with each value x is zero, we now give an interpretation to $f(x)$. If x is any number and $\Delta x > 0$, then

$$P(X \in [x, x + \Delta x]) = \int_x^{x+\Delta x} f(y)\,dy$$

which is the area under $f(x)$ between x and $x + \Delta x$, as shown in Fig. 4.3. It follows that a continuous random variable X is more likely to fall in an interval above which $f(x)$ is "large" than in an interval of the same width above which $f(x)$ is "small."

The distribution function $F(x)$ for a continuous random variable X is given by

$$F(x) = P(X \in (-\infty, x]) = \int_{-\infty}^{x} f(y)\,dy \qquad \text{for all } -\infty < x < \infty$$

Thus (under some mild technical assumptions), $f(x) = F'(x)$ [the derivative of $F(x)$]. Furthermore, if $I = [a, b]$ for any real numbers a and b such that $a < b$,

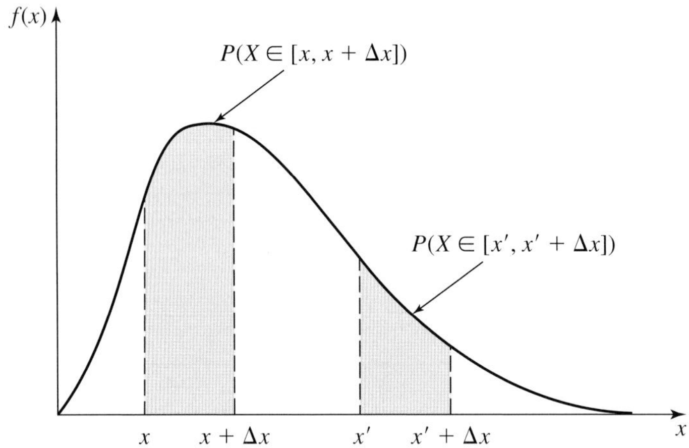

FIGURE 4.3
Interpretation of the probability density function $f(x)$.

then

$$P(X \in I) = \int_a^b f(y)\,dy = F(b) - F(a)$$

where the last equality is an application of the *fundamental theorem of calculus,* since $F'(x) = f(x)$.

EXAMPLE 4.7. A uniform random variable on the interval [0, 1] has the following probability density function:

$$f(x) = \begin{cases} 1 & \text{if } 0 \le x \le 1 \\ 0 & \text{otherwise} \end{cases}$$

Furthermore, if $0 \le x \le 1$, then

$$F(x) = \int_0^x f(y)\,dy = \int_0^x 1\,dy = x$$

[What is $F(x)$ if $x < 0$ or if $x > 1$?] Plots of $f(x)$ and $F(x)$ are given in Figs. 4.4 and 4.5, respectively.

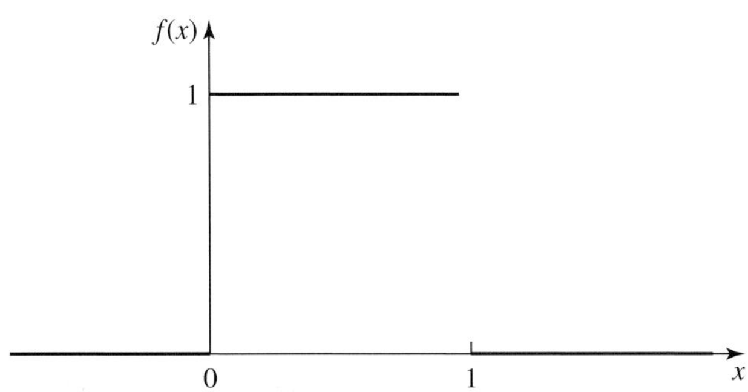

FIGURE 4.4
$f(x)$ for a uniform random variable on [0, 1].

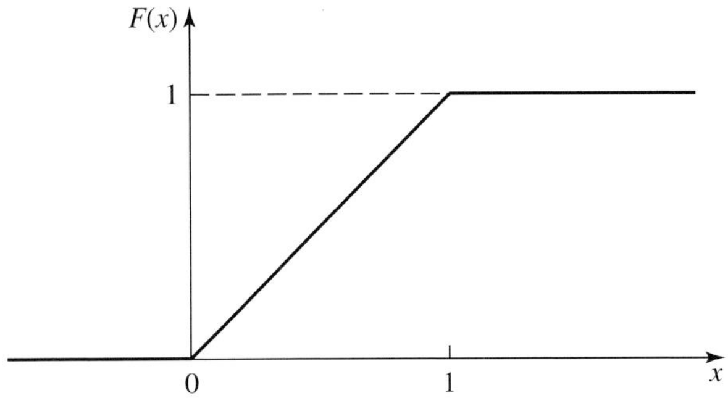

FIGURE 4.5
$F(x)$ for a uniform random variable on [0, 1].

Finally, if $0 \leq x < x + \Delta x \leq 1$, then

$$\begin{aligned} P(X \in [x, x + \Delta x]) &= \int_x^{x+\Delta x} f(y)\, dy \\ &= F(x + \Delta x) - F(x) \\ &= (x + \Delta x) - x \\ &= \Delta x \end{aligned}$$

It follows that a uniform random variable on [0, 1] is equally likely to fall in any interval of length Δx between 0 and 1, which justifies the name "uniform." The uniform random variable on [0, 1] is fundamental to simulation, since it is the basis for generating any random quantity on a computer (see Chaps. 7 and 8).

EXAMPLE 4.8. In Chap. 1 the exponential random variable was used for interarrival and service times in the queueing example and for interdemand times in the inventory example. The probability density function and distribution function for an exponential random variable with mean β are given in Figs. 4.6 and 4.7.

So far in this chapter we have considered only one random variable at a time, but in a simulation one must usually deal with n (a positive integer) random variables $X_1, X_2, \ldots, X_n$ simultaneously. For example, in the queueing model of Sec. 1.4, we were interested in the (input) service-time random variables $S_1, S_2, \ldots, S_n$ and the (output) delay random variables $D_1, D_2, \ldots, D_n$. In the discussion that follows,

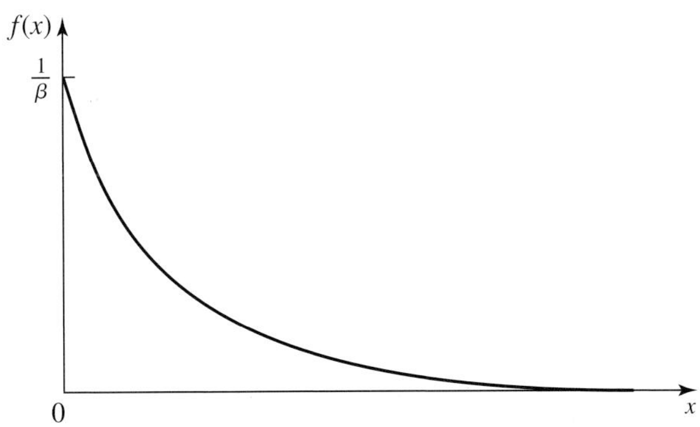

FIGURE 4.6
$f(x)$ for an exponential random variable with mean β.

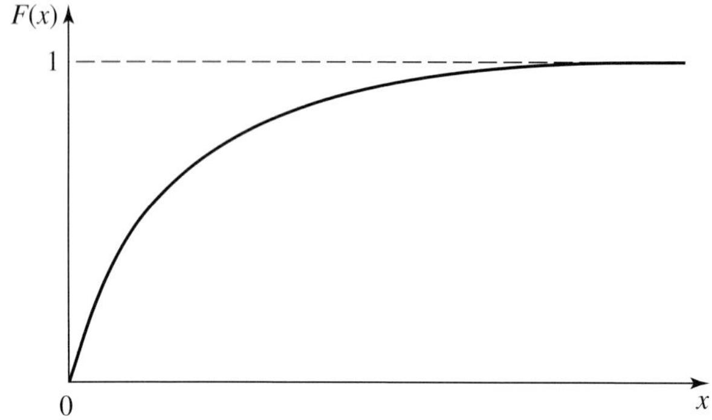

FIGURE 4.7
$F(x)$ for an exponential random variable with mean β.

we assume for expository convenience that $n = 2$ and that the two random variables in question are X and Y.

If X and Y are discrete random variables, then let

$$p(x, y) = P(X = x, Y = y) \qquad \text{for all } x, y$$

where $p(x, y)$ is called the *joint probability mass function* of X and Y. In this case, X and Y are *independent* if

$$p(x, y) = p_X(x)p_Y(y) \qquad \text{for all } x, y$$

where

$$p_X(x) = \sum_{\text{all } y} p(x, y)$$

$$p_Y(y) = \sum_{\text{all } x} p(x, y)$$

are the (marginal) probability mass functions of X and Y.

EXAMPLE 4.9. Suppose that X and Y are jointly discrete random variables with

$$p(x, y) = \begin{cases} \dfrac{xy}{27} & \text{for } x = 1, 2 \text{ and } y = 2, 3, 4 \\ 0 & \text{otherwise} \end{cases}$$

Then

$$p_X(x) = \sum_{y=2}^{4} \frac{xy}{27} = \frac{x}{3} \qquad \text{for } x = 1, 2$$

$$p_Y(y) = \sum_{x=1}^{2} \frac{xy}{27} = \frac{y}{9} \qquad \text{for } y = 2, 3, 4$$

Since $p(x, y) = xy/27 = p_X(x)p_Y(y)$ for all x, y, the random variables X and Y are independent.

EXAMPLE 4.10. Suppose that 2 cards are dealt from a deck of 52 without replacement. Let the random variables X and Y be the number of aces and kings that occur, both of which have possible values of 0, 1, 2. It can be shown that

$$p_X(1) = p_Y(1) = 2\left(\frac{4}{52}\right)\left(\frac{48}{51}\right)$$

and

$$p(1, 1) = 2\left(\frac{4}{52}\right)\left(\frac{4}{51}\right)$$

Since

$$p(1, 1) = 2\left(\frac{4}{52}\right)\left(\frac{4}{51}\right) \neq 4\left(\frac{4}{52}\right)^2\left(\frac{48}{51}\right)^2$$

it follows that X and Y are *not* independent (see Prob. 4.5).

The random variables X and Y are *jointly continuous* if there exists a nonnegative function $f(x, y)$, called the *joint probability density function* of X and Y, such that for all sets of real numbers A and B,

$$P(X \in A, Y \in B) = \int_B \int_A f(x, y)\, dx\, dy$$

In this case, X and Y are *independent* if

$$f(x, y) = f_X(x) f_Y(y) \qquad \text{for all } x, y$$

where

$$f_X(x) = \int_{-\infty}^{\infty} f(x, y)\, dy$$

$$f_Y(y) = \int_{-\infty}^{\infty} f(x, y)\, dx$$

are the (marginal) probability density functions of X and Y, respectively.

EXAMPLE 4.11. Suppose that X and Y are jointly continuous random variables with

$$f(x, y) = \begin{cases} 24xy & \text{for } x \geq 0,\ y \geq 0, \text{ and } x + y \leq 1 \\ 0 & \text{otherwise} \end{cases}$$

Then

$$f_X(x) = \int_0^{1-x} 24xy\, dy = 12xy^2 \Big|_0^{1-x} = 12x(1-x)^2 \qquad \text{for } 0 \leq x \leq 1$$

$$f_Y(y) = \int_0^{1-y} 24xy\, dx = 12yx^2 \Big|_0^{1-y} = 12y(1-y)^2 \qquad \text{for } 0 \leq y \leq 1$$

Since

$$f\left(\frac{1}{2}, \frac{1}{2}\right) = 6 \neq \left(\frac{3}{2}\right)^2 = f_X\left(\frac{1}{2}\right) f_Y\left(\frac{1}{2}\right)$$

X and Y are not independent.

Intuitively, the random variables X and Y (whether discrete or continuous) are independent if knowing the value that one random variable takes on tells us nothing about the distribution of the other. Also, if X and Y are not independent, we say that they are *dependent*.

We now consider once again the case of n random variables $X_1, X_2, \ldots, X_n$, and we discuss some characteristics of the single random variable X_i and some measures of the dependence that may exist between two random variables X_i and X_j.

The *mean* or *expected value* of the random variable X_i (where $i = 1, 2, \ldots, n$) will be denoted by μ_i or $E(X_i)$ and is defined by

$$\mu_i = \begin{cases} \displaystyle\sum_{j=1}^{\infty} x_j p_{X_i}(x_j) & \text{if } X_i \text{ is discrete} \\ \displaystyle\int_{-\infty}^{\infty} x f_{X_i}(x)\, dx & \text{if } X_i \text{ is continuous} \end{cases}$$

The mean is one measure of central tendency in the sense that it is the center of gravity [see, for example, Billingsley et al. (1986, pp. 42–43)].

EXAMPLE 4.12. For the demand-size random variable in Example 4.5, the mean is given by

$$\mu = 1\left(\frac{1}{6}\right) + 2\left(\frac{1}{3}\right) + 3\left(\frac{1}{3}\right) + 4\left(\frac{1}{6}\right) = \frac{5}{2}$$

EXAMPLE 4.13. For the uniform random variable in Example 4.7, the mean is given by

$$\mu = \int_0^1 x f(x)\, dx = \int_0^1 x\, dx = \frac{1}{2}$$

Let c or c_i denote a constant (real number). Then the following are important properties of means:

1. $E(cX) = cE(X)$.
2. $E(\sum_{i=1}^{n} c_i X_i) = \sum_{i=1}^{n} c_i E(X_i)$ *even if the* X_i*'s are dependent.*

The *median* $x_{0.5}$ of the random variable X_i, which is an alternative measure of central tendency, is defined to be the smallest value of x such that $F_{X_i}(x) \geq 0.5$. If X_i is a continuous random variable, then $F_{X_i}(x_{0.5}) = 0.5$, as shown in Fig. 4.8. The median may be a better measure of central tendency than the mean when X_i can take on very large or very small values, since extreme values can greatly affect the mean even if they are very unlikely to occur; such is not the case with the median.

EXAMPLE 4.14. Consider a discrete random variable X that takes on each of the values, 1, 2, 3, 4, and 5 with probability 0.2. Clearly, the mean and median of X are 3. Consider now a random variable Y that takes on each of the values 1, 2, 3, 4, and 100 with probability 0.2. The mean and median of Y are 22 and 3, respectively. Note that the median is insensitive to this change in the distribution.

The *mode* m of a continuous (discrete) random variable X_i, which is another alternative measure of central tendency, is defined to be that value of x that maximizes $f_{X_i}(x)[p_{X_i}(x)]$ (see Fig. 4.8). Note that the mode may not be unique for some distributions.

The *variance* of the random variable X_i will be denoted by σ_i^2 or $\text{Var}(X_i)$ and is defined by

$$\sigma_i^2 = E[(X_i - \mu_i)^2] = E(X_i^2) - \mu_i^2$$

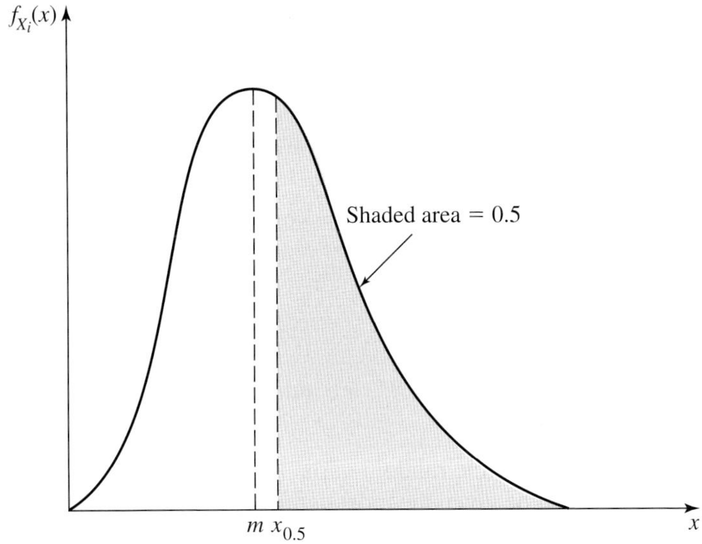

FIGURE 4.8
The median $x_{0.5}$ and mode m for a continuous random variable.

The variance is a measure of the dispersion of a random variable about its mean, as seen in Fig. 4.9. The larger the variance, the more likely the random variable is to take on values far from its mean.

EXAMPLE 4.15. For the demand-size random variable in Example 4.5, the variance is computed as follows:

$$E(X^2) = 1^2\left(\frac{1}{6}\right) + 2^2\left(\frac{1}{3}\right) + 3^2\left(\frac{1}{3}\right) + 4^2\left(\frac{1}{6}\right) = \frac{43}{6}$$

$$\text{Var}(X) = E(X^2) - \mu^2 = \frac{43}{6} - \left(\frac{5}{2}\right)^2 = \frac{11}{12}$$

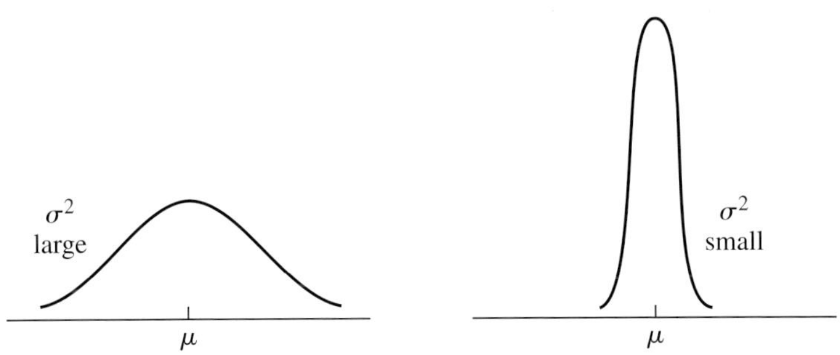

FIGURE 4.9
Density functions for continuous random variables with large and small variances.

EXAMPLE 4.16. For the uniform random variable on [0, 1] in Example 4.7, the variance is computed as follows:

$$E(X^2) = \int_0^1 x^2 f(x)\, dx = \int_0^1 x^2\, dx = \frac{1}{3}$$

$$\text{Var}(X) = E(X^2) - \mu^2 = \frac{1}{3} - \left(\frac{1}{2}\right)^2 = \frac{1}{12}$$

The variance has the following properties:

1. $\text{Var}(X) \geq 0$.
2. $\text{Var}(cX) = c^2\, \text{Var}(X)$.
3. $\text{Var}(\sum_{i=1}^n X_i) = \sum_{i=1}^n \text{Var}(X_i)$ if the X_i's are independent (or uncorrelated, as discussed below).

The *standard deviation* of the random variable X_i is defined to be $\sigma_i = \sqrt{\sigma_i^2}$. The standard deviation can be given the most definitive interpretation when X_i has a normal distribution (see Sec. 6.2.2). In particular, suppose that X_i has a normal distribution with mean μ_i and standard deviation σ_i. In this case, for example, the probability that X_i is between $\mu_i - 1.96\sigma_i$ and $\mu_i + 1.96\sigma_i$ is 0.95.

We now consider measures of dependence between two random variables. The *covariance* between the random variables X_i and X_j (where $i = 1, 2, \ldots, n$; $j = 1, 2, \ldots, n$), which is a measure of their (linear) dependence, will be denoted by C_{ij} or $\text{Cov}(X_i, X_j)$ and is defined by

$$C_{ij} = E[(X_i - \mu_i)(X_j - \mu_j)] = E(X_i X_j) - \mu_i \mu_j \qquad (4.1)$$

Note that covariances are symmetric, that is, $C_{ij} = C_{ji}$, and that if $i = j$, then $C_{ij} = C_{ii} = \sigma_i^2$.

EXAMPLE 4.17. For the jointly continuous random variables X and Y in Example 4.11, the covariance is computed as

$$\begin{aligned} E(XY) &= \int_0^1 \int_0^{1-x} xy\, f(x, y)\, dy\, dx \\ &= \int_0^1 x^2 \left(\int_0^{1-x} 24y^2\, dy \right) dx \\ &= \int_0^1 8x^2(1-x)^3\, dx \\ &= \frac{2}{15} \end{aligned}$$

$$E(X) = \int_0^1 x f_X(x)\, dx = \int_0^1 12x^2(1-x)^2\, dx = \frac{2}{5}$$

$$E(Y) = \int_0^1 y f_Y(y)\, dy = \int_0^1 12y^2(1-y)^2\, dy = \frac{2}{5}$$

Therefore,

$$\begin{aligned}\text{Cov}(X, Y) &= E(XY) - E(X)E(Y)\\ &= \frac{2}{15} - \left(\frac{2}{5}\right)\left(\frac{2}{5}\right)\\ &= -\frac{2}{75}\end{aligned}$$

If $C_{ij} = 0$, the random variables X_i and X_j are said to be *uncorrelated*. It is easy to show that if X_i and X_j are independent random variables, then $C_{ij} = 0$ (see Prob. 4.8). In general, though, the converse is not true (see Prob. 4.9). However, if X_i and X_j are jointly normally distributed random variables with $C_{ij} = 0$, then they are also independent (see Prob. 4.10).

We now give two definitions that will shed some light on the significance of the covariance C_{ij}. If $C_{ij} > 0$, then X_i and X_j are said to be *positively correlated*. In this case, $X_i > \mu_i$ and $X_j > \mu_j$ tend to occur together, and $X_i < \mu_i$ and $X_j < \mu_j$ also tend to occur together [see Eq. (4.1)]. Thus, for positively correlated random variables, if one is large, the other is likely to be large also. If $C_{ij} < 0$, then X_i and X_j are said to be *negatively correlated*. In this case, $X_i > \mu_i$ and $X_j < \mu_j$ tend to occur together, and $X_i < \mu_i$ and $X_j > \mu_j$ also tend to occur together. Thus, for negatively correlated random variables, if one is large, the other is likely to be small. We give examples of positively and negatively correlated random variables in the next section.

If $X_1, X_2, \ldots, X_n$ are simulation output data (for example, X_i might be the delay D_i for the queueing example of Sec. 1.4), we shall often need to know not only the mean μ_i and variance σ_i^2 for $i = 1, 2, \ldots, n$, but also a measure of the dependence between X_i and X_j for $i \neq j$. However, the difficulty with using C_{ij} as a measure of dependence between X_i and X_j is that it is not dimensionless, which makes its interpretation troublesome. (If X_i and X_j are in units of minutes, say, then C_{ij} is in units of minutes squared.) As a result, we use the *correlation* ρ_{ij}, defined by

$$\rho_{ij} = \frac{C_{ij}}{\sqrt{\sigma_i^2 \sigma_j^2}} \qquad \begin{aligned} i &= 1, 2, \ldots, n \\ j &= 1, 2, \ldots, n \end{aligned} \tag{4.2}$$

as our primary measure of the (linear) dependence (see Prob. 4.11) between X_i and X_j. [We shall also denote the correlation between X_i and X_j by $\text{Cor}(X_i, X_j)$.] Since the denominator in Eq. (4.2) is positive, it is clear that ρ_{ij} has the same sign as C_{ij}. Furthermore, it can be shown that $-1 \leq \rho_{ij} \leq 1$ for all i and j (see Prob. 4.12). If ρ_{ij} is close to $+1$, then X_i and X_j are highly positively correlated. On the other hand, if ρ_{ij} is close to -1, then X_i and X_j are highly negatively correlated.

EXAMPLE 4.18. For the random variables in Example 4.11, it can be shown that $\text{Var}(X) = \text{Var}(Y) = \frac{1}{25}$. Therefore,

$$\text{Cor}(X, Y) = \frac{\text{Cov}(X, Y)}{\sqrt{\text{Var}(X)\,\text{Var}(Y)}} = \frac{-\frac{2}{75}}{\frac{1}{25}} = -\frac{2}{3}$$

4.3 SIMULATION OUTPUT DATA AND STOCHASTIC PROCESSES

Since most simulation models use random variables as input, the simulation output data are themselves random, and care must be taken in drawing conclusions about the model's true characteristics, e.g., the (expected) average delay in the queueing example of Sec. 1.4. In this and the next three sections we lay the groundwork for a careful treatment of output data analysis in Chaps. 9 and 10.

A *stochastic process* is a collection of "similar" random variables ordered over time, which are all defined on a common sample space. The set of all possible values that these random variables can take on is called the *state space*. If the collection is $X_1, X_2, \ldots$, then we have a *discrete-time* stochastic process. If the collection is $\{X(t), t \geq 0\}$, then we have a *continuous-time* stochastic process.

EXAMPLE 4.19. Consider a single-server queueing system, e.g., the $M/M/1$ queue, with IID interarrival times $A_1, A_2, \ldots$, IID service times $S_1, S_2, \ldots$, and customers served in a FIFO manner. Relative to the experiment of generating the random variates $A_1, A_2, \ldots$ and $S_1, S_2, \ldots$, one can define the discrete-time stochastic process of delays in queue $D_1, D_2, \ldots$ as follows (see Prob. 4.14):

$$D_1 = 0$$

$$D_{i+1} = \max\{D_i + S_i - A_{i+1}, 0\} \qquad \text{for } i = 1, 2, \ldots$$

Thus, the simulation maps the input random variables (i.e., the A_i's and the S_i's) into the output stochastic process $D_1, D_2, \ldots$ of interest. Here, the state space is the set of nonnegative real numbers. Note that D_i and D_{i+1} are positively correlated. (Why?)

EXAMPLE 4.20. For the queueing system of Example 4.19, let $Q(t)$ be the number of customers in the queue at time t. Then $\{Q(t), t \geq 0\}$ is a continuous-time stochastic process with state space $\{0, 1, 2, \ldots\}$.

EXAMPLE 4.21. For the inventory system of Sec. 1.5, let C_i be the total cost (i.e., the sum of the ordering, holding, and shortage costs) in month i. Then $C_1, C_2, \ldots$ is a discrete-time stochastic process with state space the nonnegative real numbers.

To draw inferences about an underlying stochastic process from a set of simulation output data, one must sometimes make assumptions about the stochastic process that may not be strictly true in practice. (Without such assumptions, however, statistical analysis of the output data may not be possible.) An example of this is to assume that a stochastic process is covariance-stationary, a property that we now define. A discrete-time stochastic process $X_1, X_2, \ldots$ is said to be *covariance-stationary* if

$$\mu_i = \mu \qquad \text{for } i = 1, 2, \ldots \text{ and } -\infty < \mu < \infty$$

$$\sigma_i^2 = \sigma^2 \qquad \text{for } i = 1, 2, \ldots \text{ and } \sigma^2 < \infty$$

and $C_{i,i+j} = \text{Cov}(X_i, X_{i+j})$ is independent of i for $j = 1, 2, \ldots$.

Thus, for a covariance-stationary process, the mean and variance are stationary over time (the common mean and variance are denoted by μ and σ^2, respectively), and the covariance between two observations X_i and X_{i+j} depends only on the separation j (sometimes called the *lag*) and not on the actual time values i and $i + j$. (It is also possible to define a covariance-stationary continuous-time stochastic process $\{X(t), t \geq 0\}$ in an analogous way.)

For a covariance-stationary process, we denote the covariance and correlation between X_i and X_{i+j} by C_j and ρ_j, respectively, where

$$\rho_j = \frac{C_{i,i+j}}{\sqrt{\sigma_i^2 \sigma_{i+j}^2}} = \frac{C_j}{\sigma^2} = \frac{C_j}{C_0} \qquad \text{for } j = 0, 1, 2, \ldots$$

EXAMPLE 4.22. Consider the output process $D_1, D_2, \ldots$ for a covariance-stationary (see App. 4A for a discussion of this technical detail) $M/M/1$ queue with $\rho = \lambda/\omega < 1$ (recall that λ is the arrival rate and ω is the service rate). From results in Daley (1968), one can compute ρ_j, which we plot in Fig. 4.10 for $\rho = 0.5$ and 0.9. (Do not confuse ρ_j and ρ.) Note that the correlations ρ_j are positive and monotonically decrease to zero as j increases. In particular, $\rho_1 = 0.99$ for $\rho = 0.9$ and $\rho_1 = 0.78$ for $\rho = 0.5$. Furthermore, the convergence of ρ_j to zero is considerably slower for $\rho = 0.9$; in fact, ρ_{50} is (amazingly) 0.69. (In general, our experience indicates that output processes for queueing systems are positively correlated.)

EXAMPLE 4.23. Consider an (s, S) inventory system with zero delivery lag and backlogging. (For this inventory system, which is a simpler version of the one considered in Sec. 1.5, it is possible to compute the desired correlations analytically.) Let I_i, J_i, and Q_i denote, respectively, the amount of inventory on hand before ordering, the

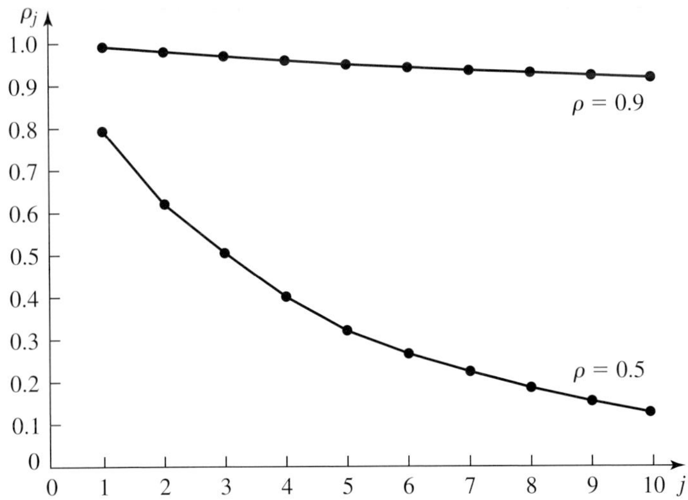

FIGURE 4.10
Correlation function ρ_j of the process $D_1, D_2, \ldots$ for the $M/M/1$ queue.

amount of inventory on hand after ordering, and the demand, each in month i. Assume that Q_i has a Poisson distribution (see Sec. 6.2.3 for further discussion) with mean 25; that is,

$$p(x) = P(Q_i = x) = \frac{e^{-25}(25)^x}{x!} \qquad \text{for } x = 0, 1, 2, \ldots$$

If $I_i < s$, we order $S - I_i$ items ($J_i = S$) and incur a cost $K + i(S - I_i)$, where $K = 32$ and $i = 3$. If $I_i \geq s$, no order is placed ($J_i = I_i$) and no ordering cost is incurred. After J_i has been determined, the demand Q_i occurs. If $J_i - Q_i \geq 0$, a holding cost $h(J_i - Q_i)$ is incurred, where $h = 1$. If $J_i - Q_i < 0$, a shortage cost $\pi(Q_i - J_i)$ is incurred, where $\pi = 5$. In either case, $I_{i+1} = J_i - Q_i$. Let C_i be the total cost in month i, and assume that $s = 17$, $S = 57$, and $I_1 = S$. From results in Wagner (1969, p. A19), one can compute ρ_j for the output process $C_1, C_2, \ldots$, which we plot in Fig. 4.11. (See App. 4A for discussion of a technical detail.) Note that ρ_2 is positive, since for this particular system one tends to order every other month, incurring a large cost each time. On the other hand, ρ_1 is negative, because if one orders in a particular month (large cost), then it is likely that no order will be placed the next month (small cost).

If $X_1, X_2, \ldots$ is a stochastic process beginning at time 0 in a simulation, then it is quite likely *not* to be covariance-stationary (see App. 4A). However, for *some* simulations $X_{k+1}, X_{k+2}, \ldots$ will be approximately covariance-stationary if k is large enough, where k is the length of the *warmup period* (see Sec. 9.5.1).

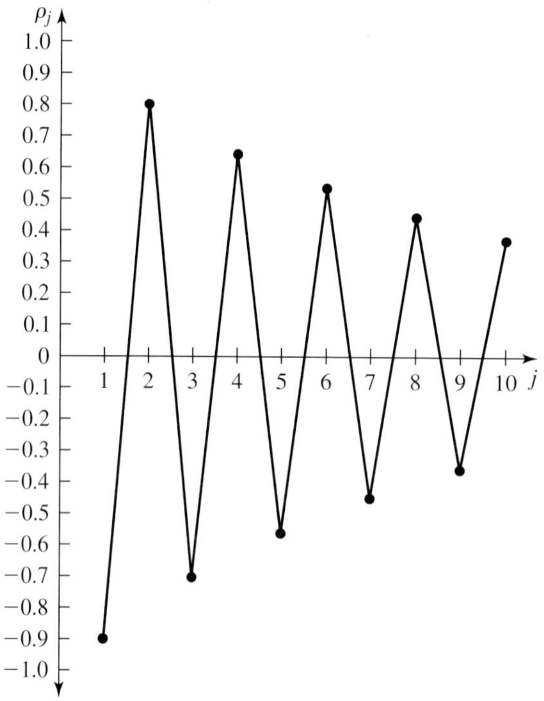

FIGURE 4.11
Correlation function ρ_j of the process $C_1, C_2, \ldots$ for an (s, S) inventory system.

4.4 ESTIMATION OF MEANS, VARIANCES, AND CORRELATIONS

Suppose that $X_1, X_2, \ldots, X_n$ are IID random variables (observations) with finite population mean μ and finite population variance σ^2 and that our primary objective is to estimate μ; the estimation of σ^2 is of secondary interest. Then the *sample mean*

$$\bar{X}(n) = \frac{\sum_{i=1}^{n} X_i}{n} \tag{4.3}$$

is an unbiased (point) estimator of μ; that is, $E[\bar{X}(n)] = \mu$ (see Prob. 4.16). [Intuitively, $\bar{X}(n)$ being an unbiased estimator of μ means that if we perform a very large number of independent experiments, each resulting in an $\bar{X}(n)$, the average of the $\bar{X}(n)$'s will be μ.] Similarly, the *sample variance*

$$S^2(n) = \frac{\sum_{i=1}^{n} [X_i - \bar{X}(n)]^2}{n-1} \tag{4.4}$$

is an unbiased estimator of σ^2, since $E[S^2(n)] = \sigma^2$ (see Prob. 4.16). Note that the estimators $\bar{X}(n)$ and $S^2(n)$ are sometimes denoted by $\hat{\mu}$ and $\hat{\sigma}^2$, respectively.

The difficulty with using $\bar{X}(n)$ as an estimator of μ without any additional information is that we have no way of assessing how close $\bar{X}(n)$ is to μ. Because $\bar{X}(n)$ is a random variable with variance $\text{Var}[\bar{X}(n)]$, on one experiment $\bar{X}(n)$ may be close to μ while on another $\bar{X}(n)$ may differ from μ by a large amount. (See Fig. 4.12, where the X_i's are assumed to be continuous random variables.) The usual way to assess the precision of $\bar{X}(n)$ as an estimator of μ is to construct a confidence interval

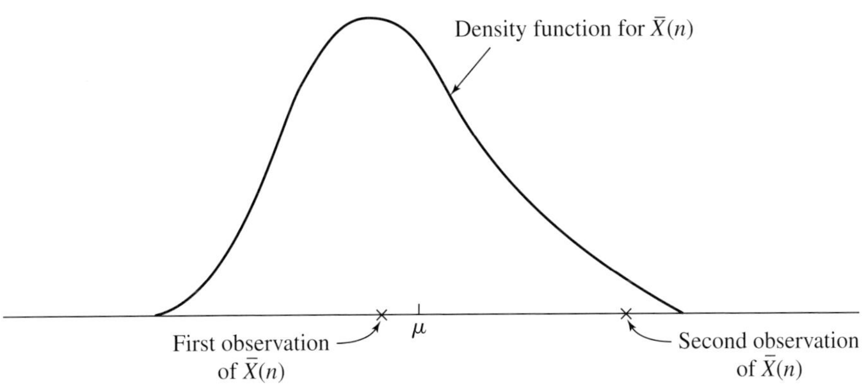

FIGURE 4.12
Two observations of the random variable $\bar{X}(n)$.

for μ, which we discuss in the next section. However, the first step in constructing a confidence interval is to estimate $\text{Var}[\overline{X}(n)]$. Since

$$\begin{aligned}\text{Var}[\overline{X}(n)] &= \text{Var}\left(\frac{1}{n}\sum_{i=1}^{n} X_i\right)\\ &= \frac{1}{n^2}\text{Var}\left(\sum_{i=1}^{n} X_i\right)\\ &= \frac{1}{n^2}\sum_{i=1}^{n}\text{Var}(X_i) \qquad \text{(because the } X_i\text{'s are independent)}\\ &= \frac{1}{n^2}n\sigma^2 = \frac{\sigma^2}{n} \end{aligned} \tag{4.5}$$

it is clear that, in general, the bigger the sample size n, the closer $\overline{X}(n)$ should be to μ (see Fig. 4.13). Furthermore, an unbiased estimator of $\text{Var}[\overline{X}(n)]$ is obtained by replacing σ^2 in Eq. (4.5) by $S^2(n)$, resulting in

$$\widehat{\text{Var}}[\overline{X}(n)] = \frac{S^2(n)}{n} = \frac{\sum_{i=1}^{n}[X_i - \overline{X}(n)]^2}{n(n-1)}$$

Observe that the expression for $\widehat{\text{Var}}[\overline{X}(n)]$ has both an n and an $n - 1$ in the denominator when it is rewritten in terms of the X_i's and $\overline{X}(n)$.

Finally, note that if the X_i's are independent, they are uncorrelated, and thus $\rho_j = 0$ for $j = 1, 2, \ldots, n - 1$.

It has been our experience that simulation output data are almost always correlated. Thus, the above discussion about IID observations is not *directly* applicable to analyzing simulation output data. To understand the dangers of treating simulation output data as if they were independent, we shall use the covariance-stationary model discussed in the last section. In particular, assume that the random variables

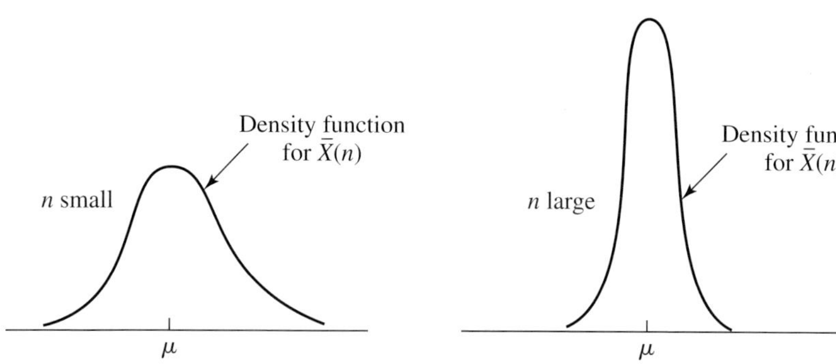

FIGURE 4.13
Distributions of $\overline{X}(n)$ for small and large n.

$X_1, X_2, \ldots, X_n$ are from a covariance-stationary stochastic process. Then it is still true that the sample mean $\overline{X}(n)$ is an unbiased estimator of μ; however, the sample variance $S^2(n)$ is no longer an unbiased estimator of σ^2. In fact, it can be shown [see Anderson (1994, p. 448)] that

$$E[S^2(n)] = \sigma^2 \left[1 - 2 \frac{\sum_{j=1}^{n-1} (1 - j/n)\rho_j}{n - 1} \right] \tag{4.6}$$

Thus, if $\rho_j > 0$ (positive correlation), as is very often the case in practice, $S^2(n)$ will have a negative bias: $E[S^2(n)] < \sigma^2$. This is important because several simulation-software products use $S^2(n)$ to estimate the variance of a set of simulation output data, which can lead to serious errors in analysis.

Let us now consider the problem of estimating the variance of the sample mean $\text{Var}[\overline{X}(n)]$ (which will be used to construct a confidence interval for μ in the next section) when $X_1, X_2, \ldots, X_n$ are from a covariance-stationary process. It can be shown (see Prob. 4.17) that

$$\text{Var}[\overline{X}(n)] = \sigma^2 \frac{\left[1 + 2 \sum_{j=1}^{n-1} (1 - j/n)\rho_j \right]}{n} \tag{4.7}$$

Thus, if one estimates $\text{Var}[\overline{X}(n)]$ from $S^2(n)/n$ (the correct expression in the IID case), which has often been done historically, there are two sources of error: the bias in $S^2(n)$ as an estimator of σ^2 and the negligence of the correlation terms in Eq. (4.7). As a matter of fact, if we combine Eq. (4.6) and Eq. (4.7), we get

$$E\left[\frac{S^2(n)}{n} \right] = \frac{[n/a(n)] - 1}{n - 1} \text{Var}[\overline{X}(n)] \tag{4.8}$$

where $a(n)$ denotes the quantity in square brackets in Eq. (4.7). If $\rho_j > 0$, then $a(n) > 1$ and $E[S^2(n)/n] < \text{Var}[\overline{X}(n)]$.

EXAMPLE 4.24. Suppose that we have the data $D_1, D_2, \ldots, D_{10}$ from the process of delays $D_1, D_2, \ldots$ for a covariance-stationary $M/M/1$ queue with $\rho = 0.9$. Then, substituting the true correlations ρ_j (where $j = 1, 2, \ldots, 9$) into Eqs. (4.6) and (4.8), we get

$$E[S^2(10)] = 0.0328\sigma^2$$

and

$$E\left[\frac{S^2(10)}{10} \right] = 0.0034 \text{ Var}[\overline{D}(10)]$$

where

$$\sigma^2 = \text{Var}(D_i), \qquad \overline{D}(10) = \frac{\sum_{i=1}^{10} D_i}{10}, \qquad \text{and} \qquad S^2(10) = \frac{\sum_{i=1}^{10} [D_i - \overline{D}(10)]^2}{9}$$

Thus, on average $S^2(10)/10$ is a gross underestimate of $\text{Var}[\overline{D}(10)]$, and we are likely to be overly optimistic about the closeness of $\overline{D}(10)$ to $\mu = E(D_i)$.

Sometimes one is interested in estimating the ρ_j's (or C_j's) from the data $X_1, X_2, \ldots, X_n$. {For example, estimates of the ρ_j's might be substituted into Eq. (4.7) to obtain a better estimate of $\text{Var}[\overline{X}(n)]$; see Sec. 9.5.3 for an application.} If this is the case, ρ_j (for $j = 1, 2, \ldots, n - 1$) can be estimated as follows:

$$\hat{\rho}_j = \frac{\hat{C}_j}{S^2(n)}, \qquad \hat{C}_j = \frac{\sum_{i=1}^{n-j} [X_i - \overline{X}(n)][X_{i+j} - \overline{X}(n)]}{n - j} \tag{4.9}$$

(Other estimators of ρ_j are also used. For example, one could replace the $n - j$ in the denominator of $\hat{C}_j$ by n.) The difficulty with the estimator $\hat{\rho}_j$ (or any other estimator of ρ_j) is that it is biased, it has a large variance unless n is very large, and it is correlated with other correlation estimators, that is, $\text{Cov}(\hat{\rho}_j, \hat{\rho}_k) \neq 0$. {In particular, $\hat{\rho}_{n-1}$ will be a poor estimator of ρ_{n-1} since it is based on the single product $[X_1 - \overline{X}(n)][X_n - \overline{X}(n)]$.} Thus, in general, "good" estimates of the ρ_j's will be difficult to obtain unless n is very large and j is small relative to n.

EXAMPLE 4.25. Suppose we have the data $D_1, D_2, \ldots, D_{100}$ from the process considered in Example 4.24. In Fig. 4.14 we plot $\hat{\rho}_j$ [as computed from Eq. (4.9)] and ρ_j for $j = 1, 2, \ldots, 10$. Note the poor quality of the correlation estimates.

Note that correlation estimates will not necessarily be zero when the X_i's are independent, since the estimator $\hat{\rho}_j$ is a random variable.

We have seen that simulation output data are correlated, and thus formulas from classical statistics based on IID observations cannot be used directly for estimating variances. However, we shall see in Chap. 9 that it is often possible to group simulation output data into new "observations" to which the formulas based on IID observations *can* be applied. Thus, the formulas in this and the next two sections based on IID observations are *indirectly* applicable to analyzing simulation output data.

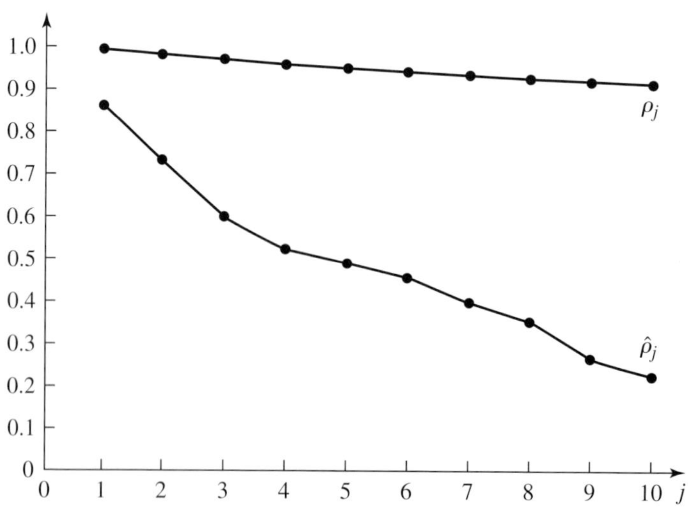

FIGURE 4.14
ρ_j and $\hat{\rho}_j$ of the process $D_1, D_2, \ldots$ for the $M/M/1$ queue with $\rho = 0.9$.

4.5
CONFIDENCE INTERVALS AND HYPOTHESIS TESTS FOR THE MEAN

Let $X_1, X_2, \ldots, X_n$ be IID random variables with finite mean μ and finite variance σ^2. (Also assume that $\sigma^2 > 0$, so that the X_i's are not degenerate random variables.) In this section we discuss how to construct a confidence interval for μ and also the complementary problem of testing the hypothesis that $\mu = \mu_0$.

We begin with a statement of the most important result in probability theory, the classical central limit theorem. Let Z_n be the random variable $[\overline{X}(n) - \mu]/\sqrt{\sigma^2/n}$, and let $F_n(z)$ be the distribution function of Z_n for a sample size of n; that is, $F_n(z) = P(Z_n \le z)$. [Note that μ and σ^2/n are the mean and variance of $\overline{X}(n)$, respectively.] Then the *central limit theorem* is as follows [see Chung (1974, p. 169) for a proof].

THEOREM 4.1. $F_n(z) \to \Phi(z)$ as $n \to \infty$, where $\Phi(z)$, the distribution function of a normal random variable with $\mu = 0$ and $\sigma^2 = 1$ (henceforth called a *standard normal random variable*; see Sec. 6.2.2), is given by

$$\Phi(z) = \frac{1}{\sqrt{2\pi}} \int_{-\infty}^{z} e^{-y^2/2}\, dy \qquad \text{for } -\infty < z < \infty$$

The theorem says, in effect, that if n is "sufficiently large," the random variable Z_n will be approximately distributed as a standard normal random variable, regardless of the underlying distribution of the X_i's. It can also be shown for large n that the sample mean $\overline{X}(n)$ is approximately distributed as a normal random variable with mean μ and variance σ^2/n.

The difficulty with using the above results in practice is that the variance σ^2 is generally unknown. However, since the sample variance $S^2(n)$ converges to σ^2 as n gets large, it can be shown that Theorem 4.1 remains true if we replace σ^2 by $S^2(n)$ in the expression for Z_n. With this change the theorem says that if n is sufficiently large, the random variable $t_n = [\overline{X}(n) - \mu]/\sqrt{S^2(n)/n}$ is approximately distributed as a standard normal random variable. It follows for large n that

$$\begin{aligned} P\left(-z_{1-\alpha/2} \le \frac{\overline{X}(n) - \mu}{\sqrt{S^2(n)/n}} \le z_{1-\alpha/2}\right) &= P\left[\overline{X}(n) - z_{1-\alpha/2}\sqrt{\frac{S^2(n)}{n}} \le \mu \le \overline{X}(n) + z_{1-\alpha/2}\sqrt{\frac{S^2(n)}{n}}\right] \\ &\approx 1 - \alpha \end{aligned} \tag{4.10}$$

where the symbol $\approx$ means "approximately equal" and $z_{1-\alpha/2}$ (for $0 < \alpha < 1$) is the upper $1 - \alpha/2$ critical point for a standard normal random variable (see Fig. 4.15 and the last line of Table T.1 of the Appendix at the back of the book). Therefore, if n is sufficiently large, an approximate $100(1 - \alpha)$ percent confidence interval for μ is given by

$$\overline{X}(n) \pm z_{1-\alpha/2}\sqrt{\frac{S^2(n)}{n}} \tag{4.11}$$

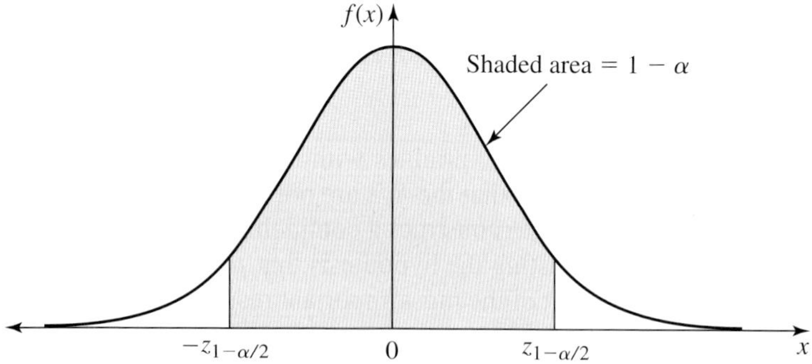

FIGURE 4.15
Density function for the standard normal distribution.

For a given set of data $X_1, X_2, \ldots, X_n$, the lower confidence-interval endpoint $l(n, \alpha) = \bar{X}(n) - z_{1-\alpha/2}\sqrt{S^2(n)/n}$ and the upper confidence-interval endpoint $u(n, \alpha) = \bar{X}(n) + z_{1-\alpha/2}\sqrt{S^2(n)/n}$ are just numbers (actually, specific realizations of random variables) and the confidence interval $[l(n, \alpha), u(n, \alpha)]$ either contains μ or does not contain μ. Thus, there is nothing probabilistic about the single confidence interval $[l(n, \alpha), u(n, \alpha)]$ *after* the data have been obtained and the interval's endpoints have been given numerical values. The correct interpretation to give to the confidence interval (4.11) is as follows [see (4.10)]: If one constructs a very large number of independent $100(1 - \alpha)$ percent confidence intervals, each based on n observations, where n is sufficiently large, the proportion of these confidence intervals that contain (cover) μ should be $1 - \alpha$. We call this proportion the *coverage* for the confidence interval.

EXAMPLE 4.26. To further amplify the correct interpretation to be given to a confidence interval, we generated 15 independent samples of size $n = 10$ from a normal distribution with mean 5 and variance 1. For each data set we constructed a 90 percent confidence interval for μ, which we know has a true value of 5. In Fig. 4.16 we plot the 15 confidence intervals vertically (the dot at the center of the confidence interval is the sample mean), and we see that all intervals other than 7 and 13 cover the mean value at height 5. In general, if we were to construct a very large number of such 90 percent confidence intervals, we would find that 90 percent of them will, in fact, contain (cover) μ.

The difficulty in using (4.11) to construct a confidence interval for μ is in knowing what "n sufficiently large" means. It turns out that the more skewed (i.e., nonsymmetric) the underlying distribution of the X_i's, the larger the value of n needed for the distribution of t_n to be closely approximated by $\Phi(z)$. (See the discussion later in this section.) If n is chosen too small, the actual coverage of a desired $100(1 - \alpha)$ percent confidence interval will generally be less than $1 - \alpha$. This is why the confidence interval given by (4.11) is stated to be only approximate.

In light of the above discussion, we now develop an alternative confidence-interval expression. If the X_i's are *normal* random variables, the random variable $t_n = [\bar{X}(n) - \mu]/\sqrt{S^2(n)/n}$ has a t distribution with $n - 1$ degrees of freedom (df)

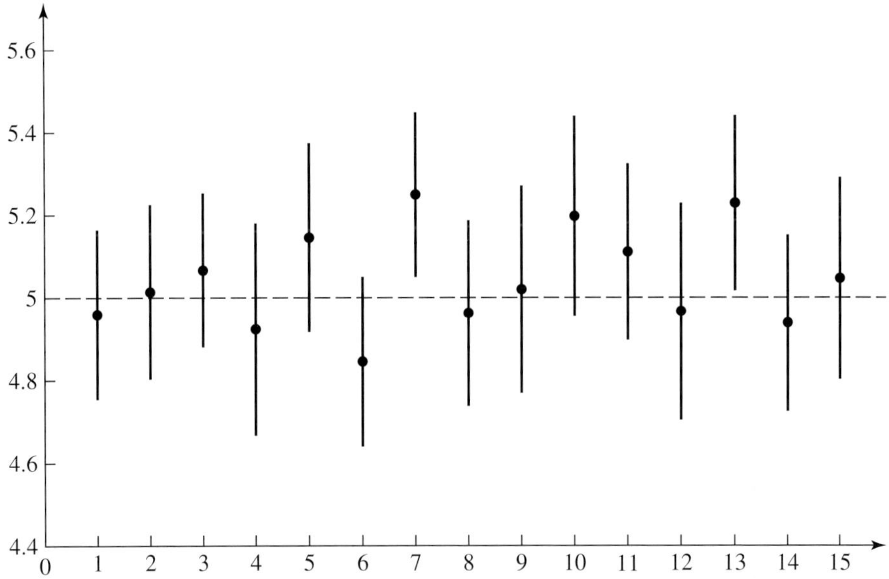

FIGURE 4.16
Confidence intervals each based on a sample of $n = 10$ observations from a normal distribution with mean 5 and variance 1.

[see, for example, Hogg and Craig (1995, pp. 181–182)], and an *exact* (for any $n \geq 2$) $100(1 - \alpha)$ percent confidence interval for μ is given by

$$\bar{X}(n) \pm t_{n-1,\,1-\alpha/2}\sqrt{\frac{S^2(n)}{n}} \tag{4.12}$$

where $t_{n-1,1-\alpha/2}$ is the upper $1 - \alpha/2$ critical point for the t distribution with $n - 1$ df. These critical points are given in Table T.1 of the Appendix at the back of the book. Plots of the density functions for the t distribution with 4 df and for the standard normal distribution are given in Fig. 4.17. Note that the t distribution is less peaked and

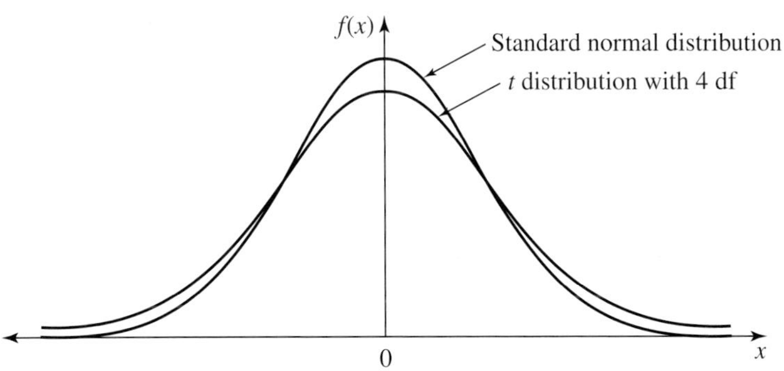

FIGURE 4.17
Density functions for the t distribution with 4 df and for the standard normal distribution.

has longer tails than the normal distribution, so, for any finite n, $t_{n-1,1-\alpha/2} > z_{1-\alpha/2}$. We call (4.12) the *t confidence interval*.

The quantity that we add to and subtract from $\bar{X}(n)$ in (4.12) to construct the confidence interval is called the *half-length* of the confidence interval. It is a measure of how precisely we know μ. It can be shown that if we increase the sample size from n to $4n$ in (4.12), then the half-length is decreased by a factor of approximately 2 (see Prob. 4.20).

In practice, the distribution of the X_i's will rarely be normal, and the confidence interval given by (4.12) will also be approximate in terms of coverage. Since $t_{n-1,1-\alpha/2} > z_{1-\alpha/2}$, the confidence interval given by (4.12) will be larger than the one given by (4.11) and will generally have coverage closer to the desired level $1 - \alpha$. For this reason, we recommend using (4.12) to construct a confidence interval for μ. Note that $t_{n-1,1-\alpha/2} \to z_{1-\alpha/2}$ as $n \to \infty$; in particular, $t_{40,0.95}$ differs from $z_{0.95}$ by less than 3 percent. However, in most of our applications of (4.12) in Chaps. 9, 10, and 12, n will be small enough for the difference between (4.11) and (4.12) to be appreciable.

EXAMPLE 4.27. Suppose that the 10 observations 1.20, 1.50, 1.68, 1.89, 0.95, 1.49, 1.58, 1.55, 0.50, and 1.09 are from a normal distribution with unknown mean μ and that our objective is to construct a 90 percent confidence interval for μ. From these data we get

$$\bar{X}(10) = 1.34 \qquad \text{and} \qquad S^2(10) = 0.17$$

which results in the following confidence interval for μ:

$$\bar{X}(10) \pm t_{9,0.95}\sqrt{\frac{S^2(10)}{10}} = 1.34 \pm 1.83\sqrt{\frac{0.17}{10}} = 1.34 \pm 0.24$$

Note that (4.12) was used to construct the confidence interval and that $t_{9,0.95}$ was taken from Table T.1. Therefore, subject to the interpretation stated above, we claim with 90 percent confidence that μ is in the interval [1.10, 1.58].

We now discuss how the coverage of the confidence interval given by (4.12) is affected by the distribution of the X_i's. In Table 4.1 we give estimated coverages for 90 percent confidence intervals based on 500 independent experiments for each of the sample sizes $n = 5$, 10, 20, and 40 and each of the distributions normal, exponential, chi square with 1 df (a standard normal random variable squared; see the discussion of the gamma distribution in Sec. 6.2.2), lognormal (e^Y, where Y is a

TABLE 4.1
Estimated coverages based on 500 experiments

Distribution	Skewness ν	$n = 5$	$n = 10$	$n = 20$	$n = 40$
Normal	0.00	0.910	0.902	0.898	0.900
Exponential	2.00	0.854	0.878	0.870	0.890
Chi square	2.83	0.810	0.830	0.848	0.890
Lognormal	6.18	0.758	0.768	0.842	0.852
Hyperexponential	6.43	0.584	0.586	0.682	0.774

standard normal random variable; see Sec. 6.2.2), and hyperexponential whose distribution function is given by

$$F(x) = 0.9F_1(x) + 0.1\,F_2(x)$$

where $F_1(x)$ and $F_2(x)$ are the distribution functions of exponential random variables with means 0.5 and 5.5, respectively. For example, the table entry for the exponential distribution and $n = 10$ was obtained as follows. Ten observations were generated from an exponential distribution with a *known* mean μ, a 90 percent confidence interval was constructed using (4.12), and it was determined whether the interval contained μ. (This constituted one experiment.) Then the whole procedure was repeated 500 times, and 0.878 is the proportion of the 500 confidence intervals that contained μ. Note that the coverage for the normal distribution and $n = 10$ is 0.902 rather than the expected 0.900, since the table is based on 500 rather than an infinite number of experiments.

Observe from the table that for a particular distribution, coverage generally gets closer to 0.90 as n gets larger, which follows from the central limit theorem (see Prob. 4.22). (The results for the exponential distribution would also probably follow this behavior if the number of experiments were larger.) Notice also that for a particular n, coverage decreases as the skewness of the distribution gets larger, where skewness is defined by

$$\nu = \frac{E[(X-\mu)^3]}{(\sigma^2)^{3/2}} \qquad -\infty < \nu < \infty$$

The skewness, which is a measure of symmetry, is equal to 0 for a symmetric distribution such as the normal. We conclude from the table that the larger the skewness of the distribution in question, the larger the sample size needed to obtain satisfactory (close to 0.90) coverage.

*We saw in Table 4.1 that there is still significant degradation in coverage probability for sample sizes as large as 40 if the data come from a highly skewed distribution such as the lognormal, which is not at all uncommon in practice. As a result we now discuss an improved confidence developed by Willink (2005), which computes an estimate of the skewness ν and uses this to obtain a confidence interval with coverage closer to the nominal value $1 - \alpha$ than that for the standard t confidence given by (4.12). Let

$$\hat{\mu}_3 = \frac{n\sum_{i=1}^{n}[X_i - \overline{X}(n)]^3}{(n-1)(n-2)}, \qquad a = \frac{\hat{\mu}_3}{6\sqrt{n}[S^2(n)]^{3/2}},$$

and

$$G(r) = \frac{[1 + 6a(r-a)]^{1/3} - 1}{2a}$$

where $\hat{\mu}_3/[S^2(n)]^{3/2}$ is an estimator for the skewness ν. Then an approximate $100(1-\alpha)$ percent confidence interval for μ is given by

$$\left[\overline{X}(n) - G(t_{n-1,1-\alpha/2})\sqrt{S^2(n)/n},\, \overline{X}(n) - G(-t_{n-1,1-\alpha/2})\sqrt{S^2(n)/n}\right] \qquad (4.13)$$

---

*The discussion of the Willink confidence interval may be skipped on a first reading.

EXAMPLE 4.28. For the data of Example 4.27, we now construct a 90 percent confidence interval for μ using the Willink confidence interval given by (4.13). We get

$$\hat{\mu}_3 = -0.062, \quad a = -0.048, \quad G(r) = \frac{[1 - 0.288(r + 0.048)]^{1/3} - 1}{-0.096}$$

and the following 90 percent confidence interval for μ:

$$[1.34 - 0.31, 1.34 + 0.20] \qquad \text{or} \qquad [1.04, 1.54]$$

In order to get an idea how much improvement in coverage probability might be obtained by using the Willink confidence interval given by (4.13) instead of the t confidence interval given by (4.12), we regenerated using different random numbers the observations for the entry in Table 4.1 corresponding to the lognormal distribution and $n = 10$. Based again on 500 experiments, the estimated coverages for the Willink and t confidence intervals were 0.872 and 0.796, respectively. Thus, the Willink confidence interval produces a coverage probability "close" to the nominal level 0.90 even for the highly skewed lognormal distribution and a sample size of only 10. On the other hand, the average half-length for the Willink confidence interval was 76 percent larger than the average half-length for the t confidence interval in this case. The decision whether to use the t or Willink confidence interval should depend on the relative importance one places on coverage close to the nominal level $1 - \alpha$ and a small half-length.

Assume that $X_1, X_2, \ldots, X_n$ are normally distributed (or are approximately so) and that we would like to test the *null hypothesis* H_0: $\mu = \mu_0$ against the *alternative hypothesis* H_1: $\mu \neq \mu_0$, where μ_0 is a fixed, hypothesized value for μ. Intuitively, we would expect that if $|\bar{X}(n) - \mu_0|$ is large [recall that $\bar{X}(n)$ is the point estimator for μ], H_0 is not likely to be true. However, to develop a test with known statistical properties, we need a statistic (a function of the X_i's) whose distribution is known when H_0 is true. It follows from the above discussion that if H_0 is true, the statistic $t_n = [\bar{X}(n) - \mu_0]/\sqrt{S^2(n)/n}$ will have a t distribution with $n - 1$ df. Therefore, consistent with our intuitive discussion above, the form of our (two-tailed) hypothesis test for H_0 is

$$\begin{bmatrix} \text{If } |t_n| > t_{n-1,1-\alpha/2}, \text{ reject } H_0 \\ \text{If } |t_n| \le t_{n-1,1-\alpha/2}, \text{ fail to reject } H_0 \end{bmatrix} \qquad (4.14)$$

The portion of the real line that corresponds to rejection of H_0, namely, the set of all x such that $|x| > t_{n-1,1-\alpha/2}$, is called the *rejection* (or critical) *region* for the test, and the probability that the statistic falls in the rejection region given that H_0 is true, which is clearly equal to α, is called the *level* (or size) of the test. Typically, an experimenter will choose the level equal to 0.05 or 0.10. We call the hypothesis test given by (4.14) the *t test*.

When one performs a hypothesis test, two types of errors can be made. If one rejects H_0 when in fact it is true, this is called a *Type I error*. The probability of Type I error is equal to the level α and is thus under the experimenter's control. If one fails to reject H_0 when it is false, this is called a *Type II error*. For a fixed level α and sample size n, the probability of a Type II error, which we denote by β, depends on

TABLE 4.2
Hypothesis-testing situations and their corresponding probabilities of occurrence

Outcome \ H_0	True	False
Reject	α	$\delta = 1 - \beta$
Fail to reject	$1 - \alpha$	β

what is actually true (other than H_0: $\mu = \mu_0$), and is usually unknown. We call $\delta = 1 - \beta$ the *power* of the test, and it is equal to the probability of rejecting H_0 when it is false. There are four different situations that can occur when one tests the null hypothesis H_0 against the alternative hypothesis H_1, and these are delineated in Table 4.2 along with their probabilities of occurrence.

Clearly, a test with high power is desirable. If α is fixed, the power can only be increased by increasing n. Since the power of a test may be low and unknown to us, this is why we say "fail to reject H_0" (instead of "accept H_0") when the statistic t_n does not lie in the rejection region. (When H_0 is not rejected, we generally do not know with any certainty whether H_0 is true or whether H_0 is false, since our test may not be powerful enough to detect any difference between H_0 and what is actually true.)

EXAMPLE 4.29. For the data of Example 4.27, suppose that we would like to test the null hypothesis H_0: $\mu = 1$ against the alternative hypothesis H_1: $\mu \neq 1$ at level $\alpha = 0.1$. Since

$$t_{10} = \frac{\bar{X}(10) - 1}{\sqrt{S^2(10)/10}} = \frac{0.34}{\sqrt{0.17/10}} = 2.65 > 1.83 = t_{9,0.95}$$

we reject H_0.

EXAMPLE 4.30. For the null hypothesis H_0: $\mu = 1$ in Example 4.29, we can estimate the power of the test when, in fact, the X_i's have a normal distribution with $\mu = 1.5$ and standard deviation $\sigma = 1$. (This is H_1.) We randomly generated 1000 independent observations of the statistic $t_{10} = [\bar{X}(10) - 1]/\sqrt{S^2(10)/10}$ under the assumption that H_1 is true. For 433 out of the 1000 observations, $|t_{10}| > 1.83$ and, therefore, the estimated power is $\hat{\delta} = 0.433$. Thus, if H_1 is true, we will only reject the null hypothesis H_0 approximately 43 percent of the time for a test at level $\alpha = 0.10$. To see what effect the sample size n has on the power of the test, we generated 1000 observations of t_{25} ($n = 25$) when H_1 is true and also 1000 observations of t_{100} ($n = 100$) when H_1 is true (all X_i's were normal). The estimated powers were $\hat{\delta} = 0.796$ and $\hat{\delta} = 0.999$, respectively. It is not surprising that the power is apparently an increasing function of n, since we would expect to have a better estimate of the true value of μ when n is large. [Note that in the case of normal sampling and a *known* standard deviation, as in this example, the power of the test can actually be computed numerically, obviating the need for simulation as done here; see, for example, Devore (2008, pp. 302–303).]

It should be mentioned that there is an intimate relationship between the confidence interval given by (4.12) and the hypothesis test given by (4.14). In particular, rejection of the null hypothesis H_0: $\mu = \mu_0$ is equivalent to μ_0 not being contained in the confidence interval for μ, assuming the same value of α for both the hypothesis test and the confidence interval (see Prob. 4.28). However, the confidence interval *also* gives you a range of possible values for μ, and in this sense it is the preferred methodology.

4.6 THE STRONG LAW OF LARGE NUMBERS

The second most important result in probability theory (after the central limit theorem) is arguably the strong law of large numbers. Let $X_1, X_2, \ldots, X_n$ be IID random variables with finite mean μ. Then the *strong law of large numbers* is as follows [see Chung (1974, p. 126) for a proof].

THEOREM 4.2. $\bar{X}(n) \rightarrow \mu$ w.p. 1 as $n \rightarrow \infty$.

The theorem says, in effect, that if one performs an infinite number of experiments, each resulting in an $\bar{X}(n)$, and n is sufficiently large, then $\bar{X}(n)$ will be arbitrarily close to μ for almost all the experiments.

EXAMPLE 4.31. Suppose that $X_1, X_2, \ldots$ are IID normal random variables with $\mu = 1$ and $\sigma^2 = 0.01$. Figure 4.18 plots the values of $\bar{X}(n)$ for various n that resulted from sampling from this distribution. Note that $\bar{X}(n)$ differed from μ by less than 1 percent for $n \geq 28$.

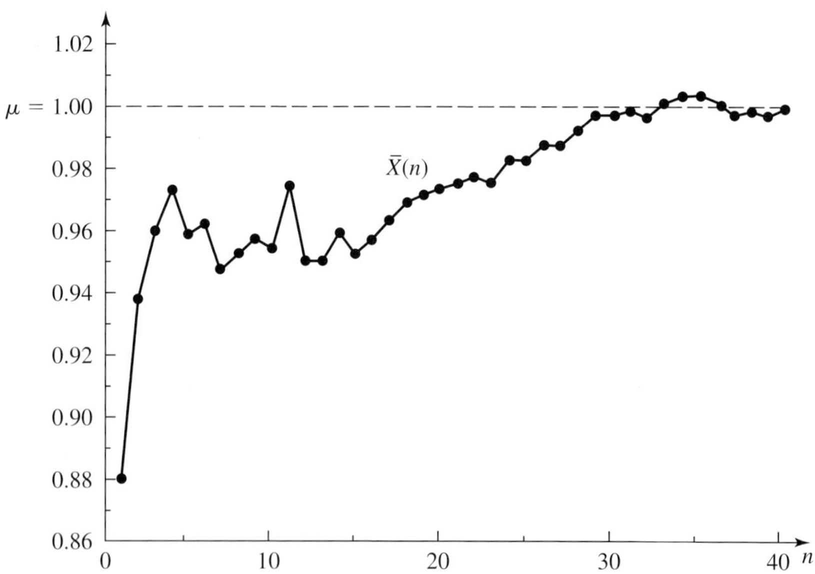

FIGURE 4.18
$\bar{X}(n)$ for various values of n when the X_i's are normal random variables with $\mu = 1$ and $\sigma^2 = 0.01$.

4.7 THE DANGER OF REPLACING A PROBABILITY DISTRIBUTION BY ITS MEAN

Simulation analysts have sometimes replaced an input probability distribution by its mean in their simulation models. This practice may be caused by a lack of understanding on the part of the analyst or by lack of information on the actual form of the distribution (e.g., only an estimate of the mean of the distribution is available). The following example illustrates the danger of this practice.

EXAMPLE 4.32. Consider a manufacturing system consisting of a single machine tool. Suppose that "raw" parts arrive to the machine with exponential interarrival times having a mean of 1 minute and that processing times at the machine are exponentially distributed with a mean of 0.99 minute. Thus, this system is an *M*/*M*/1 queue with utilization factor $\rho = 0.99$. Furthermore, it can be shown that the average delay in queue of a part in the long run is 98.01 minutes [see App. 1B or Gross et al. (2009)]. On the other hand, if we replace each distribution by its corresponding mean (i.e., if customers arrive at times 1 minute, 2 minutes, . . . and if each part has a processing time of exactly 0.99 minute), then no part is ever delayed in the queue. In general, the variances as well as the means of the input distributions affect the output measures for queueing-type systems, as noted at the end of App. 1B.

APPENDIX 4A COMMENTS ON COVARIANCE-STATIONARY PROCESSES

Consider the process $\{D_i, i \geq 1\}$ for the *M*/*M*/1 queue when no customers are present at time 0. Clearly, $D_1 = 0$, but $P(D_i > 0) > 0$ for $i = 2, 3, \ldots$. Therefore, $E(D_1) = 0$ and $E(D_i) > 0$ for $i = 2, 3, \ldots$, which implies that $\{D_i, i \geq 1\}$ is *not* covariance-stationary. However, if $\rho < 1$, it can be shown for all $x \geq 0$ that

$$P(D_i \leq x) \rightarrow (1 - \rho) + \rho(1 - e^{-(\omega - \lambda)x}) \qquad \text{as } i \rightarrow \infty \tag{4.15}$$

It follows from (4.15) and the equation for D_{i+1} in Example 4.19 that if we delete the first k observations from $D_1, D_2, \ldots$ and k is sufficiently large, then the process $D_{k+1}, D_{k+2}, \ldots$ will be (approximately) covariance-stationary. Therefore, when we say "consider the process $\{D_i, i \geq 1\}$ for the covariance-stationary *M*/*M*/1 queue," we mean that we let the *M*/*M*/1 queue "warm up" for some amount of time before observing the first delay.

Consider the process $\{C_i, i \geq 1\}$ for the inventory system of Example 4.23 when $I_1 = S$. Since $P(I_i = S) \neq 1$ for $i = 2, 3, \ldots$, it follows that $\{C_i, i \geq 1\}$ is not covariance-stationary. However, it can be shown that $P(C_i \leq x)$ converges to a limiting distribution function as $i \rightarrow \infty$ [see Wagner (1969, p. A48)]. Thus, $C_{k+1}, C_{k+2}, \ldots$ will be (approximately) covariance-stationary for k large. Furthermore, the correlations plotted in Fig. 4.11 are for an inventory system warmed up for some amount of time before the first cost is observed.

PROBLEMS

4.1. Suppose that X is a discrete random variable with probability mass function given by

$$p(1) = \tfrac{1}{10}, \quad p(2) = \tfrac{3}{10}, \quad p(3) = \tfrac{2}{10}, \quad p(4) = \tfrac{3}{10}, \quad \text{and} \quad p(5) = \tfrac{1}{10}$$

(*a*) Plot $p(x)$.
(*b*) Compute and plot $F(x)$.
(*c*) Compute $P(1.4 \le X \le 4.2)$, $E(X)$, and $\text{Var}(X)$.

4.2. Suppose that X is a continuous random variable with probability density function given by

$$f(x) = x^2 + \tfrac{2}{3}x + \tfrac{1}{3} \qquad \text{for } 0 \le x \le c$$

(*a*) What must be the value of c?
Assuming this value of c, do the following:
(*b*) Plot $f(x)$.
(*c*) Compute and plot $F(x)$.
(*d*) Compute $P(\tfrac{1}{3} \le X \le \tfrac{2}{3})$, $E(X)$, and $\text{Var}(X)$.

4.3. Suppose that X and Y are jointly discrete random variables with

$$p(x, y) = \begin{cases} \dfrac{2}{n(n+1)} & \text{for } x = 1, 2, \ldots, n \text{ and } \\ & \quad y = 1, 2, \ldots, x \\ 0 & \text{otherwise} \end{cases}$$

Compute $p_X(x)$ and $p_Y(y)$ and determine whether X and Y are independent.

4.4. Suppose that X and Y are jointly discrete random variables with

$$p(x, y) = \begin{cases} \dfrac{x+y}{30} & \text{for } x = 0, 1, 2 \text{ and } \\ & \quad y = 0, 1, 2, 3 \\ 0 & \text{otherwise} \end{cases}$$

(*a*) Compute and plot $p_X(x)$ and $p_Y(y)$.
(*b*) Are X and Y independent?
(*c*) Compute and plot $F_X(x)$ and $F_Y(y)$.
(*d*) Compute $E(X)$, $\text{Var}(X)$, $E(Y)$, $\text{Var}(Y)$, $\text{Cov}(X, Y)$, and $\text{Cor}(X, Y)$.

4.5. Are the random variables X and Y in Example 4.10 independent if the sampling of the two cards is done *with* replacement?

4.6. Suppose that X and Y are jointly continuous random variables with

$$f(x, y) = \begin{cases} 32x^3y^7 & \text{if } 0 \le x \le 1 \text{ and } 0 \le y \le 1 \\ 0 & \text{otherwise} \end{cases}$$

Compute $f_X(x)$ and $f_Y(y)$ and determine whether X and Y are independent.

4.7. Suppose that X and Y are jointly continuous random variables with

$$f(x, y) = \begin{cases} y - x & \text{if } 0 < x < 1 \text{ and } 1 < y < 2 \\ 0 & \text{otherwise} \end{cases}$$

(*a*) Compute and plot $f_X(x)$ and $f_Y(y)$.
(*b*) Are X and Y independent?

(*c*) Compute $F_X(x)$ and $F_Y(y)$.
(*d*) Compute $E(X)$, $\text{Var}(X)$, $E(Y)$, $\text{Var}(Y)$, $\text{Cov}(X, Y)$, and $\text{Cor}(X, Y)$.

4.8. If X and Y are jointly continuous random variables with joint probability density function $f(x, y)$ and X and Y are independent, show that $\text{Cov}(X, Y) = 0$. Therefore, X and Y being independent implies that $E(XY) = E(X)E(Y)$.

4.9. Suppose that X is a discrete random variable with $p_X(x) = 0.25$ for $x = -2, -1, 1, 2$. Let Y also be a discrete random variable such that $Y = X^2$. Clearly, X and Y are not independent. However, show that $\text{Cov}(X, Y) = 0$. Therefore, uncorrelated random variables are not necessarily independent.

4.10. Suppose that X_1 and X_2 are jointly normally distributed random variables with joint probability density function

$$f_{X_1, X_2}(x_1, x_2) = \frac{1}{2\pi\sqrt{\sigma_1^2\sigma_2^2(1 - \rho_{12}^2)}} e^{-q/2} \qquad \begin{array}{l}\text{for } -\infty < x_1 < \infty \\ \text{and } -\infty < x_2 < \infty\end{array}$$

where

$$q = \frac{1}{1 - \rho_{12}^2}\left[\frac{(x_1 - \mu_1)^2}{\sigma_1^2} - 2\rho_{12}\frac{(x_1 - \mu_1)(x_2 - \mu_2)}{\sqrt{\sigma_1^2\sigma_2^2}} + \frac{(x_2 - \mu_2)^2}{\sigma_2^2}\right]$$

If $\rho_{12} = 0$, show that X_1 and X_2 are independent.

4.11. Suppose that X and Y are random variables such that $Y = aX + b$ and a and b are constants. Show that

$$\text{Cor}(X, Y) = \begin{cases} +1 & \text{if } a > 0 \\ -1 & \text{if } a < 0 \end{cases}$$

This is why the correlation is said to be a measure of *linear* dependence.

4.12. If X_1 and X_2 are random variables, then $E(X_1^2)E(X_2^2) \geq [E(X_1X_2)]^2$ by *Schwarz's inequality*. Use this fact to show that $-1 \leq \rho_{12} \leq 1$.

4.13. For any random variables X_1, X_2 and any numbers a_1, a_2, show that $\text{Var}(a_1X_1 + a_2X_2) = a_1^2 \text{Var}(X_1) + 2a_1a_2 \text{Cov}(X_1, X_2) + a_2^2 \text{Var}(X_2)$.

4.14. Justify the equation for D_{i+1} in Example 4.19.

4.15. Using the equation for D_{i+1} in Example 4.19, write a C program requiring approximately 15 lines of code to simulate the *M*/*M*/1 queue with a mean interarrival time of 1 and a mean service time of 0.5. Run the program until 1000 D_i's have been observed and compute $\overline{D}(1000)$. The program should not require a simulation clock, an event list, or a timing routine.

4.16. Using the fact that $E(\sum_{i=1}^n a_iX_i) = \sum_{i=1}^n a_iE(X_i)$ for any random variables $X_1, X_2, \ldots, X_n$ and any numbers $a_1, a_2, \ldots, a_n$, show that if $X_1, X_2, \ldots, X_n$ are IID random variables with mean μ and variance σ^2, then $E[\overline{X}(n)] = \mu$ and $E[S^2(n)] = \sigma^2$. Show that the first result still holds if the X_i's are dependent.

4.17. Show that Eq. (4.7) is correct.

4.18. If $X_1, X_2, \ldots, X_n$ are IID random variables with mean μ and variance σ^2, then compute $\mathrm{Cov}[\bar{X}(n), S^2(n)]$. When will this covariance be equal to 0?

4.19. Show that the equality of the two probability statements in Eq. (4.10) is correct.

4.20. For the confidence interval given by (4.12), show that if we increase the sample size from n to $4n$, then the half-length is decreased by a factor of approximately 2.

4.21. Explain why the 90 percent confidence interval in Example 4.27 contained only 5 of the 10 observations.

4.22. For the confidence interval given by (4.12), show that the coverage approaches $1 - \alpha$ as $n \to \infty$.

4.23. Suppose that 7.3, 6.1, 3.8, 8.4, 6.9, 7.1, 5.3, 8.2, 4.9, and 5.8 are 10 observations from a distribution (not highly skewed) with unknown mean μ. Compute $\bar{X}(10)$, $S^2(10)$, and an approximate 95 percent confidence interval for μ.

4.24. For the data in Prob. 4.23, test the null hypothesis H_0: $\mu = 6$ at level $\alpha = 0.05$.

4.25. In Example 4.30 explain why the power goes to 1 as n gets large. (*Hint:* Look at what happens to the numerator and denominator in the statistic $t_n = [\bar{X}(n) - 1]/\sqrt{S^2(n)/n}$ as n gets large.)

4.26. In Example 4.30 the estimated power was 0.433 for $n = 10$ and the alternative hypothesis H_1: $\mu = 1.5$ and $\sigma = 1$.

(*a*) For $n = 10$ will the power increase or decrease if the alternative hypothesis is instead H_1: $\mu = 1.25$ and $\sigma = 1$? Substantiate your answer by randomly sampling (e.g., in Excel) from an appropriate normal distribution.

(*b*) For $n = 10$ will the power increase or decrease if the alternative hypothesis is instead H_1: $\mu = 1.5$ and $\sigma = 0.75$? Substantiate your answer by randomly sampling from an appropriate normal distribution.

4.27. A manufacturing process is supposed to produce ball bearings with a diameter of 0.5 inch. The company examines $n = 50$ ball bearings and finds that $\bar{X}(50) = 0.45$ and $S^2(n) = 0.06$. Test the null hypothesis H_0: $\mu = 0.5$ against the alternative hypothesis H_1: $\mu \neq 0.5$ at level $\alpha = 0.05$. Also, construct a 95 percent confidence interval for μ.

4.28. Show algebraically that rejection of the null hypothesis H_0: $\mu = \mu_0$ by the t test given by (4.14) is equivalent to the t confidence interval given by (4.12) not containing μ_0.

4.29. Suppose that X and Y are random variables with unknown covariance $\mathrm{Cov}(X, Y)$. If the pairs X_i, Y_i (for $i = 1, 2, \ldots, n$) are independent observations of X, Y, then show that

$$\widehat{\mathrm{Cov}}(X, Y) = \frac{\sum_{i=1}^{n} [X_i - \bar{X}(n)][Y_i - \bar{Y}(n)]}{n - 1}$$

is an unbiased estimator of $\mathrm{Cov}(X, Y)$.

4.30. A random variable X is said to have the *memoryless property* if

$$P(X > t + s|X > t) = P(X > s) \qquad \text{for all } t, s > 0$$

[The conditional probability $P(X > t + s\,|X > t)$ is the probability of the event $\{X > t + s\}$ occurring given that the event $\{X > t\}$ has occurred; see Ross (2003, chap. 3).] Show that the exponential distribution has the memoryless property.

4.31. A geometric distribution with parameter p $(0 < p < 1)$ has probability mass function

$$p(x) = p(1 - p)^x \qquad \text{for } x = 0, 1, 2, \ldots$$

Show that this distribution has the memoryless property.

4.32. Suppose that a man has k keys, one of which will open a door. Compute the expected number of keys required to open the door for the following two cases:
(*a*) The keys are tried one at a time without replacement.
(*b*) The keys are tried one at a time with replacement. (*Hint:* Condition on the outcome of the first try.)

4.33. Are the mean, median, and mode equal for every symmetric distribution?

4.34. In Example 4.32 is the long-run throughput (departure rate) larger when interarrival times and processing times are each exponentially distributed or when they are each a constant?

CHAPTER 5

Building Valid, Credible, and Appropriately Detailed Simulation Models

Recommended sections for a first reading: 5.1 through 5.5, 5.6.1

5.1 INTRODUCTION AND DEFINITIONS

One of the most difficult problems facing a simulation analyst is that of trying to determine whether a simulation model is an accurate representation of the actual system being studied, i.e., whether the model is *valid*. In this chapter we present a *practical* discussion of how to build valid and credible models. We also provide guidelines on how to determine the level of detail for a model of a complex system, also a critical and challenging issue. Information for this chapter came from a review of the existing literature, from consulting studies performed by Averill M. Law & Associates, and from the experiences of the thousands of people who have attended the author's simulation short courses since 1977. We present more than 40 examples to illustrate the concepts presented.

Important works on validation and verification include those by Balci (1998), Banks et al. (2010), Carson (1986, 2002), Feltner and Weiner (1985), Law (2009, 2011), Naylor and Finger (1967), Sargent (2012), Shannon (1975), and Van Horn (1971). References on the assessment of an existing simulation model include Fossett et al. (1991), Gass (1983), Gass and Thompson (1980), and Knepell and Arangno (1993).

We begin by defining the important terms used in this chapter, including verification, validation, and credibility. *Verification* is concerned with determining whether the "assumptions document" (see Sec. 5.4.3) has been correctly translated into a computer "program," i.e., debugging the simulation computer program. Although verification is simple in concept, debugging a large-scale simulation program is a difficult and arduous task due to the potentially large number of logical paths. Techniques for verifying a simulation computer program are discussed in Sec. 5.3.

Validation is the *process* of determining whether a simulation model is an accurate representation of the system, *for the particular objectives of the study.* [Fishman and Kiviat (1968) appear to be the first ones to have given definitions similar to these.] The following are some general perspectives on validation:

- Conceptually, if a simulation model is "valid," then it can be used to make decisions about the system similar to those that would be made if it *were* feasible and cost-effective to experiment with the system itself.
- The ease or difficulty of the validation process depends on the complexity of the system being modeled and on *whether a version of the system currently exists* (see Sec. 5.4.5). For example, a model of a neighborhood bank would be relatively easy to validate since it could be closely observed. However, a model of the effectiveness of a naval weapons system in the year 2025 would be impossible to validate completely, since the location of the battle and the nature of the enemy weapons would be unknown.
- A simulation model of a complex system can only be an *approximation* to the actual system, no matter how much effort is spent on model building. There is no such thing as absolute model validity, nor is it even desired. The more time (and hence money) that is spent on model development, the more valid the model should be in general. However, the most valid model is not necessarily the most cost-effective. For example, increasing the validity of a model beyond a certain level might be quite expensive, since extensive data collection may be required, but might not lead to significantly better insight or decisions. A famous quote by Professor George E.P. Box says, "All models are wrong, but some are useful." This means that it is *not* possible to get every detail of the system into a model, but some models are still useful for decision making.
- A simulation model should always be developed for a particular set of purposes. Indeed, a model that is valid for one purpose may not be for another.
- The measures of performance used to validate a model should include those that the decision maker will actually use for evaluating system designs.
- Validation is not something to be attempted after the simulation model has already been developed, and only if there is time and money remaining. Unfortunately, our experience indicates that this recommendation is often not followed.

EXAMPLE 5.1. An organization paid a consulting company $500,000 to perform a "simulation study." After the study was supposedly completed, a person from the client organization called and asked, "Can you tell me in *five minutes* on the phone how to validate our model?"

- Each time a simulation model is being considered for a new application, its validity should be reexamined. The current purpose may be substantially different from the original purpose, or the passage of time may have invalidated certain model parameters.

A simulation model and its results have *credibility* if the manager and other key project personnel accept them as "correct." (We will henceforth use the term "manager" to mean manager, decision maker, or client, as is appropriate to the context.) Note that a credible model is not necessarily valid, and vice versa. Also, a model can be credible and not actually used as an aid in making decisions. For example, a model could be credible but not used because of political or economic reasons. The following things help establish credibility for a model:

- The manager's understanding of and agreement with the model's assumptions (see Sec. 5.4.2)
- Demonstration that the model has been validated and verified
- The manager's ownership of and involvement with the project
- Reputation of the model developers
- A compelling animation

The U.S. Department of Defense (DoD) is a large user of simulation models, and in recent years there has been considerable interest in verification, validation, and a concept known as accreditation (VV&A). *Accreditation* [see Modeling & Simulation Coordination Office (2011)] is the official certification (by the project sponsor) that a simulation model is acceptable for a specific purpose. The main reason that accreditation is mandated within DoD is that someone must take responsibility for the decision to use a model for a particular application, since a large amount of money and people's lives may be at stake. Also, most military analyses are done with legacy models, which may have been developed for another application or by another organization. Issues that are considered in an accreditation decision include:

- Verification and validation that have been done
- Credibility of the model
- Simulation model development and use history (e.g., model developer and similar applications)
- Quality of the data that are available
- Quality of the documentation
- Known problems or limitations with the simulation model

The timing and relationships of validation, verification, and establishing credibility are shown in Fig. 5.1. The rectangles represent states of the model or the system of interest, the solid horizontal arrows correspond to the actions necessary to move from one state to another, and the curved dashed arrows show where the three major concepts are most prominently employed. The numbers below each solid arrow correspond to the steps in a sound simulation study, as discussed in Sec. 1.7. We have not attempted to illustrate feedback arcs in the figure.

Validation should be contrasted with *output analysis* (the subject of Chaps. 9 through 12), which is a statistical issue concerned with estimating a simulation *model's*

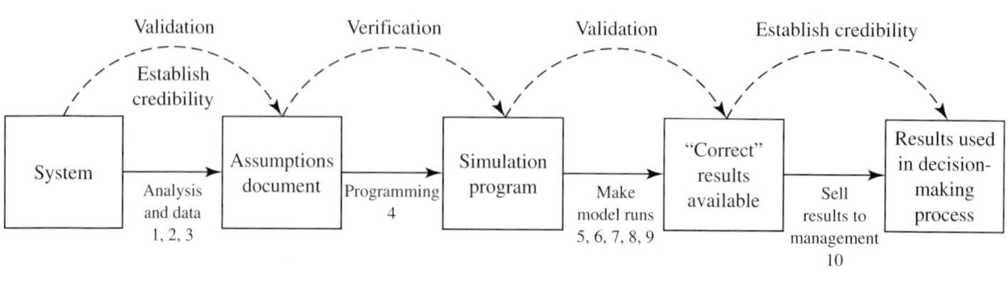

FIGURE 5.1
Timing and relationships of validation, verification, and establishing credibility.

(not necessarily the system's) true measures of performance. Topics of interest in output analysis include simulation run length, length of the warmup period (if any), and number of independent model runs (using different random numbers).

To get a better idea of the difference between validation and output analysis, suppose that we want to estimate the mean μ_S of some system. Suppose that we construct a simulation model whose corresponding mean is μ_M. We make a simulation run and obtain an estimate $\hat{\mu}_M$ of μ_M. Then the error in $\hat{\mu}_M$ as an estimate of μ_S is given by

$$\begin{aligned} \text{Error in } \hat{\mu}_M &= |\hat{\mu}_M - \mu_S| \\ &= |\hat{\mu}_M - \mu_M + \mu_M - \mu_S| \\ &\leq |\hat{\mu}_M - \mu_M| + |\mu_M - \mu_S| \qquad \text{(by the triangle inequality)} \end{aligned}$$

Validation is concerned with making the second absolute value small (in the line above), while output analysis is concerned with making the first absolute value small. Thus, to have a good estimate of the mean of the system, we have to be concerned with *both* validation and output analysis.

5.2 GUIDELINES FOR DETERMINING THE LEVEL OF MODEL DETAIL

A simulation practitioner must determine what aspects of a complex real-world system actually need to be incorporated into the simulation model and at what level of detail, and what aspects can be safely ignored. It is rarely necessary to have a one-to-one correspondence between each element of the system and each element of the model. Modeling each aspect of the system will seldom be required to make effective decisions, and might result in excessive model execution time, in missed deadlines, or in obscuring important system factors.

EXAMPLE 5.2. A dog-food manufacturer had a consulting company build a simulation model of its manufacturing line, which produced 1 million cans per day at a constant rate. Because each can of food was represented by a separate entity in the model, the model was very expensive to run and, thus, not very useful. A few years later the model was rewritten, treating the manufacturing process as a "continuous flow" (see Sec. 1.2). The new model produced accurate results and executed in a small fraction of the time necessary for the original model.

EXAMPLE 5.3. A simulation model of a 1.5-mile-long factory was built in 1985 at a cost of $250,000. However, the model was so detailed that no runs were ever made due to excessive computer memory requirements.

We now present some general guidelines for determining the level of detail required by a simulation model [see also Law (1991) and Robinson (2004, pp. 87–92)].

- Carefully define the *specific* issues to be investigated by the study and the measures of performance that will be used for evaluation. Models are not universally valid, but are designed for specific purposes. If the issues of interest have not been delineated, then it is impossible to determine the appropriate level of model detail. Since some models can accurately estimate one measure of performance but not another, it is also important to specify the performance measures of interest. For example, a simple model of a manufacturing system might accurately predict throughput (e.g., parts per day) but be inadequate for determining the required floor space for work-in-process (see Example 14.3). Finally, it is important to understand the manager's needs. A great model for the wrong problem will never be used. Problem formulation is usually done at an initial kickoff meeting with people representing all key aspects of the system being present.

EXAMPLE 5.4. A U.S. military analyst worked on a simulation model for six months without interacting with the general who requested it. At the Pentagon briefing for the study, the general walked out after 5 minutes stating, "That's not the problem I'm interested in."

- The entity moving through the simulation model does not always have to be the same as the entity moving through the corresponding system (see Example 5.5). Furthermore, it is not always necessary to model each component of the system in complete detail (see Example 5.26).

EXAMPLE 5.5. A large food manufacturer built a simulation model of its manufacturing line for snack crackers. Initially, they tried to model each cracker as a separate entity, but the computational requirements of the model made this approach infeasible. As a result, the company was forced to use a box of crackers as the entity moving through the model. The validity of this modeling approach was determined by using sensitivity analysis (see below and Example 5.25).

- Use subject-matter experts (SMEs) and sensitivity analyses to help determine the level of model detail. People who are familiar with systems similar to the one of interest are asked what components of the proposed system are likely to be the most important and, thus, need to be carefully modeled. Sensitivity analyses (see Sec. 5.4.4) can be used to determine what system factors (e.g., parameters or distributions) have the greatest impact on the desired measures of performance. Given a limited amount of time for model development, one should obviously concentrate on the most important factors.
- A mistake often made by beginning modelers is to include an excessive amount of model detail. As a result, we recommend starting with a "moderately detailed" model, which can later be embellished if needed. The adequacy of a particular version of the model is determined in part by presenting the model to SMEs and managers. Regular interaction with these people also maintains their interest in the simulation study.

EXAMPLE 5.6. We developed a simulation model of a pet-food manufacturing system, which consisted of a meat plant and a cannery. In the meat plant, meat was either ground fine or into chunks and then placed into buckets and transported to the cannery by an overhead conveyor system. In the cannery buckets are dumped into mixers that process the meat and then dispense it to filler/seamers for canning. The empty buckets are conveyed back to the meat plant for refilling. Originally, it was decided that the system producing the chunky product was relatively unimportant and, thus, it was modeled in a simple manner. However, at the structured walk-through of the model (see Sec. 5.4.3), machine operators stated that this subsystem was actually much more complex. To gain credibility with these members of the project team, we had to include machine breakdowns and contention for resources. Furthermore, after the initial model runs were made, it was necessary to make additional changes to the model suggested by a mixer operator.

- Do not have more detail in the model than is necessary to address the issues of interest, subject to the proviso that the model must have enough detail to be credible. Thus, it may sometimes be necessary to include things in a model that are not strictly required for model validity, due to credibility concerns.
- The level of model detail should be consistent with the type of data available. A model used to design a new manufacturing system will generally be less detailed than one used to fine-tune an existing system, since little or no data will be available for a proposed system.
- In virtually all simulation studies, time and money constraints are a major factor in determining the amount of model detail.
- If the number of factors (aspects of interest) for the study is large, then use a "coarse" simulation model or an analytic model to identify what factors have a significant impact on system performance. A "detailed" simulation model is then built, emphasizing these factors [see Haider, Noller, and Robey (1986) for an example]. Note that there are commercial software packages available for performing analytic analyses in application areas such as manufacturing systems and communications networks. Statistical experimental design (see Chap. 12) might also be useful for determining important factors.

5.3 VERIFICATION OF SIMULATION COMPUTER PROGRAMS

In this section we discuss eight techniques that can be used to debug the computer program of a simulation model [see Balci (1998) for additional techniques from the field of software engineering]. Some of these techniques may be used to debug any computer program, while others we believe to be unique to simulation modeling.

Technique 1

In developing a simulation model, write and debug the computer program in modules or subprograms. By way of example, for a 10,000-statement simulation model it would be poor programming practice to write the entire program before attempting any debugging. When this large, untested program is finally run, it almost certainly will not execute, and determining the location of the errors in the program will be extremely difficult. Instead, the simulation model's main program and a few of the key subprograms should be written and debugged first, perhaps representing the other required subprograms as "dummies" or "stubs." Next, additional subprograms or levels of detail should be added and debugged successively, until a model is developed that satisfactorily represents the system under study. In general, it is always better to start with a "moderately detailed" model, which is gradually made as complex as needed, than to develop "immediately" a complex model, which may turn out to be more detailed than necessary and excessively expensive to run (see Example 5.25 for further discussion).

EXAMPLE 5.7. For the multiteller bank with jockeying considered in Sec. 2.6, a good programming approach would be first to write and debug the computer program without letting customers jockey from queue to queue.

Technique 2

It is advisable in developing large simulation models to have more than one person review the computer program, since the writer of a particular subprogram may get into a mental rut and, thus, may not be a good critic. In some organizations, this idea is implemented formally and is called a *structured walk-through of the program.* For example, all members of the modeling team, say, systems analysts, programmers, etc., are assembled in a room, and each is given a copy of a particular set of subprograms to be debugged. Then the subprograms' developer goes through the programs but does not proceed from one statement to another until everyone is convinced that a statement is correct.

Technique 3

Run the simulation under a variety of settings of the input parameters, and check to see that the output is reasonable. In some cases, certain simple measures of performance may be computed exactly and used for comparison. (See the case study in Sec. 14.6.)

EXAMPLE 5.8. For many queueing systems with s servers in parallel, it can be shown that the long-run average utilization of the servers is $\rho = \lambda/(s\omega)$ (see App. 1B for notation). Thus, if the average utilization from a simulation run is close to the utilization factor ρ, there is some indication that the program may be working correctly.

Technique 4

One of the most powerful techniques that can be used to debug a discrete-event simulation program is a "trace." In a *trace,* the state of the simulated system, i.e., the contents of the event list, the state variables, certain statistical counters, etc., are displayed just after each event occurs and are compared with hand calculations to see if the program is operating as intended. In performing a trace it is desirable to evaluate each possible program path as well as the program's ability to deal with "extreme" conditions. Sometimes such a thorough evaluation may require that special (perhaps deterministic) input data be prepared for the model. Most simulation packages provide the capability to perform traces.

A batch-mode trace often produces a large volume of output, which must be checked event by event for errors. Unfortunately, some key information may be omitted from the trace (not having been requested by the analyst); or, worse yet, a particular error may not occur in the "short" debugging simulation run. Either difficulty will require that the simulation be rerun. As a result, it is usually preferable to use an interactive debugger to find programming errors.

An *interactive debugger* allows an analyst to stop the simulation at a selected point in time, and to examine and possibly change the values of certain variables. This latter capability can be used to "force" the occurrence of certain types of errors. Many modern simulation packages have an interactive debugger.

EXAMPLE 5.9. Table 5.1 shows a trace for the intuitive explanation of the single-server queue in Sec. 1.4.2. The first row of the table is a snapshot of the system just after

TABLE 5.1
Partial trace for the single-server queue considered in Sec. 1.4.2

Event	Clock	Server status	Number in queue	Times of arrival	Event list		Number of customers delayed	Total delay	Area under number-in-queue function	Area under busy function
					Arrive	Depart				
Initialization	0	0	0		0.4	∞	0	0	0	0
Arrival	0.4	1	0		1.6	2.4	1	0	0	0
Arrival	1.6	1	1	1.6	2.1	2.4	1	0	0	1.2
Arrival	2.1	1	2	1.6, 2.1	3.8	2.4	1	0	0.5	1.7
Departure	2.4	1	1	2.1	3.8	3.1	2	0.8	1.1	2.0
Departure	3.1	1	0		3.8	3.3	3	1.8	1.8	2.7
Departure	3.3	0	0		3.8	∞	3	1.8	1.8	2.9

TABLE 5.2
Theoretical values (T) and simulation estimates (S) for a simplified job-shop model ($M/E_2/1$ queue)

Average number in queue		Average utilization		Average delay in queue	
T	S	T	S	T	S
0.676	0.685	0.600	0.604	0.563	0.565

initialization at time 0, the second row is a snapshot of the system just after the first event (an arrival) has occurred, etc.

Technique 5

The model should be run, when possible, under simplifying assumptions for which its true characteristics are known or can easily be computed.

EXAMPLE 5.10. For the job-shop model presented in Sec. 2.7, it is not possible to compute the desired system characteristics analytically. Therefore, one must use simulation. To debug the simulation model, one could first run the general model of Sec. 2.7.2 with one workstation, one machine in that station, and only type 1 jobs (which have an arrival rate of $0.3/0.25 = 1.2$ jobs per hour). The resulting model is known as the $M/E_2/1$ queue and has known transient and steady-state characteristics [see Kelton (1985) and Gross et al. (2009)]. Table 5.2 gives the theoretical values of the steady-state average number in queue, average utilization, and average delay in queue, and also estimates of these quantities from a simulation run of length 2000 eight-hour days. Since the estimates are very close to the true values, we have some degree of confidence that the computer program is correct.

A more definitive test of the program can be achieved by running the general model of Sec. 2.7.2 with the original number of workstations (5), the original number of machines in each station (3, 2, 4, 3, 1), only type 1 jobs, and with exponential service times (with the same mean as the corresponding 2-Erlang service time) at each workstation. The resulting model is, in effect, four multiserver queues in series, with the first queue an $M/M/4$, the second an $M/M/3$, etc. [The interdeparture times from an $M/M/s$ queue (s is the number of servers) that has been in operation for a long time are IID exponential random variables; see Gross et al. (2009).] Furthermore, steady-state characteristics are known for the $M/M/s$ queue [see Gross et al. (2009)]. Table 5.3 gives, for each workstation,

TABLE 5.3
Theoretical values (T) and simulation estimates (S) for a simplified job-shop model (four multiserver queues in series)

Work station	Average number in queue		Average utilization		Average delay in queue	
	T	S	T	S	T	S
3	0.001	0.001	0.150	0.149	0.001	0.001
1	0.012	0.012	0.240	0.238	0.010	0.010
2	0.359	0.350	0.510	0.508	0.299	0.292
5	0.900	0.902	0.600	0.601	0.750	0.752

the theoretical values of the steady-state average number in queue, average utilization, and average delay in queue, and also estimates of these quantities from a simulation run of length 2000 eight-hour days. Once again, the simulation estimates are quite close to the theoretical values, which gives increased confidence in the program.

EXAMPLE 5.11. We developed a simulation model for a large provider of cellular phone service, where the goal was to determine the long-term availability (proportion of time up) of several alternative network configurations. Originally, we tried computing availability using analytic approaches such as continuous-time Markov chains and conditional expectation [see, for example, Ross (2003)], but we were only able to obtain results for simple cases. Therefore, we needed to use simulation, and we partially verified our simulation model by comparing the simulation and analytic results for the simple cases.

Technique 6

With some types of simulation models, it may be helpful to observe an animation of the simulation output (see Sec. 3.4.3).

EXAMPLE 5.12. A simulation model of a network of automobile traffic intersections was developed, supposedly debugged, and used for some time to study such issues as the effect of various light-sequencing policies. However, when the simulated flow of traffic was animated, it was found that simulated cars were actually colliding in the intersections; subsequent inspection of the computer program revealed several previously undetected errors.

Technique 7

Compute the sample mean and sample variance for each simulation input probability distribution, and compare them with the desired (e.g., historical) mean and variance. This suggests that values are being correctly generated from these distributions.

EXAMPLE 5.13. The parameters of gamma and Weibull distributions are defined differently in various simulation packages and books. Thus, this technique would be valuable here.

Technique 8

Use a commercial simulation package to reduce the amount of programming required. On the other hand, care must be taken when using a simulation package (particularly a recently released one), since it may contain errors of a subtle nature. Also, simulation packages contain powerful high-level macro statements, which are sometimes not well documented.

5.4 TECHNIQUES FOR INCREASING MODEL VALIDITY AND CREDIBILITY

In this section we discuss six classes of techniques for increasing the validity and credibility of a simulation model. You might review the ten steps in a sound simulation study (Sec. 1.7) before proceeding.

5.4.1 Collect High-Quality Information and Data on the System

In developing a simulation model, the analyst should make use of all existing information, including the following:

Conversations with Subject-Matter Experts

A simulation model is not an abstraction developed by an analyst working in isolation; in fact, the modeler must work closely with people who are intimately familiar with the system. There will never be one single person or document that contains all the information needed to build the model. Therefore, the analyst will have to be resourceful to obtain a complete and accurate set of information. Care must be taken to identify the true SMEs for each subsystem and to avoid obtaining biased data (see Example 5.19). Ideally, SMEs should have some knowledge of simulation modeling, so that they supply relevant information. The process of bringing all the system information together in one place is often valuable in its own right, even if a simulation study is never performed. Note that since the specifications for a system may be changing during the course of a simulation study, the modeler may have to talk to some SMEs on a continuing basis.

EXAMPLE 5.14. For a manufacturing system, the modelers should obtain information from sources such as machine operators, manufacturing and industrial engineers, maintenance personnel, schedulers, managers, vendors, and blueprints.

EXAMPLE 5.15. For a communications network, relevant people might include end-users, network designers, technology experts (e.g., for switches and satellites), system administrators, application architects, maintenance personnel, managers, and carriers.

Observations of the System

If a system similar to the one of interest exists, then data should be obtained from it for use in building the model. These data may be available from historical records or may have to be collected during a time study. Since the people who provide the data might be different from the simulation modelers, it is important that the following two principles be followed:

- The modelers need to make sure that the data requirements (type, format, amount, conditions under which they should be collected, why needed, etc.) are specified precisely to the people who provide the data.
- The modelers need to understand the process that produced the data, rather than treat the observations as just abstract numbers.

The following are five potential difficulties with data:

- Data are not representative of what one really wants to model.

EXAMPLE 5.16. The data that have been collected during a military field test may not be representative of actual combat conditions due to differences in troop behavior and lack of battlefield smoke (see also Prob. 5.1).

- Data are not of the appropriate type or format.

EXAMPLE 5.17. In modeling a manufacturing system, the largest source of randomness is usually random downtimes of a machine. Ideally, we would like data on time to failure (in terms of actual machine busy time) and time to repair of a machine. Sometimes data are available on machine breakdowns, but quite often they are not in the proper format. For example, the times to failure might be based on wall-clock time and include periods that the machine was idle or off-shift.

- Data may contain measurement, recording, or rounding errors.

EXAMPLE 5.18. Repair times for military-aircraft components were often rounded to the nearest day, making it impossible to fit a continuous probability distribution (see Chap. 6).

- Data may be "biased" because of self-interest.

EXAMPLE 5.19. The maintenance department in an automotive factory reported the reliability of certain machines to be greater than reality to make themselves look good.

- Data may have inconsistent units.

EXAMPLE 5.20. The U.S. Transportation Command transports military cargo by air, land, and sea. Sometimes there is confusion in building simulation models because the U.S. Air Force and the U.S. Army use short tons (2000 pounds) while the U.S. Navy uses long tons (2200 pounds).

Existing Theory

For example, if one is modeling a service system such as a bank and the arrival rate of customers is constant over some time period, theory tells us that the interarrival times of customers are quite likely to be IID exponential random variables; in other words, customers arrive in accordance with a Poisson process (see Sec. 6.12.1 and Example 6.4).

Relevant Results from Similar Simulation Studies

If one is building a simulation model of a military ground encounter (as has been done many times in the past), then results from similar studies should be sought out and used, if possible.

Experience and Intuition of the Modelers

It will often be necessary to use one's experience or intuition to hypothesize how certain components of a complex system operate, particularly if the system does not currently exist in some form. It is hoped that these hypotheses can be substantiated later in the simulation study.

5.4.2 Interact with the Manager on a Regular Basis

We now discuss one of the most important ideas in this chapter, whose use will increase considerably the likelihood that the completed model will be employed in the decision-making process. *It is extremely important for the modeler to interact with the manager on a regular basis throughout the course of the simulation study.* This approach has the following benefits:

- When a simulation study is initiated, there may not be a clear idea of the problem to be solved. Thus, as the study proceeds and the nature of the problem becomes clearer, this information should be conveyed to the manager, who may reformulate the study's objectives. Clearly, the greatest model for the wrong problem is invalid!
- The manager's interest and involvement in the study are maintained.
- The manager's knowledge of the system contributes to the actual validity of the model.
- The model is more credible since the manager understands and accepts the model's assumptions. As a matter of fact, it is extremely desirable to have the manager (and other important personnel) "sign off" on key model assumptions. This may cause the manager to believe, "Of course, it's a good model, since I helped develop it."

5.4.3 Maintain a Written Assumptions Document and Perform a Structured Walk-Through

Communication errors are a major reason why simulation models often contain invalid assumptions or have critical omissions. The documentation of all model concepts, assumptions, algorithms, and data summaries in a written *assumptions document* can greatly lessen this problem, and it will also enhance the credibility of the model. (Within DoD and elsewhere an assumptions document is better known as a *conceptual model.*) However, deciding on the appropriate content of an assumptions document is a less-than-obvious task that depends on the modeler's insight, knowledge of modeling principles (e.g., from operations research, probability and statistics, etc.), and experience in modeling similar types of systems. An assumptions document is not an "exact" description of how the system works, but rather a description of how it works relative to the particular issues that the model is to address. Indeed, the assumptions document is the embodiment of the simulation analyst's vision of how the system of interest should be modeled.

The assumptions document should be written to be readable by analysts, SMEs, and technically trained managers alike, and it should contain the following:

- An overview section that discusses overall project goals, the specific issues to be addressed by the simulation study, model inputs, and the performance measures for evaluation.
- A process-flow or system-layout diagram, if appropriate (see Fig. 14.31).
- Detailed descriptions of each subsystem *in bullet format* and how these subsystems interact. (Bullet format, as on this page, makes the assumptions document easier to review at the structured walk-through of the assumptions document, which is described below.)
- What simplifying assumptions were made and why. Remember that a simulation model is supposed to be a simplification or abstraction of reality.

- Limitations of the simulation model.
- Summaries of a data set such as its sample mean and a histogram. Detailed statistical analyses or other technical material should probably be placed in appendices to the report—remember that the assumptions document should be readable by technical managers.
- Sources of important or controversial information (people, books, technical papers, etc.).

The assumptions document should contain enough detail so that it is a "blueprint" for creating the simulation computer program. Additional information on assumptions documents (conceptual models) can be found in Modeling & Simulation Coordination Office (2011), Pace (2003), and Robinson (2008a,b).

As previously discussed, the simulation modeler will need to collect system information from many different people. Furthermore, these people are typically very busy dealing with the daily problems that occur within their organizations, often resulting in their giving something less than their undivided attention to the questions posed by the simulation modeler. As a result, there is a considerable danger that the simulation modeler will not obtain a complete and correct description of the system. *One way of dealing with this potential problem is to conduct a structured walk-through of the assumptions document before an audience of SMEs and managers.* Using a projection device, the simulation modeler goes through the assumptions document bullet by bullet, but not proceeding from one bullet to the next until everybody in the room is convinced that a particular bullet is correct and at an appropriate level of detail. A structured walk-through will increase both the validity and the credibility of the simulation model.

The structured walk-through ideally should be held at a remote site (e.g., a hotel meeting room), so that people give the meeting their full attention. Furthermore, it should be held prior to the beginning of programming in case major problems are uncovered at the meeting. The assumptions document should be sent to participants prior to the meeting and their comments requested. We do not, however, consider this to be a replacement for the structured walk-through itself, since people may not have the time or motivation to review the document carefully on their own. Furthermore, the interactions that take place at the actual meeting are invaluable. [Within DoD the structured walk-through of the assumptions document (conceptual model) is sometimes called *conceptual model validation*.] It is imperative that all key members of the project team be present at the structured walk-through and that they all take an active role.

It is likely that *many* model assumptions will be found to be incorrect or to be missing at the structured walk-through. Thus, any errors or omissions found in the assumptions document should be corrected before programming begins.

We now present two examples of structured walk-throughs, the first being very successful and the other producing quite surprising but still useful results.

EXAMPLE 5.21. We performed a structured walk-through in doing a simulation study for a Fortune 500 manufacturing company (see Sec. 14.6). There were nine people at the meeting, including two modelers and seven people from the client organization. The client personnel included the foreman of the machine operators, three engineers of various types, two people from the scheduling department, and a manager. The assumptions document was 19 pages long and contained approximately 160 tentative model assumptions. Each of the 160 assumptions was presented and discussed, with the whole process taking 5½ hours. The process resulted in several erroneous assumptions being discovered and corrected, a few new assumptions being added, and some level-of-detail issues being resolved. Furthermore, at the end of the meeting, all nine people felt that *they* had a valid model! In other words, they had taken *ownership* of the model.

EXAMPLE 5.22. At a structured walk-through for a transportation system, a significant percentage of the assumptions given to us by our corporate sponsor were found to be wrong by the SMEs present. (Due to the long geographic distances between the home offices of the sponsor and the SMEs, it was not possible for the SMEs to be present at the kickoff meeting for the project.) As a result, various people were assigned responsibilities to collect information on different parts of the system. The collected information was used to update the assumptions document, and a second walk-through was successfully performed. This experience pointed out the critical importance of having all key project members present at the kickoff meeting.

Some people think that the need for an assumptions document and its formal review are just common sense. However, based on talking to literally thousands of simulation practitioners, we believe that, perhaps, 75 percent of all simulation models have inadequate documentation.

5.4.4 Validate Components of the Model by Using Quantitative Techniques

The simulation analyst should use quantitative techniques whenever possible to test the validity of various components of the overall model. We now give some examples of techniques that can be used for this purpose, all of which are generally applicable.

If one has fitted a theoretical probability distribution to a set of observed data, then the adequacy of the representation can be assessed by using the graphical plots and goodness-of-fit tests discussed in Chap. 6.

As stated in Sec. 5.4.1, it is important to use appropriate data in building a model; however, it is equally important to exercise care when structuring these data. For example, if several sets of data have been observed for the "same" random phenomenon, then the correctness of merging these data can be assessed by the Kruskal-Wallis test of homogeneity of populations (see Sec. 6.13). If the data sets appear to be homogeneous, they can be merged and the combined data set used for some purpose in the simulation model.

EXAMPLE 5.23. For the manufacturing system described in the case study of Sec. 14.6, time-to-failure and time-to-repair data were collected for two "identical" machines made by the same vendor. However, the Kruskal-Wallis test showed that the two distributions were, in fact, different for the two machines. Thus, each machine was given its own time-to-failure and time-to-repair distributions in the simulation model.

An important technique for determining which model factors have a significant impact on the desired measures of performance is *sensitivity analysis*. If a particular factor appears to be important, then it needs to be modeled carefully. The following are examples of factors that could be investigated by a sensitivity analysis:

- The value of a parameter (see Example 5.24)
- The choice of a distribution
- The entity moving through the simulated system (see Example 5.25)
- The level of detail for a subsystem (see Example 5.26)
- What data are the most crucial to collect (using a "coarse" model of the system)

EXAMPLE 5.24. In a simulation study of a new system, suppose that the value of a parameter is estimated to be 0.75 as a result of conversations with SMEs. The importance of this parameter can be determined by running the simulation with 0.75 and, in addition, by running it with each of the values 0.70 and 0.80. If the three simulation runs produce approximately the same results, then the output is not sensitive to the choice of the parameter *over the range 0.70 to 0.80*. Otherwise, a better specification of the parameter is needed.

EXAMPLE 5.25. We built a simulation model for a candy-bar manufacturing line. Initially, we used a single candy bar as the basic entity moving through the model, but this resulted in excessive computer execution time. A sensitivity analysis was performed, and it was found that using one-quarter of a case of candy bars (150 candy bars) produced virtually the same simulation results for the desired performance measure, *cases produced per shift*, while reducing the execution time considerably.

EXAMPLE 5.26. We developed a simulation model of the assembly and test area for a PC manufacturing company. Later the company managers decided that they wanted to run the model on their own computers, but the memory requirements of the model were too great. As a result, we were forced to simplify greatly the model of the assembly area to save computer memory. (The main focus of the simulation study was the required capacity for the test area.) We ran the simplified simulation model (the model of the test area was unchanged) and found that the desired performance measure, *daily throughput*, differed by only 2 percent from that of the original model. [This is an example of using one model to help validate another (see Sec. 5.4.5).] Thus, a large amount of detail was unnecessary for the assembly area. Note, however, that the simplified model would not have been appropriate to study how to improve the efficiency of the assembly area. On the other hand, it may not have been necessary to model the test area in this case.

When one is performing a sensitivity analysis, it is important to use the method of common random numbers (see Sec. 11.2) to control the randomness in the simulation. Otherwise, the effect of changing one factor may be confounded with other changes (e.g., different random values from some input distribution) that inadvertently occur.

If one is trying to determine the sensitivity of the simulation output to changes in two or more factors of interest, then it is not correct, in general, to vary one factor at a time while setting the other factors to some arbitrary values. A more correct approach is to use statistical experimental design, which is discussed in Chap. 12. The effect of each factor can be formally estimated; and if the number of factors is not too large, interactions between factors can also be detected.

5.4.5 Validate the Output from the Overall Simulation Model

The most definitive test of a simulation model's validity is to establish that its output data closely resemble the output data that would be expected from the actual (proposed) system. This might be called *results validation* and, in this section, we will discuss several ways that it could be carried out.

Comparison with an Existing System

If a system similar to the proposed one now exists, then a simulation model of the existing system is developed and its output data are compared to those from the existing system itself. If the two sets of data compare "closely," then the model of the *existing* system is considered "valid." (The accuracy required from the model will depend on its intended use and the utility function of the manager.) The model is then modified so that it represents the proposed system. The greater the commonality between the existing and proposed systems, the greater our confidence in the model of the proposed system. There is no completely definitive approach for validating the model of the proposed system. If there were, there might be no need for a simulation model in the first place. If the above comparison is successful, then it has the additional benefit of providing credibility for the use of simulation (see Example 5.27). The comparison of the model and system output data could be done using numerical statistics such as the sample mean, the sample variance, and the sample correlation function. Alternatively, the assessment could be made by using graphical plots (see Example 5.30) such as histograms, distribution functions, box plots, and spider-web plots (called radar plots in Microsoft Excel).

EXAMPLE 5.27. We performed a simulation study for the corporate headquarters of a manufacturer of paper products. A particular manufacturing plant for this company currently had two machines of a certain type, and local management wanted to purchase a third machine. The goal of the study was to see whether the additional machine was really needed. To validate our model, we first simulated the existing system with two machines. The model and system throughputs for the two machines differed by 0.4 and 1.1 percent, while the machine utilizations differed by 1.7 and 11 percent. (The relatively large error of 11 percent was caused by the second machine operator's not following company policy.) Using the "validated" simulation model, we simulated the system with three machines and found that the additional machine was not necessary. Based on the *credible* simulation results, the vice president for manufacturing of the entire company rejected the plant's request for a new machine, resulting in a capital avoidance of \$1.4 million.

EXAMPLE 5.28. A U.S. Air Force test agency performed a simulation study for a wing of bombers using the Logistics Composite Model (LCOM). The ultimate goal of the study was to evaluate the effect of various proposed logistics policies on the availability of the bombers, i.e., the proportion of time that the bombers were available to fly missions. Data were available from the actual operations of the wing over a 9-month period, and they included both failure data for various aircraft components and the wing availability. To validate the model, the Air Force first simulated the 9-month period with the existing logistics policy. The model availability differed from

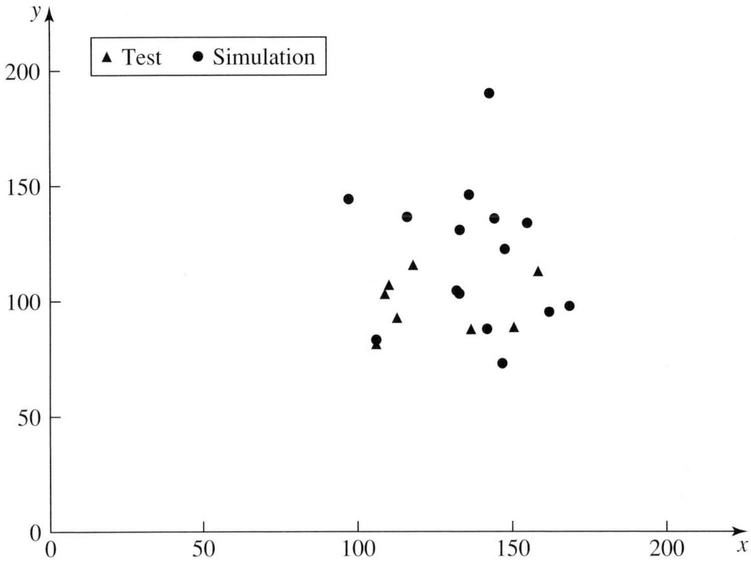

FIGURE 5.2
Impact points for the test and simulated missiles (in feet).

the historical availability by less than 3 percent, providing strong evidence for the validity of the model.

EXAMPLE 5.29. A major manufacturer of telecommunications switches submitted a prototype switch to an artificial traffic stream (e.g., exponential interarrival times) in a laboratory. A simulation model of the switch was then submitted to the same traffic stream, and comparable model and system performance measures were compared. The closeness of the respective measures gave the model developers confidence in the validity of the model.

EXAMPLE 5.30. A hypothetical new ground-to-ground missile is being developed by the U.S. Army. Eight prototype missiles were field tested for the *same* scenario (and set of environmental conditions), and their impact points in an xy coordinate system were recorded. A simulation model for the missile system was developed, 15 independent replications of the model were made for the same scenario using different random numbers, and the corresponding impact points were computed. The impact points for the test and simulated missiles (in feet) are plotted in Fig. 5.2. It appears from the figure that the simulated missiles are less accurate than the test missiles, but it would be desirable to have further substantiation. We next computed the miss distance d for each test missile and each simulated missile using the Pythagorean theorem, which states that

$$d = \sqrt{x^2 + y^2}$$

The resulting miss distances (in feet) are given in Table 5.4, where it's seen that the average miss distance for the simulated missiles is 14.7 percent larger than the average miss distance for the test missiles. A spider-web plot for the miss distances is given in Fig. 5.3.

TABLE 5.4
Miss distances *d* for the test and simulated missiles (in feet)

Missile number	Test miss distance	Simulation miss distance
1	174.45	134.60
2	146.09	194.73
3	194.72	168.14
4	149.84	178.82
5	161.93	163.78
6	165.52	186.39
7	153.62	237.20
8	133.46	187.73
9	—	197.90
10	—	173.55
11	—	166.64
12	—	199.10
13	—	168.17
14	—	204.32
15	—	191.48
Sample mean	159.95	183.50
Sample variance	355.75	545.71

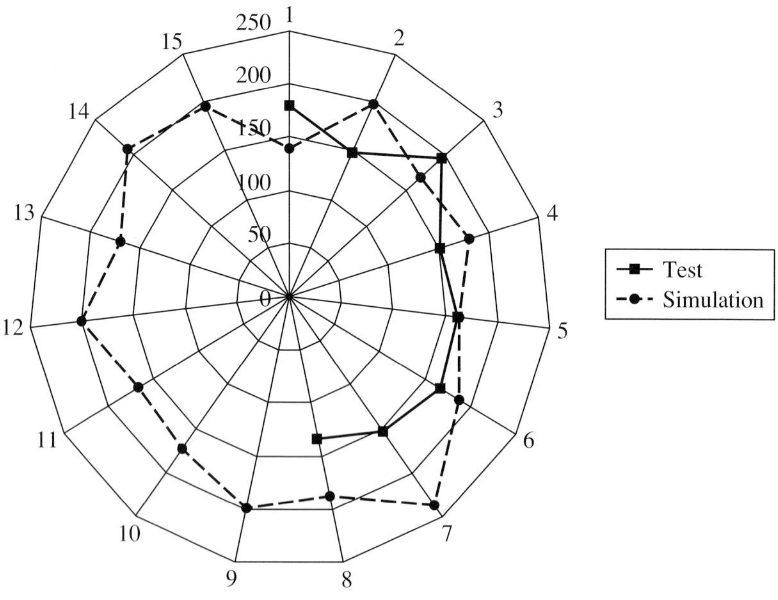

FIGURE 5.3
Spider-web plot for the test and simulation miss distances.

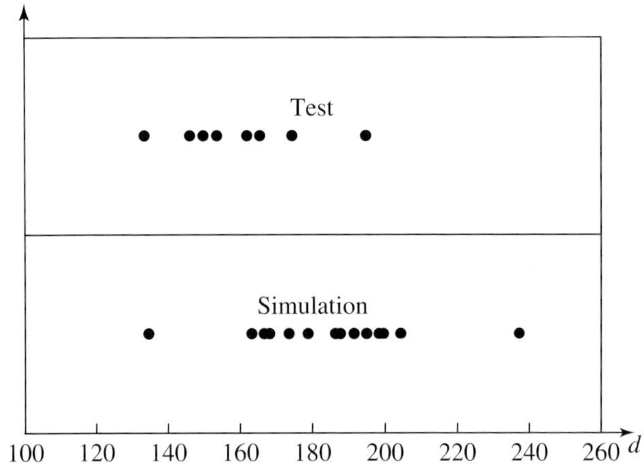

FIGURE 5.4
Dot plots for the test and simulation miss distances.

The numbers 50, 100, . . . , 250 are the miss distances, and the numbers 1, 2, . . . , 15 are the missile numbers. It is clear from this plot that the simulation miss distances are, in general, larger than the test miss distances. Dot plots for the miss distances are given in Fig. 5.4. It follows from these plots that the simulation miss distances have a larger mean (central tendency) and variance (spread) than the test miss distances. In summary, based on the sample means, the sample variances, and the three plots, it appears that the model does not provide a valid representation of the prototype missile relative to the criterion of miss distance. However, we will revisit this example in Sec. 5.6.2.

In addition to statistical procedures, one can use a *Turing test* [see Turing (1950), Schruben (1980), and Carson (1986)] to compare the output data from the model to those from the system. People knowledgeable about the system (e.g., engineers or managers) are asked to examine one or more sets of system data as well as one or more sets of model data, without knowing which sets are which. Each data set should be presented on a separate piece of paper using exactly the same format. If these SMEs can differentiate between the system and model data, their explanation of how they were able to do so is used to improve the model.

EXAMPLE 5.31. Schruben (1980) reports the use of a Turing test in a simulation study of an automobile-component factory. Data from the factory and from the simulation were put on time-study forms and reviewed at a meeting by three managers, three industrial engineers, and two factory workers. The inability of these people to agree on which data were real and which were simulated led to immediate acceptance of the simulation model.

EXAMPLE 5.32. An animation version of the Turing test was used in validating a simulation model of microscopic vehicle flow on a freeway. An animation of traffic flow from the simulation was displayed simultaneously on a large-screen monitor with an animation produced from data collected from the actual freeway. The data from the freeway were collected by a video camera mounted on an airplane.

Up to now, we have discussed validating a simulation model relative to past or present system output data; however, a perhaps more definitive test of a model is to establish its ability to predict *future* system behavior. Since models often evolve over time and are used for multiple applications (particularly legacy models within the DoD), there is often an opportunity for such *prospective* validation. For example, if a model is used to decide which version of a proposed system to build, then after the system has been built and sufficient time has elapsed for output data to be collected, these data can be compared with the predictions of the model. If there is reasonable agreement, we have increased confidence in the "validity" of the model. On the other hand, discrepancies between the two data sets should be used to update the model. Regardless of the accuracy of a model's past predictions, a model should be carefully scrutinized before each new application, since a change in purpose or the passage of time may have invalidated some aspect of the existing model. This once again points out the need for good documentation of the model.

Suppose that we compare the output data from an existing system with those from a simulation model of that system and find significant discrepancies. If these discrepancies or other information *objectively* suggests how to improve the model, then these changes should be made and the simulation rerun. If the new simulation output data compare closely with the system output data, then the model can be considered "valid."

Suppose instead that there are major discrepancies between the system and model output data, but that changes are made to the model, somewhat without justification (e.g., some parameter is "tweaked"), and the resulting output data are again compared with the system output data. This procedure, which we call *calibration* of a model, is continued until the two data sets agree closely. However, we must ask whether this procedure produces a valid model for the system, in general, or whether the model is only representative of this particular set of input data. To answer this question (in effect, to validate the model), one can use a completely independent set of system input and output data. The calibrated model might be driven by the second set of input data (in a manner similar to that described in Sec. 5.6.1) and the resulting model output data compared with the second set of system output data. This idea of using one set of data for calibration and another independent set for validation is fairly common in economics and the biological sciences. In particular, it was used by the Crown Zellerbach Corporation in developing a simulation model of tree growth. Here the system data were available from the U.S. Forest Service.

EXAMPLE 5.33. In order to make the idea of model calibration clearer, consider the *xy* data in Table 5.5, which are also plotted in Fig. 5.5. A linear regression model and a sixth-degree polynomial regression model were each fit to the data using the method of least squares, and both are also plotted in Fig. 5.5. Note that the linear model does not go through any of the seven points, but that the *calibrated* polynomial model goes through each of the points exactly. (The R^2 values are 0.97 and 1, respectively.) Thus, in this sense, the polynomial model provides a better fit to the data.

TABLE 5.5
Data for calibration example

x	y
1.1	5.5
2.3	6.1
3.2	10.1
4.5	11.7
5.9	15.1
6.4	16.8
7.1	19.4

If we use the two models to *predict* the value of y for $x' = 1.5$, then the linear and (over-fit) polynomial models give 5.46 and 2.86, respectively, with the former prediction appearing to be much more reasonable.

Comparison with Expert Opinion

Whether or not there is an existing system, SMEs should review the simulation results for reasonableness. (Care must be taken in performing this exercise, since if one knew exactly what output to expect, there would be no need for a model.) If the simulation results are consistent with perceived system behavior, then the model is said to have *face validity*.

EXAMPLE 5.34. The above idea was put to good use in the development of a simulation model of the U.S. Air Force manpower and personnel system. (This model was

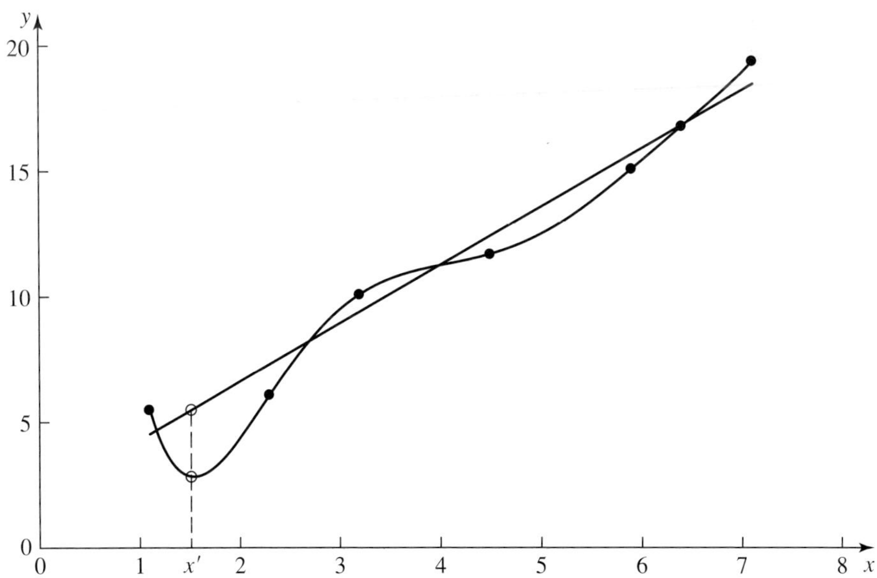

FIGURE 5.5
Linear and sixth-degree polynomial regression models fit to data, and their predictions for $x' = 1.5$.

designed to provide Air Force policy analysts with a systemwide view of the effects of various proposed personnel policies.) The model was run under the baseline personnel policy, and the results were shown to Air Force analysts and decision makers, who subsequently identified some discrepancies between the model and perceived system behavior. This information was used to improve the model, and after several additional evaluations and improvements, a model was obtained that appeared to approximate current Air Force policy closely. This exercise improved not only the validity of the model, but also its credibility.

Comparison with Another Model

Suppose that another model was developed for the same system and for a "similar" purpose, and that it is thought to be a "valid" representation. Then numerical statistics or graphical plots for the model that is currently of interest can be informally compared with the comparable statistics or graphical plots from the other model. Alternatively, the confidence-interval procedures discussed in Sec. 10.2 can be used to make a more formal comparison between the two models. It should be kept in mind that just because two models produce similar results doesn't necessarily mean that either model is valid, since both models could contain a similar error.

EXAMPLE 5.35. A defense supply center was building a new simulation model called the Performance and Requirements Impact Simulation to replace an existing model. One of the purposes of both models is to decide when to order and how much to order for each stock number. To validate the *old model,* the total dollar amount of all orders placed by the model for fiscal year 1996 was compared with the total dollar amount for the actual system for the same time period. Since these dollar amounts differed by less than 3 percent, there was a fair amount of confidence in the validity of the old model. To validate the *new model*, the two models were used to predict the total dollar amount of all orders for fiscal year 1998, and the results differed by less than 6 percent. Thus, there was reasonable confidence in the validity of the new model.

In Example 5.35, it probably would have been a good idea for the simulation analysts to also use a smaller level of aggregation for validation purposes, such as the dollar amounts for certain categories of stock numbers. (It is possible that positive errors for some categories might cancel out negative errors for other categories.) Also, it would have been interesting to compare the total dollar amounts for all orders placed by the two models in 1996.

5.4.6 Animation

An animation can be an effective way to find invalid model assumptions and to enhance the credibility of a simulation model.

EXAMPLE 5.36. A simulation model was developed for a candy packaging system. A newly promoted operations manager, who had no familiarity with the simulation model, declared, "That's my system!" upon seeing an animation of his system for the first time—the model gained instant credibility.

5.5 MANAGEMENT'S ROLE IN THE SIMULATION PROCESS

The manager of the system of interest must have a basic understanding of simulation and be aware that a successful simulation study requires a commitment of his or her *time* and resources. The following are some of the responsibilities of the manager:

- Formulating problem objectives
- Directing personnel to provide information and data to the simulation modeler and to attend the structured walk-through
- Interacting with the simulation modeler on a regular basis
- Using the simulation results as an aid in the decision-making process

Simulation studies require the use of an organization's technical personnel for some period of time. If the study is done in-house, then several company personnel may be required full-time for several months. These people often have other jobs such as being responsible for the day-to-day operations of a manufacturing system. Even if a consultant does the study, company personnel must be involved in the modeling process and may also be needed to collect data.

5.6 STATISTICAL PROCEDURES FOR COMPARING REAL-WORLD OBSERVATIONS AND SIMULATION OUTPUT DATA

In this section we present statistical procedures that might be useful for carrying out the comparison of model and system output data (see Sec. 5.4.5).

Suppose that $R_1, R_2, \ldots, R_k$ are observations from a real-world system and that $M_1, M_2, \ldots, M_l$ are output data from a corresponding simulation model (see Example 5.37). We would like to compare the two data sets in some way to determine whether the model is an accurate representation of the real-world system. The first approach that comes to mind is to use one of the classical statistical tests (t, Mann-Whitney, two-sample chi-square, two-sample Kolmogorov-Smirnov, etc.) to determine whether the underlying distributions of the two data sets can be safely regarded as being the same. [For a good discussion of these tests, which assume *IID data,* see Breiman (1973) and Conover (1999).] However, the output processes of almost all real-world systems and simulations are *nonstationary* (the distributions of the successive observations change over time) and *autocorrelated* (the observations in the process are correlated with each other), and thus none of these tests is *directly* applicable. Furthermore, we question whether hypothesis tests, as compared with constructing confidence intervals for differences, are even the appropriate statistical approach. Since the model is only an approximation to the actual system, a null hypothesis that the system and model are the "same" is clearly false. We believe that it is more useful to ask whether the differences between the system and the model are significant enough to affect any conclusions derived from the model. In Secs. 5.6.1 through 5.6.3 we discuss, respectively, inspection, confidence-interval, and time-series approaches to this comparison problem. Finally, two additional approaches based on regression analysis and bootstrapping are discussed in Sec. 5.6.4.

5.6.1 Inspection Approach

The approach that seems to be used by most simulation practitioners who attempt the aforementioned comparison is to compute one or more numerical statistics from the real-world observations and corresponding statistics from the model output data, and then compare the two sets of statistics without the use of a formal statistical procedure (see Examples 5.27 and 5.28). Examples of statistics that might be used for this purpose are the sample mean, the sample variance (see Sec. 4.4 for a discussion of the danger in using the sample variance from autocorrelated data), and the sample correlation function. (The comparison of graphical plots can also be quite useful, as we saw in Example 5.30.) The difficulty with this inspection approach, which is graphically illustrated in Example 5.37, is that each statistic is essentially a sample of size 1 from some underlying population, making this idea particularly vulnerable to the inherent randomness of the observations from both the real system and the simulation model.

EXAMPLE 5.37. To illustrate the danger of using inspection, suppose that the real-world system of interest is the $M/M/1$ queue with $\rho = 0.6$ and that the corresponding simulation model is the $M/M/1$ queue with $\rho = 0.5$; in both cases the arrival rate is 1. Suppose that the output process of interest is $D_1, D_2, \ldots$ (where D_i is the delay in queue of the ith customer) and let

$$X = \frac{\sum_{i=1}^{200} D_i}{200} \qquad \text{for the system}$$

and

$$Y = \frac{\sum_{i=1}^{200} D_i}{200} \qquad \text{for the model}$$

(Thus, the number of observations for the system, k, and for the model, l, are both equal to 200.) We shall attempt to determine how good a representation the model is for the system for comparing an estimate for $\mu_Y = E(Y) = 0.49$ [the expected average delay of the first 200 customers for the model; see Heathcote and Winer (1969) for a discussion of how to compute $E(Y)$] with an estimate of $\mu_X = E(X) = 0.87$. Table 5.6 gives the results of three independent simulation experiments, each corresponding to a possible application of the inspection approach. For each experiment, $\hat{\mu}_X$ and $\hat{\mu}_Y$ represent the sample mean of the 200 delays for the system and model, respectively, and $\hat{\mu}_X - \hat{\mu}_Y$

TABLE 5.6
Results for three experiments with the inspection approach

Experiment	$\hat{\mu}_X$	$\hat{\mu}_Y$	$\hat{\mu}_X - \hat{\mu}_Y$
1	0.90	0.70	0.20
2	0.70	0.71	−0.01
3	1.08	0.35	0.73

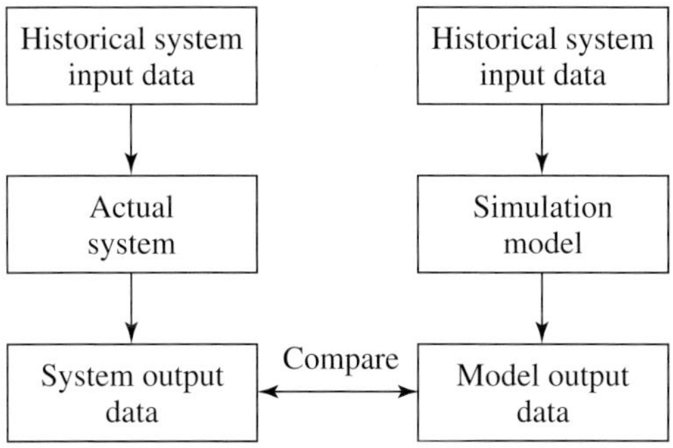

FIGURE 5.6
The correlated inspection approach.

is an estimate of $\mu_X - \mu_Y = 0.38$, which is what we are really trying to estimate. Note that $\hat{\mu}_X - \hat{\mu}_Y$ varies greatly from experiment to experiment. Also observe for experiment 2 that $\hat{\mu}_X - \hat{\mu}_Y = -0.01$, which would tend to lead one to think that the model is a good representation for the system. However, we believe that the model is really a poor representation for the system for purposes of estimation of the expected average delay in the real-world system, since μ_Y is nearly 44 percent smaller than μ_X.

Because of the inherent danger in using the *basic inspection approach* presented above, we now describe a better approach for comparing system and model output data if the system data are complete enough and in the right format. In particular, it is recommended that the system and model be compared by "driving" the model with historical system input data (e.g., actual observed interarrival times and service times), rather than samples from the input probability distributions, and then comparing the model and system outputs; see Fig. 5.6. (The system outputs are those corresponding to the historical system input data.) Thus, the system and the model experience *exactly the same observations* from the input random variables, which should result in a statistically more precise comparison. We call this idea the *correlated inspection approach*, since it generally results in comparable model and system output statistics being positively correlated. This approach is a more definitive way to validate the *assumptions of the simulation model* other than the probability distributions; the latter are validated by using the techniques of Chap. 6. (Note that a simulation that is driven by historical input data is sometimes called a *trace-driven simulation.*)

EXAMPLE 5.38. To illustrate the benefits of the correlated inspection approach, suppose that the system is the five-teller bank of Sec. 2.6 with jockeying, and the model is the same bank but without jockeying (i.e., customers never leave the line they originally join). Assume, however, that the mean service time is now 4 minutes. Let

$$X = \text{average delay in queue for system}$$

and

$$Y = \text{average delay in queue for model}$$

We will attempt to determine the accuracy of the model by comparing an estimate of the expected average delay for the model $\mu_Y = E(Y)$ with an estimate of the expected average delay for the system $\mu_X = E(X)$. Table 5.7 gives the results from the first 10 of 500

TABLE 5.7
Results for the first 10 of 500 experiments with the correlated and basic inspection approaches, and a summary for all 500

Experiment j	X_j	Y_j	Y'_j	$X_j - Y_j$	$X_j - Y'_j$
1	3.06	3.81	2.62	−0.75	0.44
2	2.79	3.37	2.05	−0.58	0.74
3	2.21	2.61	4.56	−0.40	−2.35
4	2.54	3.59	1.86	−1.05	0.68
5	9.27	11.02	2.41	−1.75	6.86
6	3.09	3.75	1.85	−0.66	1.24
7	2.50	2.84	1.13	−0.34	1.37
8	0.31	0.71	3.12	−0.40	−2.81
9	3.17	3.94	5.09	−0.77	−1.92
10	0.98	1.18	1.25	−0.20	−0.27
Sample mean of all 500	2.10	2.85	2.70	−0.75	−0.60
Sample variance of all 500	2.02	2.28	2.12	0.08	4.08

independent experiments, each corresponding to a possible application of the correlated inspection approach. There, X_j and Y_j are the average delay for the system and for the model in the jth experiment, respectively, and $X_j - Y_j$ is an estimate of $\mu_X - \mu_Y$, which is what we are really trying to estimate. (Note that X_j and Y_j use exactly the same interarrival times and service times; they differ only in the jockeying rule employed.) Also given in the table are Y'_j, the average delay for the model in the jth experiment when *independent* random numbers are used to generate the interarrival times and service times, and $X_j - Y'_j$, whose mean is also $\mu_X - \mu_Y$. [Note that X_j and Y'_j are based on independent (and thus different) realizations of the same input probability distributions.] Comparing Y'_j and X_j corresponds approximately to an application of the basic inspection approach. (In an actual application of the basic inspection approach, the input probability distributions would not be known and would have to be estimated from system input data.) Finally, the last two rows of the table give the usual sample mean and sample variance for each column computed from *all 500* experiments. Observe from the table that $X_j - Y_j$ is a much better estimator of $\mu_X - \mu_Y$ than is $X_j - Y'_j$, since it has a considerably smaller variance (0.08 versus 4.08). Thus, the difference $X - Y$ for a particular application of the correlated inspection approach is likely to be much closer to $\mu_X - \mu_Y$ than the difference $X - Y'$ for a particular application of the basic inspection approach.

We now explain more clearly why $\text{Var}(X - Y)$ is less than $\text{Var}(X - Y')$. In particular, if A and B are random variables, then it can be shown (see Prob. 4.13) that

$$\text{Var}(A - B) = \text{Var}(A) + \text{Var}(B) - 2\,\text{Cov}(A, B)$$

In the case of the basic inspection approach, $A = X$, $B = Y'$, $\text{Cov}(X, Y') = 0$ (the estimated value was 0.03; see Prob. 4.29), and thus

$$\text{Var}(X - Y') = \text{Var}(X) + \text{Var}(Y')$$

For the correlated inspection approach, $A = X$, $B = Y$, $\widehat{\text{Cov}}(X, Y) = 2.11$ [$\widehat{\text{Cor}}(X, Y) = 0.99$] and thus

$$\begin{aligned} \text{Var}(X - Y) &= \text{Var}(X) + \text{Var}(Y) - 2\,\text{Cov}(X, Y) \\ &= \text{Var}(X) + \text{Var}(Y') - 2\,\text{Cov}(X, Y) \\ &< \text{Var}(X - Y') \end{aligned}$$

assuming that the sign of the true covariance is the same as that of its estimate.

The idea of comparing a model and the corresponding system under the same statistical conditions is similar to the use of the variance-reduction technique known as common random numbers in simulation (see Sec. 11.2) and the use of blocking in statistical experimental design. It should be mentioned, however, that we do not recommend using historical system input data to drive a model for the purpose of making *production* runs (see Sec. 6.1).

EXAMPLE 5.39. The correlated inspection approach was used to help validate a simulation model of a cigarette manufacturing process at Brown & Williamson Tobacco Company [see Carson (1986) and Carson et al. (1981) for details]. The manufacturing system basically consists of a cigarette maker, a reservoir (buffer) for cigarettes, a packer, and a cartoner. The maker and packer are subject to frequent product-induced failures such as the cigarette paper's tearing. The major objective of the study was to determine the optimal capacity of the reservoir, which helps lessen the effect of the above failures.

The existing system was observed over a 4-hour period, and time-to-failure and time-to-repair data were collected for the maker and packer, as well as the total cigarette production. These times to failure and times to repair were used to drive the simulation model for a 4-hour simulation run, and the total model cigarette production was observed. The fact that the model production differed from the actual production by only 1 percent helped convince management of the model's validity.

EXAMPLE 5.40. For the freeway simulation of Example 5.32, the correlated inspection approach was used to compare the average travel time for the simulation model and the system. The model was driven by car entry times, speeds, lanes, etc., that were observed from the actual system.

In summary, we believe that the inspection approach may provide valuable insight into the adequacy of a simulation model for some simulation studies (particularly if the correlated approach can be used). As a matter of fact, for most studies it will be the only feasible statistical approach because of severe limitations on the amount of data available on the operation of the real system. However, as Example 5.37 shows, extreme care must be used in interpreting the results of this approach (especially the basic version).

5.6.2 Confidence-Interval Approach Based on Independent Data

We now describe a more reliable approach for comparing a model with the corresponding system for the situation where it is possible to collect a potentially large number of sets of data from both the system and the model. This might be the case, e.g., when the system of interest is located in a laboratory (see Example 5.29). This approach will not, however, be feasible for most military and manufacturing situations due to the paucity of real-world data.

In the spirit of terminating simulations (see Secs. 9.3 and 9.4, and Chap. 10), suppose we collect m independent sets of data from the system and n independent sets of data from the model. Let X_j be a random variable defined on the jth set of system data, and let Y_j be the same random variable defined on the jth set of model data. (For Example 5.38, X_j is the average delay in queue for the system from experiment j.) The X_j's are IID random variables (assuming that the m sets of system data are homogeneous) with mean $\mu_X = E(X_j)$, and the Y_j's are IID random variables (assuming that the n data sets for the model were produced by independent replications) with mean $\mu_Y = E(Y_j)$. We will attempt to compare the model with the system by constructing a confidence interval for $\zeta = \mu_X - \mu_Y$. We believe that constructing a confidence interval for ζ is preferable to testing the null hypothesis H_0: $\mu_X = \mu_Y$ for the following reasons:

- Since the model is only an approximation to the system, H_0 will clearly be *false* in almost all cases.
- A confidence interval provides more information than the corresponding hypothesis test. If the hypothesis test indicates that $\mu_X \neq \mu_Y$, then the confidence interval will provide this information and also give an indication of the magnitude by which μ_X differs from μ_Y. Constructing a confidence interval for ζ is a special case of the problem of comparing two systems by means of a confidence interval, as discussed in Sec. 10.2. Thus, we may construct a confidence interval for ζ by using either the paired-t approach or the Welch approach. (In the notation of Sec. 10.2, $n_1 = m$, $n_2 = n$, $X_{1j} = X_j$, and $X_{2j} = Y_j$.) The paired-t approach requires $m = n$ but allows X_j to be correlated with Y_j, which would be the case if the idea underlying the correlated inspection approach is used (see Sec. 5.6.1). The Welch approach can be used for any values of $m \geq 2$ and $n \geq 2$ but requires that the X_j's be independent of the Y_j's.

Runciman, Vagenas, and Corkal (1997) used the paired-t approach to help validate a model of underground mining operations. For their model X_j was the average number of tons of ore hauled per shift for month j ($j = 1, 2, 3$).

Suppose that we have constructed a $100(1 - \alpha)$ percent confidence interval for ζ by using either the paired-t or Welch approach, and we let $l(\alpha)$ and $u(\alpha)$ be the corresponding lower and upper confidence-interval endpoints, respectively. If $0 \notin [l(\alpha), u(\alpha)]$, then the observed difference between μ_X and μ_Y, that is, $\bar{X}(m) - \bar{Y}(n)$, is said to be *statistically significant* at level α. This is equivalent to rejecting the null hypothesis H_0: $\mu_X = \mu_Y$ in favor of the two-sided alternative hypothesis H_1: $\mu_X \neq \mu_Y$ at the same level α. If $0 \in [l(\alpha), u(\alpha)]$, any observed difference between μ_X and μ_Y is not statistically significant at level α and might be explained by sampling fluctuation. Even if the observed difference between μ_X and μ_Y is statistically significant, this need not mean that the model is, for practical purposes, an "invalid" representation of the system. For example, if $\zeta = 1$ but $\mu_X = 1000$ and $\mu_Y = 999$, then the difference that exists between the model and the system is probably of no practical consequence regardless of whether we detect statistical significance. We shall say that the difference between a model and a system is *practically significant* if the "magnitude" of the difference is large enough to invalidate any inferences about the system that would be derived from the model. Clearly, the decision as to whether the difference between a model and a system is practically significant is a subjective one, depending on such factors as the purpose of the model and the utility function of the person who is going to use the model.

If the length of the confidence interval for ζ is not small enough to decide practical significance, it will be necessary to obtain additional X_j's or Y_j's (or both). Note, however, that for the Welch approach it is not possible to make the confidence interval arbitrarily small by adding only X_j's or only Y_j's. Thus, if the number of sets of system data, m, cannot be increased, it may not be possible to determine practical significance by just making more and more replications of the model.

EXAMPLE 5.41. Suppose that X_j and Y_j are defined as in Example 5.38, and we would like to construct a 90 percent confidence interval for $\zeta = \mu_X - \mu_Y$ using the paired-t approach to determine whether the model (no jockeying) is an accurate representation of the system (with jockeying). Letting $W_j = X_j - Y_j$ and $m = n = 10$, we obtained from the first 10 rows of Table 5.7 the following:

$$\overline{W}(10) = \overline{X}(10) - \overline{Y}(10) = 2.99 - 3.68 = -0.69 \qquad \text{(point estimate for } \zeta)$$

$$\widehat{\text{Var}}[\overline{W}(10)] = \frac{\sum_{j=1}^{10} [W_j - \overline{W}(10)]^2}{(10)(9)} = 0.02$$

and the 90 percent confidence interval for ζ is

$$\overline{W}(10) \pm t_{9,0.95}\sqrt{\widehat{\text{Var}}[\overline{W}(10)]} = -0.69 \pm 0.26$$

or $[-0.95, -0.43]$. Since the interval does not contain 0, the observed difference between μ_X and μ_Y is statistically significant. It remains to decide the practical significance of such a difference.

EXAMPLE 5.42. Consider the missile system and corresponding simulation model of Example 5.30. Let

$$X_j = \text{miss distance for } j\text{th test missile } (j = 1, 2, \ldots, 8)$$

$$Y_j = \text{miss distance for } j\text{th simulated missile } (j = 1, 2, \ldots, 15)$$

Since $m = 8 \neq 15 = n$, we will use the Welch approach (see Sec. 10.2.2) to construct a 95 percent confidence interval for $\zeta = \mu_X - \mu_Y$. We get

$$\overline{X}(8) = 159.95, \qquad \overline{Y}(15) = 183.50$$

$$S_X^2(8) = 355.75, \qquad S_Y^2(15) = 545.71$$

$$\hat{f} = 17.34 \text{ (estimated degrees of freedom)}$$

and a 95 percent confidence for $\zeta = \mu_X - \mu_Y$ is

$$\overline{X}(8) - \overline{Y}(15) \pm t_{\hat{f},0.975}\sqrt{\frac{S_X^2(8)}{8} + \frac{S_Y^2(15)}{15}} = -23.55 \pm 18.97$$

or $[-42.52, -4.58]$. Since the interval does not contain 0, the observed difference between the mean miss distance for the test missile and the mean miss distance for the simulated missile is statistically significant. The practical significance of such a difference must be determined by the relevant SMEs.

Two difficulties with the above replication approach are that it may require a large amount of data (each set of output data produces only one "observation") and that it provides no information about the autocorrelation structures of the two output processes (if of interest).

5.6.3 Time-Series Approaches

In this section we briefly discuss three time-series approaches for comparing model output data with system output data. [A *time series* is a finite realization of a stochastic process. For example, the delays $D_1, D_2, \ldots, D_{200}$ from a queueing model (see Example 5.37) or system form a time series.] These approaches require only one set of each type of output data and may also yield information on the autocorrelation structures of the two output processes. Thus, the two difficulties of the replication approach mentioned above are not present here. There are, however, other significant difficulties.

The *spectral-analysis* approach [see Fishman and Kiviat (1967) and Naylor (1971, p. 247)] proceeds by computing the sample spectrum, i.e., the Fourier cosine transformation of the estimated autocovariance function, of each output process and then using existing theory to construct a confidence interval for the difference of the logarithms of the two spectra. This confidence interval can potentially be used to assess the degree of similarity of the two autocorrelation functions. Two drawbacks of this approach are that it requires that the output processes be covariance-stationary (an assumption generally not satisfied in practice), and that a high level of mathematical sophistication is required to apply it. It is also difficult to relate this type of confidence interval to the validity of the simulation model.

Spectral analysis is a nonparametric approach in that it makes no assumptions about the distributions of the observations in the time series. Hsu and Hunter (1977) suggest an alternative approach, which consists of fitting a parametric time-series model [see Box, Jenkins, and Reinsel (2008)] to each set of output data and then applying a hypothesis test to see whether the two models appear to be the same. As stated above, we believe that a hypothesis-test approach is less desirable than one based on a confidence interval.

Chen and Sargent (1987) give a method for constructing a confidence interval for the difference between the steady-state mean of a system and the corresponding steady-state mean of the simulation model, based on Schruben's standardized time-series approach (see Sec. 9.5.3). An attractive feature of the method, compared with the approach in Sec. 5.6.2, is that only one set of output data is needed from the system and one set from the model. The method does, however, require that the two sets of output data be independent and satisfy certain other assumptions.

5.6.4 Other Approaches

Kleijnen, Bettonvil, and Van Groenendaal (1998) developed a hypothesis test based on regression analysis to test the composite null hypothesis that the model mean is equal to the system mean *and* the model variance is equal to the system variance, in the case of a *trace-driven simulation model* (see Sec 5.6.1). Their test assumes that n (normally distributed) IID observations are available from the system and n (normally distributed) IID observations are available from the model, with $n \geq 3$. Therefore, it would have to be applied in the same context as in Sec. 5.6.2. They evaluate the statistical properties of the test (i.e., the probability of a Type I error and the power) by performing experiments with the $M/M/1$ queue.

Kleijnen, Cheng, and Bettonvil (2000, 2001) developed a *distribution-free* hypothesis test based on bootstrapping [see, e.g., Efron and Tibshirani (1993)] to test the null hypothesis that the model mean is equal to the system mean, in the case of a trace-driven simulation model. Their test assumes that n IID observations are available from the system and sn IID observations are available from the model, with $n \geq 3$ and s a positive integer (e.g., 10) that is chosen by the user. Therefore, it would have to be applied in the same context as in Sec. 5.6.2. They evaluate the statistical properties of the test by performing experiments with the $M/M/1$ queue and other queueing systems.

Once again, we believe that it is preferable to use a confidence interval rather than a hypothesis test to validate a simulation model.

PROBLEMS

5.1. As stated in Sec. 5.4.1, care must be taken that data collected on a system are representative of what one actually wants to model. Discuss this potential problem with regard to a study that will involve observing the efficiency of workers on an assembly line for the purpose of building a simulation model.

5.2. Discuss why validating a model of a computer system might be easier than validating a military combat model. Assume that the computer system of interest is similar to an existing one.

5.3. If one constructs a confidence interval for $\zeta = \mu_X - \mu_Y$, using the confidence-interval approach of Sec. 5.6.2, which of the following outcomes are possible?

	Statistically significant	Practically significant
(*a*)	Yes	Yes
(*b*)	Yes	No
(c)	Yes	?
(*d*)	No	Yes
(*e*)	No	No
(*f*)	No	?

TABLE 6.1
Sources of randomness for common simulation applications

Type of system	Sources of randomness
Manufacturing	Processing times, machine times to failure, machine repair times
Defense-related	Arrival times and payloads of missiles or airplanes, outcome of an engagement, miss distances for munitions
Communications	Interarrival times of messages, message types, message lengths
Transportation	Ship-loading times, interarrival times of customers to a subway

Note that none of the four histograms has a symmetric shape like that of a normal distribution, despite the fact that many simulation practitioners and simulation books widely use normal input distributions.

We saw in Sec. 4.7 that it is generally necessary to represent each source of system randomness by a probability distribution (rather than just its mean) in the simulation model. The following example shows that failure to choose the "correct" distribution can also affect the accuracy of a model's results, sometimes drastically.

EXAMPLE 6.1. A single-server queueing system (e.g., a single machine in a factory) has exponential interarrival times with a mean of 1 minute. Suppose that 200 service times are available from the system, but their underlying probability distribution is

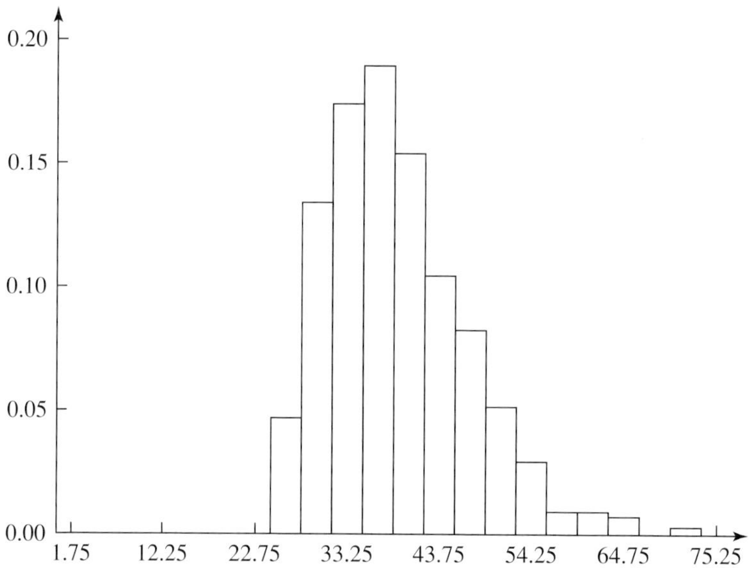

FIGURE 6.1
Histogram of 890 machine processing times for an automotive manufacturer.

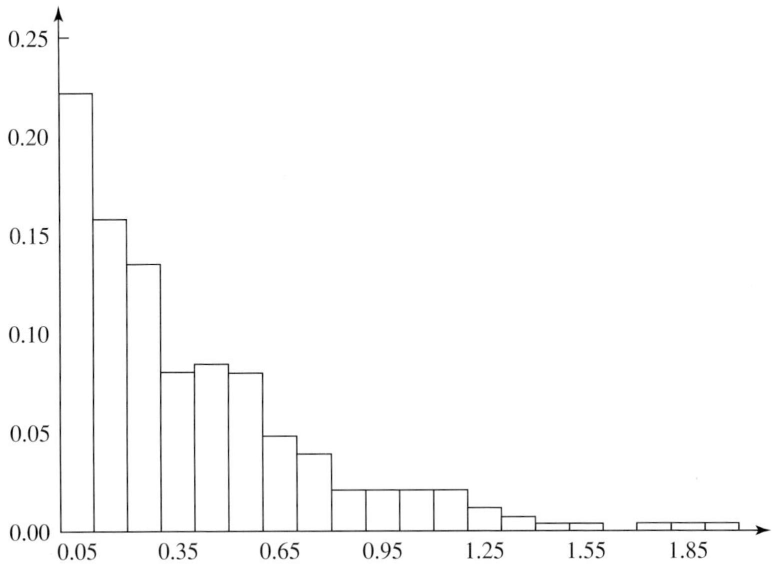

FIGURE 6.2
Histogram of 219 interarrival times to a drive-up bank.

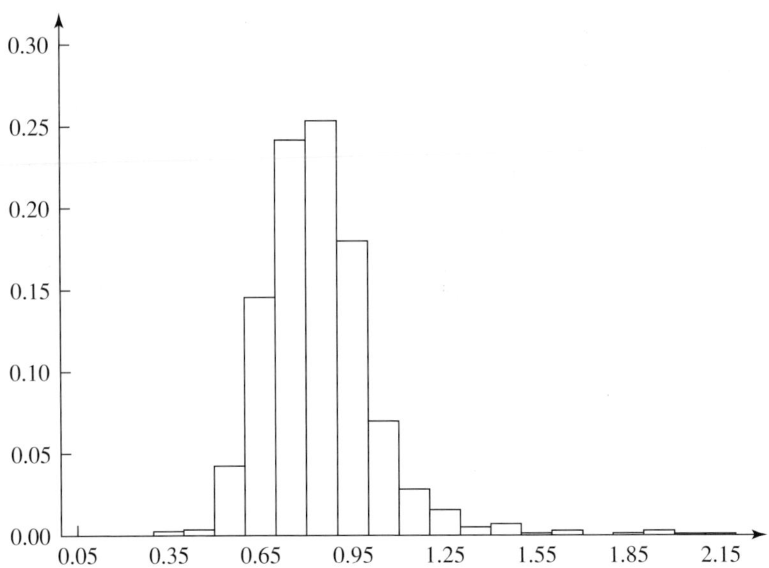

FIGURE 6.3
Histogram of 856 ship-loading times.

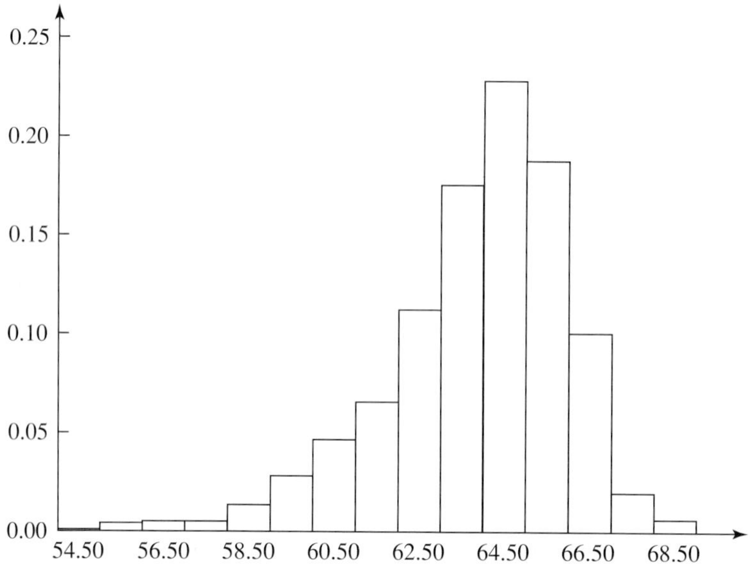

FIGURE 6.4
Histogram of the yardages for 1000 large rolls of paper for a household-products manufacturer.

unknown. Using an approach to be discussed in Sec. 6.5, we "fit" the "best" exponential, gamma, Weibull, lognormal, and normal distributions (see Sec. 6.2.2 for a discussion of these distributions) to the observed service-time data. (In the case of the exponential distribution, we chose the mean β so that the resulting distribution most closely "resembled" the available data.) We then made 100 independent simulation runs (i.e., different random numbers were used for each run, as discussed in Sec. 7.2) of the queueing system, using *each* of the five fitted distributions. (For the normal distribution, if a service time was negative, then it was generated again.) Each of the 500 simulation runs was continued until 1000 delays in queue were collected. A summary of the results from these simulation runs is given in Table 6.2. Note in the second column of the table that the average of the 100,000 delays is given for each of the service-time distributions (see Prob. 6.27). As we will see in Sec. 6.7, the Weibull distribution actually provides the best model for the service-time data. Thus, the average delay for the real system should be close to 4.36 minutes. On the other hand, the average delays for the normal and lognormal

TABLE 6.2
Simulation results for the five service-time distributions (in minutes where appropriate)

Service-time distribution	Average delay in queue	Average number in queue	Proportion of delays ≥20
Exponential	6.71	6.78	0.064
Gamma	4.54	4.60	0.019
Weibull	4.36	4.41	0.013
Lognormal	7.19	7.30	0.078
Normal	6.04	6.13	0.045

distributions are 6.04 and 7.19 minutes, respectively, corresponding to model output errors of 39 percent and 65 percent. This is particularly surprising for the lognormal distribution, since it has the same general shape (i.e., skewed to the right) as the Weibull distribution. However, it turns out that the lognormal distribution has a "thicker" right tail, which allows larger service times and delays to occur. The relative differences between the "tail probabilities" in column 4 of the table are even more significant. The choice of probability distributions can evidently have a large impact on the simulation output and, potentially, on the quality of the decisions made with the simulation results.

If it is possible to collect data on an input random variable of interest, these data can be used in one of the following approaches to specify a distribution (in increasing order of desirability):

1. The data values themselves are used directly in the simulation. For example, if the data represent service times, then one of the data values is used whenever a service time is needed in the simulation. This is sometimes called a *trace-driven simulation.*
2. The data values themselves are used to define an *empirical* distribution function (see Sec. 6.2.4) in some way. If these data represent service times, we would sample from this distribution when a service time is needed in the simulation.
3. Standard techniques of statistical inference are used to "fit" a *theoretical* distribution form (see Example 6.1), e.g., exponential or Poisson, to the data and to perform hypothesis tests to determine the goodness of fit. If a particular theoretical distribution with certain values for its parameters is a good model for the service-time data, then we would sample from this distribution when a service time is needed in the simulation.

Two drawbacks of approach 1 are that the simulation can only reproduce what has happened historically and that there is seldom enough data to make all the desired simulation runs. Approach 2 avoids these shortcomings since, at least for continuous data, any value between the minimum and maximum observed data points can be generated (see Sec. 8.3.16). Thus, approach 2 is generally preferable to approach 1. However, approach 1 does have its uses. For example, suppose that it is desired to compare a proposed material-handling system with the existing system for a distribution center. For each incoming order there is an arrival time, a list of the desired products, and a quantity for each product. Modeling a stream of orders for a certain period of time (e.g., for 1 month) will be difficult, if not impossible, using approach 2 or 3. Thus, in this case the existing and proposed systems will often be simulated using the historical order stream. Approach 1 is also recommended for *model validation* when model output for an existing system is compared with the corresponding output for the system itself. (See the discussion of the correlated inspection approach in Sec. 5.6.1.)

If a theoretical distribution can be found that fits the observed data reasonably well (approach 3), then this will generally be preferable to using an empirical distribution (approach 2) for the following reasons:

- An empirical distribution function may have certain "irregularities," particularly if only a small number of data values are available. A theoretical distribution, on the other hand, "smooths out" the data and may provide information on the overall underlying distribution.

- If empirical distributions are used in the *usual* way (see Sec. 6.2.4), it is not possible to generate values outside the range of the observed data in the simulation (see Sec. 8.3.16). This is unfortunate, since many measures of performance for simulated systems depend heavily on the probability of an "extreme" event's occurring, e.g., generation of a very large service time. With a fitted theoretical distribution, however, values outside the range of the observed data can be generated.
- There may be a compelling physical reason in some situations for using a certain theoretical distribution form as a model for a particular input random variable (see, for example, Sec. 6.12.1). Even when we are fortunate enough to have this kind of information, it is a good idea to use observed data to provide empirical support for the use of this particular distribution.
- A theoretical distribution is a compact way of representing a set of data values. Conversely, if n data values are available from a continuous distribution, then $2n$ values (e.g., data and corresponding cumulative probabilities) must be entered and stored in the computer to represent an empirical distribution in simulation packages. Thus, use of an empirical distribution will be cumbersome if the data set is large.
- A theoretical distribution is easier to change. For example, suppose that a set of interarrival times is found to be modeled well by an exponential distribution with a mean of 1 minute. If we want to determine the effect on the simulated system of increasing the arrival rate by 10 percent, then all we have to do is to change the mean of the exponential distribution to 0.909.

There are definitely situations for which no theoretical distribution will provide an adequate fit for the observed data, including the following:

- The data are a mixture of two or more heterogeneous populations (see the discussion of machine repair times in Sec. 6.4.2).
- The times to perform some task have been significantly rounded (effectively making the data discrete), and there are not enough distinct values in the sample to allow any continuous theoretical distribution to provide a good representation.

In situations where no theoretical distribution is appropriate, we recommend using an empirical distribution. Another possible drawback of theoretical distributions (e.g., lognormal) is that arbitrarily large values can be generated, albeit with a very small probability. Thus, if it is known that a random variable can never take on values larger than b, then it might be desirable to truncate the fitted theoretical distribution at b (see Sec. 6.8). For example, it might be known that a service time in a bank is extremely unlikely to exceed 15 minutes.

The remainder of this chapter discusses various topics related to the selection of input distributions. Section 6.2 discusses how theoretical distributions are parameterized, provides a compendium of relevant facts on most of the commonly used continuous and discrete distributions, and discusses how empirical distributions can be specified. In Sec. 6.3 we present techniques for determining whether the data are independent observations from some underlying distribution, which is a requirement of many of the statistical procedures in this chapter. In Secs. 6.4 through 6.6 we discuss the three basic activities in specifying a theoretical distribution on the basis of observed data. The ExpertFit distribution-fitting software and a comprehensive example are discussed in Sec. 6.7. In Sec. 6.8 we indicate how certain of the theoretical distributions, e.g., gamma, Weibull, and lognormal, can be "shifted" away from 0 to make them better fit our observed data in some cases; we also discuss truncated distributions. We treat Bézier distributions, which are a fourth way to specify a distribution based on observed data, in Sec. 6.9. In Sec. 6.10 we describe how multivariate distributions are specified and estimated when observed data are available. In Sec. 6.11 we describe several possible methods for specifying input distributions when no data are available. Several useful probabilistic models for describing the manner in which "customers" arrive to a system are given in Sec. 6.12, while in Sec. 6.13 we present techniques for determining whether observations from different sources are homogeneous and can be merged.

The graphical plots and goodness-of-fit tests presented in this chapter were developed using the ExpertFit distribution-fitting software (see Sec. 6.7).

6.2 USEFUL PROBABILITY DISTRIBUTIONS

The purpose of this section is to discuss a variety of distributions that have been found to be useful in simulation modeling and to provide a unified listing of relevant properties of these distributions [see also Forbes et al. (2011); Johnson, Kotz, and Balakrishnan (1994, 1995); and Johnson, Kotz, and Kemp (1992)]. Section 6.2.1 provides a short discussion of common methods by which continuous distributions are defined, or parameterized. Then Secs. 6.2.2 and 6.2.3 contain compilations of several continuous and discrete distributions. Finally, Sec. 6.2.4 suggests how the data themselves can be used directly to define an empirical distribution.

6.2.1 Parameterization of Continuous Distributions

For a given family of continuous distributions, e.g., normal or gamma, there are usually several alternative ways to define, or *parameterize*, the probability density function. However, if the parameters are defined correctly, they can be classified, on the basis of their physical or geometric interpretation, as being one of three basic types: location, scale, or shape parameters.

A *location parameter* γ specifies an abscissa (x axis) location point of a distribution's range of values; usually γ is the midpoint (e.g., the mean μ for a normal distribution) or lower endpoint (see Sec. 6.8) of the distribution's range. (In the latter case, location parameters are sometimes called *shift parameters*.) As γ changes, the associated distribution merely shifts left or right without otherwise changing. Also, if the distribution of a random variable X has a location parameter of 0, then the distribution of the random variable $Y = X + \gamma$ has a location parameter of γ.

A *scale parameter* β determines the scale (or unit) of measurement of the values in the range of the distribution. (The standard deviation σ is a scale parameter for the normal distribution.) A change in β compresses or expands the associated distribution without altering its basic form. Also, if the distribution of the random variable X has a scale parameter of 1, then the distribution of the random variable $Y = \beta X$ has a scale parameter of β.

A *shape parameter* α determines, distinct from location and scale, the basic form or shape of a distribution within the general family of distributions of interest. A change in α generally alters a distribution's properties (e.g., skewness) more fundamentally than a change in location or scale. Some distributions (e.g., exponential and normal) do not have a shape parameter, while others (e.g., beta) may have two.

6.2.2 Continuous Distributions

Table 6.3 gives information relevant to simulation modeling applications for 13 continuous distributions. Possible applications are given first to indicate some (certainly not all) uses of the distribution [see Hahn and Shapiro (1994) and Lawless (2003) for other applications]. Then the density function and distribution function (if it exists in simple closed form) are listed. Next is a short description of the parameters, including their possible values. The range indicates the interval where the associated random variable can take on values. Also listed are the mean (expected value), variance, and mode, i.e., the value at which the density function is maximized. MLE refers to the maximum-likelihood estimator(s) of the parameter(s), treated later in Sec. 6.5. General comments include relationships of the distribution under study to other distributions. Graphs are given of the density functions for each distribution. The notation following the name of each distribution is our abbreviation for that distribution, which includes the parameters. The symbol $\sim$ is read "is distributed as."

Note that we have included the less familiar Johnson S_B, Johnson S_U, log-logistic, Pearson type V, and Pearson type VI distributions, because we have found that these distributions often provide a better fit to data sets than standard distributions such as gamma, lognormal, and Weibull.

TABLE 6.3
Continuous distributions

Uniform	**U(a, b)**
Possible applications	Used as a "first" model for a quantity that is felt to be randomly varying between a and b but about which little else is known. The U(0, 1) distribution is essential in generating random values from all other distributions (see Chaps. 7 and 8).
Density (See Fig. 6.5)	$f(x) = \begin{cases} \dfrac{1}{b-a} & \text{if } a \le x \le b \\ 0 & \text{otherwise} \end{cases}$
Distribution	$F(x) = \begin{cases} 0 & \text{if } x < a \\ \dfrac{x-a}{b-a} & \text{if } a \le x \le b \\ 1 & \text{if } b < x \end{cases}$
Parameters	a and b real numbers with $a < b$; a is a location parameter, $b - a$ is a scale parameter

TABLE 6.3 *(continued)*

Uniform	**U(*a*, *b*)**
Range	$[a, b]$
Mean	$\dfrac{a+b}{2}$
Variance	$\dfrac{(b-a)^2}{12}$
Mode	Does not uniquely exist
MLE	$\hat{a} = \min_{1 \le i \le n} X_i$, $\hat{b} = \max_{1 \le i \le n} X_i$
Comments	1. The U(0, 1) distribution is a special case of the beta distribution (when $\alpha_1 = \alpha_2 = 1$). 2. If $X \sim$ U(0, 1) and $[x, x + \Delta x]$ is a subinterval of [0, 1] with $\Delta x \ge 0$, $$P(X \in [x, x+\Delta x]) = \int_x^{x+\Delta x} 1 dy = (x + \Delta x) - x = \Delta x$$ which justifies the name "uniform."

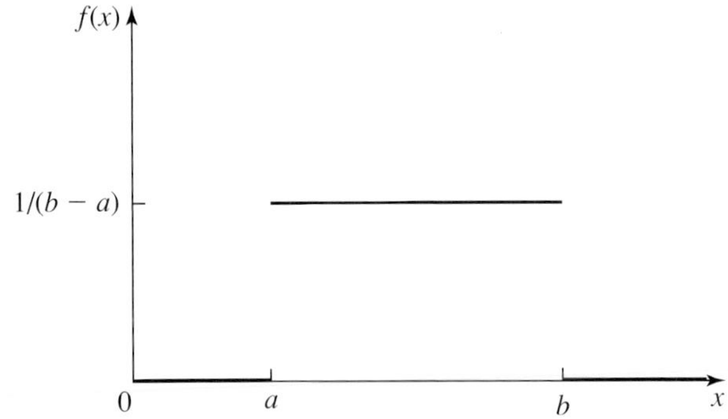

FIGURE 6.5
U(*a*, *b*) density function.

Exponential	**expo(β)**
Possible applications	Interarrival times of "customers" to a system that occur at a constant rate, time to failure of a piece of equipment.
Density (see Fig. 6.6)	$f(x) = \begin{cases} \dfrac{1}{\beta} e^{-x/\beta} & \text{if } x \ge 0 \\ 0 & \text{otherwise} \end{cases}$
Distribution	$F(x) = \begin{cases} 1 - e^{-x/\beta} & \text{if } x \ge 0 \\ 0 & \text{otherwise} \end{cases}$
Parameter	Scale parameter $\beta > 0$
Range	$[0, \infty)$
Mean	β
Variance	β^2
Mode	0

(continued)

TABLE 6.3 *(continued)*

Exponential	**expo(β)**
MLE	$\hat{\beta} = \overline{X}(n)$
Comments	1. The expo(β) distribution is a special case of both the gamma and Weibull distributions (for shape parameter $\alpha = 1$ and scale parameter β in both cases). 2. If $X_1, X_2, \ldots, X_m$ are independent expo(β) random variables, then $X_1 + X_2 + \cdots + X_m \sim$ gamma(m, β), also called the *m-Erlang(β) distribution.* 3. The exponential distribution is the only continuous distribution with the memoryless property (see Prob. 4.30).

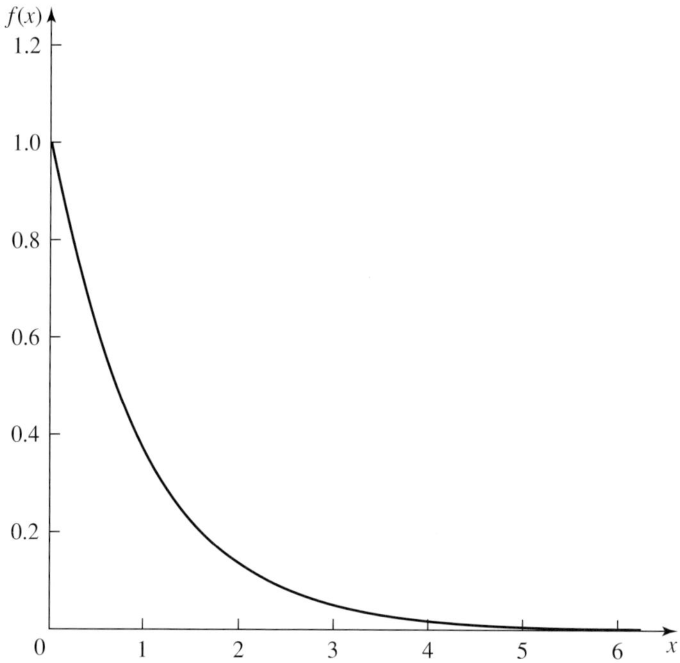

FIGURE 6.6
expo(1) density function.

Gamma	**gamma(α, β)**
Possible applications	Time to complete some task, e.g., customer service or machine repair
Density (see Fig. 6.7)	$f(x) = \begin{cases} \dfrac{\beta^{-\alpha} x^{\alpha-1} e^{-x/\beta}}{\Gamma(\alpha)} & \text{if } x > 0 \\ 0 & \text{otherwise} \end{cases}$ where $\Gamma(\alpha)$ is the *gamma function*, defined by $\Gamma(z) = \int_0^\infty t^{z-1} e^{-t} dt$ for any real number $z > 0$. Some properties of the gamma function: $\Gamma(z + 1) = z\Gamma(z)$ for any $z > 0$, $\Gamma(k + 1) = k!$ for any nonnegative integer k, $\Gamma(k + \frac{1}{2}) = \sqrt{\pi} \cdot 1 \cdot 3 \cdot 5 \cdots (2k - 1)/2^k$ for any positive integer k, $\Gamma(1/2) = \sqrt{\pi}$

TABLE 6.3 *(continued)*

Gamma	**gamma(α, β)**
Distribution	If α is not an integer, there is no closed form. If α is a positive integer, then $$F(x) = \begin{cases} 1 - e^{-x/\beta} \sum_{j=0}^{\alpha-1} \frac{(x/\beta)^j}{j!} & \text{if } x > 0 \\ 0 & \text{otherwise} \end{cases}$$
Parameters	Shape parameter $\alpha > 0$, scale parameter $\beta > 0$
Range	$[0, \infty)$
Mean	$\alpha\beta$
Variance	$\alpha\beta^2$
Mode	$\beta(\alpha - 1)$ if $\alpha \geq 1$, 0 if $\alpha < 1$
MLE	The following two equations must be satisfied: $$\ln \hat{\beta} + \Psi(\hat{\alpha}) = \frac{\sum_{i=1}^{n} \ln X_i}{n}, \qquad \hat{\alpha}\hat{\beta} = \overline{X}(n)$$ which could be solved numerically. [$\Psi(\hat{\alpha}) = \Gamma'(\hat{\alpha})/\Gamma(\hat{\alpha})$ and is called the *digamma function*; Γ' denotes the derivative of Γ.] Alternatively, approximations to $\hat{\alpha}$ and $\hat{\beta}$ can be obtained by letting $T = [\ln \overline{X}(n) - \Sigma_{i=1}^{n} \ln X_i/n]^{-1}$, using Table 6.21 (see App. 6A) to obtain $\hat{\alpha}$ as a function of T, and letting $\hat{\beta} = \overline{X}(n)/\hat{\alpha}$. [See Choi and Wette (1969) for the derivation of this procedure and of Table 6.21.]

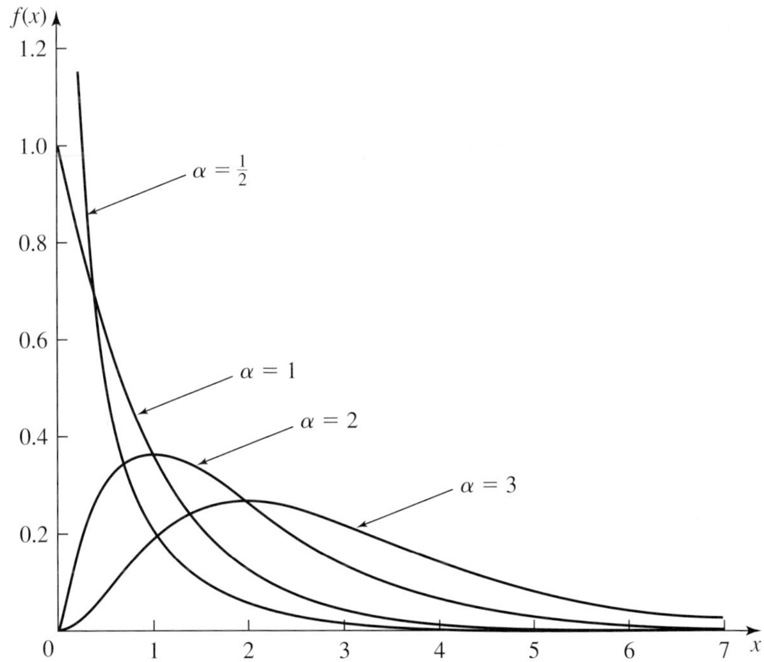

FIGURE 6.7
gamma(α, 1) density functions.

(continued)

TABLE 6.3 *(continued)*

Gamma	**gamma(α, β)**
Comments	1. The expo(β) and gamma(1, β) distributions are the same. 2. For a positive integer m, the gamma(m, β) distribution is called the m-Erlang(β) distribution. 3. The chi-square distribution with k df is the same as the gamma($k/2$, 2) distribution. 4. If $X_1, X_2, \ldots, X_m$ are independent random variables with $X_i \sim$ gamma(α_i, β), then $X_1 + X_2 + \cdots + X_m \sim$ gamma($\alpha_1 + \alpha_2 + \cdots + \alpha_m$, β). 5. If X_1 and X_2 are independent random variables with $X_i \sim$ gamma(α_i, β), then $X_1/(X_1 + X_2) \sim$ beta(α_1, α_2). 6. $X \sim$ gamma(α, β) if and only if $Y = 1/X$ has a Pearson type V distribution with shape and scale parameters α and $1/\beta$, denoted PT5(α, $1/\beta$). 7. $\lim_{x \to 0} f(x) = \begin{cases} \infty & \text{if } \alpha < 1 \\ \dfrac{1}{\beta} & \text{if } \alpha = 1 \\ 0 & \text{if } \alpha > 1 \end{cases}$

Weibull	**Weibull(α, β)**
Possible applications	Time to complete some task, time to failure of a piece of equipment; used as a rough model in the absence of data (see Sec. 6.11)
Density (see Fig. 6.8)	$f(x) = \begin{cases} \alpha\beta^{-\alpha}x^{\alpha-1}e^{-(x/\beta)^{\alpha}} & \text{if } x > 0 \\ 0 & \text{otherwise} \end{cases}$
Distribution	$F(x) = \begin{cases} 1 - e^{-(x/\beta)^{\alpha}} & \text{if } x > 0 \\ 0 & \text{otherwise} \end{cases}$
Parameters	Shape parameter $\alpha > 0$, scale parameter $\beta > 0$
Range	$[0, \infty)$
Mean	$\dfrac{\beta}{\alpha}\Gamma\left(\dfrac{1}{\alpha}\right)$
Variance	$\dfrac{\beta^2}{\alpha}\left\{2\Gamma\left(\dfrac{2}{\alpha}\right) - \dfrac{1}{\alpha}\left[\Gamma\left(\dfrac{1}{\alpha}\right)\right]^2\right\}$
Mode	$\begin{cases} \beta\left(\dfrac{\alpha-1}{\alpha}\right)^{1/\alpha} & \text{if } \alpha \ge 1 \\ 0 & \text{if } \alpha < 1 \end{cases}$
MLE	The following two equations must be satisfied: $\dfrac{\sum_{i=1}^{n} X_i^{\hat{\alpha}} \ln X_i}{\sum_{i=1}^{n} X_i^{\hat{\alpha}}} - \dfrac{1}{\hat{\alpha}} = \dfrac{\sum_{i=1}^{n} \ln X_i}{n}, \qquad \hat{\beta} = \left(\dfrac{\sum_{i=1}^{n} X_i^{\hat{\alpha}}}{n}\right)^{1/\hat{\alpha}}$ The first can be solved for $\hat{\alpha}$ numerically by Newton's method, and the second equation then gives $\hat{\beta}$ directly. The general recursive step for the Newton iterations is $\hat{\alpha}_{k+1} = \hat{\alpha}_k + \dfrac{A + 1/\hat{\alpha}_k - C_k/B_k}{1/\hat{\alpha}_k^2 + (B_k H_k - C_k^2)/B_k^2}$

TABLE 6.3 (*continued*)

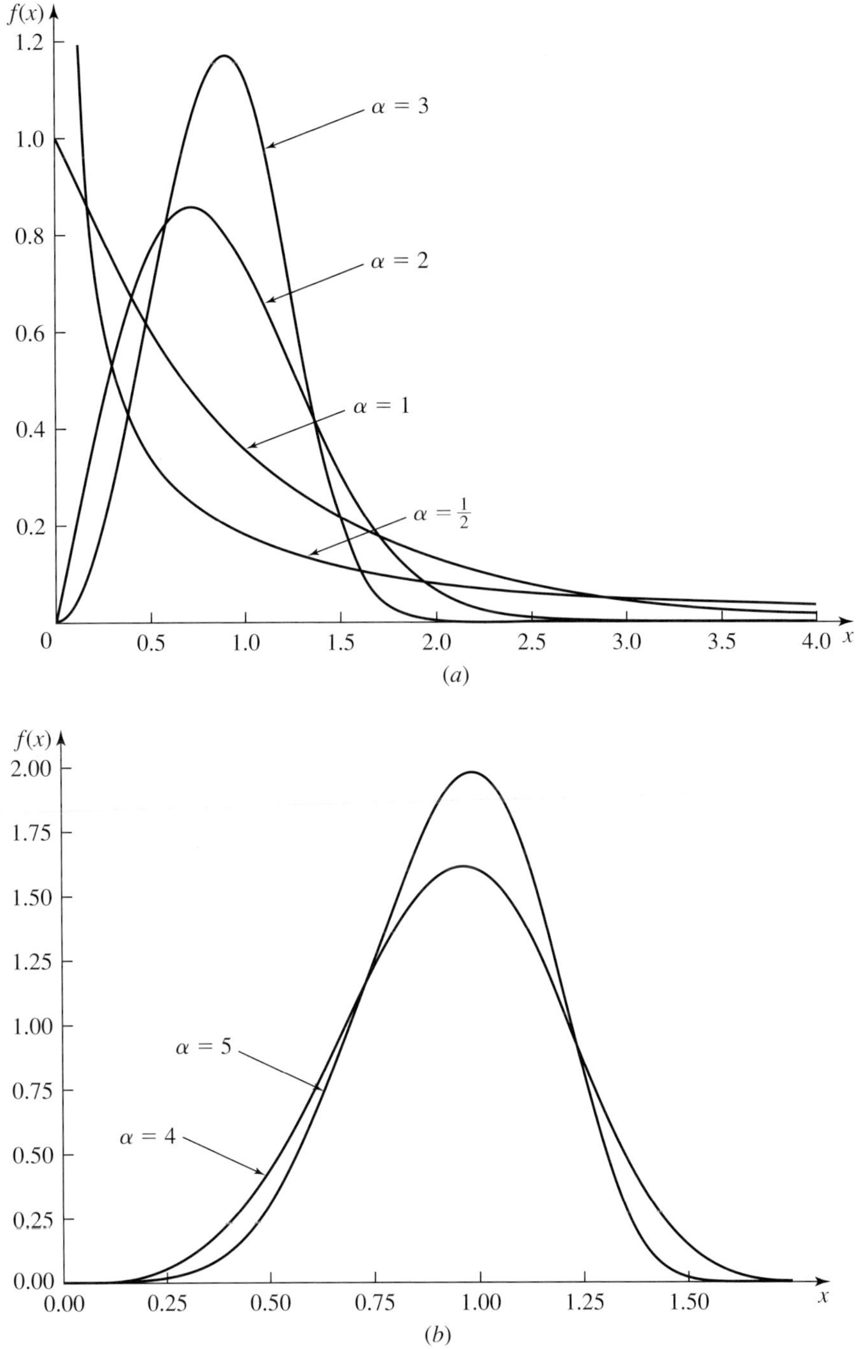

FIGURE 6.8
Weibull(α, 1) density functions.

(*continued*)

TABLE 6.3 *(continued)*

Weibull	**Weibull(α, β)**
	where $$A = \frac{\sum_{i=1}^{n} \ln X_i}{n}, \qquad B_k = \sum_{i=1}^{n} X_i^{\hat{\alpha}_k}, \qquad C_k = \sum_{i=1}^{n} X_i^{\hat{\alpha}_k} \ln X_i$$ and $$H_k = \sum_{i=1}^{n} X_i^{\hat{\alpha}_k} (\ln X_i)^2$$ [See Thoman, Bain, and Antle (1969) for these formulas, as well as for confidence intervals on the true α and β.] As a starting point for the iterations, the estimate $$\hat{\alpha}_0 = \left\{ \frac{(6/\pi^2)\left[\sum_{i=1}^{n} (\ln X_i)^2 - \left(\sum_{i=1}^{n} \ln X_i\right)^2 \Big/ n\right]}{n-1} \right\}^{-1/2}$$ [due to Menon (1963) and suggested in Thoman, Bain, and Antle (1969)] may be used. With this choice of $\hat{\alpha}_0$, it was reported in Thoman, Bain, and Antle (1969) that an average of only 3.5 Newton iterations were needed to achieve four-place accuracy.
Comments	1. The expo(β) and Weibull(1, β) distributions are the same. 2. $X \sim$ Weibull(α, β) if and only if $X^\alpha \sim$ expo(β^α) (see Prob. 6.2). 3. The (natural) logarithm of a Weibull random variable has a distribution known as the *extreme-value* or *Gumbel distribution* [see Averill M. Law & Associates (2013), Lawless (2003), and Prob. 8.1(*b*)]. 4. The Weibull(2, β) distribution is also called a *Rayleigh distribution* with parameter β, denoted Rayleigh(β). If Y and Z are independent normal random variables with mean 0 and variance β^2 (see the normal distribution), then $X = (Y^2 + Z^2)^{1/2} \sim$ Rayleigh($2^{1/2}\beta$). 5. As $\alpha \to \infty$, the Weibull distribution becomes degenerate at β. Thus, Weibull densities for large α have a sharp peak at the mode. 6. The Weibull distribution has a negative skewness when $\alpha > 3.6$ [see Fig. 6.8(*b*)]. 7. $$\lim_{x \to 0} f(x) = \begin{cases} \infty & \text{if } \alpha < 1 \\ \dfrac{1}{\beta} & \text{if } \alpha = 1 \\ 0 & \text{if } \alpha > 1 \end{cases}$$

Normal	**N(μ, σ^2)**
Possible applications	Errors of various types, e.g., in the impact point of a bomb; quantities that are the sum of a large number of other quantities (by virtue of central limit theorems)
Density (see Fig. 6.9)	$f(x) = \dfrac{1}{\sqrt{2\pi\sigma^2}} e^{-(x-\mu)^2/(2\sigma^2)}$ for all real numbers x
Distribution	No closed form
Parameters	Location parameter $\mu \in (-\infty, \infty)$, scale parameter $\sigma > 0$
Range	$(-\infty, \infty)$

TABLE 6.3 *(continued)*

Normal	**N(μ, σ^2)**
Mean	μ
Variance	σ^2
Mode	μ
MLE	$\hat{\mu} = \overline{X}(n), \qquad \hat{\sigma} = \left[\frac{n-1}{n} S^2(n)\right]^{1/2}$
Comments	1. If two jointly distributed normal random variables are uncorrelated, they are also independent. For distributions other than normal, this implication is not true in general.
	2. Suppose that the joint distribution of $X_1, X_2, \ldots, X_m$ is multivariate normal and let $\mu_i = E(X_i)$ and $C_{ij} = \text{Cov}(X_i, X_j)$. Then for any real numbers $a, b_1, b_2, \ldots, b_m$, the random variable $a + b_1X_1 + b_2X_2 + \cdots + b_mX_m$ has a normal distribution with mean $\mu = a + \sum_{i=1}^{m} b_i\mu_i$ and variance $\sigma^2 = \sum_{i=1}^{m}\sum_{j=1}^{m} b_ib_jC_{ij}$ Note that we need *not* assume independence of the X_i's. If the X_i's *are* independent, then $\sigma^2 = \sum_{i=1}^{m} b_i^2 \text{Var}(X_i)$
	3. The N(0, 1) distribution is often called the *standard* or *unit normal distribution.*
	4. If $X_1, X_2, \ldots, X_k$ are independent standard normal random variables, then $X_1^2 + X_2^2 + \cdots + X_k^2$ has a chi-square distribution with k df, which is also the gamma($k/2$, 2) distribution.

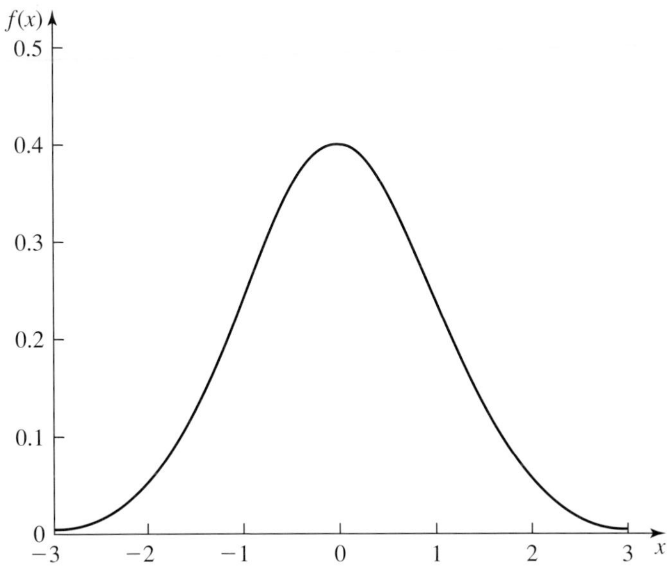

FIGURE 6.9
N(0, 1) density function.

(continued)

TABLE 6.3 *(continued)*

Normal	**N(μ, σ^2)**
	5. If $X \sim N(\mu, \sigma^2)$, then e^X has the *lognormal distribution* with scale parameter e^μ and shape parameter σ, denoted LN(μ, σ^2). 6. If $X \sim N(0, 1)$, if Y has a chi-square distribution with k df, and if X and Y are independent, then $X/\sqrt{Y/k}$ has a t distribution with k df (sometimes called *Student's t distribution*). 7. If the normal distribution is used to represent a nonnegative quantity (e.g., time), then its density should be truncated at $x = 0$ (see Sec. 6.8). 8. As $\sigma \to 0$, the normal distribution becomes degenerate at μ.

Lognormal	**LN(μ, σ^2)**
Possible applications	Time to perform some task [density takes on shapes similar to gamma(α, β) and Weibull(α, β) densities for $\alpha > 1$, but can have a large "spike" close to $x = 0$ that is often useful]; quantities that are the product of a large number of other quantities (by virtue of central limit theorem); used as a rough model in the absence of data (see Sec. 6.11)
Density (see Fig. 6.10)	$f(x) = \begin{cases} \dfrac{1}{x\sqrt{2\pi\sigma^2}} \exp \dfrac{-(\ln x - \mu)^2}{2\sigma^2} & \text{if } x > 0 \\ 0 & \text{otherwise} \end{cases}$
Distribution	No closed form
Parameters	Shape parameter $\sigma > 0$, scale parameter $e^\mu > 0$
Range	$[0, \infty)$
Mean	$e^{\mu+\sigma^2/2}$
Variance	$e^{2\mu+\sigma^2}(e^{\sigma^2} - 1)$

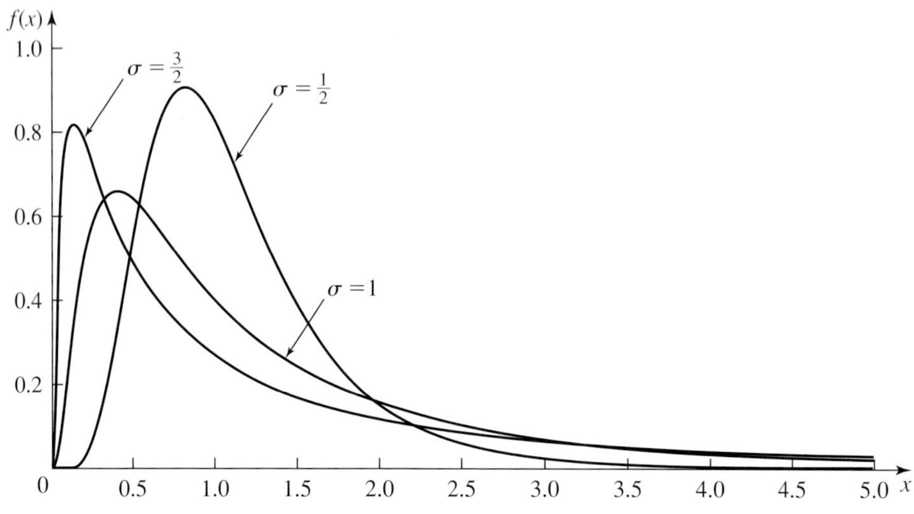

FIGURE 6.10
LN(0, σ^2) density functions.

TABLE 6.3 *(continued)*

Lognormal	**LN(μ, σ^2)**
Mode	$e^{\mu-\sigma^2}$
MLE	$\hat{\mu} = \dfrac{\sum_{i=1}^{n} \ln X_i}{n}$, $\hat{\sigma} = \left[\dfrac{\sum_{i=1}^{n} (\ln X_i - \hat{\mu})^2}{n}\right]^{1/2}$, MLE for scale parameter $= e^{\hat{\mu}}$
Comments	1. $X \sim \text{LN}(\mu, \sigma^2)$ if and only if $\ln X \sim N(\mu, \sigma^2)$. Thus, if one has data $X_1, X_2, \ldots, X_n$ that are thought to be lognormal, the logarithms of the data points $\ln X_1, \ln X_2, \ldots, \ln X_n$ can be treated as normally distributed data for purposes of hypothesizing a distribution, parameter estimation, and goodness-of-fit testing. 2. As $\sigma \to 0$, the lognormal distribution becomes degenerate at e^{μ}. Thus, lognormal densities for small σ have a sharp peak at the mode. 3. $\lim_{x \to 0} f(x) = 0$, regardless of the parameter values.

Beta	**beta(α_1, α_2)**
Possible applications	Used as a rough model in the absence of data (see Sec. 6.11); distribution of a random proportion, such as the proportion of defective items in a shipment; time to complete a task, e.g., in a PERT network
Density (see Fig. 6.11)	$f(x) = \begin{cases} \dfrac{x^{\alpha_1-1}(1-x)^{\alpha_2-1}}{B(\alpha_1,\alpha_2)} & \text{if } 0 < x < 1 \\ 0 & \text{otherwise} \end{cases}$ where $B(\alpha_1, \alpha_2)$ is the *beta function,* defined by $B(z_1, z_2) = \int_0^1 t^{z_1-1}(1-t)^{z_2-1}\,dt$ for any real numbers $z_1 > 0$ and $z_2 > 0$. Some properties of the beta function: $B(z_1, z_2) = B(z_2, z_1), \qquad B(z_1, z_2) = \dfrac{\Gamma(z_1)\Gamma(z_2)}{\Gamma(z_1 + z_2)}$
Distribution	No closed form, in general. If either α_1 or α_2 is a positive integer, a binomial expansion can be used to obtain $F(x)$, which will be a polynomial in x, and the powers of x will be, in general, positive real numbers ranging from 0 through $\alpha_1 + \alpha_2 - 1$.
Parameters	Shape parameters $\alpha_1 > 0$ and $\alpha_2 > 0$
Range	[0, 1]
Mean	$\dfrac{\alpha_1}{\alpha_1 + \alpha_2}$
Variance	$\dfrac{\alpha_1\alpha_2}{(\alpha_1 + \alpha_2)^2(\alpha_1 + \alpha_2 + 1)}$
Mode	$\begin{cases} \dfrac{\alpha_1 - 1}{\alpha_1 + \alpha_2 - 2} & \text{if } \alpha_1 > 1, \alpha_2 > 1 \\ 0 \text{ and } 1 & \text{if } \alpha_1 < 1, \alpha_2 < 1 \\ 0 & \text{if } (\alpha_1 < 1, \alpha_2 \geq 1) \text{ or if } (\alpha_1 = 1, \alpha_2 > 1) \\ 1 & \text{if } (\alpha_1 \geq 1, \alpha_2 < 1) \text{ or if } (\alpha_1 > 1, \alpha_2 = 1) \\ \text{does not uniquely exist} & \text{if } \alpha_1 = \alpha_2 = 1 \end{cases}$

(continued)

TABLE 6.3 *(continued)*

Beta	**beta(α_1, α_2)**
MLE	The following two equations must be satisfied: $\Psi(\hat{\alpha}_1) - \Psi(\hat{\alpha}_1 + \hat{\alpha}_2) = \ln G_1, \qquad \Psi(\hat{\alpha}_2) - \Psi(\hat{\alpha}_1 + \hat{\alpha}_2) = \ln G_2$ where Ψ is the digamma function, $G_1 = (\prod_{i=1}^{n} X_i)^{1/n}$, and $G_2 = [\prod_{i=1}^{n}(1 - X_i)]^{1/n}$ [see Gnanadesikan, Pinkham, and Hughes (1967)]; note that $G_1 + G_2 \leq 1$. These equations could be solved numerically [see Beckman and Tietjen (1978)], or approximations to $\hat{\alpha}_1$ and $\hat{\alpha}_2$ can be obtained from Table 6.22 (see App. 6A), which was computed for particular (G_1, G_2) pairs by modifications of the methods in Beckman and Tietjen (1978).
Comments	1. The U(0, 1) and beta(1, 1) distributions are the same. 2. If X_1 and X_2 are independent random variables with $X_i \sim$ gamma(α_i, β), then $X_1/(X_1 + X_2) \sim$ beta(α_1, α_2). 3. A beta random variable X on [0, 1] can be rescaled and relocated to obtain a beta random variable on $[a, b]$ of the same shape by the transformation $a + (b - a)X$. 4. $X \sim$ beta(α_1, α_2) if and only if $1 - X \sim$ beta(α_2, α_1). 5. $X \sim$ beta(α_1, α_2) if and only if $Y = X/(1 - X)$ has a Pearson type VI distribution with shape parameters α_1, α_2 and scale parameter 1, denoted PT6(α_1, α_2, 1).

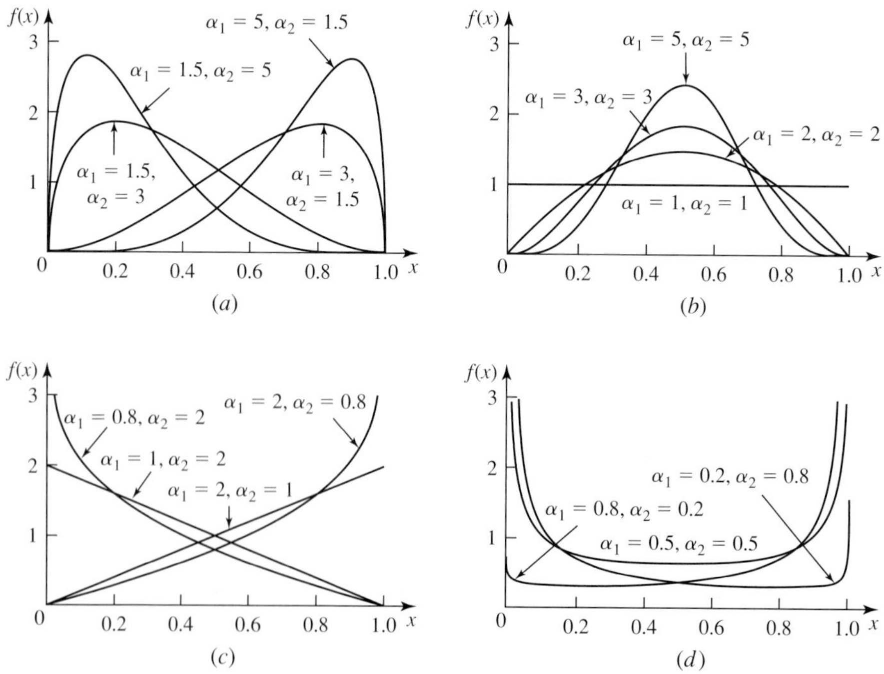

FIGURE 6.11
beta(α_1, α_2) density functions.

TABLE 6.3 *(continued)*

Beta	**beta(α_1, α_2)**
	6. The beta(1, 2) density is a left triangle, and the beta(2, 1) density is a right triangle.
	7. $\lim_{x\to 0} f(x) = \begin{cases} \infty & \text{if } \alpha_1 < 1 \\ \alpha_2 & \text{if } \alpha_1 = 1, \\ 0 & \text{if } \alpha_1 > 1 \end{cases} \qquad \lim_{x\to 1} f(x) = \begin{cases} \infty & \text{if } \alpha_2 < 1 \\ \alpha_1 & \text{if } \alpha_2 = 1 \\ 0 & \text{if } \alpha_2 > 1 \end{cases}$
	8. The density is symmetric about $x = \frac{1}{2}$ if and only if $\alpha_1 = \alpha_2$. Also, the mean and the mode are equal if and only if $\alpha_1 = \alpha_2 > 1$.

Pearson type V	**PT5(α, β)**
Possible applications	Time to perform some task (density takes on shapes similar to lognormal, but can have a larger "spike" close to $x = 0$)
Density (see Fig. 6.12)	$f(x) = \begin{cases} \dfrac{x^{-(\alpha+1)}e^{-\beta/x}}{\beta^{-\alpha}\Gamma(\alpha)} & \text{if } x > 0 \\ 0 & \text{otherwise} \end{cases}$
Distribution	$F(x) = \begin{cases} 1 - F_G\left(\dfrac{1}{x}\right) & \text{if } x > 0 \\ 0 & \text{otherwise} \end{cases}$ where $F_G(x)$ is the distribution function of a gamma(α, $1/\beta$) random variable
Parameters	Shape parameter $\alpha > 0$, scale parameter $\beta > 0$

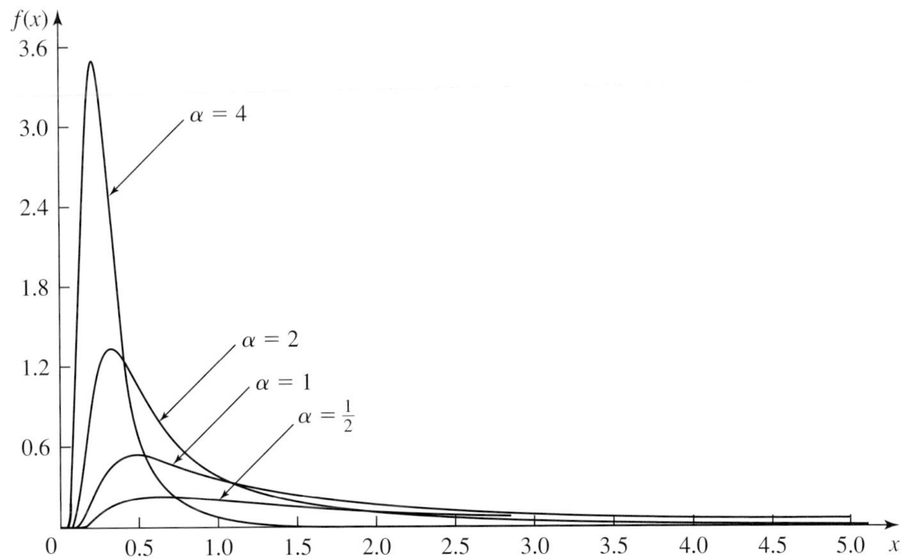

FIGURE 6.12
PT5(α, 1) density functions.

(continued)

TABLE 6.3 *(continued)*

Pearson type V	**PT5(α, β)**
Range	$[0, \infty)$
Mean	$\dfrac{\beta}{\alpha - 1}$ for $\alpha > 1$
Variance	$\dfrac{\beta^2}{(\alpha - 1)^2(\alpha - 2)}$ for $\alpha > 2$
Mode	$\dfrac{\beta}{\alpha + 1}$
MLE	If one has data $X_1, X_2, \ldots, X_n$, then fit a gamma(α_G, β_G) distribution to $1/X_1, 1/X_2, \ldots, 1/X_n$, resulting in the maximum-likelihood estimators $\hat{\alpha}_G$ and $\hat{\beta}_G$. Then the maximum-likelihood estimators for the PT5(α, β) are $\hat{\alpha} = \hat{\alpha}_G$ and $\hat{\beta} = 1/\hat{\beta}_G$ (see comment 1 below).
Comments	1. $X \sim$ PT5(α, β) if and only if $Y = 1/X \sim$ gamma(α, $1/\beta$). Thus, the Pearson type V distribution is sometimes called the *inverted gamma distribution*. 2. Note that the mean and variance exist only for certain values of the shape parameter.

Pearson type VI	**PT6(α_1, α_2, β)**
Possible applications	Time to perform some task
Density (see Fig. 6.13)	$f(x) = \begin{cases} \dfrac{(x/\beta)^{\alpha_1 - 1}}{\beta B(\alpha_1, \alpha_2)[1 + (x/\beta)]^{\alpha_1 + \alpha_2}} & \text{if } x > 0 \\ 0 & \text{otherwise} \end{cases}$
Distribution	$F(x) = \begin{cases} F_B\left(\dfrac{x}{x + \beta}\right) & \text{if } x > 0 \\ 0 & \text{otherwise} \end{cases}$ where $F_B(x)$ is the distribution function of a beta(α_1, α_2) random variable
Parameters	Shape parameters $\alpha_1 > 0$ and $\alpha_2 > 0$, scale parameter $\beta > 0$
Range	$[0, \infty)$
Mean	$\dfrac{\beta\alpha_1}{\alpha_2 - 1}$ for $\alpha_2 > 1$
Variance	$\dfrac{\beta^2\alpha_1(\alpha_1 + \alpha_2 - 1)}{(\alpha_2 - 1)^2(\alpha_2 - 2)}$ for $\alpha_2 > 2$
Mode	$\begin{cases} \dfrac{\beta(\alpha_1 - 1)}{\alpha_2 + 1} & \text{if } \alpha_1 \geq 1 \\ 0 & \text{otherwise} \end{cases}$
MLE	If one has data $X_1, X_2, \ldots, X_n$ that are thought to be PT6(α_1, α_2, 1), then fit a beta(α_1, α_2) distribution to $X_i/(1 + X_i)$ for $i = 1, 2, \ldots, n$, resulting in the maximum-likelihood estimators $\hat{\alpha}_1$ and $\hat{\alpha}_2$. Then the maximum-likelihood estimators for the PT6(α_1, α_2, 1) (note that $\beta = 1$) distribution are also $\hat{\alpha}_1$ and $\hat{\alpha}_2$ (see comment 1 below).

TABLE 6.3 *(continued)*

Pearson type VI	**PT6($\alpha_1, \alpha_2, \beta$)**
Comments	1. $X \sim$ PT6(α_1, α_2, 1) if and only if $Y = X/(1 + X) \sim$ beta(α_1, α_2). 2. If X_1 and X_2 are independent random variables with $X_1 \sim$ gamma(α_1, β) and $X_2 \sim$ gamma(α_2, 1), then $Y = X_1/X_2 \sim$ PT6($\alpha_1, \alpha_2, \beta$) (see Prob. 6.3). 3. Note that the mean and variance exist only for certain values of the shape parameter α_2.

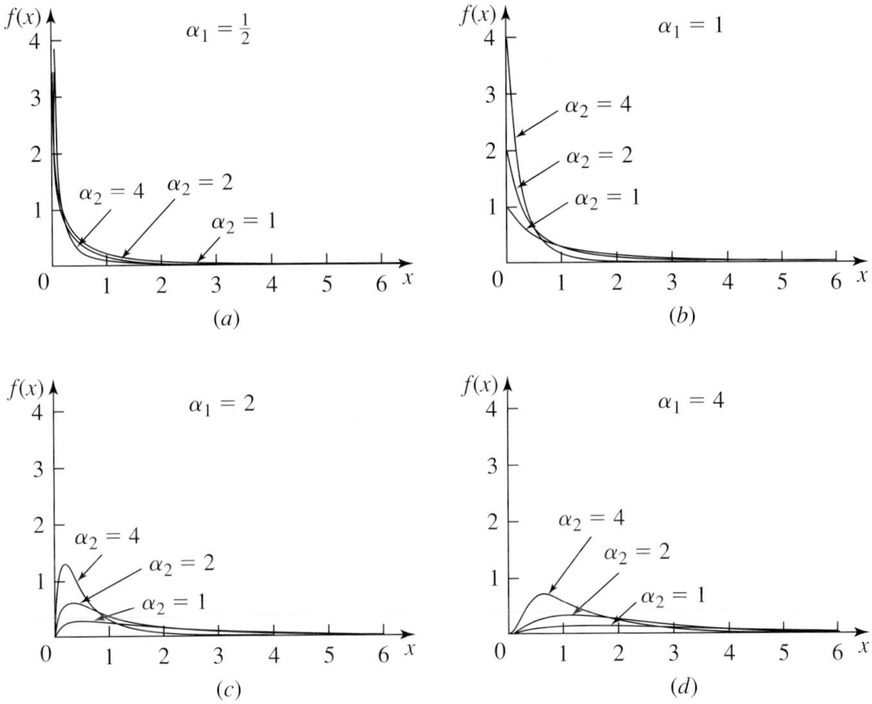

FIGURE 6.13
PT6(α_1, α_2, 1) density functions.

Log-logistic	**LL(α, β)**
Possible applications	Time to perform some task
Density (see Fig. 6.14)	$f(x) = \begin{cases} \dfrac{\alpha(x/\beta)^{\alpha-1}}{\beta[1 + (x/\beta)^\alpha]^2} & \text{if } x > 0 \\ 0 & \text{otherwise} \end{cases}$
Distribution	$F(x) = \begin{cases} \dfrac{1}{1 + (x/\beta)^{-\alpha}} & \text{if } x > 0 \\ 0 & \text{otherwise} \end{cases}$
Parameters	Shape parameter $\alpha > 0$, scale parameter $\beta > 0$

(continued)

TABLE 6.3 *(continued)*

Log-logistic	**LL(α, β)**
Range	$[0, \infty)$
Mean	$\beta\theta$ cosecant(θ) for $\alpha > 1$, where $\theta = \pi/\alpha$
Variance	$\beta^2\theta\{2$ cosecant$(2\theta) - \theta[$cosecant$(\theta)]^2\}$ for $\alpha > 2$
Mode	$\begin{cases} \beta\left(\dfrac{\alpha-1}{\alpha+1}\right)^{1/\alpha} & \text{if } \alpha > 1 \\ 0 & \text{otherwise} \end{cases}$
MLE	Let $Y_i = \ln X_i$. Solve the following two equations for $\hat{a}$ and $\hat{b}$:

$$\sum_{i=1}^{n} \left[1 + e^{(Y_i - \hat{a})/\hat{b}}\right]^{-1} = \frac{n}{2} \tag{6.1}$$

and

$$\sum_{i=1}^{n} \left(\frac{Y_i - \hat{a}}{\hat{b}}\right) \frac{1 - e^{(Y_i - \hat{a})/\hat{b}}}{1 + e^{(Y_i - \hat{a})/\hat{b}}} = n \tag{6.2}$$

Then the MLEs for the log-logistic distribution are $\hat{\alpha} = 1/\hat{a}$ and $\hat{\beta} = e^{\hat{b}}$. Johnson, Kotz, and Balakrishnan (1995, chap. 23) suggest solving Eqs. (6.1) and (6.2) by using Newton's method.

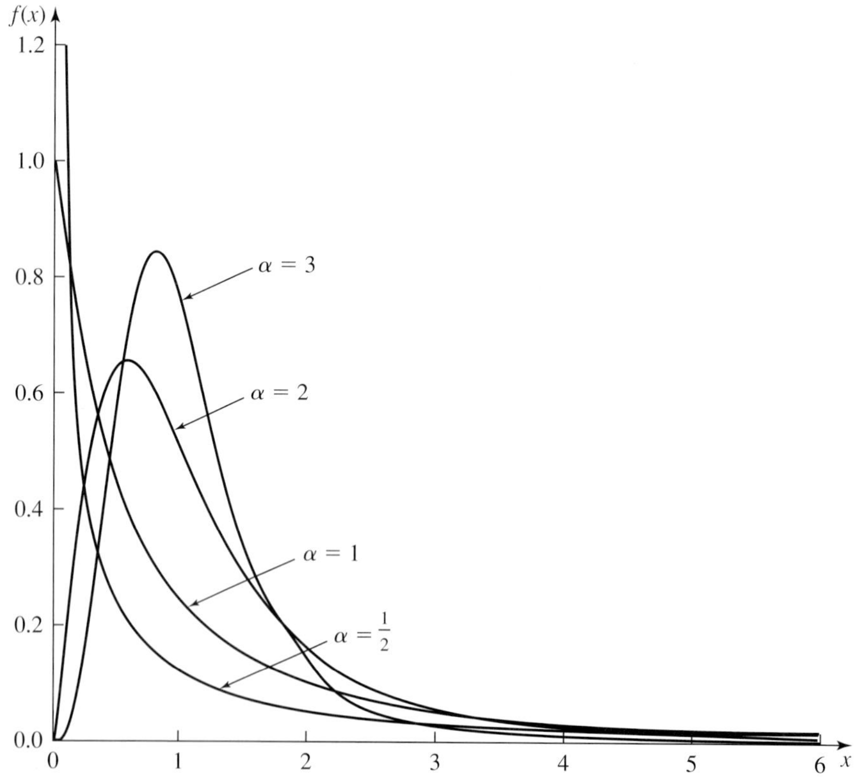

FIGURE 6.14
LL(α, 1) density functions.

TABLE 6.3 *(continued)*

Log-logistic	**LL(α, β)**
Comment	$X \sim \text{LL}(\alpha, \beta)$ if and only if $\ln X$ is distributed as a logistic distribution (see Prob. 8.1) with location parameter $\ln \beta$ and scale parameter $1/\alpha$. Thus, if one has data $X_1, X_2, \ldots, X_n$ that are thought to be log-logistic, the logarithms of the data points $\ln X_1, \ln X_2, \ldots, \ln X_n$ can be treated as having a logistic distribution for purposes of hypothesizing a distribution, parameter estimation, and goodness-of-fit testing.

Johnson S_B	**JSB(α_1, α_2, a, b)**
Density (see Fig. 6.15)	$f(x) = \begin{cases} \dfrac{\alpha_2(b-a)}{(x-a)(b-x)\sqrt{2\pi}} e^{-\frac{1}{2}\left[\alpha_1 + \alpha_2 \ln\left(\frac{x-a}{b-x}\right)\right]^2} & \text{if } a < x < b \\ 0 & \text{otherwise} \end{cases}$
Distribution	$F(x) = \begin{cases} \Phi\left[\alpha_1 + \alpha_2 \ln\left(\dfrac{x-a}{b-x}\right)\right] & \text{if } a < x < b \\ 0 & \text{otherwise} \end{cases}$ where $\Phi(x)$ is the distribution function of a normal random variable with $\mu = 0$ and $\sigma^2 = 1$
Parameters	Location parameter $a \in (-\infty, \infty)$, scale parameter $b - a$ $(b > a)$, shape parameters $\alpha_1 \in (-\infty, \infty)$ and $\alpha_2 > 0$
Range	$[a, b]$
Mean	All moments exist but are extremely complicated [see Johnson, Kotz, and Balakrishnan (1994, p. 35)]
Mode	The density is bimodal when $\alpha_2 < \dfrac{1}{\sqrt{2}}$ and $$\lvert\alpha_1\rvert < \frac{\sqrt{1-2\alpha_2^2}}{\alpha_2} - 2\alpha_2 \tanh^{-1}\left(\sqrt{1-2\alpha_2^2}\right)$$ [$\tanh^{-1}$ is the inverse hyperbolic tangent]; otherwise the density is unimodal. The equation satisfied by any mode x, other than at the endpoints of the range, is $$\frac{2(x-a)}{b-a} = 1 + \alpha_1\alpha_2 + \alpha_2^2 \ln\left(\frac{x-a}{b-x}\right)$$
Comments	1. $X \sim \text{JSB}(\alpha_1, \alpha_2, a, b)$ if and only if $$\alpha_1 + \alpha_2 \ln\left(\frac{X-a}{b-X}\right) \sim \text{N}(0, 1)$$ 2. The density function is skewed to the left, symmetric, or skewed to the right if $\alpha_1 > 0$, $\alpha_1 = 0$, or $\alpha_1 < 0$, respectively. 3. $\lim_{x \to a} f(x) = \lim_{x \to b} f(x) = 0$ for all values of α_1 and α_2. 4. The four parameters may be estimated using a number of methods [see, for example, Swain, Venkatraman, and Wilson (1988) and Slifker and Shapiro (1980)].

(continued)

TABLE 6.3 (*continued*)

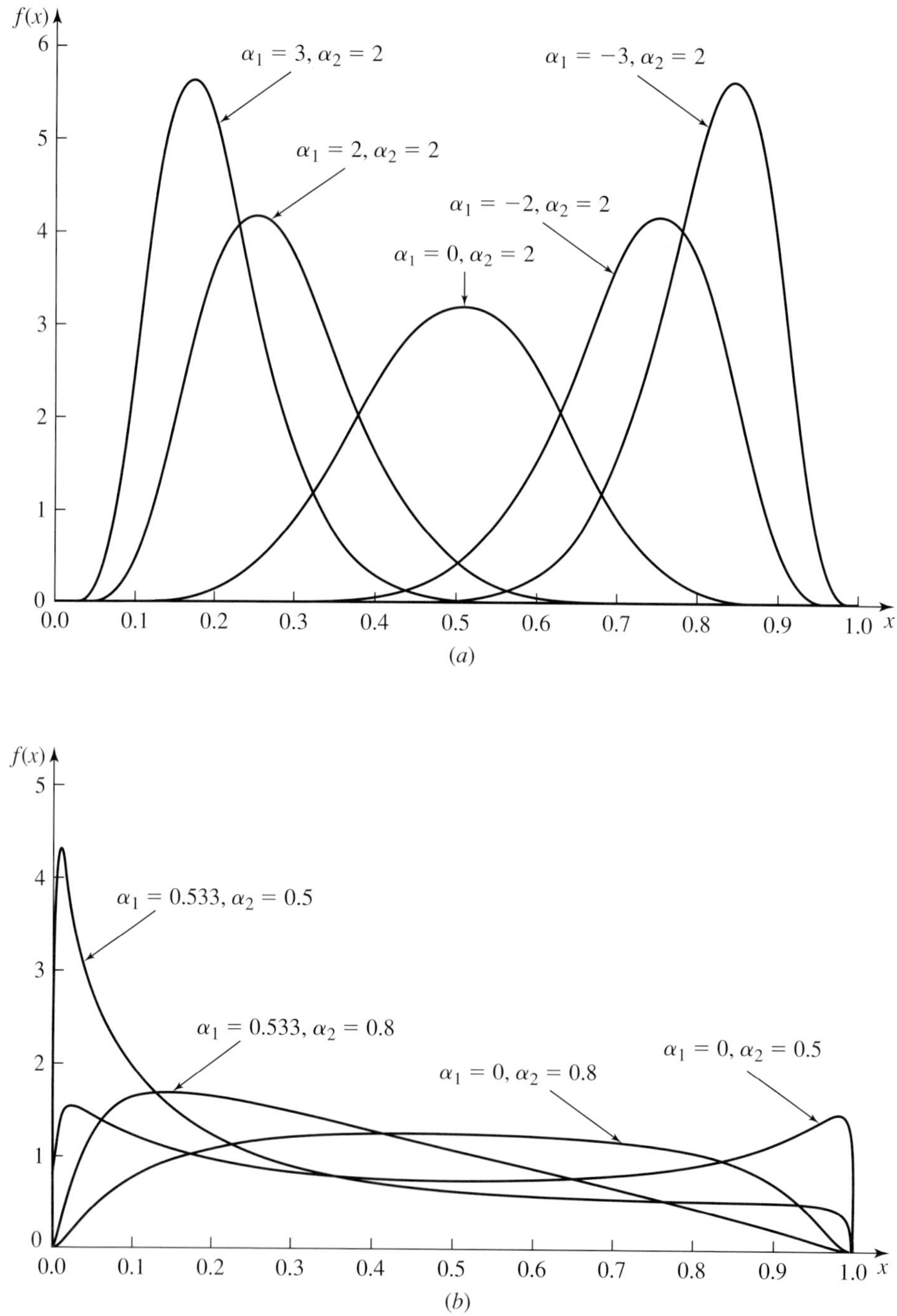

FIGURE 6.15
JSB(α_1, α_2, 0, 1) density functions.

TABLE 6.3 *(continued)*

Johnson S_U	**JSU($\alpha_1, \alpha_2, \gamma, \beta$)**
Density (see Fig. 6.16)	$f(x) = \dfrac{\alpha_2}{\sqrt{2\pi}\sqrt{(x-\gamma)^2+\beta^2}} e^{-\frac{1}{2}\left\{\alpha_1+\alpha_2 \ln\left[\frac{x-\gamma}{\beta}+\sqrt{\left(\frac{x-\gamma}{\beta}\right)^2+1}\right]\right\}^2}$ for $-\infty < x < \infty$
Distribution	$F(x) = \Phi\left\{\alpha_1 + \alpha_2 \ln\left[\dfrac{x-\gamma}{\beta} + \sqrt{\left(\dfrac{x-\gamma}{\beta}\right)^2 + 1}\right]\right\}$ for $-\infty < x < \infty$
Parameters	Location parameter $\gamma \in (-\infty, \infty)$, scale parameter $\beta > 0$, shape parameters $\alpha_1 \in (-\infty, \infty)$ and $\alpha_2 > 0$
Range	$(-\infty, \infty)$
Mean	$\gamma - \beta e^{1/(2\alpha_2^2)} \sinh\left(\dfrac{\alpha_1}{\alpha_2}\right)$, where sinh is the hyperbolic sine
Mode	The equation satisfied by the mode, other than at the endpoints of the range, is $\gamma + \beta y$, where y satisfies $y + \alpha_1\alpha_2\sqrt{y^2+1} + \alpha_2^2\sqrt{y^2+1}\ln(y + \sqrt{y^2+1}) = 0$
Comments	1. $X \sim \text{JSU}(\alpha_1, \alpha_2, \gamma, \beta)$ if and only if $\alpha_1 + \alpha_2 \ln\left[\dfrac{X-\gamma}{\beta} + \sqrt{\left(\dfrac{X-\gamma}{\beta}\right)^2 + 1}\right] \sim \text{N}(0, 1)$ 2. The density function is skewed to the left, symmetric, or skewed to the right if $\alpha_1 > 0$, $\alpha_1 = 0$, or $\alpha_1 < 0$, respectively. 3. The four parameters may be estimated by a number of methods [see, for example, Swain, Venkatraman, and Wilson (1988) and Slifker and Shapiro (1980)].

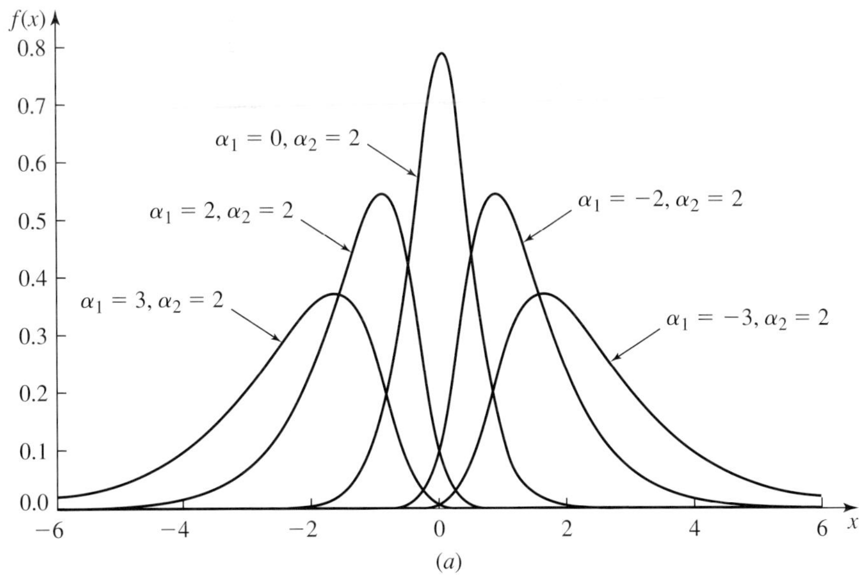

FIGURE 6.16
JSU(α_1, α_2, 0, 1) density functions.

(continued)

TABLE 6.3 *(continued)*

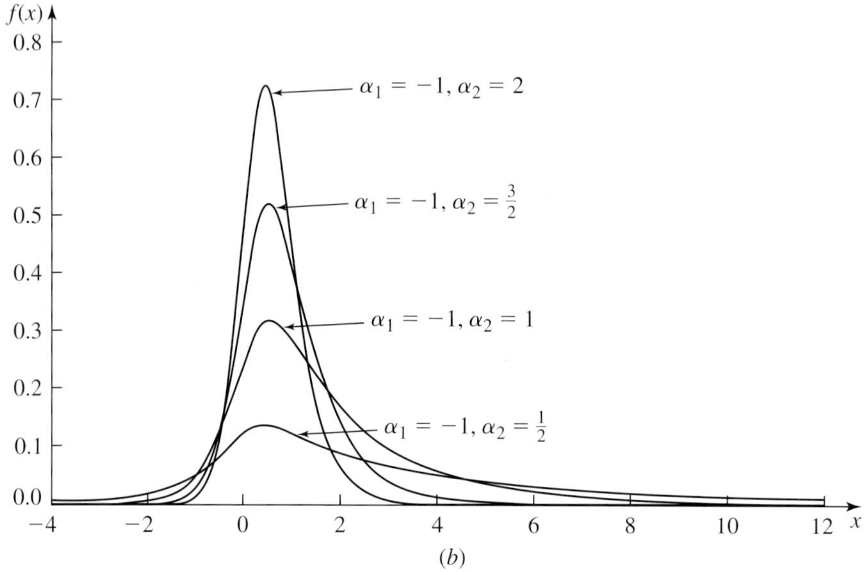

FIGURE 6.16
(continued)

Triangular	**triang(*a*, *b*, *m*)**
Possible applications	Used as a rough model in the absence of data (see Sec. 6.11)
Density (see Fig. 6.17)	$f(x) = \begin{cases} \dfrac{2(x-a)}{(b-a)(m-a)} & \text{if } a \le x \le m \\ \dfrac{2(b-x)}{(b-a)(b-m)} & \text{if } m < x \le b \\ 0 & \text{otherwise} \end{cases}$
Distribution	$F(x) = \begin{cases} 0 & \text{if } x < a \\ \dfrac{(x-a)^2}{(b-a)(m-a)} & \text{if } a \le x \le m \\ 1 - \dfrac{(b-x)^2}{(b-a)(b-m)} & \text{if } m < x \le b \\ 1 & \text{if } b < x \end{cases}$
Parameters	a, b, and m real numbers with $a < m < b$. a is a location parameter, $b - a$ is a scale parameter, m is a shape parameter
Range	$[a, b]$
Mean	$\dfrac{a + b + m}{3}$

TABLE 6.3 *(continued)*

Triangular	**triang(a, b, m)**
Variance	$\dfrac{a^2 + b^2 + m^2 - ab - am - bm}{18}$
Mode	m
MLE	Our use of the triangular distribution, as described in Sec. 6.11, is as a rough model when there are no data. Thus, MLEs are not relevant.
Comment	The limiting cases as $m \rightarrow b$ and $m \rightarrow a$ are called the *right triangular* and *left triangular distributions*, respectively, and are discussed in Prob. 8.7. For $a = 0$ and $b = 1$, both the left and right triangular distributions are special cases of the beta distribution.

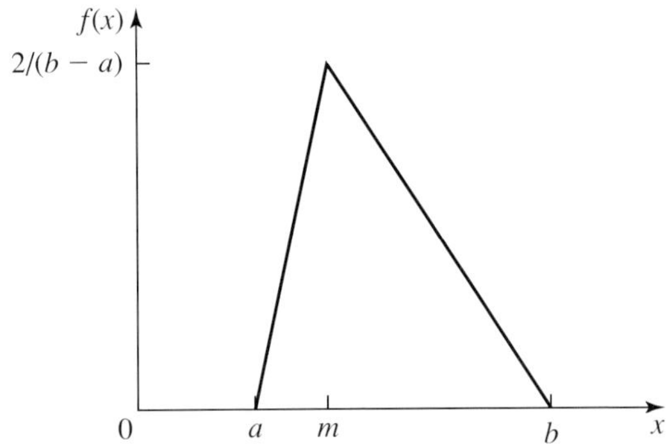

FIGURE 6.17
triang(a, b, m) density function.

6.2.3 Discrete Distributions

The descriptions of the six discrete distributions in Table 6.4 follow the same pattern as for the continuous distributions in Table 6.3.

6.2.4 Empirical Distributions

In some situations we might want to use the observed data themselves to specify directly (in some sense) a distribution, called an *empirical distribution,* from which random values are generated during the simulation, rather than fitting a theoretical distribution to the data. For example, it could happen that we simply cannot find a theoretical distribution that fits the data adequately (see Secs. 6.4 through 6.6). This section explores ways of specifying empirical distributions.

For continuous random variables, the type of empirical distribution that can be defined depends on whether we have the actual values of the individual original observations $X_1, X_2, \ldots, X_n$ rather than only the *number* of X_i's that fall into each of several specified intervals. (The latter case is called *grouped data* or *data in the form of a histogram.*) If the original data are available, we can define a continuous, piecewise-linear distribution function F by first sorting the X_i's into increasing

TABLE 6.4
Discrete distributions

Bernoulli	**Bernoulli(p)**
Possible applications	Random occurrence with two possible outcomes; used to generate other discrete random variates, e.g., binomial, geometric, and negative binomial
Mass (see Fig. 6.18)	$p(x) = \begin{cases} 1-p & \text{if } x = 0 \\ p & \text{if } x = 1 \\ 0 & \text{otherwise} \end{cases}$
Distribution	$F(x) = \begin{cases} 0 & \text{if } x < 0 \\ 1-p & \text{if } 0 \le x < 1 \\ 1 & \text{if } 1 \le x \end{cases}$
Parameter	$p \in (0, 1)$
Range	$\{0, 1\}$
Mean	p
Variance	$p(1-p)$
Mode	$\begin{cases} 0 & \text{if } p < \frac{1}{2} \\ 0 \text{ and } 1 & \text{if } p = \frac{1}{2} \\ 1 & \text{if } p > \frac{1}{2} \end{cases}$
MLE	$\hat{p} = \overline{X}(n)$
Comments	1. A Bernoulli(p) random variable X can be thought of as the outcome of an experiment that either "fails" or "succeeds." If the probability of success is p, and we let $X = 0$ if the experiment fails and $X = 1$ if it succeeds, then $X \sim$ Bernoulli(p). Such an experiment, often called a *Bernoulli trial,* provides a convenient way of relating several other discrete distributions to the Bernoulli distribution. 2. If t is a positive integer and $X_1, X_2, \ldots, X_t$ are independent Bernoulli(p) random variables, then $X_1 + X_2 + \cdots + X_t$ has the binomial distribution with parameters t and p. Thus, a binomial random variable can be thought of as the number of successes in a fixed number of independent Bernoulli trials. 3. Suppose we begin making independent replications of a Bernoulli trial with probability p of success on each trial. Then the number of failures *before* observing the first success has a geometric distribution with parameter p. For a positive integer s, the number of failures before

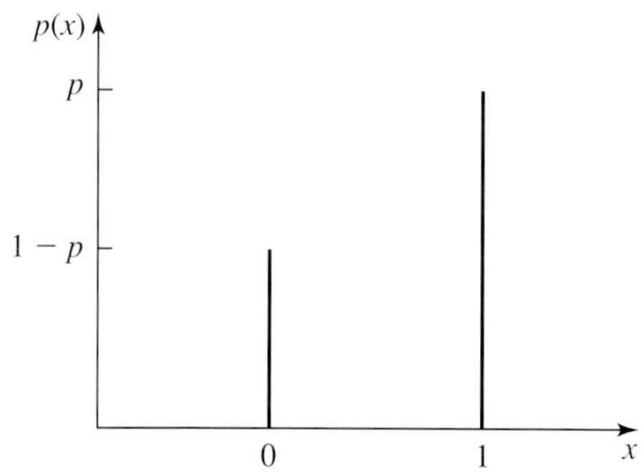

FIGURE 6.18
Bernoulli(p) mass function ($p > 0.5$ here).

TABLE 6.4 *(continued)*

Bernoulli	**Bernoulli(p)**
	observing the sth success has a negative binomial distribution with parameters s and p. 4. The Bernoulli(p) distribution is a special case of the binomial distribution (with $t = 1$ and the same value for p).

Discrete uniform	**DU(i, j)**
Possible applications	Random occurrence with several possible outcomes, each of which is equally likely; used as a "first" model for a quantity that is varying among the integers i through j but about which little else is known
Mass (see Fig. 6.19)	$p(x) = \begin{cases} \dfrac{1}{j-i+1} & \text{if } x \in \{i, i+1, \ldots, j\} \\ 0 & \text{otherwise} \end{cases}$
Distribution	$F(x) = \begin{cases} 0 & \text{if } x < i \\ \dfrac{\lfloor x \rfloor - i + 1}{j-i+1} & \text{if } i \le x \le j \\ 1 & \text{if } j < x \end{cases}$ where $\lfloor x \rfloor$ denotes the largest integer $\le x$
Parameters	i and j integers with $i \le j$; i is a location parameter, $j - i$ is a scale parameter
Range	$\{i, i+1, \ldots, j\}$
Mean	$\dfrac{i+j}{2}$
Variance	$\dfrac{(j-i+1)^2 - 1}{12}$
Mode	Does not uniquely exist
MLE	$\hat{i} = \min\limits_{1 \le k \le n} X_k, \quad \hat{j} = \max\limits_{1 \le k \le n} X_k$
Comment	The DU(0, 1) and Bernoulli($\frac{1}{2}$) distributions are the same.

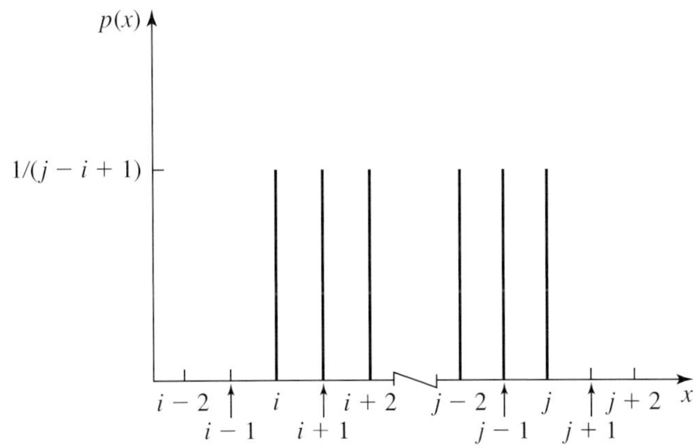

FIGURE 6.19
DU(i, j) mass function.

(continued)

TABLE 6.4 *(continued)*

Binomial	**bin(t, p)**
Possible applications	Number of successes in t independent Bernoulli trials with probability p of success on each trial; number of "defective" items in a batch of size t; number of items in a batch (e.g., a group of people) of random size; number of items demanded from an inventory
Mass (see Fig. 6.20)	$p(x) = \begin{cases} \binom{t}{x} p^x(1-p)^{t-x} & \text{if } x \in \{0, 1, \ldots, t\} \\ 0 & \text{otherwise} \end{cases}$ where $\binom{t}{x}$ is the *binomial coefficient*, defined by $\binom{t}{x} = \frac{t!}{x!(t-x)!}$
Distribution	$F(x) = \begin{cases} 0 & \text{if } x < 0 \\ \sum_{i=0}^{\lfloor x \rfloor} \binom{t}{i} p^i(1-p)^{t-i} & \text{if } 0 \le x \le t \\ 1 & \text{if } t < x \end{cases}$
Parameters	t a positive integer, $p \in (0, 1)$
Range	$\{0, 1, \ldots, t\}$

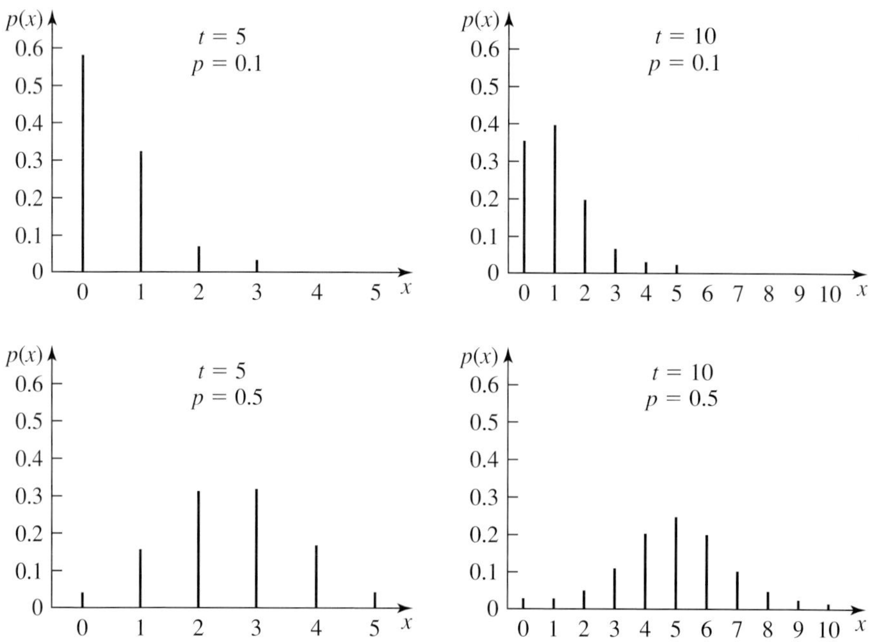

FIGURE 6.20
bin(t, p) mass functions.

TABLE 6.4 *(continued)*

Binomial	**bin(t, p)**
Mean	tp
Variance	$tp(1-p)$
Mode	$\begin{cases} p(t+1)-1 \text{ and } p(t+1) & \text{if } p(t+1) \text{ is an integer} \\ \lfloor p(t+1) \rfloor & \text{otherwise} \end{cases}$
MLE	If t is known, then $\hat{p} = \bar{X}(n)/t$. If both t and p are unknown, then $\hat{t}$ and $\hat{p}$ exist if and only if $\bar{X}(n) > (n-1)S^2(n)/n = V(n)$. Then the following approach could be taken. Let $M = \max_{1 \le i \le n} X_i$, and for $k = 0, 1, \ldots, M$, let f_k be the number of X_i's $\ge k$. Then it can be shown that $\hat{t}$ and $\hat{p}$ are the values for t and p that maximize the function $$g(t, p) = \sum_{k=1}^{M} f_k \ln(t-k+1) + nt\ln(1-p) + n\bar{X}(n)\ln\frac{p}{1-p}$$ subject to the constraints that $t \in \{M, M+1, \ldots\}$ and $0 < p < 1$. It is easy to see that for a fixed value of t, say t_0, the value of p that maximizes $g(t_0, p)$ is $\bar{X}(n)/t_0$, so $\hat{t}$ and $\hat{p}$ are the values of t and $\bar{X}(n)/t$ that lead to the largest value of $g[t, \bar{X}(n)/t]$ for $t \in \{M, M+1, \ldots, M'\}$, where M' is given by [see DeRiggi (1983)] $$M' = \left\lfloor \frac{\bar{X}(n)(M-1)}{1-[V(n)/\bar{X}(n)]} \right\rfloor$$ Note also that $g[t, \bar{X}(n)/t]$ is a unimodal function of t.
Comments	1. If $Y_1, Y_2, \ldots, Y_t$ are independent Bernoulli(p) random variables, then $Y_1 + Y_2 + \cdots + Y_t \sim \text{bin}(t, p)$. 2. If $X_1, X_2, \ldots, X_m$ are independent random variables and $X_i \sim \text{bin}(t_i, p)$, then $X_1 + X_2 + \cdots + X_m \sim \text{bin}(t_1 + t_2 + \cdots + t_m, p)$. 3. The bin($t, p$) distribution is symmetric if and only if $p = \frac{1}{2}$. 4. $X \sim \text{bin}(t, p)$ if and only if $t - X \sim \text{bin}(t, 1-p)$. 5. The bin($1, p$) and Bernoulli($p$) distributions are the same.

Geometric	**geom(p)**
Possible applications	Number of failures before the first success in a sequence of independent Bernoulli trials with probability p of success on each trial; number of items inspected before encountering the first defective item; number of items in a batch of random size; number of items demanded from an inventory
Mass (see Fig. 6.21)	$p(x) = \begin{cases} p(1-p)^x & \text{if } x \in \{0, 1, \ldots\} \\ 0 & \text{otherwise} \end{cases}$
Distribution	$F(x) = \begin{cases} 1-(1-p)^{\lfloor x \rfloor + 1} & \text{if } x \ge 0 \\ 0 & \text{otherwise} \end{cases}$
Parameter	$p \in (0, 1)$
Range	$\{0, 1, \ldots\}$
Mean	$\dfrac{1-p}{p}$

(continued)

TABLE 6.4 *(continued)*

Geometric	**geom(p)**
Variance	$\dfrac{1-p}{p^2}$
Mode	0
MLE	$\hat{p} = \dfrac{1}{\bar{X}(n) + 1}$
Comments	1. If $Y_1, Y_2, \ldots$ is a sequence of independent Bernoulli(p) random variables and $X = \min\{i: Y_i = 1\} - 1$, then $X \sim$ geom(p). 2. If $X_1, X_2, \ldots, X_s$ are independent geom(p) random variables, then $X_1 + X_2 + \cdots + X_s$ has a negative binomial distribution with parameters s and p. 3. The geometric distribution is the discrete analog of the exponential distribution, in the sense that it is the only discrete distribution with the memoryless property (see Prob. 4.31). 4. The geom(p) distribution is a special case of the negative binomial distribution (with $s = 1$ and the same value for p).

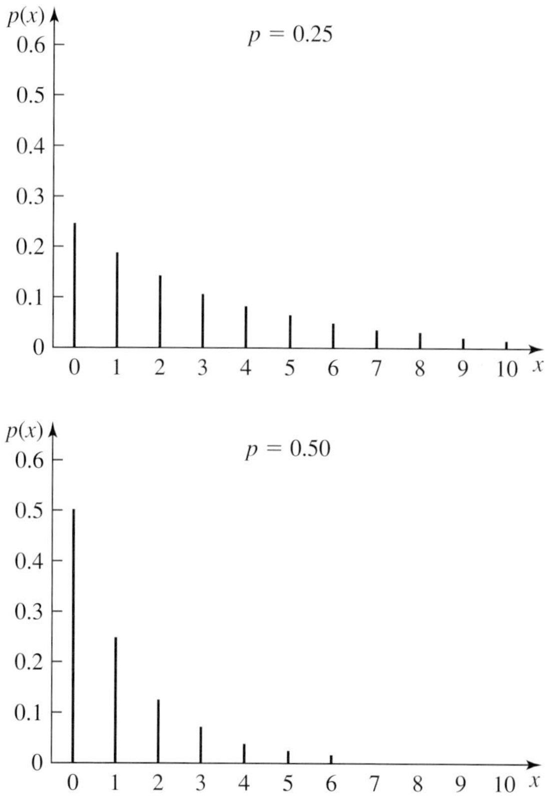

FIGURE 6.21
geom(p) mass functions.

TABLE 6.4 *(continued)*

Negative binomial	**negbin(s, p)**
Possible applications	Number of failures before the sth success in a sequence of independent Bernoulli trials with probability p of success on each trial; number of good items inspected before encountering the sth defective item; number of items in a batch of random size; number of items demanded from an inventory
Mass (see Fig. 6.22)	$p(x) = \begin{cases} \binom{s+x-1}{x} p^s(1-p)^x & \text{if } x \in \{0, 1, \ldots\} \\ 0 & \text{otherwise} \end{cases}$
Distribution	$F(x) = \begin{cases} \sum_{i=0}^{\lfloor x \rfloor} \binom{s+i-1}{i} p^s(1-p)^i & \text{if } x \geq 0 \\ 0 & \text{otherwise} \end{cases}$
Parameters	s a positive integer, $p \in (0, 1)$
Range	$\{0, 1, \ldots\}$
Mean	$\dfrac{s(1-p)}{p}$
Variance	$\dfrac{s(1-p)}{p^2}$
Mode	Let $y = [s(1-p) - 1]/p$; then $\text{Mode} = \begin{cases} y \text{ and } y+1 & \text{if } y \text{ is an integer} \\ \lfloor y \rfloor + 1 & \text{otherwise} \end{cases}$
MLE	If s is known, then $\hat{p} = s/[\overline{X}(n) + s]$. If both s and p are unknown, then $\hat{s}$ and $\hat{p}$ exist if and only if $V(n) = (n-1)S^2(n)/n > \overline{X}(n)$. Let $M = \max_{1 \leq i \leq n} X_i$, and for $k = 0, 1, \ldots, M$, let f_k be the number of X_i's $\geq k$. Then we can show that $\hat{s}$ and $\hat{p}$ are the values for s and p that maximize the function $$h(s, p) = \sum_{k=1}^{M} f_k \ln(s + k - 1) + ns \ln p + n\overline{X}(n) \ln(1-p)$$ subject to the constraints that $s \in \{1, 2, \ldots\}$ and $0 < p < 1$. For a fixed value of s, say s_0, the value of p that maximizes $h(s_0, p)$ is $s_0/[\overline{X}(n) + s_0]$, so that we could examine $h(1, 1/[\overline{X}(n) + 1]), h(2, 2/[\overline{X}(n) + 2]), \ldots$. Then $\hat{s}$ and $\hat{p}$ are chosen to be the values of s and $s/[\overline{X}(n) + s]$ that lead to the biggest observed value of $h(s, s/[\overline{X}(n) + s])$. However, since $h(s, s/[\overline{X}(n) + s])$ is a unimodal function of s [see Levin and Reeds (1977)], it is clear when to terminate the search.
Comments	1. If $Y_1, Y_2, \ldots, Y_s$ are independent geom(p) random variables, then $Y_1 + Y_2 + \cdots + Y_s \sim$ negbin(s, p). 2. If $Y_1, Y_2, \ldots$ is a sequence of independent Bernoulli(p) random variables and $X = \min\{i: \sum_{j=1}^{i} Y_j = s\} - s$, then $X \sim$ negbin(s, p). 3. If $X_1, X_2, \ldots, X_m$ are independent random variables and $X_i \sim$ negbin(s_i, p), then $X_1 + X_2 + \cdots + X_m \sim$ negbin($s_1 + s_2 + \cdots + s_m, p$). 4. The negbin(1, p) and geom(p) distributions are the same.

(continued)

TABLE 6.4 *(continued)*

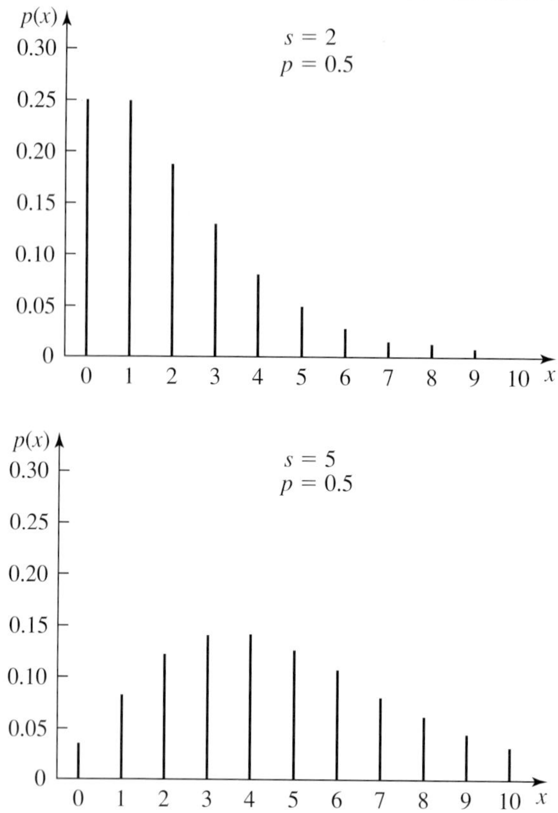

FIGURE 6.22
negbin(s, p) mass functions.

Poisson	**Poisson(λ)**
Possible applications	Number of events that occur in an interval of time when the events are occurring at a constant rate (see Sec. 6.12); number of items in a batch of random size; number of items demanded from an inventory
Mass (see Fig. 6.23)	$p(x) = \begin{cases} \dfrac{e^{-\lambda}\lambda^x}{x!} & \text{if } x \in \{0, 1, \ldots\} \\ 0 & \text{otherwise} \end{cases}$
Distribution	$F(x) = \begin{cases} 0 & \text{if } x < 0 \\ e^{-\lambda} \sum_{i=0}^{\lfloor x \rfloor} \dfrac{\lambda^i}{i!} & \text{if } x \ge 0 \end{cases}$
Parameter	$\lambda > 0$
Range	$\{0, 1, \ldots\}$
Mean	λ
Variance	λ

TABLE 6.4 *(continued)*

Poisson	Poisson(λ)
Mode	$\begin{cases} \lambda - 1 \text{ and } \lambda & \text{if } \lambda \text{ is an integer} \\ \lfloor \lambda \rfloor & \text{otherwise} \end{cases}$
MLE	$\hat{\lambda} = \bar{X}(n)$.
Comments	1. Let $Y_1, Y_2, \ldots$ be a sequence of nonnegative IID random variables, and let $X = \max\{i: \sum_{j=1}^{i} Y_j \le 1\}$. Then the distribution of the Y_i's is expo($1/\lambda$) if and only if $X \sim$ Poisson(λ). Also, if $X' = \max\{i: \sum_{j=1}^{i} Y_j \le \lambda\}$, then the Y_i's are expo(1) if and only if $X' \sim$ Poisson(λ) (see also Sec. 6.12). 2. If $X_1, X_2, \ldots, X_m$ are independent random variables and $X_i \sim$ Poisson(λ_i), then $X_1 + X_2 + \cdots + X_m \sim$ Poisson($\lambda_1 + \lambda_2 + \cdots + \lambda_m$).

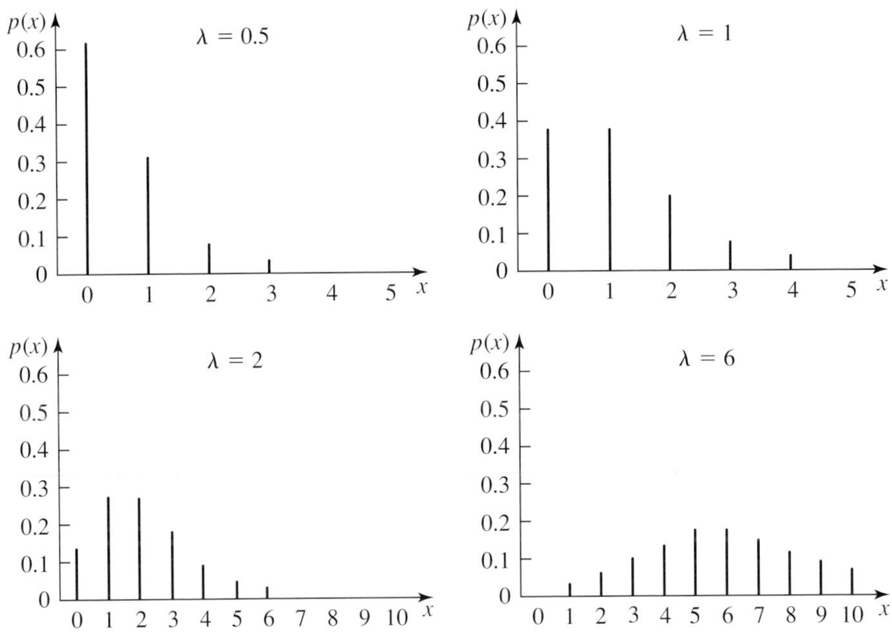

FIGURE 6.23
Poisson(λ) mass functions.

order. Let $X_{(i)}$ denote the ith smallest of the X_j's, so that $X_{(1)} \le X_{(2)} \le \cdots \le X_{(n)}$. Then F is given by

$$F(x) = \begin{cases} 0 & \text{if } x < X_{(1)} \\ \dfrac{i-1}{n-1} + \dfrac{x - X_{(i)}}{(n-1)(X_{(i+1)} - X_{(i)})} & \text{if } X_{(i)} \le x < X_{(i+1)} \\ & \quad \text{for } i = 1, 2, \ldots, n-1 \\ 1 & \text{if } X_{(n)} \le x \end{cases}$$

Figure 6.24 gives an illustration for $n = 6$. Note that $F(x)$ rises most rapidly over those ranges of x in which the X_i's are most densely distributed, as desired.

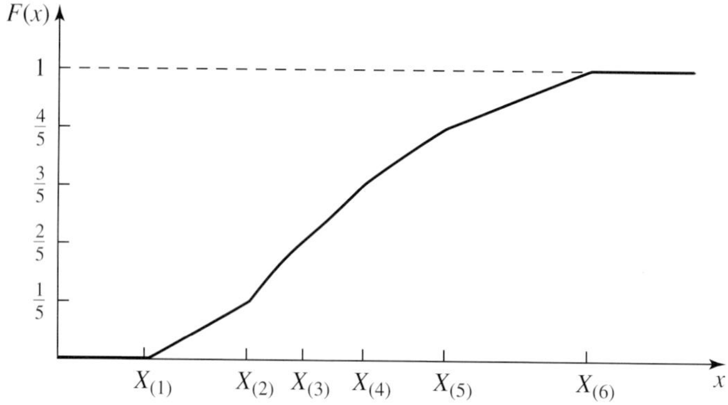

FIGURE 6.24
Continuous, piecewise-linear empirical distribution function from original data.

Also, for each i, $F(X_{(i)}) = (i-1)/(n-1)$, which is approximately (for large n) the proportion of the X_j's that are *less than* $X_{(i)}$; this is also the way we would like a *continuous* distribution function to behave. (See Prob. 6.5 for a discussion of another way to define F.) However, one clear disadvantage of specifying this particular empirical distribution is that random values generated from it during a simulation run can never be less than $X_{(1)}$ or greater than $X_{(n)}$ (see Sec. 8.3.16). Also, the mean of $F(x)$ is not equal to the sample mean $\bar{X}(n)$ of the X_i's (see Prob. 6.6).

If, however, the data are grouped, then a different approach must be taken since we do not know the values of the individual X_i's. Suppose that the n X_i's are grouped into k adjacent intervals $[a_0, a_1), [a_1, a_2), \ldots, [a_{k-1}, a_k)$, so that the jth interval contains n_j observations, where $n_1 + n_2 + \cdots + n_k = n$. (Often the a_j's will be equally spaced, but we need not make this assumption.) A reasonable piecewise-linear empirical distribution function G could be specified by first letting $G(a_0) = 0$ and $G(a_j) = (n_1 + n_2 + \cdots + n_j)/n$ for $j = 1, 2, \ldots, k$. Then, interpolating linearly between the a_j's, we define

$$G(x) = \begin{cases} 0 & \text{if } x < a_0 \\ G(a_{j-1}) + \dfrac{x - a_{j-1}}{a_j - a_{j-1}} [G(a_j) - G(a_{j-1})] & \text{if } a_{j-1} \le x < a_j \\ & \quad \text{for } j = 1, 2, \ldots, k \\ 1 & \text{if } a_k \le x \end{cases}$$

Figure 6.25 illustrates this specification of an empirical distribution for $k = 4$. In this case, $G(a_j)$ is the proportion of the X_i's that are less than a_j, and $G(x)$ rises most rapidly over ranges of x where the observations are most dense. The random values generated from this distribution, however, will still be bounded both below (by a_0) and above (by a_k); see Sec. 8.3.16.

In practice, many continuous distributions are skewed to the right and have a density with a shape similar to that in Fig. 6.26. Thus, if the sample size n is not very large, we are likely to have few, if any, observations from the right tail of the true underlying distribution (since these tail probabilities are usually small). Moreover, the above empirical distributions do not allow random values to be generated

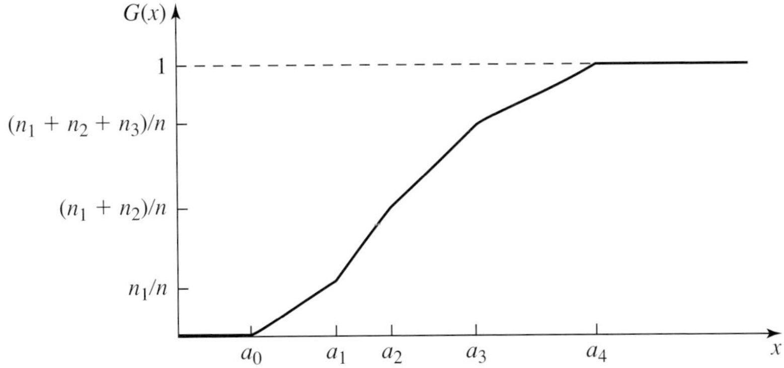

FIGURE 6.25
Continuous, piecewise-linear empirical distribution function from grouped data.

beyond the largest observation. On the other hand, very large generated values can have a significant impact on the disposition of a simulation run. For example, a large service time can cause considerable congestion in a queueing-type system. As a result, Bratley, Fox, and Schrage (1987, pp. 131–133, 150–151) suggest appending an exponential distribution to the right side of the empirical distribution, which allows values larger than $X_{(n)}$ to be generated.

For discrete data, it is quite simple to define an empirical distribution, provided that the original data values $X_1, X_2, \ldots, X_n$ are available. For each possible value x, an empirical mass function $p(x)$ can be defined to be the proportion of the X_i's that are equal to x. For grouped discrete data we could define a mass function such that the *sum* of the $p(x)$'s over all possible values of x in an interval is equal to the

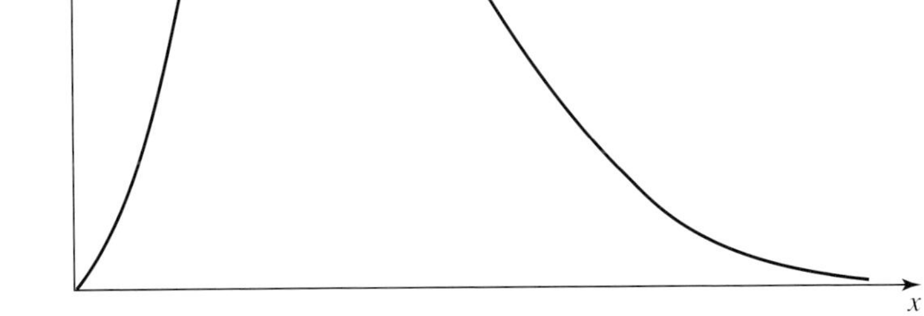

FIGURE 6.26
Typical density function experienced in practice.

proportion of the X_i's in that interval. How the individual $p(x)$'s are allocated for the possible values of x within an interval is essentially arbitrary.

6.3 TECHNIQUES FOR ASSESSING SAMPLE INDEPENDENCE

An important assumption made by many of the statistical techniques discussed in this chapter is that the observations $X_1, X_2, \ldots, X_n$ are an *independent* (or *random*) sample from some underlying distribution. For example, maximum-likelihood estimation (see Sec. 6.5) and chi-square tests (see Sec. 6.6.2) assume independence. If the assumption of independence is not satisfied, then these statistical techniques may not be valid. However, even when the data are not independent, heuristic techniques such as histograms can still be used.

Sometimes observations collected over time are dependent. For example, suppose that $X_1, X_2, \ldots$ represent hourly temperatures in a certain city starting at noon on a particular day. We would not expect these data to be independent, since hourly temperatures close together in time should be positively correlated. As a second example, consider the single-server queueing system in Sec. 1.4. Let $X_1, X_2, \ldots$ be the delays in queue of the successive customers arriving to the system. If the arrival rate of customers is close to the service rate, the system will be congested and the X_i's will be highly positively correlated (see Sec. 4.3).

We now describe two graphical techniques for informally assessing whether the data $X_1, X_2, \ldots, X_n$ (listed in time order of collection) are independent. The *correlation plot* is a graph of the sample correlation $\hat{\rho}_j$ (see Sec. 4.4) for $j = 1, 2, \ldots, l$ (l is a positive integer). The sample correlation $\hat{\rho}_j$ is an estimate of the true correlation ρ_j between two observations that are j observations apart in time. (Note that $-1 \le \rho_j \le 1$.) If the observations $X_1, X_2, \ldots, X_n$ are independent, then $\rho_j = 0$ for $j = 1, 2, \ldots, n - 1$. However, the $\hat{\rho}_j$'s will not be exactly zero even when the X_i's are independent, since $\hat{\rho}_j$ is an observation of a random variable whose mean is not equal to 0 (see Sec. 4.4). If the $\hat{\rho}_j$'s differ from 0 by a significant amount, then this is strong evidence that the X_i's are not independent.

The *scatter diagram* of the observations $X_1, X_2, \ldots, X_n$ is a plot of the pairs (X_i, X_{i+1}) for $i = 1, 2, \ldots, n - 1$. Suppose for simplicity that the X_i's are nonnegative. If the X_i's are independent, one would expect the points (X_i, X_{i+1}) to be scattered randomly throughout the first quadrant of the (X_i, X_{i+1}) plane. The nature of the scattering will, however, depend on the underlying distributions of the X_i's. If the X_i's are positively correlated, then the points will tend to lie along a line with positive slope in the first quadrant. If the X_i's are negatively correlated, then the points will tend to lie along a line with negative slope in the first quadrant.

EXAMPLE 6.2. In Figs. 6.27 and 6.28 we give the correlation plot and scatter diagram for 100 *independent* observations from an exponential distribution with a mean of 1. Note in Fig. 6.27 that the sample correlations are close to 0, but have absolute values as large as 0.16. The scattering of the points in Fig. 6.28 substantiates the independence of the exponential data.

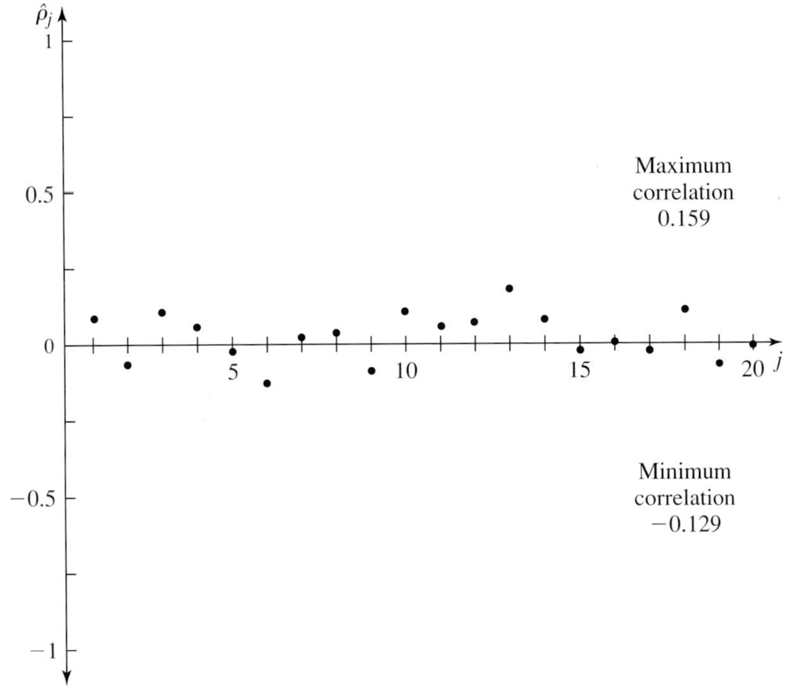

FIGURE 6.27
Correlation plot for independent exponential data.

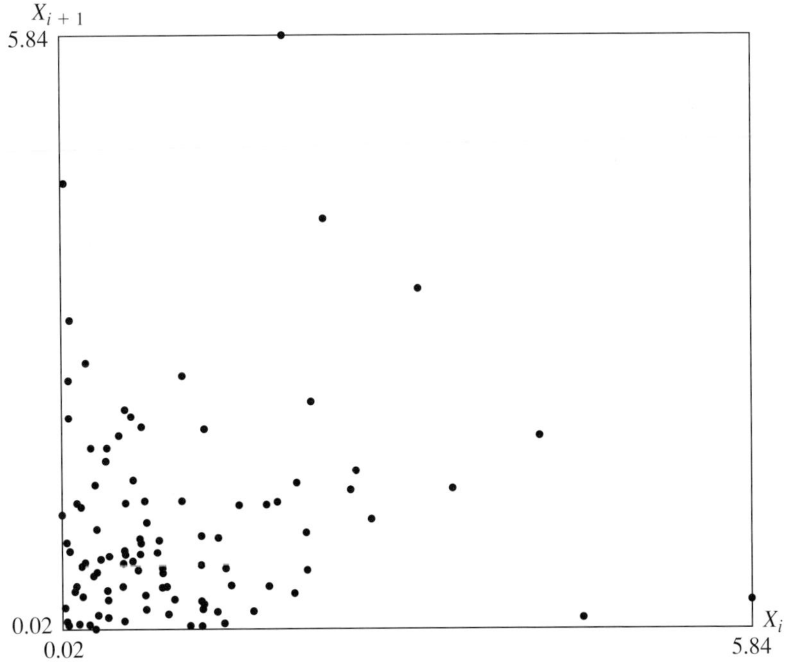

FIGURE 6.28
Scatter diagram for independent exponential data.

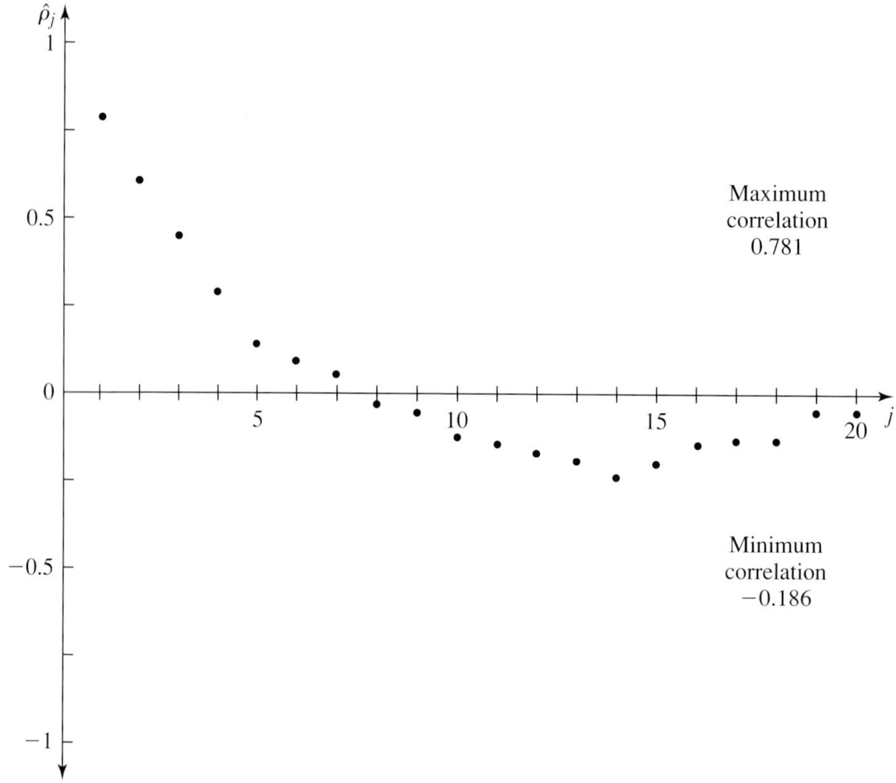

FIGURE 6.29
Correlation plot for correlated queueing data.

EXAMPLE 6.3. In Figs. 6.29 and 6.30 we present the correlation plot and scatter diagram for 100 delays in queue from an *M/M/*1 queueing system (see Sec. 1.4.3) with utilization factor $\rho = 0.8$. Note that the $\hat{\rho}_j$'s are large for small values of j and that the points in the scatter diagram tend to lie along a line with positive slope. These facts are consistent with our statement that delays in queue are positively correlated.

There are also several nonparametric (i.e., no assumptions are made about the distributions of the X_i's) statistical tests that can be used to test formally whether $X_1, X_2, \ldots, X_n$ are independent. Bartels (1982) proposes a rank version of von Neumann's ratio as a test statistic for independence and provides the necessary critical values to carry out the test. However, one potential drawback is that the test assumes that there are no "ties" in the data, where a tie means $X_i = X_j$ for $i \neq j$. This requirement will generally not be met for discrete data, and may not even be satisfied for continuous data if they are recorded with only a few decimal places of accuracy. (See the interarrival times in Table 6.7.) Bartels states that his critical values may still be reasonably accurate if the number of ties is small.

There are several versions of the runs test [see, for example, Sec. 7.4.1 and Gibbons (1985)], which can also be used to assess the independence of the X_i's.

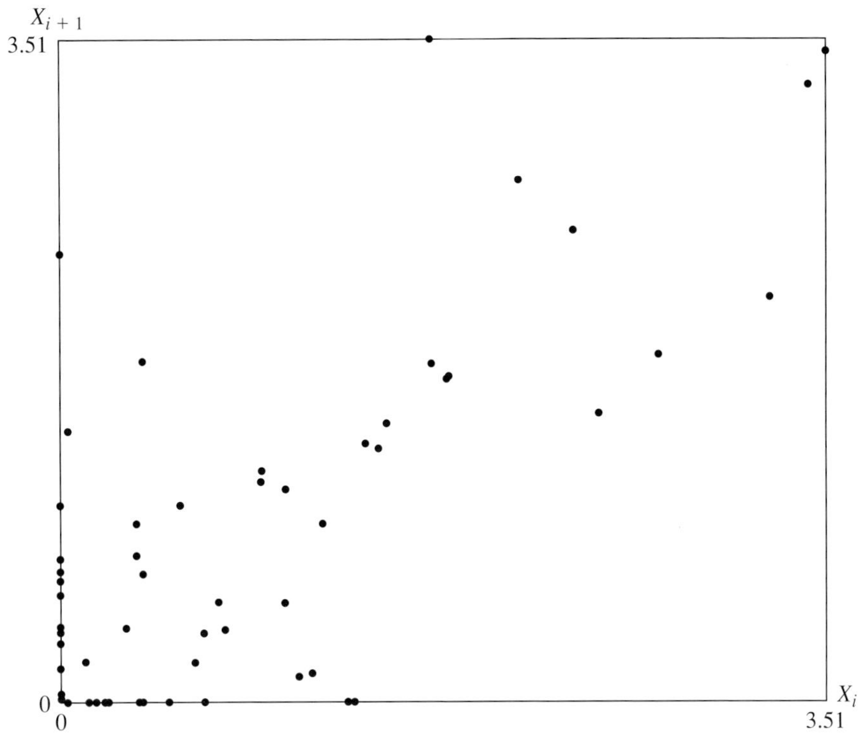

FIGURE 6.30
Scatter diagram for correlated queueing data.

They should have less difficulty with ties than the rank von Neumann test, since runs tests require only that $X_i \neq X_{i+1}$ for $i = 1, 2, \ldots, n - 1$. On the other hand, Bartels showed empirically that the rank von Neumann test is considerably more powerful than one of the runs tests against certain types of alternatives to the X_i's being independent.

6.4 ACTIVITY I: HYPOTHESIZING FAMILIES OF DISTRIBUTIONS

The first step in selecting a particular input distribution is to decide what general families—e.g., exponential, normal, or Poisson—appear to be appropriate on the basis of their shapes, without worrying (yet) about the specific parameter values for these families. This section describes some general techniques that can be used to *hypothesize* families of distributions that might be representative of a simulation input random variable.

In some situations, use can be made of *prior knowledge* about a certain random variable's role in a system to select a modeling distribution or at least rule out some distributions; this is done on theoretical grounds and does not require any data at all. For example, if we feel that customers arrive to a service facility one at a time, at a constant rate, and so that the numbers of customers arriving in disjoint time intervals are independent, then there are theoretical reasons (see Sec. 6.12.1) for postulating that the interarrival times are IID exponential random variables. Recall also that several discrete distributions—binomial, geometric, and negative binomial—were developed from a physical model. Often the range of a distribution rules it out as a modeling distribution. Service times, for example, should not be generated directly from a normal distribution (at least in principle), since a random value from *any* normal distribution can be negative. The proportion of defective items in a large batch should not be assumed to have a gamma distribution, since proportions must be between 0 and 1, whereas gamma random variables have no upper bound. Prior information should be used whenever available, but confirming the postulated distribution with data is also strongly recommended.

In practice, we seldom have enough of this kind of theoretical prior information to select a single distribution, and the task of hypothesizing a distribution family from observed data is somewhat less structured. In the remainder of this section, we discuss various *heuristics*, or guidelines, that can be used to help one choose appropriate families of distributions.

6.4.1 Summary Statistics

Some distributions are characterized at least partially by functions of their *true* parameters. In Table 6.5 we give a number of such functions, formulas to estimate these functions from IID data $X_1, X_2, \ldots, X_n$ [these estimates are called *summary* (or *descriptive*) statistics], an indication of whether they are applicable to continuous (C) or discrete (D) data, and comments about their interpretation or use. (We have included the sample minimum and maximum because of their utility, even though they may not be a direct function of a distribution's parameters.) Further discussion of many of these functions may be found in Chap. 4.

These functions might be used in some cases to suggest an appropriate distribution family. For a symmetric continuous distribution (e.g., normal), the mean μ is equal to the median $x_{0.5}$. (For a symmetric discrete distribution, the population mean and median may be only approximately equal; see the definition of the median in Sec. 4.2.) Thus, if the estimates $\overline{X}(n)$ and $\hat{x}_{0.5}(n)$ are "almost equal," this is some indication that the underlying distribution may be symmetric. One should keep in mind that $\overline{X}(n)$ and $\hat{x}_{0.5}(n)$ are observations of random variables, and thus their relationship does not necessarily provide definitive information about the true relationship between μ and $x_{0.5}$.

The *coefficient of variation* cv can sometimes provide useful information about the form of a continuous distribution. In particular, cv $=$ 1 for the exponential distribution, regardless of the scale parameter β. Thus, $\widehat{\text{cv}}(n)$ being close to 1 suggests that the underlying distribution is exponential. For the gamma and Weibull distributions, cv is greater than, equal to, or less than 1 when the shape parameter α is less than, equal to, or greater than 1, respectively. Furthermore, these distributions

TABLE 6.5
Useful summary statistics

Function	Sample estimate (summary statistic)	Continuous (C) or discrete (D)	Comments
Minimum, maximum	$X_{(1)}, X_{(n)}$	C, D	$[X_{(1)}, X_{(n)}]$ is a rough estimate of the range
Mean μ	$\bar{X}(n)$	C, D	Measure of central tendency
Median $x_{0.5}$	$\hat{x}_{0.5}(n) = \begin{cases} X_{((n+1)/2)} & \text{if } n \text{ is odd} \\ [X_{(n/2)} + X_{((n/2)+1)}]/2 & \text{if } n \text{ is even} \end{cases}$	C, D	Alternative measure of central tendency
Variance σ^2	$S^2(n)$	C, D	Measure of variability
Coefficient of variation, $\text{cv} = \frac{\sqrt{\sigma^2}}{\mu}$	$\widehat{\text{cv}}(n) = \frac{\sqrt{S^2(n)}}{\bar{X}(n)}$	C	Alternative measure of variability
Lexis ratio, $\tau = \frac{\sigma^2}{\mu}$	$\hat{\tau}(n) = \frac{S^2(n)}{\bar{X}(n)}$	D	Alternative measure of variability
Skewness, $\nu = \frac{E[(X - \mu)^3]}{(\sigma^2)^{3/2}}$	$\hat{\nu}(n) = \frac{n^2}{(n-1)(n-2)} \frac{\sum_{i=1}^{n} [X_i - \bar{X}(n)]^3/n}{[S^2(n)]^{3/2}}$	C, D	Measure of symmetry

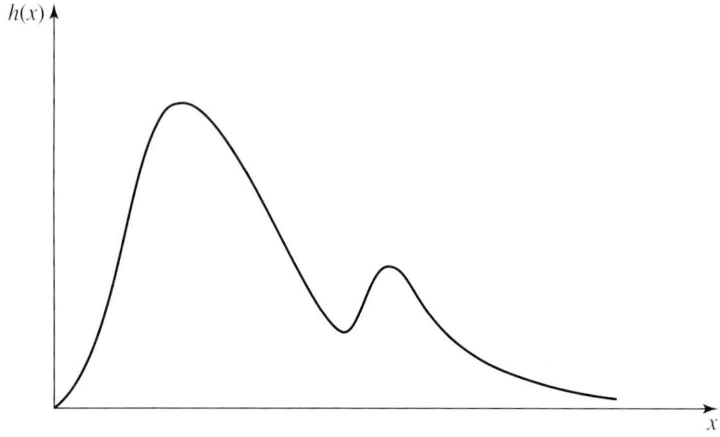

FIGURE 6.31
Histogram corresponding to a density function with two local modes.

However, in this case we need not make any arbitrary subjective decisions about interval width and placement.

There are certain situations in which the histogram will have several local modes (or "humps"), in which case none of the standard distributions discussed in Sec. 6.2 may provide an adequate representation. In Fig. 6.31 we give such an example, which might represent (continuous) times to repair some machine collected over a 1-year period. There are two types of breakdowns for the machine. Most of the breakdowns are minor, and the corresponding repair time is relatively small; this case corresponds to the left hump in Fig. 6.31. A small proportion of the breakdowns are major and have large repair times, since spare parts need to be ordered. This results in the right hump in Fig. 6.31. If the observed repair times can be separated into these two cases (corresponding to minor and major repairs), with p_j being the proportion of observations for case j ($j = 1, 2$), then a density $f_j(x)$ is fit to the class j observations ($j = 1, 2$) using the methods discussed in Secs. 6.4 through 6.6. Thus, the overall repair-time density $f(x)$ is given by

$$f(x) = p_1 f_1(x) + p_2 f_2(x)$$

and random repair times can be generated from $f(x)$ during a simulation by using the composition technique (see Sec. 8.2.2). See Sec. 6.9 and Prob. 6.8 for alternative methods for modeling a histogram with several modes.

6.4.3 Quantile Summaries and Box Plots

The *quantile summary* [see, for example, Tukey (1970)] is a synopsis of the sample that is useful for determining whether the underlying probability density function or probability mass function is symmetric or skewed to the right or to the left. It is applicable to either continuous or discrete data sets; however, for expository convenience we will explain it only for the continuous case.

TABLE 6.6
Structure of the quantile summary for the sample $X_1, X_2, \ldots, X_n$

Quantile	Depth	Sample value(s)		Midpoint
Median	$i = (n + 1)/2$	$X_{(i)}$		$X_{(i)}$
Quartiles	$j = (\lfloor i \rfloor + 1)/2$	$X_{(j)}$	$X_{(n-j+1)}$	$[X_{(j)} + X_{(n-j+1)}]/2$
Octiles	$k = (\lfloor j \rfloor + 1)/2$	$X_{(k)}$	$X_{(n-k+1)}$	$[X_{(k)} + X_{(n-k+1)}]/2$
Extremes	1	$X_{(1)}$	$X_{(n)}$	$[X_{(1)} + X_{(n)}]/2$

Suppose that $F(x)$ is the distribution function for a continuous random variable. Suppose further that $F(x)$ is continuous and strictly increasing when $0 < F(x) < 1$. [This means that if $x_1 < x_2$ and $0 < F(x_1) \leq F(x_2) < 1$, then in fact $F(x_1) < F(x_2)$.] For $0 < q < 1$, the *q-quantile* of $F(x)$ is that number x_q such that $F(x_q) = q$. If F^{-1} denotes the inverse of $F(x)$, then $x_q = F^{-1}(q)$. $\{F^{-1}$ is that function such that $F[F^{-1}(x)] = F^{-1}[F(x)] = x.\}$ Here we are particularly interested in the median $x_{0.5}$, the lower and upper quartiles $x_{0.25}$ and $x_{0.75}$, and the lower and upper octiles $x_{0.125}$ and $x_{0.875}$. A quantile summary for the sample $X_1, X_2, \ldots, X_n$ has a form that is given in Table 6.6.

In Table 6.6, if the "depth" subscript l (l is equal to i, j, or k) is halfway between the integers m and $m' = m + 1$, then $X_{(l)}$ is defined to be the average of $X_{(m)}$ and $X_{(m')}$. The value $X_{(i)}$ is an estimate of the median, $X_{(j)}$ and $X_{(n-j+1)}$ are estimates of the quartiles, and $X_{(k)}$ and $X_{(n-k+1)}$ are estimates of the octiles. If the underlying distribution of the X_i's is symmetric, then the four midpoints should be approximately equal. On the other hand, if the underlying distribution of the X_i's is skewed to the right (left), then the four midpoints (from the top to the bottom of the table) should be increasing (decreasing).

A *box plot* is a graphical representation of the quantile summary (see Fig. 6.33). Fifty percent of the observations fall within the horizontal boundaries of the box $[x_{0.25}, x_{0.75}]$. (In some books, box plots do not contain octiles.)

The following two examples illustrate the use of the techniques discussed in Sec. 6.4.

EXAMPLE 6.4. A simulation model was developed for a drive-up banking facility, and data were collected on the arrival pattern for cars. Over a fixed 90-minute interval, 220 cars arrived, and we noted the (continuous) interarrival time X_i (in minutes) between cars i and $i + 1$, for $i = 1, 2, \ldots, 219$. Table 6.7 lists these $n = 219$ interarrival times after they have been sorted into increasing order. The numbers of cars arriving in the six consecutive 15-minute intervals were counted and found to be approximately equal, suggesting that the arrival rate is somewhat constant over *this* 90-minute interval. Furthermore, cars arrive one at a time, and there is no reason to believe that the numbers of arrivals in disjoint intervals are not independent. Thus, on theoretical grounds (see Sec. 6.12.1) we postulate that the interarrival times are exponential. To substantiate this hypothesis, we first look at the summary statistics given in Table 6.8. Since $\overline{X}(219) = 0.399 > 0.270 = \hat{x}_{0.5}(219)$ and $\hat{\nu}(219) = 1.478$, this suggests that the underlying distribution is skewed to the right, rather than symmetric. Furthermore, $\widehat{\text{cv}}(219) = 0.953$, which is close to the theoretical value of 1 for the exponential distribution. Next we made three different histograms of the data, using $b_0 = 0$ in each case and $\Delta b = 0.050$, 0.075, and 0.100, as shown in Fig. 6.32 (see also Fig. 6.2). The smoothest-looking

TABLE 6.7
n = 219 interarrival times (minutes) sorted into increasing order

0.01	0.06	0.12	0.23	0.38	0.53	0.88
0.01	0.07	0.12	0.23	0.38	0.53	0.88
0.01	0.07	0.12	0.24	0.38	0.54	0.90
0.01	0.07	0.13	0.25	0.39	0.54	0.93
0.01	0.07	0.13	0.25	0.40	0.55	0.93
0.01	0.07	0.14	0.25	0.40	0.55	0.95
0.01	0.07	0.14	0.25	0.41	0.56	0.97
0.01	0.07	0.14	0.25	0.41	0.57	1.03
0.02	0.07	0.14	0.26	0.43	0.57	1.05
0.02	0.07	0.15	0.26	0.43	0.60	1.05
0.03	0.07	0.15	0.26	0.43	0.61	1.06
0.03	0.08	0.15	0.26	0.44	0.61	1.09
0.03	0.08	0.15	0.26	0.45	0.63	1.10
0.04	0.08	0.15	0.27	0.45	0.63	1.11
0.04	0.08	0.15	0.28	0.46	0.64	1.12
0.04	0.09	0.17	0.28	0.47	0.65	1.17
0.04	0.09	0.18	0.29	0.47	0.65	1.18
0.04	0.10	0.19	0.29	0.47	0.65	1.24
0.04	0.10	0.19	0.30	0.48	0.69	1.24
0.05	0.10	0.19	0.31	0.49	0.69	1.28
0.05	0.10	0.20	0.31	0.49	0.70	1.33
0.05	0.10	0.21	0.32	0.49	0.72	1.38
0.05	0.10	0.21	0.35	0.49	0.72	1.44
0.05	0.10	0.21	0.35	0.50	0.72	1.51
0.05	0.10	0.21	0.35	0.50	0.74	1.72
0.05	0.10	0.21	0.36	0.50	0.75	1.83
0.05	0.11	0.22	0.36	0.51	0.76	1.96
0.05	0.11	0.22	0.36	0.51	0.77	
0.05	0.11	0.22	0.37	0.51	0.79	
0.06	0.11	0.23	0.37	0.52	0.84	
0.06	0.11	0.23	0.38	0.52	0.86	
0.06	0.12	0.23	0.38	0.53	0.87	

TABLE 6.8
Summary statistics for the interarrival-time data

Summary statistic	Value
Minimum	0.010
Maximum	1.960
Mean	0.399
Median	0.270
Variance	0.144
Coefficient of variation	0.953
Skewness	1.478

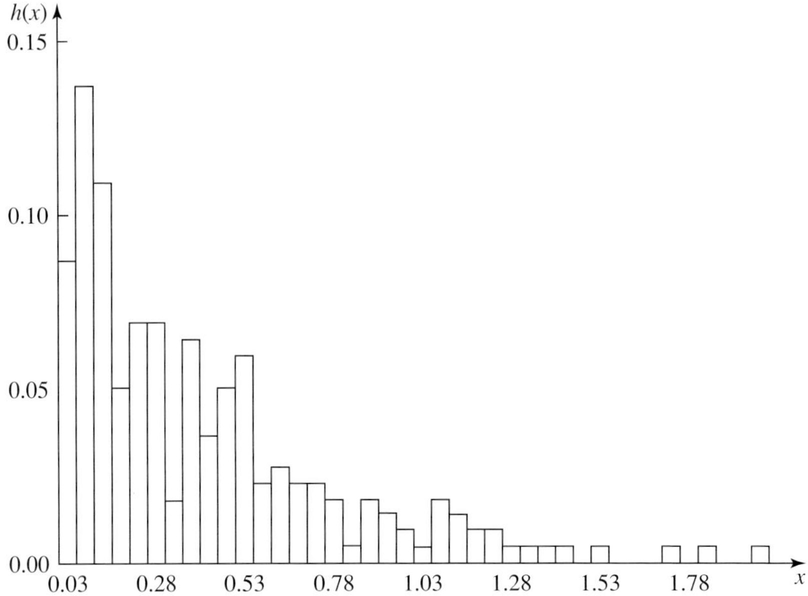

(a)

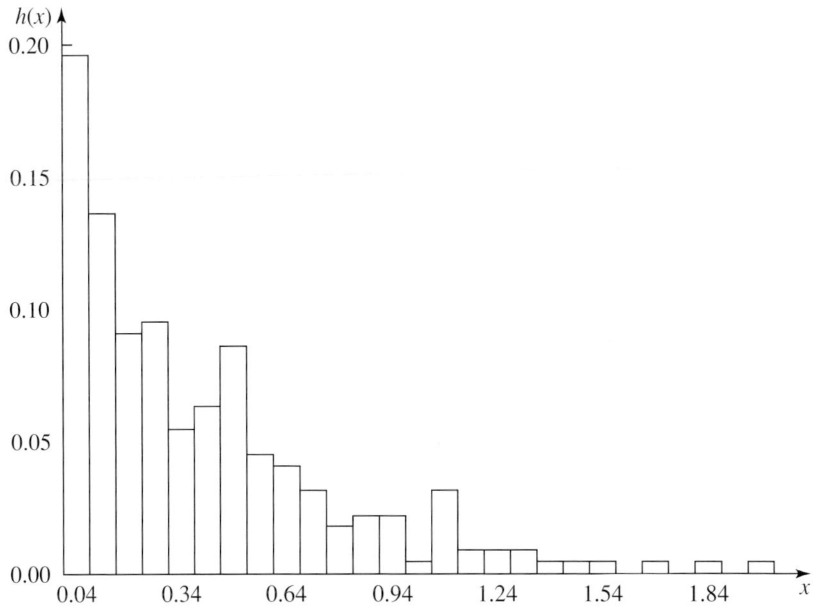

(b)

FIGURE 6.32
Histograms of the interarrival-time data in Table 6.7: (a) $\Delta b = 0.050$; (b) $\Delta b = 0.075$; (c) $\Delta b = 0.100$.

(continued)

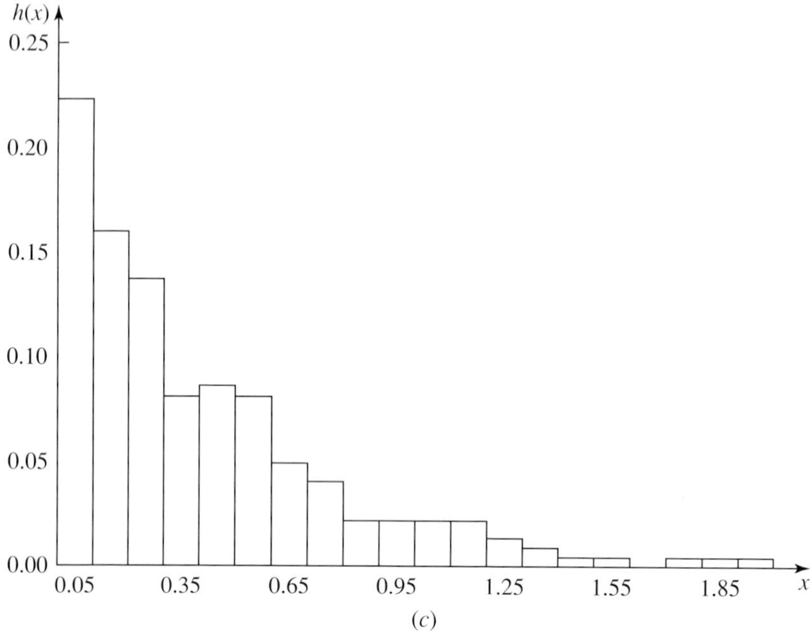

FIGURE 6.32
(*continued*)

histogram appears to be for $\Delta b = 0.100$ and its shape resembles that of an exponential density. (Note that Sturges's rule gives $k = 8$ and $\Delta b = 0.250$, resulting in overaggregation of the data.) Finally, in Fig. 6.33 we give the quantile summary and box plot for the interarrival times. The increasing midpoints and the elongated nature of the right side of the box plot reaffirm that the underlying distribution is exponential. In summary, for both theoretical and empirical reasons, we hypothesize that the interarrival times are exponential.

Quantile	Depth	Sample value(s)			Midpoint
Median	110		0.270		0.270
Quartiles	55.5	0.100		0.545	0.323
Octiles	28	0.050		0.870	0.460
Extremes	1	0.010		1.960	0.985

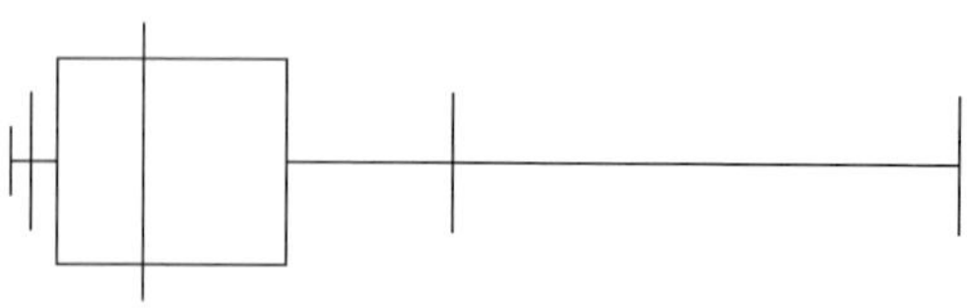

FIGURE 6.33
Quantile summary and box plot for the interarrival-time data.

TABLE 6.9
Values and counts for n = 156 demand sizes arranged into increasing order

0(59),	1(26),	2(24),	3(18),	4(12),
5(5),	6(4),	7(3),	9(3),	11(2)

TABLE 6.10
Summary statistics for the demand-size data

Summary statistic	Value
Minimum	0.000
Maximum	11.000
Mean	1.891
Median	1.000
Variance	5.285
Lexis ratio	2.795
Skewness	1.687

EXAMPLE 6.5. Table 6.9 gives the values and counts for $n = 156$ observations on the (discrete) number of items demanded in a week from an inventory over a 3-year period, arranged into increasing order. Rather than giving all the individual values, we give the frequency counts; 59 X_i's were equal to 0, 26 X_i's were equal to 1, etc. Summary statistics and a histogram for these data are given in Table 6.10 and Fig. 6.34, respectively.

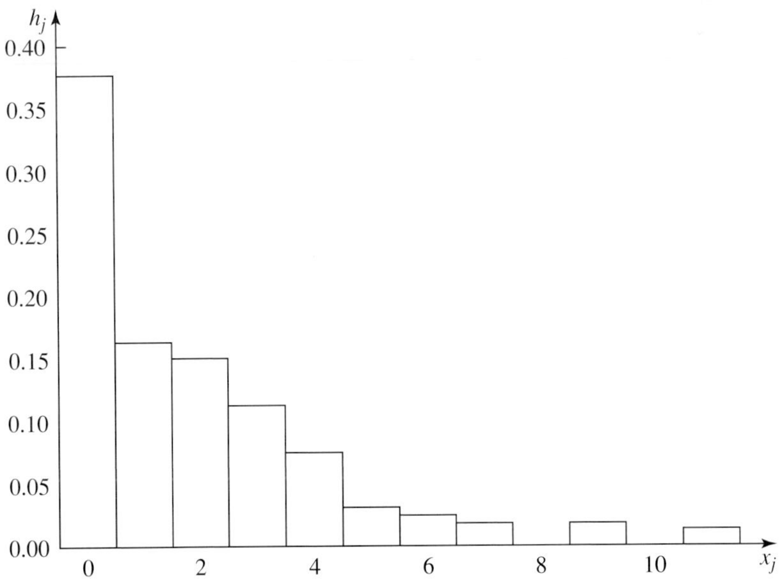

FIGURE 6.34
Histogram of the demand-size data in Table 6.9.

Since the lexis ratio $\hat{\tau}(156) = 2.795$, the binomial and Poisson distributions do not seem likely models. Furthermore, the large positive value of the skewness $\hat{\nu}(156) = 1.687$ would appear to rule out the discrete uniform distribution that is symmetric. Therefore, the possible discrete models (of those considered in this book) are the geometric and negative binomial distributions, with the former being a special case of the latter when $s = 1$. However, based on the monotonically decreasing histogram in Fig. 6.34 (and the mass functions in Fig. 6.21), we hypothesize that the demand data are from a geometric distribution.

6.5
ACTIVITY II: ESTIMATION OF PARAMETERS

After one or more candidate families of distributions have been hypothesized in Activity I, we must somehow specify the values of their parameters in order to have completely specified distributions for possible use in the simulation. Our IID data $X_1, X_2, \ldots, X_n$ were used to help us hypothesize distributions, and these same data can also be used to estimate their parameters. When data are used directly in this way to specify a numerical value for an unknown parameter, we say that we are *estimating* that parameter from the data.

An *estimator* is a numerical function of the data. There are many ways to specify the form of an estimator for a particular parameter of a given distribution, and many alternative ways to evaluate the quality of an estimator. We shall consider explicitly only one type, *maximum-likelihood estimators* (MLEs), for three reasons: (1) MLEs have several desirable properties often not enjoyed by alternative methods of estimation, e.g., least-squares estimators, unbiased estimators, and the method of moments; (2) the use of MLEs turns out to be important in justifying the chi-square goodness-of-fit test (see Sec. 6.6.2); and (3) the central idea of maximum-likelihood estimation has a strong intuitive appeal.

The basis for MLEs is most easily understood in the discrete case. Suppose that we have hypothesized a discrete distribution for our data that has one unknown parameter θ. Let $p_\theta(x)$ denote the probability mass function for this distribution, so that the parameter θ is part of the notation. *Given that we have already observed* the IID data $X_1, X_2, \ldots, X_n$, we define the *likelihood function* $L(\theta)$ as follows:

$$L(\theta) = p_\theta(X_1)p_\theta(X_2) \cdots p_\theta(X_n)$$

Now $L(\theta)$, which is just the joint probability mass function since the data are independent (see Sec. 4.2), gives the probability (likelihood) of obtaining our observed data if θ is the value of the unknown parameter. Then the MLE of the unknown value of θ, which we denote by $\hat{\theta}$, is defined to be the value of θ that maximizes $L(\theta)$; that is, $L(\hat{\theta}) \geq L(\theta)$ for all possible values of θ. Thus, $\hat{\theta}$ "best explains" the data we have collected. In the continuous case, MLEs do not have quite as simple an intuitive explanation, since the probability that a continuous random variable *equals* any fixed number is always 0 [see Prob. 6.26 and Breiman (1973, pp. 67–68) for intuitive justification of MLEs in the continuous case]. Nevertheless, MLEs for continuous distributions are defined analogously to the discrete case. If $f_\theta(x)$ denotes the hypothesized density function (again we assume that there is only one unknown parameter θ), the likelihood function is given by

$$L(\theta) = f_\theta(X_1)f_\theta(X_2)\cdots f_\theta(X_n)$$

The MLE $\hat{\theta}$ of θ is defined to be the value of θ that maximizes $L(\theta)$ over all permissible values of θ. The following two examples show how to compute MLEs for the distributions hypothesized earlier in Examples 6.4 and 6.5.

EXAMPLE 6.6. For the exponential distribution, $\theta = \beta$ ($\beta > 0$) and $f_\beta(x) = (1/\beta)e^{-x/\beta}$ for $x \geq 0$. The likelihood function is

$$\begin{aligned} L(\beta) &= \left(\frac{1}{\beta}e^{-X_1/\beta}\right)\left(\frac{1}{\beta}e^{-X_2/\beta}\right)\cdots\left(\frac{1}{\beta}e^{-X_n/\beta}\right) \\ &= \beta^{-n}\exp\left(-\frac{1}{\beta}\sum_{i=1}^{n} X_i\right) \end{aligned}$$

and we seek the value of β that maximizes $L(\beta)$ over all $\beta > 0$. This task is more easily accomplished if, instead of working directly with $L(\beta)$, we work with its logarithm. Thus, we define the *log-likelihood function* as

$$l(\beta) = \ln L(\beta) = -n\ln\beta - \frac{1}{\beta}\sum_{i=1}^{n} X_i$$

Since the logarithm function is strictly increasing, maximizing $L(\beta)$ is equivalent to maximizing $l(\beta)$, which is much easier; that is, $\hat{\beta}$ maximizes $L(\beta)$ if and only if $\hat{\beta}$ maximizes $l(\beta)$. Standard differential calculus can be used to maximize $l(\beta)$ by setting its derivative to zero and solving for β. That is,

$$\frac{dl}{d\beta} = \frac{-n}{\beta} + \frac{1}{\beta^2}\sum_{i=1}^{n} X_i$$

which equals zero if and only if $\beta = \sum_{i=1}^{n} X_i/n = \overline{X}(n)$. To make sure that $\beta = \overline{X}(n)$ is a maximizer of $l(\beta)$ (as opposed to a minimizer or an inflection point), a sufficient (but not necessary) condition is that $d^2l/d\beta^2$, evaluated at $\beta = \overline{X}(n)$, be negative. But

$$\frac{d^2l}{d\beta^2} = \frac{n}{\beta^2} - \frac{2}{\beta^3}\sum_{i=1}^{n} X_i$$

which is easily seen to be negative when $\beta = \overline{X}(n)$ since the X_i's are positive. Thus, the MLE of β is $\hat{\beta} = \overline{X}(n)$. Notice that the MLE is quite natural here, since β is the mean of the hypothesized distribution and the MLE is the *sample* mean. For the data of Example 6.4, $\hat{\beta} = \overline{X}(219) = 0.399$.

EXAMPLE 6.7. The discrete data of Example 6.5 were hypothesized to come from a geometric distribution. Here $\theta = p$ ($0 < p < 1$) and $p_p(x) = p(1-p)^x$ for $x = 0, 1, \ldots$. The likelihood function is

$$L(p) = p^n(1-p)^{\sum_{i=1}^{n} X_i}$$

which is again amenable to the logarithmic transformation to obtain

$$l(p) = \ln L(p) = n\ln p + \sum_{i=1}^{n} X_i \ln(1-p)$$

Differentiating $l(p)$, we get

$$\frac{dl}{dp} = \frac{n}{p} - \frac{\sum_{i=1}^{n} X_i}{1 - p}$$

which equals zero if and only if $p = 1/[\overline{X}(n) + 1]$. To make sure that this is a maximizer, note that

$$\frac{d^2l}{dp^2} = -\frac{n}{p^2} - \frac{\sum_{i=1}^{n} X_i}{(1 - p)^2} < 0$$

for any valid p. Thus, the MLE of p is $\hat{p} = 1/[\overline{X}(n) + 1]$, which is intuitively appealing (see Prob. 6.9). For the demand-size data of Example 6.5, $\hat{p} = 0.346$.

The above two examples illustrate two important practical tools for deriving MLEs, namely, the use of the log-likelihood function and setting its derivative (with respect to the parameter being estimated) equal to zero to find the MLE. While these tools are often useful in finding MLEs, the reader should be cautioned against assuming that finding a MLE is always a simple matter of setting a derivative to zero and solving easily for $\hat{\theta}$. For some distributions, neither the log-likelihood function nor differentiation is useful; probably the best-known example is the uniform distribution (see Prob. 6.10). For other distributions, both tools are useful, but solving $dl/d\theta = 0$ cannot be accomplished by simple algebra, and numerical methods must be used; the gamma, Weibull, and beta distributions are (multiparameter) examples of this general situation. We refer the reader to Breiman (1973, pp. 65–84) for examples of techniques used to find MLEs for a variety of distributions.

We have said that MLEs have several desirable statistical properties, some of which are as follows [see Breiman (1973, pp. 85–88) and Kendall and Stuart (1979, chap. 18)]:

1. For most of the common distributions, the MLE is unique; that is, $L(\hat{\theta})$ is *strictly* greater than $L(\theta)$ for any other value of θ.
2. Although MLEs need not be unbiased, in general, the asymptotic distribution (as $n \to \infty$) of $\hat{\theta}$ has mean equal to θ (see property 4 below).
3. MLEs are *invariant*; that is, if $\phi = h(\theta)$ for some function h, then the MLE of ϕ is $h(\hat{\theta})$. (Unbiasedness is not invariant.) For example, the variance of an expo(β) random variable is β^2, so the MLE of this variance is $[\overline{X}(n)]^2$.
4. MLEs are asymptotically normally distributed; that is, $\sqrt{n}(\hat{\theta} - \theta) \xrightarrow{\mathcal{D}} N(0, \delta(\theta))$, where $\delta(\theta) = -n/E(d^2l/d\theta^2)$ (the expectation is with respect to X_i, assuming that X_i has the hypothesized distribution) and $\xrightarrow{\mathcal{D}}$ denotes convergence in distribution. Furthermore, if $\tilde{\theta}$ is any other estimator such that $\sqrt{n}(\tilde{\theta} - \theta) \xrightarrow{\mathcal{D}} N(0, \sigma^2)$, then $\delta(\theta) \le \sigma^2$. (Thus, MLEs are called *best asymptotically normal.*)
5. MLEs are *strongly consistent*; that is, $\lim_{n\to\infty} \hat{\theta} = \theta$ (w.p. 1).

The proofs of these and other properties sometimes require additional mild "regularity" assumptions; see Kendall and Stuart (1979).

Property 4 is of special interest, since it allows us to establish an approximate confidence interval for θ. If we define $\delta(\theta)$ as in property 4 above, it can be shown that

$$\frac{\hat{\theta} - \theta}{\sqrt{\delta(\hat{\theta})/n}} \xrightarrow{\mathcal{D}} \text{N}(0, 1)$$

as $n \to \infty$. Thus, for large n an approximate $100(1 - \alpha)$ percent confidence interval for θ is

$$\hat{\theta} \pm z_{1-\alpha/2}\sqrt{\frac{\delta(\hat{\theta})}{n}} \tag{6.3}$$

EXAMPLE 6.8. Construct a 90 percent confidence interval for the parameter p of the geometric distribution, and specialize it to the data of Example 6.5. It is easy to show that

$$E\left[\frac{d^2l}{dp^2}\right] = -\frac{n}{p^2} - \frac{n(1-p)/p}{(1-p)^2} = -\frac{n}{p^2(1-p)}$$

so that $\delta(p) = p^2(1 - p)$ and, for large n, an approximate 90 percent confidence interval for p is given by

$$\hat{p} \pm 1.645\sqrt{\frac{\hat{p}^2(1-\hat{p})}{n}}$$

For the data of Example 6.5, we get 0.346 ± 0.037.

This suggests a way of checking how sensitive a simulation output measure of performance is to a particular input parameter. The simulation could be run for θ set at, say, the left endpoint, the center ($\hat{\theta}$), and the right endpoint of the confidence interval in (6.3). If the measure of performance appeared to be insensitive to values of θ in this range, we could feel confident that we have an adequate estimate of θ for our purposes. On the other hand, if the simulation appeared to be sensitive to θ, we might seek a better estimate of θ; this would usually entail collecting more data.

The general form of the above problem may be stated as follows. A simulation model's performance measures depend on the choice of input probability distributions and their associated parameters. When we choose the distributions to use for a simulation model, we generally don't know with absolute certainty whether these are the correct distributions to use, and this lack of complete knowledge results in what we might call *model uncertainty*. Also, given that certain input distributions have been selected, we typically do not know with complete certainty what parameters to use for these distributions, and we might call this *parameter uncertainty*. (Parameters are typically *estimated* from observed data or are specified *subjectively* based on expert opinion.) The term *input-model uncertainty* is used to refer to these two issues collectively. Ideally, we would like to have a method for constructing a confidence interval for a simulation performance measure that takes into account *both* the sampling variability of the simulation model (see Chap. 9) and input-model uncertainty. Henderson (2003) says that such a method should be understandable by the simulation practitioner, based on sound statistical procedures, relatively easy to implement, and computationally efficient.

There have been a number of methods suggested for addressing the problem of input-model uncertainty, including the following [see Barton (2012) and Henderson (2003)]:

- Bayesian model averaging [Chick (2001), Zouaoui and Wilson (2003, 2004)]
- Delta-method approaches [Cheng and Holland (1997, 1998, 2004)]
- Metamodel-assisted bootstrapping [Barton et al. (2013), Chapter 12]; see Cheng (2006) and Efron and Tibshirani (1993) for a discussion of bootstrap resampling
- Nonparametric bootstrapping [Barton and Schruben (1993, 2001)]
- Quick method based on a random-effects model [Ankenman and Nelson (2012)]

Unfortunately, most of these methods are reasonably complicated and make assumptions that may not always be satisfied in practice [see Barton (2012) and Barton et al. (2013)]. For example, Bayesian model averaging and the delta-method approaches assume that the family (or families) of distributions (but not the parameter values) that best represents a source of system randomness is known in advance, which is unlikely to be true in most real-world applications.

So far, we have explicitly treated only distributions with a single unknown parameter. If a distribution has several parameters, we can define MLEs of these parameters in a natural way. For instance, the gamma distribution has two parameters (α and β), and the likelihood function is defined to be

$$L(\alpha, \beta) = \frac{\beta^{-n\alpha}\left(\prod_{i=1}^{n} X_i\right)^{\alpha-1} \exp\left[-(1/\beta)\sum_{i=1}^{n} X_i\right]}{[\Gamma(\alpha)]^n}$$

The MLEs $\hat{\alpha}$ and $\hat{\beta}$ of the unknown values of α and β are defined to be the values of α and β that (jointly) maximize $L(\alpha, \beta)$. [Finding $\hat{\alpha}$ and $\hat{\beta}$ usually proceeds by letting $l(\alpha, \beta) = \ln L(\alpha, \beta)$ and trying to solve the equations $\partial l/\partial\alpha = 0$ and $\partial l/\partial\beta = 0$ simultaneously for α and β.] Analogs of the properties of MLEs listed above also hold in this multiparameter case. Unfortunately, the process of finding MLEs when there are several parameters is usually quite difficult. (The normal distribution is a notable exception.)

For each of the distributions in Secs. 6.2.2 (except for the Johnson S_B, Johnson S_U, and triangular distributions) and 6.2.3, we listed either formulas for the MLEs or a method for obtaining them numerically. For the gamma MLEs, Table 6.21 can be used with standard linear interpolation. For the beta MLEs, Table 6.22 can be used; one could either simply pick $(\hat{\alpha}_1, \hat{\alpha}_2)$ corresponding to the closest table values of G_1 and G_2 or devise a scheme for two-dimensional interpolation.

6.6 ACTIVITY III: DETERMINING HOW REPRESENTATIVE THE FITTED DISTRIBUTIONS ARE

After determining one or more probability distributions that might fit our observed data in Activities I and II, we must now closely examine these distributions to see how well they represent the true underlying distribution for our data. If several of these distributions are "representative," we must also determine which distribution provides the best fit. In general, none of our fitted distributions will probably be *exactly* correct. What we are really trying to do is to determine a distribution that is accurate enough for the intended purposes of the model.

In this section we discuss both heuristic procedures and goodness-of-fit hypothesis tests for determining the "quality" of fitted distributions.

6.6.1 Heuristic Procedures

We will discuss five heuristic or graphical procedures for comparing fitted distributions with the true underlying distribution; several additional techniques can be found in Averill M. Law & Associates (2013).

Density-Histogram Plots and Frequency Comparisons

For continuous data, a *density-histogram plot* can be made by plotting $\Delta b\,\hat{f}(x)$ over the histogram $h(x)$ and looking for similarities. [Recall that the area under $h(x)$ is Δb.] A *frequency comparison* is an alternative graphical comparison of a histogram of the data with the density function $\hat{f}(x)$ of a fitted distribution. Let $[b_0, b_1), [b_1, b_2), \ldots, [b_{k-1}, b_k)$ be a set of k histogram intervals each with width $\Delta b = b_j - b_{j-1}$. Let h_j be the *observed* proportion of the X_i's in the jth interval $[b_{j-1}, b_j)$ and let r_j be the *expected* proportion of the n observations that would fall in the jth interval if the fitted distribution were in fact the true one; i.e., r_j is given by (see Prob. 6.13)

$$r_j = \int_{b_{j-1}}^{b_j} \hat{f}(x)\,dx \tag{6.4}$$

Then the frequency comparison is made by plotting both h_j and r_j in the jth histogram interval for $j = 1, 2, \ldots, k$.

For discrete data, a *frequency comparison* is a graphical comparison of a histogram of the data with the mass function $\hat{p}(x)$ of a fitted distribution. Let h_j be the observed proportion of the X_i's that are equal to x_j, and let r_j be the expected proportion of the n observations that would be equal to x_j if the fitted distribution were in fact the true one, i.e., $r_j = \hat{p}(x_j)$. Then the frequency comparison is made by plotting both h_j and r_j versus x_j for all relevant values of x_j.

For either the continuous or discrete case, if the fitted distribution is a good representation for the true underlying distribution of the data (and if the sample size n is sufficiently large), then r_j and h_j should closely agree.

EXAMPLE 6.9. For the interarrival-time data of Example 6.4, we hypothesized an exponential distribution and obtained the MLE $\hat{\beta} = 0.399$ in Example 6.6. Thus, the density of the fitted distribution is

$$\hat{f}(x) = \begin{cases} 2.506e^{-x/0.399} & \text{if } x \geq 0 \\ 0 & \text{otherwise} \end{cases}$$

For the histogram in Fig. 6.32(*c*), we give a density-histogram plot in Fig. 6.35.

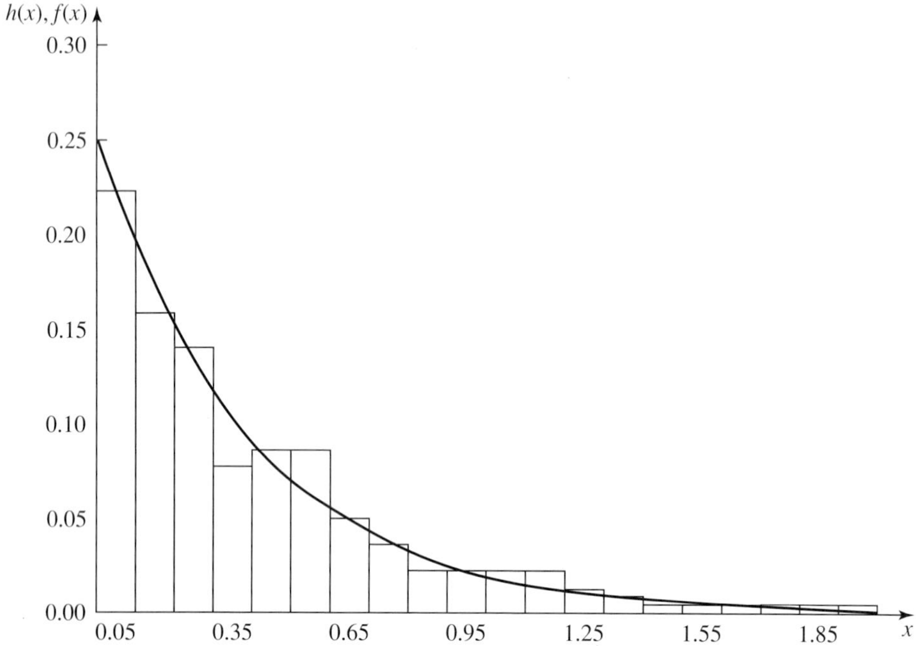

FIGURE 6.35
Density-histogram plot for the fitted exponential distribution and the interarrival-time data.

EXAMPLE 6.10. The demand-size data of Example 6.5 were hypothesized to have come from a geometric distribution, and the MLE of the parameter p was found in Example 6.7 to be $\hat{p} = 0.346$. Thus, the mass function of the fitted distribution is

$$\hat{p}(x) = \begin{cases} 0.346(0.654)^x & \text{if } x = 0, 1, 2, \ldots \\ 0 & \text{otherwise} \end{cases}$$

For the histogram in Fig. 6.34, $r_j = \hat{p}(x_j) = \hat{p}(j - 1)$ for $j = 1, 2, \ldots, 12$, and the frequency comparison is given in Fig. 6.36, where the h_j's are represented by the white vertical bars and the r_j's by the gray vertical bars. Once again, the agreement is good except possibly for $x_2 = 1$.

Distribution-Function-Differences Plots

The density-histogram plot can be thought of as a comparison of the individual probabilities of the fitted distribution and of the individual probabilities of the true underlying distribution. We can also make a graphical comparison of the cumulative probabilities (distribution functions). Define a (new) empirical distribution function $F_n(x)$ as follows:

$$F_n(x) = \frac{\text{number of } X_i\text{'s} \le x}{n} \tag{6.5}$$

which is the proportion of the observations that are less than or equal to x. Then we could plot $\hat{F}(x)$ (the distribution function of the fitted distribution) and $F_n(x)$ on the

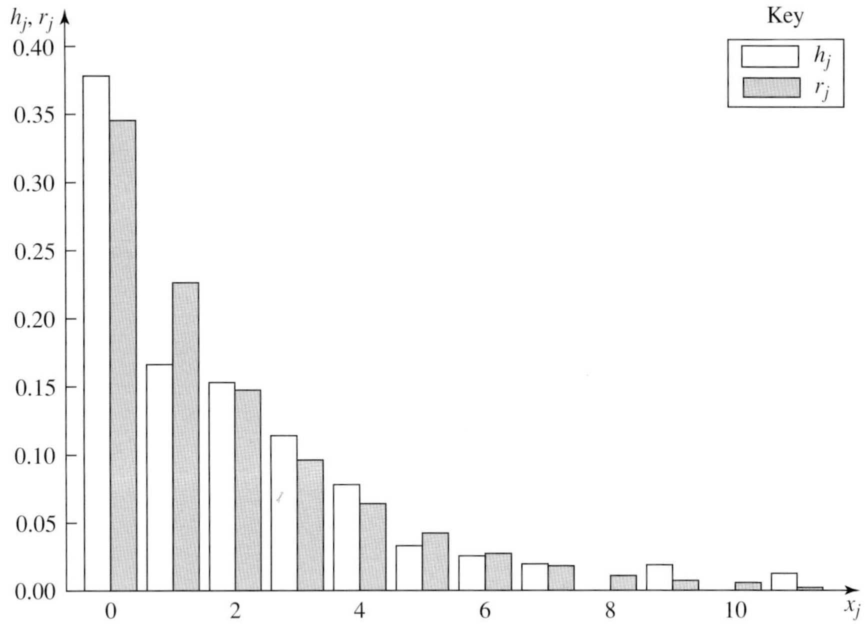

FIGURE 6.36
Frequency comparison for the fitted geometric distribution and the demand-size data.

same graph and look for similarities. However, distribution functions generally do not have as characteristic an appearance as density or mass functions do. In fact, many distribution functions have some sort of "S" shape, and eyeballing for differences or similarities in S-shaped curves is somewhat perplexing. We therefore define the *distribution-function-differences plot* to be a plot of the differences between $\hat{F}(x)$ and $F_n(x)$, over the range of the data. If the fitted distribution is a perfect fit and the sample size is infinite, then this plot will be a horizontal line at height 0. Thus, the greater the vertical deviations from this line, the worse the quality of fit. Many fitted distributions that are bad in an absolute sense have large deviations at the lower end of the range of the data.

EXAMPLE 6.11. A distribution-function-differences plot for the interarrival-time data of Example 6.4 and the fitted exponential distribution is given in Fig. 6.37. This plot indicates a good fit except possibly at the lower end of the range of the observed data. (The dotted horizontal lines are error bounds that depend on the sample size n. If a differences plot crosses these lines, then this is a strong indication of a bad fit. These error bounds were determined from the differences for each of the 35,000 data sets discussed in Sec. 6.7.)

EXAMPLE 6.12. A distribution-function-differences plot for the demand-size data of Example 6.5 and the fitted geometric distribution is given in Fig. 6.38. This plot indicates a good fit except possibly at the lower end of the range of the observed data.

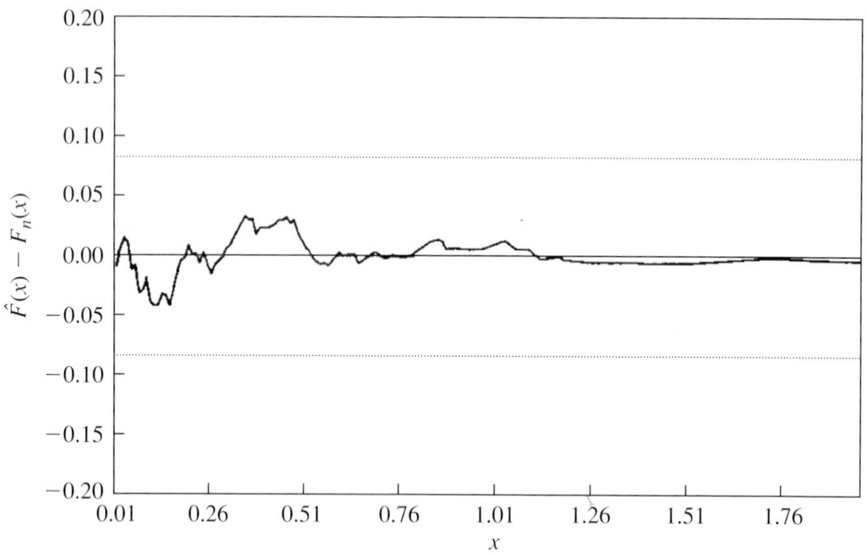

FIGURE 6.37
Distribution-function-differences plot for the fitted exponential distribution and the interarrival-time data.

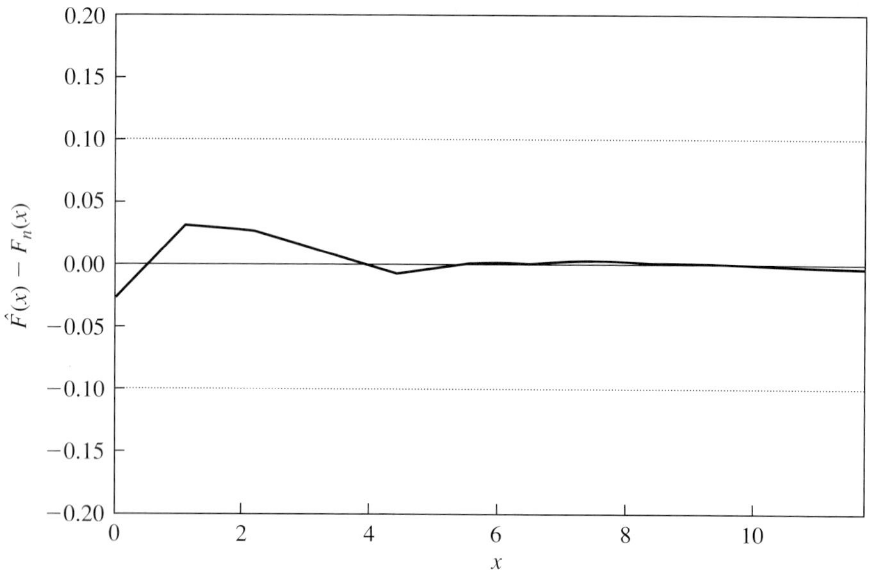

FIGURE 6.38
Distribution-function-differences plot for the fitted geometric distribution and the demand-size data.

Probability Plots

A probability plot can be thought of as another graphical comparison of an estimate of the true distribution function of our data $X_1, X_2, \ldots, X_n$ with the distribution function of a fitted distribution. There are many kinds (and uses) of probability plots, only two of which we describe here; see Barnett (1975), Hahn and Shapiro (1994), and Wilk and Gnanadesikan (1968) for additional discussions.

As in Sec. 6.2.4, let $X_{(i)}$ be the ith smallest of the X_j's, sometimes called the ith *order statistic* of the X_j's. A reasonable estimate of the distribution function $F(x)$ of a random variable X is $F_n(x)$, which was defined by Eq. (6.5). Note that $F_n(X_{(i)}) = i/n$. For purposes of probability plotting, however, it turns out to be somewhat inconvenient to have $F_n(X_{(n)}) = 1$, that is, to have an empirical distribution function that is equal to 1 for a finite value of x (see Prob. 6.14). We therefore will use the following empirical distribution function here:

$$\tilde{F}_n(X_{(i)}) = F_n(X_{(i)}) - \frac{0.5}{n} = \frac{i - 0.5}{n}$$

for $i = 1, 2, \ldots, n$. [Clearly, for moderately large n, this adjustment is quite small. Other adjustments have been suggested, such as $i/(n + 1)$.] A straightforward procedure would then be to plot the n points $(X_{(1)}, 0.5/n)$, $(X_{(2)}, 1.5/n), \ldots,$ $(X_{(n)}, (n - 0.5)/n)$, compare this result with a plot of the distribution function of a distribution being considered as a model for the data, and look for similarities. However, as stated above, many distribution functions have some sort of "S" shape, and eyeballing S-shaped curves for similarities or differences is difficult. Most of us, however, *can* recognize whether a set of plotted points appears to lie more or less along a *straight* line, and probability-plotting techniques reduce the problem of comparing distribution functions to one of looking for a straight line.

Let $q_i = (i - 0.5)/n$ for $i = 1, 2, \ldots, n$, so that $0 < q_i < 1$. For any *continuous* data set (see Prob. 6.15), a *quantile–quantile (Q–Q) plot* (see Sec. 6.4.3 for the definition of a quantile) is a graph of the q_i-quantile of a fitted (model) distribution function $\hat{F}(x)$, namely, $x_{q_i}^M = \hat{F}^{-1}(q_i)$, versus the q_i-quantile of the empirical distribution function $\tilde{F}_n(x)$, namely, $x_{q_i}^S = \tilde{F}_n^{-1}(q_i) = X_{(i)}$, for $i = 1, 2, \ldots, n$. The definition of a Q–Q plot is illustrated in Fig. 6.39, where we have represented $\tilde{F}_n(x)$ as a smooth curve for convenience. Corresponding to each ordinate value q are the two quantiles x_q^M and x_q^S.

If $\hat{F}(x)$ is the same distribution as the true underlying distribution $F(x)$, and if the sample size n is large, then $\hat{F}(x)$ and $\tilde{F}_n(x)$ will be close together and the Q–Q plot will be approximately linear with an intercept of 0 and a slope of 1. Even if $\hat{F}(x)$ is the correct distribution, there will be departures from linearity for small to moderate sample sizes.

A *probability–probability (P–P) plot* is a graph of the model probability $\hat{F}(X_{(i)})$ versus the sample probability $\tilde{F}_n(X_{(i)}) = q_i$, for $i = 1, 2, \ldots, n$; it is valid for both continuous and discrete data sets. This definition is also illustrated in Fig. 6.39. Corresponding to each abscissa value p are the two probabilities $\hat{F}(p)$ and $\tilde{F}_n(p)$. If

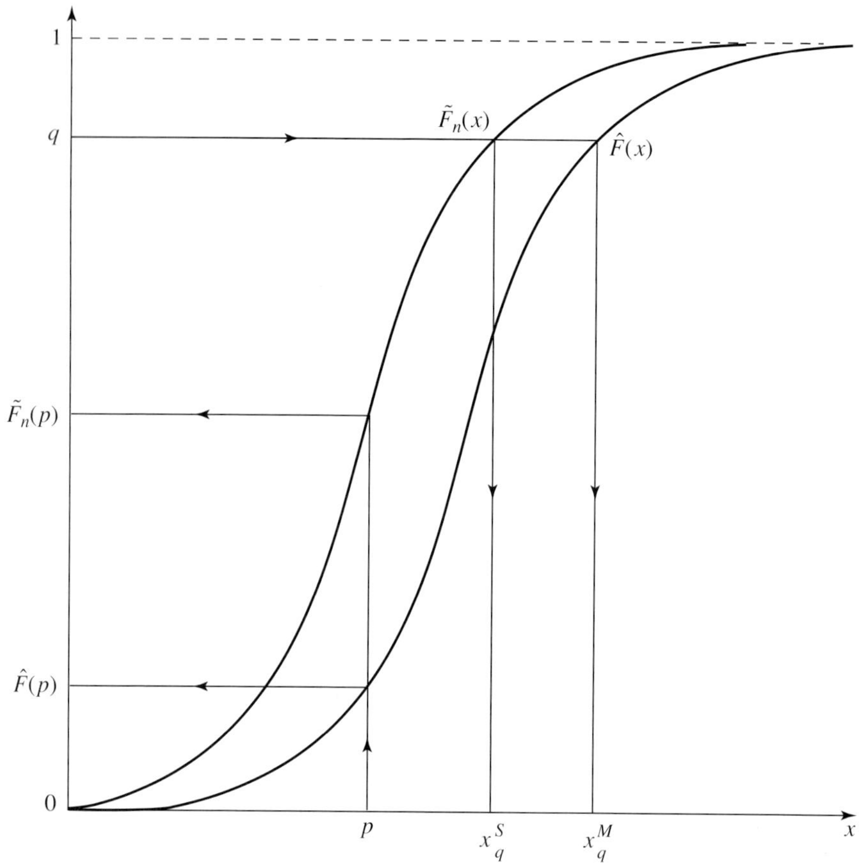

FIGURE 6.39
Definitions of *Q–Q* and *P–P* plots.

$\hat{F}(x)$ and $\tilde{F}_n(x)$ are close together, then the *P–P* plot will also be approximately linear with an intercept of 0 and a slope of 1.

The *Q–Q* plot will amplify differences that exist between the tails of the model distribution function $\hat{F}(x)$ and the tails of the empirical distribution function $\tilde{F}_n(x)$, whereas the *P–P* plot will amplify differences between the middle of $\hat{F}(x)$ and the middle of $\tilde{F}_n(x)$. The difference between the right tails of the distribution functions in Fig. 6.40 is amplified by the *Q–Q* plot but not the *P–P* plot. On the other hand, the difference between the "middles" of the two distribution functions in Fig. 6.41 is amplified by the *P–P* plot.

The above formulations of *Q–Q* and *P–P* plots implicitly assumed that the X_i's were distinct (no ties); this certainly will not always be the case. To modify the definitions when the X_i's may not be distinct, let $Y_1, Y_2, \ldots, Y_l$ be the distinct values in the sample $X_1, X_2, \ldots, X_n$ arranged in increasing order,

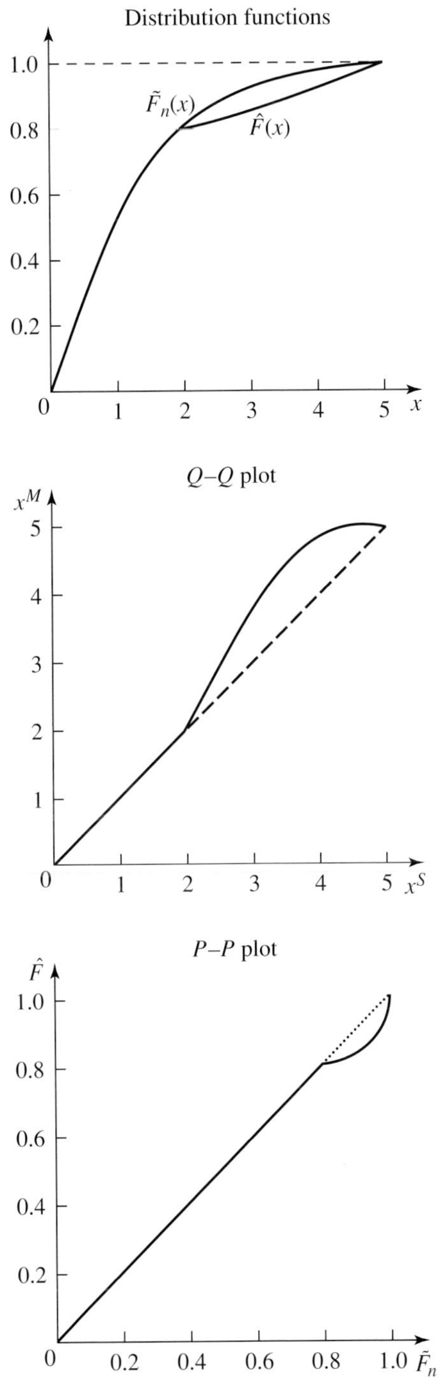

FIGURE 6.40
The difference between the right tails of $\hat{F}(x)$ and $\tilde{F}_n(x)$ amplified by the *Q–Q* plot.

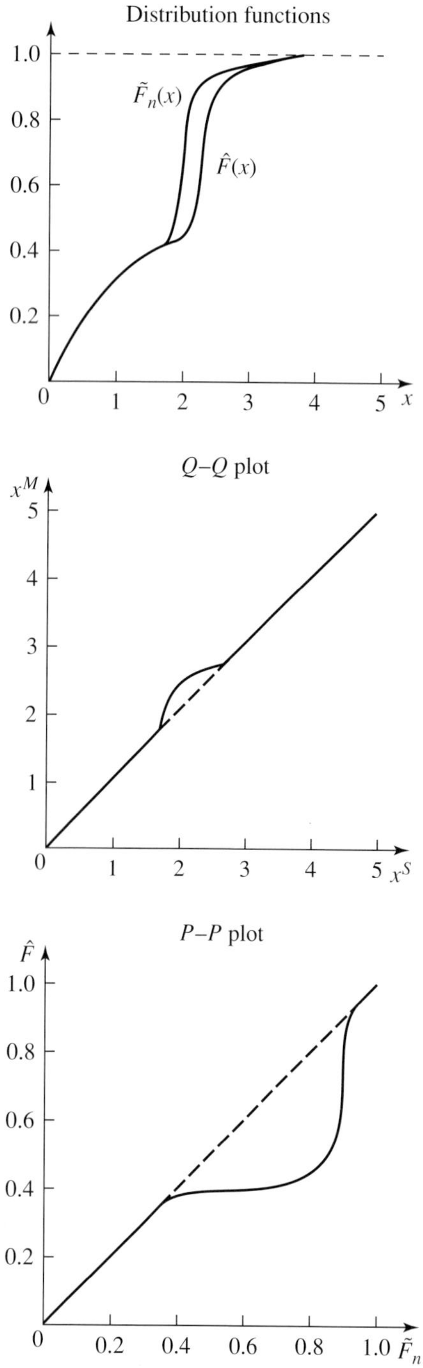

FIGURE 6.41
The difference between the "middles" of $\hat{F}(x)$ and $\tilde{F}_n(x)$ amplified by the P–P plot.

TABLE 6.11
Approaches for computing $\hat{F}$ or $\hat{F}^{-1}$ for certain mathematically intractable distributions

	$\hat{F}$	$\hat{F}^{-1}$
Gamma	See Bhattacharjee (1970)	See Best and Roberts (1975)
Normal	See Milton and Hotchkiss (1969)	See Moro (1995)
Lognormal	Fit a normal distribution to $Y_i = \ln X_i$ for $i = 1, 2, \ldots, n$; see Sec. 6.2.2	Same as $\hat{F}$
Beta	See Bosten and Battiste (1974)	See Cran, Martin, and Thomas (1977)
Pearson type V	Fit a gamma distribution to $Y_i = 1/X_i$ for $i = 1, 2, \ldots, n$; see Sec. 6.2.2	Same as $\hat{F}$
Pearson type VI	Fit a beta distribution to $Y_i = X_i/(1 + X_i)$ for $i = 1, 2, \ldots, n$; see Sec. 6.2.2	Same as $\hat{F}$
Johnson S_B	See the normal distribution	Same as $\hat{F}$
Johnson S_U	See the normal distribution	Same as $\hat{F}$

where $l \leq n$. (If the X_i's are distinct, then $Y_i = X_{(i)}$ for $i = 1, 2, \ldots, n$.) Let q_i' be defined by

$$q_i' = (\text{proportion of } X_j\text{'s} \leq Y_i) - \frac{0.5}{n}$$

In other words, $q_i' = \tilde{F}_n(Y_i)$. Then q_i' replaces q_i and Y_i replaces $X_{(i)}$ in the definitions of *Q–Q* and *P–P* plots.

The construction of a *Q–Q* plot requires the calculation of the model quantile $\hat{F}^{-1}(q_i)$. For the uniform, exponential, Weibull, and log-logistic distributions, there is no problem, since a closed-form expression for $\hat{F}^{-1}$ is available. For the other continuous distributions, we give in Table 6.11 either a transformation for addressing the problem or a reference to a numerical approximation for $\hat{F}^{-1}$. Also given in Table 6.11 are similar prescriptions for computing the model probability $\hat{F}(X_{(i)})$, which is required for a *P–P* plot. Functions for computing $\hat{F}$ or $\hat{F}^{-1}$ are also available in the IMSL Statistical Library [Rogue Wave (2013)], and the ExpertFit statistical package (see Sec. 6.7) performs *Q–Q* and *P–P* plots automatically.

EXAMPLE 6.13. A *Q–Q* plot for the fitted exponential distribution and the interarrival-time data is given in Fig. 6.42. The plot is fairly linear except for large values of q_i'. This is not uncommon, since the *Q–Q* plot will amplify small differences between $\hat{F}(x)$ and $\tilde{F}_n(x)$ when they are both close to 1. The corresponding *P–P* plot is given in Fig. 6.43. Its linearity indicates that the middle of the fitted exponential agrees closely with the middle of the true underlying distribution.

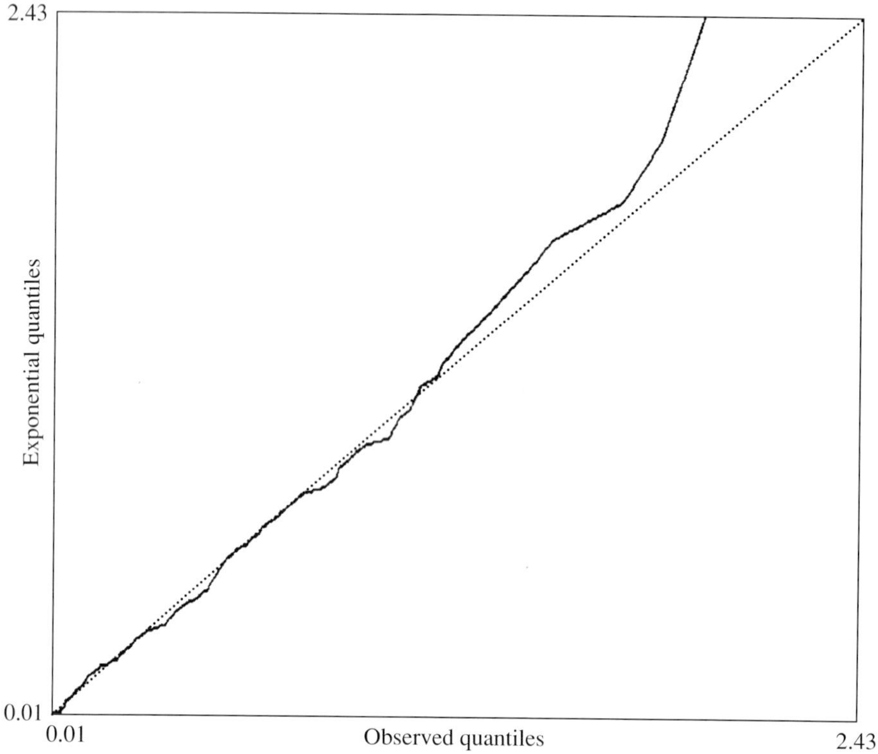

FIGURE 6.42
Q–Q plot for exponential distribution and interarrival-time data.

EXAMPLE 6.14. The *P–P* plot for the fitted geometric distribution and the demand-size data is given in Fig. 6.44. Once again we find the *P–P* plot to be reasonably linear, indicating agreement between the geometric and true distributions.

6.6.2 Goodness-of-Fit Tests

A *goodness-of-fit test* is a statistical hypothesis test (see Sec. 4.5) that is used to assess formally whether the observations $X_1, X_2, \ldots, X_n$ are an independent sample from a particular distribution with distribution function $\hat{F}$. That is, a goodness-of-fit test can be used to test the following null hypothesis:

$$H_0\text{: The } X_i\text{'s are IID random variables with distribution function } \hat{F}$$

Before proceeding with a discussion of several specific goodness-of-fit tests, we feel compelled to comment on the formal structure and properties of these tests. First, failure to reject H_0 should *not* be interpreted as "accepting H_0 as being true."

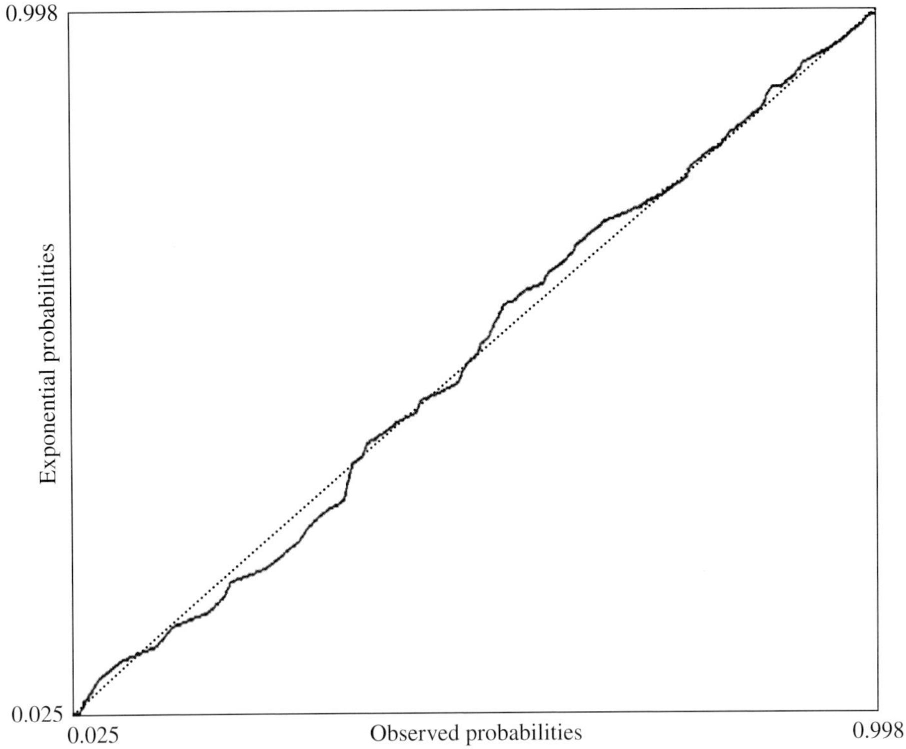

FIGURE 6.43
P–P plot for exponential distribution and interarrival-time data.

These tests are often not very powerful for small to moderate sample sizes n; that is, they are not very sensitive to subtle disagreements between the data and the fitted distribution. Instead, they should be regarded as a systematic approach for detecting fairly gross differences. On the other hand, if n is very large, then these tests will almost always reject H_0 [see Gibbons (1985, p. 76)]. Since H_0 is virtually never *exactly* true, even a minute departure from the hypothesized distribution will be detected for large n. This is an unfortunate property of these tests, since it is usually sufficient to have a distribution that is "nearly" correct.

Chi-Square Tests

The oldest goodness-of-fit hypothesis test is the *chi-square test*, which dates back at least to the paper of K. Pearson (1900). As we shall see, a chi-square test may be thought of as a more formal comparison of a histogram with the fitted density or mass function (see the frequency comparison in Sec. 6.6.1).

To compute the chi-square test statistic in either the continuous or discrete case, we must first divide the entire range of the fitted distribution into k adjacent intervals

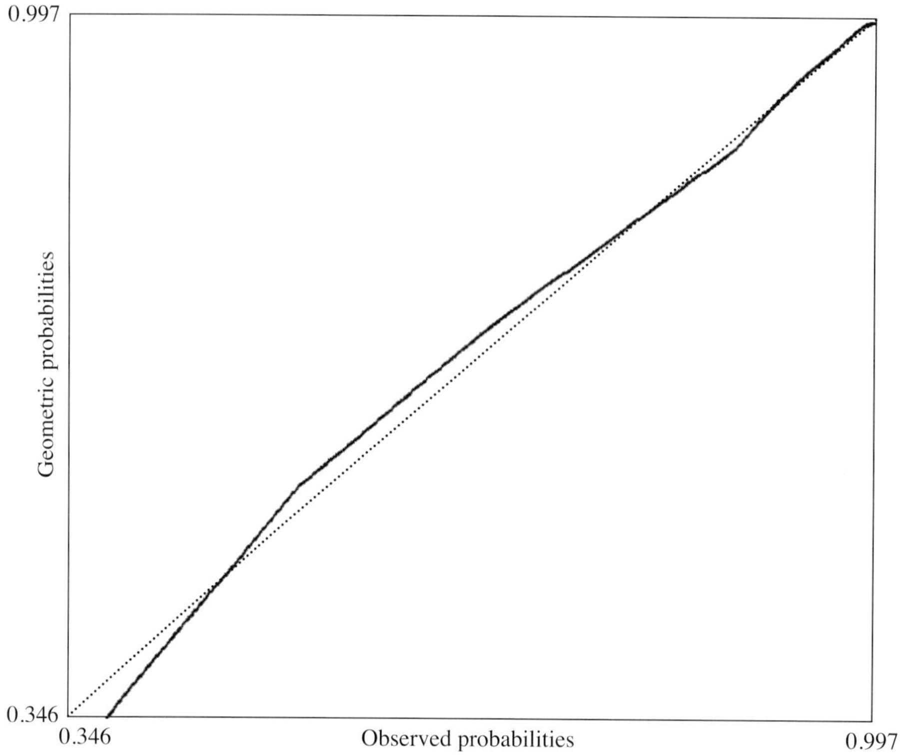

FIGURE 6.44
P–P plot for geometric distribution and demand-size data.

$[a_0, a_1), [a_1, a_2), \ldots, [a_{k-1}, a_k)$, where it could be that $a_0 = -\infty$, in which case the first interval is $(-\infty, a_1)$, or $a_k = +\infty$, or both. Then we tally

$$N_j = \text{number of } X_i\text{'s in the } j\text{th interval } [a_{j-1}, a_j)$$

for $j = 1, 2, \ldots, k$. (Note that $\sum_{j=1}^{k} N_j = n$.) Next, we compute the expected *proportion* p_j of the X_i's that would fall in the jth interval if we were sampling from the fitted distribution. In the continuous case,

$$p_j = \int_{a_{j-1}}^{a_j} \hat{f}(x)\, dx$$

where $\hat{f}$ is the density of the fitted distribution. For discrete data,

$$p_j = \sum_{a_{j-1} \le x_i < a_j} \hat{p}(x_i)$$

where $\hat{p}$ is the mass function of the fitted distribution. Finally, the test statistic is

$$\chi^2 = \sum_{j=1}^{k} \frac{(N_j - np_j)^2}{np_j}$$

Since np_j is the expected number of the n X_i's that would fall in the jth interval if H_0 were true (see Prob. 6.17), we would expect χ^2 to be small if the fit were good. Therefore, we reject H_0 if χ^2 is too large. The precise form of the test depends on whether we have estimated any of the parameters of the fitted distribution from our data.

First, suppose that all parameters of the fitted distribution are known; that is, we specified the fitted distribution without making use of the data in any way. [This all-parameters-known case might appear to be of little practical use, but there are at least two applications for it in simulation: (1) In the Poisson-process test (later in this section), we test to see whether times of arrival can be regarded as being IID U(0, T) random variables, where T is a constant independent of the data; and (2) in empirical testing of random-number generators (Sec. 7.4.1), we test for a U(0, 1) distribution.] Then if H_0 is true, χ^2 converges in distribution (as $n \rightarrow \infty$) to a chi-square distribution with $k - 1$ df, which is the same as the gamma[$(k - 1)/2$, 2] distribution. Thus, for large n, a test with *approximate* level α is obtained by rejecting H_0 if $\chi^2 > \chi^2_{k-1,1-\alpha}$ (see Fig. 6.45), where $\chi^2_{k-1,1-\alpha}$ is the upper $1 - \alpha$ critical point for a chi-square distribution with $k - 1$ df. (Values for $\chi^2_{k-1,1-\alpha}$ can be found in Table T.2 at the end of the book.) Note that the chi-square test is only *valid*, i.e., is of level α, asymptotically as $n \rightarrow \infty$.

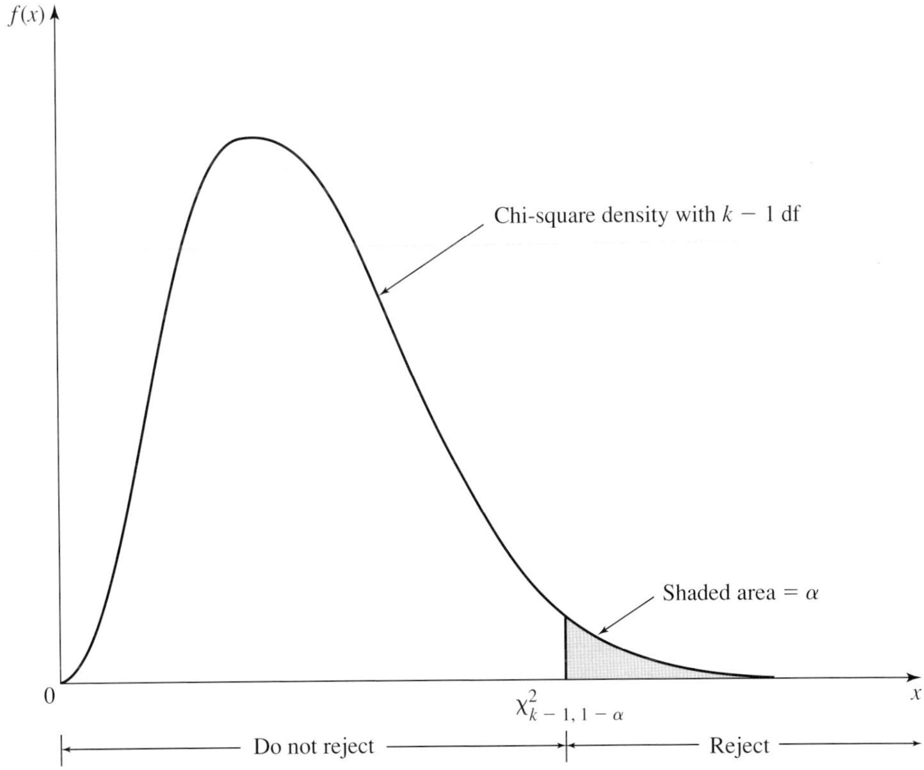

FIGURE 6.45
The chi-square test when all parameters are known.

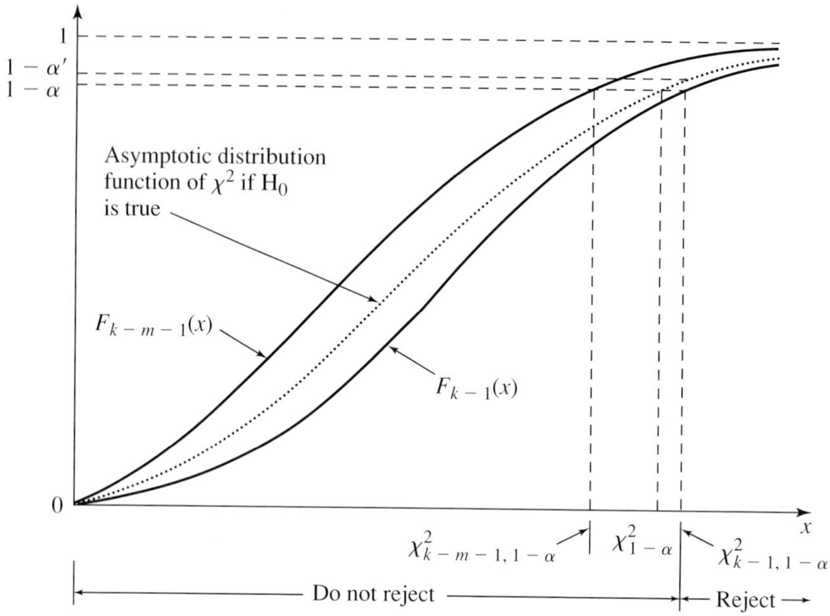

FIGURE 6.46
The chi-square test when m parameters are estimated by their MLEs.

Second, suppose that in order to specify the fitted distribution, we had to estimate m parameters ($m \geq 1$) from the data. When MLEs are used, Chernoff and Lehmann (1954) showed that if H_0 is true, then as $n \to \infty$ the distribution function of χ^2 converges to a distribution function that lies *between* the distribution functions of chi-square distributions with $k - 1$ and $k - m - 1$ df. (See Fig. 6.46, where F_{k-1} and F_{k-m-1} represent the distribution functions of chi-square distributions with $k - 1$ and $k - m - 1$ df, respectively, and the dotted distribution function is the one to which the distribution function of χ^2 converges as $n \to \infty$.) If we let $\chi^2_{1-\alpha}$ be the upper $1 - \alpha$ critical point of the asymptotic distribution of χ^2, then

$$\chi^2_{k-m-1,1-\alpha} \leq \chi^2_{1-\alpha} \leq \chi^2_{k-1,1-\alpha}$$

as shown in Fig. 6.46; unfortunately, the value of $\chi^2_{1-\alpha}$ will not be known in general. It is clear that we should reject H_0 if $\chi^2 > \chi^2_{k-1,1-\alpha}$ and we should not reject H_0 if $\chi^2 < \chi^2_{k-m-1,1-\alpha}$; an ambiguous situation occurs when

$$\chi^2_{k-m-1,1-\alpha} \leq \chi^2 \leq \chi^2_{k-1,1-\alpha}$$

It is often recommended that we reject H_0 only if $\chi^2 > \chi^2_{k-1,1-\alpha}$, since this is *conservative*; that is, the actual probability α' of committing a Type I error [rejecting H_0 when it is true (see Sec. 4.5)] is at *least* as small as the *stated* probability α (see Fig. 6.46). This choice, however, will entail loss of power (probability of rejecting a false H_0) of the test. Usually, m will be no more than 2, and if k is fairly large, the difference between $\chi^2_{k-m-1,1-\alpha}$ and $\chi^2_{k-1,1-\alpha}$ will not be too great. Thus, we reject H_0 if (and only if) $\chi^2 > \chi^2_{k-1,1-\alpha}$, as in the all-parameters-known case. The rejection region for χ^2 is indicated in Fig. 6.46.

The most troublesome aspect of carrying out a chi-square test is choosing the number and size of the intervals. This is a difficult problem, and no definitive prescription can be given that is guaranteed to produce good results in terms of validity (actual level of the test close to the desired level α) and high power for all alternative distributions and all sample sizes. There are, however, a few guidelines that are often followed. First, some of the ambiguity in interval selection is eliminated if the intervals are chosen so that $p_1 = p_2 = \cdots = p_k$, which is called the *equiprobable approach*. In the continuous case, this might be inconvenient to do for some distributions since the distribution function of the fitted distribution must be inverted (see Example 6.15 below). Furthermore, for discrete distributions, we will generally be able to make the p_j's only approximately equal (see Example 6.16).

We now discuss how to choose the intervals to ensure "validity" of the test. Let $a = \min_{1 \le j \le k} np_j$, and let $y(5)$ be the number of np_j's less than 5. Based on extensive theoretical and empirical investigations (for the all-parameters-known case), Yarnold (1970) states that the chi-square test will be approximately valid if $k \ge 3$ and $a \ge 5y(5)/k$. For equiprobable intervals, these conditions will be satisfied if $k \ge 3$ and $np_j \ge 5$ for all j.

We now turn our attention to the power of the chi-square test. A test is said to be *unbiased* if it is more likely to reject H_0 when it is false than when it is true or, in other words, power is greater than the probability of a Type I error. A test without this property would certainly be undesirable. It can be shown that the chi-square test is always unbiased for the equiprobable approach [see Kendall and Stuart (1979, pp. 455–461)]. If the np_j's are not equal (and many are small), it is possible to obtain a valid test that is highly biased [see Haberman (1988)].

In general, there is no rule for choosing the intervals so that high power is obtained for all alternative distributions. For a particular null distribution, a fixed sample size n, and the equiprobable approach, Kallenberg, Oosterhoff, and Schriever (1985) showed empirically that power is an increasing function of the number of intervals k for some alternative distributions, and a decreasing function of k for other alternative distributions. Surprisingly, they also found in certain cases that the power was greater when the np_j's were smaller in the tails (see Prob. 6.18).

In the absence of a definitive guideline for choosing the intervals, we recommend the equiprobable approach and $np_j \ge 5$ for all j in the continuous case. This guarantees a valid and unbiased test. In the discrete case, we suggest making the np_j's approximately equal and all at least 5. The lack of a clear prescription for interval selection is the major drawback of the chi-square test. In some situations entirely different conclusions can be reached from the *same* data set depending on how the intervals are specified, as illustrated in Example 6.17. The chi-square test nevertheless remains in wide use, since it can be applied to any hypothesized distribution; as we shall see below, other goodness-of-fit tests do not enjoy such a wide range of applicability.

TABLE 6.12
A chi-square goodness-of-fit test for the interarrival-time data

j	Interval	N_j	np_j	$\frac{(N_j - np_j)^2}{np_j}$
1	[0, 0.020)	8	10.950	0.795
2	[0.020, 0.042)	11	10.950	0.000
3	[0.042, 0.065)	14	10.950	0.850
4	[0.065, 0.089)	14	10.950	0.850
5	[0.089, 0.115)	16	10.950	2.329
6	[0.115, 0.142)	10	10.950	0.082
7	[0.142, 0.172)	7	10.950	1.425
8	[0.172, 0.204)	5	10.950	3.233
9	[0.204, 0.239)	13	10.950	0.384
10	[0.239, 0.277)	12	10.950	0.101
11	[0.277, 0.319)	7	10.950	1.425
12	[0.319, 0.366)	7	10.950	1.425
13	[0.366, 0.419)	12	10.950	0.101
14	[0.419, 0.480)	10	10.950	0.082
15	[0.480, 0.553)	20	10.950	7.480
16	[0.553, 0.642)	9	10.950	0.347
17	[0.642, 0.757)	11	10.950	0.000
18	[0.757, 0.919)	9	10.950	0.347
19	[0.919, 1.195)	14	10.950	0.850
20	[1.195, ∞)	10	10.950	0.082
				$\chi^2 = 22.188$

EXAMPLE 6.15. We now use a chi-square test to compare the $n = 219$ interarrival times of Table 6.7 with the fitted exponential distribution having distribution function $\hat{F}(x) = 1 - e^{-x/0.399}$ for $x \geq 0$. If we form, say, $k = 20$ intervals with $p_j = 1/k = 0.05$ for $j = 1, 2, \ldots, 20$, then $np_j = (219)(0.05) = 10.950$, so that this satisfies the guidelines that the intervals be chosen with equal p_j's and $np_j \geq 5$. In this case, it is easy to find the a_j's, since $\hat{F}$ can be inverted. That is, we set $a_0 = 0$ and $a_{20} = \infty$, and for $j = 1, 2, \ldots, 19$ we want a_j to satisfy $\hat{F}(a_j) = j/20$; this is equivalent to setting $a_j = -0.399 \ln(1 - j/20)$ for $j = 1, 2, \ldots, 19$ since $a_j = \hat{F}^{-1}(j/20)$. (For continuous distributions such as the normal, gamma, and beta, the inverse of the distribution function does not have a simple closed form. In these cases, however, F^{-1} can be evaluated by numerical methods; consult the references given in Table 6.11.) The computations for the test are given in Table 6.12, and the value of the test statistic is $\chi^2 = 22.188$. Referring to Table T.2, we see that $\chi^2_{19,0.90} = 27.204$, which is not exceeded by χ^2, so we would not reject H_0 at the $\alpha = 0.10$ level. (Note that we would also not reject H_0 for certain larger values of α such as 0.25.) Thus, this test gives us no reason to conclude that our data are poorly fitted by the expo(0.399) distribution.

EXAMPLE 6.16. As an illustration of the chi-square test in the discrete case, we test how well the fitted geom(0.346) distribution agrees with the demand-size data of Table 6.9. As is usually the case for discrete distributions, we cannot make the p_j's exactly equal, but by grouping together adjacent points on which the mass function $\hat{p}(x)$ is defined (here, the nonnegative integers), we can define intervals that make the p_j's roughly the same. One way to do this is to note that the mode of the fitted distribution is 0; thus, $\hat{p}(0) = 0.346$ is the largest value of the mass function. The large value for the

TABLE 6.13
A chi-square goodness-of-fit test for the demand-size data

j	Interval	N_j	np_j	$\frac{(N_j - np_j)^2}{np_j}$
1	$\{0\}$	59	53.960	0.471
2	$\{1, 2\}$	50	58.382	1.203
3	$\{3, 4, \ldots\}$	47	43.658	0.256
				$\chi^2 = 1.930$

mode limits our choice of intervals, and we end up with the three intervals given in Table 6.13, where the calculations for the chi-square test are also presented. In particular, $\chi^2 = 1.930$, which is less than the critical value $\chi^2_{2,0.90} = 4.605$. Thus, we would not reject H_0 at the $\alpha = 0.10$ level, and we have no reason to believe that the demand-size data are not fitted well by a geom(0.346) distribution.

EXAMPLE 6.17. If we fit the log-logistic distribution to the 856 ship-loading times of Fig. 6.3, then we obtain the MLEs $\hat{\alpha} = 8.841$ and $\hat{\beta} = 0.822$ for the shape and scale parameters, respectively. We now perform a chi-square test at level $\alpha = 0.1$ using $k = 10$, 20, and 40 equiprobable intervals, with the results given in Table 6.14. (Note that all three choices for k satisfy the recommendation that $np_j \geq 5$.) We see that the log-logistic distribution is rejected for 20 intervals, but is not rejected for 10 or 40 intervals.

Kolmogorov-Smirnov Tests

As we just saw, chi-square tests can be thought of as a more formal comparison of a histogram of the data with the density or mass function of the fitted distribution. We also identified a real difficulty in using a chi-square test in the continuous case, namely, that of deciding how to specify the intervals. *Kolmogorov-Smirnov* (K-S) *tests* for goodness of fit, on the other hand, compare an empirical *distribution* function with the *distribution* function $\hat{F}$ of the hypothesized distribution. As we shall see, K-S tests do not require us to group the data in any way, so no information is lost; this also eliminates the troublesome problem of interval specification. Another advantage of K-S tests is that they are valid (exactly) for any sample size n (in the all-parameters-known case), whereas chi-square tests are valid only in an asymptotic sense. Finally, K-S tests tend to be more powerful than chi-square tests against many alternative distributions; see, for example, Stephens (1974).

TABLE 6.14
Chi-square goodness-of-fit tests for the ship-loading data

k	Statistic	Critical value	Result of test
10	11.383	14.684	Do not reject
20	27.645	27.204	Reject
40	50.542	50.660	Do not reject

Nevertheless, K-S tests do have some drawbacks, at least at present. Most seriously, their range of applicability is more limited than that for chi-square tests. First, for discrete data, the required critical values are not readily available and must be computed using a complicated set of formulas [see Conover (1999, pp. 435–437), Gleser (1985), and Pettitt and Stephens (1977)]. Second, the *original* form of the K-S test is valid only if *all* the parameters of the hypothesized distribution are *known* and the distribution is continuous; i.e., the parameters cannot have been estimated from the data. However, the K-S test has been extended to allow for estimation of the parameters in the cases of normal (lognormal), exponential, Weibull, and log-logistic distributions. Although the K-S test in its original (all-parameters-known) form has often been applied directly for any continuous distribution with estimated parameters and for discrete distributions, this will, in fact, produce a conservative test [see Conover (1999, pp. 432, 442)]. That is, the probability of a Type I error will be smaller than specified, with a corresponding loss of power.

To define the K-S statistic, we will use the empirical distribution function $F_n(x)$ defined by Eq. (6.5), which is a (right-continuous) step function such that $F_n(X_{(i)}) = i/n$ for $i = 1, 2, \ldots, n$ (see Prob. 6.19). If $\hat{F}(x)$ is the fitted distribution function, a natural assessment of goodness of fit is some kind of measure of the closeness between the functions F_n and $\hat{F}$. The K-S test statistic D_n is simply the *largest* (vertical) distance between $F_n(x)$ and $\hat{F}(x)$ *for all values of x* and is defined formally by

$$D_n = \sup_x \{|F_n(x) - \hat{F}(x)|\}$$

[The "sup" of a set of numbers A is the smallest value that is greater than or equal to all members of A. The "sup" is used here instead of the more familiar "max" since, in some cases, the maximum may not be well defined. For example, if $A = (0, 1)$, there is no maximum but the "sup" is 1.] The statistic D_n can be computed by calculating

$$D_n^+ = \max_{1 \le i \le n} \left\{ \frac{i}{n} - \hat{F}(X_{(i)}) \right\}, \qquad D_n^- = \max_{1 \le i \le n} \left\{ \hat{F}(X_{(i)}) - \frac{i-1}{n} \right\}$$

and finally letting

$$D_n = \max\{D_n^+, D_n^-\}$$

An example is given in Fig. 6.47 for $n = 4$, where $D_n = D_n^+$. [*Beware!* Incorrect computational formulas are often given for D_n. In particular, one sometimes sees

$$D'_n = \max_{1 \le i \le n} \left\{ \left| \frac{i}{n} - \hat{F}(X_{(i)}) \right| \right\}$$

as a "formula" for D_n. For the situation of Fig. 6.47, it *is* true that $D'_n = D_n$. Consider, however, Fig. 6.48, where $D'_n = \hat{F}(X_{(2)}) - \frac{2}{4}$ but the correct value for D_n is $\hat{F}(X_{(2)}) - \frac{1}{4}$, which occurs *just before* $x = X_{(2)}$. Clearly, $D'_n \ne D_n$ in this case.] Direct computation of D_n^+ and D_n^- requires sorting the data to obtain the $X_{(i)}$'s. However, Gonzalez, Sahni, and Franta (1977) provide an algorithm for computing D_n^+ and D_n^- without sorting.

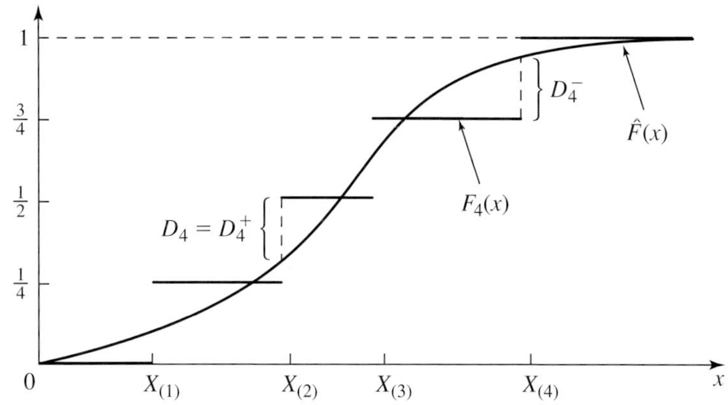

FIGURE 6.47
Geometric meaning of the K-S test statistic D_n for $n = 4$.

Clearly, a large value of D_n indicates a poor fit, so that the form of the test is to reject the null hypothesis H_0 if D_n exceeds some constant $d_{n,1-\alpha}$, where α is the specified level of the test. The numerical value of the critical point $d_{n,1-\alpha}$ depends on how the hypothesized distribution was specified, and we must distinguish several cases.

Case 1

If *all parameters of* $\hat{F}$ *are known*, i.e., none of the parameters of $\hat{F}$ is estimated in any way from the data, the distribution of D_n does not depend on $\hat{F}$, assuming (of course) that $\hat{F}$ is continuous. This rather remarkable fact means that a single table of values for $d_{n,1-\alpha}$ will suffice for all continuous distribution forms; these tables are widely available [see, for example, Owen (1962)]. Stephens (1974) devised an

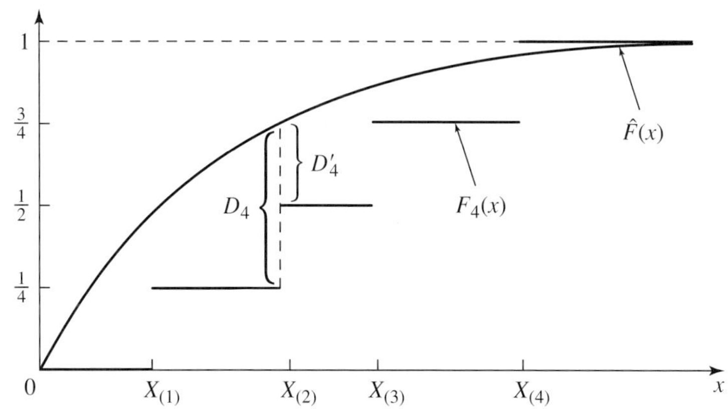

FIGURE 6.48
An example in which the K-S test statistic D_n is not equal to D'_n.

TABLE 6.15
Modified critical values $c_{1-\alpha}$, $c'_{1-\alpha}$, and $c''_{1-\alpha}$ for adjusted K-S test statistics

		$1-\alpha$				
Case	**Adjusted test statistic**	**0.850**	**0.900**	**0.950**	**0.975**	**0.990**
All parameters known	$\left(\sqrt{n} + 0.12 + \frac{0.11}{\sqrt{n}}\right)D_n$	1.138	1.224	1.358	1.480	1.628
$N(\bar{X}(n), S^2(n))$	$\left(\sqrt{n} - 0.01 + \frac{0.85}{\sqrt{n}}\right)D_n$	0.775	0.819	0.895	0.955	1.035
$\text{expo}(\bar{X}(n))$	$\left(D_n - \frac{0.2}{n}\right)\left(\sqrt{n} + 0.26 + \frac{0.5}{\sqrt{n}}\right)$	0.926	0.990	1.094	1.190	1.308

accurate approximation that eliminates the need for all but a tiny table; instead of testing for $D_n > d_{n,1-\alpha}$, we reject H_0 if

$$\left(\sqrt{n} + 0.12 + \frac{0.11}{\sqrt{n}}\right)D_n > c_{1-\alpha}$$

where values for $c_{1-\alpha}$ (which do not depend on n) are given in the all-parameters-known row of Table 6.15. This all-parameters-known case is the original form of the K-S test.

Case 2

Suppose that the hypothesized distribution is $N(\mu, \sigma^2)$ with both μ and σ^2 unknown. We can estimate μ and σ^2 by $\bar{X}(n)$ and $S^2(n)$, respectively, and define the distribution function $\hat{F}$ to be that of the $N(\bar{X}(n), S^2(n))$ distribution; i.e., let $\hat{F}(x) = \Phi\{[x - \bar{X}(n)]/\sqrt{S^2(n)}\}$, where Φ is the distribution function of the standard normal distribution. Using this $\hat{F}$ (which *has* estimated parameters), D_n is computed in the same way, but different critical points must be used. Lilliefors (1967) estimated (via Monte Carlo simulation) the critical points of D_n as a function of n and $1 - \alpha$. Stephens (1974) performed further Monte Carlo simulations and provided an accurate approximation that obviates the need for large tables; namely, we reject H_0 if

$$\left(\sqrt{n} - 0.01 + \frac{0.85}{\sqrt{n}}\right)D_n > c'_{1-\alpha}$$

where values for $c'_{1-\alpha}$ are given in the $N(\bar{X}(n), S^2(n))$ row of Table 6.15. (This case includes a K-S test for the lognormal distribution if the X_i's are the *logarithms* of the basic data points we have hypothesized to have a lognormal distribution; see Sec. 6.2.2.)

Case 3

Suppose the hypothesized distribution is expo(β) with β unknown. Now β is estimated by its MLE $\bar{X}(n)$, and we define $\hat{F}$ to be the expo($\bar{X}(n)$) distribution function; that is, $\hat{F}(x) = 1 - e^{-x/\bar{X}(n)}$ for $x \geq 0$. In this case, critical points for D_n were originally estimated by Lilliefors (1969) in a Monte Carlo study, and exact tables

TABLE 6.16
Modified critical values $c^*_{1-\alpha}$ for the K-S test for the Weibull distribution

	$1-\alpha$			
n	**0.900**	**0.950**	**0.975**	**0.990**
10	0.760	0.819	0.880	0.944
20	0.779	0.843	0.907	0.973
50	0.790	0.856	0.922	0.988
∞	0.803	0.874	0.939	1.007

were later obtained by Durbin (1975) [see also Margolin and Maurer (1976)]. Stephens's (1974) approximation in this case is to reject H_0 if

$$\left(D_n - \frac{0.2}{n}\right)\left(\sqrt{n} + 0.26 + \frac{0.5}{\sqrt{n}}\right) > c''_{1-\alpha}$$

where $c''_{1-\alpha}$ can be found in the expo($\overline{X}(n)$) row of Table 6.15.

Case 4

Suppose the hypothesized distribution is Weibull with both shape parameter α and scale parameter β unknown; we estimate these parameters by their respective MLEs $\hat{\alpha}$ and $\hat{\beta}$. (See the discussion of the Weibull MLEs in Sec. 6.2.2.) And $\hat{F}$ is taken to be the Weibull($\hat{\alpha}$, $\hat{\beta}$) distribution function $\hat{F}(x) = 1 - \exp[-(x/\hat{\beta})^{\hat{\alpha}}]$ for $x \geq 0$, and D_n is computed in the usual fashion. Then H_0 is rejected if the adjusted K-S statistic $\sqrt{n}D_n$ is greater than the modified critical value $c^*_{1-\alpha}$ [see Chandra, Singpurwalla, and Stephens (1981)] given in Table 6.16. Note that critical values are available only for certain sample sizes n, and that the critical values for $n = 50$ and ∞ (an extremely large sample size) are, fortunately, very similar. [Critical values for other n less than 50 are given by Littell, McClave, and Offen (1979).]

Case 5

Suppose that the hypothesized distribution is log-logistic with both shape parameter α and scale parameter β unknown. Let the X_i's here be the *logarithms* of the basic data points. Estimate the parameters by their respective MLEs $\hat{\alpha}$ and $\hat{\beta}$ based on the X_i's (see Sec. 6.2.2). Also $\hat{F}(x)$ is taken to be the logistic distribution function

$$\hat{F}(x) = \left(1 + e^{[-(x-\ln\hat{\beta})]\hat{\alpha}}\right)^{-1} \qquad \text{for } -\infty < x < \infty$$

and D_n is computed in the usual fashion. Then H_0 is rejected if the adjusted K-S statistic $\sqrt{n}D_n$ is greater than the modified critical value $c^\dagger_{1-\alpha}$ [see Stephens (1979)] given in Table 6.17. Note that the critical values are available only for certain sample sizes n, and that the critical values for $n = 50$ and ∞ are, fortunately, very similar.

EXAMPLE 6.18. In Example 6.15 we used a chi-square test to check the goodness of fit of the fitted expo(0.399) distribution for the interarrival-time data of Table 6.7. We can also apply a K-S test with $\hat{F}(x) = 1 - e^{-x/0.399}$ for $x \geq 0$, by using Case 3 above.

TABLE 6.17
Modified critical values $c^{\dagger}_{1-\alpha}$ for the K-S test for the log-logistic distribution

	$1-\alpha$			
n	**0.900**	**0.950**	**0.975**	**0.990**
10	0.679	0.730	0.774	0.823
20	0.698	0.755	0.800	0.854
50	0.708	0.770	0.817	0.873
∞	0.715	0.780	0.827	0.886

Using the formulas for D^+_{219} and D^-_{219}, we found that $D_{219} = 0.047$, so that the adjusted test statistic is

$$\left(D_{219} - \frac{0.2}{219}\right)\left(\sqrt{219} + 0.26 + \frac{0.5}{\sqrt{219}}\right) = 0.696$$

Since 0.696 is less than $0.990 = c''_{0.90}$ (from the last row of Table 6.15), we do not reject H_0 at the $\alpha = 0.10$ level.

Note that critical values for the K-S test in the case of the gamma distribution with estimated parameters have been published by Tadikamalla (1990), but, unfortunately, the largest sample size considered is 40.

Anderson-Darling Tests*

One possible drawback of K-S tests is that they give the same weight to the difference $|F_n(x) - \hat{F}(x)|$ for every value of x, whereas many distributions of interest differ primarily in their tails. The *Anderson-Darling* (A-D) *test* [see Anderson and Darling (1954)], on the other hand, is designed to detect discrepancies in the tails and has higher power than the K-S test against many alternative distributions [see Stephens (1974)]. The A-D statistic A^2_n is defined by

$$A^2_n = n\int_{-\infty}^{\infty} [F_n(x) - \hat{F}(x)]^2\,\psi(x)\hat{f}(x)\,dx$$

where the *weight function* $\psi(x) = 1/\{\hat{F}(x)[1 - \hat{F}(x)]\}$. Thus, A^2_n is just the weighted average of the squared differences $[F_n(x) - \hat{F}(x)]^2$, and the weights are the largest for $\hat{F}(x)$ close to 1 (right tail) and $\hat{F}(x)$ close to 0 (left tail). If we let $Z_i = \hat{F}(X_{(i)})$ for $i = 1, 2, \ldots, n$, then it can be shown that

$$A^2_n = \left(-\left\{\sum_{i=1}^{n} (2i - 1)[\ln Z_i + \ln(1 - Z_{n+1-i})]\right\}/n\right) - n$$

which is the form of the statistic used for actual computations. Since A^2_n is a "weighted distance," the form of the test is to reject the null hypothesis H_0 if A^2_n exceeds some critical value $a_{n,1-\alpha}$, where α is the level of the test.

*Skip this section on the first reading.

TABLE 6.18
Modified critical values for adjusted A-D test statistics

		$1-\alpha$			
Case	**Adjusted test statistic**	**0.900**	**0.950**	**0.975**	**0.990**
All parameters known	A_n^2 for $n \geq 5$	1.933	2.492	3.070	3.857
$N(\overline{X}(n), S^2(n))$	$\left(1+\frac{4}{n}-\frac{25}{n^2}\right)A_n^2$	0.632	0.751	0.870	1.029
$\text{Expo}(\overline{X}(n))$	$\left(1+\frac{0.6}{n}\right)A_n^2$	1.062	1.321	1.591	1.959
$\text{Weibull}(\hat{\alpha}, \hat{\beta})$	$\left(1+\frac{0.2}{\sqrt{n}}\right)A_n^2$	0.637	0.757	0.877	1.038
$\text{Log-logistic}(\hat{\alpha}, \hat{\beta})$	$\left(1+\frac{0.25}{\sqrt{n}}\right)A_n^2$	0.563	0.660	0.769	0.906

Critical values $a_{n,1-\alpha}$ are available for the A-D test for the same five continuous distributions [see Stephens (1974, 1976, 1977, 1979) and D'Agostino and Stephens (1986, p. 134)] as for the K-S test. [See Gleser (1985) for a discussion of the discrete case.] Furthermore, $\hat{F}(x)$ is computed in the same manner as before; see Example 6.19 below. Performance of the A-D test is facilitated by the use of adjusted test statistics (except for the all-parameters-known case) and modified critical values, which are given in Table 6.18. If the adjusted test statistic is greater than the modified critical value, then H_0 is rejected.

D'Agostino and Stephens (1986, pp. 151–156) give a procedure for performing an A-D test for the gamma distribution, where the critical values are obtained by interpolating in a table. An A-D test can also be performed for the Pearson type V distribution by using the fact that if X has a Pearson type V distribution, then $1/X$ has a gamma distribution (see Sec. 6.2.2). Cheng and Currie (2009) show how bootstrapping can be used to estimate critical values for the A-D test in the case of distributions with no published tables.

EXAMPLE 6.19. We can use Case 3 of the A-D test to see whether the fitted exponential distribution $\hat{F}(x) = 1 - e^{-x/0.399}$ provides a good model for the interarrival-time data at level $\alpha = 0.10$. We found that $A_{219}^2 = 0.558$, so that the adjusted test statistic is

$$\left(1+\frac{0.6}{219}\right)A_{219}^2 = 0.560$$

Since 0.560 is less than the modified critical value 1.062 (from the third row of Table 6.18), we do not reject H_0 at level 0.10.

Poisson-Process Tests*

Suppose that we observe a Poisson process (see Sec. 6.12.1) for a *fixed* interval of time $[0, T]$, where T is a constant that is decided upon before we start our

*Skip this section on the first reading.

observation. Let n be the number of events we observe in the interval $[0, T]$, and let t_i be the time of the ith event for $i = 1, 2, \ldots, n$. {Thus, $0 \leq t_1 \leq t_2 \leq \cdots \leq t_n \leq T$. If $t_n < T$, then no events occurred in the interval $(t_n, T]$.} Then the joint distribution of $t_1, t_2, \ldots, t_n$ is related to the U(0, T) distribution in the following way. Assume that $Y_1, Y_2, \ldots, Y_n$ (the same n as above) are IID random variables with the U(0, T) distribution, and let $Y_{(1)}, Y_{(2)}, \ldots, Y_{(n)}$ be their corresponding order statistics (see Sec. 6.2.4). Then a property of the Poisson process is that $t_1, t_2, \ldots, t_n$ have the same joint distribution as $Y_{(1)}, Y_{(2)}, \ldots, Y_{(n)}$. [See Ross (2003, p. 303) for a proof.]

One way of interpreting this property is that if someone simply showed us the *values* of $t_1, t_2, \ldots, t_n$ without telling us that t_i was obtained as the time of the ith event in some sequence of events, it would appear (in a statistical sense) that these n numbers had been obtained by taking a sample of n IID random values from the U(0, T) distribution and then sorting them into increasing order. Alternatively, one could think of this property as saying that if we consider $t_1, t_2, \ldots, t_n$ as unordered random variables, they are IID with the U(0, T) distribution. This is why we sometimes see a Poisson process described as one in which events occur "at random," since the instants at which events occur are uniformly distributed over time.

In any case, this property provides us with a different way of testing the null hypothesis that an observed sequence of events was generated by a Poisson process. (We have already seen one way this hypothesis can be tested, namely, testing whether the interevent times appear to be IID exponential random variables; see Sec. 6.12.1 and Examples 6.15, 6.18, and 6.19.) We simply test whether the event times $t_1, t_2, \ldots, t_n$ appear to be IID U(0, T) random variables using any applicable testing procedure.

EXAMPLE 6.20. The interarrival-time data of Table 6.7 were collected over a fixed 90-minute period, and $n = 220$ arrivals were recorded during this interval. (It was decided beforehand to start observing the process at exactly 5 P.M., rather than at the first time after 5:00 when an arrival happened to take place. Also, data collection terminated promptly at 6:30 P.M., regardless of any arrivals that occurred later. It is important for the validity of this test that the data collection be designed in this way, i.e., independent of the actual event times.) The times of arrivals were $t_1 = 1.53$, $t_2 = 1.98, \ldots, t_{220} = 88.91$ (in minutes after 5 P.M.). To test whether these numbers can be regarded as being independent with the U(0,90) distribution, we used the *all-parameters-known* cases of the chi-square and K-S tests. [The density and distribution functions of the fitted distribution are, respectively, $\hat{f}(x) = 1/90$ and $\hat{F}(x) = x/90$, for $0 \leq x \leq 90$. Note also that our "data" points are already sorted, conveniently.] We carried out a chi-square test with the $k = 17$ equal-size intervals $[0, 5.294), [5.294, 10.588), \ldots, [84.706, 90]$, so that $np_j = 220/17 = 12.941$ for $j = 1, 2, \ldots, 17$. The resulting value of χ^2 was 13.827, and since $\chi^2_{16,0.90} = 23.542$, we cannot reject the null hypothesis that the arrivals occurred in accordance with a Poisson process at level 0.10. The K-S test resulted in $D_{220} = 0.045$, and the value of the adjusted test statistic from the all-parameters-known row of Table 6.15 is thus 0.673. Since this is well below $c_{0.90} = 1.224$, once again we cannot reject the null hypothesis at level 0.10.

6.7
THE ExpertFit SOFTWARE AND AN EXTENDED EXAMPLE

Performing the statistical procedures discussed in this chapter can, in some cases, be difficult, time-consuming, and prone to error. For example, the chi-square test with equiprobable intervals requires the availability of the inverse of the distribution function, which is not available in closed form for some distributions (e.g., normal and gamma). Thus, in these cases a numerical approximation to the inverse of the distribution function would have to be obtained and programmed. Also, the K-S test is often misstated or misapplied in textbooks and software packages. These considerations led to the development of the ExpertFit distribution-fitting software.

The commercial versions of ExpertFit [see Averill M. Law & Associates (2013)] will automatically and accurately determine which of 40 probability distributions best represents a data set. The selected distribution is then put into the proper format for direct input to a large number of different simulation packages. ExpertFit contains the following four modules that are used sequentially to determine the best distribution:

- "Data" reads or imports data into ExpertFit, displays summary statistics, and makes histograms; makes correlation plots and scatter diagrams; and performs the Kruskal-Wallis test for homogeneity of data sets (see Sec. 6.13).
- "Models" fits distributions to the data by using the method of maximum likelihood, ranks the distributions in terms of quality of fit, and determines whether the "best" distribution is actually good enough to use in a simulation model. (Otherwise, it recommends the use of an empirical distribution.)
- "Comparisons" compares the best distribution(s) to the data to further determine the quality of fit, using density-histogram plots, distribution-function-differences plots, probability plots, goodness-of-fit tests, etc.
- "Applications" displays and computes characteristics of a fitted distribution such as the density function, moments, probabilities, and quantiles; it also puts the selected distribution into the proper format for a chosen simulation package.

ExpertFit has the following documentation:

- Context-sensitive help for all menus and all results tables and graphs
- Online feature index and tutorials (see the "Help" pull-down menu in the Menu Bar at the top of the screen)
- User's Guide with eight complete examples

There is a Student Version of ExpertFit on the book's website, www.mhhe.com/law, that can be used to analyze most data sets corresponding to the examples and problems in this chapter. It cannot, however, be used to analyze your own data sets.

We now use ExpertFit to perform a comprehensive analysis of the $n = 200$ service times of Example 6.1. However, for expository convenience we limit our analysis to the exponential, gamma, Weibull, lognormal, log-logistic, Pearson type V, Pearson type VI, and normal distributions. In Table 6.19 we present the "Data Summary" (i.e., summary statistics) for the service times, and Fig. 6.49 is a corresponding histogram based on $k = 12$ intervals of width $\Delta b = 0.2$. (The interval width was

TABLE 6.19
Data summary for the service-time data

Data characteristic	Value
Source file	EXAMPLE61
Observation type	Real valued
Number of observations	200
Minimum observation	0.054
Maximum observation	2.131
Mean	0.888
Median	0.849
Variance	0.210
Coefficient of variation	0.515
Skewness	0.513

determined by trial and error.) The shape of the histogram strongly suggests that the underlying distribution is skewed to the right, which tends to rule out the normal distribution. This is supported by noting that $\bar{X}(200) = 0.888 > 0.849 = \hat{x}_{0.5}(200)$ and $\hat{\nu}(200) = 0.513 > 0$. Furthermore, $\widehat{cv}(200) = 0.515$ makes it fairly unlikely that the true distribution could be exponential, which has a coefficient of variation of 1; this conclusion is supported by the shape of the histogram.

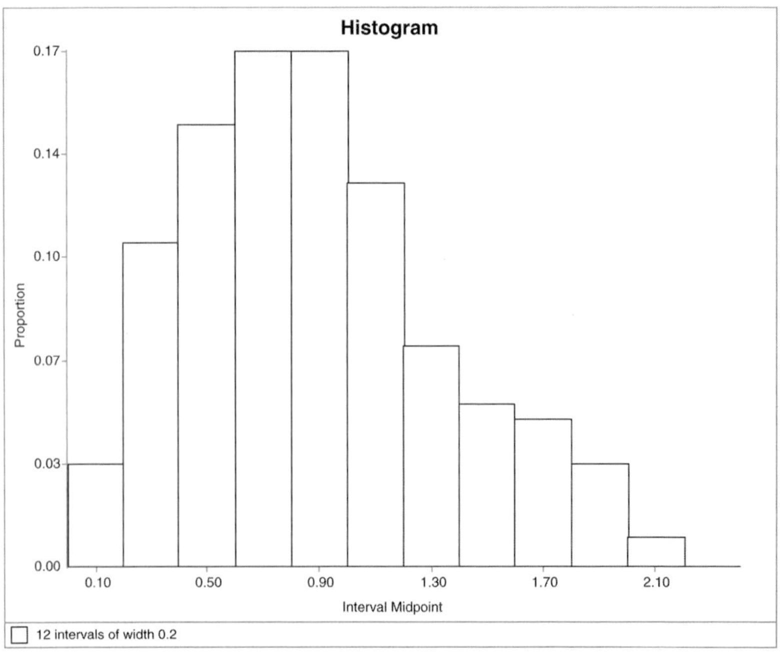

FIGURE 6.49
Histogram of 200 service times with $\Delta b = 0.2$.

Relative Evaluation of Candidate Models

Model	Relative Score	Parameters	
1 - Weibull	100.00	Location	0.00000
		Scale	1.00342
		Shape	2.04472
2 - Gamma	83.33	Location	0.00000
		Scale	0.27318
		Shape	3.25198
3 - Log-Logistic	62.50	Location	0.00000
		Scale	0.79528
		Shape	2.91443

7 models are defined with scores between 0.00 and 100.00

Absolute Evaluation of Model 1 - Weibull

Evaluation: Good

Suggestion: Additional evaluations using Comparisons Tab might be informative.
See Help for more information.

Additional Information about Model 1 - Weibull

"Error" in the model mean relative to the sample mean -5.8399e-4 = 0.07%

FIGURE 6.50
ExpertFit results screen for the service-time data.

The "Automated Fitting" option, which is in the Models module, was then used to fit, rank, and evaluate the specified distributions other than the normal distribution automatically. The normal distribution was not automatically fit to the data, since it can take on negative values that are inconsistent with the range of service times. (If desired, the normal distribution could be fit to this data set manually by using "Fit Individual Models" in the Models module.) The resulting ExpertFit results screen is shown in Fig. 6.50. From the "Relative Evaluation of Candidate Models," it can be seen that the Weibull distribution is ranked first and received a "Relative Score" (see below) of 100.00 followed by the gamma distribution and the log-logistic distribution with Relative Scores of 83.33 and 62.50, respectively. The maximum-likelihood estimates for the best-fitting Weibull distribution are $\hat{\alpha} = 2.045$ and $\hat{\beta} = 1.003$.

Even if a distribution is ranked first, this does not necessarily mean that it is good enough to use in a simulation. However, since the "Absolute Evaluation" is "Good," there is no current evidence for not using the Weibull distribution. On the other hand, it is prudent to obtain further confirmation using the Comparisons module. If the highest-ranked distribution receives an Absolute Evaluation of "Bad," then it is not suitable for use in a simulation model and ExpertFit will recommend the use of an empirical distribution (see Sec. 6.2.4).

The ExpertFit ranking and evaluation algorithm was developed as follows. We had 15 heuristics that were thought to have some ability to discriminate between a good-fitting and bad-fitting distribution. (The chi-square statistic was not considered because it depends on an arbitrary choice of intervals.) To determine which of these heuristics was actually the best, a random sample of size n was generated from a known "parent" distribution, and each of the 15 heuristics was applied to see if it could, in fact, choose the correct distribution. This was repeated for 200 independent samples, giving an estimated probability that each heuristic would pick the parent distribution for the specified sample size. This whole process was repeated for 175 parent distribution/sample-size pairs, resulting in several heuristics that appeared to be superior. These heuristics were combined to give the overall algorithm for ranking the fitted distributions and for computing the relative scores. The 35,000 generated data sets were also used to develop the rules for determining the Absolute Evaluations.

The ranking screen also shows that the error in the mean of the Weibull distribution relative to the sample mean is only 0.07 percent.

As suggested by the Absolute Evaluation, we will now try to obtain additional confirmation for the Weibull distribution by using graphical plots and goodness-of-fit tests. In Fig. 6.51 we give density-histogram plots for the Weibull and gamma

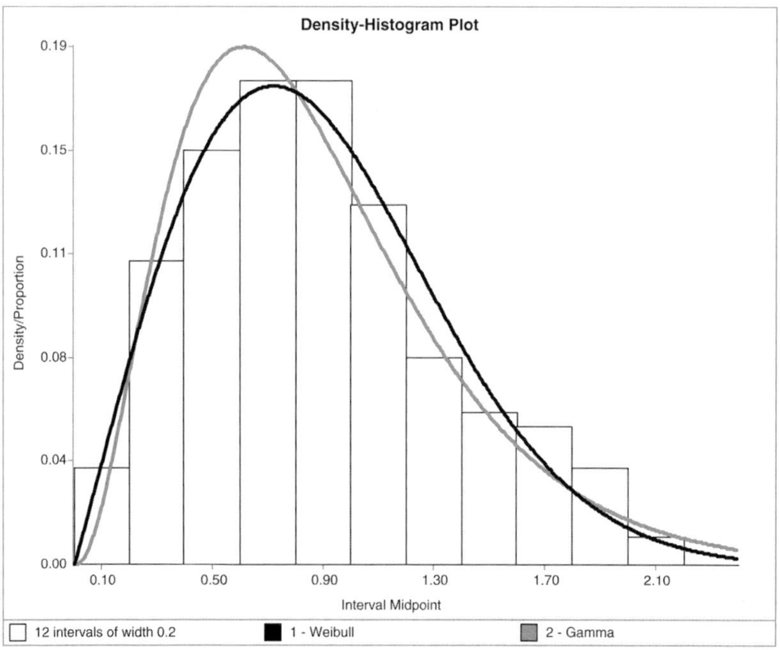

FIGURE 6.51
Density-histogram plots for the service-time data and the Weibull and gamma distributions.

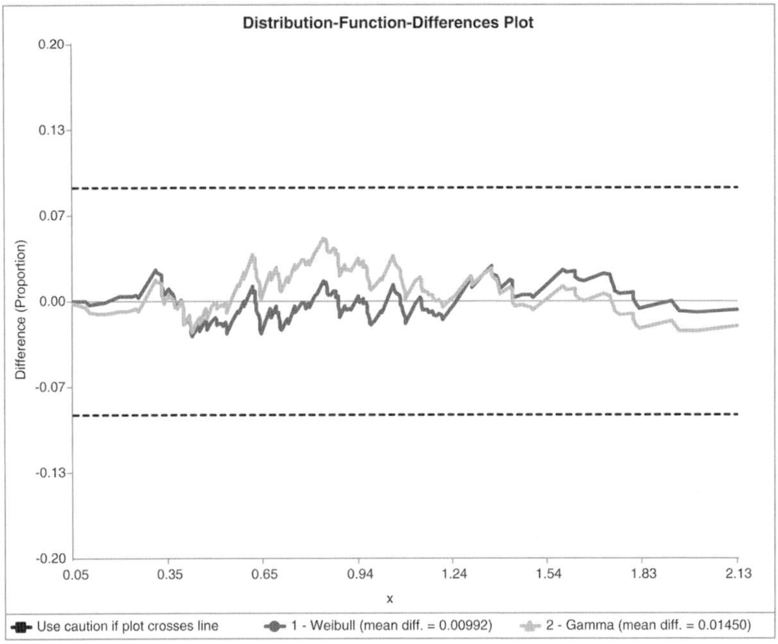

FIGURE 6.52
Distribution-function-differences plots for the service-time data and the Weibull and gamma distributions.

distributions (see also the Color Plates). It can be seen that the Weibull distribution matches the histogram well and that the gamma distribution is clearly inferior. Figure 6.52 gives distribution-function-differences plots for the two distributions and, once again, the superiority of the Weibull distribution can be seen (see the Color Plates). The *P–P* plots in Fig. 6.53 also show that the Weibull distribution is preferable.

We next performed an equiprobable chi-square test for the Weibull distribution at level $\alpha = 0.05$ using $k = 20$ intervals. The chi-square statistic was 15.6, which is less than the critical value 30.144; therefore, this particular chi-square test gives us no reason to reject the Weibull distribution. The adjusted test statistic for the K-S test was 0.428, which is less than the $\alpha = 0.05$ modified critical value 0.874. Once again we have no reason to reject the Weibull distribution. Finally, the test statistic for the A-D test was 0.264, which is less than the $\alpha = 0.05$ critical value 0.746, giving us no reason to reject the Weibull distribution.

Thus, based on the Absolute Evaluation, the graphical plots, and the goodness-of-fit tests, there is no reason to think that the Weibull distribution is not a good representation for the service-time data.

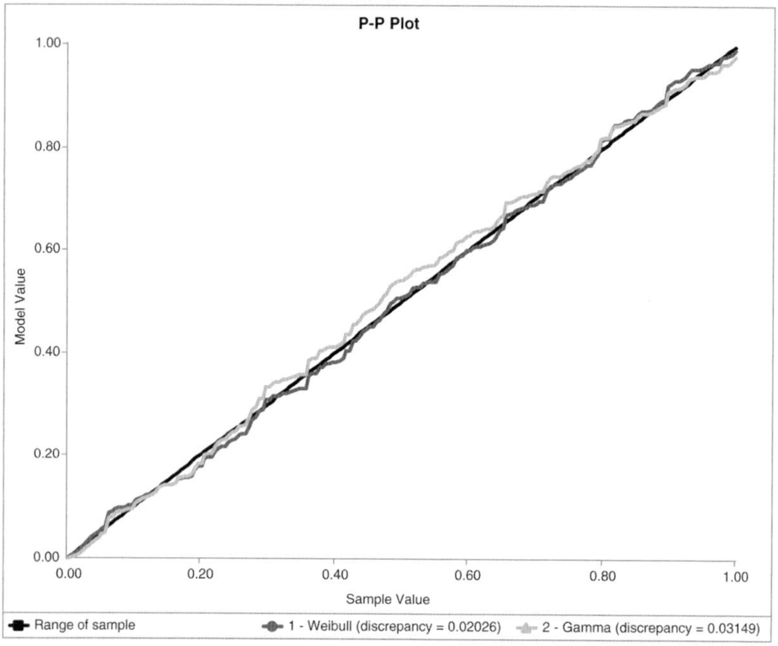

FIGURE 6.53
P–P plots for the service-time data and the Weibull and gamma distributions.

6.8 SHIFTED AND TRUNCATED DISTRIBUTIONS

The exponential, gamma, Weibull, lognormal, Pearson type V, Pearson type VI, and log-logistic distributions, discussed in Sec. 6.2.2, have range $[0, \infty)$. Thus, if the random variable X has any of these distributions, it can take on arbitrarily small positive values. However, frequently in practice if X represents the time to complete some task (such as customer service), it is simply impossible for X to be less than some fixed positive number. For example, in a bank it is probably not possible to serve anyone in less than, say, 30 seconds; this will be reflected in the service-time data we might collect on the bank's operation. Thus, in reality $P(X < 30 \text{ seconds}) = 0$; however, for a fitted gamma distribution, for instance, there is a *positive* probability of generating a random value that is less than 30 seconds. Thus, it would appear that a modification of these distribution forms would provide a more realistic model and might result in a better fit *in some cases*.

This change can be effected by *shifting* the distribution some distance to the right. What this really amounts to is generalizing the density function of the distribution in question to include a location parameter (see Sec. 6.2.1).

For example, the gamma distribution shifted to the right by an amount $\gamma > 0$ has density

$$f(x) = \begin{cases} \dfrac{\beta^{-\alpha}(x-\gamma)^{\alpha-1} e^{-(x-\gamma)/\beta}}{\Gamma(\alpha)} & \text{if } x > \gamma \\ 0 & \text{otherwise} \end{cases}$$

which has the same shape and scale parameters as the gamma (α, β) distribution but is shifted γ units to the right. (This is often called the *three-parameter gamma distribution.*) Shifted versions of the other distributions discussed above are defined similarly, by replacing x by $x - \gamma$ in the density functions and their domains of definition. The range of these shifted distributions is $[\gamma, \infty)$.

With these shifted distributions, we then have to estimate γ as well as the other parameters. In theory, this can be done by finding the MLE for γ in addition to the MLEs for the original parameters. For the shifted exponential, $\hat{\gamma}$ and $\hat{\beta}$ are relatively easy to find (see Prob. 6.12). However, finding MLEs for the three-parameter distributions is considerably more problematic. For example, in the case of the gamma, Weibull, and lognormal distributions, it is known that (global) MLEs are not well defined [see Cheng and Amin (1983), Cohen and Whitten (1980), and Zanakis (1979a)]. That is, the likelihood function L can be made infinite by choosing $\hat{\gamma} = X_{(1)}$ (the smallest observation in the sample), which results in inadmissible values for the other parameters. A simple approach to the three-parameter estimation problem is first to estimate the location parameter γ by

$$\tilde{\gamma} = \frac{X_{(1)}X_{(n)} - X_{(k)}^2}{X_{(1)} + X_{(n)} - 2X_{(k)}}$$

where k is the smallest integer in $\{2, 3, \ldots, n-1\}$ such that $X_{(k)} > X_{(1)}$ [see Dubey (1967)]. It can be shown that $\tilde{\gamma} < X_{(1)}$ if and only if $X_{(k)} < [X_{(1)} + X_{(n)}]/2$, which is very likely to occur; see Prob. 6.23. [Zanakis (1979b) has shown empirically the accuracy of $\tilde{\gamma}$ for the Weibull distribution.] Given the value $\tilde{\gamma}$, we next define X_i' as follows:

$$X_i' = X_i - \tilde{\gamma} \geq 0 \qquad \text{for } i = 1, 2, \ldots, n$$

Finally, MLE estimators of the scale and shape parameters are obtained by applying the usual two-parameter MLE procedures to the observations $X_1', X_2', \ldots, X_n'$.

EXAMPLE 6.21. In Fig. 6.54, we give a histogram (with $\Delta b = 0.2$) of the times (in hours) to unload $n = 808$ coal trains, each consisting of approximately 110 cars. (Figure 6.54 is actually a density-histogram plot.) The shape of the histogram suggests that a fitted distribution would require a positive location parameter. Since $X_{(1)} = 3.37$, $X_{(2)} = 3.68$, and $X_{(808)} = 6.32$, we get $\hat{\gamma} = 3.329$. The values $X_i' = X_i - 3.329$ for $i = 1, 2, \ldots, 808$ were then used to obtain the MLEs $\hat{\alpha} = 7.451$ and $\hat{\beta} = 1.271$ for the log-logistic distribution, whose density function is also given in Fig. 6.54. In general, the agreement between the shifted log-logistic density function and the histogram seems quite good.

In some situations a fitted distribution might provide a good model for observed data generally, but other information says that, for instance, no value can be larger

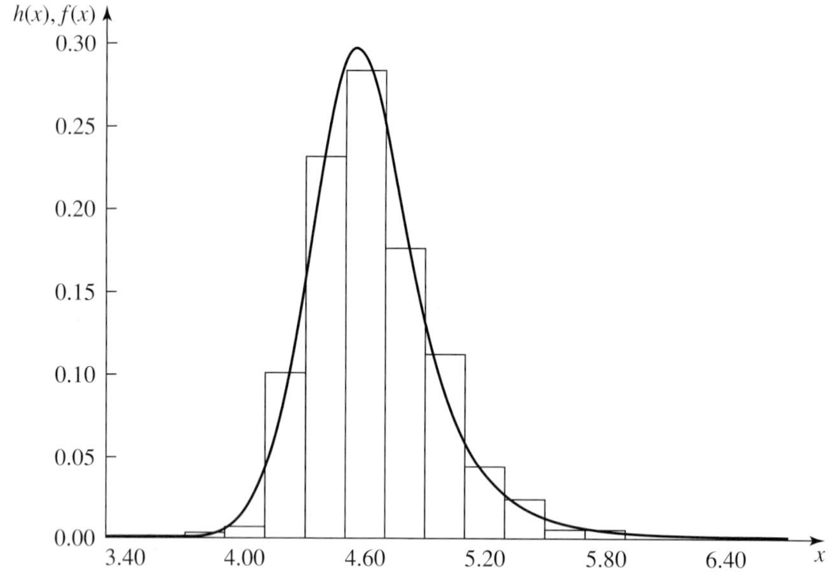

FIGURE 6.54
Density-histogram plot for the train-unloading data and the fitted log-logistic distribution.

than some finite constant $b > 0$. If the range of the fitted density f is $[0, \infty)$, this is incompatible with the upper limit b, so we might instead use a truncated density

$$f^*(x) = f(x)/F(b) \text{ for } 0 \leq x \leq b \text{ (and 0 otherwise), where } F(b) = \int_0^b f(x)\, dx < 1.$$

A method to generate random values from f^* is given in Sec. 8.2.1.

EXAMPLE 6.22. If a gamma distribution is found to provide a good model for service times in a bank, the density function might be truncated above $b = 15$ minutes if larger values than this are extremely unlikely.

6.9 BÉZIER DISTRIBUTIONS

There is a fourth approach [Wagner and Wilson (1996a, 1996b)] for specifying a probability distribution that models a set of observed data $X_1, X_2, \ldots, X_n$ (see Sec. 6.1 for the other three approaches). If X is a continuous random variable with finite range $[a, b]$ and a distribution function $F(x)$ having any shape, then $F(x)$ can be approximated arbitrarily closely by a *Bézier distribution* function with sufficiently high degree m. Let $\{\mathbf{p}_0, \mathbf{p}_1, \ldots, \mathbf{p}_m\}$ be a set of *control points*, where

$\mathbf{p}_i = (y_i, z_i)$ $(i = 1, 2, \ldots, m - 1)$, $\mathbf{p}_0 = (a, 0)$, and $\mathbf{p}_m = (b, 1)$. The Bézier distribution function $\mathbf{P}(t)$ is given parametrically by

$$\mathbf{P}(t) = \sum_{i=0}^{m} B_{m,i}(t)\mathbf{p}_i \qquad \text{for } t \in [0, 1] \tag{6.6}$$

where

$$B_{m,i}(t) = \frac{m!}{i!(m - i)!} t^i(1 - t)^{m-i}$$

Let $\mathbf{y}$ be the vector of y_i's, and let $\mathbf{z}$ be the vector of z_i's. Furthermore, let $F_n(x)$ be the empirical distribution function defined by Eq. (6.5), and let $F(x; m, \mathbf{y}, \mathbf{z})$ be the Bézier distribution function given by Eq. (6.6). For fixed m, $F(x; m, \mathbf{y}, \mathbf{z})$ is fit to the X_i's by using a suitable optimization technique (e.g., least-squares estimation) to find the minimum distance between $F_n(x)$ and $F(x; m, \mathbf{y}, \mathbf{z})$ over all possible $\mathbf{y}$ and $\mathbf{z}$, and subject to certain constraints. (The optimization determines $\mathbf{p}_i$ for $i = 1, 2, \ldots, m - 1$.)

A Bézier distribution is an alternative to an empirical distribution for modeling a data set that is not represented well by a standard theoretical distribution. Furthermore, a software package for fitting Bézier distributions has been developed by Wagner and Wilson. There is, however, a difficulty in using Bézier distributions, at least at present. Bézier distributions are not implemented in most simulation packages, and doing so on one's own could be difficult in some software.

6.10
SPECIFYING MULTIVARIATE DISTRIBUTIONS, CORRELATIONS, AND STOCHASTIC PROCESSES

So far in this chapter we have considered only the specification and estimation of the distribution of a single, univariate random variable at a time. If the simulation model needs input of only such scalar random variables, and if they are all independent of each other across the model, then repeated application to each input of the methods we've discussed up to now in this chapter will suffice. Indeed, this is the standard mode of operation in most simulation projects, and it is the one supported by most simulation packages.

There are systems, however, in which the input random variables are statistically related to each other in some way:

- Some of the input random variables together form a random *vector* with some multivariate (or joint) probability distribution (see Sec. 4.2) to be specified by the modeler.
- In other cases we may not want (or be able) to go quite so far as to specify the complete multivariate distribution, but nonetheless suspect that there could be *correlation* between different input random variables having their own individual, or *marginal,* distributions, without knowledge or specification of the complete multivariate distribution. We would like our inputs to reflect this correlation even if we can't specify the entire multivariate distribution.

- In yet other cases, we may want to specify an entire input stochastic process (see Sec. 4.3) in which the marginal distribution of the individual random variables composing the process is to be specified, as well as the autocorrelations between them out through some desired lag. This could be regarded as an infinite-dimensional input random vector.

It is easy to think of physical situations where such input might occur:

- Consider a maintenance shop that can be modeled as a tandem queue with two service stations. At the first station, incoming parts are inspected, and any defects are marked for repair at the second station. Since a badly damaged part would probably require above-average times for both inspection and repair, we might expect the two service times for a given part to be positively correlated. Mitchell et al. (1977) found that ignoring this correlation in modeling a system can lead to serious inaccuracies in simulation results.
- In a model of a communications system, the sizes of (and perhaps interarrival times between) arriving messages could form a stochastic process with some stationary marginal univariate distribution of message size, as well as some kind of correlation out through several lags. For instance, it could be that large messages tend to come in groups, as do small messages, resulting in positive autocorrelation within the message-size input process. Livny et al. (1993) show that autocorrelation in either the service-time or interarrival-time input process of a simple $M/M/1$ queue can have a major effect on the output performance measures.
- In a model of an inventory or production system, the stream of incoming orders could display negative lag-one autocorrelation if a large order in one period tends to be followed by a small order in the next period, and vice versa.

Thus, if the modeler has evidence of some kind of statistical relationship between a simulation's various scalar input random variables, or if an input stream is a process over time that exhibits autocorrelation within itself, then consideration might be given to modeling these relationships and generating them during the simulation to avoid possible problems with model validity.

In the remainder of this section we briefly discuss some of these issues with regard to specification and estimation [see the book chapter by Biller and Ghosh (2006) for a comprehensive discussion], and in Sec. 8.5 we discuss generating the corresponding observations for input to the simulation as it runs. In Sec. 6.12 we take up the related issue of modeling arrival processes; in Sec. 8.6 we discuss generation methods for such processes. Many of these issues are discussed in Leemis (2004) and in Sec. 5 of Nelson and Yamnitsky (1998).

6.10.1 Specifying Multivariate Distributions

Let $\mathbf{X} = (X_1, X_2, \ldots, X_d)^T$ be an input random vector of dimension d (A^T denotes the transpose of a vector or matrix A, so that $\mathbf{X}$ is a $d \times 1$ column vector). For instance, in the maintenance-shop example above, $d = 2$ (in which case $\mathbf{X}$ is called *bivariate*), X_1 is the inspection time of a part, and X_2 is the subsequent repair time of that *same* part. Let $\mathbf{X}_k = (X_{1k}, X_{2k}, \ldots, X_{dk})^T$ be the kth of n IID observations on this d-dimensional random vector; in the maintenance shop we would have n pairs

$$\begin{pmatrix} X_{11} \\ X_{21} \end{pmatrix}, \begin{pmatrix} X_{12} \\ X_{22} \end{pmatrix}, \ldots, \begin{pmatrix} X_{1n} \\ X_{2n} \end{pmatrix}$$

of observed data corresponding to the inspection and repair times of n different parts, and we would further want to be able to generate such a sequence of 2-vectors as input to the simulation.

Note that while we allow correlation *within* the components of a specific $\mathbf{X}_k$, we are assuming here that the component random variables *across* different $\mathbf{X}_k$'s are independent, i.e., that the random vectors $\mathbf{X}_1, \mathbf{X}_2, \ldots, \mathbf{X}_n$ are independent of each other. In the maintenance-shop situation this means that while the inspection and repair times of a given part may be related, there is no relation between either of these times across different parts—the parts are assumed to behave independently of each other. [In Sec. 6.10.3, we allow autocorrelation in the $\{\mathbf{X}_1, \mathbf{X}_2, \ldots\}$ sequence, but mostly in the univariate (scalar) case $d = 1$.]

The *multivariate* (or *joint*) *distribution function* of the random vector $\mathbf{X}$ is defined as

$$F(\mathbf{x}) = P(\mathbf{X} \le \mathbf{x}) = P(X_1 \le x_1, X_2 \le x_2, \ldots, X_d \le x_d)$$

for any fixed d-vector $\mathbf{x} = (x_1, x_2, \ldots, x_d)^T$. This includes all the cases of continuous, discrete, or mixed individual marginal distributions. In addition to implying the marginal distributions, all the information about relationships between the individual component random variables is embodied in the multivariate distribution function, including their correlations.

As with univariate scalar random variables, there are a variety of multivariate distributions that have been developed and parameterized in various ways and into various families; see Chap. XI of Devroye (1986), Johnson (1987), Johnson et al. (1997), and Kotz et al. (2000). However, it may be difficult or impractical to estimate the entire multivariate distribution of a random vector from observed data, particularly if the sample size n is not large. Thus, we restrict ourselves in the remainder of this subsection to certain special cases of multivariate-distribution estimation that have been found useful in simulation, and we discuss in Sec. 6.10.2 what can be done if our estimation goals are more modest than that of specifying the entire multivariate distribution. And since our interest is ultimately in simulation input, we must also pay attention to how realizations of such random vectors can be generated, as discussed in Sec. 8.5.

Multivariate Normal

This is probably the best-known special case of a multivariate distribution. While this distribution might have somewhat limited direct utility as a simulation-input model since all its marginal distributions are symmetric and have infinite tails in both directions, it does serve as a springboard to other more useful input-modeling distributions.

The multivariate normal density function (see Sec. 4.2) is defined as

$$f(\mathbf{x}) = (2\pi)^{-n/2}|\Sigma|^{-1/2}\exp\left[-\frac{(\mathbf{x}-\boldsymbol{\mu})^T\Sigma^{-1}(\mathbf{x}-\boldsymbol{\mu})}{2}\right]$$

for any vector $\mathbf{x}$ in d-dimensional real space. Here, $\boldsymbol{\mu} = (\mu_1, \mu_2, \ldots, \mu_d)^T$ is the mean vector, Σ is the covariance matrix with (i, j)th entry $\sigma_{ij} = \sigma_{ji} = \text{Cov}(X_i, X_j)$ (so Σ is symmetric and positive definite), $|\Sigma|$ is the determinant of Σ, and Σ^{-1} is the matrix inverse of Σ. The marginal distribution of X_i is $\text{N}(\mu_i, \sigma_{ii})$. We denote the multivariate normal distribution as $\text{N}_d(\boldsymbol{\mu}, \Sigma)$.

The *correlation coefficient* between X_i and X_j is $\rho_{ij} = \sigma_{ij}/\sqrt{\sigma_{ii}\sigma_{jj}} = \rho_{ji}$, which is always between -1 and $+1$. Thus, since $\sigma_{ij} = \sigma_{ji} = \rho_{ij}\sqrt{\sigma_{ii}\sigma_{jj}}$, an alternative parameterization of the multivariate normal distribution would be to replace Σ by the parameters σ_{ii} and ρ_{ij} for $i = 1, 2, \ldots, d$ and $j = i + 1, i + 2, \ldots, d$.

Note that in the multivariate-normal case, the entire joint distribution is uniquely determined by the marginal distributions and the correlation coefficients. This is generally not true for other, non-normal multivariate distributions; i.e., there could be several different joint distributions that result in the same set of marginal distributions and correlations.

To fit a multivariate normal distribution to observed d-dimensional data $\mathbf{X}_1$, $\mathbf{X}_2, \ldots, \mathbf{X}_n$, the mean vector $\boldsymbol{\mu}$ is estimated by the MLE

$$\hat{\boldsymbol{\mu}} = \overline{\mathbf{X}} = (\overline{X}_1, \overline{X}_2, \ldots, \overline{X}_d)^T \tag{6.7}$$

where $\overline{X}_i = \sum_{k=1}^{n} X_{ik}/n$, and the covariance matrix Σ is estimated by the $d \times d$ matrix $\hat{\Sigma}$ whose (i, j)th entry is

$$\hat{\sigma}_{ij} = \frac{\sum_{k=1}^{n}(X_{ik} - \overline{X}_i)(X_{jk} - \overline{X}_j)}{n} \tag{6.8}$$

The correlation coefficient ρ_{ij} is estimated by the MLE

$$\hat{\rho}_{ij} = \frac{\hat{\sigma}_{ij}}{\sqrt{\hat{\sigma}_{ii}\hat{\sigma}_{jj}}} = \hat{\rho}_{ji} \tag{6.9}$$

With a multivariate normal distribution so estimated, generation from it is possible by methods given in Sec. 8.5.2.

Multivariate Lognormal

This multivariate distribution affords the modeler positively skewed marginal distributions on $[0, \infty)$ with the possibility of correlation between them.

Rather than giving the explicit definition of its full joint density function, it is more useful for simulation purposes to describe the multivariate lognormal in terms of its transformational relation to the multivariate normal. We say that $\mathbf{X} = (X_1, X_2, \ldots, X_d)^T$ has a multivariate lognormal distribution if and only if

$$\mathbf{Y} = (Y_1, Y_2, \ldots, Y_d)^T = (\ln X_1, \ln X_2, \ldots, \ln X_d)^T$$

has a multivariate normal distribution $N_d(\boldsymbol{\mu}, \Sigma)$; see Jones and Miller (1966) and Johnson and Ramberg (1978). Put another way, the multivariate lognormal random vector **X** can be represented as

$$\mathbf{X} = \left(e^{Y_1}, e^{Y_2}, \ldots, e^{Y_d}\right)^T$$

where **Y** is multivariate normal $N_d(\boldsymbol{\mu}, \Sigma)$. The marginal distribution of X_i is univariate lognormal $LN(\mu_i, \sigma_{ii})$ where μ_i is the ith element of $\boldsymbol{\mu}$ and σ_{ii} is the ith diagonal entry in Σ.

Since the multivariate normal random vector **Y** in the above logarithmic transformation of **X** has mean vector $\boldsymbol{\mu} = (\mu_1, \mu_2, \ldots, \mu_d)^T$ and covariance matrix Σ with (i, j)th entry σ_{ij} (so the correlation coefficients are $\rho_{ij} = \sigma_{ij}/\sqrt{\sigma_{ii}\sigma_{jj}}$), it turns out that

$$E(X_i) = e^{\mu_i + \sigma_{ii}/2} \tag{6.10}$$

$$\mathrm{Var}(X_i) = e^{2\mu_i + \sigma_{ii}}(e^{\sigma_{ii}} - 1) \tag{6.11}$$

and

$$\mathrm{Cov}(X_i, X_j) = (e^{\sigma_{ij}} - 1)\exp\left(\mu_i + \mu_j + \frac{\sigma_{ii} + \sigma_{jj}}{2}\right) \tag{6.12}$$

This implies that the correlation coefficient between X_i and X_j is

$$\mathrm{Cor}(X_i, X_j) = \frac{e^{\sigma_{ij}} - 1}{\sqrt{(e^{\sigma_{ii}} - 1)(e^{\sigma_{jj}} - 1)}} \tag{6.13}$$

Note that $\boldsymbol{\mu}$ and Σ are *not* the mean vector and covariance matrix of the multivariate lognormal random vector **X**, but rather are the mean and covariance of the corresponding multivariate normal random vector **Y**. The mean vector and covariance matrix (and correlations) of **X** are given by Eqs. (6.10) through (6.13) above.

To fit a multivariate lognormal distribution to a sample $\mathbf{X}_1, \mathbf{X}_2, \ldots, \mathbf{X}_n$ of d-dimensional vectors, take the natural logarithm of each component scalar observation in each observed data vector to get the data vectors $\mathbf{Y}_1, \mathbf{Y}_2, \ldots, \mathbf{Y}_n$; treat these $\mathbf{Y}_k$'s as multivariate normal with unknown mean vector $\boldsymbol{\mu}$ and covariance matrix Σ; and estimate $\boldsymbol{\mu}$ and Σ, respectively, by Eqs. (6.7) and (6.8) above.

Generation from a fitted multivariate lognormal distribution is discussed in Sec. 8.5.2.

Multivariate Johnson Translation System

The univariate Johnson translation system, which includes the normal, lognormal, Johnson S_B (see Sec. 6.2.2), and Johnson S_U distributions, affords considerable flexibility in terms of range and shape of fitted distributions. This family of distributions has been extended to the multivariate case; see Chap. 5 of Johnson (1987), Stanfield et al. (1996), and Wilson (1997).

As in the univariate case, the multivariate Johnson translation system permits great flexibility in terms of range and shape to obtain good fits to a wide variety of observed multivariate data vectors, certainly far more flexibility than given by the multivariate normal or lognormal distributions discussed above. In particular, in the method developed by Stanfield et al. (1996), the first four moments of the marginal distributions from the fitted multivariate distribution match those of the observed data, and the correlation structure in the fitted distribution matches the empirical correlations as well. Fitting such a distribution to observed data involves several steps and uses methods to fit univariate Johnson distributions; for details on this fitting procedure, as well as generating random vectors from the fitted multivariate Johnson distribution, see Stanfield et al. (1996).

Bivariate Bézier

Univariate Bézier distributions, as described in Sec. 6.9, have been extended to the bivariate case ($d = 2$ dimensions) by Wagner and Wilson (1995). Software is also described there that allows graphical interactive adjustment of the fitted distribution; in addition, generating random vectors is discussed there. Further results and methods concerning bivariate Bézier distributions can be found in Wagner and Wilson (1996a).

Extension of Bézier distributions to three or more dimensions is described by Wagner and Wilson (1995) as "feasible but cumbersome."

6.10.2 Specifying Arbitrary Marginal Distributions and Correlations

In Sec. 6.10.1 we discussed several cases where a complete multivariate distribution might be specified to model the joint behavior of d possibly related input random variables that together compose an input random vector. In each of these cases, the fitted member of the multivariate distribution family involved (normal, lognormal, Johnson, or Bézier) determined the correlation between pairs of the component random variables in the vector, as well as their marginal distributions; it also imposed a more general and complete description of the joint variation of the component random variables as embodied in the joint density function itself.

Sometimes we need greater flexibility than that. We may want to allow for possible correlation between various pairs of input random variables to our simulation model, yet not impose an overall multivariate distribution forcing the fitted marginal distributions all to be members of the same family. In other words, we would like to be free to specify arbitrary univariate distributions to model the input random variables separately, as described in Secs. 6.1 through 6.9, yet also estimate correlations between them quite apart from their marginal distributions. In fact, we might even want some of the component input random variables to be continuous, others to be discrete, and still others to be mixed continuous-discrete, yet still allowing for correlations between them.

A very simple, and fairly obvious, procedure for doing this is just to fit distributions to each of the univariate random variables involved, one at a time and in isolation from the others, and then to estimate suspected correlations between pairs of input random variables by Eq. (6.9) above. Gather these random variables together into an input random vector, which then by construction has the desired univariate marginal distributions and desired correlation structure. However, it is important to note that this procedure does not specify, or "control," the resulting joint distribution of the random vector as a whole—in fact, we generally won't even know what this joint distribution is. Thus, the suggested procedure allows for greater flexibility on the marginal distributions and correlations, but exerts less overall control. Another caution is that the form and parameters of the marginal distributions can impose restrictions on what correlations are possible; see Whitt (1976).

While specification of such a situation seems, at least in principle, relatively straightforward, we need to make sure that whatever we specify here can be generated from during the simulation. We discuss this in Sec. 8.5.5, based on work in Hill and Reilly (1994) and Cario et al. (2002).

6.10.3 Specifying Stochastic Processes

As mentioned earlier, there are situations in which a sequence of input random variables on the same phenomenon are appropriately modeled as being draws from the same (marginal) distribution, yet might exhibit some autocorrelation between themselves within the sequence. For instance, if $\{X_1, X_2, \ldots\}$ denote the sizes of successive messages arriving to a communications node, the X_i's might be from the same (stationary) distribution, but $\text{Cor}(X_i, X_{i+l})$ could be nonzero for lags $l = 1, 2, \ldots, p$, where the longest autocorrelation lag p would be specified as part of the modeling activity. In this case, the X_i's are identically distributed, but they are not independent and so form a stationary stochastic process with possible autocorrelation out through lag p. As mentioned earlier, such autocorrelation in an input stream can have a major impact on a simulation's results, as demonstrated by Livny et al. (1993).

In this subsection we briefly describe some models for this situation, and in Sec. 8.5.6 we discuss how realizations from such models can be generated as input to the simulation. Except for VARTA processes, we consider only the case where the points X_i in the process are univariate (scalar) random variables, rather than being themselves multivariate random vectors.

AR and ARMA Processes

Standard *autoregressive* (AR) or *autoregressive moving-average* (ARMA) models, developed in Box et al. (2008) for time-series data analysis, might first come to mind for modeling an input time series. While there are many different parameterizations of these processes in the literature, one version of a stationary AR(p) model with mean μ is

$$X_i = \mu + \phi_1(X_{i-1} - \mu) + \phi_2(X_{i-2} - \mu) + \cdots + \phi_p(X_{i-p} - \mu) + \varepsilon_i \quad (6.14)$$

where the ε_i's are IID normal random variables with mean 0 and variance chosen to control $\text{Var}(X_i)$, and the ϕ_i's are constants that must obey a condition for the X_i's to have a stationary marginal distribution. The definition of ARMA models adds weighted proportions of past values of the ε_i's to the above recursion [see Box et al. (2008) for complete details].

To fit such models to observed data, a linear-regression approach is taken to estimate the unknown parameters of the process. The marginal distribution of the X_i's is generally restricted to being normal, however, making this model of limited direct use in simulation-input modeling since the range is infinite in both directions. AR processes do serve, however, as "base" processes for ARTA models discussed below, which are more flexible and useful as simulation input process models.

Gamma Processes

These processes, developed by Lewis et al. (1989), yield marginal distributions having a gamma distribution, as well as autocorrelation between points within the process. They are constructed by a kind of autoregressive operation, similar in spirit to the normal AR processes described in Eq. (6.14) above. This includes the case of exponential marginals, known as *exponential autoregressive* (EAR) processes.

ARTA Processes

Cario and Nelson (1996) developed *autoregressive-to-anything* (ARTA) processes, which seek to model any stationary marginal distribution and any autocorrelation structure. ARTA processes can exactly match the desired autocorrelation structure out to a specified lag p, as well as the desired stationary marginal distribution; in addition, they are specified by an automated procedure requiring no subjective interactive manipulation.

To define an ARTA process, start by specifying a standard stationary AR process $\{Z_i\}$ with N(0, 1) marginal distribution ($\{Z_i\}$ is called the *base process*). Then define the final input process to the simulation as

$$X_i = F^{-1}[\Phi(Z_i)] \tag{6.15}$$

where F^{-1} is the inverse of the desired stationary marginal distribution F and Φ denotes the N(0, 1) distribution function. Since $\Phi(Z_i)$ has a U(0, 1) distribution by a basic result known as the *probability integral transform* [see, e.g., Mood, Graybill, and Boes (1974, pp. 202–203)], applying F^{-1} to this U(0, 1) random variable results in one that has distribution function F. Thus, it is clear that the marginal distribution of X_i will be the desired F.

The principal work in specifying the desired ARTA process, however, is to specify the autocorrelation structure of the base process $\{Z_i\}$ so that the resulting final input process $\{X_i\}$ will exhibit the autocorrelation structure desired. Cario and Nelson (1998) developed numerical methods to do so, as well as a software package to carry out the calculations. The software assumes that the marginal distribution and the autocorrelations for the $\{X_i\}$ process are *given,* although it will compute sample autocorrelations from a set of observed time-series data if desired.

Biller and Nelson (2005, 2008) present a statistical methodology and software for fitting an ARTA process with marginal distributions from the Johnson translation system (see Sec. 6.10.1) to a set of observed univariate time-series data.

VARTA Processes

Biller and Nelson (2003) provided a methodology for modeling and generating stationary multivariate stochastic processes $\{\mathbf{X}_1, \mathbf{X}_2, \ldots\}$, which they call *vector-autoregressive-to-anything* (VARTA) processes. Let $\mathbf{X}_i = (X_{1i}, X_{2i}, \ldots, X_{d,i})^T$ be the input random vector of dimension d at time i, for $i = 1, 2, \ldots$. Let F_j be the distribution function of $X_{j,i}$ for $j = 1, 2, \ldots, d$ and $i = 1, 2, \ldots$. Also, let $\rho_{j,k,l}(\mathbf{X}) = \text{Cor}(X_{j,i}, X_{k,i+l})$ for $j,k = 1, 2, \ldots, d$ and lag $l = 0, 1, \ldots, p$, where $\rho_{j,j,0}(\mathbf{X}) = 1$. Their methodology assumes that F_j is a *given* member of the Johnson translation system and that the correlations $\rho_{j,k,l}(\mathbf{X})$ are *specified.* (In general, F_j will be different for each value of j.)

The principal work in specifying the desired VARTA process is to specify the autocorrelation structure of a Gaussian vector-autoregressive base process $\{\mathbf{Z}_i\}$ so that the resulting final input process $\{\mathbf{X}_i\}$ will exhibit the autocorrelation structure desired.

Biller (2009) generalizes VARTA processes using copula theory to allow representing dependence structures that arise in situations where extreme component realizations occur together.

6.11 SELECTING A DISTRIBUTION IN THE ABSENCE OF DATA

In some simulation studies it may not be possible to collect data on the random variables of interest, so the techniques of Secs. 6.4 through 6.6 are not applicable to the problem of selecting corresponding probability distributions. For example, if the system being studied does not currently exist in some form, then collecting data from the system is obviously not possible. This difficulty can also arise for existing systems, if the number of required probability distributions is large and the time available for the simulation study prohibits the necessary data collection and analysis. Also, sometimes data are collected by an automated data-collection system, which doesn't provide the data in a suitable format. In this section we discuss four heuristic procedures for choosing a distribution in the absence of data.

Let us assume that the random quantity of interest is a continuous random variable X. It will also be useful to think of this random variable as being the time to perform some task, e.g., the time required to repair a piece of equipment when it fails. The first step in using the triangular-distribution or beta-distribution approaches is to identify an interval $[a, b]$ (where a and b are real numbers such that $a < b$) in which it is felt that X will lie with probability close to 1; that is, $P(a \le X \le b) \approx 1$. To obtain *subjective* estimates of a and b, subject-matter experts (SMEs) are asked for their most optimistic and pessimistic estimates, respectively, of the time to perform the task. Once an interval $[a, b]$ has been identified subjectively, the next step is to place a probability density function on $[a, b]$ that is thought to be representative of X.

In the triangular-distribution approach, the SMEs are also asked for their subjective estimate of the most-likely time to perform the task. This most-likely value m is the mode of the distribution of X. Given a, b, and m, the random variable X is then considered to have a triangular distribution (see Sec. 6.2.2) on the interval $[a, b]$ with mode m. A graph of a triangular density function is given in Fig. 6.17. Furthermore, an algorithm for generating a triangular random variate is given in Sec. 8.3.15.

One difficulty with the triangular approach is that it requires subjective estimates of the absolute minimum and maximum possible values a and b, which can be problematic. For example, is the value b the maximum over the next 3 months or the maximum over a lifetime? A second major problem with the triangular distribution is that it cannot have a long right tail, as is often the case with density functions for the time to perform some task. [Alternative triangular distributions are discussed in Keefer and Bodily (1983).]

A second approach to placing a density function on $[a, b]$ is to assume that the random variable X has a beta distribution (see Sec. 6.2.2) on this interval with shape parameters α_1 and α_2. This approach offers greater modeling flexibility because of the variety of shapes that the beta density function can assume (see Fig. 6.11). On the other hand, it is not clear how to choose the parameters α_1 and α_2 so as to specify the distribution completely. We can suggest several possible ideas. If one is willing to assume that X is equally likely to take on any value between a and b, choose $\alpha_1 = \alpha_2 = 1$, which results in the U(a, b) distribution (see Fig. 6.11). (This model might be used if very little is known about the random variable X other than its range $[a, b]$.) An alternative idea, which we feel is generally more realistic, is to assume that the density function of X is skewed to the right. (Our experience with real-world data indicates that density functions corresponding to a task time usually have this shape.) This density shape corresponds to $\alpha_2 > \alpha_1 > 1$ in the beta distribution (see Fig. 6.11). Furthermore, such a beta distribution has a mean μ and a mode m, given by

$$\mu = a + \frac{\alpha_1(b-a)}{\alpha_1 + \alpha_2} \quad \text{and} \quad m = a + \frac{(\alpha_1 - 1)(b-a)}{\alpha_1 + \alpha_2 - 2}$$

Given subjective estimates of μ and m, these equations can be solved to obtain the following estimates of α_1 and α_2:

$$\tilde{\alpha}_1 = \frac{(\mu - a)(2m - a - b)}{(m - \mu)(b - a)} \quad \text{and} \quad \tilde{\alpha}_2 = \frac{(b - \mu)\tilde{\alpha}_1}{\mu - a}$$

Note, however, that μ must be greater than m for the density to be skewed to the right; if $\mu < m$, it will be skewed to the left. Algorithms for generating a beta random variate are given in Sec. 8.3.8.

A difficulty with the second idea for specifying a beta distribution is that some SMEs will have trouble differentiating between the mean and the mode of a distribution. Keefer and Bodily (1983) suggest alternative ways of specifying the parameters of a beta distribution.

People sometimes use the triangular or beta distribution to model a source of randomness even when it is feasible to collect and analyze the necessary data. This might be done just because the analyst doesn't want to be bothered collecting data, or because the analyst doesn't understand the importance of choosing an appropriate distribution. Example 6.23 shows that the cavalier use of the triangular (or beta) distribution can sometimes result in very erroneous results.

EXAMPLE 6.23. Consider a single-server queueing system with exponential interarrival times with mean 1 and lognormal service times with mean 0.9 and variance 1.39 ($\mu = -0.605$ and $\sigma^2 = 1$), as shown in Fig. 6.55. However, the service-time distribution is actually *unknown* to the analyst, and he first tries to approximate this distribution by a triangular distribution with $a = 0$, $m = 0.2$, and $b = 1.97$ (the 0.9-quantile for the lognormal distribution). Note that a and m have been guessed correctly. Using the formula for the steady-state average delay in queue d for an $M/G/1$ queue in App. 1B, it can be shown that $d = 11.02$ for the lognormal distribution, but $d = 1.30$ for this triangular distribution. Thus, approximating the lognormal distribution by this triangular distribution results in an 88.2 percent error (see Table 6.20 and Fig. 6.55).

Alternatively, suppose the analyst tries to approximate the unknown lognormal distribution by a triangular distribution with $a = 0$, $m = 0.2$, and a mean of 0.9 (correct),

TABLE 6.20
Approximating a lognormal distribution by triangular or beta distributions

Service-time distribution	Steady-state average delay in queue, *d*	Percent error
Lognormal(−0.605, 1)	11.02	0
Triangular(0, 1.97, 0.2)	1.30	88.2
Triangular(0, 2.5, 0.2)	5.66	48.7
2.5 Beta(1.08, 1.92)	5.85	46.9

which results in $b = 2.5$. [The mean of a triangular distribution is $(a + b + m)/3$.] In this case, $d = 5.66$, which is still an error of 48.7 percent.

Finally, suppose that the analyst tries to approximate the lognormal distribution by a beta distribution with $a = 0$, $b = 2.5$, $\mu = 0.9$, and $m = 0.2$ (the same as for the second triangular distribution), resulting in $\tilde{\alpha}_1 = 1.08$ and $\tilde{\alpha}_2 = 1.92$. In this case, $d = 5.85$, which is a 46.7 percent error.

In summary, we have seen that approximating an unknown distribution by a triangular or beta distribution can result in a large error in the simulation output.

*Because of the shortcomings of the triangular and beta approaches, we now develop two new models for representing a task time in the absence of data that are

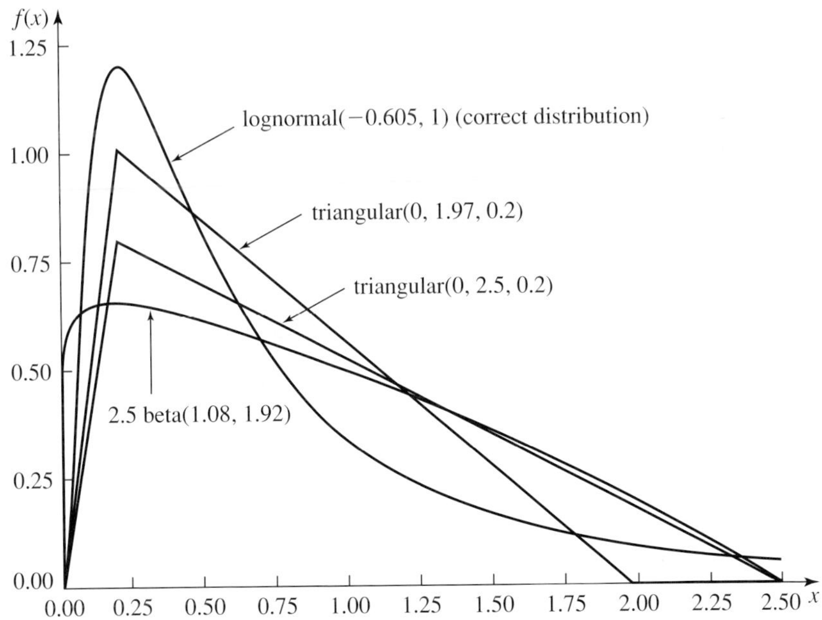

FIGURE 6.55
Lognormal distribution and approximating triangular and beta distributions.

*Skip the remainder of this section on the first reading.

based on the lognormal and Weibull distributions. These models require subjective estimates of the location parameter γ, the most-likely task time m, and the q-quantile ($100q$th percentile) x_q, of the task-time distribution. The location parameter γ plays a role similar to that played by the minimum value a above, but now X must be greater than γ. We also assume that $0 \le \gamma < m < x_q < \infty$.

We begin with the lognormal distribution. If Y has normal distribution with mean μ and variance σ^2, then $V = e^Y$ has a (two-parameter) lognormal distribution with scale parameter e^μ ($e^\mu > 0$) (see Sec. 6.2.2) and shape parameter σ ($\sigma > 0$). If $X = V + \gamma$, then X has a three-parameter lognormal distribution (see Sec. 6.8) with location parameter γ, scale parameter e^μ, and shape parameter σ, denoted by $\text{LN}(\gamma, \mu, \sigma^2)$. It follows from the discussion of the lognormal distribution in Sec. 6.2.2 that the mode of X is given by

$$m = \gamma + e^{\mu - \sigma^2} \tag{6.16}$$

Furthermore, it can be shown that (see Prob. 6.28)

$$x_q = \gamma + e^{\mu + z_q \sigma} \tag{6.17}$$

where z_q is the q-quantile of a N(0,1) random variable.

If we substitute e^μ from Eq. (6.16) into Eq. (6.17), then we get the following quadratic equation in σ:

$$\sigma^2 + z_q\sigma + c = 0$$

where $c = \ln[(m - \gamma)/(x_q - \gamma)] < 0$. Solving this equation for σ gives the following expression for σ:

$$\sigma = \frac{-z_q \pm \sqrt{z_q^2 - 4c}}{2}$$

Since σ must be positive, we take the "+" root and get the following estimate $\tilde{\sigma}$ for the shape parameter σ:

$$\tilde{\sigma} = \frac{-z_q + \sqrt{z_q^2 - 4c}}{2} \tag{6.18}$$

Substituting $\tilde{\sigma}$ into (6.16), we get the following estimate $\tilde{\mu}$ for μ:

$$\tilde{\mu} = \ln(m - \gamma) + (\tilde{\sigma})^2 \tag{6.19}$$

EXAMPLE 6.24. Suppose that we want a lognormal distribution with a location parameter of $\gamma = 1$, a most-likely value of $m = 4$, and a 0.9-quantile (90th percentile) of $x_{0.9} = 10$. From Eqs. (6.18) and (6.19), we get $\tilde{\sigma} = 0.588$ and $\tilde{\mu} = 1.444$, and the resulting lognormal density function is shown in Fig. 6.56.

We now consider the Weibull distribution. Suppose that the random variable Y has a (two-parameter) Weibull distribution with shape parameter α ($\alpha > 0$) and scale parameter β ($\beta > 0$). We will further assume that $\alpha > 1$, so that the mode is greater than zero. If $X = Y + \gamma$, then X has a three-parameter Weibull distribution (see Sec. 6.8) with location parameter γ, shape parameter α, and scale parameter β, denoted by Weibull(γ, α, β). The mode of X is given by (see Sec. 6.2.2)

$$m = \gamma + \beta\left(\frac{\alpha - 1}{\alpha}\right)^{1/\alpha}$$

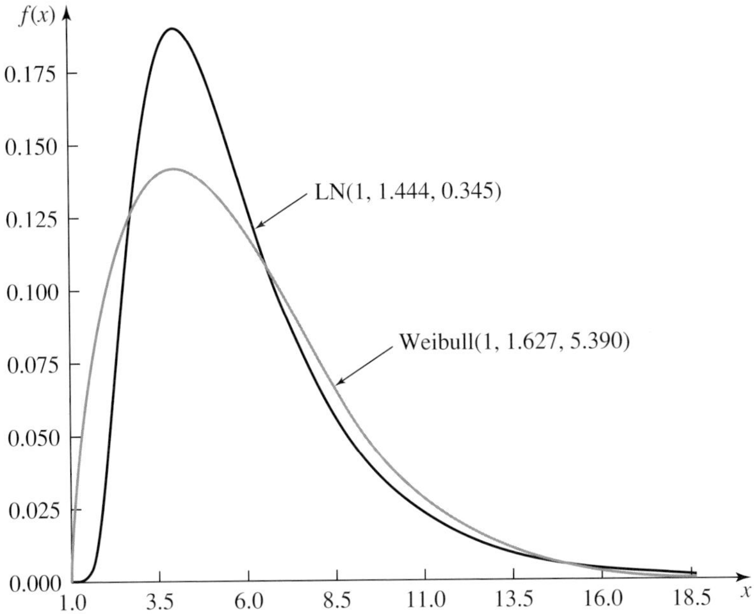

FIGURE 6.56
Specified lognormal and Weibull distributions.

which can be rewritten as

$$\beta = \frac{m - \gamma}{[(\alpha - 1)/\alpha]^{1/\alpha}} \tag{6.20}$$

Furthermore, the distribution function of X evaluated at x_q, $F_X(x_q)$, is given by (see Sec. 6.8)

$$F_X(x_q) = 1 - e^{-[(x_q - \gamma)/\beta]^\alpha} = q$$

which can be rewritten as

$$\beta = \frac{x_q - \gamma}{\{\ln[1/(1 - q)]\}^{1/\alpha}} \tag{6.21}$$

Equating Eqs. (6.20) and (6.21) gives the following expression in α:

$$\frac{m - \gamma}{x_q - \gamma} = \left\{\frac{\alpha - 1}{\alpha \ln[1/(1 - q)]}\right\}^{1/\alpha} \tag{6.22}$$

This equation cannot be solved in closed form, but can be solved iteratively by using Newton's method [see, e.g., Press et al. (2007)] to obtain an estimate $\tilde{\alpha}$ of the shape parameter α (see Prob. 6.29). Then $\tilde{\alpha}$ can be substituted into Eq. (6.20) to get an estimate $\tilde{\beta}$ of the scale parameter β:

$$\tilde{\beta} = \frac{m - \gamma}{[(\tilde{\alpha} - 1)/\tilde{\alpha}]^{1/\tilde{\alpha}}} \tag{6.23}$$

EXAMPLE 6.25. Suppose that we want a Weibull distribution with a location parameter of $\gamma = 1$, a most-likely value of $m = 4$, and a 0.9-quantile of $x_{0.9} = 10$. From Eqs. (6.22) and (6.23), we get $\tilde{\alpha} = 1.627$ and $\tilde{\beta} = 5.390$, and the resulting Weibull density function is also shown in Fig. 6.56. Note that the calculation of the estimates $\tilde{\alpha}$ and $\tilde{\beta}$ was done using ExpertFit (see Sec. 6.7).

The lognormal and Weibull distributions can take on arbitrary large values, albeit with a very small probability. Thus, if it is known that the corresponding random variable can never take on values larger than $b(b > x_q)$, then it might be desirable to truncate the distribution at b (see Sec. 6.8).

Note that it is also possible to specify a triangular distribution based on subjective estimates of a (the minimum value), m, and x_q (see Prob. 6.30).

6.12 MODELS OF ARRIVAL PROCESSES

In many simulations we need to generate a sequence of random points in time $0 = t_0 \le t_1 \le t_2 \le \cdots$, such that the ith event of some kind occurs at time t_i $(i = 1, 2, \ldots)$ and the distribution of the event times $\{t_i\}$ follows some specified form. Let $N(t) = \max\{i: t_i \le t\}$ be the number of events to occur at or before time t for $t \ge 0$. We call the stochastic process $\{N(t), t \ge 0\}$ an *arrival process* since, for our purposes, the events of interest are usually arrivals of customers to a service facility of some kind. In what follows, we call $A_i = t_i - t_{i-1}$ (where $i = 1, 2, \ldots$) the *interarrival time* between the $(i - 1)$st and ith customers.

In Sec. 6.12.1 we discuss the Poisson process, which is an arrival process for which the A_i's are IID exponential random variables. The Poisson process is probably the most commonly used model for the arrival process of customers to a queueing system. Section 6.12.2 discusses the nonstationary Poisson process, which is often used as a model of the arrival process to a system when the arrival rate varies with time. Finally, in Sec. 6.12.3 we describe an approach to modeling arrival processes where each event is really the arrival of a "batch" of customers.

A general reference for this section is Çinlar (1975, Chap. 4).

6.12.1 Poisson Processes

In this section we define a Poisson process, state some of its important properties, and in the course of doing so explain why the interarrival times for many real-world systems closely resemble IID exponential random variables.

The stochastic process $\{N(t), t \ge 0\}$ is said to be a *Poisson process* if:

1. Customers arrive one at a time.
2. $N(t + s) - N(t)$ (the number of arrivals in the time interval $(t, t + s]$) is independent of $\{N(u), 0 \le u \le t\}$.
3. The distribution of $N(t + s) - N(t)$ is independent of t for all $t, s \ge 0$.

Properties 1 and 2 are characteristic of many actual arrival processes. Property 1 would not hold if customers arrived in batches; see Sec. 6.12.3. Property 2 says that the number of arrivals in the interval $(t, t + s]$ is independent of the number of arrivals in the earlier time interval $[0, t]$ and also of the times at which these arrivals occur. This property could be violated if, for example, a large number of arrivals in $[0, t]$ caused some customers arriving in $(t, t + s]$ to balk, i.e., to go away immediately without being served, because they find the system highly congested. Property 3, on the other hand, will be violated by many real-life arrival processes since it implies that the arrival rate of customers does not depend on the time of day, etc. If, however, the time period of interest for the system is relatively short, say, a 1- or 2-hour period of peak demand, we have found that for many systems (but certainly not all) the arrival rate is reasonably constant over this interval and the Poisson process is a good model for the process during this interval. (See Theorem 6.2 below and then Example 6.4.)

The following theorem, proved in Çinlar (1975, pp. 74–76), explains where the Poisson process gets its name.

THEOREM 6.1. If $\{N(t), t \geq 0\}$ is a Poisson process, then the number of arrivals in any time interval of length s is a Poisson random variable with parameter λs (where λ is a positive real number). That is,

$$P[N(t + s) - N(t) = k] = \frac{e^{-\lambda s}(\lambda s)^k}{k!} \qquad \text{for } k = 0, 1, 2, \ldots \text{ and } t, s \geq 0$$

Therefore, $E[N(s)] = \lambda s$ (see Sec. 6.2.3) and, in particular, $E[N(1)] = \lambda$. Thus, λ is the expected number of arrivals in any interval of length 1. We call λ the *rate* of the process.

We now see that the interarrival times for a Poisson process are IID exponential random variables; see Çinlar (1975, pp. 79–80).

THEOREM 6.2. If $\{N(t), t \geq 0\}$ is a Poisson process with rate λ, then its corresponding interarrival times $A_1, A_2, \ldots$ are IID exponential random variables with mean $1/\lambda$.

This result together with our above discussion explains why we have found that interarrival times during a restricted time period are often approximately IID exponential random variables. For example, recall that the interarrival times of cars for the drive-up bank of Example 6.4 were found to be approximately exponential during a 90-minute period.

The converse of Theorem 6.2 is also true. Namely, if the interarrival times $A_1, A_2, \ldots$ for an arrival process $\{N(t), t \geq 0\}$ are IID exponential random variables with mean $1/\lambda$, then $\{N(t), t \geq 0\}$ is a Poisson process with rate λ [Çinlar (1975, p. 80)].

6.12.2 Nonstationary Poisson Processes

Let $\lambda(t)$ be the arrival rate of customers to some system at time t. [See below for some insight into the meaning of $\lambda(t)$.] If customers arrive at the system in accordance with a Poisson process with constant rate λ, then $\lambda(t) = \lambda$ for all $t \geq 0$. However, for many real-world systems, $\lambda(t)$ is actually a function of t. For example, the arrival rate of customers to a fast-food restaurant will be larger during the noon rush hour than in the middle of the afternoon. Also, traffic on a freeway will be heavier during the morning and evening rush hours. If the arrival rate $\lambda(t)$ does in fact change with time, then the interarrival times $A_1, A_2, \ldots$ are *not* identically distributed; thus, it is not appropriate to fit a single probability distribution to the A_i's by using the techniques discussed in Secs. 6.4 through 6.6. In this section we discuss a commonly used model for arrival processes with time-varying arrival rates.

The stochastic process $\{N(t), t \geq 0\}$ is said to be a *nonstationary Poisson process* if:

1. Customers arrive one at a time.
2. $N(t + s) - N(t)$ is independent of $\{N(u), 0 \leq u \leq t\}$.

Thus, for a nonstationary Poisson process, customers must still arrive one at a time, and the numbers of arrivals in disjoint intervals are independent, but now the arrival rate $\lambda(t)$ is allowed to be a function of time.

Let $\Lambda(t) = E[N(t)]$ for all $t \geq 0$. If $\Lambda(t)$ is differentiable for a particular value of t, we formally define $\lambda(t)$ as

$$\lambda(t) = \frac{d}{dt}\Lambda(t)$$

Intuitively, $\lambda(t)$ will be large in intervals for which the expected number of arrivals is large. We call $\Lambda(t)$ and $\lambda(t)$ the *expectation function* and the *rate function*, respectively, for the nonstationary Poisson process.

The following theorem shows that the number of arrivals in the interval $(t, t + s]$ for a nonstationary Poisson process is a Poisson random variable whose parameter depends on *both t* and s.

THEOREM 6.3. If $\{N(t), t \geq 0\}$ is a nonstationary Poisson process with continuous expectation function $\Lambda(t)$, then

$$P[N(t + s) - N(t) = k] = \frac{e^{-b(t,s)}[b(t, s)]^k}{k!} \qquad \text{for } k = 0, 1, 2, \ldots \text{ and } t, s \geq 0$$

where $b(t, s) = \Lambda(t + s) - \Lambda(t) = \int_t^{t+s}\lambda(y)dy$, the last equality holding if $d\Lambda(t)/dt$ is bounded on $[t, t + s]$ and if $d\Lambda(t)/dt$ exists and is continuous for all but finitely many points in $[t, t + s]$ (see Prob. 6.25).

We have not yet addressed the question of how to estimate $\lambda(t)$ [or $\Lambda(t)$] from a set of observations on an arrival process of interest. The following example gives a heuristic but practical approach, and other approaches are briefly discussed after the example.

EXAMPLE 6.26. A simulation model was developed for a xerographic copy shop, and data were collected on the times of arrival of customers between 11 A.M. and 1 P.M. for eight different days. From observing the characteristics of the arriving customers, it was felt that properties 1 and 2 for the nonstationary Poisson process were applicable and, in addition, that $\lambda(t)$ varied over the 2-hour interval. To obtain an estimate of $\lambda(t)$, the 2-hour interval was divided into the following 12 subintervals:

$$[11{:}00, 11{:}10), [11{:}10, 11{:}20), \ldots, [12{:}40, 12{:}50), [12{:}50, 1{:}00)$$

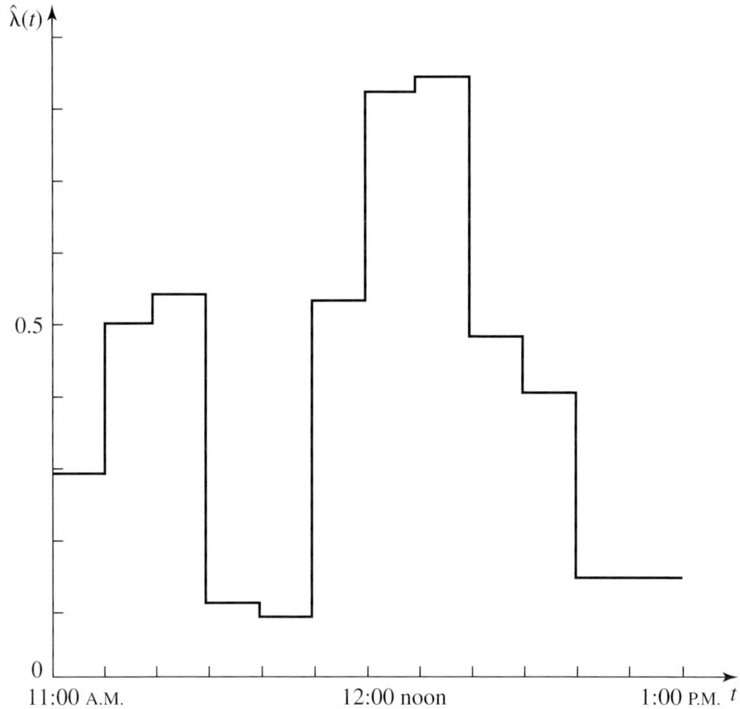

FIGURE 6.57
Plot of the estimated rate function $\hat{\lambda}(t)$ in customers per minute for the arrival process to a copy shop between 11 A.M. and 1 P.M.

For each day, the number of arrivals in each of these subintervals was determined. Then, for each subinterval, the average number of arrivals in that subinterval over the 8 days was computed. These 12 averages are estimates of the expected numbers of arrivals in the corresponding subintervals. Finally, for each subinterval, the average number of arrivals in that subinterval was divided by the subinterval length, 10 minutes, to obtain an estimate of the arrival rate for that subinterval. The estimated arrival rate $\hat{\lambda}(t)$ (in customers per minute) is plotted in Fig. 6.57. Note that the estimated arrival rate varies substantially over the 2-hour period.

One might legitimately ask how we decided on these subintervals of length 10 minutes. Actually, we computed estimates of $\lambda(t)$ in the above manner for subintervals of length 5, 10, and 15 minutes. The estimate of $\lambda(t)$ based on subintervals of length 5 minutes was rejected because it was felt that the corresponding plot of $\hat{\lambda}(t)$ was too ragged; i.e., a subinterval length of 5 minutes was too small. On the other hand, the estimate of $\lambda(t)$ based on subintervals of length 15 minutes was not chosen because the corresponding plot of $\hat{\lambda}(t)$ seemed too "smooth," meaning that information on the true nature of $\lambda(t)$ was being lost. In general, the problem of choosing a subinterval length here is similar to that of choosing the interval width for a histogram (see Sec. 6.4.2).

While the piecewise-constant method of specifying $\lambda(t)$ in Example 6.26 is certainly quite simple and fairly flexible, it does require somewhat arbitrary judgment about the boundaries and widths of the constant-rate time intervals. Other methods for specifying and estimating $\lambda(t)$ [or, alternatively, $\Lambda(t)$] have been developed, which we briefly mention here:

- Several authors have proposed procedures where the estimated rate function $\hat{\lambda}(t)$ is specified to be a generalization of what was done in Example 6.26, in terms of allowing for piecewise-linear or piecewise-polynomial forms. These include Kao and Chang (1988), Lewis and Shedler (1976), and Klein and Roberts (1984).
- Leemis (1991) developed an intuitive and simple nonparametric method to specify a piecewise-linear estimate of the expectation function $\Lambda(t)$, where the breakpoints are determined by the observed arrival times in a superposition of several realizations of the process. He shows that the estimator converges, with probability 1, to the true underlying expectation function as the number of observed realizations increases, and also derives a confidence band around the true $\Lambda(t)$ that could be useful in input-specification sensitivity analysis. Since the estimated $\Lambda(t)$ is piecewise linear, generating observations (see Sec. 8.6.2) is simple and efficient. A generalization of this method is given in Arkin and Leemis (2000).
- A different approach to specifying and estimating the rate function $\lambda(t)$ is to assume that it has some specific parametric (functional) form that is general enough in structure and has a sufficient number of parameters to allow it to fit observed data well. The parametric form should allow for trends and cycles, and should admit rigorous statistical methods for parameter estimation, such as maximum-likelihood or least-squares methods. Such functions, together with software for estimation and generation, are developed in Lee et al. (1991), Johnson et al. (1994a, 1994b), Kuhl, Damerji, and Wilson (1997), Kuhl, Wilson, and Johnson (1997), and Kuhl and Wilson (2000).
- Kuhl and Wilson (2001) and Kuhl et al. (2006) give a combined nonparametric/parametric approach and software for estimating an expectation function $\Lambda(t)$ of a nonstationary Poisson process with a long-run trend or cyclic effects that may exhibit nontrigonometric characteristics.
- Gerhardt and Nelson (2009) provide methodologies for modeling nonstationary arrival processes that are more or less variable than a nonstationary Poisson process.

6.12.3 Batch Arrivals

For some real-world systems, customers arrive in *batches*, or groups, so that property 1 of the Poisson process and of the nonstationary Poisson process is violated. For example, people arriving at a sporting event or at a cafeteria often come in batches. We now consider how one might model such an arrival process.

Let $N(t)$ now be the number of *batches* of individual customers that have arrived by time t. By applying the techniques discussed previously in this chapter to the times of arrivals of the successive batches, we can develop a model for the process $\{N(t), t \geq 0\}$. For example, if the interarrival times of batches appear to be approximately IID exponential random variables, $\{N(t), t \geq 0\}$ can be modeled as a Poisson process. Next, we fit a discrete distribution to the sizes of the successive batches; the batch sizes will be positive integers. Thus, for the original arrival process, it is assumed that batches of customers arrive in accordance with the arrival process $\{N(t), t \geq 0\}$ and that the number of customers in each batch is a random variable with the fitted discrete distribution.

The above informal discussion can be made more precise. If $X(t)$ is the total number of individual customers to arrive by time t, and if B_i is the number of customers in the ith batch, then $X(t)$ is given by

$$X(t) = \sum_{i=1}^{N(t)} B_i \qquad \text{for } t \geq 0$$

If the B_i's are assumed to be IID random variables that are also independent of $\{N(t), t \geq 0\}$, and if $\{N(t), t \geq 0\}$ is a Poisson process, then the stochastic process $\{X(t), t \geq 0\}$ is said to be a *compound Poisson process.*

6.13 ASSESSING THE HOMOGENEITY OF DIFFERENT DATA SETS

Sometimes an analyst collects k sets of observations on a random phenomenon independently and would like to know whether these data sets are homogeneous and thus can be merged. For example, it might be of interest to know whether service times of customers in a bank collected on different days are homogeneous. If they are, then the service times from the different days can be merged and the combined sample used to find *the* service-time distribution. Otherwise, more than one service-time distribution is needed. In this section, we discuss the Kruskal-Wallis hypothesis test for homogeneity. It is a nonparametric test since no assumptions are made about the distributions of the data.

Suppose that we have k independent samples of possibly different sizes, and that the samples themselves are independent. Denote the ith sample of size n_i by X_{i1}, $X_{i2}, \ldots, X_{in_i}$ for $i = 1, 2, \ldots, k$; and let n denote the total number of observations

$$n = \sum_{i=1}^{k} n_i$$

Then we would like to test the null hypothesis

H_0: All the population distribution functions are identical

against the alternative hypothesis

H_1: At least one of the populations tends to yield larger observations than at least one of the other populations

To construct the Kruskal-Wallis (K-W) statistic, assign rank 1 to the smallest of the n observations, rank 2 to the second smallest, and so on to the largest of the

n observations, which receives rank n. Let $R(X_{ij})$ represent the rank assigned to X_{ij}, and let R_i be the sum of the ranks assigned to the ith sample, that is,

$$R_i = \sum_{j=1}^{n_i} R(X_{ij}) \qquad \text{for } i = 1, 2, \ldots, k$$

Then the K-W test statistic T is defined as

$$T = \frac{12}{n(n+1)} \sum_{i=1}^{k} \frac{R_i^2}{n_i} - 3(n+1)$$

We reject the null hypothesis H_0 at level α if $T > \chi^2_{k-1,1-\alpha}$, where $\chi^2_{k-1,1-\alpha}$ is the upper $1 - \alpha$ critical value for a chi-square distribution with $k - 1$ degrees of freedom. The above expression for T assumes that no two observations are equal. If this is not the case, then a different expression for T must be used [see Conover (1999, pp. 288–290)].

EXAMPLE 6.27. A simulation model was developed for the hub operations of an overnight air-delivery service for the purpose of determining the amount of unloading equipment required. The model included provision for the fact that planes may arrive before or after their scheduled arrival times. Data were available on the actual times of arrival for two different incoming flight numbers (each corresponding to a different origin city) for 57 different days. (Each flight number arrives once a day, 5 days a week.) Let X_{ij} be the scheduled time of arrival minus the actual time of arrival (in minutes) for day j and flight number i, for $j = 1, 2, \ldots, 57$ and $i = 1, 2$. If $X_{ij} < 0$, then flight number i was late on day j. We want to perform a K-W test to determine whether the X_{1j}'s and X_{2j}'s are homogeneous, i.e., whether the arrival patterns for the two flight numbers are similar. We computed the K-W statistic and obtained $T = 4.317$, which is greater than the critical value $2.706 = \chi^2_{1,0.90}$. Therefore, we rejected the null hypothesis at level $\alpha = 0.10$, and the arrival patterns for the two flight numbers had to be modeled separately. The observed differences were to a large extent due to different weather conditions in the two origin cities.

APPENDIX 6A TABLES OF MLEs FOR THE GAMMA AND BETA DISTRIBUTIONS

TABLE 6.21
$\hat{\alpha}$ as a function of T, gamma distribution

T	$\hat{\alpha}$	T	$\hat{\alpha}$	T	$\hat{\alpha}$	T	$\hat{\alpha}$
0.01	0.010	1.40	0.827	5.00	2.655	13.00	6.662
0.02	0.019	1.50	0.879	5.20	2.755	13.50	6.912
0.03	0.027	1.60	0.931	5.40	2.856	14.00	7.163
0.04	0.036	1.70	0.983	5.60	2.956	14.50	7.413
0.05	0.044	1.80	1.035	5.80	3.057	15.00	7.663
0.06	0.052	1.90	1.086	6.00	3.157	15.50	7.913
0.07	0.060	2.00	1.138	6.20	3.257	16.00	8.163

(continued)

TABLE 6.21 (*continued*)

T	$\hat{\alpha}$	T	$\hat{\alpha}$	T	$\hat{\alpha}$	T	$\hat{\alpha}$
0.08	0.068	2.10	1.189	6.40	3.357	16.50	8.413
0.09	0.076	2.20	1.240	6.60	3.458	17.00	8.663
0.10	0.083	2.30	1.291	6.80	3.558	17.50	8.913
0.11	0.090	2.40	1.342	7.00	3.658	18.00	9.163
0.12	0.098	2.50	1.393	7.20	3.759	18.50	9.414
0.13	0.105	2.60	1.444	7.40	3.859	19.00	9.664
0.14	0.112	2.70	1.495	7.60	3.959	19.50	9.914
0.15	0.119	2.80	1.546	7.80	4.059	20.00	10.164
0.16	0.126	2.90	1.596	8.00	4.159	20.50	10.414
0.17	0.133	3.00	1.647	8.20	4.260	21.00	10.664
0.18	0.140	3.10	1.698	8.40	4.360	21.50	10.914
0.19	0.147	3.20	1.748	8.60	4.460	22.00	11.164
0.20	0.153	3.30	1.799	8.80	4.560	22.50	11.414
0.30	0.218	3.40	1.849	9.00	4.660	23.00	11.664
0.40	0.279	3.50	1.900	9.20	4.760	23.50	11.914
0.50	0.338	3.60	1.950	9.40	4.860	24.00	12.164
0.60	0.396	3.70	2.001	9.60	4.961	24.50	12.414
0.70	0.452	3.80	2.051	9.80	5.061	25.00	12.664
0.80	0.507	3.90	2.101	10.00	5.161	30.00	15.165
0.90	0.562	4.00	2.152	10.50	5.411	35.00	17.665
1.00	0.616	4.20	2.253	11.00	5.661	40.00	20.165
1.10	0.669	4.40	2.353	11.50	5.912	45.00	22.665
1.20	0.722	4.60	2.454	12.00	6.162	50.00	25.166
1.30	0.775	4.80	2.554	12.50	6.412		

TABLE 6.22

$\hat{\alpha}_1$ and $\hat{\alpha}_2$ as functions of G_1 and G_2, beta distribution

If $G_1 \leq G_2$, use the first line of labels; if $G_2 \leq G_1$, use the second line of labels

G_1 G_2	G_2 G_1	$\hat{\alpha}_1$ $\hat{\alpha}_2$	$\hat{\alpha}_2$ $\hat{\alpha}_1$	G_1 G_2	G_2 G_1	$\hat{\alpha}_1$ $\hat{\alpha}_2$	$\hat{\alpha}_2$ $\hat{\alpha}_1$
0.01	0.01	0.112	0.112	0.15	0.35	0.405	0.563
0.01	0.05	0.126	0.157	0.15	0.40	0.432	0.653
0.01	0.10	0.135	0.192	0.15	0.45	0.464	0.762
0.01	0.15	0.141	0.223	0.15	0.50	0.502	0.903
0.01	0.20	0.147	0.254	0.15	0.55	0.550	1.090
0.01	0.25	0.152	0.285	0.15	0.60	0.612	1.353
0.01	0.30	0.157	0.318	0.15	0.65	0.701	1.752
0.01	0.35	0.163	0.354	0.15	0.70	0.842	2.429
0.01	0.40	0.168	0.395	0.15	0.75	1.111	3.810
0.01	0.45	0.173	0.441	0.15	0.80	1.884	8.026
0.01	0.50	0.179	0.495	0.15	0.84	7.908	42.014

(*continued*)

TABLE 6.22 *(continued)*

G_1 / G_2	G_2 / G_1	$\hat{\alpha}_1$ / $\hat{\alpha}_2$	$\hat{\alpha}_2$ / $\hat{\alpha}_1$	G_1 / G_2	G_2 / G_1	$\hat{\alpha}_1$ / $\hat{\alpha}_2$	$\hat{\alpha}_2$ / $\hat{\alpha}_1$
0.01	0.55	0.185	0.559	0.20	0.20	0.395	0.395
0.01	0.60	0.192	0.639	0.20	0.25	0.424	0.461
0.01	0.65	0.200	0.741	0.20	0.30	0.456	0.537
0.01	0.70	0.210	0.877	0.20	0.35	0.491	0.626
0.01	0.75	0.221	1.072	0.20	0.40	0.531	0.735
0.01	0.80	0.237	1.376	0.20	0.45	0.579	0.873
0.01	0.85	0.259	1.920	0.20	0.50	0.640	1.057
0.01	0.90	0.299	3.162	0.20	0.55	0.720	1.314
0.01	0.95	0.407	8.232	0.20	0.60	0.834	1.701
0.01	0.98	0.850	42.126	0.20	0.65	1.016	2.352
0.05	0.05	0.180	0.180	0.20	0.70	1.367	3.669
0.05	0.10	0.195	0.223	0.20	0.75	2.388	7.654
0.05	0.15	0.207	0.263	0.20	0.79	10.407	39.649
0.05	0.20	0.217	0.302	0.25	0.25	0.500	0.500
0.05	0.25	0.228	0.343	0.25	0.30	0.543	0.588
0.05	0.30	0.238	0.387	0.25	0.35	0.592	0.695
0.05	0.35	0.248	0.437	0.25	0.40	0.651	0.830
0.05	0.40	0.259	0.494	0.25	0.45	0.724	1.007
0.05	0.45	0.271	0.560	0.25	0.50	0.822	1.254
0.05	0.50	0.284	0.640	0.25	0.55	0.962	1.624
0.05	0.55	0.299	0.739	0.25	0.60	1.186	2.243
0.05	0.60	0.317	0.867	0.25	0.65	1.620	3.486
0.05	0.65	0.338	1.037	0.25	0.70	2.889	7.230
0.05	0.70	0.366	1.280	0.25	0.74	12.905	37.229
0.05	0.75	0.403	1.655	0.30	0.30	0.647	0.647
0.05	0.80	0.461	2.305	0.30	0.35	0.717	0.777
0.05	0.85	0.566	3.682	0.30	0.40	0.804	0.947
0.05	0.90	0.849	8.130	0.30	0.45	0.920	1.182
0.05	0.94	2.898	45.901	0.30	0.50	1.086	1.532
0.10	0.10	0.245	0.245	0.30	0.55	1.352	2.115
0.10	0.15	0.262	0.291	0.30	0.60	1.869	3.280
0.10	0.20	0.278	0.337	0.30	0.65	3.387	6.779
0.10	0.25	0.294	0.386	0.30	0.69	15.402	34.780
0.10	0.30	0.310	0.441	0.35	0.35	0.879	0.879
0.10	0.35	0.327	0.503	0.35	0.40	1.013	1.101
0.10	0.40	0.345	0.576	0.35	0.45	1.205	1.430
0.10	0.45	0.365	0.663	0.35	0.50	1.514	1.975
0.10	0.50	0.389	0.770	0.35	0.55	2.115	3.060
0.10	0.55	0.417	0.909	0.35	0.60	3.883	6.313
0.10	0.60	0.451	1.093	0.35	0.64	17.897	32.315
0.10	0.65	0.497	1.356	0.40	0.40	1.320	1.320
0.10	0.70	0.560	1.756	0.40	0.45	1.673	1.827
0.10	0.75	0.660	2.443	0.40	0.50	2.358	2.832
0.10	0.80	0.846	3.864	0.40	0.55	4.376	5.837
0.10	0.85	1.374	8.277	0.40	0.59	20.391	29.841
0.10	0.89	5.406	44.239	0.45	0.45	2.597	2.597
0.15	0.15	0.314	0.314	0.45	0.50	4.867	5.354
0.15	0.20	0.335	0.367	0.45	0.54	22.882	27.359
0.15	0.25	0.357	0.424	0.49	0.49	12.620	12.620
0.15	0.30	0.380	0.489	0.49	0.50	24.873	25.371

PROBLEMS

6.1. Suppose that a man's job is to install 98 rivets in the right wing of an airplane under construction. If the random variable T is the total time required for one airplane, then what is the approximate distribution of T?

6.2. Prove comment 2 for the Weibull distribution in Table 6.3.

6.3. Prove comment 2 for the Pearson type VI distribution in Table 6.3.

6.4. Consider a four-parameter Pearson type VI distribution with shape parameters α_1 and α_2, scale parameter β, and location parameter γ. If $\alpha_1 = 1$, $\gamma = \beta = c > 0$, then the resulting density is

$$f(x) = \alpha_2 x^{-(\alpha_2+1)} c^{\alpha_2} \qquad \text{for } x > c$$

which is the density function of a *Pareto distribution* with parameters c and α_2, denoted Pareto(c, α_2). Show that $X \sim$ Pareto(c, α_2) if and only if $Y = \ln X \sim$ expo($\ln c$, $1/\alpha_2$), an exponential distribution with location parameter $\ln c$ and scale parameter $1/\alpha_2$.

6.5. For the empirical distribution given by $F(x)$ in Sec. 6.2.4, discuss the merit of defining $F(X_{(i)}) = i/n$ for $i = 1, 2, \ldots, n$, which seems like an intuitive definition. In this case, how would you define $F(x)$ for $0 \le x < X_{(1)}$?

6.6. Compute the expectation of the empirical distribution given by $F(x)$ in Sec. 6.2.4.

6.7. For discrete distributions, prove that the histogram (Sec. 6.4.2) is an unbiased estimator of the (unknown) mass function; i.e., show that $E(h_j) = p(x_j)$ for all j. *Hint:* For j fixed, define

$$Y_i = \begin{cases} 1 & \text{if } X_i = x_j \\ 0 & \text{otherwise} \end{cases} \qquad \text{for } i = 1, 2, \ldots, n$$

6.8. Suppose that the histogram of your observed data has several local modes (see Fig. 6.31), but that it is not possible to break the data into natural groups with a different probability distribution fitting each group. Describe an alternative approach for modeling your data.

6.9. For a geometric distribution with parameter p, explain why the MLE $\hat{p} = 1/[\bar{X}(n) + 1]$ is intuitive.

6.10. For each of the following distributions, derive formulas for the MLEs of the indicated parameters. Assume that we have IID data $X_1, X_2, \ldots, X_n$ from the distribution in question.
(*a*) U(0, b), MLE for b
(*b*) U(a, 0), MLE for a
(*c*) U(a, b), joint MLEs for a and b
(*d*) N(μ, σ^2), joint MLEs for μ and σ
(*e*) LN(μ, σ^2), joint MLEs for μ and σ
(*f*) Bernoulli(p), MLE for p
(*g*) DU(i, j), joint MLEs for i and j

(*h*) bin(t, p), MLE for p assuming that t is known
(*i*) negbin(s, p), MLE for p assuming that s is known
(*j*) U($\theta - 0.5, \theta + 0.5$), MLE for θ

6.11. For a Poisson distribution with parameter λ, derive an approximate $100(1 - \alpha)$ percent confidence interval for λ given the data $X_1, X_2, \ldots, X_n$. Use the asymptotic normality of the MLE $\hat{\lambda}$.

6.12. Consider the shifted (two-parameter) exponential distribution, which has density function

$$f(x) = \begin{cases} \dfrac{1}{\beta} e^{-(x-\gamma)/\beta} & \text{if } x \geq \gamma \\ 0 & \text{otherwise} \end{cases}$$

for $\beta > 0$ and any real number γ. Given a sample $X_1, X_2, \ldots, X_n$ of IID random values from this distribution, find formulas for the joint MLEs $\hat{\gamma}$ and $\hat{\beta}$. *Hint:* Remember that γ cannot exceed any X_i.

6.13. For a frequency comparison, show that r_j as given by Eq. (6.4) is actually the expected proportion of the n observations that would fall in the jth interval if the fitted distribution were in fact the true one.

6.14. For *Q–Q* plots, why it is inconvenient to have an empirical distribution function $\tilde{F}_n(x)$ such that $\tilde{F}_n(X_{(n)}) = 1$?

6.15. What difficulty arises when you try to define a *Q–Q* plot for a discrete distribution?

6.16. Suppose that the true distribution function $F(x)$ and the fitted distribution function $\hat{F}(x)$ are the same. For what distribution $F(x)$ will the *Q–Q* and *P–P* plots be essentially the same if the sample size n is large?

6.17. Suppose that the random variable M_j is the number of the n X_i's that would fall in the jth interval $[a_{j-1}, a_j)$ for a chi-square test if the fitted distribution were in fact the true one. What is the distribution of M_j, and what is its mean?

6.18. For the chi-square test, explain intuitively why Kallenberg, Oosterhoff, and Schriever (1985) found in certain cases that power was greater when the np_j's were smaller in the tails rather than all being equal.

6.19. Let $F_n(x)$ be the empirical distribution function used for the K-S test. Show that $F_n(x) \to F(x)$ as $n \to \infty$ (w.p. 1) for all x, where $F(x)$ is the true underlying distribution function.

6.20. Assume for the following analyses that each data set consists of IID observations from a continuous distribution. Use the Student Version of ExpertFit (see www.mhhe.com/law) to analyze these data (included in ExpertFit), following the steps in Sec. 6.7 (i.e., data summary, histogram, fitting and ranking distributions, density-histogram plot, distribution-function-differences plot, *P–P* plot, chi-square test, K-S test, and A-D test). Use a level of $\alpha = 0.05$ for the tests.
(*a*) 91 laboratory-processing times
(*b*) 1000 paper-roll yardages (use second-best model so tests are applicable)

(*c*) 218 post-office service times (use second-best model so tests are applicable)
(*d*) 1592 times at an automated-teller machine (ATM)
(*e*) 694 machine-repair times
(*f*) 3035 post-anesthesia recovery times

6.21. Assume for the following analyses that each data set consists of IID observations from a discrete distribution. Use the Student Version of ExpertFit to analyze these data, performing the following steps: data summary, histogram, fitting and ranking distributions, frequency-comparison plot, distribution-function-differences plot, *P–P* plot, and chi-square test. (K-S and A-D tests are not applicable to discrete data.) Use a level of $\alpha = 0.05$ for the test.
(*a*) 369 university test scores
(*b*) 200 deaths per corps per year by horse kick in the Prussian army in the late 1800s

6.22. There are two sets of IID machine-repair times named PROB622a and PROB622b. (The machines are from the same vendor.) Use the Student Version of ExpertFit (with "Advanced Mode") to perform the Kruskal-Wallis test (see Sec. 6.13) at level $\alpha = 0.05$ to determine whether the data sets are homogeneous.

6.23. For the location parameter estimator $\tilde{\gamma}$ in Sec. 6.8, show that $\tilde{\gamma} < X_{(1)}$ if and only if $X_{(k)} < [X_{(1)} + X_{(n)}]/2$.

6.24. Let $\text{LN}(\gamma, \mu, \sigma^2)$ denote the shifted (three-parameter) lognormal distribution, which has density

$$f(x) = \begin{cases} \dfrac{1}{(x-\gamma)\sqrt{2\pi\sigma^2}} \exp \dfrac{-[\ln(x-\gamma)-\mu]^2}{2\sigma^2} & \text{if } x > \gamma \\ 0 & \text{otherwise} \end{cases}$$

for $\sigma > 0$ and any real numbers γ and μ. [Thus, $\text{LN}(0, \mu, \sigma^2)$ is the original $\text{LN}(\mu, \sigma^2)$ distribution.]
(*a*) Verify that $X \sim \text{LN}(\gamma, \mu, \sigma^2)$ if and only if $X - \gamma \sim \text{LN}(\mu, \sigma^2)$.
(*b*) Show that for a fixed, known value of γ, the MLEs of μ and σ in the $\text{LN}(\gamma, \mu, \sigma^2)$ distribution are

$$\hat{\mu} = \frac{\sum_{i=1}^{n} \ln(X_i - \gamma)}{n} \quad \text{and} \quad \hat{\sigma} = \left\{ \frac{\sum_{i=1}^{n} [\ln(X_i - \gamma) - \hat{\mu}]^2}{n} \right\}^{1/2}$$

i.e., we simply shift the data by an amount $-\gamma$ and then treat them as being (unshifted) lognormal data.

6.25. For Theorem 6.3 in Sec. 6.12.2, explain intuitively why the expected number of arrivals in the interval $(t, t+s]$, $b(t, s)$, should be equal to $\int_t^{t+s} \lambda(y)\, dy$.

6.26. Provide an intuitive motivation for the definition of MLEs in the continuous case (see Sec. 6.5) by going through steps (*a*) through (*c*) below. As before, the observed data are $X_1, X_2, \ldots, X_n$, and are IID realizations of a random variable X with density f_θ. Bear in mind that the X_i's have already been observed, so are to be regarded as fixed numbers rather than variables.
(*a*) Let ε be a small (but strictly positive) real number, and define the phrase "getting a value of X near X_i" to be the event $\{X_i - \varepsilon < X < X_i + \varepsilon\}$. Use the mean-value

the following chapter treats methods of transforming them to obtain variates from other distributions, and realizations of various processes.

The methodology of generating random numbers has a long and interesting history; see Hull and Dobell (1962), Morgan (1984, pp. 51–56), and Dudewicz (1975) for entertaining accounts. The earliest methods were essentially carried out by hand, such as casting lots (Matthew 27 : 35), throwing dice, dealing out cards, or drawing numbered balls from a "well-stirred urn." Many lotteries are still operated in this way, as is well known by American males who were of draft age in the late 1960s and early 1970s. In the early twentieth century, statisticians joined gamblers in their interest in random numbers, and mechanized devices were built to generate random numbers more quickly; in the late 1930s, Kendall and Babington-Smith (1938) used a rapidly spinning disk to prepare a table of 100,000 random digits. Some time later, electric circuits based on randomly pulsating vacuum tubes were developed that delivered random digits at rates of up to 50 per second. One such random-number machine, the Electronic Random Number Indicator Equipment (ERNIE), was used by the British General Post Office to pick the winners in the Premium Savings Bond lottery [see Thomson (1959)]. Another electronic device was used by the Rand Corporation (1955) to generate a table of a million random digits. Many other schemes have been contrived, such as picking numbers "randomly" out of phone books or census reports, or using digits in an expansion of π to 100,000 decimal places. There has been more recent interest in building and testing physical random-number "machines"; for example, Miyatake et al. (1983) describe a device based on counting gamma rays.

As computers (and simulation) became more widely used, increasing attention was paid to methods of random-number generation compatible with the way computers work. One possibility would be to hook up an electronic random-number machine, such as ERNIE, directly to the computer. This has several disadvantages, chiefly that we could not reproduce a previously generated random-number stream exactly. (The desirability of being able to do this is discussed later in this section.) Another alternative would be to read in a table, such as the Rand Corporation table, but this would entail either large memory requirements or a lot of time for relatively slow input operations. (Also, it is not at all uncommon for a modern large-scale simulation to use far more than a million random *numbers*, each of which would require several individual random *digits*.) Therefore, research in the 1940s and 1950s turned to *numerical* or *arithmetic* ways to generate "random" numbers. These methods are sequential, with each new number being determined by one or several of its predecessors according to a fixed mathematical formula. The first such arithmetic generator, proposed by von Neumann and Metropolis in the 1940s, is the famous *midsquare method*, an example of which follows.

EXAMPLE 7.1. Start with a four-digit positive integer Z_0 and square it to obtain an integer with up to eight digits; if necessary, append zeros to the left to make it exactly eight digits. Take the *middle four* digits of this eight-digit number as the next four-digit number, Z_1. Place a decimal point at the left of Z_1 to obtain the first "U(0, 1) random number," U_1. Then let Z_2 be the middle four digits of Z_1^2 and let U_2 be Z_2 with a decimal point at the left, and so on. Table 7.1 lists the first few Z_i's and U_i's for $Z_0 = 7182$ (the first four digits to the right of the decimal point in the number e).

TABLE 7.1
The midsquare method

i	Z_i	U_i	Z_i^2
0	7182	—	51,581,124
1	5811	0.5811	33,767,721
2	7677	0.7677	58,936,329
3	9363	0.9363	87,665,769
4	6657	0.6657	44,315,649
5	3156	0.3156	09,960,336
.	.	.	.
.	.	.	.
.	.	.	.

Intuitively the midsquare method seems to provide a good scrambling of one number to obtain the next, and so we might think that such a haphazard rule would provide a fairly good way of generating random numbers. In fact, it does not work very well at all. One serious problem (among others) is that it has a strong tendency to degenerate fairly rapidly to zero, where it will stay forever. (Continue Table 7.1 for just a few more steps, or try $Z_0 = 1009$, the first four digits from the Rand Corporation tables.) This illustrates the danger in assuming that a good random-number generator will always be obtained by doing something strange and nefarious to one number to obtain the next.

A more fundamental objection to the midsquare method is that it is not "random" at all, in the sense of being unpredictable. Indeed, if we know one number, the next is completely determined since the rule to obtain it is fixed; actually, when Z_0 is specified, the *whole sequence* of Z_i's and U_i's is determined. This objection applies to all arithmetic generators (the only kind we consider in the rest of this chapter), and arguing about it usually leads one quickly into mystical discussions about the true nature of truly random numbers. (Sometimes arithmetic generators are called *pseudorandom*, an awkward term that we avoid, even though it is probably more accurate.) Indeed, in an oft-quoted quip, John von Neumann (1951) declared that:

> Any one who considers arithmetical methods of producing random digits is, of course, in a state of sin. For, as has been pointed out several times, there is no such thing as a random number—there are only methods to produce random numbers, and a strict arithmetic procedure of course is not such a method. . . . We are here dealing with mere "cooking recipes" for making digits. . . .

It is seldom stated, however, that von Neumann goes on in the same paragraph to say, less gloomily, that these "recipes"

> . . . probably . . . can not be justified, but should merely be judged by their results. Some statistical study of the digits generated by a given recipe should be made, but exhaustive tests are impractical. If the digits work well on one problem, they seem usually to be successful with others of the same type.

This more practical attitude was shared by Lehmer (1951), who developed what is probably still the most widely used class of techniques for random-number generation (discussed in Sec. 7.2); he viewed the idea of an arithmetic random-number generator as

> . . . a vague notion embodying the idea of a sequence in which each term is unpredictable to the uninitiated and whose digits pass a certain number of tests traditional with statisticians and depending somewhat on the use to which the sequence is to be put.

More formal definitions of "randomness" in an axiomatic sense are cited by Ripley (1987, p. 19); Niederreiter (1978) argues that statistical randomness may not even be desirable, and that other properties of the generated numbers, such as "evenness" of the distribution of points, are more important in some applications, such as Monte Carlo integration. We agree with most writers that arithmetic generators, if designed carefully, can produce numbers that *appear* to be independent draws from the U(0, 1) distribution, in that they pass a series of statistical tests (see Sec. 7.4). This is a useful definition of "random numbers," to which we subscribe.

A "good" arithmetic random-number generator should possess several properties:

1. Above all, the numbers produced should appear to be distributed uniformly on [0, 1] and should not exhibit any correlation with each other; otherwise, the simulation's results may be completely invalid.
2. From a practical standpoint, we would naturally like the generator to be fast and avoid the need for a lot of storage.
3. We would like to be able to reproduce a given stream of random numbers exactly, for at least two reasons. First, this can sometimes make debugging or verification of the computer program easier. More important, we might want to use *identical* random numbers in simulating different systems in order to obtain a more precise comparison; Sec. 11.2 discusses this in detail.
4. There should be provision in the generator for easily producing separate "streams" of random numbers. As we shall see, a stream is simply a subsegment of the numbers produced by the generator, with one stream beginning where the previous stream ends. We can think of the different streams as being separate and independent generators (provided that we do not use up a whole stream, whose length is typically chosen to be a very large number). Thus, the user can "dedicate" a particular stream to a particular source of randomness in the simulation. We did this, for example, in the single-server queueing model of Sec. 2.4, where stream 1 was used for generating interarrival times and stream 2 for generating service times. Using separate streams for separate purposes facilitates reproducibility and comparability of simulation results. While this idea has obvious intuitive appeal, there is probabilistic foundation in support of it as well, as discussed in Sec. 11.2. Further advantages of having streams available are discussed in other parts of Chap. 11. The ability to create separate streams for a generator is facilitated if there is an efficient way to jump from the ith random number to the $(i + k)$th random number for large values of k.
5. We would like the generator to be portable, i.e., to produce the same sequence of random numbers (at least up to machine accuracy) for all standard compilers and computers (see Sec. 7.2.2).

Most of the commonly used generators are quite fast, require very little storage, and can easily reproduce a given sequence of random numbers, so that points 2 and 3 above are almost universally met. Furthermore, most generators now have the facility for multiple streams in some way, especially those generators included in modern simulation packages, satisfying point 4. Unfortunately, there are also some generators that fail to satisfy the uniformity and independence criteria of point 1 above, which are absolutely necessary if one hopes to obtain correct simulation results. For example, L'Ecuyer and Simard (2007) report several instances of published generators' displaying very poor performance.

In Sec. 7.2 we discuss the most common kind of generator, while Sec. 7.3 discusses some alternative methods. Section 7.4 discusses how one can test a given random-number generator for the desired statistical properties. Finally, Apps. 7A and 7B contain portable computer code for two random-number generators in C. The first generator was used for the examples in Chaps. 1 and 2. The second generator is known to have better statistical properties and is recommended for real-world applications.

The subject of random-number generation is a complicated one, involving such disparate disciplines as abstract algebra and number theory, on one hand, and systems programming and computer hardware engineering, on the other. General references on random-number generators are the books by Fishman (1996, 2001, 2006), Gentle (2010), Knuth (1998a), and Tezuka (1995) and, in addition, the book chapters by L'Ecuyer (2006, 2012).

7.2 LINEAR CONGRUENTIAL GENERATORS

Many random-number generators in use today are *linear congruential generators* (LCGs), introduced by Lehmer (1951). A sequence of integers $Z_1, Z_2, \ldots$ is defined by the recursive formula

$$Z_i = (aZ_{i-1} + c)(\text{mod } m) \tag{7.1}$$

where m (the *modulus*), a (the *multiplier*), c (the *increment*), and Z_0 (the *seed*) are nonnegative integers. Thus, Eq. (7.1) says that to obtain Z_i, divide $aZ_{i-1} + c$ by m and let Z_i be the *remainder* of this division. Therefore, $0 \le Z_i \le m - 1$, and to obtain the desired random numbers U_i (for $i = 1, 2, \ldots$) on [0, 1], we let $U_i = Z_i/m$. We shall concentrate our attention for the most part on the Z_i's, although the precise nature of the division of Z_i by m should be paid attention to due to differences in the way various computers and compilers handle floating-point arithmetic. In addition to nonnegativity, the integers m, a, c, and Z_0 should satisfy $0 < m$, $a < m$, $c < m$, and $Z_0 < m$.

Immediately, two objections could be raised against LCGs. The first objection is one common to all (pseudo) random-number generators, namely, that the Z_i's defined by Eq. (7.1) are not really random at all. In fact, one can show by mathematical induction that for $i = 1, 2, \ldots,$

$$Z_i = \left[a^i Z_0 + \frac{c(a^i - 1)}{a - 1}\right] (\text{mod } m)$$

so that *every* Z_i is completely determined by m, a, c, and Z_0. However, by careful choice of these four parameters we try to induce behavior in the Z_i's that makes the corresponding U_i's *appear* to be IID U(0, 1) random variates when subjected to a variety of tests (see Sec. 7.4).

The second objection to LCGs might be that the U_i's can take on only the rational values $0, 1/m, 2/m, \ldots, (m-1)/m$; in fact, the U_i's might actually take on only a fraction of these values, depending on the specification of the constants m, a, c, and Z_0, as well as on the nature of the floating-point division by m. Thus there is no possibility of getting a value of U_i between, say, $0.1/m$ and $0.9/m$, whereas this *should* occur with probability $0.8/m > 0$. As we shall see, the modulus m is usually chosen to be very large, say 10^9 or more, so that the points in [0, 1] where the U_i's can fall are very dense; for $m \geq 10^9$, there are at least a billion possible values.

EXAMPLE 7.2. Consider the LCG defined by $m = 16$, $a = 5$, $c = 3$, and $Z_0 = 7$. Table 7.2 gives Z_i and U_i (to three decimal places) for $i = 1, 2, \ldots, 19$. Note that $Z_{17} = Z_1 = 6$, $Z_{18} = Z_2 = 1$, and so on. That is, from $i = 17$ through 32, we shall obtain *exactly* the same values of Z_i (and hence U_i) that we did from $i = 1$ through 16, and in *exactly* the same order. (We do not seriously suggest that anyone use this generator since m is so small; it only illustrates the arithmetic of LCGs.)

The "looping" behavior of the LCG in Example 7.2 is inevitable. By the definition in Eq. (7.1), whenever Z_i takes on a value it has had previously, exactly the same sequence of values is generated, and this cycle repeats itself endlessly. The length of a cycle is called the *period* of a generator. For LCGs, Z_i depends *only* on the previous integer Z_{i-1}, and since $0 \leq Z_i \leq m - 1$, it is clear that the period is at most m; if it is in fact m, the LCG is said to have *full period.* (The LCG in Example 7.2 has full period.) Clearly, if a generator is full-period, any choice of the initial seed Z_0 from $\{0, 1, \ldots, m - 1\}$ will produce the entire cycle in some order. If, however, a generator has less than full period, the cycle length could in fact depend on the particular value of Z_0 chosen, in which case we should really refer to the period of the *seed* for this generator.

Since large-scale simulation projects can use millions of random numbers, it is manifestly desirable to have LCGs with long periods. Furthermore, it is comforting to have full-period LCGs, since we are assured that every integer between 0 and $m - 1$ will occur exactly once in each cycle, which should contribute to the uniformity of the U_i's. (Even full-period LCGs, however, can exhibit nonuniform behavior in segments within a cycle. For example, if we generate only $m/2$ consecutive Z_i's,

TABLE 7.2
The LCG $Z_i = (5Z_{i-1} + 3)(\text{mod } 16)$ with $Z_0 = 7$

i	Z_i	U_i	i	Z_i	U_i	i	Z_i	U_i	i	Z_i	U_i
0	7	—	5	10	0.625	10	9	0.563	15	4	0.250
1	6	0.375	6	5	0.313	11	0	0.000	16	7	0.438
2	1	0.063	7	12	0.750	12	3	0.188	17	6	0.375
3	8	0.500	8	15	0.938	13	2	0.125	18	1	0.063
4	11	0.688	9	14	0.875	14	13	0.813	19	8	0.500

they may leave large gaps in the sequence $0, 1, \ldots, m - 1$ of possible values.) Thus, it is useful to know how to choose m, a, and c so that the corresponding LCG will have full period. The following theorem, proved by Hull and Dobell (1962), gives such a characterization.

THEOREM 7.1. The LCG defined in Eq. (7.1) has full period if and only if the following three conditions hold:

(*a*) The only positive integer that (exactly) divides both m and c is 1.
(*b*) If q is a prime number (divisible by only itself and 1) that divides m, then q divides $a - 1$.
(*c*) If 4 divides m, then 4 divides $a - 1$.

[Condition (*a*) in Theorem 7.1 is often stated as "c is relatively prime to m."]

Obtaining a full (or at least a long) period is just one desirable property for a good LCG; as indicated in Sec. 7.1, we also want good statistical properties (such as apparent independence), computational and storage efficiency, reproducibility, facilities for separate streams, and portability (see Sec. 7.2.2). Reproducibility is simple, for we must only remember the initial seed used, Z_0, and initiate the generator with this value again to obtain the same sequence of U_i's exactly. Also, we can easily resume generating the Z_i's at any point in the sequence by saving the final Z_i obtained previously and using it as the new seed; this is a common way to obtain nonoverlapping, "independent" sequences of random numbers.

Streams are typically set up in a LCG by simply specifying the initial seed for each stream. For example, if we want streams of length 1,000,000 each, we set Z_0 for the first stream to some value, then use $Z_{1,000,000}$ as the seed for the second stream, $Z_{2,000,000}$ as the seed for the third stream, and so on. Thus, we see that streams are actually nonoverlapping adjacent subsequences of *the single* sequence of random numbers being generated; if we were to use more than 1,000,000 random numbers from one stream in the above example, we would be encroaching on the beginning of the next stream, which might already have been used for something else, resulting in unwanted correlation.

In the remainder of this section we consider the choice of parameters for obtaining good LCGs and identify some poor LCGs that are still in use. Because of condition (*a*) in Theorem 7.1, LCGs tend to behave differently for $c > 0$ (called *mixed* LCGs) than for $c = 0$ (called *multiplicative* LCGs).

7.2.1 Mixed Generators

For $c > 0$, condition (*a*) in Theorem 7.1 is possible, so we might be able to obtain full period m, as we now discuss. For a large period and high density of the U_i's on [0, 1], we want m to be large. Furthermore, in the early days of computer simulation when computers were relatively slow, dividing by m to obtain the remainder in Eq. (7.1) was a relatively slow arithmetic operation, and it was desirable to avoid having to do this division explicitly. A choice of m that is good in all these respects is $m = 2^b$, where b is the number of bits (*bi*nary digi*ts*) in a word on the computer being used that are available for actual data storage. For example, most computers and compilers have 32-bit words, the leftmost bit being a sign bit, so $b = 31$ and $m = 2^{31} > 2.1$ billion. Furthermore, choosing $m = 2^b$ does allow us to avoid explicit division by m on most computers by taking advantage of *integer overflow.* The largest integer that can be represented is $2^b - 1$, and any attempt to store a larger integer W (with, say, $h > b$ bits) will result in loss of the left (most significant) $h - b$ bits of this oversized integer. What remains in the retained b bits is precisely $W(\text{mod } 2^b)$.

With the choice of $m = 2^b$, Theorem 7.1 says that we shall obtain a full period if c is odd and $a - 1$ is divisible by 4. Furthermore, Z_0 can be any integer between 0 and $m - 1$ without affecting the period. We will, however, focus on multiplicative LCGs in the remainder of Sec. 7.2, because they are much more widely used.

7.2.2 Multiplicative Generators

Multiplicative LCGs are advantageous in that the addition of c is not needed, but they cannot have full period since condition (a) of Theorem 7.1 cannot be satisfied (because, for example, m is positive and divides both m and $c = 0$). As we shall see, however, it is possible to obtain period $m - 1$ if m and a are chosen carefully.

As with mixed generators, it's still computationally efficient to choose $m = 2^b$ and thus avoid explicit division. However, it can be shown [see, for example, Knuth (1998a, p. 20)] that in this case the period is at most 2^{b-2}, that is, only *one-fourth* of the integers 0 through $m - 1$ can be obtained as values for the Z_i's. (In fact, the period is 2^{b-2} if Z_0 is odd and a is of the form $8k + 3$ or $8k + 5$ for some $k = 0, 1, \ldots$.) Furthermore, we generally shall not know *where* these $m/4$ integers will fall; i.e., there might be unacceptably large gaps in the Z_i's obtained. Additionally, if we choose a to be of the form $2^l + j$ (so that the multiplication of Z_{i-1} by a is replaced by a shift and j adds), poor statistical properties can be induced. The generator usually known as RANDU is of this form ($m = 2^{31}$, $a = 2^{16} + 3 = 65{,}539$, $c = 0$) and has been shown to have very undesirable statistical properties (see Sec. 7.4). Even if one does not choose $a = 2^l + j$, using $m = 2^b$ in multiplicative LCGs is probably not a good idea, if only because of the shorter period of $m/4$ and the resulting possibility of gaps.

Because of these difficulties associated with choosing $m = 2^b$ in multiplicative LCGs, attention was paid to finding other ways of specifying m. Such a method, which has proved to be quite successful, was reported by Hutchinson (1966), who attributed the idea to Lehmer. Instead of letting $m = 2^b$, it was proposed that m be the largest prime number that is less than 2^b. For example, in the case of $b = 31$, the largest prime that is less than 2^{31} is, very agreeably, $2^{31} - 1 = 2{,}147{,}483{,}647$. Now for m prime, it can be shown that the period is $m - 1$ if a is a *primitive element modulo m*; that is, the smallest integer l for which $a^l - 1$ is divisible by m is $l = m - 1$; see Knuth (1998a, p. 20). With m and a chosen in this way, we obtain each integer $1, 2, \ldots, m - 1$ exactly once in each cycle, so that Z_0 can be any integer from 1 through $m - 1$ and a period of $m - 1$ will still result. These are called *prime modulus multiplicative LCGs* (PMMLCGs).

Two issues immediately arise concerning PMMLCGs: (1) How does one obtain a primitive element modulo m? Although Knuth (1998a, pp. 20–21) gives some characterizations, the task is quite complicated from a computational standpoint. We shall, in essence, finesse this point by discussing below two widely used PMMLCGs. (2) Since we are not choosing $m = 2^b$, we can no longer use the integer overflow mechanism directly to effect division modulo m. A technique for avoiding explicit division in this case, which also uses a type of overflow, was given by Payne, Rabung, and Bogyo (1969) and has been called *simulated division*. Marse and Roberts' portable generator, which we discuss below, uses simulated division.

Considerable work has been directed toward identifying good multipliers a for PMMLCGs that are primitive elements modulo $m^* = 2^{31} - 1$, which result in a period of $m^* - 1$. In an important set of papers, Fishman and Moore (1982, 1986) evaluated *all* multipliers a that are primitive elements modulo m^*, numbering some 534 million. They used both empirical and theoretical tests (see Sec. 7.4 below), and they identified several multipliers that perform well according to a number of fairly stringent criteria.

Two particular values of a that have been widely used for the modulus m^* are $a_1 = 7^5 = 16{,}807$ and $a_2 = 630{,}360{,}016$, both of which are primitive elements modulo m^*. [However, neither value of a was found by Fishman and Moore to be among the best (see Sec. 7.4.2).] The multiplier a_1 was originally suggested by Lewis, Goodman, and Miller (1969), and it was used by Schrage (1979) in a clever FORTRAN implementation using simulated division. The importance of Schrage's code was that it provided at that time a reasonably good and portable random-number generator.

The multiplier a_2, suggested originally by Payne, Rabung, and Bogyo (1969), was found by Fishman and Moore to yield statistical performance better than does a_1 (see Sec. 7.4.2). Marse and Roberts (1983) provided a highly portable FORTRAN routine for this multiplier, and a C version of this generator is given in App. 7A. This is the generator that we used for all the examples in Chaps. 1 and 2, and it is the one built into the simlib package in Chap. 2.

The PMMLCG with $m = m^* = 2^{31} - 1$ and $a = a_2 = 630{,}360{,}016$ may provide acceptable results for some applications, particularly if the required number of random numbers is not too large. However, many experts [see, e.g., L'Ecuyer, Simard, Chen, and Kelton (2002) and Gentle (2010, p. 21)] recommend that LCGs with a modulus of around 2^{31} should no longer be used as the random-number generator in a general-purpose software package (e.g., for discrete-event simulation). Not only can the period of the generator be exhausted in a few minutes on many computers, but, more importantly, the relatively poor statistical properties of these generators can bias simulation results for sample sizes that are *much smaller* than the period of the generator. For example, L'Ecuyer and Simard (2001) found using the birthday spacings test that the PMMLCGs with modulus m^* and multipliers a_1 or a_2 exhibit a certain departure from what would be expected in a sample of independent observations from the U(0, 1) distribution if the number of observations in the sample is approximately 8 times the *cube root* of the period of the generator. (As the sample size gets larger, the power of the test increases, eventually detecting the fact that the U_i's are not truly uniformly distributed.) Thus, the "safe sample size" of these generators is actually approximately 10,000 [see also L'Ecuyer et al. (2000)].

If a random-number generator with a larger period and better statistical properties is desired, then the combined multiple recursive generator of L'Ecuyer (Sec. 7.3.2), the Mersenne twister (Sec. 7.3.3), or the WELL generator (Sec. 7.3.3) should be considered.

7.3 OTHER KINDS OF GENERATORS

Although LCGs are probably the most widely used and best understood kind of random-number generator, there are many alternative types. (We have already seen one alternative in Sec. 7.1, the midsquare method, which is not recommended.) Most of these other generators have been developed in an attempt to obtain longer periods and better statistical properties. Our treatment in this section is meant not to be an exhaustive compendium of all kinds of generators, but only to indicate some of the main alternatives to LCGs.

7.3.1 More General Congruences

LCGs can be thought of as a special case of generators defined by

$$Z_i = g(Z_{i-1}, Z_{i-2}, \ldots)(\text{mod } m) \tag{7.2}$$

where g is a fixed deterministic function of previous Z_j's. As with LCGs, the Z_i's defined by Eq. (7.2) lie between 0 and $m - 1$, and the U(0, 1) random numbers are given by $U_i = Z_i/m$. [For LCGs, the function g is, of course, $g(Z_{i-1}, Z_{i-2}, \ldots) = aZ_{i-1} + c$.] Here we briefly discuss a few of these kinds of generators and refer the reader to Knuth (1998a, pp. 26–36) or L'Ecuyer (2012) for a more detailed discussion.

One obvious generalization of LCGs would be to let $g(Z_{i-1}, Z_{i-2}, \ldots) = a'Z_{i-1}^2 + aZ_{i-1} + c$, which produces a *quadratic* congruential generator. A special case that has received some attention is when $a' = a = 1$, $c = 0$, and m is a power of 2; although this particular generator turns out to be a close relative of the mid-square method (see Sec. 7.1), it has better statistical properties. Since Z_i still depends only on Z_{i-1} (and not on earlier Z_j's), and since $0 \leq Z_i \leq m - 1$, the period of quadratic congruential generators is at most m, as for LCGs.

A different choice of the function g is to maintain linearity but to use earlier Z_j's; this gives rise to generators called *multiple recursive generators* (MRGs) and defined by

$$g(Z_{i-1}, Z_{i-2}, \ldots) = a_1 Z_{i-1} + a_2 Z_{i-2} + \cdots + a_q Z_{i-q} \tag{7.3}$$

where $a_1, a_2, \ldots, a_q$ are constants. A period as large as $m^q - 1$ then becomes possible if the parameters are chosen properly [see Knuth (1998a, pp. 29–30)]. L'Ecuyer, Blouin, and Couture (1993) investigated such generators, and included a generalization of the spectral test (see Sec. 7.4.2) for their evaluation; they also identified several specific generators of this type that perform well, and give portable implementations. Additional attention to generators with g of the form in Eq. (7.3) used in Eq. (7.2) has focused on g's defined as $Z_{i-1} + Z_{i-q}$, which includes the old Fibonacci generator

$$Z_i = (Z_{i-1} + Z_{i-2})(\text{mod } m)$$

This generator tends to have a period in excess of m but is completely unacceptable from a statistical standpoint; see Prob. 7.12.

7.3.2 Composite Generators

Several researchers have developed methods that take two or more *separate* generators and combine them in some way to generate the final random numbers. It is hoped that this *composite* generator will exhibit a longer period and better statistical behavior than any of the simple generators composing it. The disadvantage in using a composite generator is, of course, that the cost of obtaining each U_i is more than that of using one of the simple generators alone.

Perhaps the earliest kind of composite generators used a second LCG to *shuffle* the output from the first LCG; they were developed by MacLaren and Marsaglia (1965) and extended by Marsaglia and Bray (1968), Grosenbaugh (1969), and Nance and Overstreet (1975). Initially, a vector $\mathbf{V} = (V_1, V_2, \ldots, V_k)$ is filled sequentially with the first k U_i's from the first LCG ($k = 128$ was originally suggested). Then the second LCG is used to generate a random integer I distributed uniformly on the integers $1, 2, \ldots, k$ (see Sec. 8.4.2), and V_I is returned as the first U(0, 1) variate; the first LCG then replaces this Ith location in $\mathbf{V}$ with its next U_i, and the second LCG randomly chooses the next returned random number from this updated $\mathbf{V}$, etc. Shuffling has a natural intuitive appeal, especially since we would expect it to break up any correlation and greatly extend the period. Indeed, MacLaren and Marsaglia obtained a shuffling generator with very good statistical behavior even though the two individual LCGs were quite poor. In a subsequent evaluation of shuffling, Nance and Overstreet (1978) confirm that shuffling one bad LCG by another bad LCG can result in a good composite generator, e.g., by extending the period when used on computers with short word lengths, but that little is accomplished by shuffling a good LCG. In addition, they found that a vector of length $k = 2$ works as well as much larger vectors.

Several variations on this shuffling scheme have been considered; Bays and Durham (1976) and Gebhardt (1967) propose shuffling a generator by itself rather than by another generator. Atkinson (1980) also reported that simply applying a *fixed* permutation (rather than a random shuffling) of the output of LCGs ". . . removes the effect of all but the worst generators, and very appreciably alleviates the damage that even a dreadful generator can cause."

Despite these apparent advantages of rearranging a simple generator's output in some way, there is not as much known about shuffled generators; for example, one cannot jump into an arbitrary point of a shuffled generator's output sequence without generating all the intermediate values, whereas this is possible for LCGs.

Another way to combine two generators is discussed and evaluated by L'Ecuyer (1988) [see also L'Ecuyer and Tezuka (1991)]. In simplified form, the idea is to let $\{Z_{1i}\}$ and $\{Z_{2i}\}$ denote the integer sequences generated by two different LCGs with different moduli, then let $Z_i = (Z_{1i} - Z_{2i})(\text{mod } m)$ for some integer m, and finally set $U_i = Z_i/m$. This idea could clearly be extended to more than two generators, and has several advantages; the period is very long (at least 10^{18} in one example given by L'Ecuyer), the multipliers in each of the component generators can be small (thus promoting portability and usability on virtually any computer), the resulting generator is quite fast, and the statistical properties of these generators also appear to be very good.

One very appealing class of generators is obtained by combining MRGs (discussed in Sec. 7.3.1) in a particular way, and was developed and studied by L'Ecuyer (1996a, 1999a). In general, J different MRGs [using the function g from Eq. (7.3) in the recursion (7.2)] are implemented simultaneously to form the sequences $\{Z_{1,i}\}$, $\{Z_{2,i}\}, \ldots, \{Z_{J,i}\}$. Letting m_1 be the modulus m from Eq. (7.2) used in the first of these MRGs, and letting $\delta_1, \delta_2, \ldots, \delta_J$ be specified constants, we define

$$Y_i = (\delta_1 Z_{1,i} + \delta_2 Z_{2,i} + \cdots + \delta_J Z_{J,i})(\text{mod } m_1)$$

and finally return $U_i = Y_i/m_1$ as the ith random number for use in the simulation. Although the parameters for these kinds of generators must be chosen very carefully, extremely long periods and exceptionally good statistical properties are possible. L'Ecuyer (1999a) carried out an extensive search for good parameter settings and supplied small, portable, and fast C code for several recommended cases; the simplest of these cases, where $J = 2$ MRGs are combined, is defined by

$$\begin{aligned} Z_{1,i} &= (1{,}403{,}580 Z_{1,i-2} - 810{,}728 Z_{1,i-3})[\text{mod } (2^{32} - 209)] \\ Z_{2,i} &= (527{,}612 Z_{2,i-1} - 1{,}370{,}589 Z_{2,i-3})[\text{mod } (2^{32} - 22{,}853)] \\ Y_i &= (Z_{1,i} - Z_{2,i})[\text{mod } (2^{32} - 209)] \\ U_i &= \frac{Y_i}{2^{32} - 209} \end{aligned}$$

and has a period of approximately 2^{191} (which is about 3.1×10^{57}) as well as excellent statistical properties through dimension 45 (see Sec. 7.4.2). (This generator is denoted by MRG32k3a in the literature.) Note that for this generator, the seed is actually a 6-vector $(Z_{1,0}, Z_{1,1}, Z_{1,2}, Z_{2,0}, Z_{2,1}, Z_{2,2})$ and the first returned random number would be indexed as U_3. In App. 7B we give a portable C-code implementation for this particular generator, which supports a large number of streams spaced very far apart.

This generator with many large streams and substreams is implemented in the Arena [Kelton et al. (2010, p. 518)], AutoMod [Banks (2004, p. 367)], and WITNESS [Lanner (2013)] simulation packages. (Substreams are nonoverlapping adjacent subsequences of the random numbers in a stream.) If one is making multiple replications of their simulation model, these packages will automatically move to the beginning of the next substream for each stream at the beginning of replications 2, 3, ... This can help synchronize the random numbers across the different system configurations of interest when using the variance-reduction technique called common random numbers (see Sec. 11.2.3).

Wichmann and Hill (1982) proposed the following idea for combining three generators, again striving for long period, portability, speed, and usability on small computers (as well as statistical adequacy). If U_{1i}, U_{2i}, and U_{3i} are the ith random numbers produced by three separate generators, then let U_i be the fractional part (i.e., ignore any digits to the left of the decimal point) of $U_{1i} + U_{2i} + U_{3i}$; see Prob. 7.13 for the underlying motivation. This indeed produces a very long period [although not as long as claimed in the original paper; see Wichmann and Hill (1984)] and is highly portable and efficient. It was later pointed out by McLeod (1985), however, that their code may have numerical difficulties in some computer architectures. Zeisel (1986) subsequently showed that this generator is identical to a multiplicative LCG, but that this equivalent LCG has a very large modulus and multiplier; thus, the Wichmann-Hill generator turned out to be a way to implement a multiplicative LCG with very large parameters on even the smallest computers. The Wichmann-Hill generator is implemented in Microsoft Excel 2010.

There are many conceivable ways to combine individual random-number generators, some of which we have reviewed above. Others are discussed by Collins (1987), Fishman (1996, pp. 634–645), Gentle (2010, pp. 46–51), and L'Ecuyer (1994b).

7.3.3 Feedback Shift Register Generators

Several interesting kinds of generators have been developed on the basis of a paper by Tausworthe (1965). These generators, which are related to cryptographic methods, operate directly on bits to form random numbers.

Define a sequence $b_1, b_2, \ldots$ of binary digits by the recurrence

$$b_i = (c_1 b_{i-1} + c_2 b_{i-2} + \cdots + c_q b_{i-q}) (\text{mod } 2) \tag{7.4}$$

where $c_1, c_2, \ldots, c_{q-1}$ are constants that are equal to 0 or 1 and $c_q = 1$. Note the similarity between the recurrence for b_i and Eq. (7.3). In most applications of *Tausworthe generators*, only two of the c_j coefficients are nonzero for computational simplicity, in which case Eq. (7.4) becomes

$$b_i = (b_{i-r} + b_{i-q}) (\text{mod } 2) \tag{7.5}$$

for integers r and q satisfying $0 < r < q$. Execution of Eq. (7.5) is expedited by noting that addition modulo 2 is equivalent to the *exclusive-or* instruction on bits. That is, Eq. (7.5) can be expressed as

$$b_i = \begin{cases} 0 & \text{if } b_{i-r} = b_{i-q} \\ 1 & \text{if } b_{i-r} \neq b_{i-q} \end{cases}$$

which is denoted by $b_i = b_{i-r} \oplus b_{i-q}$. To initialize the $\{b_i\}$ sequence, $b_1, b_2, \ldots, b_q$ must be specified somehow; this is akin to specifying the seed Z_0 for LCGs.

To form a sequence of binary integers $W_1, W_2, \ldots$, we string together l consecutive b_i's and consider this as a *number in base* 2. That is,

$$W_1 = b_1 b_2 \cdots b_l$$

and

$$W_i = b_{(i-1)l+1} b_{(i-1)l+2} \cdots b_{il} \qquad \text{for } i = 2, 3, \ldots$$

Note that the recurrence for the W_i's is the same as the recurrence for the b_i's given by Eq. (7.5), namely

$$W_i = W_{i-r} \oplus W_{i-q} \tag{7.6}$$

where the exclusive-or operation is performed bitwise. The ith U(0, 1) random number U_i is then defined by

$$U_i = \frac{W_i}{2^l} \qquad \text{for } i = 1, 2, \ldots$$

The maximum period of the $\{b_i\}$ sequence is $2^q - 1$, since $b_{i-1}, b_{i-2}, \ldots, b_{i-q}$ can take on 2^q different possible states and the occurrence of the q-tuple $0, 0, \ldots, 0$ would cause the $\{b_i\}$ sequence to stay in that state forever. Let

$$f(x) = x^q + c_1 x^{q-1} + \cdots + c_{q-1} x + 1$$

be the characteristic polynomial of the recurrence given by Eq. (7.4). Tausworthe (1965) showed that the period of the b_i's is, in fact, $2^q - 1$ if and only if the polynomial $f(x)$ is *primitive* [see Knuth (1998a, pp. 29–30)] over the Galois field $\mathcal{F}_2$, which is the set $\{0, 1\}$ on which the binary operations of addition and multiplication modulo 2 are defined. If l is relatively prime to $2^q - 1$, then the period of the W_i's (and the U_i's) will also be $2^q - 1$. Thus, for a computer with 31 bits for actual data storage, the maximum period is $2^{31} - 1$, which is the same as that for a LCG.

EXAMPLE 7.3. Let $r = 3$ and $q = 5$ in Eq. (7.5), and let $b_1 = b_2 = \cdots = b_5 = 1$. Thus, for $i \geq 6$, b_i is the "exclusive-or" of b_{i-3} with b_{i-5}. In this case, $f(x)$ is the trinomial $x^5 + x^2 + 1$, which is, in fact, primitive over $\mathcal{F}_2$. The first 40 b_i's are then

1111100011011101010000100101100111110001

Note that the period of the bits is $31 = 2^5 - 1$, since b_{32} through b_{36} are the same as b_1 through b_5. If $l = 4$ (which is relatively prime to 31), then the following sequence of W_i's is obtained:

15, 8, 13, 13, 4, 2, 5, 9, 15, 1, . . .

which also has a period of 31 (see Prob. 7.15). The corresponding U_i's are obtained by dividing the W_i's by $16 = 2^4$.

The original motivation for suggesting that the b_i's be used as a source of U(0, 1) random numbers came from the observation that the recurrence given by Eq. (7.4) can be implemented on a binary computer using a switching circuit called a *linear feedback shift register* (LFSR). This is an array of q bits that is shifted, say, to the left one position at a time, with the bit shifted out on the left combined with other bits in the array to form the new rightmost bit. Because of the relationship between the recurrence (7.4) and a feedback shift register, Tausworthe generators are also called *LFSR generators.*

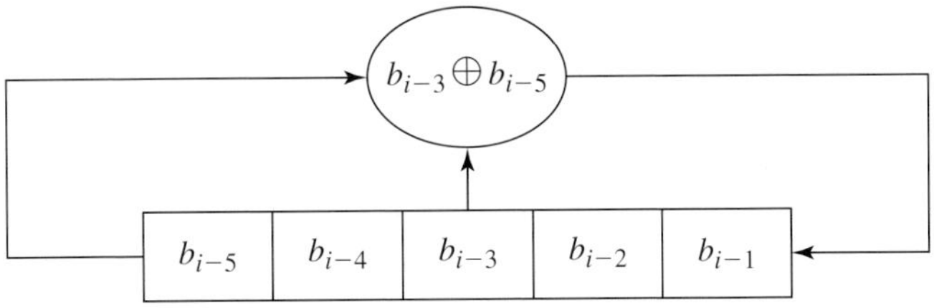

FIGURE 7.1
A LFSR corresponding to the recurrence (7.5) with $r = 3$ and $q = 5$.

EXAMPLE 7.4. The generator discussed in Example 7.3 can be represented by the LFSR shown in Fig. 7.1. The bits b_{i-3} and b_{i-5} are combined using the exclusive-or operation to produce a new bit that goes into the rightmost location (i.e., the one that previously contained bit b_{i-1}) of the array. The bit that was in the leftmost location of the array (i.e., b_{i-5}) is removed from the array. The values of b_{i-5}, b_{i-4}, b_{i-3}, b_{i-2}, and b_{i-1} for $i = 6, 7, \ldots, 15$ are given in Table 7.3.

Unfortunately, LFSR generators are known to have statistical deficiencies, as discussed by Matsumoto and Kurita (1996) and Tezuka (1995). However, L'Ecuyer (1996b, 1999b) considered combined LFSR generators, which have better statistical properties and a larger period.

Lewis and Payne (1973) introduced a modification of the LFSR generator that they called a *generalized feedback shift register* (GFSR) generator. To obtain a sequence of l-bit binary integers $Y_1, Y_2, \ldots$, the sequence of bits $b_1, b_2, \ldots$ produced by Eq. (7.5) is used to fill the first (leftmost) binary position of the integers being formed. Then the same sequence of bits, but with a delay of d, is used to fill the second binary position of the integers. That is, the bits $b_{1+d}, b_{2+d}, \ldots$ are used for the second binary position. Finally, bits $b_{1+(l-1)d}, b_{2+(l-1)d}, \ldots$ are used to fill the lth binary position of the integers. The period of the Y_i's will be $2^q - 1$ if $Y_1, Y_2, \ldots, Y_q$

TABLE 7.3
Successive states of the LFSR for $r = 3$ and $q = 5$

i	$b_{i-5}^{\dagger}$	b_{i-4}	$b_{i-3}^{\dagger}$	b_{i-2}	b_{i-1}
6	1	1	1	1	1
7	1	1	1	1	0
8	1	1	1	0	0
9	1	1	0	0	0
10	1	0	0	0	1
11	0	0	0	1	1
12	0	0	1	1	0
13	0	1	1	0	1
14	1	1	0	1	1
15	1	0	1	0	1

†Source of bits.

TABLE 7.4
GFSR generator with $r = 3, q = 5, l = 4$, and $d = 6$

i	Y_i	i	Y_i	i	Y_i
1	1011 = 11	13	1100 = 12	25	0010 = 2
2	1010 = 10	14	1000 = 8	26	1001 = 9
3	1010 = 10	15	0011 = 3	27	0101 = 5
4	1100 = 12	16	1001 = 9	28	1101 = 13
5	1110 = 14	17	0011 = 3	29	1110 = 14
6	0001 = 1	18	1111 = 15	30	0111 = 7
7	0110 = 6	19	0001 = 1	31	0100 = 4
8	0100 = 4	20	0000 = 0	32	1011 = 11
9	1101 = 13	21	0110 = 6	33	1010 = 10
10	1000 = 8	22	0010 = 2	34	1010 = 10
11	0101 = 5	23	1111 = 15	35	1100 = 12
12	1011 = 11	24	0111 = 7	36	1110 = 14

are linearly independent; that is, $a_1Y_1 + a_2Y_2 + \cdots + a_qY_q = 0$ for $a_j = 0$ or 1 implies that all a_j's are 0. Note also that the Y_i's satisfy the recurrence

$$Y_i = Y_{i-r} \oplus Y_{i-q} \tag{7.7}$$

where the exclusive-or operation is performed bitwise.

The following example illustrates in detail how a GFSR generator works.

EXAMPLE 7.5. For the LFSR generator of Example 7.3, $l = 4$, and a delay of $d = 6$, we give the Y_i's produced by the resulting GFSR generator in Table 7.4. Note that the period of the Y_i's is 31, since Y_{32} through Y_{36} are the same as Y_1 through Y_5. Each of the integers 1 through 15 occurs *twice* and 0 occurs once in the period of length 31.

Because of the parallel nature of the binary positions in the Y_i's, a GFSR generator can have l equal to the word size of the computer, regardless of the relationship between l and q. If $l < q$, then there will be many repeated Y_i's but the period will still be $2^q - 1$. Thus, a very long period can be obtained on an l-bit computer by taking q very large. For example, Fushimi (1990) considered a variant of a GFSR generator that has a period of $2^{521} - 1$.

Matsumoto and Kurita (1992, 1994) introduced the idea of a *twisted GFSR* (TGFSR) *generator*, where the recurrence (7.7) is replaced by

$$\mathbf{Y}_i = \mathbf{Y}_{i-r} \oplus A\mathbf{Y}_{i-q} \tag{7.8}$$

where the $\mathbf{Y}_i$'s are now considered as $l \times 1$ vectors and A is an $l \times l$ matrix, both of which consist of 0s and 1s. [If A is the identity matrix, then recurrence (7.8) is the same as recurrence (7.7).] With suitable choices for r, q, and A, a TGFSR generator can have a maximum period of $2^{ql} - 1$ as compared with $2^q - 1$ for a GFSR generator (both require ql bits to store the state of the generator). Matsumoto and Kurita (1994) discuss how to choose A so that a TGFSR generator has good statistical properties. The *Mersenne twister* [see Matsumoto and Nishimura (1998)], which is denoted by MT19937 in the literature, is a variant of the TGFSR generator with an astonishing period of $2^{19,937} - 1$ as well as excellent statistical properties through dimension 623 (see Sec. 7.4.2). It has become quite popular in general, and it has also been implemented in the Simio [Simio (2013)] and SIMUL8 [SIMUL8 (2013)] simulation packages. It is called the Mersenne twister because $2^{19,937} - 1$ is a *Mersenne prime*, i.e., a prime number of the form $2^p - 1$. (Note that $m^* = 2^{31} - 1$ is also a prime number.)

Panneton et al. (2006) showed that *if* the Mersenne twister happened to start in an initial state with only a few bits set to 1, then the average value of the U_i's produced over the next few thousand steps is likely to be *much less than 0.5*. They went on to develop a class of similar generators, called *well-equidistributed long-period linear* (WELL), that have a large period (e.g., $2^{19,937}$), excellent statistical properties, and less dependence on a bad initial state. See the survey paper by L'Ecuyer and Panneton (2009).

7.4 TESTING RANDOM-NUMBER GENERATORS

As we have seen in Secs. 7.1 through 7.3, all random-number generators currently used in computer simulation are actually completely deterministic. Thus, we can only hope that the U_i's generated *appear* as if they *were* IID U(0, 1) random variates. In this section we discuss several tests to which a random-number generator can be subjected to ascertain how well the generated U_i's do (or can) resemble values of true IID U(0, 1) random variates.

Most computers have a "canned" random-number generator as part of the available software. Before such a generator is actually used in a simulation, we strongly recommend that one identify exactly what kind of generator it is and what its numerical parameters are. Unless a generator is one of the "good" ones identified (and tested) somewhere in the literature (or is one of the specific generators recommended above), the responsible analyst should subject it (at least) to the empirical tests discussed below.

There are two quite different kinds of tests, which we discuss separately in Secs. 7.4.1 and 7.4.2. *Empirical* tests are the usual kinds of statistical tests and are based on the actual U_i's produced by a generator. *Theoretical* tests are not tests in the statistical sense, but use the numerical parameters of a generator to assess it globally without actually generating any U_i's at all.

7.4.1 Empirical Tests

Perhaps the most direct way to test a generator is to *use* it to generate some U_i's, which are then examined statistically to see how closely they resemble IID U(0, 1) random variates. We discuss four such empirical tests; several others are treated in Knuth (1998a, pp. 41–75), L'Ecuyer et al. (2000), and L'Ecuyer and Simard (2001, 2007).

The first test is designed to check whether the U_i's appear to be uniformly distributed between 0 and 1, and it is a special case of a test we have seen before (in Sec. 6.6.2), the chi-square test with all parameters known. We divide [0, 1] into k subintervals of equal length and generate $U_1, U_2, \ldots, U_n$. (As a general rule, k should be at least 100 here.) For $j = 1, 2, \ldots, k$, let f_j be the number of the U_i's that are in the jth subinterval, and let

$$\chi^2 = \frac{k}{n} \sum_{j=1}^{k} \left(f_j - \frac{n}{k} \right)^2$$

Then for large n, χ^2 will have an approximate chi-square distribution with $k - 1$ df under the null hypothesis that the U_i's are IID U(0, 1) random variables. Thus, we reject this hypothesis at level α if $\chi^2 > \chi^2_{k-1,1-\alpha}$, where $\chi^2_{k-1,1-\alpha}$ is the upper $1 - \alpha$ critical point of the chi-square distribution with $k - 1$ df. [For the large values of k likely to be encountered here, we can use the approximation

$$\chi^2_{k-1,1-\alpha} \approx (k-1) \left[1 - \frac{2}{9(k-1)} + z_{1-\alpha} \sqrt{\frac{2}{9(k-1)}} \right]^3$$

where $z_{1-\alpha}$ is the upper $1 - \alpha$ critical point of the N(0, 1) distribution.]

EXAMPLE 7.6. We applied the chi-square test of uniformity to the PMMLCG $Z_i = 630{,}360{,}016 Z_{i-1} (\text{mod}\, 2^{31} - 1)$, as implemented in App. 7A, using stream 1 with the default seed. We took $k = 2^{12} = 4096$ (so that the most significant 12 bits of the U_i's are being examined for uniformity) and let $n = 2^{15} = 32{,}768$. We obtained $\chi^2 = 4141.0$; using the above approximation for the critical point, $\chi^2_{4095,0.95} \approx 4245.0$, so the null hypothesis of uniformity is not rejected at level $\alpha = 0.05$. Therefore, *these particular* 32,768 U_i's produced by this generator do not behave in a way that is significantly different from what would be expected from truly IID U(0, 1) random variables, so far as this chi-square test can ascertain.

Our second empirical test, the *serial test*, is really just a generalization of the chi-square test to higher dimensions. If the U_i's were really IID U(0, 1) random variates, the nonoverlapping d-tuples

$$\mathbf{U}_1 = (U_1, U_2, \ldots, U_d), \qquad \mathbf{U}_2 = (U_{d+1}, U_{d+2}, \ldots, U_{2d}), \qquad \ldots$$

should be IID random *vectors* distributed uniformly on the d-dimensional unit hypercube, $[0, 1]^d$. Divide [0, 1] into k subintervals of equal size and generate $\mathbf{U}_1, \mathbf{U}_2, \ldots, \mathbf{U}_n$ (requiring nd U_i's). Let $f_{j_1 j_2 \cdots j_d}$ be the number of $\mathbf{U}_i$'s having first component in subinterval j_1, second component in subinterval j_2, etc. (It is easier to tally the $f_{j_1 j_2 \cdots j_d}$'s than might be expected; see Prob. 7.7.) If we let

$$\chi^2(d) = \frac{k^d}{n} \sum_{j_1=1}^{k} \sum_{j_2=1}^{k} \cdots \sum_{j_d=1}^{k} \left(f_{j_1 j_2 \cdots j_d} - \frac{n}{k^d} \right)^2$$

then $\chi^2(d)$ will have an approximate chi-square distribution with $k^d - 1$ df. [See L'Ecuyer, Simard, and Weggenkittl (2002) for further discussion of the serial test.] The test for d-dimensional uniformity is carried out exactly as for the one-dimensional chi-square test above.

EXAMPLE 7.7. For $d = 2$, we tested the null hypothesis that the pairs (U_1, U_2), $(U_3, U_4), \ldots, (U_{2n-1}, U_{2n})$ are IID random vectors distributed uniformly over the unit square. We used the generator in App. 7A, but starting with stream 2, and generated

$n = 32{,}768$ pairs of U_i's. We took $k = 64$, so that the degrees of freedom were again $4095 = 64^2 - 1$ and the level $\alpha = 0.05$ critical value was the same, 4245.0. The value of $\chi^2(2)$ was 4016.5, indicating acceptable uniformity in two dimensions for the first two-thirds of stream 2 (recall from Sec. 2.3 that the streams are of length 100,000 U_i's, and we used $2n = 65{,}536$ of them here). For $d = 3$, we used stream 3, took $k = 16$ (keeping the degrees of freedom as $4095 = 16^3 - 1$ and the level $\alpha = 0.05$ critical value at 4245.0), and generated $n = 32{,}768$ nonoverlapping *triples of* U_i's. And $\chi^2(3)$ was 4174.5, again indicating acceptable uniformity in three dimensions.

Why should we care about this kind of uniformity in *higher* dimensions? If the individual U_i's are correlated, the distribution of the d-vectors $\mathbf{U}_i$ will deviate from d-dimensional uniformity; thus, the serial test provides an indirect check on the assumption that the individual U_i's are independent. For example, if adjacent U_i's tend to be positively correlated, the pairs (U_i, U_{i+1}) will tend to cluster around the southwest-northeast diagonal in the unit square, and $\chi^2(2)$ should pick this up. Finally, it should be apparent that the serial test for $d > 3$ could require a lot of memory to tally the k^d values of $f_{j_1 j_2 \cdots j_d}$. (Choosing $k = 16$ in Example 7.7 when $d = 3$ is probably not a sufficiently fine division of [0, 1].)

The third empirical test we consider, the *runs* (or *runs-up*) *test*, is a more direct test of the independence assumption. (In fact, it is a test of independence *only*; i.e., we are not testing for uniformity in particular.) We examine the U_i sequence (or, equivalently, the Z_i sequence) for unbroken subsequences of maximal length within which the U_i's increase monotonically; such a subsequence is called a *run up*. For example, consider the following sequence $U_1, U_2, \ldots, U_{10}$: 0.86, 0.11, 0.23, 0.03, 0.13, 0.06, 0.55, 0.64, 0.87, 0.10. The sequence starts with a run up of length 1 (0.86), followed by a run up of length 2 (0.11, 0.23), then another run up of length 2 (0.03, 0.13), then a run up of length 4 (0.06, 0.55, 0.64, 0.87), and finally another run up of length 1 (0.10). From a sequence of n U_i's, we count the number of runs up of length 1, 2, 3, 4, 5, and ≥ 6, and then define

$$r_i = \begin{cases} \text{number of runs up of length } i & \text{for } i = 1, 2, \ldots, 5 \\ \text{number of runs up of length} \geq 6 & \text{for } i = 6 \end{cases}$$

(See Prob. 7.8 for an algorithm to tally the r_i's. For the 10 U_i's above, $r_1 = 2$, $r_2 = 2$, $r_3 = 0$, $r_4 = 1$, $r_5 = 0$, and $r_6 = 0$.) The test statistic is then

$$R = \frac{1}{n} \sum_{i=1}^{6} \sum_{j=1}^{6} a_{ij}(r_i - nb_i)(r_j - nb_j)$$

where a_{ij} is the (i, j)th element of the matrix

$$\begin{bmatrix} 4{,}529.4 & 9{,}044.9 & 13{,}568 & 18{,}091 & 22{,}615 & 27{,}892 \\ 9{,}044.9 & 18{,}097 & 27{,}139 & 36{,}187 & 45{,}234 & 55{,}789 \\ 13{,}568 & 27{,}139 & 40{,}721 & 54{,}281 & 67{,}852 & 83{,}685 \\ 18{,}091 & 36{,}187 & 54{,}281 & 72{,}414 & 90{,}470 & 111{,}580 \\ 22{,}615 & 45{,}234 & 67{,}852 & 90{,}470 & 113{,}262 & 139{,}476 \\ 27{,}892 & 55{,}789 & 83{,}685 & 111{,}580 & 139{,}476 & 172{,}860 \end{bmatrix}$$

and the b_i's are given by

$$(b_1, b_2, \ldots, b_6) = \left(\tfrac{1}{6}, \tfrac{5}{24}, \tfrac{11}{120}, \tfrac{19}{720}, \tfrac{29}{5040}, \tfrac{1}{840}\right)$$

[See Knuth (1998a, pp. 66–69) for derivation of these constants.* The a_{ij}'s given above are accurate to five significant digits.] For large n (Knuth recommends $n \geq 4000$), R will have an approximate chi-square distribution with 6 df, under the null hypothesis that the U_i's are IID random variables.

EXAMPLE 7.8. We subjected stream 4 of the generator in App. 7A to the runs-up test, using $n = 5000$, and obtained $(r_1, r_2, \ldots, r_6) = (808, 1026, 448, 139, 43, 4)$, leading to a value of $R = 9.3$. Since $\chi^2_{6,0.95} = 12.6$, we do not reject the hypothesis of independence at level $\alpha = 0.05$.

The runs-up test can be reversed in the obvious way to obtain a runs-down test; the a_{ij} and b_i constants are the same. Since runs tests look solely for independence (and not specifically for uniformity), it would probably be a good idea to apply a runs test *before* performing the chi-square or serial tests, since the last two tests implicitly assume independence.

The final type of empirical test we consider is a direct way to assess whether the generated U_i's exhibit discernible correlation: Simply compute an estimate of the correlation at lags $j = 1, 2, \ldots, l$ for some value of l. Recall from Sec. 4.3 that the correlation at lag j in a sequence $X_1, X_2, \ldots$ of random variables is defined as $\rho_j = C_j/C_0$, where

$$C_j = \text{Cov}(X_i, X_{i+j}) = E(X_i X_{i+j}) - E(X_i)E(X_{i+j})$$

is the covariance between entries in the sequence separated by j; note that $C_0 = \text{Var}(X_i)$. (It is assumed here that the process is covariance-stationary; see Sec. 4.3.) In our case, we are interested in $X_i = U_i$, and under the hypothesis that the U_i's are uniformly distributed on [0, 1], we have $E(U_i) = \frac{1}{2}$ and $\text{Var}(U_i) = \frac{1}{12}$, so that $C_j = E(U_i U_{i+j}) - \frac{1}{4}$ and $C_0 = \frac{1}{12}$. Thus, $\rho_j = 12E(U_i U_{i+j}) - 3$ in this case. From a sequence $U_1, U_2, \ldots, U_n$ of generated values, an estimate of ρ_j can thus be obtained by estimating $E(U_i U_{i+j})$ directly from U_1, U_{1+j}, U_{1+2j}, etc., to obtain

$$\hat{\rho}_j = \frac{12}{h+1} \sum_{k=0}^{h} U_{1+kj} U_{1+(k+1)j} - 3$$

where $h = \lfloor (n-1)/j \rfloor - 1$. Under the further assumption that the U_i's are independent, it turns out [see, for example, Banks et al. (2010, p. 292)] that

$$\text{Var}(\hat{\rho}_j) = \frac{13h + 7}{(h+1)^2}$$

*Knuth, D. E., *The Art of Computer Programming*, Vol. 2, p. 67, © 1998, 1981 Pearson Education, Inc. Reproduced by permission of Pearson Education, Inc. All rights reserved.

Under the null hypothesis that $\rho_j = 0$ and assuming that n is large, it can be shown that the test statistic

$$A_j = \frac{\hat{\rho}_j}{\sqrt{\text{Var}(\hat{\rho}_j)}}$$

has an approximate standard normal distribution. This provides a test of zero lag j correlation at level α, by rejecting this hypothesis if $|A_j| > z_{1-\alpha/2}$. The test should probably be carried out for several values of j, since it could be, for instance, that there is no appreciable correlation at lags 1 or 2, but there is dependence between the U_i's at lag 3, due to some anomaly of the generator.

EXAMPLE 7.9. We tested streams 5 through 10 of the generator in App. 7A for correlation at lags 1 through 6, respectively, taking $n = 5000$ in each case; i.e., we tested stream 5 for lag 1 correlation, stream 6 for lag 2 correlation, etc. The values of $A_1, A_2, \ldots, A_6$ were 0.90, -1.03, -0.12, -1.32, 0.39, and 0.76, respectively, none of which is significantly different from 0 in comparison with the N(0, 1) distribution, at level $\alpha = 0.05$. Thus, the first 5000 values in these streams do not exhibit observable autocorrelation at these lags.

As mentioned above, these are just four of the many possible empirical tests. For example, the Kolmogorov-Smirnov test discussed in Sec. 6.6.2 (for the case with all parameters known) could be applied instead of the chi-square test for one-dimensional uniformity. Also, the birthday spacings test was used by L'Ecuyer and Simard (2001) in their testing of LCGs with modulus $m = 2^{31} - 1$ and multipliers a_1 and a_2 (see Sec. 7.2.2), and it was found that these generators failed the test for a sample size of approximately $n = 10{,}000$. They also applied the test to the generators MRG32k3a and MT19937, and uniformity was not rejected for sample sizes up to and including $n = 262{,}144$. Several empirical tests have been developed around the idea that the generator in question is used to simulate a relatively simple stochastic system with *known* (population) performance measures that the simulation estimates. The simulated results are compared in some way with the known exact "answers," perhaps by means of a chi-square test. A simple application of this idea is seen in Prob. 7.10; Rudolph and Hawkins (1976) test several generators by using them to simulate Markov processes. In general, we feel that as many empirical tests should be performed as are practicable. In this regard, it should be mentioned that there are several comprehensive test suites for evaluating random-number generators. These include DIEHARD [Marsaglia (1995)], the NIST Test Suite [Rukhin et al. (2001)], and *TestU01* [L'Ecuyer and Simard (2007)], with the last package containing more than 100 empirical tests. These test suites are also described in Gentle (2010, pp. 79–85).

Lest the reader be left with the impression that the empirical tests we have presented in this section have no discriminative power at all, we subjected the infamous generator RANDU [defined by $Z_i = 65{,}539Z_{i-1} (\text{mod } 2^{31})$], with seed $Z_0 = 123{,}456{,}789$, to the same tests as in Examples 7.6 through 7.9. The test statistics were as follows:

Chi-square test:	$\chi^2 = 4{,}202.0$
Serial tests:	$\chi^2(2) = 4{,}202.3$
	$\chi^2(3) = 16{,}252.3$
Runs-up test:	$R = 6.3$
Correlation tests:	All A_j's were insignificant

While uniformity appears acceptable on [0, 1] and on the unit square, note the enormous value of the three-dimensional serial test statistic, indicating a severe problem for this generator in terms of uniformity on the unit cube. RANDU is a fatally flawed generator, due primarily to its utter failure in three dimensions; we shall see why in Sec. 7.4.2.

One potential disadvantage of empirical tests is that they are only *local*; i.e., only that segment of a cycle (for LCGs, for example) that was actually used to generate the U_i's for the test is examined, so we cannot say anything about how the generator might perform in other segments of the cycle. On the other hand, this local nature of empirical tests can be advantageous, since it might allow us to examine the actual random numbers that will be used later in a simulation. (Often we can calculate ahead of time how many random numbers will be used in a simulation, or at least get a conservative estimate, by analyzing the model's operation and the techniques used for generating the necessary random variates.) Then this entire random-number stream can be tested empirically, one would hope without excessive cost. (The tests in Examples 7.6 through 7.9 were all done together in a single program that took just a few seconds on an old, modest computer.) A more global empirical test could be performed by replicating an entire test several times and statistically comparing the observed values of the test statistics against the distribution under the null hypothesis; Fishman (1978, pp. 371–372) suggests this approach. For example, the runs-up test of Example 7.8 could be done, say, 100 times using 100 separate random-number streams from the same generator, each of length 5000. This would result in 100 independent values for R, which could then be compared with the chi-square distribution with 6 df using, for example, the K-S test with all parameters known.

7.4.2 Theoretical Tests

We now discuss theoretical tests for random-number generators. Since these tests are quite sophisticated and mathematically complex, we shall describe them somewhat qualitatively; for detailed accounts see Fishman (1996, pp. 607–628), Fishman (2006, pp. 119–123, 133–134, 140–141), Knuth (1998a, pp. 80–115), and L'Ecuyer (1998, pp. 106–114). As mentioned earlier, theoretical tests do not require that we generate any U_i's at all but are *a priori* in that they indicate how well a generator *can* perform by looking at its structure and defining constants. Theoretical tests also differ from empirical tests in that they are *global*; i.e., a generator's behavior over its *entire* cycle is examined. As we mentioned at the end of Sec. 7.4.1, it is debatable whether local or global tests are preferable; global tests have a natural appeal but do not generally indicate how well a specific segment of a cycle will behave.

It is sometimes possible to compute the "sample" mean, variance, and correlations over an entire cycle directly from the constants defining the generator. Many of these results are quoted by Kennedy and Gentle (1980, pp. 139–143). For example, in a full-period LCG, the average of the U_i's, taken over an entire cycle, is

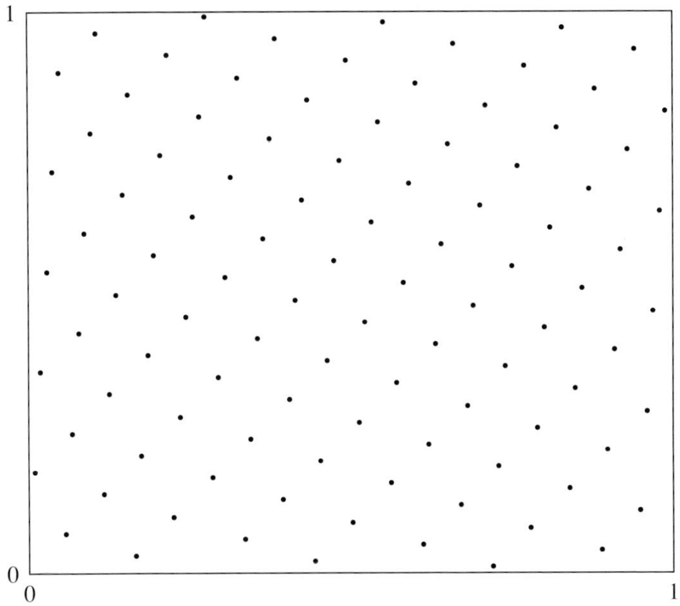

FIGURE 7.2
Two-dimensional lattice structure for the full-period LCG with $m = 101$ and $a = 18$.

$\frac{1}{2} - 1/(2m)$, which is seen to be very close to the desired $\frac{1}{2}$ if m is one of the large values (in the billions) typically used; see Prob. 7.14. Similarly, we can compute the "sample" variance of the U_i's over a full cycle and get $\frac{1}{12} - 1/(12m^2)$, which is close to $\frac{1}{12}$, the variance of the U(0, 1) distribution. Kennedy and Gentle also discuss "sample" correlations for LCGs. Although such formulas may seem comforting, they can be misleading; e.g., the result for the full-period LCG sample lag 1 correlation suggests that, to minimize this value, a be chosen close to $\sqrt{m}$, which turns out to be a poor choice from the standpoint of other important statistical considerations.

The best-known theoretical tests are based on the rather upsetting observation by Marsaglia (1968) that "random numbers fall mainly in the planes." That is, if U_1, $U_2, \ldots$ is a sequence of random numbers generated by a LCG, the overlapping d-tuples $(U_1, U_2, \ldots, U_d)$, $(U_2, U_3, \ldots, U_{d+1}), \ldots$ will all fall on a relatively small number of $(d-1)$-dimensional hyperplanes passing through the d-dimensional unit hypercube $[0, 1]^d$. For example, if $d = 2$, the pairs (U_1, U_2), $(U_2, U_3), \ldots$ will be arranged in a "lattice" fashion along several different families of parallel lines going through the unit square. The lines within a family are parallel to each other, but lines from different families are not parallel.

In Figs. 7.2 and 7.3, we display all possible pairs (U_i, U_{i+1}) for the full-period multiplicative LCGs $Z_i = 18Z_{i-1} (\text{mod } 101)$ and $Z_i = 2Z_{i-1} (\text{mod } 101)$, respectively.

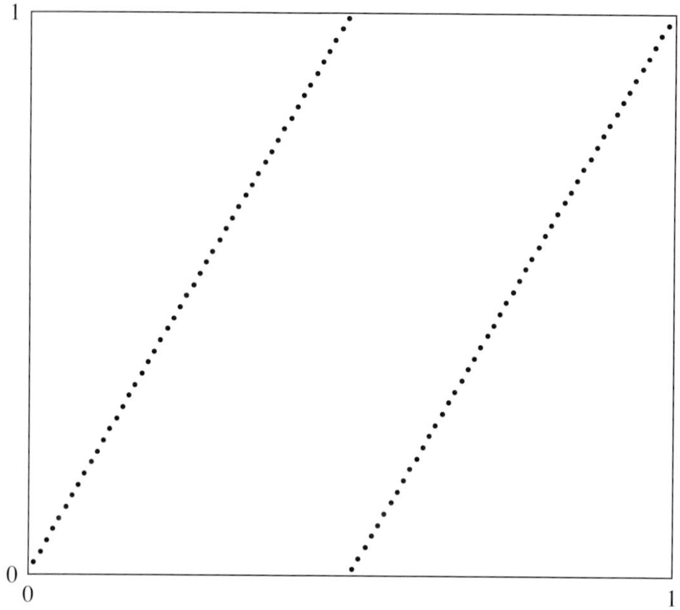

FIGURE 7.3
Two-dimensional lattice structure for the full-period LCG with $m = 101$ and $a = 2$.

(The period is 100 in each case, since the modulus $m = 101$ is prime and each value of the multiplier a is a primitive element modulo m.) While the apparent regularity in Fig. 7.2 certainly does not seem very "random," it may not be too disturbing since the pairs seem to fill up the unit square fairly well, or at least as well as could be expected with such a small modulus. On the other hand, all 100 pairs in Fig. 7.3 fall on just two parallel lines, which is definitely anxiety-provoking. Since there are large areas of the unit square where we can never realize a pair of U_i's, a simulation using such a generator would almost certainly produce invalid results.

The same difficulties occur in three dimensions. In Fig. 7.4, 2000 triples (U_i, U_{i+1}, U_{i+2}) produced by the infamous multiplicative LCG generator RANDU ($m = 2^{31}$ and $a = 65{,}539$) are displayed, viewed from a particular point outside of the unit cube. Note that all triples of U_i's fall on *only* 15 parallel planes passing through the unit cube. (In general, all the roughly half-billion triples across the period fall on these same planes.) This explains the horrific performance of RANDU on the three-dimensional serial test noted at the end of Sec. 7.4.1.

Among all families of parallel hyperplanes that cover all overlapping d-tuples $(U_i, U_{i+1}, \ldots, U_{i+d-1})$, take the one for which adjacent hyperplanes are farthest apart and denote this distance by $\delta_d(m, a)$. The idea of computing $\delta_d(m, a)$ was suggested by Coveyou and MacPherson (1967) and is typically called the *spectral test.* If $\delta_d(m, a)$ is small, then we would expect that the corresponding generator would be able to uniformly fill up the d-dimensional unit hypercube $[0, 1]^d$.

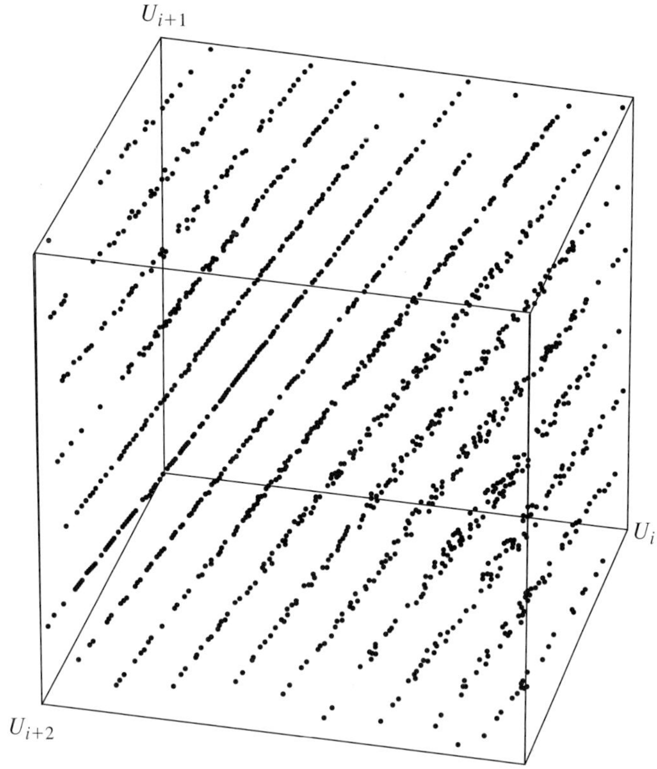

FIGURE 7.4
Three-dimensional lattice structure for 2000 triples from the multiplicative LCG RANDU with $m = 2^{31}$ and $a = 65{,}539$.

For LCGs it is possible to compute a theoretical lower bound $\delta_d^*(m)$ on $\delta_d(m, a)$, which is given by the following:

$$\delta_d(m, a) \ge \delta_d^*(m) = \frac{1}{\gamma_d m^{1/d}} \quad \text{for all } a$$

where γ_d is a constant whose exact value is known only for $d \le 8$. We can then define the following figures of merit for a LCG:

$$S_d(m, a) = \frac{\delta_d^*(m)}{\delta_d(m, a)}$$

and

$$M_8(m, a) = \min_{2 \le d \le 8} S_d(m, a)$$

These figures of merit will be between 0 and 1, with values close to 1 being desirable. Methods for performing the spectral test [i.e., for computing $\delta_d(m, a)$] are discussed by Knuth (1998a, pp. 98–104) and L'Ecuyer and Couture (1997).

TABLE 7.5
The results of the spectral test for some LCGs

Figure of merit	Generator: $m = 2^{31} - 1$, $a = a_1 = 16{,}807$	$m = 2^{31} - 1$, $a = a_2 = 630{,}360{,}016$	$m = 2^{31} - 1$, $a = 742{,}938{,}285$	$m = 2^{31}$, $a = 65{,}539$
$S_2(m, a)$	0.338	0.821	0.867	0.931
$S_3(m, a)$	0.441	0.432	0.861	0.012
$S_4(m, a)$	0.575	0.783	0.863	0.060
$S_5(m, a)$	0.736	0.802	0.832	0.157
$S_6(m, a)$	0.645	0.570	0.834	0.293
$S_7(m, a)$	0.571	0.676	0.624	0.453
$S_8(m, a)$	0.610	0.721	0.707	0.617
$M_8(m, a)$	0.338	0.432	0.624	0.012

Values of $S_d(m, a)$ and $M_8(m, a)$ are given in Table 7.5 for several well-known LCGs. The LCGs in columns 2 and 3 with multipliers a_1 and a_2 were discussed in Sec. 7.2.2, and it's seen that the latter generator is superior relative to the spectral test. The generator in column 4 with $a = 742{,}938{,}285$ was found by Fishman and Moore (1986) in an exhaustive search to be the best relative to the criterion $M_6(2^{31} - 1, a)$. Finally, in column 5 are the results of the spectral test for RANDU; its poor behavior in $d = 3$ dimensions is clearly reflected in the value $S_3(2^{31}, 65{,}539) = 0.012$.

7.4.3 Some General Observations on Testing

The number, variety, and range of complexity of tests for random-number generators are truly bewildering. To make matters worse, there has been (and probably always will be) considerable controversy over which tests are best, whether theoretical tests are really more definitive than empirical tests, and so on. Indeed, no amount of testing can ever absolutely convince everyone that some particular generator is absolutely "the best." One piece of advice that is often offered, however, is that a random-number generator should be tested in a way that is consistent with its intended use. This would entail, for example, examining the behavior of pairs of U_i's (perhaps with the two-dimensional serial test) if random numbers are naturally used in pairs in the simulation itself. In a broader sense, this advice would imply that one should be more careful in choosing and testing a random-number generator if the simulation in which it will be used is very costly, requires high-precision results, or is a particularly critical component of a larger study.

APPENDIX 7A
PORTABLE C CODE FOR A PMMLCG

Here we present computer code in C to implement the PMMLCG defined by modulus $m = m^* = 2^{31} - 1 = 2{,}147{,}483{,}647$ and multiplier $a = a_2 = 630{,}360{,}016$, discussed at the end of Sec. 7.2.2. The code shown here can be downloaded from www.mhhe.com/law. This code is based closely on the FORTRAN code of Marse and Roberts (1983), and it requires that integers between $-m^*$ and m^* be represented and computed correctly. This generator has 100 different streams that are spaced 100,000 apart.

It is generally *not* recommended that this generator be used for serious real-world applications, since the combined MRG in App. 7B has much better statistical properties.

Figure 7.5 gives code for an ANSI-standard C (i.e., using function prototyping) version of this generator, in three functions, as detailed in the comments. Figure 7.6 gives a header file (lcgrand.h) that the user must #include to declare the functions. We have used this code on a variety of computers and compilers, and it was used in the C examples in Chaps. 1 and 2.

```
/* Prime modulus multiplicative linear congruential generator
   Z[i] = (630360016 * Z[i-1]) (mod(pow(2,31) - 1)), based on Marse and Roberts'
   portable FORTRAN random-number generator UNIRAN.  Multiple (100) streams are
   supported, with seeds spaced 100,000 apart.  Throughout, input argument
   "stream" must be an int giving the desired stream number.  The header file
   lcgrand.h must be included in the calling program (#include "lcgrand.h")
   before using these functions.

   Usage: (Three functions)

   1. To obtain the next U(0,1) random number from stream "stream," execute
          u = lcgrand(stream);
      where lcgrand is a float function.  The float variable u will contain the
      next random number.

   2. To set the seed for stream "stream" to a desired value zset, execute
          lcgrandst(zset, stream);
      where lcgrandst is a void function and zset must be a long set to the
      desired seed, a number between 1 and 2147483646 (inclusive).  Default
      seeds for all 100 streams are given in the code.

   3. To get the current (most recently used) integer in the sequence being
      generated for stream "stream" into the long variable zget, execute
          zget = lcgrandgt(stream);
      where lcgrandgt is a long function. */

/* Define the constants. */

#define MODLUS 2147483647
#define MULT1       24112
#define MULT2       26143

/* Set the default seeds for all 100 streams. */
```

FIGURE 7.5
C code for the PMMLCG with $m = 2^{31} - 1$ and $a = 630{,}360{,}016$ based on Marse and Roberts (1983).

```
static long zrng[] =
{         1,
 1973272912, 281629770,  20006270,1280689831,2096730329,1933576050,
  913566091, 246780520,1363774876, 604901985,1511192140,1259851944,
  824064364, 150493284, 242708531,  75253171,1964472944,1202299975,
  233217322,1911216000, 726370533, 403498145, 993232223,1103205531,
  762430696,1922803170,1385516923,  76271663, 413682397, 726466604,
  336157058,1432650381,1120463904, 595778810, 877722890,1046574445,
   68911991,2088367019, 748545416, 622401386,2122378830, 640690903,
 1774806513,2132545692,2079249579,  78130110, 852776735,1187867272,
 1351423507,1645973084,1997049139, 922510944,2045512870, 898585771,
  243649545,1004818771, 773686062, 403188473, 372279877,1901633463,
  498067494,2087759558, 493157915, 597104727,1530940798,1814496276,
  536444882,1663153658, 855503735,  67784357,1432404475, 619691088,
  119025595, 880802310, 176192644,1116780070, 277854671,1366580350,
 1142483975,2026948561,1053920743, 786262391,1792203830,1494667770,
 1923011392,1433700034,1244184613,1147297105, 539712780,1545929719,
  190641742,1645390429, 264907697, 620389253,1502074852, 927711160,
  364849192,2049576050, 638580085, 547070247 };
/* Generate the next random number. */

float lcgrand(int stream)
{
    long zi, lowprd, hi31;

    zi     = zrng[stream];
    lowprd = (zi & 65535) * MULT1;
    hi31   = (zi >> 16) * MULT1 + (lowprd >> 16);
    zi     = ((lowprd & 65535) - MODLUS) +
             ((hi31 & 32767) << 16) + (hi31 >> 15);
    if (zi < 0) zi += MODLUS;
    lowprd = (zi & 65535) * MULT2;
    hi31   = (zi >> 16) * MULT2 + (lowprd >> 16);
    zi     = ((lowprd & 65535) - MODLUS) +
             ((hi31 & 32767) << 16) + (hi31 >> 15);
    if (zi < 0) zi += MODLUS;
    zrng[stream] = zi;
    return (zi >> 7 | 1) / 16777216.0;
}


void lcgrandst (long zset, int stream) /* Set the current zrng for stream
                                          "stream" to zset. */
{
    zrng[stream] = zset;
}


long lcgrandgt (int stream) /* Return the current zrng for stream "stream". */
{
    return zrng[stream];
}
```

FIGURE 7.5
(*continued*)

```
/* The following 3 declarations are for use of the random-number generator
   lcgrand and the associated functions lcgrandst and lcgrandgt for seed
   management.  This file (named lcgrand.h) should be included in any program
   using these functions by executing
       #include "lcgrand.h"
   before referencing the functions. */

float lcgrand(int stream);
void  lcgrandst(long zset, int stream);
long  lcgrandgt(int stream);
```

FIGURE 7.6
C header file (lcgrand.h) to accompany the C code in Fig. 7.5.

APPENDIX 7B
PORTABLE C CODE FOR A COMBINED MRG

Here we present an ANSI-standard C function, mrand, that implements the combined MRG specified in Sec. 7.3.2, taken from L'Ecuyer (1999a), and which supports multiple streams (up to 10,000) with seed vectors spaced 10^{16} (ten quadrillion) apart. This code requires that all integers between -2^{53} and 2^{53} be represented exactly in floating point, which will be satisfied in the (common) situation of a 32-bit word-length machine and a C compiler that conforms to the IEEE standard for floating-point storage and arithmetic. All codes shown here can be downloaded from www.mhhe.com/law.

Figure 7.7 gives the code for this generator, in three functions, as described in the comments in the code. Figure 7.8 gives a header file (mrand.h) that the user must #include before the main function in the calling program. Figure 7.9 gives the first 23 and last 4 lines (showing the seed vectors for streams 1–20 and 9998–10,000) of the file mrand_seeds.h, which contains seed vectors for the 10,000 streams spaced 10^{16}

```
/* Combined MRG from Sec. 7.3.2, from L'Ecuyer (1999a).  Multiple
   (10,000) streams are supported, with seed vectors spaced
   10,000,000,000,000,000 apart.  Throughout, input argument "stream"
   must be an int giving the desired stream number.  The header file
   mrand_seeds.h is included here, so must be available in the
   appropriate directory.  The header file mrand.h must be included in
   the calling program (#include "mrand.h") before using these
   functions.

   Usage: (Three functions)

   1. To obtain the next U(0,1) random number from stream "stream,"
      execute
          u = mrand(stream);
      where mrand is a double function.  The double variable u will
      contain the next random number.

   2. To set the seed vector for stream "stream" to a desired 6-vector,
      execute
          mrandst(zset, stream);
      where mrandst is a void function and zset must be a double
      vector with positions 0 through 5 set to the desired
      stream 6-vector, as described in Sec. 7.3.2.

   3. To get the current (most recently used) 6-vector of integers in
      the sequences (to use, e.g., as the seed for a subsequent
      independent replication), into positions 0 through 5 of the
      double vector zget, execute
          mrandgt(zget, stream);
      where mrandgt is void function.  */

#include "mrand_seeds.h"
#define norm   2.328306549295728e-10  /* 1.0/(m1+1) */
#define norm2  2.328318825240738e-10  /* 1.0/(m2+1) */
#define m1     4294967087.0
#define m2     4294944443.0

/* Generate the next random number. */
```

FIGURE 7.7
C code for the combined MRG specified in Sec. 7.3.2, based on L'Ecuyer (1999a).

```
double mrand(int stream)
{
    long k;
    double p,
           s10 = drng[stream][0], s11 = drng[stream][1], s12 = drng[stream][2],
           s20 = drng[stream][3], s21 = drng[stream][4], s22 = drng[stream][5];

    p = 1403580.0 * s11 - 810728.0 * s10;
    k = p / m1;  p -= k*m1;  if (p < 0.0) p += m1;
    s10 = s11;   s11 = s12;  s12 = p;

    p = 527612.0 * s22 - 1370589.0 * s20;
    k = p / m2;  p -= k*m2;  if (p < 0.0) p += m2;
    s20 = s21;   s21 = s22;  s22 = p;

    drng[stream][0] = s10;  drng[stream][1] = s11;  drng[stream][2] = s12;
    drng[stream][3] = s20;  drng[stream][4] = s21;  drng[stream][5] = s22;

    if (s12 <= s22) return ((s12 - s22 + m1) * norm);
    else return ((s12 - s22) * norm);
}

/* Set seed vector for stream "stream". */

void mrandst(double* seed, int stream)
{
int i;
    for (i = 0; i <= 5; ++i) drng[stream][i] = seed[i];
}

/* Get seed vector for stream "stream". */

void mrandgt(double* seed, int stream)
{
int i;
    for (i = 0; i <= 5; ++i) seed[i] = drng[stream][i];
}
```

FIGURE 7.7
(*continued*)

```
/* Header file "mrand.h" to be included by programs using mrand.c */

double mrand(int stream);
void mrandst(double* seed, int stream);
void mrandgt(double* seed, int stream);
```

FIGURE 7.8
C header file (mrand.h) to accompany the C code in Fig. 7.7.

apart. We have used these codes on a variety of computers and compilers successfully, though some compilers might issue harmless warnings about the size of the numbers in mrand.h (such warnings can usually be turned off by a compiler switch like -w on some UNIX C compilers). Also, the calling program might have to load a mathematical library (e.g., the -lm switch on UNIX C compilers).

Codes for this generator in C, C++, and Java, which allow for substreams (see Sec. 7.3.2), can be downloaded from www.iro.umontreal.ca/~lecuyer. [See also L'Ecuyer, Simard, Chen, and Kelton (2002).]

```
/* Header file "mrand_seeds.h" included by mrand.c */

static double drng[][6] =
{
          0,           0,           1,           0,           0,           1,
 1772212344,  1374954571,  2377447708,   540628578,  1843308759,   549575061,
 2602294560,  1764491502,  3872775590,  4089362440,  2683806282,   437563332,
  376810349,  1545165407,  3443838735,  3650079346,  1898051052,  2606578666,
 1847817841,  3038743716,  2014183350,  2883836363,  3242147124,  1955620878,
 1075987441,  3468627582,  2694529948,   368150488,  2026479331,  2067041056,
  134547324,  4246812979,  1700384422,  2358888058,    83616724,  3045736624,
 2816844169,   885735878,  1824365395,  2629582008,  3405363962,  1835381773,
  675808621,   434584068,  4021752986,  3831444678,  4193349505,  2833414845,
 2876117643,  1466108979,   163986545,  1530526354,    68578399,  1111539974,
  411040508,   544377427,  2887694751,   702892456,   758163486,  2462939166,
 3631741414,  3388407961,  1205439229,   581001230,  3728119407,    94602786,
 4267066799,  3221182590,  2432930550,   813784585,  1980232156,  2376040999,
 1601564418,  2988901653,  4114588926,  2447029331,  4071707675,  3696447685,
 3878417653,  2549122180,  1351098226,  3888036970,  1344540382,  2430069028,
  197118588,  1885407936,   576504243,   439732583,   103559440,  3361573194,
 4024454184,  2530169746,  2135879297,  2516366026,   260078159,  2905856966,
 2331743881,  2059737664,   186644977,   401315249,    72328980,  1082588425,
  694808921,  2851138195,  1756125381,  1738505503,  2662188364,  3598740668,
 2834735415,  2017577369,  3257393066,  3823680297,  2315410613,   637316697,
 4132025555,  3700940887,   838767760,  2818574268,  1375004287,  2172829019,
.
.
.
  560024289,  1830276631,   144885590,  1556615741,  1597610225,  1856413969,
 1031792556,  1844191084,  1441357589,  3147919604,   199001354,  2555043119,
 2023049680,  4184669824,  4074523931,   252765086,  3328098427,  1480103038
};
```

FIGURE 7.9
Excerpt from seed-vector file (mrand_seeds.h) to accompany the C codes in Figs. 7.7 and 7.8 (complete file can be downloaded from www.mhhe.com/law).

PROBLEMS

7.1. For the LCG of Example 7.2 find Z_{500}, using only pencil and paper.

7.2. For the following multiplicative LCGs, compute Z_i for enough values of $i \geq 1$ to cover an entire cycle:
(*a*) $Z_i - (11Z_{i-1})(\text{mod } 16), Z_0 = 1$
(*b*) $Z_i = (11Z_{i-1})(\text{mod } 16), Z_0 = 2$
(*c*) $Z_i = (2Z_{i-1})(\text{mod } 13), Z_0 = 1$
(*d*) $Z_i = (3Z_{i-1})(\text{mod } 13), Z_0 = 1$

Note that (*a*) and (*b*) have m of the form 2^b; (*c*) is a PMMLCG, for which $a = 2$ is a primitive element modulo $m = 13$.

7.3. Without actually computing any Z_i's, determine which of the following mixed LCGs have full period:
(*a*) $Z_i = (13Z_{i-1} + 13)(\text{mod } 16)$
(*b*) $Z_i = (12Z_{i-1} + 13)(\text{mod } 16)$
(*c*) $Z_i = (13Z_{i-1} + 12)(\text{mod } 16)$
(*d*) $Z_i = (Z_{i-1} + 12)(\text{mod } 13)$

7.4. For the four mixed LCGs in Prob. 7.3, compute Z_i for enough values of $i \geq 1$ to cover an entire cycle; let $Z_0 = 1$ in each case. Comment on the results.

7.5. (*a*) Implement the PMMLCG $Z_i = 630{,}360{,}016Z_{i-1} (\bmod 2^{31} - 1)$ on your computer, using the Marse-Roberts code in App. 7A.

(*b*) Repeat the empirical tests of Examples 7.6 through 7.9 with this generator, and compare your results with those given in the examples.

7.6. Use the multiplicative LCG in part (*a*) of Prob. 7.2 to shuffle the output from the mixed LCG in part (*d*) of Prob. 7.3, using a vector **V** of length 2. Let the seed for both LCGs be 1, and list the first 100 values of **V**, I, and V_I. Identify the period and comment generally on the results.

7.7. For the chi-square test of uniformity, verify the following algorithm for computing $f_1, f_2, \ldots, f_k$:

```
Set f_j = 0 for j = 1,2, . . . , k
For i = 1, . . . , n do
    Generate U_i
    Set J = ⌈kU_i⌉
    Replace f_J by f_J + 1
End do
```

(For a real number x, $\lceil x \rceil$ denotes the smallest integer that is greater than or equal to x.) Generalize this algorithm to compute the test statistic for a general d-dimensional serial test.

7.8. Show that the following algorithm correctly computes $r_1, r_2, \ldots, r_6$ for the runs-up test, from the generated numbers $U_1, U_2, \ldots, U_n$:

```
Set r_j = 0 for j = 1, . . . , 6
Generate U_1, set A = U_1, and set J = 1
For i = 2, . . . , n do
    Generate U_i and set B = U_i
    If A ≥ B then
        Set J = min(J,6)
        Replace r_J by r_J + 1
        Set J = 1
    Else
        Replace J by J + 1
    End if
    Replace A by B
End do
Set J = min(J,6)
Replace r_J by r_J + 1
```

7.9. Subject the canned random-number generator on your computer to the chi-square test, two- and three-dimensional serial tests, the runs-up test, and correlation tests at lags $1, 2, \ldots, 5$. Use the same values for n, k, and α that were used in Examples 7.6 through 7.9. (If your generator does not pass these tests, we suggest that you exercise caution in using it until you can obtain more information on it, either from the literature or from your own further testing.)

7.10. A general approach to testing a random-number generator empirically is to use it to simulate a *simple* stochastic model and obtain estimates of *known* parameters; a standard test is then used to compare the estimate(s) against the known parameter(s). For example, we know that in throwing two fair dice independently, the sum of the two outcomes will be 2, 3, . . . , 12 with respective probabilities $\frac{1}{36}$, $\frac{1}{18}$, $\frac{1}{12}$, $\frac{1}{9}$, $\frac{5}{36}$, $\frac{1}{6}$, $\frac{5}{36}$, $\frac{1}{9}$, $\frac{1}{12}$, $\frac{1}{18}$, and $\frac{1}{36}$. Simulate 1000 independent throws of a pair of independent fair dice, and compare the observed proportion of 2s, 3s, . . . , 12s with the known probabilities, using an appropriate test from Chap. 6. Use the canned generator on your computer or one of the generators in App. 7A or 7B.

7.11. For the LCG in part (*d*) of Prob. 7.3, plot the pairs (U_1, U_2), (U_2, U_3), . . . and observe the lattice structure obtained. Note that this LCG has full period.

7.12. Consider the Fibonacci generator discussed in Sec. 7.3.1.

(*a*) Show that this generator can never produce the following arrangement of three consecutive output values: $U_{i-2} < U_i < U_{i-1}$.

(*b*) Show that the arrangement in (*a*) should occur with probability $\frac{1}{6}$ for a "perfect" random-number generator.

This points out a gross defect in the generator, as noted by Bratley, Fox, and Schrage (1987), who credit U. Dieter with having noticed this.

7.13. Suppose that $U_1, U_2, \ldots, U_k$ are IID U(0, 1) random variables. Show that the fractional part (i.e., ignoring anything to the left of the decimal point) of $U_1 + U_2 + \cdots + U_k$ is also uniformly distributed on the interval [0, 1]. [This property motivated the composite generator of Wichmann and Hill (1982).]

7.14. Show that the average of the U_i's taken over an entire cycle of a full-period LCG is $\frac{1}{2} - 1/(2m)$. [*Hint:* for a positive integer k, *Euler's formula* states that $1 + 2 + \cdots + k = k(k + 1)/2$.]

7.15. For Example 7.3, use Eq. (7.6) to show that the period of the W_i's is 31.

CHAPTER 8

Generating Random Variates

Recommended sections for a first reading: 8.1 and 8.2

8.1 INTRODUCTION

A simulation that has any random aspects at all must involve sampling, or *generating*, random variates from probability distributions. As in Chap. 7, we use the phrase "generating a random variate" to refer to the activity of obtaining an observation on (or a realization of) a random variable from the desired distribution. These distributions are often specified as a result of fitting some appropriate distributional form, e.g., exponential, gamma, or Poisson, to observed data, as discussed in Chap. 6. In this chapter we assume that a distribution has already been specified somehow (including the values of the parameters), and we address the issue of how we can generate random variates with this distribution in order to run the simulation model. For example, the queueing-type models discussed in Sec. 1.4 and Chap. 2 required generation of interarrival and service times to drive the simulation through time, and the inventory model of Sec. 1.5 needed randomly generated demand sizes at the times when a demand occurred.

As we shall see in this chapter, the basic ingredient needed for *every* method of generating random variates from *any* distribution or random process is a source of IID U(0, 1) random variates. For this reason it is essential that a statistically reliable U(0, 1) random-number generator be available. Most computer installations and simulation packages have a convenient random-number generator but some of them (especially the older ones) do not perform adequately (see Chap. 7). Without an acceptable random-number generator, it is impossible to generate random variates correctly from any distribution. In the rest of this chapter, we therefore assume that a good source of random numbers is available.

There are usually several alternative algorithms that can be used for generating random variates from a given distribution, and several factors should be considered when choosing which algorithm to use in a particular simulation study. Unfortunately, these different factors often conflict with each other, so the analyst's judgment of which algorithm to use must involve a number of tradeoffs. All we can do here is raise some of the pertinent questions.

The first issue is *exactness*. We feel that, if possible, one should use an algorithm that results in random variates with exactly the desired distribution, within the unavoidable external limitations of machine accuracy and exactness of the U(0, 1) random-number generator. Efficient and exact algorithms are now available for all of the commonly used distributions, obviating the need to consider any older, approximate methods. [Many of these approximations, e.g., the well-known technique of obtaining a "normal" random variate as 6 less than the sum of 12 U(0, 1) random variates, are based on the central limit theorem.] On the other hand, the practitioner may argue that a specified distribution is really only an approximation to reality anyway, so that an approximate generation method should suffice; since this depends on the situation and is often difficult to quantify, we still prefer to use an exact method.

Given that we have a choice, then, of alternative exact algorithms, we would clearly like to use one that is *efficient*, in terms of both storage space and execution time. Some algorithms require *storage* of a large number of constants or of large tables, which could prove troublesome or at least inconvenient. As for execution time, there are really two factors. Obviously, we hope that we can accomplish the generation of each random variate in a small amount of time; this is called the *marginal execution time*. Second, some algorithms have to do some initial computing to specify constants or tables that depend on the particular distribution and parameters; the time required to do this is called the *setup time*. In most simulations, we shall be generating a large number of random variates from a given distribution, so that marginal execution time is likely to be more important than setup time. If the parameters of a distribution change often or randomly during the course of the simulation, however, setup time could become an important consideration.

A somewhat subjective issue in choosing an algorithm is its overall *complexity*, including conceptual as well as implementational factors. One must ask whether the potential gain in efficiency that might be experienced by using a more complicated algorithm is worth the extra effort to understand and implement it. This issue should be considered relative to the purpose in implementing a method for random-variate generation; a more efficient but more complex algorithm might be appropriate for use as permanent software but not for a "one-time" simulation model.

Finally, there are a few issues of a more technical nature. Some algorithms rely on a source of random variates from distributions other than U(0, 1), which is undesirable, other things being equal. Another technical issue is that a given algorithm may be efficient for some parameter values but costly for others. We would like to have algorithms that are efficient for all parameter values (sometimes called *robustness* of the algorithm); see Devroye (1988). One last technical point is relevant if we want to use certain kinds of variance-reduction techniques in order to obtain better (less variable) estimates (see Chap. 11 and also Chaps. 10 and 12). Two commonly used variance-reduction techniques (common random numbers and antithetic variates) require synchronization of the basic U(0, 1) input random variates used in the simulation of the system(s) under study, and this synchronization is more easily accomplished for certain types of random-variate generation algorithms. In particular, the general inverse-transform approach can be very helpful in facilitating the desired synchronization and variance reduction; Sec. 8.2.1 treats this point more precisely.

There are a number of comprehensive references on random-variate generation, including Dagpunar (1988), Devroye (1986), Fishman (1996), Gentle (2010), Hörmann et al. (2004), and Johnson (1987). There are also several computer packages that provide good capabilities for generating random variates from a wide variety of distributions, such as the IMSL routines [Rogue Wave (2013)] and the C codes in secs. 7.1 and 7.3 of Press et al. (2007).

The remainder of this chapter is organized as follows. In Sec. 8.2 we survey the most important general approaches for random-variate generation, including examples and general discussions of the relative merits of the various approaches. In Secs. 8.3 and 8.4 we present algorithms for generating random variates from particular continuous and discrete distributions that have been found useful in simulation. Finally, in Secs. 8.5 and 8.6 we discuss two more specialized topics: generating correlated random variates and generating realizations of both stationary and non-stationary arrival processes.

8.2 GENERAL APPROACHES TO GENERATING RANDOM VARIATES

There are many techniques for generating random variates, and the particular algorithm used must, of course, depend on the distribution from which we wish to generate; however, nearly all these techniques can be classified according to their theoretical basis. In this section we discuss these general approaches.

8.2.1 Inverse Transform

Suppose that we wish to generate a random variate X that is continuous (see Sec. 4.2) and has distribution function F that is continuous and strictly increasing when $0 < F(x) < 1$. [This means that if $x_1 < x_2$ and $0 < F(x_1) \leq F(x_2) < 1$, then in fact $F(x_1) < F(x_2)$.] Let F^{-1} denote the inverse of the function F. Then an algorithm for generating a random variate X having distribution function F is as follows (recall that $\sim$ is read "is distributed as"):

1. Generate $U \sim$ U(0, 1).
2. Return $X = F^{-1}(U)$.

Note that $F^{-1}(U)$ will always be defined, since $0 \leq U \leq 1$ and the range of F is [0, 1]. Figure 8.1 illustrates the algorithm graphically, where the random variable

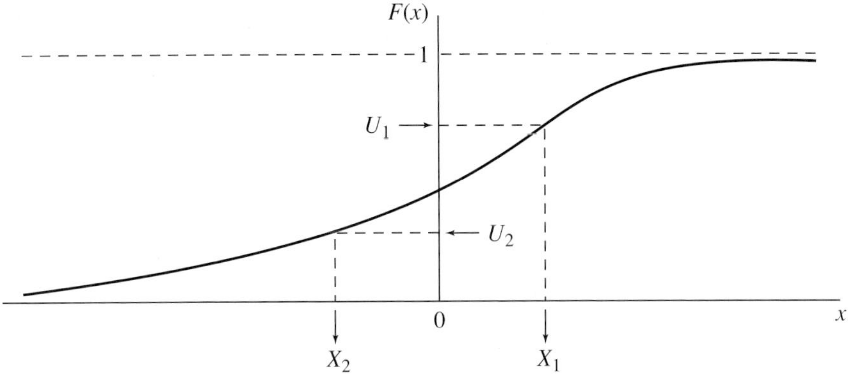

FIGURE 8.1
Inverse-transform method for continuous random variables.

corresponding to this distribution function can take on either positive or negative values; the particular value of U determines which will be the case. In the figure, the random number U_1 results in the positive random variate X_1, while the random number U_2 leads to the negative variate X_2.

To show that the value X returned by the above algorithm, called the general *inverse-transform method*, has the desired distribution F, we must show that for any real number x, $P(X \leq x) = F(x)$. Since F is invertible, we have

$$P(X \leq x) = P(F^{-1}(U) \leq x) = P(U \leq F(x)) = F(x)$$

where the last equality follows since $U \sim U(0, 1)$ and $0 \leq F(x) \leq 1$. (See the discussion of the uniform distribution in Sec. 6.2.2.)

EXAMPLE 8.1. Let X have the exponential distribution with mean β (see Sec. 6.2.2). The distribution function is

$$F(x) = \begin{cases} 1 - e^{-x/\beta} & \text{if } x \geq 0 \\ 0 & \text{otherwise} \end{cases}$$

so to find F^{-1}, we set $u = F(x)$ and solve for x to obtain

$$F^{-1}(u) = -\beta \ln (1 - u)$$

Thus, to generate the desired random variate, we first generate a $U \sim U(0, 1)$ and then let $X = -\beta \ln U$. [It is possible in this case to use U instead of $1 - U$, since $1 - U$ and U have the same U(0, 1) distribution. This saves a subtraction.]

In the above example, we replaced $1 - U$ by U for the sake of a perhaps minor gain in efficiency. However, replacing $1 - U$ by U in situations like this results in negative correlation of the X's with the U's, rather than positive correlation. Also, it is not true that wherever a "$1 - U$" appears in a variate-generation algorithm it can be replaced by a "U," as illustrated in Sec. 8.3.15.

The inverse-transform method's validity in the continuous case was demonstrated mathematically above, but there is also a strong intuitive appeal. The density function $f(x)$ of a continuous random variable may be interpreted as the relative chance of observing variates on different parts of the range; on regions of the x axis above which $f(x)$ is high we expect to observe a lot of variates, and where $f(x)$ is low we should find only a few. For example, Fig. 8.2*b* shows the density function for the Weibull distribution with shape parameter $\alpha = 1.5$ and scale parameter $\beta = 6$ (see Sec. 6.2.2 for definition of this distribution), and we would expect that many generated variates would fall between, say, $x = 2$ and $x = 5$, but not many between 13 and 16. Figure 8.2*a* shows the corresponding distribution function, $F(x)$. Since the density is the derivative of the distribution function [that is, $f(x) = F'(x)$], we can view $f(x)$ as the "slope function" of $F(x)$; that is, $f(x)$ is the slope of F at x. Thus, F rises most steeply for values of x where $f(x)$ is large (e.g., for x between 2 and 5), and, conversely, F is relatively flat in regions where $f(x)$ is small (e.g., for x between 13 and 16). Now, the inverse-transform method says to take the random number U, which should be evenly (uniformly) spread on the interval [0, 1] on the vertical axis of the plot for $F(x)$, and "read across and down." More U's will hit the steep parts of $F(x)$ than the flat parts, thus concentrating the X's under those regions where $F(x)$ is steep—which are precisely those regions where $f(x)$ is high. The interval [0.25, 0.30] on the vertical axis in Fig. 8.2*a* should contain about 5 percent of the U's, which lead to X's in the relatively narrow region [2.6, 3.0] on the x axis; thus, about 5 percent of the X's will be in this region. On the other hand, the interval [0.93, 0.98] on the vertical axis, which is the same size as [0.25, 0.30] and thus contains about 5 percent of the U's as well, leads to X's in the large interval [11.5, 14.9] on the x axis; here we will also find about 5 percent of the X's, but spread out sparsely over a much larger interval.

Figure 8.3 shows the algorithm in action, with 50 X's being generated (using the random-number generator from App. 7A with stream 1). The U's are plotted on the vertical axis of Fig. 8.3*a*, and the X's corresponding to them are obtained by following the dashed lines across and down. Note that the U's on the vertical axis are fairly evenly spread, but the X's on the horizontal axis are indeed more dense where the density function $f(x)$ is high, and become more spread out where $f(x)$ is low. Thus, the inverse-transform method essentially deforms the uniform distribution of the U's to result in a distribution of the X's in accordance with the desired density.

The inverse-transform method can also be used when X is discrete. Here the distribution function is

$$F(x) = P(X \le x) = \sum_{x_i \le x} p(x_i)$$

where $p(x_i)$ is the probability mass function

$$p(x_i) = P(X = x_i)$$

(We assume that X can take on only the values $x_1, x_2, \ldots$ where $x_1 < x_2 < \cdots$.) Then the algorithm is as follows:

1. Generate $U \sim U(0, 1)$.
2. Determine the smallest positive integer I such that $U \le F(x_I)$, and return $X = x_I$.

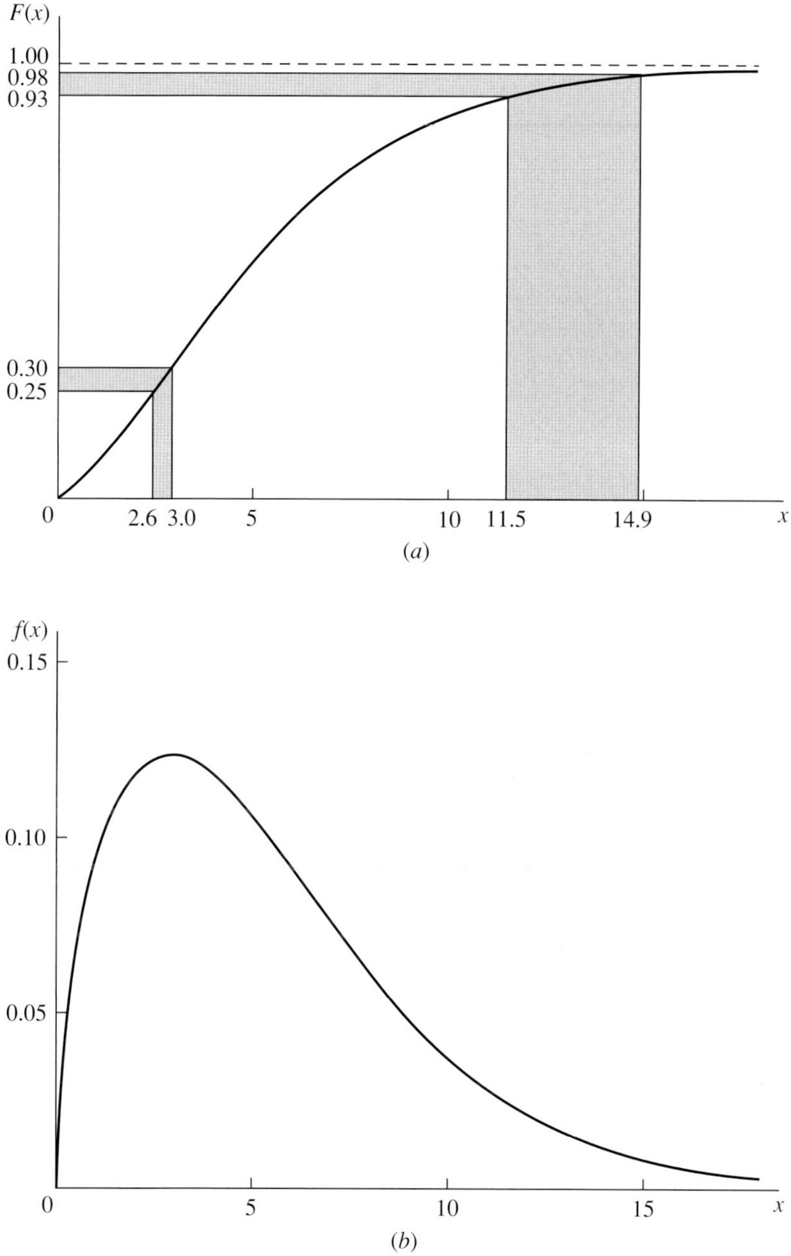

FIGURE 8.2
(*a*) Intervals for *U* and *X*, inverse transform for Weibull(1.5, 6) distribution;
(*b*) density for Weibull(1.5, 6) distribution.

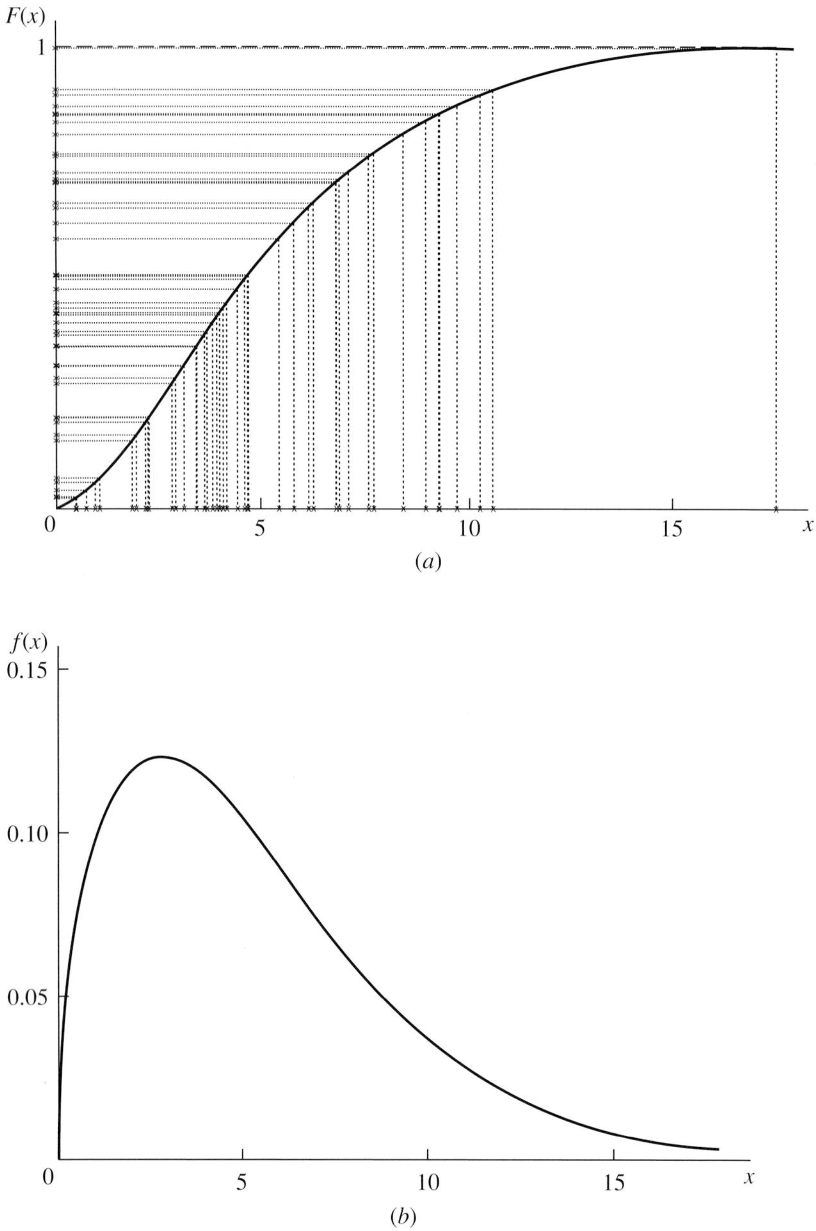

FIGURE 8.3
(*a*) Sample of 50 *U*'s and *X*'s, inverse transform for Weibull(1.5, 6) distribution; (*b*) density for Weibull(1.5, 6) distribution.

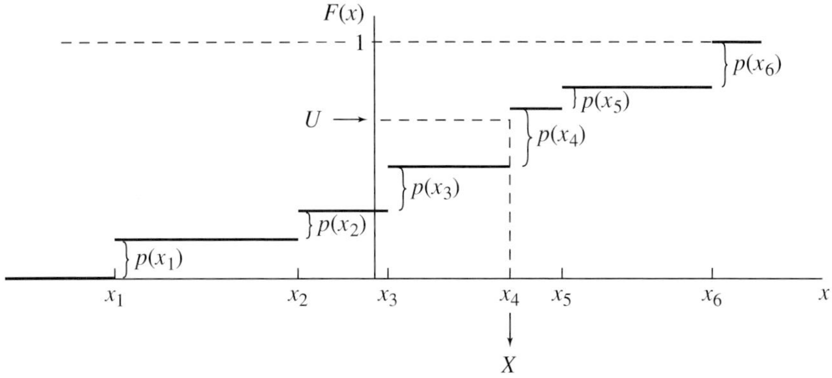

FIGURE 8.4
Inverse-transform method for discrete random variables.

Figure 8.4 illustrates the method, where we generate $X = x_4$ in this case. Although this algorithm might not seem related to the inverse-transform method for continuous random variates, the similarity between Figs. 8.1 and 8.4 is apparent.

To verify that the discrete inverse-transform method is valid, we need to show that $P(X = x_i) = p(x_i)$ for all i. For $i = 1$, we get $X = x_1$ if and only if $U \le F(x_1) = p(x_1)$, since we have arranged the x_i's in increasing order. Since $U \sim \text{U}(0, 1)$, $P(X = x_1) = p(x_1)$, as desired. For $i \ge 2$, the algorithm sets $X = x_i$ if and only if $F(x_{i-1}) < U \le F(x_i)$, since the i chosen by the algorithm is the smallest positive integer such that $U \le F(x_i)$. Further, since $U \sim \text{U}(0, 1)$ and $0 \le F(x_{i-1}) < F(x_i) \le 1$,

$$P(X = x_i) = P[F(x_{i-1}) < U \le F(x_i)] = F(x_i) - F(x_{i-1})(= p(x_i)$$

EXAMPLE 8.2. Recall the inventory example of Sec. 1.5, where the demand-size random variable X is discrete, taking on the values 1, 2, 3, 4 with respective probabilities $\frac{1}{6}$, $\frac{1}{3}$, $\frac{1}{3}$, $\frac{1}{6}$; the distribution function F is given in Fig. 4.2. To generate an X, first generate $U \sim \text{U}(0, 1)$ and set X to either 1, 2, 3, or 4, depending on the subinterval in [0, 1] into which U falls. If $U \le \frac{1}{6}$, then let $X = 1$; if $\frac{1}{6} < U \le \frac{1}{2}$, let $X = 2$; if $\frac{1}{2} < U \le \frac{5}{6}$, let $X = 3$; finally, if $\frac{5}{6} < U$, let $X = 4$.

Although both Fig. 8.4 and Example 8.2 deal with discrete random variables taking on only finitely many values, the discrete inverse-transform method can also be used directly as stated to generate random variates with an infinite range, e.g., the Poisson, geometric, or negative binomial.

The discrete inverse-transform method, when written as in Example 8.2, is really quite intuitive. We split the unit interval into contiguous subintervals of width $p(x_1), p(x_2), \ldots$ and assign X according to whichever of these subintervals contains the generated U. For example, U will fall in the second subinterval with probability $p(x_2)$, in which case we let $X = x_2$. The efficiency of the algorithm will depend on how we look for the subinterval that contains a given U. The simplest approach would be to start at the left and move up; first check whether $U \le p(x_1)$, in which case we return $X = x_1$. If $U > p(x_1)$, check whether $U \le p(x_1) + p(x_2)$, in which case we return $X = x_2$, etc. The number of comparisons needed to determine a value for X is thus dependent on U and the $p(x_i)$'s. If, for example, the first several $p(x_i)$'s are very small, the probability is high that we will have to do a large number of comparisons before the algorithm terminates. This suggests that we might be well advised to perform this search in a more sophisticated manner, using appropriate sorting and searching techniques from the computer-science literature [see, for example, Knuth (1998b)]. One simple improvement would be first to check whether U lies in the widest subinterval, since this would be the single most-likely case. If not, we would check the second widest subinterval, etc. This method would be particularly useful when some $p(x_i)$ values are considerably greater than others and there are many x_i's; see Prob. 8.2 for more on this idea. See also Chen and Asau (1974) and Fishman and Moore (1984) for very efficient search methods using the idea of *indexing*.

Generalization, Advantages, and Disadvantages of the Inverse-Transform Method

Both the continuous and discrete versions of the inverse-transform method can be combined, at least formally, into the more general form

$$X = \min\{x: F(x) \geq U\}$$

which has the added advantage of being valid for distributions that are *mixed*, i.e., have both continuous and discrete components, as well as for continuous distribution functions with flat spots. To check that the above is valid in the continuous case, note in Fig. 8.1 that the set $\{x: F(x) \geq U_1\}$ is the interval $[X_1, \infty)$, which has minimum X_1. In the discrete case, we see in Fig. 8.4 that $\{x: F(x) \geq U\} = [x_4, \infty)$, which has minimum x_4. Figure 8.5 shows a mixed distribution with two jump

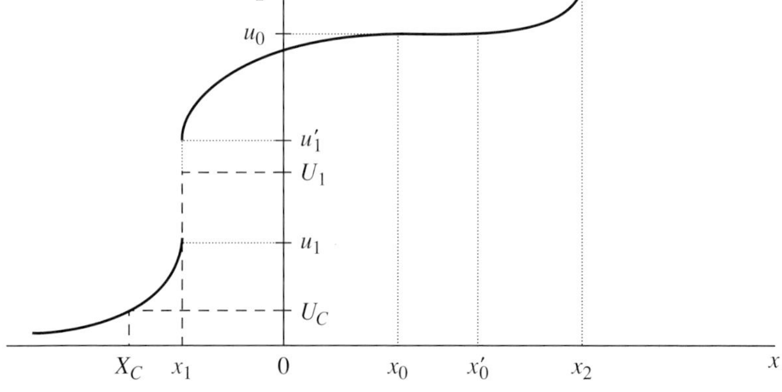

FIGURE 8.5
Inverse-transform method for a mixed distribution.

discontinuities and a flat spot; in this case the associated random variable X should satisfy $P(X = x_1) = u_1' - u_1$ (jump at x_1), $P(X = x_2) = u_2' - u_2$ (jump at x_2), and $P(x_0 \leq X \leq x_0') = 0$ (flat spot between x_0 and x_0'). For the continuous component, note that

$$X = \min\{x\colon F(x) \geq U_C\} = \min[X_C, \infty) = X_C$$

as expected. For the jump discontinuity at x_1, we get, for $u_1 \leq U_1 \leq u_1'$,

$$X = \min\{x\colon F(x) \geq U_1\} = \min[x_1, \infty) = x_1$$

which will occur with probability $u_1' - u_1$, as desired; the jump at x_2 is similar. For the flat spot, we will generate a variate X in (x_0, x_0') only if we generate a random number U that is *equal* to u_0; as U represents a continuous random variable, this occurs with probability 0, although in practice the finite accuracy of the generated random number U could result in $U = u_0$. Thus, this more general statement of the inverse-transform method handles any continuous, discrete, or mixed distribution. How it is actually implemented, though, will of course depend heavily on the distribution desired.

Let us now consider some general advantages and disadvantages of the inverse-transform method in both the continuous and discrete cases. One possible impediment to use of this method in the continuous case is the need to evaluate $F^{-1}(U)$. Since we might not be able to write a formula for F^{-1} in closed form for the desired distribution (e.g., the normal and gamma distributions), simple use of the method, as in Example 8.1, might not be possible. However, even if F^{-1} does not have a simple closed-form expression, we might be able to use numerical methods, e.g., a power-series expansion, to evaluate F^{-1}. (See, e.g., the discussion in Sec. 8.3 concerning the generation of gamma, normal, and beta random variates.) These numerical methods can yield arbitrary accuracy, so in particular can match the accuracy inherent in machine roundoff error; in this sense, they are exact for all practical purposes. However, Devroye (1986, pp. 31–35) points out that it may be difficult to specify an acceptable stopping rule for some distributions, especially those whose range is infinite. Kennedy and Gentle (1980, chap. 5) provide a comprehensive survey of numerical methods for computing distribution functions and their inverses; see also Abramowitz and Stegun (1964, chap. 26) and Press et al. (2007, chap. 6). The IMSL library [Rogue Wave (2013)] includes routines to compute most of the common distribution functions and their inverses, using carefully chosen algorithms. As an alternative to approximating F^{-1} numerically, Marsaglia (1984) proposes that a function g be found that is "close" to F^{-1} and is easy to evaluate; then X is generated as $g(Y)$, where Y has a particular distribution that is "close" to U(0, 1). Marsaglia called this method the *exact-approximation method* [see also Fishman (1996, pp. 185–187)].

Hörmann and Leydold (2003) proposed a general adaptive method for constructing a highly accurate Hermite interpolation for F^{-1} in the case of continuous distributions. Based on a one-time setup, their method produces moderate-size tables for the interpolation points and coefficients. Generating random variates using these tables is then very fast. The code for their method is available in a public-domain library called UNURAN.

A second potential disadvantage is that for a given distribution the inverse-transform method may not be the fastest way to generate the corresponding random variate; in Secs. 8.3 and 8.4 we discuss the efficiency of alternative algorithms for each distribution considered.

Despite these possible drawbacks, there are some important advantages in using the inverse-transform method. The first is to facilitate variance-reduction techniques (see Chap. 11) that rely on inducing correlation between random variates; examples of such techniques are common random numbers and antithetic variates. If F_1 and F_2 are two distribution functions, then $X_1 = F_1^{-1}(U_1)$ and $X_2 = F_2^{-1}(U_2)$ will be random variates with respective distribution functions F_1 and F_2, where U_1 and U_2 are random numbers. If U_1 and U_2 are independent, then of course X_1 and X_2 will be independent as well. However, if we let $U_2 = U_1$, then the correlation between X_1 and X_2 is made as positive as possible, and taking $U_2 = 1 - U_1$ (which, recall, is also distributed uniformly over [0, 1]) makes the correlation between X_1 and X_2 as negative as possible. Thus, the inverse-transform method induces the strongest correlation (of either sign) between the generated random variates, which we hope will propagate through the simulation model to induce the strongest possible correlation in the output, thereby contributing to the success of the variance-reduction technique. [It is possible, however, to induce correlation in random variates generated by methods other than the inverse-transform method; see Schmeiser and Kachitvichyanukul (1990)]. On a more pragmatic level, inverse transform eases application of variance-reduction techniques since we always need exactly one random number to produce one value of the desired X. (Other methods to be discussed later may require several random numbers to obtain a single value of X, or the number of random numbers might itself be random, as in the acceptance-rejection method.) This observation is important since proper implementation for many variance-reduction techniques requires some sort of synchronization of the input random numbers between different simulation runs. If the inverse-transform technique is used, synchronization is easier to achieve.

The second advantage concerns ease of generating from truncated distributions (see Sec. 6.8). In the continuous case, suppose that we have a density f with corresponding distribution function F. For $a < b$ (with the possibility that $a = -\infty$ or $b = +\infty$), we define the *truncated density*

$$f^*(x) = \begin{cases} \dfrac{f(x)}{F(b) - F(a)} & \text{if } a \le x \le b \\ 0 & \text{otherwise} \end{cases}$$

which has corresponding *truncated distribution function*

$$F^*(x) = \begin{cases} 0 & \text{if } x < a \\ \dfrac{F(x) - F(a)}{F(b) - F(a)} & \text{if } a \le x \le b \\ 1 & \text{if } b < x \end{cases}$$

(The discrete case is analogous.) Then an algorithm for generating an X having distribution function F^* is as follows:

1. Generate $U \sim U(0, 1)$.
2. Let $V = F(a) + [F(b) - F(a)]U$.
3. Return $X = F^{-1}(V)$.

We leave it as an exercise (Prob. 8.3) to show that the X defined by this algorithm indeed has distribution function F^*. Note that the inverse-transform idea is really used twice: first in step 2 to distribute V uniformly between $F(a)$ and $F(b)$ and then in step 3 to obtain X. (See Prob. 8.3 for another way to generate X and Prob. 8.4 for a different type of truncation, which results in a distribution function that is *not* the same as F^*.)

Finally, the inverse-transform method can be quite useful for generating order statistics. Suppose that $Y_1, Y_2, \ldots, Y_n$ are IID with common distribution function F and that for $i = 1, 2, \ldots, n$, $Y_{(i)}$ denotes the ith smallest of the Y_j's. Recall from Chap. 6 that $Y_{(i)}$ is called the ith order statistic from a sample of size n. [Order statistics have been useful in simulation when one is concerned with the reliability, or *lifetime*, of some system having components subject to failure. If Y_j is the lifetime of the jth component, then $Y_{(1)}$ is the lifetime of a system consisting of n such components connected in series and $Y_{(n)}$ is the lifetime of the system if the components are connected in parallel.] One direct way of generating $X = Y_{(i)}$ is first to generate n IID variates $Y_1, Y_2, \ldots, Y_n$ with distribution function F, then sort them into increasing order, and finally set X to the ith value of the Y_j's after sorting. This method, however, requires generating n separate variates with distribution function F and then sorting them, which can be slow if n is large. As an alternative, we can use the following algorithm to generate $X = Y_{(i)}$:

1. Generate $V \sim \text{beta}(i, n - i + 1)$.
2. Return $X = F^{-1}(V)$.

The validity of this algorithm is established in Prob. 8.5. Note that step 1 requires generating from a beta distribution, which we discuss below in Sec. 8.3.8. No sorting is required, and we need to evaluate F^{-1} only once; this is particularly advantageous if n is large or evaluating F^{-1} is slow. Two important special cases are generating either the minimum or maximum of the n Y_j's, where step 1 becomes particularly simple. For the minimum, $i = 1$ and V in step 1 can be defined by $V = 1 - U^{1/n}$, where $U \sim U(0, 1)$. For the maximum, $i = n$ and we can set $V = U^{1/n}$ in step 1. (See Prob. 8.5 for verification in these two special cases.) For more on generating order statistics, see Ramberg and Tadikamalla (1978), Schmeiser (1978a, 1978b), and Schucany (1972).

8.2.2 Composition

The *composition* technique applies when the distribution function F from which we wish to generate can be expressed as a convex combination of other distribution functions $F_1, F_2, \ldots$. We would hope to be able to sample from the F_j's more easily than from the original F.

Specifically, we assume that for all x, $F(x)$ can be written as

$$F(x) = \sum_{j=1}^{\infty} p_j F_j(x)$$

where $p_j \geq 0$, $\sum_{j=1}^{\infty} p_j = 1$, and each F_j is a distribution function. (Although we have written this combination as an infinite sum, there may be a k such that $p_k > 0$ but $p_j = 0$ for $j > k$, in which case the sum is actually finite.) Equivalently, if X has density f that can be written as

$$f(x) = \sum_{j=1}^{\infty} p_j f_j(x)$$

where the f_j's are other densities, the method of composition still applies; the discrete case is analogous. The general composition algorithm, then, is as follows:

1. Generate a positive random integer J such that

$$P(J = j) = p_j \qquad \text{for } j = 1, 2, \ldots$$

2. Return X with distribution function F_J.

Step 1 can be thought of as choosing the distribution function F_j with probability p_j and could be accomplished, for example, by the discrete inverse-transform method. Given that $J = j$, generating X in step 2 should be done, of course, independently of J. By conditioning on the value of J generated in step 1, we can easily see that the X returned by the algorithm will have distribution function F [see, for example, Ross (2003, chap. 3)]:

$$P(X \leq x) = \sum_{j=1}^{\infty} P(X \leq x \mid J = j)P(J = j) = \sum_{j=1}^{\infty} F_j(x)p_j = F(x)$$

Sometimes we can give a geometric interpretation to the composition method. For a continuous random variable X with density f, for example, we might be able to divide the area under f into regions of areas $p_1, p_2, \ldots$, corresponding to the decomposition of f into its convex-combination representation. Then we can think of step 1 as choosing a region and step 2 as generating from the distribution corresponding to the chosen region. The following two examples allow this kind of geometric interpretation.

EXAMPLE 8.3. The *double-exponential* (or *Laplace*) *distribution* has density $f(x) = 0.5e^{-|x|}$ for all real x; this density is plotted in Fig. 8.6. From the plot we see that except for the normalizing factor 0.5, $f(x)$ is two exponential densities placed back to back; this suggests the use of composition. Indeed, we can express the density as

$$f(x) = 0.5e^{x}I_{(-\infty,0)}(x) + 0.5e^{-x}I_{[0,\infty)}(x)$$

where I_A denotes the *indicator function* of the set A, defined by

$$I_A(x) = \begin{cases} 1 & \text{if } x \in A \\ 0 & \text{otherwise} \end{cases}$$

Thus, $f(x)$ is a convex combination of $f_1(x) = e^x I_{(-\infty,0)}(x)$ and $f_2(x) = e^{-x} I_{[0,\infty)}(x)$, both of which are densities, and $p_1 = p_2 = 0.5$. Therefore, we can generate an X with density f by

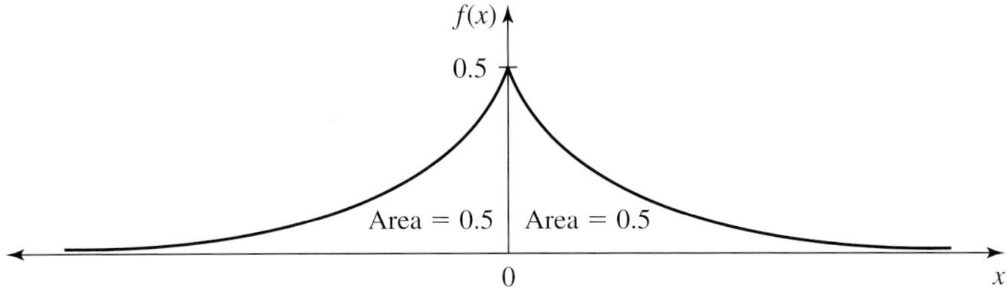

FIGURE 8.6
Double-exponential density.

composition. First generate U_1 and U_2 as IID U(0, 1). If $U_1 \le 0.5$, return $X = \ln U_2$. On the other hand, if $U_1 > 0.5$, return $X = -\ln U_2$. Note that we are essentially generating an exponential random variate with mean 1 and then changing its sign with probability 0.5. Alternatively, we are generating from the left half of the density in Fig. 8.6 with probability equal to the corresponding area (0.5) and from the right half with probability 0.5.

Note that in Example 8.3, step 2 of the general composition algorithm was accomplished by means of the inverse-transform method for exponential random variates; this illustrates how different general approaches for generating random variates might be combined. Also, we see that *two* random numbers are required to generate a single X in this example; in general, we shall need *at least two* random numbers to use the composition method. (The reader may find it interesting to compare Example 8.3 with the inverse-transform method for generating a double-exponential random variate; see Prob. 8.6.)

In Example 8.3 we obtained the representation for f by dividing the area below the density with a vertical line, namely, the ordinate axis. In the following example, we make a horizontal division instead.

EXAMPLE 8.4. For $0 < a < 1$, the *right-trapezoidal distribution* has density

$$f(x) = \begin{cases} a + 2(1 - a)x & \text{if } 0 \le x \le 1 \\ 0 & \text{otherwise} \end{cases}$$

(see Fig. 8.7). As suggested by the dashed lines, we can think of dividing the area under f into a rectangle having area a and a right triangle with area $1 - a$. Now $f(x)$ can be decomposed as

$$f(x) = aI_{[0,1]}(x) + (1 - a)2xI_{[0,1]}(x)$$

so that $f_1(x) = I_{[0,1]}(x)$, which is simply the U(0, 1) density, and $f_2(x) = 2xI_{[0,1]}(x)$ is a right-triangular density. Clearly, $p_1 = a$ and $p_2 = 1 - a$. The composition method thus calls for generating $U_1 \sim$ U(0, 1) and checking whether $U_1 \le a$. If so, generate an independent $U_2 \sim$ U(0, 1), and return $X = U_2$. If $U_1 > a$, however, we must generate from the right-triangular distribution. This can be accomplished either by generating $U_2 \sim$ U(0, 1) and returning $X = \sqrt{U_2}$, or by generating U_2 and U_3 distributed as IID U(0, 1) and returning $X = \max\{U_2, U_3\}$ (see Prob. 8.7). Since the time to take a square root is probably greater than that required to generate an extra U(0, 1) random variate *and* to perform a comparison, the latter method would appear to be a faster way of generating an X with density f_2.

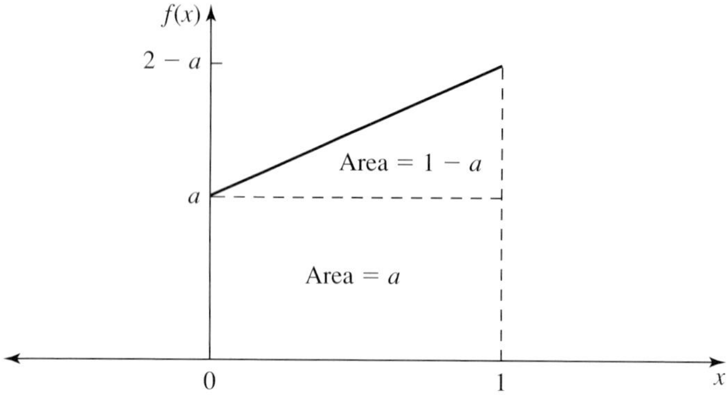

FIGURE 8.7
Right-trapezoidal density.

Again, the reader is encouraged to develop the inverse-transform method for generating a random variate from the right-trapezoidal distribution in Example 8.4. Note that especially if a is large, the composition method will be faster than the inverse transform, since the latter *always* requires that a square root be taken, while it is quite likely (with probability a) that the former will simply return $X = U_2 \sim$ U(0, 1). This increase in speed must be played off by the analyst against the possible disadvantage of having to generate two or three random numbers to obtain one value of X. Trapezoidal distributions like that in Example 8.4 play an important role in the efficient methods developed by Schmeiser and Lal (1980) for generating gamma random variates and for beta generation in Schmeiser and Babu (1980).

Composition methods (also called "mixture" methods) are further analyzed by Peterson and Kronmal (1982), who show as well that many specific variate-generation methods can actually be expressed as a composition of some sort. An interesting technique that is related closely to composition, the *acceptance-complement method*, was proposed by Kronmal and Peterson (1981, 1982); Devroye (1986, pp. 75–81) further discusses this and associated methods.

8.2.3 Convolution

For several important distributions, the desired random variable X can be expressed as a sum of other random variables that are IID and can be generated more readily than direct generation of X. We assume that there are IID random variables Y_1, $Y_2, \ldots, Y_m$ (for fixed m) such that $Y_1 + Y_2 + \cdots + Y_m$ has the same distribution as X; hence we write

$$X = Y_1 + Y_2 + \cdots + Y_m$$

The name of this method, *convolution*, comes from terminology in stochastic processes, where the distribution of X is called the *m-fold convolution* of the distribution of a Y_j. The reader should take care not to confuse this situation with the method of composition. Here we assume that the *random variable* X can be represented as a sum of other *random variables*, whereas the assumption behind the method of composition is that the *distribution function* of X is a (weighted) sum of other *distribution functions*; the two situations are fundamentally different.

The algorithm for generating the desired random variate X is quite intuitive (let F be the distribution function of X and G be the distribution function of a Y_j):

1. Generate $Y_1, Y_2, \ldots, Y_m$ IID each with distribution function G.
2. Return $X = Y_1 + Y_2 + \cdots + Y_m$.

To demonstrate the validity of this algorithm, recall that we assumed that X and $Y_1 + Y_2 + \cdots + Y_m$ have the same distribution function, namely, F. Thus,

$$P(X \leq x) = P(Y_1 + Y_2 + \cdots + Y_m \leq x) = F(x)$$

EXAMPLE 8.5. The m-Erlang random variable X with mean β can be defined as the sum of m IID exponential random variables with common mean β/m. Thus, to generate X, we can first generate $Y_1, Y_2, \ldots, Y_m$ as IID exponential with mean β/m (see Example 8.1), then return $X = Y_1 + Y_2 + \cdots + Y_m$. (See Sec. 8.3.3 for an improvement in efficiency of this algorithm.)

The convolution method, when it can be used, is very simple, provided that we can generate the required Y_j's easily. However, depending on the particular parameters of the distribution of X, it may not be the most efficient way. For example, to generate an m-Erlang random variate by the convolution method (as in Example 8.5) when m is large could be very slow. In this case it would be better to recall that the m-Erlang distribution is a special case of the gamma distribution (see Sec. 6.2.2) and to use a general method for generating gamma random variates (see Sec. 8.3.4). See also Devroye (1988).

Convolution is really an example of a more general idea, that of transforming some intermediate random variates into a final variate that has the desired distribution; the transformation with convolution is just adding, and the intermediate variates are IID. There are many other ways to transform intermediate variates, some of which are discussed in Sec. 8.2.6, as well as in Secs. 8.3 and 8.4.

8.2.4 Acceptance-Rejection

The three approaches for generating random variates discussed so far (inverse transform, composition, and convolution) might be called *direct* in the sense that they deal directly with the distribution or random variable desired. The *acceptance-rejection method* is less direct in its approach and can be useful when the direct methods fail or are inefficient. Our discussion is for the continuous case, where we want to generate X having distribution function F and density f; the discrete case is exactly analogous and is treated in Prob. 8.9. The underlying idea dates back to at least von Neumann (1951).

The acceptance-rejection method requires that we specify a function t, called the *majorizing function*, such that $t(x) \geq f(x)$ for all x. Now t will not, in general, be a density since

$$c = \int_{-\infty}^{\infty} t(x)\, dx \geq \int_{-\infty}^{\infty} f(x)\, dx = 1$$

but the function $r(x) = t(x)/c$ clearly *is* a density. (We assume that t is such that $c < \infty$.) We must be able to generate (easily and quickly, we hope) a random variate Y having density r. The general algorithm follows:

1. Generate Y having density r.
2. Generate $U \sim$ U(0, 1), independent of Y.
3. If $U \leq f(Y)/t(Y)$, return $X = Y$. Otherwise, go back to step 1 and try again.

The algorithm continues looping back to step 1 until finally we generate a (Y, U) pair in steps 1 and 2 for which $U \leq f(Y)/t(Y)$, when we "accept" the value Y for X. Since demonstrating the validity of this algorithm is more complicated than for the three previous methods, we refer the reader to App. 8A for a proof.

EXAMPLE 8.6. The beta(4, 3) distribution (on the unit interval) has density

$$f(x) = \begin{cases} 60x^3(1-x)^2 & \text{if } 0 \leq x \leq 1 \\ 0 & \text{otherwise} \end{cases}$$

[Since the distribution function $F(x)$ is a sixth-degree polynomial, the inverse-transform approach would not be simple, involving numerical methods to find polynomial roots.] By standard differential calculus, i.e., setting $df/dx = 0$, we see that the maximum value of $f(x)$ occurs at $x = 0.6$, where $f(0.6) = 2.0736$ (exactly). Thus, if we define

$$t(x) = \begin{cases} 2.0736 & \text{if } 0 \leq x \leq 1 \\ 0 & \text{otherwise} \end{cases}$$

then t majorizes f. Next, $c = \int_0^1 2.0736\, dx = 2.0736$, so that $r(x)$ is just the U(0, 1) density. The functions f, t, and r are shown in Fig. 8.8. The algorithm first generates Y and U as IID U(0, 1) random variates in steps 1 and 2; then in step 3 we check whether

$$U \leq \frac{60\, Y^3(1-Y)^2}{2.0736}$$

If so, we return $X = Y$; otherwise, we reject Y and go back to step 1.

Note that in the preceding example, X is bounded on an interval (the unit interval in this case), and so we were able to choose t to be constant over this interval, which in turn led to r's being a uniform density. The acceptance-rejection method is often stated *only* for such bounded random variables X and *only* for this uniform choice of r; our treatment is more general.

The acceptance-rejection algorithm above seems curious to say the least, and the proof of its validity in App. 8A adds little insight. There is, however, a natural intuition to the method. Figure 8.9 presents again the $f(x)$ and $t(x)$ curves from Example 8.6, and in addition shows the algorithm in action. We generated 50 X's from the beta(4, 3) distribution by acceptance-rejection (using stream 2 of the

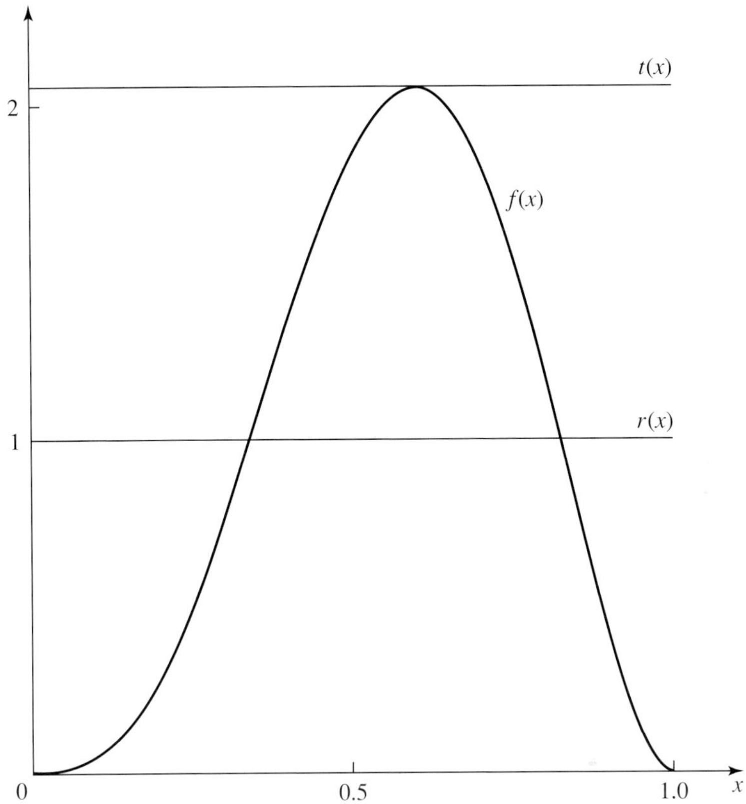

FIGURE 8.8
$f(x)$, $t(x)$, and $r(x)$ for the acceptance-rejection method, beta(4, 3) distribution.

random-number generator in App. 7A), which are marked by crosses on the x axis. On the $t(x)$ curve at the top of the graph we also mark the location of all the Y's generated in step 1 of the algorithm, regardless of whether they ended up being accepted as X's; 50 of these Y's were accepted and made it down to the x axis. The uniformity of the Y's on the $t(x)$ curve is evident, and the higher concentration of the X's on the x axis where $f(x)$ is high is also clear. For those Y's falling in regions where $f(x)$ is low (e.g., x near 0 or 1), $f(Y)/t(Y)$ is small, and as this is the probability of accepting Y as an X, most of such Y's will be rejected. This can be seen in Fig. 8.9 for small (near 0) and large (near 1) values of Y where $f(x)$ is small. On the other hand, Y values where $f(x)$ is high (e.g., near $x = 0.6$) will probably be kept, since $f(Y)/t(Y)$ is nearly 1; thus, most of the Y's around $x = 0.6$ are accepted as X's and make it down to the x axis. In this way, the algorithm "thins out" the Y's from the $r(x)$ density where $t(x)$ is much larger than $f(x)$, but retains most of the Y's where $t(x)$ is only a little higher than $f(x)$. The result is that the concentration of the Y's from $r(x)$ is altered to agree with the desired density $f(x)$.

The principle of acceptance-rejection is quite general, and looking at the above algorithm in a slightly different way clarifies how it can be extended to generation

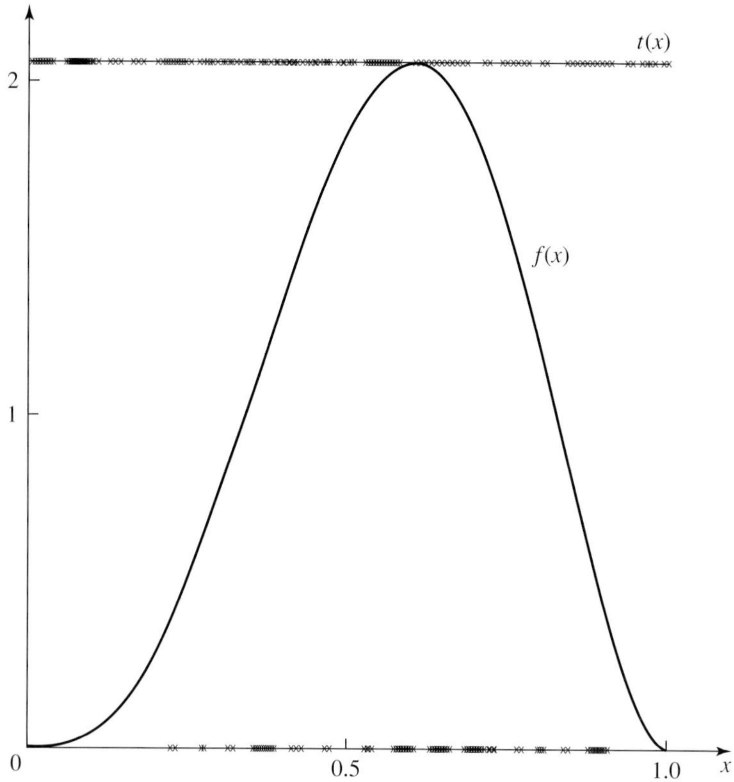

FIGURE 8.9
Sample of 50 X's (on horizontal axis) and the required Y's [on the $t(x)$ line], acceptance-rejection method for beta(4, 3) distribution.

of random points in higher-dimensional spaces; this is important, for example, in Monte Carlo estimation of multiple integrals (see Sec. 13.5). The acceptance condition in step 3 of the algorithm can obviously be restated as $Ut(Y) \leq f(Y)$, which means geometrically that Y will be accepted as an X if the point $(Y, Ut(Y))$ falls under the curve for the density f. Figure 8.10 shows this for the same Y values as in Fig. 8.9, with the dots being the points $(Y, Ut(Y))$ and the 50 accepted values of X again being marked by crosses on the x axis. By accepting the Y values for those $(Y, Ut(Y))$ points falling under the $f(x)$ curve, it is intuitive that the accepted X's will be more dense on the x axis where $f(x)$ is high, since it is more likely that the uniformly distributed dots will be under $f(x)$ there. While in this particular example the rectangular nature of the region under $t(x)$ makes the uniformity of the points $(Y, Ut(Y))$ clear, the same is true for regions of any shape, and in any dimension. The challenge is to find a way of efficiently generating points uniformly in an arbitrary nonrectangular region; Smith (1984) discusses this, and proposes a more efficient alternative to acceptance-rejection in high-dimensional spaces.

Although acceptance-rejection generates a value of X with the desired distribution regardless of the choice of the majorizing function t, this choice will play an

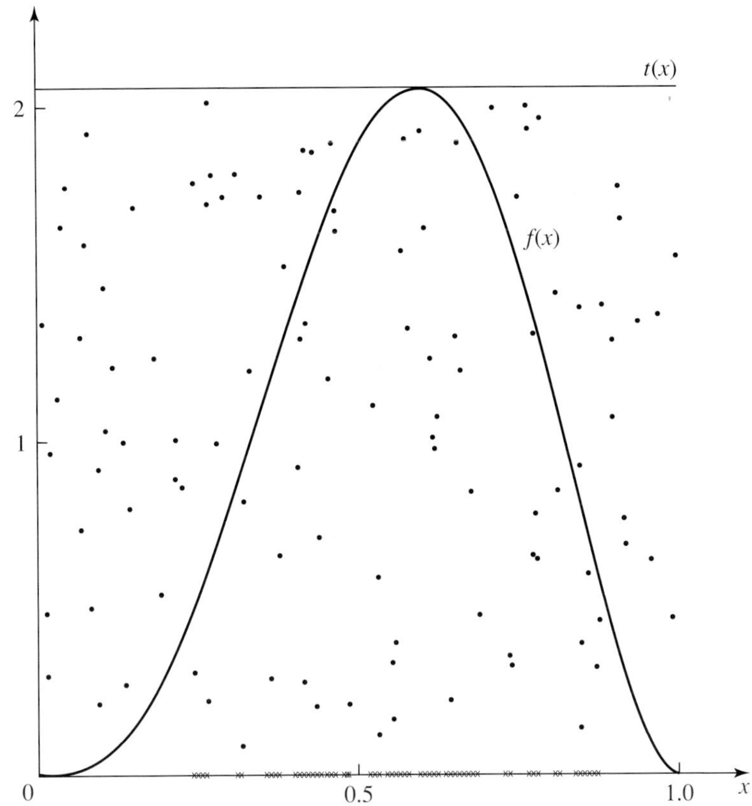

FIGURE 8.10
Sample of 50 X's (on horizontal axis) and the required $(Y, Ut(Y))$ pairs, acceptance-rejection method for beta(4, 3) distribution.

important role in its efficiency in two ways. First, since step 1 requires generating Y with density $t(x)/c$, we want to choose t so that this can be accomplished rapidly. (The uniform t chosen in Example 8.6 certainly satisfies this wish.) Second, we hope that the probability of rejection in step 3 can be made small, since we have to start all over if this rejection occurs. In App. 8A we show that on any given iteration through the algorithm, the probability of acceptance in step 3 is $1/c$; we therefore would like to choose t so that c is small. Thus, we want to find a t that fits closely above f, bringing c closer to 1, its lower bound. Intuitively, a t that is only a little above f leads to a density r that will be close to f, so that the Y values generated from r in step 1 are from a distribution that is almost correct, and so we should accept most of them. (From this standpoint, then, we see that the uniform choice of t in Example 8.6 might not be so wise after all, since it does not fit down on top of f very snugly. Since $c = 2.0736$, the probability of acceptance is only about 0.48, lower than we might like.) These two goals, ease of generation from $t(x)/c$ and a small value of c, may well conflict with each other, so the choice of t is by no means obvious and deserves care. Considerable research has been aimed at identifying good choices for t for a given distribution; see, for example, Ahrens and Dieter (1972, 1974), Atkinson (1979b), Atkinson and Whittaker (1976), Schmeiser (1980a, 1980b), Schmeiser and Babu (1980), Schmeiser and Lal (1980), Schmeiser and Shalaby (1980), and Tadikamalla (1978). One popular method of finding a suitable t is *first* to specify $r(x)$ to be some common density, e.g., a normal or double exponential, then find the smallest c such that $t(x) = cr(x) \geq f(x)$ for all x.

EXAMPLE 8.7. Consider once again the beta(4, 3) distribution from Example 8.6, but now with a more elaborate majorizing function in an attempt to raise the probability of acceptance without unduly burdening the generation of Y's from $r(x)$; we do this along the lines of Schmeiser and Shalaby (1980). For this density, there are two *inflection points* [i.e., values of x above which $f(x)$ switches from convex to concave, or vice versa], which can be found by solving $f''(x) = 0$ for those values of x between 0 and 1; the solutions are $x = 0.36$ and $x = 0.84$ (to two decimals). Checking the signs of $f''(x)$ on the three regions of [0, 1] created by these two inflection points, we find that $f(x)$ is convex on [0, 0.36], concave on [0.36, 0.84], and again convex on [0.84, 1]. By the definition of convexity, a line from the point (0, 0) to the point (0.36, $f(0.36)$) will lie above $f(x)$; similarly, the line connecting (0.84, $f(0.84)$) with the point (1, 0) will be above $f(x)$. Over the concave region, we simply place a horizontal line at height 2.0736, the maximum of $f(x)$. This leads to the piecewise-linear majorizing function $t(x)$ shown in Fig. 8.11; adding up the areas of the

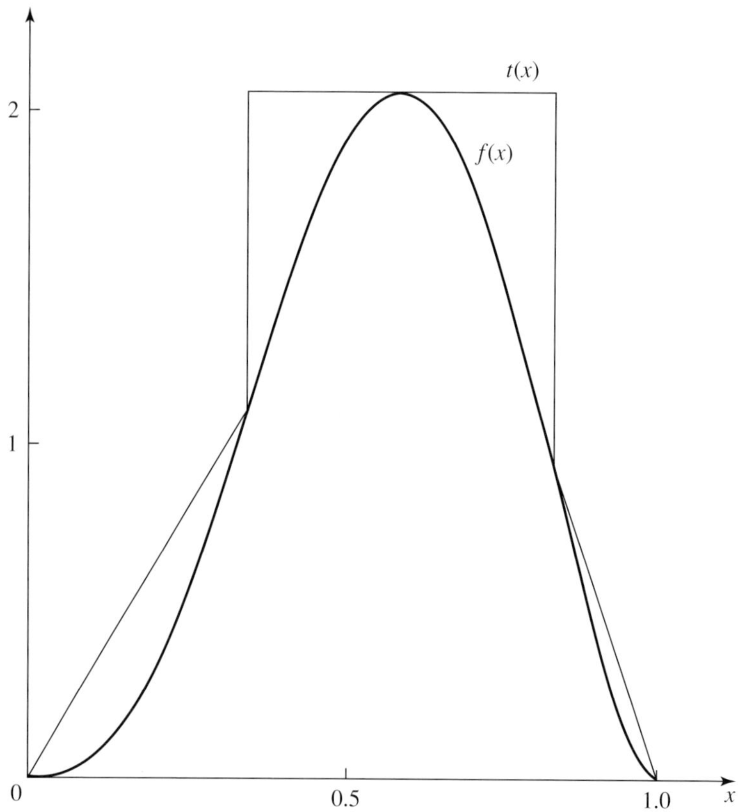

FIGURE 8.11
$f(x)$ and piecewise-linear majorizing function $t(x)$, acceptance-rejection method for beta(4, 3) distribution.

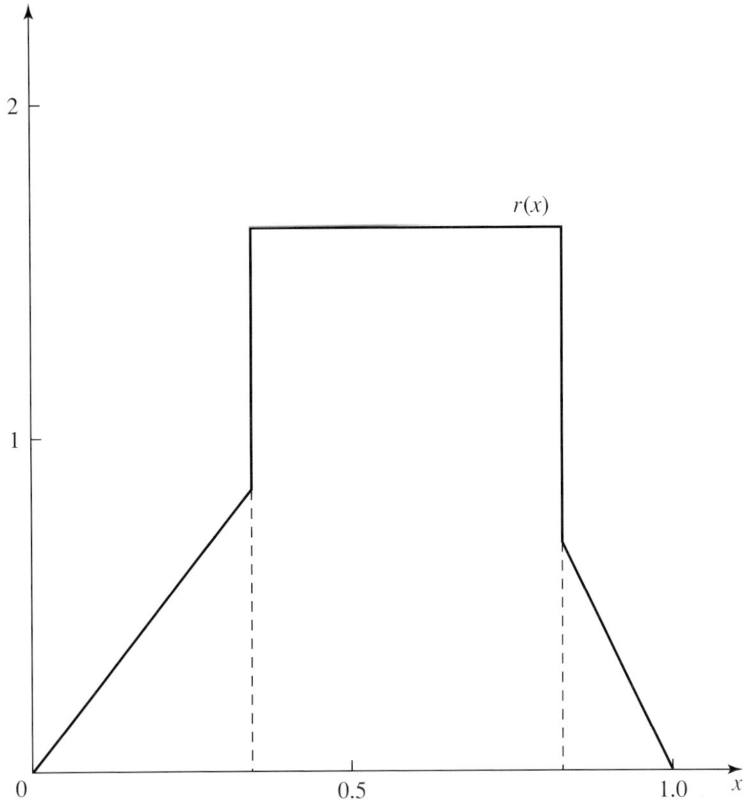

FIGURE 8.12
$r(x)$ corresponding to the piecewise-linear majorizing function $t(x)$ in Fig. 8.11.

two triangles and the rectangle, we get $c = 1.28$, so that the probability of acceptance on a given pass through the algorithm is 0.78, being considerably better than the 0.48 acceptance probability when using the simple uniform majorizing function in Example 8.6. However, it now becomes more difficult to generate values from the density $r(x)$, which is plotted in Fig. 8.12; this is a typical tradeoff in specifying a majorizing function. As suggested in Fig. 8.12, generating from $r(x)$ can be done using composition, dividing the area under $r(x)$ into three regions, each corresponding to a density from which generation is easy; see Prob. 8.16. Thus, we would really be combining three different generation techniques here: inverse transform [for the component densities of $r(x)$], composition [for $r(x)$], and finally acceptance-rejection [for $f(x)$]. In comparison with Example 8.6, whether the higher acceptance probability justifies the increased work to generate a Y is not clear, and may depend on several factors, such as the particular parameters, code efficiency, as well as the programming language, compiler, and hardware.

There have been many variations of and modifications to the general acceptance-rejection method, mostly to improve speed. For example, Hörmann and Derflinger (1996) give a version for generating from discrete distributions (including those with infinite tails), which uses a continuous majorizing function and avoids generating a separate random number to decide between acceptance and rejection.

8.2.5 Ratio of Uniforms

Let $f(x)$ be the density function corresponding to a continuous random variable X, from which we would like to generate random variates. The *ratio-of-uniforms method*, which is due to Kinderman and Monahan (1977), is based on a curious relationship among the random variables U, V, and V/U. Let p be a positive real number. If (U, V) is uniformly distributed over the set

$$S = \left\{(u, v): 0 \le u \le \sqrt{pf\left(\frac{v}{u}\right)}\right\}$$

then V/U has density function f, which we will now show. The joint density function of U and V is given by

$$f_{U,V}(u, v) = \frac{1}{s} \qquad \text{for } (u, v) \in S$$

where s is the area of the set S. Let $Y = U$ and $Z = V/U$. The Jacobian, J, of this transformation is given by the following determinant:

$$J = \begin{vmatrix} \dfrac{\partial u}{\partial y} & \dfrac{\partial u}{\partial z} \\[2ex] \dfrac{\partial v}{\partial y} & \dfrac{\partial v}{\partial z} \end{vmatrix} = \begin{vmatrix} 1 & 0 \\ z & y \end{vmatrix} = y$$

Therefore, the joint distribution of Y and Z is [see, e.g., DeGroot (1975, pp. 133–136)]

$$f_{Y,Z}(y, z) = |J|\, f_{U,V}(u, v) = \frac{y}{s} \qquad \text{for } 0 \le y \le \sqrt{pf(z)} \text{ and } 0 < z < \infty$$

so that the density function of Z is

$$f_Z(z) = \int_0^{\sqrt{pf(z)}} f_{Y,Z}(y, z)\, dy = \int_0^{\sqrt{pf(z)}} \frac{y}{s}\, dy = \frac{p}{2s} f(z)$$

Since $f_Z(z)$ and $f(z)$ must both integrate to 1, it follows that $s = p/2$ and that $Z = V/U$ has density $f(x)$ as desired.

To generate (u, v) uniformly in S, we may choose a majorizing region T that contains S, generate a point (u, v) uniformly in T, and accept this point if

$$u^2 \le pf\left(\frac{v}{u}\right)$$

Otherwise, we generate a new point in T and try again, etc. Hopefully, it should be easy to generate a point uniformly in the region T.

The boundary of the acceptance region S is defined parametrically by the following equations (see Prob. 8.19):

$$u(z) = \sqrt{pf(z)} \quad \text{and} \quad v(z) = z\sqrt{pf(z)} \tag{8.1}$$

If $f(x)$ and $x^2 f(x)$ are bounded, then a good choice of T is the rectangle

$$T = \{(u, v) : 0 \le u \le u^* \text{ and } v_* \le v \le v^*\}$$

where

$$u^* = \sup_z u(z) = \sup_z \sqrt{pf(z)}$$
$$v_* = \inf_z v(z) = \inf_z z\sqrt{pf(z)}$$
$$v^* = \sup_z v(z) = \sup_z z\sqrt{pf(z)}$$

[The supremum (sup) of the set (0, 1) is 1, but the maximum doesn't exist. The definition of the infimum (inf) is analogous.] With this choice of the majorizing region T, a formal statement of the ratio-of-uniforms method is as follows:

1. Generate $U \sim \text{U}(0, u^*)$ and $V \sim \text{U}(v_*, v^*)$ independently.
2. Set $Z = V/U$.
3. If $U^2 \le pf(Z)$, then return Z. Otherwise, go back to step 1.

If t is the area of the region T, then the probability of accepting a particular Z is

$$\frac{s}{t} = \frac{p/2}{u^*(v^* - v_*)}$$

and the mean number of passes through steps 1 through 3 until a Z is accepted is the inverse of the above ratio.

EXAMPLE 8.8. Suppose that $f(x) = 3x^2$ for $0 \le x \le 1$ [a beta(3, 1) distribution (see Sec. 6.2.2)] and $p = 1/3$. Then

$$S = \left\{(u, v) : 0 \le u \le \frac{v}{u}, 0 \le \frac{v}{u} \le 1\right\}$$
$$s = \frac{1}{6}$$
$$u^* = 1, \quad v_* = 0, \quad v^* = 1$$

We generated 2000 points (u, v) uniformly in the square T (with area $t = 1$), and 330 of these points satisfied the stopping rule stated in the definition of S. Note that $330/2000 = 0.165$, which is approximately equal to $s/t = \frac{1}{6}/1 = 0.167$. A plot of these 330 accepted points is given in Fig. 8.13. The sample mean and sample variance of the 330 selected points were 0.763 and 0.0395, respectively, while the true mean and variance of the beta(3, 1) distribution are 0.750 and 0.0375. Note that the acceptance region S is bounded above and below by the curves $v = u$ and $v = u^2$, respectively (see Prob. 8.20).

The rectangle T had a probability of acceptance of $1/6$ in Example 8.8. We could choose a majorizing region T that is closer in shape to the acceptance region S so that the ratio s/t is brought closer to 1 (see Prob. 8.21). However, this gain in efficiency has to be traded off with the potentially greater difficulty of generating a point uniformly in a more complicated majorizing region. Cheng and Feast (1979) give a fast algorithm for generating from a gamma distribution, where T is a parallelogram. Leydold (2000) develops fast ratio-of-uniforms algorithms that use polygonal majorizing regions and are applicable to a large class of distributions.

Stadlober (1990) shows that the ratio-of-uniforms method is, in fact, an acceptance-rejection method. He also extends the ratio-of-uniforms method to

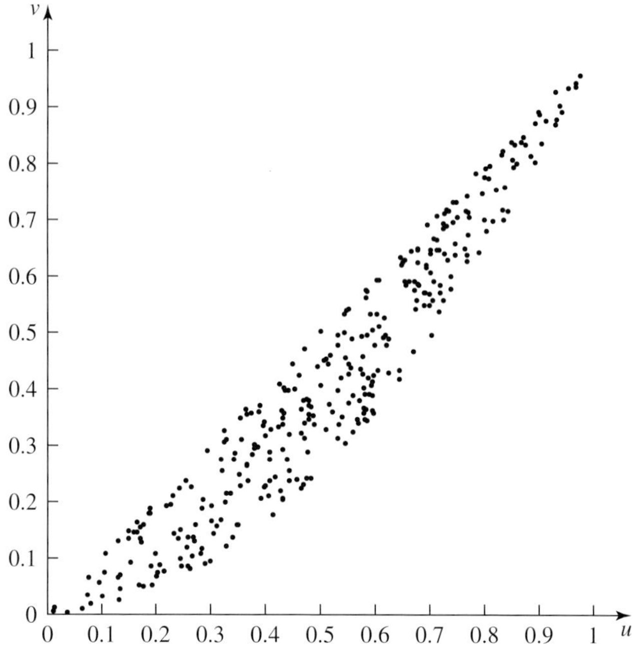

FIGURE 8.13
Accepted points for the ratio-of-uniforms method.

discrete distributions, while Wakefield et al. (1991) and Stefănescu and Văduva (1987) consider multivariate distributions.

8.2.6 Special Properties

Although most methods for generating random variates can be classified into one of the five approaches discussed so far in Sec. 8.2, some techniques simply rely on some *special property* of the desired distribution function F or the random variable X. Frequently, the special property will take the form of representing X in terms of other random variables that are more easily generated; in this sense the method of convolution is a "special" special property. The following four examples are based on normal-theory random variables (see Secs. 8.3 and 8.4 for other examples that have nothing to do with the normal distribution).

EXAMPLE 8.9. If $Y \sim N(0, 1)$ (the standard normal distribution), then Y^2 has a chi-square distribution with 1 df. (We write $X \sim \chi_k^2$ to mean that X has a chi-square distribution with k df.) Thus, to generate $X \sim \chi_1^2$, generate $Y \sim N(0, 1)$ (see Sec. 8.3.6), and return $X = Y^2$.

EXAMPLE 8.10. If $Z_1, Z_2, \ldots, Z_k$ are IID χ_1^2 random variables, then $X = Z_1 + Z_2 + \cdots + Z_k \sim \chi_k^2$. Thus, to generate $X \sim \chi_k^2$, first generate $Y_1, Y_2, \ldots, Y_k$ as

IID N(0, 1) random variates, and then return $X = Y_1^2 + Y_2^2 + \cdots + Y_k^2$ (see Example 8.9). Since for large k this may be quite slow, we might want to exploit the fact that the χ_k^2 distribution is a gamma distribution with shape parameter $\alpha = k/2$ and scale parameter $\beta = 2$. Then X can be obtained directly from the gamma-generation methods discussed in Sec. 8.3.4.

EXAMPLE 8.11. If $Y \sim \text{N}(0, 1)$, $Z \sim \chi_k^2$, and Y and Z are independent, then $X = Y/\sqrt{Z/k}$ is said to have *Student's t distribution* with k df, which we denote $X \sim t_k$. Thus, to generate $X \sim t_k$, we generate $Y \sim \text{N}(0, 1)$ and $Z \sim \chi_k^2$ independently of Y (see Example 8.10), and return $X = Y/\sqrt{Z/k}$.

EXAMPLE 8.12. If $Z_1 \sim \chi_{k_1}^2$, $Z_2 \sim \chi_{k_2}^2$, and Z_1 and Z_2 are independent, then

$$X = \frac{Z_1/k_1}{Z_2/k_2}$$

is said to have an *F distribution* with (k_1, k_2) df, denoted $X \sim F_{k_1,k_2}$. We thus generate $Z_1 \sim \chi_{k_1}^2$ and $Z_2 \sim \chi_{k_2}^2$ independently, and return $X = (Z_1/k_1)/(Z_2/k_2)$.

For some continuous distributions, it is possible to transform the density function so that it is easy to construct majorizing functions for use with the acceptance-rejection method. In particular, Hörmann (1995) suggested the *transformed density rejection method* for generating random variates from a continuous distribution with density f. The idea is to transform f by a strictly increasing function T so that $T(f(x))$ is concave, in which case we say that f is *T-concave*. [A function g is said to be *concave* if

$$\frac{g(x_1) + g(x_2)}{2} < g\left(\frac{x_1 + x_2}{2}\right)$$

for $x_1 < x_2$.] Since $T(f(x))$ is a concave function, a majorizing function for $T(f(x))$ can be constructed easily as the minimum of several tangents. Then T^{-1} is used to transform the majorizing function back to the original scale. This results in a majorizing function for the density f, and random variates can be generated from f by the acceptance-rejection method. If $T(x) = -1/\sqrt{x}$, then a large number of distributions are T-concave, including the beta, exponential, gamma, lognormal, normal, and Weibull distributions. (For some distributions, there are restrictions on the values of the parameters.) Since transformed density rejection is applicable to a large class of distributions, it is sometimes called a *universal* method [see Hörmann et al. (2004)].

8.3 GENERATING CONTINUOUS RANDOM VARIATES

In this section we discuss particular algorithms for generating random variates from several commonly occurring continuous distributions; Sec. 8.4 contains a similar treatment for discrete random variates. Although there may be several different algorithms for generating from a given distribution, we explicitly present only one technique in each case and provide references for other algorithms that may be better in some sense, e.g., in terms of speed at the expense of increased setup cost and greater complexity. In deciding which algorithm to present, we have tried to choose those that are simple to describe and implement, and are reasonably efficient as well. We also give only exact (up to machine accuracy) methods, as opposed to approximations. If speed is critically important, however, we urge the reader to pursue the various references given for the desired distribution. For definitions of density functions, mass functions, and distribution functions, see Secs. 6.2.2 and 6.2.3.

8.3.1 Uniform

The distribution function of a U(a, b) random variable is easily inverted by solving $u = F(x)$ for x to obtain, for $0 \leq u \leq 1$,

$$x = F^{-1}(u) = a + (b - a)u$$

Thus, we can use the inverse-transform method to generate X:

1. Generate $U \sim$ U(0, 1).
2. Return $X = a + (b - a)U$.

If many X values are to be generated, the constant $b - a$ should, of course, be computed beforehand and stored for use in the algorithm.

8.3.2 Exponential

The exponential random variable with mean $\beta > 0$ was considered in Example 8.1, where we derived the following inverse-transform algorithm:

1. Generate $U \sim$ U(0, 1).
2. Return $X = -\beta \ln U$.

[Recall that the U in step 2 would be $1 - U$ instead if we wanted a literal version of $X = F^{-1}(U)$ in order to make the correlation between the X's and U's positive.] This is certainly a simple technique and has all the advantages of the inverse-transform method discussed in Sec. 8.2.1. It is also reasonably fast, with most of the computing time's being taken up in evaluating the logarithm. In the experiments of Ahrens and Dieter (1972), this method was the fastest of the four algorithms considered if programming in FORTRAN, with some 72 percent of the time taken up by the logarithm evaluation. If one is willing to program in a lower-level language, however, there are other methods that avoid the logarithm and are faster, although considerably more complex and involving various amounts of preliminary setup; see von Neumann (1951), Marsaglia (1961), and MacLaren, Marsaglia, and Bray (1964). We refer the interested reader to Ahrens and Dieter (1972) and to Fishman (1978, pp. 402–410) for further discussion.

8.3.3 *m*-Erlang

As discussed in Example 8.5, if X is an m-Erlang random variable with mean β, we can write $X = Y_1 + Y_2 + \cdots + Y_m$, where the Y_i's are IID exponential random variables, each with mean β/m. This led to the convolution algorithm described in Example 8.5. Its efficiency can be improved, however, as follows. If we use the inverse-transform method of Sec. 8.3.2 to generate the exponential Y_i's [$Y_i = (-\beta/m) \ln U_i$, where $U_1, U_2, \ldots, U_m$ are IID U(0, 1) random variates], then

$$X = \sum_{i=1}^{m} Y_i = \sum_{i=1}^{m} \frac{-\beta}{m} \ln U_i = \frac{-\beta}{m} \ln\left(\prod_{i=1}^{m} U_i\right)$$

so that we need to evaluate only one logarithm (rather than m logarithms). Then the statement of the algorithm is as follows:

1. Generate $U_1, U_2, \ldots, U_m$ as IID U(0, 1).
2. Return $X = \dfrac{-\beta}{m} \ln\left(\prod_{i=1}^{m} U_i\right)$.

(Again, one should compute β/m beforehand and store it for repeated use.) This algorithm is really a combination of the composition and inverse-transform methods.

Since we must generate m random numbers and perform m multiplications, the execution time of the algorithm is approximately proportional to m. Therefore, one might look for an alternative method when m is large. Fortunately, the m-Erlang distribution is a special case of the gamma distribution (with shape parameter α equal to the integer m), so that we can use one of the methods for generating gamma random variates here as well (see Sec. 8.3.4 for discussion of gamma generation). The precise threshold for m beyond which one should switch to general gamma generation will depend on the method used for generating a gamma random variate as well as on languages, compilers, and hardware; preliminary experimentation in one's particular situation might prove worthwhile. [For the gamma generator of Sec. 8.3.4 in the case $\alpha > 1$, timing experiments in Cheng (1977) indicate that using his general gamma generator becomes faster than the above m-Erlang algorithm for $m \geq 10$, approximately.] Another potential problem with using the above algorithm, especially for large m, is that $\prod_{i=1}^{m} U_i$ might get close to zero, which could lead to numerical difficulties when its logarithm is taken.

8.3.4 Gamma

General gamma random variates are more complicated to generate than the three types of random variates considered so far in this section, since the distribution function has no simple closed form for which we could try to find an inverse. First note that given $X \sim \text{gamma}(\alpha, 1)$, we can obtain, for any $\beta > 0$, a gamma(α, β) random variate X' by letting $X' = \beta X$, so that it is sufficient to restrict attention to generating from the gamma(α, 1) distribution. Furthermore, recall that the gamma(1, 1) distribution is just the exponential distribution with mean 1, so that we need consider only $0 < \alpha < 1$ and $\alpha > 1$. Since the available algorithms for generating gamma random variates are for the most part valid in only one of these ranges of α, we shall discuss them separately. [Tadikamalla and Johnson (1981) provide a comprehensive review of gamma variate generation methods that were available at that time.]

We first consider the case $0 < \alpha < 1$. (Note that if $\alpha = 0.5$, we have a rescaled χ_1^2 distribution and X can be easily generated using Example 8.9; the algorithm stated below is nevertheless valid for $\alpha = 0.5$.) Atkinson and Pearce (1976) tested three alterative algorithms for this case, and we present one of them, due to Ahrens and Dieter (1974). [The algorithm of Forsythe (1972) was usually the fastest in the comparisons in Atkinson and Pearce (1976), but it is considerably more complicated.] This algorithm, denoted GS in Ahrens and Dieter (1974), is an acceptance-rejection technique, with majorizing function

$$t(x) = \begin{cases} 0 & \text{if } x \le 0 \\ \dfrac{x^{\alpha-1}}{\Gamma(\alpha)} & \text{if } 0 < x \le 1 \\ \dfrac{e^{-x}}{\Gamma(\alpha)} & \text{if } 1 < x \end{cases}$$

Thus, $c = \int_0^\infty t(x)\,dx = b/[\alpha\Gamma(\alpha)]$, where $b = (e + \alpha)/e > 1$, which yields the density $r(x) = t(x)/c$ as

$$r(x) = \begin{cases} 0 & \text{if } x \le 0 \\ \dfrac{\alpha x^{\alpha-1}}{b} & \text{if } 0 < x \le 1 \\ \dfrac{\alpha e^{-x}}{b} & \text{if } 1 < x \end{cases}$$

Generating a random variate Y with density $r(x)$ can be done by the inverse-transform method; the distribution function corresponding to r is

$$R(x) = \int_0^x r(y)\,dy = \begin{cases} \dfrac{x^\alpha}{b} & \text{if } 0 \le x \le 1 \\ 1 - \dfrac{\alpha e^{-x}}{b} & \text{if } 1 < x \end{cases}$$

which can be inverted to obtain

$$R^{-1}(u) = \begin{cases} (bu)^{1/\alpha} & \text{if } u \le \dfrac{1}{b} \\ -\ln \dfrac{b(1-u)}{\alpha} & \text{otherwise} \end{cases}$$

Thus, to generate Y with density r, we first generate $U_1 \sim \text{U}(0, 1)$. If $U_1 \leq 1/b$, we set $Y = (bU_1)^{1/\alpha}$; in this case, $Y \leq 1$. Otherwise, if $U_1 > 1/b$, set $Y = -\ln [b(1 - U_1)/\alpha]$, which will be greater than 1. Noting that

$$\frac{f(Y)}{t(Y)} = \begin{cases} e^{-Y} & \text{if } 0 \leq Y \leq 1 \\ Y^{\alpha-1} & \text{if } 1 < Y \end{cases}$$

we obtain the final algorithm [$b = (e + \alpha)/e$ must be computed beforehand]:

1. Generate $U_1 \sim \text{U}(0, 1)$, and let $P = bU_1$. If $P > 1$, go to step 3. Otherwise, proceed to step 2.
2. Let $Y = P^{1/\alpha}$, and generate $U_2 \sim \text{U}(0, 1)$. If $U_2 \leq e^{-Y}$, return $X = Y$. Otherwise, go back to step 1.
3. Let $Y = -\ln [(b - P)/\alpha]$ and generate $U_2 \sim \text{U}(0, 1)$. If $U_2 \leq Y^{\alpha-1}$, return $X = Y$. Otherwise, go back to step 1.

We now consider the case $\alpha > 1$, where there are several good algorithms. In view of timing experiments by Schmeiser and Lal (1980) and Cheng and Feast (1979), we will present a modified acceptance-rejection method due to Cheng (1977), who calls this the GB algorithm. This algorithm has a "capped" execution time; i.e., its execution time is bounded as $\alpha \to \infty$ and in fact appears to become faster as α grows. (The modification of the general acceptance-rejection method consists of adding a faster pretest for acceptance.) To obtain a majorizing function $t(x)$, first let $\lambda = \sqrt{2\alpha - 1}$, $\mu = \alpha^\lambda$, and $c = 4\alpha^\alpha e^{-\alpha}/[\lambda\Gamma(\alpha)]$. Then define $t(x) = cr(x)$, where

$$r(x) = \begin{cases} \dfrac{\lambda \mu x^{\lambda-1}}{(\mu + x^\lambda)^2} & \text{if } x > 0 \\ 0 & \text{otherwise} \end{cases}$$

The distribution function corresponding to the density $r(x)$ is

$$R(x) = \begin{cases} \dfrac{x^\lambda}{\mu + x^\lambda} & \text{if } x \geq 0 \\ 0 & \text{otherwise} \end{cases}$$

which is easily inverted to obtain

$$R^{-1}(u) = \left(\frac{\mu u}{1 - u}\right)^{1/\lambda} \qquad \text{for } 0 < u < 1$$

To verify that $t(x)$ indeed majorizes $f(x)$, see Cheng (1977). Note that this is an example of obtaining a majorizing function by first specifying a known distribution [$R(x)$ is actually the log-logistic distribution function (see Sec. 8.3.11) with shape parameter λ, scale parameter $\mu^{1/\lambda}$, and location parameter 0] and then rescaling the density $r(x)$ to majorize $f(x)$. Thus, we use the inverse-transform method to generate Y with density r. After adding an advantageous pretest for acceptance and streamlining for computational efficiency, Cheng (1977) recommends the following algorithm (the prespecified constants are $a = 1/\sqrt{2\alpha - 1}$, $b = \alpha - \ln 4$, $q = \alpha + 1/a$, $\theta = 4.5$, and $d = 1 + \ln \theta$):

1. Generate U_1 and U_2 as IID U(0, 1).
2. Let $V = a \ln [U_1/(1 - U_1)]$, $Y = \alpha e^V$, $Z = U_1^2 U_2$, and $W = b + qV - Y$.
3. If $W + d - \theta Z \geq 0$, return $X = Y$. Otherwise, proceed to step 4.
4. If $W \geq \ln Z$, return $X = Y$. Otherwise, go back to step 1.

Step 3 is the added pretest, which (if passed) avoids computing the logarithm in the regular acceptance-rejection test in step 4. (If step 3 were removed, the algorithm would still be valid and would just be the literal acceptance-rejection method.)

As mentioned above, there are several other good algorithms that could be used when $\alpha > 1$. Schmeiser and Lal (1980) present another acceptance-rejection method with $t(x)$ piecewise linear in the "body" of $f(x)$ and exponential in the tails; their algorithm was roughly twice as fast as the one we chose to present above, for α ranging from 1.0001 through 1000. However, their algorithm is more complicated and requires additional time to set up the necessary constants for a given value of α. This is typical of the tradeoffs the analyst must consider in choosing among alternative variate-generation algorithms.

Finally, we consider direct use of the inverse-transform method to generate gamma random variates. Since neither the gamma distribution function nor its inverse has a simple closed form, we must resort to numerical methods. Best and Roberts (1975) give a numerical procedure for inverting the distribution function of a chi-square random variable with degrees of freedom that need not be an integer, so is applicable for gamma generation for any $\alpha > 0$. [If $Y \sim \chi_\nu^2$ where $\nu > 0$ need not be an integer, then $Y \sim \text{gamma}(\nu/2, 2)$. If we want $X \sim \text{gamma}(\alpha, 1)$, first generate $Y \sim \chi_{2\alpha}^2$, and then return $X = Y/2$.] An IMSL routine [Rogue Wave (2013)] is available to invert the chi-square distribution function. Press et al. (2007, sec. 6.2) give C codes to evaluate the chi-square distribution function (a reparameterization of what's known as the *incomplete gamma function*), which would then have to be numerically inverted by a root-finding algorithm, which they discuss in their chap. 9.

8.3.5 Weibull

The Weibull distribution function is easily inverted to obtain

$$F^{-1}(u) = \beta[-\ln(1 - u)]^{1/\alpha}$$

which leads to the following inverse-transform algorithm:

1. Generate $U \sim \text{U}(0, 1)$.
2. Return $X = \beta(-\ln U)^{1/\alpha}$.

Again we are exploiting the fact that U and $1 - U$ have the same U(0, 1) distribution, so that in step 2, U should be replaced by $1 - U$ if the literal inverse-transform method is desired. This algorithm can also be justified by noting that if Y has an exponential distribution with mean β^α, then $Y^{1/\alpha} \sim$ Weibull(α, β); see Sec. 6.2.2.

8.3.6 Normal

First note that given $X \sim$ N(0, 1), we can obtain $X' \sim$ N(μ, σ^2) by setting $X' = \mu + \sigma X$, so that we can restrict attention to generating standard normal random variates. Efficiency is important, since the normal density has often been used to provide majorizing functions for acceptance-rejection generation of random variates from other distributions, e.g., Ahrens and Dieter's (1974) gamma and beta generators. Normal random variates can also be transformed directly into random variates from other distributions, e.g., the lognormal. Also, statisticians seeking to estimate empirically, in a Monte Carlo study, the null distribution of a test statistic for normality will need an efficient source of normal random variates. [See, for example, Filliben (1975), Lilliefors (1967), or Shapiro and Wilk (1965).]

One of the early methods for generating N(0, 1) random variates, due to Box and Muller (1958), is evidently still in use despite the availability of much faster algorithms. It does have the advantage, however, of maintaining a one-to-one correspondence between the random numbers used and the N(0, 1) random variates produced; it may thus prove useful for maintaining synchronization in the use of common random numbers or antithetic variates as a variance-reduction technique (see Secs. 11.2 and 11.3). The method simply says to generate U_1 and U_2 as IID U(0, 1), then set $X_1 = \sqrt{-2 \ln U_1} \cos 2\pi U_2$ and $X_2 = \sqrt{-2 \ln U_1} \sin 2\pi U_2$. Then X_1 and X_2 are IID N(0, 1) random variates. Since we obtain the desired random variates in pairs, we could, on odd-numbered calls to the subprogram, actually compute X_1 and X_2 as just described, but return only X_1, saving X_2 for immediate return on the next (even-numbered) call. Thus, we use *two* random numbers to produce *two* N(0, 1) random variates. While this method is valid in principle, i.e., if U_1 and U_2 are truly IID U(0, 1) random variables, there is a serious difficulty if U_1 and U_2 are actually adjacent random numbers produced by a linear congruential generator (see Sec. 7.2), as they might be in practice. Due to the fact that U_2 would depend on U_1 according to the recursion in Eq. (7.1) in Sec. 7.2, it can be shown that the generated variates X_1 and X_2 must fall on a spiral in (X_1, X_2) space, rather than being truly independently normally distributed; see, for example, Bratley, Fox, and Schrage (1987, pp. 223–224). Thus, the Box-Muller method should not be used with a single stream of a linear congruential generator; it might be possible to use separate streams or a composite generator instead, e.g., the combined multiple recursive generator in App. 7B, but one of the methods described below for normal variate generation should probably be used instead.

An improvement to the Box and Muller method, which eliminates the trigonometric calculations and was described in Marsaglia and Bray (1964), has become known as the *polar method*. It relies on a special property of the normal distribution and was found by Atkinson and Pearce (1976) to be between 9 and 31 percent faster in FORTRAN programming than the Box and Muller method, depending on the machine used. [Ahrens and Dieter (1972) experienced a 27 percent reduction in time.] The polar method, which also generates N(0, 1) random variates in pairs, is as follows:

1. Generate U_1 and U_2 as IID U(0, 1); let $V_i = 2U_i - 1$ for $i = 1, 2$; and let $W = V_1^2 + V_2^2$.
2. If $W > 1$, go back to step 1. Otherwise, let $Y = \sqrt{(-2 \ln W)/W}$, $X_1 = V_1Y$, and $X_2 = V_2Y$. Then X_1 and X_2 are IID N(0, 1) random variates.

Since a "rejection" of U_1 and U_2 can occur in step 2 (with probability $1 - \pi/4$, by Prob. 8.12), the polar method will require a random number of U(0, 1) random variates to generate each pair of N(0, 1) random variates. More recently, a very fast algorithm for generating N(0, 1) random variates was developed by Kinderman and Ramage (1976), which is more complicated but required 30 percent less time than the polar method in their FORTRAN experiments.

For direct use of the inverse-transform method in normal generation, one must use a numerical method, since neither the normal distribution function nor its inverse has a simple closed-form expression. Such a method is given by Moro (1995). Also, the IMSL [Rogue Wave (2013)] library has routines to invert the standard normal distribution function.

8.3.7 Lognormal

A special property of the lognormal distribution, namely, that if $Y \sim N(\mu, \sigma^2)$, then $e^Y \sim LN(\mu, \sigma^2)$, is used to obtain the following algorithm:

1. Generate $Y \sim N(\mu, \sigma^2)$.
2. Return $X = e^Y$.

To accomplish step 1, any method discussed in Sec. 8.3.6 for normal generation can be used.

Note that μ and σ^2 are *not* the mean and variance of the LN(μ, σ^2) distribution. In fact, if $X \sim LN(\mu, \sigma^2)$ and we let $\mu' = E(X)$ and $\sigma'^2 = \text{Var}(X)$, then it turns out that $\mu' = e^{\mu+\sigma^2/2}$ and $\sigma'^2 = e^{2\mu+\sigma^2}(e^{\sigma^2} - 1)$. Thus, if we want to generate a lognormal random variate X with *given* mean $\mu' = E(X)$ and *given* variance $\sigma'^2 = \text{Var}(X)$, we should solve for μ and σ^2 in terms of μ' and σ'^2 first, *before* generating the intermediate normal random variate Y. The formulas are easily obtained as

$$\mu = E(Y) = \ln \frac{\mu'^2}{\sqrt{\mu'^2 + \sigma'^2}}$$

and

$$\sigma^2 = \text{Var}(Y) = \ln\left(1 + \frac{\sigma'^2}{\mu'^2}\right)$$

8.3.8 Beta

First note that we can obtain $X' \sim \text{beta}(\alpha_1, \alpha_2)$ on the interval $[a, b]$ for $a < b$ by setting $X' = a + (b - a)X$, where $X \sim \text{beta}(\alpha_1, \alpha_2)$ on the interval [0, 1], so that it is sufficient to consider only the latter case, which we henceforth call *the* beta(α_1, α_2) distribution.

Some properties of the beta(α_1, α_2) distribution for certain (α_1, α_2) combinations facilitate generating beta random variates. First, if $X \sim$ beta(α_1, α_2), then $1 - X \sim$ beta(α_2, α_1), so that we can readily generate a beta(α_2, α_1) random variate if we can obtain a beta(α_1, α_2) random variate easily. One such situation occurs when either α_1 or α_2 is equal to 1. If $\alpha_2 = 1$, for example, then for $0 \le x \le 1$ we have $f(x) = \alpha_1 x^{\alpha_1 - 1}$, so the distribution function is $F(x) = x^{\alpha_1}$, and we can easily generate $X \sim$ beta(α_1, 1) by the inverse-transform method, i.e., by returning $X = U^{1/\alpha_1}$, for $U \sim$ U(0, 1). Finally, the beta(1, 1) distribution is simply U(0, 1).

A general method for generating a beta(α_1, α_2) random variate for any $\alpha_1 > 0$ and $\alpha_2 > 0$ is a result of the fact that if $Y_1 \sim$ gamma(α_1, 1), $Y_2 \sim$ gamma(α_2, 1), and Y_1 and Y_2 are independent, then $Y_1/(Y_1 + Y_2) \sim$ beta(α_1, α_2). This leads to the following algorithm:

1. Generate $Y_1 \sim$ gamma(α_1, 1) and $Y_2 \sim$ gamma(α_2, 1) independent of Y_1.
2. Return $X = Y_1/(Y_1 + Y_2)$.

Generating the two gamma random variates Y_1 and Y_2 can be done by any appropriate algorithm for gamma generation (see Sec. 8.3.4), so that we must take care to check whether α_1 and α_2 are less than or greater than 1.

This method is quite convenient, in that it is essentially done provided that we have gamma(α, 1) generators for all $\alpha > 0$; its efficiency will, of course, depend on the speed of the chosen gamma generators. There are, however, considerably faster (and more complicated, as usual) algorithms for generating from the beta distribution directly. For $\alpha_1 > 1$ and $\alpha_2 > 1$, Schmeiser and Babu (1980) present a very fast acceptance-rejection method, where the majorizing function is piecewise linear over the center of $f(x)$ and exponential over the tails; a fast acceptance pretest is specified by a piecewise-linear function $b(x)$ that minorizes (i.e., is always below) $f(x)$. If $\alpha_1 < 1$ or $\alpha_2 < 1$ (or both), algorithms for generating beta(α_1, α_2) random variates directly are given by Atkinson and Whittaker (1976, 1979), Cheng (1978), and Jöhnk (1964). Cheng's (1978) method BA is quite simple and is valid as well for any $\alpha_1 > 0$, $\alpha_2 > 0$ combination; the same is true for the algorithms of Atkinson (1979a) and Jöhnk (1964).

The inverse-transform method for generating beta random variates must rely on numerical methods, as was the case for the gamma and normal distributions. Cran, Martin, and Thomas (1977) give such a method with a FORTRAN program, and IMSL [Rogue Wave (2013)] routines are also available. Press et al. (2007, sec. 6.4) give C codes to evaluate the beta distribution function (also known as the *incomplete beta function*), which would then have to be numerically inverted by a root-finding algorithm, which they discuss in their chap. 9.

8.3.9 Pearson Type V

As noted in Sec. 6.2.2, $X \sim$ PT5(α, β) if and only if $1/X \sim$ gamma(α, $1/\beta$), which leads to the following special-property algorithm:

1. Generate $Y \sim$ gamma(α, $1/\beta$).
2. Return $X = 1/Y$.

Any method from Sec. 8.3.4 for gamma generation could be used, taking care to note whether $\alpha < 1$, $\alpha = 1$, or $\alpha > 1$. To use the inverse-transform method, we note from Sec. 6.2.2 that the PT5(α, β) distribution function is $F(x) = 1 - F_G(1/x)$ for $x > 0$, where F_G is the gamma(α, $1/\beta$) distribution function. Setting $F(X) = U$ thus leads to $X = 1/F_G^{-1}(1 - U)$ as the literal inverse-transform method, or to $X = 1/F_G^{-1}(U)$ if we want to exploit the fact that $1 - U$ and U have the same U(0, 1) distribution. In any case, we would generally have to use a numerical method to evaluate F_G^{-1}, as discussed in Sec. 8.3.4.

8.3.10 Pearson Type VI

From Sec. 6.2.2, we note that if $Y_1 \sim$ gamma(α_1, β) and $Y_2 \sim$ gamma(α_2, 1), and Y_1 and Y_2 are independent, then $Y_1/Y_2 \sim$ PT6(α_1, α_2, β); this leads directly to:

1. Generate $Y_1 \sim$ gamma(α_1, β) and $Y_2 \sim$ gamma(α_2, 1) independent of Y_1.
2. Return $X = Y_1/Y_2$.

Any method from Sec. 8.3.4 for gamma generation could be used, checking whether $\alpha < 1$, $\alpha = 1$, or $\alpha > 1$. To use the inverse-transform method, note from Sec. 6.2.2 that the PT6(α_1, α_2, β) distribution function is $F(x) = F_B(x/(x + \beta))$ for $x > 0$, where F_B is the beta(α_1, α_2) distribution function. Setting $F(X) = U$ thus leads to $X = \beta F_B^{-1}(U)/[1 - F_B^{-1}(U)]$, where $F_B^{-1}(U)$ would generally have to be evaluated by a numerical method, as discussed in Sec. 8.3.8.

8.3.11 Log-Logistic

The log-logistic distribution function can be inverted to obtain

$$F^{-1}(u) = \beta\left(\frac{u}{1 - u}\right)^{1/\alpha}$$

which leads to the inverse-transform algorithm:

1. Generate $U \sim$ U(0, 1).
2. Return $X = \beta[U/(1 - U)]^{1/\alpha}$.

8.3.12 Johnson Bounded

$X \sim$ JSB(α_1, α_2, a, b) if and only if $Z = \alpha_1 + \alpha_2 \ln[(X - a)/(b - X)] \sim$ N(0, 1), and we can solve this equation for X in terms of Z to get the following special-property algorithm:

1. Generate $Z \sim$ N(0, 1).
2. Let $Y = \exp[(Z - \alpha_1)/\alpha_2]$.
3. Return $X = (a + bY)/(Y + 1)$.

Any method from Sec. 8.3.6 for standard normal generation can be used to generate Z in step 1.

8.3.13 Johnson Unbounded

$X \sim \text{JSU}(\alpha_1, \alpha_2, \gamma, \beta)$ if and only if

$$Z = \alpha_1 + \alpha_2 \ln\left[\frac{X-\gamma}{\beta} + \sqrt{\left(\frac{X-\gamma}{\beta}\right)^2 + 1}\right] \sim \text{N}(0, 1)$$

and we can solve this equation for X in terms of Z to get the following special-property algorithm:

1. Generate $Z \sim \text{N}(0, 1)$.
2. Let $Y = \exp[(Z - \alpha_1)/\alpha_2]$.
3. Return $X = \gamma + (\beta/2)(Y - 1/Y)$.

Any method from Sec. 8.3.6 for standard normal generation can be used to generate Z in step 1. An alternative statement of the algorithm is $X = \gamma + \beta \sinh[(Z - \alpha_1)/\alpha_2]$ where Z is as in step 1.

8.3.14 Bézier

Random variates from fitted Bézier distributions, as discussed in Sec. 6.9, can be generated by a numerical inverse-transform method given by Wagner and Wilson (1996b), which requires a root-finding algorithm as part of its operation.

8.3.15 Triangular

First notice that if we have $X \sim \text{triang}[0, 1, (m - a)/(b - a)]$, then $X' = a + (b - a)X \sim \text{triang}(a, b, m)$, so we can restrict attention to triang(0, 1, m) random variables, where $0 < m < 1$. (For the limiting cases $m = 0$ or $m = 1$, giving rise to a left or right triangle, see Prob. 8.7.) The distribution function is easily inverted to obtain, for $0 \le u \le 1$,

$$F^{-1}(u) = \begin{cases} \sqrt{mu} & \text{if } 0 \le u \le m \\ 1 - \sqrt{(1-m)(1-u)} & \text{if } m < u \le 1 \end{cases}$$

Therefore, we can state the following inverse-transform algorithm for generating $X \sim \text{triang}(0, 1, m)$:

1. Generate $U \sim \text{U}(0, 1)$.
2. If $U \le m$, return $X = \sqrt{mU}$. Otherwise, return $X = 1 - \sqrt{(1-m)(1-U)}$.

(Note that if $U > m$ in step 2, we *cannot* replace the $1 - U$ in the formula for X by U. Why?) For an alternative method of generating a triangular random variate (by composition), see Prob. 8.13.

8.3.16 Empirical Distributions

In this section we give algorithms for generating random variates from the continuous empirical distribution functions F and G defined in Sec. 6.2.4. In both cases, the inverse-transform approach can be used.

First suppose that we have the original individual observations, which we use to define the empirical distribution function $F(x)$ given in Sec. 6.2.4 (see also Fig. 6.24). Although an inverse-transform algorithm might at first appear to involve some kind of a search, the fact that the "corners" of F occur precisely at levels $0, 1/(n-1), 2/(n-1), \ldots, (n-2)/(n-1)$, and 1 allows us to avoid an explicit search. We leave it to the reader to verify that the following algorithm *is* the inverse-transform method:

1. Generate $U \sim U(0, 1)$, let $P = (n-1)U$, and let $I = \lfloor P \rfloor + 1$.
2. Return $X = X_{(I)} + (P - I + 1)(X_{(I+1)} - X_{(I)})$.

Note that the $X_{(i)}$'s must be stored and that storing a separate array containing the values of $X_{(I+1)} - X_{(I)}$ would eliminate a subtraction in step 2. Also, the values of X generated will always be between $X_{(1)}$ and $X_{(n)}$; this limitation is a possible disadvantage of specifying an empirical distribution in this way. The lack of a search makes the marginal execution time of this algorithm essentially independent of n, although large n entails more storage and setup time for sorting the X_i's.

Now suppose that our data are grouped; that is, we have k adjacent intervals $[a_0, a_1), [a_1, a_2), \ldots, [a_{k-1}, a_k]$, and the jth interval contains n_j observations, with $n_1 + n_2 + \cdots + n_k = n$. In this case, we defined an empirical distribution function $G(x)$ in Sec. 6.2.4 (see also Fig. 6.25), and the following inverse-transform algorithm generates a random variate with this distribution:

1. Generate $U \sim U(0, 1)$.
2. Find the nonnegative integer J ($0 \le J \le k-1$) such that $G(a_J) \le U < G(a_{J+1})$, and return $X = a_J + [U - G(a_J)](a_{J+1} - a_J)/[G(a_{J+1}) - G(a_J)]$.

Note that the J found in step 2 satisfies $G(a_J) < G(a_{J+1})$, so that no X can be generated in an interval for which $n_j = 0$. (Also, it is clear that $a_0 \le X \le a_k$.) Determining J in step 2 could be done by a straightforward left-to-right search or by a search starting with the value of j for which $G(a_{j+1}) - G(a_j)$ is largest, then next largest, etc. As an alternative that avoids the search entirely (at the expense of extra storage), we could initially define a vector $(m_1, m_2, \ldots, m_n)$ by setting the first n_1 m_i's to 0, the next n_2 m_i's to 1, etc., with the last n_k m_i's being set to $k-1$. (If some n_j is 0, no m_i's are set to $j-1$. For example, if $k \ge 3$ and $n_1 > 0$, $n_2 = 0$, and $n_3 > 0$, the first n_1 m_i's are set to 0 and the *next* n_3 m_i's are set to 2.) Then the value of J in step 2 can be determined by setting $L = \lfloor nU \rfloor + 1$ and letting $J = m_L$. Whether or not this is worthwhile depends on the particular characteristics of the data and on the importance of any computational speed that might be gained relative to the extra storage and programming effort. Finally, Chen and Asau (1974) give another method for determining J in step 2, based on preliminary calculations that reduce the range of search for a given U; it requires only 10 extra memory locations. (Their treatment is for a discrete empirical distribution function but can also be applied to the present case.)

The empirical/exponential distribution mentioned briefly in Sec. 6.2.4 can also be inverted so that the inverse-transform method can be used; an explicit algorithm is given in Bratley, Fox, and Schrage (1987, p. 151).

8.4 GENERATING DISCRETE RANDOM VARIATES

This section discusses particular algorithms for generating random variates from various discrete distributions that might be useful in a simulation study. As in Sec. 8.3, we usually present for each distribution one algorithm that is fairly simple to implement and reasonably efficient. References will be made to alternative algorithms that might be faster, usually at the expense of greater complexity.

The discrete inverse-transform method, as described in Sec. 8.2.1, can be used for any discrete distribution, whether the range of possible values is finite or (countably) infinite. Many of the algorithms presented in this section *are* the discrete inverse-transform method, although in some cases this fact is very well disguised due to the particular way the required search is performed, which often takes advantage of the special form of the probability mass function. As was the case for continuous random variates, however, the inverse-transform method may not be the most efficient way to generate a random variate from a given distribution.

One other general approach should be mentioned here, which can be used for generating *any* discrete random variate having a *finite* range of values. This is the *alias method*, developed by Walker (1977) and refined by Kronmal and Peterson (1979); it is very general and efficient, but it does require some initial setup as well as extra storage. We discuss the alias method in greater detail in Sec. 8.4.3, but the reader should keep in mind that it is applicable to *any* discrete distribution with a finite range (such as the binomial). For an infinite range, the alias method can be used indirectly in conjunction with the general composition approach (see Sec. 8.2.2); this is also discussed in Sec. 8.4.3.

In addition to the alias method, there are some other general discrete-variate generation ideas; see, for example, Shanthikumar (1985) and Peterson and Kronmal (1983).

A final comment concerns the apparent loss of generality in considering below only distributions that have range $S_n = \{0, 1, 2, \ldots, n\}$ or $S = \{0, 1, 2, \ldots\}$, which may appear to be more restrictive than our original definition of a discrete random variable having general range $T_n = \{x_1, x_2, \ldots, x_n\}$ or $T = \{x_1, x_2, \ldots\}$. However, no generality is actually lost. If we really want a random variate X with mass function $p(x_i)$ and general range T_n (or T), we can first generate a random variate I with range S_{n-1} (or S) such that $P(I = i - 1) = p(x_i)$ for $i = 1, 2, \ldots, n$

(or $i = 1, 2, \ldots$). Then the random variate $X = x_{I+1}$ is returned and has the desired distribution. (Given I, x_{I+1} could be determined from a stored table of the x_i's or from a formula that computes x_i as a function of i.)

8.4.1 Bernoulli

The following algorithm is quite intuitive and is equivalent to the inverse-transform method (if the roles of U and $1 - U$ are reversed):

1. Generate $U \sim U(0, 1)$.
2. If $U \leq p$, return $X = 1$. Otherwise, return $X = 0$.

8.4.2 Discrete Uniform

Again, the straightforward intuitive algorithm given below is (exactly) the inverse-transform method:

1. Generate $U \sim U(0, 1)$.
2. Return $X = i + \lfloor (j - i + 1)U \rfloor$.

Note that no search is required. The constant $j - i + 1$ should, of course, be computed ahead of time and stored.

8.4.3 Arbitrary Discrete Distribution

Consider the very general situation in which we have *any* probability mass function $p(0), p(1), p(2), \ldots$ on the nonnegative integers S, and we want to generate a discrete random variate X with the corresponding distribution. The $p(i)$'s could have been specified theoretically by some distributional form or empirically from a data set directly. The case of finite range S_n is included here by setting $p(i) = 0$ for all $i \geq n + 1$. (Note that this formulation includes *every* special discrete distribution form.)

The direct inverse-transform method, for either the finite- or infinite-range case, is as follows (define the empty sum to be 0):

1. Generate $U \sim U(0, 1)$.
2. Return the nonnegative integer $X = I$ satisfying

$$\sum_{j=0}^{I-1} p(j) \leq U < \sum_{j=0}^{I} p(j)$$

Note that this algorithm will never return a value $X = i$ for which $p(i) = 0$, since the strict inequality between the two summations in step 2 would be impossible. Step 2 does require a search, which may be time consuming. As an alternative, we could initially sort the $p(i)$'s into decreasing order so that the search would be likely to terminate after a smaller number of comparisons; see Prob. 8.2 for an example.

Due to the generality of the present situation, we present three other methods that are useful when the desired random variable has *finite* range S_n. The first of these methods assumes that each $p(i)$ is exactly equal to a q-place decimal; for exposition we take the case $q = 2$, so that $p(i)$ is of the form $0.01k_i$ for some integer $k_i \in \{0, 1, \ldots, 100\}$ $(i = 0, 1, 2, \ldots, n)$, and $\sum_{i=0}^{n} k_i = 100$. We initialize a vector $(m_1, m_2, \ldots, m_{100})$ by setting the first k_0 m_j's to 0, the next k_1 m_j's to 1, etc., and the last k_n m_j's to n. (If $k_i = 0$ for some i, no m_j's are set to i.) Then an algorithm for generating the desired random variate X is as follows:

1. Generate $J \sim \text{DU}(1, 100)$.
2. Return $X = m_J$.

(See Sec. 8.4.2 to accomplish step 1.) Note that this method requires 10^q extra storage locations and an array reference in step 2; it *is*, however, the inverse-transform method provided that J is generated by the algorithm in Sec. 8.4.2. If three or four decimal places are needed to specify the $p(i)$'s exactly, the value of 100 in step 1 would be replaced by 1000 or 10,000, respectively, and the storage requirements would also grow by one or two orders of magnitude. Even if the $p(i)$'s are not *exactly* q-place decimals for some small value of q, the analyst might be able to obtain sufficient accuracy by rounding the $p(i)$'s to the nearest hundredth or thousandth; this is an attractive alternative especially when the $p(i)$'s are proportions obtained directly from data, and may not be accurate beyond two or three decimal places anyway. When rounding the $p(i)$'s, however, it is important to remember that they must sum exactly to 1.

The above idea is certainly fast, but it could require large tables if we need high precision in the probabilities. Marsaglia (1963) proposed another kind of table-based algorithm requiring less storage and only slightly more time. For example, consider the distribution

$$p(0) = 0.15, \qquad p(1) = 0.20, \qquad p(2) = 0.37, \qquad p(3) = 0.28$$

Then the idea of the preceding paragraph would require a vector of length 100 to store 15 0s, 20 1s, 37 2s, and 28 3s. Instead, define *two* vectors—one for the "tenths" place and the other for the "hundredths" place. To fill up the tenths vector, look only at the tenths place in the probabilities, and put in that many copies of the associated i (for $i = 0, 1, 2, 3$), so we would take one 0, two 1s, three 2s, and two 3s to get

$$0\ 1\ 1\ 2\ 2\ 2\ 3\ 3$$

Similarly, the hundredths vector is

$$0\ 0\ 0\ 0\ 0\ 2\ 2\ 2\ 2\ 2\ 2\ 2\ 3\ 3\ 3\ 3\ 3\ 3\ 3\ 3$$

corresponding to the hundredths place in the probabilities; thus, there are 28 storage locations in all (as opposed to 100 for the earlier table method). To generate an X, pick the tenths vector with probability equal to one-tenth the sum of the digits in the probabilities' tenths places, i.e., with probability

$$\frac{1 + 2 + 3 + 2}{10} = 0.8$$

and then choose one of the eight members of the tenths vector at random (equiprobably) as the returned X. On the other hand, we choose the hundredths vector with probability equal to $\frac{1}{100}$ of the sum of the digits in the hundredths place in the original probabilities, i.e., with probability

$$\frac{5 + 0 + 7 + 8}{100} = 0.2$$

and then choose one of the 20 entries in the hundredths vector at random to return as the value of X. It is easy to see that this method is valid; for example,

$$\begin{aligned} P(X = 2) &= P(X = 2 \mid \text{choose tenths vector})P(\text{choose tenths vector}) \\ &\quad + P(X = 2 \mid \text{choose hundredths vector})P(\text{choose hundredths vector}) \\ &= \tfrac{3}{8}(0.8) + \tfrac{7}{20}(0.2) \\ &= 0.37 \end{aligned}$$

as required. The storage advantage of Marsaglia's tables becomes more marked as the number of decimal places in the probabilities increases; in his original example there were three-place decimals, so the direct table method of the preceding paragraph would require 1000 storage locations; the three vectors (tenths, hundredths, and thousandths) in this example required only 91 locations.

The third attractive technique to use when X has range S_n is the alias method mentioned earlier. The method requires that we initially calculate two arrays of length $n + 1$ each, from the given $p(i)$'s. The first array contains what are called the *cutoff values* $F_i \in [0, 1]$ for $i = 0, 1, \ldots, n$, and the second array gives the *aliases* $L_i \in S_n$ for $i = 0, 1, \ldots, n$; two algorithms for computing valid cutoff values and aliases from the $p(i)$'s are given in App. 8B. (The cutoff values and aliases are not unique, and indeed the two algorithms in App. 8B may produce different results for the same distribution; both will result in a valid variate-generation algorithm, however.) Then the alias method is as follows:

1. Generate $I \sim \text{DU}(0, n)$ and $U \sim \text{U}(0, 1)$ independent of I.
2. If $U \leq F_I$, return $X = I$. Otherwise, return $X = L_I$.

Thus, step 2 involves a kind of "rejection," but upon rejecting I we need *not* start over but only return I's alias L_I, rather than I itself. The cutoff values are seen to be the probabilities with which we return I rather than its alias. There is only one comparison needed to generate each X, and we need exactly two random numbers for each X if I is generated as in Sec. 8.4.2. (See Prob. 8.17 for a way to accomplish step 1 with only *one* random number.) Although the setup is not complicated, storing the cutoffs and aliases does require $2(n + 1)$ extra storage locations; Kronmal and Peterson (1979) discuss a way to cut the storage in half (see Prob. 8.18). In any case, storage is of order n, which is regarded as the principal weakness of the alias method if n could be very large.

EXAMPLE 8.13. Consider a random variable on $S_3 = \{0, 1, 2, 3\}$ with probability mass function $p(0) = 0.1$, $p(1) = 0.4$, $p(2) = 0.2$, and $p(3) = 0.3$. Applying the first algorithm in App. 8B leads to the following setup:

i	0	1	2	3
$p(i)$	0.1	0.4	0.2	0.3
F_i	0.4	0.0	0.8	0.0
L_i	1	1	3	3

For instance, if step 1 of the algorithm produces $I = 2$, the probability is $F_2 = 0.8$ that we would keep $X = I = 2$, and with probability $1 - F_2 = 0.2$ we would return $X = L_2 = 3$ instead. Thus, since 2 is not the alias of anything else (i.e., none of the other L_i's is equal to 2), the algorithm returns $X = 2$ if and only if $I = 2$ in step 1 and $U \leq 0.8$ in step 2, so that

$$\begin{aligned} P(X = 2) &= P(I = 2 \text{ and } U \leq 0.8) \\ &= P(I = 2)P(U \leq 0.8) \\ &= 0.25 \times 0.8 \\ &= 0.2 \end{aligned}$$

which is equal to $p(2)$, as desired. (The second equality in the above follows since U and I are generated independently.) On the other hand, the algorithm can return $X = 3$ in two different (and mutually exclusive) ways: if $I = 3$, then since $F_3 = 0$ we will always return $X = L_3 = 3$; and if $I = 2$ we will return $X = L_2 = 3$ with probability $1 - F_2 = 0.2$. Thus,

$$\begin{aligned} P(X = 3) &= P(I = 3) + P(I = 2 \text{ and } U > F_2) \\ &= 0.25 + (0.25 \times 0.2) \\ &= 0.3 \end{aligned}$$

which is $p(3)$. The reader is encouraged to verify that the algorithm is correct for $i = 0$ and 1 as well. Figure 8.14 illustrates the method's rationale. Figure 8.14*a* shows bars whose (total) height is $1/(n + 1) = 0.25$, and thus is the probability mass function of I generated in step 1. The shaded areas in the bars represent the probability mass that is moved by the method, and the number in each shaded area is the value L_i that will be returned as X. Thus, if step 1 generates $I = 0$, there is a probability of $1 - F_0 = 0.6$ that this I will be changed into its alias, $L_0 = 1$, for the returned X; the shaded area in the bar above 0 is of height $0.6 \times 0.25 = 0.15$, or 60 percent of that bar. Similarly, the fraction $1 - F_2 = 0.2$ of the 0.25-high bar (resulting in a shaded area of height $0.2 \times 0.25 = 0.05$) above 2 represents the chance that a generated $I = 2$ will be changed into $X = L_2 = 3$. Note that the entire bars above 1 and 3 are shaded, since F_1 and F_3 are both zero; however, the indicated values are their own aliases, so they do not really get moved. Figure 8.14*b* shows the probability mass function of the returned X after the shaded areas (probabilities) are moved to their destination values, and it is seen to equal the desired probabilities $p(i)$.

Although the alias method is limited to discrete random variables with a finite range, it can be used indirectly for discrete distributions with an infinite range, such as the geometric, negative binomial, or Poisson, by combining it with the general

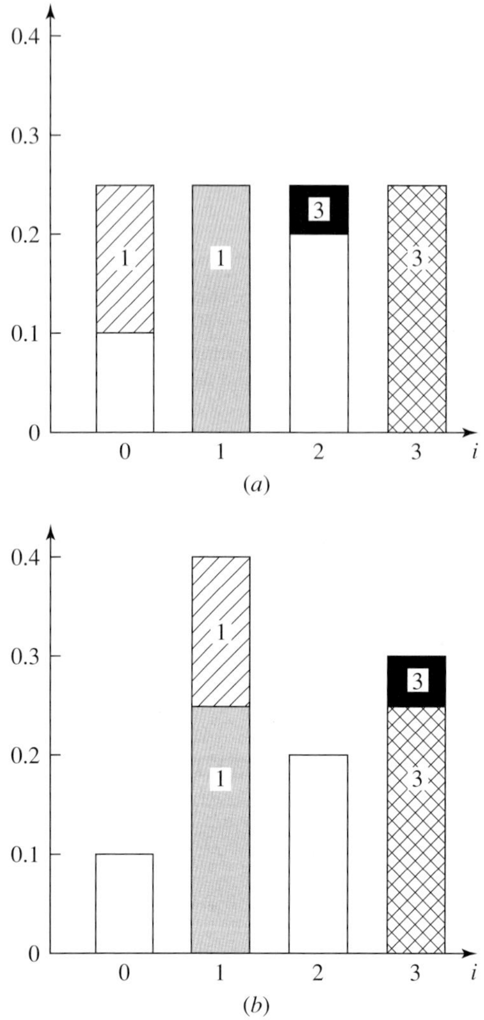

FIGURE 8.14
Setup for the alias method in Example 8.13.

composition method. For example, if X can be any nonnegative integer, we can examine the $p(i)$'s to find an n such that $q = \sum_{i=0}^{n} p(i)$ is close to 1, so that the probability is high that $X \in S_n$. Since for any i we can write

$$p(i) = q\left[\frac{p(i)}{q} I_{S_n}(i)\right] + (1 - q)\left\{\frac{p(i)}{1 - q}[1 - I_{S_n}(i)]\right\}$$

we obtain the following general algorithm:

1. Generate $U \sim$ U(0, 1). If $U \leq q$, go to step 2. Otherwise, go to step 3.
2. Use the alias method to return X on S_n with probability mass function $p(i)/q$ for $i = 0, 1, \ldots, n$.
3. Use any other method to return X on $\{n + 1, n + 2, \ldots\}$ with probability mass function $p(i)/(1 - q)$ for $i = n + 1, n + 2, \ldots$.

In step 3, we could use the inverse-transform method, for example. Since n was chosen to make q close to 1, we would expect to avoid step 3 most of the time.

Finally, we note that all the table-based methods discussed above, as well as the alias method, require some effort in an initial setup stage. Thus, they could be unattractive if the probability mass function changes frequently over time as the simulation proceeds. An efficient method for general discrete-variate generation in this case was developed by Rajasekaran and Ross (1993).

8.4.4 Binomial

To generate a bin(t, p) random variate, recall from Sec. 6.2.3 that the sum of t IID Bernoulli(p) random variables has the bin(t, p) distribution. This relation leads to the following convolution algorithm:

1. Generate $Y_1, Y_2, \ldots, Y_t$ as IID Bernoulli(p) random variates.
2. Return $X = Y_1 + Y_2 + \cdots + Y_t$.

Since the execution time of this algorithm is proportional to t, we might want to look for an alternative if t is large. One possibility would be the direct inverse-transform method with an efficient search. Another alternative is the alias method (see Sec. 8.4.3), since the range of X is finite. Finally, algorithms specific to the binomial distribution that are efficient for large t are discussed by Ahrens and Dieter (1974) and Kachitvichyanukul and Schmeiser (1988).

8.4.5 Geometric

The following algorithm is equivalent to the inverse-transform method if we replace U by $1 - U$ in step 2 (see Prob. 8.14):

1. Generate $U \sim$ U(0, 1).
2. Return $X = \lfloor \ln U / \ln (1 - p) \rfloor$.

The constant $\ln (1 - p)$ should, of course, be computed beforehand. If p is near 0, $\ln (1 - p)$ will also be near zero, so that double-precision arithmetic should be considered to avoid excessive roundoff error in the division in step 2. For p near 1, $\ln (1 - p)$ will be a large negative number, which also could cause numerical difficulties; fortunately, for large p it is more efficient to use an altogether different algorithm based on the relationship between geometric and Bernoulli random variables described in Sec. 6.2.3 (see Prob. 8.14).

8.4.6 Negative Binomial

The relation between the negbin(s, p) and geom(p) distributions in Sec. 6.2.3 leads to the following convolution algorithm:

1. Generate $Y_1, Y_2, \ldots, Y_s$ as IID geom(p) random variates.
2. Return $X = Y_1 + Y_2 + \cdots + Y_s$.

This is simple, but its execution time is proportional to s. For large s, consideration might be given to an alternative method discussed in Fishman (1978), which makes use of a special relationship between the negative binomial, gamma, and Poisson distributions; its efficiency depends on the ability to generate rapidly from the gamma and Poisson distributions. Other alternatives are discussed in Ahrens and Dieter (1974).

8.4.7 Poisson

Our algorithm for generating Poisson(λ) random variates is based essentially on the relationship between the Poisson(λ) and expo($1/\lambda$) distributions stated in Sec. 6.2.3. The algorithm is as follows:

1. Let $a = e^{-\lambda}$, $b = 1$, and $i = 0$.
2. Generate $U_{i+1} \sim U(0, 1)$ and replace b by bU_{i+1}. If $b < a$, return $X = i$. Otherwise, go to step 3.
3. Replace i by $i + 1$ and go back to step 2.

The algorithm is justified by noting that $X = i$ if and only if

$$\sum_{j=1}^{i} Y_j \leq 1 < \sum_{j=1}^{i+1} Y_j$$

where $Y_j = (-1/\lambda) \ln U_j \sim \text{expo}(1/\lambda)$ and the Y_j's are independent. That is, $X = \max\{i: \sum_{j=1}^{i} Y_j \leq 1\}$, so that $X \sim \text{Poisson}(\lambda)$ by the first comment in the description of the Poisson distribution in Table 6.4.

Unfortunately, this algorithm becomes slow as λ increases, since a large λ means that $a = e^{-\lambda}$ is smaller, requiring more executions of step 2 to bring the cumulative product of the U_{i+1}'s down under a. [In fact, since X is 1 less than the number of U_{i+1}'s required, the expected number of executions of step 2 is $E(X) + 1 = \lambda + 1$, so that execution time grows with λ in an essentially linear fashion.] One alternative would be to use the alias method in concert with the composition approach (since the range of X is infinite), as described in Sec. 8.4.3. Another possibility would be the inverse-transform method with an efficient search. Atkinson (1979b, 1979c) examined several such search procedures and reported that an indexed search similar to the method of Chen and Asau (1974), discussed earlier in Sec. 8.3.16, performed well. (This search procedure, called PQM by Atkinson, requires a small amount of setup and extra storage but is still quite simple to implement.) Other fast methods of generating Poisson variates are given by Devroye (1981) and by Schmeiser and Kachitvichyanukul (1981).

8.5
GENERATING RANDOM VECTORS, CORRELATED RANDOM VARIATES, AND STOCHASTIC PROCESSES

So far in this chapter we have really considered generation of only a single random variate at a time from various *univariate distributions*. Applying one of these algorithms repeatedly with independent sets of random numbers produces a sequence of IID random variates from the desired distribution.

In some simulation models, however, we may want to generate a random *vector* $\mathbf{X} = (X_1, X_2, \ldots, X_d)^T$ from a specified *joint* (or *multivariate*) *distribution*, where the individual components of the vector might not be independent. (A^T denotes the transpose of a vector or matrix A.) Even if we cannot specify the exact, full joint distribution of $X_1, X_2, \ldots, X_d$, we might want to generate them so that the individual X_i's have specified univariate distributions (called the *marginal distributions* of the X_i's) and so that the correlations, ρ_{ij}, between X_i and X_j are specified by the modeler. In Sec. 6.10 we discussed the need for modeling these situations, and in this section we give examples of methods for generating such correlated random variates and processes in some specific cases. There are several other problems related to generating correlated random variates that we do not discuss explicitly, e.g., generating from a multivariate exponential distribution; we refer the reader to Johnson (1987), Johnson, Wang, and Ramberg (1984), Fishman (1973a, 1978), Mitchell and Paulson (1979), Marshall and Olkin (1967), and Devroye (1997).

8.5.1 Using Conditional Distributions

Suppose that we have a fully specified joint distribution function $F_{X_1, X_2, \ldots, X_d}(x_1, x_2, \ldots, x_d)$ from which we would like to generate a random vector $\mathbf{X} = (X_1, X_2, \ldots, X_d)^T$. Also assume that for $i = 2, 3, \ldots, d$ we can obtain the *conditional distribution* of X_i given that $X_j = x_j$ for $j = 1, 2, \ldots, i - 1$; denote the conditional distribution function by $F_i(x_i | x_1, x_2, \ldots, x_{i-1})$. [See any probability text, such as Mood, Graybill, and Boes (1974, chap. IV) or Ross (2003, chap. 3) for a discussion of conditional distributions.] In addition, let $F_{X_i}(x_i)$ be the marginal distribution function of X_i for $i = 1, 2, \ldots, d$. Then a general algorithm for generating a random vector $\mathbf{X}$ with joint distribution function $F_{X_1, X_2, \ldots, X_d}$ is as follows:

1. Generate X_1 with distribution function F_{X_1}.
2. Generate X_2 with distribution function $F_2(\cdot | X_1)$.
3. Generate X_3 with distribution function $F_3(\cdot | X_1, X_2)$.

.
.
.

***d*.** Generate X_d with distribution function $F_d(\cdot | X_1, X_2, \ldots, X_{d-1})$.
***d* + 1.** Return $\mathbf{X} = (X_1, X_2, \ldots, X_d)^T$.

Note that in steps 2 through d the conditional distributions used are those with the previously generated X_i's; for example, if x_1 is the value generated for X_1 in step 1, the conditional distribution function used in step 2 is $F_2(\cdot | x_1)$, etc. Proof of the validity of this algorithm relies on the definition of conditional distributions and is left to the reader.

As general as this approach may be, its practical utility is probably quite limited. Not only is specification of the entire joint distribution required, but also derivation of all the required marginal and conditional distributions must be carried out. Such a level of detail is probably rarely obtainable in a complicated simulation.

8.5.2 Multivariate Normal and Multivariate Lognormal

The d-dimensional multivariate normal distribution with mean vector $\boldsymbol{\mu} = (\mu_1, \mu_2, \ldots, \mu_d)^T$ and covariance matrix Σ, where the (i, j)th entry is σ_{ij}, has joint density function given in Sec. 6.10.1. Although the conditional-distribution approach of Sec. 8.5.1 can be applied, a simpler method due to Scheuer and Stoller (1962) is available, which uses a special property of the multivariate normal distribution. Since Σ is symmetric and positive definite, we can factor it uniquely as $\Sigma = CC^T$ (called the *Cholesky decomposition*), where the $d \times d$ matrix C is lower triangular. Algorithms to compute C can be found in Fishman (1973a, p. 217), in Press et al. (2007, sec. 2.9), or among the IMSL routines [Rogue Wave (2013)]. If c_{ij} is the (i, j)th element of C, an algorithm for generating the desired multivariate normal vector $\mathbf{X}$ is as follows:

1. Generate $Z_1, Z_2, \ldots, Z_d$ as IID N(0, 1) random variates.
2. For $i = 1, 2, \ldots, d$, let $X_i = \mu_i + \sum_{j=1}^{i} c_{ij} Z_j$ and return $\mathbf{X} = (X_1, X_2, \ldots, X_d)^T$.

To accomplish the univariate normal generation in step 1, see Sec. 8.3.6. In matrix notation, if we let $\mathbf{Z} = (Z_1, Z_2, \ldots, Z_d)^T$, the algorithm is just $\mathbf{X} = \boldsymbol{\mu} + C\mathbf{Z}$; note the similarity with the transformation $X' = \mu + \sigma X$ for generating $X' \sim \mathrm{N}(\mu, \sigma^2)$ given $X \sim \mathrm{N}(0, 1)$.

The multivariate lognormal random vector from Jones and Miller (1966) and Johnson and Ramberg (1978), as discussed in Sec. 6.10.1, can be represented as $\mathbf{X} = (e^{Y_1}, e^{Y_2}, \ldots, e^{Y_d})^T$, where $\mathbf{Y} = (Y_1, Y_2, \ldots, Y_d)^T \sim \mathrm{N}_d(\boldsymbol{\mu}, \Sigma)$. This relation defines the vector generation algorithm:

1. Generate $\mathbf{Y} = (Y_1, Y_2, \ldots, Y_d)^T \sim \mathrm{N}_d(\boldsymbol{\mu}, \Sigma)$.
2. Return $\mathbf{X} = (e^{Y_1}, e^{Y_2}, \ldots, e^{Y_d})^T$.

Note that $\boldsymbol{\mu}$ and Σ are *not* the mean vector and covariance matrix of the desired multivariate lognormal random vector $\mathbf{X}$, but rather are the mean and covariance matrix of the corresponding multivariate normal random vector $\mathbf{Y}$. Formulas for the expected values and variances of the X_i's, as well as the covariances and correlations between them, were given by Eqs. (6.10) to (6.13) in Sec. 6.10.1, and are functions of and $\boldsymbol{\mu}$ and Σ, the mean vector and covariance matrix of the multivariate normal random vector $\mathbf{Y}$. Thus, if we want to generate an observation from a lognormal random vector $\mathbf{X}$ with *given* mean vector $\boldsymbol{\mu}' = E(\mathbf{X}) = (\mu_1', \mu_2', \ldots, \mu_d')^T$ and *given* covariance matrix Σ' with (i, j)th entry $\sigma_{ij}' = \mathrm{Cov}(X_i, X_j)$, we should solve for $\boldsymbol{\mu}$ and Σ in terms of $\boldsymbol{\mu}'$ and Σ' first, before generating the intermediate multivariate normal random vector $\mathbf{Y}$. The formulas are easily obtained with the ith element of $\boldsymbol{\mu}$ being

$$\mu_i = E(Y_i) = \ln\left(\frac{\mu_i'^2}{\sqrt{\mu_i'^2 + \sigma_i'^2}}\right)$$

and the (i, j)th entry of Σ being

$$\sigma_{ij} = \text{Cov}(Y_i, Y_j) = \ln\left(1 + \frac{\sigma'_{ij}}{|\mu'_i \mu'_j|}\right)$$

8.5.3 Correlated Gamma Random Variates

We now come to a case where we cannot write the entire joint distribution but only specify the marginal distributions (gamma) and the correlations between the component random variables of the **X** vector. Indeed, there is not even agreement about what the "multivariate gamma" distribution should be. Unlike the multivariate normal case, specification of the marginal distributions and the correlation matrix does not completely determine the joint distribution here.

The problem, then, is as follows. For a given set of shape parameters $\alpha_1, \alpha_2, \ldots, \alpha_d$, scale parameters $\beta_1, \beta_2, \ldots, \beta_d$, and correlations ρ_{ij} ($i = 1, 2, \ldots, d$; $j = 1, 2, \ldots, d$), we want to generate a random vector $\mathbf{X} = (X_1, X_2, \ldots, X_d)^T$ so that $X_i \sim \text{gamma}(\alpha_i, \beta_i)$ and $\text{Cor}(X_i, X_j) = \rho_{ij}$. An immediate difficulty is that not all ρ_{ij} values between -1 and $+1$ are theoretically consistent with a given set of α_i's; that is, the α_i's place a limitation on the possible ρ_{ij}'s [see Schmeiser and Lal (1982)]. The next difficulty is that, even for a set of α_i's and ρ_{ij}'s that *are* theoretically possible, there might not be an algorithm that will do the job. For this reason, we must be content with generating correlated gamma random variates in some restricted cases.

One situation in which there *is* a simple algorithm is the bivariate case, $d = 2$. A further restriction is that $\rho = \rho_{12} \geq 0$, that is, positive correlation, and yet another restriction is that $\rho \leq \min\{\alpha_1, \alpha_2\}/\sqrt{\alpha_1 \alpha_2}$. Nevertheless, this does include many useful situations, especially when α_1 and α_2 are close together. (If $\alpha_1 = \alpha_2$, the upper bound on ρ is removed.) Notice that any two positively correlated exponential random variates are included by setting $\alpha_1 = \alpha_2 = 1$. The algorithm, using a general technique developed by Arnold (1967), relies on a special property of gamma distributions:

1. Generate $Y_1 \sim \text{gamma}(\alpha_1 - \rho\sqrt{\alpha_1 \alpha_2}, 1)$.
2. Generate $Y_2 \sim \text{gamma}(\alpha_2 - \rho\sqrt{\alpha_1 \alpha_2}, 1)$ independent of Y_1.
3. Generate $Y_3 \sim \text{gamma}(\rho\sqrt{\alpha_1 \alpha_2}, 1)$ independent of Y_1 and Y_2.
4. Return $X_1 = \beta_1(Y_1 + Y_3)$ and $X_2 = \beta_2(Y_2 + Y_3)$.

This technique is known as *trivariate reduction*, since the three random variates Y_1, Y_2, and Y_3 are "reduced" to the two final random variates X_1 and X_2. Note that the algorithm does not control the joint distribution of X_1 and X_2; this point is addressed by Schmeiser and Lal (1982).

Correlated gamma random variates can also be generated in some less restrictive cases. Schmeiser and Lal (1982) give algorithms for generating bivariate gamma random vectors with any theoretically possible correlation, either positive or negative. Ronning (1977) treats the general multivariate case ($d \geq 2$) but again restricts consideration to certain positive correlations. Lewis (1983) gives a method for generating negatively correlated gamma variates that have the same shape and scale parameters.

8.5.4 Generating from Multivariate Families

Multivariate versions of the Johnson translation system, discussed in Sec. 6.10.1, can be generated by inverse-transform methods given by Stanfield et al. (1996). The generated vectors will then match the empirical marginal moments from the sample data, and will have correlations between the coordinates that are close to their sample counterparts as long as the marginal distributions are not heavily skewed.

As mentioned in Sec. 6.10.1, Bézier distributions have been generalized to the bivariate case. Wagner and Wilson (1995) give algorithms for generating samples from the corresponding random vectors based on the conditional-distribution method of Sec. 8.5.1. Extension of Bézier distributions to three or more dimensions is described by Wagner and Wilson (1995) as "feasible but cumbersome." Further results and methods concerning bivariate Bézier distributions can be found in Wagner and Wilson (1996a).

8.5.5 Generating Random Vectors with Arbitrarily Specified Marginal Distributions and Correlations

In Sec. 6.10.2 we noted the need to model some input random variables as a random vector with fairly arbitrary marginal distributions and correlation structure, rather than specifying and controlling their entire joint distribution as a member of some multivariate parametric family like normal, lognormal, Johnson, or Bézier. The individual marginal distributions need not be members of the same parametric family; we may even want to specify them to be of different types—continuous, discrete, or mixed. The only constraint is that the correlation structure between them be internally consistent with the form and parameters of the marginal distributions, as discussed by Whitt (1976), i.e., that the correlation structure specified be *feasible*. The modeling flexibility and marginal-distribution-fitting ease of such a setup has obvious appeal, but the question then becomes how to generate observations on random variables with such arbitrary specified marginals and correlations. In the remainder of this subsection, we mention two methods that address this issue.

Hill and Reilly (1994) describe a technique applicable when the marginal distributions are either all discrete or all continuous, involving composition (or random mixing) of distributions known to exhibit the most extreme feasible correlations to achieve the final correlation structure desired. They present specific examples through dimension $d = 3$ when the marginal distributions are uniform, exponential, and discrete uniform.

Cario et al. (2002) develop a method called *normal to anything* (NORTA). In this approach, we transform a multivariate normal random vector to one having a specified set of marginal distributions (including the case where some marginals are continuous, others are discrete, and still others are mixed continuous-discrete) and any feasible correlation structure. Let F_i denote the ith of the d marginal distribution functions desired for the final generated vector $\mathbf{X} = (X_1, X_2, \ldots, X_d)^T$, and let $\rho_{ij}(\mathbf{X}) = \mathrm{Cor}(X_i, X_j)$ be the desired correlations between the components of $\mathbf{X}$. Initially, a standard multivariate normal random vector $\mathbf{Z} = (Z_1, Z_2, \ldots, Z_d)^T$ is generated (see Sec. 8.5.2) with $Z_i \sim N(0, 1)$ and correlations $\rho_{ij}(\mathbf{Z}) = \text{Cor}(Z_i, Z_j)$; specification of the $\rho_{ij}(\mathbf{Z})$'s is discussed below. Letting Φ denote the N(0, 1) distribution function, the ith component of $\mathbf{X}$ is then generated as $X_i = F_i^{-1}[\Phi(Z_i)]$. Since $\Phi(Z_i) \sim U(0, 1)$ [by a basic result known as the *probability integral transform*, as discussed by Mood, Graybill, and Boes (1974, pp. 202–203), for instance], it is clear that X_i will have the desired marginal distribution F_i by the validity of the inverse-transform method for variate generation. The main task in NORTA generation, then, is to find the correlations $\rho_{ij}(\mathbf{Z})$ between the Z_i's that induce the desired correlations $\rho_{ij}(\mathbf{X})$ between the generated X_i's. Cario et al. (2002) give numerical methods for doing so in general, and indicate that these methods are fairly efficient [see also Chen (2001)]. Also, the N(0, 1) distribution function Φ would need to be evaluated numerically, but there are efficient methods for doing this to high accuracy; see, e.g., chap. 26 of Abramowitz and Stegun (1964). Finally, evaluating the inverse distribution function F_i^{-1} could, depending on its form, require a numerical method or search. Thus, NORTA vector generation does require some internal numerical-method computation, though in most cases the burden should not be too great, particularly in comparison with the work involved in a large, complex dynamic simulation. On the other hand, the benefit of NORTA vector generation is its generality and flexibility within a single framework.

Ghosh and Henderson (2002) show that there are sets of marginal distributions with feasible correlation matrix for $d \geq 3$ that the NORTA method cannot generate. In such cases, they show how to modify the initialization phase of the NORTA method so that it will exactly match the marginals and approximately match the desired correlations [see also Ghosh and Henderson (2003, 2009)].

8.5.6 Generating Stochastic Processes

As mentioned in Sec. 6.10.3, some applications require that we generate observations of the "same" random variable as it is observed through time. For example, we might want to generate a sequence of processing times of parts on a machine, or the sizes of incoming messages in a telecommunications system. If the observations of this random variable are assumed to be IID, we just repeatedly sample independently from the appropriate univariate distribution, as discussed in Secs. 8.1 through 8.4.

But if there is some kind of dependence between successive observations (or between observations spaced more than a single time lag apart), this method will not account for correlation to the possible detriment of model validity; see Livny et al. (1993), for example. In parallel to our discussion in Sec. 6.10.3 of specifying and fitting input stochastic processes, we discuss in this subsection how such processes can be generated for a simulation.

AR and ARMA Processes

Autoregressive (AR) and *autoregressive moving-average* (ARMA) models are generated quite obviously from their very definition, given for the case of an AR(p) process in Eq. (6.14) of Sec. 6.10.3. The process must be initialized in a specific way to obtain stationarity; see Box et al. (2008) for complete details. Thus, to generate an AR(p) process, the defining recursion in Eq. (6.14) is simply implemented mechanistically, and generation of the normally distributed ε_i's proceeds by any method from Sec. 8.3.6. The autocorrelation structure of the generated process is implied by the weighting parameters in the recursion. The marginal distribution of the X_i's is normal, which limits direct application of these processes as simulation input models.

Gamma Processes

Lewis et al. (1989) discuss generation from these processes, including *exponential autoregressive* (EAR) processes. As mentioned in Sec. 6.10.3, the result is an autocorrelated process with gamma marginals, and an autoregressive-type recursive definition and generation procedure.

ARTA Processes

Autoregressive-to-anything (ARTA) processes, developed by Cario and Nelson (1996, 1998) and described in Sec. 6.10.3, allow the modeler to achieve any desired stationary marginal distribution for the generated process, as well as the desired autocorrelation structure out to any specified lag p. The generation of a specified ARTA process proceeds by generating a stationary AR(p) *base process* $\{Z_i\}$ with N(0, 1) marginals, and then transforming it to the desired $\{X_i\}$ input process via Eq. (6.15) in Sec. 6.10.3. As mentioned there, the autocorrelation of the base $\{Z_i\}$ process is determined so that, after the transformation in Eq. (6.15), the autocorrelation structure of $\{X_i\}$ is as desired. The methodology for this is developed in Cario and Nelson (1996), and software for both specification and generation is discussed in Cario and Nelson (1998).

VARTA Processes

Vector-autoregressive-to-anything (VARTA) processes, which were developed by Biller and Nelson (2003) and described in Sec. 6.10.3, provide a methodology for modeling and generating stationary multivariate stochastic processes $\{\mathbf{X}_1, \mathbf{X}_2, \ldots\}$.

8.6 GENERATING ARRIVAL PROCESSES

In this section, we show how to generate the times of arrival $t_1, t_2, \ldots$ for the arrival processes discussed in Sec. 6.12.

8.6.1 Poisson Processes

The (stationary) Poisson process with rate $\lambda > 0$, discussed in Sec. 6.12.1, has the property that the interarrival times $A_i = t_i - t_{i-1}$ (where $i = 1, 2, \ldots$) are IID exponential random variables with common mean $1/\lambda$. Thus, we can generate the t_i's recursively as follows (assume that t_{i-1} has been determined and we want to generate the next arrival time t_i):

1. Generate $U \sim$ U(0, 1) independent of any previous random variates.
2. Return $t_i = t_{i-1} - (1/\lambda) \ln U$.

The recursion starts by computing t_1 (recall that $t_0 = 0$).

This algorithm can be easily modified to generate any arrival process where the interarrival times are IID random variables, whether or not they are exponential. Step 2 would just add an independently generated interarrival time to t_{i-1} in order to get t_i; the form of step 2 as given above is simply a special case for exponential interarrival times.

8.6.2 Nonstationary Poisson Processes

We now discuss how to generate arrival times that follow a nonstationary Poisson process (see Sec. 6.12.2).

It is tempting to modify the algorithm of Sec. 8.6.1 to generate t_i given t_{i-1} by substituting $\lambda(t_{i-1})$ in step 2 for λ. However, this would be incorrect, as can be seen from Fig. 8.15. (This figure might represent traffic arrival rates at an intersection over a 24-hour day.) If $t_{i-1} = 5$, for example, this erroneous "algorithm" would tend to generate a large interarrival time before t_i, since $\lambda(5)$ is low compared with $\lambda(t)$ for t between 6 and 9. Thus, we would miss this upcoming rise in the arrival rate and would not generate the high traffic density associated with the morning rush; indeed, if t_i turned out to be 11, we would miss the morning rush altogether. Kaminsky and Rumpf (1977) illustrate the danger in using other more sophisticated approximations.

Care must be taken, then, to generate a nonstationary Poisson process in a valid way. A general and simple method proposed by Lewis and Shedler (1979), known as *thinning*, can be used. We present a special case of the thinning algorithm that works when $\lambda^* = \max_t\{\lambda(t)\}$ is finite. Briefly, we generate a stationary Poisson process with constant rate λ^* and arrival times $\{t_i^*\}$ (using, for example, the algorithm of Sec. 8.6.1), then "thin out" the t_i^*'s by throwing away (rejecting) each t_i^* as an arrival with probability $1 - \lambda(t_i^*)/\lambda^*$. Thus, we are more likely to accept t_i^* as an arrival if $\lambda(t_i^*)$ is high, yielding the desired property that arrivals will occur more frequently in intervals for which $\lambda(t)$ is high. An equivalent algorithm, in a more

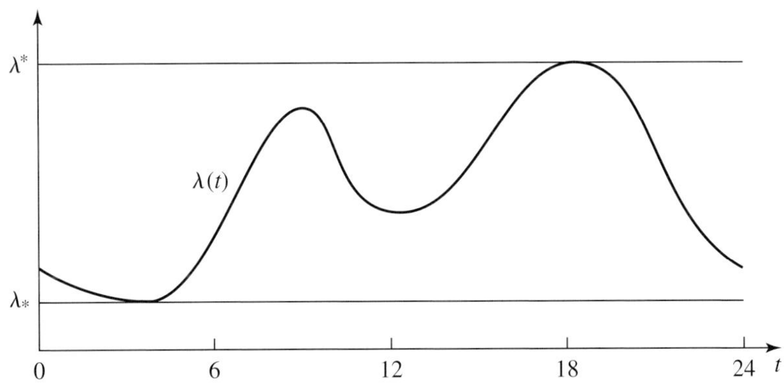

FIGURE 8.15
Nonstationary Poisson process.

convenient recursive form, is as follows (again we assume that t_{i-1} has been validly generated and we want to generate the next arrival time t_i):

1. Set $t = t_{i-1}$.
2. Generate U_1 and U_2 as IID U(0, 1) independent of any previous random variates.
3. Replace t by $t - (1/\lambda^*) \ln U_1$.
4. If $U_2 \leq \lambda(t)/\lambda^*$, return $t_i = t$. Otherwise, go back to step 2.

(Once again the algorithm is started by computing t_1.) If the evaluation of $\lambda(t)$ is slow [which might be the case if, for example, $\lambda(t)$ is a complicated function involving exponential and trigonometric calculations], computation time might be saved in step 4 by adding an acceptance pretest; i.e., the current value for t is automatically accepted as the next arrival time if $U_2 \leq \lambda_*/\lambda^*$, where $\lambda_* = \min_t\{\lambda(t)\}$. This would be useful especially when $\lambda(t)$ is fairly flat.

EXAMPLE 8.14. Recall Example 6.26, where $\lambda(t)$ was specified empirically from data to be the piecewise-constant function plotted in Fig. 6.57. This rate function is plotted again in Fig. 8.16, along with $\lambda_* = 0.09$ and $\lambda^* = 0.84$ as indicated. Values of $\{t_i^*\}$ from the stationary Poisson process at rate λ^* were generated (using stream 3 of the random-number generator in App. 7A), and are marked by the crosses on the λ^* line; these indeed appear to be distributed uniformly along the line, as would be expected (see Poisson Process Tests in Sec. 6.6). The t_i^*'s were then thinned out, as specified by the algorithm, and the "accepted" arrivals are marked with crosses on the t axis. As desired, these actual arrivals are few and far between when $\lambda(t)$ is low (e.g., between

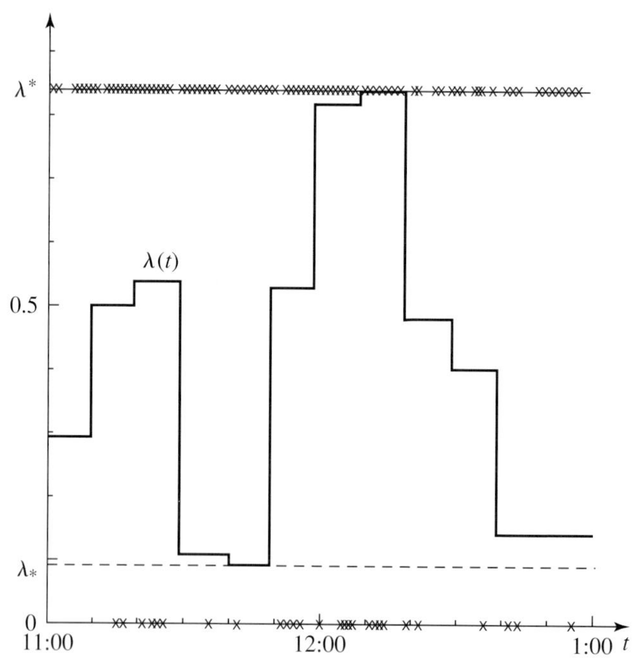

FIGURE 8.16
Generating a nonstationary Poisson process by thinning.

11:30 and 11:50), since most of the t_i^*'s were thinned out. On the other hand, most t_i^*'s were retained as actual arrivals during peak arrival periods (e.g., from 12:00 to 12:20). Note the similarity between Fig. 8.16 and Fig. 8.9, which exemplifies another "thinning" idea, the acceptance-rejection method for random-variate generation.

Although the thinning algorithm is simple, it might be inefficient in some cases. For example, if $\lambda(t)$ is relatively low except for a few high and narrow peaks, λ^* will be a lot larger than $\lambda(t)$ most of the time, resulting in thinning out most of the t_i^*'s. In such cases, a more general thinning algorithm with a nonconstant λ^* curve could be used [see Lewis and Shedler (1979)].

There is a different and older method, treated, for example, by Çinlar (1975, pp. 94–101), and is the analog of the inverse-transform method of random-variate generation, just as the thinning algorithm is analogous to the acceptance-rejection method for variate generation. Recall from Sec. 6.12.2 that the expectation function is

$$\Lambda(t) = \int_0^t \lambda(y)\, dy$$

which will always be a continuous function of t, since it is an indefinite integral; $\Lambda(t)$ is the expected number of arrivals between time 0 and time t. Then a nonstationary Poisson process with expectation function Λ can be generated by first generating Poisson arrival times $\{t_i'\}$ at rate 1, and then setting $t_i = \Lambda^{-1}(t_i')$, where Λ^{-1} is the inverse of the function Λ. Note that *all* of the rate 1 arrival times t_i' are used, in contrast with the thinning method. A recursive version of this algorithm is

1. Generate $U \sim U(0, 1)$.
2. Set $t_i' = t_{i-1}' - \ln U$.
3. Return $t_i = \Lambda^{-1}(t_i')$.

EXAMPLE 8.15. Figure 8.17*a* plots the expectation function $\Lambda(t)$ corresponding to the rate function $\lambda(t)$ from Fig. 8.16; for comparison purposes, $\lambda(t)$ is redrawn in Fig. 8.17*b*. Note that $\Lambda(t)$ is piecewise linear, since $\lambda(t)$ was specified to be piecewise constant. Also, $\Lambda(t)$ rises most steeply for those values of t where $\lambda(t)$ is highest, i.e., where arrivals should occur rapidly. The times t_i' for the stationary rate 1 Poisson process are plotted on the vertical axis of the plot for $\Lambda(t)$, and do appear to be fairly uniformly spread. Following the dashed lines across to $\Lambda(t)$ and down (i.e., taking Λ^{-1} of the t_i''s) leads to the actual arrival times t_i, marked on the t axis of the plot. The concentration of the t_i's where $\lambda(t)$ is high [and $\Lambda(t)$ is steep, thus "catching" many t_i''s] seems evident, such as between 12:00 and 12:20, and the spreading out of the t_i's during the low-arrival period of 11:30 to 11:50 is also clear. Thus, applying Λ^{-1} to the uniformly spread t_i''s on the vertical axis has the effect of deforming their uniformity to agree with the nonstationarity of the arrival process, just as applying F^{-1} to the uniform U's in the inverse-transform variate-generation algorithm deformed them to agree with the density f. Indeed, there is a strong similarity between Figs. 8.17 and 8.3.

This second algorithm for generating a nonstationary Poisson process does, however, require inversion of Λ, which could be difficult. (In Example 8.15, this could be accomplished easily by a short search and linear interpolation, since Λ was piecewise linear.) This must be traded off against the "wasting" of generated t_i^*'s in the thinning algorithm, which can become particularly inefficient if the rate function

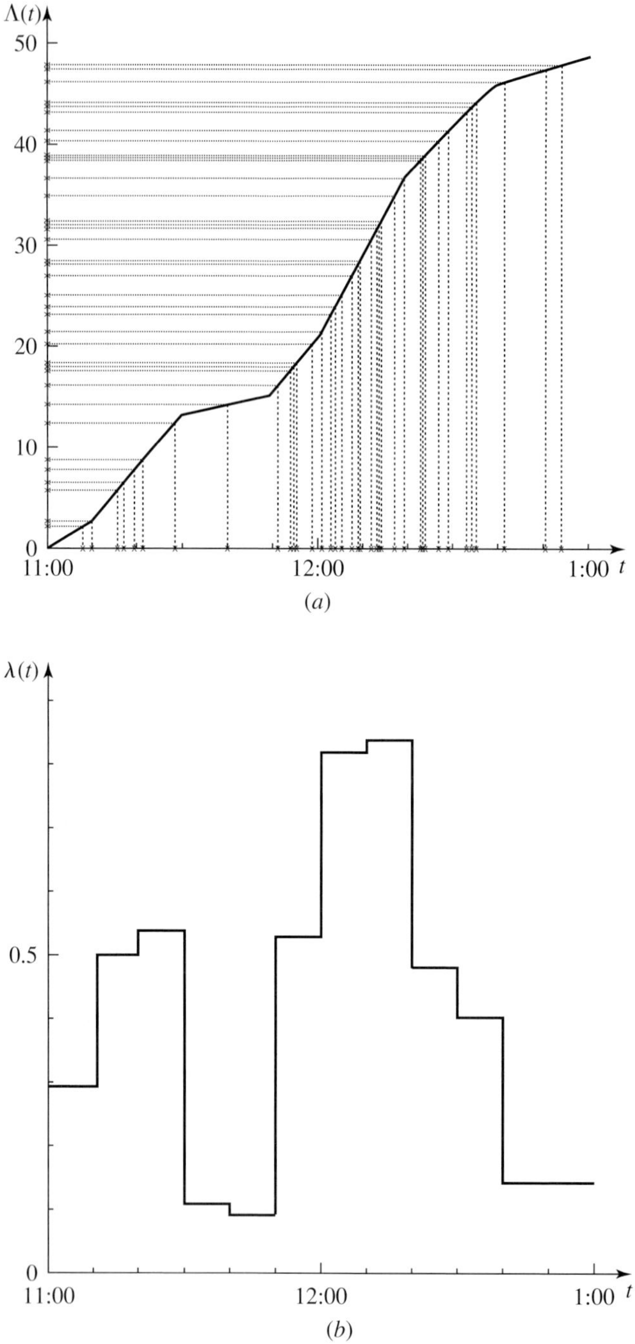

FIGURE 8.17
Generating a nonstationary Poisson process by inverting the expectation function: (*a*) $\Lambda(t)$ and generated arrival times; (*b*) $\lambda(t)$.

$\lambda(t)$ has one or more tall narrow spikes. For more on comparison of these and other methods, see Lewis and Shedler (1979).

Finally, we note that it is sometimes possible to exploit some special feature of the rate function $\lambda(t)$ or cumulative rate function $\Lambda(t)$ to achieve an efficient algorithm. This is the case for some of the specific estimation methods referenced at the end of Sec. 6.12.2, and the interested reader is referred to the original papers for details.

8.6.3 Batch Arrivals

Consider an arrival process where the ith batch of customers arrives at time t_i and the number of customers in this batch is a discrete random variable B_i. Assume that the B_i's are IID and, in addition, are independent of the t_i's. Then a general recursive algorithm for generating this arrival process is as follows:

1. Generate the next arrival time t_i.
2. Generate the discrete random variate B_i independently of any previous B_j's and also independently of $t_1, t_2, \ldots, t_i$.
3. Return the information that B_i customers are arriving at time t_i.

Note that the arrival times $\{t_i\}$ are arbitrary; in particular, they could be from a nonstationary Poisson process.

APPENDIX 8A
VALIDITY OF THE ACCEPTANCE-REJECTION METHOD

We demonstrate here that the acceptance-rejection method for continuous random variables (Sec. 8.2.4) is valid by showing that for any x, $P(X \leq x) = \int_{-\infty}^{x} f(y)dy$.

Let A denote the event that acceptance occurs in step 3 of the algorithm. Now X is defined only on the event (or set) A, which is a *subset* of the entire space on which Y and U (of steps 1 and 2) are defined. Thus, *unconditional* probability statements about X alone are really *conditional* probability statements (conditioned on A) about Y and U. Since, given that A occurs we have $X = Y$, we can write

$$P(X \leq x) = P(Y \leq x|A) \tag{8.2}$$

We shall evaluate the right side of Eq. (8.2) directly.

By the definition of conditional probability,

$$P(Y \leq x|A) = \frac{P(A, Y \leq x)}{P(A)} \tag{8.3}$$

We shall solve explicitly for the two probabilities on the right side of Eq. (8.3). To do this, it will be convenient first to note that for any y,

$$P(A|Y = y) = P\left[U \leq \frac{f(y)}{t(y)}\right] = \frac{f(y)}{t(y)} \tag{8.4}$$

where the first equality follows since U is independent of Y and the second equality since $U \sim U(0, 1)$ and $f(y) \leq t(y)$.

We now use Eq. (8.4) to show that

$$\begin{aligned} P(A, Y \leq x) &= \int_{-\infty}^{x} P(A, Y \leq x \mid Y = y) r(y)\, dy \\ &= \int_{-\infty}^{x} P(A \mid Y = y) \frac{t(y)}{c}\, dy \\ &= \frac{1}{c} \int_{-\infty}^{x} f(y)\, dy \end{aligned} \tag{8.5}$$

Next, we note that $P(A) = \int_{-\infty}^{\infty} P(A \mid Y = y) r(y)\, dy = 1/c$ [by Eq. (8.4) and the fact that f is a density, so integrates to 1]. This, together with Eqs. (8.5), (8.3), and (8.2), yields the desired result.

APPENDIX 8B
SETUP FOR THE ALIAS METHOD

There are at least two different algorithms for computing the cutoff values F_i and the aliases L_i in the setup for the alias method in Sec. 8.4.3; they do not in general lead to the same sets of cutoff values and aliases for a given distribution, but both will be valid. Originally, Walker (1977) gave the following algorithm in an explicit FORTRAN program:

1. Set $L_i = i$, $F_i = 0$, and $b_i = p(i) - 1/(n + 1)$, for $i = 0, 1, \ldots, n$.
2. For $i = 0, 1, \ldots, n$, do the following steps:
  a. Let $c = \min\{b_0, b_1, \ldots, b_n\}$ and let k be the index of this minimal b_j. (Ties can be broken arbitrarily.)
  b. Let $d = \max\{b_0, b_1, \ldots, b_n\}$ and let m be the index of this maximal b_j. (Ties can be broken arbitrarily.)
  c. If $\sum_{j=0}^{n} |b_j| < \epsilon$, stop the algorithm.
  d. Let $L_k = m$, $F_k = 1 + c(n + 1)$, $b_k = 0$, and $b_m = c + d$.

Note that if the condition in step 2c is satisfied at some point, the rest of the range of i in step 2 will not be completed. This condition in step 2c should theoretically be for equality of the summation to 0, but insisting on this could cause numerical difficulties in floating-point arithmetic; in the above, ϵ is a small positive number such as 10^{-5}.

While the above algorithm is easy to implement in any programming language, Kronmal and Peterson (1979) gave a more efficient algorithm using set operations:

1. Set $F_i = (n + 1)\, p(i)$ for $i = 0, 1, \ldots, n$.
2. Define the sets $G = \{i: F_i \geq 1\}$ and $S = \{i: F_i < 1\}$.
3. Do the following steps until S becomes empty:
  a. Remove an element k from G and remove an element m from S.
  b. Set $L_m = k$ and replace F_k by $F_k - 1 + F_m$.
  c. If $F_k < 1$, put k into S; otherwise, put k back into G.

This algorithm will leave at least one L_i undefined, but the corresponding F_i values will be equal to 1, so these aliases will never be used in the variate-generation algorithm. Implementing the sets G and S in this second algorithm could be accomplished in many ways, such as a simple push/pop stack or by using a linked-list structure as discussed in Chap. 2.

The second algorithm is more efficient, since in the first algorithm steps 2a and 2b each require a search of $n + 1$ elements, while no such search is required in the second algorithm; this could be important if n is large. However, we should note that numerical difficulties can occur in the second algorithm if the $p(i)$'s do not sum *exactly* to 1; this could occur if, for instance, the $p(i)$'s are proportions corresponding to frequency counts from data, complete with roundoff error. We experienced failure of the second algorithm (using several different set implementations) when the sum of the $p(i)$'s differed from 1 by as little as 10^{-5}.

PROBLEMS

8.1. Give algorithms for generating random variates with the following densities:

(*a*) Cauchy

$$f(x) = \left\{\pi\beta\left[1 + \left(\frac{x-\gamma}{\beta}\right)^2\right]\right\}^{-1} \quad \text{where } -\infty < \gamma < \infty, \quad \beta > 0, \quad -\infty < x < \infty$$

(*b*) Gumbel (or extreme value)

$$f(x) = \frac{1}{\beta}\exp\left[-e^{-(x-\gamma)/\beta} - \frac{x-\gamma}{\beta}\right] \quad \text{where } -\infty < \gamma < \infty, \quad \beta > 0, \quad -\infty < x < \infty$$

(*c*) Logistic

$$f(x) = \frac{(1/\beta)e^{-(x-\gamma)/\beta}}{[1 + e^{-(x-\gamma)/\beta}]^2} \quad \text{where } -\infty < \gamma < \infty, \quad \beta > 0, \quad -\infty < x < \infty$$

(*d*) Pareto

$$f(x) = \frac{\alpha_2 c^{\alpha_2}}{x^{\alpha_2+1}} \quad \text{where } c > 0, \quad \alpha_2 > 0, \quad x > c$$

For $\gamma = 0$ and $\beta = 1$ in each of (*a*), (*b*), and (*c*), use your algorithms to generate IID random variates $X_1, X_2, \ldots, X_{5000}$ and write out $\bar{X}(n) = \sum_{i=1}^{n} X_i/n$ for $n = 50, 100, 150, \ldots, 5000$ to verify empirically the strong law of large numbers (Sec. 4.6), i.e., that $\bar{X}(n)$ converges to $E(X_i)$ (if it exists); do the same for (*d*) with $c = 1$ and $\alpha_2 = 2$.

8.2. Let X be discrete with probability mass function $p(1) = 0.05$, $p(2) = 0.05$, $p(3) = 0.1$, $p(4) = 0.1$, $p(5) = 0.6$, and $p(6) = 0.1$, and for $i = 1, 2, \ldots, 6$, let $q(i) = p(1) + p(2) + \cdots + p(i)$. Convince yourself that the following algorithm is explicitly the discrete inverse-transform method with a simple left-to-right search:

1. Generate $U \sim U(0, 1)$ and set $i = 1$.
2. If $U \leq q(i)$, return $X = i$. Otherwise, go to step 3.
3. Replace i by $i + 1$ and go back to step 2.

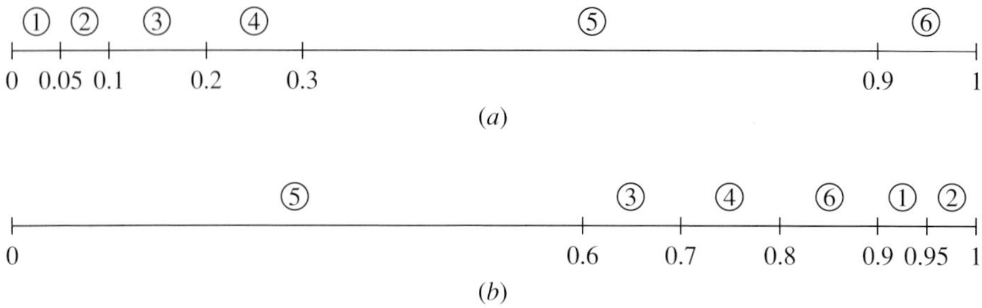

FIGURE 8.18
Representation of the two algorithms in Prob. 8.2.

Let N be the number of times step 2 is executed (so that N is also the number of comparisons). Show that N has the same distribution as X, so $E(N) = E(X) = 4.45$. This algorithm can be represented as in Fig. 8.18*a*, where the circled numbers are the values to which X is set if U falls in the interval directly below them and the search is left-to-right.

Alternatively, we could first sort the $p(i)$'s into decreasing order and form a *coding vector* $i'(i)$, as follows. Let $q'(1) = 0.6$, $q'(2) = 0.7$, $q'(3) = 0.8$, $q'(4) = 0.9$, $q'(5) = 0.95$, and $q'(6) = 1$; also let $i'(1) = 5$, $i'(2) = 3$, $i'(3) = 4$, $i'(4) = 6$, $i'(5) = 1$, and $i'(6) = 2$. Show that the following algorithm is valid:

1′. Generate $U \sim$ U(0, 1) and set $i = 1$.
2′. If $U \leq q'(i)$, return $X = i'(i)$. Otherwise, go to step 3′.
3′. Replace i by $i + 1$ and go back to step 2′.

If N' is the number of comparisons for this second algorithm, show that $E(N') = 2.05$, which is less than half of $E(N)$. This saving in marginal execution time will depend on the particular distribution and must be weighed against the extra setup time and storage for the coding vector $i'(i)$. This second algorithm can be represented as in Fig. 8.18*b*.

8.3. Recall the truncated distribution function F^* and the algorithm for generating from it, as given in Sec. 8.2.1.
(*a*) Show that the algorithm stated in Sec. 8.2.1 is valid when F is continuous and strictly increasing.
(*b*) Show that the following algorithm is also valid for generating X with distribution function F^* (assume again that F is continuous and strictly increasing):

1. Generate $U \sim$ U(0, 1).
2. If $F(a) \leq U \leq F(b)$, return $X = F^{-1}(U)$. Otherwise, go back to step 1.

Which algorithm do you think is "better"? In what sense? Under what conditions?

8.4. A truncation of a distribution function F can be defined differently from the F^* of Sec. 8.2.1. Again for $a < b$, define the distribution function

$$\tilde{F}(x) = \begin{cases} 0 & \text{if } x < a \\ F(x) & \text{if } a \leq x < b \\ 1 & \text{if } b \leq x \end{cases}$$

Find a method for generating from the distribution function $\tilde{F}$, assuming that we already have a method for generating from F. Demonstrate the validity of your algorithm.

8.5. Show that the algorithm in Sec. 8.2.1 for generating the ith order statistic is valid when F is strictly increasing. [*Hint:* Use the fact that if $U_1, U_2, \ldots, U_n$ are IID U(0, 1), then $U_{(i)} \sim \text{beta}(i, n - i + 1)$.] Verify directly that for $i = 1$ and $i = n$ it is valid to let $V = 1 - U^{1/n}$ and $V = U^{1/n}$, respectively.

8.6. Derive the inverse-transform algorithm for the double-exponential distribution of Example 8.3, and compare it with the composition algorithm as given in the example. Which would you prefer?

8.7. For $a < b$, the *right-triangular distribution* has density function

$$f_R(x) = \begin{cases} \dfrac{2(x-a)}{(b-a)^2} & \text{if } a \le x \le b \\ 0 & \text{otherwise} \end{cases}$$

and the *left-triangular distribution* has density function

$$f_L(x) = \begin{cases} \dfrac{2(b-x)}{(b-a)^2} & \text{if } a \le x \le b \\ 0 & \text{otherwise} \end{cases}$$

These distributions are denoted by RT(a, b) and LT(a, b), respectively.

(*a*) Show that if $X \sim \text{RT}(0, 1)$, then $X' = a + (b - a)X \sim \text{RT}(a, b)$; verify the same relation between LT(0, 1) and LT(a, b). Thus it is sufficient to generate from RT(0, 1) and LT(0, 1).

(*b*) Show that if $X \sim \text{RT}(0, 1)$, then $1 - X \sim \text{LT}(0, 1)$. Thus it is enough to restrict our attention further to generating from RT(0, 1).

(*c*) Derive the inverse-transform algorithm for generating from RT(0, 1). Despite the result in (*b*), also derive the inverse-transform algorithm for generating directly from LT(0, 1).

(*d*) As an alternative to the inverse-transform method, show that if U_1 and U_2 are IID U(0, 1) random variables, then $\max\{U_1, U_2\} \sim \text{RT}(0, 1)$. Do you think that this is better than the inverse-transform method? In what sense? (See Example 8.4.)

8.8. In each of the following cases, give an algorithm that uses exactly *one* random number for generating a random variate with the same distribution as X.

(*a*) $X = \min\{U_1, U_2\}$, where U_1 and U_2 are IID U(0, 1).

(*b*) $X = \max\{U_1, U_2\}$, where U_1 and U_2 are IID U(0, 1).

(*c*) $X = \min\{Y_1, Y_2\}$, where Y_1 and Y_2 are IID exponential with common mean β.

Compare (*a*) and (*b*) with Prob. 8.7. Compare your one-U algorithms in (*a*) through (*c*) with the direct ones of actually generating the U_i's or Y_i's and then taking the minimum or maximum.

8.9. The general acceptance-rejection method of Sec. 8.2.4 has the following discrete analog. Let X be discrete with probability mass function $p(x_i)$ for $i = 0, \pm 1, \pm 2, \ldots$, let the majorizing function be $t(x_i) \ge p(x_i)$ for all i, let $c = \sum_{i=-\infty}^{\infty} t(x_i)$, and let $r(x_i) = t(x_i)/c$ for $i = 0, \pm 1, \pm 2, \ldots$.

1′. Generate Y having probability mass function r.
2′. Generate $U \sim \text{U}(0, 1)$, independent of Y.
3′. If $U \le p(Y)/t(Y)$, return $X = Y$. Otherwise, go back to step 1′ and try again.

Show that this algorithm is valid by following steps similar to those in App. 8A. What considerations are important in choosing the function $t(x_i)$?

8.10. For the general acceptance-rejection method (either continuous, as in Sec. 8.2.4, or discrete, as in Prob. 8.9) find the distribution of the number of (Y, U) pairs that are rejected before acceptance occurs. What is the expected number of rejections?

8.11. Give inverse-transform, composition, and acceptance-rejection algorithms for generating from each of the following densities. Discuss which algorithm is preferable for each density. (First plot the densities.)

(*a*)

$$f(x) = \begin{cases} \dfrac{3x^2}{2} & \text{if } -1 \le x \le 1 \\ 0 & \text{otherwise} \end{cases}$$

(*b*) For $0 < a < \frac{1}{2}$,

$$f(x) = \begin{cases} 0 & \text{if } x \le 0 \\ \dfrac{x}{a(1-a)} & \text{if } 0 \le x \le a \\ \dfrac{1}{1-a} & \text{if } a \le x \le 1-a \\ \dfrac{1-x}{a(1-a)} & \text{if } 1-a \le x \le 1 \\ 0 & \text{if } 1 \le x \end{cases}$$

8.12. Recall the polar method of Sec. 8.3.6 for generating N(0, 1) random variates. Show that the probability of "acceptance" of W in step 2 is $\pi/4$, and find the distribution of the number of "rejections" of W before "acceptance" finally occurs. What is the expected number of executions of step 1?

8.13. Give a composition algorithm for generating from the triang(0, 1, m) distribution ($0 < m < 1$) of Sec. 8.3.15. Compare it with the inverse-transform algorithm in Sec. 8.3.15. (*Hint:* See Prob. 8.7.)

8.14. (*a*) Demonstrate the validity of the algorithm given in Sec. 8.4.5 for generating from the geom(p) distribution. (*Hint:* For a real number x and an integer i, $\lfloor x \rfloor = i$ if and only if $i \le x < i + 1$.) Also verify (with $1 - U$ in place of U) that this *is* the inverse-transform algorithm.

(*b*) Show that the following algorithm is also valid for generating $X \sim$ geom(p):

1. Let $i = 0$.
2. Generate $U \sim$ U(0, 1) independent of any previously generated U(0, 1) random variates.
3. If $U \le p$, return $X = i$. Otherwise, replace i by $i + 1$ and go back to step 2.

Note that if p is large (close to 1), this algorithm is an attractive alternative to the one given in Sec. 8.4.5, since no logarithms are required and early termination is likely.

8.15. Recall the shifted exponential, gamma, Weibull, lognormal, Pearson types V and VI, and log-logistic distributions discussed in Sec. 6.8. Assuming the ability to generate random variates from the original (unshifted) versions of these distributions, give a general algorithm for generating random variates from the shifted versions. (Assume that the shift parameter γ is specified.)

8.16. Give an explicit algorithm for generating a variate Y from the density $r(x)$ in Example 8.7; $r(x)$ is plotted in Fig. 8.12. (See also Prob. 8.7.)

8.17. The alias method, as stated in Sec. 8.4.3, requires generating at least two U(0, 1) random numbers—one to generate I in step 1 and the other to determine whether I or its alias is returned in step 2. Show that the following version of the alias method, which requires only one random number, is also valid:

1. Generate $U \sim$ U(0, 1).
2. Let $V = (n + 1)U$, $I = \lfloor V \rfloor$, and $U' = V - I$.
3. If $U' \leq F_I$, return $X = I$. Otherwise, return $X = L_I$.

[*Hint:* What is the joint distribution of I and U'? Although this "trick" does reduce the number of random numbers generated, it is probably not a good idea, since it depends on the low-order (least significant) bits of $V - I$ being "random," which may be doubtful for many (pseudo) random-number generators.]

8.18. The setup algorithms in App. 8B for the alias method produce cutoff values F_i that could actually be equal to 1; this will occur for at least one i if the second algorithm is used.
(*a*) Find a way to alter the cutoff and alias values so that every F_i will be strictly less than 1.
(*b*) With the F_i's all being strictly less than 1, find a way to reduce the storage requirements from $2(n + 1)$ to $n + 1$ by combining the L_i and F_i arrays into a single array of length $n + 1$. Restate the alias algorithm from Sec. 8.4.3 so that it works with this one-array method of holding the aliases and cutoff values.

8.19. For the ratio-of-uniforms method, show that the formulas for $u(z)$ and $v(z)$ in Eq. (8.1) are correct.

8.20. Show that the acceptance region S in Example 8.8 is bounded above and below by the curves $v = u$ and $v = u^2$, respectively.

8.21. Develop a majorizing region T that is closer in shape to the acceptance region S for Example 8.8. What is s/t? Give an algorithm for generating points uniformly in T.

8.22. Develop a ratio-of-uniforms algorithm for the standard normal distribution. Draw the acceptance region S. What is s/t?

8.23. The standard Kumaraswamy distribution has the following density function

$$f(x) = \alpha_1\alpha_2 x^{\alpha_1 - 1}(1 - x^{\alpha_1})^{\alpha_2 - 1} \qquad \text{for } 0 < x < 1$$

where $\alpha_1 > 0$ and $\alpha_2 > 0$ are shape parameters. Develop an algorithm for generating random variates from this distribution.

CHAPTER 9

Output Data Analysis for a Single System

Recommended sections for a first reading: 9.1 through 9.3, 9.4.1, 9.4.3, 9.5.1, 9.5.2, 9.8

9.1 INTRODUCTION

In many simulation studies a great deal of time and money is spent on model development and "programming," but little effort is made to analyze the simulation output data appropriately. As a matter of fact, a common mode of operation is to make a single simulation run of somewhat arbitrary length and then to treat the resulting simulation estimates as the "true" model characteristics. Since random samples from probability distributions are typically used to drive a simulation model through time, these estimates are just particular realizations of random variables that may have large variances. As a result, these estimates could, in a particular simulation run, differ greatly from the corresponding true characteristics for the model. The net effect is, of course, that there could be a significant probability of making erroneous inferences about the system under study.

Historically, there are several reasons why output data analyses have not been conducted in an appropriate manner. First, some users have the unfortunate impression that simulation is largely an exercise in computer programming, albeit a complicated one. Consequently some simulation "studies" begin with construction of an assumptions document (see Sec. 5.4.3) and subsequent "programming," and end with a single run of the simulation to produce the "answers." In fact, however, a simulation is a computer-based statistical sampling experiment. Thus if the results of a simulation study are to have any meaning, appropriate statistical techniques must be used to design and analyze the simulation experiments. A second reason for inadequate statistical analyses is that the output processes of virtually all simulations are nonstationary and autocorrelated (see Sec. 5.6). Thus, classical statistical techniques based on IID observations are not *directly* applicable. At present, there are still several output-analysis problems for which there is no completely accepted solution, and the methods that are available are often complicated to apply (see, for example, Sec. 9.5.4). Another impediment to obtaining precise estimates of a model's true parameters or characteristics is the computer time needed to collect the necessary amount of simulation output data. This difficulty often occurs in the simulation of large-scale military problems or high-speed communications networks.

We now describe more precisely the random nature of simulation output. Let Y_1, $Y_2, \ldots$ be an output stochastic process (see Sec. 4.3) from a *single* simulation run. For example, Y_i might be the throughput (production) in the ith hour for a manufacturing system. The Y_i's are random variables that will, in general, be neither independent nor identically distributed. Thus, most of the formulas of Chap. 4, which assume independence [e.g., the confidence interval given by (4.12)], do not apply *directly*.

Let $y_{11}, y_{12}, \ldots, y_{1m}$ be a realization of the random variables $Y_1, Y_2, \ldots, Y_m$ resulting from making a simulation run of length m observations using the random numbers $u_{11}, u_{12}, \ldots$. (The ith random number used in the jth run is denoted u_{ji}.) If we run the simulation with a different set of random numbers $u_{21}, u_{22}, \ldots$, then we will obtain a different realization $y_{21}, y_{22}, \ldots, y_{2m}$ of the random variables $Y_1, Y_2, \ldots, Y_m$. (The two realizations are not the same since the different random numbers used in the two runs produce different samples from the input probability distributions.) In general, suppose that we make n independent replications (runs) of the simulation (i.e., different random numbers are used for each replication, the statistical counters are reset at the beginning of each replication, and each replication uses the same initial conditions; see Sec. 9.4.3) of length m, resulting in the observations:

$$
\begin{array}{ccccc}
y_{11}, & \ldots, & y_{1i}, & \ldots, & y_{1m} \\
y_{21}, & \ldots, & y_{2i}, & \ldots, & y_{2m} \\
\vdots & & \vdots & & \vdots \\
y_{n1}, & \ldots, & y_{ni}, & \ldots, & y_{nm}
\end{array}
$$

The observations from a particular replication (row) are clearly not IID. However, note that $y_{1i}, y_{2i}, \ldots, y_{ni}$ (from the ith column) are IID observations of the random variable Y_i, for $i = 1, 2, \ldots, m$. This *independence across runs* (see Prob. 9.1) is the key to the relatively simple output-data-analysis methods described in later sections of this chapter. Then, roughly speaking, the goal of output analysis is to use the observations y_{ji} ($i = 1, 2, \ldots, m$; $j = 1, 2, \ldots, n$) to draw inferences about the (distributions of the) random variables $Y_1, Y_2, \ldots, Y_m$. For example, $\bar{y}_i(n) = \sum_{j=1}^{n} y_{ji}/n$ is an unbiased estimate of $E(Y_i)$.

EXAMPLE 9.1. Consider a bank with five tellers and one queue, which opens its doors at 9 A.M., closes its doors at 5 P.M., but stays open until all customers in the bank at 5 P.M. have been served. Assume that customers arrive in accordance with a Poisson process at rate 1 per minute (i.e., IID exponential interarrival times with mean 1 minute), that service times are IID exponential random variables with mean 4 minutes, and that customers are served in a FIFO manner. Table 9.1 shows several typical output statistics from 10 independent replications of a simulation of the bank, assuming that no

TABLE 9.1
Results for 10 independent replications of the bank model

Replication	Number served	Finish time (hours)	Average delay in queue (minutes)	Average queue length	Proportion of customers delayed < 5 minutes
1	484	8.12	1.53	1.52	0.917
2	475	8.14	1.66	1.62	0.916
3	484	8.19	1.24	1.23	0.952
4	483	8.03	2.34	2.34	0.822
5	455	8.03	2.00	1.89	0.840
6	461	8.32	1.69	1.56	0.866
7	451	8.09	2.69	2.50	0.783
8	486	8.19	2.86	2.83	0.782
9	502	8.15	1.70	1.74	0.873
10	475	8.24	2.60	2.50	0.779

customers are present initially. Note that results from various replications can be quite different. Thus, one run clearly does not produce "the answers."

Our goal in this chapter is to discuss methods for statistical analysis of simulation output data and to present the material with a practical focus that should be accessible to a reader having a basic understanding of probability and statistics. (Reviewing Chap. 4 might be advisable before reading this chapter.) We will discuss what we believe are all the important methods for output analysis; however, the emphasis will be on statistical procedures that are relatively easy to understand and implement, have been shown to perform well in practice, and have applicability to real-world problems.

In Secs. 9.2 and 9.3 we discuss types of simulations with regard to output analysis, and also measures of performance or parameters θ for each type. Sections 9.4 through 9.6 show how to get a point estimator $\hat{\theta}$ and confidence interval for each type of parameter θ, with the confidence interval typically requiring an estimate of the variance of $\hat{\theta}$, namely, $\widehat{\text{Var}}(\hat{\theta})$. Each of the analysis methods discussed may suffer from one or both of the following problems:

1. $\hat{\theta}$ is not an unbiased estimator of θ, that is, $E(\hat{\theta}) \neq \theta$; see, for example, Sec. 9.5.1.
2. $\widehat{\text{Var}}(\hat{\theta})$ is not an unbiased estimator of $\text{Var}(\hat{\theta})$; see, for example, Sec. 9.5.3.

Section 9.7 extends the above analysis to confidence-interval construction for several different parameters simultaneously. Finally, in Sec. 9.8 we show how time plots of important variables may provide insight into a system's dynamic behavior.

We will not attempt to give every reference on the subject of output-data analysis, since literally hundreds of papers on the subject have been written. A very comprehensive set of references up to 1983 is given in the survey paper by Law (1983); also see the survey paper by Pawlikowski (1990) and the book chapters by Alexopoulos and Seila (1998) and by Welch (1983). Most of the recent papers have been published in the journals *Transactions on Modeling and Computer Simulation, Operations Research, and INFORMS Journal on Computing*, or in the *Proceedings of the Winter Simulation Conference* (held every December).

9.2 TRANSIENT AND STEADY-STATE BEHAVIOR OF A STOCHASTIC PROCESS

Consider the output stochastic process $Y_1, Y_2, \ldots$. Let $F_i(y \mid I) = P(Y_i \le y \mid I)$ for $i = 1, 2, \ldots$, where y is a real number and I represents the initial conditions used to start the simulation at time 0. [The conditional probability $P(Y_i \le y \mid I)$ is the probability that the event $\{Y_i \le y\}$ occurs *given* the initial conditions I.] For a manufacturing system, I might specify the number of jobs present, and whether each machine is busy or idle, at time 0. We call $F_i(y \mid I)$ the *transient distribution* of the output process at (discrete) time i for initial conditions I. Note that $F_i(y \mid I)$ will, in general, be different for each value of i and each set of initial conditions I. The density functions for the transient distributions corresponding to the random variables Y_{i_1}, Y_{i_2}, Y_{i_3}, and Y_{i_4} are shown in Fig. 9.1 for a particular set of initial conditions I and increasing time indices i_1, i_2, i_3, and i_4, where it is assumed that the random variable Y_{i_j} has density function $f_{Y_{i_j}}$. The density $f_{Y_{i_j}}$ specifies how the random variable Y_{i_j} can vary from one replication to another. In particular, suppose that we make a very large number of replications, n, of the simulation and observe the stochastic process $Y_1, Y_2, \ldots$ on each one. If we make a histogram of the n observed values of the random variable Y_{i_j}, then this histogram (when appropriately scaled) will look very much like the density $f_{Y_{i_j}}$.

For fixed y and I, the probabilities $F_1(y \mid I), F_2(y \mid I), \ldots$ are just a sequence of numbers. *If* $F_i(y \mid I) \to F(y)$ as $i \to \infty$ for all y and for any initial conditions I, then $F(y)$ is called the *steady-state distribution* of the output process $Y_1, Y_2, \ldots$. Strictly speaking, the steady-state distribution $F(y)$ is only obtained in the limit as $i \to \infty$. In practice,

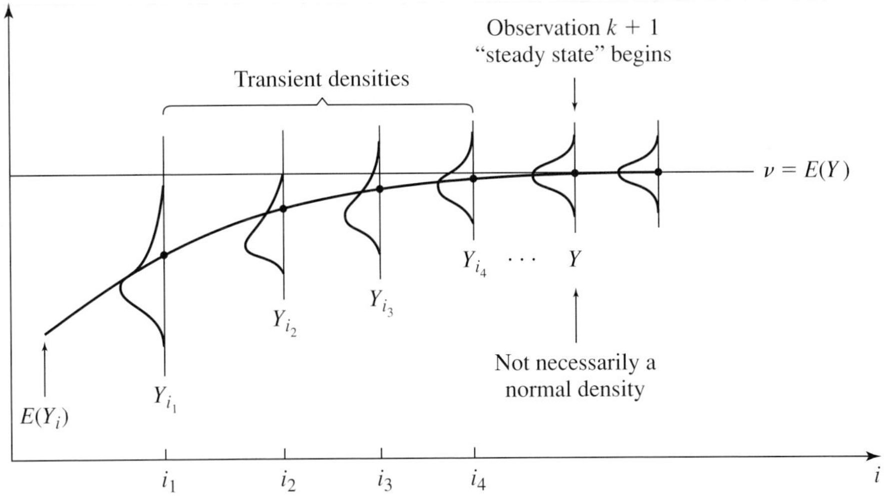

FIGURE 9.1
Transient and steady-state density functions for a particular stochastic process $Y_1, Y_2, \ldots$ and initial conditions I.

however, there will often be a finite time index, say, $k + 1$, such that the distributions from this point on will be approximately the same as each other; "steady state" is figuratively said to start at time $k + 1$ as shown in Fig. 9.1. Note that steady state does *not* mean that the random variables $Y_{k+1}, Y_{k+2}, \ldots$ will all take on the same value in a particular simulation run; rather, it means that they will all have approximately the same *distribution*. Furthermore, these random variables will not be independent, but will approximately constitute a covariance-stationary stochastic process (see Sec. 4.3). See Welch (1983) for an excellent discussion of transient and steady-state distributions.

The steady-state distribution $F(y)$ does not depend on the initial conditions I; however, the rate of convergence of the transient distributions $F_i(y|I)$ to $F(y)$ does, as the following example shows.

EXAMPLE 9.2. Consider the stochastic process $D_1, D_2, \ldots$ for the $M/M/1$ queue with $\rho = 0.9$ ($\lambda = 1$, $\omega = 10/9$), where D_i is the delay in queue of the ith customer. In Fig. 9.2 we plot the convergence of the transient mean $E(D_i)$ to the steady-state mean

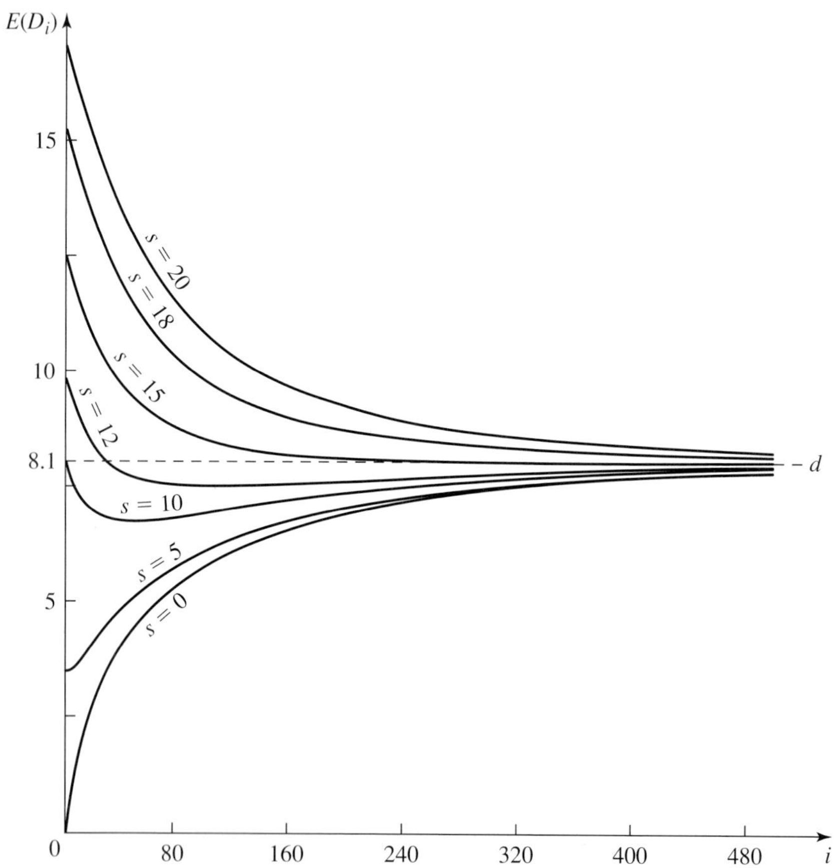

FIGURE 9.2
$E(D_i)$ as a function of i and the number in system at time 0, s, for the $M/M/1$ queue with $\rho = 0.9$.

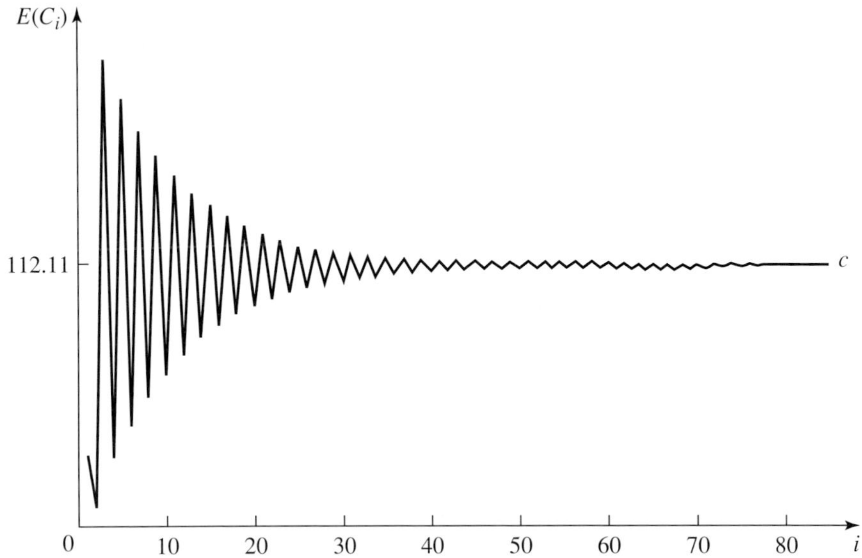

FIGURE 9.3
$E(C_i)$ as a function of i for the (s, S) inventory system.

$d = E(D) = 8.1$ as i gets large for various values of the number in system at time 0, s. (The random variable D has the steady-state delay in queue distribution.) Note that the convergence of $E(D_i)$ to d is, surprisingly, much faster for $s = 15$ than for $s = 0$ (see Prob. 9.11). The values for $E(D_i)$ were derived in Kelton and Law (1985); see also Kelton (1985) and Murray and Kelton (1988). The distribution function of D is given by (4.15) in App. 4A.

EXAMPLE 9.3. Consider the stochastic process $C_1, C_2, \ldots$ for the inventory problem of Example 4.23, where C_i is the total cost in the ith month. In Fig. 9.3 we plot the convergence of $E(C_i)$ to the steady-state mean $c = E(C) = 112.11$ [see Wagner (1969, p. A19)] as i gets large for an initial inventory level of 57. Note that the convergence is clearly not monotone.

In Examples 9.2 and 9.3 we plotted the convergence of the *expected value* $E(Y_i)$ to the steady-state mean $E(Y)$. It should be remembered, however, that the entire *distribution* of Y_i is also converging to the distribution of Y as i gets large.

9.3 TYPES OF SIMULATIONS WITH REGARD TO OUTPUT ANALYSIS

The options available in designing and analyzing simulation experiments depend on the type of simulation at hand, as depicted in Fig. 9.4. Simulations may be either terminating or nonterminating, depending on whether there is an obvious way for

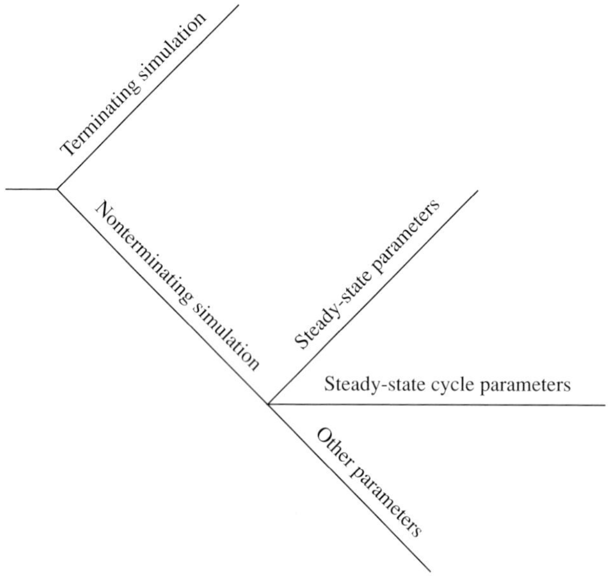

FIGURE 9.4
Types of simulations with regard to output analysis.

determining the run length. Furthermore, measures of performance or parameters for nonterminating simulations may be of several types, as shown in the figure. These concepts are defined more precisely below.

A *terminating simulation* is one for which there is a "natural" event E that specifies the length of each run (replication). Since different runs use independent random numbers and the same initialization rule, this implies that comparable random variables from the different runs are IID (see Sec. 9.4). The event E often occurs at a time point when the system is "cleaned out" (see Example 9.4), at a time point beyond which no useful information is obtained (see Example 9.5), or at a time point specified by management mandate (see Example 9.8). It is specified before any runs are made, and the time of occurrence of E for a particular run may be a random variable. Since the *initial conditions for a terminating simulation generally affect the desired measures of performance*, these conditions should be representative of those for the actual system (see Sec. 9.4.3).

EXAMPLE 9.4. A retail/commercial establishment, e.g., a bank, closes each evening. If the establishment is open from 9 A.M. to 5 P.M., the objective of a simulation might be to estimate some measure of the quality of customer service over the period beginning at 9 A.M. and ending when the last customer who entered before the doors closed at 5 P.M. has been served. In this case E = {at least 8 hours of simulated time have elapsed and the system is empty}, and the initial conditions for the simulation are the number of customers present at time 0 (see Sec. 9.4.3).

EXAMPLE 9.5. Consider a military ground confrontation between a blue force and a red force. Relative to some initial force strengths, the goal of a simulation might be to determine the (final) force strengths when the battle ends. In this case $E = \{$either the blue force or the red force has "won" the battle$\}$. An example of a condition that would end the battle is one side losing 30 percent of its force, since this side would no longer be considered viable. The choice of initial conditions, e.g., the number of troops and tanks for each force, for the simulation is generally not a problem here, since they are specified by the military scenario under consideration.

EXAMPLE 9.6. An aerospace manufacturer receives a contract to produce 100 airplanes, which must be delivered within 18 months. The company would like to simulate various manufacturing configurations to see which one can meet the delivery deadline at least cost. In this case $E = \{100$ airplanes have been completed$\}$.

EXAMPLE 9.7. Consider a manufacturing company that operates 16 hours a day (two shifts) with work in process carrying over from one day to the next. Would this qualify as a terminating simulation with $E = \{16$ hours of simulated time have elapsed$\}$? No, since this manufacturing operation is essentially a continuous process, with the ending conditions for one day being the initial conditions for the next day.

EXAMPLE 9.8. A company that sells a single product would like to decide how many items to have in inventory during a planning horizon of 120 months (see Sec. 1.5). Given some initial inventory level, the objective might be to determine how much to order each month so as to minimize the expected average cost per month of operating the inventory system. In this case $E = \{120$ months have been simulated$\}$, and the simulation is initialized with the current inventory level.

A *nonterminating simulation* is one for which there is no natural event E to specify the length of a run. This often occurs when we are designing a new system or changing an existing system, and we are interested in the behavior of the system in the long run when it is operating "normally." Unfortunately, "in the long run" doesn't naturally translate into a terminating event E. A measure of performance for such a simulation is said to be a *steady-state parameter* if it is a characteristic of the steady-state distribution of some output stochastic process $Y_1, Y_2, \ldots$. In Fig. 9.1, if the random variable Y has the steady-state distribution, then we might be interested in estimating the steady-state mean $\nu = E(Y)$ or a probability $P(Y \leq y)$ for some real number y.

EXAMPLE 9.9. Consider a company that is going to build a new manufacturing system and would like to determine the long-run (steady-state) mean hourly throughput of their system after it has been running long enough for the workers to know their jobs and for mechanical difficulties to have been worked out. Assume that:

(*a*) The system will operate 16 hours a day for 5 days a week.
(*b*) There is negligible loss of production at the end of one shift or at the beginning of the next shift (see Prob. 9.3).
(*c*) There are no breaks (e.g., lunch) that shut down production at specified times each day.

This system could be simulated by "pasting together" 16-hour days, thus ignoring the system idle time at the end of each day and on the weekend. Let N_i be the number of parts manufactured in the ith hour. If the stochastic process $N_1, N_2, \ldots$ has a steady-state distribution with corresponding random variable N, then we are interested in estimating the mean $\nu = E(N)$ (see Prob. 9.4).

It should be mentioned that stochastic processes for most *real* systems do not have steady-state distributions, since the characteristics of the system change over time. For example, in a manufacturing system the production-scheduling rules and the facility layout (e.g., number and location of machines) may change from time to time. On the other hand, a simulation model (which is an abstraction of reality) may have steady-state distributions, since characteristics of the *model* are often assumed not to change over time. When we have new information on the characteristics of the system, we can redo our steady-state analysis.

If, in Example 9.9, the manufacturing company wanted to know the time required for the system to go from startup to operating in a "normal" manner, this would be a terminating simulation with terminating event $E = \{$simulated system is running "normally"$\}$ (if such can be defined). *Thus, a simulation for a particular system might be either terminating or nonterminating, depending on the objectives of the simulation study.*

EXAMPLE 9.10. Consider a simulation model for a communications network that does not currently exist. Since there are typically no representative data available on the arrival mechanism for messages, it is common to assume that messages arrive in accordance with a Poisson process with *constant* rate equal to the *predicted* arrival rate of messages during the period of peak loading. (When the system is actually built, the arrival rate will vary as a function of time, and the period of peak loading may be relatively short.) Since the state of the system during "normal operation" is unknown, initial conditions must be chosen somewhat arbitrarily (e.g., no messages present at time 0). Then the goal is to run the simulation long enough so that the arbitrary choice of initial conditions is no longer having a significant effect on the estimated measures of performance (e.g., mean end-to-end delay of a message).

In performing the above steady-state analysis of the proposed communications network, we are essentially trying to determine how the network will respond to a peak load of infinite duration. If, however, the peak period in the actual network is short or if the arrival rate before the peak period is considerably lower than the peak rate, our analysis may overestimate the congestion level during the peak period in the network. This might result in purchasing a network configuration that is more powerful than actually needed.

Consider a stochastic process $Y_1, Y_2, \ldots$ for a nonterminating simulation that does not have a steady-state distribution. Suppose that we divide the time axis into equal-length, contiguous time intervals called *cycles*. (For example, in a manufacturing system a cycle might be an 8-hour shift.) Let Y_i^C be a random variable defined on the ith cycle, and assume that $Y_1^C, Y_2^C, \ldots$ are comparable. Suppose that the process $Y_1^C, Y_2^C, \ldots$ has a steady-state distribution F^C and that $Y^C \sim F^C$. Then a measure of performance is said to be a *steady-state cycle parameter* if it is a characteristic of Y^C such as the mean $\nu^C = E(Y^C)$. Thus, a steady-state cycle parameter is just a steady-state parameter of the appropriate cycle process $Y_1^C, Y_2^C, \ldots$.

EXAMPLE 9.11. Suppose for the manufacturing system in Example 9.9 that there is a half-hour lunch break at the beginning of the fifth hour in each 8-hour shift. Then the process of hourly throughputs $N_1, N_2, \ldots$ has no steady-state distribution (see Prob. 9.6). Let N_i^C be the average hourly throughput in the ith 8-hour shift (cycle). Then we might be interested in estimating the steady-state expected average hourly throughput over a cycle, $\nu^C = E(N^C)$, which is a steady-state cycle parameter.

EXAMPLE 9.12. Consider a call center for an airline. Suppose that the arrival rate of calls to the system varies with the time of day and day of the week, but assume that the pattern of arrival rates is identical from week to week. Let D_i be the delay experienced by the ith arriving call. The stochastic process $D_1, D_2, \ldots$ does not have a steady-state distribution. Let D_i^C be the average delay over the ith week. Then we might be interested in estimating the steady-state expected average delay over a week, $\nu^C = E(D^C)$.

For a nonterminating simulation, suppose that the stochastic process $Y_1, Y_2, \ldots$ does not have a steady-state distribution, and that there is no appropriate cycle definition such that the corresponding process $Y_1^C, Y_2^C, \ldots$ has a steady-state distribution. This can occur, for example, if the parameters for the model continue to change over time. In Example 9.12, if the arrival rate of calls changes from week to week and from year to year, then steady-state (cycle) parameters will probably not be well defined. In these cases, however, there will typically be a fixed amount of data describing how input parameters change over time. This provides, in effect, a terminating event E for the simulation and, thus, the analysis techniques for terminating simulations in Sec. 9.4 are appropriate. This is why we do not treat this situation as a separate case later in the chapter. Measures of performance or parameters for such simulations usually change over time and are included in the category "Other parameters" in Fig. 9.4.

EXAMPLE 9.13. Consider the manufacturing system of Example 5.26. There was a 3-month build schedule available from marketing, which described the types and numbers of computers to be produced each week. The schedule changed from week to week because of changing sales and the introduction of new computers. In this case, weekly or monthly throughputs did not have steady-state distributions. We therefore performed a terminating simulation of length 3 months and estimated the mean throughput for each week.

9.4 STATISTICAL ANALYSIS FOR TERMINATING SIMULATIONS

Suppose that we make n independent replications of a terminating simulation, where each replication is terminated by the event E and is begun with the "same" initial conditions (see Sec. 9.4.3). The independence of replications is accomplished by using different random numbers for each replication. (For a discussion of how this can easily be accomplished if the n replications are made in more than one execution, see Sec. 7.2.) Assume for simplicity that there is a single measure of performance of interest. (This assumption is dropped in Sec. 9.7.) Let X_j be a random variable defined on the jth replication for $j = 1, 2, \ldots, n$; it is assumed that the X_j's are comparable for different replications. Then the X_j's are IID random variables. For the bank of Examples 9.1 and 9.4, X_j might be the average delay $\sum_{i=1}^{N} D_i/N$ over a day (see column 4 in Table 9.1) from the jth replication, where N (a random variable) is the number of customers served in a day. For the combat model of Example 9.5, X_j might be the number of red tanks destroyed on the jth replication. Finally, for the inventory system of Example 9.8, X_j could be the average cost $\sum_{i=1}^{120} C_i/120$ from the jth replication.

9.4.1 Estimating Means

Suppose that we would like to obtain a point estimate and confidence interval for the mean $\mu = E(X)$, where X is a random variable defined on a replication as described above. Make n independent replications of the simulation and let X_1, $X_2, \ldots, X_n$ be the resulting IID random variables. Then, by substituting the X_j's into (4.3) and (4.12), we get that $\overline{X}(n)$ is an unbiased point estimator for μ, and an approximate $100(1 - \alpha)$ percent $(0 < \alpha < 1)$ confidence interval for μ is given by

$$\overline{X}(n) \pm t_{n-1,1-\alpha/2}\sqrt{\frac{S^2(n)}{n}} \tag{9.1}$$

where the sample variance $S^2(n)$ is given by Eq. (4.4). We will call the confidence interval based on (9.1) the *fixed-sample-size procedure*. [See also the Willink confidence interval given by (4.13).]

EXAMPLE 9.14. For the bank of Example 9.1, suppose that we want to obtain a point estimate and an approximate 90 percent confidence interval for the expected average delay of a customer over a day, which is given by

$$E(X) = E\left(\frac{\sum_{i=1}^{N} D_i}{N}\right)$$

(Note that we estimate the expected *average* delay, since each delay has, in general, a different mean.) From the 10 replications given in Table 9.1 we obtained

$$\overline{X}(10) = 2.03, \qquad S^2(10) = 0.31$$

and

$$\overline{X}(10) \pm t_{9,0.95}\sqrt{\frac{S^2(10)}{10}} = 2.03 \pm 0.32$$

Thus, subject to the correct interpretation to be given to confidence intervals (see Sec. 4.5), we can claim with approximately 90 percent confidence that $E(X)$ is contained in the interval [1.71, 2.35] minutes.

EXAMPLE 9.15. For the inventory system of Sec. 1.5 and Example 9.8, suppose that we want to obtain a point estimate and an approximate 95 percent confidence interval for the expected average cost over the 120-month planning horizon, which is given by

$$E(X) = E\left(\frac{\sum_{i=1}^{120} C_i}{120}\right)$$

We made 10 independent replications and obtained the following X_j's:

129.35	127.11	124.03	122.13	120.44
118.39	130.17	129.77	125.52	133.75

which resulted in

$$\bar{X}(10) = 126.07, \qquad S^2(10) = 23.55$$

and the 95 percent confidence interval

$$126.07 \pm 3.47 \qquad \text{or, alternatively,} \qquad [122.60, 129.54]$$

Note that the estimated coefficient of variation (see Table 6.5), a measure of variability, is 0.04 for the inventory system and 0.27 for the bank model. Thus the X_j's for the bank model are inherently more variable than those for the inventory system.

EXAMPLE 9.16. For the bank of Example 9.1, suppose that we would like to obtain a point estimate and an approximate 90 percent confidence interval for the expected proportion of customers with a delay less than 5 minutes over a day, which is given by

$$E(X) = E\left(\frac{\sum_{i=1}^{N} I_i(0, 5)}{N}\right)$$

where the *indicator function* $I_i(0, 5)$ is defined as

$$I_i(0, 5) = \begin{cases} 1 & \text{if } D_i < 5 \\ 0 & \text{otherwise} \end{cases}$$

for $i = 1, 2, \ldots, N$. From the last column of Table 9.1, we obtained

$$\bar{X}(10) = 0.853, \qquad S^2(10) = 0.004$$

and the 90 percent confidence interval

$$0.853 \pm 0.036 \qquad \text{or} \qquad [0.817, 0.889]$$

The correctness of the confidence interval given by (9.1) (in terms of having coverage close to $1 - \alpha$) depends on the assumption that the X_j's are normal random variables (or on n being "sufficiently large"); this is why we called the confidence intervals in Examples 9.14, 9.15, and 9.16 *approximate*. Since this assumption will rarely be satisfied in practice, we now use several simple stochastic models with *known* means to investigate empirically the robustness of the confidence interval to departures from normality. Our goal is to provide the simulation practitioner with some guidance as to how well the confidence interval will perform, in terms of coverage, in practice.

We first performed 500 independent simulation experiments for the $M/M/1$ queue with $\rho = 0.9$. For each experiment we considered $n = 5, 10, 20, 40$, and for each n we used (9.1) to construct an approximate 90 percent confidence interval for

$$d(25|s = 0) = E\left(\left.\frac{\sum_{i=1}^{25} D_i}{25}\right| s = 0\right) = 2.12$$

TABLE 9.2
Fixed-sample-size results for $d(25|s = 0) = 2.12$ based on 500 experiments, $M/M/1$ queue with $\rho = 0.9$

n	Estimated coverage	Average of (confidence-interval half-length)/$\overline{X}(n)$
5	0.880 ± 0.024	0.67
10	0.864 ± 0.025	0.44
20	0.886 ± 0.023	0.30
40	0.914 ± 0.021	0.21

where s is the number of customers present at time 0 [see Kelton and Law (1985) and Example 9.2]. Table 9.2 gives the proportion, $\hat{p}$, of the 500 confidence intervals that covered the true $d(25|s = 0)$, a 90 percent confidence interval for the true coverage p [the proportion of a very large number of confidence intervals that would cover $d(25|s = 0)$], and the average value of the confidence-interval half-length [that is, $t_{n-1,1-\alpha/2}\sqrt{S^2(n)/n}$] divided by the point estimate $\overline{X}(n)$ over the 500 experiments, which is a measure of the precision of the confidence interval; see below for further discussion. The 90 percent confidence interval for the true coverage is computed from

$$\hat{p} \pm z_{0.95}\sqrt{\frac{\hat{p}(1 - \hat{p})}{500}}$$

and is based on the fact that $(\hat{p} - p)/\sqrt{\hat{p}(1 - \hat{p})/500}$ is approximately distributed as a standard normal random variable [see, e.g., Hogg and Craig (1995, pp. 254–255)]. It is recommended that this confidence interval for p only be used if $n\hat{p} \geq 10$ and $n(1 - \hat{p}) \geq 10$. If this is not the case in a particular situation, then the *score* confidence interval [Devore (2008, p. 266)] might be used instead.

From Table 9.2 it can be seen that 86.4 percent of the 500 confidence intervals based on $n = 10$ replications covered $d(25|s = 0)$, and we know with approximately 90 percent confidence that the true coverage for $n = 10$ is between 0.839 and 0.889. Considering that a simulation model is always just an approximation to the corresponding real-world system, we believe that the estimated coverages presented in Table 9.2 are close enough to the desired 0.9 to be useful. Note also from the last column of the table that four times as many replications are required to increase the precision of the confidence interval by a factor of approximately 2. This is not surprising since there is a $\sqrt{n}$ in the denominator of the expression for the confidence-interval half-length in (9.1).

To show that the confidence interval given by (9.1) does not always produce coverages close to $1 - \alpha$, we considered a second example. A reliability model consisting of three components will function as long as component 1 works and either component 2 or 3 works. If G is the time to failure of the whole system and G_i is the time to failure of component i (where $i = 1, 2, 3$), then $G = \min\{G_1, \max\{G_2, G_3\}\}$. We further assume that the G_i's are independent random variables and that each G_i has a Weibull distribution with shape parameter 0.5 and scale parameter 1 (see Sec. 6.2.2). This particular Weibull distribution is extremely skewed and

TABLE 9.3
Fixed-sample-size results for $E(G \mid \text{all components new}) = 0.78$ based on 500 experiments, reliability model

n	Estimated coverage	Average of (confidence-interval half-length)/$\bar{X}(n)$
5	0.708 ± 0.033	1.16
10	0.750 ± 0.032	0.82
20	0.800 ± 0.029	0.60
40	0.840 ± 0.027	0.44

non-normal. Once again we performed 500 independent simulation experiments; for each experiment we considered $n = 5, 10, 20, 40$, and for each n we used (9.1) to construct a 90 percent confidence interval for $E(G \mid \text{all components new}) = 0.78$ (which was calculated by analytic reasoning). The results from these experiments are given in Table 9.3. Note that for small values of n there is significant coverage degradation. Also, as n gets large, the coverage appears to be approaching 0.9, as guaranteed by the central limit theorem. The Willink confidence interval could possibly be used for this model unless n is "large."

We can see from Tables 9.2 and 9.3 that the coverage actually obtained from the confidence interval given by (9.1) depends on the simulation model under consideration (actually, on the distribution of the resulting X_j's) and also on the sample size n. It is therefore natural to ask why the confidence interval worked better for the $M/M/1$ queue than it did for the reliability model. To answer this question, we first performed 500 independent simulation experiments for the $M/M/1$ queue with $\rho = 0.9$ and $s = 0$ ($n = 1$), and we observed $\sum_{i=1}^{25} D_i/25$ on each replication. A histogram of the 500 average delays is given in Fig. 9.5, and the sample skewness was 1.64 (see

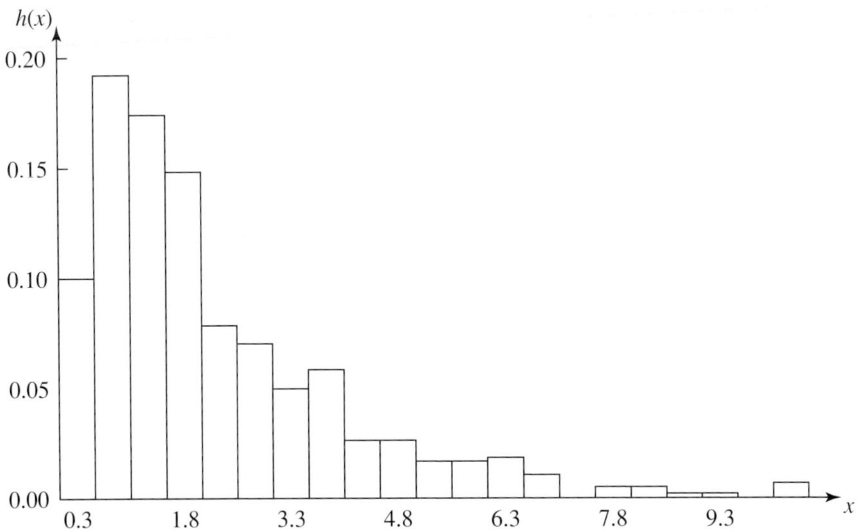

FIGURE 9.5
Histogram of 500 average delays (each based on 25 individual delays) for the $M/M/1$ queue with $\rho = 0.9$.

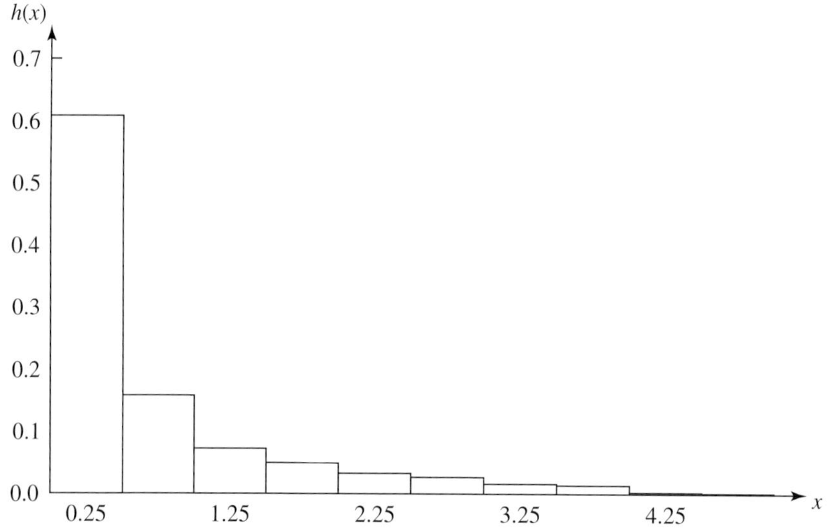

FIGURE 9.6
Histogram of 500 times to failure for the reliability model.

Tables 4.1 and 6.5). Although the histogram indicates that average delay is not normally distributed, it does show that the distribution of average delay is not extremely skewed. (For example, an exponential distribution has a skewness of 2.) We next performed 500 independent experiments for the reliability model and observed the time to failure G on each replication. A histogram of the 500 values of G is given in Fig. 9.6, and the estimated skewness was 3.64. Thus, the distribution of time to failure is considerably more non-normal than the distribution of average delay. These results shed some light on why the coverages for the $M/M/1$ queue are closer to 0.9 than for the reliability model.

The reader might wonder why average delay is more normally distributed than time to failure. Note that an X_j for the $M/M/1$ queue is actually an average of 25 individual delays, while an X_j for the reliability model is computed from the three individual times to failure by a formula involving a minimum and a maximum. There are central limit theorems for certain types of correlated data that state that averages of these data become approximately normally distributed as the number of points in the average gets large. To show this for the $M/M/1$ queue, we performed 500 independent experiments and observed $\sum_{i=1}^{6400} D_i/6400$ on each replication. A histogram of the 500 average delays (each based on 6400 individual delays) is given in Fig. 9.7, and the estimated skewness was 1.07. (The skewness of a normal distribution is 0.) Clearly, the histogram in Fig. 9.7 is closer to a normal distribution than the histogram in Fig. 9.5.

We therefore expect that if X_j is the average of a large number of individual observations (even though correlated), the degradation in coverage of the confidence interval may not be severe. Our experience indicates that many real-world simulations produce X_j's of this type.

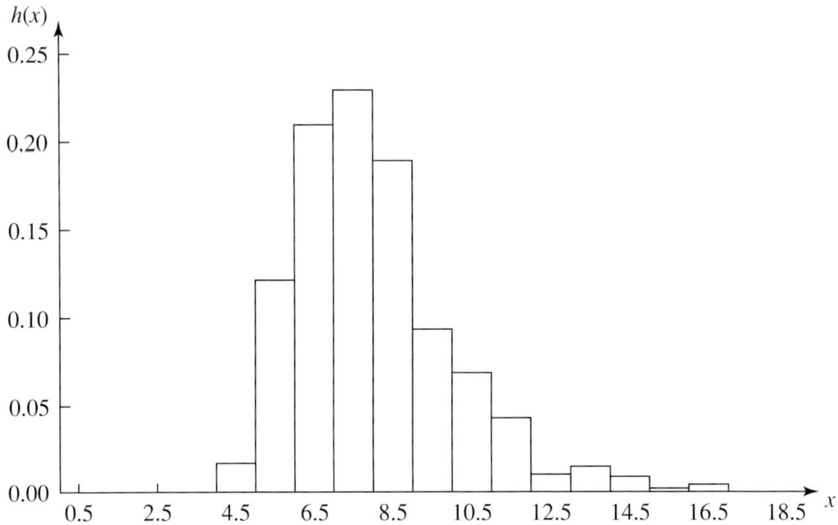

FIGURE 9.7
Histogram of 500 average delays (each based on 6400 individual delays) for the $M/M/1$ queue with $\rho = 0.9$.

Obtaining a Specified Precision

One disadvantage of the fixed-sample-size procedure based on n replications is that the analyst has no control over the confidence-interval half-length [or the precision of $\overline{X}(n)$]; for fixed n, the half-length will depend on Var(X), the population variance of the X_j's. In what follows we discuss procedures for determining the number of replications required to estimate the mean $\mu = E(X)$ with a specified error or precision.

We begin by defining two ways of measuring the error in the estimate $\overline{X}$. (The dependence on n is suppressed, since the number of replications may be a random variable.) If the estimate $\overline{X}$ is such that $|\overline{X} - \mu| = \beta$, then we say that $\overline{X}$ has an *absolute error* of β. If we make replications of a simulation until the half-length of the $100(1 - \alpha)$ percent confidence interval given by (9.1) is less than or equal to β (where $\beta > 0$), then

$$\begin{aligned} 1 - \alpha &\approx P(\overline{X} - \text{half-length} \le \mu \le \overline{X} + \text{half-length}) \\ &= P(|\overline{X} - \mu| \le \text{half-length}) \\ &\le P(|\overline{X} - \mu| \le \beta) \end{aligned}$$

[If A and B are events with A being a subset of B, then $P(A) \le P(B)$.] Thus, $\overline{X}$ has an absolute error of at most β with a probability of approximately $1 - \alpha$. In other words, if we construct 100 independent 90 percent confidence intervals using the above stopping rule, we would expect $\overline{X}$ to have an absolute error of at most β in about 90 out of the 100 cases; in about 10 cases the absolute error would be greater than β.

Suppose that we have constructed a confidence interval for μ based on a fixed number of replications n. If we assume that our estimate $S^2(n)$ of the population variance will not change (appreciably) as the number of replications increases, an *approximate* expression for the total number of replications, $n_a^*(\beta)$, required to obtain an absolute error of β is given by

$$n_a^*(\beta) = \min\left\{i \geq n: t_{i-1,1-\alpha/2}\sqrt{\frac{S^2(n)}{i}} \leq \beta\right\} \tag{9.2}$$

(The colon ":" is read "such that.") We can determine $n_a^*(\beta)$ by iteratively increasing i by 1 until a value of i is obtained for which $t_{i-1,1-\alpha/2}\sqrt{S^2(n)/i} \leq \beta$. [Alternatively, $n_a^*(\beta)$ can be approximated as the smallest integer i satisfying $i \geq S^2(n)(z_{1-\alpha/2}/\beta)^2$.] If $n_a^*(\beta) > n$ and if we make $n_a^*(\beta) - n$ additional replications of the simulation, then the estimate $\overline{X}$ based on all $n_a^*(\beta)$ replications should have an absolute error of approximately β. The accuracy of Eq. (9.2) depends on how close the variance estimate $S^2(n)$ is to $\text{Var}(X)$.

EXAMPLE 9.17. For the bank of Example 9.14, suppose that we would like to estimate the expected average delay with an absolute error of 0.25 minute and a confidence level of 90 percent. From the 10 available replications, we get

$$n_a^*(0.25) = \min\left\{i \geq 10: t_{i-1,0.95}\sqrt{\frac{0.31}{i}} \leq 0.25\right\} = 16$$

We now discuss another way of measuring the error in $\overline{X}$. Assume now that $\mu \neq 0$. If the estimate $\overline{X}$ is such that $|\overline{X} - \mu|/|\mu| = \gamma$, then we say that $\overline{X}$ has a *relative error* of γ, or that the *percentage error* in $\overline{X}$ is 100γ percent. Suppose that we make replications of a simulation until the half-length of the confidence interval given by (9.1), divided by $|\overline{X}|$, is less than or equal to $\gamma (0 < \gamma < 1)$. This ratio is an estimate of the actual relative error. Then

$$\begin{aligned}
1 - \alpha &\approx P(|\overline{X} - \mu|/|\overline{X}| \leq \text{half-length}/|\overline{X}|) \\
&\leq P(|\overline{X} - \mu| \leq \gamma|\overline{X}|) && [(\text{half-length}/|\overline{X}|) \leq \gamma] \\
&= P(|\overline{X} - \mu| \leq \gamma|\overline{X} - \mu + \mu|) && (\text{add, subtract } \mu) \\
&\leq P(|\overline{X} - \mu| \leq \gamma(|\overline{X} - \mu| + |\mu|)) && (\text{triangle inequality}) \\
&= P((1 - \gamma)|\overline{X} - \mu| \leq \gamma|\mu|) && (\text{algebra}) \\
&= P(|\overline{X} - \mu|/|\mu| \leq \gamma/(1 - \gamma)) && (\text{algebra})
\end{aligned}$$

Thus, $\overline{X}$ has a relative error of at most $\gamma/(1 - \gamma)$ with a probability of approximately $1 - \alpha$. In other words, if we construct 100 independent 90 percent confidence intervals using the above stopping rule, we would expect $\overline{X}$ to have a relative error of at most $\gamma/(1 - \gamma)$ in about 90 of the 100 cases; in about 10 cases the relative error would be greater than $\gamma/(1 - \gamma)$. Note that we get a relative error of $\gamma/(1 - \gamma)$ rather than the desired γ, since we *estimate* $|\mu|$ by $|\overline{X}|$.

Suppose once again that we have constructed a confidence interval for μ based on a fixed number of replications n. If we assume that our estimates of both the population mean and population variance will not change (appreciably) as the number of replications increases, an *approximate* expression for the number of replications, $n_r^*(\gamma)$, required to obtain a relative error of γ is given by

$$n_r^*(\gamma) = \min\left\{ i \ge n\colon \frac{t_{i-1,1-\alpha/2}\sqrt{S^2(n)/i}}{|\overline{X}(n)|} \le \gamma' \right\} \tag{9.3}$$

where $\gamma' = \gamma/(1 + \gamma)$ is the "adjusted" relative error needed to get an *actual* relative error of γ. {Again, $n_r^*(\gamma)$ is approximated as the smallest integer i satisfying $i \ge S^2(n)[z_{1-\alpha/2}/(\gamma'\overline{X}(n))]^2$.} If $n_r^*(\gamma) > n$ and if we make $n_r^*(\gamma) - n$ additional replications of the simulation, then the estimate $\overline{X}$ based on all $n_r^*(\gamma)$ replications should have a relative error of approximately γ.

EXAMPLE 9.18. For the bank of Example 9.14, suppose that we would like to estimate the expected average delay with a relative error of 0.10 and a confidence level of 90 percent. From the 10 available replications, we get

$$n_r^*(0.10) = \min\left\{ i \ge 10\colon \frac{t_{i-1,0.95}\sqrt{0.31/i}}{2.03} \le 0.09 \right\} = 27$$

where $\gamma' = 0.1/(1 + 0.1) = 0.09$.

The difficulty with using Eq. (9.3) directly to obtain an estimate $\overline{X}$ with a relative error of γ is that $\overline{X}(n)$ and $S^2(n)$ may not be precise estimates of their corresponding population parameters. If $n_r^*(\gamma)$ is greater than the number of replications actually required, then a significant number of unnecessary replications may be made, resulting in a waste of computer resources. Conversely, if $n_r^*(\gamma)$ is too small, then an estimate $\overline{X}$ based on $n_r^*(\gamma)$ replications may not be as precise as we think. We now present a *sequential* procedure (new replications are added one at a time) for obtaining an estimate of μ with a specified relative error that takes only as many replications as are actually needed. The procedure assumes that $X_1, X_2, \ldots$ is a sequence of IID random variables that need not be normal.

The specific objective of the procedure is to obtain an estimate of μ with a relative error of $\gamma (0 < \gamma < 1)$ and a confidence level of $100(1 - \alpha)$ percent. Choose an initial number of replications $n_0 \ge 10$ and let

$$\delta(n, \alpha) = t_{n-1,1-\alpha/2}\sqrt{\frac{S^2(n)}{n}}$$

be the usual confidence-interval half-length. Then the sequential procedure is as follows:

0. Make n_0 replications of the simulation and set $n = n_0$.
1. Compute $\overline{X}(n)$ and $\delta(n, \alpha)$ from $X_1, X_2, \ldots, X_n$.
2. If $\delta(n, \alpha)/|\overline{X}(n)| \le \gamma'$, use $\overline{X}(n)$ as the point estimate for μ and stop. Equivalently,

$$I(\alpha, \gamma) = [\overline{X}(n) - \delta(n, \alpha), \overline{X}(n) + \delta(n, \alpha)] \tag{9.4}$$

is an approximate $100(1 - \alpha)$ percent confidence interval for μ with the desired precision. Otherwise, replace n by $n + 1$, make an additional replication of the simulation, and go to step 1.

Note that the procedure computes a new estimate of $\text{Var}(X)$ after *each* replication is obtained, and that the total number of replications required by the procedure is a random variable.

EXAMPLE 9.19. For the bank of Example 9.14, suppose that we would like to obtain an estimate of the expected average delay with a relative error of $\gamma = 0.1$ and a confidence level of 90 percent. Using the previous $n_0 = 10$ replications as a starting point, we obtained

$$\text{Number of replications at termination} = 74$$

$$\bar{X}(74) = 1.76, \qquad S^2(74) = 0.67$$

$$\text{90 percent confidence interval: } [1.60, 1.92]$$

Note that the number of replications actually required, 74, is considerably larger than the 27 predicted in Example 9.18, due mostly to the imprecise variance estimate based on 10 replications.

Although the sequential procedure described above is intuitively appealing, the question naturally arises as to how well it performs in terms of producing a confidence interval with coverage close to the desired $1 - \alpha$. In Law, Kelton, and Koenig (1981), it is shown that if $\mu \neq 0$ [and $0 < \text{Var}(X) < \infty$], then the coverage of the confidence interval given by Eq. (9.4) will be arbitrarily close to $1 - \alpha$, provided the desired relative error is sufficiently close to 0. Based on sampling from a large number of stochastic models and probability distributions (including the *M/M/*1 queue and the above reliability model) for which the true values of μ are known, our recommendation is to use the sequential procedure with $n_0 \geq 10$ and $\gamma \leq 0.15$. It was found that if these recommendations are followed, the estimated coverage (based on 500 independent experiments for each model) for a desired 90 percent confidence interval was never less than 0.864.

Analogous to the sequential procedure described above is a sequential procedure due to Chow and Robbins (1965) for constructing a $100(1 - \alpha)$ percent confidence interval for μ with a small absolute error β. Furthermore, it can be shown that the coverage actually produced by the procedure will be arbitrarily close to $1 - \alpha$ provided the desired absolute error β is sufficiently close to 0. However, since the meaning of "*absolute error* sufficiently small" is extremely model-dependent, and since the coverage results in Law (1980) indicate that the procedure is very sensitive to the choice of β, we do not recommend the use of the Chow and Robbins procedure in general.

Recommended Use of the Procedures

We now make our recommendations on the use of the fixed-sample-size and sequential procedures for terminating simulations. If one is performing an exploratory experiment where the precision of the confidence interval may not be overwhelmingly important, we recommend using the fixed-sample-size procedure. However, if the X_j's are highly non-normal and the number of replications n is too small, the actual coverage of the constructed confidence interval may be somewhat lower than desired. In this case consider the use of the Willink confidence interval.

From an exploratory experiment consisting of n replications, one can estimate the execution time per replication and the population variance of the X_j's, and then obtain from Eq. (9.2) a *rough estimate* of the number of replications, $n_a^*(\beta)$, required to estimate μ with a desired absolute error β. Alternatively, one can obtain from Eq. (9.3) a *rough estimate* of the number of replications, $n_r^*(\gamma)$, required to estimate μ with a desired relative error γ. Sometimes the choice of β or γ may have to be tempered by the execution time associated with the required number of replications. If it is finally decided to construct a confidence interval with a small relative error γ, we recommend use of the sequential procedure with $\gamma \le 0.15$ and $n_0 \ge 10$. If one wants a confidence interval with a relative error γ greater than 0.15, we recommend several successive applications of the fixed-sample-size approach. In particular, one might estimate $n_r^*(\gamma)$, collect, say $[n_r^*(\gamma) - n]/2$ more replications, and then use (9.1) to construct a confidence interval based on the existing $[n + n_r^*(\gamma)]/2$ replications. If the estimated relative error of the resulting confidence interval is still greater than γ', then $n_r^*(\gamma)$ can be reestimated based on a new variance estimate, and some portion of the necessary additional replications may be collected, etc. To construct a confidence interval with a small absolute error β, we once again recommend several successive applications of the fixed-sample-size approach.

Regardless of the time per replication, we recommend always making at least three to five replications of a stochastic simulation to assess the variability of the X_j's. If this is not possible due to time considerations, then the simulation study should probably not be done at all.

9.4.2 Estimating Other Measures of Performance

In this section we discuss estimating measures of performance other than means. As the following example shows, comparing two or more systems by some sort of mean system response may result in misleading conclusions.

EXAMPLE 9.20. Consider the bank of Example 9.14, where the utilization factor $\rho = \lambda/(5\omega) = 0.8$. We compare the policy of having one queue for each teller (and jockeying) with the policy of having one queue feed all tellers on the basis of *expected average delay in queue* (see Example 9.14) and *expected time-average number of customers in queue*, which is defined by

$$E\left[\frac{\int_0^T Q(t)\,dt}{T}\right]$$

where $Q(t)$ is the number of customers in queue at time t and T is the bank's operating time ($T \ge 8$ hours). Table 9.4 gives the results of making one simulation run of each policy. [These simulation runs were performed so that the time of arrival of the ith customer ($i = 1, 2, \ldots, N$) was identical for both policies and so that the service time of

TABLE 9.4
Simulation results for the two bank policies: averages

	Estimates	
Measure of performance	**Five queues**	**One queue**
Expected operating time, hours	8.14	8.14
Expected average delay, minutes	5.57	5.57
Expected average number in queue	5.52	5.52

the ith customer to begin service ($i = 1, 2, \ldots, N$) was the same for both policies.] Thus, on the basis of "average system response," it would appear that the two policies are equivalent. However, this is clearly not the case. Since customers need not be served in the order of their arrival with the multiqueue policy, we would expect this policy to result in greater variability of a customer's delay. Table 9.5 gives estimates, computed from the same two simulation runs used above, of the expected proportion of customers with a delay in the interval [0, 5) (in minutes), the expected proportion of customers with a delay in [5, 10), . . . , the expected proportion of customers with a delay in [40, 45) for both policies. (We did not estimate variances from these runs since, as pointed out in Sec. 4.4, variance estimates computed from correlated simulation output data are highly biased.) Observe from Table 9.5 that a customer is more likely to have a large delay with the multiqueue policy than with the single-queue policy. In particular, if 480 customers arrive in a day (the expected number), then 33 and 6 of them would be expected to have delays greater than or equal to 20 minutes for the five-queue and one-queue policies, respectively. (For larger values of ρ, the differences between the two policies would be even greater.) This observation together with the greater equitability of the single-queue policy has probably led many organizations, e.g., banks and airlines, to adopt this policy.

We conclude from the above example that comparing alternative systems or policies on the basis of average system behavior alone can sometimes result in misleading conclusions and, furthermore, that proportions can be a useful measure of system performance. In Example 9.16 we showed how to obtain a point estimate

TABLE 9.5
Simulation results for the two bank policies: proportions

	Estimates of expected proportions of delays in interval	
Interval (minutes)	**Five queues**	**One queue**
[0, 5)	0.626	0.597
[5, 10)	0.182	0.188
[10, 15)	0.076	0.107
[15, 20)	0.047	0.095
[20, 25)	0.031	0.013
[25, 30)	0.020	0
[30, 35)	0.015	0
[35, 40)	0.003	0
[40, 45)	0	0

and a confidence interval for an expected proportion. In this section we show how to perform similar analyses for probabilities and quantiles in the context of terminating simulations.

Let X be a random variable defined on a replication as described in Sec. 9.4.1. Suppose that we would like to estimate the probability $p = P(X \in B)$, where B is a set of real numbers. {For example, B could be the interval $[20, \infty)$ in Example 9.20.} Make n independent replications and let $X_1, X_2, \ldots, X_n$ be the resulting IID random variables. Let S be the number of X_j's that fall in the set B. Then S has a binomial distribution (see Sec. 6.2.3) with parameters n and p, and an unbiased point estimator for p is given by

$$\hat{p} = \frac{S}{n}$$

Furthermore, if n is "sufficiently large," then an approximate $100(1 - \alpha)$ percent confidence interval for p is given by

$$\hat{p} \pm z_{1-\alpha/2}\sqrt{\frac{\hat{p}(1 - \hat{p})}{n}}$$

[see Devore (2008, p. 266) for an alternative confidence interval and also Prob. 9.9].

EXAMPLE 9.21. For the bank of Example 9.14, suppose that we would like to get a point estimate and approximate 90 percent confidence interval for

$$p = P(X \le 15) \qquad \text{where } X = \max_{0 \le t \le T} Q(t)$$

In this case, $B = [0, 15]$. We made 100 independent replications of the bank simulation and obtained $\hat{p} = 0.77$. Thus, for approximately 77 out of every 100 days, we expect the maximum queue length during a day to be less than or equal to 15 customers. We also obtained the following approximate 90 percent confidence interval for p:

$$0.77 \pm 0.07 \qquad \text{or, alternatively,} \qquad [0.70, 0.84]$$

Suppose now that we would like to estimate the q-quantile (100qth percentile) x_q of the distribution of the random variable X (see Sec. 6.4.3 for the definition). For example, the 0.5-quantile is the median. If $X_{(1)}, X_{(2)}, \ldots, X_{(n)}$ are the order statistics corresponding to the X_j's from n independent replications, then a point estimator for x_q is the sample q-quantile $\hat{x}_q$, which is given by

$$\hat{x}_q = \begin{cases} X_{(nq)} & \text{if } nq \text{ is an integer} \\ X_{(\lfloor nq+1 \rfloor)} & \text{otherwise} \end{cases}$$

Let r and s be positive integers that satisfy $1 \le r < s \le n$. If n is "sufficiently large," then a $100(1 - \alpha)$ percent confidence interval for x_q is given by [see Conover (1999, pp. 143–148)]

$$P(X_{(r)} \le x_q \le X_{(s)}) \ge 1 - \alpha$$

where

$$r = \lceil nq + z_{\alpha/2}\sqrt{nq(1 - q)} \rceil$$

and

$$s = \lceil nq + z_{1-\alpha/2}\sqrt{nq(1 - q)} \rceil$$

The greater than or equal to sign in the confidence-interval expression becomes an equal sign if X is a continuous random variable.

EXAMPLE 9.22. For the bank of Example 9.14, suppose that we would like to decide how large a lobby is needed to accommodate customers waiting in the queue. If we let X be the maximum queue length as defined in Example 9.21, then we might want to build a lobby large enough to hold $x_{0.95}$ customers, the 0.95-quantile of X. From the 100 replications in the previous example, we obtained $\hat{x}_{0.95} = X_{(95)} = 20$. Thus, if the lobby has room for 20 customers waiting in queue, this will be sufficient for approximately 95 out of every 100 days. Furthermore, an approximate 90 percent confidence interval for $x_{0.95}$ is $[X_{(91)}, X_{(99)}] = [19, 23]$. (For this problem, X is a discrete random variable, so that the confidence level is approximate.)

The interested reader may also want to consult Conover (1999, pp. 150–155) for a discussion of a *tolerance interval*, which is an interval that contains a specified proportion of the *values* of the random variable X (and does so with a certain prescribed confidence level).

9.4.3 Choosing Initial Conditions

As stated in Sec. 9.3, the measures of performance for a terminating simulation depend explicitly on the state of the system at time 0; thus, care must be taken in choosing appropriate initial conditions. Let us illustrate this potential problem by means of an example. Suppose that we would like to estimate the expected average delay of all customers who arrive and complete their delays between 12 noon and 1 P.M. (the busiest period) in a bank. Since the bank will probably be quite congested at noon, starting the simulation then with no customers present (the usual initial conditions for a queueing simulation) will cause our estimate of expected average delay to be biased low. We now discuss two heuristic approaches to this problem, the first of which appears to be used widely (see Sec. 9.5.1).

For the first approach, let us assume that the bank opens at 9 A.M. with no customers present. Then we can start the simulation at 9 A.M. with no customers present and run it for 4 simulated hours. In estimating the desired expected average delay, we use only the delays of those customers who arrive and complete their delays between noon and 1 P.M. The evolution of the simulation between 9 A.M. and noon (the "warmup period") determines the appropriate conditions for the simulation at noon. A disadvantage of this approach is that 3 hours of simulated time are not used directly in the estimate. As a result, one might compromise and start the simulation at some other time, say 11 A.M., with no customers present. However, there is no guarantee that the conditions in the simulation at noon will be representative of the actual conditions in the bank at noon.

An alternative approach is to collect data on the number of customers present in the bank at noon for several different days. Let $\hat{p}_i$ be the proportion of these days that i customers ($i = 0, 1, \ldots$) are present at noon. Then we simulate the bank from noon to 1 P.M. with the number of customers present at noon being randomly chosen from the distribution $\{\hat{p}_i\}$. (All customers who are being served at noon might be assumed to be just beginning their services. Starting all services fresh at noon results in an approximation to the actual situation in the bank, since the customers who are in the process of being served at noon would have partially completed their services. However, the effect of this approximation should be negligible for a simulation of length 1 hour.)

If more than one simulation run from noon to 1 P.M. is desired, then a different sample from $\{\hat{p}_i\}$ is drawn for each run. The X_j's that result from these runs are still IID, since the initial conditions for each run are chosen independently from the same distribution.

9.5 STATISTICAL ANALYSIS FOR STEADY-STATE PARAMETERS

Let $Y_1, Y_2, \ldots$ be an output stochastic process from a single run of a nonterminating simulation. Suppose that $P(Y_i \le y) = F_i(y) \to F(y) = P(Y \le y)$ as $i \to \infty$, where Y is the steady-state random variable of interest with distribution function F. (We have suppressed in our notation the dependence of F_i on the initial conditions I.) Then ϕ is a steady-state parameter if it is a characteristic of Y such as $E(Y)$, $P(Y \le y)$, or a quantile of Y. One difficulty in estimating ϕ is that the distribution function of Y_i (for $i = 1, 2, \ldots$) is different from F, since it will generally not be possible to choose I to be representative of "steady-state behavior." This causes an estimator of ϕ based on the observations $Y_1, Y_2, \ldots, Y_m$ not to be "representative." For example, the sample mean $\overline{Y}(m)$ will be a biased estimator of $\nu = E(Y)$ for all finite values of m. The problem we have just described is called the *problem of the initial transient* or the *startup problem* in the simulation literature.

EXAMPLE 9.23. To illustrate the startup problem more succinctly, consider the process of delays $D_1, D_2, \ldots$ for the $M/M/1$ queue with $\rho < 1$ (see Example 9.2). From queueing theory, it is possible to show that

$$P(D_i \le y) \to P(D \le y) = (1 - \rho) + \rho\left[1 - e^{-(\omega-\lambda)y}\right] \qquad \text{as } i \to \infty$$

If the number of customers s present at time 0 is 0, then $D_1 = 0$ and $E(D_i) \ne E(D) = d$ for any i. On the other hand, if s is chosen in accordance with the steady-state number in system distribution [see, for example, Gross et al. (2009)], then for all i, $P(D_i \le y) = P(D \le y)$ and $E(D_i) = d$ (see Prob. 9.11). Thus, there is no initial transient in this case.

In practice, the steady-state distribution will not be known and the above initialization technique will not be possible. Techniques for dealing with the startup problem in practice are discussed in the next section.

9.5.1 The Problem of the Initial Transient

Suppose that we want to estimate the steady-state mean $\nu = E(Y)$, which is also generally defined by

$$\nu = \lim_{i\to\infty} E(Y_i)$$

Thus, the transient means converge to the steady-state mean. The most serious consequence of the problem of the initial transient is probably that $E[\overline{Y}(m)] \neq \nu$ for any m [see Law (1983, pp. 1010–1012) for further discussion]. The technique most often suggested for dealing with this problem is called *warming up the model* or *initial-data deletion*. The idea is to delete some number of observations from the beginning of a run and to use only the remaining observations to estimate ν. For example, given the observations $Y_1, Y_2, \ldots, Y_m$, it is often suggested to use

$$\overline{Y}(m, l) = \frac{\sum_{i=l+1}^{m} Y_i}{m - l}$$

($1 \leq l \leq m - 1$) rather than $\overline{Y}(m)$ as an estimator of ν. In general, one would expect $\overline{Y}(m, l)$ to be less biased than $\overline{Y}(m)$, since the observations near the "beginning" of the simulation may not be very representative of steady-state behavior due to the choice of initial conditions. [If $\hat{\theta}$ is an estimator for a parameter θ, then the bias in $\hat{\theta}$ is $\text{Bias}(\hat{\theta}) = E(\hat{\theta}) - \theta$.] For example, this is true for the process $D_1, D_2, \ldots$ in the case of an $M/M/1$ queue with $s = 0$, since $E(D_i)$ increases monotonically to d as $i \to \infty$ (see Fig. 9.2). Fishman (1972) showed that this is also the case for a first-order autoregressive [AR(1)] process (see Sec. 6.10.3).

Some authors, however, have questioned the efficacy of initial-data deletion [see, for example, Grassmann (2011)], so we first look at the point estimator $\overline{Y}(m, l)$ more carefully. Although $\overline{Y}(m, l)$ will generally be less biased than $\overline{Y}(m)$, it will often have a larger variance, as was shown by Fishman (1972) for an AR(1) process. However, probably the most commonly used overall measure of point-estimator quality is mean-squared error [see Pasupathy and Schmeiser (2010)]. Blomqvist (1970) showed for the $M/M/1$ queue (and certain other queueing systems) with m sufficiently large, that zero is the value of l that minimizes the mean-squared error of $\overline{D}(m, l)$, which is defined by

$$\text{MSE}[\overline{D}(m, l)] = E\{[\overline{D}(m, l) - d]^2\} = \{\text{Bias}[\overline{D}(m, l)]\}^2 + \text{Var}[\overline{D}(m, l)]$$

On the other hand, Snell and Schruben (1979) and Kelton (1980) showed for a AR(1) process that deletion may either increase or decrease mean-squared error, depending on m, l, and the values of the process parameters. As one might suspect, deletion most significantly reduced mean-squared error when the initialization bias was high and the autocorrelation (see Sec. 5.6) was heavy, causing the bias to dissipate slowly. In these cases, the value of l that minimized $\text{MSE}[\overline{Y}(m, l)]$ decreased as m increased. This observation is consistent with Blomqvist's result that for very large values of m, deletion is not advisable for the mean-squared-error performance measure.

Another criterion that is used for evaluating the efficacy of deletion is confidence-interval quality, which is the one that we prefer. [We believe that one should always construct a confidence interval for ν; otherwise, we have no explicit way of knowing how close $\overline{Y}(m, l)$ is to ν.] The replication/deletion approach for constructing a confidence interval for ν, which is discussed in Sec. 9.5.2, is based on making n independent "short" replications of the process $Y_1, Y_2, \ldots$ of length m observations and deleting the first l observations from each replication. Let $\overline{Y}_j(m, l)$ be the sample mean of the final $m - l$ observations in the jth replication, for $j = 1, 2, \ldots, n$. Then the $\overline{Y}_j(m, l)$'s play the same role as the X_j's in the confidence interval given by (4.12). In order for the replication/deletion approach to produce confidence intervals with acceptable coverage, it is *critical* that m and l be chosen so that $E[\overline{Y}_j(m, l)] \approx \nu$, i.e., that $\overline{Y}_j(m, l)$ is an approximately *unbiased estimator* for ν [see Law (1977)].

Suppose now that we make one "long" run of length m observations, resulting in the observations $Y_1, Y_2, \ldots, Y_m$. There are a number of methods for constructing a confidence interval for ν based on this one-replication scenario (see Sec. 9.5.3). For example, the method of batch means, which is the most widely used of these approaches, divides the m observations into n batches of size k ($m = nk$). Let $\overline{Y}_j(k)$ be the sample (or batch) mean of the k observations in the jth batch, for $j = 1, 2, \ldots, n$. Then the $\overline{Y}_j(k)$'s play the same role as the X_j's in the confidence interval given by (4.12). In order for the batch-means method to produce confidence intervals with acceptable coverage, k must be chosen large enough so that the $\overline{Y}_j(k)$'s are approximately *uncorrelated*. Results in Law (1977), Law and Carson (1979), and Law and Kelton (1984), suggest that batch means (and the other methods of Sec. 9.5.3) will produce confidence intervals with acceptable coverage *without a warmup period* (i.e., $l = 0$), provided that m is "moderate" in value. For instance, in the case of an $M/M/1$ queue with $\rho = 0.9$ and $s = 0$, batch means achieved a coverage of 0.865 for a nominal 90 percent confidence interval for d based on $m = 12{,}800$ and $n = 5$ batches of size 2560 [Law (1977)]. Apparently, if m is large enough, then the observations from the initial transient get "washed out" by the remaining "steady-state" observations.

Thus, in terms of confidence-interval coverage, the need for an effective warmup period appears to be much more important when using the replication/deletion approach, which is based on multiple "short" replications. Thus, we will focus on the replication/deletion approach and its need for an unbiased point estimator in our discussion of the problem of the initial transient that follows.

The question naturally arises as to how to choose the *warmup period* (or deletion amount) l. We would like to pick l (and m) such that $E[\overline{Y}(m, l)] \approx \nu$. If l and m are chosen too small, then $E[\overline{Y}(m, l)]$ may be significantly different from ν. On the other hand, if l is chosen larger than necessary, then $\overline{Y}(m, l)$ will probably have an unnecessarily large variance. There have been a number of methods suggested in the literature for choosing l. However, Gafarian, Ancker, and Morisaku (1978) found that none of the methods available at that time performed well in practice. Kelton and Law (1983) developed an algorithm for choosing l (and m) that worked well {that is, $E[\overline{Y}(m, l)] \approx \nu$} for a wide variety of stochastic models. However, a theoretical limitation of the procedure is that it basically makes the assumption that $E(Y_i)$ is a monotone function of i.

A simple and general technique for determining l is a graphical procedure due to Welch (1981, 1983). Its specific goal is to determine a time index l such that $E(Y_i) \approx \nu$ for $i > l$, where l is the warmup period. [This is equivalent to determining when the transient mean curve $E(Y_i)$ (for $i = 1, 2, \ldots$) "flattens out" at level ν; see Fig. 9.1.] In general, it is very difficult to determine l from a single replication due to the inherent variability of the process $Y_1, Y_2, \ldots$ (see Fig. 9.10 below).

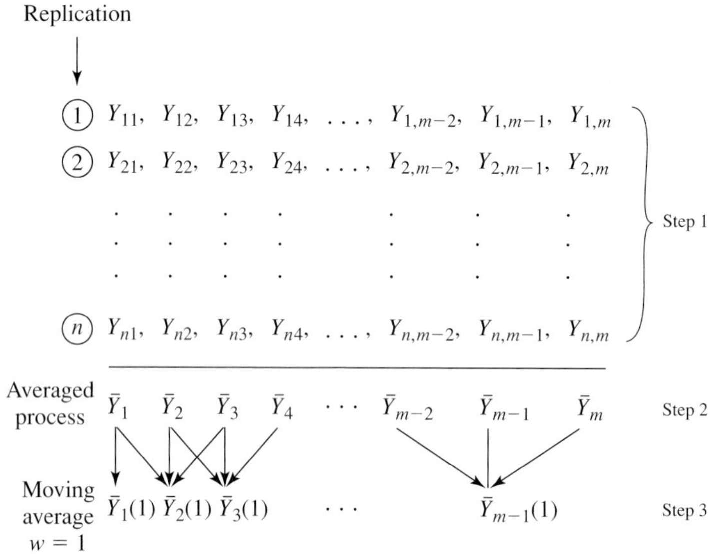

FIGURE 9.8
Averaged process and moving average with $w = 1$ based on n replications of length m.

As a result, Welch's procedure is based on making n independent replications of the simulation and employing the following four steps:

1. Make n replications of the simulation ($n \geq 5$), each of length m (where m is large). Let Y_{ji} be the ith observation from the jth replication ($j = 1, 2, \ldots, n$; $i = 1, 2, \ldots, m$), as shown in Fig. 9.8.
2. Let $\bar{Y}_i = \sum_{j=1}^{n} Y_{ji}/n$ for $i = 1, 2, \ldots, m$ (see Fig. 9.8). The averaged process $\bar{Y}_1, \bar{Y}_2, \ldots$ has means $E(\bar{Y}_i) = E(Y_i)$ and variances $\text{Var}(\bar{Y}_i) = \text{Var}(Y_i)/n$ (see Prob. 9.12). Thus, the averaged process has the same transient mean curve as the original process, but its plot has only $(1/n)$th the variance.
3. To smooth out the high-frequency oscillations in $\bar{Y}_1, \bar{Y}_2, \ldots$ (but leave the low-frequency oscillations or long-run trend of interest), we further define the *moving average* $\bar{Y}_i(w)$ (where w is the *window* and is a positive integer such that $w \leq \lfloor m/4 \rfloor$) as follows:

$$\bar{Y}_i(w) = \begin{cases} \dfrac{\sum_{s=-w}^{w} \bar{Y}_{i+s}}{2w+1} & \text{if } i = w+1, \ldots, m-w \\[2ex] \dfrac{\sum_{s=-(i-1)}^{i-1} \bar{Y}_{i+s}}{2i-1} & \text{if } i = 1, \ldots, w \end{cases}$$

Thus, if i is not too close to the beginning of the replications, then $\bar{Y}_i(w)$ is just the simple average of $2w + 1$ observations of the averaged process centered at observation i (see Fig. 9.8). It is called a moving average since i moves through time.

4. Plot $\overline{Y}_i(w)$ for $i = 1, 2, \ldots, m - w$ and choose l to be that value of i beyond which $\overline{Y}_1(w), \overline{Y}_2(w), \ldots$ appears to have converged. See Welch (1983, p. 292) for an aid in determining convergence.

The following example illustrates the calculation of the moving average.

EXAMPLE 9.24. For simplicity, assume that $m = 10$, $w = 2$, $\overline{Y}_i = i$ for $i = 1, 2, \ldots, 5$, and $\overline{Y}_i = 6$ for $i = 6, 7, \ldots, 10$. Then

$$\overline{Y}_1(2) = 1 \qquad \overline{Y}_2(2) = 2 \qquad \overline{Y}_3(2) = 3$$

$$\overline{Y}_4(2) = 4 \qquad \overline{Y}_5(2) = 4.8 \qquad \overline{Y}_6(2) = 5.4$$

$$\overline{Y}_7(2) = 5.8 \qquad \overline{Y}_8(2) = 6$$

Before giving examples of applying Welch's procedure to actual stochastic models, we make the following recommendations on choosing the parameters n, m, and w:

- Initially, make $n = 5$ or 10 replications (depending on model execution time), with m as large as practical. In particular, m should be much larger than the anticipated value of l (see Sec. 9.5.2) and also large enough to allow infrequent events (e.g., machine breakdowns) to occur a reasonable number of times.
- Plot $\overline{Y}_i(w)$ for several values of the window w and choose the smallest value of w (if any) for which the corresponding plot is "reasonably smooth." Use this plot to determine the length of the warmup period l. [Choosing w is like choosing the interval width Δb for a histogram (see Sec. 6.4.2). If w is too small, the plot of $\overline{Y}_i(w)$ will be "ragged." If w is too large, then the $\overline{Y}_i$ observations will be overaggregated and we will not have a good idea of the shape of the transient mean curve, $E(Y_i)$ for $i = 1, 2, \ldots$.]
- If no value of w in step 3 is satisfactory, make 5 or 10 additional replications of length m. Repeat step 2 using all available replications. [For a fixed value of w, the plot of $\overline{Y}_i(w)$ will get "smoother" as the number of replications increases. Why?]

The major difficulty in applying Welch's procedure in practice is that the required number of replications, n, may be relatively large if the process $Y_1, Y_2, \ldots$ is highly variable [see Alexopoulos and Seila (1998, p. 240)]. Also, the choice of l is somewhat subjective.

EXAMPLE 9.25. A small factory consists of a machining center and inspection station in series, as shown in Fig. 9.9. Unfinished parts arrive to the factory with exponential interarrival times having a mean of 1 minute. Processing times at the machine are uniform on the interval [0.65, 0.70] minute, and subsequent inspection times at the inspection

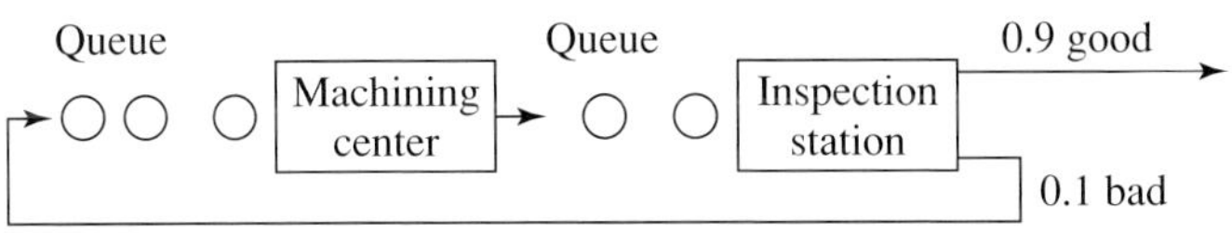

FIGURE 9.9
Small factory consisting of a machining center and an inspection station.

station are uniform on the interval [0.75, 0.80] minute. Ninety percent of inspected parts are "good" and are sent to shipping; 10 percent of the parts are "bad" and are sent back to the machine for rework. (Both queues are assumed to have infinite capacity.) The machining center is subject to randomly occurring breakdowns. In particular, a new (or freshly repaired) machine will break down after an exponential amount of *calendar* time with a mean of 6 hours (see Sec. 14.4.2). Repair times are uniform on the interval [8, 12] minutes. If a part is being processed when the machine breaks down, then the machine continues where it left off upon the completion of repair. Assume that the factory is initially empty and idle, and is open 8 hours per day.

Consider the stochastic process $N_1, N_2, \ldots,$ where N_i is the number of parts produced in the ith hour. Suppose that we want to determine the warmup period l so that we can eventually estimate the steady-state mean hourly throughput $\nu = E(N)$ (see Example 9.30). We made $n = 10$ independent replications of the simulation each of length $m = 160$ hours (or 20 days). In Fig. 9.10 we plot the averaged process $\overline{N}_i$ for $i = 1, 2, \ldots, 160$. It is clear that further smoothing of the plot is necessary, and that one replication, in general, is not sufficient to estimate l. In Figs. 9.11*a* and 9.11*b* we plot the moving average $\overline{N}_i(w)$ for both $w = 20$ and $w = 30$. From the plot for $w = 30$ (which is smoother), we chose a warmup period of $l = 24$ hours. Note that it is better to choose l too large rather than too small, since our goal is to have $E(Y_i)$ close to ν for $i > l$. (We choose to tolerate slightly higher variance in order to be more certain that our point estimator for ν will have a small bias.)

EXAMPLE 9.26. Consider a simple model of a Signaling System Number 7 (SS7) network that is used for setting up and tearing down of telephone calls, and for processing of "800" calls. (The actual calls are transmitted on an associated circuit-switched

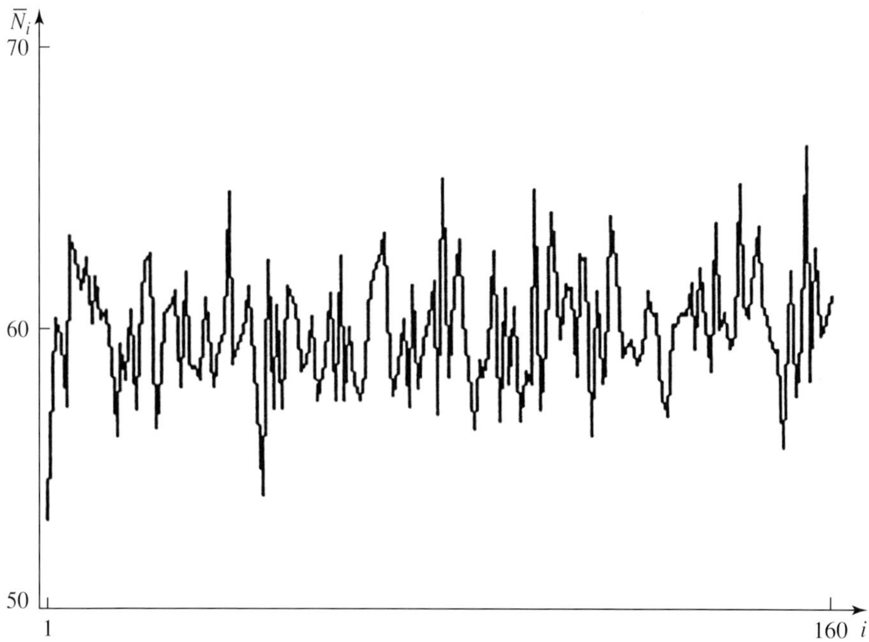

FIGURE 9.10
Averaged process for hourly throughputs, small factory.

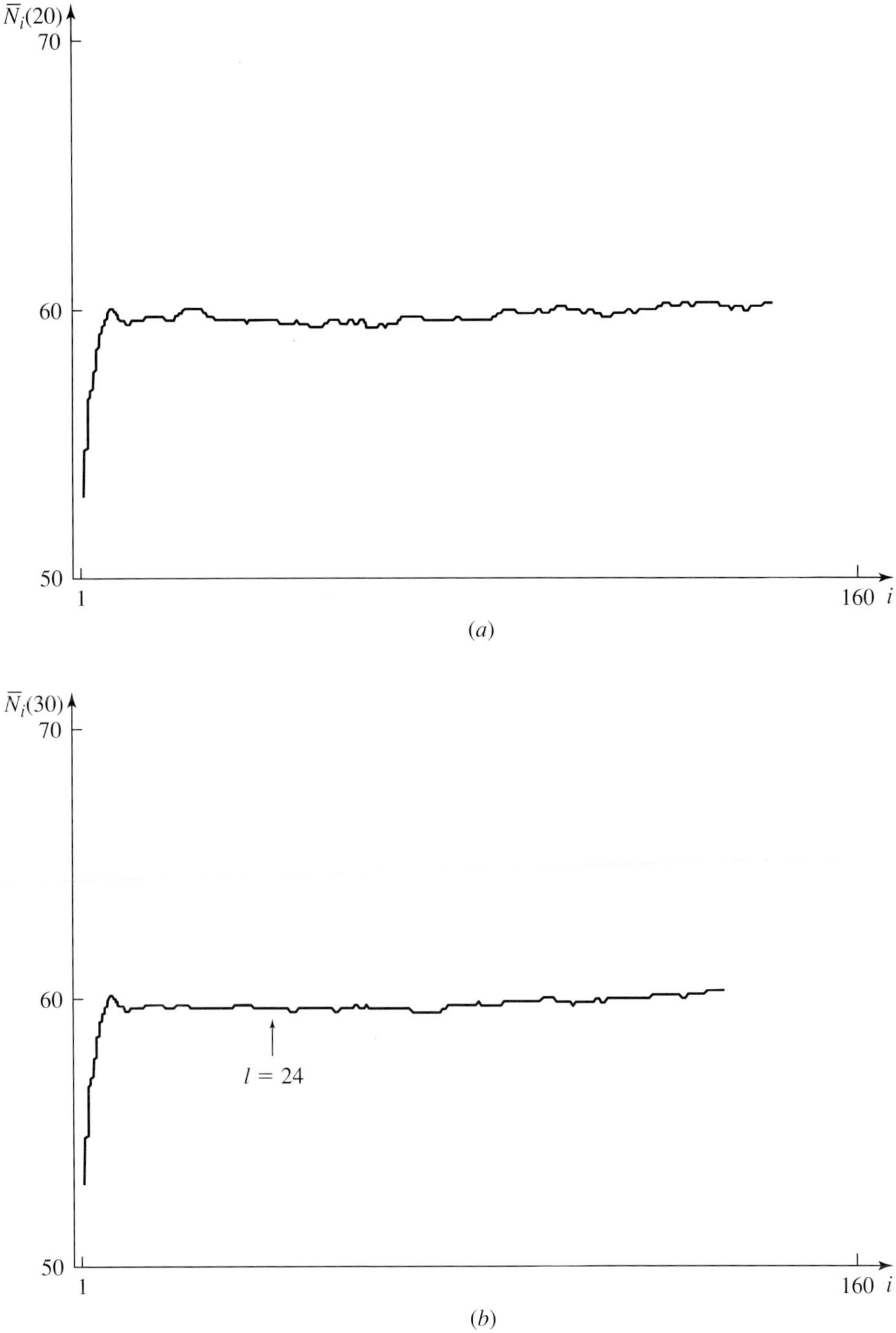

FIGURE 9.11
Moving averages for hourly throughputs, small factory: (*a*) $w = 20$; (*b*) $w = 30$.

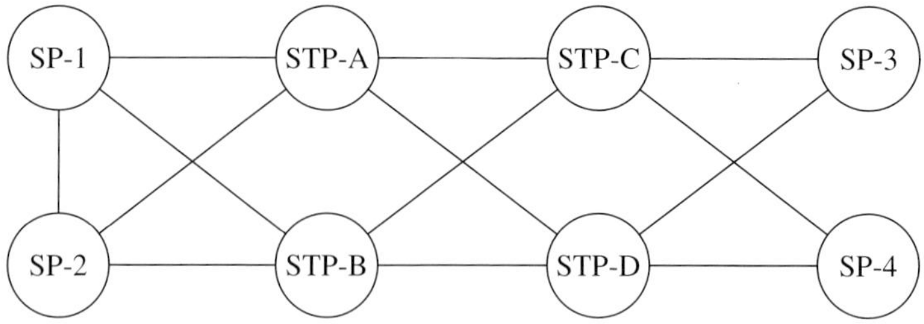

Note: Each line segment represents two links.

FIGURE 9.12
Topology of the SS7 network.

network.) The network consists of four Signaling Points (denoted SP-1, . . . , SP-4), two Signal Transfer Point pairs (STP-A/STP-B and STP-C/STP-D), and pairs (see Prob. 9.33) of 56 kilobits per second, full-duplex (bidirectional) links as shown in Fig. 9.12. (A line segment in Fig. 9.12 corresponds to two links.) The links from node SP-1 to node STP-A are denoted by 1-A, the links from STP-A to STP-C are denoted by A-C, etc. There is a system requirement that the utilization of each STP and link cannot exceed 0.4. (This requirement is necessary in the actual network to allow extra capacity in case a resource breaks down; however, we do *not* model breakdowns here.)

Each SP sends messages (signals) to each of the other SPs in accordance with a Poisson process (i.e., exponential interarrival times) with rates given in Table 9.6. The length of a message is a discrete uniform random variable in the range 23 to 29 bytes. Each message also includes a 7-byte routing label (containing the source and destination nodes) when it is sent over a link.

Each STP (SP) contains three (two) parallel processors (see Prob. 9.34) that are fed by a single input queue, and there is an output queue for each link that emanates from the node. A message must be processed on one of the processors in a node, and processing times are a constant 2.5 milliseconds.

The initial links used to send a message from one node to another are given in Table 9.7. When two links are available, each one is chosen with a probability of 0.5.

Consider the stochastic process $E_1, E_2, \ldots$, where E_i is the end-to-end delay (i.e., the time to go from a source SP to a destination SP) of the ith completed message. Suppose that we want to determine the warmup period l so that we can eventually estimate the steady-state mean $\nu = E(E)$ (see Example 9.31). [The symbol $E(E)$ is the expected value of the steady-state random variable E.] We made $n = 5$ independent replications of the simulation, each of length $m = 10$ seconds. In Fig. 9.13 we plot the end-to-end delay moving average $\overline{E}_i(w)$ for $w = 600$. [Note that the number of E_i observations in a 10-second simulation run is a random variable with approximate mean 12,400, since the

TABLE 9.6
Traffic rates (in messages per minute) from one SP to another SP

Node	SP-1	SP-2	SP-3	SP-4
SP-1		9600	7200	4800
SP-2	8000		4800	7200
SP-3	6400	4800		6400
SP-4	4800	5600	4800	

TABLE 9.7
Initial links used (see Fig. 9.12) in going from one node (row) to another node (column)

Node	SP-1	SP-2	SP-3	SP-4
SP-1		1-2	1-A, 1-B	1-A, 1-B
SP-2	1-2		2-A, 2-B	2-A, 2-B
SP-3	3-C, 3-D	3-C, 3-D		3-C, 3-D
SP-4	4-C, 4-D	4-C, 4-D	4-C, 4-D	

Node	SP-1	SP-2	SP-3	SP-4
STP-A	1-A	2-A	A-C, A-D	A-C, A-D
STP-B	1-B	2-B	B-C, B-D	B-C, B-D
STP-C	A-C, B-C	A-C, B-C	3-C	4-C
STP-D	A-D, B-D	A-D, B-D	3-D	4-D

overall arrival rate is 1240 messages per second and the system is stable (see Prob. 9.35). Therefore, for our analysis we used the minimum number of observations for any one of the 5 runs, which was 12,306. However, $\overline{E}_i(w)$ is only plotted for $i = 1, 2, \ldots, 9920$ (a multiple of 1240) in Fig. 9.13.] From the plot, we conservatively chose a warmup period of $l = 6200$ (5×1240) end-to-end delays. However, for the construction of a confidence interval in Example 9.31, we will actually use a warmup period of 5 seconds, since the run length m is in units of seconds.

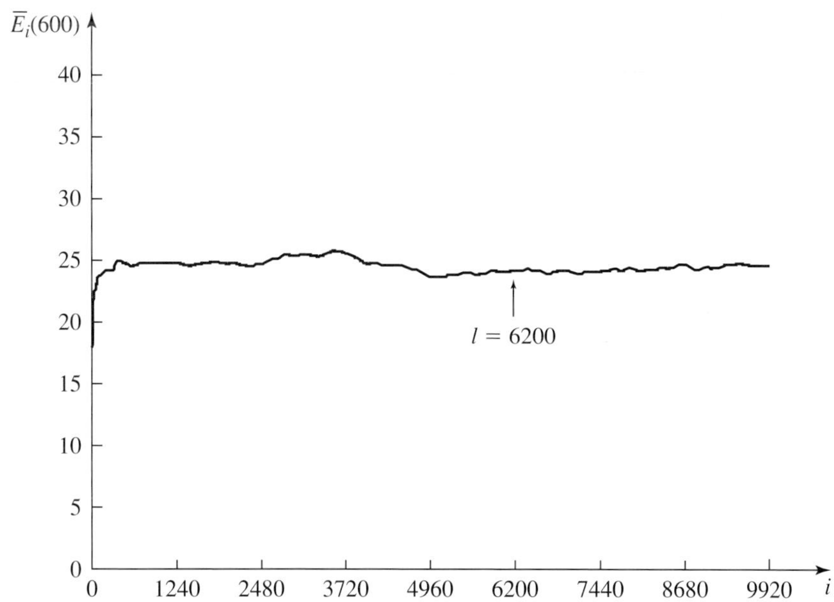

FIGURE 9.13
Moving average with $w = 600$ for end-to-end delays, SS7 network.

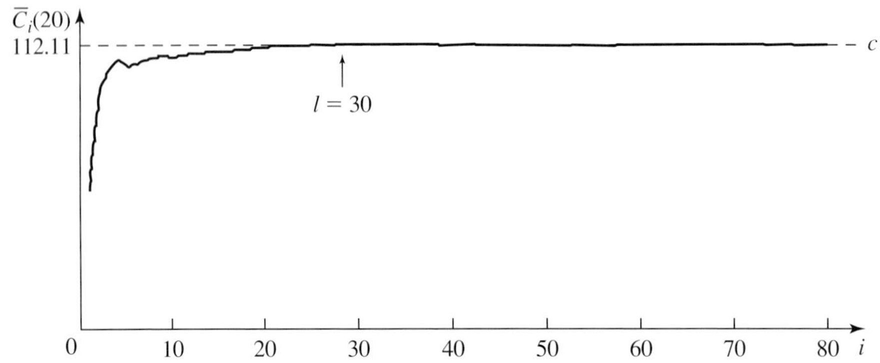

FIGURE 9.14
Moving average with $w = 20$ for monthly costs, inventory system.

EXAMPLE 9.27. Consider the process $C_1, C_2, \ldots$ for the inventory system of Example 9.3. Suppose that we want to determine the warmup period l in order to estimate the steady-state mean cost per month $c = E(C) = 112.11$. We made $n = 10$ independent replications of the simulation of length $m = 100$ months. In Fig. 9.14 we plot the moving average $\overline{C}_i(w)$ for $w = 20$, from which we chose a warmup period of $l = 30$ months.

Additional applications of Welch's procedure are given in Chaps. 10 through 12 and 14. Note also that a version of Welch's procedure is available in the manufacturing-oriented simulation package AutoMod [see Banks (2004)].

White (1997) introduced a procedure for determining a warmup period or deletion amount called MSER (*M*arginal *S*tandard *E*rror *R*ules), which is based on minimizing mean-squared error. Let $\overline{Y}(m, l)$ be as defined above and let

$$S^2(m, l) = \frac{\sum_{i=l+1}^{m} [Y_i - \overline{Y}(m, l)]^2}{m - l}$$

be the sample variance of $Y_{l+1}, Y_{l+2}, \ldots, Y_m$ if we divide by $m - l$ rather than the usual $m - l - 1$. Define the MSER(m, l) statistic as

$$\text{MSER}(m, l) = \frac{S^2(m, l)}{m - l}$$

If the Y_i's *were* IID and $S^2(m, l)$ had an $m - l - 1$ in the denominator, then the MSER(m, l) statistic would be an unbiased estimator of the variance of $\overline{Y}(m, l)$ [the square of the *standard error* of $\overline{Y}(m, l)$]. Then the optimal deletion amount, l^*, is that value of l that minimizes MSER(m, l) over the values $l = 0, 1, \ldots, m - 1$, which is often written as

$$l^* = \underset{l=0,1,\ldots,m-1}{\arg\min} \ \text{MSER}(m, l) \tag{9.5}$$

where "arg" is an abbreviation for argument. Pasupathy and Schmeiser (2010) show that MSER(m, l) is asymptotically (as m goes to infinity) proportional to the mean-squared error MSE[$\overline{Y}(m, l)$] for every l. Therefore, for large m the value of l that minimizes MSER(m, l) will tend to lie close to the value of l that minimizes MSE[$\overline{Y}(m, l)$]. Although MSER is explicitly designed to minimize mean-squared error, it is also stated by its proponents to be a procedure for reducing the bias in $\overline{Y}(m, l)$ [see Hoad et al. (2009, p. 9) and Franklin and White (2008, p. 545)].

White et al. (2000) discuss a variant of MSER called MSER-k. Let

$$Z_j = \frac{\sum_{i=1}^{k} Y_{k(j-1)+i}}{k} \qquad \text{for } j = 1, 2, \ldots, \lfloor m/k \rfloor$$

Then MSER-k applies the rule given by Eq. (9.5) to the batch averages Z_j's rather than to the Y_i's, where MSER-1 is, of course, the same as MSER. In practice, MSER-5 is typically used rather than MSER, since the former operates on "smoother" data. Also, if $l^* > \lfloor m/k \rfloor/2$ (half the number of batches), then l^* is rejected as a valid warmup period. In this case, m should be increased and MSER-5 applied to the new set of batch averages, etc. Note that the choices $k = 5$ and $\lfloor m/k \rfloor/2$ are somewhat arbitrary, but have been found to work fairly well in practice. Finally, Hoad et al. (2009) recommend that MSER-5 be applied to data averaged over five replications rather than to data from one replication (see Example 9.28). Additional papers that discuss MSER-5 are Mokashi et al. (2010) and Sanchez and White (2011).

EXAMPLE 9.28. Consider the delay-in-queue process $D_1, D_2, \ldots$ for the $M/M/1$ queue with $\rho = 0.9$ ($\lambda = 1$, $\omega = 10/9$) and initial conditions $s = 0$. We made $n = 5$ independent replications of length $m = 65{,}000$ observations and applied MSER-5 to the averaged process $\overline{D}_1, \overline{D}_2, \ldots, \overline{D}_{65{,}000}$ (see Sec. 9.5.1 for the definition of $\overline{D}_i$). MSER-5 chose a warmup period of $l^* = 3$ batches, resulting in a total deletion amount of 15 observations. (All calculations were performed using an Excel macro graciously provided by Professor Katy Hoad of the University of Warwick; it allows m to have a maximum value of 65,536.) The fact that l^* is close to 0 is not surprising given the result of Blomqvist discussed earlier in this section. A plot of the MSER-5 statistic as a function of the batch number, l, is given Fig. 9.15, where it can be seen that $l = 3$ does, in fact, minimize the MSER-5 statistic. It can also be seen from Fig. 9.2 that MSER-5 failed to delete a large amount of biased data.

In order to see how sensitive the optimal deletion amount l^* might be to the value of m, we repeated the above analysis using subsets of the existing 65,000 observations of size 1000, 5000, 10,000, 20,000, and 40,000. For each of the five subset sizes, l^* was equal to 3 or 4.

To see the effect of the batch size k on the selected warmup period, we applied MSER-1 (i.e., $k = 1$) to the $n = 5$ replications of length $m = 65{,}000$ and obtained $l^* = 16$, resulting in a total deletion amount of 16 observations (compared to a deletion amount of 15 above).

EXAMPLE 9.29 Consider again the SS7 network of Example 9.26, where we had $n = 5$ replications of length $m = 12{,}306$ observations. We applied MSER-5 to the averaged process $\overline{E}_1, \overline{E}_2, \ldots, \overline{E}_{12{,}306}$ and obtained a warmup period of $l^* = 2$ batches, resulting in a total deletion amount of 10 observations. (Recall from Example 9.26 that Welch's procedure called for a warmup period of 6200 observations.) A plot of the MSER-5

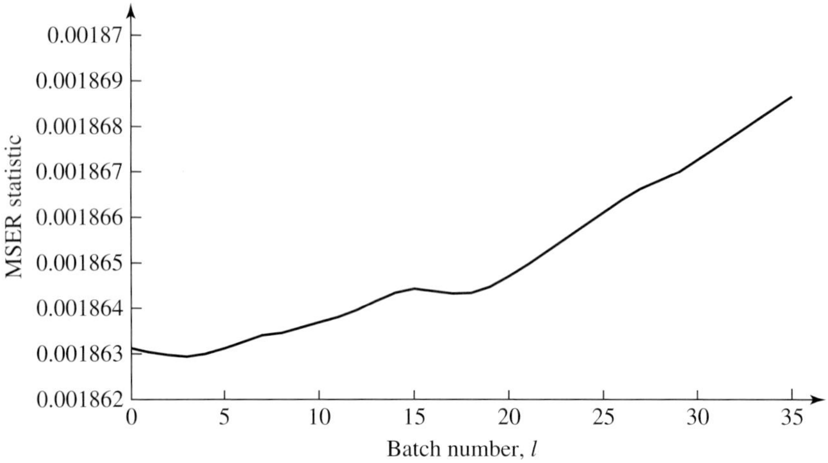

FIGURE 9.15
Plot of MSER-5 statistic as a function of the batch number, l, $M/M/1$ queue with $\rho = 0.9$.

statistic as a function of the batch number, l, is given in Fig. 9.16, where it can be seen that $l = 2$ minimizes the MSER-5 statistic. It appears from Fig. 9.13 that MSER-5 failed to delete a large amount of biased data.

In order to see how sensitive the optimal deletion amount l^* might be to the value of m, we repeated the above analysis using subsets of the existing 12,306 observations of size 1000, 2000, 4000, and 8000. For each of the four subset sizes, l^* was equal to 2.

Based on the two examples presented above (and several others not shown), it appears that MSER may fail to delete a significant amount of highly biased data for some simulation models.

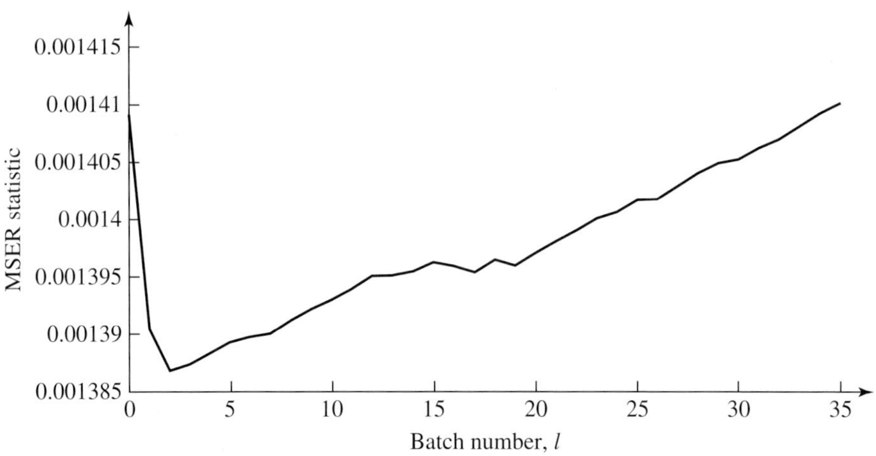

FIGURE 9.16
Plot of MSER-5 statistic as a function of the batch number, l, SS7 network.

Schruben (1982) developed a very general procedure based on standardized time series (see Sec. 9.5.3) for determining whether the observations $Y_{s+1}, Y_{s+2}, \ldots,$ Y_{s+t} (where s need not be zero) contain initialization bias with respect to the steady-state mean $\nu = E(Y)$, that is, whether $E(Y_i) \neq \nu$ for at least one i (where $s + 1 \leq i \leq s + t$). As the procedure is constituted, it is not an algorithm for determining a deletion amount l, but rather a test to determine whether a set of observations contains initialization bias. For example, it could be applied to the truncated averaged process $\overline{Y}_{l+1}, \overline{Y}_{l+2}, \ldots, \overline{Y}_m$ resulting from applying Welch's procedure, in order to determine if there is significant remaining bias. Schruben tested his procedure on several stochastic models with a known value of ν, and found that it had high power in detecting initialization bias [see also Glynn (1995)]. Variations of this initialization-bias test are given in Schruben, Singh, and Tierney (1983) and in Goldsman, Schruben, and Swain (1994). Additionally, Vassilacopoulos (1989) proposed a rank test for accessing the presence of initialization bias. Limited testing on the *M*/*M*/*s* queue produced encouraging results. Finally, comprehensive lists of references on the problem of the initial transient can be found in Hoad et al. (2009) and Pasupathy and Schmeiser (2010).

In Example 9.23 we saw that initializing the *M*/*M*/1 queue with the steady-state number in system distribution resulted in the process $D_1, D_2, \ldots$ not having an initial transient. This suggests trying to estimate the steady-state distribution from a "pilot" run, and then independently sampling from this estimated distribution in order to determine the initial conditions for each production run. Kelton (1989) applied this idea to several queueing systems and also a computer model, where in each case the state of the system is an integer-valued random variable. He found that random initialization reduced the severity and duration of the initial transient period as compared with starting the simulation in a fixed state (e.g., no one present in a queueing system). This technique would be harder to apply, however, in the case of many real-world simulations, where the state of the system has a multivariate distribution [see Murray (1988) and Law (1983, p. 1016) for further discussion]. Glynn (1988) discusses a related method where a one-time pass through the "transient period" is used to specify the starting conditions for subsequent replications.

9.5.2 Replication/Deletion Approach for Means

Suppose that we want to estimate the steady-state mean $\nu = E(Y)$ of the process $Y_1,$ $Y_2, \ldots$. There are six fundamental approaches for addressing this problem, which are discussed in this and the next section. We will for the most part, however, concentrate on one of these, the replication/deletion approach, for the following reasons:

1. If properly applied, this approach should give reasonably good statistical performance.
2. It is the easiest approach to understand and implement. (This is very important in practice due to the time constraints of many simulation projects and because many analysts do not have the statistical background necessary to use some of the more complicated analysis approaches.)

3. This approach applies to all types of output parameters (i.e., Secs. 9.4 through 9.6).
4. It can easily be used to estimate several different parameters for the same simulation model (see Sec. 9.7).
5. This approach can be used to compare different system configurations, as discussed in Chap. 10.
6. Multiple replications can be made simultaneously on different cores within a single computer or on different computers on a network, provided that the software being used for simulation supports this.

We now present the *replication/deletion approach* for obtaining a point estimate and confidence interval for ν. The analysis is similar to that for terminating simulations except that now only those observations beyond the warmup period l in each replication are used to form the estimates. Specifically, suppose that we make n' replications of the simulation each of length m' observations, where m' is much larger than the warmup period l determined by Welch's graphical method (see Sec. 9.5.1). Let Y_{ji} be as defined before and let X_j be given by

$$X_j = \frac{\sum_{i=l+1}^{m'} Y_{ji}}{m' - l} \qquad \text{for } j = 1, 2, \ldots, n'$$

(Note that X_j uses only those observations from the jth replication corresponding to "steady state," namely, $Y_{j,l+1}, Y_{j,l+2}, \ldots, Y_{j,m'}$.) Then the X_j's are IID random variables with $E(X_j) \approx \nu$ (see Prob. 9.15), $\overline{X}(n')$ is an approximately unbiased point estimator for ν, and an approximate $100(1 - \alpha)$ percent confidence interval for ν is given by

$$\overline{X}(n') \pm t_{n'-1,1-\alpha/2}\sqrt{\frac{S^2(n')}{n'}} \tag{9.6}$$

where $\overline{X}(n')$ and $S^2(n')$ are computed from Eqs. (4.3) and (4.4), respectively.

One legitimate objection that might be levied against the replication/deletion approach is that it uses one set of n replications (the pilot runs) to determine the warmup period l, and then uses *only* the last $m' - l$ observations from a different set of n' replications (production runs) to perform the actual analyses. However, this is usually not a problem due to the relatively low cost of computer time.

In some situations, it should be possible to use the initial n pilot runs of length m observations both to determine l and to construct a confidence interval. In particular, if m is substantially larger than the selected value of the warmup period l, then it is probably safe to use the "initial" runs for both purposes. Since Welch's graphical method is only approximate, a "small" number of observations beyond the warmup period l might contain significant bias relative to ν. However, if m is much larger than l, these biased observations will have little effect on the overall quality (i.e., lack of bias) of X_j (based on $m - l$ observations) or $\overline{X}(n)$. Strictly speaking, however, it is more correct statistically to base the replication/deletion approach on two independent sets of replications (see Prob. 9.16 and Example 9.31).

EXAMPLE 9.30. For the manufacturing system of Example 9.25, suppose that we would like to obtain a point estimate and 90 percent confidence interval for the steady-state mean hourly throughput $\nu = E(N)$. From the $n = 10$ replications of length $m = 160$ hours used there, we specified a warmup period of $l = 24$ hours. Since $m = 160$ is much larger than $l = 24$, we will use these same replications to construct a confidence interval. Let

$$X_j = \frac{\sum_{i=25}^{160} N_{ji}}{136} \qquad \text{for } j = 1, 2, \ldots, 10$$

Then a point estimate and 90 percent confidence interval for ν are given by

$$\hat{\nu} = \overline{X}(10) = 59.97$$

and

$$\overline{X}(10) \pm t_{9,0.95}\sqrt{\frac{0.62}{10}} = 59.97 \pm 0.46$$

Thus, in the long run we would expect the small factory to produce an average of about 60 parts per hour. Does this throughput seem reasonable? (See Prob. 9.17.)

EXAMPLE 9.31. For the SS7 network of Example 9.26, suppose that we would like to obtain a point estimate and 95 percent confidence interval for the steady-state mean end-to-end delay $\nu = E(E)$. For this example, we made $n' = 5$ *new* independent replications of the simulation of length $m' = 65$ seconds and used the previously determined warmup period of $l = 5$ seconds. Let X_j be the average end-to-end delay of all messages that are completed in the interval [5, 65] seconds for replication j. Then a point estimate and 95 percent confidence interval for ν (in milliseconds) are given by

$$\hat{\nu} = \overline{X}(5) = 24.11$$

and

$$\overline{X}(5) \pm t_{4,0.975}\sqrt{\frac{0.0114}{5}} = 24.11 \pm 0.13$$

From these five replications, we also found that the utilization of each STP and link was less than 0.4, as expected. In particular, the utilization of STP-A was 0.316, and the utilization of link 1-2 was 0.377. Do these values seem reasonable? (See Prob. 9.36.)

The half-length of the replication/deletion confidence interval given by (9.6) depends on the variance of X_j, $\text{Var}(X_j)$, which will be unknown when the first n replications are made. Therefore, if we make a fixed number of replications of the simulation, the resulting confidence-interval half-length may or may not be small enough for a particular purpose. We know, however, that the half-length can be decreased by a factor of approximately 2 by making 4 times as many replications. See also the discussion of "Obtaining a Specified Precision" in Sec. 9.4.1.

A criticism that is sometimes made about the replication/deletion approach is that a $100(1 - \alpha)$ percent confidence interval is actually being constructed for $E(X_j)$ rather than for ν [i.e., $\overline{X}(n')$ is a biased estimator of ν]. As a result, if we make a large number of replications n' in an effort to make the confidence-interval half-length small, then the coverage of the confidence interval might be much less than the desired $1 - \alpha$. However, since a simulation model is only an approximation to the corresponding real-world system, we feel that for many, if not most, models it is sufficient to estimate $E(X_j)$, provided that it is "close" to ν. This should be the case if we choose the run length m' sufficiently large and use Welch's procedure to choose a *conservative* warmup period l.

9.5.3 Other Approaches for Means

In this section we present a more comprehensive discussion of procedures for constructing a point estimate and a confidence interval for the steady-state mean $\nu = E(Y)$ of a simulation output process $Y_1, Y_2, \ldots$. The following definitions of ν are usually equivalent:

$$\nu = \lim_{i \to \infty} E(Y_i)$$

and

$$\nu = \lim_{m \to \infty} \frac{\sum_{i=1}^{m} Y_i}{m} \qquad \text{(w.p. 1)}$$

General references on this subject include Alexopoulos, Goldsman, and Serfozo (2006), Banks et al. (2010), Bratley, Fox, and Schrage (1987), Fishman (1978, 2001), Law (1983), and Welch (1983).

Two general strategies have been suggested in the simulation literature for constructing a point estimate and confidence interval for ν:

1. *Fixed-sample-size procedures.* A single simulation run of an *arbitrary* fixed length is made, and then one of a number of available procedures is used to construct a confidence interval from the available data.
2. *Sequential procedures.* The length of a single simulation run is sequentially increased until an "acceptable" confidence interval can be constructed. There are several techniques for deciding when to stop the simulation run.

Fixed-Sample-Size Procedures

There have been six fixed-sample-size procedures suggested in the literature [see Law (1983) and Law and Kelton (1984) for surveys]. The replication/deletion approach, which was discussed in Sec. 9.5.2, is based on n independent "short" replications of length m observations. It tends to suffer from bias in the point estimator $\hat{\nu}$ (see Sec. 9.1). The five other approaches are based on one "long" replication, and tend to have a problem with bias in the estimator $\widehat{\text{Var}}(\hat{\nu})$ of the variance of the point estimator $\hat{\nu}$. Properties of the six approaches are given in Table 9.8, and details of the five new approaches are now presented.

The method of *batch means*, like the replication/deletion approach, seeks to obtain independent observations so that the formulas of Chap. 4 can be used to obtain a confidence interval. However, since the batch-means method is based on a

TABLE 9.8
Properties of steady-state estimation procedures

Approach	Number of replications	Most serious bias problem	Potential difficulties
Replication/deletion	n ($n \geq 2$)	$\hat{\nu}$	Choice of warmup period, l
Batch means	1	$\widehat{\mathrm{Var}}(\hat{\nu})$	Choice of batch size, k, to obtain uncorrelated batch means
Autoregressive	1	$\widehat{\mathrm{Var}}(\hat{\nu})$	Quality of autoregressive model
Spectral	1	$\widehat{\mathrm{Var}}(\hat{\nu})$	Choice of number of covariance lags, q
Regenerative	1	$\widehat{\mathrm{Var}}(\hat{\nu})$	Existence of cycles with "small" mean length
Standardized time series	1	$\widehat{\mathrm{Var}}(\hat{\nu})$	Choice of batch size, k

single long run, it has to go through the "transient period" only once. Assume that $Y_1, Y_2, \ldots$ is a covariance-stationary process (see Sec. 4.3) with $E(Y_i) = \nu$ for all i. (Alternatively, suppose that the first l observations have been deleted and we are dealing with $Y_{l+1}, Y_{l+2}, \ldots$. If ν exists, in general $Y_{l+1}, Y_{l+2}, \ldots$ will be approximately covariance-stationary if l is large enough.) Suppose that we make a simulation run of length m and then divide the resulting observations $Y_1, Y_2, \ldots, Y_m$ into n batches of length k. (Assume that $m = nk$.) Thus, batch 1 consists of observations $Y_1, \ldots, Y_k$, batch 2 consists of observations $Y_{k+1}, \ldots, Y_{2k}$, etc. Let $\overline{Y}_j(k)$ (where $j = 1, 2, \ldots, n$) be the sample (or batch) mean of the k observations in the jth batch, and let $\overline{\overline{Y}}(n, k) = \sum_{j=1}^{n} \overline{Y}_j(k)/n = \sum_{i=1}^{m} Y_i/m$ be the grand sample mean. We shall use $\overline{\overline{Y}}(n, k)$ as our point estimator for ν. [The $\overline{Y}_j(k)$'s will eventually play the same role for batch means as the X_j's did for the replication/deletion approach in Sec. 9.5.2.]

If the process $Y_1, Y_2, \ldots$ satisfies some additional conditions in addition to being covariance-stationary, then, for a fixed number of batches n, Steiger and Wilson (2001) show that the $\overline{Y}_j(k)$'s are asymptotically (as $k \to \infty$) distributed as independent normal random variables with mean ν. Therefore, if the batch size k is large enough, it is reasonable to treat the $\overline{Y}_j(k)$'s as if they were IID normal random variables with mean ν. Then a point estimate and approximate $100(1 - \alpha)$ percent confidence interval for ν are obtained by substituting $X_j = \overline{Y}_j(k)$ into (4.3), (4.4), and (4.12).

The major source of error for batch means lies in choosing the batch size k too small, which results in the $\overline{Y}_j(k)$'s possibly being highly correlated and $S^2(n)/n$ being a severely biased estimator of $\mathrm{Var}[\overline{X}(n)] = \mathrm{Var}[\overline{\overline{Y}}(n, k)]$; see Sec. 4.4. In particular, if the Y_i's are positively correlated (as is often the case in practice), the $\overline{Y}_j(k)$'s will be too, giving a variance estimator that is biased low and a confidence interval that is too small. Thus, the confidence interval will cover ν with a probability that is lower than the desired $1 - \alpha$.

There have been several variations of batch means proposed in the literature. Meketon and Schmeiser (1984) introduced the method of *overlapping batch means* (OBM), where $\overline{\overline{Y}}(n, k)$ is once again the point estimator for ν but the expression for $\widehat{\text{Var}}[\overline{\overline{Y}}(n, k)]$ involves all $m - k + 1$ batch means of size k. In particular, batch 1 consists of observations $Y_1, \ldots, Y_k$, batch 2 consists of observations $Y_2, \ldots, Y_{k+1}$, etc. Let $\overline{Y}_j(k)$ (where $j = 1, 2, \ldots, m - k + 1$) be the sample (or batch) mean of the k observations in the jth batch; the $\overline{Y}_j(k)$'s will, in general, be highly correlated. Then the OBM-based estimator of $\text{Var}[\overline{\overline{Y}}(n, k)]$ is given by

$$\widehat{\text{Var}}_O[\overline{\overline{Y}}(n, k)] = \frac{k \sum_{j=1}^{m-k+1} [\overline{Y}_j(k) - \overline{\overline{Y}}(n, k)]^2}{(m - k + 1)(m - k)}$$

and an approximate $100(1 - \alpha)$ percent confidence interval for ν is

$$\overline{\overline{Y}}(n, k) \pm t_{f,1-\alpha/2}\sqrt{\widehat{\text{Var}}_O[\overline{\overline{Y}}(n, k)]}$$

where the degrees of freedom, f, for the t distribution is discussed in Alexopoulos, Goldsman, and Serfozo (2006). Empirical results for the OBM confidence interval can be found in Sargent, Kang, and Goldsman (1992).

Bischak, Kelton, and Pollak (1993) studied the idea of *weighted batch means*, where a weight of w_i is assigned to the ith observation in a batch and the w_i's sum to 1. In the usual batch-means approach, $w_i = 1/k$ for all i. Fox, Goldsman, and Swain (1991) consider the idea of *spaced batch means*, where a spacer of size s is inserted between the batches used for the actual analysis to reduce the correlations among the $\overline{Y}_j(k)$'s.

Tafazzoli et al. (2011) propose N-Skart. It accounts for skewness in the batch means by using the Willink confidence interval given by (4.13) and it makes a correlation adjustment to the half-length of the confidence interval based on the estimated lag-one correlation between the batch means.

Argon and Andradóttir (2006) introduced the method of *replicated batch means*, which is based on making a "small" number, r, of replications of length m, and then breaking each replication into n batches of length k ($m = nk$). The sample mean of the r replication averages is used as a point estimator for ν, and the rn batch means are used to construct a variance estimator. This method includes replication as a special case when $n = 1$, and it includes batch means as a special case when $r = 1$. Other papers that discuss batch means in general are by Alexopoulos and Goldsman (2004); Alexopoulos, Goldsman, and Serfozo (2006); Damerdji (1994); Fishman and Yarberry (1997); Sargent, Kang, and Goldsman (1992); Schmeiser (1982); Schmeiser and Song (1996); and Song and Schmeiser (1995). Sequential procedures based on batch means are discussed at the end of this section.

Rather than attempt to achieve independence, the two methods we discuss next use estimates of the autocorrelation structure of the underlying stochastic process to obtain an estimate of the variance of the sample mean and ultimately to construct a confidence interval for ν. Assume that we have the observations $Y_1, Y_2, \ldots, Y_m$ from a single replication of the simulation and let $\overline{Y}(m) = \sum_{i=1}^{m} Y_i/m$ be our point estimator for ν. The *autoregressive method*, developed by Fishman (1971, 1973a, 1978), assumes that the process $Y_1, Y_2, \ldots$ is covariance-stationary with $E(Y_i) = \nu$ and can be represented by the pth-order autoregressive model

$$\sum_{j=0}^{p} b_j(Y_{i-j} - \nu) = \epsilon_i \tag{9.7}$$

where $b_0 = 1$ and $\{\epsilon_i\}$ is a sequence of uncorrelated random variables with common mean 0 and variance σ_ϵ^2. For known autoregressive order p and

$$\sum_{j=-\infty}^{\infty} |C_j| < \infty \tag{9.8}$$

it is possible to show that $m \operatorname{Var}[\overline{Y}(m)] \rightarrow \sigma_\epsilon^2/(\sum_{j=0}^{p} b_j)^2$ as $m \rightarrow \infty$. Based on estimating the covariances C_j from the observations $Y_1, \ldots, Y_m$, Fishman (1973a) gives a procedure for determining the order p and obtaining estimates $\hat{b}_j$ (where $j = 1, 2, \ldots, \hat{p}$) and $\hat{\sigma}_\epsilon^2$, where $\hat{p}$ is the estimated order. Let $\hat{b} = 1 + \sum_{j=1}^{\hat{p}} \hat{b}_j$. Then, for large m, an estimate of $\operatorname{Var}[\overline{Y}(m)]$ and an approximate $100(1 - \alpha)$ percent confidence interval for ν are given by

$$\widehat{\operatorname{Var}}[\overline{Y}(m)] = \frac{\hat{\sigma}_\epsilon^2}{m(\hat{b})^2}$$

and

$$\overline{Y}(m) \pm t_{\hat{f},1-\alpha/2} \sqrt{\widehat{\operatorname{Var}}[\overline{Y}(m)]}$$

where an expression for the estimated df $\hat{f}$ is given by

$$\hat{f} = \frac{m\hat{b}}{2\sum_{j=0}^{\hat{p}} (\hat{p} - 2j)\hat{b}_j}$$

Yuan and Nelson (1994) give an alternative approach for estimating the autoregressive order p and the df f. Their approach gives better coverage than Fishman's approach for the *M*/*M*/1 queue with $\rho = 0.9$.

A major concern in using these approaches is whether the autoregressive model provides a good representation for an arbitrary stochastic process. Schriber and Andrews (1984) give a generalization of the autoregressive method that allows for moving-average components as well.

The method of *spectrum analysis* also assumes that the process $Y_1, Y_2, \ldots$ is covariance-stationary with $E(Y_i) = \nu$, but does not make any further assumptions such as that given by Eq. (9.7). Under this stationarity assumption, it is possible to show that

$$\operatorname{Var}[\overline{Y}(m)] = \frac{C_0 + 2\sum_{j=1}^{m-1} (1 - j/m)C_j}{m} \tag{9.9}$$

[which is essentially the same as Eq. (4.7)], and the method of spectrum analysis uses this relationship as a starting point for estimating $\operatorname{Var}[\overline{Y}(m)]$. The name of this method is based on the fact that, provided (9.8) holds, we have $m\,\text{Var}[\overline{Y}(m)] \to 2\pi g(0)$ as $m \to \infty$, where $g(\tau)$ is called the *spectrum* of the process at frequency τ, and is defined by the Fourier transform $g(\tau) = (2\pi)^{-1}\sum_{j=-\infty}^{\infty} C_j \exp(-i\tau j)$ for $|\tau| \leq \pi$ and $i = \sqrt{-1}$. Thus, for large m, $\text{Var}[\overline{Y}(m)] \approx 2\pi g(0)/m$ and the problem of estimating $\text{Var}[\overline{Y}(m)]$ can be viewed as that of estimating the spectrum at zero frequency.

An estimator of $\text{Var}[\overline{Y}(m)]$ that immediately presents itself is obtained by simply replacing C_j in Eq. (9.9) by an estimate $\hat{C}_j$ computed from $Y_1, Y_2, \ldots, Y_m$ and Eq. (4.9). However, for large m and j near m, C_j will generally be nearly zero, but $\hat{C}_j$ will have a large variance since it will be based on only a few observations. As a result, several authors have suggested estimators of the following form:

$$\widehat{\text{Var}}[\overline{Y}(m)] = \frac{\hat{C}_0 + 2\sum_{j=1}^{q-1} W_q(j)\hat{C}_j}{m}$$

where q (which determines the number of $\hat{C}_j$'s in the estimator) must be specified and the weighting function $W_q(j)$ is designed to improve the sampling properties of $\widehat{\text{Var}}[\overline{Y}(m)]$. Then an approximate $100(1 - \alpha)$ percent confidence interval for ν is given by

$$\overline{Y}(m) \pm t_{f,1-\alpha/2}\sqrt{\widehat{\text{Var}}[\overline{Y}(m)]}$$

where f depends on m, q, and the choice of weighting function [see Fishman (1969, 1973a) and Law and Kelton (1984)]. Welch (1987) discusses the relationships among batch means, overlapping batch means, and spectrum analysis.

This technique is complicated, requiring a fairly sophisticated background on the part of the analyst. Moreover, there is no definitive procedure for choosing the value of q. Additional discussions of spectral methods may be found in Damerdji (1991), Heidelberger and Welch (1981a, 1981b, 1983), Lada and Wilson (2006a), and Lada et al. (2007).

The *regenerative method* is an altogether different approach to simulation and thus leads to different approaches to constructing a confidence interval for ν. The idea is to identify random times at which the process probabilistically "starts over," i.e., regenerates, and to use these regeneration points to obtain independent random variables to which classical statistical analysis can be applied to form point and interval estimates for ν. This method was developed simultaneously by Crane and Iglehart (1974a, 1974b, 1975) and by Fishman (1973b, 1974); we follow the presentation of the former authors.

Assume for the output process $Y_1, Y_2, \ldots$ that there is a sequence of random indices $1 \leq B_1 < B_2 < \cdots$, called *regeneration points*, at which the process starts over probabilistically; i.e., the distribution of the process $\{Y_{B_j+i-1}, i = 1, 2, \ldots\}$ is the same for each $j = 1, 2, \ldots$, and the process from each B_j on is assumed to be independent of the process prior to B_j. The portion of the process between two successive B_j's is called a *regeneration cycle*, and it can be shown that successive cycles are IID replicas of each other. In particular, comparable random variables defined over the successive cycles are IID. Let $N_j = B_{j+1} - B_j$ for $j = 1, 2, \ldots$ and assume that $E(N_j) < \infty$. If $Z_j = \sum_{i=B_j}^{B_{j+1}-1} Y_i$, the random vectors $\mathbf{U}_j = (Z_j, N_j)^T$

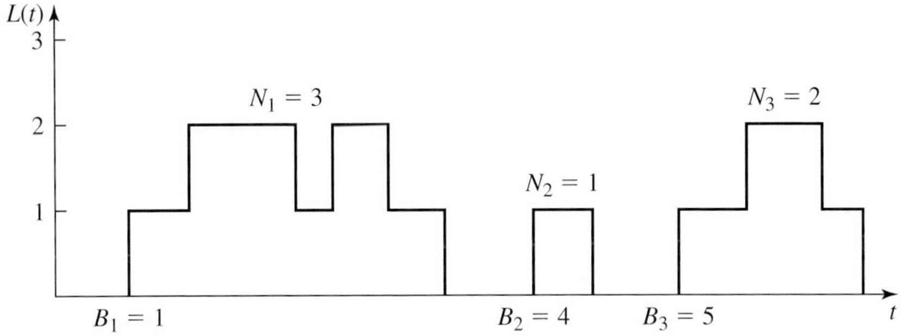

FIGURE 9.17
A realization of the number-in-system process $\{L(t), t \geq 0\}$ for a single-server queue.

(where $\mathbf{A}^T$ is the transpose of the vector $\mathbf{A}$) are IID, and provided that $E(|Z_j|) < \infty$, the steady-state mean ν is given (see Prob. 9.21) by

$$\nu = \frac{E(Z)}{E(N)}$$

EXAMPLE 9.32. Consider the output process of delays $D_1, D_2, \ldots$ for a single-server queue with IID interarrival times, IID service times, customers served in a FIFO manner, and $\rho < 1$. The indices of those customers who arrive to find the system completely empty are regeneration points (see Fig. 9.17). Let N_j be the total number of customers served in the jth cycle and let $Z_j = \sum_{i=B_j}^{B_{j+1}-1} D_i$ be the total delay of all customers served in the jth cycle. Then the steady-state mean delay d is given by $d = E(Z)/E(N)$.

Note that the indices of customers who arrive to find l customers present ($l \geq 1$ and fixed) will not, in general, be regeneration points for the process $D_1, D_2, \ldots$. This is because the distribution of the remaining service time of the customer in service will be different for successive customers who arrive to find l customers present. However, if service times are exponential random variables, these indices *are* regeneration points due to the memoryless property of the exponential distribution (see Probs. 4.26 and 9.22).

We now discuss how to obtain a point estimator and a confidence interval for ν using the regenerative method. Suppose that we simulate the process $Y_1, Y_2, \ldots$ for exactly n' regeneration cycles, resulting in the following data:

$$Z_1, Z_2, \ldots, Z_{n'}$$

$$N_1, N_2, \ldots, N_{n'}$$

Each of these sequences consists of IID random variables. In general, however, Z_j and N_j are not independent. A point estimator for ν is then given by

$$\hat{\nu}(n') = \frac{\bar{Z}(n')}{\bar{N}(n')}$$

Although $\bar{Z}(n')$ and $\bar{N}(n')$ are unbiased estimators of $E(Z)$ and $E(N)$, respectively, $\hat{\nu}(n')$ is *not* an unbiased estimator of ν (see App. 9A). It is true, however, that $\hat{\nu}(n')$ is a *strongly consistent estimator* of ν, that is, $\hat{\nu}(n') \rightarrow \nu$ as $n' \rightarrow \infty$ (w.p. 1); see Prob. 9.21.

Let the covariance matrix of the vector $\mathbf{U}_j = (Z_j, N_j)^T$ be

$$\Sigma = \begin{bmatrix} \sigma_{11} & \sigma_{12} \\ \sigma_{12} & \sigma_{22} \end{bmatrix}$$

for example, $\sigma_{12} = E\{[Z_j - E(Z_j)][N_j - E(N_j)]\}$, and let $V_j = Z_j - \nu N_j$. Then the V_j's are IID random variables with mean 0 and variance $\sigma_V^2 = \sigma_{11} - 2\nu\sigma_{12} + \nu^2\sigma_{22}$ (see Prob. 4.13). Therefore, if $0 < \sigma_V^2 < \infty$, it follows from the classical central limit theorem (see Theorem 4.1 in Sec. 4.5) that

$$\frac{\overline{V}(n')}{\sqrt{\sigma_V^2/n'}} \xrightarrow{\mathfrak{D}} \mathrm{N}(0, 1) \qquad \text{as } n' \to \infty \tag{9.10}$$

where $\xrightarrow{\mathfrak{D}}$ denotes convergence in distribution. Let

$$\hat{\Sigma}(n') = \begin{bmatrix} \hat{\sigma}_{11}(n') & \hat{\sigma}_{12}(n') \\ \hat{\sigma}_{12}(n') & \hat{\sigma}_{22}(n') \end{bmatrix} = \frac{\sum_{j=1}^{n'} [\mathbf{U}_j - \overline{\mathbf{U}}(n')][\mathbf{U}_j - \overline{\mathbf{U}}(n')]^T}{n' - 1}$$

be the estimated covariance matrix and let

$$\hat{\sigma}_V^2(n') = \hat{\sigma}_{11}(n') - 2\hat{\nu}(n')\hat{\sigma}_{12}(n') + [\hat{\nu}(n')]^2\hat{\sigma}_{22}(n')$$

be the estimate of σ_V^2 based on n' regeneration cycles. It can be shown that $\hat{\sigma}_V^2(n') \to \sigma_V^2$ as $n' \to \infty$ (w.p. 1). Consequently, we can replace σ_V^2 in (9.10) by $\hat{\sigma}_V^2(n')$ [see Chung (1974, p. 93)], and dividing through the ratio by $\overline{N}(n')$ yields

$$\frac{\hat{\nu}(n') - \nu}{\sqrt{\hat{\sigma}_V^2(n')/\{n'[\overline{N}(n')]^2\}}} \xrightarrow{\mathfrak{D}} \mathrm{N}(0, 1) \qquad \text{as } n' \to \infty$$

Therefore, if the number of cycles n' is sufficiently large, an approximate (in terms of coverage) $100(1 - \alpha)$ percent confidence interval for ν is given by

$$\hat{\nu}(n') \pm \frac{z_{1-\alpha/2}\sqrt{\hat{\sigma}_V^2(n')/n'}}{\overline{N}(n')} \tag{9.11}$$

We call this regenerative approach to constructing a confidence interval for ν the *classical approach* (C). For an alternative regenerative approach to constructing a confidence interval for ν, known as the *jackknife approach* (J), see App. 9A.

The difficulty with using the regenerative method in practice is that real-world simulations may not have regeneration points, or (even if they do) the expected cycle length may be so large that only a very few cycles can be simulated [in which case the confidence interval given by (9.11) will not be valid]. For example, suppose one wants to estimate by simulation the steady-state mean total delay in queue for a network consisting of k queueing systems in series. [A customer departing from queueing system i (where $i = 1, 2, \ldots, k - 1$) proceeds to queueing system $i + 1$.] Then regeneration points for the process $D_1, D_2, \ldots$ (where D_i is the total delay of the ith customer to arrive) are the indices of those customers who arrive at the first queueing system to find the *entire* network empty. If the queueing systems composing the network are highly utilized, as is typical, regeneration points for the network will be few and far between. A more complete discussion of the regenerative method may be found in Crane and Lemoine (1977), Henderson and Glynn (2001), and Shedler (1993).

The *standardized time series method* [see Schruben (1983a)] assumes that the process $Y_1, Y_2, \ldots$ is strictly stationary with $E(Y_i) = \nu$ for all i and is also phi-mixing. *Strictly stationary* means that the joint distribution of $Y_{i_1+j}, Y_{i_2+j}, \ldots, Y_{i_n+j}$ is independent of j for all time indices $i_1, i_2, \ldots, i_n$. (If ν exists, then, in general, $Y_{l+1}, Y_{l+2}, \ldots$ should be approximately strictly stationary if l is large enough.) Roughly speaking, $Y_1, Y_2, \ldots$ is *phi-mixing* if Y_i and Y_{i+j} become essentially independent as j becomes large [see Billingsley (1999) for a precise definition]. Suppose that we make one simulation run of length m and divide $Y_1, Y_2, \ldots, Y_m$ into n batches of size k (where $m = nk$). Let $\bar{Y}_j(k)$ be the sample mean of the k observations in the jth batch. The grand sample mean $\bar{Y}(m)$ is the point estimator for ν. Furthermore, if m is large, then $\bar{Y}(m)$ will be approximately normally distributed with mean ν and variance τ^2/m, where

$$\tau^2 = \lim_{m\to\infty} m \operatorname{Var}[\bar{Y}(m)]$$

and is called the *variance parameter*. [See Alexopoulos et al. (2007a, 2007b), Antonini et al. (2009), Alexopoulos et al. (2010), and Meterelliyoz et al. (2012) for recent papers on estimating τ^2.] Let

$$A = \left(\frac{12}{k^3 - k}\right)\sum_{j=1}^{n}\left\{\sum_{s=1}^{k}\sum_{i=1}^{s}[\bar{Y}_j(k) - Y_{i+(j-1)k}]\right\}^2$$

For a fixed number of batches n, A will be asymptotically (as $k \to \infty$) distributed as τ^2 times a chi-square random variable with n df and asymptotically independent of $\bar{Y}(m)$. Therefore, for k large, we can treat

$$\frac{[\bar{Y}(m) - \nu]/\sqrt{\tau^2/m}}{\sqrt{(A/\tau^2)/n}} = \frac{\bar{Y}(m) - \nu}{\sqrt{A/(mn)}}$$

as having a t distribution with n df, and an approximate $100(1 - \alpha)$ percent confidence interval for ν is given by

$$\bar{Y}(m) \pm t_{n,1-\alpha/2}\sqrt{A/(mn)}$$

The major source of error for standardized time series is choosing the batch size k too small [see Schruben (1983a) for details]. It should be noted that this approach is based on the same underlying theory as Schruben's test for initialization bias discussed in Sec. 9.5.1. Additional references for standardized time series, including alternative confidence-interval formulations, are Glynn and Iglehart (1990), Goldsman, Meketon, and Schruben (1990), Goldsman and Schruben (1984, 1990), and Sargent, Kang, and Goldsman (1992).

Since the five fixed-sample-size confidence-interval approaches presented in this section depend on assumptions that will not be strictly satisfied in an actual simulation, it is of interest to see how these approaches perform in practice. We first present the results from 400 independent simulation experiments for the *M*/*M*/1 queue with $\rho = 0.8$ ($\lambda = 1$ and $\omega = \frac{5}{4}$), where in each experiment our goal was to construct a 90 percent confidence interval for the steady-state mean delay $d = 3.2$ using all five procedures. Not knowing how to select definitively the total sample size m for batch means (B), the autoregressive method (A), spectrum analysis (SA), and standardized times series (STS), we arbitrarily chose $m = 320$, 640, 1280, and 2560. For the regenerative method (R), it can be shown that $E(N) = 1/(1 - \rho) = 5$ for the $M/M/1$ queue with $\rho = 0.8$ (see Prob. 9.25). We therefore chose the number of regeneration cycles $n' = 64$, 128, 256, and 512 so that, on the average, all procedures used the same number of observations, that is, $m = n'E(N)$. Furthermore, we considered both the classical and jackknifed regenerative confidence intervals. For batch means and standardized time series, we chose the number of batches $n = 5$, 10, and 20. The df f for spectrum analysis was chosen so that $f + 1 = n$, where f is related to the number of covariance estimates q in the variance expression by $q = 1.33m/f$ [see Law and Kelton (1984) for details]. Table 9.9 gives the proportion of the 400 confidence intervals that covered d for each of the 48 cases discussed above. [All results are taken from Law and Kelton (1984), except those for standardized time series, which were graciously provided by Professor David Goldsman of Georgia Tech.] For example, in the case of $m = 320$ and $n = 5$ for batch means (i.e., each confidence interval was based on five batches of size 64), 69 percent of the 400 confidence intervals covered d, falling considerably short of the desired 90 percent. (Note that for fixed m, the estimated coverage for batch means decreases as n increases. This is because as n increases, the batch means become more correlated, resulting in a more biased estimate of the variance of the sample mean.)

We next present the results from 200 independent simulation experiments for the time-shared computer model with 35 terminals [see Law and Kelton (1984)], which was discussed in Sec. 2.5. Our objective was to construct 90 percent confidence intervals for the steady-state mean response time $r = 8.25$ [see Adiri and Avi-Itzhak (1969)]. We chose m and n as above and, since $E(N) \approx 32$ for the computer model, we took $n' = 10$, 20, 40, and 80. Table 9.10 gives the proportion of the 200 confidence intervals that covered r for each of 36 cases (results for standardized time series were not available). Even though the computer model is physically much more complex than the $M/M/1$ queue, it can be seen from Table 9.10 that batch means with $n = 5$ produces an estimated coverage very close to 0.90 for m as small as 640. Thus, the $M/M/1$ queue with $\rho = 0.8$ is much more difficult statistically, despite its very simple structure. These two examples illustrate that one cannot infer anything about the statistical behavior of the output data by looking at how "complex" the model's structure might be.

From the empirical results presented in Tables 9.9 and 9.10 and also those in Law (1977), Law and Kelton (1984), and Sargent, Kang, and Goldsman (1992), we came to the following conclusions with regard to fixed-sample-size procedures:

1. If the total sample size m (or n') is chosen too small, the actual coverages of *all* existing fixed-sample-size procedures (including replication/deletion) may be considerably lower than desired. This is really not surprising, since a steady-state parameter is defined as a limit as the length of the simulation (total number of observations) goes to infinity.

TABLE 9.9

Estimated coverages based on 400 experiments, *M/M/*1 queue with $\rho = 0.8$

	B			STS			SA			A	R	
	n			*n*			$f+1$				Method	
$m(n')$	5	10	20	5	10	20	5	10	20		C	J
320 (64)	0.690	0.598	0.490	0.520	0.340	0.208	0.713	0.625	0.538	0.688	0.560	0.670
640 (128)	0.723	0.708	0.588	0.628	0.485	0.318	0.760	0.735	0.645	0.723	0.683	0.728
1280 (256)	0.780	0.740	0.705	0.730	0.645	0.485	0.783	0.770	0.745	0.753	0.705	0.748
2560 (512)	0.798	0.803	0.753	0.798	0.725	0.598	0.833	0.808	0.773	0.755	0.745	0.763

TABLE 9.10

Estimated coverages based on 200 experiments, time-shared computer model

	B			SA			A	R	
	n			$f+1$				Method	
$m(n')$	5	10	20	5	10	20		C	J
320 (10)	0.860	0.780	0.670	0.880	0.815	0.720	0.680	0.545	0.725
640 (20)	0.890	0.855	0.790	0.870	0.870	0.820	0.805	0.730	0.830
1280 (40)	0.910	0.885	0.880	0.910	0.910	0.905	0.890	0.830	0.865
2560 (80)	0.905	0.875	0.895	0.910	0.885	0.900	0.885	0.870	0.915

2. The "appropriate" choice of m (or n') would appear to be extremely model-dependent and thus impossible to choose arbitrarily. For the method of batch means with $n = 5$, $m = 640$ gave good results for the computer model; however, even for m as large as 2560, we did not obtain good results for the $M/M/1$ queue.
3. For m fixed, the methods of batch means, standardized time series, and spectrum analysis will achieve the best coverage for n and f small.

Sequential Procedures

We now discuss procedures that sequentially determine the length of a single simulation run needed to construct an acceptable confidence interval for the steady-state mean ν. The need for such sequential procedures is evident from the fixed-sample-size results reported above. Specifically, no procedure in which the run length is fixed before the simulation begins can generally be relied upon to produce a confidence interval that covers ν with the desired probability $1 - \alpha$, if the fixed run length is too small for the system being simulated.

In addition to the problem of coverage, an analyst might want to determine a run length large enough to obtain an estimate of ν with a specified absolute error β or relative error γ (see Sec. 9.4.1). It will seldom be possible to know in advance even the order of magnitude of the run length needed to meet these goals for a given simulation problem, so some sort of procedure to increase the run length iteratively would seem to be in order.

Law and Kelton (1982) and Law (1983) surveyed the sequential procedures available at those times and found three that appeared to perform well in terms of achieved coverage if the specified absolute or relative error was small enough. In particular, Fishman (1977) developed a procedure based on the regenerative method and an absolute-error stopping rule. Law and Kelton found that it achieved acceptable coverage for 9 out of 10 stochastic models tested if $\beta = 0.075\ \nu$. Fishman's procedure has the disadvantage of being based on the regenerative method, which we feel limits its application to real-world problems. Also, specifying an appropriate value for β in practice may be troublesome, since ν will, of course, be unknown.

Law and Carson (1979) developed a procedure based on batch means and a relative-error stopping rule. For a fixed number of batches $n = 40$, the batch size k is increased until the resulting batch means are approximately uncorrelated and the corresponding confidence interval satisfies the specified relative error. However, at a particular iteration, 400 batch means each based on $k/10$ observations are actually used to determine whether the corresponding 40 batch means, each based on k observations, are uncorrelated. This scheme was necessary because correlation estimators are generally biased and for small n have a large variance. The Law and Carson (L&C) procedure does not test the batch means to see whether they are approximately normally distributed. However, since $n = 40$ and each batch mean is an average of many individual observations, this is probably not a major issue in general (see Table 4.1).

They applied their procedure to 14 stochastic models for which ν can be computed analytically. For each model, they tried to construct a 90 percent confidence

TABLE 9.11
Estimated coverage, 90 percent confidence interval for true coverage, and average sample size when constructing nominal 90 percent confidence intervals with $\gamma = 0.075$, batch-means procedures

Model	L&C	ASAP3	SBatch	Skart
$M/M/1$, $\rho = 0.8$	0.87 ± 0.06 75,648	0.868 ± 0.028 72,060	0.903 ± 0.024 89,434	0.912 ± 0.014 82,508
$M/M/1$ LIFO, $\rho = 0.8$	0.84 ± 0.06 74,624	0.875 ± 0.027 68,325	0.888 ± 0.016 97,172	0.916 ± 0.014 81,441
$M/H_2/1$, $\rho = 0.8$	0.90 ± 0.05 229,632	0.900 ± 0.025 228,482	0.896 ± 0.025 254,400	0.913 ± 0.015 255,363
$M/M/1/M/1$, $\rho = 0.8$	0.87 ± 0.06 49,920	0.913 ± 0.023 58,844	0.931 ± 0.013 55,398	0.909 ± 0.016 58,573
Central-server model 3	0.88 ± 0.05 3740	0.870 ± 0.026 18,447	0.921 ± 0.014 85,842	0.873 ± 0.017 12,231
Experiments	100	400	1000	1000

interval with a relative error of $\gamma = 0.075$, and they carried out 100 independent experiments. (In general, we believe that if someone is going to use a sequential procedure, then they will choose $\gamma \le 0.1$. Otherwise, they will use a fixed-sample-size procedure.) Note that the L&C procedure does not explicitly address the startup problem (e.g., no warmup period is used).

In Table 9.11 we give for the L&C procedure the proportion, $\hat{p}$, of the 100 confidence intervals that contained ν, a 90 percent confidence interval for the true coverage p, and the average run length (sample size) at termination, respectively, for five of the tested models. The 90 percent confidence interval for the true coverage p was computed from $\hat{p} \pm z_{0.95}\sqrt{\hat{p}(1 - \hat{p})/100}$ (see Sec. 9.4.2). The results in the first four rows of Table 9.11 are for the delay-in-queue process for the $M/M/1$ queue, the $M/M/1$ LIFO queue, the $M/H_2/1$ queue [hyperexponential service times with cv $= 2$; see Law (1974) for the exact definition], and the $M/M/1/M/1$ queue (two $M/M/1$ queues in series), respectively; for each model, $\rho = 0.8$. The fifth row of Table 9.11 is for the response-time process for a simple model of a computer system, which Law and Carson call central-server model 3. The last row in Table 9.11 gives the number of independent experiments used in the evaluation of each procedure.

Heidelberger and Welch (1983) developed a procedure (denoted H&W) based on spectral methods and a relative-error stopping rule, which uses regression techniques to estimate the spectrum at zero frequency. Their procedure requires the user to specify a maximum sample size, so some of the confidence intervals produced may not satisfy the relative-error requirement. For the response-time process for two models of computer systems, they tried to construct a 90 percent confidence interval for ν, and they carried out 50 independent experiments [see Heidelberger and Welch (1981b)]. Let $\hat{p}$ be the proportion of confidence intervals *satisfying the precision requirement* that cover ν. For $\gamma = 0.05$ they obtained $\hat{p}$ equal to 0.88 and

TABLE 9.12

Estimated coverage, 90 percent confidence interval for true coverage, and average sample size when constructing nominal 90 percent confidence intervals with $\gamma = 0.075$, spectral procedures

Model	H&W	WASSP
$M/M/1$, $\rho = 0.8$	0.790 ± 0.034 77,971	0.885 ± 0.026 117,540
$M/M/1$ LIFO, $\rho = 0.8$	0.795 ± 0.033 80,098	0.902 ± 0.024 152,355
$M/H_2/1$, $\rho = 0.8$	0.780 ± 0.034 233,430	0.910 ± 0.024 330,580
$M/M/1/M/1$, $\rho = 0.8$	0.803 ± 0.033 52,700	0.890 ± 0.026 82,680
Central-server model 3	0.880 ± 0.027 12,562	0.930 ± 0.021 79,188
Experiments	400	400

0.84 for the two models. Additional empirical results for the H&W procedure are given in Table 9.12 above.

Steiger et al. (2005) proposed a modified version of the *A*utomated *S*imulation *A*nalysis *P*rocedure [Steiger and Wilson (2002)], called ASAP3, which is based on the method of batch means. It operates as follows: The batch size is incrementally increased until spaced groups of four adjacent batch means pass a test for multivariate normality (see Sec. 6.10.1), where the spacer preceding each group also consists of four adjacent batch means. Then after skipping the first spacer as the warmup period, ASAP3 fits an AR(1) process to the *nonspaced* batch means. If necessary, the batch size is further increased until the autoregressive parameter ϕ in the AR(1) model does not exceed 0.8. Next, ASAP3 uses a modified t confidence interval based on the AR(1) parameter estimates to account for the remaining correlations in the batch means. Note that unlike the L&C procedure, ASAP3 does *not* try to obtain uncorrelated batch means. For each model they tried to construct a 90 percent confidence interval for ν with a relative error of $\gamma = 0.075$, and they carried out 400 independent experiments, with the results given in Table 9.11. Additional performance results for ASAP3 are given in Tafazzoli et al. (2011).

Lada et al. (2008) introduced SBatch (*S*paced *Batch* means) for constructing a confidence interval for a steady-state mean. SBatch uses a randomness test and a normality test to iteratively determine the size s of a spacer proceeding each batch and the batch size k so that the resulting spaced batch means are approximately IID normal random variables. To check for any residual correlation between the spaced batch means, SBatch tests the lag-one correlation of the spaced batch means to make sure that it does not exceed 0.8. Each time the correlation test is failed, the batch size is increased, additional observations are obtained from the simulation, a new set of spaced batch means is computed, and the correlation test is repeated for the new set of spaced batch means.

Once the correlation test is passed, SBatch constructs a correlation-adjusted confidence interval for ν using the current set of spaced batch means as follows: The center of the confidence interval is the average of *all* observations beyond the first spacer (the warmup period), and the half-length uses the sample variance of the spaced batch means and a correlation adjustment based on the estimated lag-one correlation [see Eq. (4.9)] between the spaced batch means. For each model they tried to construct a 90 percent confidence interval for ν with a relative error of $\gamma = 0.075$, and they carried out 1000 independent experiments, with the results given in Table 9.11. (We would like to thank Dr. Emily Lada, Dr. Ali Tafazzoli, and Professor James Wilson for supplying some of results presented in Table 9.11.) Additional results for SBatch are given in Tafazzoli et al. (2011).

Tafazzoli and Wilson (2011) developed a procedure that they called Skart (*Sk*ewness- and *a*uto*r*egression-adjusted Student's *t* analysis). [See also Tafazzoli et al. (2011).] Skart addresses the startup problem by successively applying a randomness test to spaced batch means with progressively increasing batch sizes and inter-batch spacer sizes. When the test is finally passed with a batch size k and a spacer size dk (d a nonnegative integer), the warmup period is taken to be $l = dk$.

For the data beyond the warmup period l, Skart computes and uses n' *nonspaced* batch means with batch size k. Since the batch means will, in general, be skewed, Skart uses (4.13) [by Willink (2005)] to construct a confidence interval for the steady-state mean ν, with the batch means' playing the role of the X_i's. The "center" of the nonsymmetric confidence interval is the sample mean of the batch means, and the half-length uses the sample variance of the batch means and a correlation adjustment based on the estimated lag-one correlation between the batch means. For each model they tried to construct a 90 percent confidence interval for ν with a relative error of $\gamma = 0.075$, and they carried out 1000 independent experiments, with the results given in Table 9.11.

Lada and Wilson (2006a) developed WASSP (*WA*velet-based *S*equential *S*pectral *P*rocedure) that also uses a relative-error stopping rule. Lada and Wilson (2006b) tested WASSP and H&W on the same five models discussed above. They performed 400 independent experiments and attempted to construct 90 percent confidence intervals for ν with a relative error of $\gamma = 0.075$, with the results given in Table 9.12. Based on the coverage results in Table 9.12 and in Lada et al. (2007), which we believe are more important than average sample sizes, we conclude that WASSP is superior to H&W. Additional results for WASSP can be found in Tafazzoli et al. (2011).

We do, however, believe that the ASAP3, SBatch, and Skart are preferable to WASSP, since the latter procedure generally requires much larger average sample sizes. Also, WASSP is more complicated since it requires 21 steps as compared to, for example, the 13 steps employed by Skart. (If a particular step for one of these procedures requires p substeps, then we consider the overall step as actually consisting of p steps.) Using the results in Table 9.11 and also those in Tables 1 and 6 of Tafazzoli et al. (2011), we believe that Skart provides the best overall results among the ASAP3, SBatch, and Skart procedures using coverage and average sample size as the criteria for comparison.

However, we believe that the L&C procedure is also worthy of some consideration, since it provided satisfactory performance on 14 stochastic models, albeit based on only 100 experiments per model (compared to 1000 experiments for Skart). It is also the simplest of all sequential procedures discussed here, requiring only five steps. This is very important if a procedure has to be programmed from scratch for a particular application. Finally, Chen and Kelton (2009) present an additional sequential procedure based on batch means, but only limited and noncomparable experimental results are given.

If one wants to construct a confidence interval for a steady-state mean ν that is likely to have coverage close to $1 - \alpha$ and to require a "reasonable" sample size, then one might consider the use of the Skart or L&C procedures with a relative error of $\gamma = 0.075$ or smaller. These two procedures have been tested on a large number of stochastic models and generally produced good results in terms of estimated coverage and average sample size. The reader should be aware, however, that these procedures are more complicated to understand and implement than, say, the replication/deletion approach of Sec. 9.5.2. They may also require larger sample sizes and will probably not easily generalize to the common situation of multiple measures of performance [see Sec. 9.7 and Tafazzoli et al. (2011)].

It might be noted that Glynn and Whitt (1992b) give sufficient conditions for a sequential procedure to be asymptotically valid, i.e., produce a coverage of $1 - \alpha$ as the run length goes to infinity.

9.5.4 Estimating Other Measures of Performance

As we saw in Sec. 9.4.2, the mean does not always provide us with an appropriate measure of system performance. We thus consider the estimation of steady-state parameters ϕ other than the mean $\nu = E(Y)$.

Suppose that we would like to estimate the steady-state probability $p = P(Y \in B)$, where B is a set of real numbers. By way of example, for a communications network we might want to determine the steady-state probability that the end-to-end delay of a message is less than or equal to 5 seconds ($B = \{$all real numbers $\leq 5\}$). Estimating the probability p, as it turns out, is just a special case of estimating the mean ν, as we now see. Let the steady-state random variable Z be defined by

$$Z = \begin{cases} 1 & \text{if } Y \in B \\ 0 & \text{otherwise} \end{cases}$$

Then

$$\begin{aligned} P(Y \in B) &= P(Z = 1) = 1 \cdot P(Z = 1) + 0 \cdot P(Z = 0) \\ &= E(Z) \end{aligned}$$

Thus, estimating p is equivalent to estimating the steady-state mean $E(Z)$, which has been discussed in Secs. 9.5.2 and 9.5.3. In particular, let

$$Z_i = \begin{cases} 1 & \text{if } Y_i \in B \\ 0 & \text{otherwise} \end{cases}$$

for $i = 1, 2, \ldots$, where $Y_1, Y_2, \ldots$ is the original stochastic process of interest. Then, for example, the replication/deletion approach could be applied to the output process $Z_1, Z_2, \ldots$ to obtain a point estimate and confidence interval for $E(Z) = p$. Note that the warmup period for the (binary) process $Z_1, Z_2, \ldots$ may be different from that for the original process $Y_1, Y_2, \ldots$.

Another parameter of the steady-state distribution of considerable interest is the q-quantile, y_q, which was defined in Sec. 6.4.3. That is, y_q is the value of y such that $P(Y \leq y_q) = q$, where Y is the steady-state random variable. For example, in the case of the communications network discussed above, it might be desired to estimate the 0.9-quantile of the steady-state end-to-end delay distribution. Estimating quantiles is both conceptually and computationally (in terms of the number of observations required to obtain a specified precision) a more difficult problem than estimating the steady-state mean. Furthermore, most procedures for estimating quantiles are based on order statistics and require storage and sorting of the observations.

There have been several procedures proposed for estimating quantiles based on batch means (or extensions), spectral, and regenerative methods [see Law (1983) and Heidelberger and Lewis (1984)]. One drawback of these procedures is that they are all based on a fixed sample size, which must be chosen somewhat arbitrarily. If this sample size is chosen too small, the coverage of the resulting confidence interval will be somewhat less than desired.

Raatikainen (1990) proposed a procedure for estimating quantiles based on the P^2 algorithm of Jain and Chlamtac (1985), which does not require storing and sorting the observations. It is a sequential procedure based on a spectral method and a relative-error stopping rule. Raatikainen tested his procedure on several stochastic models of computer systems and appeared to obtain good results in terms of coverage. The procedure is, however, difficult to implement.

Chen and Kelton (2006) proposed two sequential procedures—*zoom in* (ZI) and *quasi-independent* (QI)—for constructing a confidence interval for a quantile. They tested their procedures on the delay-in-queue process for the $M/M/1$ and $M/M/2$ queues, performing 100 independent experiments in each case. By way of example, suppose that the goal is to construct a 95 percent confidence interval for the 0.9-quantile for the $M/M/1$ queue with $\rho = 0.9$. The ZI procedure had an estimated coverage of 1.00 and an average sample size at termination of approximately 12,464,000. On the other hand, the QI procedure had an estimated coverage of 0.95 and an average sample size of approximately 14,793,000.

Alexopoulos et al. (2012) studied the feasibility of developing a sequential procedure to construct point estimators and confidence intervals for quantiles based on nonoverlapping batches. (The batched quantiles become approximately independent.) Their results are encouraging in terms of the sample sizes that will be required.

9.6 STATISTICAL ANALYSIS FOR STEADY-STATE CYCLE PARAMETERS

Suppose that the output process $Y_1, Y_2, \ldots$ does not have a steady-state distribution. Assume, on the other hand, that there is an appropriate cycle definition so that the process $Y_1^C, Y_2^C, \ldots$ has a steady-state distribution F^C, where Y_i^C is the random variable defined on the ith cycle (see Sec. 9.3). If $Y^C \sim F^C$, then we are interested in estimating some characteristic of Y^C such as the mean $\nu^C = E(Y^C)$ or the probability $P(Y^C \leq y)$. Clearly, estimating a steady-state cycle parameter is just a special case of estimating a steady-state parameter, so all of the techniques of Sec. 9.5 apply, except to the *cycle* random variables Y_i^C's rather than to the original Y_i's. For example, we could use Welch's method to identify a warmup period and then apply the replication/deletion approach to obtain a point estimate and confidence interval for ν^C.

EXAMPLE 9.33. Consider once again the small factory of Example 9.25 but suppose that there is a half-hour lunch break that starts 4 hours into each 8-hour shift. This break stops the inspection process, but unfinished parts continue to arrive and to be processed by the unmanned machine. If N_i is the throughput in the ith hour, then the process $N_1, N_2, \ldots$ does not have a steady-state distribution (see Example 9.11). We might, however, expect that it is periodic with a cycle length of 8 hours. To substantiate this, we made $n = 10$ replications of length $m = 160$ hours (20 shifts). From the plot of the averaged process $\overline{N}_i$ (where $i = 1, 2, \ldots, 160$) in Fig. 9.18, we see that the process $N_1, N_2, \ldots$ does indeed appear to have a cycle of length 8 hours.

Let N_i^C be the average production in the ith 8-hour cycle and assume that $N_1^C, N_2^C, \ldots$ has a steady-state distribution. Suppose that we want to obtain a point estimate and a 99 percent confidence interval for the steady-state expected average production over a shift, $\nu^C = E(N^C)$, using the replication/deletion approach. Let N_{ji}^C be the average production in the ith cycle of our jth available replication ($j = 1, 2, \ldots, 10$; $i = 1, 2, \ldots, 20$), and let $\overline{N}_i^C$ for $i = 1, 2, \ldots, 20$ be the corresponding averaged process (that is, $\overline{N}_i^C = \sum_{j=1}^{10} N_{ji}^C/10$), which is plotted in Fig. 9.19. We conclude from this plot that further smoothing is desirable. As a result, we plot the moving average $\overline{N}_i^C(w)$ (from Welch's procedure) for both $w = 3$ and $w = 6$ shifts in Figs. 9.20*a* and 9.20*b*. From the plot for $w = 6$ (which is smoother), we chose a warmup period of $l = 5$ shifts or 40 hours. (Compare this l with that obtained in Example 9.25.)

Let

$$X_j^C = \frac{\sum_{i=6}^{20} N_{ji}^C}{15} \qquad \text{for } j = 1, 2, \ldots, 10$$

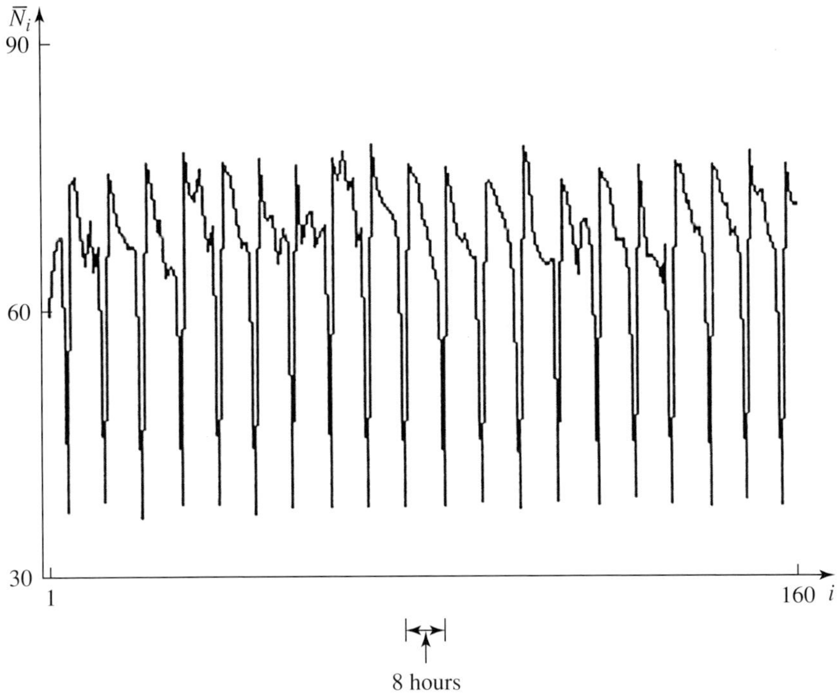

FIGURE 9.18
Averaged process for hourly throughputs, small factory with lunch breaks.

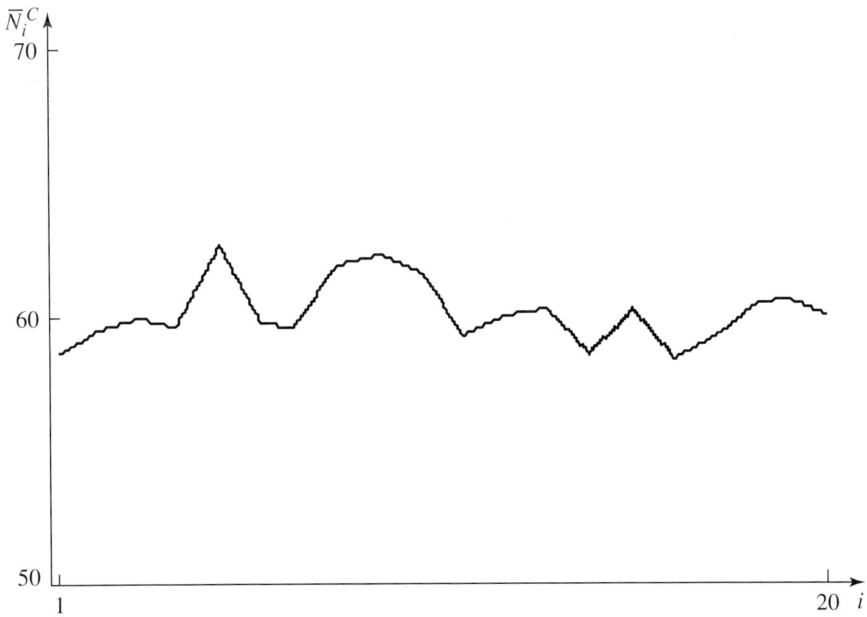

FIGURE 9.19
Averaged process for average hourly throughputs over a shift, small factory with lunch breaks.

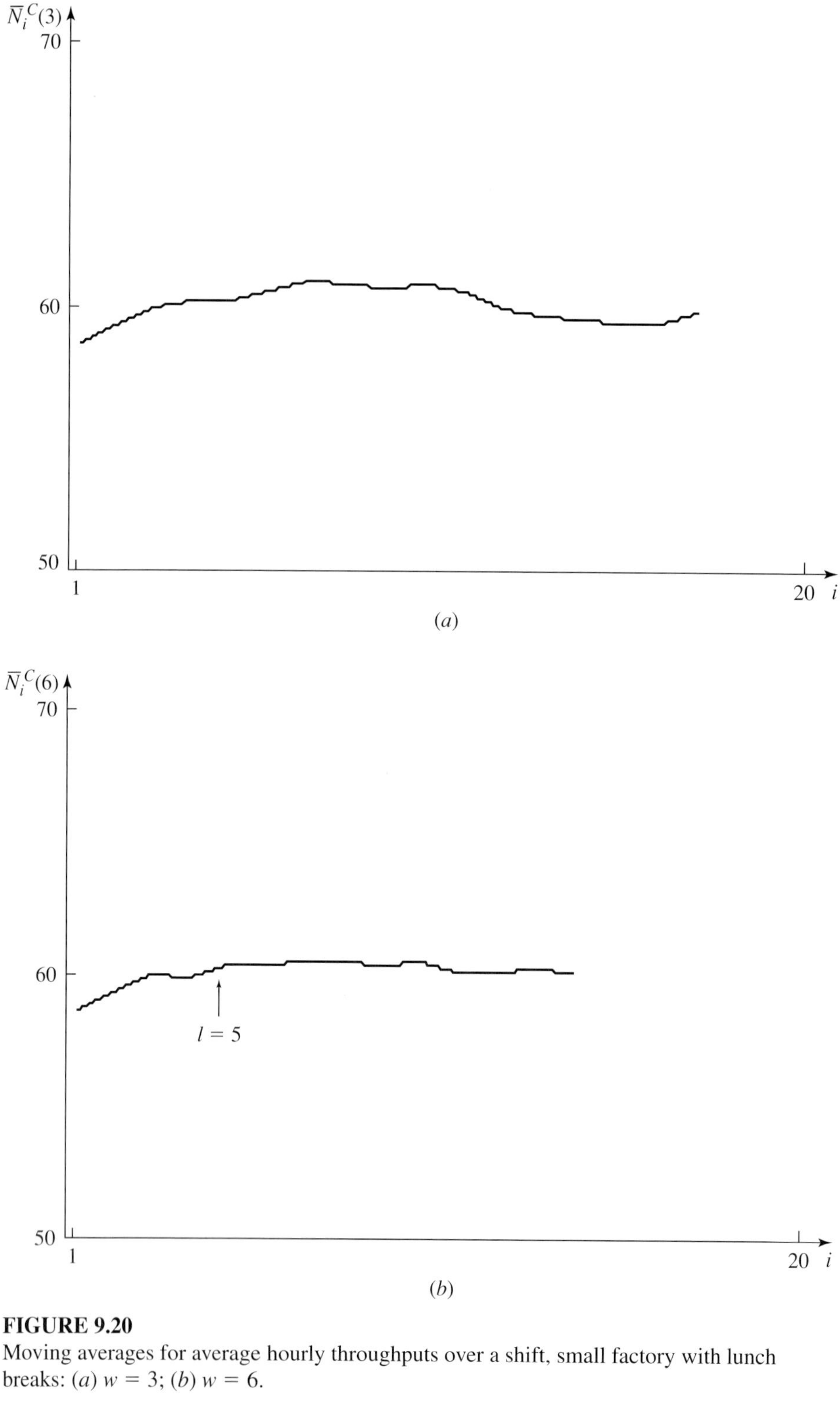

FIGURE 9.20
Moving averages for average hourly throughputs over a shift, small factory with lunch breaks: (*a*) $w = 3$; (*b*) $w = 6$.

Then a point estimate and 99 percent confidence interval for ν^C are given by

$$\hat{\nu}^C = \overline{X}^C(10) = 60.24$$

and
$$X^C(10) \pm t_{9,0.995}\sqrt{\frac{0.79}{10}} = 60.24 \pm 0.91$$

which also contains 60 (see Prob. 9.27).

9.7 MULTIPLE MEASURES OF PERFORMANCE

In Secs. 9.4 through 9.6 we presented procedures for constructing a confidence interval for a single measure of performance. However, for most real-world simulations several measures of performance are of interest simultaneously. Suppose that I_s is a $100(1 - \alpha_s)$ percent confidence interval for the measure of performance μ_s (where $s = 1, 2, \ldots, k$). (The μ_s's may all be measures of performance for a terminating simulation or may all be measures for a nonterminating simulation.) Then the probability that *all* k confidence intervals *simultaneously* contain their respective true measures satisfies (see Prob. 9.31)

$$P(\mu_s \in I_s \text{ for all } s = 1, 2, \ldots, k) \geq 1 - \sum_{s=1}^{k} \alpha_s \tag{9.12}$$

whether or not the I_s's are independent. This result, known as the *Bonferroni inequality*, has serious implications for a simulation study. For example, suppose that one constructs 90 percent confidence intervals, that is, $\alpha_s = 0.1$ for all s, for 10 different measures of performance. Then the probability that each of the 10 confidence intervals contains its true measure can only be claimed to be greater than or equal to *zero*. Thus, one must be careful in interpreting the results from such a study. The difficulty we have just described is known in the statistics literature as the *multiple-comparisons problem*.

We now describe a practical solution to the above problem when the value of k is small. If one wants the overall confidence level associated with k confidence intervals to be at least $100(1 - \alpha)$ percent, choose the α_s's so that $\sum_{s=1}^{k} \alpha_s = \alpha$. (Note that the α_s's do *not* have to be equal. Thus, α_s's corresponding to more important measures could be chosen smaller.) Therefore, one could construct ten 99 percent confidence intervals and have the overall confidence level be *at least* 90 percent. The difficulty with this solution is that the confidence intervals will be larger than they were originally if a fixed-sample-size procedure is used, or more data will be required for a specified set of k relative errors if a sequential procedure is used. For this reason, we recommend that k be no larger than about 10.

If one has a very large number of measures of performance, the only recourse available is to construct the usual 90 percent or 95 percent confidence intervals but to be aware that one or more of these confidence intervals probably does not contain its true measure.

TABLE 9.13

Results of making 10 replications of the bank model with five tellers and one queue

Measure of performance	Point estimate	96.667% confidence interval
$E\left[\dfrac{\int_0^T Q(t)\,dt}{T}\right]$	1.97	[1.55, 2.40]
$E\left(\dfrac{\sum_{i=1}^{N} D_i}{N}\right)$	2.03	[1.59, 2.47]
$E\left[\dfrac{\sum_{i=1}^{N} I_i(0, 5)}{N}\right]$	0.85	[0.80, 0.90]

EXAMPLE 9.34. Consider the bank of Example 9.1 with five tellers and one queue. Table 9.13 gives the results of using these 10 replications of the (terminating) simulation and (9.1) to construct 96.667 percent confidence intervals for each of the measures of performance

$$E\left[\frac{\int_0^T Q(t)\,dt}{T}\right], \quad E\left(\frac{\sum_{i=1}^{N} D_i}{N}\right), \quad E\left[\frac{\sum_{i=1}^{N} I_i(0, 5)}{N}\right]$$

so that the overall confidence level is at least 90 percent (see Prob. 9.38).

EXAMPLE 9.35. Suppose for the small factory of Example 9.25 that we would like to obtain point estimates and confidence intervals for both the steady-state mean hourly throughput ν_N and the steady-state mean time in system of a part ν_T, with the overall confidence level being at least 90 percent. Therefore, we will make the confidence level of each individual interval 95 percent. Using the 10 replications from Example 9.30, we plotted the moving average $\overline{T}_i(w)$ ($i = 1, 2, \ldots$) for the time-in-system process T_1, $T_2, \ldots$ in order to determine its warmup period. (Here T_i is the time in system of the ith departing part.) Since this plot was highly variable, we made an additional 10 replications of length 160 hours and used the entire 20 replications for our analysis. In Fig. 9.21*a* we plot the hourly throughput moving average $\overline{N}_i(w)$ for $w = 30$, and in Fig. 9.21*b* we plot the time-in-system moving average $\overline{T}_i(w)$ for $w = 1200$. (Note that the number of T_i observations in a 160-hour simulation run is a random variable with approximate mean 9600. Therefore, for our analysis we used the minimum number of observations for any one of the 20 runs, which was 9407.) From Figs. 9.21*a* and 9.21*b*, we decided on warmup periods of $l_N = 24$ hours and $l_T = 2286$ times, respectively. Note, however, that 2286 times corresponds to approximately 38 hours. Since 24 and 2286 are much smaller than 160 and 9407, respectively, we will use these same replications to construct our confidence intervals.

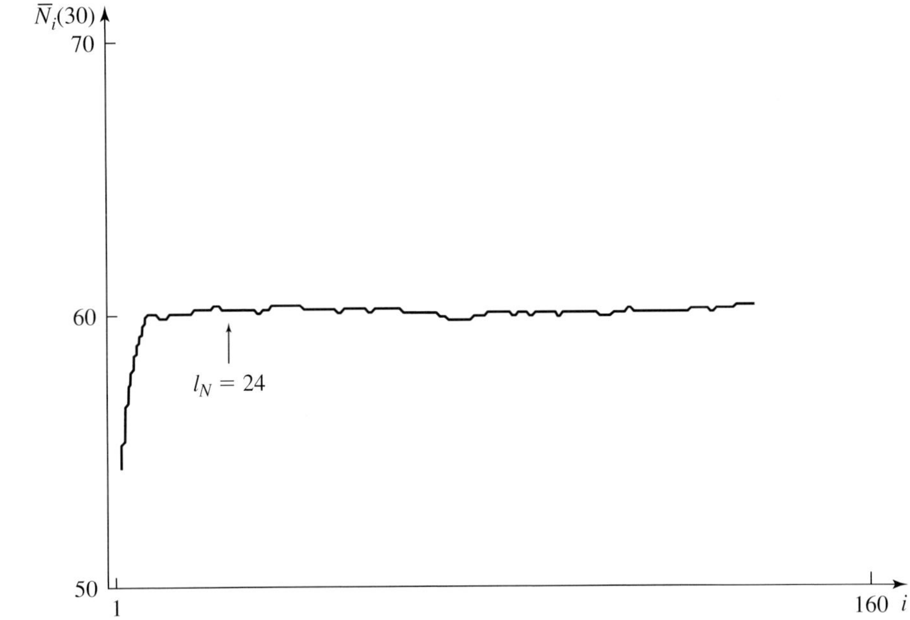

(*a*)

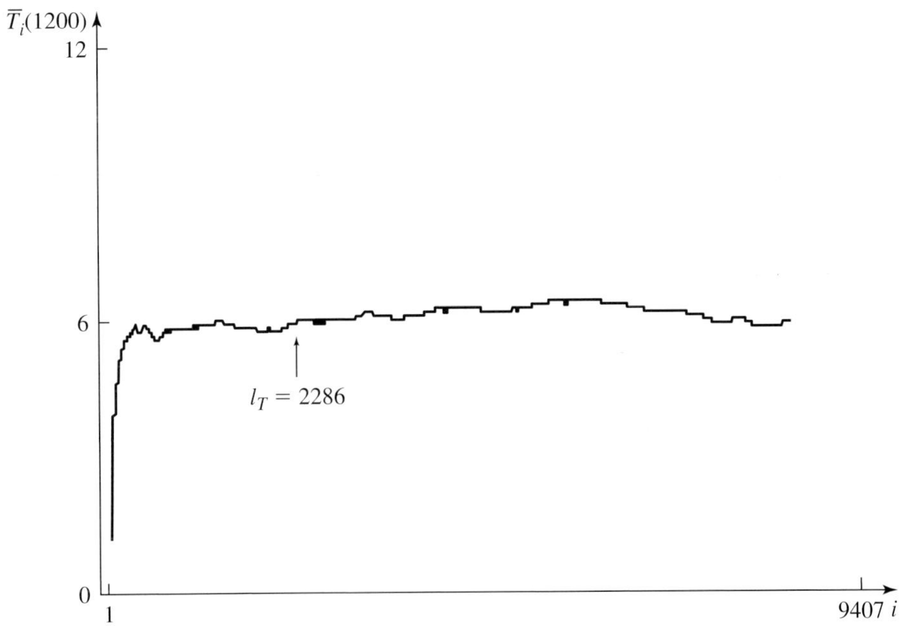

(*b*)

FIGURE 9.21
Moving averages for small factory: (*a*) $w = 30$ for hourly throughputs; (*b*) $w = 1200$ for times in system.

Let

$$X_j = \frac{\sum_{i=25}^{160} N_{ji}}{136} \qquad \text{for } j = 1, 2, \ldots, 20$$
$$Y_j = \frac{\sum_{i=2287}^{9407} T_{ji}}{7121}$$

Then point estimates and 95 percent confidence intervals for ν_N and ν_T are given by

$$\hat{\nu}_N = \overline{X}(20) = 60.03, \qquad \hat{\nu}_T = \overline{Y}(20) = 6.16 \text{ minutes}$$

and

$$\overline{X}(10) \pm t_{19,0.975}\sqrt{\frac{0.70}{20}} = 60.03 \pm 0.39$$

$$\overline{Y}(10) \pm t_{19,0.975}\sqrt{\frac{0.55}{20}} = 6.16 \pm 0.35$$

Thus, we are at least 90 percent confident that ν_N and ν_T are simultaneously in the intervals [59.64, 60.42] and [5.81, 6.51], respectively.

Additional methods for constructing confidence intervals (or regions) for multiple measures of performance are surveyed by Charnes (1995).

9.8 TIME PLOTS OF IMPORTANT VARIABLES

In this chapter we have seen how to construct point estimates and confidence intervals for several different measures of performance, with an emphasis on mean system response. Although these measures are clearly quite useful, there are situations where we need a better indication of how system performance changes dynamically over time. This is particularly true when characteristics of the system (e.g., number of available workers) vary as a function of time. Animation (see Sec. 3.4.3) can provide considerable insight into the short-term dynamic behavior of a system, but it does not give us an easily interpreted record of system performance over the entire length of the simulation. On the other hand, plotting one or more key variables over the duration of the simulation is an easy way to gain an understanding of long-run dynamic system behavior. For example, a graph of queue size over time can provide information on whether the corresponding server (or servers) has sufficient processing capacity and also on the required floor space or capacity for the queue. The following example illustrates the use of time plots, with additional applications being given in Chap. 14 (see also Prob. 9.28).

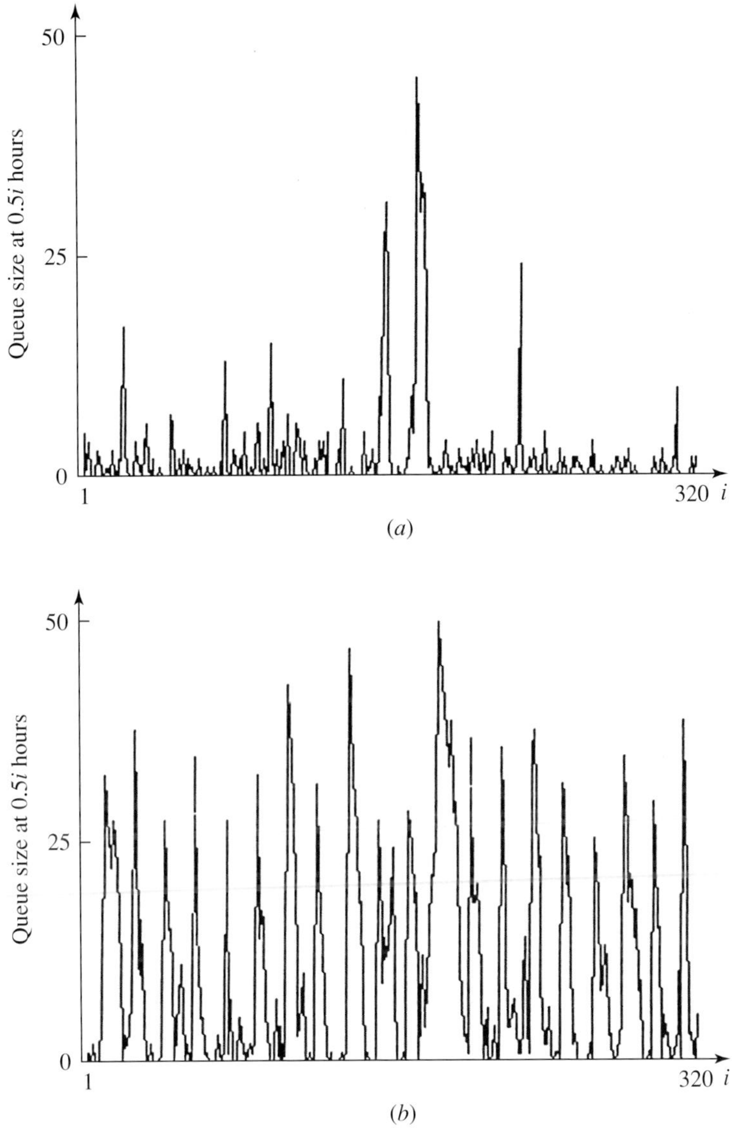

FIGURE 9.22
Time plots for number in queue in time increments of 30 minutes (run 1), small factory: (*a*) machine queue; (*b*) inspector queue.

EXAMPLE 9.36. Consider the small factory with lunch breaks discussed in Example 9.33. In Figs. 9.22*a* and 9.22*b*, we plot the numbers in the machine and inspector queues sampled in 30-minute increments of time, respectively, based on the first of the 10 available simulation replications. Note the periodic behavior of the inspector plot due to the half-hour lunch break.

APPENDIX 9A
RATIOS OF EXPECTATIONS AND JACKKNIFE ESTIMATORS

Much of this chapter has been concerned with estimating the expectation of a single random variable X, namely, $E(X)$. However, as the following examples show, there are many situations in simulation where it is of interest to estimate the ratio of two expectations, such as $E(Y)/E(X)$:

1. For the regenerative method, we saw in Sec. 9.5.3 that steady-state parameters can be expressed as the ratio of two expectations.
2. For the combat simulation of Example 9.5, it is sometimes of interest to estimate $E(R)/E(B)$, where R and B are the numbers of red losses and blue losses in a battle.
3. For the bank simulation of Example 9.14, let $P = \sum_{i=1}^{N} D_i$ be the total delay of all customers served in a day. Then it is of interest to estimate $E(P/N)$, which can be interpreted as the expectation of the average delay of a customer where the expectation is taken with respect to all possible days. However, it may also be of interest to estimate the long-run average delay of all customers, which can be shown to be equal to $E(P)/E(N)$.

Estimators of ratios of expectations, however, are usually biased. We now discuss a method of obtaining a less biased point estimator, as well as an alternative confidence interval.

Suppose that we want to estimate the ratio $\phi = E(Y)/E(X)$ from the data $Y_1, Y_2, \ldots, Y_n$ and $X_1, X_2, \ldots, X_n$, where the X_i's are IID random variables, the Y_i's are IID random variables, and $\text{Cov}(Y_i, X_j) = 0$ for $i \neq j$. The classical point estimator of ϕ is given by $\hat{\phi}_C(n) = \bar{Y}(n)/\bar{X}(n)$; see the discussion of the regenerative method in Sec. 9.5.3 for the classical confidence interval for ϕ. We now discuss the jackknife approach to point and interval estimation of ϕ [see Iglehart (1975) and Miller (1974)]. First define

$$\theta_g = n\hat{\phi}_C(n) - (n-1)\frac{\sum_{\substack{j=1\\ j\neq g}}^{n} Y_j}{\sum_{\substack{j=1\\ j\neq g}}^{n} X_j} \qquad \text{for } g = 1, 2, \ldots, n$$

Then the jackknife point estimator for ϕ is given by $\hat{\phi}_J(n) = \sum_{g=1}^{n} \theta_g/n$, which is, in general, less biased than $\hat{\phi}_C(n)$. Let

$$\hat{\sigma}_J^2(n) = \frac{\sum_{g=1}^{n} [\theta_g - \hat{\phi}_J(n)]^2}{n-1}$$

Then it can be shown [see Miller (1974)] that

$$\frac{\hat{\phi}_J(n) - \phi}{\sqrt{\hat{\sigma}_J^2(n)/n}} \xrightarrow{\mathcal{D}} \text{N}(0, 1) \qquad \text{as } n \to \infty$$

which gives the jackknife $100(1-\alpha)$ percent confidence interval $\hat{\phi}_J(n) \pm z_{1-\alpha/2}\sqrt{\hat{\sigma}_J^2(n)/n}$ for ϕ. (See Sec. 9.5.3 for some empirical results on the relative performance of the classical and jackknife confidence intervals.)

PROBLEMS

9.1. Argue heuristically that comparable output random variables from replications using different random numbers should be independent.

9.2. Consider a machine that works for an exponential amount of time having mean $1/\lambda$ before breaking down. Suppose that it takes an exponential amount of time having mean $1/\omega$ to repair the machine. Let $Y(t)$ be the state of the machine at time t for $t \geq 0$, where

$$Y(t) = \begin{cases} 1 & \text{if the machine is working at time } t \\ 0 & \text{otherwise} \end{cases}$$

Then $\{Y(t), t \geq 0\}$ is a continuous-time stochastic process. Furthermore, it can be shown that [see Ross (2003, pp. 364–366)]

$$P(Y(t) = 1 | Y(0) = 1) = \frac{\lambda}{\lambda + \omega} e^{-(\lambda+\omega)t} + \frac{\omega}{\lambda + \omega}$$

and

$$P(Y(t) = 1 | Y(0) = 0) = -\frac{\omega}{\lambda + \omega} e^{-(\lambda+\omega)t} + \frac{\omega}{\lambda + \omega}$$

Thus, the distribution of $Y(t)$ depends on both t and $Y(0)$. By letting $t \to \infty$ in these equations, compute the steady-state distribution of $Y(t)$. Does it depend on $Y(0)$?

9.3. In Example 9.9, suppose that condition (*b*) is violated. In particular, suppose that it takes workers 20 minutes to put their tools away at the end of a shift and it takes the new workers 20 minutes to set up their tools at the beginning of the next shift. Does $N_1, N_2, \ldots$ have a steady-state distribution?

9.4. Suppose in Example 9.9 that we would like to estimate the steady-state mean total time in system of a part. Does our approach to simulating the manufacturing system present a problem?

9.5. Why is determining the required number of tellers for a bank different from determining the hardware requirements for a computer or communications system (see Example 9.10)?

9.6. In Example 9.11, why doesn't the process of hourly throughputs $N_1, N_2, \ldots$ have a steady-state distribution?

9.7. For the following systems, state whether you think a terminating or nonterminating simulation would be more appropriate. In the terminating cases, state the terminating event E. In the nonterminating cases, would the parameter of interest be a steady-state parameter or a steady-state cycle parameter?

(*a*) Consider a telephone system for which an arriving call may experience a delay before obtaining a line. Suppose that the goal is to estimate the mean delay of the 100th arriving call, $E(D_{100})$.

(*b*) Consider a military inventory system (see Sec. 1.5) during peacetime, which is assumed to have a long duration. Assume that system parameters (e.g., the interdemand time distribution) do not change over time and we are interested in the output process $C_1, C_2, \ldots$, where C_i is the total cost in the ith month. Suppose further that we want a measure of mean cost.

(*c*) Consider a manufacturing system for food products. A production schedule is issued, the system produces product for 13 days, and then the system is completely cleaned out on the fourteenth day. Then a new production schedule is issued and the 2-week cycle is repeated, etc. The goal is to estimate the mean throughput over a cycle.

(*d*) Consider an air freight company that provides overnight delivery of packages. Aircraft loaded with packages start arriving at the hub operations at approximately 11 P.M. The packages are unloaded and then sorted in a warehouse according to the destination Zip code. Packages with similar Zip codes are placed on one aircraft, and the last plane departs at approximately 5 A.M. It is desired to estimate the mean (across departing planes) amount of time that planes are late in departing.

(*e*) Consider a manufacturing system that operates in a similar manner 7 days a week. Suppose, however, that 6 machines operate during the first two shifts in each day, but only 4 machines operate during the third shift. Let $N_1, N_2, \ldots$ be the output process of interest, where N_i is the number of parts produced in the ith shift. We are interested in a measure of mean throughput. Does your answer depend on the relationship between the arrival rate and the service rate of an individual machine?

9.8. For the small factory of Example 9.25, suppose that the system operates 24 hours a day for 5 days and then is completely cleaned out. Thus, we have a terminating simulation of length 120 hours. Make five independent replications and construct a point estimate and 95 percent confidence interval for the mean weekly throughput. Approximately how many replications would be required to obtain an absolute error of 50? A relative error of 5 percent?

9.9. Let p be a probability of interest for a terminating simulation, as discussed in Sec. 9.4.2. Define IID random variables $Y_1, Y_2, \ldots, Y_n$ such that $\hat{p} = \overline{Y}(n)$ and use these Y_j's in (4.3), (4.4), and (4.12) to derive one possible confidence interval for p. Show that the variance estimate given by Eq. (4.4) can be written as $\hat{p}(1 - \hat{p})/(n - 1)$.

9.10. Consider the bank of Example 9.1. Use the data from the 10 replications in Table 9.1 to construct a point estimate for the median (i.e., 0.5-quantile) of the distribution of the average delay over a day. How does this estimate compare with the sample mean in Example 9.14?

9.11. For the $M/M/1$ queue with $\rho < 1$ of Example 9.23, suppose that the number of customers present when the first customer arrives has the following discrete distribution:

$$p(x) = (1 - \rho)\rho^x \qquad \text{for } x = 0, 1, \ldots$$

which is the steady-state distribution of the number of customers in the system. Compute the distribution function of D_1 and its mean. In this case, it can also be shown that D_i for $i \geq 2$ has this same distribution.

9.12. For Welch's procedure in Sec. 9.5.1, show that $E(\overline{Y}_i) = E(Y_i)$ and $\text{Var}(\overline{Y}_i) = \text{Var}(Y_i)/n$.

9.13. Assume that $Y_1, Y_2, \ldots$ is a covariance-stationary process and that $\rho_i < 1$ for $i \geq 1$. Show for Welch's procedure that $\text{Var}[\overline{Y}_i(w)] < \text{Var}(\overline{Y}_i)$.

9.14. Suppose that $Y_1, Y_2, \ldots$ is an output process with steady-state mean ν and that $\overline{Y}(m)$ is the usual sample mean based on m observations. Consider plotting $\overline{Y}(m)$ as a function of m and let l' be the point beyond which $\overline{Y}(m)$ does not change appreciably. Is l' a good warmup period in the sense that $E(Y_i) \approx \nu$ for $i > l'$ and also that l' is not excessively large? Why?

9.15. Consider the replication/deletion approach of Sec. 9.5.2. Show that $E(X_j) \approx \nu$. Give two reasons why the confidence interval given by (9.6) is only approximate in terms of coverage.

9.16. Consider the replication/deletion approach in Sec. 9.5.2 based on using the same set of replications to determine the warmup period l and to construct a confidence interval. Are the resulting X_j's truly independent?

9.17. For the small factory of Example 9.30, what should the steady-state mean hourly throughput be if the system is well defined in the sense that $\rho < 1$ for both the machine and the inspector?

9.18. Consider a continuous-time stochastic process such as $\{Q(t), t \geq 0\}$, where $Q(t)$ is the number of customers in queue at time t. Suppose that we would like to estimate the steady-state time-average number in queue, Q (see App. 1B for one definition), using the method of batch means based on one simulation run of length m time units. Discuss two approaches for getting *exactly* m basic discrete observations $Q_1, Q_2, \ldots, Q_m$ for use in the method of batch means. The m Q_i's will be batched to form n batch means.

9.19. If $Y_1, Y_2, \ldots$ is a covariance-stationary process, show for the method of batch means that $C_i(k) = \text{Cov}[\overline{Y}_j(k), \overline{Y}_{j+i}(k)]$ is given by

$$C_i(k) = \sum_{l=-(k-1)}^{k-1} \frac{(1 - |l|/k)\, C_{ik+l}}{k} \qquad \text{where } C_l = \text{Cov}(Y_i, Y_{i+l})$$

9.20. Let $Y_1, Y_2, \ldots$ be a covariance-stationary process. For the method of batch means, let $\rho_i(k) = \text{Cor}[\overline{Y}_j(k), \overline{Y}_{j+i}(k)]$ and let $b(n, k)$ be such that $E\{\widehat{\text{Var}}[\overline{\overline{Y}}(n, k)]\} = b(n, k) \cdot \text{Var}[\overline{\overline{Y}}(n, k)]$. Show that $\rho_i(k) \to 0$ (for $i = 1, 2, \ldots, n - 1$) as $k \to \infty$ implies that $E\{\widehat{\text{Var}}[\overline{\overline{Y}}(n, k)]\} \to \text{Var}[\overline{\overline{Y}}(n, k)]$ as $k \to \infty$. *Hint:* First show that

$$b(n, k) = \frac{\left\{ n \Big/ \left[1 + 2 \sum_{i=1}^{n-1} (1 - i/n)\, \rho_i(k) \right] \right\} - 1}{n - 1}$$

9.21. For the regenerative method, show that $\nu = E(Z)/E(N)$. [*Hint:* Observe that

$$\frac{\sum_{j=1}^{n'} Z_j}{\sum_{j=1}^{n'} N_j} = \frac{\sum_{i=1}^{M(n')} Y_i}{M(n')}$$

where n' is the number of regeneration cycles and $M(n')$ is the total number of observations (a random variable) in the n' cycles. Let $n' \to \infty$ and apply the strong law of large numbers (see Sec. 4.6) to both sides of the above equation.] Also conclude that $\hat{\nu}(n') = \bar{Z}(n')/\bar{N}(n') \to \nu$ as $n' \to \infty$ (w.p. 1), so that $\hat{\nu}(n')$ is a strongly consistent estimator of ν. (See the definitions of ν in Sec. 9.5.3.)

9.22. For the queueing system considered in Example 9.32, are the indices of those customers who depart and leave exactly l customers behind ($l \geq 0$ and fixed) regeneration points for the process $D_1, D_2, \ldots$? If not, under what circumstances would they be?

9.23. For the inventory example of Sec. 1.5, identify a sequence of regeneration points for the monthly-cost process. Repeat assuming that the interdemand times are not exponential random variables.

9.24. Suppose that $\hat{\nu}(n')$ is the (biased) regenerative point estimator for the steady-state mean ν based on simulating the process $Y_1, Y_2, \ldots$ for n' regeneration cycles. Do you think that it is advisable to have a warmup period of l cycles to reduce the point estimator bias?

9.25. Consider an $M/M/1$ queue with $\rho < 1$, and let the number of customers served in a cycle, N, be as defined in Example 9.32. By conditioning on whether the second customer arrives before or after the first customer departs, show that $E(N) = 1/(1 - \rho)$.

9.26. For Example 9.33, compute the utilization factor ρ for both the machine and the inspector. What arrival rate should be used? Is this system well defined in the sense that $\rho < 1$ in both cases?

9.27. In Example 9.33, what should be the value for ν^C if the system is well defined?

9.28. A manufacturing system consists of two machines in parallel and a single queue. Jobs arrive with exponential interarrival times at a rate of 10 per hour, and each machine has exponential processing times at a rate of 8 per hour. During the first 16 hours of each day both machines are operational, but only one machine is used during the final 8 hours.

(*a*) Determine whether the system is well defined by computing the utilization factor ρ and comparing it with 1.

(*b*) Let N_i be the throughput for the ith hour. Does $N_1, N_2, \ldots$ have a steady-state distribution?

(*c*) Make 10 replications of the simulation of length 480 hours (20 days) each. Plot the averaged process $\bar{N}_1, \bar{N}_2, \ldots, \bar{N}_{480}$.

(*d*) Let M_i be the throughput for the ith 24-hour day. Use the data from part (*c*) and the replication/deletion approach to construct a point estimate and 90 percent confidence interval for the steady-state mean daily throughput $\nu = E(M) = 240$.

9.29. For the system in Prob. 9.28, make one replication of length 200 days and let M_i be as previously defined. Use the M_i's and the method of batch means to construct a point estimate and a 90 percent confidence interval for $\nu = 240$ based on $n = 10$ batches and also on $n = 5$ batches.

9.30. Repeat Prob. 9.29 using standardized time series rather than batch means.

9.31. Let E_s be an event that occurs with probability $1 - \alpha_s$ for $s = 1, 2, \ldots, k$. Then prove that

$$P\left(\bigcap_{s=1}^{k} E_s\right) \geq 1 - \sum_{s=1}^{k} \alpha_s$$

where $\bigcap_{s=1}^{k} E_s$ is the intersection of the events $E_1, E_2, \ldots, E_k$. Do not assume that the E_s's are independent. [This result is called the *Bonferroni inequality*; see (9.12).] *Hint:* The proof is by mathematical induction. That is, first show that $P(E_1 \cap E_2) \geq 1 - \alpha_1 - \alpha_2$. Then show that if

$$P\left(\bigcap_{s=1}^{k-1} E_s\right) \geq 1 - \sum_{s=1}^{k-1} \alpha_s$$

is true, the desired result is also true.

9.32. For Example 9.21, compute the approximate number of replications required to reduce the half-length of the confidence interval for p to 0.05.

9.33. For Example 9.26, show that there must be two links between SP-1 and SP-2 so that the utilization of this link group does not exceed 0.4.

9.34. For Example 9.26, show that STP-A must contain three processors so that its utilization does not exceed 0.4. Also show that SP-1 must contain two processors so that its utilization is less than 1.

9.35. For Example 9.26, show that the overall arrival rate of messages is 1240 per second.

9.36. For Example 9.31, does the utilization of 0.316 for STP-A seem reasonable? What about the utilization of 0.377 for link 1-2?

9.37. Suppose that one constructs k $100(1 - \alpha)$ percent confidence intervals from the same set of replications (see Sec. 9.7), so the confidence intervals are *dependent.* Derive an expression for the expected number of confidence intervals that do *not* contain their respective true measures of performance.

9.38. If the 10 replications and subsequent analysis corresponding to Table 9.13 were performed independently by 100 different banks, what could be said about the confidence intervals for approximately 90 of the banks?

CHAPTER 10

Comparing Alternative System Configurations

Recommended sections for a first reading: 10.1 through 10.3, 10.4.1

10.1 INTRODUCTION

In Chap. 9 we saw the importance of applying appropriate statistical analyses to the output from a simulation model of a *single* system. In this chapter we discuss statistical analyses of the output from several *different* simulation models that might represent competing system designs or alternative operating policies. This is a very important subject, since the real utility of simulation lies in comparing such alternatives before implementation. As the following example illustrates, appropriate statistical methods are essential if we are to avoid making serious errors leading to fallacious conclusions and, ultimately, poor decisions. We hope that this example will demonstrate the danger inherent in making decisions based on the output from a *single* run (or replication) of each alternative system.

EXAMPLE 10.1. A bank planning to install an automated teller station must choose between buying one Zippytel machine or two Klunkytel machines. Although one Zippy costs twice as much to purchase, install, and operate as one Klunky, the Zippy works twice as fast. Since the total cost to the bank is thus the same regardless of its decision, the managers would like to install the system that will provide the best service.

From available data, it appears that during a certain rush period, customers arrive one at a time according to a Poisson process with rate 1 per minute. The Zippy could provide service times that are IID exponential random variables with mean 0.9 minute. Alternatively, if two Klunkys are installed, each will yield service times that are IID exponential random variables with mean 1.8 minutes; in this case a single FIFO queue will be formed instead of two separate lines. Thus, we are comparing an $M/M/1$ queue with an $M/M/2$ queue, each with utilization factor $\rho = 0.9$, as shown in Fig. 10.1. The

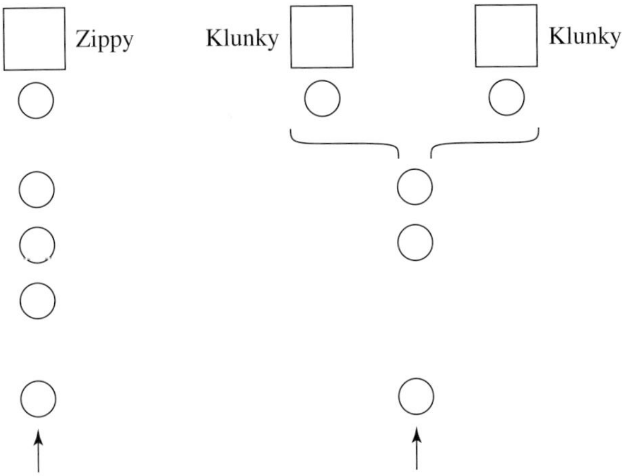

FIGURE 10.1
One Zippy or two Klunkys?

performance measure of interest is the expected average delay in queue of the first 100 customers, assuming that the first customer arrives to an empty and idle system; we denote these (expected) quantities by $d_Z(100)$ and $d_K(100)$ for the one-Zippy and two-Klunky cases, respectively. (The bank decided to ignore customer service times, since waiting in line is the most irritating part of the experience and customers are reasonably pacified as long as they are being served; see Prob. 10.1 for further consideration of this issue.) The bank's intrepid systems analyst decided to make a simulation run of length 100 customer delays for each system (using independent random numbers) and to use the average of the 100 delays in each case to infer whether $d_Z(100)$ or $d_K(100)$ is smaller, and thus make a recommendation.

How likely is it that the analyst will make the right recommendation? To find out, we performed 100 independent experiments of the analyst's entire scheme and noted how many times the best system would have been recommended. (The number of experiments, 100, has no relationship to the number of customers in a replication, which is also 100.) The best system is actually the two-Klunky installation, since $d_Z(100) = 4.13$ and $d_K(100) = 3.70$. [These values were determined from the queueing-theoretic results in Kelton and Law (1985).] Our experiment was, thus, to perform 100 independent pairs of independent simulations of the two systems, and average the delays in each simulation to obtain $\hat{d}_Z(100)$ and $\hat{d}_K(100)$, say, and then recommend the Zippy or Klunky system according as $\hat{d}_Z(100)$ or $\hat{d}_K(100)$ was smaller; some of the results are in Table 10.1. In only 48 of our 100 experiments was $\hat{d}_K(100) < \hat{d}_Z(100)$, so the analyst would not really appear to have any better chance of making the right decision than making the wrong one.

We have an uneasy feeling that many simulation studies are carried out in a manner similar to that described in Example 10.1. The difficulty is that the simulation output data are stochastic, so comparing the two systems on the basis of only a single run of each is a very unreliable approach.

The following example indicates how the comparison in Example 10.1 could be improved.

EXAMPLE 10.2. To illuminate the problem with the one-run-of-each approach in Example 10.1, we plotted all 100 $\hat{d}_Z(100)$'s and $\hat{d}_K(100)$'s in the "$n = 1$" pair of

TABLE 10.1
Testing the analyst's decision rule

Experiment	$\hat{d}_Z(100)$	$\hat{d}_K(100)$	Recommendation	
1	3.80	4.60	Zippy	(wrong)
2	3.17	8.37	Zippy	(wrong)
3	3.96	4.18	Zippy	(wrong)
4	1.91	5.77	Zippy	(wrong)
5	1.71	2.23	Zippy	(wrong)
6	6.16	4.72	Klunky	(right)
7	5.67	1.39	Klunky	(right)
⋮	⋮	⋮	⋮	
98	8.40	9.39	Zippy	(wrong)
99	7.70	1.54	Klunky	(right)
100	4.64	1.17	Klunky	(right)

horizontal dot plots in Fig. 10.2; each circle (solid or hollow) represents the average of the 100 delays in a single simulation, positioned according to the scale at the bottom. Even though the *expected* average delay for the two-Klunky system is smaller than that for the one-Zippy system, the distributions of the *observed* average delays overlap substantially. This accounts for the distressingly large probability of making the wrong choice noted at the end of Example 10.1.

Instead, we could make some number, n, of complete independent replications of each alternative system, and compare the systems on the basis of their averages across replications. Specifically, let X_{1j} be the average of the 100 delays in the one-Zippy system on the jth independent replication of this system, and let X_{2j} be the average of the 100 delays in the two-Klunky system on its jth replication, for $j = 1, 2, \ldots, n$. (We also made the simulations so that the X_{1j}'s and the X_{2j}'s are independent.) Then if $\bar{X}_1(n)$ and

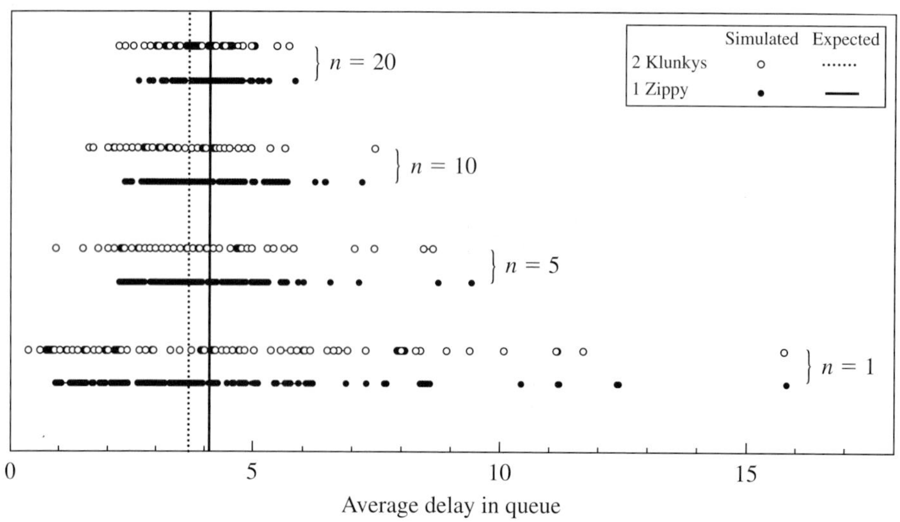

FIGURE 10.2
One Zippy vs. two Klunkys, as described in Examples 10.1 and 10.2.

TABLE 10.2
Proportion of wrong recommendations in the n-replication method of Example 10.2

n	Proportion of experiments favoring the one-Zippy system
1	0.52
5	0.43
10	0.38
20	0.34

$\overline{X}_2(n)$ are the sample means of the X_{1j}'s and X_{2j}'s, respectively, we would recommend the system with the smaller $\overline{X}_i(n)$. (The method of Example 10.1 is thus a special case, taking $n = 1$.) Table 10.2 shows the proportion of 100 independent pairs of n-replication averages in which the one-Zippy system appeared better, i.e., would result in the wrong recommendation, for $n = 1$, 5, 10, and 20. The chance of making an error falls as n increases, but at a corresponding higher cost of simulating. The four pairs of plots in Fig. 10.2 also indicate that as n rises, the distributions of the n-replication averages (each circle represents such an average) tighten up around their expectations, but there is still considerable overlap even for $n = 20$, where the proportion of incorrect recommendations is still 0.34.

Examples 10.1 and 10.2 illustrate the need for careful design and analysis of comparative simulations. Indeed, even with $n = 20$ replications of each system design, Example 10.2 indicates that there is substantial room for error. One way of sharpening the comparison will be discussed in Sec. 11.2, and the above examples will be reworked in that context; see Example 11.3 in Sec. 11.2.4.

Note that both Examples 10.1 and 10.2 dealt with terminating simulations (see Secs. 9.3 and 9.4). As we shall see in this chapter, a basic requirement for using many statistical methods for comparing alternative configurations is the ability to collect IID observations with expectation equal to the desired measure of performance. For terminating simulations, this is easily accomplished by simply making independent replications; e.g., a basic unit of observation in Examples 10.1 and 10.2 was the average of the 100 delays in a single *entire* replication of the model. If we want to compare alternative systems on the basis of steady-state behavior (see Secs. 9.3 and 9.5), however, the situation becomes more complicated since we cannot easily obtain IID observations having expectation (approximately) equal to the desired steady-state measure of performance. There are different ways of dealing with steady-state comparisons, which will be discussed throughout the chapter, specifically in Secs. 10.2.4 and 10.4.3.

Our purpose in this chapter is to present several different types of comparison and selection problems that have been found useful in simulation, together with appropriate statistical procedures for their solution, and numerical examples. We assume for this chapter that the various alternative systems are simply *given*. In many situations care should be taken in choosing *which* particular system variants to simulate; see Chap. 12 for discussion of how to choose appropriate alternative systems for comparison.

In Sec. 10.2 we treat the special but important case of comparing just two systems by constructing a confidence interval for the difference between their performance measures. These ideas are extended in Sec. 10.3 to confidence-interval comparisons of more than two systems. Section 10.4 introduces some procedures for selecting the "best" of several alternative systems, as well as for choosing a subset of the alternatives that contains the "best" system. Appendixes 10A and 10B treat certain technical issues related to the selection procedures of Sec. 10.4.

10.2 CONFIDENCE INTERVALS FOR THE DIFFERENCE BETWEEN THE EXPECTED RESPONSES OF TWO SYSTEMS

Here we consider the special case of comparing two systems on the basis of some performance measure, or expected *response*. We effect this comparison by forming a confidence interval for the *difference* in the two expectations, rather than by doing a hypothesis test to see whether the observed difference is significantly different from zero. Whereas a test results in only a "reject" or "fail-to-reject" conclusion, a confidence interval gives us this information (according as the interval misses or contains zero, respectively) as well as quantifies how much the expectations differ, if at all. (In many cases, the two expectations will be different. Thus, the null hypothesis of equality of expectations is false.) Also, we shall take a parametric, i.e., normal-theory, approach here, even though nonparametric analogues could be used instead [see, for example, Conover (1999, pp. 281–283)]. The parametric approach is simple and familiar, and moreover should be quite robust in this context, since troublesome skewness (see Sec. 9.4.1) in the underlying distributions of the output random variables should be ameliorated upon subtraction (assuming the two output distributions are skewed in the same direction).

For $i = 1, 2$, let $X_{i1}, X_{i2}, \ldots, X_{in_i}$ be a sample of n_i IID observations from system i, and let $\mu_i = E(X_{ij})$ be the expected response of interest; we want to construct a confidence interval for $\zeta = \mu_1 - \mu_2$. Whether or not X_{1j} and X_{2j} are independent depends on how the simulations are executed, and could determine which of the two confidence-interval approaches discussed in Secs. 10.2.1 and 10.2.2 is used.

10.2.1 A Paired-*t* Confidence Interval

If $n_1 = n_2$ ($=n$, say), or we are willing to discard some observations from the system on which we actually have more data, we can pair X_{1j} with X_{2j} to define $Z_j = X_{1j} - X_{2j}$, for $j = 1, 2, \ldots, n$. Then the Z_j's are IID random variables and $E(Z_j) = \zeta$, the quantity for which we want to construct a confidence interval. Thus, we can let

$$\bar{Z}(n) = \frac{\sum_{j=1}^{n} Z_j}{n}$$

and

$$\widehat{\text{Var}}[\overline{Z}(n)] = \frac{\sum_{j=1}^{n} [Z_j - \overline{Z}(n)]^2}{n(n-1)}$$

and form the (approximate) $100(1 - \alpha)$ percent confidence interval

$$\overline{Z}(n) \pm t_{n-1,1-\alpha/2}\sqrt{\widehat{\text{Var}}[\overline{Z}(n)]} \tag{10.1}$$

If the Z_j's are normally distributed, this confidence interval is exact, i.e., it covers ζ with probability $1 - \alpha$; otherwise, we rely on the central limit theorem (see Sec. 4.5), which implies that this coverage probability will be *near* $1 - \alpha$ for large n. An important point here is that we did *not* have to assume that X_{1j} and X_{2j} are independent; nor did we have to assume that $\text{Var}(X_{1j}) = \text{Var}(X_{2j})$. Allowing positive correlation between X_{1j} and X_{2j} can be of great importance, since this leads to a reduction in $\text{Var}(Z_j)$ (see Prob. 4.13) and thus to a smaller confidence interval. Section 11.2 discusses a method (*common random numbers*) that can often induce this positive correlation between the observations on the different systems. The confidence interval in (10.1) will be called the *paired-t confidence interval*, and in its derivation we essentially reduced the two-system problem to one involving a single sample, namely, the Z_j's. In this sense, the paired-t approach is the same as the method discussed in Sec. 9.4.1 for analysis of a single system. (Thus, the sequential confidence-interval procedures of Sec. 9.4.1 could be applied here.) It is important to note that the X_{ij}'s are random variables defined over an entire *replication*; for example, X_{1j} might be the average of the 100 delays on the jth replication of the Zippytel system of Example 10.2; it is *not* the delay of some individual customer.

EXAMPLE 10.3. For the inventory model of Sec. 1.5, suppose we want to compare two different (s, S) policies in terms of their effect on the expected average total cost per month for the first 120 months of operation, where we assume that the initial inventory level is 60. For the first policy $(s, S) = (20, 40)$, and the second policy sets $(s, S) = (20, 80)$. Here, X_{ij} is the average total cost per month of policy i on the jth independent replication. We made the runs for policy 1 and policy 2 independently of each other and made $n = n_1 = n_2 = 5$ independent replications of the model under each policy; Table 10.3 contains the results. Using the paired-t approach, we obtained $\overline{Z}(5) = 4.98$ and $\widehat{\text{Var}}[\overline{Z}(5)] = 2.44$, leading to the (approximate) 90 percent confidence interval

TABLE 10.3
Average total cost per month for five independent replications of two inventory policies, and the differences

j	X_{1j}	X_{2j}	Z_j
1	126.97	118.21	8.76
2	124.31	120.22	4.09
3	126.68	122.45	4.23
4	122.66	122.68	−0.02
5	127.23	119.40	7.83

[1.65, 8.31] for $\zeta = \mu_1 - \mu_2$. Thus, with approximately 90 percent confidence, we can say that μ_1 differs from μ_2, and it furthermore appears that policy 2 is superior, since it leads to a lower average operating cost (between 1.65 and 8.31 lower, which would *not* have been evident from a hypothesis test). We must use the word "approximate" to describe the confidence level, since $n_1 = n_2 = 5$ may or may not be "large" enough for this model for the central limit theorem to have taken effect. (See also the discussion in Sec. 10.4.1.)

10.2.2 A Modified Two-Sample-*t* Confidence Interval

A second approach to forming a confidence interval for ζ does not pair up the observations from the two systems, so n_1 can now be different from n_2. Assume that the X_{1j}'s are normally distributed, the X_{2j}'s are normally distributed, and that the X_{1j}'s are independent of the X_{2j}'s. Normality should not be a problem in many cases, since X_{ij} will be an average of many individual observations (e.g., the average cost in Example 10.3). We will use an old but reliable approximate solution in this situation due to Welch (1938). As usual, let

$$\overline{X}_i(n_i) = \frac{\sum_{j=1}^{n_i} X_{ij}}{n_i}$$

and

$$S_i^2(n_i) = \frac{\sum_{j=1}^{n_i} [X_{ij} - \overline{X}_i(n_i)]^2}{n_i - 1}$$

for $i = 1, 2$. Then compute the *estimated* degrees of freedom

$$\hat{f} = \frac{[S_1^2(n_1)/n_1 + S_2^2(n_2)/n_2]^2}{[S_1^2(n_1)/n_1]^2/(n_1 - 1) + [S_2^2(n_2)/n_2]^2/(n_2 - 1)}$$

and use

$$\overline{X}_1(n_1) - \overline{X}_2(n_2) \pm t_{\hat{f},1-\alpha/2}\sqrt{\frac{S_1^2(n_1)}{n_1} + \frac{S_2^2(n_2)}{n_2}} \qquad (10.2)$$

as an approximate $100(1 - \alpha)$ percent confidence interval for ζ. Since $\hat{f}$ will not, in general, be an integer, interpolation in printed t tables will probably be necessary, though statistical software usually allows for noninteger degrees of freedom. The confidence interval given by (10.2), which we will call the *Welch confidence interval*, can also be used to validate a simulation model of an existing system (see Sec. 5.6.2). If "system 1" is the real-world system on which we have physically collected data and "system 2" is the corresponding simulation model from which we have simulation output data, it is likely that n_1 will be far less than n_2. Finally, if we are comparing two simulated systems and want a "small" confidence interval, a sequential procedure due to Robbins, Simons, and Starr (1967) can be used, which is efficient in the sense of minimizing the final value of $n_1 + n_2$. It is also asymptotically correct in the sense that the confidence interval will have approximately the correct coverage probability as the prespecified confidence-interval width becomes small.

EXAMPLE 10.4. Since the runs for the two different inventory policies of Example 10.3 were done independently, we can apply the Welch approach to form an approximate 90 percent confidence interval for ζ; we use the same X_{ij} data as given in Table 10.3. We get $\bar{X}_1(5) = 125.57$, $\bar{X}_2(5) = 120.59$, $S_1^2(5) = 4.00$, $S_2^2(5) = 3.76$, and $\hat{f} = 7.99$. Interpolating in printed t tables leads to $t_{7.99,0.95} = 1.860$. Thus, the Welch confidence interval is [2.66, 7.30].

10.2.3 Contrasting the Two Methods

Since the inventory data of Table 10.3 were collected so that $n_1 = n_2$ and the X_{1j}'s were independent of the X_{2j}'s, we could apply either the paired-t or Welch approach to construct a confidence interval for ζ. It happened that the confidence interval for the Welch approach was smaller in this case, but in general we will not know which confidence interval will be smaller.

The choice of either the paired-t or the Welch approach will usually be made according to the situation. One consideration is that using *common random numbers* (CRN) (see Sec. 11.2) for simulating the two systems can often lead to a considerable reduction in $\text{Var}(Z_j)$ and, thus, to a much smaller confidence interval; this implies that $n_1 = n_2$ and that X_{1j} and X_{2j} will not be independent, so the paired-t approach is required.

On the other hand, if $n_1 \neq n_2$ (and we want to use all the available data), the Welch approach should be used. This requires independence of the X_{1j}'s from the X_{2j}'s and so in particular would preclude the use of CRN. Note that assuring independence of the results from the two systems by using separate random numbers across the systems may actually require explicit action, since the default setup in most simulation packages is that the same random-number streams and seeds (see Sec. 7.2) are used unless specified otherwise. Thus, by default, the two systems would actually use the same random numbers, though not necessarily properly synchronized (see Sec. 11.2.3), rendering the Welch approach invalid.

10.2.4 Comparisons Based on Steady-State Measures of Performance

As mentioned in Sec. 10.1, the basic ingredient for most comparison techniques is a sample of IID observations with expectation equal to the performance measure on which the comparison is to be made. The examples so far in this chapter have all been terminating simulations, so such observations come naturally by simply replicating the simulation some number of times.

In other cases, however, we might want to compare two (or more) systems on the basis of a steady-state measure of performance (see Secs. 9.3 and 9.5). Here we can no longer simply replicate the models, since initialization effects may bias the output, as discussed in Sec. 9.5.1. Thus, it is more difficult to effect a valid comparison based on steady-state performance measures, and many of the concerns discussed in Sec. 9.5 arise. The following two examples illustrate how the replication/deletion approach for steady-state analysis, as described in Sec. 9.5.2, can be adapted to the problem of constructing a confidence interval for the difference between two steady-state means.

EXAMPLE 10.5. The manufacturing company in Example 9.25 is thinking of buying a new piece of inspection equipment that will reduce inspection times by 10 percent, so that they would be distributed uniformly between 0.675 minute and 0.720 minute. A simulation study could help determine whether this change will significantly reduce the *steady-state* mean time in system. Let T_{ijp} be the time in system of the pth departing part in the jth replication ($j = 1, 2, \ldots, n$) for system i ($i = 1$ and 2 for the original and proposed systems, respectively). Let l_i and m_i be the length of the warmup period and the minimum number of T_{ijp}'s in any replication, both for system i. Using the data from Example 9.35, we have $n = 20$, $l_1 = 2286$, and $m_1 = 9407$. We next make 20 replications of length 160 hours for the proposed system ($i = 2$), and the moving average $\overline{T}_{2p}(1300)$ is plotted in Fig. 10.3. From these runs and the plot, we determined that $l_2 = 2093$ and $m_2 = 9434$. Let

$$X_{ij} = \frac{\sum_{p=l_i+1}^{m_i} T_{ijp}}{m_i - l_i} \qquad \text{for } i = 1, 2$$

and $Z_j = X_{1j} - X_{2j}$ for $j = 1, 2, \ldots, 20$. Also, let ν_i be the steady-state mean time in system for system i. Then, from the 20 replications of each system, we used (10.1) to

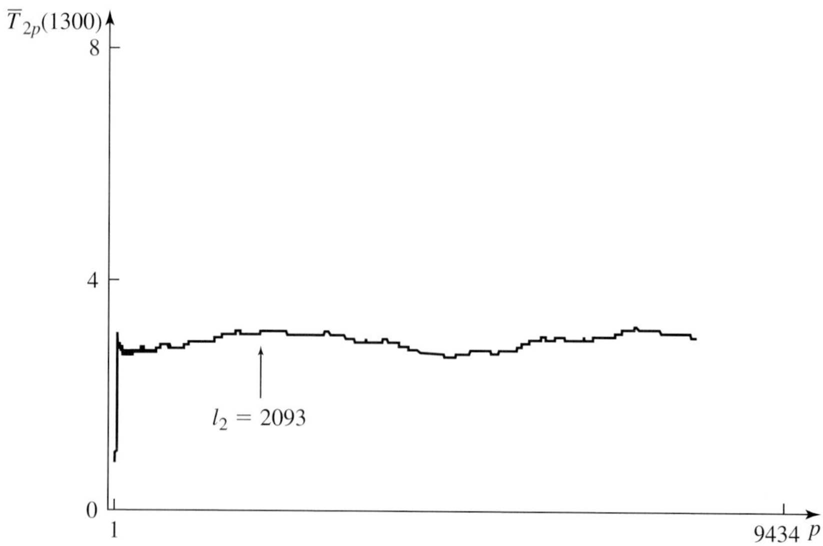

FIGURE 10.3
Time-in-system moving average ($w = 1300$) for the proposed system.

obtain 2.36 ± 0.31 as an approximate 90 percent confidence interval for $\nu_1 - \nu_2$. Thus, since this confidence interval does not contain zero, the difference between the two steady-state mean system times appears to be statistically significant, and represents a decrease of about 38 percent (3.80 vs. 6.16). (Recall that the mean inspection time was reduced by only 10 percent; see Prob. 10.9.)

EXAMPLE 10.6. Consider again the communications network of Examples 9.26 and 9.31. Recall that if two links emanate from a node, then each one is chosen with a probability of 0.5. A new routing policy has been proposed in which a message is routed to that link with the smallest total number of messages present (in transmission plus in queue). In the case of a tie, each link is chosen with a probability of 0.5. We made five independent replications of each policy of length $m = 65$ seconds and used a warmup period of length $l = 5$ seconds (see Example 9.26); the replications for the two policies were also made independently of each other and of the replications used to determine the warmup period. Let X_{ij} be the average end-to-end delay of all messages that were completed in the time interval [5, 65] seconds for policy i ($i = 1$ and 2 for the original and proposed routing policies, respectively) on replication j ($j = 1, 2, \ldots, 5$), and let $Z_j = X_{1j} - X_{2j}$. Also, let ν_i be the steady-state mean end-to-end delay for policy i. Then we used Eq. (10.1) to obtain [−0.12, 0.31] (in millisecond) as an approximate 90 percent confidence interval for $\nu_1 - \nu_2$. Since the confidence interval contains 0, the difference between the two steady-state means is not statistically significant. We will revisit this example in Sec. 11.2.

The approach used in Examples 10.5 and 10.6 basically attempted to use the replication/deletion approach to obtain IID observations for each system with mean equal to the respective steady-state measure of performance. Several of the other single-system methods for steady-state analysis discussed in Sec. 9.5.3 could also be considered. For example, if the warmup period is long, we might want to use batch means on each alternative system as a different approach toward obtaining IID unbiased observations. Since the critical factor for success of the batch-means approach is eliminating correlation between batches, we must take care to define the batches appropriately, as discussed in Sec. 9.5.3. Another possibility would be Chen and Sargent's (1987) two-model adaptation of the standardized time-series approach (see Sec. 9.5.3).

10.3 CONFIDENCE INTERVALS FOR COMPARING MORE THAN TWO SYSTEMS

If there are just two systems to compare, the methods in Sec. 10.2 provide ways of constructing confidence intervals for the difference between their performance measures. In many studies, however, there may be more than two systems, but we can still use a confidence-interval approach.

We will be making several confidence-interval statements simultaneously, so their individual levels will have to be adjusted upward so that the *overall* confidence level of all intervals' covering their respective targets is at the desired level $1 - \alpha$. We will use the Bonferroni inequality [see (9.12) in Sec. 9.7] to ensure that the overall confidence level is *at least* $1 - \alpha$. Recall, the Bonferroni inequality implies that if we want to make some number c of confidence-interval statements, then we should make each separate interval at level $1 - \alpha/c$, so that the overall confidence level associated with all intervals' covering their targets will be at least $1 - \alpha$. For instance, if we want to make $c = 10$ intervals and get an overall confidence level of $100(1 - \alpha)$ percent $= 90$ percent, we must make each individual interval at the 99 percent level. Clearly, for large c, this implies that the individual intervals may become quite wide.

Although there are many goals that could be formulated for comparing the means of k systems, we will focus primarily, in Secs. 10.3.1 and 10.3.2, on two problems: comparisons with a "standard," and all pairwise comparisons. In Sec. 10.3.3 we briefly describe a different goal, in which we compare each system with the best of the other systems. For other problems and procedures, see Hochberg and Tamane (1987), Hsu (1996), Goldsman and Nelson (1998), and Swisher et al. (2003).

10.3.1 Comparisons with a Standard

Suppose that one of the model variants is a "standard," perhaps representing the existing system or policy. If we call the standard system 1 and the other variants systems 2, 3, . . . , k, the goal is to construct $k - 1$ confidence intervals for the $k - 1$ differences $\mu_2 - \mu_1, \mu_3 - \mu_1, \ldots, \mu_k - \mu_1$, with overall confidence level $1 - \alpha$. Thus, we are making $c = k - 1$ individual intervals, so they should each be constructed at level $1 - \alpha/(k - 1)$. Then we can say (with a confidence level of at least $1 - \alpha$) that for all $i = 2, 3, \ldots, k$, system i differs from the standard if the interval for $\mu_i - \mu_1$ misses 0, and that system i is not significantly different from the standard if this interval contains 0.

EXAMPLE 10.7. Table 10.4 defines $k = 5$ different (s, S) policies for the inventory system of Sec. 1.5; policies 1 and 2 are those used in Examples 10.3 and 10.4. Suppose that policy 1, where $(s, S) = (20, 40)$, is the current policy, and the other four policies are being considered as possible alternatives.

Which of these would differ from the standard? To find out, we made five independent replications of each policy, with the runs for the different policies being independent

TABLE 10.4
The five alternative (s, S) inventory policies

Policy (i)	s	S
1	20	40
2	20	80
3	40	60
4	40	100
5	60	100

TABLE 10.5
Average total cost per month for five independent replications of each of the five inventory policies, with sample means and variances

j	X_{1j}	X_{2j}	X_{3j}	X_{4j}	X_{5j}
1	126.97	118.21	120.77	131.64	141.09
2	124.31	120.22	129.32	137.07	143.86
3	126.68	122.45	120.61	129.91	144.30
4	122.66	122.68	123.65	129.97	141.72
5	127.23	119.40	127.34	131.08	142.61
Mean	125.57	120.59	124.34	131.93	142.72
Variance	4.00	3.76	15.23	8.79	1.87

of each other as well. The individual-replication results appear in Table 10.5, along with the sample means and variances (of the X_{ij}'s) for each policy. Since there are $k - 1 = 4$ intervals to construct, we made each interval at level 97.5 percent to yield an overall confidence level of at least 90 percent. Table 10.6 shows the differences in the sample means, as well as 97.5 percent confidence intervals for $\mu_i - \mu_1$, for $i = 2, 3, 4,$ and 5. For illustration, we used both the paired-t (Sec. 10.2.1) and Welch (Sec. 10.2.2) approaches to confidence-interval formation, which are both valid since the runs for the different models were independent. The asterisks indicate those intervals not containing zero, i.e., corresponding to those alternative systems that appear to differ from the standard. Note that the two approaches for forming the individual intervals may lead to different conclusions; e.g., the paired-t interval for $\mu_2 - \mu_1$ does not indicate a difference (see Prob. 10.10), whereas the Welch interval does. Furthermore, neither method is dominant in terms of interval smallness. At any rate, it does appear that models 4 and 5 are significantly different (actually, worse, since the output is an operating cost) than the standard, and that model 3 is not different from the standard. It is not clear from these results whether model 2 differs from the standard.

Implicit in the above example and discussion is that the individual confidence intervals have the correct probability $[1 - \alpha/(k - 1)$ in this case] of covering their respective targets. Thus, we should bear in mind the robustness concerns of Sec. 9.4.1. Also, since the Bonferroni inequality is quite general, it does not matter how the individual confidence intervals are formed; they need not result from the same number of replications of each model, nor must they be independent. For example, we could

TABLE 10.6
Individual 97.5 percent confidence intervals for all comparisons with the standard system ($\mu_i - \mu_1, i = 2, 3, 4, 5$); * denotes a significant difference

		Paired-t		Welch	
i	$\bar{X}_i - \bar{X}_1$	Half-length	Interval	Half-length	Interval
2	−4.98	5.45	(−10.44, 0.48)	3.54	(−8.52, −1.44)*
3	−1.23	7.58	(−8.80, 6.34)	6.21	(−7.44, 4.97)
4	6.36	6.08	(0.27, 12.46)*	4.55	(1.82, 10.91)*
5	17.15	3.67	(13.48, 20.81)*	6.15	(14.07, 20.22)*

attempt to reduce the intervals' widths by making more replications of high-variance models, or by using CRN (Sec. 11.2) to reduce the variances of the paired differences. In addition, the above approach could be used for steady-state comparisons by using a technique for constructing individual confidence intervals for steady-state differences, as discussed in Sec. 10.2.4, with the individual confidence levels adjusted upward by the Bonferroni inequality. Finally, one can always resolve ambiguities (confidence intervals covering zero, as occurred in three of the eight intervals in Table 10.6) by making more replications (or longer runs); the rate of decrease of the intervals' widths, however, may be slow as additional simulation is done—to cut an interval width in half generally requires about four times as many replications.

10.3.2 All Pairwise Comparisons

In some studies, we might want to compare each system with every other system to detect and quantify any significant pairwise differences. For example, there may not be an existing system, and all k alternatives represent possible implementations that should be treated in the same way. One approach would be to form confidence intervals for the differences $\mu_{i_2} - \mu_{i_1}$, for all i_1 and i_2 between 1 and k, with $i_1 < i_2$. Here, there will be $k(k - 1)/2$ individual intervals, so each must be made at level $1 - \alpha/[k(k - 1)/2]$ in order to have a confidence level of at least $1 - \alpha$ for all the intervals together.

EXAMPLE 10.8. Now suppose that the five inventory policies in Table 10.4 are all to be compared against each other, using the data in Table 10.5. Since there are $5(5 - 1)/2 = 10$ possible pairs, we must make each individual interval at level 99 percent in order to achieve 90 percent overall confidence. Table 10.7 gives the resulting

TABLE 10.7
Individual 99 percent confidence intervals for all pairwise comparisons ($\mu_{i_2} - \mu_{i_1}$ for $i_1 < i_2$); * denotes a significant difference

		Paired-t			
		i_2			
		2	3	4	5
i_1	1	-4.98 ± 7.18	-1.23 ± 9.99	6.36 ± 8.01	17.15 ± 4.83*
	2		3.75 ± 9.58	11.34 ± 8.38*	22.12 ± 3.80*
	3			7.60 ± 5.66*	18.38 ± 7.73*
	4				10.78 ± 5.85*
		Welch			
		i_2			
		2	3	4	5
i_1	1	-4.98 ± 4.36*	-1.23 ± 7.91	6.36 ± 5.60*	17.15 ± 3.80*
	2		3.75 ± 7.86	11.34 ± 5.88*	22.12 ± 3.72*
	3			7.60 ± 7.67	18.38 ± 8.51*
	4				10.78 ± 5.89*

99 percent intervals, using both the paired-t and Welch approaches, with asterisks indicating those intervals missing zero, i.e., those pairs of systems that appear to have different expected operating costs. Once again, note that the two approaches do not always agree in terms of which differences are significant, and neither approach gives intervals with uniformly smaller half-lengths. Furthermore, it is possible to arrive at apparent contradictions in the conclusions. For instance, using the Welch approach we would conclude that neither μ_1 nor μ_2 differs significantly from μ_3, so that we might (crudely) want to say something like "$\mu_1 = \mu_3 = \mu_2$" and thus think logically that "$\mu_1 = \mu_2$." But the confidence interval for $\mu_2 - \mu_1$ misses zero, indicating that we *cannot* regard μ_1 as being equal to μ_2. The problem here is that we dare not interpret the confidence-interval statements as constituting "proof" of equality or inequality; in the above discussion we just could not resolve a difference between either μ_1 or μ_2 in comparison with μ_3, but we could detect a difference between μ_1 and μ_2. Such apparent contradictions become less likely as the intervals become smaller, which could occur by making more replications of the systems or perhaps by using CRN, discussed in Sec. 11.2.

As at the end of Sec. 10.3.1, we note the importance of ensuring the validity of the individual confidence intervals, the possibility of using CRN across the different models, and of taking the above approach for steady-state comparisons by using an appropriate steady-state methodology for the individual intervals.

10.3.3 Multiple Comparisons with the Best

Finally, we mention another kind of comparison goal that forms simultaneous confidence intervals for the differences between the means of each of the k alternatives and that of the best of the other alternatives, even though we do not know which of the others really is the best. This is known as *multiple comparisons with the best* (MCB), and it has as its objective to form k simultaneous confidence intervals on $\mu_i - \min_{l \neq i} \mu_l$ for $i = 1, 2, \ldots, k$, assuming that smaller means are better (if larger is better, then "min" is replaced by "max").

Hsu (1984) gives a technique for addressing the MCB goal, and Hochberg and Tamane (1987) and Hsu (1996) are comprehensive books on multiple-comparison procedures. Nelson (1993) gives a treatment of MCB that allows the use of CRN (see Sec. 11.2) for improved efficiency. Damerdji and Nakayama (1999), Nakayama (1997, 2000), and Yuan and Nelson (1993) address the steady-state MCB problem.

While MCB is useful in its own right, it is also intimately related to the ranking-and-selection procedures discussed in Sec. 10.4.1 [see Nelson and Matejcik (1995)].

10.4 RANKING AND SELECTION

In this section we consider goals that are different—and more ambitious—than simply making a comparison between several alternative systems. In Sec. 10.4.1 we describe procedures whose goal is to select one of the k systems as being the best one, in some sense, and to control the probability that the selected system really *is* the best one. Section 10.4.2 considers a different goal, picking a subset of m of the k systems so that this selected subset contains the best system, again with a specified probability. (The validity of two of these selection procedures is considered in App. 10A.) Further problems and methods are discussed in Sec. 10.4.3, including the issue of ranking and selection based on steady-state measures of performance.

10.4.1 Selecting the Best of *k* Systems

As in Secs. 10.2 and 10.3, let X_{ij} be the random variable of interest from the jth replication of the ith system, and let $\mu_i = E(X_{ij})$. For this selection problem, as well as that in Sec. 10.4.2, the X_{ij}'s are assumed to be independent for different replications of the ith system. Except for the Nelson and Matejcik (1995) procedure discussed later in this section, the replications for different systems are also to be made independently. For example X_{ij} could be the average total cost per month for the jth replication of policy i for the inventory model of Examples 10.7 and 10.8.

Let μ_{i_l} be the lth smallest of the μ_i's, so that $\mu_{i_1} \le \mu_{i_2} \le \cdots \le \mu_{i_k}$. Our goal in this section is to select a system with the *smallest* expected response, μ_{i_1}. (If we want the *largest* mean μ_{i_k}, the signs of the X_{ij}'s and μ_i's can simply be reversed.) Let "CS" denote this event of "correct selection."

The inherent randomness of the observed X_{ij}'s implies that we can never be *absolutely* sure that we shall make the CS, but we would like to be able to prespecify the *probability* of CS. Further, if μ_{i_1} and μ_{i_2} are actually very close together, we might not care if we erroneously choose system i_2 (the one with mean μ_{i_2}), so that we want a method that avoids making a large number of replications to resolve this unimportant difference. The exact problem formulation, then, is that we want $P(\text{CS}) \ge P^*$ provided that $\mu_{i_2} - \mu_{i_1} \ge d^*$, where the minimal CS probability $P^* > 1/k$ and the "indifference" amount $d^* > 0$ are both specified by the analyst. It is natural to ask what happens if $\mu_{i_2} - \mu_{i_1} < d^*$. (The value d^* is the smallest actual difference that we care about detecting.) The procedure stated below has the nice property that, with probability at least P^*, the expected response of the *selected* system will be no larger than $\mu_{i_1} + d^*$ [see sec. 18.2.3 in Kim and Nelson (2006a)]. Thus, we are protected (with probability at least P^*) against selecting a system with mean that is more than d^* worse than that of the best system (see Fig. 10.4).

The statistical procedure for solving this problem, developed by Dudewicz and Dalal (1975), involves "two-stage" sampling from each of the k systems. In the first stage we make a fixed number of replications of each system, then use the resulting variance estimates to determine how many more replications from each system are necessary in a second stage of sampling in order to reach a decision. It must be assumed that the X_{ij}'s are normally distributed, but (importantly) we need *not* assume that the values of $\sigma_i^2 = \text{Var}(X_{ij})$ are known; nor do we have to assume that the σ_i^2's are the same for different i's. [Assuming known or equal variances (see Table 10.5)

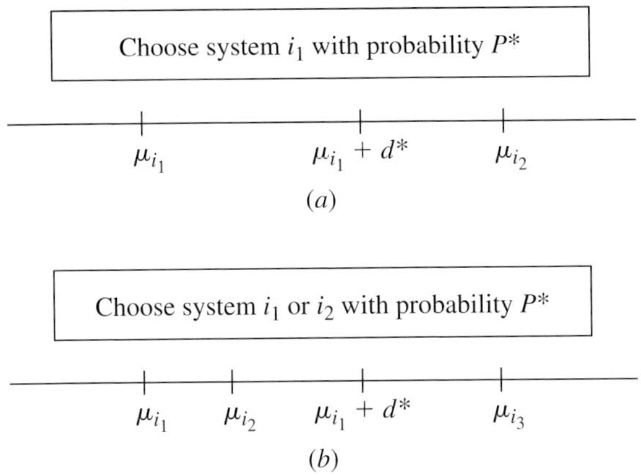

FIGURE 10.4
Selected system(s): (*a*) $\mu_{i_2} > \mu_{i_1} + d^*$; (*b*) $\mu_{i_2} < \mu_{i_1} + d^*$ and $\mu_{i_3} > \mu_{i_1} + d^*$.

is very unrealistic when simulating real systems.] The procedure's performance should be robust to departures from the normality assumption, especially if the X_{ij}'s are averages. (We have verified this robustness when X_{ij} is the average of a fixed number of delays in queue for an *M*/*M*/1 queueing system.)

In the first-stage sampling, we make $n_0 \geq 2$ replications of each of the k systems and define the first-stage sample means and variances

$$\overline{X}_i^{(1)}(n_0) = \frac{\sum_{j=1}^{n_0} X_{ij}}{n_0}$$

and

$$S_i^2(n_0) = \frac{\sum_{j=1}^{n_0} [X_{ij} - \overline{X}_i^{(1)}(n_0)]^2}{n_0 - 1}$$

for $i = 1, 2, \ldots, k$. Then we compute the total sample size N_i needed for system i as

$$N_i = \max\left\{n_0 + 1, \left\lceil \frac{h_1^2 S_i^2(n_0)}{(d^*)^2} \right\rceil\right\} \tag{10.3}$$

where $\lceil x \rceil$ is the smallest integer that is greater than or equal to the real number x, and h_1 (which depends on k, P^*, and n_0) is a constant that can be obtained from Table 10.11 in App. 10B. Next, we make $N_i - n_0$ *more* replications of system i ($i = 1, 2, \ldots, k$) and obtain the second-stage sample means

$$\overline{X}_i^{(2)}(N_i - n_0) = \frac{\sum_{j=n_0+1}^{N_i} X_{ij}}{N_i - n_0}$$

Then define the weights

$$W_{i1} = \frac{n_0}{N_i}\left\{1 + \sqrt{1 - \frac{N_i}{n_0}\left[1 - \frac{(N_i - n_0)(d^*)^2}{h_1^2 S_i^2(n_0)}\right]}\right\}$$

and $W_{i2} = 1 - W_{i1}$, for $i = 1, 2, \ldots, k$. Finally, define the weighted sample means

$$\tilde{X}_i(N_i) = W_{i1}\overline{X}_i^{(1)}(n_0) + W_{i2}\overline{X}_i^{(2)}(N_i - n_0)$$

and select the system with the smallest $\tilde{X}_i(N_i)$. (See App. 10A for an explanation of the seemingly bizarre definition of W_{i1}.)

The choices of P^* and d^* depend on the analyst's goals and the particular systems under study; specifying them might be tempered by the computing cost of obtaining a large N_i associated with a large P^* or small d^*. However, choosing n_0 is more troublesome, and we can only say, on the basis of our experiments and various statements in the literature, that n_0 be at least 20. If n_0 is too small, we might get a poor estimate $S_i^2(n_0)$ of σ_i^2; in particular, it could be that $S_i^2(n_0)$ is much greater than σ_i^2, leading to an unnecessarily large value of N_i. On the other hand, if n_0 is too large, we could "overshoot" the necessary numbers of replications for some of the systems, which is wasteful. Table 10.11, in App. 10B, gives values of h_1 for $P^* = 0.90$ and 0.95, $n_0 = 20$ and 40, and for $k = 2, 3, \ldots, 10$. If values of h_1 are needed for other P^*, n_0, or k values, we refer the reader to Dudewicz and Dalal (1975) or Koenig and Law (1985).

EXAMPLE 10.9. For the inventory model of Sec. 1.5 (and Examples 10.7 and 10.8), suppose that we want to compare the $k = 5$ different (s, S) policies, as given in Table 10.4, on the basis of their corresponding expected average total costs per month for the first 120 months of operation, which we denote by μ_i for the ith policy. Our goal is to select a system with the smallest μ_i and to be $100P^* = 90$ percent sure that we have made the correct selection provided that $\mu_{i_2} - \mu_{i_1} \geq d^* = 1$. We made $n_0 = 20$ initial independent replications of each system, so that $h_1 = 2.747$ from Table 10.11. The results of the first-stage sampling are given in the $\overline{X}_i^{(1)}(20)$ and $S_i^2(20)$ columns of Table 10.8. From the $S_i^2(20)$'s, h_1, and d^*, we next computed the total sample size N_i for each system, as shown in Table 10.8. Then we made $N_i - 20$ additional replications for each policy, i.e., 90 more replications for policy 1, 41 more for policy 2, etc., and computed the second-stage sample means $\overline{X}_i^{(2)}(N_i - 20)$, as shown. Finally, we calculated the weights W_{i1} and W_{i2} for each system and the weighted sample means $\tilde{X}_i(N_i)$. Since $\tilde{X}_2(N_2)$ is the smallest weighted sample mean, we select policy 2 ($s = 20$ and $S = 80$) as being the lowest-cost configuration. Note from the $S_i^2(20)$ and N_i columns of Table 10.8 that

TABLE 10.8
Selecting the best of the five inventory policies

i	$\overline{X}_i^{(1)}(20)$	$S_i^2(20)$	N_i	$\overline{X}_i^{(2)}(N_i - 20)$	W_{i1}	W_{i2}	$\tilde{X}_i(N_i)$
1	126.48	14.52	110	124.45	0.21	0.79	124.87
2	121.92	7.96	61	121.63	0.39	0.61	121.74
3	127.16	9.45	72	126.11	0.32	0.68	126.44
4	130.71	8.25	63	132.03	0.37	0.63	131.54
5	144.07	6.20	47	144.83	0.46	0.54	144.48

the procedure calls for a higher value of the final N_i if the variance estimate $S_i^2(20)$ is high; this is simply reflecting the fact that we need more data on the more variable systems. Note that if $d^* = 2$, then 28, 21, 21, 21, and 21 total replications are required for policies 1 through 5, respectively.

There is another popular procedure for selecting the best of k systems that is due to Rinott (1978) (denoted $\mathcal{R}$). It uses the usual sample means (based on all first-stage and second-stage replications) from the k systems to make its selection, whereas the Dudewicz and Dalal ($\mathcal{DD}$) procedure uses the weighted sample means from the k systems. However, the $\mathcal{DD}$ procedure generally requires fewer replications than the computationally simpler $\mathcal{R}$ procedure, since h_1 is smaller than the comparable "h value" for the $\mathcal{R}$ procedure.

*The $\mathcal{DD}$ and $\mathcal{R}$ procedures discussed above for selecting the best system assume that the k systems are simulated independently. However, in some cases it might be advantageous (in terms of the sample sizes required to make the correct selection) to use CRN in simulating the k systems. In this regard, Nelson and Matejcik (1995) introduced a two-stage procedure (denoted $\mathcal{NM}$) for selecting the best system that explicitly allows for the use of CRN. Let Σ denote the covariance matrix (see Sec. 6.10.1) of the random variables $X_{1j}, X_{2j}, \ldots, X_{kj}$. The $\mathcal{NM}$ procedure assumes that Σ has a particular structure called *sphericity*, which is defined by

$$\Sigma = \begin{bmatrix} 2\psi_1 + \tau^2 & \psi_1 + \psi_2 & \cdots & \psi_1 + \psi_k \\ \psi_2 + \psi_1 & 2\psi_2 + \tau^2 & \cdots & \psi_2 + \psi_k \\ \vdots & \vdots & & \vdots \\ \psi_k + \psi_1 & \psi_k + \psi_2 & \cdots & 2\psi_k + \tau^2 \end{bmatrix}$$

where the ψ_i's and τ^2 are constants, and $\tau^2 > \sqrt{k\Sigma_{i=1}^k \psi_i^2} - \Sigma_{i=1}^k \psi_i$ is required to make Σ positive definite. Sphericity implies that $\text{Var}(X_{ij} - X_{lj}) = 2\tau^2$ for $i \neq l$ (see Prob. 10.11). This means that the variances of all pairwise differences across the systems are equal, even though the marginal variances and covariances may be unequal.

As for the $\mathcal{DD}$ procedure, let n_0 be the first-stage sample size, d^* the indifference amount, and $P^* = 1 - \alpha$ the probability of correct selection. Also, let $g = T^{1-\alpha}_{k-1,(k-1)(n_0-1),0.5}$ be the $(1 - \alpha)$-quantile of the maximum of a $(k - 1)$-dimensional multivariate t distribution with $(k - 1)(n_0 - 1)$ degrees of freedom and a common correlation of 0.5. Values of g are given in table B.3 of Bechhofer et al. (1995) and in table 4 of Hochberg and Tamhane (1987). Then the following is a statement of the $\mathcal{NM}$ procedure:

1. In the first-stage sampling, make $n_0 \geq 2$ independent replications of the ith system using CRN across the k systems (for $i = 1, 2, \ldots, k$).

*The remainder of this section may be skipped on a first reading.

2. Based on the assumption of sphericity, compute the sample variance of the pairwise differences as

$$S^2 = \frac{2\sum_{i=1}^{k}\sum_{j=1}^{n_0}(X_{ij} - \overline{X}_{i\cdot} - \overline{X}_{\cdot j} + \overline{X}_{\cdot\cdot})^2}{(k-1)(n_0-1)}$$

where $\overline{X}_{i\cdot}$ denotes the sample mean of $X_{i1}, X_{i2}, \ldots, X_{in_0}$; $\overline{X}_{\cdot j}$ denotes the sample mean of $X_{1j}, X_{2j}, \ldots, X_{kj}$, etc. (see Prob. 10.12).

3. Compute the total required sample size N (constant for all k systems) as

$$N = \max\left\{n_0, \left\lceil \frac{g^2S^2}{(d^*)^2} \right\rceil\right\} \tag{10.4}$$

4. In the second-stage sampling, make $N - n_0$ independent replications of the ith system using CRN across the k systems (for $i = 1, 2, \ldots, k$).
5. Compute the overall sample mean for the ith system as

$$\overline{X}_i(N) = \frac{\sum_{j=1}^{N} X_{ij}}{N} \qquad \text{for } i = 1, 2, \ldots, k$$

6. Select the system with the smallest $\overline{X}_i(N)$ as being the best alternative.

Nelson and Matejcik show that the probability of correct selection for the $\mathcal{NM}$ procedure is at least P^* when $\mu_{i_2} - \mu_{i_1} \geq d^*$, provided that Σ satisfies the property of sphericity. If $\mu_{i_2} - \mu_{i_1} < d^*$, then a system is returned whose mean is within d^* of the best mean. They also show that their procedure is robust to departures from sphericity when the covariances σ_{ij} are nonnegative, which is the assumed effect of CRN.

EXAMPLE 10.10. Consider the problem of selecting the best of the five inventory policies in Example 10.9, where $100P^* = 90$ percent and $d^* = 1$. We made $n_0 = 20$ first-stage independent replications for each of the five policies using partial CRN as described in Example 11.7; specifically, we made the interdemand times and demand sizes the same across the policies, but generated the delivery lags independently. From the resulting X_{ij}'s, we found that $S^2 = 3.71$ and computed the required total sample size N as

$$N = \max\left\{n_0, \left\lceil \frac{g^2S^2}{(d^*)^2} \right\rceil\right\} = \max\left\{20, \frac{(1.86)^2(3.71)}{(1)^2}\right\} = 20$$

where the value of $g = 1.86$ was taken from table B.3 of Bechhofer et al. (1995). Since $N = 20 = n_0$, it was not necessary to make any second-stage replications. Furthermore, since the five first-stage sample means (i.e., the $\overline{X}_{i\cdot}$'s) were 125.64, 121.48, 126.16, 131.61, and 144.52, respectively, we once again selected policy 2 as being the best. Note that the $\mathcal{NM}$ procedure using CRN required 100 total replications to select policy

2 as being the best, whereas the $\mathcal{DD}$ procedure required a total of 353 independent replications in Example 10.9. Thus, the $\mathcal{NM}$ procedure reduced the computational effort by approximately 72 percent.

In Sec. 10.3.3 we briefly discussed multiple comparisons with the best (MCB), which has the objective of forming k simultaneous confidence intervals on $\mu_i - \min_{l \neq i} \mu_l$ for $i = 1, 2, \ldots, k$. Nelson and Matejcik (1995) showed that the output of most indifference-zone procedures (e.g., $\mathcal{DD}$ and $\mathcal{NM}$) can be used to construct MCB confidence intervals, and simultaneously guarantee both the correct selection and the coverage of the MCB differences with overall confidence level P^*. This approach allows one to pick the system with the smallest mean and to draw inferences about the differences between the means of the systems, which may facilitate decision making based on a secondary criterion. For example, if the mean of the second-best system does not differ much from the mean of the best system, then it may be desirable to choose the second-best system because of political or economic reasons.

To make these ideas more concrete, consider once again the $\mathcal{NM}$ procedure. Then the following seventh step can be appended to their procedure:

7. For $i = 1, 2, \ldots, k$, construct the MCB confidence interval for $\mu_i - \min_{l \neq i} \mu_l$ as

$$[-(\bar{X}_{i\cdot} - \min_{l \neq i} \bar{X}_{l\cdot} - d^*)^-, (\bar{X}_{i\cdot} - \min_{l \neq i} \bar{X}_{l\cdot} + d^*)^+]$$

where $-x^- = \min(0, x)$ and $x^+ = \max(0, x)$.

EXAMPLE 10.11. For the five inventory policies of Example 10.10, the calculations for the MCB confidence intervals are given in Table 10.9. Overall we are at least 90 percent confident that policy 2 is the best *and* that the five confidence intervals contain their respective MCB differences. From the second confidence interval, we conclude that policy 2 is no worse than the other policies (the upper endpoint is 0), and it may be as much as \$5.16 less expensive than the others (the lower endpoint is −5.16). The other confidence intervals tell us that policies 1, 3, 4, and 5 are no better than policy 2 (the lower endpoints of their intervals are 0) and may be as much as \$5.16, \$5.68, \$11.13, and \$24.04 more expensive, respectively.

The $\mathcal{DD}$ and $\mathcal{NM}$ procedures are typically used when the number of alternative systems, k, is 20 or fewer. These procedures are designed to produce the desired

TABLE 10.9
MCB confidence intervals for the five inventory policies

i	Lower MCB endpoint	$\bar{X}_{i\cdot} - \min_{l \neq i} \bar{X}_{l\cdot}$	Upper MCB endpoint
1	0	4.16	5.16
2	−5.16	−4.16	0
3	0	4.68	5.68
4	0	10.13	11.13
5	0	23.04	24.04

probability of correct selection, P^*, when $\mu_{i_1} + d^* = \mu_{i_2} = \cdots = \mu_{i_k}$ (see App. 10A), an arrangement of the μ_i's known as the *least-favorable configuration* (LFC). This is the worst-case situation in that it makes the best system as hard to distinguish from the others as possible, given that it's at least d^* better than everything else. {This assumption is made because it makes the calculation of N_i or N [see Eqs. (10.3) and (10.4), respectively] independent of the true and sample means.} Thus, when k is "large" and the μ_i's differ widely, the $\mathscr{D}\mathscr{D}$ and $\mathscr{N}\mathscr{M}$ procedures may prescribe larger sample sizes than needed to deliver the desired probability of correct selection. As a result of these considerations, Nelson et al. (2001) introduced a screen-and-select procedure (denoted $\mathscr{N}\mathscr{S}\mathscr{G}\mathscr{S}$) for use when k is large. The screening stage first produces a subset (of random size) that excludes clearly inferior systems. Then in the succeeding selection stage an indifference-zone procedure (e.g., $\mathscr{D}\mathscr{D}$ or $\mathscr{N}\mathscr{M}$) is applied to the set of remaining systems to choose the "best" system, and the combined procedure guarantees an overall probability of correct selection. Because no selection-stage observations are collected on inferior systems, the combined procedure may require fewer observations than the use of an indifference-zone procedure alone. The screening part of this procedure has been implemented in the Process Analyzer for the Arena simulation package (see Sec. 3.5.1).

10.4.2 Selecting a Subset of Size *m* Containing the Best of *k* Systems

Now we consider a different kind of selection problem, that of selecting a subset of exactly m of the k systems (m is prespecified) so that, with probability at least P^*, the selected subset will contain a system with the smallest mean response μ_{i_1}. This could be a useful goal in the initial stages of a simulation study, where there may be a large number (k) of alternative systems and we would like to perform an initial screening to eliminate those that appear to be clearly inferior. Thus, we could avoid expending a large amount of computer time getting precise estimates of the behavior of these inferior systems.

We define X_{ij}, μ_i, μ_{i_l}, and σ_i^2 as in Sec. 10.4.1. Here we assume that all X_{ij}'s are independent and normal (CRN is not allowed), and for fixed i, $X_{i1}, X_{i2}, \ldots$ are IID; the σ_i^2's are unknown and need not be equal. Here, correct selection (CS) is defined to mean that the subset of size m that is selected contains a system with mean μ_{i_1} and we want $P(\text{CS}) \geq P^*$ provided that $\mu_{i_2} - \mu_{i_1} \geq d^*$; here we must have $1 \leq m \leq k - 1$, $P^* > m/k$, and $d^* > 0$. (If $\mu_{i_2} - \mu_{i_1} < d^*$, then with probability at least P^*, the subset selected will contain a system with expected response that is no larger than $\mu_{i_1} + d^*$.)

The procedure is very similar to the $\mathscr{D}\mathscr{D}$ procedure of Sec. 10.4.1, and has been derived by Koenig and Law (1985). We take a first-stage sample of $n_0 \geq 2$ replications from each system and define $\bar{X}_i^{(1)}(n_0)$ and $S_i^2(n_0)$ for $i = 1, 2, \ldots, k$ exactly as in Sec. 10.4.1. Next we compute the total number of replications, N_i, needed for the ith system exactly as in Eq. (10.3), except that h_1 is replaced by h_2 (which depends on m as well as on k, P^*, and n_0), as found in Table 10.12 in App. 10B. [For values of h_2 that might be needed for other P^*, n_0, k, or m values, see Koenig and Law

TABLE 10.10
Selecting a subset of size 3 containing the best of the 5 inventory policies

i	$\overline{X}_i^{(1)}(20)$	$S_i^2(20)$	N_i	$\overline{X}_i^{(2)}(N_i - 20)$	W_{i1}	W_{i2}	$\tilde{X}_i(N_i)$
1	124.71	17.16	27	125.64	0.80	0.20	124.89
2	121.20	12.64	21	125.69	1.01	−0.01	121.15
3	125.57	9.07	21	123.51	1.10	−0.10	125.78
4	132.39	6.22	21	133.37	1.18	−0.18	132.21
5	144.27	4.23	21	143.67	1.27	−0.27	144.43

(1985).] Then we make $N_i - n_0$ more replications, form the second-stage sample means $\overline{X}_i^{(2)}(N_i - n_0)$, weights W_{i1} and W_{i2}, and weighted sample means $\tilde{X}_i(N_i)$, exactly as in Sec. 10.4.1. Finally, we define the selected subset to consist of the m systems corresponding to the m smallest values of the $\tilde{X}_i(N_i)$'s.

EXAMPLE 10.12. Consider again our five inventory systems of Example 10.9, as defined in Table 10.4. Now, however, suppose that we want to select a subset of size $m = 3$ from among the $k = 5$ systems and be assured with confidence level at least $P^* = 0.90$ that the selected subset contains the best (least-cost) system provided that $\mu_{i_2} - \mu_{i_1} \geq d^* = 1$. Again we made $n_0 = 20$ initial replications of each system (independent of those used in Example 10.9); the complete results for the subset-selection procedure are given in Table 10.10. (From Table 10.12, $h_2 = 1.243$.) The subset selected consists of policies 1, 2, and 3.

Comparing the value of $h_2(= 1.243)$ used here with that of $h_1(= 2.747)$ used in Example 10.9, we see from the form of Eq. (10.3) that the more modest goal of selecting a subset of size 3 *containing* the best system requires considerably fewer replications on average than does the more ambitious goal of selecting *the* best system. (In fact, the selection problem of Sec. 10.4.1 is really just a special case of the present subset-selection problem, with $m = 1$.) This effect exemplifies what we meant at the beginning of this section by referring to this subset-selection problem as a relatively inexpensive initial "screening."

10.4.3 Additional Problems and Methods

In Sec. 10.4.1 we discussed the indifference-zone approach for selecting the system with the smallest mean out of k systems, so that the probability of correct selection $P(\text{CS}) \geq P^*$. One problem with this approach is that it does not make use of any sample-mean information from the first stage in deciding how many replications to make in the second stage, which seems inefficient. We now discuss two other *general* approaches to this ranking-and-selection problem. Chen et al. (2000) discuss the *optimal computing budget allocation* ($\mathscr{OCBA}$) multistage (sequential) approach for maximizing the probability of correct selection given that a total budget B of replications is available to simulate the k systems. They show that the number of replications allocated to system i should be proportional to the square of the noise-to-signal ratio, where the noise refers to the sample standard deviation for system i and the signal refers to the difference between system i's sample mean and the minimum sample mean. At stage 0 of their approach, n_0 replications of each system are made, and the corresponding sample means and variances are computed. (The budget B is reduced by $k \cdot n_0$ replications.) Then at stage l (for $l = 1, 2, \ldots$), a total of Δ replications is allocated to the k systems, with $\Delta_i^l (\Delta_i^l \geq 0)$ being the allocation to system i and $\sum_{i=1}^{k} \Delta_i^l = \Delta$. (Note that the total allocation Δ is the same at each stage $l \geq 1$.) The values of the Δ_i^l's are chosen to maximize a Bayesian approximation to the P(CS), and the optimization algorithm uses the latest values for the sample means and variances in its computations. Then the specified Δ_i^l additional replications are made for system i, and the sample mean and variance are recomputed using all available replications at stage l. This iterative process is continued until the remaining budget of replications reaches a value of 0. (The overall budget is reduced by Δ replications at each stage.) At this point, the system with the smallest overall sample mean is chosen as best. [See Chen et al. (2010) for a detailed algorithm.]

The $\mathscr{OCBA}$ approach and the two-stage $\mathscr{R}$ procedure were both applied to the inventory model of Example 10.9, but with a planning horizon of 60 rather than 120 months to increase the variability of the performance measure, average cost per month. Using $n_0 = 5$, $\Delta = 10$, $P^* = 0.90$, and $d^* = 3.08$ $(= \mu_{i_2} - \mu_{i_1})$, the $\mathscr{R}$ procedure required an average of 118.8 replications and achieved an estimated P(CS) of 0.967 (based on 10,000 independent experiments). On the other hand, the $\mathscr{OCBA}$ approach achieved an estimated P(CS) of 0.969 with an average budget of $B = 65$ replications, which is a 45.3 percent reduction in computational effort. In general, the $\mathscr{OCBA}$ approach may achieve greater computational efficiency when there is a larger number of systems, because it will then have more flexibility in allocating the computing budget.

It should be noted that the goal of the $\mathscr{OCBA}$ procedure is to *maximize* the P(CS) for a specified computing budget B. However, for a particular value of B it does *not* guarantee that a particular P(CS) (e.g., 0.90) will be achieved. Additional references for $\mathscr{OCBA}$ are Chen (1996), and Chen & Lee (2011).

Chick (1997) proposes a third general approach to ranking and selection problems, which is based on Bayesian decision-theoretic ideas. Chick and Inoue (2001a) introduce a new two-stage procedure that allocates replications to maximize the *expected* probability of correct selection, rather than to achieve a specified P(CS) in the conservative LFC, which is the goal of indifference-zone approaches. They also introduce a second two-stage procedure that allocates replications to reduce the expected opportunity cost of potentially incorrect decisions. (Both procedures use first-stage sample-mean information in determining how many replications to make in the second stage.) They tested these procedures along with the two-stage $\mathscr{R}$ and $\mathscr{NSGS}$ procedures on the inventory model with a 60-month planning horizon, and found that the new procedures achieved a higher estimated P(CS). Chick and Inoue (2001b) propose analogues of these procedures that allow the use of CRN. Additional references for these Bayesian *value of information procedures* ($\mathscr{VIP}$) are Chick (2006), Chick and Frazier (2012), and Chick and Gans (2009).

Several additional ranking-and-selection procedures that use first-stage sample-mean information in determining sample sizes are discussed by Chen and Kelton (2005).

A reasonably complete and easy-to-read survey on ranking and selection (as well as on multiple-comparison procedures) can be found in Swisher et al. (2003). Other general-purpose references are Bechhofer et al. (1995), Goldsman and Nelson (1998), and Kim and Nelson (2006a). Applications of selection procedures are described in Gray and Goldsman (1988) and Swisher et al. (2003).

Boesel et al. (2003) and Pichitlamken et al. (2006) use ranking-and-selection methods to provide a statistical guarantee that the system configuration returned by a heuristic search method attempting to find an optimal system configuration (see Sec. 12.5) is at least the best of the configurations actually simulated. The sequential-selection-with-memory procedure discussed in the latter paper has been implemented in the OptQuest optimization package (see Sec. 12.5.2).

Subset Selection

The procedures in Sec. 10.1 and 10.2 used an indifference-zone approach, where the analyst prespecifies an amount d^* representing a threshold below which errors resulting from incorrect selection are deemed inconsequential. The result was the selection of a fixed, prespecified number (perhaps 1) of the alternatives as "good" in some sense. This was extended to selecting a subset of size m of the k systems that contains the *m best* of the systems by Koenig and Law (1985). An $\mathcal{OCBA}$ procedure for solving this problem is discussed in Chen et al. (2008). See also the paper by Chen (2009).

On the other hand, Gupta (1956, 1965) developed a procedure producing a subset of *random* size that contains the best system, with prespecified probability P^*, without specifying an indifference amount (i.e., setting $d^* = 0$). Although the size of the selected subset is not controlled, this could be a useful first step in screening out those of a large number of alternatives that are clearly not inferior. Gupta and Santner (1973) and Santner (1975) extended this method to allow for prespecifying the maximum size m of the selected subset, and they also showed the relationship of this method to indifference-zone approaches. A major limitation of these procedures in simulation is that they assume known and equal variances, which is unlikely to be satisfied in practice. Sullivan and Wilson (1989) developed a much more general restricted-subset-selection procedure that allows for unknown and unequal variances, as well as specification of an indifference amount. In all these formulations, the advantage of defining m as the *maximum* size of the selected subset, instead of insisting that *exactly m* alternatives be selected, is that far fewer than m systems could be chosen in situations where it is fairly clear that only a few of the systems could be the best. Finally, as discussed in Sec. 10.4.1, Nelson et al. (2001) combine a subset-selection procedure with indifference-zone approaches to obtain the $\mathcal{NSGS}$ procedure, which has greater statistical efficiency.

Fully Sequential Procedures

The ranking-and-selection procedures discussed in Secs. 10.4.1 and 10.4.2 involved two-stage sampling, where a variance estimate was computed from the first-stage observations and used to determine the number of additional observations required in the second stage. One drawback of this approach is that if the first-stage variance estimate happens to be a lot larger than the actual variance, a perhaps unnecessarily large amount of sampling in the second stage will be prescribed. As a result, *fully sequential* procedures have been proposed, where a *single* "observation" (e.g., the average response over an entire replication) is taken from each alternative system that is still in the running at the current stage of sampling, and inferior systems are eliminated from further consideration until a best system is identified. The goal of such procedures is to reduce the number of observations required to choose the best system with a specified probability of correct selection.

Kim and Nelson (2001) developed an indifference-zone-based fully sequential procedure (denoted $\mathcal{KN}$) that assumes the ability to collect IID normal observations from each system, and allows the use of CRN across the alternative systems. Kim and Nelson (2007) applied the $\mathcal{R}$ and $\mathcal{KN}$ procedures to the inventory problem of Sec. 10.4.1 with a planning horizon of 30 months, and they used $n_0 = 10$, $P^* = 0.95$, and $\delta^* = 1$. The $\mathcal{R}$ procedure required 1556 replications for the two stages and the $\mathcal{KN}$ procedure required a total of 232 replications for all stages. (The $\mathcal{DD}$ procedure would require 1423 replications for this problem.)

A shortcoming of sequential procedures is the time and effort required to switch among the simulations corresponding to the alternative systems. In this regard, Hong and Nelson (2005) developed a sequential procedure that is designed to balance the cost of sampling and switching. Also, the $\mathcal{KN}$ procedure has been implemented in the Simio simulation package (see Sec. 3.5.3).

The $\mathcal{OCBA}$ procedures discussed above are sequential (multistage), where a total of Δ replications (observations) are allocated to the k systems at each stage. (For the inventory example discussed at the beginning of this section, $\Delta = 10$ observations were allocated at each stage to the $k = 5$ inventory policies.)

Criteria Other Than Expectations

The comparison and selection methods we have considered have all been based on looking at an *expected* system response, e.g., the expected average delay in queue or the expected average operating cost per month. However, in some situations other criteria may be more appropriate. Goldsman (1984a, 1984b) describes an inventory system where policy 1 results in a profit of 1000 with probability 0.001 and a profit of 0 with probability 0.999; policy 2, on the other hand, always gives profit 0.999. Thus, the expected profits from policies 1 and 2 are 1 and 0.999, respectively, so that policy 1 would be preferable on this basis. However, policy 2 will yield higher profit (0.999 instead of 0) with probability 0.999, so it could be considered preferable even though its expected profit is lower. Thus, we might reconsider what we regard as the "best" system, defining it to be the one that has the largest probability of producing a "good" outcome.

Goldsman (1984a, 1984b) surveys indifference-zone methods with this goal in mind, while Chen (1988) considers this problem from a subset-selection perspective. Miller et al. (1998) propose a procedure for this problem that requires smaller sample sizes to achieve a specified probability of correct selection. See Kim and Nelson (2006a) for additional discussion of this problem. Also see Chick and Inoue (2001a) and He et al. (2007) for additional discussions of selection criteria.

Correlation Between Alternatives

We saw in Sec. 10.4.1 that the use of CRN across the simulated systems can reduce the number of observations required to achieve a specified probability of correct selection. In particular, for the inventory problem, the $\mathcal{NM}$ procedure with CRN required 72 percent fewer replications than the $\mathcal{DD}$ procedure, which requires the systems of interest to be simulated independently. The $\mathcal{KN}$ procedure of Kim and Nelson (2001) also allows the use of CRN. Additionally, Fu et al. (2007) and Peng et al. (2013) discuss $\mathcal{OCBA}$ procedures that allow the use of CRN.

It is important that the common-random-numbers technique, in fact, induce the desired positive correlation between the output responses, $X_{1j}, X_{2j}, \ldots, X_{kj}$, for the k systems, and not "backfire" to induce negative correlation (see Sec. 11.2); Koenig and Law (1982) observed backfiring in testing selection procedures on inventory models, resulting in significant degradation in correct-selection probabilities.

Correlation Within an Alternative

Another type of independence that we have been assuming is for the observations from a particular alternative system. This poses no difficulty when the simulation is terminating, since we simply make independent replications of the model, and each replication produces an unbiased estimate for the desired expected response. However, in the case of a steady-state parameter for a nonterminating simulation (see Sec. 9.3), such unbiased independent observations do not come as easily. One approach to selection for steady-state parameters would be to use the replication/deletion approach to produce X_{ij}'s that are independent and approximately unbiased for the steady-state mean of system i, as was done in Examples 10.5 and 10.6. Another possibility would be to make a single long run of system i and then let X_{ij} be the sample mean of the observations in the jth batch within this run (see the discussion of batch means in Sec. 9.5.3); the critical issue here is how to choose the batch size so that the batch means are approximately uncorrelated. Additionally, Goldsman et al. (2002) developed a sequential procedure (denoted $\mathcal{KN}$++) based on one long run of each system, where *basic* observations (e.g., the delays in queue of individual customers) from each system are added one at a time. This procedure does not allow the use of CRN. The asymptotic validity of the $\mathcal{KN}$++ procedure is shown in Kim and Nelson (2006b).

Constraints on Secondary Performance Measures

There has been a fair amount of recent interest in *constrained ranking and selection*, where the goal is to find which of k systems has the smallest (largest) mean response subject to constraints on secondary mean responses (performance measures). For example, in scheduling surgery for a hospital the goal might be to minimize the mean idle time of resources, subject to an upper bound on the mean waiting time of patients. Papers that address such problems include Andradóttir and Kim (2010), Healey et al. (2013), Hunter and Pasupathy (2013), Lee et al. (2012), and Pujowidanto et al. (2009).

APPENDIX 10A VALIDITY OF THE SELECTION PROCEDURES

The purpose of this appendix is to give a brief indication of how the procedures of Secs. 10.4.1 and 10.4.2 (except the $\mathcal{NM}$ procedure) are justified and how the values for h_1 and h_2 in App. 10B were computed. For a more complete discussion, we refer the interested reader to Dudewicz and Dalal (1975) and Koenig and Law (1985).

Both procedures are based on the fact that for $i = 1, 2, \ldots, k$,

$$T_i = \frac{\tilde{X}_i(N_i) - \mu_i}{d^*/h}$$

has a t distribution with $n_0 - 1$ df, where h is either h_1 or h_2 depending on which selection procedure is used; the T_i's are also independent. The rather curious form of the expression for the weight W_{i1} was chosen specifically to make $\tilde{X}_i(N_i)$ such that T_i *would* have this t distribution. [Other ways of defining W_{i1} and $\tilde{X}_i(N_i)$ also result in the T_i's having this t distribution; see Dudewicz and Dalal (1975).]

For the selection problem of Sec. 10.4.1 assume that $\mu_{i_2} - \mu_{i_1} \geq d^*$. Then correct selection occurs if and only if $\tilde{X}_{i_1}(N_{i_1})$ is the smallest of the $\tilde{X}_i(N_i)$'s (where i_1 is the index of a system with smallest expected response, μ_{i_1}). Thus if we let f and F denote the density and distribution function, respectively, of the t distribution with $n_0 - 1$ df, we can write

$$\begin{aligned} P(\text{CS}) &= P[\tilde{X}_{i_1}(N_{i_1}) < \tilde{X}_{i_l}(N_{i_l}) \text{ for } l = 2, 3, \ldots, k] \\ &= P\left[\frac{\tilde{X}_{i_1}(N_{i_1}) - \mu_{i_1}}{d^*/h_1} \leq \frac{\tilde{X}_{i_l}(N_{i_l}) - \mu_{i_l}}{d^*/h_1} + \frac{\mu_{i_l} - \mu_{i_1}}{d^*/h_1} \text{ for } l = 2, 3, \ldots, k\right] \\ &= P\left(T_{i_l} \geq T_{i_1} - \frac{\mu_{i_l} - \mu_{i_1}}{d^*/h_1} \text{ for } l = 2, 3, \ldots, k\right) \\ &= \int_{-\infty}^{\infty} \prod_{l=2}^{k} F\left(\frac{\mu_{i_l} - \mu_{i_1}}{d^*/h_1} - t\right) f(t)\, dt \end{aligned} \tag{10.5}$$

[The last line in Eq. (10.5) follows by conditioning on $T_{i_1} = t$ and by the independence of the T_i's.] Now since we assumed that $\mu_{i_2} - \mu_{i_1} \geq d^*$ and the μ_{i_l}'s are increasing with l, we know that $\mu_{i_l} - \mu_{i_1} \geq d^*$ for $l = 2, 3, \ldots, k$. Thus, since F is monotone increasing, Eq. (10.5) yields (after a change of variable in the integral)

$$P(\text{CS}) \geq \int_{-\infty}^{\infty} [F(t + h_1)]^{k-1} f(t)\, dt \tag{10.6}$$

and equality holds in (10.6) exactly when $\mu_{i_1} + d^* = \mu_{i_2} = \cdots = \mu_{i_k}$, an arrangement of the μ_i's called the LFC. Table 10.11 was thus obtained by setting the integral on the right-hand side of (10.6) to P^* and solving (numerically) for h_1.

Demonstrating the validity of the subset-selection procedure of Sec. 10.4.2 is more complicated but follows a similar line of reasoning. We can show [see Koenig and Law (1985)] ultimately that

$$P(\text{CS}) \geq (k-m)\binom{k-1}{k-m}\int_{-\infty}^{\infty} F(t+h_2)[F(t)]^{m-1}[F(-t)]^{k-m-1}f(t)\,dt$$

and we equate the right-hand side to P^* to solve for h_2, as given in Table 10.12. The LFC for this problem [in which case $P(\text{CS}) = P^*$] is the same as that for the problem in Sec. 10.4.1.

APPENDIX 10B
CONSTANTS FOR THE SELECTION PROCEDURES

TABLE 10.11
Values of h_1 for the procedure of Sec. 10.4.1

P^*	n_0	$k = 2$	$k = 3$	$k = 4$	$k = 5$	$k = 6$	$k = 7$	$k = 8$	$k = 9$	$k = 10$
0.90	20	1.896	2.342	2.583	2.747	2.870	2.969	3.051	3.121	3.182
0.90	40	1.852	2.283	2.514	2.669	2.785	2.878	2.954	3.019	3.076
0.95	20	2.453	2.872	3.101	3.258	3.377	3.472	3.551	3.619	3.679
0.95	40	2.386	2.786	3.003	3.150	3.260	3.349	3.422	3.484	3.539

TABLE 10.12
Values of h_2 for the procedure of Sec. 10.4.2
For $m = 1$, use Table 10.11

m	$k = 3$	$k = 4$	$k = 5$	$k = 6$	$k = 7$	$k = 8$	$k = 9$	$k = 10$
				$P^* = 0.90$, $n_0 = 20$				
2	1.137	1.601	1.860	2.039	2.174	2.282	2.373	2.450
3		0.782	1.243	1.507	1.690	1.830	1.943	2.038
4			0.556	1.012	1.276	1.461	1.603	1.718
5				0.392	0.843	1.105	1.291	1.434
6					0.265	0.711	0.971	1.156
7						0.162	0.603	0.861
8							0.075	0.512
9								†
				$P^* = 0.90$, $n_0 = 40$				
2	1.114	1.570	1.825	1.999	2.131	2.237	2.324	2.399
3		0.763	1.219	1.479	1.660	1.798	1.909	2.002
4			0.541	0.991	1.251	1.434	1.575	1.688
5				0.381	0.824	1.083	1.266	1.408
6					0.257	0.693	0.950	1.133
7						0.156	0.587	0.841
8							0.072	0.497
9								†

(continued)

TABLE 10.12 *(continued)*

m	$k = 3$	$k = 4$	$k = 5$	$k = 6$	$k = 7$	$k = 8$	$k = 9$	$k = 10$
				$P^* = 0.95, n_0 = 20$				
2	1.631	2.071	2.321	2.494	2.625	2.731	2.819	2.894
3		1.256	1.697	1.952	2.131	2.267	2.378	2.470
4			1.021	1.458	1.714	1.894	2.033	2.146
5				0.852	1.284	1.539	1.720	1.860
6					0.721	1.149	1.402	1.583
7						0.615	1.038	1.290
8							0.526	0.945
9								0.449
				$P^* = 0.95, n_0 = 40$				
2	1.591	2.023	2.267	2.435	2.563	2.665	2.750	2.823
3		1.222	1.656	1.907	2.082	2.217	2.325	2.415
4			0.990	1.420	1.672	1.850	1.987	2.098
5				0.824	1.248	1.499	1.678	1.816
6					0.695	1.114	1.363	1.541
7						0.591	1.004	1.252
8							0.505	0.913
9								0.430

† Recall that for this selection problem we must have $P^* > m/k$. [If $P^* = 0.90$, $m = 9$, and $k = 10$, we can obtain $P(\text{CS}) = P^*$ by selecting nine systems at random, without any data collection at all.]

PROBLEMS

10.1. In Examples 10.1 and 10.2, what if the bank *did* want to count the service times, in addition to the delays in queue? That is, suppose that the performance measure is the expected average total time in system of the first 100 customers, instead of the expected average delay in queue. What is the "best" system in this case? Which criterion do you think is more appropriate? Discuss.

10.2. Consider the two systems of Example 10.1, with the same initial conditions and performance measures given there; let $\zeta = d_Z(100) - d_K(100)$.

(*a*) Make $n_1 = n_2 = 5$ independent replications of each system and construct an approximate 90 percent confidence interval for ζ. (Perform the simulations for the two systems independently of each other.) Use the paired-t approach.

(*b*) Make $n_1 = 5$ replications of the Zippytel system and $n_2 = 10$ replications of the Klunkytel system, and construct an approximate 90 percent confidence interval for ζ. (Again make the runs of the two systems independently.)

(*c*) Use the $\mathcal{DD}$ procedure of Sec. 10.4.1 to select the best of the $k = 2$ systems. Let $n_0 = 20$, $P^* = 0.90$, and $d^* = 0.4$.

10.3. For the time-shared computer model of Sec. 2.5, suppose that the company is considering a change in the service quantum length q in an effort to reduce the *steady-state*

mean response time of a job; the values for q under consideration are 0.05, 0.10, 0.20, and 0.40. Assume that there are $n = 35$ terminals and that the other parameters and initial conditions are the same as those in Sec. 2.5. To obtain IID observations with expectation approximately equal to the steady-state mean response time of a job, it is felt that warming up the models for 50 response times is adequate, after which the next 640 response times are averaged to obtain a basic X_{ij} observation; independent replications of these 690 response times are then made as needed. Use an appropriate selection procedure from Secs. 10.4.1 and 10.4.2 (other than the $\mathcal{NM}$ procedure) with $n_0 = 20$, $P^* = 0.90$, and $d^* = 0.7$ to solve each of the following problems.
(*a*) Select the best of the four values for q.
(*b*) Select two values of q, one of which is the best.

10.4. For the job-shop model of Sec. 2.7, we can now carry out a better analysis for the question of deciding which workstation should be given an additional machine. (See Sec. 2.7.3 and note from Fig. 2.46 that, on the basis of a single replication of the existing system, workstations 1, 2, and 4 appear to be the three most congested stations.) Use the $\mathcal{DD}$ procedure of Sec. 10.4.1 to recommend whether a machine should be added to station 1, 2, or 4, assuming that these are the only three possibilities; let $n_0 = 20$, $P^* = 0.90$, and $d^* = 1$. Use the *steady-state* expected overall average job total delay as the measure of performance; to obtain the X_{ij} observations, warm up the model for 10 eight-hour days and use the data from the next 90 days, as in Prob. 2.7. Compare your conclusions with those at the end of Sec. 2.7.3. From the moral of Example 10.1, how might this entire study be improved?

10.5. Consider the original time-shared computer model of Sec. 2.5 and the alternative processing policy described in Prob. 2.18, both with $n = 35$ terminals. Use the $\mathcal{DD}$ procedure of Sec. 10.4.1 with $n_0 = 20$ to recommend which processing policy results in the smallest steady-state mean response time of a job. To obtain the X_{ij}'s here, warm up the model for 50 response times, then use the average of the next 640 response times, and replicate as needed. Choose your own P^* and d^*, perhaps based on cost considerations, or your own feeling about what constitutes an "important" difference in mean response time.

10.6. For the manufacturing shop of Prob. 1.22, use the selection procedure of Sec. 10.4.2 to choose three out of the five values of s (the number of repairmen), one of which results in the smallest expected average cost per hour. Use $n_0 = 20$, $P^* = 0.90$, and $d^* = 5$.

10.7. For the four alternatives of Prob. 10.3, construct confidence intervals for all comparisons with the current ($q = 0.10$) system, using an overall confidence level of 90 percent. Make as many replications as you think are needed to get meaningful results.

10.8. For the manufacturing shop of Probs. 1.22 and 10.6, form confidence intervals for all pairwise differences of the expected average costs per hour for the five values of s; use an overall confidence level of 0.90. Replicate as needed to get meaningful results.

10.9. For Example 10.5 the mean inspection time was reduced by only 10 percent. How, then, could the steady-state mean time in system be reduced by 38 percent?

10.10. In Example 10.3, the difference between μ_1 and μ_2 was statistically significant, but in Example 10.7 it was not. Why are the outcomes different?

10.11. Show that sphericity implies that $\text{Var}(X_{ij} - X_{lj}) = 2\tau^2$ for $i \neq l$ (see Sec. 10.4.1).

10.12. Consider the $\mathcal{NM}$ procedure of Sec. 10.4.1. Assume that $X_{1j}, X_{2j}, \ldots, X_{kj}$ (for $j = 1, 2, \ldots, n_0$) has a multivariate normal distribution with covariance matrix Σ, which has the property of sphericity. Then it can be shown [see Lemma 2 in Nelson and Matejcik (1995)] that S^2 is distributed as $2\tau^2\chi^2_{(k-1)(n_0-1)}/[(k-1)(n_0-1)]$, where χ^2_ν is a chi-square random variable with ν degrees of freedom. Under these assumptions, show that S^2 is an unbiased estimator of $\text{Var}(X_{ij} - X_{lj}) = 2\tau^2$.

CHAPTER 11

Variance-Reduction Techniques

Recommended sections for a first reading: 11.1, 11.2

11.1 INTRODUCTION

One of the points we have tried to emphasize throughout this book is that simulations driven by random inputs will produce random output. Thus, appropriate statistical techniques applied to simulation output data are imperative if the results are to be properly analyzed, interpreted, and used (see Chaps. 9, 10, and 12). Since large-scale simulations may require great amounts of computer time and storage, appropriate statistical analyses (possibly requiring multiple replications of the model, for example) can become quite costly. Sometimes the cost of even a modest statistical analysis of the output can be so high that the precision of the results, perhaps measured by confidence-interval width, will be unacceptably poor. The analyst should therefore try to use any means possible to increase the simulation's efficiency.

Of course, "efficiency" mandates careful programming to expedite execution and minimize storage requirements. In this chapter, however, we focus on *statistical* efficiency, as measured by the *variances* of the output random variables from a simulation. If we can somehow reduce the variance of an output random variable of interest (such as average delay in queue or average cost per month in an inventory system) without disturbing its expectation, we can obtain greater precision, e.g., smaller confidence intervals, for the same amount of simulating, or, alternatively, achieve a desired precision with less simulating. Sometimes such a *variance-reduction technique* (VRT), properly applied, can make the difference between an impossibly expensive simulation project and a frugal, useful one.

As we shall see, the method of applying VRTs usually depends on the particular model (or models) of interest. Therefore, a thorough understanding of the workings of the model(s) is required for proper use of VRTs. Furthermore, it is generally impossible to know beforehand how great a variance reduction might be realized, or (worse) whether the variance will be reduced at all in comparison with straightforward simulation. However, preliminary runs could be made (if affordable) to compare the results of applying a VRT with those from straightforward simulation. Finally, some VRTs themselves will increase computing cost, and this decrease in computational efficiency must be traded off against the potential gain in statistical efficiency [see Glynn and Whitt (1992a) and Prob. 11.1]. Almost all VRTs require *some* extra effort on the part of the analyst (if only to understand the technique) and this, as always, must be considered.

VRTs were developed originally in the early days of computers, to be applied in Monte Carlo simulations or distribution sampling [see Sec. 13.5, as well as Hammersley and Handscomb (1964) and Morgan (1984, chap. 7)]. However, many of these original VRTs have been found not to be directly applicable to simulations of complex dynamic systems.

In the remainder of this chapter we will discuss in some detail five general types of VRTs that would appear to have the most promise of successful application to a wide variety of simulations. We refer the reader to Kleijnen (1974), Morgan (1984, chap. 7), and Bratley, Fox, and Schrage (1987, chap. 2) for detailed discussions of other VRTs, such as stratified sampling and importance sampling (see also Sec. 11.6). There is a very large literature on VRTs, and we do not attempt an exhaustive treatment here. Fortunately, there are several comprehensive surveys that provide useful ways of classifying VRTs and also contain extensive bibliographies; Wilson (1984), Nelson (1985, 1986, 1987a, 1987c), L'Ecuyer (1994a), and Kleijnen (1998, sec. 6.3.5 and app. 6.2) are particularly recommended to the reader interested in going further with this subject. In addition, special issues of the journals *Management Science* (Volume 35, Number 11, November 1989, edited by G. S. Fishman) and the *Association for Computing Machinery (ACM) Transactions on Modeling and Computer Simulation* (Volume 3, Number 3, July 1993, edited by P. Glasserman and P. Heidelberger), were devoted to research on VRTs. While our discussion will focus on the different VRTs by themselves, it is possible to use them together; see Kwon and Tew (1994), Avramidis and Wilson (1996), and Yang and Liou (1996).

11.2 COMMON RANDOM NUMBERS

The first VRT we consider, *common random numbers* (CRN), is actually different from the others in that it applies when we are comparing two or more alternative system configurations (see Chap. 10) instead of investigating a single configuration. Despite its simplicity, CRN is the most useful and popular VRT of all. In fact, as mentioned at the end of Sec. 10.2.3, the default setup in most simulation packages is that the same random-number streams and seeds (see Sec. 7.2) are used unless specified otherwise. Thus, by default, the two configurations would actually use the same random numbers, though not necessarily properly synchronized (see Sec. 11.2.3), which is critical for the success of CRN.

11.2.1 Rationale

The basic idea is that we should compare the alternative configurations "under similar experimental conditions" so that we can be more confident that any observed differences in performance are due to differences in the system configurations rather than to fluctuations of the "experimental conditions." In simulation, these "experimental conditions" are the generated random variates that are used to drive the models through simulated time. In queueing simulations, for instance, these would include interarrival times and service times of customers; in inventory simulations we might include interdemand times and demand sizes. The name of this technique stems from the possibility in many situations of using the *same* basic U(0, 1) random numbers (see Chap. 7) to drive each of the alternative configurations through time. As we shall see later in this section, however, certain programming techniques are often needed to facilitate proper implementation of CRN. In the terminology of classical experimental design, CRN is a form of *blocking*, i.e., "comparing like with like." CRN has also been called *correlated sampling*.

To see the rationale for CRN more clearly, consider the case of *two* alternative configurations, as in Sec. 10.2, where X_{1j} and X_{2j} are the observations from the first and second configurations on the jth independent replication, and we want to estimate $\zeta = \mu_1 - \mu_2 = E(X_{1j}) - E(X_{2j})$. If we make n replications of each system and let $Z_j = X_{1j} - X_{2j}$ for $j = 1, 2, \ldots, n$, then $E(Z_j) = \zeta$ so

$$\bar{Z}(n) = \frac{\sum_{j=1}^{n} Z_j}{n}$$

is an unbiased estimator of ζ. Since the Z_j's are IID random variables,

$$\text{Var}[\bar{Z}(n)] = \frac{\text{Var}(Z_j)}{n} = \frac{\text{Var}(X_{1j}) + \text{Var}(X_{2j}) - 2\,\text{Cov}(X_{1j}, X_{2j})}{n}$$

[see Eq. (4.5) and Prob. 4.13]. If the simulations of the two different configurations are done independently, i.e., with different random numbers, X_{1j} and X_{2j} will be independent, so that $\text{Cov}(X_{1j}, X_{2j}) = 0$. On the other hand, if we could somehow do the simulations of configurations 1 and 2 so that X_{1j} and X_{2j} are *positively* correlated, then $\text{Cov}(X_{1j}, X_{2j}) > 0$, so that the variance of our estimator $\bar{Z}(n)$ is reduced. Thus, when $\bar{Z}(n)$ is observed in a particular simulation experiment, its value should be closer to ζ. CRN is a technique where we try to induce this positive correlation by using (carefully, as discussed in Sec. 11.2.3 below) the *same* random numbers to simulate both configurations. (This does not change the probability distributions of X_{1j} and X_{2j} and, in particular, their means and variances.) What makes this possible is the deterministic, reproducible nature of random-number generators (see Sec. 7.1); irreproducible gimmicks such as seeding the random-number generator by the square root of the computer's clock value would generally preclude the use of CRN as well as many other valuable VRTs.

11.2.2 Applicability

Unfortunately, there is no completely general proof that CRN "works," i.e., that it will always reduce the variance. Even if it does work, we usually will not know beforehand how great a reduction in variance we might experience. The efficacy of CRN depends wholly on the particular models being compared, and its use presupposes the analyst's (perhaps implicit) belief that the different models will respond "similarly" to large or small values of the random variates driving the models. For example, we would expect that smaller interarrival times for several designs of a queueing facility would result in longer delays and queues for *each* system.

There are, however, some classes of models for which CRN's success *is* guaranteed. Heidelberger and Iglehart (1979) showed this for certain types of regenerative simulations, and Bratley, Fox, and Schrage (1987, chap. 2) derive results indicating conditions under which CRN will work. See also Gal, Rubinstein, and Ziv (1984), Rubinstein, Samorodnitsky, and Shaked (1985), and Glasserman and Yao (1992) for additional results of this type.

Figure 11.1 schematically illustrates the concept in principle, where the horizontal axis shows possible values of a *particular* U_k used for a *particular* purpose in both of the simulations; for instance, this U_k might be used to generate a service time. The curves indicate how the results of the simulations might react, all other things being equal, to possible values of this U_k. In either of the two situations in the top row of plots, both X_{1j} and X_{2j} react monotonically in the same direction to U_k, and we would expect CRN to induce the desired positive correlation, and thus reduce the variance. In the bottom two plots, however, X_{1j} and X_{2j} react in opposite directions to U_k, so CRN could induce negative correlation and thus "backfire," leading to $\text{Cov}(X_{1j}, X_{2j}) < 0$ and an actual *increase* in the variance. Problem 11.2 considers a specific instance of this issue.

Usually, random numbers are first used to generate variates from other distributions (see Chap. 8), which are then used to drive the simulation models. In order to give CRN the best chance of working, we should thus try first to ensure that the generated variates themselves react monotonically to the U_k's in this intermediate variate-generation step; we then must assume that the measures of performance react monotonically to the generated variates. For this reason, the inverse-transform method of variate generation (Sec. 8.2.1) is recommended, since it guarantees monotonicity of the generated input variates to the random numbers; it further provides the strongest possible positive correlation among all variate-generation methods [see Bratley et al. (1987, pp. 53–54) or Whitt (1976)]. Since the inverse-transform method can be slow, however, for some distributions (perhaps involving numerical methods to invert the distribution function), its computational inefficiency could offset its statistical efficiency. For this reason,

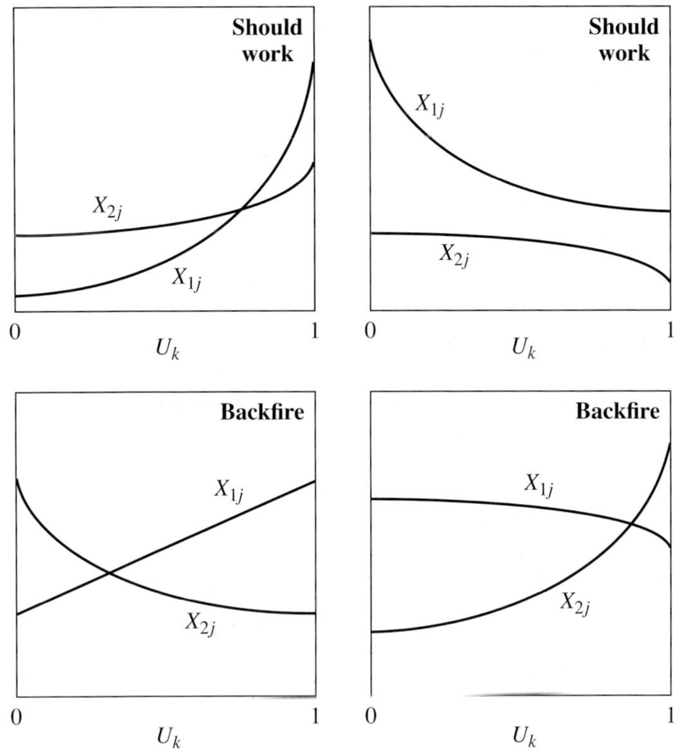

FIGURE 11.1
Model responses for CRN to work (top row) and backfire (bottom row).

Schmeiser and Kachitvichyanukul (1990) developed faster non-inverse-transform methods that still induce positive correlation in the generated variates, as required for CRN to work.

If affordable, a small pilot study could provide a preliminary check on the efficacy of CRN for the alternative configurations. In the case of two configurations, make n replications of each, *using* CRN, to obtain output observations X_{1j} and X_{2j} for $j = 1, 2, \ldots, n$. Let $S_1^2(n)$ and $S_2^2(n)$ be the sample variances [using Eq. (4.4)] of the X_{1j}'s and X_{2j}'s, respectively, and let $S_Z^2(n)$ be the sample variance of the differences, $Z_j = X_{1j} - X_{2j}$; since the runs were made using CRN, $S_Z^2(n)$ is an unbiased estimator of the variance of a Z_j under CRN. Regardless of the fact that we used CRN, $S_1^2(n)$ is unbiased for $\text{Var}(X_{1j})$ and $S_2^2(n)$ is unbiased for $\text{Var}(X_{2j})$, so $S_1^2(n) + S_2^2(n)$ is an unbiased estimator of the variance of a Z_j if we *were* to make the runs without CRN. Thus, if CRN is working, we would expect to observe that $S_Z^2(n) < S_1^2(n) + S_2^2(n)$, and the difference estimates how much CRN is reducing the variance of a Z_j. Of course, any extra programming that might be necessary to implement CRN would have to be done for such a pilot study, whether or not CRN is ultimately adopted. While there are some examples of CRN's backfiring, as observed by Wright and Ramsay (1979) and Koenig and Law (1982) for inventory simulations, we feel that CRN is generally a valuable tool that should be given serious consideration by an analyst faced with the task of comparing two or more alternative configurations.

Another possible drawback to CRN is that formal statistical analyses can be complicated by the induced correlation. Adaptations for standard analysis-of-variance tests in the presence of this correlation are discussed by Heikes, Montgomery, and Rardin (1976) and by Kleijnen (1979). Further issues regarding statistical analysis in the presence of CRN-induced correlation are discussed by Nelson (1987b), who also deals with similar problems created by the antithetic-variates VRT treated in Sec. 11.3. Nozari, Arnold, and Pegden (1987) address the issue of statistical analysis in the general framework of Schruben and Margolin (1978) for correlation induction in simulation experiments, and Tew and Wilson (1992) develop tests for applicability of their methods. Nelson and Hsu (1993) consider CRN with the MCB procedure of Sec. 10.3.3, and Kleijnen (1992) discusses the effect of CRN on regression metamodels of simulations (described in Sec. 12.4). See also the discussion in Sec. 10.4.3 under the heading "Correlation Between Alternatives," relating to CRN in ranking-and-selection procedures.

11.2.3 Synchronization

To implement CRN properly, we must match up, or *synchronize*, the random numbers across the different system configurations on a particular replication. *Ideally*, a specific random number used for a specific purpose in one configuration is used for *exactly the same* purpose in all other configurations. For instance, if a specific U_k is used in the first of two alternative queueing configurations to generate a specific service time, then it should be used in the second configuration to generate the same service time (rather than an interarrival time or some other service time) as well; otherwise, the benefit of CRN could be lost, or (worse) backfiring might occur. In particular, it is generally *not* enough just to start off the simulations of all configurations with the same seed of a random-number stream, which results in all simulations using the same random numbers $U_1, U_2, \ldots$. This is illustrated by the following example.

EXAMPLE 11.1. Recall the two competing designs for the automated teller machine of Examples 10.1 and 10.2. The first configuration (one Zippytel machine) is an $M/M/1$ queue, and the second (two Klunkytels) is an $M/M/2$ queue, both with utilization factor $\rho = 0.9$. The performance measure of interest is the expected average delay in queue for the first 100 customers given that the first customer finds the system empty and idle. Thus, X_{ij} is the average delay in the $M/M/i$ queue on the jth replication, for $i = 1, 2$. In Examples 10.1 and 10.2, we generated X_{1j} and X_{2j} independently for the 100 independent replications, but we could have used CRN.

In an attempt to do so, we used a single random-number stream (see Secs. 2.3 and 7.1) to generate both interarrival and service times, and we simply reset the stream's seed back to its original value before simulating the second configuration. For the

TABLE 11.1
Use of the first five random numbers for the *M/M/1* and *M/M/2* simulations

Random number	Usage in *M/M/1*	Time of usage	Usage in *M/M/2*	Time of usage
U_1	A_1	0	A_1	0
U_2	A_2	A_1	A_2	A_1
U_3	S_1	A_1	S_1	A_1
U_4	A_3	$A_1 + A_2$	A_3	$A_1 + A_2$
U_5	A_4	$A_1 + A_2 + A_3$	S_2	$A_1 + A_2$

M/M/1 case, the program logic of Sec. 1.4 was used. In particular, when a customer arrives, we first generate the time of arrival of the next customer. If the server is idle when a customer arrives, then we generate the customer's service time immediately and schedule the departure event for this customer. On the other hand, if the server is busy, then the arriving customer joins the queue and we do *not* generate his or her service time until the customer enters service, after a delay in queue. The *M/M/2* queue was programmed similarly. To see how the usage of random numbers can get out of synchronization, suppose, e.g., that customers 2 and 3 arrive before customer 1 departs. In Table 11.1 we give the usage of the first five random numbers for the two simulations, as well as the time that these random numbers are used. The random number U_1 is used at time 0 in both simulations to generate A_1, so that the time of the first arrival can be scheduled into the event list. The first customer arrives in both simulations at time A_1, and the random number U_2 is then used to generate A_2 and to schedule the arrival of the second customer. Since there is an idle server in both simulations when the first customer arrives, U_3 is used to generate S_1 and to schedule the time of departure of the first customer. The second customer arrives at time $A_1 + A_2$ (before the first customer departs), at which time U_4 is used to generate A_3. Since there is an idle server when the second customer arrives for the *M/M/2* simulation, U_5 is used at this time to generate S_2. However, in the *M/M/1* simulation, there is no available server when the second customer arrives, and so this customer joins the queue and his or her service time is not generated at this time. The next event in this simulation is the arrival of the third customer at time $A_1 + A_2 + A_3$, at which time U_5 is used to generate A_4. Thus, U_5 is used to generate A_4 and S_2 in the *M/M/1* and *M/M/2* simulations, respectively, and the usage of the random numbers is no longer synchronized.

In Table 11.2 we show how the interarrival times and service times are actually generated from the U_k's. (Recall from Sec. 8.3.2 that an exponential random variate is generated as minus the desired mean times the natural log of a random number.) Note from this table that the correlation between the first service time for the *M/M/1* queue and the first service time for the *M/M/2* queue is a perfect +1 (see Prob. 4.11), which is highly desirable. On the other hand, the correlation between A_4 for the *M/M/1* queue and S_2 for the *M/M/2* queue is also +1. Thus, a large value of U_5 will make A_4 small and tend to make X_{1j} larger for the *M/M/1* queue. On the other hand, a large value of U_5 will make S_2 small and tend to make X_{2j} smaller for the *M/M/2* queue. This is not the intended effect.

Thus, we cannot in general expect CRN to be implemented properly if we merely recycle the same random numbers without paying attention to how they are

TABLE 11.2
Computation of the A_k's and the S_k's for the $M/M/1$ and $M/M/2$ queues

Random number	$M/M/1$ queue	$M/M/2$ queue
U_1	$A_1 = -\ln U_1$	$A_1 = -\ln U_1$
U_2	$A_2 = -\ln U_2$	$A_2 = -\ln U_2$
U_3	$S_1 = -0.9 \ln U_3$	$S_1 = -1.8 \ln U_3$
U_4	$A_3 = -\ln U_4$	$A_3 = -\ln U_4$
U_5	$A_4 = -\ln U_5$	$S_2 = -1.8 \ln U_5$

used. The poor synchronization in Example 11.1 is due in part to the particular way we programmed the simulations. We did not, however, consciously try to destroy the synchronization, but wrote code in a way that seems reasonable and is in fact correct. The issue of coding for correct synchronization is considered below and in Example 11.4, which also illustrates the statistical consequences of ignoring synchronization.

How difficult it is to maintain proper synchronization in general depends entirely on the model structure and parameters, and on the methods used to generate the random variates needed in the simulations. Several programming "tricks" could be considered to maintain synchronization in a given simulation:

- If there are multiple streams of random numbers available (see Secs. 2.3 and 7.1), or if there are several different random-number generators operating simultaneously, we could "dedicate" a stream (or generator) to producing the random numbers for each particular type of input random variate. In a queueing simulation, for instance, one stream could be dedicated to generating the interarrival times, and a different stream could be dedicated to service times. Stream dedication is generally a good idea, and most simulation packages have facility for separate random-number streams. (The number of different streams readily available, however, may not be entirely adequate for large simulations.) Moreover, since streams are usually just adjacent segments of a single random-number generator's output and thus have a particular length, care should be taken to avoid overlapping them when doing long simulations or when replicating intensively. A back-of-the-envelope calculation might indicate roughly how many random numbers will be used from a stream, and appropriate assignments can then be made. For example, in a simple single-server queueing simulation where about 5000 customers are expected to pass through the system, each will need an interarrival time and a service time. If the inverse-transform method (see Sec. 8.2.1) is used to generate all these variates, we would need about 5000 random numbers from each stream; if we were to replicate the simulation 30 times, we would go through some 150,000 random numbers from each stream. If the streams are, say, 100,000 long and we dedicated stream 1 to interarrival times and stream 2 to service times (as usual), we see that the last 50,000 random numbers used for the interarrival times would actually be the same as the first 50,000 used for the service times, destroying the replications' independence:

Stream 1	Stream 2	Stream 3
$U_1 \cdots\cdots U_{100,000}$	$U_{100,001} \cdots\cdots U_{200,000}$	$U_{200,001} \cdots\cdots U_{300,000}$

Interarrival Times

Service Times

The remedy is, of course, to skip some stream assignments: Keep stream 1 (and the first half of stream 2) for the interarrival times, and use, for example, stream 6 (and the first half of stream 7) for the service times.

- The inverse-transform method for generating random variates (see Sec. 8.2.1) can facilitate synchronization since we always need *exactly* one random number to produce each value of the desired random variable. By contrast, the acceptance-rejection method (Sec. 8.2.4), for example, uses a *random* number of U(0, 1) random numbers to produce a single value of the desired random variable. The inverse-transform method, moreover, monotonically transforms the random numbers (see Sec. 11.2.2), and induces the strongest possible positive correlation between the generated variates that then serve as input to the simulations, as discussed in Sec. 8.2.1; this correlation will hopefully propagate through to the simulation output to yield the strongest variance reduction.
- It might be helpful to "waste" some random numbers at certain points in simulating some models. Problem 11.4 gives such an example.
- In some queueing simulations we could generate all of the service requirements of a customer at the time of arrival instead of when the customer actually needs them, and store them as attributes of the customer. Example 11.5 below illustrates this idea for implementing CRN for the alternative job-shop models of Sec. 2.7.3. Also, this approach would have ensured synchronization of the $M/M/1$ vs. $M/M/2$ systems in Example 11.1, preventing the mix-up of random-number usage depicted in Table 11.1. However, this approach could have the practical disadvantage of requiring a lot of computer memory if there are many attributes per entity and the number of concurrent entities in the simulation becomes large. And the difficulty of taking this approach will generally depend on the model's particular logic; for instance, if there is an inspection of entities at some juncture in the model with the possibility of multiple failures and feedback loops, it might not be clear how to pre-generate and store as attributes all of the inspection times that *might* be required for such an entity (see Prob. 11.19).

It is important when using CRN with multiple replications to make sure that the random numbers are synchronized across the different models for replications beyond just the first one, as will be illustrated by the following example.

EXAMPLE 11.2. Consider the inventory model of Sec. 1.5, and suppose we want to compare the results for $(s, S) = (20, 40)$, which we call model 1, vs. $(s, S) = (20, 100)$, which we call model 2. There are three sources of randomness: the times between successive demands, the sizes of those demands, and the delivery lag when an order is placed to the supplier. If we dedicate stream 1 to generating interdemand times, stream 2 to generating demand sizes, and stream 3 to generating delivery lags, we will ensure proper synchronization of all random-number usage across models 1 and 2 in replication 1. Furthermore, due to the nature and logic of this model, we will be using the same *number* of random numbers from stream 1 to generate the interdemand times for both models 1 and 2, and the same *number* of random numbers from stream 2 to generate the demand sizes for both models. However, since the reorder point s is 20 for both models, and the order-up-to level S is only 40 for model 1 but 100 for model 2, the order amounts in model 1 will tend to be considerably smaller than in model 2, so we will be placing more (small) orders in model 1 than in model 2, requiring generation of more delivery lags in model 1 than in model 2. As a result, we will use up more of stream 3 in simulating model 1 than we will use in simulating model 2. So if we begin replication 2 of both models where streams 1, 2, and 3 left off after finishing the first replications of models 1 and 2, we will indeed get proper synchronization across the models for the interdemand times (stream 1) and demand sizes (stream 2), but not for the delivery lags (stream 3); thus, we will not have synchronization for delivery lags across the two models for replication 2 and beyond. One possible remedy is to abandon streams 1, 2, and 3 after the first replication, and start the second replication with (say) streams 4, 5, and 6 for interdemand times, demand sizes, and delivery lags, respectively, then move on to streams 7, 8, and 9 for replication 3, etc. Assuming that we do not use up more than a whole stream for any source of randomness on any replication, and that we have enough random-number streams available to carry out the desired number of replications, this will bring the delivery lags back into proper synchronization for all replications, possibly strengthening the effect of CRN. What is another remedy that requires fewer streams (see Prob. 11.17)? Example 11.7 discusses whether delivery lags *should*, in fact, be the same across the two models.

It might be mentioned that the Arena [Kelton et al. (2010, p. 518)], AutoMod [Banks (2004, p. 367)], and WITNESS [Lanner (2013)] simulation packages have special features for facilitating synchronization beyond the first replication (see Sec. 7.3.2).

Even if one is armed with programming tricks such as those discussed above, it may simply be impossible to attain full synchronization across all configurations under study. Also, the extra programming effort, computation time, or storage requirements needed for full synchronization might not be worth the realized variance reduction. Thus, we might consider synchronizing *some* of the input random variates and generating others independently across the various configurations. For instance, it might be convenient to synchronize interarrival times but not service times in a complicated network of queues. In the final analysis, the benefit of using common random numbers and the degree to which we synchronize depend on the situation.

11.2.4 Some Examples

Since the applicability, power, and appropriate synchronization methods for CRN can be quite model-dependent, we will present several examples of its use in particular situations.

EXAMPLE 11.3. We now rework the $M/M/1$ vs. $M/M/2$ comparison of Example 11.1, but this time we synchronize correctly and present the actual simulation results. Using separate streams to implement CRN, we estimated the effect of various degrees of synchronization in four sequences of 100 pairs of simulations each. In the first sequence,

TABLE 11.3
Statistical results of CRN for the *M/M/1* queue vs. the *M/M/2* queue

	I	A	S	A & S
$S^2(100)$	18.00	9.02	8.80	0.07
90% confidence-interval half-length	0.70	0.49	0.49	0.04
$\hat{p}$	0.52	0.37	0.40	0.03
$\widehat{\text{Cor}}(X_{1j}, X_{2j})$	−0.17	0.33	0.44	0.995

denoted "I" in Table 11.3, all runs were independent; i.e., CRN was not used at all. In the second sequence ("A" in Table 11.3), the interarrival times for the two models were generated using CRN, but we generated the service times independently. For the third sequence ("S"), the interarrival times were independent but the service times were generated using CRN, so both systems experienced the "same" ordered sequence of arriving service demands, with those for the *M/M/2* being exactly twice as great as those for the *M/M/1*. Finally, the fourth sequence ("A & S") was fully synchronized, matching up both interarrival and service times. We can think of these four schemes in physical terms like this:

I	Different customers (in terms of their service requirements) arrive to the two configurations, and at different times.
A	Different customers arrive to the two configurations, but at the same times.
S	The same customers arrive to the two configurations, but at different times.
A & S	The same customers arrive at the same times to both configurations. (The *i*th customer to arrive is the *i*th customer to begin service for both systems, since there is a single queue.)

From the 100 pairs of simulations in each of the four cases we estimated $\text{Var}(Z_j)$ by the usual unbiased variance estimator $S^2(100)$, from Eq. (4.4) applied to the Z_j's. From this, the half-length of a nominal 90 percent confidence interval for ζ is $1.645\sqrt{S^2(100)/100}$. We computed as well the proportion $\hat{p}$ of the 100 pairs for which the "wrong" decision would be made, i.e., when $X_{1j} < X_{2j}$ [since $E(X_{1j}) > E(X_{2j})$, as discussed in Example 10.1]. As a more direct check on whether CRN is inducing the desired positive correlation, we also estimated the correlation between X_{1j} and X_{2j} by

$$\widehat{\text{Cor}}(X_{1j}, X_{2j}) = \frac{\frac{1}{99}\sum_{j=1}^{100}[X_{1j} - \bar{X}_1(100)][X_{2j} - \bar{X}_2(100)]}{\sqrt{S_1^2(100)S_2^2(100)}}$$

where $\bar{X}_i(100)$ is the sample mean of the X_{ij}'s over j, and $S_i^2(100)$ is the sample variance of the X_{ij}'s over j (see Prob. 4.29).

It is clear from Table 11.3 that the estimated variance reduction attained by full synchronization (A & S) compared with independent sampling (I) is quite significant here, being a reduction of over 99 percent, probably since the two systems are quite similar. Accordingly, the confidence-interval half-length fell from 0.70 (I) to 0.04 (A & S), a reduction of almost 95 percent. Looked at another way, we ask how many replications of each system under independent sampling we would need in order to achieve a precision in our estimator $\bar{Z}(n)$ for ζ (perhaps measured by confidence-interval half-length) equal to that from fully synchronized CRN. If we made n_I replications of each system under independent sampling, the half-length would be approximately proportional to $\sqrt{18.00/n_I}$ (ignoring degrees of freedom); on the other hand, if we made n_C replications of each system under completely synchronized CRN, the half-length would be approximately proportional to $\sqrt{0.07/n_C}$. Equating the two square roots, we find that $n_I/n_C = 257.14$; i.e., we would need more than 250 times as many replications under independent sampling to get the same precision we would get with fully synchronized CRN.

The estimated probability of making the wrong decision is reduced from 52 percent to 3 percent (see Example 10.1). Looking at the estimated correlations, we see that fully synchronized CRN induced an extremely strong correlation between the two configurations' output measures, explaining the large reduction in variance. For the two partial synchronization schemes, we experienced weaker (but still positive) correlations, and correspondingly weaker variance reductions and only limited drops in $\hat{p}$.

The effect of CRN (completely synchronized) in this example can be expressed graphically in several ways. In Fig. 11.2*a* are the individual-replication results for the

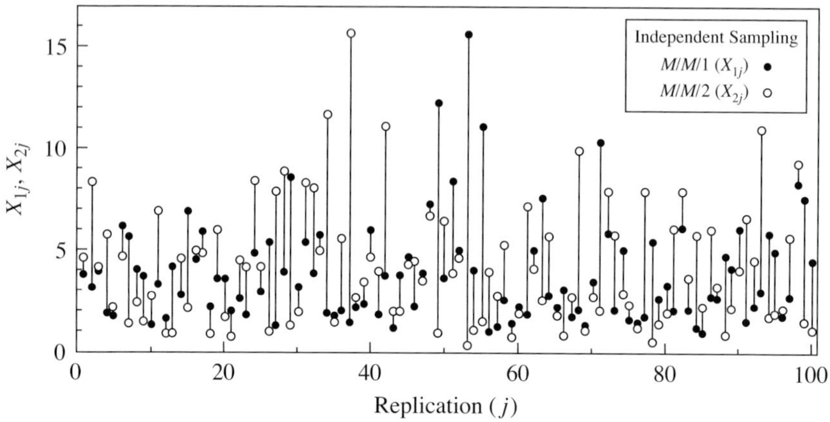

(*a*)

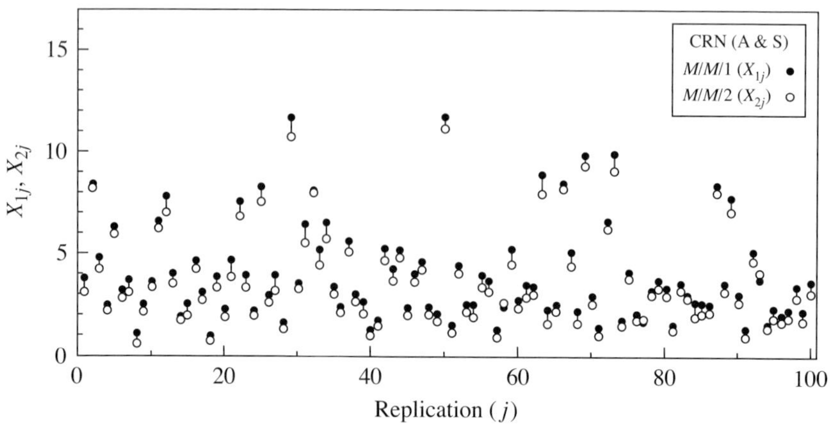

(*b*)

FIGURE 11.2
*M/M/*1 vs. *M/M/*2: individual replications.

100 pairs of runs under independent sampling, versus the replication number. The solid circles are the average delays in queue for the *M/M/*1 model (X_{1j}'s), and the hollow circles are for the *M/M/*2 case (X_{2j}'s); for each fixed j, X_{1j} and X_{2j} are connected by a vertical line, whose length is thus $|Z_j|$. Note in particular that there are 52 pairs for which the hollow circle (*M/M/*2) is at the top of a line and the solid circle (*M/M/*1) is at the bottom, which is the wrong order (in terms of their expectations), and corresponds to $\hat{p} = 0.52$ in the "I" column of Table 11.3. Figure 11.2*b* does likewise, but under completely synchronized CRN. The better-behaved nature of the Z_j's is apparent, with none of the very long vertical lines that appear in Fig. 11.2*a*, and with the line lengths being much more consistent within themselves. This is because the variance of $|X_{1j} - X_{2j}|$ is smaller when there is positive correlation, since a large value of X_{1j} tends to be accompanied by a large value of X_{2j}, and small values of X_{1j} and X_{2j} tend to occur together as well. Moreover, there are only three cases in Fig. 11.2*b* where a line has the *M/M/*2 hollow circle at the top and the *M/M/*1 solid circle at the bottom, corresponding to $\hat{p} = 0.03$ in the "A & S" column of Table 11.3.

A direct way of seeing the correlation that CRN induced in this example is shown in Fig. 11.3, where we plot the pairs (X_{1j}, X_{2j}) for both independent sampling (hollow triangles) and completely synchronized CRN (solid triangles). While there is no apparent pattern in the independent pairs, we note an extremely straight (and positively sloping) alignment of the CRN pairs, corresponding to the very strong positive correlation estimate (0.995) in the "A & S" column of Table 11.3.

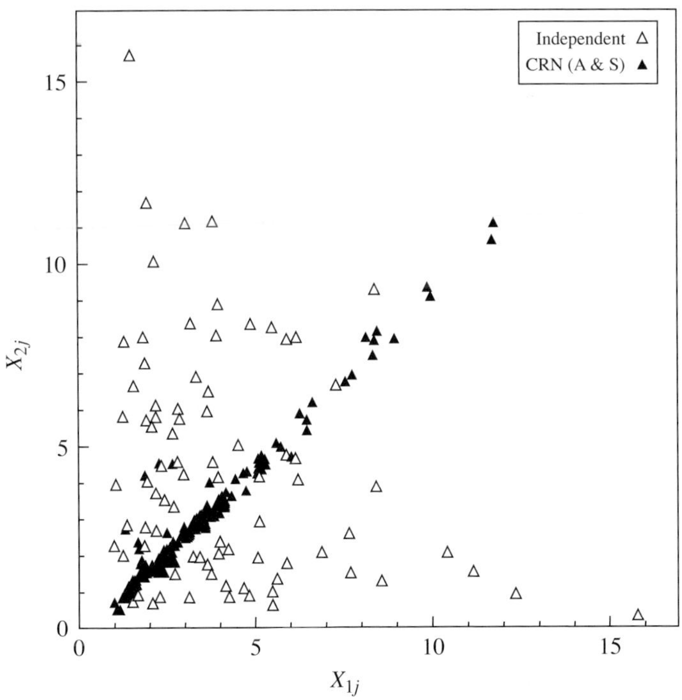

FIGURE 11.3
Correlation plot of *M/M/*2 average delays (vertical axis) vs. *M/M/*1 average delays (horizontal axis).

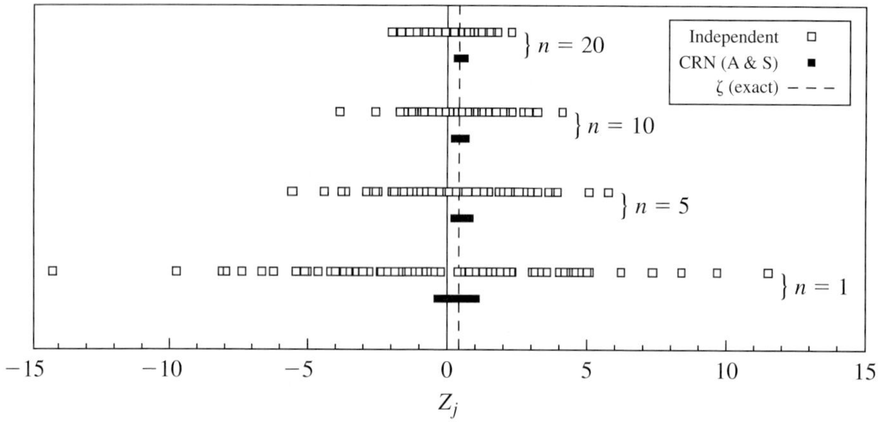

FIGURE 11.4
*M/M/*1 vs. *M/M/*2: differences.

In the "$n = 1$" pair of dot plots at the bottom of Fig. 11.4, each square represents a Z_j, plotted according to the scale shown at the bottom, with the hollow squares being the results of independent sampling, and the solid squares (which run together in the plot) being the results of fully synchronized CRN. The spread of the CRN Z_j's about their expectation (ζ) is much narrower than for the independent-sampling case. We also show in Fig. 11.4 plots of 100 observations on $\bar{Z}(n)$ for $n = 5$, 10, and 20, plotted on the same scale (these correspond to the similar cases in Fig. 10.2 in the case of independent sampling). It is striking to note that we do much better in terms of spread for CRN with $n = 1$ than we do for independent sampling for n as high as 20. Thus, CRN here gave us much better results than we could have gotten by spending more than 20 times as much with independent sampling!

Unlike Example 11.1, we implemented CRN in Example 11.3 with proper synchronization techniques, using separate streams for the two different sources of randomness. The next example illustrates the statistical importance of maintaining proper synchronization.

EXAMPLE 11.4. We reran the experiments of Example 11.3, supposedly using the full "A & S" CRN, except this time we generally ignored synchronization. Our codes are all still "correct," i.e., faithfully simulate the two models, and represent programs that one could actually write, without malice aforethought to disrupt synchronization intentionally. In "Code 1" we generated service requirements upon arrival, and we used the same random-number stream throughout. As it happens, this still results in proper synchronization, as evidenced in Table 11.4. (The numbers differ from the "A & S" column of Table 11.3 since separate streams were used there.) "Code 2" of Table 11.4 uses a single stream but does not generate the service times upon arrival, waiting until a customer enters service to generate the service time; in this case, the random numbers will get mixed up in terms of their usage, as demonstrated in Example 11.1. As seen in Table 11.4, the results are not much better than the "I" case in Table 11.3, since we have lost the benefit (apparently nearly all) of CRN. "Code 3" is the same as Code 2, except that the next interarrival time is generated at the end of the arrival subprogram (see Sec. 1.4), representing yet another valid but nonsynchronized code; again, no benefit is seen.

TABLE 11.4
Statistical results of properly (Code 1) and improperly (Codes 2 and 3) synchronized CRN for the *M/M/*1 queue vs. the *M/M/*2 queue

	Code 1	Code 2	Code 3
$S^2(100)$	0.07	16.80	12.00
90% confidence-interval half-length	0.04	0.67	0.57
$\hat{p}$	0.07	0.43	0.42
$\widehat{\text{Cor}}(X_{1j}, X_{2j})$	0.997	0.02	−0.03

The examples so far in this chapter (except 11.2) have involved the same *M/M/*1 vs. *M/M/*2 configurations. These are very simple systems for which properly synchronized CRN is relatively easy to implement. They are also quite similar to each other, probably accounting for the dramatic variance reductions through CRN that we have seen. The next two examples involve models that are considerably more complicated, and consider as well using CRN for steady-state parameters (see Secs. 9.3 and 9.5).

EXAMPLE 11.5. In the manufacturing-system model of Sec. 2.7, recall the discussion at the end of Sec. 2.7.3. As in the last three rows of Table 2.1, let configurations 1, 2, and 3 be, respectively, the manufacturing system obtained by adding a machine to station 1, 2, and 4; and let ν_i be the *steady-state* expected overall average job total delay in configuration i for $i = 1, 2$, and 3. Suppose that we want to estimate $\zeta_{12} = \nu_1 - \nu_2$, $\zeta_{13} = \nu_1 - \nu_3$, and $\zeta_{23} = \nu_2 - \nu_3$ by making simulations of length 100 eight-hour days of each of the three configurations but using the first 10 of these 100 days as a warmup period and collecting data on only the last 90 days (see Prob. 2.7). Let X_{ij} be the overall average job total delay over these 90 days for configuration i as observed on the jth replication, and let $Z_{12j} = X_{1j} - X_{2j}$, $Z_{13j} = X_{1j} - X_{3j}$, and $Z_{23j} = X_{2j} - X_{3j}$. We assume that the 10-day warmup period is sufficient, so that $E(Z_{i_1 i_2 j}) \approx \zeta_{i_1 i_2}$.

We made the runs of the different configurations completely independent of each other (denoted "I" in Table 11.5 below), and also used CRN across the three configurations, as follows. For each configuration, we used the same interarrival times for the jobs and made the sequence of job types the same. Further, when a job arrived at the system and its type was determined, we immediately generated its service requirements that will be needed later as it moves along its route through the system and stored them as additional attributes of this job. Thus, when a job entered service at a particular station, its service time was taken from its appropriate attribute for this station. In this way, we

TABLE 11.5
CRN for the three manufacturing-system configurations

	I	CRN	Variance reduction (%)
$S_{12}^2(10)$	6.27	1.46	77
$S_{13}^2(10)$	10.40	2.35	77
$S_{23}^2(10)$	23.08	0.87	96

used synchronized CRN for all sources of randomness. Note also that in this example all types of random variates are generated at the same instant in simulated time (when a job arrives), so a *single* random-number stream could have been used for all sources of randomness.

Let $S^2_{i_1 i_2}(10)$ be the usual unbiased estimator of $\text{Var}(Z_{i_1 i_2 j})$, which we computed from 10 independent replications using both independent sampling and CRN, as given in Table 11.5. Here, CRN led to variance reductions ranging from 77 percent to 96 percent, depending on which two configurations are being compared. In terms of the required number of replications to achieve a desired confidence-interval half-width, we can proceed as in Example 11.3 to find that independent sampling would need 4.29 ($= 6.27/1.46$) times as many replications as CRN to compare configurations 1 and 2, 4.43 times as many for configurations 1 and 3, and more than 26 times as many if we are interested in the difference between configurations 2 and 3.

EXAMPLE 11.6. In Example 10.5 we compared two configurations of the manufacturing facility from Example 9.25. In the second configuration, the mean inspection time was smaller. We are again interested in the steady-state mean time in system of parts, so we followed the replication/deletion approach (Sec. 9.5.2) and made moving-average plots for both configurations as in Fig. 10.3. Again letting l_i and m_i be the length (in parts) of the warmup period and the minimum replication length for configuration i, we obtained $m_1 = m_2 = 9445$, $l_1 = 1929$, and $l_2 = 1796$. As in Example 10.5, we made $n = 20$ independent pairs of runs, but we now used separate streams to synchronize the random numbers for all six sources of randomness in this model [interarrival times, machine processing times, inspection times, good/bad decisions, machine operating (up) times, and machine repair (down) times]. Again, we formed a 90 percent confidence interval for the difference between the steady-state mean times in system from these 20 replications, and obtained 1.98 ± 0.18; recall that in Example 10.5 the corresponding interval was 2.36 ± 0.31, from 20 replications of each configuration that were close to the same length and from which close to the same amount of initial data were deleted. Thus, CRN reduced the size of the confidence interval on the difference between the performance measures by 42 percent of its original size, corresponding to an estimated variance reduction of 66 percent. As more direct evidence that CRN is working properly, we estimated the correlation (see Example 11.3) between X_{1j} and X_{2j} to be 0.98.

The next pair of examples of CRN involves an inventory model, for which complete synchronization of all sources of randomness is of debatable correctness; thus, we generated some inputs using properly synchronized CRN and others independently.

EXAMPLE 11.7. For the inventory model (defined in Sec. 1.5) that we considered in Example 10.3, recall that (s, S) was (20, 40) for configuration 1, and was (20, 80) for configuration 2. For each configuration we can arrange for demands of the same size to occur at the same times; i.e., we use CRN (via separate streams) for the demand-size and interdemand-time sources of randomness. Due to the different values of S, however, orders will generally be placed at different times and for different amounts for the two policies, and so the number of orders placed will also differ under the two policies. Thus, it is not clear how we could reasonably match up the delivery-lag random variates (or whether it even makes sense to match them up), so we just generated them independently across the configurations. (In Example 11.2 we attempted to synchronize the delivery lags to illustrate how the random numbers could get out of synchronization on replications 2, 3 . . . .)

As in Example 10.3, we made $n = 5$ independent pairs of simulations, but here with (partial) CRN as just described. We obtained $\bar{Z}(5) = 3.95$ and $\widehat{\text{Var}}[\bar{Z}(5)] = 0.27$, so that the paired-$t$ 90 percent confidence interval is [2.84, 5.06]. Comparing this with the independent-sampling results of Example 10.3, the estimated variance is reduced by about 89 percent, and the confidence-interval half-length is some 67 percent smaller. Thus, it would take about 45 replications of each system under independent sampling to get a confidence interval as small as the one we got from partial CRN with only 5 replications of each.

The following example illustrates how the multiple confidence-interval methods described in Sec. 10.3 can be sharpened with CRN.

EXAMPLE 11.8. Consider now the five different policy configurations defined in Table 10.4. As in Example 10.7, we first regard policy 1, where $(s, S) = (20, 40)$, as the standard against which the other four are to be compared. We reran the analysis of Example 10.7, again with $n = 5$ replications of each policy configuration, but now using the partial CRN sampling plan described in Example 11.7, across all five policies. Desiring overall confidence of at least 90 percent, we used the Bonferroni inequality (see Sec. 10.3) to form four individual 97.5 percent confidence intervals for $\mu_i - \mu_1$, exactly as described in Example 10.7; here, however, CRN implies that the results on a given replication (j) across the five policies are not independent, precluding use of the Welch approach to confidence-interval formation. Thus, Table 11.6 contains only the paired-t intervals corresponding to Table 10.6. The half-lengths obtained here are all quite a bit smaller than those in Table 10.6. Moreover, comparing the paired-t approaches only, CRN enabled us to identify one more statistically significant difference (between policy 2 and the standard) than we were able to in Example 10.7.

We can also effect the all-pairwise-comparisons analysis of Sec. 10.3.2 using CRN; this was done with independent sampling in Example 10.8, with the results given in Table 10.7. Since there are now 10 individual confidence intervals, we make each at level 99 percent to attain overall confidence of at least 90 percent. The intervals resulting from CRN (again, only the paired-t approach is valid) in Table 11.7 indicate once again that CRN markedly reduced confidence-interval length in all cases except one ($i_2 = 5, i_1 = 2$). In this case the paired-t interval under independent sampling (22.12 ± 3.80) from Table 10.7 is smaller than the CRN interval (23.64 ± 5.02) from Table 11.7. Looking back at Table 10.7, the interval in this case was the smallest one observed, possibly due to simple sampling fluctuation, and at any rate the difference is significant both there and here. Perhaps more important, we see in Table 11.7 that 8 of the 10 CRN-based intervals miss zero (indicating a statistically significant difference between the

TABLE 11.6
Individual 97.5 percent confidence intervals for all comparisons with the standard policy ($\mu_i - \mu_1, i = 2, 3, 4, 5$) using CRN; * denotes a significant difference

		Paired-t	
i	$\bar{X}_i - \bar{X}_1$	Half-length	Interval
2	−3.95	1.83	(−5.78, −2.12)*
3	1.02	2.65	(−1.63, 3.68)
4	5.94	1.41	(4.53, 7.35)*
5	19.69	2.28	(17.41, 21.97)*

TABLE 11.7

Individual 99 percent confidence intervals for all pairwise comparisons ($\mu_{i_2} - \mu_{i_1}$ for $i_1 < i_2$) using CRN; * denotes a significant difference

		Paired-*t*			
		i_2			
		2	3	4	5
i_1	1	−3.95 ± 2.41*	1.02 ± 3.49	5.94 ± 1.86*	19.69 ± 3.00*
	2		4.97 ± 5.62	9.89 ± 3.68*	23.64 ± 5.02*
	3			4.92 ± 2.39*	18.67 ± 1.69*
	4				13.75 ± 2.03*

corresponding configurations), whereas only 6 or 7 of the 10 in Table 10.7 (depending on the approach) missed zero. Thus, with no more sampling we were able to sharpen our comparisons among these policies.

EXAMPLE 11.9. Consider again the problem of comparing the original and proposed routing policies for the communications network of Example 10.6. We once again made five independent replications of each policy of length $m = 65$ seconds and used a warmup period of length $l = 5$ seconds, but now partial CRN was used across the two policies. For each configuration, we generated outgoing messages for a particular SP at the same times, and with the messages having the same sizes and destinations. However, when each of two links had to be chosen with a probability of 0.5, we used different random numbers for the two configurations. We used (10.1) to obtain [0.05, 0.12] (in millisecond) as an approximate 90 percent confidence interval for $\nu_1 - \nu_2$. Since the confidence interval does not contain 0, the difference in the two steady-state means *is* statistically significant, whereas it was not in Example 10.6. Furthermore, the sample variance of the Z_j's has been reduced by about 97 percent, the confidence-interval half-length is some 83 percent smaller, and the estimated correlation (see Example 11.3) between X_{1j} and X_{2j} is 0.94.

In summary, we have found that we could realize at least partial synchronization across the different system configurations in many real-world simulation studies that we have performed.

11.3 ANTITHETIC VARIATES

Antithetic variates (AV) is a VRT that is applicable to simulating a *single* system, as are the rest of the VRTs in this chapter. As in CRN, we try to induce correlation between separate runs, but now we seek *negative* correlation.

The central idea, dating back at least to Hammersley and Morton (1956) in the context of Monte Carlo simulation, is to make *pairs* of runs of the model such that a "small" observation on one of the runs in a pair tends to be offset by a "large" observation on the other one; i.e., the two observations are negatively correlated. Then if we use the *average* of the two observations in the pair as a basic data point for analysis, it will tend to be closer to the common expectation μ of an observation (which we want to estimate) than it would be if the two observations in the pair were independent.

In its simplest form, AV tries to induce this negative correlation by using *complementary* random numbers to drive the two runs in a pair. That is, if U_k is a particular random number used *for a particular purpose* (e.g., to generate the ith service time) in the first run, we use $1 - U_k$ *for this same purpose* in the second run. It is valid to use $1 - U_k$ instead of simply a direct draw from the random-number generator, since $U \sim U(0, 1)$ implies that $1 - U \sim U(0, 1)$ as well.

An important point is that the use of a U_k in one replication and its complement $1 - U_k$ in the paired replication must be synchronized, i.e., used for the same purpose; the benefit of AV could otherwise be lost, or it could even backfire. For instance, if U_k happens to be large and is used via the (literal) inverse-transform method to generate a service time, this would result in a large service time and have the effect of increasing the queue's congestion in the first run of the pair. In this case, $1 - U_k$ would be small, so if it were used erroneously to generate an interarrival time in the second run, this interarrival time would be small and would increase congestion on that run as well, which is the opposite of the intended effect. Most of the programming tricks mentioned in Sec. 11.2 for synchronizing random numbers, such as random-number stream dedication, using the inverse-transform method of variate generation wherever possible, judicious wasting of random numbers, pre-generation, and advancing the stream numbers across multiple replications, can be used here as well. Moreover, we could consider "partial" AV, generating some inputs antithetically and others independently within a pair if full synchronization proves too difficult or there does not seem to be a sensible way to use AV for all inputs (see Example 11.12 below). To be sure, then, it is *not* enough just to go through the simulation code and replace each "U" with a "$1 - U$."

As with CRN, there is a mathematical basis for AV. Suppose that we make *n pairs* of runs of the simulation resulting in observations $(X_1^{(1)}, X_1^{(2)}), \ldots, (X_n^{(1)}, X_n^{(2)})$, where $X_j^{(1)}$ is from the first run (using just the "U"s) of the jth pair, and $X_j^{(2)}$ is from the antithetic run (using the "$1 - U$"s, properly synchronized) of the jth pair. Both $X_j^{(1)}$ and $X_j^{(2)}$ are legitimate observations of the simulation model, so that $E(X_j^{(1)}) = E(X_j^{(2)}) = \mu$. Also, each pair is independent of every other pair; i.e., for $j_1 \neq j_2$, $X_{j_1}^{(l_1)}$ and $X_{j_2}^{(l_2)}$ are independent, regardless of whether l_1 and l_2 are equal. (Note that the total number of replications is thus $2n$.) For $j = 1, 2, \ldots, n$, let $X_j = (X_j^{(1)} + X_j^{(2)})/2$, and let the average of the X_j's, $\overline{X}(n)$, be the (unbiased) point estimator of $\mu = E(X_j^{(l)}) = E(X_j) = E[\overline{X}(n)]$. Then since the X_j's are IID,

$$\text{Var}[\overline{X}(n)] = \frac{\text{Var}(X_j)}{n} = \frac{\text{Var}(X_j^{(1)}) + \text{Var}(X_j^{(2)}) + 2\,\text{Cov}(X_j^{(1)}, X_j^{(2)})}{4n}$$

If the two runs within a pair were made independently, then $\text{Cov}(X_j^{(1)}, X_j^{(2)}) = 0$. On the other hand, if we could indeed induce negative correlation between $X_j^{(1)}$ and $X_j^{(2)}$, then $\text{Cov}(X_j^{(1)}, X_j^{(2)}) < 0$, which reduces $\text{Var}[\overline{X}(n)]$; this is the goal of AV.

Yet another feature that AV shares with CRN is that we cannot be completely sure that it will work, and its feasibility and efficacy are perhaps even more model-dependent than for CRN. In some cases, however, AV has been shown analytically to lead to variance reductions, although the magnitude of the reduction is not known; see Andréasson (1972), George (1977), Hammersley and Handscomb (1964), Mitchell (1973), Wilson (1979), Rubinstein, Samorodnitsky, and Shaked (1985), and Bratley, Fox, and Schrage (1987, chap. 2). In general, we cannot know beforehand how great a variance reduction might be achieved. A pilot study like that described for CRN might be useful to assess whether AV is a good idea in a specific case.

The fundamental requirement that a model should satisfy for AV to work is that its response to a random number used for a particular purpose be monotonic, in either direction. In most queueing-type models, for instance, a large random number used to generate a service time (via the literal inverse-transform method) will produce a large service time and lead to increased congestion; thus, we would expect that the response of congestion measures to random numbers used to generate service times would be monotonically increasing. Backfiring of AV could occur, for example, if a model's response were large for small U_k's, smaller for U_k's near 0.5, and then rose again for large U_k's (see Prob. 11.3). We urge the analyst to provide some kind of evidence that AV *will* work, either by arguing from "physical" properties of the model's structure or by initial experimentation. As with CRN, the inverse-transform method of generating a model's input variates is suggested in order to promote the required monotonicity by ensuring it at least in this intermediate variate-generation step. Franta (1975) gives examples of the failure of AV if other methods are used, but Schmeiser and Kachitvichyanukul (1990) develop fast non-inverse-transform methods that *do* lead to the desired negative correlation at this intermediate level.

EXAMPLE 11.10. Consider the $M/M/1$ queue with $\rho = 0.9$, as in Examples 11.1, 11.3, and 11.4, so that now an "observation" $X_j^{(l)}$ is the average of 100 customer delays. From the model's structure it seems reasonable to assume that large interarrival times would tend to make $X_j^{(l)}$ smaller (and vice versa), and large service times would generally result in a larger $X_j^{(l)}$. Further, if we use the method of Sec. 8.3.2 to generate the exponential interarrival-time and service-time variates, we would expect AV to work. We made $n = 100$ independent pairs of runs using both independent sampling within a pair [so $\text{Cov}(X_j^{(1)}, X_j^{(2)}) = 0$], as well as using AV, synchronizing by dedicating separate random-number streams to generating the interarrival and service times. The results are in Table 11.8, and show that AV reduced the estimated variance $S^2(100)$ of an X_j by 60 percent. If we used the 100 X_j's to form an approximate 90 percent confidence interval for μ, it would have a half-length of 0.36 under independent sampling, which would be reduced to 0.23 under AV, a reduction of 36 percent. That AV is inducing the desired negative correlation is confirmed by noting the estimated correlation of -0.52 between $X_j^{(1)}$ and $X_j^{(2)}$ in the AV case. Note that the extra cost of AV over independent sampling is negligible here, since AV requires almost no extra programming and only

TABLE 11.8
Statistical results for AV in the case of the *M/M/*1 queue

	Independent	AV
$S^2(100)$	4.84	1.94
90% confidence-interval half-length	0.36	0.23
$\widehat{\text{Cor}}(X_j^{(1)}, X_j^{(2)})$	−0.07	−0.52

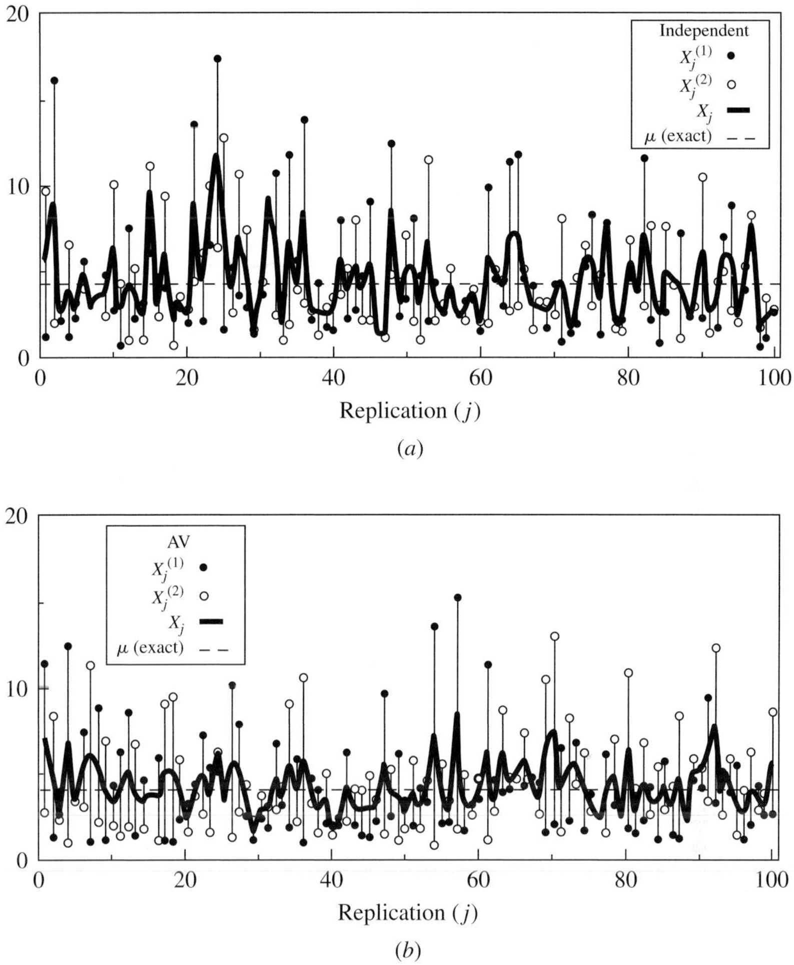

FIGURE 11.5
Individual replications of the *M*/*M*/1 queue: (*a*) independent sampling; (*b*) AV.

the subtraction of the random numbers from 1; both methods required 200 separate simulation runs.

Figure 11.5*a* shows the individual values of the independently sampled $X_j^{(1)}$'s (solid circles) and the $X_j^{(2)}$'s (hollow circles) for each j. The heavy line connects the values of X_j across j. Figure 11.5*b* does likewise, except for the fact that AV was used, and we see that the heavy line appears somewhat less twitchy, indicating the lower variance of the X_j's in the AV case. We can also see in Fig. 11.5*b* that under AV there appears to be a tendency for an $X_j^{(1)}$ on one side of the dashed line (at height μ) to be offset by an $X_j^{(2)}$ on the other side of the line, while this is less so in the independent-sampling plot in Fig. 11.5*a*. The lower variability of the X_j's under AV is confirmed more clearly in Fig. 11.6, where their narrower spread is evident. Finally, Fig. 11.7 gives a correlation plot of the pairs $(X_j^{(1)}, X_j^{(2)})$ under both independent sampling (hollow triangles) and AV (solid triangles). There does appear to be some negative correlation in the AV case, since the solid triangles show some tendency to slope downward.

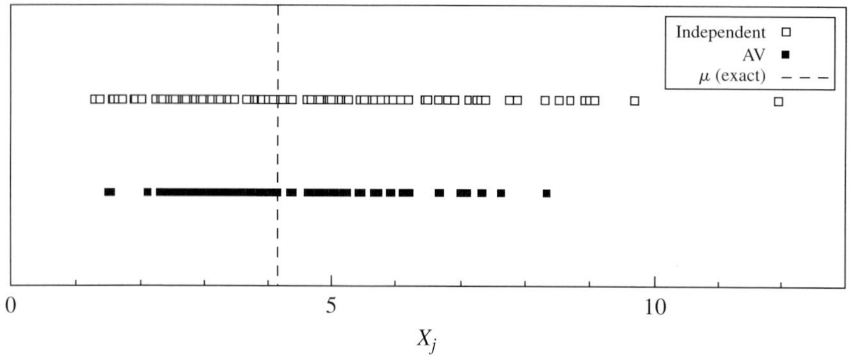

FIGURE 11.6
Within-pair averages for the *M*/*M*/1 queue with independent sampling and AV.

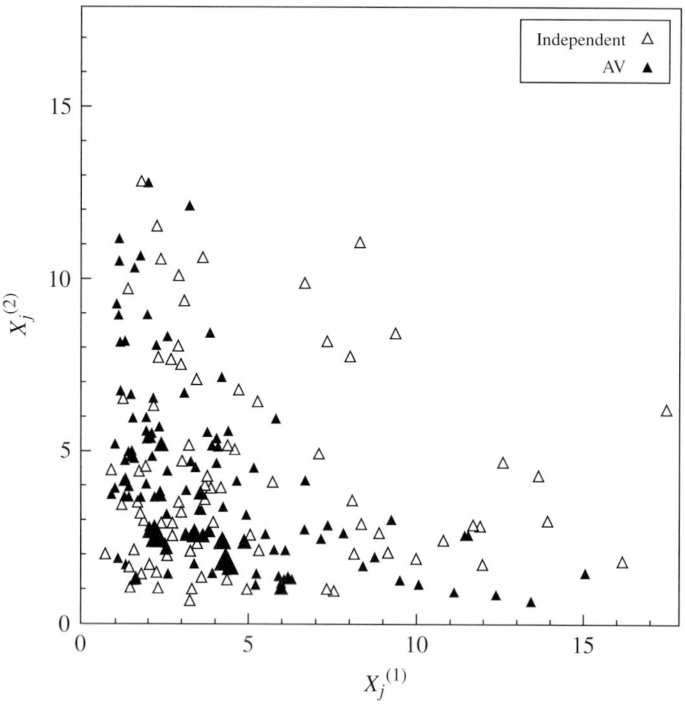

FIGURE 11.7
Correlation plot for pairs of runs of the *M*/*M*/1 queue with independent sampling and AV.

The magnitude of the correlation induced by AV in Example 11.10 was not as strong as we observed in using CRN to compare the *M*/*M*/1 and *M*/*M*/2 queues in Example 11.3, and so the variance reduction from AV was weaker than that obtained via CRN. This is a good illustration of how a VRT's success generally depends on model characteristics. In Example 11.3 the only difference in the input variates to the two configurations (under fully synchronized CRN, called "A & S" there) was that the service times for the *M*/*M*/2 queue were in every case exactly twice those for the *M*/*M*/1 queue, and were thus *linearly* related (see Prob. 4.11). In the AV scheme of Example 11.10, however, the input variates for the first and second runs of a pair were not linearly related, coming basically down to using $\ln U$ vs. $\ln(1 - U)$, where U is a random number, since exponential variate generation was done by taking natural logarithms of random numbers, as described in Sec. 8.3.2. In both the CRN and AV examples, the input variates are then transformed nonlinearly by the simulation model itself. Remembering that covariances and correlations, which figure prominently in the variance-reduction amount for both CRN and AV, measure *linear* relationships only, we see that the greater linearity in the CRN application of Example 11.3 evidently accounts for the stronger variance reduction than that observed in the less linear AV application of Example 11.10.

EXAMPLE 11.11. In the particular case of applying AV to queueing simulations, Page (1965) suggested another type of antithetic sampling that does not involve substituting $1 - U$ for U in the second of a pair of runs. Since performance measures for queueing systems usually react to large interarrival times oppositely from the way they react to large service times, Page suggested that the random numbers used to generate the interarrival times in the first run of a pair be used instead to generate the service times in the second run, and vice versa. Implementing this idea on the *M*/*M*/1 model of Example 11.10, we experienced a variance reduction of 65 percent. This general method of interchanging the use of random numbers might be useful in inducing negative correlation for other types of models as well.

Our last example of AV illustrates its use in a nonqueueing model, and for which only partial synchronization is meaningful.

EXAMPLE 11.12. Although somewhat more work is needed to see a physical rationale for response monotonicity and the potential success of AV (see Prob. 11.5), it can also be applied to the inventory model of Sec. 1.5. Take the case $(s, S) = (20, 40)$, and assume the same parameters and output variables as in Example 11.7. Also as done in Example 11.7, we shall apply AV to only the interdemand times and the demand sizes, and generate the delivery lags independently between the two runs of a pair. Again we made $n = 100$ independent pairs of runs, first making $X_j^{(1)}$ and $X_j^{(2)}$ independent, and obtained 8.55 as an estimate of $\text{Var}(X_j)$, whereas the comparable variance estimate under AV was 3.26, a reduction of some 62 percent. Thus we see that an AV scheme that is only partially synchronized can still yield worthwhile variance reductions.

Due to the similarities between CRN and AV, the idea reasonably comes to mind of using them together when several alternative system configurations are to be compared. At first it would appear that we might obtain stronger variance reductions by using AV for each configuration separately and CRN across the different configurations. However, upon closer examination [see Kleijnen (1974, pp. 207–238), and Prob. 11.11] we find that if both AV and CRN work properly, i.e., induce correlations of the desired sign, certain "cross covariances" (specifically, the covariance between the first run of an antithetic pair of runs for configuration 1 and the second run of the corresponding antithetic pair for configuration 2, and vice versa) enter the relevant variance expression with the *wrong* sign, which might *increase* the variance. Thus, it is by no means clear that combining AV with CRN for comparing alternative system configurations is a good idea. Schruben and Margolin (1978) and Schruben (1979) consider in more generality the issue of random-number assignment in correlation-induction strategies for variance reduction in a variety of simulation experiments.

More general versions of AV have been developed, in terms of both the quantities to be estimated (other than expectations) as well as in the method to induce the desired negative correlation (other than using complementary random numbers); see Cheng (1982, 1984), Fishman and Huang (1983), and Wilson (1983) for specifics. A potential side benefit of AV was noted by Nelson (1990b), who showed that AV (combined with control variates, discussed in Sec. 11.4) can improve both point- and interval-estimator performance when initialization bias is present. Avramidis and Wilson (1998) use AV to improve estimators of quantiles (see Sec. 9.4.2).

11.4 CONTROL VARIATES

Like CRN and AV, the method of *control variates* (CV) attempts to take advantage of correlation between certain random variables to obtain a variance reduction. Depending on the specific type of CV technique used, this correlation might arise naturally during the course of a simulation, or might be induced by using CRN in an auxiliary simulation.

In principle, at least, there is an appealing intuition to CV. Let X be an output random variable, such as the average of the first 100 customer delays in queue, and assume we want to estimate $\mu = E(X)$. Suppose that Y is another random variable involved in the simulation that is thought to be correlated with X (either positively or negatively), and that we *know* the value of $\nu = E(Y)$. For instance, Y could be the average of the service times of the first 99 customers who complete their service in the queueing model mentioned above, so we would know its expectation since we generated the service-time variates from some known input distribution. (Problem 11.12 mentions a subtle issue in this regard concerning the precise definition of Y.) It is reasonable to suspect that larger-than-average service times (i.e., $Y > \nu$) tend to lead to longer-than-average delays ($X > \mu$) and vice versa; i.e., Y is correlated with X, in this case positively. Thus if we run a simulation and notice that $Y > \nu$ (which we can tell for sure since we know ν), we might suspect that X is above its expectation μ as well (although we would not know this for sure unless the correlation between Y and X were perfect), and accordingly adjust X downward by some amount. If it turned out, on the other hand, that $Y < \nu$, we would suspect that $X < \mu$ as well and so adjust it upward instead. In this way, we use our knowledge of Y's expectation to pull X (down or up) toward *its* expectation μ, thus reducing its variability about μ from one run to the next. We call Y a *control variate* for X since it is used to adjust X, or partially "control" it.

Unlike CRN and AV, the success of CV does *not* depend on the correlation being of a particular sign. If Y and X were negatively correlated, which we might imagine if Y were the average of the first 100 generated *interarrival* times in the example of the preceding paragraph (widely separated arrivals tend to produce lower congestion levels), we would simply adjust X *upward* if $Y > \nu$ and *downward* if $Y < \nu$.

To carry out the above idea, we must quantify the amount of the upward or downward adjustment to X. It is convenient to express this amount in terms of the deviation, $Y - \nu$, of Y from its expectation ν. Let a be a constant (to be determined below) that has the same sign as the correlation between Y and X. In the earlier example where X is the average queueing delay and Y is the average service time, a would thus be some positive number. We use a to scale (magnify or shrink) the deviation $Y - \nu$ to arrive at an adjustment to X and thus define the "controlled" estimator

$$X_C = X - a(Y - \nu)$$

Note that if Y and X are positively correlated, so that $a > 0$, we would adjust X downward whenever $Y > \nu$ and upward when $Y < \nu$, as desired; the opposite is true when Y and X are negatively correlated, in which case $a < 0$.

Since $E(X) = \mu$ and $E(Y) = \nu$, it is clear that for any real number a, $E(X_C) = \mu$; that is, X_C is an unbiased estimator of μ that might have lower variance than X. Specifically,

$$\text{Var}(X_C) = \text{Var}(X) + a^2\,\text{Var}(Y) - 2a\,\text{Cov}(X, Y) \tag{11.1}$$

so that X_C is less variable than X if and only if

$$2a\,\text{Cov}(X, Y) > a^2\,\text{Var}(Y)$$

which may or may not be true, depending on the choice of Y and a. In many treatments of CV, only the special cases $a = 1$ [if we think that $\text{Cov}(X, Y) > 0$] or $a = -1$ [if we feel that $\text{Cov}(X, Y) < 0$] are considered, but this requires the more stringent condition that $|\text{Cov}(X, Y)| > \text{Var}(Y)/2$ for a variance reduction to be realized. Thus, simply setting $a = \pm 1$ places the entire burden for success upon the choice of Y; by allowing other values for a we can do better.

To find the "best" value of a for a given Y, we can view the right-hand side of Eq. (11.1) as a function $g(a)$ of a and set its derivative to zero; i.e.,

$$\frac{dg}{da} = 2a\,\text{Var}(Y) - 2\,\text{Cov}(X, Y) = 0$$

and solve for the optimal (variance-minimizing) value

$$a^* = \frac{\text{Cov}(X, Y)}{\text{Var}(Y)} \tag{11.2}$$

[$d^2g/da^2 = 2\,\text{Var}(Y)$, which is of course positive, a sufficient condition for a^* to be a minimizer of $g(a)$, as opposed to a maximizer or an inflection point.] One of the implications of Eq. (11.2) is that if Y is strongly correlated with X, that is, $|\text{Cov}(X, Y)|$ is large, the value of a^* is increased, and so we are willing to make more drastic adjustments to X since we feel more confident about what Y's deviation from ν is telling us about what X's deviation from μ might be. Also, if Y is itself less variable, that is, $\text{Var}(Y)$ is small, we may get a larger value of a^* (and a more drastic adjustment to X) since we have more confidence in the precision of the observed value of Y itself.

Plugging a^* from Eq. (11.2) into the right-hand side of Eq. (11.1), we get that the minimum-variance *adjusted* (or *controlled*) estimator X_C^* over all choices of a has variance

$$\text{Var}(X_C^*) = \text{Var}(X) - \frac{[\text{Cov}(X, Y)]^2}{\text{Var}(Y)} = (1 - \rho_{XY}^2)\,\text{Var}(X)$$

where ρ_{XY} is the correlation between X and Y. Thus, using the optimal value a^* for a, the optimally controlled estimator X_C^* can never be more variable than the uncontrolled X, and will in fact have lower variance if Y is *at all* correlated with X. Moreover, the stronger the correlation between X and Y, the greater the variance reduction—in the extreme, as $\rho_{XY} \to \pm 1$, we see in fact that $\text{Var}(X_C^*) \to 0$. Intuitively, this says that if the correlation between Y and X were nearly perfect (± 1), we could control X almost exactly to μ every time, thereby eliminating practically all of its variance.

In practice, though, things are not quite so rosy. Depending on the source and nature of the control variate Y, we may or may not know the value of $\text{Var}(Y)$, and we will certainly not know $\text{Cov}(X, Y)$, making it impossible to find the exact value of a^*. Accordingly, several methods have been proposed to estimate a^* from simulation runs, and we next describe one of the simpler of these, due to Lavenberg, Moeller, and Welch (1982) and Lavenberg and Welch (1981), which can also be used to form a confidence interval for μ. [As stated, the method applies to terminating simulations (see Sec. 9.3) that are simply replicated, although it might be applicable to steady-state parameters by using the replication/deletion approach of Sec. 9.5.2 or by replacing the replication averages by batch means, as discussed in Sec. 9.5.3.]

The method simply replaces $\text{Cov}(X, Y)$ and $\text{Var}(Y)$ in Eq. (11.2) by their sample estimators. Suppose that we make n independent replications to obtain the n IID observations $X_1, X_2, \ldots, X_n$ on X and the n IID observations $Y_1, Y_2, \ldots, Y_n$ on Y. Let $\bar{X}(n)$ and $\bar{Y}(n)$ be the sample means of the X_j's and Y_j's, respectively, and let $S_Y^2(n)$ be the unbiased sample variance of the Y_j's. The covariance between X and Y is estimated by (see Prob. 4.29)

$$\hat{C}_{XY}(n) = \frac{\sum_{j=1}^{n} [X_j - \bar{X}(n)][Y_j - \bar{Y}(n)]}{n - 1}$$

and the estimator for a^* is then

$$\hat{a}^*(n) = \frac{\hat{C}_{XY}(n)}{S_Y^2(n)}$$

to arrive at the final point estimator for μ,

$$\overline{X}_C^*(n) = \overline{X}(n) - \hat{a}^*(n)[\overline{Y}(n) - \nu]$$

Immediately, we must note that since the constant a^* has been replaced by the random variable $\hat{a}^*(n)$, which is generally *not* independent of $\overline{Y}(n)$ (having been computed from the same simulation output data), we cannot blithely take expectations across the factors in the second term of $\overline{X}_C^*(n)$. Unfortunately, then, $\overline{X}_C^*(n)$, unlike X_C and X_C^*, will in general be biased for μ. The severity of this bias, as well as the amount of variance reduction that might be obtained from this scheme, are investigated by Lavenberg, Moeller, and Welch (1982).

Alternative estimators of a^*, based on jackknifing to reduce the bias in $\overline{X}_C^*(n)$, are discussed by Kleijnen (1974) as well as by Lavenberg, Moeller, and Welch (1982). Cheng and Feast (1980) and Bauer (1987) consider CV problems when we know the variance of the control variate. Nelson (1989, 1990a) considers CV with batch means for steady-state simulation, and surveys and evaluates several alternative approaches to dealing with the problem of point-estimator bias, as well as related problems; Yang and Nelson (1992) extend this analysis to multivariate batch means in conjunction with CV. Avramidis and Wilson (1993) discuss splitting up the simulation output data to estimate a^*.

EXAMPLE 11.13. To solidify the example we have been discussing informally in this section, let X be the average delay in queue of the first 100 customers arriving to an $M/M/1$ queue that starts out empty and idle, has mean interarrival time 1 minute, and mean service time 0.9 minute; this is the same model we have used in Examples 11.1, 11.3, 11.4, 11.10, and 11.11. As a control variate for X, let Y be the average of the 99 service times that would be needed to complete a replication of this model; since the simulation ends when the 100th service time begins, its value will have no impact on the output and so is not included in Y. Since Y is thus the average of a *fixed* number (see Prob. 11.12) of IID service times that have expectation 0.9, $\nu = E(Y) = 0.9$ as well.

We made $n = 10$ independent replications and observed the 10 X_j's and 10 corresponding Y_j's given in Table 11.9. From these data, $\overline{X}(10) = 3.78$ and $\overline{Y}(10) = 0.89$;

TABLE 11.9
Average delays (X_j's) and average service times (Y_j's) using CV for the $M/M/1$ queue

j	X_j	Y_j
1	13.84	0.92
2	3.18	0.95
3	2.26	0.88
4	2.76	0.89
5	4.33	0.93
6	1.35	0.81
7	1.82	0.84
8	3.01	0.92
9	1.68	0.85
10	3.60	0.88

thus, the average service time is a bit lower than its expectation $\nu = 0.9$, and the average delay in queue is also low compared to its expectation $\mu = 4.13$ (which we actually know in this artificial example), as suggested at the beginning of this section. Further, we got $S_X^2(10) = 13.33$, $S_Y^2(10) = 0.002$, and $\hat{C}_{XY}(10) = 0.07$, leading to an estimated value of 0.43 for the correlation between X and Y, confirming our feeling that they should be positively correlated. Finally, we get $\hat{a}^*(10) = 35.00$ and so $\overline{X}_C^*(10) = 4.13$, which is indeed closer to μ than is the uncontrolled estimator $\overline{X}(10) = 3.78$.

To see whether $\text{Var}[\overline{X}_C^*(10)]$ is in fact smaller than $\text{Var}[\overline{X}(10)]$, we repeated the entire 10-replication experiment of the preceding paragraph 100 times, getting 100 independent observations on both $\overline{X}(10)$ and $\overline{X}_C^*(10)$. From these data we estimated $\text{Var}[\overline{X}(10)]$ to be 0.99, whereas our estimate of $\text{Var}[\overline{X}_C^*(10)]$ was 0.66, a reduction of a third. The correlation between $\overline{X}(10)$ and $\overline{Y}(10)$ was estimated to be 0.67, which is positive, as anticipated. At the same time, we estimated from the 100 observations on $\overline{X}_C^*(10)$ that a 95 percent confidence interval for $E[\overline{X}_C^*(10)]$ is 4.18 ± 0.16, which contains μ, indicating that whatever bias in the controlled estimator was introduced by estimating a^* by $\hat{a}^*(10)$ is evidently not noticeable in this case.

In Example 11.13 we chose the average of the service times as our control variate, but, as the following two examples show, the issue of what to use as a control variate is by no means clear.

EXAMPLE 11.14. We repeated the experiments of Example 11.13 but used instead as a control variate Y the average of the first 100 *interarrival* times. We can be sure that there will always be at least this many and thus get a control variate based on a *fixed* number of generated interarrival times (see Prob. 11.12), so we know that $E(Y) = 1$. Carrying out a set of 100 experiments of $n = 10$ replications each, as described in Example 11.13, we estimated $\text{Var}[\overline{X}_C^*(10)]$ based on this control variate to be 0.89, a reduction of only 10 percent in comparison with the estimated variance of 0.99 for $\overline{X}(10)$. Thus, it appears that our original choice of the average service time as a control variate was a better idea than using the average interarrival time.

EXAMPLE 11.15. Could we somehow make use of both? Let $Y^{(1)}$ be the average-service-time control variate used in Example 11.13, and let $Y^{(2)}$ be the average-interarrival-time control variate used in Example 11.14. Then, since $\text{Cov}(X, Y^{(1)})$ and $\text{Cov}(X, Y^{(2)})$ probably have opposite signs, we could perhaps incorporate information from both if we define a new control variate $Y = Y^{(1)} - Y^{(2)}$; we anticipate that $\text{Cov}(X, Y) > 0$, being supported by both $Y^{(1)}$ and $Y^{(2)}$. Indeed, when using this scheme in 100 new experiments of $n = 10$ replications each, the estimated correlation between $\overline{X}(10)$ and $\overline{Y}(10)$ was 0.77, and the estimate of the variance of the controlled estimator was 0.56, being a 43 percent reduction in variance from the 0.99 figure for the uncontrolled estimator, and better than either $Y^{(1)}$ or $Y^{(2)}$ alone. However, there was evidently some point-estimator bias introduced in this case, as a 95 percent confidence interval for $E[\overline{X}_C^*(10)]$ was 4.38 ± 0.15, which misses $\mu = 4.13$; whether or not this is worrisome depends on how one chooses to trade off bias against variance in the point estimator.

There were really two different control variates in Example 11.15 that we were able to combine in a sensible way to get a single control variate. However, why did we subtract them rather than divide one by the other? Or, why not let $Y = Y^{(1)} - 2Y^{(2)}$ instead? In complex models there will be many potential control variates available, and it could be difficult to suggest the best way to roll them all into one. Moreover, even if we could combine them in a reasonable way, we might not be using their information to our best advantage. In Example 11.15, we let *the* control variate $Y = Y^{(1)} - Y^{(2)}$, so that the controlled estimator is

$$\begin{aligned} X_C &= X - a(Y - \nu) \\ &= X - a(Y^{(1)} - \nu^{(1)}) - a(-Y^{(2)} + \nu^{(2)}) \end{aligned}$$

where $\nu^{(l)} = E(Y^{(l)})$. In this formulation, then, we are forcing both individual control variates ($Y^{(1)}$ and $-Y^{(2)}$) to enter the adjustment using the *same* coefficient, a, which may not be the best use of their information. A logical modification would be to allow the two control variates to have different weights, and redefine

$$X_C = X - a_1(Y^{(1)} - \nu^{(1)}) - a_2(Y^{(2)} - \nu^{(2)})$$

We could then derive (and estimate) the weights a_1 and a_2 that minimize Var(X_C), as we did before when there was just a single control variate.

This idea is easily generalized to the case where we have m control variates $Y^{(1)}, \ldots, Y^{(m)}$ with respective known expectations $\nu^{(1)}, \ldots, \nu^{(m)}$. The general (linearly) controlled estimator is

$$X_C = X - \sum_{l=1}^{m} a_l(Y^{(l)} - \nu^{(l)})$$

where the a_l's are real numbers to be determined (and estimated). Allowing for correlation not only between X and the control variates but also between the control variates themselves, we get

$$\begin{aligned} \text{Var}(X_C) = \text{Var}(X) &+ \sum_{l=1}^{m} a_l^2 \text{Var}(Y^{(l)}) - 2\sum_{l=1}^{m} a_l \text{Cov}(X, Y^{(l)}) \\ &+ 2\sum_{l_1=2}^{m} \sum_{l_2=1}^{l_1-1} a_{l_1} a_{l_2} \text{Cov}(Y^{(l_1)}, Y^{(l_2)}) \end{aligned} \tag{11.3}$$

Taking partial derivatives of the right-hand side of Eq. (11.3) with respect to each of the a_l's and equating them to zero leads to a set of m linear equations to solve for the m variance-minimizing weights (see Prob. 11.13). As in the case of a single control variate, these optimal weights must be estimated, and bias introduction in the controlled estimator is again a possibility. Lavenberg and Welch (1981) and Nelson (1990a) discuss these and related problems. The estimates of the optimal weights turn out to be identical to least-squares estimates of the coefficients in a certain linear-regression model, and so CV is sometimes referred to as *regression sampling*.

We close this section with a brief discussion of finding and selecting control variates. As we have seen, a good control variate should be strongly correlated with the output random variable X, in order to give us a lot of information about X and to make a good adjustment to it. We would also like the control variates themselves to have low variance. Finding such control variates could proceed by an analysis of the model's structure, or through initial experimentation. With these goals in mind, three general sources of control variates have been suggested:

- *Internal.* Input random variates, or simple functions of them (such as averages), are often used as control variates. All the control variates used in Examples 11.13

through 11.15 were internal. Their expectations will generally be known (see the caveat of Prob. 11.12), and a simple analysis of their role in the model could suggest how they might be correlated with the output random variable. Most important, internal control variates must be essentially generated anyway to run the simulation, so they add basically nothing to the simulation's cost; thus, they will prove worthwhile even if they do not reduce the variance greatly (see Prob. 11.1 for an economic model of the efficacy of VRTs). Detailed accounts of various kinds of internal CV applications can be found in Iglehart and Lewis (1979), Lavenberg, Moeller, and Sauer (1979), Lavenberg, Moeller, and Welch (1982), and Wilson and Pritsker (1984a, 1984b).

- *External.* Presumably, we are simulating since we cannot compute $\mu = E(X)$ analytically. Perhaps, though, if we altered the model by making some additional simplifying assumptions, we *would* be able to compute the expectation ν of the simplified model's output random variable Y. While we may be unwilling to make these simplifying assumptions in our actual model since they could materially impair the model's validity, Y could serve as a control variate for X. We would then simulate the simplified model alongside the actual model, using CRN (Sec. 11.2), and hope that Y is correlated with X, presumably positively. Unlike internal CV, this approach is *not* costless since it involves a second simulation to get the control variate; thus, the correlation between Y and X would have to be stronger for external CV to pay off than would be the case if Y were an internal CV. Examples of external CV can be found in Burt, Gaver, and Perlas (1970), Gaver and Shedler (1971), Gaver and Thompson (1973), Schmeiser and Taaffe (1994), Nelson et al. (1997), and Irish et al. (2003), as well as in Prob. 11.14.
- *Using multiple estimators.* In some situations we may have several unbiased estimators $X^{(1)}, \ldots, X^{(k)}$ for μ, where the $X^{(i)}$'s may or may not be independent. This might arise, for instance, when we can use the method of indirect estimation, to be discussed in Sec. 11.5. If $b_1, \ldots, b_k$ are any real numbers (not necessarily positive) that sum to 1, then

$$X_C = \sum_{i=1}^{k} b_i X^{(i)}$$

is also unbiased for μ. Since $b_1 = 1 - \sum_{i=2}^{k} b_i$, we can express X_C as

$$\begin{aligned} X_C &= \left(1 - \sum_{i=2}^{k} b_i\right) X^{(1)} + \sum_{i=2}^{k} b_i X^{(i)} \\ &= X^{(1)} - \sum_{i=2}^{k} b_i (X^{(1)} - X^{(i)}) \end{aligned}$$

so that we can view $Y_i = X^{(1)} - X^{(i)}$, for $i = 2, 3, \ldots, k$, as $k - 1$ control variates for $X^{(1)}$.

As can be seen from the above, there may be a very large number of possible control variates for a complex model. However, it is not necessarily a good idea to use them all, since the variance reduction they may bring is accompanied by variance contributions associated with the need to estimate the optimal a_i's. Bauer and

Wilson (1992) propose a method for selecting the best subset from the available control variates, under a variety of assumptions about what we know concerning their variances and covariances. See also Rubinstein and Marcus (1985), Venkatraman and Wilson (1986), and Porta Nova and Wilson (1993).

Our discussion of control variates has centered on estimation of means. For a discussion of using CV to sharpen estimators of probabilities and quantiles, as described in Sec. 9.4.2, see Hsu and Nelson (1990) and Hesterberg and Nelson (1998).

11.5 INDIRECT ESTIMATION

This VRT has been developed for queueing-type simulations when the quantities to be estimated are steady-state performance measures, such as d, w, Q, and L (see App. 1B). Proofs that variance reductions are obtained have been given for these kinds of models [see Law (1974, 1975), Carson and Law (1980), and Glynn and Whitt (1989)], but the idea might be applicable to other situations as well; again, initial experimentation could reveal whether worthwhile variance reductions are being experienced. The basic tools are the theoretical relations between d, w, Q, and L given in App. 1B.

Let D_i and W_i, respectively, be the delay in queue and the total wait in system of the ith customer arriving to a $GI/G/s$ queue. Thus, if S_i is the service time of the ith customer, $W_i = D_i + S_i$. Also, let $Q(t)$ and $L(t)$, respectively, be the number of customers in queue and in system at time t. From a simulation run in which a fixed number n of customers complete their service and which lasts for $T(n)$ units of simulated time, the *direct* estimators of d, w, Q, and L are, respectively,

$$\hat{d}(n) = \frac{1}{n}\sum_{i=1}^{n} D_i, \qquad \hat{w}(n) = \frac{1}{n}\sum_{i=1}^{n} W_i$$

$$\hat{Q}(n) = \frac{1}{T(n)}\int_0^{T(n)} Q(t)\,dt, \qquad \hat{L}(n) = \frac{1}{T(n)}\int_0^{T(n)} L(t)\,dt$$

Now $\hat{w}(n) = \hat{d}(n) + \bar{S}(n)$, where $\bar{S}(n) = \sum_{i=1}^{n} S_i/n$ and $E[\bar{S}(n)] = E(S)$, the known expected service time. Thus, an alternative estimator of w might be

$$\tilde{w}(n) = \hat{d}(n) + E(S)$$

i.e., we replace the estimator $\bar{S}(n)$ by its *known* (and zero-variance) expectation $E(S)$. We call $\tilde{w}(n)$ an *indirect* estimator of w, and it seems reasonable to suspect that $\tilde{w}(n)$ might be less variable than $\hat{w}(n)$, since the random term $\bar{S}(n)$ in $\hat{w}(n)$ is replaced by the fixed number $E(S)$ to obtain $\tilde{w}(n)$. For any $GI/G/s$ queue and for any n, this is indeed the case, as shown by Law (1974), although the proof is not as simple as it might seem since $\bar{S}(n)$ and $\hat{d}(n)$ are not independent. Thus, the indirect estimator $\tilde{w}(n)$ is better than the more obvious direct estimator.

The variance reduction of the previous paragraph is suggested by the *additive* relation $w = d + E(S)$, and it seems intuitive that there is no point in using the random variable $\bar{S}(n)$ in the estimator of w when we could use its expectation $E(S)$ instead, thereby avoiding an additional source of variation. What is perhaps not so intuitive is that better indirect estimators of Q and L can be obtained from the *multiplicative* relations in the two conservation equations

$$Q = \lambda d \tag{11.4}$$

$$L = \lambda w \tag{11.5}$$

where λ is the arrival rate (see App. 1B), which would again be known in a simulation. An indirect estimator of Q that Eq. (11.4) suggests is

$$\tilde{Q}(n) = \lambda\,\hat{d}(n)$$

and it is shown by Carson (1978) and Carson and Law (1980) that *asymptotically* [as both n and $T(n)$ become infinite] $\tilde{Q}(n)$ has smaller variance than the direct estimator $\hat{Q}(n)$. Similarly, using Eq. (11.5) and the superior indirect estimator $\tilde{w}(n)$ of w, we can show that the indirect estimator

$$\tilde{L}(n) = \lambda\tilde{w}(n) = \lambda[\hat{d}(n) + E(S)]$$

asymptotically has smaller variance than the direct estimator $\hat{L}(n)$. Thus we see that it is better to estimate w, Q, and L by simple deterministic functions of $\hat{d}(n)$ than to estimate them directly. This is one of the reasons we have emphasized estimation of the delay in queue in our examples throughout this book. Another appeal of indirect estimation is that only the delays $D_1, D_2, \ldots$, and not W_i, $Q(t)$, or $L(t)$, need be collected during the simulation, even if we really want to estimate w, Q, or L.

EXAMPLE 11.16. The exact asymptotic variance reductions obtained by estimating Q (for example) indirectly with $\tilde{Q}(n)$ rather than directly with $\hat{Q}(n)$ can be calculated for $M/G/1$ queues [see Law (1974)]. Table 11.10 gives these reductions (in percent) for exponential, 4-Erlang, and hyperexponential (see Sec. 4.5) service times, and for $\rho = 0.5$, 0.7, and 0.9.

One weakness of the above indirect-estimation technique is that as $\rho \to 1$, the variance reductions decrease to 0. This is evident in reading across each row of Table 11.10, and was shown analytically for the $M/G/1$ queue by Law (1974). But since highly congested systems are also highly variable, it is in this case that we need variance reduction the most. A more general use of indirect estimators developed by Carson (1978), which is related to techniques devised by Heidelberger (1980), does better for ρ near 1, and generally achieves stronger variance reductions. Again taking the example of estimating Q, we note that there are two estimators

TABLE 11.10
Exact asymptotic variance reductions for indirect estimation of Q, $M/G/1$ queue

	Reduction, percent		
Service-time distribution	$\rho = 0.5$	$\rho = 0.7$	$\rho = 0.9$
Exponential	15	11	4
4-Erlang	22	17	7
Hyperexponential	4	3	2

$\hat{Q}(n)$ and $\tilde{Q}(n)$ that could be combined to get a linear-combination estimator $Q(a_1, a_2, n) = a_1\hat{Q}(n) + a_2\tilde{Q}(n)$, where $a_1 + a_2 = 1$; it is not necessary that both a_1 and a_2 be nonnegative. Then a_1 and a_2 could be chosen to minimize Var$[Q(a_1, a_2, n)]$ subject to the constraint that $a_1 + a_2 = 1$. Note that $Q(1, 0, n) = \hat{Q}(n)$ and $Q(0, 1, n) = \tilde{Q}(n)$, so that this technique includes both the direct and indirect estimators as special cases; thus, for the optimal (a_1, a_2), $\text{Var}[Q(a_1, a_2, n)] \leq \min\{\text{Var}[\hat{Q}(n)], \text{Var}[\tilde{Q}(n)]\}$. As with CV (Sec. 11.4), however, the optimal (a_1, a_2) must be estimated. Carson (1978) gives an asymptotically valid way to do this, based on the regenerative method, and also allows more than two alternative estimators; see the discussion on using multiple estimators in Sec. 11.4. His analytical and empirical studies indicate that variance reductions of at least 40 percent, in comparison with direct estimators, are often achieved.

Additional papers that discuss indirect estimation are by Srikant and Whitt (1999) and Wang and Wolff (2003, 2005).

11.6 CONDITIONING

The final VRT we consider, *conditioning*, shares a feature with indirect estimation in that we exploit some special property of a model to replace an *estimate* of a quantity by its *exact analytical* value. In removing this source of variability, we hope that the final output random variable will be more stable, although there is no absolute guarantee of this; again, pilot studies comparing the conditioning technique with straightforward simulation could indicate whether and to what extent the variance is being reduced. The general conditioning technique as we shall discuss it is in the same spirit as the "conditional Monte Carlo" method treated by Hammersley and Handscomb (1964).

As usual, let X be an output random variable, such as the delay in queue of a customer, whose expectation μ we want to estimate. Suppose that there is some other random variable Z such that, given any particular possible value z for Z, we can analytically compute the *conditional expectation* $E(X|Z = z)$. Note that $E(X|Z = z)$ is a (known) deterministic function of the real number z, but $E(X|Z)$ is a random variable that is this same function of the random variable Z. Then by conditioning on Z [see, e.g., Ross (2003, p. 106)], we see that $\mu = E(X) = E_Z[E(X|Z)]$ (the outer expectation is denoted E_Z since it is taken with respect to the distribution of Z), so that the random variable $E(X|Z)$ is also unbiased for μ. For instance, if Z is discrete with probability mass function $p(z) = P(Z = z)$, then

$$E_Z[E(X|Z)] = \sum_z E(X|Z = z)p(z)$$

where we assume that the $p(z)$'s are unknown. Further,

$$\text{Var}_Z[E(X|Z)] = \text{Var}(X) - E_Z[\text{Var}(X|Z)] \leq \text{Var}(X) \tag{11.6}$$

[see Ross (2003, p. 118), for example], indicating that if we observe the random variable $E(X|Z)$ (as computed from an observation z on Z), instead of observing X directly, we will get a smaller variance. In other words, it is suggested that we simulate to get a random observation z on Z (since its distribution is not known), plug this observation into the known formula for $E(X|Z = z)$, and use *this* as a basic observation; of course, this entire scheme could then be replicated some number of times in the case of a terminating simulation.

Naturally, the trick here is specifying a random variable Z so that:

- Z can be easily and efficiently generated, since we still have to simulate it.
- $E(X|Z = z)$ as a function of z can be computed analytically and efficiently for any possible value of z that Z can take on.
- $E_Z[\text{Var}(X|Z)]$ is large, thus soaking up a lot of Var(X) in Eq. (11.6). In words, $E_Z[\text{Var}(X|Z)]$ is the mean conditional variance of X over the possible values for Z, and since we have a formula for $E(X|Z = z)$ we never have to simulate X given Z, so we are not affected by its variance.

Since this VRT is so heavily model-dependent, our illustrations describe two successful implementations from the literature. The following example, taken from Lavenberg and Welch (1979), illustrates conditioning to obtain variance reductions in estimates of several expected delays in a queueing network.

EXAMPLE 11.17. A time-shared computer model has a single CPU and 15 terminals, as well as a disk drive and a tape drive, as shown in Fig. 11.8. At each terminal sits a user who "thinks" for an exponential amount of time with mean 100 seconds, and then sends a job to the computer where it may join a FIFO queue for the CPU. Each job entering the CPU occupies it for an exponential amount of time with mean 1 second. A job leaving the CPU is finished with probability 0.20 and returns to its terminal to begin another think time; on the other hand, it may need to access the disk drive (with probability 0.72) or the tape drive (probability 0.08) instead. A job going to the disk drive potentially waits in a FIFO queue there, then occupies the drive for an exponential amount of time S_D with mean 1.39 seconds, after which it must go back to the CPU. Similarly, a job going from the CPU to the tape drive faces a FIFO queue there, uses the drive for an exponential amount of time S_T with mean 12.50 seconds, and then returns to the CPU. All think times, service times, and branching decisions are independent, and all jobs are initially in the think state at their terminals. The goal is to estimate d_C, d_D, and d_T, the steady-state expected delays in queue of jobs at the CPU, disk drive, and tape drive, respectively. For this purpose, the run length was taken to be the time required for 400 jobs to be processed and sent back to their terminals.

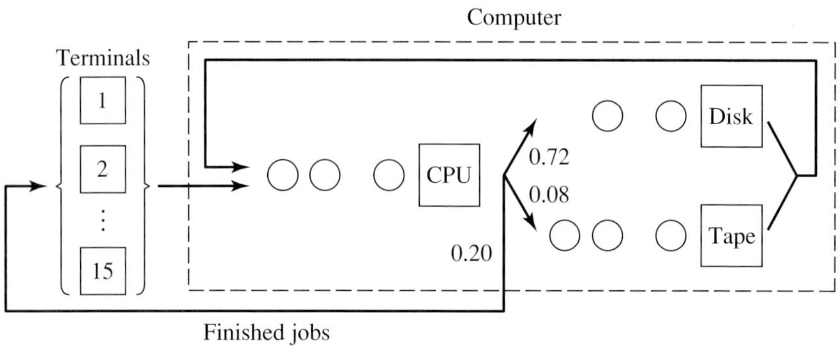

FIGURE 11.8
The time-shared computer model of Example 11.17.

Straightforward simulation could be used to obtain estimates of these steady-state expected delays by simply using the averages of the delays observed in each of the three queues. However, the number of observations of tape-drive delays could be quite low, since only about 8 percent of the jobs exiting the CPU go there; thus, the straightforward estimator of d_T, being based on relatively little data, could be highly variable.

We can obtain a different estimate of d_T by observing the total number N_T of jobs at the tape drive (in queue and in service) at the instant *each* job leaves the CPU, regardless of where it is going. *Given* that a job leaving the CPU *would* go to the tape drive, its expected delay in queue there *would be* $E(S_T)N_T = 12.50N_T$ seconds. (Since the job in service, if any, at the tape drive has an exponential service time, its *remaining* service time is also exponential with mean 12.50, due to the memoryless property of the exponential distribution, as described in Prob. 4.30. Conditioning is still possible for nonexponential service times but requires more information.) In this way we get an observation on tape-drive delays from *every* job leaving the CPU rather than from just the 8 percent that really go there. Moreover, we use the exact value of $E(S_T) = 12.50$ rather than draws of the random variable S_T that would be generated in a straightforward simulation. The observed values of $12.50N_T$ are averaged to get an improved estimate of d_T. This approach is valid since jobs leaving the CPU "see" the same state regardless of whether they actually go to the tape drive.

In terms of our earlier general discussion, we are simulating to observe values of $Z = N_T$ whenever a job leaves the CPU, and $E(\text{delay in tape-drive queue} \mid N_T = z) = 12.50z$, a known deterministic function, given that $N_T = z$. However, the final output variable, the *average* delay in the tape-drive queue, is a more complicated consequence of the entire dynamic simulation, so that Eq. (11.6) does not apply overall. We still hope, though, that some of this "local" variance reduction will propagate through the model's dynamics.

Similarly, for each job leaving the CPU we could condition on its going to the disk drive, and take $1.39N_D$ as an observation on a disk-drive delay, where N_D is the observed number of jobs in queue and in service at the disk drive at this moment. This will also increase the number of observations, but not as dramatically as for the tape drive since nearly three-fourths of the jobs exiting the CPU go to the disk drive anyway. However, we use the known expectation of a disk-drive service time S_D, rather than random observations on it.

Finally, by conditioning on N_C = the total number of jobs at the CPU whenever a job leaves either its terminal, the disk drive, or the tape drive, we can average the values of $1N_C$ (since the mean CPU time is 1 second) to try to get a better estimate of d_C; this does not generate any extra imaginary CPU visits since all such jobs will go to the CPU anyway, but it does allow us to exploit knowledge of the expected CPU service time.

In 100 independent replications, estimated variance reductions of 19, 28, and 56 percent were observed in the estimates of d_C, d_D, and d_T, respectively, in comparison with straightforward simulation. As anticipated, the greatest benefit was for the tape-drive queue, where the conditioning technique led to some 12 times as many observations as observed in the straightforward simulation. Seven other versions of this model were also simulated in which second moments were estimated as well, and variance reductions from conditioning were between 9 and 86 percent, depending on the model and what was being estimated. The additional computing time in the conditioning approach was negligible.

As the preceding example shows, the conditioning VRT requires careful analysis of the model's probabilistic structure. Also, the success was evidently due not only to exploiting knowledge of an analytic formula for conditional expectations, but in addition to increasing the number of observations of a "rare" event artificially, in this case a job's going to the tape drive. These comments apply as well to the success of conditioning in the following example, due to Carter and Ignall (1975).

EXAMPLE 11.18. A simulation model was developed to compare alternative policies for dispatching fire trucks in the Bronx. Certain fires are classified as "serious," since there is considerable danger that lives will be lost and property damage will be high unless the fire department is able to respond quickly with enough fire trucks. The goal of the simulation was to estimate the expected response time to a serious fire under a given dispatching policy.

Historical data indicated that about 1 of 30 fires is serious. Thus, the model would have to progress through about 30 simulated fires to get a single observation on the response time to a serious fire, which could lead to very long and expensive runs to generate enough serious fires to get a good estimate of the expected response time to them. However, the model's specific structure was such that, given the state of the system (the location of all fire trucks) at any instant, the *true* expected response time to a serious fire could be calculated analytically, should one occur at that instant. Further, the probabilistic assumptions (serious fires occur according to a Poisson process) justified conditioning on the event of a serious fire at *every* instant when the system state was observed regardless of whether a serious fire really did occur [see Wolff (1982)]. Thus, the simulation was interrupted periodically to observe the system state, the expected response time to a serious fire, given the current state, was calculated and recorded, and the simulation was resumed. The final estimator was the average of these conditional expected response times and included many more terms than the number of serious fires actually simulated.

In terms of the general discussion, the purpose of the simulation was to observe a vector Z of locations of fire trucks, and E(response time to a serious fire $| Z = z$) was analytically known as a function of z, so did not have to be estimated in the simulation. The increased frequency of the (imaginary) serious fires over that actually observed is an additional benefit of the approach.

The variance of the estimated expected response time was reduced by some 95 percent with this conditioning approach, in comparison with straightforward simulation. The conditional-expectation approach was somewhat more expensive, but even accounting for this the variance reduction was 92 percent for the same computational effort.

Note that in dynamic simulations, Eq. (11.6) applies directly only to a single random variable and may not be applicable to the simulation's overall output random variables (e.g., the average delay in queue of 1000 customers), so a variance reduction is not guaranteed.

There are several other examples of using the conditioning approach as a VRT that might be helpful. Carter and Ignall (1975) also consider an inventory model where the event on which conditioning occurs is a shortage, which seldom occurs but which has a large impact on system performance when it does happen. Burt and Garman (1971) considered simulation of stochastic PERT networks and conditioned on certain task times that are common to more than one path through the network; in their use of conditioning, the concept of artificially increasing the frequency of a rare event is not present. Further VRTs based on conditioning in stochastic network simulations are discussed by Garman (1972) and by Sigal, Pritsker, and Solberg (1979). A generalization of the method was proposed by Minh (1989) for situations where $E(X|Z = z)$ may be unknown for some values of z.

Nakayama (1994a, 1994b), Heidelberger (1995), Shahabuddin (1994, 1995), Glasserman and Liu (1996), Glasserman et al. (1999), and Nicola et al. (2001) discuss a variety of VRTs, including importance sampling. This latter VRT can be used to estimate the probability of a rare but important event, such as the breakdown of a highly reliable communications network or a buffer overflow in a queueing system.

PROBLEMS

11.1. Some VRTs are nearly costless (e.g., CRN), but others could entail considerable extra cost (e.g., external CV), and this must be taken into account when deciding whether a particular VRT is worth it. Let V_0 be the appropriate variance measure with a straightforward simulation (without using a VRT) and let V_1 be the corresponding variance measure using a particular VRT. Also, let C_0 and C_1 be the costs of making a particular number of runs of a particular length with the straightforward and VRT approaches, respectively. Find conditions on V_0, V_1, C_0, and C_1 for which the VRT would be advisable.

11.2. In Sec. 11.2.2, and specifically in Fig. 11.1, we considered the question of whether CRN would induce the desired positive correlation for a given pair of alternative configurations, or whether it might backfire. Consider the following simple Monte Carlo examples, where U represents a random number:

(1) $X_{1j} = U^2$ and $X_{2j} = U^3$
(2) $X_{1j} = U^2$ and $X_{2j} = (1 - U)^3$

(*a*) Sketch the graphs of the responses in both examples.
(*b*) For each example, analytically find $\text{Cov}(X_{1j}, X_{2j})$.
(*c*) For each example, analytically calculate $\text{Var}(X_{1j} - X_{2j})$ under both independent sampling and CRN.
(*d*) Confirm your calculations in (*b*) and (*c*) empirically by designing and carrying out a small simulation study.

11.3. In Sec. 11.3 we discussed the conditions under which AV would work or backfire. Consider the following simple Monte Carlo examples, where U represents a random number:

(1) $X_j = U^2$
(2) $X_j = 4(U - 0.5)^2$

(*a*) Sketch the graph of the response in both examples.
(*b*) For each example, analytically find $\text{Cov}(X_j^{(1)}, X_j^{(2)})$.
(*c*) For each example, analytically calculate $\text{Var}[(X_j^{(1)} + X_j^{(2)})/2]$ under both independent sampling and AV.
(*d*) Confirm your calculations in (*b*) and (*c*) empirically by designing and carrying out a small simulation study.

11.4. Consider the queueing model in Fig. 11.9. Customers arrive according to a Poisson process at rate 1 per minute and face a FIFO queue for server 1, who provides

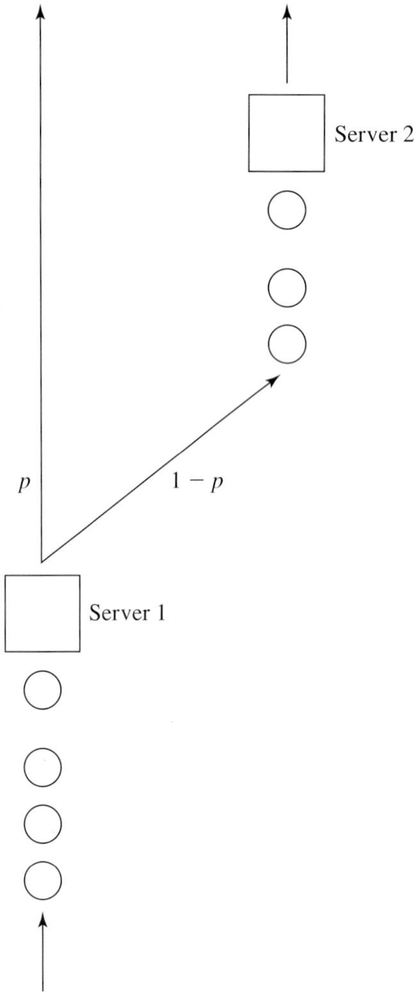

FIGURE 11.9
The queueing model of Prob. 11.4.

exponential service with mean 0.7 minute. Upon exiting server 1, customers leave with probability p, and go to server 2 with probability $1 - p$. Server 2 is also fed by a FIFO queue, and provides exponential service with mean 0.9 minute. All service times, interarrival times, and routing decisions are independent, the system is initially empty and idle, and it runs until 100 customers have finished their total delay in queue(s); the total delay in queues of a customer visiting server 2 is the sum of his or her delays in the two queues. The performance measure is the expected average total delay in queue(s) of the first 100 customers to complete their total delay in queue(s).

(*a*) Suppose there are two configurations of this system, with p being either 0.3 or 0.8. Make 10 replications of each system using both independent sampling and CRN, and compare the estimated variances of the resulting estimate of the difference between the performance measures. Take care to maintain proper synchronization when using CRN.

(*b*) For $p = 0.3$, make five pairs of runs using both independent sampling and AV within a pair, and compare the estimated variances of the estimated performance measure. Again, pay attention to synchronization.

11.5. Recall the inventory simulation of Sec. 1.5, as used in Example 11.12 to illustrate AV. There are three sources of randomness (interdemand times, demand sizes, and delivery lags), and three cost components (ordering, holding, and shortage). Analyze this model, as programmed in Sec. 1.5, to provide a rationale for AV. Specifically, see what the effect of a small (or large) random number would be on each of the three types of costs if it is used to generate each of the three types of input random variables. For example, suppose that a small U is used to generate an interdemand time. Would this tend to make the ordering cost generally large or small, other things being equal?

11.6. Recall the bank model of Sec. 2.6, and suppose that the bank's management would like an estimate of the effect of adding a sixth teller *and* of adding a seventh teller (in comparison with the current configuration of five tellers) that is better than the results in Fig. 2.36. Use CRN to do this, and make enough replications of the three systems to obtain what you feel are sufficiently precise estimates of the differences in the expectations of the average delays in queue. Consider generating customer service times when the customer arrives, rather than when he or she enters service.

11.7. Recall the harbor model of Prob. 2.19.

(*a*) Consider using AV for the model as stated originally. Specifically, which input random variates should be generated antithetically, and how could proper synchronization be maintained?

(*b*) Suppose that thought is being given to replacing the two existing cranes with two faster ones. Specifically, single-crane unloading times for a ship would be distributed uniformly between 0.2 and 1.0 day; everything else remains the same. Discuss proper application and implementation of CRN to compare the original system with the proposed new one.

(*c*) Carry out the comparative simulations, using both independent sampling and CRN, and replicate as needed to estimate the variance reduction (if any) achieved by CRN.

11.8. Discuss the use of CRN to compare job-processing policies (*a*) and (*b*) for the computer model of Prob. 2.20.

11.9. For the two priority policies in the computer model of Prob. 2.22, use CRN to sharpen the comparison between the expected average delay in queue under each policy.

11.10. Consider two $M/G/1$ queues with exponential service times in the first queue and gamma service times in the second, but with the same mean service time. Discuss problems of synchronization of the random numbers in implementing CRN to compare these two queues on the basis, say, of the expected average delay of the first 100 customers given empty and idle initial conditions. Sections 8.2.1 and 8.3.4 may be of use.

11.11. In comparing two system configurations, consider using AV and CRN together, i.e., use AV within a pair of runs of each configuration, and CRN across the configurations. To simplify things, suppose we make just one pair of runs of each configuration, shown schematically below:

	Primary run		*Antithetic run*
Configuration 1:	$X_1^{(1)}$	←AV→	$X_1^{(2)}$
	↑ CRN ↓		↑ CRN ↓
Configuration 2:	$X_2^{(1)}$	←AV→	$X_2^{(2)}$

The estimator of $\zeta = E(X_1^{(l)} - X_2^{(l)})$ is $Z = (X_1^{(1)} + X_1^{(2)})/2 - (X_2^{(1)} + X_2^{(2)})/2$.

(*a*) Find an expression for Var(Z) in terms of the variances and covariances corresponding to the four runs in the above schematic.

(*b*) Assume that both CRN and AV work on their own, i.e., induce correlations of the desired signs. Does the combined scheme then work? That is, do we know that this scheme will reduce Var(Z) in comparison to independent sampling throughout? Explain.

11.12. If $Y_1, Y_2, \ldots$ is a sequence of IID random variables and N is a positive integer-valued random variable that may depend on the Y_i's in some way, then the sample mean of N Y_i's may *not* be unbiased for $\mu = E(Y_i)$. Use this fact to explain why we were careful in the CV examples in Sec. 11.4 to define the CV Y as the average of a *fixed* number of IID random variables, such as interarrival or service times, rather than letting Y be the average of all the interarrival or service times generated by the time the simulation ends.

11.13. For the general linear CV method with m control variates, the variance of the controlled estimator was given in Eq. (11.3), where the weights a_l must be specified.

(*a*) Find the optimal (i.e., variance-minimizing) weights for the cases $m = 2$ and 3.

(*b*) Assuming that the control variates are uncorrelated with each other, find the optimal weights for any m.

(*c*) For both cases (*a*) and (*b*) above, give a method for estimating the optimal weights. If we know the variances of the control variates (as we might if they are just averages of input variates), could your estimators be improved? In (*a*), what if we also know the covariances between the control variates?

11.14. Suppose that we want to estimate the expected average delay in queue of the first 100 customers in a FIFO *M*/*G*/1 queue where the initial conditions are empty and idle, the mean interarrival time is 1 minute, and service times have a Weibull distribution with shape parameter $\alpha = 2$ and scale parameter $\beta = 1.8/\sqrt{\pi}$ minutes. Thus, the mean service time is $\beta\Gamma[(1/\alpha) + 1] = (1.8/\sqrt{\pi})(\sqrt{\pi}/2) = 0.9$ minute (see Sec. 6.2.2), and the utilization factor is $\rho = 0.9$. (See Sec. 8.3.5 for Weibull-variate generation, which is easily done by the inverse-transform method.) As an external control variate, we could use CRN to simulate the *M*/*M*/1 queue for 100 customers with the same mean interarrival and service times, which is precisely the model of Example 11.13, and use the fact that the *known* expected average delay in queue for this

$M/M/1$ queue is 4.13. Use the estimation technique given in Sec. 11.4 to estimate the optimal weight a^* from $n = 10$ replications, and repeat the whole process 100 times to estimate the variance reduction in comparison with straightforward simulation of this $M/G/1$ queue. Is the variance reduction worthwhile, or should the computing time needed to simulate the $M/M/1$ queue be devoted instead to making additional direct replications of this $M/G/1$ queue?

11.15. Discuss proper use of AV for the time-shared computer model of Sec. 2.5. For alternative designs of this model (such as buying a faster CPU or changing the service quantum), how could CRN be appropriately applied for making comparative simulations?

11.16. Does allowing jockeying as described in the multiteller bank of Sec. 2.6 affect customers' average delay in queue(s)? To find out, regard the original model (with jockeying) as "configuration 1" and define "configuration 2" to be this same model but without any jockeying allowed; assume five tellers in each case. Use dedicated streams to facilitate CRN—stream 1 for interarrival times and stream 2 for service times. However, it is not exactly obvious how we should generate the service times from stream 2; there are (at least) the following two possibilities:

(*a*) A customer's service time is generated when he arrives and is stored with him as an attribute. This corresponds physically to the idea of forcing the "same" customers (in terms of their service demands on the tellers) to arrive to both configurations at the same times.

(*b*) Generate a service time from stream 2 only when a customer begins service. In this case, the two configurations will not see the same customers, but the ordered sequence of service times begun for both configurations will be identical.

Carry out a simulation experiment to investigate whether (*a*) or (*b*) is a better way to implement CRN, in terms of the variance of the estimator of the difference between the expected average delay in queue(s) in the two configurations.

11.17. Suppose that we want to make five replications of the two inventory models of Example 11.2. If we use streams 1, 2, and 3 for replication 1, streams 4, 5, and 6 for replication 2, etc., then a total of 15 streams will be required for the five replications. How could we maintain synchronization for the five replications using only seven streams? How about using three streams?

11.18. Why is the correlation between X_{1j} and X_{2j} equal to -0.17 for the independent case ("I") in Table 11.3, since independent random variables are uncorrelated (see Prob. 4.8)?

11.19. Consider the small factory of Example 9.25 where the probability of a bad part was 0.10. Suppose that the company is considering a new manufacturing process that will lower the probability of a bad part to 0.05. The company wants to compare the two manufacturing processes on the basis of the steady-state mean time in system, and it decides to make 10 independent replications of each process of length 12,400 minutes with a warmup period of 2400 minutes (40 hours). Let X_{ij} be the average time in system for process i ($i = 1, 2$ for the original and proposed processes, respectively) over the last 10,000 minutes on replication j ($j = 1, 2, \ldots, 10$), and let $Z_j = X_{1j} - X_{2j}$.

Compute the sample variance of the Z_j's for each of the following cases of synchronization:

(*a*) The two manufacturing processes are simulated completely independently (no synchronization).

(*b*) Only interarrival times of new parts are synchronized.

(*c*) Only times to failure and repair times for the machine are synchronized.

(*d*) Only processing times and inspection times of a part on its first pass through the system (if more than one pass is required) are synchronized.

Compute the variance reductions corresponding to cases (*b*), (*c*), and (*d*), using case (*a*) as the base case. What random variates are the most important to synchronize?

11.20. In Example 11.7, how could we get the same interdemand times and demand sizes for the two policies, using only one random-number stream?

CHAPTER 12

Experimental Design and Optimization

Recommended sections for a first reading: 12.1, 12.2, 12.3

12.1 INTRODUCTION

This chapter provides an introduction to the use of statistical experimental design and optimization techniques when the "experiment" is the execution of a computer simulation model. As in Chap. 10, we shall discuss simulations of alternative system configurations and examine and compare their results. In Chap. 10, on one hand, we assumed that the various system configurations were simply *given*, having been specified as *the* alternatives, perhaps based on physical constraints, contractual obligations, or political considerations. In this chapter, on the other hand, we deal with a situation in which there is less structure in the goal of the simulation study; we might want to find out which of possibly many parameters and structural assumptions have the greatest effect on a performance measure, or which set of model specifications appears to lead to optimal performance. For these broader (and more ambitious) objectives, we may not be able to carry out formal statistical analyses like those of Chap. 10 or make such precise probabilistic statements at the end of our analyses.

In experimental-design terminology, the input parameters and structural assumptions composing a model are called *factors*, and output performance measures are called *responses*. The decision as to which parameters and structural assumptions are considered fixed aspects of a model and which are experimental factors depends on the goals of the study rather than on the inherent form of the model. Also, in simulation studies there are usually several different responses or performance measures of interest.

TABLE 12.1
Examples of factors and responses

System	Possible factors	Quantitative or qualitative?	Possible responses
Inventory system	Reorder point Order-up-to level	Quantitative Quantitative	Average cost per month, average number of items in inventory
Manufacturing system	Number of machines Number of forklifts Forklift dispatching rule	Quantitative Quantitative Qualitative	Average time in system, throughput, average queue size
Communications network	Nodes of nodes Number of links Routing policy	Quantitative Quantitative Qualitative	Average end-to-end delay, throughput

Factors can be either *quantitative* or *qualitative* (sometimes called *categorical*). Quantitative factors naturally assume numerical values, while qualitative factors represent structural assumptions that are not naturally quantified; see Table 12.1 for some examples.

We can also classify factors in simulation experiments as being *controllable* or *uncontrollable*, depending on whether they represent action options to managers of the corresponding real-world system. Usually, we shall focus on controllable factors in simulation experiments, since they are most relevant to decisions that must be made about implementation of real-world systems. However, uncontrollable factors might also be of interest in simulation experiments; e.g., we might want to assess how a 10 percent increase in the arrival rate of customers would affect congestion. In a mathematical-modeling activity such as simulation, we do, after all, get to control *everything*, regardless of actual real-world controllability.

The major goal of experimental design in simulation is to determine which factors have the greatest effect on a response, and to do so with the least amount of simulating. This is often called *factor screening* or *sensitivity analysis* (see Sec. 5.4.4). Carefully designed experiments are much more efficient than a hit-or-miss sequence of runs in which we simply try a number of alternative configurations unsystematically to see what happens. The 2^k factorial designs and the 2^{k-p} fractional factorial designs that we consider in Secs. 12.2 and 12.3, respectively, are particularly useful in the early stages of experimentation, when we might be in the dark about which factors are important and how they affect the responses.

After we learn more about which factors really matter and how they appear to be affecting the responses, we can then develop a *metamodel* or *response surface* based on the important factors to accomplish the following:

- *Predict* the model response for system configurations that were not simulated, since the execution time for the simulation model is large
- Find that combination of input-factor values that *optimizes* (i.e., minimizes or maximizes, as appropriate) a response, using what is called *response-surface methodology*

Metamodels, which are discussed in Sec. 12.4, usually take the form of a regression equation that relates the model response to one or more input factors.

This chapter is not meant to be a complete treatment of experimental design, which is a major topic in the field of statistics. In fact, there are whole books on the design of experiments and response-surface methodology, including those by Barton (1999), Box and Draper (2008), Box, Hunter, and Hunter (2005), Montgomery (2013), Myers et al. (2009), and Wu and Hamada (2009). References that discuss experimental design in the context of simulation include Barton (2010), Cheng and Kleijnen (1999), Cioppa and Lucas (2007), Kleijnen (1998, 2007, 2008), Kleijnen et al. (2005), Sanchez and Sanchez (2005), and Sanchez and Wan (2012).

In Sec. 12.5 we discuss in greater generality techniques that have been used to optimize the performance of a simulated system. Our emphasis will be on methods (i.e., metaheuristics) that are used in optimization packages integrated into commercial simulation software.

Although one can think of simulation experiments as just an instance of experimentation in general, there are some advantageous characteristics of simulation that distinguish it from the usual physical manufacturing, laboratory, or agricultural experiments traditionally used as examples in the experiment-design literature:

- As mentioned earlier, we have the opportunity to control factors such as customer arrival rates that are in reality uncontrollable. Thus, we can investigate many more kinds of contingencies than we could in a physical experiment with the system.
- Another aspect of enhanced control over simulation experiments stems from the deterministic nature of random-number generators (see Chap. 7). In simulation experiments, then, we can control the basic source of variability, unlike the situation in physical experiments. Thus, we might be able to use the variance-reduction technique common random numbers (Sec. 11.2) to sharpen our conclusions, although care must be taken to avoid potential backfiring (see the discussion following Example 12.3 as well as Prob. 12.3).
- In most physical experiments it is prudent to *randomize* the run order of factor combinations to protect against systematic bias contributed by experimental conditions, such as a steady rise in ambient laboratory temperature during a sequence of biological experiments that are not thermally insulated. Randomizing in simulation experimentation is not necessary, assuming that the random-number generator is working properly.
- For some physical experiments, it is only possible to make one replication for each combination of factor levels, due to time or cost considerations. Then, to determine whether a particular factor has a statistically significant impact on the response, it is necessary to make the, perhaps questionable, assumption that the response for each factor-level combination has the same variance. However, for many (if not most) simulation models it is now possible (because of computer speeds) to make multiple replications for each input-factor combination, resulting in a simple procedure for determining statistical significance.

12.2
2^k FACTORIAL DESIGNS

If a model has only one factor, the experimental design is conceptually simple: We just run the simulation at various values, or *levels*, of the factor, perhaps forming a confidence interval for the expected response at each of the factor levels. For quantitative factors, a graph of the response as a function of the factor level may be useful. In the case of terminating simulations (Sec. 9.4), we would make some number n of independent replications at each factor level. At the minimum there would be two factor levels, and we would thus need $2n$ replications.

Now suppose that there are k ($k \geq 2$) factors and we want to get an initial estimate of how each factor affects the response. We might also want to determine if the factors *interact* with one another, i.e., whether the effect of one factor on the response depends on the levels of the others. One way to measure the effect of a particular factor would be to fix the levels of the *other* $k - 1$ factors at some set of values and make simulation runs at each of two levels of the factor of interest to see how the response reacts to changes in this single factor. The whole process is then repeated to examine each of the other factors, one a time. This strategy, which is called the *one-factor-at-a-time* (OFAT) *approach*, is quite inefficient in terms of the number of simulation runs needed to obtain a specified precision [see Montgomery (2013, pp. 4–5, 186–187)]. More importantly, it does not allow us to measure any interactions; indeed, it assumes that there are no interactions, which is often not the case in simulation applications.

EXAMPLE 12.1. Suppose that we have two factors A and B. Let the baseline levels of these factors be A^- and B^-. Also, let A^+ and B^+ be proposed levels for these factors. Then the OFAT method would specify simulating the following *three* combinations of A and B:

$$A^-, B^-$$
$$A^+, B^-$$
$$A^-, B^+$$

resulting in the responses $R(A^-, B^-)$, $R(A^+, B^-)$, and $R(A^-, B^+)$. Then the effect on the response of changing factor A from A^- to A^+ would be computed as

$$R(A^+, B^-) - R(A^-, B^-) \tag{12.1}$$

However, this calculation is based *only* on factor B being at its B^- level. It could be, though, that the effect on the response of changing factor A would be quite different if factor B were at its B^+ level (i.e., if the factors interact); see Example 12.3 for a numerical example. (A similar discussion applies to factor B.)

If we had also simulated the combination A^+, B^+ resulting in the response $R(A^+, B^+)$, then the effect on the response of changing factor A could also be computed as

$$R(A^+, B^+) - R(A^-, B^+) \tag{12.2}$$

However, this last calculation would *not* actually be possible under the OFAT strategy, since A^+, B^+ would not have been simulated. For 2^2 factorial designs, which will be discussed next, the average of the differences given by Eqs. (12.1) and (12.2) will be used to estimate the effect on the response of moving factor A from its A^- level to its A^+ level.

A much more economical strategy for determining the effects of factors on the response with which we can also measure interactions, called a 2^k *factorial design*, requires that we choose just *two* levels for each factor and then calls for simulation runs at each of the 2^k possible factor-level combinations, which are sometimes called *design points*. Usually, we associate a minus sign with one level of a factor and a plus sign with the other; which sign is associated with which level is arbitrary, but for quantitative factors it will be less confusing if we use a minus sign to denote the lower numerical value. The levels, which should be chosen in consultation with subject-matter experts, should be far enough apart that we would expect to see a difference in the response, but not so separated that nonsensical configurations are obtained. Because we are using only two levels for each factor, we assume that the response is approximately linear (or at least monotonic) over the range of the factor. [If the response is nonmonotonic (e.g., in the shape of a parabola) over the range, then we might be misled into thinking that the factor has no effect on the response.] We will discuss a method for testing the linearity assumption in Sec. 12.4.

The form of a 2^k factorial design can be compactly represented in tabular form, as in Table 12.2 for $k = 3$. The variable R_i for $i = 1, 2, \ldots, 8$ is the value of the response when running the simulation with the ith combination of factor levels. For instance, R_6 is the response resulting from running the simulation with factors 1 and 3 at their respective "+" levels and factor 2 at its "−" level. We shall see later that writing down this array, called the *design matrix*, facilitates calculation of the factor effects and interactions.

The *main effect* of factor j, denoted by e_j, is the *average change* in the response due to moving factor j from its "−" level to its "+" level while holding all other factors fixed. This average is taken over all combinations of the other factor levels in the design. It is important to realize that a main effect is computed relative to the *current* design and factor levels only, and we cannot generally extrapolate beyond this unless other conditions (e.g., no interactions) are satisfied. These limitations on the interpretation of main effects are discussed later in this section.

For the 2^3 factorial design of Table 12.2, the main effect of factor 1 is thus

$$e_1 = \frac{(R_2 - R_1) + (R_4 - R_3) + (R_6 - R_5) + (R_8 - R_7)}{4}$$

TABLE 12.2
Design matrix for a 2^3 factorial design

Factor combination (design point)	Factor 1	Factor 2	Factor 3	Response
1	−	−	−	R_1
2	+	−	−	R_2
3	−	+	−	R_3
4	+	+	−	R_4
5	−	−	+	R_5
6	+	−	+	R_6
7	−	+	+	R_7
8	+	+	+	R_8

Note that at design points 1 and 2, factors 2 and 3 remain fixed, as they do at design points 3 and 4, 5 and 6, as well as 7 and 8. The main effect of factor 2 is

$$e_2 = \frac{(R_3 - R_1) + (R_4 - R_2) + (R_7 - R_5) + (R_8 - R_6)}{4}$$

and that of factor 3 is

$$e_3 = \frac{(R_5 - R_1) + (R_6 - R_2) + (R_7 - R_3) + (R_8 - R_4)}{4}$$

Looking at Table 12.2 and the above expressions for the e_j's leads to an alternative way of defining main effects, as well as a simpler way of computing them. Namely, e_j is the *difference* between the average response when factor j is at its "+" level and the average response when it is at its "−" level. [See Montgomery (2013, p. 243) for a geometric interpretation of main effects.] Thus, to compute e_j, we simply apply the signs in the "Factor j" column to the corresponding R_i's, add them up, and divide by 2^{k-1}. (In other words, if we interpret the "+" signs and "−" signs in the design matrix as $+1$ and -1, respectively, we take the dot product of the "Factor j" column with the "Response" column and then divide by 2^{k-1}.) For example, in the 2^3 factorial design of Table 12.2,

$$e_2 = \frac{-R_1 - R_2 + R_3 + R_4 - R_5 - R_6 + R_7 + R_8}{4}$$

which is identical to the earlier expression for e_2.

The main effects measure the average change in the response due to a change in an individual factor, with this average being taken over all possible combinations of the other $k - 1$ factors (numbering 2^{k-1}). It could be, though, that the effect of factor j_1 depends in some way on the level of some other factor j_2, in which case these two factors are said to *interact*. A measure of the interaction is the difference between the average effect of factor j_1 when factor j_2 is at its "+" level (and all other factors other than j_1 and j_2 are held constant) and the average effect of factor j_1 when factor j_2 is at its "−" level. By convention *one-half* of this difference is called the *two-factor (two-way) interaction effect* and denoted by $e_{j_1 j_2}$. It is also called the $j_1 \times j_2$ *interaction*. For example, in the design of Table 12.2 we have

$$e_{12} = \frac{1}{2}\left[\frac{(R_4 - R_3) + (R_8 - R_7)}{2} - \frac{(R_2 - R_1) + (R_6 - R_5)}{2}\right]$$

$$e_{13} = \frac{1}{2}\left[\frac{(R_6 - R_5) + (R_8 - R_7)}{2} - \frac{(R_2 - R_1) + (R_4 - R_3)}{2}\right]$$

and

$$e_{23} = \frac{1}{2}\left[\frac{(R_7 - R_5) + (R_8 - R_6)}{2} - \frac{(R_3 - R_1) + (R_4 - R_2)}{2}\right]$$

To see that the formula for e_{13}, for example, measures the quantity described in words above, note from the design matrix in Table 12.2 that factor 3 is always at its "+" level for design points 5, 6, 7, and 8, and that factor 1 moves from its "−" to its "+" level between design points 5 and 6 (where all other factors, in this example just factor 2, remain fixed at the "−" level), as well as between design points 7 and 8 (where factor 2 is fixed at the "+" level). Thus, the first fraction inside the square brackets in the above expression for e_{13} is the average effect of moving factor 1 from its "−" to its "+" level when factor 3 is held at its "+" level. Similarly, the second fraction inside the square brackets is the average effect of moving factor 1 from its "−" to its "+" level (design points 1 to 2, and 3 to 4) when factor 3 is held at its "−" level. The difference between these two fractions, then, is the difference in the effect that factor 1 has on the response depending on whether factor 3 is at its "+" or "−" level; one-half of this difference is the definition of the interaction effect between factors 1 and 3.

As with main effects, there is an easier way to compute interaction effects, based on the design matrix. If we rearrange the above expression for e_{13}, for instance, so that the R_i's appear in increasing order of the i's, we get

$$e_{13} = \frac{R_1 - R_2 + R_3 - R_4 - R_5 + R_6 - R_7 + R_8}{4}$$

Now if we create a new column labeled "1 × 3" of 8 signs by "multiplying" the ith sign in the "Factor 1" column by the ith sign in the "Factor 3" column (the product of like signs is a "+" and the product of opposite signs is a "−"), we get a column of signs that gives us precisely the signs of the R_i's used to form e_{13}; as with main effects, the divisor is 2^{k-1}. Thus, the interaction effect between factors 1 and 3 can be thought of as the difference between the average response when factors 1 and 3 are at the same (both "+" or both "−") level and the average response when they are at opposite levels. (We leave it to the reader to compute e_{12} and e_{23} in this way.) Note that two-factor interaction effects are completely symmetric; for example, $e_{12} = e_{21}$, $e_{23} = e_{32}$, etc.

Although interpretation becomes more difficult, we can define and compute three- and higher-factor interaction effects, all the way up to a k-factor interaction. For example, in the 2^3 factorial design of Table 12.2, the three-factor interaction is one-half the difference between the two-factor interaction effect between factors 1 and 2 when factor 3 is at its "+" level and the two-factor interaction effect between factors 1 and 2 when factor 3 is at its "−" level. That is,

$$\begin{aligned} e_{123} &= \frac{1}{2}\left[\frac{(R_8 - R_7) - (R_6 - R_5)}{2} - \frac{(R_4 - R_3) - (R_2 - R_1)}{2}\right] \\ &= \frac{-R_1 + R_2 + R_3 - R_4 + R_5 - R_6 - R_7 + R_8}{4} \end{aligned}$$

The second expression for e_{123} is obtained by multiplying the ith signs from the columns for factors 1, 2, and 3 in Table 12.2 and applying them to the R_i's; the denominator is once again 2^{k-1}. Three- and higher-factor interaction effects are also symmetric: $e_{123} = e_{132} = e_{213}$, etc.

If two- or higher-factor interactions appear to be present, then the main effect of each factor involved in such a significant interaction *cannot* be interpreted as simply the effect in general of moving that factor from its "−" to its "+" level, since

TABLE 12.3

Coding chart for *s* and *d* in the inventory model

Factor	−	+
s	20	60
d	10	50

the magnitude and possibly the sign of the change in the response depend on the level of at least one other factor.

EXAMPLE 12.2. It is convenient to reparameterize the inventory model of Sec. 1.5 slightly in terms of the ordering policy. Specifically, we let s be the *reorder point* as before, but instead of ordering "up to S" we will view our decision in terms of the *difference* $d = S - s$. In other words, our experimental factors are s and d, and our interest is in how they affect the expected average total operating cost; of course, S is just $s + d$. The "low" and "high" levels we chose for these factors are given in the *coding chart* in Table 12.3. [If we had used the original parameters s and S in the coding chart, then we would have obtained nonsensical inventory policies such as (20, 10).] The design matrix and corresponding response values are given in Table 12.4, together with an extra column giving the signs to be applied in computing the $s \times d$ interaction. Each R_i is the average cost per month from a single 120-month replication; we used independent random-number streams for each separate R_i. The main effects are

$$e_s = \frac{-144.16 + 144.50 - 119.99 + 147.00}{2} = 13.68$$

and

$$e_d = \frac{-144.16 - 144.50 + 119.99 + 147.00}{2} = -10.84$$

and the $s \times d$ interaction effect is

$$e_{sd} = \frac{144.16 - 144.50 - 119.99 + 147.00}{2} = 13.34$$

Thus, the average effect of raising s from 20 to 60 was to increase the monthly cost by 13.68, and raising d from 10 to 50 decreased the monthly cost by an average of 10.84. Therefore, it appears that the smaller value of s and the larger value of d would be preferable, since lower monthly costs are desired. Since the $s \times d$ interaction is positive, there is further indication that lower costs are observed by setting s and d at opposite

TABLE 12.4

Design matrix and simulation results for the 2^2 factorial design on *s* and *d* for the inventory model

Factor combination (design point)	*s*	*d*	*s* × *d*	Response
1	−	−	+	144.16
2	+	−	−	144.50
3	−	+	−	119.99
4	+	+	+	147.00

levels. However, if this interaction really is present in a significant way (a question addressed in Example 12.3 below), then the effect that s has on the response depends on the level of d, and vice versa.

Since the R_i's are random variables, the observed effects are random also. To find out whether the effects are "real," as opposed to being explainable by sampling fluctuation, we must determine if the effects are statistically significant. This is often addressed in the experimental-design literature by performing an *analysis of variance* [see, e.g., Montgomery (2013, pp. 245–249)], which assumes that the response has the same population variance for each design point. However, as we will see in Examples 12.3 and 12.4, this is very often *not* a good assumption in simulation modeling. We will, therefore, take the simple approach of replicating the *whole design* n times to obtain n IID values of each effect. These values can then be used to construct confidence intervals for the *expected* effects. For example, let e_j^i be the observed main effect of factor j on replication i, for $i = 1, 2, \ldots, n$. Let

$$\bar{e}_j(n) = \frac{\sum_{i=1}^{n} e_j^i}{n}$$

and

$$S_j^2(n) = \frac{\sum_{i=1}^{n} [e_j^i - \bar{e}_j(n)]^2}{n-1}$$

Then an approximate $100(1 - \alpha)$ percent confidence interval for the expected main effect $E(e_j)$ is given by [see (4.12)]

$$\bar{e}_j(n) \pm t_{n-1,1-\alpha/2}\sqrt{S_j^2(n)/n}$$

If the confidence interval for $E(e_j)$ does not contain 0, we conclude that the effect is statistically significant; otherwise, we have no statistical evidence that it is actually present. Note that whether an effect is statistically significant depends on the number of replications, n, and the confidence level, $1 - \alpha$. We can construct a confidence interval for an expected interaction effect in a similar manner. We must also keep in mind that *statistical* significance of an effect does not necessarily imply that its magnitude is *practically* significant.

EXAMPLE 12.3. We replicated the entire 2^2 factorial design of the inventory model in Example 12.2 $n = 10$ times, and Table 12.5 gives the sample mean and variance of the

TABLE 12.5
Sample means and variances of the responses for the inventory model

Design point	Sample mean	Sample variance
$s = 20, d = 10$	135.71	22.24
$s = 60, d = 10$	143.94	2.26
$s = 20, d = 50$	119.45	15.07
$s = 60, d = 50$	148.17	1.60

TABLE 12.6
96.667 percent confidence intervals for the expected effects, inventory model

Expected effect	96.667 percent confidence interval
$E(e_s)$	18.47 ± 2.58
$E(e_d)$	-6.02 ± 2.47
$E(e_{sd})$	10.25 ± 2.88

responses across the 10 replications for each of the four design points. Note that the largest and smallest sample variances differ by a factor of approximately 14. Based on the 10 independent replicates of each of the three effects that we obtained, Table 12.6 gives 96.667 percent confidence intervals for $E(e_s)$, $E(e_d)$, and $E(e_{sd})$, so that the overall confidence level is at least 90 percent by Bonferroni's inequality (see Sec. 9.7). All effects appear to be real since their confidence intervals do not contain zero.

In Figs. 12.1*a* and 12.1*b* we give *main-effect plots* for s and d. For each plot, the average cost at a particular level ("−" or "+") for the factor of interest is the average of the sample means in Table 12.5 over the two levels of the other factor. (Thus, 127.58 in Fig. 12.1*a* is the average of 135.71 and 119.45.) If we could interpret these main effects literally, we would expect the average cost per month to increase by 18.47 when we move s from 20 to 60, and to decrease by 6.02 when we move d from 10 to 50. However, since there is a significant interaction between s and d, these main effects are actually of *limited value.*

In Fig. 12.2 we give the *interaction plot* for s and d, where the presence of a significant interaction is indicated by the *nonparallel lines* [see Eq. (12.8)]. In particular, when $d = 10$, moving s from 20 to 60 increases the average cost by 8.23 (see Table 12.5). However, when $d = 50$, moving s from 20 to 60 increases the average cost by 28.72. Note that one-half of the difference between 28.72 and 8.23 is 10.25, which is $\bar{e}_{sd}(10)$ (the average of the 10 interaction effects). Note also that the OFAT approach would give 8.23 as the increase in average cost resulting from moving s from 20 to 60, whereas we got 18.47 from the 2^2 factorial design.

We conclude from Fig. 12.2 that both s and d have a significant effect on the average cost per month. However, the actual numerical change in the average cost due to changing s depends on the level of d, and vice versa; this will be discussed further in Sec. 12.4.

In Examples 12.2 and 12.3 we carried out the simulations across the four different factor combinations independently. Since we are dealing with four different configurations here, we could have used instead common random numbers (CRN) (see Sec. 11.2) across all four of them in an attempt to reduce the half-lengths of the confidence intervals for the expected effects. However, the situation here is not as simple as that in Sec. 11.2. If CRN in fact "works" and induces the desired positive correlations between the responses of the different configurations, certain covariances enter the expression for the variance of an effect with the wrong sign; the variance could thus increase or decrease depending on the relative magnitudes of the covariances and on which effect is involved (see Prob. 12.3). We reran the experiments in Example 12.3 using CRN and found that the confidence-interval

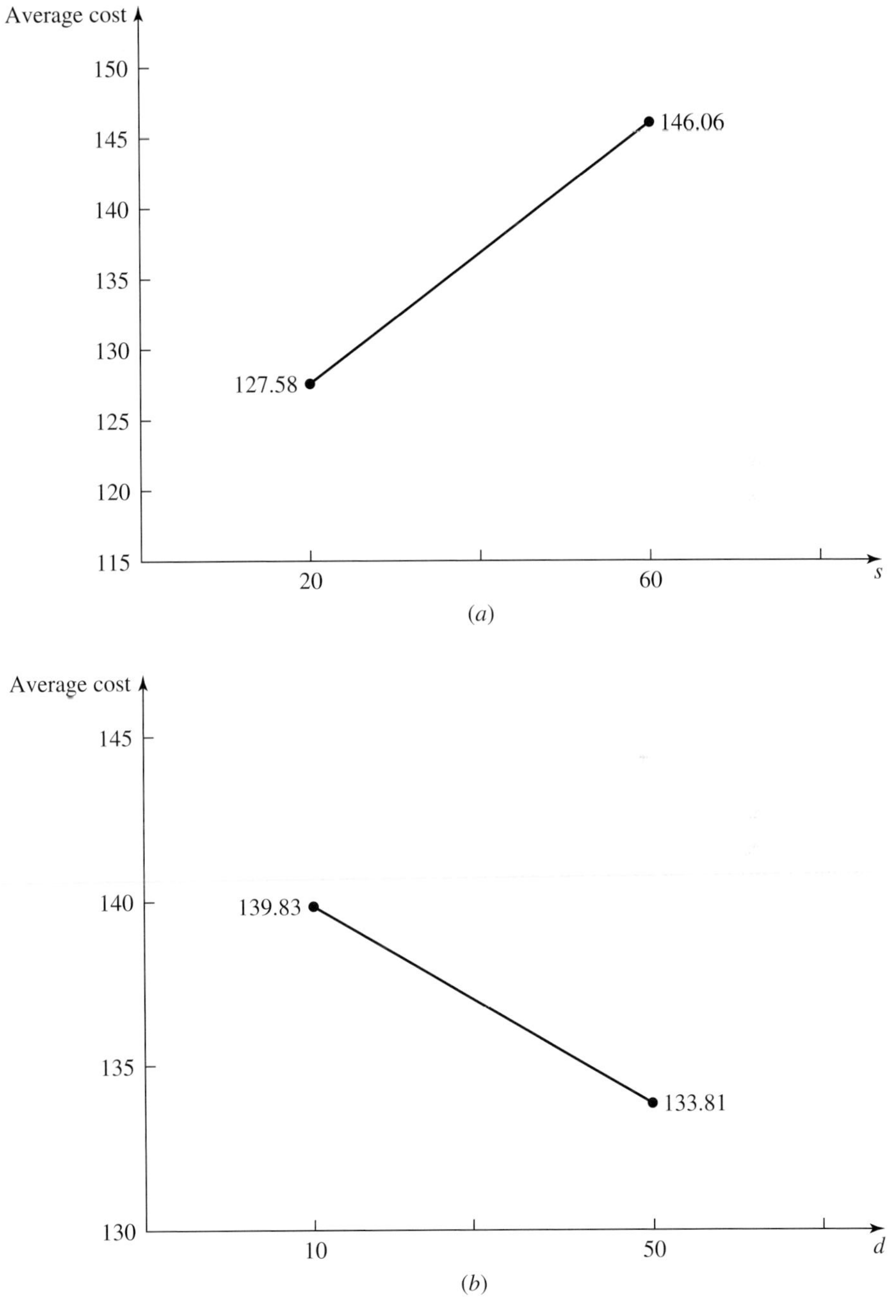

FIGURE 12.1
Main-effect plots for inventory model: (*a*) factor *s*; (*b*) factor *d*.

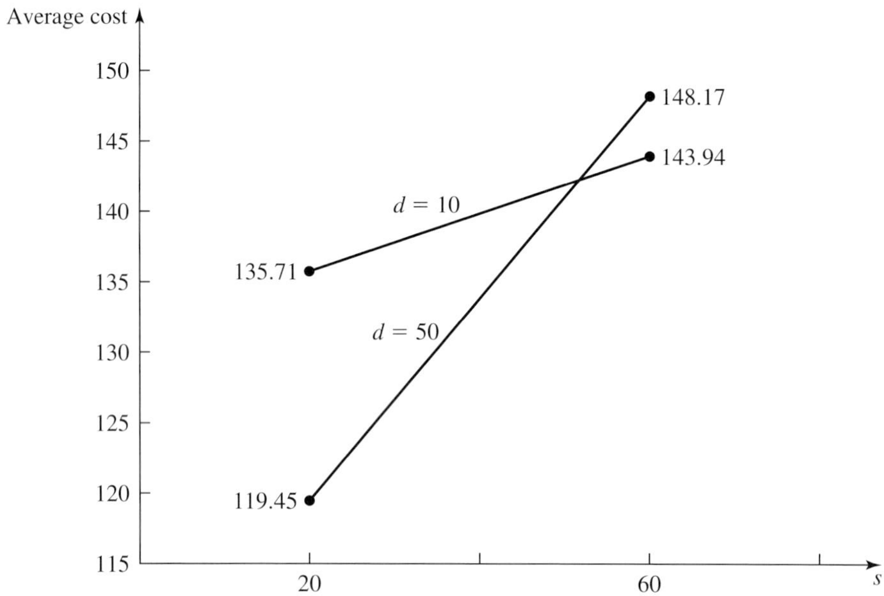

FIGURE 12.2
Interaction plot for factors s and d, inventory model.

half-lengths for $E(e_s)$, $E(e_d)$, and $E(e_{sd})$ were reduced to 1.31, 0.68, and 0.46, respectively. This phenomenon is an instance of the whole issue of random-number allocation in simulation raised originally by Schruben and Margolin (1978); see also Donohue et al. (1992, 1995) and Hussey et al. (1987).

Our next example in this section concerns a model with six factors, and it illustrates the computational effort required when applying 2^k factorial designs to problems with a larger number of factors.

EXAMPLE 12.4. In Example 9.25 a model of a small factory was introduced in which parts arrive for machining and then go on to be inspected; parts failing inspection are returned to the machining station for rework (see Fig. 9.9). The machine also experiences breakdowns and then must undergo repair. The model runs for 160 hours, from which the first 40 hours are deleted (see Example 9.35) to allow the model to warm up to steady state. We take as our response the average time a part spends in the system. We do not consider throughput, since it will be 60 parts per hour for any well-defined (i.e., stable in the long run) system configuration. Parts arrive according to a Poisson process at rate 1 per minute, which we assume is uncontrollable and will not include in our design as an experimental factor. There are six other factors that could be controllable, as given in Table 12.7. For each factor, the "−" level is the current situation, as described in Example 9.25, and the "+" level represents what is felt would be an improvement in terms of reducing the average time in system of parts. Note that in all but one case the numerical parameters at the "+" level are actually smaller than their counterparts at the "−" level, violating our earlier advice; but by coding in this way each main effect will be the consequence of the corresponding purported improvement.

TABLE 12.7
Factor coding, small-factory model (all times are in minutes)

Factor number	Factor description	− (current)	+ (improved)
1	Machining times	U(0.65, 0.70)	U(0.585, 0.630)
2	Inspection times	U(0.75, 0.80)	U(0.675, 0.720)
3	Machine uptimes	expo(360)	expo(396)
4	Machine repair times	U(8, 12)	U(7.2, 10.8)
5	Probability of a bad part	0.10	0.09
6	Queue disciplines (both)	FIFO	Shortest job first

Factors 1 through 5 are quantitative, and the "+" level in each case constitutes a 10 percent improvement; factor 6 is qualitative and represents changing the discipline in each of the two queues from FIFO to shortest job first in terms of their actual machining or inspection times.

Table 12.8 is the complete design matrix for the 2^6 factorial design, and requires 64 different design points. We replicated this entire design $n = 5$ times to get confidence intervals on the expected effects, as in Example 12.3, so there were in all 320 simulation runs for the experiment. It turned out to be most convenient to use CRN across all 64 design points.

Figure 12.3 plots the responses from individual replications (in minutes) as the small dots, so there are five of them distributed vertically over each design point. The large dots show the average of the five replications at each design point, and the horizontal line gives the overall average of the responses, i.e., the average of all 320 individual-replication results. Several observations can be made directly from this graph:

- There is a strong and consistent pairing of the large dots—two "high" values, followed by two "low" values, then two "high" values, etc. Looking back at the design matrix in Table 12.8, we see that the pattern follows the level changes of factor 2, the inspection-time factor. What seems clear (and will be confirmed formally below with the effects computations) is that decreasing the inspection times produces a consistent and appreciable improvement in the response.
- Within each group of two large dots, the second one is lower. Factor 1 (machining times) is the one that changes level at every point, so we see that average time in system could be reduced by decreasing the machining times.
- Within each block of 16 large dots, the second eight are lower than the first eight. Factor 4 (machine repair times) is the one that changes level every eight points, so we see that improved performance could be expected from reducing machine downtimes.
- Within each block of 32 large dots, the second 16 are lower, indicating the benefit of reducing the probability of a part's failing inspection (factor 5, which switches level after 16 design points).
- The results from design points 33 through 64 seem to be nearly an exact copy of those from design points 1 through 32; the only difference between the factor settings in these two groups is the queue discipline applied to each of the queues (factor 6). Thus, it appears that this factor is quite unimportant.

TABLE 12.8
Design matrix for the 2^6 factorial design, small-factory model

Design point	Factor number 1	2	3	4	5	6	Design point	Factor number 1	2	3	4	5	6
1	−	−	−	−	−	−	33	−	−	−	−	−	+
2	+	−	−	−	−	−	34	+	−	−	−	−	+
3	−	+	−	−	−	−	35	−	+	−	−	−	+
4	+	+	−	−	−	−	36	+	+	−	−	−	+
5	−	−	+	−	−	−	37	−	−	+	−	−	+
6	+	−	+	−	−	−	38	+	−	+	−	−	+
7	−	+	+	−	−	−	39	−	+	+	−	−	+
8	+	+	+	−	−	−	40	+	+	+	−	−	+
9	−	−	−	+	−	−	41	−	−	−	+	−	+
10	+	−	−	+	−	−	42	+	−	−	+	−	+
11	−	+	−	+	−	−	43	−	+	−	+	−	+
12	+	+	−	+	−	−	44	+	+	−	+	−	+
13	−	−	+	+	−	−	45	−	−	+	+	−	+
14	+	−	+	+	−	−	46	+	−	+	+	−	+
15	−	+	+	+	−	−	47	−	+	+	+	−	+
16	+	+	+	+	−	−	48	+	+	+	+	−	+
17	−	−	−	−	+	−	49	−	−	−	−	+	+
18	+	−	−	−	+	−	50	+	−	−	−	+	+
19	−	+	−	−	+	−	51	−	+	−	−	+	+
20	+	+	−	−	+	−	52	+	+	−	−	+	+
21	−	−	+	−	+	−	53	−	−	+	−	+	+
22	+	−	+	−	+	−	54	+	−	+	−	+	+
23	−	+	+	−	+	−	55	−	+	+	−	+	+
24	+	+	+	−	+	−	56	+	+	+	−	+	+
25	−	−	−	+	+	−	57	−	−	−	+	+	+
26	+	−	−	+	+	−	58	+	−	−	+	+	+
27	−	+	−	+	+	−	59	−	+	−	+	+	+
28	+	+	−	+	+	−	60	+	+	−	+	+	+
29	−	−	+	+	+	−	61	−	−	+	+	+	+
30	+	−	+	+	+	−	62	+	−	+	+	+	+
31	−	+	+	+	+	−	63	−	+	+	+	+	+
32	+	+	+	+	+	−	64	+	+	+	+	+	+

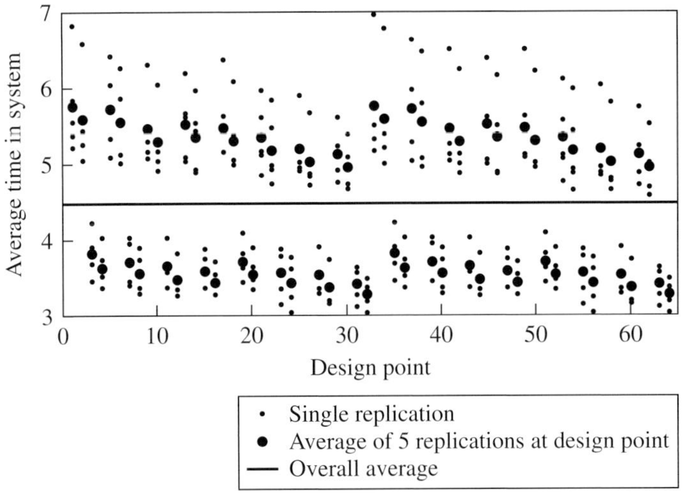

FIGURE 12.3
Experimental design for small factory: individual-replication and average-over-replications results.

- The variance of the five responses (small dots) for a particular design point is larger when the average of the five responses (large dots) is large, which occurs above the "Overall average" horizontal line. In particular, the sample variances for design points 1 (all factors at their "−" levels) and 64 (all factors at their "+" levels) are 0.413 and 0.034, respectively. (Actually, the largest sample variance is 0.550, which occurs at design point 33; this is 16 times larger than the smallest sample variance of 0.034.) Thus, we see for this problem that the variance of the response is *not* constant across the 64 design points, which is a fundamental assumption of the analysis of variance.

While the above observations are valuable, we should confirm them formally and also attempt to quantify the effects. Table 12.9 [$E(e_j)$ is the expected main effect for

TABLE 12.9
90 percent confidence intervals for the expected main effects (in minutes), small-factory model

Expected main effect	90 percent confidence interval
$E(e_1)$	-0.17 ± 0.03
$E(e_2)$	-1.83 ± 0.29
$E(e_3)$	-0.07 ± 0.10
$E(e_4)$	-0.20 ± 0.09
$E(e_5)$	-0.23 ± 0.11
$E(e_6)$	-0.01 ± 0.05

TABLE 12.10
90 percent confidence intervals for the expected interaction effects (in minutes), small-factory model

Expected interaction effect	90 percent confidence interval	Expected interaction effect	90 percent confidence interval
$E(e_{12})$	0.008 ± 0.013	$E(e_{26})$	-0.001 ± 0.047
$E(e_{13})$	0.012 ± 0.015	$E(e_{34})$	0.029 ± 0.054
$E(e_{14})$	-0.001 ± 0.008	$E(e_{35})$	-0.040 ± 0.017
$E(e_{15})$	0.003 ± 0.007	$E(e_{36})$	-0.001 ± 0.003
$E(e_{16})$	-0.004 ± 0.001	$E(e_{45})$	-0.004 ± 0.008
$E(e_{23})$	-0.026 ± 0.107	$E(e_{46})$	0.0018 ± 0.0019
$E(e_{24})$	0.050 ± 0.034	$E(e_{56})$	-0.001 ± 0.005
$E(e_{25})$	0.103 ± 0.056	—	—

factor j] and Table 12.10 [$E(e_{j_1 j_2})$ is the expected interaction effect between factors j_1 and j_2] give 90 percent confidence intervals for the 6 expected main effects and 15 expected interaction effects (in minutes), respectively, and in Fig. 12.4 we plot these confidence intervals. (We did not use the Bonferroni inequality to adjust the confidence levels, since there are a total of 21 confidence intervals.) Although we computed three- and higher-way interactions (including the six-way interaction) as well, we do not give them here since they were all extremely close to zero. Actually, we see from Table 12.10 and Fig. 12.4 that the two-way interactions are either not statistically significant (11 out of 15) or are "small" in magnitude. Indeed, this lack of important interactions is what allows direct interpretation of the main-effects estimates, which we discuss next.

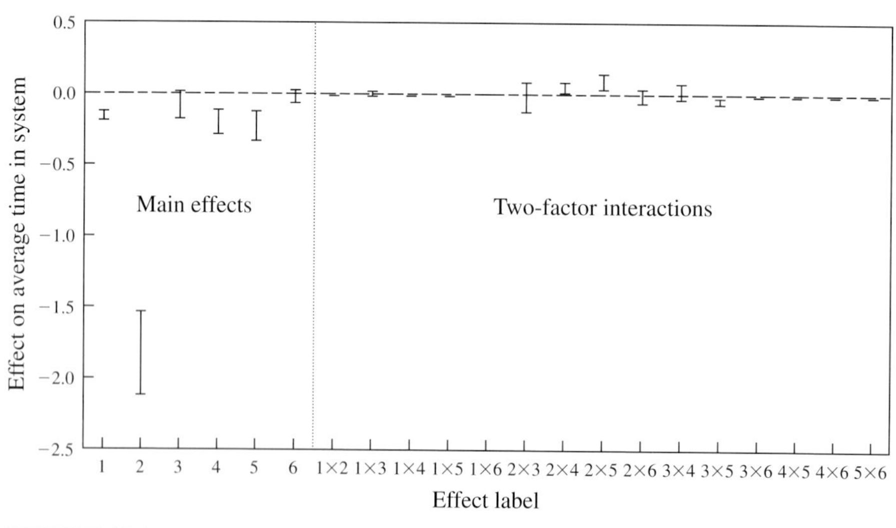

FIGURE 12.4
Experimental design for small factory: main effects and two-factor interactions.

The greatest reduction in average time in system (1.83 minutes) can be obtained by reducing inspection times (factor 2). Beyond that, it would seem that improving quality (factor 5), reducing machine repair times (factor 4), or reducing machining times (factor 1) would be the next best step to take. Factor 3 (machine uptimes) is not statistically significant (its confidence interval contains 0 in Table 12.9) and is small in magnitude, so effort should not go to improving the machine's reliability. Factor 6 (queue discipline) is not statistically significant and very small in magnitude, so it's certainly not worthwhile to change the queue discipline. In any future analysis of this system [e.g., an attempt to find the optimal values of the factors (see Sec. 12.5)], factors 4 and 6 can be set to their "−" levels and probably not considered again, thereby reducing the size of the problem to just four factors.

There were four two-way interaction effects that were statistically significant, with the 2 × 5 interaction having the largest magnitude (0.10). However, even this interaction is of little practical consequence.

Since we did not find any important interactions, a main effect *can* be regarded as the change in average time in system that results from moving the corresponding factor from its "−" level to its "+" level (see Sec. 12.4 for further discussion). However, it is probably *not* safe to assume that a main-effect estimate is an accurate portrayal of what happens to the response in general when the factor is moved by the *amount* of the difference from its "−" to its "+" level, starting from *any* initial value. For example, the probability of a bad part (factor 5) was 0.10 at its "−" level and 0.09 at its "+" level, a change of −0.01 when moving from "−" to "+". Thus, due to the absence of important interactions, we will interpret the main-effect estimate of factor 5 as the change in the response if we move this factor from 0.10 to 0.09. However, it is probably *not* safe to say that this same main-effect estimate is an accurate portrayal of what would happen to the response if we were to move this factor by the same −0.01, starting from *any* value (say, moving it from 0.99 to 0.98, or from 0.43 to 0.42), unless we were willing to make the somewhat risky assumption that the response remains linear well outside the range of the factor levels that we actually considered in our experiment. We just do not have any direct knowledge about the response outside of the range of the factor levels we chose (in this example, 0.10 to 0.09), and it is thus questionable to extrapolate our results and conclusions out to those unexplored regions where we did not experiment.

EXAMPLE 12.5. Consider the predator-prey model of Sec. 13.2.1, which you should read in detail before proceeding. The five factors of interest are given in the coding chart in Table 12.11, along with their abbreviations and their "−" and "+" levels. The response is the average number of wolves alive over a horizon of 2000 time points. We

TABLE 12.11
Coding chart for the predator-prey model

Factor number	Factor description	−	+
1	Sheep gain in energy (SG)	3	5
2	Sheep reproduction rate (SR)	3	5
3	Wolf gain in energy (WG)	15	25
4	Wolf reproduction rate (WR)	4	6
5	Grass regrowth time (RT)	15	35

TABLE 12.12
95 percent confidence intervals for the expected main effects (in wolves), predator-prey model

Expected main effect	95 percent confidence interval
$E(e_1)$	45.99 ± 6.35
$E(e_2)$	27.33 ± 1.52
$E(e_3)$	26.12 ± 5.58
$E(e_4)$	-1.38 ± 7.40
$E(e_5)$	-12.15 ± 3.28

performed a 2^5 factorial design and made $n = 5$ replications at each design point using the NetLogo (2013) simulation package. (Independent random numbers were used for each of the 32 design points.) We give approximate 95 percent confidence intervals for the expected main effects in Table 12.12. All main effects except for wolf reproduction rate are "large" and statistically significant.

We give 95 percent confidence intervals for the expected two-factor, three-factor, and four-factor interaction effects in Tables 12.13 through 12.15, respectively. (The five-factor interaction effect is not statistically significant.) Note that five of the ten

TABLE 12.13
95 percent confidence intervals for the expected two-factor interaction effects (in wolves), predator-prey model

Expected two-factor interaction effect	95 percent confidence interval	Expected two-factor interaction effect	95 percent confidence interval
$E(e_{12})$	16.21 ± 2.22	$E(e_{24})$	1.09 ± 4.34
$E(e_{13})$	-23.40 ± 6.46	$E(e_{25})$	-4.90 ± 5.69
$E(e_{14})$	-2.28 ± 6.20	$E(e_{34})$	-1.84 ± 6.74
$E(e_{15})$	12.08 ± 1.69	$E(e_{35})$	5.33 ± 3.66
$E(e_{23})$	12.28 ± 1.92	$E(e_{45})$	0.77 ± 4.21

TABLE 12.14
95 percent confidence intervals for the expected three-factor interaction effects (in wolves), predator-prey model

Expected three-factor interaction effect	95 percent confidence interval	Expected three-factor interaction effect	95 percent confidence interval
$E(e_{123})$	2.06 ± 2.71	$E(e_{145})$	-0.13 ± 3.63
$E(e_{124})$	-0.56 ± 4.98	$E(e_{234})$	0.99 ± 4.34
$E(e_{125})$	-0.73 ± 4.46	$E(e_{235})$	-0.81 ± 5.56
$E(e_{134})$	-3.45 ± 5.90	$E(e_{245})$	2.53 ± 8.09
$E(e_{135})$	28.21 ± 2.08	$E(e_{345})$	0.31 ± 4.59

TABLE 12.15
95 percent confidence intervals for the expected four-factor interaction effects (in wolves), predator-prey model

Expected four-factor interaction effect	95 percent confidence interval
$E(e_{1234})$	-0.89 ± 4.88
$E(e_{1235})$	2.78 ± 3.78
$E(e_{1245})$	1.63 ± 7.30
$E(e_{1345})$	0.20 ± 3.77
$E(e_{2345})$	1.93 ± 8.34

two-factor interaction effects are statistically significant and some are large in magnitude. Observe also that the $1 \times 3 \times 5$ interaction effect is large (i.e., 28.21) and statistically significant. This can also be seen in the *cube plot* shown in Fig. 12.5, where SR = 4 and WR = 5. The numbers in "boxes" at the vertices of the cube are the average responses across the five replications for the corresponding design points. It is clear from the plot that the three factors do work together to determine the response. This shows that three-factor interactions can, in fact, be large for some models, contrary to what is often assumed for fractional factorial designs (see Sec. 12.3). On the other hand, the four-way interaction effects are not statistically significant, although several are somewhat different than zero.

Finally, note for this model that the sample variances for the 32 design points varied from a minimum of 0.028 to a maximum of 2261.35, a factor of 80,763 difference!

It should be mentioned that a factor can be important even if the magnitude of its main effect is small, which is illustrated by the following example.

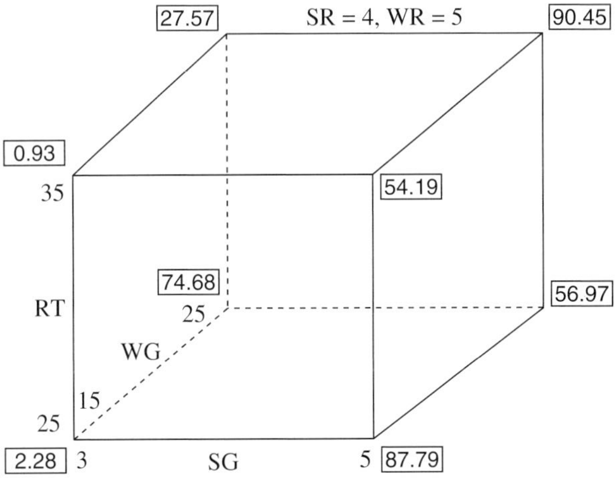

FIGURE 12.5
Cube plot for factors SG, WG, and RT, predator-prey model.

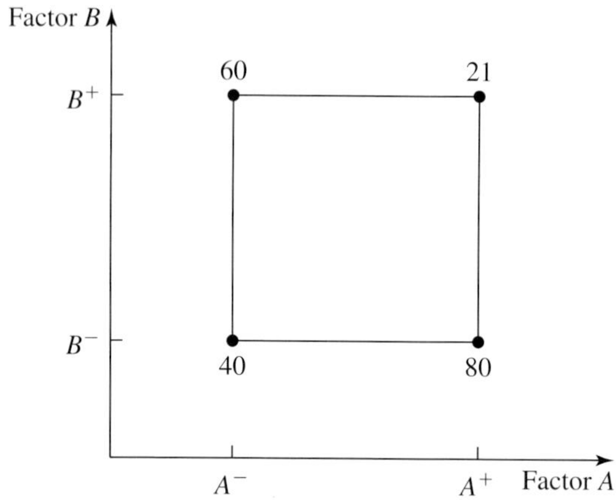

FIGURE 12.6
A 2^2 factorial design with the resulting responses.

EXAMPLE 12.6. Suppose that we have two factors A and B with "−" levels A^- and B^- and "+" levels A^+ and B^+. The responses at the four design points are given in Fig. 12.6. Then the main effects of factors A and B are

$$e_A = \frac{(80 - 40) + (21 - 60)}{2} = 0.5$$

and

$$e_B = \frac{(60 - 40) + (21 - 80)}{2} = -19.5$$

If factor B is at its B^+ level, then the response decreases by 39 when A is moved from its A^- level to its A^+ level. On the other hand, if factor B is at its B^- level, then the response increases by 40 when A is moved from its A^- level to its A^+ level. Thus, the $A \times B$ interaction effect is

$$e_{AB} = \frac{-39 - 40}{2} = -39.5$$

Since $e_A = 0.5$ is small, at first glance we might conclude that factor A has essentially no effect on the response. In fact, moving factor A from its A^- level to its A^+ level *does* have a significant impact on the response, but the amount of the change depends on the level of factor B. Thus, we see that the importance of a particular factor can be hidden in the presence of a significant interaction.

Our examples in this section illustrate the experimental-design methods we have described, but the reader might find it interesting to peruse accounts of applications of these methods (as well as those in the next section) in simulation projects, such as by Hood and Welch (1992), Kang et al. (2006), Kumar and Nottestad (2006), Porcaro (1996), and Posadas and Paulo (2003). We might mention as well that the 2^k factorial designs considered in this section and the 2^{k-p} fractional factorial designs presented in the next section have been implemented in the AutoStat package that is an option for the AutoMod simulation software [see Applied (2013)]. Also, factorial designs are available in the ExtendSim simulation software (see Sec. 3.5.2). There are also several statistical software packages that provide excellent capabilities for experimental design, including Design-Expert [Stat-Ease (2013)], JMP [SAS (2013)], and Minitab [Minitab (2013)].

12.3
2^{k-p} FRACTIONAL FACTORIAL DESIGNS

Our experiment with the manufacturing model of Example 12.4 involved six factors and required considerable computational effort. It is easy to imagine a more complicated version of this model in which we might be interested in dozens of factors. In such a case, a full 2^k factorial design would quickly become unmanageable. For instance, $k = 11$ factors would lead to $2^{11} = 2048$ design points, and if we wanted to make $n = 5$ replications at each design point (certainly a modest sample size from a statistical viewpoint), there would be 10,240 replications in all. If each replication took, say, 1 minute of computer time (a modest amount of time for many real-world simulation models), we would need more than a full week of round-the-clock computing to run the experiment.

In this section we first discuss 2^{k-p} fractional factorial designs, which are widely used to "screen out" an important subset of k factors of interest, with generally less computational effort than would be required by a full factorial design; typically, fractional factorial designs have been used with 15 or fewer factors. We then review the literature on other types of screening designs that could be considered when the number of factors is much larger. The hope with screening designs is that we can quickly determine some of the factors as being important, fix the other factors at some reasonable levels, and thus forget about them in follow-up studies that pay more attention to the factors that *do* matter. In particular, reducing the number of factors likewise reduces the dimensionality of the search space for optimum-seeking methods discussed in Sec. 12.5, which is a great computational benefit when using such methods.

Fractional factorial designs provide a way to get good estimates of the main effects and often two-factor interactions at a fraction of the computational effort required by a full 2^k factorial design. Basically, a 2^{k-p} fractional factorial design is constructed by choosing a certain subset (of size 2^{k-p}) of all the 2^k possible design points and then running the simulation for only these chosen points. Since only $1/2^p$ of the possible 2^k factor combinations are actually run, we sometimes speak of a "half fraction" if $p = 1$, a "quarter fraction" if $p = 2$, and so on. Clearly, we would like p to be large from a computational viewpoint, but a larger p may also result in less information from the experiment, as one might expect.

The important issue of *which* 2^{k-p} of the possible 2^k combinations to choose is an involved issue whose thorough explanation is best left to the experimental-design literature [see, e.g., Montgomery (2013, chap. 8)]. We can nevertheless give a relatively simple "cookbook" procedure to use in many situations.

To do so requires that we first discuss the idea of *confounding* in 2^{k-p} fractional factorial designs. It will turn out that in such a design we may wind up with exactly the same algebraic expression for several different effects. For instance, in a 2^{4-1} half fraction, it could be that the formulas for the main effect e_4 and the three-way interaction effect e_{123} are identical; in this case we say that the main effect of factor 4 is *confounded* or *aliased* with the three-way interaction effect between factors 1, 2, and 3. What this really means is that the common formula for e_4 and e_{123} is an unbiased estimator for $E(e_4) + E(e_{123})$. We say that e_4 and e_{123} are *aliases* of each other, and we denote this by $e_4 = e_{123}$. Now if we are willing to assume that $E(e_{123}) = 0$ or is negligible in comparison with $E(e_4)$, then e_4 is an unbiased (or nearly so) estimator of $E(e_4)$. It often happens that higher-way interactions *do* turn out to be small in comparison with main effects or perhaps two-way interactions (as we indeed noted in Example 12.4), so such an assumption may actually be warranted. Trouble may arise, though, in cases where two-way interactions are confounded with each other; e.g., the formulas for e_{12} and e_{34} could be identical, in which case this common expression is an unbiased estimator for $E(e_{12}) + E(e_{34})$ and we may feel uncomfortable assuming that either of the two-way interactions is zero. Worse, we may have a main effect confounded with a two-way interaction, which makes the main-effect estimate of limited value if the two-way interaction is present (which we cannot easily determine because two-way interactions are confounded with main effects, with each other, and with higher-way interactions). In general, the larger the value of p, the more pervasive the confounding problem.

One way to quantify the overall severity of confounding is through the concept of the *resolution* of a particular 2^{k-p} fractional factorial design. It is guaranteed that two effects are not confounded with each other if the sum of their "ways" is strictly less than the design's resolution; for this purpose main effects are regarded as "one-way" effects. The most commonly used fractional factorial designs in physical experiments are resolutions III, IV, and V (resolutions are denoted by Roman numerals), and their definitions are given in Table 12.16. For instance, in a resolution IV design, no main effect is confounded with any other main effect *or* with any two-way interaction ($1 + 2 < 4$), but two-way interactions are aliased with each other ($2 + 2 = 4$). Thus, assuming that three-way (and higher-way) interactions are negligible, resolution IV designs allow us to obtain "clear" main-effects estimates. Notationally, the resolution is attached as a subscript: 2_{IV}^{6-2}, 2_{V}^{5-1}, etc. We will also be interested in resolution VI and VII designs (see Table 12.17), whose definitions should be clear.

Once we have determined the number of factors k and the desired resolution, we need to construct the design, i.e., identify p and which 2^{k-p} rows of the full

TABLE 12.16
Definitions of resolution III, IV, and V fractional factorial designs

Resolution	Definition
III	No main effect is confounded with any other main effect, but main effects are confounded with two-way interactions and some two-way interactions may be confounded with each other.
IV	No main effect is confounded with any other main effect *or* with any two-way interaction, but two-way interactions are aliased with each other.
V	No main effect or two-way interaction is confounded with any other main effect or two-way interaction.

TABLE 12.17
Rules for constructing 2^{k-p} fractional factorial designs

	Factors (k)						
Runs	**3**	**4**	**5**	**6**	**7**	**8**	**9**
4	2^{3-1}_{III} $3 = \pm 12$						
8		2^{4-1}_{IV} $4 = \pm 123$	2^{5-2}_{III} $4 = \pm 12$ $5 = \pm 13$	2^{6-3}_{III} $4 = \pm 12$ $5 = \pm 13$ $6 = \pm 23$	2^{7-4}_{III} $4 = \pm 12$ $5 = \pm 13$ $6 = \pm 23$ $7 = \pm 123$		
16			2^{5-1}_{V} $5 = \pm 1234$	2^{6-2}_{IV} $5 = \pm 123$ $6 = \pm 234$	2^{7-3}_{IV} $5 = \pm 123$ $6 = \pm 234$ $7 = \pm 134$	2^{8-4}_{IV} $5 = \pm 234$ $6 = \pm 134$ $7 = \pm 123$ $8 = \pm 124$	2^{9-5}_{III} $5 = \pm 123$ $6 = \pm 234$ $7 = \pm 134$ $8 = \pm 124$ $9 = \pm 1234$
32				2^{6-1}_{VI} $6 = \pm 12345$	2^{7-2}_{IV} $6 = \pm 1234$ $7 = \pm 1245$	2^{8-3}_{IV} $6 = \pm 123$ $7 = \pm 124$ $8 = \pm 2345$	2^{9-4}_{IV} $6 = \pm 2345$ $7 = \pm 1345$ $8 = \pm 1245$ $9 = \pm 1235$
64					2^{7-1}_{VII} $7 = \pm 123456$	2^{8-2}_{V} $7 = \pm 1234$ $8 = \pm 1256$	2^{9-3}_{IV} $7 = \pm 1234$ $8 = \pm 1356$ $9 = \pm 3456$
128							2^{9-2}_{VI} $8 = \pm 13467$ $9 = \pm 23567$

2^k factorial design matrix to use. The first step is to write out a full 2^{k-p} factorial design matrix in factors 1, 2, . . . , $k - p$, as in Tables 12.2 and 12.8. (This basic design matrix has the required number of rows, namely, 2^{k-p}.) The remaining p columns (for factors $k - p + 1, \ldots, k$) are then determined by "multiplying" certain of the first $k - p$ columns together according to the rules given in Table 12.17 [which is excerpted from Montgomery (2013, p. 342)], where "multiplying columns" means that corresponding entries of each column are multiplied together and the product of like signs is a "+" while the product of different signs is a "−," exactly as we did in computing interactions in full factorial designs. The required number of runs (design points) for a particular 2^{k-p} design is also given in Table 12.17.

For example, to construct a 2^{8-2}_{V} design (a quarter fraction in $k = 8$ factors) described in Table 12.17, we first write out a full 2^6 factorial design in factors 1, 2, . . . , 6, and we then define the column for factor 7 to be the product of columns 1, 2, 3, and 4; the column for factor 8 is the product of columns 1, 2, 5, and 6. (Note that we could have reversed the signs of either or both of columns 7 or 8, taking instead the "−" option in the "±" specification in Table 12.17; this flexibility could prove useful in simulation if, for instance, always taking the "+" option leads to model configurations that are costly to run.) The main effect of factor j is then computed as in full factorial designs: Apply the signs of the column for factor j to the corresponding numbers in the response column and add them up; this is divided, though, by 2^{k-p-1} rather than 2^{k-1}. Interactions are also computed as before: Multiply the columns for the involved factors together, apply the resulting signs to the response column, add them up, and divide by 2^{k-p-1}; when computing interactions, we should remember that not all of them are clear of confounding due to the limited design resolution.

A few comments are in order before we give an example that uses fractional factorial designs:

- That the designs defined by this procedure are actually of the indicated resolution is not immediately obvious; the interested reader should see Montgomery (2013, chap. 8.) We can begin to see why, though, by looking at the definition, say, of the 2_{V}^{8-2} design in Table 12.17 (taking the "+" option for both factors 7 and 8). If we were to construct this design and then decide to compute the four-factor interaction e_{1234}, we would obviously get a formula identical to that for e_7, since this is precisely how the column for factor 7 was defined. Thus, the main effect of factor 7 is confounded with this four-way interaction, but not with a three-way interaction since four separate factors were used in the definition of its column in the design matrix. All this is consistent with what is meant by a resolution V design.
- There may not be a design of the desired resolution for a particular k. For example, there is not a resolution V design for $k = 6$. However, in this case we could use a 2_{VI}^{6-1} design (resolution VI with $p = 1$), which would require 32 design points (see Table 12.17). Note also that Table 12.17 is extended out to $k = 15$ factors in Montgomery.

EXAMPLE 12.7. We reconsider the small-factory model of Example 12.4 using the 2_{VI}^{6-1} design from Table 12.17, taking the "+" option for factor 6. The resulting design matrix is given in Table 12.18. A main effect is not aliased with any other main effect or with any two-way, three-way, or four-way interaction, and a two-way interaction is not aliased with any other two-way interaction or any three-way interaction. Since we already made five replications for these 32 design points in Example 12.4, we used the same responses to compute estimates of main effects and two-way interactions based on the 2_{VI}^{6-1} design. We give approximate 90 percent confidence intervals for the expected main effects in Table 12.19. These estimates are identical to their full-factorial counterparts in Table 12.9 to two decimal places. (The magnitude of the largest five-way interaction in the analysis of Example 12.4 was 0.0009.) Approximate 90 percent confidence intervals for the expected two-factor interaction effects are given in Table 12.20. These estimates are very similar to those from the factorial design in Table 12.10. (The magnitude of the largest four-way interaction in the analysis of Example 12.4 was 0.002.) Thus, we came to the same conclusions from our 32-run resolution VI fractional factorial design as we did from the 64 design points of our full 2^6 factorial design.

The next example shows that things do not necessarily work out completely well when we use a fractional factorial design rather than a full factorial design and there happens to be a significant three-factor interaction present.

TABLE 12.18
The 2_{VI}^{6-1} design matrix

	Factor number					
Design point	**1**	**2**	**3**	**4**	**5**	**6**
1	–	–	–	–	–	–
2	+	–	–	–	–	+
3	–	+	–	–	–	+
4	+	+	–	–	–	–
5	–	–	+	–	–	+
6	+	–	+	–	–	–
7	–	+	+	–	–	–
8	+	+	+	–	–	+
9	–	–	–	+	–	+
10	+	–	–	+	–	–
11	–	+	–	+	–	–
12	+	+	–	+	–	+
13	–	–	+	+	–	–
14	+	–	+	+	–	+
15	–	+	+	+	–	+
16	+	+	+	+	–	–
17	–	–	–	–	+	+
18	+	–	–	–	+	–
19	–	+	–	–	+	–
20	+	+	–	–	+	+
21	–	–	+	–	+	–
22	+	–	+	–	+	+
23	–	+	+	–	+	+
24	+	+	+	–	+	–
25	–	–	–	+	+	–
26	+	–	–	+	+	+
27	–	+	–	+	+	+
28	+	+	–	+	+	–
29	–	–	+	+	+	+
30	+	–	+	+	+	–
31	–	+	+	+	+	–
32	+	+	+	+	+	+

EXAMPLE 12.8. Consider again the predator-prey model of Example 12.5, where we performed a 2^5 factorial design. Recall from Table 12.15 that the four-factor interaction effects differed somewhat from zero, although they were not statistically significant. We now perform a 2_{V}^{5-1} fractional factorial design (see Table 12.17) using the response data from Example 12.5. Main effects are now confounded with four-factor interaction effects and two-factor interaction effects are confounded with three-factor interaction effects. The *biased* main-effect estimates are given in column 2

TABLE 12.19
90 percent confidence intervals for the expected main effects (in minutes) for a 2_{VI}^{6-1} fractional factorial design, small-factory model

Expected main effect	90 percent confidence interval
$E(e_1)$	-0.17 ± 0.03
$E(e_2)$	-1.83 ± 0.29
$E(e_3)$	-0.07 ± 0.10
$E(e_4)$	-0.20 ± 0.09
$E(e_5)$	-0.23 ± 0.11
$E(e_6)$	-0.01 ± 0.05

of Table 12.21. In column 3 are the unbiased main-effect estimates from the factorial design (Table 12.12). Finally, in column 4 are unbiased estimates of the corresponding four-factor interaction effects from the factorial design (Table 12.15). (Main effects and four-factor interaction effects are unbiased for the factorial design.) For example, the 1.93 in column 4 of row 2 is an unbiased estimate of $E(e_{2345})$. Note for a particular data row in Table 12.21 that the sum of the numbers in columns 3 and 4 is equal to the number in column 2 (as expected). Thus, the resolution V fractional factorial design gave us "slightly" biased estimates of the main effects because of the nonzero four-factor interaction effects. [However, the estimate of $E(e_4)$ was actually of the wrong sign.] It did, however, still identify factors 1, 2, and 3 as being the most important.

On the other hand, the resolution V design estimated $E(e_{24})$ to be 29.30, whereas the *unbiased* estimate from the factorial design was 1.09 (Table 12.13)! This is because the unbiased estimate of $E(e_{135})$ was 28.21 for the factorial design (Table 12.14).

As we just saw in Examples 12.7 and 12.8, fractional factorial designs *may* be an effective tool for screening out a subset of the k factors that are the "drivers" for a simulation model, with a reduction in the computational effort as compared with full factorial designs. [There are also minimum-run resolution V designs for six or

TABLE 12.20
90 percent confidence intervals for expected interaction effects (in minutes) for a 2_{VI}^{6-1} fractional factorial design, small-factory model

Expected interaction effect	90 percent confidence interval	Expected interaction effect	90 percent confidence interval
$E(e_{12})$	0.008 ± 0.013	$E(e_{26})$	-0.001 ± 0.051
$E(e_{13})$	0.012 ± 0.015	$E(e_{34})$	0.028 ± 0.054
$E(e_{14})$	-0.001 ± 0.008	$E(e_{35})$	-0.040 ± 0.017
$E(e_{15})$	0.003 ± 0.007	$E(e_{36})$	-0.002 ± 0.004
$E(e_{16})$	-0.001 ± 0.009	$E(e_{45})$	-0.005 ± 0.008
$E(e_{23})$	-0.026 ± 0.107	$E(e_{46})$	0.000 ± 0.003
$E(e_{24})$	0.050 ± 0.034	$E(e_{56})$	0.000 ± 0.009
$E(e_{25})$	0.103 ± 0.056	–	–

TABLE 12.21
Comparison of main-effect point estimates from the factorial and fractional factorial designs, predator-prey model

Expected main effect	Point estimate from fractional factorial design (biased)	Point estimate from factorial design (Table 12.12)	Point estimate of corresponding four-factor interaction effect (Table 12.15)
$E(e_1)$	47.92	45.99	1.93
$E(e_2)$	27.53	27.33	0.20
$E(e_3)$	27.75	26.12	1.63
$E(e_4)$	1.40	−1.38	2.78
$E(e_5)$	−13.04	−12.15	−0.89

more factors than can reduce the computational requirements even further; see Montgomery (2013, pp. 100–102).] Returning to our 11-factor example at the beginning of this section, we could, e.g., construct a 2_{V}^{11-4} design that would provide us with unbiased estimates of main effects and two-factor interactions. This would require only 128 design points rather than 2048; using the earlier figure of 1 minute per run, we could replicate this $n = 5$ times in 10 hours and 40 minutes, rather than taking the entire week needed for the full design.

Occasionally, we may have a simulation model with a large number of factors whose impact on a response needs to be determined. If a fractional factorial design is not computationally feasible, then we could try to reduce the (effective) number of factors k. Such an effort could be quite beneficial, since the computational requirements for a factor-effect investigation grow exponentially in k for 2^k and 2^{k-p} designs. One way to accomplish this would be to use a screening design such as *sequential bifurcation* [see Bettonvil and Kleijnen (1997), Cheng (1997), Kleijnen et al. (2006), Sanchez et al. (2009), and Wan et al. (2006, 2010)] or a *sequential factorial design* [see Shen and Wan (2009) and Shen et al. (2010)]. For the sequential-bifurcation methods, all factors are initially in a single group, which is tested to see whether the group of factors has a significant effect on the response. If this group is important, then it is broken into two subgroups and each of these is tested for significance. The procedure continues in this way, with each unimportant group being eliminated from further consideration and each important group being broken into two smaller groups. Eventually, all factors that are not in discarded groups are tested individually for significance. To keep the main effects for the factors in a group from canceling each other out, sequential bifurcation assumes that the "−" level and "+" level for each factor are chosen so that the expected response is larger at the "+" level than at the "−" level. The ability to choose the levels for a factor in this way requires that the direction (but not the magnitude) of the effect be known. On the other hand, sequential-factorial-design methods do not require the direction of an effect to be known and can detect significant interactions, which sequential bifurcation cannot do. Additional screening methods are surveyed in Campolongo et al. (2000), Dean and Lewis (2006), and Trocine and Malone (2001). Screening designs are most effective when there is a large number of factors and the percentage of them that are significant is relatively small.

The methods described so far in this section are applicable to physical experiments and so certainly to simulation experiments as well. In a dynamic simulation, however, there are opportunities for approaches that are not possible with static models or physical experiments. One such idea, developed originally by Schruben and Cogliano (1987), is to oscillate the different input-parameter values during the course of the simulation, each at a different frequency. The output process is then examined to see which input parameters' oscillation frequencies can be detected in the output. While an important factor's oscillation will produce noticeable oscillation in the output at the corresponding frequency, those oscillations of unimportant factors will not be apparent. In this way, Schruben and Cogliano were able to pick out the important factors in several test models with substantially less simulating than that required by conventional experimental-design approaches; Sanchez and Schruben (1987) present a detailed example of using this approach to identify important factors in the African-port model of Prob. 2.23. These kinds of *frequency-domain methods* have been further studied by Jacobson et al. (1991), Sanchez and Sanchez (1991), Sargent and Som (1992), Morrice and Schruben (1993a, 1993b), Morrice and Bardhan (1995), and Hazra, Morrice, and Park (1997).

12.4 RESPONSE SURFACES AND METAMODELS

In Secs. 12.2 and 12.3 we discussed experimental designs that can be used to screen out a subset of the k factors that have a significant impact on the response. In some cases we might want to take these *important* factors and build a metamodel of how the simulation transforms a particular set of input-factor values into the output response. This metamodel, which usually takes the form of a first- or second-order regression equation, can then be used to *predict* the response for other factor-level combinations of interest, since the cost of simulating a large number of system configurations for some models might be prohibitive. We can also use the metamodel to find a set of factor values that *optimizes* (maximizes or minimizes, as appropriate) the response. Books that discuss metamodeling and response surfaces in general are Box and Draper (2008) and Myers et al. (2009). Metamodeling in the context of simulation is discussed in Barton (2009), Barton and Meckesheimer (2006), Friedman (1996), Kleijnen (2007, 2009), Poropudas and Virtanen (2011), and Sanchez and Wan (2012). Applications of metamodeling in simulation are presented by Hood and Welch (1993), Kumar and Nottestad (2006), Sanchez et al. (2012), Watson et al. (1998), and Zeimer and Tew (1995).

The remainder of this section is organized as follows. In Sec. 12.4.1 we give an introduction to regression-based metamodeling and then apply this methodology to the inventory model discussed earlier. Then in Sec. 12.4.2 we develop a metamodel for the predator-prey model using a central composite design and a quadratic regression model. Finally, in Sec. 12.4.3 we discuss space-filling designs and Kriging, the latter being an alternative to regression for constructing a metamodel. These methodologies are also used to develop a metamodel for the predator-prey model, and the regression and Kriging approaches are compared.

12.4.1 Introduction and Analysis of the Inventory Model

We begin our discussion of metamodeling using the inventory model of Examples 12.2 and 12.3, where all effects were found to be statistically significant. Let $E[R(s, d)]$ denote the expected average cost per month for particular values of the reorder point, s, and the difference, d. Then in a 2^2 factorial design, we are in fact assuming that $E[R(s, d)]$ can be represented by the following *regression model* [see Montgomery (2013, chap. 10)]:

$$E[R(s, d)] = \beta_0 + \beta_s x_s + \beta_d x_d + \beta_{sd} x_s x_d \tag{12.3}$$

where β_0, β_s, β_d, and β_{sd} are coefficients, and x_s and x_d are *coded variables* for the factors that we now define. In particular, let $\bar{s}$ and $\bar{d}$ be the average values of s and d (called the *natural variables* for the factors) in Table 12.3; that is, $\bar{s} = 40$ and $\bar{d} = 30$. Also, let Δs and Δd be the differences between the "−" and "+" levels for s and d, respectively, so that $\Delta s = 40$ and $\Delta d = 40$. Then the coded variables for s and d are defined by (see Prob. 12.9)

$$x_s = \frac{2(s - \bar{s})}{\Delta s} = \frac{s - 40}{20} \tag{12.4}$$

and

$$x_d = \frac{2(d - \bar{d})}{\Delta d} = \frac{d - 30}{20} \tag{12.5}$$

Note that Eq. (12.4) maps $s = 20$ into $x_s = -1$ and $s = 60$ into $x_s = +1$. Similarly, Eq. (12.5) maps $d = 10$ into $x_d = -1$ and $d = 50$ into $x_d = +1$. Coded variables are commonly used in experimental design because the effect on the response of a change in a factor is always measured relative to the range −1 to +1.

Suppose that $\bar{e}_s(10)$, $\bar{e}_d(10)$, and $\bar{e}_{sd}(10)$ are the effects estimates from the $n = 10$ independent replications of Example 12.3. Also, let $\bar{R}_F(10)$ be the average response over the four factorial (denoted by F) design points and over the 10 replications. [Thus, $\bar{R}_F(10)$ is the average of the 40 individual responses.] Then *least-squares estimators* [see Montgomery (2013, pp. 280–282)] of β_0, β_s, β_d, and β_{sd} are given by

$$\hat{\beta}_0 = \bar{R}_F(10), \quad \hat{\beta}_s = \frac{\bar{e}_s(10)}{2}, \quad \hat{\beta}_d = \frac{\bar{e}_d(10)}{2}, \quad \hat{\beta}_{sd} = \frac{\bar{e}_{sd}(10)}{2} \tag{12.6}$$

Note that Eq. (12.6) provides an alternative way to compute the effects estimates by using the regression-analysis capabilities of any standard statistics package: Transform the natural-variable values to their corresponding coded-variable values by using Eqs. (12.4) and (12.5), fit the model (12.3) by using these values and the responses, and then double the corresponding least-squares estimates of the coefficients by using Eq. (12.6). The reason that a regression coefficient (other than $\hat{\beta}_0$) is one-half of the effect estimate is that a regression coefficient measures the effect of a unit change in x on the mean $E[R(s, d)]$, while the effect estimate is based on a two-unit change (from −1 to +1).

Substituting the estimated coefficients from Eq. (12.6) into the model (12.3), we obtained the following *fitted* regression model in the coded variables x_s and x_d:

$$\hat{R}(s, d) = 136.819 + 9.237x_s - 3.009x_d + 5.123x_s x_d \tag{12.7}$$

Note that the coefficients 9.237, −3.009, and 5.123 are, in fact, one-half of the effects estimates in Table 12.6 (up to roundoff). Putting x_s and x_d as given by Eqs. (12.4) and (12.5) into the model given by Eq. (12.7), we get the following equivalent regression model in the natural variables *s* and *d*:

$$\hat{R}(s, d) = 138.226 + 0.078s - 0.663d + 0.013sd \tag{12.8}$$

Equation (12.8) is a model of how the simulation transforms the input parameters *s* and *d* into the output response $\hat{R}(s, d)$, and it is called a *metamodel* (i.e., a model of the simulation model). We plot $\hat{R}(s, d)$ as given by Eq. (12.8) in Fig. 12.7*a*; this plot was made using the Design-Expert experimental design

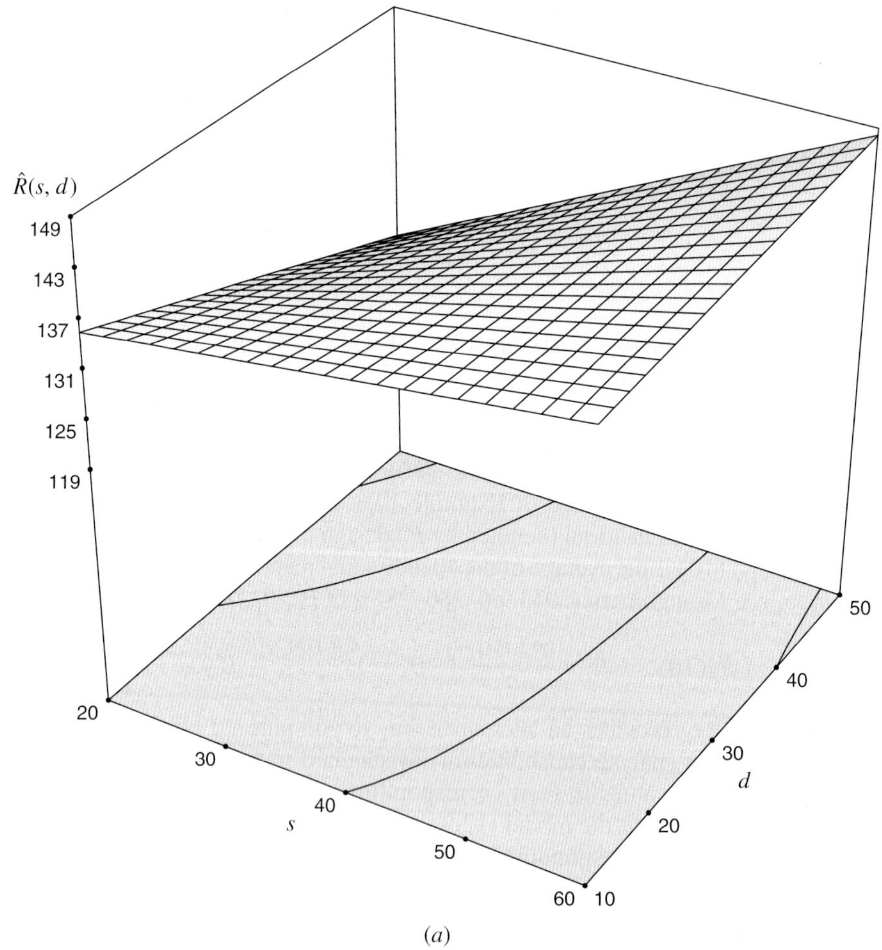

(*a*)

FIGURE 12.7
(*a*) Response-surface plot and (*b*) contour plot of the metamodel from the 2^2 factorial design, inventory model.

(*continued*)

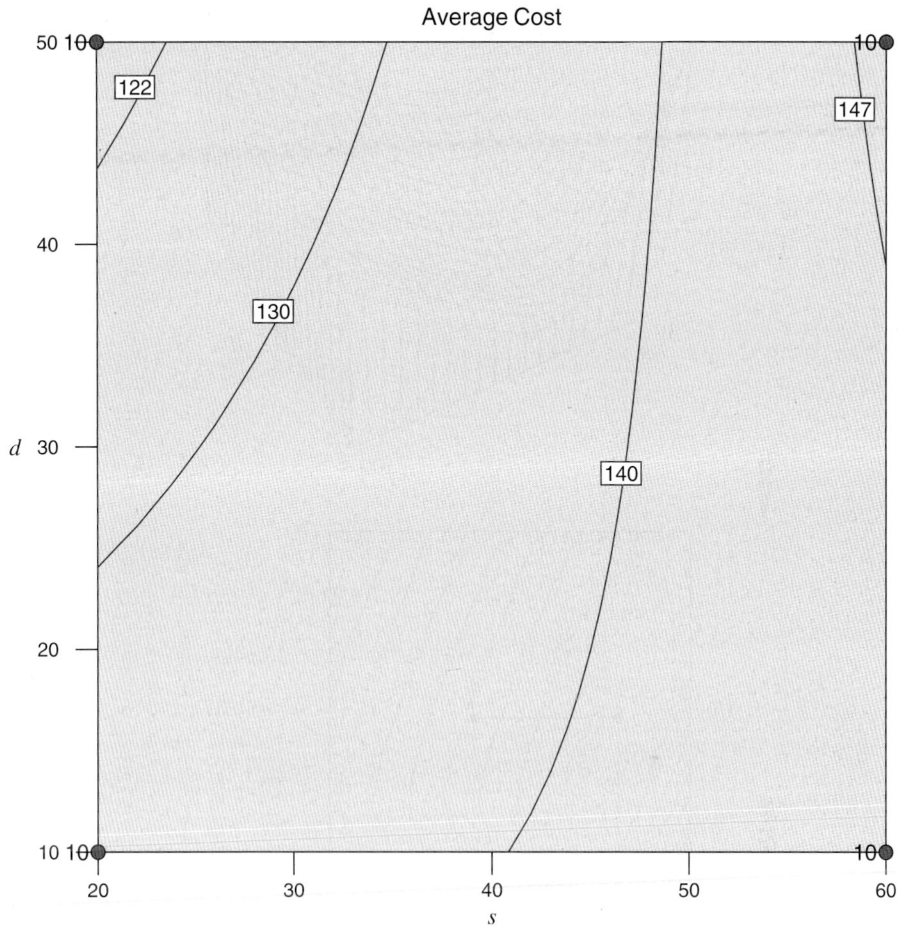

(*b*)

FIGURE 12.7
(*continued*)

software [see Stat-Ease (2013)]. This plot, which is called a *response surface*, is a "twisted plane" because of the interaction term in Eq. (12.8). Note that if the coefficient of *sd* in Eq. (12.8) were 0, then the effect of *s* on the response would not depend on *d*, and vice versa; i.e., there would be *no interaction* between *s* and *d*. In Fig. 12.7*b* we give a *contour plot* of the response surface, where all (*s*, *d*) points along a particular contour line would produce approximately the same average-response value. The design points from Table 12.3 are shown as large dots, and the value at the side of a dot is the corresponding number of replications (in this case 10).

The metamodel (12.8) could be regarded as a proxy for the full simulation model's response surface; all we would need is a pocket calculator or spreadsheet to evaluate it for any (*s*, *d*) pair of interest. We must remember, though, that Eq. (12.8)

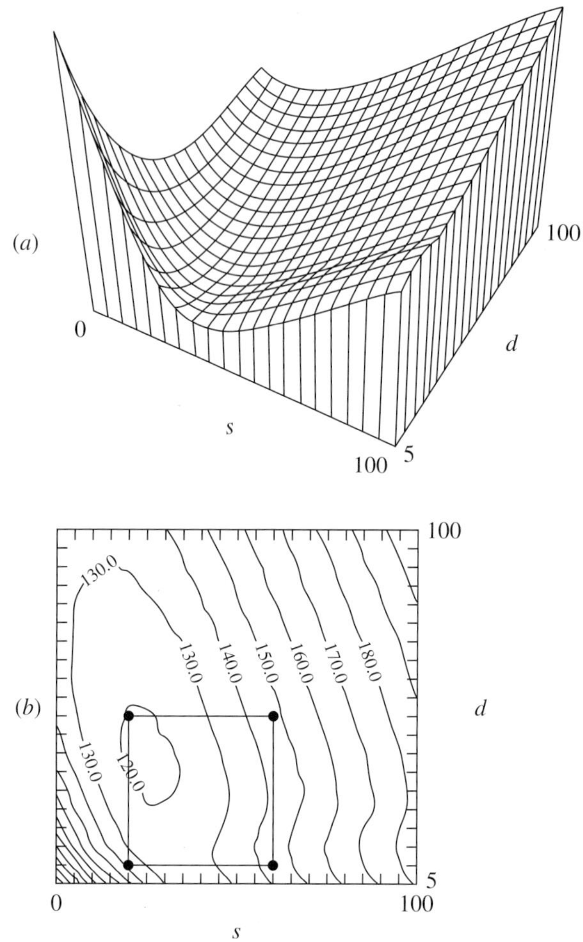

FIGURE 12.8
(a) Response-surface plot and (b) contour plot from direct simulation of the inventory model.

is just an approximation to the actual simulation and may thus be inaccurate, especially far from the values of s and d that provided the data on which it is based. A metamodel, after all, is itself a model, and as such may or may not be valid relative to the simulation model.

To get an idea how accurate an approximation Eq. (12.8) might be to the actual simulation model, we made $n = 10$ independent replications of the simulation for all 420 combinations of $s = 0, 5, 10, \ldots, 100$ and $d = 5, 10, 15, \ldots, 100$. Figure 12.8$a$ gives a response-surface plot based on the average of the simulation-generated values of $R(s, d)$ across the 10 replications. The corresponding contour plot is given in Fig. 12.8b, with the four design points from Example 12.3 marked as large dots.

If we compare the contour plot from Fig. 12.7*b* to the corresponding area of the contour plot of Fig. 12.8*b*, we can see that the metamodel given by Eq. (12.8) is a good approximation to the "true" response surface near the four points where data were actually collected; however, it does *not* provide an adequate representation in the "interior" of the data-collection area. Notice also from Fig. 12.8*b* that the lowest average cost appears to be somewhere between \$110 and \$120 per month, which would be achieved by taking s to be about 25 and d to be between 35 and 40 (S between 60 and 65).

To generate the data for the response surface in Fig. 12.8*a*, we had to make 4200 separate simulation replications, not the sort of thing one could do in practice with a large-scale model. Indeed, a single replication of some simulations can take hours to execute on a powerful computer.

The regression model given by Eq. (12.3) assumes that the response is a *linear* function in the factor effects. However, in some cases the simulation model's response might be better represented by the following *quadratic* (or second-order) regression model:

$$E[R(s, d)] = \beta_0 + \beta_s x_s + \beta_d x_d + \beta_{sd} x_s x_d + \beta_{ss} x_s^2 + \beta_{dd} x_d^2 \qquad (12.9)$$

To determine *in practice* whether the model given by Eq. (12.3) is a good approximation to the simulation model's response surface (since plots similar to those in Figs. 12.8*a* and 12.8*b* would *not* be available in an actual application) or whether the second-order model given by Eq. (12.9) is necessary, we made $n = 10$ independent replications of the simulation at the *center point* (denoted by C), $x_s = 0$ and $x_d = 0$ (or, equivalently, $s = 40$ and $d = 30$), and we obtained an average response of $\bar{R}_C(10) = 122.95$. Substituting $x_s = 0$ and $x_d = 0$ into Eq. (12.7) gives $\bar{R}_F(10) = 136.82$, which is the *predicted* average response for the model at the center point. Thus, we get a difference of $\bar{R}_F(10) - \bar{R}_C(10) = 13.87$, which seems large in Fig. 12.9, where we graphically show the relationship between the two average responses at the center point. [If Eq. (12.8) were a good approximation for the average simulation response in the "interior" of the data-collection area, then $\bar{R}_C(10)$ should be close to the plane defined by Eq. (12.8).]

To see whether the difference 13.87 is statistically significant, we constructed a 90 percent confidence interval [using Eq. (10.1)] for $E(R_F) - E(R_C)$ and obtained 13.87 ± 1.47. Since the confidence interval does not contain 0, the difference is, in fact, statistically significant. Thus, it appears that quadratic (or higher-order) curvature *is* present and the second-order model given by Eq. (12.9) should be considered.

Unfortunately, we cannot uniquely estimate the six required coefficients in Eq. (12.9) because we have only collected data from five independent design points (i.e., four from the 2^2 factorial design and one at the center point). Therefore, we will augment our five existing points with four *axial points.* The resulting design, called a *central composite design* (CCD) and shown in Fig. 12.10, will be used to fit the second-order model. Note that all design points other than the center point lie on a circle centered at the origin and having a radius of $\sqrt{2}$. An experimental design with this property is called *rotatable*, which means that the variance of the predicted

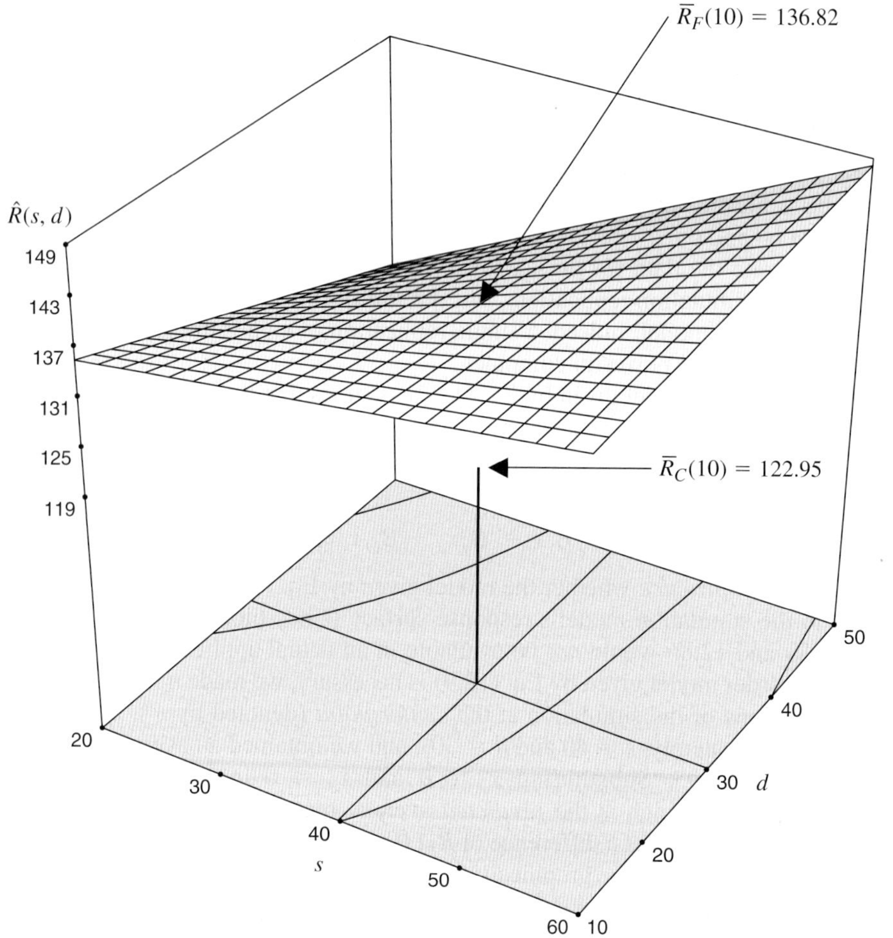

FIGURE 12.9
Response-surface plot of the metamodel [Eq. (12.8)] from the 2^2 factorial design and the average simulation response at the center point, inventory model.

response is the same for all points that are at the same distance from the design center. We made $n = 10$ independent replications of the simulation for each of the four axial points, with the results presented in Table 12.22. (All nine design points for the CCD were simulated independently.) From the data for all nine design points, we obtained by using Design-Expert the following fitted second-order model in the coded variables:

$$\hat{R}(s, d) = 122.848 + 8.268x_s - 0.973x_d + 4.627x_s x_d + 9.368x_s^2 + 3.510x_d^2 \quad (12.10)$$

The equivalent second-order model in the natural variables is

$$\hat{R}(s, d) = 167.020 - 1.807s - 1.038d + 0.012sd + 0.023s^2 + 0.009d^2 \quad (12.11)$$

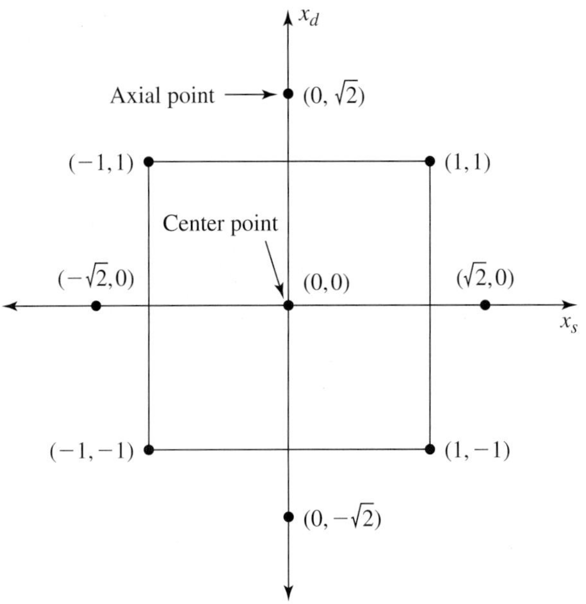

FIGURE 12.10
Central composite design.

Substituting $x_s = 0$ and $x_d = 0$ into Eq. (12.10), we get 122.85, which is very close to the average simulation response, $\overline{R}_C(10) = 122.95$, at the center point. In Fig. 12.11*a* we give the response-surface plot defined by Eq. (12.11), and in Fig. 12.11*b* we give the corresponding contour plot (see also the Color Plates). If we compare this contour plot with the comparable area in Fig. 12.8*b*, it is clear that the second-order model is a better approximation to the "true" response surface than is the model given by Eq. (12.8).

To further check the quality of fit provided by the second-order model, we first computed the adjusted coefficient of determination [see, for example, Montgomery (2013, pp. 248–251)], R^2_{adjusted}, and got the fairly large value of 0.864. However, in *general* a large value of R^2_{adjusted} (or R^2) does *not* necessarily mean that the regression model fits the response data well or that it is a good metamodel (see Prob. 12.10)! We then made $n = 10$ replications of the simulation at the *new* design points $s = 50$, $d = 40$ ($x_s = 0.5, x_d = 0.5$) and $s = 30$, $d = 20$ ($x_s = -0.5, x_d = -0.5$), and got average

TABLE 12.22
Sample means of the responses for the four axial points, inventory model

Axial point (in natural variables)	Sample mean
$s = 12, d = 30$	129.65
$s = 68, d = 30$	150.35
$s = 40, d = 2$	125.55
$s = 40, d = 58$	130.48

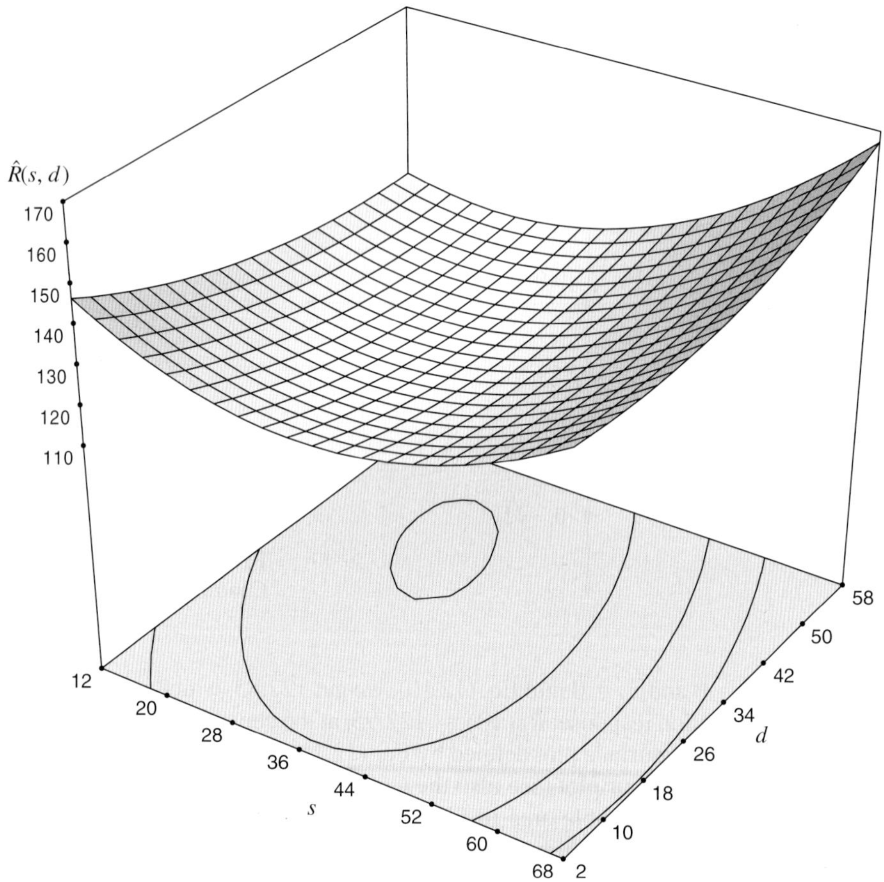

FIGURE 12.11
(*a*) Response-surface plot and (*b*) contour plot of the second-order metamodel from the central composite design, inventory model.

(*continued*)

responses of 132.74 and 119.02, respectively. Substituting the coded-variable values into Eq. (12.10), we got predicted expected responses of 130.87 and 123.58, which correspond to metamodel errors of 1.41 and 3.83 percent, respectively. Since the second-order metamodel appears to be "valid," we could now use it to predict the average responses at other design points *within* our area of experimentation [see Kleijnen and Sargent (2000) and Kleijnen and Deflandre (2006) for a discussion of additional validation techniques].

We now discuss the classical approach to finding the values of s and d that give the minimum average response over our area of experimentation. (A more comprehensive discussion of optimization is given in Sec. 12.5.) Going back to the 2^2 factorial design in Example 12.3, we fit a first-order regression model

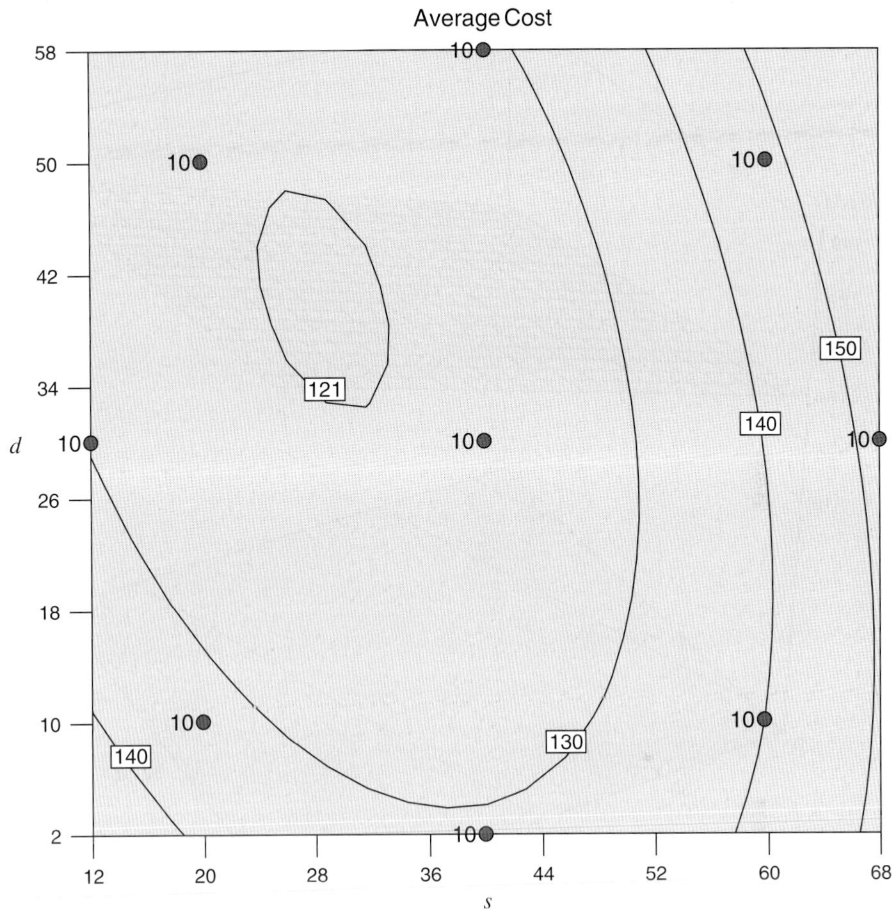

(*b*)

FIGURE 12.11
(*continued*)

(i.e., no interaction term or second-order terms) in s and d to the 40 individual responses and obtained

$$\hat{R}(s, d) = 122.857 + 0.462s - 0.150d \tag{12.12}$$

whose response-surface plot and contour plot are given in Figs. 12.12*a* and 12.12*b*. As an overall metamodel for the simulation's response surface, Eq. (12.12) is clearly very poor, but this is not the use to which we wish to put it. Instead, we can think of Eq. (12.12) as a *local* linear approximation to the expected response surface, and ask in what direction we should move from the center of the design (i.e., $s = 40$, $d = 30$) to decrease the metamodel's height most rapidly. (Decreasing is desirable in this example, since the response is a cost.) From

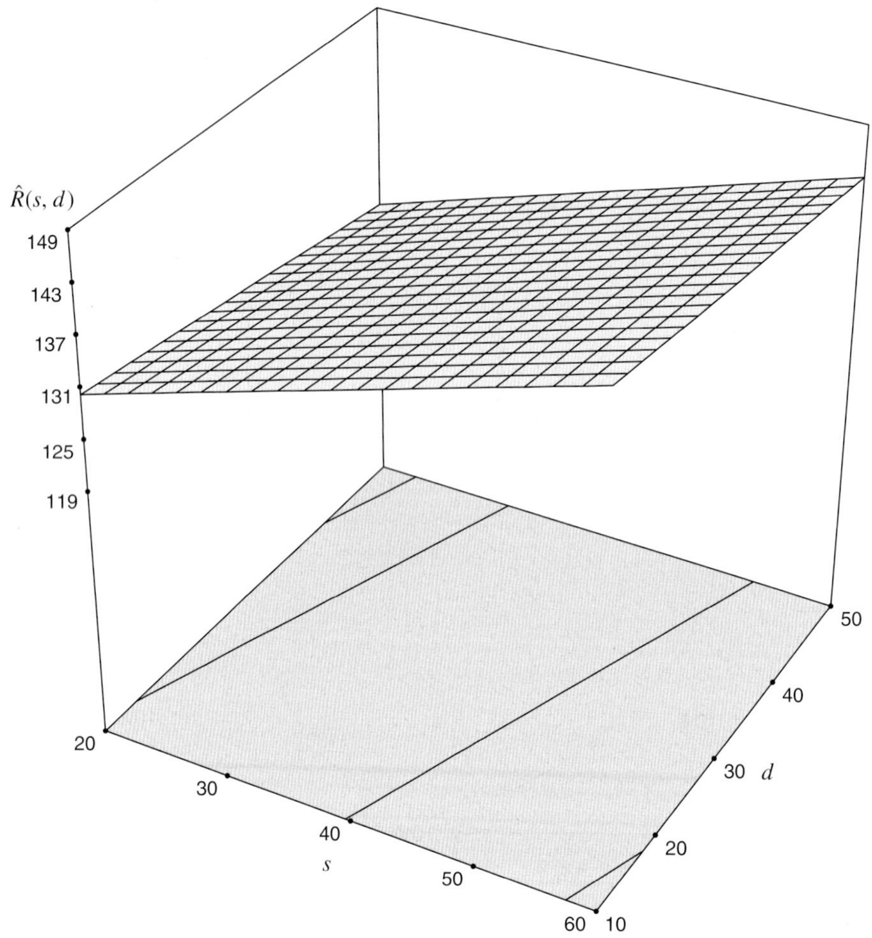

(a)

FIGURE 12.12
(a) Response-surface plot and (b) contour plot of the first-order metamodel from the 2^2 factorial design, inventory model; (c) contour plot from direct simulation (arrows indicate search direction).

(*continued*)

calculus, we know that the direction of *steepest descent* is in the direction of the negative of the vector of partial derivatives (i.e., the gradient) for the metamodel, i.e., in the direction $(-0.462, 0.150)$ in this case. The arrow emanating from the center point of the design in Fig. 12.12*b* indicates this direction, which is perpendicular to the contours of the metamodel. In terms of the "true" contour plot in Fig. 12.12*c*, it indeed seems to indicate a good direction in which to move. We could then move along this line, picking values of s and d on it (or near it, since they must be integers in this model), running the simulation at each point, and continuing as long as the response continues to fall. When it begins to rise, we could stop, perform another 2^2 factorial design, fit another linear model, and pick

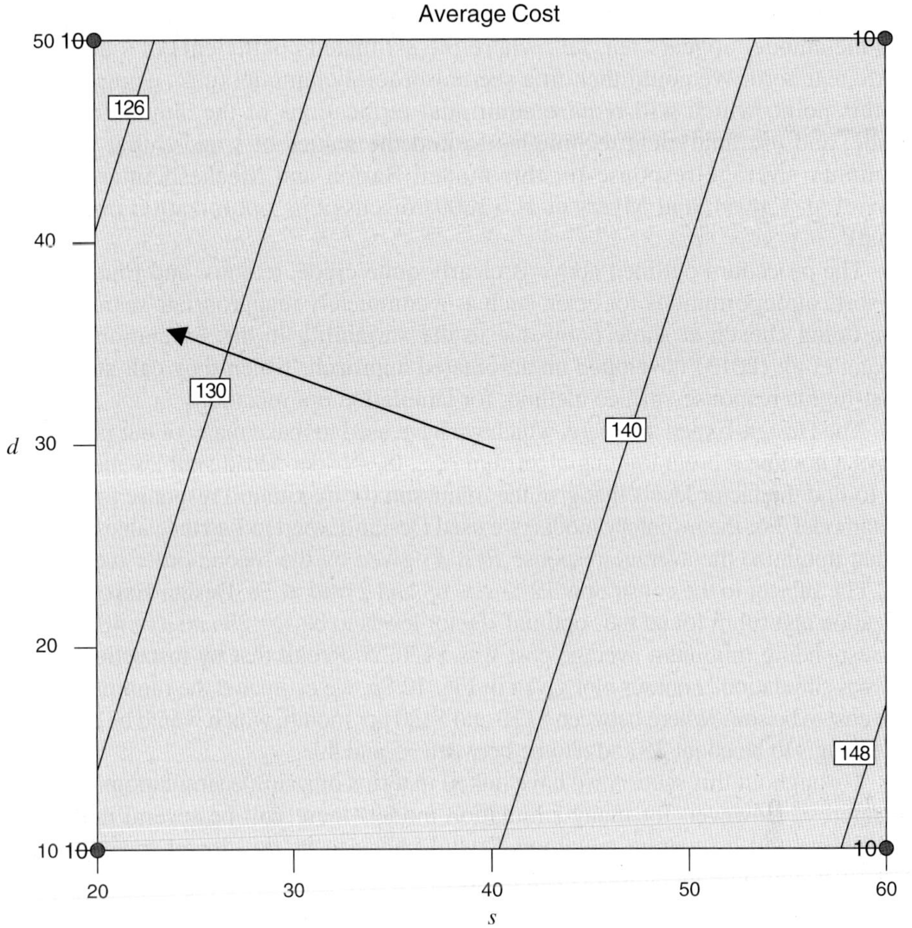

(b)

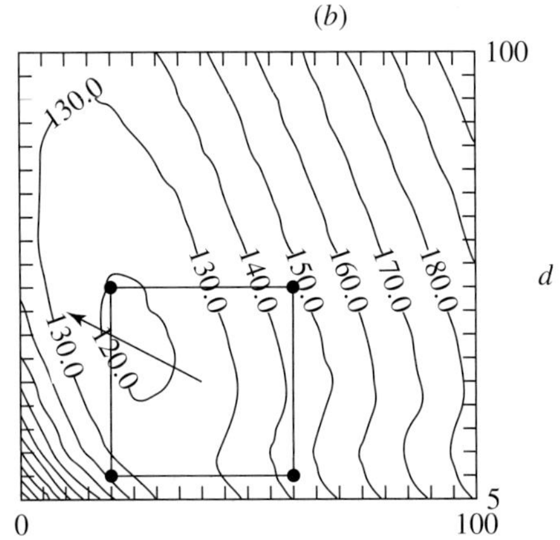

(c)

FIGURE 12.12
(*continued*)

a new search direction. The process could continue until we reach a point where the metamodel appears flat, i.e., where the estimated coefficients of s and d are both near zero. We could then fit a second-order metamodel (e.g., using a CCD) at this point, which will require additional replications of the simulation to be made, and use analytical techniques to find the values of s and d that give the minimum average response for this model. Barton and Meckesheimer (2006), Box et al. (2005), and Myers et al. (2009) discuss this optimization process in detail.

The procedure outlined above is clearly quite crude, tedious, and fraught with all sorts of opportunities for error, such as a completely inappropriate search direction being chosen at some point due to the variability in the simulation output. Chang et al. (2013) developed an automated approach, which they call stochastic trust-region response-surface method, for simulation optimization.

The Design-Expert software, which we have used to make many of our plots, employs a nonlinear programming algorithm (i.e., the Nelder-Mead simplex method) to try to find the factor levels that give the minimum (or maximum) response for a fitted metamodel. For the inventory model, we used Design-Expert to find the values of s and d that minimize the average response $\hat{R}(s, d)$ given by the second-order metamodel (12.11), subject to the constraints $12 \leq s \leq 68$ and $2 \leq d \leq 58$. Design-Expert's optimization algorithm found the "optimal" factor levels to be $s = 29$ and $d = 40$, and the corresponding minimum average cost was \$120.25. Recall that by inspection of the "direct-simulation" contour plot given in Fig. 12.8*b*, we estimated the minimum average cost to be somewhere between \$110 and \$120 per month, which would be achieved by taking s to be about 25 and d to be between 35 and 40.

Throughout this section we have talked in terms of a single simulation response of interest. However, for many simulation models there will be several important responses, and a separate metamodel would have to be developed for each one. However, multiple metamodels can be fit by using the same set of simulation runs if (1) all factors that are significant for any of the responses are included in the design and (2) all responses are recorded for each run. See Angün et al. (2009) for further discussion of multiple responses.

12.4.2 Analysis of the Predator-Prey Model

We now develop a quadratic metamodel for the predator-prey model using a face-centered CCD, which puts each axial point on the face of the "cube" rather than outside of it [see Montgomery (2013, pp. 501–503)]. We use a face-centered CCD rather than a rotatable one because we want to stay within the original factor-level ranges. An illustration of a face-centered CCD for $k = 2$ is given in Figure 12.13.

In order to get greater statistical precision in the estimates of the factor effects, we made $n = 30$ *new* replications at each of required 43 design points (i.e., $32 = 2^5$ factorial points, $10 = 2(5)$ axial points, and 1 center point), rather than using the existing response data from Sec. 12.2. Let x_i be the coded variable corresponding to the ith factor, for $i = 1, 2, \ldots, 5$ (e.g., x_1 is the coded variable corresponding to the

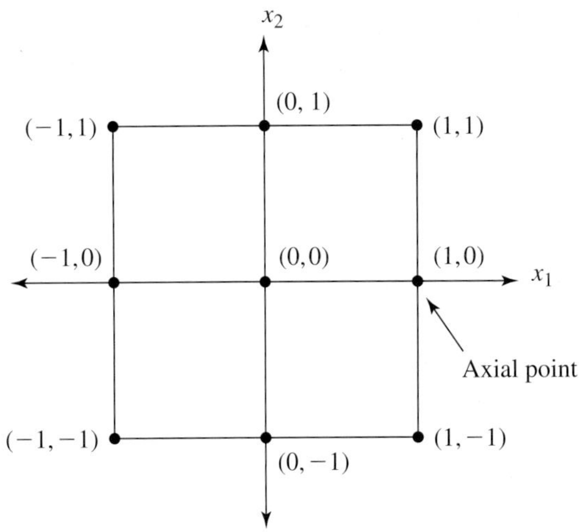

FIGURE 12.13
Face-centered central composite design for $k = 2$.

first factor, SG). Using stepwise regression [see, for example, Montgomery and Runger (2011, pp. 499–501)], we obtained the following fitted quadratic regression model in the coded variables:

$$\begin{aligned}\hat{R} = {} & 73.04 + 24.13x_1 + 14.02x_2 + 14.61x_3 - 1.18x_4 - 7.21x_5 \\ & + 8.18x_1x_2 - 11.29x_1x_3 - 1.32x_1x_4 + 5.47x_1x_5 + 6.03x_2x_3 \\ & - 2.83x_2x_5 - 1.37x_3x_4 + 2.10x_3x_5 - 18.47x_1^2 - 9.02x_3^2 + 4.06x_4^2\end{aligned} \tag{12.13}$$

Note that the terms x_2x_4, x_4x_5, x_2^2, and x_5^2 are not in the model because the stepwise-regression algorithm found them not to be statistically significant. (By leaving these four unimportant terms out of the model, we get a more *parsimonious* representation.) Observe also that x_4 (corresponding to WR) *is* included in the model, apparently because the 30 replications used here allow smaller factor effects to be detected. A response-surface plot for the factors SG and WG is given in Fig. 12.14 (SR = 4, WR = 5, and RT = 30). Note from the plot that the metamodel can take on *negative values* when SG is close to 3 and WG is close to 15. The value of R^2_{adjusted} for this model is 0.823, which is reasonably large but also misleading (see Table 12.23).

A plot of the predicted expected response versus the average simulation response is given in Fig. 12.15. If the model given by Eq. (12.13) were a perfect fit, then the plotted points would all fall on a line with a slope of 1 and an intercept of 0 (shown).

To assess the quality of fit provided by Eq. (12.13), we randomly generated 20 *new* design points over the experimental region specified by the factor levels given in Table 12.11. For each of these design points, we made $n = 30$ independent replications of the simulation and computed the average simulation response across the replications. In Table 12.23 we give for the first three of these design points the average simulation response, the predicted expected response from Eq. (12.13), and the percentage error in the prediction relative to the simulation average. (The

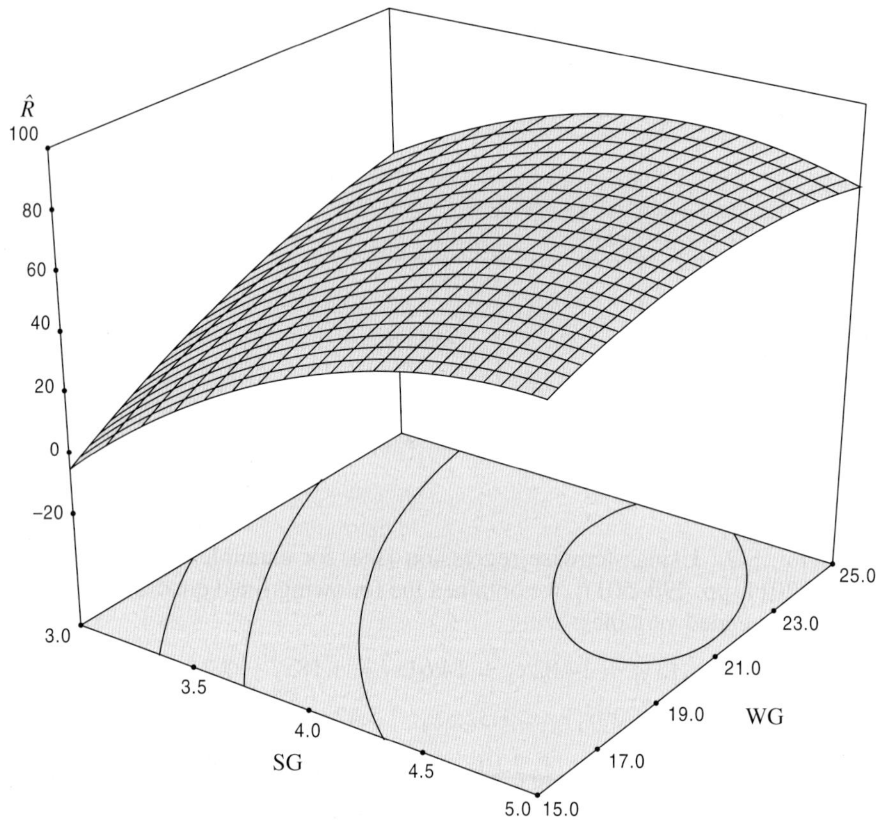

FIGURE 12.14
Response-surface plot for the face-centered central composite design, predator-prey model.

remaining 17 design points will be discussed in Sec. 12.4.3). As can be seen from the table, the quality of the model estimates is quite poor, particularly for the first design point. We conclude that the metamodel given by Eq. (12.13) is *not* valid.

The problem with a CCD (rotatable or face centered) is that only the center point is placed in the "interior" of the experimental region, rather than having the design points "uniformly sprinkled" throughout. We will address this problem in

TABLE 12.23
Comparison of the model prediction and simulation average for three new design points, predator-prey model

SG	SR	WG	WR	RT	Model prediction	Simulation average	Percentage error
4.37	3.11	15	5.89	32.37	50.87	30.94	64.41
4.47	3.21	22.37	5.16	34.47	64.76	70.35	7.95
5	3.53	19.74	4.21	30.26	72.64	82.32	11.76

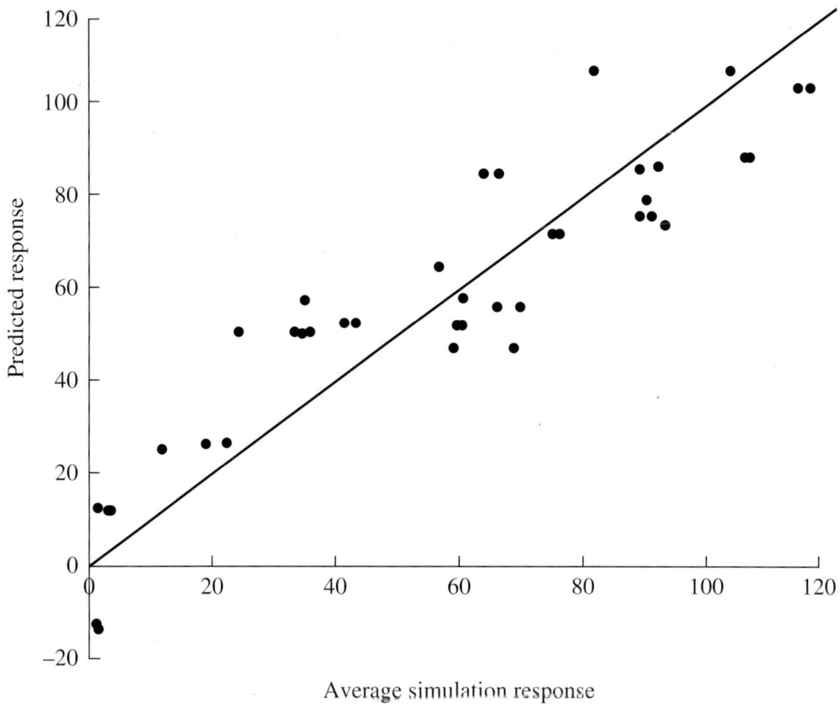

FIGURE 12.15
Predicted expected response versus average simulation response for face-centered central composite design, predator-prey model.

Sec. 12.4.3 when we introduce the concept of space-filling designs. Additionally, CCDs may be unaffordable even for a moderate value of k, since they require $2^k + 2k + 1$ design points. For example, if $k = 10$, then $1045 = 2^{10} + 2(10) + 1$ design points are needed. (For $k \geq 5$ factors, it is possible to replace the 2^k "core" points by a fractional factorial design.)

12.4.3 Space-Filling Designs and Kriging

The goal of *space-filling designs* (SFDs), which were developed for *deterministic* computer models (e.g., in finite element analysis or computational fluid dynamics), is to spread the design points "uniformly" throughout the experimental region. They require the factors to be continuous variables or discrete variables with potentially a large number of different levels. There are many types of SFDs, including Latin hypercube designs, sphere-packing designs, and uniform designs [see Santner et al. (2003, chaps. 5 and 6), Hernandez et al. (2012), Montgomery (2013, chap. 11), and Cioppa and Lucas (2007)]. We will, however, focus on Latin hypercube designs in this discussion, which are supported by JMP [SAS (2013)] and MATLAB [MathWorks (2013)].

TABLE 12.24
Design matrix for a Latin hypercube design with $k = 2$ and $m = 5$

Design point	Factor 1	Factor 2	Response
1	−0.5	0	R_1
2	1	−1	R_2
3	0.5	1	R_3
4	−1	0.5	R_4
5	0	−0.5	R_5

In a *Latin hypercube design* (LHD) the design matrix has m rows and k columns, where m is the desired number of design points (levels for each factor). For a particular column (factor), the m levels $l_1, l_2, \ldots, l_m$ are equally spaced and can be coded as

$$l_1 = -1$$

$$l_i = l_{i-1} + \frac{2}{m-1} \qquad \text{for } i = 2, 3, \ldots, m$$

Then each column is randomly permuted independently of every other column. For example, suppose $k = 2$ and $m = 5$. Then an example design matrix is given in Table 12.24. A rule of thumb for choosing the number of design points is $m = 10k$ [see Loeppky et al. (2009)].

Consider once again the predator-prey model of Sec. 12.4.2. We will develop a metamodel based on a LHD that relates the response R to the coded variables $x_1, x_2, \ldots, x_5$. We used JMP to generate the design matrix for a LHD with $m = 50 = 10(5)$ design points. A projection of these design points onto the (x_1, x_3) plane is given in Fig. 12.16. We then made $n = 30$ replications for each design point and averaged across the replications. These 50 *averages* were used as the data to construct a metamodel.

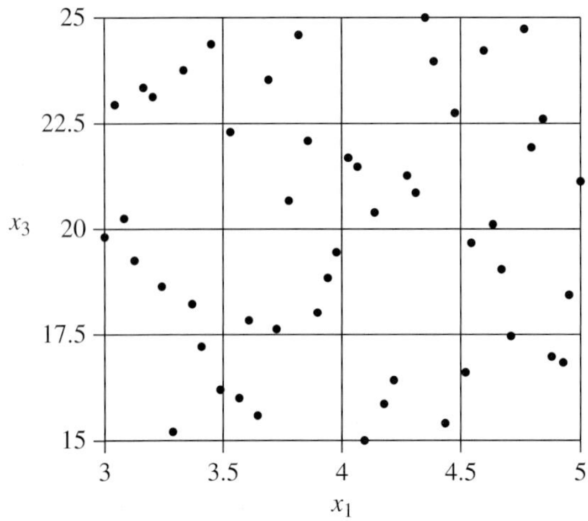

FIGURE 12.16
Projection of the 50 design points from a Latin hypercube design onto the (x_1, x_3) plane.

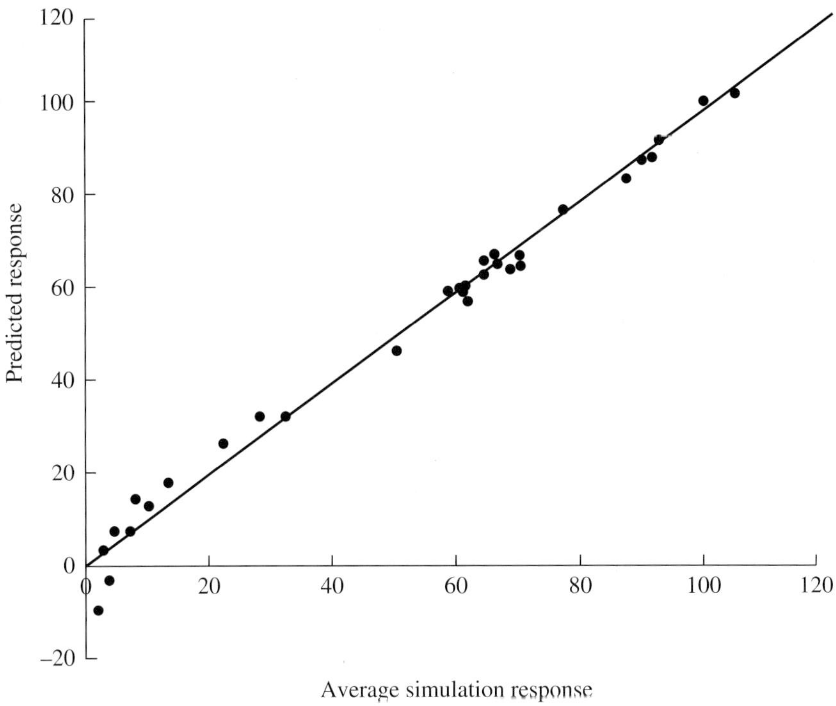

FIGURE 12.17
Predicted expected response versus the average simulation response for the Latin hypercube design, predator-prey model.

Using stepwise regression, we obtained the following fitted quadratic regression model in the coded variables:

$$\begin{aligned}\hat{R} = {} & 71.61 + 37.47x_1 + 13.47x_2 + 27.62x_3 - 17.20x_5 \\ & + 8.82x_1x_2 - 18.82x_1x_3 + 13.43x_1x_5 + 5.76x_2x_3 \\ & - 4.11x_2x_5 + 10.97x_3x_5 - 19.30x_1^2 - 10.07x_3^2\end{aligned} \tag{12.14}$$

Note that there are 13 terms in the model given by Eq. (12.14), as compared to the 17 terms in the model given by Eq. (12.13), the latter being based on a CCD. The value of R^2_{adjusted} for Eq. (12.14) is 0.988. Observe also x_4 (WR) is now *not* in the model. The plot of the predicted expected response versus the average simulation response in Fig. 12.17 indicates that the metamodel given by Eq. (12.14) fits the response data *very well*, except at the two design points where it gives negative values. However, these two points only represent 4 percent of the total number of design points. Moreover the quality of the fit for the LHD is much better than for the CCD in Fig. 12.15. A contour plot for SG and WG is given in Fig. 12.18 (SR = 4, WR = 5, and RT = 30).

"Interaction Profiles" for the metamodel given by Eq. (12.14) produced by JMP are given in Fig. 12.19. Because of the interactions for this model, the impact on the

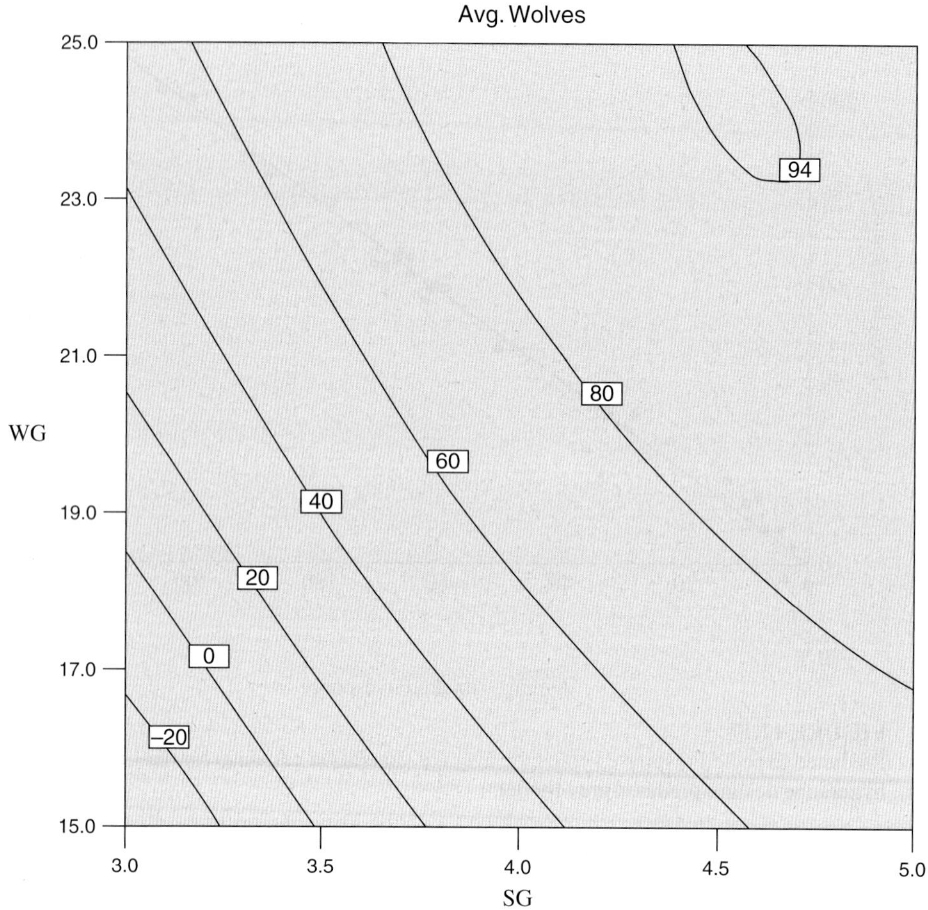

FIGURE 12.18
Contour plot for factors SG and WG for the Latin hypercube design, predator-prey model.

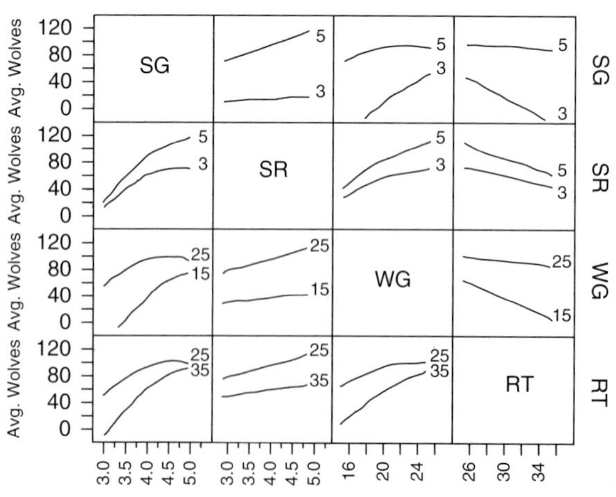

FIGURE 12.19
Interaction Profiles for the metamodel based on the Latin hypercube design, predator-prey model.

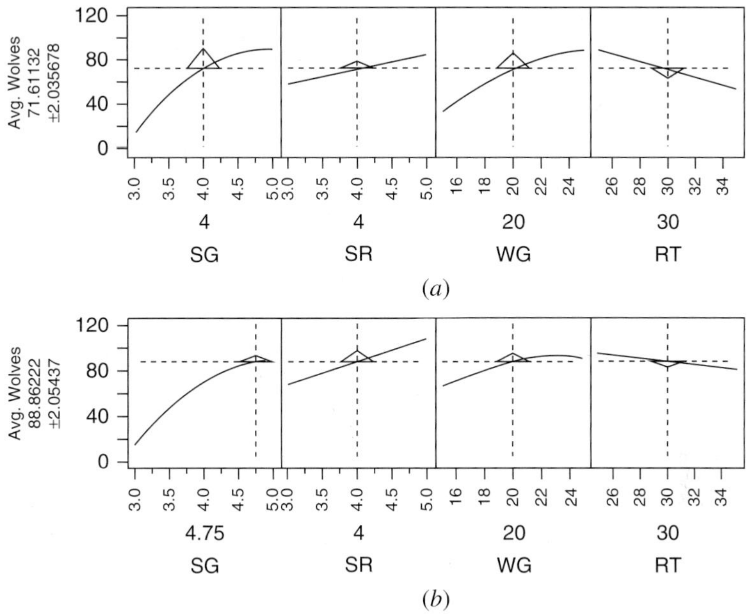

FIGURE 12.20
Prediction Profiler for the Latin hypercube design: (*a*) SG = 4; (*b*) SG = 4.75.

response of changing a particular factor (i.e., the factor's importance) depends on the reference point in the design space. In Figure 12.20*a* we show the "Prediction Profiler" from JMP at the reference point SG = 4, SR = 4, WG = 20, and RT = 30. (WR is not in the model and is set to 5.) For each of the four factors, the vertical dotted line is its current value, the horizontal dotted line is the predicted response (71.61) from the model given by Eq. (12.14), and the solid line passing through the intersection of the two dotted lines at the reference point shows how the predicted response changes as the factor is moved over its range while the *other factors are held fixed.* The derivative of the predicted response (i.e., its rate of change) at the reference point is denoted by the size and direction of the superimposed triangle. The factors SG and WG have the largest triangles and, thus, are the most important at this reference point.

In Figure 12.20*b* we show the Prediction Profiler at the reference point SG = 4.75, SR = 4, WG = 20, and RT = 30. At this reference point, the factors SR and WG appear to be the most important.

*Low-order regression models are typically used to develop a metamodel for data obtained from a relatively small experimental area, i.e., they are *local* approximations. On the other hand, *Kriging* or *Gaussian process modeling* has traditionally been used to fit *global* metamodels, particularly for deterministic computer models. However, during the last 10 years there has been an interest in applying Kriging to

*The remainder of this section may be skipped on a first reading.

response data from stochastic discrete-event simulation models, which has been spearheaded by Professor Jack Kleijnen of Tilburg University. We give an introduction to this use of Kriging in the discussion that follows. General references on Kriging are Cressie (1993), Sacks et al. (1989), and Santner et al. (2003), while references specifically for stochastic simulation are Ankenman et al. (2010), Kleijnen (2007, 2009), and Staum (2009).

Let $\mathbf{x} = (x_1, x_2, \ldots, x_k)$ denote a point in our k-dimensional experimental region ($\mathbf{x}$ denotes a vector). Then a *Kriging model* or *Gaussian process model* (GPM) is defined by

$$Y(\mathbf{x}) = \mu + Z(\mathbf{x}) \tag{12.15}$$

where μ is the average value of the response Y over the experimental region and $Z(\mathbf{x})$ is a Gaussian random process with mean 0, variance σ^2, and correlation matrix $\mathbf{R}(\boldsymbol{\theta})[\boldsymbol{\theta} = (\theta_1, \theta_2, \ldots, \theta_k)$ is a vector of nonnegative scale parameters]. (A random process is a generalization of a stochastic process, which has $k = 1$ and is indexed on time.) For any points $\mathbf{x}_1, \mathbf{x}_2, \ldots, \mathbf{x}_m$ ($m \geq 1$), this implies that the vector $[Z(\mathbf{x}_1), Z(\mathbf{x}_2), \ldots, Z(\mathbf{x}_m)]$ has a multivariate normal distribution with marginal mean 0, marginal variance σ^2, and correlation matrix $\mathbf{R}(\boldsymbol{\theta})$ (see Sec. 6.10.1). In particular, for the points $\mathbf{x}_i = (x_{i1}, x_{i2}, \ldots, x_{ik})$ and $\mathbf{x}_j = (x_{j1}, x_{j2}, \ldots, x_{jk})$, we assume that the correlation between x_{is} and x_{js} is of the form $e^{-\theta_s(x_{is}-x_{js})^2}$, which dies out more quickly for large values of θ_s. We further assume that the correlation between the points $\mathbf{x}_i$ and $\mathbf{x}_j$, $\mathrm{r}(\mathbf{x}_i, \mathbf{x}_j)$, is given by the product

$$\mathrm{r}(\mathbf{x}_i, \mathbf{x}_j) = \prod_{s=1}^{k} e^{-\theta_s(x_{is}-x_{js})^2} = e^{-\sum_{s=1}^{k}\theta_s(x_{is}-x_{js})^2}$$

which is the (i, j)th entry in the correlation matrix $\mathbf{R}(\boldsymbol{\theta})$. Note that the correlation $\mathrm{r}(\mathbf{x}_i, \mathbf{x}_j)$ decreases as $\mathbf{x}_i$ and $\mathbf{x}_j$ become further apart.

Suppose that we run the simulation model at the m design points $\mathbf{x}_1, \mathbf{x}_2, \ldots, \mathbf{x}_m$ and let $\mathbf{Y}^T = [Y_1, Y_2, \ldots, Y_m]$ be the corresponding responses. For a new design point $\mathbf{x}*$, the predicted value of $Y(\mathbf{x}*)$ is then computed from

$$\hat{Y}(\mathbf{x}*) = \hat{\mu} + \mathbf{r}^T(\mathbf{x}*)\mathbf{R}(\hat{\boldsymbol{\theta}})^{-1}(\mathbf{Y} - \mathbf{1}\hat{\mu}) \tag{12.16}$$

where $\hat{\mu}$ and $\hat{\boldsymbol{\theta}}$ are the maximum-likelihood estimators of μ and $\boldsymbol{\theta}$ [see Santner et al. (2003, pp. 65–66)] computed from $\mathbf{Y}^T$, $\mathbf{R}(\hat{\boldsymbol{\theta}})^{-1}$ is the inverse of the matrix $\mathbf{R}(\hat{\boldsymbol{\theta}})$, $\mathbf{1}$ is a $m \times 1$ vector of 1s, and

$$\mathbf{r}^T(\mathbf{x}*) = [\mathrm{r}(\mathbf{x}*, \mathbf{x}_1), \mathrm{r}(\mathbf{x}*, \mathbf{x}_2), \ldots, \mathrm{r}(\mathbf{x}*, \mathbf{x}_m)]$$

The prediction equation given by Eq. (12.16) will contain one model term for each of the m design points. It will also interpolate *exactly* at $\mathbf{x}_i$ (for $i = 1, 2, \ldots, m$), i.e., $\hat{Y}(\mathbf{x}_i) = Y_i$. Note that JMP and MATLAB [Lophaven et al. (2002)] will fit and provide predictions from a GPM.

Kriging can be viewed as an approach to *interpolation* in a random process. In particular, it can be shown that

$$\hat{Y}(\mathbf{x}*) = \sum_{i=1}^{m} \lambda_i(\mathbf{x}*)Y_i$$

where the weights $\lambda_i(\mathbf{x}*)$ depend on the new design point $\mathbf{x}*$ and satisfy

$$\sum_{i=1}^{m} \lambda_i(\mathbf{x}*) = 1$$

Kriging was developed during the 1950s by D.G. Krige in South Africa as a way of predicting the amount of gold at a new site, given the amounts of gold at certain existing sites.

Consider again the predator-prey model discussed earlier in this section, where the simulation was run at $m = 50$ design points. Let Y_i be the average response across the $n = 30$ replications for design point i. The estimated parameters for the GPM computed from the Y_i's by JMP are

$$\hat{\mu} = 51.872, \hat{\sigma}^2 = 1778.361, \hat{\boldsymbol{\theta}} = [0.441, 0.050, 0.015, 0.013, 0.006]$$

Let $\mathbf{x}* = (\text{SG, SR, WG, WR, RT})$. Then the first part of the resulting prediction equation is

$$\begin{aligned}\hat{Y}(\mathbf{x}*) = 51.872 - 222.418 \exp\{-[0.441(\text{SG} - 4.27)^2 \\ + 0.050(\text{SR} - 4.80)^2 + 0.015(\text{WG} - 21.33)^2 + 0.013(\text{WR} - 4.73)^2 \\ + 0.006(\text{RT} - 32.96)^2]\} + \cdots\end{aligned}$$

We do not give a plot of predicted expected response versus average simulation response (similar to Fig. 12.17) for this metamodel since we know a priori that all plotted points will fall on a line with a slope of 1 and an intercept of 0 [i.e., $\hat{Y}(\mathbf{x}_i) = Y_i$].

If there is a lot of random variation in the simulation output, then it might be better to have the GPM *smooth* the response data rather than interpolate it exactly, because in the standard case discussed above the GPM is essentially fitting the "noise" in the data. (Recall that GPM has been traditionally used for deterministic computer models.) This smoothing can be accomplished in JMP by using a so-called "nugget parameter" [see Ankenman et al. (2010), Kleijnen (2009), and Staum (2009)], which amounts to adding a random error term ε with variance σ_ε^2 to Eq. (12.15), where $Z(\mathbf{x})$ and ε are independent. We used JMP to fit a GPM with a nugget parameter to the Y_i's and the estimated parameters were

$$\hat{\mu} = 13.314, \hat{\sigma}^2 = 4469.058, \text{Nugget} = 8.231, \hat{\boldsymbol{\theta}} = [0.171, 0.015, 0.004, 0, 0.002]$$

where "Nugget" is an estimate of σ_ε^2. A plot of the predicted expected response from the resulting metamodel versus the average simulation response is given in Fig. 12.21. By comparing Figs. 12.17 and 12.21, we can see that the GPM with a nugget parameter provides better predictions of the responses at the two design points with negative ordinate values than does the regression model.

We have constructed four different metamodels for the predator-prey model: (1) A regression model based on a 43-design-point CCD; (2) A regression model based on a 50-design-point LHD; (3) A GPM based on the same 50-design-point LHD; and (4) A GPM *with a nugget parameter* based on the same 50-design-point LHD. In order to determine the general predictive ability of these metamodels (i.e., to validate them), we randomly generated 20 *new* design points over the experimental

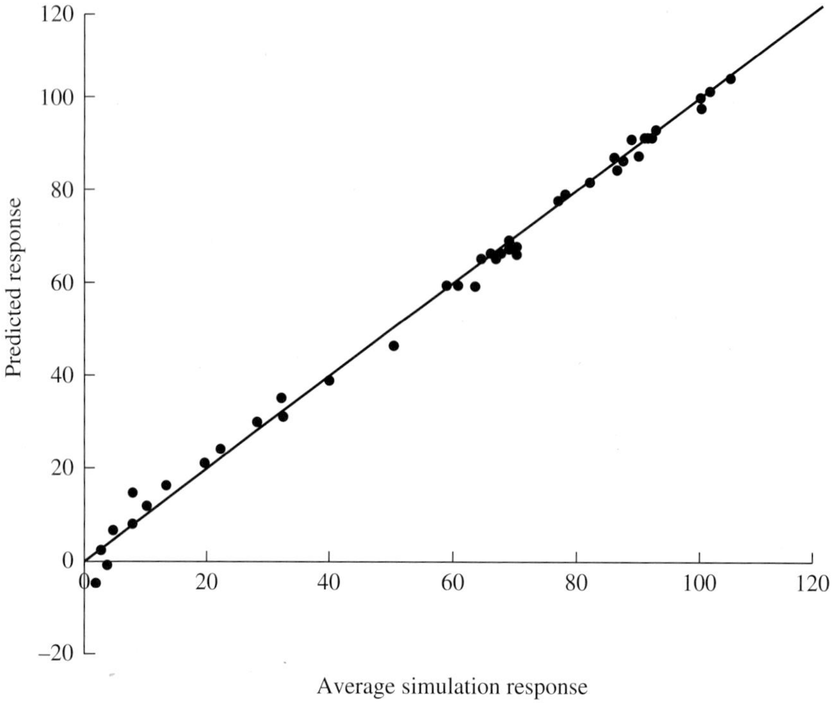

FIGURE 12.21
Predicted expected response versus the average simulation response for the Gaussian process model with nugget parameter, predator-prey model.

region specified by the factor levels given in Table 12.11. For each of these design points, we made $n = 30$ independent replications of the simulation and computed the average response across the replications. (We discussed the first three of these new design points in Sec. 12.4.2.) For two of the 20 design points, the average simulation response was small (less than 11), and all metamodels give negative values for their predicted responses. In these two cases, it is reasonable to take the predicted responses to be zero. For the remaining 18 design points, we computed, for each metamodel, the percentage error in the predicted response relative to the average simulation response. We present in Table 12.25 the mean and maximum of the percentage errors for the 18 design points. For example, the mean and maximum

TABLE 12.25
Percentage errors for 18 of the 20 new design points

Error	Regression model for a 43-point CCD	Regression model for a 50-point LHD	GPM for a 50-point LHD	GPM with nugget for a 50-point LHD
Mean	15.30	3.30	4.69	3.56
Maximum	64.41	10.77	21.55	9.83

percentage errors across the 18 design points for the GPM were 4.69 and 21.55 percent, respectively. (Recall that for two of the original 50 design points, all four metamodels gave negative values for their predicted responses.)

From the results in Table 12.25, we came to the following conclusions for the predator-prey model:

- A (space-filling) LHD is far superior to a CCD, which is *not* valid for this simulation model.
- The GPM with a nugget parameter (smoothed) provides a better representation than the standard GPM (exact interpolation for the original design points).
- The regression metamodel based on a LHD and the GPM with a nugget parameter based on a LHD provide the best overall representations for the predator-prey model.

It should be mentioned that Ankenman et al. (2010) developed a GPM for stochastic simulations that allows the variance for the corresponding Gaussian random process to be different at each design point. This methodology can be implemented in MATLAB using software that is available at the website www.stochastickriging.net. The effect of common random numbers on GPM has been studied by Chen, Ankenman, and Nelson (2010).

12.5 SIMULATION-BASED OPTIMIZATION

The ultimate, perhaps, in analyzing a simulation model is to find a combination of the input factors that optimizes a key output performance measure. For example, there may be an output of direct economic importance, such as a profit or cost, which we would like to maximize or minimize over all possible values of the input factors.

In general, the input factors of interest could include discrete quantitative variables such as the number of machines at a workstation in a manufacturing system, continuous quantitative variables such as the mean processing time for a machine, or qualitative variables such as the choice of a queue discipline. Although it would be possible in a simulation study to seek optimal values of both controllable and uncontrollable input factors, the primary focus in most applications is on input factors that are controllable as part of a facility design or an operational policy.

At first glance, this optimization goal might seem quite similar to the goals of selecting a best system, as discussed in Sec. 10.4. There, however, we assumed that the alternative system configurations of interest were simply *given* and that there were a relatively small number of alternatives (e.g., 20 or fewer). This is the typical situation in many simulation studies. But now we are in a much less structured situation where we have to decide *what* alternative system configurations to simulate as well as how to evaluate and compare their results. Since we are potentially looking at all possible combinations of a large number of input factors, the number of alternative configurations to simulate and compare could literally be in the hundreds of thousands.

It is helpful to think of this problem in terms of classical mathematical optimization, e.g., linear or nonlinear programming. We have an output performance measure from the simulation, say R, whose value depends on the values of input factors, say $v_1, v_2, \ldots, v_k$; these input factors are the *decision variables* for the optimization problem. Since R is the output from a simulation, it will generally be a random variable subject to variance. The goal is to maximize or minimize the objective function $E[R(v_1, v_2, \ldots, v_k)]$ over all possible combinations of $v_1, v_2, \ldots, v_k$. There may be constraints on the input-factor combinations, such as range constraints of the form

$$l_i \le v_i \le u_i$$

for constants l_i (lower bound) and u_i (upper bound), as well as more general constraints, perhaps p linear constraints of the form

$$a_{j1}v_1 + a_{j2}v_2 + \cdots + a_{jk}v_k \le c_j$$

for constants a_{ji} and c_j, for $j = 1, 2, \ldots, p$. For instance, if v_1, v_2, v_3, and v_4 are the numbers of machines of types 1, 2, 3, and 4 that we need to decide to buy, a_{1i} is the cost of a machine of type i, and c_1 is the amount budgeted for machine purchases, then in choosing the values of the v_i's we would have to obey the machine-budget constraint

$$a_{11}v_1 + a_{12}v_2 + a_{13}v_3 + a_{14}v_4 \le c_1$$

In general, if the output R is, say, profit that we would seek to maximize, the problem can be formally stated as

$$\max_{v_1, v_2, \ldots, v_k} E[R(v_1, v_2, \ldots, v_k)]$$

subject to

$$\begin{gathered} l_1 \le v_1 \le u_1 \\ l_2 \le v_2 \le u_2 \\ \vdots \\ l_k \le v_k \le u_k \\ a_{11}v_1 + a_{12}v_2 + \cdots + a_{1k}v_k \le c_1 \\ a_{21}v_1 + a_{22}v_2 + \cdots + a_{2k}v_k \le c_2 \\ \vdots \\ a_{p1}v_1 + a_{p2}v_2 + \cdots + a_{pk}v_k \le c_p \end{gathered}$$

Solving such a problem in a real simulation context will usually be truly daunting. First, as in any optimization problem, if the number of decision variables (input factors in the simulation) k is large, we are looking for an optimal point in k-dimensional space; of course, a lot of mathematical-programming research spanning decades has been devoted to solving such problems. Second, in simulation we cannot evaluate the objective function by simply plugging a set of possible decision-variable values into a simple closed-form formula—indeed, the entire simulation itself must be run to produce an observation of the output R in the above notation. Finally, in a stochastic simulation we cannot evaluate the objective function exactly due to randomness in the output; one way to ameliorate this problem is to replicate the simulation, say, n times at a set of input-factor values of interest and use the average value of R across these replications, $\overline{R}$, as an estimate of the objective function at that point, with larger n leading to a better estimate (and, of course, to greater computational effort).

Nonetheless, there has been considerable recent research devoted to finding methods to optimize a simulation, some of which will be mentioned in Secs. 12.5.1 and 12.5.2. And we have seen some of these methods developed into practical optimization packages that work together with simulation software (see Chap. 3) to search the factor space intelligently in seeking a point that optimizes an objective function; in Sec. 12.5.2 we discuss some of these optimization packages. Clearly, seeking an optimal system configuration will usually be a computationally intensive activity, and work on both methods and software for optimizing simulations has naturally been aided in recent years by advances in computer hardware, a trend that we expect will continue.

Despite the challenges from both the theoretical and practical sides, finding even an approximately optimal system configuration holds the potential of great payoffs in practice, so interest and activity in this topic are high. There have been a number of applications of various methods and software reported in the literature; some examples are as follows:

- Emergency-room operations [Fu et al. (2005)]
- Automobile manufacturing [Spieckermann et al. (2000)]
- Management of a production-inventory system [Kapuściński and Tayur (1998)]

12.5.1 Optimum-Seeking Methods

Researchers have proposed and developed many different methods that attempt to optimize a simulation by searching through the space of possible input-factor combinations. These search procedures vary widely in terms of how they work and what information they require (e.g., whether they require estimates of derivatives along the way). However, these procedures can generally be classified as being one of the following approaches:

- Metaheuristics such as genetic algorithms, simulated annealing, and tabu search (see Sec. 12.5.2)
- Response-surface methodology (see Sec. 12.4)
- Ordinal optimization [Ho et al. (2000), Ho, Sreenivas, and Vakili (1992)]
- Gradient-based procedures [Fu (2006, 2008), Glasserman (1991), Ho and Cao (1991), Rubinstein and Shapiro (1993), Spall (2003)]
- Random search [Andradóttir (2006), Andradóttir and Prudius (2010)]
- Sample-path optimization [Gürkan et al. (1999), Kim, Pasupathy, and Henderson (2013), Robinson (1996)]

However, our focus in this chapter will be on *metaheuristics*, which are methods that guide other search heuristics to keep them from being trapped at a local optimum [see Blum and Roli (2003) for other definitions]. Several of these methods have actually been implemented in commercial simulation-software packages, as will be discussed in Sec. 12.5.2.

There are a number of good surveys and handbooks on simulation optimization, including those by Andradóttir (1998), Fu (2002, 2013), Fu, Glover, and April (2005), Ólaffson and Kim (2002), Swisher et al. (2004), and Tekin and Sabuncuoglu (2004). Papers that discuss new methodologies for simulation optimization are Boesel, Nelson, and Ishii (2003), Hong and Nelson (2006), Hu, Fu, and Marcus (2007), Kabirian and Ólaffson (2011), Shi and Ólaffson (2000), and Xu, Nelson, and Hong (2013).

12.5.2 Optimum-Seeking Packages Interfaced with Simulation Software

As noted in Sec. 12.5.1, many methods have been proposed to search for a combination of inputs to a simulation model that will optimize an objective function. Such methods involve simulating a sequence of system configurations, with the results from simulating earlier configurations being used to suggest promising new directions to search through the space of possible input-factor combinations, leading to configurations that we hope will give better system performance. There is thus the very practical issue of how to manage such a sequence of system configurations; clearly, doing this by manually running different system configurations, with the results suggesting the next configuration, is not workable, given the large number of configurations that will probably need to be simulated. However, based on the availability of faster PCs and improved heuristic optimization search techniques, most discrete-event simulation-software vendors have now integrated optimum-seeking packages into their simulation software.

The goal of an optimum-seeking package (for brevity, we will call these *optimization packages*, but it should be remembered that they do not guarantee a true optimum) is to orchestrate the simulation of a sequence of system configurations (each configuration corresponds to particular settings of the input decision variables or factors) so that a system configuration is eventually obtained that provides a near-optimal solution. Such a solution should, of course, be obtained with the least amount of simulating possible. The interactions between the optimization package and the simulation model are shown in Fig. 12.22. The optimization package first instructs the simulation model to make one or more replications of an initial system configuration. (This initial configuration can be chosen by the user based on system knowledge, or it can be specified by the optimization package.) The results (objective-function values) from these replications are fed back into the optimization package, which then uses its built-in search algorithm to decide on an additional configuration to simulate, etc. This process is continued until the optimization package's stopping rule has been satisfied.

The operational setup of Fig. 12.22 is indeed convenient, and it makes it workable to simulate an optimum-seeking sequence of system configurations in the context of the chosen simulation software. But it is important to remember that the results are not guaranteed to be absolutely optimal, for all the reasons discussed at the beginning of Sec. 12.5. Furthermore, optimization packages require that the user

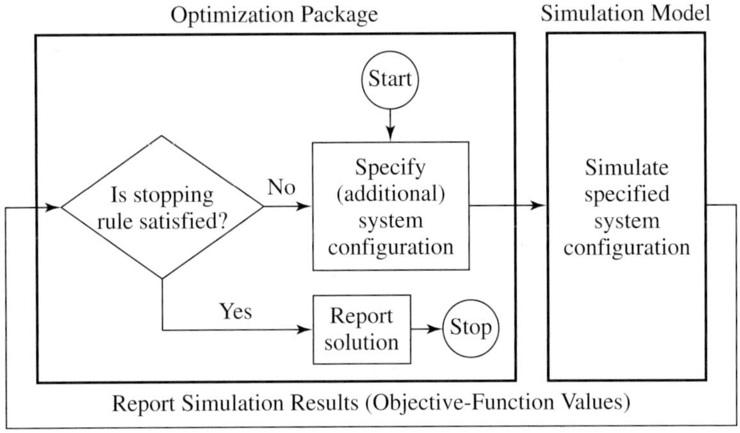

FIGURE 12.22
Interactions between an optimization package and a simulation model.

specify a number of options and parameters, and it may not be obvious how to do so in a given situation—but the results will probably depend on how one chooses such specifications. Despite these cautions, we feel that such packages will often find a near-optimal model configuration, or in any case a configuration that is likely to be superior to what an analyst could find "by hand" in a time-consuming, hit-or-miss sequence of system configurations.

The following are some features that would be desirable for an optimization package to possess:

- The two most important features are the quality of the solution obtained (although this will be essentially impossible to benchmark in practice since the true optimum will not be known) and the amount of execution time to get to it. The total execution time depends on the number of system configurations that need to be simulated, as well as the execution time per configuration. The latter execution time depends on the speed of the simulation software used (see Sec. 3.4.1) and how fast the simulation software can get the needed simulation results back to the optimization package when simulation of a configuration has finished.
- During execution, a dynamic display of important information should be made available, including a plot of the best objective-function value through the current configuration, as well as the objective-function value, system configuration, and configuration number for the m best system configurations, where m is user-specified.
- Linear constraints on the decision variables should be allowed as part of the problem formulation. It would be better yet if *nonlinear* constraints such as $v_1^2 + v_1 v_2 \le c$ could be included, where v_1 and v_2 are decision variables and c is a constant.
- It might be useful if one could specify a constraint on an *output* random variable; e.g., one might want to consider only system configurations for which the observed utilization of a workstation is below 0.8. The feasibility of a particular configuration relative to constraints on the output random variables can be checked only *after* the simulation model is run for this configuration.

- The optimization package should include several stopping rules, such as no improvement for a specified number of configurations, a specified number of configurations have been completed, a specified amount of wall-clock time has elapsed, and exhaustive enumeration (if the number of system configurations is relatively small).
- A confidence interval for the expected value of the objective function should be provided for each of the m best system configurations.
- The estimator $\bar{R}$ of the objective function may be more variable for some system configurations than for others, so we would like to make more replications for the higher-variance configurations in order to estimate the objective function with the same precision for all configurations. For example, a simulation model of a workstation with two machines will generally have a larger variance than a simulation model of the same workstation with three machines, since the utilization of the workstation will be larger in the former case. Therefore, the number of replications for a particular system configuration should ideally depend on a variance estimate computed from a small number of initial replications; the sequential procedure of Sec. 9.4.1 might be useful in this regard.
- The simulation software that is being used with the optimization package should reset the seeds for all random-number streams back to their default values before each configuration is simulated, in order to promote the use of the variance-reduction technique common random numbers (see Sec. 11.2).
- Since optimization problems may require a large amount of execution time, it should be possible to make the required replications for a particular configuration simultaneously on different computers or different cores within a single computer.

Table 12.26 lists several optimization packages available at this writing, their vendors, the simulation-software products that they support, and the search procedures used. As can be seen, the five packages use different search heuristics, including evolution strategies [Bäck (1996), Bäck and Schwefel (1993), and Schwefel (1995)], genetic algorithms [Michalewicz (2013)], neural networks [Bishop (1995) and Haykin (2009)], scatter search [Laguna (2002) and Laguna and Marti (2003)],

TABLE 12.26
Optimization packages

Package	Vendor	Simulation-software products supported	Search procedures used
AutoStat	Applied Materials	AutoMod, AutoSched	Evolution strategies
ExtendSim Optimizer	Imagine That, Inc.	ExtendSim	Evolution strategies
OptQuest	OptTek Systems, Inc.	AnyLogic, Arena, FlexSim, Simio, SIMUL8	Scatter search, tabu search, neural networks
SimRunner	ProModel Corp.	MedModel, ProModel, ServiceModel	Evolution strategies, genetic algorithms
WITNESS Optimizer	Lanner Group, Inc.	WITNESS	Simulated annealing, tabu search

simulated annealing [Eglese (1990) and Henderson et al. (2003)], and tabu search [Glover and Laguna (1997, 2002)]. While we cannot go into great detail on how these packages work, we will give a brief discussion of OptQuest and the WITNESS Optimizer, which we will use in our examples below.

OptQuest [Laguna (2011)] uses an implementation of scatter search (a population-based metaheuristic) as its primary search procedure, with tabu search and neural networks playing a secondary role. One available stopping rule lets the optimization algorithm run until a user-specified number of configurations (*NC*) have been completed. A second option runs the optimizer for a specified amount of time, while a third, called *Automatic Stop*, is much more sophisticated and too complicated to succinctly describe here. OptQuest also provides the following features:

- Linear and nonlinear constraints on decision variables and on output random variables
- An option to allow the number of replications for a particular configuration to depend on a variance estimate
- Ranking-and-selection methods to provide a statistical guarantee that the best system configuration returned by OptQuest is at least the best of the configurations actually simulated (see Sec. 10.4.3)
- Support for multi-objective simulation

The WITNESS Optimizer [see Lanner (2013)] uses simulated annealing and tabu search in its primary search procedure, which is called *Adaptive Thermostatistical Simulated Annealing* [see Debuse et al. (1999)]. The stopping rule has two user-specified parameters: the maximum number of configurations (*MC*) and the number of configurations for which there is no improvement (*CNI*) in the value of the objective function. For example, suppose that $MC = 500$, $CNI = 100$, and the objective-function value at configuration j is the best up to that point. Then the algorithm will terminate at configuration $j + 100$ if none of the objective-function values at configurations $j + 1, j + 2, \ldots, j + 100$ is better than that at configuration j; however, the algorithm will never go beyond 500 configurations. There is also an all-possible-combinations stopping rule, which is useful for small problems (see Example 12.10). The WITNESS Optimizer also has the following features:

- Allows linear constraints on decision variables
- Calculates the number of feasible configurations for an optimization problem, even when constraints have been specified
- Provides a mechanism for evaluating the replication-to-replication variability of the objective function for a particular configuration
- Results tables can be exported to Minitab for further analysis

EXAMPLE 12.9. Consider the inventory problem of Example 12.2, but now with decision variables (or factors) s and S. Let $R(s, S)$ be the average cost per month over the planning horizon of 120 months corresponding to a particular (s, S) pair. Suppose that the possible values for s are $0, 1, \ldots, 99$, and the possible values for S are $1, 2, \ldots, 100$. However, S must be larger than s. Then a formal statement of our optimization problem is as follows:

$$\min_{s,S} E[R(s, S)]$$

subject to the range constraints

$$s \in \{0, 1, \ldots, 99\}$$
$$S \in \{1, 2, \ldots, 100\}$$

and to the general linear constraint

$$S - s \geq 1$$

Thus, there are 5050 = 100(101)/2 feasible combinations of the two decision variables.

We used the OptQuest optimization package as implemented in the Arena simulation software (see Sec. 3.5.1) to perform the optimization, with $n = 10$ replications (of length 120 months) per configuration, a stopping rule of $NC = 200$, and $s = 20$ and $S = 40$ as the starting configuration (see Example 10.3). The best solution found by OptQuest was $s = 27$ and $S = 61$, and the corresponding average cost per month was \$118.47, which was realized on the 137th configuration. Note that these values of s and S are quite consistent with the values of s and d that appear to give the minimum average cost per month for the contour plot of Fig. 12.8*b*. (In Fig. 12.8*b* the parameters s and d were each varied in increments of 5.) Moreover, the 137 configurations required to obtain the "optimal" solution represent only 2.7 percent of the 5050 feasible combinations of s and S.

Let $\overline{R}_i$ be the average cost across the 10 replications for the ith configuration that was simulated, and let $m_i = \min\{\overline{R}_1, \overline{R}_2, \ldots, \overline{R}_i\}$. (Thus, m_i is a nonincreasing function of i.) In Fig. 12.23 we plot m_i for $i = 1, 2, \ldots, 200$, and it can be seen from the figure that m_i does not decrease much beyond $i = 19$.

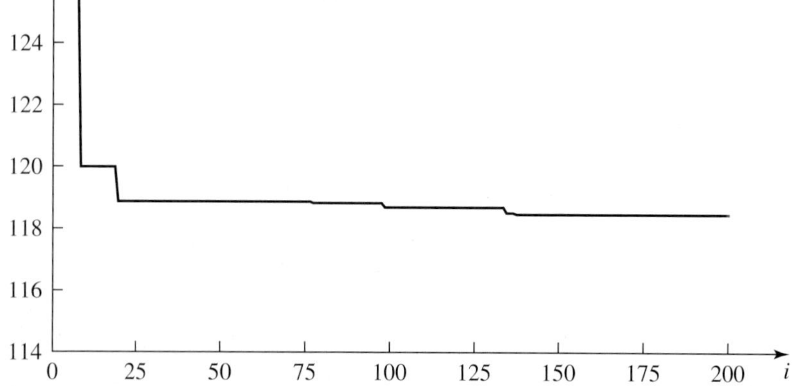

FIGURE 12.23
Minimum average cost per month at configuration i, m_i, for the (s, S) inventory system.

EXAMPLE 12.10. Consider a manufacturing line consisting of four workstations, three finite-size buffers (queues), and an infinite supply of blank parts, as shown in Fig. 12.24. A part is processed at stations 1 through 4 in succession (with each station adding value) and then exits the system. Processing times on a machine at a particular station are exponentially distributed with means given in Table 12.27. When a machine at station 1, 2, or 3 finishes its current part, it will push the part into the downstream buffer, unless all positions in the buffer are occupied. In this case the completing machine becomes *blocked* and cannot process another part until a buffer position is freed up. A machine at station 1 can never be idle (only busy or blocked), because there is always a blank part waiting to be processed. A machine at stations 2 and 3 can be busy, idle, or blocked, while a machine at station 4 can only be busy or idle.

There are seven decision variables for this problem. Let v_i (for $i = 1, 2, 3, 4$) be the number of machines at station i, and let v_i (for $i = 5, 6, 7$) be the number of buffer positions in buffer $i - 3$. We are interested in determining what values of v_1 through v_7 will maximize the expected profit for a 30-day period. In particular, suppose that the manufacturing company receives \$200 for each part that it sells. Suppose further that it costs \$25,000 to use a machine at any station for 30 days. (In general, machines at different stations would have different costs.) Also, it costs \$1000 to use a buffer position for 30 days, because of the floor-space requirements. Assume that the company is considering buying between 1 and 3 machines for each station (i.e., $l_i = 1$ and $u_i = 3$ for $i = 1, 2, 3, 4$) and between 1 and 10 positions for each buffer (i.e., $l_i = 1$ and $u_i = 10$ for $i = 5, 6, 7$). Thus, there are $81{,}000 = 3^4 \cdot 10^3$ different combinations of the seven decision variables. Let N (a random variable whose distribution depends on the values of the decision variables) be the number of parts produced (i.e., the throughput) for 30 days. Then the profit for a 30-day period, $R(v_1, v_2, \ldots, v_7)$, is given by

$$R(v_1, v_2, \ldots, v_7) = 200N - 25{,}000 \sum_{i=1}^{4} v_i - 1000 \sum_{i=5}^{7} v_i$$

and our optimization problem can be stated formally as

$$\max_{v_1, v_2, \ldots, v_7} \; E[R(v_1, v_2, \ldots, v_7)]$$

subject to the range constraints

$$v_i \in \{1, 2, 3\} \qquad \text{for } i = 1, 2, 3, 4$$
$$v_i \in \{1, 2, \ldots, 10\} \qquad \text{for } i = 5, 6, 7$$

We used the WITNESS Optimizer to perform the optimization, with $n = 5$ replications per configuration, a stopping rule of $MC = 500$ and $CNI = 100$, and $v_i = 2$

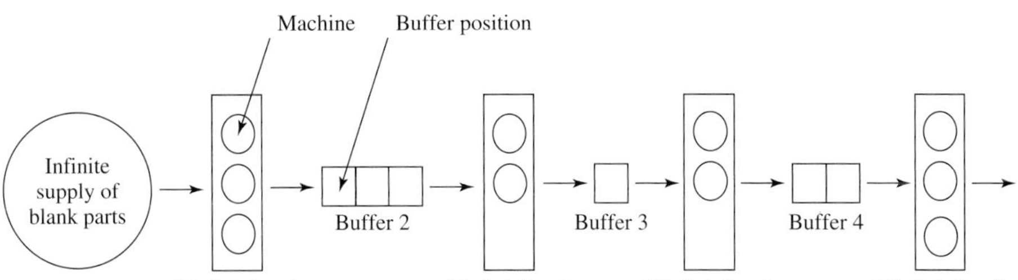

FIGURE 12.24
Layout for the manufacturing line.

TABLE 12.27
Mean processing time for a machine at each of the four stations, manufacturing line

Workstation	Mean processing time for a machine (in hours)
1	0.33333
2	0.50000
3	0.20000
4	0.25000

(for $i = 1, 2, 3, 4$) and $v_i = 6$ (for $i = 5, 6, 7$) as the starting configuration. Since we are interested in the steady-state behavior of the manufacturing line, each replication was of length 40 days with the first 10 days' being a warmup period. The adequacy of a 10-day warmup period was determined by applying Welch's graphical procedure (see Sec. 9.5.1) to several configurations of the system, with 10 days' being much larger than the warmup periods actually required for these configurations. (Strictly speaking, each of the 81,000 different configurations of the system might require a different warmup period.) The best solution found by the WITNESS Optimizer was $v_1 = 3$, $v_2 = 3$, $v_3 = 2$, $v_4 = 2$, $v_5 = 7$, $v_6 = 8$, and $v_7 = 3$, and the corresponding average profit was \$578,400, which was realized on the 124th configuration. Note that 124 configurations represent only 0.15 percent of the 81,000 possible combinations of the seven decision variables.

Let $\bar{R}_i$ be the average profit across the five replications for the ith configuration that was simulated, and let $M_i = \max\{\bar{R}_1, \bar{R}_2, \ldots, \bar{R}_i\}$. (Thus, M_i is a nondecreasing function of i.) In Fig. 12.25 we plot M_i for $i = 1, 2, \ldots, 150$ and also an estimate of the optimal expected profit, as discussed below.

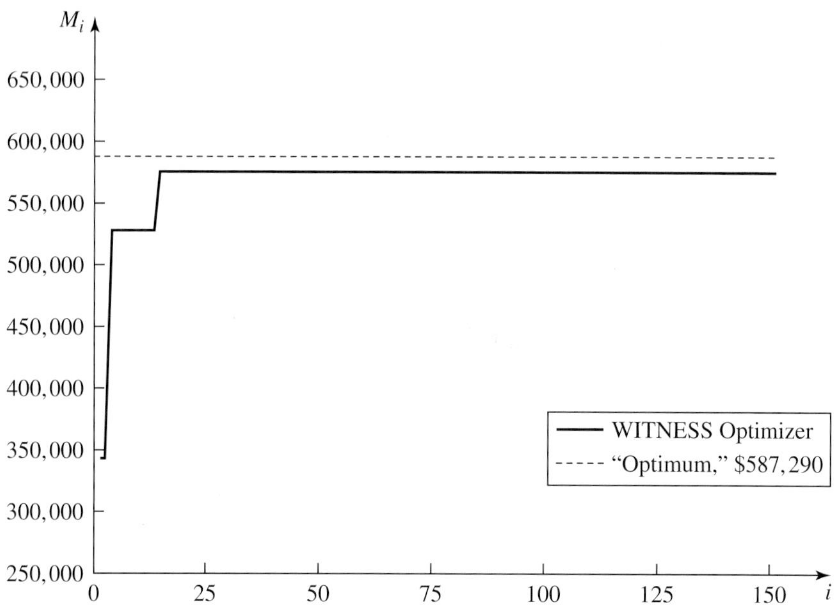

FIGURE 12.25
Maximum average profit at configuration i, M_i, for the manufacturing line.

It is natural to ask how close \$578,400 might be to the true optimal expected profit for this problem. To address this question, we used the all-possible-combinations option in the WITNESS Optimizer to make $n = 5$ replications for each of the 81,000 configurations of the manufacturing line. We found for each of the top 200 configurations (the number we tracked) that $v_1 = 3$, $v_2 = 3$, $v_3 = 2$, and $v_4 = 2$. Using these settings for v_1 through v_4, we then made $n = 100$ replications for each of the 1000 combinations of v_5, v_6, and v_7. The best combination of these three decision variables turned out to be $v_5 = 7$, $v_6 = 9$, and $v_7 = 4$, and the corresponding average profit was \$587,290. (However, there were three other configurations with an average profit greater than \$587,000.) Thus, the average profit of \$578,400 obtained by the WITNESS Optimizer differs from the "optimal" expected profit of \$587,290 by approximately 1.5 percent. (For a real-world simulation model with a "reasonable" execution time per replication, an exhaustive enumeration as discussed here would not be possible.)

EXAMPLE 12.11. Consider once again the manufacturing line of Example 12.10, but suppose now that each machine is subject to randomly occurring breakdowns. In particular, the (busy) time to failure of a machine (see Sec. 14.4.2) has an exponential distribution with mean 10 hours, and the time to repair of a machine has a gamma distribution with mean 0.5 hour and a shape parameter of 2 (see Sec. 6.2.2). Furthermore, the repair of a machine requires the availability of a mechanic; a machine that breaks down when a mechanic is not available joins a FIFO mechanic queue. Each mechanic costs the manufacturing company \$4000 in salary and benefits for 30 days, and the company is considering hiring one or two mechanics.

There are eight decision variables for this problem, with v_8 being the number of mechanics to hire ($l_8 = 1$ and $u_8 = 2$). Thus, there are 162,000 combinations of the eight decision variables. We once again used the WITNESS Optimizer to perform the optimization, with $n = 5$ replications per configuration, $MC = 500$ and $CNI = 100$, and $v_i = 2$ (for $i = 1, 2, 3, 4$), $v_i = 6$ (for $i = 5, 6, 7$), and $v_8 = 1$ as the starting configuration. The best solution found was $v_1 = 3$, $v_2 = 3$, $v_3 = 2$, $v_4 = 2$, $v_5 = 9$, $v_6 = 10$, $v_7 = 5$, and $v_8 = 2$, and the corresponding average profit was \$528,880, which was realized on the 218th configuration. The average profit here is less than that in Example 12.10, because the machines are available for less time to produce parts and each mechanic must be paid \$4000.

For the simple inventory and manufacturing systems in Examples 12.9 through 12.11, the optimization packages seem to provide very good results in terms of selecting configurations close to the optimal solutions and doing so in an efficient manner. However, this was partially a result of our experimenting with different settings for the stopping rules (i.e., *NC* and *CNI*) and the number of replications per configuration, n. Choosing these parameters for a real-world application is not an easy task, since there are currently no definitive prescriptions available. On one hand, it is important for the optimization package to explore a large enough part of the search space, which bodes for a "large" value of *NC* or *CNI*. On the other hand, n must be chosen large enough that a sufficiently precise estimate of $E[R(v_1, v_2, \ldots, v_k)]$ is obtained for a particular configuration $v_1, v_2, \ldots, v_k$. Otherwise, the optimization algorithm could proceed in a completely inappropriate direction in the search space. (In this regard, it is advisable to perform some preliminary experiments to determine a reasonable value for n.) If one can only make a fixed number of model replications in attempting to find a near-optimal solution, then these two goals (i.e., explore many configurations versus many replications per configuration) may be in conflict with each other.

Another current impediment to the use of simulation-based optimization is the execution time per replication for certain applications. For example, it is not uncommon to have large execution times for some simulation models of military systems and communications networks. However, this difficulty should become less severe as computers continue to get faster. On the other hand, this will be partially offset by people modeling larger and more complex systems. Finally, the goal of many simulation studies is to compare a *small* number of system configurations (e.g., the existing system and several proposed alternatives), which is not consistent with the optimization problem formulated above.

Despite the current difficulties with simulation-based optimization, we believe that it can be quite a valuable tool when one needs a systematic and efficient method to determine which of a large number of system configurations leads to a near-optimal value for an objective function.

PROBLEMS

12.1. Recall the model of the manufacturing system in Prob. 1.22 with five machines that are subject to breakdowns, and s repairmen. Suppose that the shop has not yet been built and that in addition to deciding how many repairmen to hire, management has the following two decisions to make:

(*a*) There is a higher-quality "deluxe" machine on the market that is more reliable, in that it will run for an amount of time that is an exponential random variable with mean 16 hours (rather than the 8 hours for the standard machine). However, the higher price of these deluxe machines means that it costs the shop \$100 (rather than \$50) for each hour that each deluxe machine is broken down. Since deluxe machines work no faster, the shop will still need five of them. Assume also that the shop cannot purchase some of each kind of machine, i.e., the machines must be either all standard or all deluxe.

(*b*) Instead of hiring the standard repairmen, the managers have the option of hiring a team of better-trained "expert" repairmen, who would have to be paid \$15 an hour (rather than the \$10 an hour for the standard repairmen) but who can repair a broken machine (regardless of whether it is standard or deluxe) in an exponential amount of time with a mean of 1.5 hours (rather than 2 hours). The repairmen hired must be either all standard or all expert.

Use the coding in Table 12.28 to perform a full 2^3 factorial experiment, replicate $n = 5$ times, and compute 90 percent confidence intervals for all expected main and interaction effects. Each simulation run is for 800 hours and begins with all five machines in working order. Make all runs independently. What are your conclusions?

TABLE 12.28
Coding chart for the generalized machine-breakdown model

Factor	−	+
s	2	4
Machine type	Standard	Deluxe
Repairman type	Standard	Expert

12.2. For the time-shared computer model of Sec. 2.5, suppose that consideration is being given to adjusting the service quantum length q (as in Prob. 10.3) as well as to adopting the alternative processing policy discussed in Probs. 2.18 and 10.5. Perform a 2^2 factorial experiment with these two factors ($q = 0.05$ or 0.40, and the processing policy either as described originally in Sec. 2.5 or as in Prob. 2.18), running the model for 500 job completions (without warming it up), using 35 terminals with all terminals initially in the think state. Make $n = 5$ replications for each design point, and construct 90 percent confidence intervals for the expected main and interaction effects; the design points should be simulated independently.

12.3. Consider using common random numbers (CRN) across all four design points of the full 2^2 factorial design on the inventory model in Examples 12.2 and 12.3. Let $C_{12} = \text{Cov}(R_1, R_2)$, $C_{13} = \text{Cov}(R_1, R_3)$, etc., and assume that CRN "works," i.e., all the covariances between the R_i's are positive.

(*a*) Find expressions for the variances of both main effects as well as the interaction effect in terms of these covariances and the variances of the R_i's. What can you conclude about whether CRN reduces the variances of the estimators for the expected effects?

(*b*) Suppose that we are interested primarily in getting precise estimates of the expected main effects and care less about the expected interaction effect. Suggest an alternative random-number-assignment strategy that would do this. What happens to the precision of the estimate for the expected interaction effect?

12.4. Consider the communications network of Example 9.26, where there were two processors in each SP (Signaling Point). At which SP should a third processor be added to reduce the average end-to-end delay by the greatest amount? Perform a 2^4 factorial design with $n = 10$ replications at each of the 16 design points; the different system configurations should be simulated using CRN (see Example 11.9). All replications should be of length 62 seconds, with the first 2 seconds' being a warmup period. Construct 90 percent confidence intervals for the expected main and two-factor interaction effects. Which effects are statistically significant?

12.5. Consider a queueing system with five single-server stations in series, each with its own FIFO queue. Suppose that interarrival times to the system (at station 1) are exponential with a mean of 10 minutes. Suppose further that all service times are exponentially distributed, with the mean service times at stations 1 through 5 being 8, 6, 9, 7, and 5 minutes, respectively. The system is initially empty and idle, and it runs for exactly 100,000 minutes.

(*a*) At what station should a second server be added to reduce the average time in system by the greatest amount? Perform a 2_{V}^{5-1} fractional factorial design with $n = 10$ replications at each of the 16 design points; the different system configurations should be simulated using CRN. Construct 90 percent confidence intervals for the expected main and two-factor interaction effects. Which effects are statistically significant?

(*b*) For the original system with one server at each station, compute the utilization factor for each station (see App. 1B). Do these five values shed any light on your results from part (*a*)?

(*c*) How could we answer the question in part (*a*) by simulating only a "small" number of design points?

12.6. Consider the manufacturing line of Example 12.10, where the optimal numbers of machines in workstations 1 through 4 turned out to be 3, 3, 2, and 2, respectively.
(*a*) Why do you think that it is optimal to have 3 rather than 2 machines in station 2?
(*b*) Given that there should be 3 machines in station 2, why should there *not* be 3 machines in station 3?
(*c*) Given that there should be 3 machines in station 2, why should there *not* be 2 machines in station 1? (If there were 2 and 3 machines in stations 1 and 2, respectively, then both stations would have the same *potential* processing rate of 6 per hour.)

12.7. Consider once again the manufacturing line of Example 12.10, where the optimal values for v_5 and v_6 turned out to be 7 and 9, respectively (using exhaustive enumeration).
(*a*) Why do you think that v_5 is "relatively large" (i.e., closer to 10 than to 1)?
(*b*) Why do you think that v_6 is "relatively large"?

12.8. We constructed twenty-one 90 percent confidence intervals for expected effects in Example 12.4, all based on the *same* set of $n = 5$ replications. Compute the expected number of confidence intervals that will *not* contain their respective expected effects.

12.9. Derive Eq. (12.4) from first principles.

12.10. The second-order metamodel for the inventory model given by Eq. (12.10) had $R^2_{\text{adusted}} = 0.864$ and seemed to provide a reasonably good representation of the "true" response surface shown in Fig. 12.8. On the other hand, the metamodel given by Eq. (12.7) had $R^2_{\text{adusted}} = 0.923$ but provided a poor representation of the true response surface. How is this possible given the widespread reliance on R^2 statistics?

12.11. Consider a generalization of the inventory model of Examples 12.2 and 12.3 in which there are two new factors. The first of these is the inventory-evaluation interval m, which is the number of months between successive evaluations of the inventory level to determine whether an order will be placed. In the original model $m = 1$, but consideration is being given to changing m to 2, that is, evaluating only at the beginning of every *other* month. The second new factor arose since the supplier has introduced an "express" delivery option. Originally, if Z items were ordered, the ordering cost was $32 + 3Z$ and the delivery lag was uniformly distributed between 0.5 and 1 month. With express delivery, the supplier will cut the delivery time in half (distributed uniformly between 0.25 and 0.5 month) but will charge $48 + 4Z$ instead. The delivery priority P is thus either "normal" or "express" and is a qualitative factor. In this generalized model, then, there are $k = 4$ factors whose levels are given in the following coding chart:

Factor	−	+
s	20	60
d	10	50
m	1	2
P	Normal	Express

Make $n = 10$ replications of the 2^4 factorial design and construct 95 percent confidence intervals for the expected main and interaction effects. Does changing the inventory-evaluation interval, m, have much impact on average cost? (*Hint:* Look at the two-way interactions.) Is it worth using the express-delivery option?

CHAPTER 13

Agent-Based Simulation and System Dynamics

Recommended sections for a first reading: 13.1 through 13.3

13.1 INTRODUCTION

In this chapter we discuss types of simulation other than traditional discrete-event simulation (DES). The emphasis will be on dynamic simulation models, which represent a system as it evolves over time. There are two major types of dynamic simulation models, namely, DES (discussed in Chapters 1 through 12) and continuous simulation. Recall that in a DES the state variables change instantaneously at a countable number of separate points in time. These points in time are the ones at which an event occurs, where an event is (usually) an occurrence that immediately changes the state of the system (e.g., an arrival or a departure). However, we also use dummy "events," which may not actually change the state of the system, for purposes such as scheduling an inventory evaluation (see Sec. 1.5) and closing the doors of a bank at 5 P.M. (see Sec. 2.6). There are two major approaches for advancing the clock in DES: next-event time advance (NETA) and fixed-increment time advance (FITA), with the former approach being the most commonly used. (See App. 1A for a discussion of FITA.) Also, FITA can be realized when using the NETA approach by scheduling dummy events to occur every Δt time units. (See Sec. 13.2.2 for further discussion of time-advance mechanisms.)

The rest of the chapter is organized as follows. In Sec. 13.2 we will discuss agent-based simulation, which as we will see, is a variation of DES. Then in Sec. 13.3 we discuss continuous simulation, which is a dynamic simulation model where the state variables change continuously with respect to time. An important special

EXAMPLE 13.2. Consider a version of the "Boids" bird-flocking model [Reynolds (1987)] where agents (Boids) use the following three simple rules:

- Cohesion—each agent steers toward the average position of "local" (or nearby) agents
- Separation—each agent steers to avoid crowding local agents
- Alignment—each agent steers toward the average heading of local agents

For a particular agent, another agent is considered to be local if it is within a certain specified distance. Even with agents just applying these three simple rules relative to other agents in their neighborhood, *leaderless* flocks develop, which is considered by many to be an example of emergent behavior. This flocking behavior is illustrated in Fig. 13.1, which was produced using the NetLogo software (2013).

We believe that it is not necessary for an ABS to exhibit novel emergent behavior for it to provide useful insights about the system being simulated. Furthermore, general DES *can* also exhibit emergent behavior, such as unexpected bottlenecks, deadlocks, and oscillations.

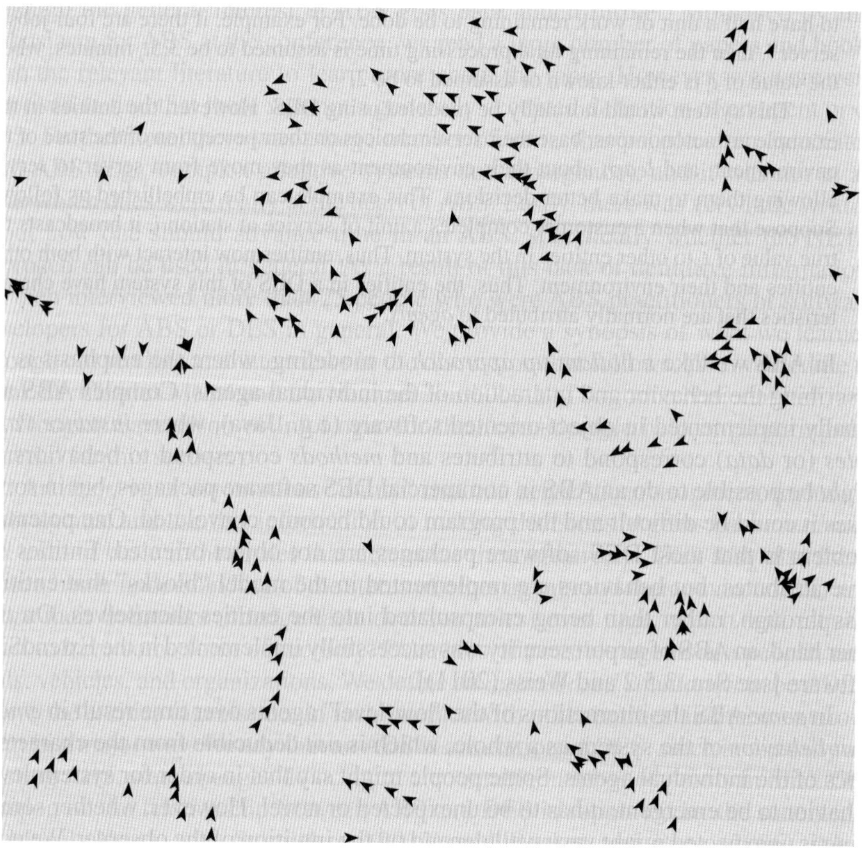

FIGURE 13.1
Leaderless flocks produced by the Boids model.

The following are some situations when an ABS might be used:

- When the "system" has entities that naturally interact with each other and their environment
- When it is important for entities to learn and to adapt their behavior
- When the movement of entities depends on situational awareness (*perception* of its environment), rather than being "scripted"

The last situation is particularly important for defense applications. For example, consider a simulation model of land combat. Historically, in many models the movement of soldiers was largely scripted. For example, a soldier might start at its "flag," move to the first waypoint on a predetermined path, move to its second waypoint, etc., regardless of the disposition of the battle. On the other hand, in an ABS the movement and actions of an agent (soldier) can depend on "personality" characteristics of the agent (e.g., the propensity of an agent to move toward friendly agents or away from enemy agents). Furthermore, these characteristics may change in response to an event in the simulation, such as the agent being shot at.

We now discuss the importance of some additional terms that are often associated with an ABS or agents, including complex adaptive systems, adaptation, and simple rules based on local information. (We discussed above that emergence is a term commonly linked to ABS.) The field of ABS has been greatly influenced by the discipline of complex adaptive systems. A *complex adaptive system* (CAS) is a system of interacting agents whose collective behavior exhibits adaptation, self-organization, and emergence. (Something is *self-organizing* if, left to itself, it tends to become more organized.) Examples of CAS in the real world are the stock market, social insect and ant colonies, the ecosystem, manufacturing businesses, and the brain. Since ABS have been widely used to study real-world CAS, in particular, artificial life [see Holland (1995) and Macal (2009)], there is an impression among some people that ABS should primarily be used for modeling such systems. However, we do not believe that this is the case. For example, there are many important books [e.g., Epstein and Axtell (1996) and Gilbert and Troitzsch (2005)] and papers that make little or no mention of CAS. Also, just because CAS exhibit adaptive behavior does *not* necessarily mean that all agents must do the same. [See, for example, Macal and North (2010), who say that agents *may* exhibit adaptive behavior.] Moreover, it is sometimes stated that agents should use simple rules that are only based on "local" information, as was the case in the Boids model of Example 13.2. [See also Epstein and Axtell (1996, p. 24) for a model where the "rationality" of an agent was *artificially* limited.] However, if this modeling philosophy is strictly adhered to, then how does one know whether the results of such a simulation model are representative of the system that one is *really* trying to model? Einstein is said to have stated, "Make things as simple as possible, but not simpler." In general, one should have enough detail in a simulation model so that any conclusions drawn from the model results would be similar to those that would be obtained if it *were* feasible and cost-effective to experiment with the system itself.

There are four main simulation packages or toolkits designed specifically for performing ABS, three of which require object-oriented programming in Java. The need for programming to build ABS should not be too surprising when you consider the diversity and complexity of the behaviors that an agent might have. A description of the major features of these packages follows.

AnyLogic [AnyLogic (2013), Grigoryev and Borshchev (2012)] is a commercial simulation-software package, marketed by The AnyLogic Company, that supports ABS, DES, and system dynamics (see Sec. 13.3.1), or a combination of the three. The behaviors for agents are developed by using state charts, process flowcharts, or system dynamics equations, and can be extended by writing Java code. The NETA and FITA approaches for time management are both supported. Agents can move and interact on grids, continuous space, networks, or maps from a geographic information system (GIS).

MASON (2013) is a free, open source toolkit that provides core services for developing ABS; it was developed at George Mason University. It uses the NETA approach for time advance and has an optional suite of visualization tools in two or three dimensions. MASON models can be built on grids, continuous space, networks, and GIS. MASON has a 300-page Users Manual, which states on page 8 that "MASON expects significant Java knowledge out of its users."

NetLogo (2013) is a free, open source software package for developing ABS and basic system dynamics models that was developed by Professor Uri Wilensky (1999) at Northwestern University. Models are developed using a dialect of the Logo programming language that has been extended to support agents. It is easy to learn, has excellent documentation, and includes a "Models Library" with a large number of example simulation models. NetLogo models have an interface that can include buttons, switches, slider bars, counters, plots, and animation. Models can be built on grids, continuous space, networks, or maps from a GIS, but only the FITA approach for time management is supported.

The NetLogo "BehaviorSpace" tool allows one to *automatically* make multiple replications for each of a number of different settings for the model input parameters using multiple processor cores. (For the predator-prey model of Example 12.5 and Sec. 13.2.1, the input parameters are sheep gain in energy, sheep reproduction rate, wolf gain in energy, wolf reproduction rate, and grass regrowth time.) Additional NetLogo models can in found in Railsback and Grimm (2012).

Repast Simphony [Argonne (2013), North et al. (2013)] is a free, open source software environment for building and analyzing ABS, which was developed at Argonne National Lab and the University of Chicago. Models can be built using Java code, point-and-click flowcharts, point-and-click state charts, or the ReLogo dialect of the Logo programming language, with the latter being able to import NetLogo models. System dynamics models can also be created visually, by programming, or imported from the Vensim software (see Sec. 13.3.1). All of these options can be seamlessly integrated into a single model and compiled into platform-independent Java.

Repast Simphony Java is used by modelers who wish to have maximum control over the details of their model, while ReLogo is employed to quickly develop simulation models without the need to learn the details of Java. State charts and flowcharts provide modelers with graphical tools to define agent behaviors. Standard Java can be included in ReLogo code, state charts, or flowcharts for model customization, but is usually not required.

Repast Simphony supports both the NETA and FITA approaches, and models can be built on grids, continuous space, networks, or maps from a GIS. A variety of libraries are included for representing agent behavior, including neural networks and genetic algorithms. Repast Simphony has a parameter-sweep system (similar to the "BehaviorSpace" tool in NetLogo) with a graphical user interface. Repast Simphony includes a set of example models along with a variety of tutorials, manuals, and other documentation.

Repast Simphony models, including those that use ReLogo, share a common core architecture with Repast for High Performance Computing [Collier and North (2013)], which is a library that supports model execution on supercomputers.

ABS has been applied to many application areas, including defense [Brown et al. (2004), Cioppa et al. (2004), Hill et al. (2004), Ilachinski (2004), McIntosh et al. (2007), SEAS (2013)], economics [Economist (2010)], epidemiology [Bagni et al. (2002), Epstein (2009)], games {e.g., *Sim City* [Lew (1989)]}, homeland security including crowd evacuations [Beeker and Page (2006), Carley et al. (2006), Samuelson (2007a,b)], logistics [Bonabeau and Meyer (2001)], manufacturing [Nilsson and Darley (2006)], movies {e.g., *Lord of the Rings* [Economist (2009)]}, transportation [Bonabeau (2002)], social sciences [Epstein (2007), Epstein and Axtell (1996)], and supply chains [Siebel and Kellam (2003)]. Additional applications of ABS are discussed in Heath, Hill, and Ciarallo (2009); Macal and North (2010, 2011); and Macal, North, and Samuelson (2013).

A list of some significant milestones in the history of ABS is given in Table 13.1. Important general references on ABS are Bonabeau (2002); Epstein and Axtell (1996); Gilbert and Troitzsch (2005); Macal and North (2010); Macal, North, and Samuelson (2013); North and Macal (2007); and the article "Agent-based model" in Wikipedia (2013).

13.2.1 Detailed Examples

Our first example demonstrates the complex *nonlinear* behavior that can result from agent interactions. Consider a *predator-prey model* that comes from the NetLogo simulation software "Models Library" [see Wilensky (1997)]. (There are also predator-prey examples written in AnyLogic and Repast Simphony.) Wolves and sheep interact on an ecosystem consisting of a 51×51 grid of grass patches of length one unit on each side. Initially, each patch is alive (green) with a probability of 0.5 and dead (brown) with a probability of 0.5. The following are the default model assumptions:

- Initially, there are 100 sheep and 50 wolves randomly placed on the grid, with each animal having a random heading. (More than one animal can be on a patch.)
- Each sheep initially has an amount of energy that is uniformly distributed on the set $\{0, 1, \ldots, 7\}$.
- Each wolf initially has an amount of energy that is uniformly distributed on the set $\{0, 1, \ldots, 39\}$.
- Each animal moves forward one unit (but not necessarily to a new patch) for each tick of an integer-valued simulation clock (i.e., the FITA approach).

TABLE 13.1
Some significant milestones in the history of agent-based simulation

Date	Milestone
1970	The *Game of Life* is a cellular automaton that exhibits complex and very interesting emergent patterns. It was developed by Conway [Gardner (1970)] and is considered an important precursor to ABS.
1971	Schelling (1971) developed his housing-segregation ABS, where coins represented agents and the environment was a checkerboard. He showed that significant long-term segregation can emerge that is not necessarily consistent with the objectives of the individual agents.
1984	The Santa Fe Institute was founded to study complex adaptive systems, and it also played a major role in the development of agent-based simulation.
1986	The BOIDS bird-flocking model, a classical example of emergence, was created by Reynolds (1987) (see Example 13.2).
1994	SWARM [Minar et al. (1996)] was the first programming language for performing ABS and was developed at the Santa Fe Institute. It was initially used for modeling CAS, in particular, artificial life [Macal (2009)].
1994	The System Effectiveness Analysis Simulation (SEAS) for modeling space and C4ISR systems was developed for the U.S. Air Force [SEAS (2013)], and is still widely used today.
1996	The groundbreaking Sugarscape ABS was developed by Epstein and Axtell (1996). It studied how entire artificial societies can be grown from the ground up by agents interacting on a grid-based environment where "sugar" grows.
1999	The NetLogo agent-based simulation programming language was developed by Uri Wilensky at Northwestern University.
2000	The Repast toolkit was created at the University of Chicago, and it is now further developed at Argonne National Lab.
2000	The AnyLogic multi-paradigm simulation package was released in St. Petersburg, Russia, by XJ Technologies, which has changed its name to The AnyLogic Company.
2009	Parker and Epstein developed the Global-Scale Agent Model (GSAM), which can simulate worldwide epidemics and include up to *6.5 billion people* [see Epstein (2009) and Parker and Epstein (2011)].

- A sheep gains 4 units of energy for each patch of green grass that it eats, and loses 1 unit for each step it takes.
- A wolf gains 20 units of energy for each sheep that it eats, and loses 1 unit for each step it takes.
- An animal dies if it has less than 0 units of energy.
- Each time a sheep moves it will have an offspring with a probability of 0.04, which will get half of its energy.
- Each time a wolf moves it will have an offspring with a probability of 0.05, which will get half of its energy.
- Each time an animal moves its new heading is its old heading plus a random value from a symmetric triangular distribution (see Sec. 6.2.2) on the interval [−50, 50] degrees, which represents its "cone of vision."
- A new offspring has a heading that is uniformly distributed on the interval [0, 360] degrees, with 0 degrees' being north and degrees' increasing clockwise.

- In general, it takes 30 time units for brown grass to regrow. However, initially the regrowth times are independent and uniform on the set {0, 1, . . . , 29} time units.
- At each time step, a wolf will randomly select a sheep (if any) on its patch to eat.

Figure 13.2 presents a plot of the sheep, wolf, and green-grass/4 populations for a simulation run of length 1000 time units. (We plot the number of green patches of grass divided by four, so that all three populations can effectively use the same vertical axis.) For this scenario the populations appear to be in *equilibrium*. In Figure 13.3 we plot the population sizes for wolf gain in energy equal to 30 and the other parameters unchanged. Note the wider population swings. Figure 13.4 is a plot of the population sizes for grass regrowth time equal to 10 and the other parameters set at their default values (see also the Color Plates). Since the grass grows back more quickly, we would expect there to be more sheep, which should, in turn, also result in more wolves. Note, however, that the wolf population dies out fairly quickly, after which the green-grass and sheep populations reach a new equilibrium! Why does this unexpected result occur (see Prob. 13.1)?

In Figure 13.5 we plot the average (*over 500 independent replications*) sheep and wolf population sizes at time 1000 as a function of the *grass regrowth time*. Note the bizarre behavior for regrowth time between approximately 15 and 25! (Originally, we ran the simulation for values of regrowth time between 10 and 50 in increments of 2.5, but we later added results for regrowth time equal to 18.75 and 21.25.)

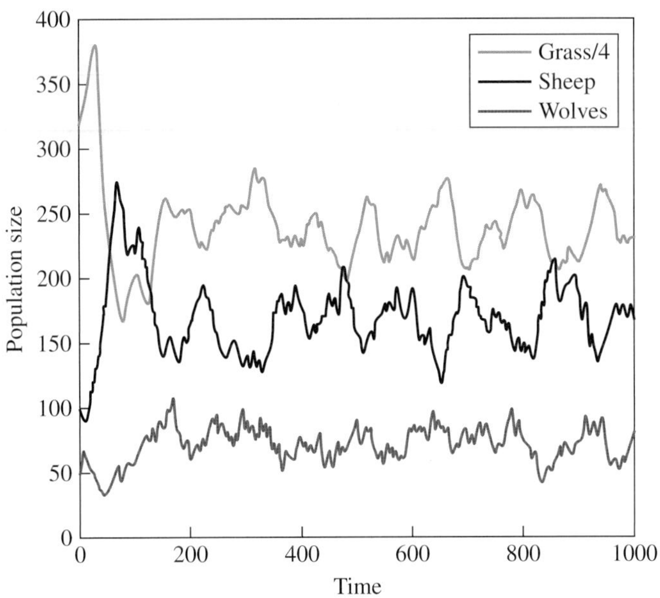

FIGURE 13.2
Population sizes as a function of time for the default parameter values, predator-prey model.

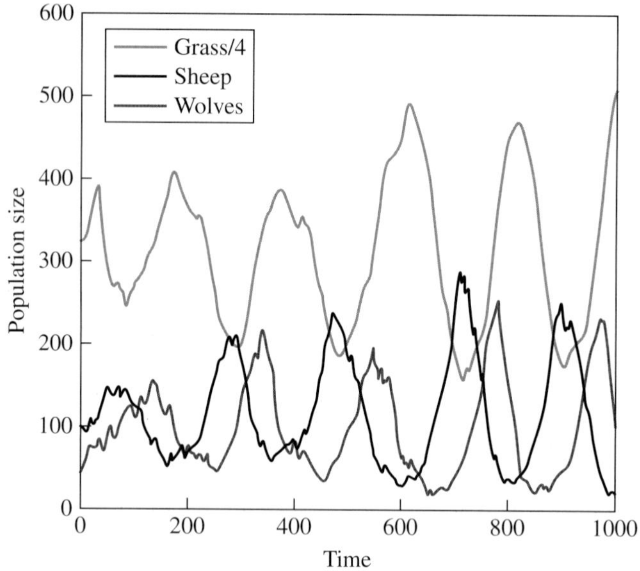

FIGURE 13.3
Population sizes as a function of time for wolf gain equal to 30, predator-prey model.

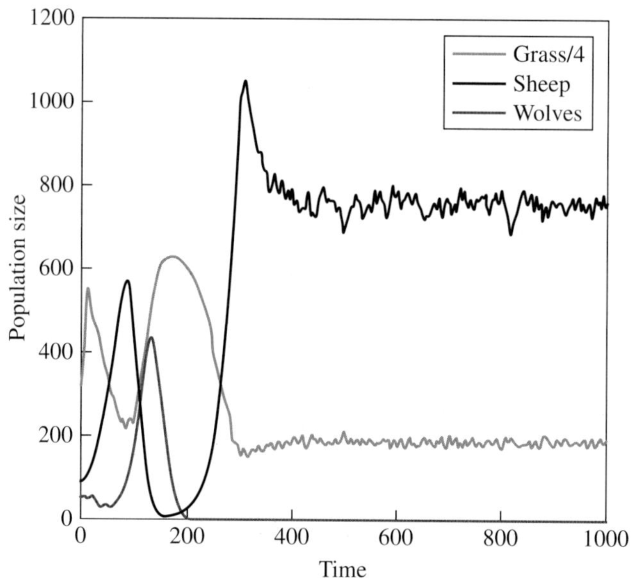

FIGURE 13.4
Population sizes as a function of time for grass regrowth time equal to 10, predator-prey model.

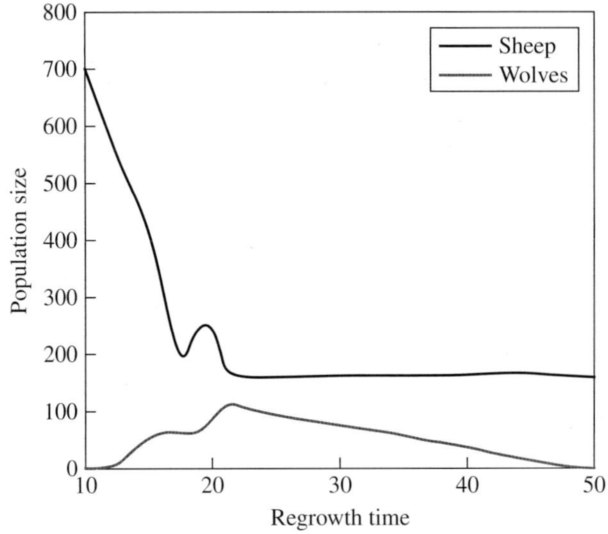

FIGURE 13.5
Average population sizes at time 1000 as a function of grass regrowth time, predator-prey model.

Our second example is simple, but it illustrates how agents can *learn* as the simulation moves through time. Consider a model of people shopping for products that can be found in Gilbert and Troitzsch (2005, pp. 182–190).* There are 10 shoppers and 12 stores each randomly placed on a 35×35 grid of patches. Each store sells a unique product and each shopper has a set of 10 randomly generated products (duplicates are possible) that it wants to buy. We will discuss three versions of the model that have increasing levels of agent sophistication.

Version 1

If there is a store with a needed product on the same patch as the shopper, then the shopper buys the product. In either case, the shopper then moves forward one unit in a *random* direction. After each shopper gets its turn to buy a needed product, the clock is incremented by one time unit (i.e., the FITA approach is used). If there is at least one shopper that still has a product to buy, then another cycle of each shopper getting a turn to buy begins. The simulation is run until each shopper has bought all of the products it needs, and then the current value of the clock is recorded.

One hundred independent replications of the model were made with different random numbers and it was found that the *average* time at termination over the 100 replications (the number used by Gilbert and Troitzsch) was 14,310. This large value is not surprising since each shopper is performing a "random walk."

*Gilbert N. and K.G. Troitzsch, *Simulation for the Social Scientist*, 2d ed., © 2005, *Reproduced with the kind permission of Open University Press. All rights reserved.*

Version 2

We now add the ability for shoppers to *perceive* their environment. When a shopper gets a turn to buy a product, it first places on a running list the (x, y) coordinates and products of all stores in the surrounding eight patches. (This is called its *Moore neighborhood*). As in Version 1, if there is a store with a needed product on the same patch as the shopper, then the shopper buys the product and moves forward one unit in a random direction. Otherwise, the shopper moves forward one unit in the direction of the closest store with a needed product on its list (if any). If there is no store on the shopper's list with a needed product, then the shopper moves forward one unit in a random direction. For Version 2, the average value of time at termination was 6983, a 51 percent reduction compared to Version 1.

Version 3

We now allow shoppers to *communicate* with each other. In particular, if two shoppers are on the same patch, they exchange the (x, y) coordinates and products on their respective lists. For Version 3, the average value of time at termination was 2013, which is an 86 percent reduction relative to Version 1.

13.2.2 Time-Advance Mechanisms for ABS

As discussed in Sec. 13.1, there are two major approaches for advancing time in a DES, namely, NETA and FITA. Historically, *virtually all* ABS have used the latter approach. There are probably two reasons for this. The first is historical legacy, since (nearly) all of the early ABS used the FITA approach, including well-known models such as Conway's *Game of Life* [Gardner (1970)], Schelling's segregation model [Schelling (1971)], and the Sugarscape model [Epstein and Axtell (1996)], and the tradition appears to have continued. Also, some people feel that it is simply not possible to use the NETA approach effectively for ABS. To wit, since many agent interactions may take place in some ABS, it might be necessary to *cancel and reschedule* certain events that have already been placed into the event list to occur at some future time. This could, of course, be potentially *inefficient*. The following hypothetical example illustrates the possible difficulties in using the NETA approach for ABS.

EXAMPLE 13.3. Consider a hypothetical environment consisting of a 50×50 grid of cells of length 100 feet on each side. Initially, each cell is green (denoted by white in Figs. 13.6 and 13.7) with a probability of 0.8 and red (denoted by grey) with a probability of 0.2, independent of all other cells. The amount of time that a cell is green before turning red is uniform on the discrete set $\{70, 71, \ldots, 90\}$ minutes, and thus has a mean of 80 minutes. The amount of time that a cell is red before turning green is uniform on the set $\{10, 11, \ldots, 30\}$ minutes, and has a mean of 20 minutes.

Suppose 100 agents "live" on the grid and that they move at a speed of 60 feet per minute. Initially, each agent is randomly placed on the grid and has a heading that is uniformly distributed on the discrete set $\{0, 90, 180, 270\}$ degrees, with 0 degrees' being north and degrees' increasing clockwise. More than one agent can be on a particular cell. An agent can "look" into the next cell and determine its color. Agents use the following movement rules:

- An agent will begin moving at its specified heading if it starts on a green cell.
- If an agent starts on a red cell, it will wait until the cell turns green to begin moving.
- If an agent is moving through a cell and reaches its "edge," then it will only enter the *next* cell if it is green. Otherwise, it will stop and wait until the latter cell turns green. (The right edge of a particular cell is the same as the left edge of the cell on its right, etc.)
- If an agent is traveling through a cell when it turns red, then it will *stop immediately*. It will not start moving again until the cell turns green.
- When an agent reaches one of the edges of the *grid*, it is destroyed and its total time in the simulation is computed. The simulation is to be run until all agents have been destroyed, at which time the average time in the "system" for the 100 agents is computed.

Suppose that we want to use the NETA approach to simulate this system. When an agent is to start moving from the "middle" of a cell, we schedule its time of arrival at the forward edge of the *current* cell into the event list (see Fig. 13.6). If an agent reaches the edge of its current cell and the next cell is green, then we schedule its time of arrival at the far edge of the *next* cell into the event list (see Fig. 13.7). If the next cell is red, then the agent stops until it turns green. If an agent is traveling through a cell when it turns red, then the event corresponding to the agent's arriving at the forward edge of the cell is *canceled* from the event list. When the cell again turns green, the time of arrival of the agent at the forward edge of the cell is *rescheduled* into the event list.

Further discussion of this example and numerical results can be found in Macal and North (2008).

Despite the need to cancel and reschedule events as in the above example, Dr. Charles Macal (2013) and Dr. Michael North, co-developers of Repast Symphony,

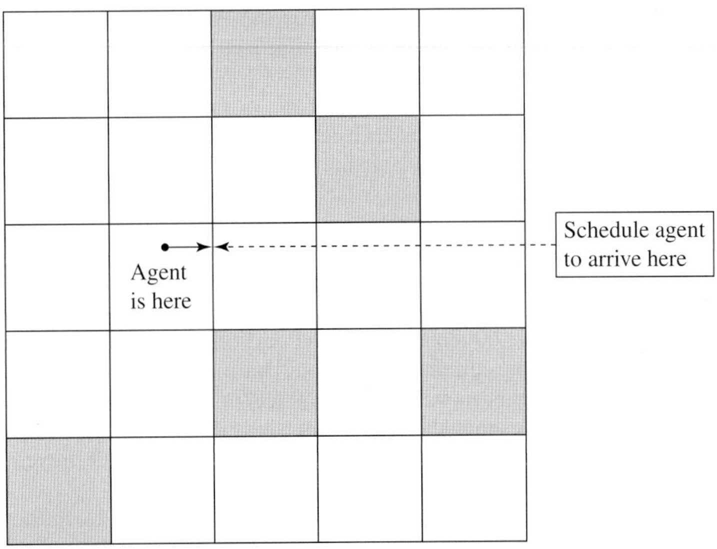

FIGURE 13.6
Movement of an agent when it is in the "middle" of a green cell.

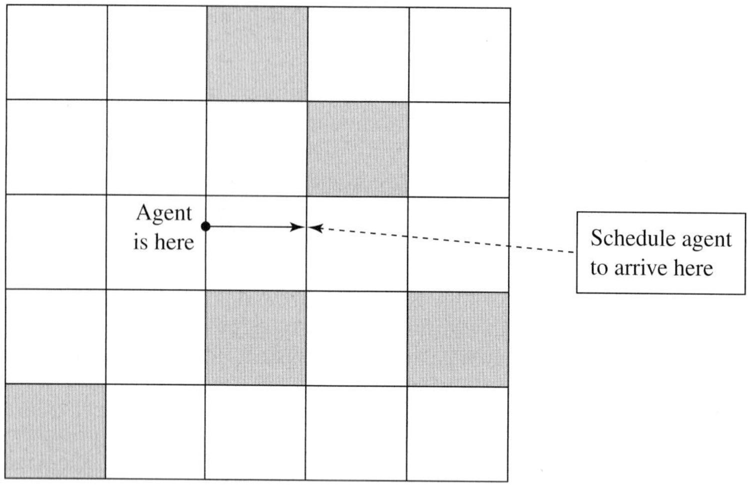

FIGURE 13.7
Movement of an agent when it is at the "edge" of a cell and the next cell is green.

and Dr. Andrei Borshchev (2013), developer of AnyLogic, feel that it *is* generally possible to efficiently use the NETA approach for implementing ABS, and they *recommend* its use. There may, however, be certain models where it is advantageous to use both the NETA and FITA approaches.

EXAMPLE 13.4. *(continuation of Example 13.3)* We now discuss some of the potential problems associated with using the FITA approach for ABS. At each time step, we will check whether to update the states of the cells before we check whether to move the agents. Suppose, for example, that we choose Δt to be 1 minute, and consider what must be done to update the cells and agents at each time step.

Cells

This choice of Δt guarantees that each cell will change state at the appropriate time. However, we will need to perform a large number of (unnecessary) checks to determine when state changes actually take place, which is *computationally inefficient.*

Agents

If an agent is more than 60 feet from the forward edge of the cell, then it will move 60 feet. If an agent is less than 60 feet from the forward edge of the cell and the next cell is *green*, then it will move 60 feet and be in the next cell. If the next cell is *red*, then it will move to the edge of the current cell and stop. This introduces an *error* into the simulation results, since an agent moves less than 60 feet in one minute, causing its time in system to be larger than it should be. If an agent is less than 60 feet from the edge of the *grid* when it begins moving, then it will move to the edge and be destroyed. This will also overestimate its time in the simulation.

Suppose that we change Δt to a value of 2 minutes in order to cut down on the number of unnecessary checks to see if the states of the cells need to be updated. Then, among other problems, the states of the cells (i.e., whether they are green or red) are not always updated when they should be. In general, different values of Δt may produce different results for an ABS, and it might not be clear what is the best choice for Δt [see Buss and Al Rowaei (2010)].

Another potential difficulty with the FITA approach is the need to check many agents "simultaneously" at a particular point in time to see whether they need updating, and the order to do so might not be obvious. In this case, it is probably a good idea to randomize the order in which agents are checked at each time step.

In summary, the use of the FITA approach may introduce errors into the simulation results, and employing a smaller Δt to ameliorate this problem will cause the model to execute more slowly.

13.2.3 Summary of ABS

The essence of ABS is autonomous agents sensing their environment including other agents and using this information in making decisions. Although ABS would appear to be a variation of DES, this in no way diminishes the value of ABS for studying systems with complex behaviors. The interactions of the low-level agents over time will sometimes result in the emergence of novel system-level behavior, but this is *not* required for an ABS to produce useful results.

13.3 CONTINUOUS SIMULATION

Continuous simulation concerns the modeling over time of a system by a representation in which the state variables change continuously with respect to time. Typically, continuous simulation models involve differential equations that give relationships for the rates of change of the state variables with time. If the differential equations are particularly simple, they can be solved analytically to give the values of the state variables for all values of time as a function of the values of the state variables at time 0 (see Example 13.6). For most continuous models analytic solutions are not possible, however, and numerical analysis techniques, e.g., Runge-Kutta integration, are used to integrate the differential equations numerically (using a small time step), given specific values for the state variables at time 0. Thus, the integration of differential equations for continuous simulation and the FITA approach for DES (see App. 1A) both use time steps. However, the critical distinction is that continuous simulation uses equation-computed updates to the state variables, while a DES schedules events to update the state variables.

Several simulation products such as SIMULINK (MathWorks), acslX (AEgis Technologies), and Dymola (Dassault Systemes) have been specifically designed for building continuous simulation models. In addition, the discrete-event simulation packages Arena [see Kelton et al. (2010)] and ExtendSim [Imagine (2013)] have continuous modeling capabilities. These two simulation packages have the added advantage of allowing both discrete and continuous components simultaneously in one model (see Sec. 13.4). Readers interested in applications of continuous simulation may wish to consult the journals *SIMULATION: Transactions of the Society for Modeling and Simulation International* and *System Dynamics Review*.

13.3.1 System Dynamics

System dynamics is a type of *continuous* simulation that is used for designing and improving policies or strategies in business, government, and the military. (It is a *top-down approach* to modeling a system.) System dynamics models look at systems at a more aggregate level and are used to make more strategic decisions than most DES models. The majority of system dynamics models are *deterministic*, but it is possible for them to have random components. System dynamics was created by Professor Jay Forrester at MIT in the 1950s. The commercial simulation products AnyLogic (The AnyLogic Company), *iThink* (isee systems), Powersim (Powersim Software), and Vensim (Ventana Systems) are commonly used to develop and analyze system dynamics models. More information on system dynamics can be obtained from the book by Sterman (2001) and the System Dynamics Society, which publishes the journal *System Dynamics Review*.

The following are the three key components of a system dynamics model that we will use in our examples below:

- A *stock* is an accumulation of a "resource." Examples are a population of people or animals, an inventory of a product, or the level of oil in a reserve (continuous variable). Stocks are denoted by rectangles (or containers) in a *stock and flow diagram* (see Fig. 13.8).
- A *flow* is a stream of a resource into or out of a stock. Flows are denoted by thick, double-line arrows (or pipes) with a superimposed butterfly valve that controls the *rate* of flow through the pipe.
- An *information link* brings information from a stock (or a variable) to the valve of a flow, and it is typically denoted by a thin curved arrow.

EXAMPLE 13.5. In Sec. 13.2.1 we considered an ABS version of a predator-prey system. We now consider a system dynamics model of what might be called the *classical* predator-prey system, which is formulated using differential equations. An environment

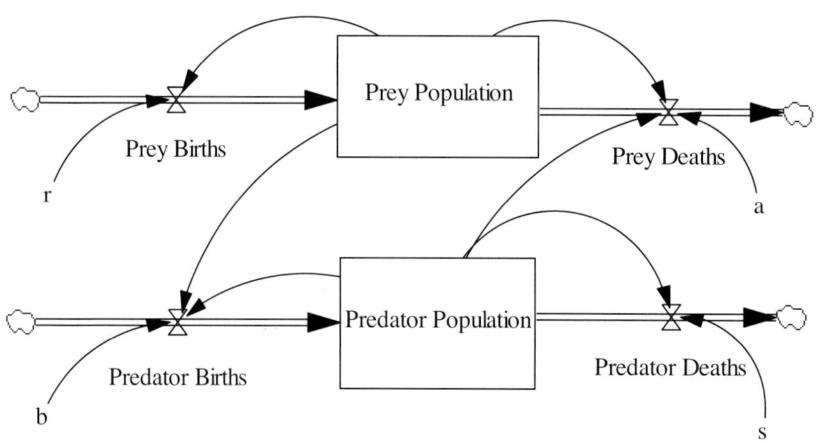

FIGURE 13.8
Stock and flow diagram for the continuous predator-prey model.

consists of two populations, predators and prey, which interact with each other. The prey are passive, but the predators depend on the prey as their source of food. (For example, the predators might be sharks and the prey might be food fish or, alternatively, the predators could be lynx and the prey could be hares.) Let $x(t)$ and $y(t)$ denote, respectively, the numbers of individuals in the prey and predator populations at time t. Suppose there is an ample supply of food for the prey and, in the absence of predators, that their rate of growth is $rx(t)$ for some positive r. (We can think of r as the natural birth rate minus the natural death rate.) Because of the interaction between the predators and prey, it is reasonable to assume that the death rate of the prey due to interaction is proportional to the product of the two population sizes, $x(t)y(t)$. Therefore, the overall rate of change of the prey population, dx/dt, is given by

$$\frac{dx}{dt} = rx(t) - ax(t)y(t) \tag{13.1}$$

where a is a positive constant of proportionality. Since the predators depend on the prey for their very existence, the rate of change of the predators in the absence of prey is $-sy(t)$ for some positive s. Furthermore, the interaction between the two populations causes the predator population to increase at a rate that is also proportional to $x(t)y(t)$. Thus, the overall rate of change of the predator population, dy/dt, is

$$\frac{dy}{dt} = -sy(t) + bx(t)y(t) \tag{13.2}$$

where b is a positive constant. Equations (13.1) and (13.2) are known as the Lotka-Volterra equations [see Lotka (1925) and Volterra (1931)].

Given initial conditions $x(0) > 0$ and $y(0) > 0$, the solution of the model given by Eqs. (13.1) and (13.2) has the interesting property that $x(t) > 0$ and $y(t) > 0$ for all $t \geq 0$ [see Braun (1975)]. Thus, the prey population can never be completely extinguished by the predators. The solution $\{x(t), y(t)\}$ is also a periodic function of time. That is, there is a $T > 0$ such that $x(t + nT) = x(t)$ and $y(t + nT) = y(t)$ for all positive integers n. This result is not unexpected. As the predator population increases, the prey population decreases. This causes a decrease in the rate of increase of the predators, which eventually results in a decrease in the number of predators. This in turn causes the number of prey to increase, etc.

Consider the particular values $r = 1$, $a = 0.035$, $s = 0.017$, $b = 1$ and the initial population sizes $x(0) = 100$ and $y(0) = 15$. We now develop a system dynamics model for this predator-prey problem using the Vensim software [see Ventana (2013)]. In Fig. 13.8 we show the stock and flow diagram, where $x(t)$ and $y(t)$ are represented by the stocks (called "Box Variables" in Vensim) "Prey Population" and "Predator Population," respectively. The birth and death rates of the Prey Population are represented by the flows (called "Rates" in Vensim) "Prey Births" and "Prey Deaths," whereas the comparable rates for the Predator Population are called "Predator Births" and "Predator Deaths." If, for example, you double-click on the flow, Prey Deaths, then you will effectively see the following equation displayed:

$$\text{Prey Deaths} = a \times \text{Prey Population} \times \text{Predator Population}$$

The information links (called "Arrows" in Vensim) are denoted by curved arrows in the stock and flow diagram, and the constants r, a, s, and b are represented in Vensim by "Variables" with the same names. If, say, you double-click on the Variable, r, then 1 will, of course, be displayed.

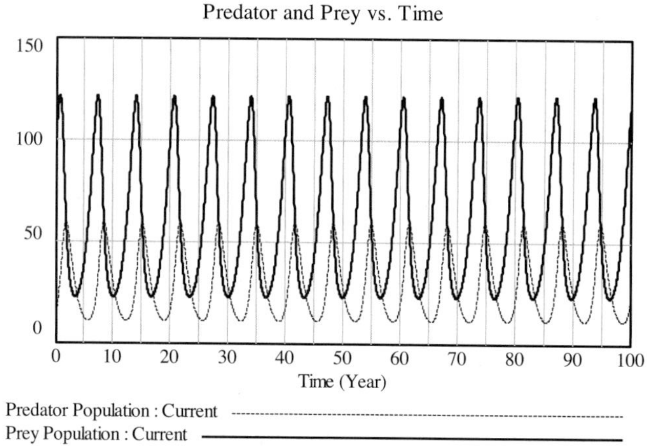

FIGURE 13.9
Population sizes as a function of time, continuous predator-prey model.

We ran the simulation for 100 years and in Fig. 13.9 we plot $x(t)$ and $y(t)$ as a function of t, where the periodicity of $\{x(t), y(t)\}$ can be clearly seen (see also the Color Plates). Note also that plot of $y(t)$ lags that for $x(t)$. Figure 13.10 presents a *phase plot* for the predator-prey model with the specified parameters, that is, a plot of $\{x(t), y(t)\}$ for $t \geq 0$. It can be seen that all plotted points fall on an "egg-shaped" closed curve, which is due to the periodic nature of the solution.

EXAMPLE 13.6. We now consider a model of aimed-fire combat due to Frederick Lanchester (1916), who applied it to aerial warfare during WWI [see also MacKay (2006) and Artelli and Deckro (2008)]. *Aimed-fire combat* describes a situation where

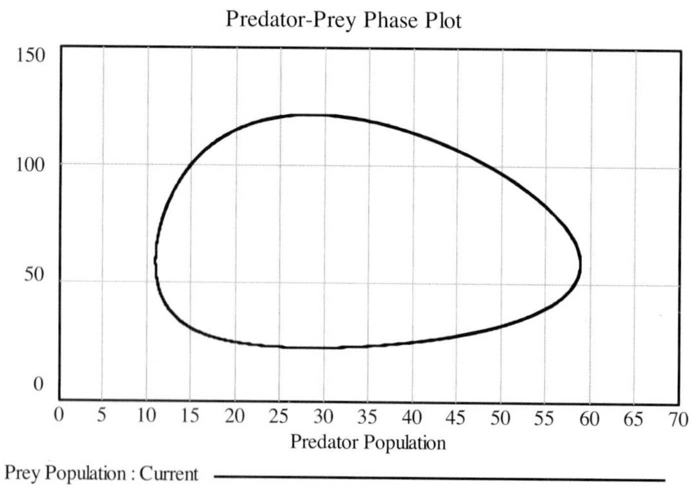

FIGURE 13.10
Phase plot for the continuous predator-prey model.

the shooter is directly aiming at an enemy. If the enemy is destroyed, the shooter moves his fire to a new target. Thus, as targets are eliminated, the firepower of the shooters becomes more and more concentrated on those targets that remain. Possible applications of aimed fire are rifle duals, tank combat, and air-to-air combat. Aimed fire is to be contrasted with unaimed-fire combat where the shooter fires into an *area*, with a possible application being artillery fire.

Let $b(t)$ and $r(t)$ denote, respectively, the numbers of blue units and red units "alive" at time t. Suppose that the *attrition* rate of the blue force at time t is proportional to $r(t)$. Thus, the rate of change of the blue force, db/dt, is given by

$$\frac{db}{dt} = -\alpha r(t) \quad \text{for } b(t) > 0 \tag{13.3}$$

where $\alpha > 0$ is called the *fighting effectiveness of the red force*. Similarly, the rate of change of the red force, dr/dt, is given by

$$\frac{dr}{dt} = -\beta b(t) \quad \text{for } r(t) > 0 \tag{13.4}$$

where $\beta > 0$ is called the *fighting effectiveness of the blue force*. Of course, $b(t)$ and $r(t)$ must be nonnegative. Equations (13.3) and (13.4) are called the *Lanchester (aimed-fire) equations*.

Consider the particular values $\alpha = 0.1$, $\beta = 0.4$ and the initial force strengths $b(0) = 175$, $r(0) = 300$. Who will win the battle? To find out we built a Vensim model of the Lanchester equations as given by Eqs. (13.3) and (13.4), with the stock and flow diagram given in Fig. 13.11. The equation inside of the "Blue Deaths" flow is effectively

$$\text{Blue Deaths} = \begin{cases} \text{Alpha} \times \text{Red Force} & \text{if Blue Force} > 0 \\ 0 & \text{otherwise} \end{cases}$$

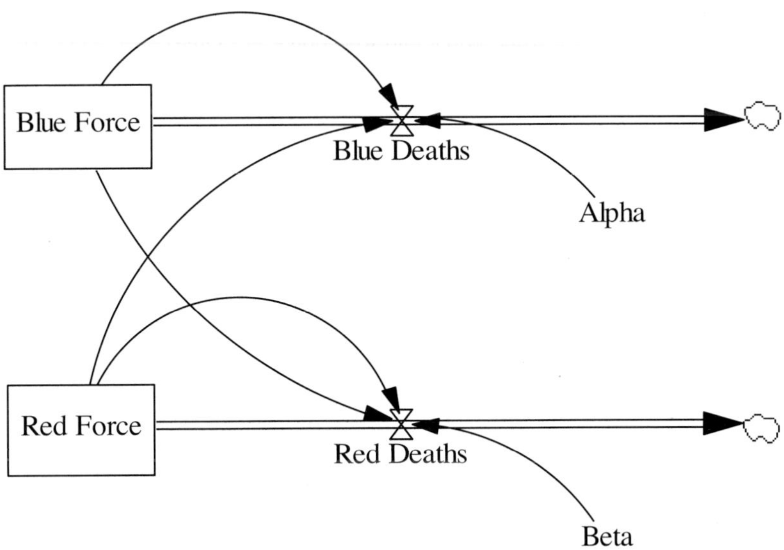

FIGURE 13.11
Stock and flow diagram for the Lanchester equations.

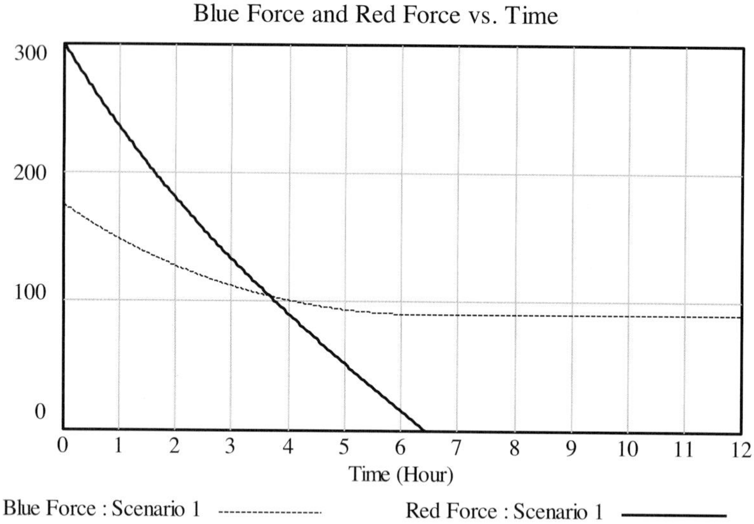

FIGURE 13.12
Force sizes as a function of time for $b(0) = 175$, Lanchester equations.

We ran the simulation for 12 hours and a plot of $b(t)$ and $r(t)$ as a function of t is given in Fig. 13.12, where it can be seen that the blue force wins the battle. What if we change $b(0)$ to 125? The resulting plot of $b(t)$ and $r(t)$ versus t is given in Fig. 13.13, where we see that the red force now wins the battle.

One might legitimately ask whether there is an analytic result involving $b(0)$, $r(0)$, α, and β that will tell us who will the battle without having to run the simulation. It turns

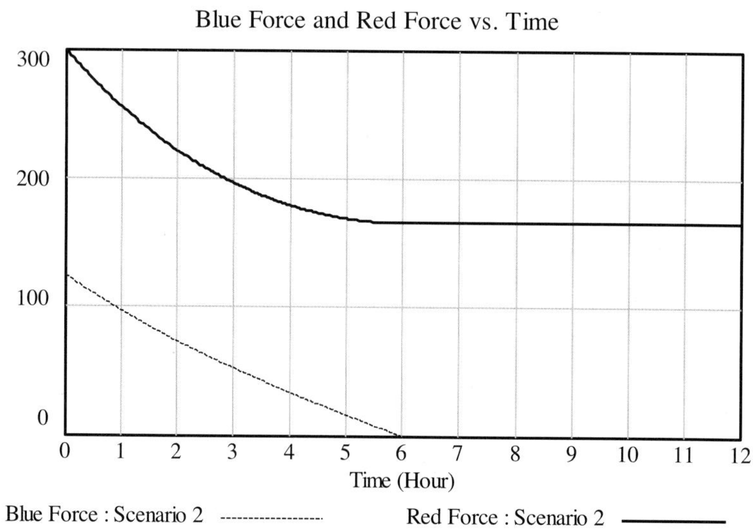

FIGURE 13.13
Force sizes as a function of time for $b(0) = 125$, Lanchester equations.

out [see Taylor (1983)] that if $b(0)/r(0) > \sqrt{\alpha/\beta}$, then the *blue force* will win the battle at time t_{end}, which is given by

$$t_{\text{end}} = \frac{1}{2\sqrt{\alpha\beta}} \ln \left(\frac{1 + \dfrac{r(0)}{b(0)}\sqrt{\dfrac{\alpha}{\beta}}}{1 - \dfrac{r(0)}{b(0)}\sqrt{\dfrac{\alpha}{\beta}}} \right)$$

and the final force sizes will be

$$b(t_{\text{end}}) = \sqrt{[b(0)]^2 - \frac{\alpha}{\beta}[r(0)]^2}, \quad r(t_{\text{end}}) = 0$$

Thus, if $b(0) = 175$, $r(0) = 300$, $\alpha = 0.1$, and $\beta = 0.4$ as in Fig. 13.12, we get $b(0)/r(0) = 0.58 > 0.50 = \sqrt{\alpha/\beta}$, $t_{\text{end}} = 6.41$ hours, $b(t_{\text{end}}) = 90.14$, and $r(t_{\text{end}}) = 0$. On the other hand, the *red force* will win the battle if $b(0)/r(0) < \sqrt{\alpha/\beta}$. Finally, if $b(0)/r(0) = \sqrt{\alpha/\beta}$, then $b(t)$ and $r(t)$ will both approach 0 as t goes to infinity.

13.4
COMBINED DISCRETE-CONTINUOUS SIMULATION

Since some systems are neither completely discrete nor completely continuous, the need may arise to construct a model with aspects of both discrete-event and continuous simulation, resulting in a *combined discrete-continuous* simulation. Pritsker (1995, pp. 61–62) describes the three fundamental types of interactions that can occur between discretely changing and continuously changing state variables:

- A discrete event may cause a discrete change in the value of a continuous state variable.
- A discrete event may cause the relationship governing a continuous state variable to change at a particular time.
- A continuous state variable achieving a threshold value may cause a discrete event to occur or to be scheduled.

Combined discrete-continuous simulation models can be built in Arena [Kelton et al. (2010)] and ExtendSim [Imagine (2013)].

The following example of a combined discrete-continuous simulation is a brief description of a model described in detail by Pritsker (1995, pp. 354–364), who also provides other examples of this type of simulation.

EXAMPLE 13.7. Tankers carrying crude oil arrive at a single unloading dock, supplying a storage tank that in turn feeds a refinery through a pipeline. An unloading tanker delivers oil to the storage tank at a specified constant rate. (Tankers that arrive when the dock is busy form a queue.) The storage tank supplies oil to the refinery at a different specified rate. The dock is open from 6 A.M. to midnight and, because of safety considerations, unloading of tankers ceases when the dock is closed.

The discrete events for this (simplified) model are the arrival of a tanker for unloading, closing the dock at midnight, and opening the dock at 6 A.M. The levels of oil in the unloading tanker and in the storage tank are given by continuous state variables whose rates of change are described by *differential equations* [see Pritsker (1995, pp. 354–364) for details]. Unloading the tanker is considered complete when the level of oil in the tanker is less than 5 percent of its capacity, but unloading must be temporarily stopped if the level of oil in the storage tank reaches its capacity. Unloading can be resumed when the level of oil in the tank decreases to 80 percent of its capacity. If the level of oil in the tank ever falls below 5000 barrels, the refinery must be shut down temporarily. To avoid frequent startups and shutdowns of the refinery, the tank does not resume supplying oil to the refinery until the tank once again contains 50,000 barrels. Each of the five events concerning the levels of oil, e.g., the level of oil in the tanker falling below 5 percent of the tanker's capacity, is what Pritsker calls a *state event*. Unlike discrete events, state events are not scheduled but occur when a continuous state variable crosses a threshold.

13.5 MONTE CARLO SIMULATION

We define *Monte Carlo simulation* as a scheme employing random numbers, that is, U(0, 1) random variates, which is used for solving certain stochastic or deterministic problems. Thus, a stochastic discrete-event simulation is included in this definition. The name "Monte Carlo" simulation or method originated during World War II, when this approach was applied to problems related to the development of the atomic bomb. For a more detailed discussion of Monte Carlo simulation, see Hammersley and Handscomb (1964), Halton (1970), Rubinstein (1981, 1992), Morgan (1984), Fishman (1996, 2006), Rubinstein et al. (1998), Glasserman (2004), and Rubinstein and Kroese (2008). The following example illustrates the application of Monte Carlo simulation to a *deterministic* problem.

EXAMPLE 13.8. Suppose that we want to evaluate the integral

$$I = \int_a^b g(x)dx$$

where $g(x)$ is a real-valued function that is not analytically integrable. (In practice, Monte Carlo simulation would probably not be used to evaluate a single integral, since there are more efficient numerical-analysis techniques for this purpose. It is more likely to be used on a multiple-integral problem with an ill-behaved integrand.) To see how this problem can be approached by Monte Carlo simulation, let Y be the random variable $(b - a)g(X)$, where X is a continuous random variable distributed uniformly on $[a, b]$ [denoted by U(a, b)]. Then the expected value of Y is

$$\begin{aligned} E(Y) &= E[(b - a)g(X)] \\ &= (b - a)E[g(X)] \\ &= (b - a)\int_a^b g(x)f_X(x)dx \\ &= (b - a)\frac{\int_a^b g(x)dx}{b - a} \\ &= I \end{aligned}$$

TABLE 13.2
$\bar{Y}(n)$ for various values of n resulting from applying Monte Carlo simulation to the estimation of the integral $\int_0^\pi \sin x\, dx = 2$

n	10	20	40	80	160
$\bar{Y}(n)$	2.213	1.951	1.948	1.989	1.993

where $f_X(x) = 1/(b - a)$ is the probability density function of a U(a, b) random variable (see Sec. 6.2.2). [For justification of the third equality, see, for example, Ross (2003, p. 45).] Thus, the problem of evaluating the integral has been reduced to one of estimating the expected value $E(Y)$. In particular, we shall estimate $E(Y) = I$ by the sample mean

$$\bar{Y}(n) = \frac{\sum_{i=1}^{n} Y_i}{n} = (b - a)\frac{\sum_{i=1}^{n} g(X_i)}{n}$$

where $X_1, X_2, \ldots, X_n$ are IID U(a, b) random variables. {It is instructive to think of $\bar{Y}(n)$ as an estimate of the area of the rectangle that has a base of length $(b - a)$ and a height $I/(b - a)$, which is the continuous average of $g(x)$ over $[a, b]$.} Furthermore, it can be shown that $E[\bar{Y}(n)] = I$, that is, $\bar{Y}(n)$ is an unbiased estimator of I, and $\text{Var}[\bar{Y}(n)] = \text{Var}(Y)/n$ (see Sec. 4.4). Assuming that Var(Y) is finite, it follows that $\bar{Y}(n)$ will be arbitrarily close to I for sufficiently large n (with probability 1) (see Sec. 4.6).

To illustrate the above scheme numerically, suppose that we would like to evaluate the integral

$$I = \int_0^\pi \sin x\, dx$$

which can be shown by elementary calculus to have a value of 2. Table 13.2 shows the results of applying Monte Carlo simulation to the estimation of this integral for various values of n.

EXAMPLE 13.9. We now use Monte Carlo simulation to estimate the characteristics of a stochastic system. Consider the system that is shown in Fig. 13.14, where it is desired to send a signal from A to B. Each of the five components is subject to random failures, and the components fail independently of each other. Let Y be the time to failure of the entire system and let X_i be the time to failure of component i, for $i = 1, 2, \ldots, 5$.

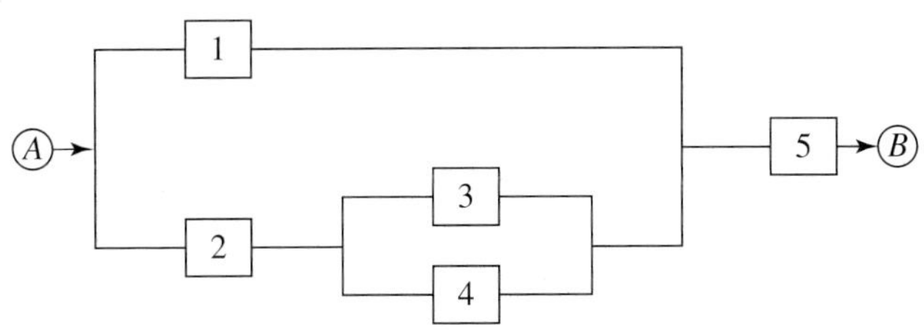

FIGURE 13.14
Layout of the five-component system.

TABLE 13.3
Means for the five components (in days)

i	β_i
1	10
2	8
3	7
4	5
5	6

We assume that X_i is exponentially distributed with mean β_i days, with the β_i's given in Table 13.3. It can be shown that (see Prob. 13.5)

$$Y = \min(\max\{X_1, \min[X_2, \max(X_3, X_4)]\}, X_5) \tag{13.5}$$

Recall from Sec. 8.3.2 that we can generate a random variate X_i from an exponential distribution with mean β_i using the following expression:

$$X_i = -\beta_i \ln U$$

where $U \sim$ U(0, 1). Thus, it takes five random numbers to generate one random variate from the distribution of Y. We generated Y_j for $j = 1, 2, \ldots, 25{,}000$ from Eq. (13.5) and obtained $\bar{Y}(25{,}000) = 4.33$ days, which is an unbiased estimate of the expected time to failure, $E(Y)$. Suppose that we are also interested in estimating the probability that the system will function for at least seven days, i.e., $p_7 = P(Y \geq 7$ days). Let the indicator function $I_j(7, \infty)$ be defined as

$$I_j(7, \infty) = \begin{cases} 1 & \text{if } Y_j \geq 7 \\ 0 & \text{otherwise} \end{cases}$$

for $j = 1, 2, \ldots, 25{,}000$. Then an unbiased estimate of p_7 is given by

$$\hat{p}_7 = \frac{\sum_{j=1}^{25{,}000} I_j(7, \infty)}{25{,}000} = 0.19$$

Finally, we give a histogram of the 25,000 Y_j's in Fig. 13.15.

Monte Carlo simulation is widely used to solve certain problems in statistics that are not analytically tractable. For example, it has been applied to estimate the critical values or the power of a new hypothesis test. Determining the critical values for the Kolmogorov-Smirnov test for normality, discussed in Sec. 6.6, is such an application. The advanced reader might also enjoy perusing the technical journals *Communications in Statistics* (Simulation and Computation), *Journal of Statistical Computation and Simulation*, and *Technometrics*, all of which contain many examples of this type of Monte Carlo simulation.

Finally, the procedures discussed in Sec. 9.4 can be used to determine the sample size n required to obtain a specified precision in a Monte Carlo simulation study.

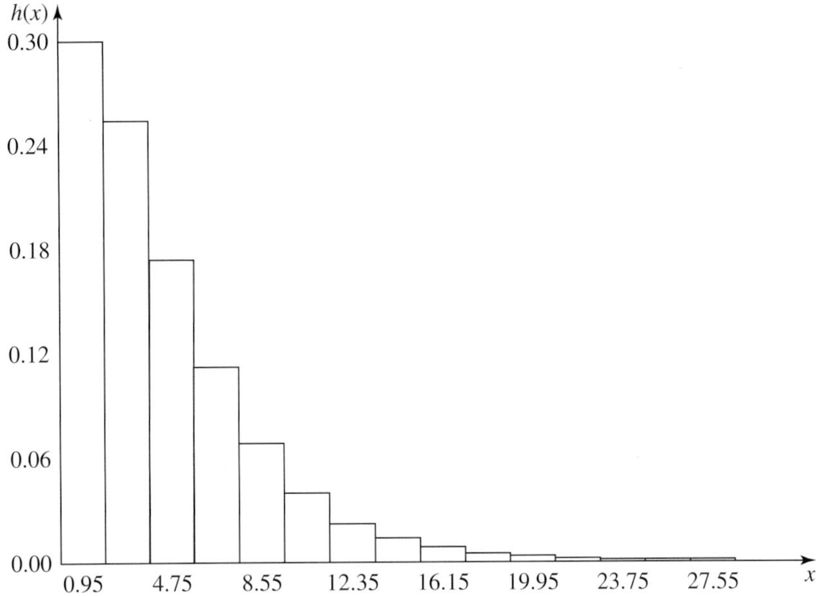

FIGURE 13.15
Histogram of 25,000 times to failure for the five-component system.

13.6 SPREADSHEET SIMULATION

Discrete-event simulation and Monte Carlo simulation can sometimes be done in spreadsheets such as Excel if the problem of interest is not too complex. In this regard, Excel provides a random-number generator, the ability to generate random values from some basic probability distributions (e.g., normal, uniform, binomial, and Poisson), summary statistics (e.g., mean and variance), and graphical plots such as a histogram. However, according to Seila (2005), spreadsheets have the following important limitations:

- Only simple data structures are available.
- Complex algorithms are difficult to implement.
- Spreadsheet simulations may have longer execution times than simulations built in a discrete-event simulation package.
- Data storage is limited.

The ease of performing a spreadsheet simulation is facilitated by using the well-known spreadsheet add-ins @Risk (Palisade Corporation), Crystal Ball (Oracle Corporation), and Risk Solver (Frontline Systems Inc.). They provide additional probability distributions, an easy mechanism for making independent replications of a spreadsheet simulation, and features for performing sensitivity analysis.

Spreadsheet simulations are widely used for performing risk analyses in application areas such as finance, manufacturing, project management, and oil and gas discovery. Additional information on spreadsheet simulation can be found in the books by Evans and Olson (2002), Seila et al. (2003), and Winston and Albright (2011).

EXAMPLE 13.10. Consider the simple (s, S) inventory system of Example 4.23. If the random variable Y is the average total cost per month over the first 12 months, then we are interested in estimating the expected value $E(Y)$, which is given by

$$E(Y) = E\left[\frac{\sum_{i=1}^{12} C_i}{12}\right] = \frac{\sum_{i=1}^{12} E(C_i)}{12}$$

In order to estimate $E(Y)$, we developed a spreadsheet simulation in Excel and performed 1000 replications using independent random numbers. The sample mean and sample variance of the 1000 observations of Y were 99.34 and 28.04, respectively. [Note that the steady-state expected total cost per month is 112.11 (see Example 9.3).] In Fig. 13.16 we give a histogram of the 1000 observations of Y, using an interval width of 3. This simulation of the inventory system is a discrete-event simulation using the FITA approach with $\Delta t = 1$ month.

Note that the Monte Carlo simulation of the five-component system in Example 13.9 was also performed using an Excel spreadsheet.

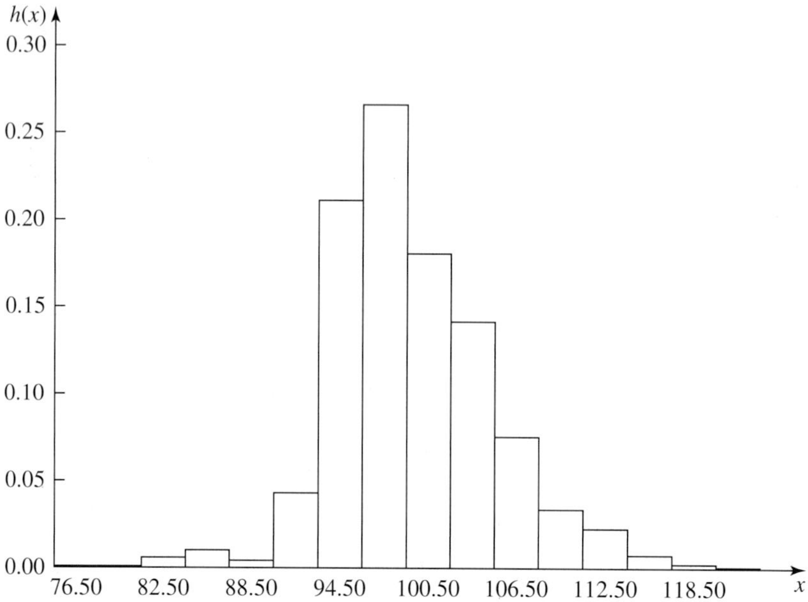

FIGURE 13.16
Histogram of 1000 observations of the average total cost per month over the first 12 months, simple (s, S) inventory system.

PROBLEMS

13.1. Download a free copy of NetLogo from the website http://ccl.northwestern.edu/netlogo/. In the "Models Library" open the model "Wolf Sheep Predation" (see the category "Biology") and turn on the "grass?" switch. Use the model to determine why the wolf population goes to 0 fairly quickly when the grass regrowth time is set to 10 (see Fig. 13.4).

13.2. For the wolf sheep predation model of Sec. 13.2.1, make 100 replications with the initial number of wolves equal to 50 (the default) and 100 replications with the initial number of wolves equal to 75, and all other parameters at their default values (use the "BehaviorSpace" option in the "Tools" menu at the top of the screen). Let μ_i be the expected final number of wolves for $i = 50, 75$. Construct a 95 percent confidence interval for $\mu_{50} - \mu_{75}$ using the Welch confidence interval (see Sec. 10.2.2). What do you conclude?

13.3. For the system of Example 13.3, suppose that the amount of time that a cell is green before turning red is exponentially distributed with a mean of 80 minutes. Also assume that the amount of time that a cell is red before turning green is exponentially distributed with a mean of 20 minutes. Discuss the difficulty in choosing Δt for the FITA approach.

13.4. For scenario 2 [i.e., $b(0) = 125$] in Example 13.6, what are the values of t_{end} and $r(t_{\text{end}})$?

13.5. Explain why the expression for Y in Eq. (13.5) is correct?

13.6. For the five-component system of Example 13.9, which of the following three options will increase the mean time to failure the most?
(*a*) Replace component 1 with two such components in parallel.
(*b*) Replace component 2 with two such components in parallel.
(*c*) Replace component 5 with two such components in parallel.
For each option, use Monte Carlo simulation with $n = 25{,}000$. Let μ_i be the mean time to failure if component i is duplicated, for $i = 1, 2, 5$. Using the Welch approach and the Bonferroni inequality (see Sec. 9.7), construct confidence intervals for $\mu_1 - \mu_2$, $\mu_1 - \mu_5$, and $\mu_2 - \mu_5$ so that the overall confidence level is at least 95 percent.

13.7. Perform a Monte Carlo simulation to estimate the value of the constant π. *Hint:* Consider a square with each side having a length of 1. Inscribe a circle inside of the square with a radius of 1/2. Then the ratio of the area of the circle to the area of the square is $\pi/4$. Use $n = 25{,}000$ random numbers to obtain your estimate.

Appendix

TABLE T.1

Critical points $t_{\nu,\gamma}$ for the t distribution with ν df, and z_γ for the standard normal distribution

$\gamma = P(T_\nu \le t_{\nu,\gamma})$, where T_ν is a random variable having the t distribution with ν df; the last row, where $\nu = \infty$, gives the normal critical points satisfying $\gamma = P(Z \le z_\gamma)$, where Z is a standard normal random variable

	γ															
ν	0.6000	0.7000	0.8000	0.9000	0.9333	0.9500	0.9600	0.9667	0.9750	0.9800	0.9833	0.9875	0.9900	0.9917	0.9938	0.9950
1	0.325	0.727	1.376	3.078	4.702	6.314	7.916	9.524	12.706	15.895	19.043	25.452	31.821	38.342	51.334	63.657
2	0.289	0.617	1.061	1.886	2.456	2.920	3.320	3.679	4.303	4.849	5.334	6.205	6.965	7.665	8.897	9.925
3	0.277	0.584	0.978	1.638	2.045	2.353	2.605	2.823	3.182	3.482	3.738	4.177	4.541	4.864	5.408	5.841
4	0.271	0.569	0.941	1.533	1.879	2.132	2.333	2.502	2.776	2.999	3.184	3.495	3.747	3.966	4.325	4.604
5	0.267	0.559	0.920	1.476	1.790	2.015	2.191	2.337	2.571	2.757	2.910	3.163	3.365	3.538	3.818	4.032
6	0.265	0.553	0.906	1.440	1.735	1.943	2.104	2.237	2.447	2.612	2.748	2.969	3.143	3.291	3.528	3.707
7	0.263	0.549	0.896	1.415	1.698	1.895	2.046	2.170	2.365	2.517	2.640	2.841	2.998	3.130	3.341	3.499
8	0.262	0.546	0.889	1.397	1.670	1.860	2.004	2.122	2.306	2.449	2.565	2.752	2.896	3.018	3.211	3.355
9	0.261	0.543	0.883	1.383	1.650	1.833	1.973	2.086	2.262	2.398	2.508	2.685	2.821	2.936	3.116	3.250
10	0.260	0.542	0.879	1.372	1.634	1.812	1.948	2.058	2.228	2.359	2.465	2.634	2.764	2.872	3.043	3.169
11	0.260	0.540	0.876	1.363	1.621	1.796	1.928	2.036	2.201	2.328	2.430	2.593	2.718	2.822	2.985	3.106
12	0.259	0.539	0.873	1.356	1.610	1.782	1.912	2.017	2.179	2.303	2.402	2.560	2.681	2.782	2.939	3.055
13	0.259	0.538	0.870	1.350	1.601	1.771	1.899	2.002	2.160	2.282	2.379	2.533	2.650	2.748	2.900	3.012
14	0.258	0.537	0.868	1.345	1.593	1.761	1.887	1.989	2.145	2.264	2.359	2.510	2.624	2.720	2.868	2.977
15	0.258	0.536	0.866	1.341	1.587	1.753	1.878	1.978	2.131	2.249	2.342	2.490	2.602	2.696	2.841	2.947
16	0.258	0.535	0.865	1.337	1.581	1.746	1.869	1.968	2.120	2.235	2.327	2.473	2.583	2.675	2.817	2.921
17	0.257	0.534	0.863	1.333	1.576	1.740	1.862	1.960	2.110	2.224	2.315	2.458	2.567	2.657	2.796	2.898
18	0.257	0.534	0.862	1.330	1.572	1.734	1.855	1.953	2.101	2.214	2.303	2.445	2.552	2.641	2.778	2.878
19	0.257	0.533	0.861	1.328	1.568	1.729	1.850	1.946	2.093	2.205	2.293	2.433	2.539	2.627	2.762	2.861
20	0.257	0.533	0.860	1.325	1.564	1.725	1.844	1.940	2.086	2.197	2.285	2.423	2.528	2.614	2.748	2.845
21	0.257	0.532	0.859	1.323	1.561	1.721	1.840	1.935	2.080	2.189	2.277	2.414	2.518	2.603	2.735	2.831
22	0.256	0.532	0.858	1.321	1.558	1.717	1.835	1.930	2.074	2.183	2.269	2.405	2.508	2.593	2.724	2.819
23	0.256	0.532	0.858	1.319	1.556	1.714	1.832	1.926	2.069	2.177	2.263	2.398	2.500	2.584	2.713	2.807
24	0.256	0.531	0.857	1.318	1.553	1.711	1.828	1.922	2.064	2.172	2.257	2.391	2.492	2.575	2.704	2.797
25	0.256	0.531	0.856	1.316	1.551	1.708	1.825	1.918	2.060	2.167	2.251	2.385	2.485	2.568	2.695	2.787
26	0.256	0.531	0.856	1.315	1.549	1.706	1.822	1.915	2.056	2.162	2.246	2.379	2.479	2.561	2.687	2.779
27	0.256	0.531	0.855	1.314	1.547	1.703	1.819	1.912	2.052	2.158	2.242	2.373	2.473	2.554	2.680	2.771
28	0.256	0.530	0.855	1.313	1.546	1.701	1.817	1.909	2.048	2.154	2.237	2.368	2.467	2.548	2.673	2.763
29	0.256	0.530	0.854	1.311	1.544	1.699	1.814	1.906	2.045	2.150	2.233	2.364	2.462	2.543	2.667	2.756
30	0.256	0.530	0.854	1.310	1.543	1.697	1.812	1.904	2.042	2.147	2.230	2.360	2.457	2.537	2.661	2.750
40	0.255	0.529	0.851	1.303	1.532	1.684	1.796	1.886	2.021	2.123	2.203	2.329	2.423	2.501	2.619	2.704
50	0.255	0.528	0.849	1.299	1.526	1.676	1.787	1.875	2.009	2.109	2.188	2.311	2.403	2.479	2.594	2.678
75	0.254	0.527	0.846	1.293	1.517	1.665	1.775	1.861	1.992	2.090	2.167	2.287	2.377	2.450	2.562	2.643
100	0.254	0.526	0.845	1.290	1.513	1.660	1.769	1.855	1.984	2.081	2.157	2.276	2.364	2.436	2.547	2.626
∞	0.253	0.524	0.842	1.282	1.501	1.645	1.751	1.834	1.960	2.054	2.127	2.241	2.326	2.395	2.501	2.576

TABLE T.2

Critical points $\chi^2_{\nu,\gamma}$ for the chi-square distribution with ν df

$\gamma = P(Y_\nu \leq \chi^2_{\nu,\gamma})$ where Y_ν has a chi-square distribution with ν df; for large ν, use the approximation for $\chi^2_{\nu,\gamma}$ in Sec. 7.4.1

	γ						
ν	**0.250**	**0.500**	**0.750**	**0.900**	**0.950**	**0.975**	**0.990**
1	0.102	0.455	1.323	2.706	3.841	5.024	6.635
2	0.575	1.386	2.773	4.605	5.991	7.378	9.210
3	1.213	2.366	4.108	6.251	7.815	9.348	11.345
4	1.923	3.357	5.385	7.779	9.488	11.143	13.277
5	2.675	4.351	6.626	9.236	11.070	12.833	15.086
6	3.455	5.348	7.841	10.645	12.592	14.449	16.812
7	4.255	6.346	9.037	12.017	14.067	16.013	18.475
8	5.071	7.344	10.219	13.362	15.507	17.535	20.090
9	5.899	8.343	11.389	14.684	16.919	19.023	21.666
10	6.737	9.342	12.549	15.987	18.307	20.483	23.209
11	7.584	10.341	13.701	17.275	19.675	21.920	24.725
12	8.438	11.340	14.845	18.549	21.026	23.337	26.217
13	9.299	12.340	15.984	19.812	22.362	24.736	27.688
14	10.165	13.339	17.117	21.064	23.685	26.119	29.141
15	11.037	14.339	18.245	22.307	24.996	27.488	30.578
16	11.912	15.338	19.369	23.542	26.296	28.845	32.000
17	12.792	16.338	20.489	24.769	27.587	30.191	33.409
18	13.675	17.338	21.605	25.989	28.869	31.526	34.805
19	14.562	18.338	22.718	27.204	30.144	32.852	36.191
20	15.452	19.337	23.828	28.412	31.410	34.170	37.566
21	16.344	20.337	24.935	29.615	32.671	35.479	38.932
22	17.240	21.337	26.039	30.813	33.924	36.781	40.289
23	18.137	22.337	27.141	32.007	35.172	38.076	41.638
24	19.037	23.337	28.241	33.196	36.415	39.364	42.980
25	19.939	24.337	29.339	34.382	37.652	40.646	44.314
26	20.843	25.336	30.435	35.563	38.885	41.923	45.642
27	21.749	26.336	31.528	36.741	40.113	43.195	46.963
28	22.657	27.336	32.620	37.916	41.337	44.461	48.278
29	23.567	28.336	33.711	39.087	42.557	45.722	49.588
30	24.478	29.336	34.800	40.256	43.773	46.979	50.892
40	33.660	39.335	45.616	51.805	55.758	59.342	63.691
50	42.942	49.335	56.334	63.167	67.505	71.420	76.154
75	66.417	74.334	82.858	91.061	96.217	100.839	106.393
100	90.133	99.334	109.141	118.498	124.342	129.561	135.807

References

Abramowitz, M., and I.A. Stegun, eds.: *Handbook of Mathematical Functions with Formulas, Graphs, and Mathematical Tables,* National Bureau of Standards, Washington, D.C. (1964).

Adiri, I., and B. Avi-Itzhak: A Time-Sharing Queue with a Finite Number of Customers, *J. Assoc. Comput. Mach., 16:* 315–323 (1969).

Ahrens, J.H., and U. Dieter: Computer Methods for Sampling from the Exponential and Normal Distributions, *Commun. Assoc. Comput. Mach., 15:* 873–882 (1972).

Ahrens, J.H., and U. Dieter: Computer Methods for Sampling from Gamma, Beta, Poisson, and Binomial Distributions, *Computing, 12:* 223–246 (1974).

Alexopoulos, C., C. Antonini, D. Goldsman, and M. Meterelliyoz: Performance of Folded Variance Estimators for Simulation, *Assoc. Comput. Mach. Trans. Modeling and Comput. Simul., 20,* No. 3, Article 11 (2010).

Alexopoulos, C., N.T. Argon, D. Goldsman, N.M. Steiger, G. Tokol, and J.R. Wilson: Efficient Computation of Overlapping Variance Estimators for Simulation, *INFORMS J. Comput., 19:* 314–327 (2007a).

Alexopoulos, C., N.T. Argon, D. Goldsman, G. Tokol, and J.R. Wilson: Overlapping Variance Estimators for Simulation, *Operations Res., 55:* 1090–1103 (2007b).

Alexopoulos, C., and D. Goldsman: To Batch or Not to Batch, *Assoc. Comput. Mach. Trans. Modeling and Comput. Simul., 14:* 76–114 (2004).

Alexopoulos, C., D. Goldsman, and R.F. Serfozo: Stationary Processes: Statistical Estimation, *Encyclopedia of Statistical Sciences,* 2d ed., N. Balakrishnan, C. Read, and B. Vidakovic, eds., John Wiley, New York (2006).

Alexopoulos, C., D. Goldsman, and J.R. Wilson: A New Perspective on Batched Quantile Estimation, *Proc. 2012 Winter Simulation Conference,* Berlin, Germany (2012).

Alexopoulos, C., and A.F. Seila: Output Data Analysis, in *Handbook of Simulation,* J. Banks, ed., John Wiley, New York (1998).

Alspaugh, C., T.A. Hepner, C. Tran, W. Youm, A.K. Legaspi, S. Ferenci, R.M. Fujimoto, and M. Choi: Navy NETWARS Interoperability Efforts, *Proceedings of the Spring 2004 Simulation Interoperability Workshop,* Arlington, Virginia (2004).

Anderson, T.W.: *The Statistical Analysis of Time Series,* John Wiley, New York (1994).

Anderson, T.W., and D.A. Darling: A Test of Goodness of Fit, *J. Am. Statist. Assoc., 49:* 765–769 (1954).

Andradóttir, S.: Simulation Optimization, in *Handbook of Simulation,* J. Banks, ed., John Wiley, New York (1998).

Andradóttir, S.: An Overview of Simulation Optimization via Random Search, in *Handbooks in Operations Research and Management Science: Simulation,* S.G. Henderson and B.L. Nelson, eds., Elsevier, New York (2006).

Andradóttir, S., and S.-H. Kim: Fully-Sequential Procedures for Comparing Constrained Systems Via Simulation, *Naval Res. Logistics, 57:* 403–421 (2010).

Andradóttir, S., and A.A. Prudius: Adaptive Random Search for Continuous Simulation Optimization, *Naval Res. Logistics, 57:* 583–604 (2010).

Andréasson, I.J.: Antithetic Methods in Queueing Simulations, Roy. Inst. Technol. Dept. Comput. Sci. Tech. Rep. NA 72.58, Stockholm (1972).

Angün, E., D. ven Hertog, G. Gürkan, and J.P.C. Kleijnen: Response Surface Methodology with Stochastic Constraints for Expensive Simulation, *J. Operational Res. Soc., 60:* 735–746 (2009).

Ankenman, B.E., and B.L. Nelson: A Quick Assessment of Input Uncertainty, *Proc. 2012 Winter Simulation Conference*, Berlin, Germany (2012).

Ankenman, B.E., B.L. Nelson, and J. Staum: Stochastic Kriging for Simulation Metamodeling, *Operations Res., 58:* 371–382 (2010).

Antonini, C., C. Alexopoulos, D. Goldsman, and J.R. Wilson: Area Variance Estimators for Simulation Using Folded Standardized Time Series, *IIE Trans., 41:* 134–144 (2009).

AnyLogic Company, The: AnyLogic simulation software, www.anylogic.com (2013).

Applied Materials, Inc.: AutoMod simulation software, www.automod.com (2013).

Argon, N.T., and S. Andradóttir: Replicated Batch Means for Steady-State Simulations, *Naval Res. Logistics, 53:* 508–524 (2006).

Argonne National Lab: Repast simulation software, repast.sourceforge.net (2013).

Arkin, B.L., and L.M. Leemis: Nonparametric Estimation of the Cumulative Intensity Function for a Nonhomogeneous Poisson Process from Overlapping Realizations, *Management Sci., 46:* 989–998 (2000).

Arnold, B.C.: A Note on Multivariate Distributions with Specified Marginals, *J. Am. Statist. Assoc., 62:* 1460–1461 (1967).

Artelli, M.J., and R.F. Deckro: Modeling the Lancaster Laws with System Dynamics, *J. of Defense Modeling and Simulation, 5:* 1–20 (2008).

Atkinson, A.C.: A Family of Switching Algorithms for the Computer Generation of Beta Random Variables, *Biometrika, 66:* 141–145 (1979a).

Atkinson, A.C.: The Computer Generation of Poisson Random Variables, *Appl. Statist., 28:* 29–35 (1979b).

Atkinson, A.C.: Recent Developments in the Computer Generation of Poisson Random Variables, *Appl. Statist., 28:* 260–263 (1979c).

Atkinson, A.C.: Tests of Pseudo-random Numbers, *Appl. Statist., 29:* 164–171 (1980).

Atkinson, A.C., and M.C. Pearce: The Computer Generation of Beta, Gamma, and Normal Random Variables, *J. Roy. Statist. Soc., A139:* 431–448 (1976).

Atkinson, A.C., and J. Whittaker: A Switching Algorithm for the Generation of Beta Random Variables with at Least One Parameter Less than 1, *J. Roy. Statist. Soc., A139:* 462–467 (1976).

Atkinson, A.C., and J. Whittaker: The Generation of Beta Random Variables with One Parameter Greater than and One Parameter Less than 1, *Appl. Statist., 28:* 90–93 (1979).

Averill M. Law & Associates, Inc.: *ExpertFit User's Guide,* Tucson, Arizona (2013).

Avramidis, A.N., and J.R. Wilson: A Splitting Scheme for Control Variates, *Operations Res. Letters, 14:* 187–198 (1993).

Avramidis, A.N., and J.R. Wilson: Integrated Variance Reduction Strategies for Simulation, *Operations Res., 44:* 327–346 (1996).

Avramidis, A.N., and J.R. Wilson: Correlation-Induction Techniques for Estimating Quantiles in Simulation Experiments, *Operations Res., 46:* 574–591 (1998).

Bäck, T.: *Evolutionary Algorithms in Theory and Practice: Evolution Strategies, Evolutionary Programming, and Genetic Algorithms,* Oxford University Press, New York (1996).

Bäck, T., and H.-P. Schwefel: An Overview of Evolutionary Algorithms for Parameter Optimization, *Evolutionary Computation, 1:* 1–23 (1993).

Bagni, R., R. Berchi, and P. Cariello: A Comparison of Simulation Models Applied to Epidemics, *J. of Artificial Societies and Social Simulation, 5,* http://jasss.soc.surrey.ac.uk/5/3/5.html (June 2002).

Balci, O.: Verification, Validation and Testing, in *Handbook of Simulation,* J. Banks, ed., John Wiley, New York (1998).

Banks, J.: *Getting Started with AutoMod,* 2d ed., Brooks Automation, Inc., Chelmsford, Massachusetts (2004).

Banks, J., J.S. Carson, B.L. Nelson, and D.M. Nicol: *Discrete-Event System Simulation,* 5th ed., Prentice-Hall, Upper Saddle River, New Jersey (2010).

Barnett, V.: Probability Plotting Methods and Order Statistics, *Appl. Statist., 24:* 95–108 (1975).

Bartels, R.: The Rank Version of von Neumann's Ratio Test for Randomness, *J. Am. Statist. Assoc., 77:* 40–46 (1982).

Barton, R.R.: *Graphical Methods for Design of Experiments,* Springer, New York (1999).

Barton, R.R.: Simulation Optimization Using Metamodels, *Proc. 2009 Winter Simulation Conference,* Austin, Texas, pp. 230–238 (2009).

Barton, R.R.: Simulation Experiment Design, *Proc. 2010 Winter Simulation Conference,* Baltimore, Maryland, pp. 75–86 (2010).

Barton, R.R.: Tutorial: Input Uncertainty in Output Analysis, *Proc. 2012 Winter Simulation Conference,* Berlin, Germany (2012).

Barton, R.R., and M. Meckesheimer: Metamodel-Based Simulation Optimization, in *Handbooks in Operations Research and Management Science: Simulation,* S.G. Henderson and B.L. Nelson, eds., Elsevier, New York (2006).

Barton, R.R., B.L. Nelson, and W. Xie: Quantifying Input Uncertainty via Simulation Confidence Intervals, to appear in *INFORMS J. Comput.* (2013).

Barton, R.R., and L.W. Schruben: Uniform and Bootstrap Resampling of Empirical Distributions, *Proc. 1993 Winter Simulation Conference,* Los Angeles, pp. 503–508 (1993).

Barton, R.R., and L.W. Schruben: Resampling Methods for Input Modeling, *Proc. 2001 Winter Simulation Conference,* Washington, D.C., pp. 372–378 (2001).

Bauer, K.W.: Control Variate Selection for Multiresponse Simulation, Ph.D. Dissertation, School of Industrial Engineering, Purdue University, West Lafayette, Indiana (1987).

Bauer, K.W., and J.R. Wilson: Control-Variate Selection Criteria, *Naval Res. Logist., 39*: 307–321 (1992).

Bays, C., and S.D. Durham: Improving a Poor Random Number Generator, *Assoc. Comput. Mach. Trans. Math. Soft., 2:* 59–64 (1976).

Beaverstock, M.C., A. Greenwood, E. Lavery, and W.B. Nordgren: *Applied Simulation: Modeling and Analysis Using FlexSim,* 3d ed., FlexSim Software Products, Orem, Utah (2013).

Bechhofer, R.E., T.J. Santner, and D. Goldsman: *Design and Analysis for Statistical Selection, Screening and Multiple Comparisons,* John Wiley, New York (1995).

Beckman, R.J., and G.L. Tietjen: Maximum Likelihood Estimation for the Beta Distribution, *J. Statist. Comput. Simul., 7:* 253–258 (1978).

Beeker, E.R., and E.H. Page: A Case Study of the Development and Use of a MANA-Based Federation for Studying U.S. Border Operations, *Proc. of the 2006 Winter Simulation Conference,* pp. 841–847, Monterey, California (2006).

Bertsekas, D.P., and R. Gallager: *Data Networks,* 2d ed., Prentice-Hall, Englewood Cliffs, New Jersey (1992).

Best, D.J., and D.E. Roberts: The Percentage Points of the χ^2 Distribution, *Appl. Statist., 24:* 385–388 (1975).

Bettonvil, B., and J.P.C. Kleijnen, Searching for Important Factors in Simulation Models with Many Factors: Sequential Bifurcation, *Eur. J. Operational Res., 96:* 180–194 (1997).

Bhattacharjee, G.P.: Algorithm AS32: The Incomplete Gamma Integral, *Appl. Statist., 19:* 285–287 (1970).

Biller, B.: Copula-Based Multivariate Input Models for Stochastic Simulation, *Operations Res., 57:* 878–892 (2009).

Biller, B., and S. Ghosh: Multivariate Input Processes, in *Handbooks in Operations Research and Management Science: Simulation,* S.G. Henderson and B.L. Nelson, eds., Elsevier, New York (2006).

Biller, B., and B.L. Nelson: Modeling and Generating Multivariate Time-Series Input Processes Using a Vector Autoregressive Technique, *Assoc. Comput. Mach. Trans. Modeling and Comput. Simul., 13:* 211–237 (2003).

Biller, B., and B.L. Nelson: Fitting Times-Series Input Processes for Simulation, *Operations Res., 53:* 549–559 (2005).

Biller, B., and B.L. Nelson: Evaluation of the ARTAFIT Method for Fitting Time-Series Input Processes for Simulation, *INFORMS J. Comput., 20:* 485–498 (2008).

Billingsley, P.: *Convergence of Probability Measures,* 2d ed., John Wiley, New York (1999).

Billingsley, P., D.J. Croft, D.V. Huntsberger, and C.J. Watson: *Statistical Inference for Management and Economics,* 3d ed., Allyn & Bacon, Boston (1986).

Bischak, D.P., W.D. Kelton, and S.M. Pollack: Weighted Batch Means for Confidence Intervals in Steady-State Simulations, *Management Sci., 39:* 1002–1019 (1993).

Bishop, C.M.: *Neural Networks for Pattern Recognition,* Oxford University Press, New York (1995).

Blomqvist, N.: On the Transient Behaviour of the GI/G/1 Waiting-Times, *Skand. Aktuarietidskr.,* 118–129 (1970).

Blum, C., and A. Roli (2003): Metaheuristics and Combinatorial Optimization: Overview and Conceptual Comparison, *Assoc. Comput. Mach. Comp. Surveys, 5:* 208–308 (2003).

Bodoh, D.J., and F. Wieland: Performance Experiments with the High Level Architecture and the Total Airport and Airspace Model (TAAM), *Proc. of the 17th Workshop on Parallel and Distributed Simulation,* San Diego, pp. 31–39 (2003).

Boesel, J., B.L. Nelson, and N. Ishii: A Framework for Simulation-Optimization Software, *IIE Trans., 35:* 221–229 (2003).

Boesel, J., B.L. Nelson, and S.-H. Kim: Using Ranking and Selection to "Clean Up" after Simulation Optimization, *Operations Res., 51:* 814–825 (2003).

Bonabeau, E.: Agent-Based Modeling: Methods and Techniques for Simulating Human Systems, *Proc. of the National Academy of Sciences, 99:* 7280–7287 (May 2002).

Bonabeau, E., and C. Meyer: Swarm Intelligence: A Whole New Way to Think about Business, *Harvard Business Review,* 107–114 (May 2001).

Borshchev, A.: Personal Communication (2013).

Bosten, N.E., and E.L. Battiste: Remark on Algorithm 179, *Commun. Assoc. Comput. Mach., 17:* 156–157 (1974).

Box, G.E.P., and N.R. Draper: *Response Surfaces, Mixtures, and Ridge Analyses,* 2d ed., John Wiley, New York (2008).

Box, G.E.P., J.S. Hunter, and W.G. Hunter: *Statistics for Experimenters: Design, Innovation, and Discovery,* 2d ed., John Wiley, Hoboken, New Jersey (2005).

Box, G.E.P., G.M. Jenkins, and G.C. Reinsel: *Time Series Analysis: Forecasting and Control,* 4th ed., John Wiley, New York (2009).

Box, G.E.P., and M.E. Muller: A Note on the Generation of Random Normal Deviates, *Ann. Math. Statist., 29:* 610–611 (1958).

Bratley, P., B.L. Fox, and L.E. Schrage: *A Guide to Simulation,* 2d ed., Springer-Verlag, New York (1987).

Braun, M.: *Differential Equations and Their Applications,* Applied Mathematical Sciences, Vol. 15, Springer-Verlag, New York (1975).

Breiman, L.: *Statistics: With a View Toward Applications,* Houghton Mifflin, Boston (1973).

Brown, L.P., T.M. Cioppa, and T.W. Lucas: Agent-Based Simulations Supporting Military Analysis, *Phalanx, 37:* 29–32 (September 2004).

Brown, R.: Calendar Queues: A Fast O(1) Priority Queue Implementation for the Simulation Event Set Problem, *Commun. Assoc. Comput. Mach., 31:* 1220–1227 (1988).

Bryant, R.E.: Simulation of Packet Communication Architecture Computer Systems, *MIT-LCSTR-188,* Massachusetts Institute of Technology, Cambridge, Massachusetts (1977).

Burt, J.M., Jr., and M.B. Garman: Conditional Monte Carlo: A Simulation Technique for Stochastic Network Analysis, *Management Sci., 18:* 207–217 (1971).

Burt, J.M., Jr., D.P. Gaver, and M. Perlas: Simple Stochastic Networks: Some Problems and Procedures, *Naval Res. Logist. Quart., 17:* 439–459 (1970).

Buss, A.H.: Modeling with Event Graphs, *Proc. 1996 Winter Simulation Conference,* San Diego, pp. 153–160 (1996).

Buss, A., and A.A. Rowaei: A Comparison of Discrete Event and Discrete Time, *Proc. of the 2010 Winter Simulation Conference*, pp. 1468–1477, Baltimore, Maryland (2010).

Campolongo, F., J.P.C. Kleijnen, and T. Andres: Screening Methods, in *Sensitivity Analysis,* A. Saltelli, K. Chan, and E.M. Scott, eds., John Wiley, New York (2000).

Cario, M.C., and B.L. Nelson: Autoregressive to Anything: Time-Series Input Processes for Simulation, *Operations Res. Letters, 19:* 51–58 (1996).

Cario, M.C., and B.L. Nelson: Numerical Methods for Fitting and Simulating Autoregressive-To-Anything Processes, *INFORMS J. Comput., 10:* 72–81 (1998).

Cario, M.C., B.L. Nelson, S.D. Roberts, and J.R. Wilson: Modeling and Generating Random Vectors with Arbitrary Marginal Distributions and Correlation Matrix, Technical Report, Dept. of Industrial Engineering and Management Sciences, Northwestern University, Evanston, Illinois (2002).

Carley, K.M., D.B. Fridsma, E. Casman, A. Yahja, N. Altman, L.-C. Chen, B. Kaminsky, and D. Nave: Biowar: Scalable Agent-Based Model of Bioattacks, *IEEE Trans. on Systems, Man, and Cybernetics, Part A, 36:* 252–265 (2006).

Carson, J.S.: Variance Reduction Techniques for Simulated Queueing Processes, Univ. Wisconsin Dept. Ind. Eng. Tech. Rep. 78-8, Madison, Wisconsin (1978).

Carson J.S.: Convincing Users of Model's Validity Is Challenging Aspect of Modeler's Job, *Ind. Eng., 18:* 74–85 (June 1986).

Carson, J.S.: Model Verification and Validation, *Proc. 2002 Winter Simulation Conference,* San Diego, pp. 42–58 (2002).

Carson, J.S., and A.M. Law: Conservation Equations and Variance Reduction in Queueing Simulations, *Operations Res., 28:* 535–546 (1980).

Carson, J.S., N. Wilson, D. Caroll, and C.H. Wysocki: A Discrete Simulation Model of a Cigarette Fabrication Process, *Proc. Twelfth Modeling and Simulation Conference,* University of Pittsburgh, pp. 683–689 (1981).

Carter, G., and E.J. Ignall: Virtual Measures: A Variance Reduction Technique for Simulation, *Management Sci., 21:* 607–616 (1975).

Chandra, M., N.D. Singpurwalla, and M.A. Stephens: Kolmogorov Statistics for Tests of Fit for the Extreme-Value and Weibull Distributions, *J. Am. Statist. Assoc., 76:* 729–731 (1981).

Chandy, K.M., and J. Misra: Distributed Simulation: A Case Study in Design and Verification of Distributed Programs, *IEEE Trans. Software Eng., SE-5:* 440–452 (1979).

Chang, K.-H., L.J. Hong, and H. Wan: Stochastic Trust-Region Response-Surface Method (STRONG)—A New Response-Surface Framework for Simulation Optimization, *INFORMS J. Comput., 25:* 230–243 (2013).

Charnes, J.S.: Analyzing Multivariate Output, *Proc. 1995 Winter Simulation Conference,* Washington, D.C., pp. 201–208 (1995).

Chen, B.-C., and R.G. Sargent: Using Standardized Time Series to Estimate the Difference between Two Stationary Stochastic Processes, *Operations Res., 35:* 428–436 (1987).

Chen, C.-H.: A Lower Bound for the Correct Subset-Selection Probability and Its Application to Discrete-Event System Simulations, *IEEE Trans. Auto. Cont., 41:* 1227–1231 (1996).

Chen, C.-H., D. He, M. Fu, and L.H. Lee: Efficient Simulation Budget Allocation for Selecting an Optimal Subset, *INFORMS J. Comput., 20:* 579–595 (2008).

Chen, C.-H., and L.H. Lee: Stochastic Simulation Optimization: An Optimal Computing Budget Allocation, World Scientific Publishing, Singapore (2011).

Chen, C.-H., J. Lin, E. Yücesan, and S.E. Chick: Simulation Budget Allocation for Further Enhancing the Efficiency of Ordinal Optimization, *Disc. Event Dyn. Syst: Theory App., 10:* 251–270 (2000).

Chen, C.-H., E. Yücesan, L. Dai, and H.C. Chen: Optimal Budget Allocation for Discrete-Event Simulation Experiments, *IIE Trans., 42:* 60–70 (2010).

Chen, E.J.: Subset Selection Procedures, *J. of Simulation, 3:* 202–210 (2009).

Chen, E.J., and W.D. Kelton: Sequential Selection Procedures: Using Sample Means to Improve Efficiency, *Eur. J. Operational Research, 166:* 133–153 (2005).

Chen, E.J., and W.D. Kelton: Quantile and Tolerance-Interval Estimation in Simulation, *Eur. J. Operational Res., 168:* 520–540 (2006).

Chen, E.J., and W.D. Kelton: Confidence Interval Estimation Using Quasi-Independent Sequences, *IIE Trans., 42:* 83–93 (2009).

Chen, H.: Initialization for NORTA: Generation of Random Vectors with Specified Marginals and Correlations, *INFORMS J. Comput., 13:* 312–331 (2001).

Chen, H., and Y. Asau: On Generating Random Variates from an Empirical Distribution, *AIIE Trans., 6:* 163–166 (1974).

Chen, P.: On Selecting the Best of k Systems: An Expository Survey of Subset-Selection Multinomial Procedures, *Proc. 1988 Winter Simulation Conference,* San Diego, pp. 440–444 (1988).

Chen, X., B.E. Ankenman, and B.L. Nelson: The Effects of Common Random Numbers on Stochastic Kriging Metamodels, *Assoc. Comput. Mach. Trans. Modeling and Comput. Simul., 22,* No. 2, Article 7 (2010).

Cheng, R.C.H.: The Generation of Gamma Variables with Non-integral Shape Parameter, *Appl. Statist., 26:* 71–75 (1977).

Cheng, R.C.H.: Generating Beta Variates with Nonintegral Shape Parameters, *Commun. Assoc. Comput. Mach., 21:* 317–322 (1978).

Cheng, R.C.H.: The Use of Antithetic Variates in Computer Simulations, *J. Operational Res. Soc., 33:* 229–237 (1982).

Cheng, R.C.H.: Antithetic Variate Methods for Simulation of Processes with Peaks and Troughs, *Eur. J. Operational Res., 15:* 227–236 (1984).

Cheng, R.C.H.: Searching for Important Factors: Sequential Bifurcation under Uncertainty, *Proc. 1997 Winter Simulation Conference,* Atlanta, pp. 275–280 (1997).

Cheng, R.C.H.: Resampling Methods, in *Handbooks in Operations Research and Management Science: Simulation,* S.G. Henderson and B.L. Nelson, eds., Elsevier, New York (2006).

Cheng, R.C.H., and N.A.K. Amin: Estimating Parameters in Continuous Univariate Distributions with a Shifted Origin, *J. Roy. Statist. Soc. B, 45:* 394–403 (1983).

Cheng, R.C.H., and C.S.M. Currie: Resampling Methods of Analysis in Simulation Studies, *Proc. of the 2009 Winter Simulation Conference*, pp. 45–59, Austin, Texas (2009).

Cheng, R.C.H., and G.M. Feast: Some Simple Gamma Variate Generators, *Appl. Statist., 28:* 290–295 (1979).

Cheng, R.C.H., and G.M. Feast: Control Variates with Known Mean and Variance, *J. Operational Res. Soc., 31:* 51–56 (1980).

Cheng, R.C.H., and W. Holland: Sensitivity of Computer Simulation Experiments to Errors in Input Data, *J. Statist. Comput. Simul., 57:* 219–241 (1997).

Cheng, R.C.H., and W. Holland: Two-Point Methods for Assessing Variability in Simulation Output, *J. Statist. Comput. Simul., 60:* 183–205 (1998).

Cheng, R.C.H., and W. Holland: Calculation of Confidence Intervals for Simulation Output, *Assoc. Comput. Mach. Trans. Modeling and Comput. Simul., 14:* 344–362 (2004).

Cheng, R.C.H., and J.P.C. Kleijnen: Improved Design of Queueing Simulation Experiments with Highly Heteroscedastic Responses, *Operations Res., 47:* 762–777 (1999).

Chernoff, H., and E.L. Lehmann: The Use of Maximum Likelihood Estimates in χ^2 Tests for Goodness of Fit, *Ann. Math. Statist., 25:* 579–586 (1954).

Chick, S.E.: Selecting the Best System: A Decision-Theoretic Approach, *Proc. 1997 Winter Simulation Conference,* Atlanta, pp. 326–333 (1997).

Chick, S.E.: Input Distribution Selection for Simulation Experiments: Accounting for Input Uncertainty, *Operations Res., 49:* 744–758 (2001).

Chick, S.E.: Subjective Probability and Bayesian Methodology, in *Handbooks in Operations Research and Management Science: Simulation,* S.G. Henderson and B.L. Nelson, eds., Elsevier, New York (2006).

Chick, S.E., and P. Frazier: Sequential Sampling with Economics of Selection Procedures, *Management Sci., 58:* 550–569 (2012).

Chick, S.E., and N. Gans: Economic Analysis of Simulation Selection Problems, *Management Sci., 55:* 421–437 (2009).

Chick, S.E., and K. Inoue: New Procedures to Select the Best Simulated System Using Common Random Numbers, *Management Sci., 47:* 1133–1149 (2001a).

Chick, S.E., and K. Inoue: New Two-Stage and Sequential Procedures for Selecting the Best Simulated System, *Operations Res., 49:* 732–744 (2001b).

Choi, S.C., and R. Wette: Maximum Likelihood Estimation of the Parameters of the Gamma Distribution and Their Bias, *Technometrics, 11:* 683–690 (1969).

Chow, Y.S., and H. Robbins: On the Asymptotic Theory of Fixed-Width Sequential Confidence Intervals for the Mean, *Ann. Math. Statist., 36:* 457–462 (1965).

Chung, K., J. Sang, and V. Rego: A Performance Comparison of Event Calendar Algorithms: An Empirical Approach, *Software—Practice and Experience, 23:* 1107–1138 (1993).

Chung, K.L.: *A Course in Probability Theory,* 2d ed., Academic Press, New York (1974).

Çinlar, E.: *Introduction to Stochastic Processes,* Prentice-Hall, Englewood Cliffs, New Jersey (1975).

Cioppa, T.M., and T.W. Lucas: Efficient Nearly Orthogonal and Space-Filling Latin Hypercubes, *Technometrics, 49:* 45–55 (2007).

Cioppa, T.M., T.W. Lucas, and S.M. Sanchez: Military Applications of Agent-Based Simulations, *Proc. of the 2004 Winter Simulation Conference,* pp. 171–180, Washington, D.C. (2004).

Cohen, A.C., and B.J. Whitten: Estimation in the Three-Parameter Lognormal Distribution, *J. Am. Statist. Assoc., 75:* 399–404 (1980).

Collier, N.T., and M.J. North: Parallel Agent-Based Simulation with Repast for High Performance Computing, to appear in *SIMULATION* (2013).

Collins, B.J.: Compound Random Number Generators, *J. Am. Statist. Assoc., 82:* 525–527 (1987).

Comfort, J.C.: The Simulation of a Microprocessor-Based Event Set Processor, *Proc. 14th Annual Simulation Symposium,* pp. 17–33 (1981).

Conover, W.J.: *Practical Nonparametric Statistics,* 3d ed., John Wiley, New York (1999).

Coveyou, R.R., and R.D. MacPherson: Fourier Analysis of Uniform Random Number Generators, *J. Assoc. Comput. Mach., 14:* 100–119 (1967).

Cran, G.W., K.J. Martin, and G.E. Thomas: A Remark on Algorithm AS63: The Incomplete Beta Integral, AS64: Inverse of the Incomplete Beta Function Ratio, *Appl. Statist., 26:* 111–114 (1977).

Crane, M.A., and D.L. Iglehart: Simulating Stable Stochastic Systems, I: General Multiserver Queues, *J. Assoc. Comput. Mach., 21:* 103–113 (1974a).

Crane, M.A., and D.L. Iglehart: Simulating Stable Stochastic Systems, II: Markov Chains, *J. Assoc. Comput. Mach., 21:* 114–123 (1974b).

Crane, M.A., and D.L. Iglehart: Simulating Stable Stochastic Systems, III: Regenerative Processes and Discrete-Event Simulations, *Operations Res., 23:* 33–45 (1975).

Crane, M.A., and A.J. Lemoine: *An Introduction to the Regenerative Method for Simulation Analysis,* Lecture Notes in Control and Information Sciences, Vol. 4, Springer-Verlag, New York (1977).

Cressie, N.A.C.: *Statistics for Spatial Data,* Revised Edition, John Wiley, New York (1993).

D'Agostino, R.B., and M.A. Stephens: *Goodness-of-Fit Tests,* Marcel Dekker, New York (1986).

Dagpunar, J.: *Principles of Random Variate Generation,* Clarendon Press, Oxford, England (1988).

Dahmann, J.S., R.M. Fujimoto, and R.M. Weatherly: The DoD High Level Architecture: An Update, *Proc. 1998 Winter Simulation Conference,* pp. 797–804, Washington, D.C. (1998).

Daley, D.J.: The Serial Correlation Coefficients of Waiting Times in a Stationary Single Server Queue, *J. Austr. Math. Soc., 8:* 683–699 (1968).

Damerdji, H.: Strong Consistency and Other Properties of the Spectral Variance Estimator, *Management Sci., 37:* 1424–1440 (1991).

Damerdji, H.: Strong Consistency of the Variance Estimator in Steady-State Simulation Output Analysis, *Math. of Operations Res., 19:* 494–512 (1994).

Damerdji, H., and M.K. Nakayama: Two-Stage Multiple Comparison Procedures for Steady-State Simulations, *Assoc. Comput. Mach. Trans. Modeling and Comput. Simul., 9:* 1–30 (1999).

Dean, A.M., and S.M. Lewis: *Screening: Methods for Experimentation in Industry, Drug Discovery, and Genetics,* Springer, New York (2006).

Debuse, J.C.W., V.J. Rayward-Smith, and G.D. Smith: Parameter Optimisation for a Discrete Event Simulator, *J. Comp. and Indust. Eng., 37:* 181–184 (1999).

DeGroot, M.H.: *Probability and Statistics,* Addison-Wesley, Reading, Massachusetts (1975).

DeRiggi, D.F.: Unimodality of Likelihood Functions for the Binomial Distribution, *J. Am. Statist. Assoc., 78:* 181–183 (1983).

Devore, J.L.: *Probability and Statistics for Engineering and the Sciences,* 7th ed., Brooks/Cole, Belmont, California (2008).

Devroye, L.: The Computer Generation of Poisson Random Variables, *Computing, 26:* 197–207 (1981).

Devroye, L.: *Non-Uniform Random Variate Generation,* Springer-Verlag, New York (1986).

Devroye, L.: Generating Sums in Constant Average Time, *Proc. 1988 Winter Simulation Conference,* San Diego, pp. 425–431 (1988).

Devroye, L.: Random Variate Generation for Multivariate Unimodal Densities, *Assoc. Comput. Mach. Trans. Modeling and Comput. Simul., 7:* 447–477 (1997).

Donohue, J.M., E.C. Houck, and R.H. Myers: Simulation Designs for Quadratic Response Surface Models in the Presence of Model Misspecification, *Management Sci., 38:* 1765–1791 (1992).

Donohue, J.M., E.C. Houck, and R.H. Myers: Simulation Designs for the Estimation of Quadratic Response Surface Gradients in the Presence of Model Misspecification, *Management Sci., 41:* 244–262 (1995).

Dubey, S.D.: On Some Permissible Estimators of the Location Parameter of the Weibull and Certain Other Distributions, *Technometrics, 9:* 293–307 (1967).

Dudewicz, E.J.: Random Numbers: The Need, the History, the Generators, in *Statistical Distributions in Scientific Work 2,* G.P. Patil, S. Kotz, and J.K. Ord, eds., D. Reidel, Dordrecht, The Netherlands (1975). [Also reprinted in *Modern Design and Analysis of Discrete-Event Computer Simulations,* E.J. Dudewicz and Z.A. Karian, eds., IEEE Computer Society (1985).]

Dudewicz, E.J., and S.R. Dalal: Allocation of Observations in Ranking and Selection with Unequal Variances, *Sankhya, B37:* 28–78 (1975).

Durbin, J.: Kolmogorov-Smirnov Tests When Parameters Are Estimated with Applications to Tests of Exponentiality and Tests on Spacings, *Biometrika, 62:* 5–22 (1975).

Economist, The: Software: Simulating the Behaviour of Crowds of People, or Swarms of Animals, Has Both Frivolous and Important Uses, www.economist.com/node/13174313 (March 7, 2009).

Economist, The: Agents of Change, www.economist.com/node/16636121 (July 24, 2010).

Efron, B., and R.J. Tibshirani: *Introduction to the Bootstrap,* Chapman and Hall, New York (1993).

Eglese, R.W.: Simulated Annealing: A Tool for Operational Research, *Eur. J. Operational Res., 46:* 271–281 (1990).

Epstein, J.M.: *Generative Social Science: Studies in Agent-Based Computational Modeling,* Princeton University Press, Princeton, New Jersey (2007).

Epstein, J.M.: Modeling to Contain Pandemics, *Nature, 460:* 687 (August 2009).

Epstein, J.M., and R. Axtell: *Growing Artificial Societies: Social Science from the Bottom Up,* MIT Press, Cambridge, Massachusetts (1996).

Evans, J.R., and D.L. Olson: *Introduction to Simulation and Risk Analysis,* 2d ed., Prentice Hall, Englewood Cliffs, New Jersey (2002).

Feltner, C.E., and S.A. Weiner: Models, Myths and Mysteries in Manufacturing, *Ind. Eng., 17:* 66–76 (July 1985).

Filliben, J.J.: The Probability Plot Correlation Coefficient Test for Normality, *Technometrics, 17:* 111–117 (1975).

Fishman G.S.: *Spectral Methods in Econometrics,* Harvard University Press, Cambridge, Massachusetts (1969).

Fishman, G.S.: Estimating Sample Size in Computer Simulation Experiments, *Management Sci., 18:* 21–38 (1971).

Fishman, G.S.: Bias Considerations in Simulation Experiments, *Operations Res., 20:* 785–790 (1972).

Fishman, G.S.: *Concepts and Methods in Discrete Event Digital Simulation,* John Wiley, New York (1973a).

Fishman, G.S.: Statistical Analysis for Queueing Simulations, *Management Sci., 20:* 363–369 (1973b).

Fishman, G.S.: Estimation in Multiserver Queueing Simulations, *Operations Res., 22:* 72–78 (1974).

Fishman, G.S.: Achieving Specific Accuracy in Simulation Output Analysis, *Commun. Assoc. Comput. Mach., 20:* 310–315 (1977).

Fishman, G.S.: *Principles of Discrete Event Simulation,* John Wiley, New York (1978).

Fishman, G.S.: *Monte Carlo: Concepts, Algorithms, and Applications,* Springer Verlag, New York (1996).

Fishman, G.S.: *Discrete-Event Simulation,* Springer, New York (2001).

Fishman, G.S.: *A First Course in Monte Carlo,* Duxbury Press, Pacific Grove, California (2006).

Fishman, G.S., and B.D. Huang: Antithetic Variates Revisited, *Commun. Assoc. Comput. Mach., 26:* 964–971 (1983).

Fishman, G.S., and P.J. Kiviat: The Analysis of Simulation-Generated Time Series, *Management Sci., 13:* 525–557 (1967).

Fishman, G.S., and P.J. Kiviat: The Statistics of Discrete-Event Simulation, *Simulation, 10:* 185–195 (1968).

Fishman, G.S., and L.R. Moore: A Statistical Evaluation of Multiplicative Congruential Random Number Generators with Modulus $2^{31} - 1$, *J. Am. Statist. Assoc., 77:* 129–136 (1982).

Fishman, G.S., and L.R. Moore: Sampling from a Discrete Distribution While Preserving Monotonicity, *Am. Statistician, 38:* 219–223 (1984).

Fishman, G.S., and L.R. Moore: An Exhaustive Analysis of Multiplicative Congruential Random Number Generators with Modulus $2^{31} - 1$, *SIAM J. Sci. Stat. Comput., 7:* 24–45 (1986).

Fishman, G.S., and L.S. Yarberry: An Implementation of the Batch Means Method, *INFORMS J. Comput., 9:* 296–310 (1997).

FlexSim Software Products, Inc.: FlexSim Healthcare simulation software, www.flexsim.com (2013).

FlexSim Software Products, Inc.: FlexSim simulation software, www.flexsim.com (2013).

Forbes, C., M. Evans, N. Hastings, and B. Peacock: *Statistical Distributions,* 4th ed., John Wiley, New York (2011).

Forsythe, G.E.: von Neumann's Comparison Method for Random Sampling from the Normal and Other Distributions, *Math. Comput., 26:* 817–826 (1972).

Fossett, F.A., D. Harrison, H. Weintrob, and S.I. Gass: An Assessment Procedure for Simulation Models: A Case Study, *Operations Res., 39:* 710–723 (1991).

Fox, B.L., D. Goldsman, and J.J. Swain: Spaced Batch Means, *Operations Res. Letters, 10:* 255–263 (1991).

Franklin, W.W., and K.P. White: Stationarity Tests and MSER-5: Exploring the Intuition Behind Mean-Squared-Error-Reduction in Detecting and Correcting Initialization Bias, *Proc. 2008 Winter Simulation Conference*, Miami, Florida, pp. 541–546 (2008).

Franta, W.R.: A Note on Random Variate Generators and Antithetic Sampling, *INFOR, 13:* 112–117 (1975).

Friedman, L.W.: *The Simulation Metamodel,* Kluwer Academic Publishers, Dordrecht, The Netherlands (1996).

Fu, M.C.: Optimization for Simulation: Theory vs. Practice, *INFORMS J. Comput., 14:* 192–215 (2002).

Fu, M.C.: Gradient Estimation, in *Handbooks in Operations Research and Management Science: Simulation,* S.G. Henderson and B.L. Nelson, eds., Elsevier, New York (2006).

Fu, M.C.: What You Should Know about Simulation and Derivatives, *Naval Res. Logistics, 55:* 723–736 (2008).

Fu, M.C.: *Handbook on Simulation Optimization*, Springer, New York (2013).

Fu, M.C., F.W. Glover, and J. April: Simulation Optimization: A Review, New Developments, and Applications, *Proc. 2005 Winter Simulation Conference,* Orlando (2005).

Fu, M.C., J.H. Hu, C.-H. Chen, and X. Xiong: Simulation Allocation for Determining the Best Design in the Presence of Correlated Sampling, *INFORMS J. Comput., 19:* 101–111 (2007).

Fujimoto, R.M.: Parallel and Distributed Simulation, in *Handbook of Simulation,* J. Banks, ed., John Wiley, New York (1998).

Fujimoto, R.M.: *Parallel and Distributed Simulation Systems,* John Wiley, New York (2000).

Fujimoto, R.M.: *Distributed Simulation Systems, Proc. 2003 Winter Simulation Conference,* New Orleans, pp. 124–134 (2003).

Fujimoto, R.M., K. Perumalla, A. Park, H. Wu, M.H. Ammar, and G.F. Riley: Large-Scale Network Simulation: How Big? How Fast?, *Proc. of the 11th International Workshop on the Modeling, Analysis, and Simulation of Computer and Telecommunication Systems,* pp. 116–125, Orlando (2003).

Fushimi, M.: Random Number Generation with the Recursion $X_t = X_{t-3p} \oplus X_{t-3q}$, *J. of Comput. and App. Math., 31:* 105–118 (1990).

Gafarian, A.V., C.J. Ancker, Jr., and F. Morisaku: Evaluation of Commonly Used Rules for Detecting "Steady-State" in Computer Simulation, *Naval Res. Logist. Quart., 25:* 511–529 (1978).

Gal, S., R.Y. Rubinstein, and A. Ziv: On the Optimality and Efficiency of Common Random Numbers, *Math. Comput. Simul., 26:* 502–512 (1984).

Gardner, M.: The Fantastic Combinations of John Conway's New Solitaire Game "Life," *Scientific American, 223:* 120–123 (1970).

Garman, M.B.: More on Conditioned Sampling in the Simulation of Stochastic Networks, *Management Sci., 19:* 90–95 (1972).

Gass, S.I.: Decision-Aiding Models Validation, Assessment, and Related Issues in Policy Analysis, *Operations Res., 31:* 603–631 (1983).

Gass, S.I., and B.W. Thompson: Guidelines for Model Evaluation: An Abridged Version of the U.S. General Accounting Office Exposure Draft, *Operations Res., 28:* 431–439 (1980).

Gaver, D.P., and G.S. Shedler: Control Variable Methods in the Simulation of a Model of a Multiprogrammed Computer System, *Naval Res. Logist. Quart., 18:* 435–450 (1971).

Gaver, D.P., and G.L. Thompson: *Programming and Probability Models,* Wadsworth, Monterey, California (1973).

Gebhardt, F.: Generating Pseudo-random Numbers by Shuffling a Fibonacci Sequence, *Math. Comput., 21:* 708–709 (1967).

Gentle, J. E.: *Random Number Generation and Monte Carlo Methods,* 3d ed., Springer, New York (2010).

George, L.L.: Variance Reduction for a Replacement Process, *Simulation, 29:* 65–74 (1977).

Gerhardt, I., and B.L. Nelson: Transforming Renewal Processes for Simulation of Nonstationary Arrival Processes, *INFORMS J. Comput., 21:* 630–640 (2009).

Ghosh, S., and S.G. Henderson: Chessboard Distributions and Random Vectors with Specified Marginals and Covariance Matrix, *Operations Res., 50:* 820–834 (2002).

Ghosh, S., and S.G. Henderson: Behavior of the NORTA Method for Correlated Random Vector Generation as the Dimension Increases, *Assoc. Comput. Mach. Trans. Modeling and Comput. Simul.,13:* 276–294 (2003).

Ghosh, S., and S.G. Henderson: Corrigendum: Behavior of the NORTA Method for Correlated Random Vector Generation as the Dimension Increases, *Assoc. Comput. Mach. Trans. Modeling and Comput. Simul., 19,* No. 4, Article 20 (2009).

Gibbons, J.D.: *Nonparametric Methods for Quantitative Analysis,* 2d ed., American Sciences Press, Columbus, Ohio (1985).

Gilbert, N., and K.G. Troitzsch: *Simulation for the Social Scientist*, 2d ed., Open University Press, Maidenhead, England (2005).

Glasserman, P.: *Gradient Estimation via Perturbation Analysis,* Kluwer Academic Publishers, Boston (1991).

Glasserman, P: *Monte Carlo Methods in Financial Engineering,* Springer, New York (2004).

Glasserman, P., P. Heidelberger, P. Shahabuddin, and T. Zajic: Multilevel Splitting for Estimating Rare Event Probabilities, *Operations Res., 47:* 585–600 (1999).

Glasserman, P., and T.-W. Liu: Rare-Event Simulation for Multistage Production-Inventory Systems, *Management Sci., 42:* 1291–1307 (1996).

Glasserman, P., and D.D. Yao: Some Guidelines and Guarantees for Common Random Numbers, *Management Sci., 38:* 884–908 (1992).

Gleser, L.J.: Exact Power of Goodness-of-Fit Tests of Kolmogorov Type for Discontinuous Distributions, *J. Am. Statist. Assoc., 80:* 954–958 (1985).

Glover, F., and M. Laguna: *Tabu Search,* Kluwer Academic Publishers, New York (1997).

Glover, F., and M. Laguna: Tabu Search, in the *Handbook of Applied Optimization,* pp. 194–208, P.M. Pardalos and M.G.C. Resende, eds., Oxford University Press, New York (2002).

Glynn, P.W.: A Non-Rectangular Sampling Plan for Estimating Steady-State Means, *Proc. of the 6th Army Conference on Applied Mathematics and Computing,* pp. 965–978 (1988).

Glynn, P.W.: Some New Results on the Initial Transient Problem, *Proc. 1995 Winter Simulation Conference,* Arlington, Virginia, pp. 165–170 (1995).

Glynn, P.W., and D.L. Iglehart: The Theory of Standardized Time Series, *Math. Operations Res., 15:* 1–16 (1990).

Glynn, P.W., and W. Whitt: Indirect Estimation via $L = \lambda w$, *Operations Res., 37:* 82–103 (1989).

Glynn, P.W., and W. Whitt: The Asymptotic Efficiency of Simulation Estimators, *Operations Res., 40:* 505–520 (1992a).

Glynn, P.W., and W. Whitt: The Asymptotic Validity of Sequential Stopping Rules for Stochastic Simulations, *Ann. of Applied Probability, 2:* 180–198 (1992b).

Gnanadesikan, R., R.S. Pinkham, and L.P. Hughes: Maximum Likelihood Estimation of the Parameters of the Beta Distribution from Smallest Order Statistics, *Technometrics, 9:* 607–620 (1967).

Goldsman, D.: On Selecting the Best of *k* Systems: An Expository Survey of Indifference-Zone Multinomial Procedures, *Proc. 1984 Winter Simulation Conference,* Dallas, pp. 107–112 (1984a).

Goldsman, D.: A Multinomial Ranking and Selection Procedure: Simulation and Applications, *Proc. 1984 Winter Simulation Conference,* Dallas, pp. 259–264 (1984b).

Goldsman, D., S.-H. Kim, W.S. Marshall, and B.L. Nelson: Ranking and Selection for Steady-State Simulation: Procedures and Perspectives, *INFORMS J. Comput., 14:* 2–19 (2002).

Goldsman, D., M. Meketon, and L.W. Schruben: Properties of Standardized Time Series Weighted Area Variance Estimators, *Management Sci., 36:* 602–612 (1990).

Goldsman, D., and B.L. Nelson: Comparing Systems via Simulation, in *Handbook of Simulation,* J. Banks, ed., John Wiley, New York (1998).

Goldsman, D., and L.W. Schruben: Asymptotic Properties of Some Confidence Interval Estimators for Simulation Output, *Management Sci., 30:* 1217–1225 (1984).

Goldsman, D., and L.W. Schruben: New Confidence Interval Estimators Using Standardized Time Series, *Management Sci., 36:* 393–397 (1990).

Goldsman, D., L.W. Schruben, and J.J. Swain: Tests for Transient Means in Simulated Times Series, *Naval Research Logistics, 41:* 171–187 (1994).

Gonzalez, T., S. Sahni, and W.R. Franta: An Efficient Algorithm for the Kolmogorov-Smirnov and Lilliefors Tests, *Assoc. Comput. Mach. Trans. Math. Software, 3:* 60–64 (1977).

Grassman, W.K.: Rethinking the Initialization Bias Problem in Steady-State Discrete Event Simulation, *Proc. 2011 Winter Simulation Conference,* Phoenix, Arizona, pp. 593–599 (2011).

Gray, D., and D. Goldsman: Indifference-Zone Selection Procedures for Choosing the Best Airspace Configuration, *Proc. 1988 Winter Simulation Conference,* San Diego, pp. 445–450 (1988).

Grigoryev, I., and A. Borshchev: *AnyLogic 6 in Three Days: A Quick Course in Simulation Modeling,* AnyLogic North America, Lisle, Illinois (2012).

Grosenbaugh, L.R.: More on Fortran Random Number Generators, *Commun. Assoc. Comput. Mach., 12*: 639 (1969).

Gross, D., J.F. Shortle, J.M. Thompson, and C.M. Harris: *Fundamentals of Queueing Theory,* 4th ed., John Wiley, New York (2009).

Gupta, S.S.: On a Decision Rule for a Problem in Ranking Means, Mimeograph Series No. 150, Institute of Statistics, University of North Carolina, Chapel Hill (1956).

Gupta, S.S.: On Some Multiple Decision (Selection and Ranking) Rules, *Technometrics, 7:* 225–245 (1965).

Gupta, S.S., and T.J. Santner: On Selection and Ranking Procedures—A Restricted Subset Selection Rule, *Proc. 39th Session of the International Statistical Institute,* Vienna, Vol. 1 (1973).

Gupta, U.G.: Using Citation Analysis to Explore the Intellectual Base, Knowledge Dissemination, and Research Impact of *Interfaces* (1970–1992), *Interfaces, 27:* 85–101 (1997).

Gürkan, G., A.Y. Özge, and S.M. Robinson: Sample-Path Solution of Stochastic Variational Inequalities, *Math. Programming, 84:* 313–333 (1999).

Haberman, S.J.: A Warning on the Use of Chi-Squared Statistics with Frequency Tables with Small Expected Cell Counts, *J. Am. Statist. Assoc., 83:* 555–560 (1988).

Hahn, G.J, and S.S. Shapiro: *Statistical Models in Engineering,* John Wiley, New York (1994).

Haider, S.W., D.G. Noller, and T.B. Robey: Experiences with Analytic and Simulation Modeling for a Factory of the Future Project at IBM, *Proc. 1986 Winter Simulation Conference,* Washington, D.C., pp. 641–648 (1986).

Halton, J.H.: A Retrospective and Prospective Survey of the Monte Carlo Method, *SIAM Rev., 12:* 1–63 (1970).

Hammersley, J.M., and D.C. Handscomb: *Monte Carlo Methods,* Methuen, London (1964).

Hammersley, J.M., and K.W. Morton: A New Monte Carlo Technique: Antithetic Variates, *Proc. Camb. Phil. Soc., 52:* 449–475 (1956).

Harrell, C.R., B.K. Ghosh, and R.O. Bowden: *Simulation Using ProModel,* 3d ed. McGraw-Hill, New York (2012).

Haykin, S.O.: *Neural Networks and Learning Machines*, 3d ed., Prentice Hall, Upper Saddle River, New Jersey (2009).

Hazra, M.M., D.J. Morrice, and S.K. Park: A Simulation Clock-Based Solution to the Frequency Domain Experiment Indexing Problem, *IIE Trans., 29:* 769–782 (1997).

He, D., S.E. Chick, and C.-H. Chen: The Opportunity Cost and OCBA Selection Procedures in Ordinal Optimization, *IEEE Trans. on Systems, Man, and Cybernetics—Part C, 37:* 951–961 (2007).

Healey, C., S. Andradóttir, and S.-H. Kim: Efficient Comparison of Constrained Systems Using Dormancy, *Eur. J. Operational Research, 224:* 340–352 (2013).

Heath, B.L., R.R. Hill, and F. Ciarello: A Survey of Agent-Based Modeling Practices (January 1998 to July 2008), *J. of Artificial Societies and Social Simulation, 12,* http://jasss.soc.surrey.ac.uk/12/4/9.html (2009).

Heathcote, C.R., and P. Winer: An Approximation to the Moments of Waiting Times, *Operations Res., 17:* 175–186 (1969).

Heidelberger, P.: Variance Reduction Techniques for the Simulation of Markov Processes, I: Multiple Estimates, *IBM J. Res. Develop., 24:* 570–581 (1980).

Heidelberger, P.: Fast Simulation of Rare Events in Queueing and Reliability Models, *Assoc. Comput. Mach. Trans. Modeling and Comput. Simul., 5:* 43–85 (1995).

Heidelberger, P., and D.L. Iglehart: Comparing Stochastic Systems Using Regenerative Simulation with Common Random Numbers, *Adv. Appl. Prob., 11:* 804–819 (1979).

Heidelberger, P., and P.A.W. Lewis: Quantile Estimation in Dependent Sequences, *Operations Res., 32:* 185–209 (1984).

Heidelberger, P., and P.D. Welch: Adaptive Spectral Methods for Simulation Output Analysis, *IBM J. Res. Develop., 25:* 860–876 (1981a).

Heidelberger, P., and P.D. Welch: A Spectral Method for Confidence Interval Generation and Run Length Control in Simulations, *Commun. Assoc. Comput. Mach., 24:* 233–245 (1981b).

Heidelberger, P., and P.D. Welch: Simulation Run Length Control in the Presence of an Initial Transient, *Operations Res., 31:* 1109–1144 (1983).

Heikes, R.G., D.C. Montgomery, and R.L. Rardin: Using Common Random Numbers in Simulation Experiments—An Approach to Statistical Analysis, *Simulation, 25:* 81–85 (1976).

Henderson, D., S.H. Jacobson, and A.W. Johnson: The Theory and Practice of Simulated Annealing, in *Handbook of Metaheuristics,* F. Glover and G. Kochenberger, eds., Springer, New York (2003).

Henderson, S.G.: Input Model Uncertainty: Why Do We Care and What Should We Do about It?, *Proc. 2003 Winter Simulation Conference,* New Orleans, pp. 90–100 (2003).

Henderson, S.G., and P.W. Glynn: Regenerative Steady-State Simulation of Discrete-Event Systems, *Assoc. Comput. Mach. Trans. Modeling and Comput. Simul., 11:* 313–345 (2001).

Henriksen, J.O.: An Improved Events List Algorithm, *Proc. 1977 Winter Simulation Conference,* San Diego, California, pp. 547–557 (1977).

Henriksen, J.O.: Event List Management—A Tutorial, *Proc. 1983 Winter Simulation Conference,* Washington, D.C., pp. 543–551 (1983).

Hernandez, A.S., T.W. Lucas, and M. Carlyle: Constructing Nearly Orthogonal Latin Hypercubes for Any Nonsaturated Run-Variable Combination, *Assoc. Comput. Mach. Trans. Modeling and Comput. Simul., 22,* No. 4, Article 20 (2012).

Hesterberg, T.C., and B.L. Nelson: Control Variates for Probability and Quantile Estimation, *Management Sci., 44:* 1295–1312 (1998).

Hill, R.R., L.E. Champagne, and J.C. Price: Using Agent-based Simulation and Game Theory to Examine the WWII Bay of Biscayne U-Boat Campaign, *J. of Defense Modeling and Simulation, 1*: 99–109 (2004).

Hill, R.R., and C.H. Reilly: Composition for Multivariate Random Variables, *Proc. 1994 Winter Simulation Conference,* Orlando, pp. 332–339 (1994).

Ho, Y.C., and X.R. Cao: *Discrete Event Dynamic Systems and Perturbation Analysis,* Kluwer Academic Publishers, Amsterdam (1991).

Ho, Y.C., C.G. Cassandras, C.H. Chen, and L.Y. Dai: Ordinal Optimization and Simulation, *J. Operational Res. Soc., 51:* 490–500 (2000).

Ho, Y.C., R. Sreenivas, and P. Vakili: Ordinal Optimization of Discrete Event Dynamic Systems, *Discrete Event Dynamic Systems: Theory and Applications, 2:* 61–88 (1992).

Hoad, K.A., S. Robinson, and R. Davies: Automating Warm-Up Length Estimation, *J. Operational Res. Soc., 61:* 1389–1403 (2009).

Hoaglin, D.C., F. Mosteller, and J.W. Tukey: *Understanding Robust and Exploratory Data Analysis,* John Wiley, New York (1983).

Hochberg, Y., and A.C. Tamhane: *Multiple Comparison Procedures,* John Wiley, New York (1987).

Hogg, R.V., and A.F. Craig: *Introduction to Mathematical Statistics,* 5th ed., Prentice-Hall, Upper Saddle River, New Jersey (1995).

Holland, J.H.: *Hidden Order: How Adaptation Builds Complexity*, Basic Books, New York (1995).

Hong, L.J., and B.L. Nelson: The Tradeoff between Sampling and Switching: New Sequential Procedures for Indifference-Zone Selection, *IIE Trans., 37:* 623–634 (2005).

Hong, L.J., and B.L. Nelson: Discrete Optimization via Simulation Using COMPASS, *Operations Res., 54:* 115–129 (2006).

Hood, S.J., and P.D. Welch: Experimental Design Issues in Simulation with Examples from Semiconductor Manufacturing, *Proc. 1992 Winter Simulation Conference,* Washington, D.C., pp. 255–263 (1992).

Hood, S.J., and P.D. Welch: Response Surface Methodology and Its Application in Simulation, *Proc. 1993 Winter Simulation Conference,* Los Angeles, pp. 115–122 (1993).

Hopp, W.J., and M.L. Spearman: *Factory Physics*, 3d ed., Waveland Press, Long Grove, Illinois (2011).

Hörmann, W.: A Rejection Technique for Sampling from T-Concave Distributions, *Assoc. Comput. Mach. Trans. Math. Software, 21:* 182–193 (1995).

Hörmann, W., and G. Derflinger: Rejection-Inversion to Generate Variates from Monotone Discrete Distributions, *Assoc. Comput. Mach. Trans. Modeling and Comput. Simul., 6:* 169–184 (1996).

Hörmann, W., and J. Leydold: Continuous Random Variate Generation by Fast Numerical Inversion, *Assoc. Comput. Mach. Trans. Modeling and Comput. Simul., 13:* 347–362 (2003).

Hörmann, W., J. Leydold, and G. Derflinger: *Automatic Nonuniform Random Variate Generation,* Springer-Verlag, New York (2004).

Hsu, D.A., and J.S. Hunter: Analysis of Simulation-Generated Responses Using Autoregressive Models, *Management Sci., 24:* 181–190 (1977).

Hsu, J.C.: Constrained Two-Sided Simultaneous Confidence Intervals for Multiple Comparisons with the Best, *Ann. Statist., 12:* 1136–1144 (1984).

Hsu, J.C.: *Multiple Comparisons: Theory and Methods,* Chapman & Hall, London, England (1996).

Hsu, J.C., and B.L. Nelson: Control Variates for Quantile Estimation, *Management Sci., 36:* 835–851 (1990).

Hu, J., M.C. Fu, and S.I. Marcus: A Model Reference Adaptive Search Method for Global Optimization, *Operations Res., 55:* 549–568 (2007).

Hull, T.E., and A.R. Dobell: Random Number Generators, *SIAM Rev., 4:* 230–254 (1962).

Hunter, S.R., and R. Pasupathy: Optimal Sampling Laws for Stochastically Constrained Simulation Optimization on Finite Sets, to appear in *INFORMS J. Comput.* (2013).

Hussey, J.R., R.H. Myers, and E.C. Houck: Correlated Simulation Experiments in First-Order Response Surface Designs, *Operations Res., 35:* 744–758 (1987).

Hutchinson, D.W.: A New Uniform Pseudorandom Number Generator, *Commun. Assoc. Comput. Mach., 9:* 432–433 (1966).

Iglehart, D.L.: Simulating Stable Stochastic Systems, V: Comparison of Ratio Estimators, *Naval Res. Logist. Quart., 22:* 553–565 (1975).

Iglehart, D.L., and P.W. Lewis: Regenerative Simulation with Internal Controls, *J. Assoc. Comput. Mach., 26:* 271–282 (1979).

Ilachinski, A.: *Artificial War: Multiagent-Based Simulation of Combat,* World Scientific Publishing Company, Singapore (2004).

Imagine That, Inc.: ExtendSim simulation software, www.extendsim.com (2013).

INCONTROL Simulation Solutions, Enterprise Dynamics simulation software, www.incontrolsim.com (2013).

Irish, T.H., D.C. Dietz, and K.W. Bauer, Jr.: Replicative Use of an External Analytical Model in Simulation Variance Reduction, *IIE Trans., 35:* 879–894 (2003).

Jacobson, S.H., A.H. Buss, and L.W. Schruben: Driving Frequency Selection for Frequency Domain Simulation Experiments, *Operations Res., 39:* 917–924 (1991).

Jain, R., and I. Chlamtac: The P^2 Algorithm for Dynamic Calculation of Quantiles and Histograms without Storing Observations, *Commun. Assoc. Comput. Mach., 28:* 1076–1085 (1985).

Jefferson, D.R.: Virtual Time, *Assoc. Comput. Mach. Trans. Programming Languages and Systems, 7:* 404–425 (1985).

Joanes, D.N., and C.A. Gill: Comparing Measures of Sample Skewness and Kurtosis, *The Statistician, 47:* 183–189 (1998).

Jöhnk, M.D.: Erzeugung von Betaverteilten und Gammaverteilten Zufallszahlen, *Metrika, 8:* 5–15 (1964).

Johnson, M.A., S. Lee, and J.R. Wilson: Experimental Evaluation of a Procedure for Estimating Nonhomogeneous Poisson Processes Having Cyclic Behavior, *ORSA J. Comput., 6:* 356–368 (1994a).

Johnson, M.A., S. Lee, and J.R. Wilson: NPPMLE and NPPSIM: Software for Estimating and Simulating Nonhomogeneous Poisson Processes Having Cyclic Behavior, *Operations Res. Letters, 15:* 273–282 (1994b).

Johnson, M.E.: *Multivariate Statistical Simulation,* John Wiley, New York (1987).

Johnson, M.E., and J.S. Ramberg: Transformations of the Multivariate Normal Distribution with Applications to Simulation, Los Alamos Sci. Lab. Tech. Rep. LA-UR-77-2595, Los Alamos, New Mexico (1978).

Johnson, M.E., C. Wang, and J.S. Ramberg: Generation of Continuous Multivariate Distributions for Statistical Applications, *Am. J. Math. and Management Sci., 4:* 96–119 (1984).

Johnson, N.L., S. Kotz, and N. Balakrishnan, *Continuous Univariate Distributions,* Volume 1, 2d ed., Houghton Mifflin, Boston (1994).

Johnson, N.L., S. Kotz, and N. Balakrishnan, *Continuous Univariate Distributions,* Volume 2, 2d ed., Houghton Mifflin, Boston (1995).

Johnson, N.L., S. Kotz, and N. Balakrishnan: *Discrete Multivariate Distributions,* John Wiley, New York (1997).

Johnson, N.L., S. Kotz, and A.W. Kemp: *Univariate Discrete Distributions*, 2d ed., Houghton Mifflin, Boston (1992).

Joines, J.A., and S.D. Roberts: Object-Oriented Simulation, in *Handbook of Simulation,* J. Banks, ed., John Wiley, New York (1998).

Jones, D.W.: An Empirical Comparison of Priority-Queue and Event-Set Implementations, *Commun. Assoc. Comput. Mach., 29:* 300–311 (1986).

Jones, R.M., and K.S. Miller: On the Multivariate Lognormal Distribution, *J. Indust. Math., 16:* 63–76 (1966).

Kabirian, A., and S. Ólafsson: Continuous Optimization via Simulation Using Golden Region Search, *Eur. J. Operational Res., 208:* 19–27 (2011).

Kachitvichyanukul, V., and B.W. Schmeiser: Binomial Random Variate Generation, *Commun. Assoc. Comput. Mach., 31:* 216–222 (1988).

Kallenberg, W.C.M., J. Oosterhoff, and B.F. Schriever: The Number of Classes in Chi-Squared Goodness-of-Fit Tests, *J. Am. Statist. Assoc., 80:* 959–968 (1985).

Kaminsky, F.C., and D.L. Rumpf: Simulating Nonstationary Poisson Processes: A Comparison of Alternatives Including the Correct Approach, *Simulation, 29:* 17–20 (1977).

Kang, K., K.H. Doerr, and S.M. Sanchez: A Design of Experiments Approach to Readiness Risk Analysis, *Proc. 2006 Winter Simulation Conference,* Monterey, California, pp. 1332–1339 (2006).

Kao, E.P.C., and S.L. Chang: Modeling Time-Dependent Arrivals to Service Systems: A Case in Using a Piecewise-Polynomial Rate Function in a Nonhomogeneous Poisson Process, *Management Sci., 34:* 1367–1379 (1988).

Kapuściński, R., and S. Tayur: A Capacitated Production-Inventory Model with Periodic Demand, *Operations Res., 46:* 899–911 (1998).

Keefer, D.L., and S.E. Bodily: Three-Point Approximations for Continuous Random Variables, *Management Sci., 29:* 595–609 (1983).

Kelton, W.D.: The Startup Problem in Discrete-Event Simulation, Technical Report 80-1, Dept. of Industrial Engineering, University of Wisconsin, Madison, Wisconsin (1980).

Kelton, W.D.: Transient Exponential-Erlang Queues and Steady-State Simulation, *Commun. Assoc. Comput. Mach., 28:* 741–749 (1985).

Kelton, W.D.: Random Initialization Methods in Simulation, *IIE Trans., 21:* 355–367 (1989).

Kelton, W.D., and A.M. Law: A New Approach for Dealing with the Startup Problem in Discrete Event Simulation, *Naval Res. Logist. Quart., 30:* 641–658 (1983).

Kelton, W.D., and A.M. Law: The Transient Behavior of the *M/M/s* Queue, with Implications for Steady-State Simulation, *Operations Res., 33:* 378–396 (1985).

Kelton, W.D., R.P. Sadowski, and N.B. Swets: *Simulation with Arena,* 5th ed., McGraw-Hill, New York (2010).

Kelton, W.D., J.S. Smith, D.T. Sturrock: *Simio & Simulation: Modeling, Analysis, Applications*, 2d ed., McGraw-Hill Learning Solutions, Indianapolis, Indiana (2011).

Kendall, M.G., and B. Babington-Smith: Randomness and Random Sampling Numbers, *J. Roy. Statist. Soc., 101A:* 147–166 (1938).

Kendall, M.G., and A. Stuart: *The Advanced Theory of Statistics,* Vol. 2, 4th ed., Griffin, London (1979).

Kendall, M.G., A. Stuart, and J.K. Ord: *The Advanced Theory of Statistics,* Vol. 1, 5th ed., Oxford University Press, New York (1987).

Kennedy, W.J., Jr., and J.E. Gentle: *Statistical Computing,* Marcel Dekker, New York (1980).

Kernighan, B.W., and D.M. Ritchie: *The C Programming Language,* 2d ed., Prentice-Hall, Englewood Cliffs, New Jersey (1988).

Kim, S., R. Pasupathy, and S.G. Henderson: A Guide to Sample-Average Approximation, in *Handbook on Simulation Optimization*, M.C. Fu, ed., Springer, New York (2013).

Kim, S.-H., and B.L. Nelson: A Fully Sequential Procedure for Indifference-Zone Selection in Simulation, *Assoc. Comput. Mach. Trans. Modeling and Comput. Simul., 11:* 251–273 (2001).

Kim, S.-H., and B.L. Nelson: Selecting the Best System, in *Elsevier Handbooks in Operations Research and Management Science,* H.G. Henderson and B.L. Nelson, eds., Elsevier, New York (2006a).

Kim, S.-H., and B.L. Nelson: On the Asymptotic Validity of Fully Sequential Selection Procedures for Steady-State Simulation, *Operations Res., 54:* 475–488 (2006b).

Kim, S.-H., and B.L. Nelson: Recent Advances in Ranking and Selection, *Proc. 2007 Winter Simulation Conference*, Washington, D.C., pp. 162–172 (2007).

Kinderman, A.J., and J.F. Monahan: Computer Generation of Random Variables Using the Ratio of Uniform Deviates, *Assoc. Comput. Mach. Trans. Math. Software, 3:* 257–260 (1977).

Kinderman, A.J., and J.G. Ramage: Computer Generation of Normal Random Variables, *J. Am. Statist. Assoc., 71:* 893–896 (1976).

Kleijnen, J.P.C.: *Statistical Techniques in Simulation,* Pt. I, Marcel Dekker, New York (1974).

Kleijnen, J.P.C.: Analysis of Simulation with Common Random Numbers: A Note on Heikes et al. (1976), *Simuletter, 11:* 7–13 (1979).

Kleijnen, J.P.C.: Regression Metamodels for Simulation with Common Random Numbers: Comparison of Validation Tests and Confidence Intervals, *Management Sci., 38:* 1164–1185 (1992).

Kleijnen, J.P.C.: Experimental Design for Sensitivity Analysis, Optimization, and Validation of Simulation Models, in *Handbook of Simulation,* J. Banks, ed., John Wiley, New York (1998).

Kleijnen, J.P.C.: *Design and Analysis of Simulation Experiments*, Springer, New York (2007).

Kleijnen, J.P.C.: Design of Experiments: Overview, *Proc. 2008 Winter Simulation Conference,* Miami, Florida, pp. 479–488 (2008).

Kleijnen, J.P.C.: Kriging Metamodeling in Simulation: A Review, *Eur. J. Operational Res., 192:* 707–716 (2009).

Kleijnen, J.P.C., B. Bettonvil, and F. Persson: Screening for the Important Factors in Large Discrete-Event Simulation Models: Sequential Bifurcation and Its Applications, in *Screening: Methods for Experimentation in Industry, Drug Discovery, and Genetics,* A.M. Dean and S.M. Lewis, eds., Springer, New York (2006).

Kleijnen, J.P.C., B. Bettonvil, and W. Van Groenendaal: Validation of Trace-Driven Simulation Models: A Novel Regression Test, *Management Sci., 44:* 812–819 (1998).

Kleijnen, J.P.C., R.C.H. Cheng, and B. Bettonvil: Validation of Trace-Driven Simulation Models: More on Bootstrap Techniques, *Proc. 2000 Winter Simulation Conference,* Orlando, pp. 882–892 (2000).

Kleijnen, J.P.C., R.C.H. Cheng, and B. Bettonvil: Validation of Trace-Driven Simulation Models: Bootstrap Tests, *Management Sci., 47:* 1533–1538 (2001).

Kleijnen, J.P.C., and D. Deflandre: Validation of Regression Metamodels in Simulation: Bootstrap Approach, *Eur. J. Operational Res., 170:* 120–131 (2006).

Kleijnen, J.P.C., S.M. Sanchez, T.W. Lucas, and T.M. Cioppa: A User's Guide to the Brave New World of Designing Simulation Experiments, *INFORMS J. Comput., 17:* 263–289 (2005).

Kleijnen, J.P.C., and R.G. Sargent: A Methodology for Fitting and Validating Metamodels in Simulation, *Eur. J. Operational Res., 120:* 14–29 (2000).

Klein, R.W., and S.D. Roberts: A Time-Varying Poisson Arrival Process Generator, *Simulation, 43*: 193–195 (1984).

Knepell, P.L., and D.C. Arangno: *Simulation Validation: A Confidence Assessment Methodology,* IEEE Computer Society Press, Los Alamitos, California (1993).

Knuth, D.E.: *The Art of Computer Programming, Vol. 1: Fundamental Algorithms,* 3d ed., Addison-Wesley, Reading, Massachusetts (1997).

Knuth, D.E.: *The Art of Computer Programming, Vol. 2: Seminumerical Algorithms,* 3d ed., Addison-Wesley, Reading, Massachusetts (1998a).

Knuth, D.E.: *The Art of Computer Programming, Vol. 3: Sorting and Searching,* 2d ed., Addison-Wesley, Reading, Massachusetts (1998b).

Koenig, L.W., and A.M. Law: A Procedure for Selecting a Subset of Size m Containing the l Best of k Independent Normal Populations, with Applications to Simulation, Tech. Rep. 82-9, Department of Management Information Systems, University of Arizona, Tucson (1982).

Koenig, L.W., and A.M. Law: A Procedure for Selecting a Subset of Size m Containing the l Best of k Independent Normal Populations, *Commun. Statist.—Simulation and Computation, 14:* 719–734 (1985).

Kotz, S., N. Balakrishnan, and N.L. Johnson: *Continuous Multivariate Distributions, Vol. 1, Models and Applications,* 2d ed., Wiley, New York (2000).

Kronmal, R.A., and A.V. Peterson, Jr.: On the Alias Method for Generating Random Variables from a Discrete Distribution, *Am. Statistician, 33:* 214–218 (1979).

Kronmal, R.A., and A.V. Peterson, Jr.: A Variant of the Acceptance-Rejection Method for Computer Generation of Random Variables, *J. Am. Statist. Assoc., 76:* 446–451 (1981).

Kronmal, R.A., and A.V. Peterson, Jr.: Corrigenda, *J. Am. Statist. Assoc., 77:* 954 (1982).

Kuhl, M.E., H. Damerdji, and J.R. Wilson: Estimating and Simulating Poisson Processes with Trends or Asymmetric Cyclic Effects, *Proc. 1997 Winter Simulation Conference,* Atlanta, pp. 287–295 (1997).

Kuhl, M.E., S.G. Sumant, and J.R. Wilson: An Automated Multiresolution Procedure for Modeling Complex Arrival Processes, *INFORMS J. Comput., 18:* 3–18 (2006).

Kuhl, F.S., R.M. Weatherly, and J.S. Dahmann: *Creating Computer Simulation Systems: An Introduction to the High Level Architecture,* Prentice-Hall, Upper Saddle River, New Jersey (2000).

Kuhl, M.E., and J.M. Wilson: Least Squares Estimation of Nonhomogeneous Poisson Processes, *J. Statist. Comput. Simul., 67:* 75–108 (2000).

Kuhl, M.E., and J.M. Wilson: Modeling and Simulating Poisson Processes Having Trends or Nontrigonometric Cyclic Effects, *Eur. J. Operational Res., 133:* 566–582 (2001).

Kuhl, M.E., J.R. Wilson, and M.A. Johnson: Estimating and Simulating Poisson Processes Having Trends or Multiple Periodicities, *IIE Trans., 29:* 201–211 (1997).

Kumar, S., and D.A. Nottestad: Capacity Design: An Application Using Discrete-Event Simulation and Designed Experiments, *IIE Trans., 38:* 729–736 (2006).

Kwon, C., and J.D. Tew: Strategies for Combining Antithetic Variates and Control Variates in Designed Simulation Experiments, *Management Sci., 40:* 1021–1034 (1994).

Lada, E.K., N.M. Steiger, and J.R. Wilson: Performance Evaluation of Recent Procedures for Steady-State Simulation Analysis, *IIE Trans., 38:* 711–727 (2006).

Lada, E.K., N.M. Steiger, and J.R. Wilson: SBatch: A Spaced Batch Means Procedure for Steady-State Simulation Analysis, *J. of Simulation, 2:* 170–185 (2008).

Lada, E.K., and J.R. Wilson: A Wavelet-Based Spectral Procedure for Steady-State Simulation Analysis, *Eur. J. Operational Res., 174:* 1769–1801 (2006a).

Lada, E.K., and J.R. Wilson: Performance Evaluation of Spectral Procedures for Simulation Analysis, *Proc. 2006 Winter Simulation Conference*, Monterey, California, pp. 198–207 (2006b).

Lada, E.K., J.R. Wilson, N.M. Steiger, and J.A. Joines: Performance of a Wavelet-Based Spectral Procedure for Steady-State Simulation Analysis, *INFORMS J. Comput., 19:* 150–160 (2007).

Laguna, M.: Scatter Search, in the *Handbook of Applied Optimization,* pp. 183–193, P.M. Pardalos and M.G.C. Resende, eds., Oxford University Press, New York (2002).

Laguna, M.: OptQuest: Optimization of Complex Systems, www.opttek.com, OptTek Systems, Inc., Boulder, Colorado (2011).

Laguna, M., and R. Marti: *Scatter Search: Methodology and Implementations in C,* Kluwer Academic Publishers, Boston (2003).

Lanchester, F.W.: *Aircraft in Warfare: the Dawn of the Fourth Arm*, Constable and Company Ltd., London (1916).

Lane, M.S., A.H. Mansour, and J.L. Harpell: Operations Research Techniques: A Longitudinal Update 1973–1988, *Interfaces, 23:* 63–68 (1993).

Lanner Group Ltd.: WITNESS simulation software, www.lanner.com (2013).

Lavenberg, S.S., T.L. Moeller, and C.H. Sauer: Concomitant Control Variables Applied to the Regenerative Simulation of Queueing Systems, *Operations Res., 27:* 134–160 (1979).

Lavenberg, S.S., T.L. Moeller, and P.D. Welch: Statistical Results on Control Variables with Application to Queueing Network Simulation, *Operations Res., 30:* 182–202 (1982).

Lavenberg, S.S., and P.D. Welch: Using Conditional Expectation to Reduce Variance in Discrete-Event Simulation, *Proc. 1979 Winter Simulation Conference,* San Diego, pp. 291–294 (1979).

Lavenberg, S.S., and P.D. Welch: A Perspective on the Use of Control Variables to Increase the Efficiency of Monte Carlo Simulations, *Management Sci., 27:* 322–335 (1981).

Law, A.M.: Efficient Estimators for Simulated Queueing Systems, *Univ. California Operations Res. Center ORC 74-7,* Berkeley (1974).

Law, A.M.: Efficient Estimators for Simulated Queueing Systems, *Management Sci., 22:* 30–41 (1975).

Law, A.M.: Confidence Intervals in Discrete-Event Simulation: A Comparison of Replication and Batch Means, *Naval Res. Logist. Quart., 24:* 667–678 (1977).

Law, A.M.: Statistical Analysis of the Output Data from Terminating Simulations, *Naval Res. Logist. Quart., 27:* 131–143 (1980).

Law, A.M.: Statistical Analysis of Simulation Output Data, *Operations Res., 31:* 983–1029 (1983).

Law, A.M.: Simulation Model's Level of Detail Determines Effectiveness, *Ind. Eng., 23:* 16, 18 (October 1991).

Law, A.M.: How to Conduct a Successful Simulation Study, *Proc. 2003 Winter Simulation Conference,* New Orleans, pp. 66–70 (2003).

Law, A.M.: How to Build Valid and Credible Simulation Models, *Proc. 2009 Winter Simulation Conference,* Austin, Texas, pp. 24–33 (2009).

Law, A.M.: A Practitioner's Perspective on Simulation Validation, VV&A Recommended Practices Guide, Modeling & Simulation Coordination Office, http://vva.msco.mil, Alexandria, Virginia (2011).

Law, A.M., and J.S. Carson: A Sequential Procedure for Determining the Length of a Steady-State Simulation, *Operations Res., 27:* 1011–1025 (1979).

Law, A.M., and W.D. Kelton: Confidence Intervals for Steady-State Simulations, II: A Survey of Sequential Procedures, *Management Sci., 28:* 550–562 (1982).

Law, A.M., and W.D. Kelton: Confidence Intervals for Steady-State Simulations, I: A Survey of Fixed Sample Size Procedures, *Operations Res., 32:* 1221–1239 (1984).

Law, A.M., W.D. Kelton, and L.W. Koenig: Relative Width Sequential Confidence Intervals for the Mean, *Commun. Statist., B10:* 29–39 (1981).

Law, A.M., and M.G. McComas: How Simulation Pays Off, *Manuf. Eng., 100:* 37–39 (February 1988).

Law, A.M., and M.G. McComas: Pitfalls to Avoid in the Simulation of Manufacturing Systems, *Ind. Eng., 21:* 28–31 (May 1989).

Lawless, J.F.: Statistical Models and Methods for Lifetime Data, 2d ed., John Wiley, New York (2003).

L'Ecuyer, P.: Efficient and Portable Combined Random Number Generators, *Commun. Assoc. Comput. Mach., 31:* 742–749 and 774 (1988).

L'Ecuyer, P.: Efficiency Improvement and Variance Reduction, *Proc. 1994 Winter Simulation Conference,* Orlando, pp. 122–132 (1994a).

L'Ecuyer, P.: Uniform Random Number Generation, *Annals of Operations Res., 53:* 77–120 (1994b).

L'Ecuyer, P.: Combined Multiple Recursive Random Number Generators, *Operations Res., 44:* 816–822 (1996a).

L'Ecuyer, P.: Maximally Equidistributed Combined Tausworthe Generators, *Math. of Computation, 65:* 203–213 (1996b).

L'Ecuyer, P.: Random Number Generation, in *Handbook of Simulation,* J. Banks, ed., John Wiley, New York (1998).

L'Ecuyer, P.: Good Parameters and Implementations for Combined Multiple Recursive Random Number Generators, *Operations Res., 47:* 159–164 (1999a).

L'Ecuyer, P.: Tables of Maximally Equidistributed Combined LFSR Generators, *Math. of Computation, 68:* 261–269 (1999b).

L'Ecuyer, P.: Uniform Random Number Generation, in *Handbooks in Operations Research and Management Science: Simulation,* S.G. Henderson and B.L. Nelson, eds., Elsevier, New York (2006).

L'Ecuyer, P.: Random Number Generation, in *Handbook of Computational Statistics,* 2d ed., J.E. Gentle, W. Härdle, and Y. Mori, eds., Springer, New York (2012).

L'Ecuyer, P., F. Blouin, and R. Couture: A Search for Good Multiple Recursive Random Number Generators, *Assoc. Comput. Mach. Trans. Modeling and Comput. Simul., 17:* 98–111 (1993).

L'Ecuyer, P., J.-F. Cordeau, and R. Simard: Close-Point Spatial Tests and Their Application to Random Number Generators, *Operations Res., 48:* 308–317 (2000).

L'Ecuyer, P., and F. Panneton: F_2 Linear Random Number Generators, in *Advancing the Frontiers of Simulation: A Festschrift in Honor of George Samuel Fishman,* C. Alexopoulos, D. Goldsman, and J.R. Wilson, eds., Springer, New York (2009).

L'Ecuyer, P., and R. Simard: On the Performance of Birthday Spacings Tests with Certain Families of Random Number Generators, *Math. and Comp. in Simul., 55:* 131–137 (2001).

L'Ecuyer, P., and R. Simard: TESTU01: A C Library for Empirical Testing of Random-Number Generators, *Assoc. Comput. Mach. Trans. Math. Software, 33,* No. 4, Article 22 (2007).

L'Ecuyer, P., R. Simard, E.J. Chen, and W.D. Kelton: An Object-Oriented Random-Number Package with Many Long Streams and Substreams, *Operations Res., 50:* 1073–1075 (2002).

L'Ecuyer, P., R. Simard, and S. Wegenkittl: Sparse Serial Tests of Uniformity for Random Number Generators, *SIAM J. Scientific Computing, 24:* 652–668 (2002).

L'Ecuyer, P., and S. Tezuka: Structural Properties for Two Classes of Combined Random Number Generators, *Math. of Computation, 57:* 735–746 (1991).

Lee, L.H., N.A. Pujowidianto, L.-W. Li, C.-H. Chen, and C.M. Yap: Approximate Simulation Budget Allocation for Selecting the Best System in the Presence of Stochastic Constraints, *IEEE Trans. on Auto. Cont., 57:* 2940–2945 (2012).

Lee, S., J.R. Wilson, and M.M. Crawford: Modeling and Simulation of a Nonhomogeneous Poisson Process Having Cyclic Behavior, *Commun. Statist., B20:* 777–809 (1991).

Leemis, L.: Nonparametric Estimation of the Cumulative Intensity Function for a Nonhomogeneous Poisson Process, *Management Sci., 37:* 886–900 (1991).

Leemis, L.: Building Credible Input Models, *Proc. 2004 Winter Simulation Conference,* Washington, D.C., pp. 29–40 (2004).

Lehmer, D.H.: Mathematical Methods in Large-Scale Computing Units, *Ann. Comput. Lab. Harvard Univ., 26:* 141–146 (1951).

Levasseur, J.A.: The Case for Object-Oriented Simulation, *OR/MS Today, 23:* 65–67 (August 1996).

Levin, B., and J. Reeds: Compound Multinomial Likelihood Functions Are Unimodal: Proof of a Conjecture of I.J. Good, *Ann. Statist., 5:* 79–87 (1977).

Lew, J.: Making City Planning a Game, *The New York Times* (June 15, 1989).

Lewis, P.A.W.: Generating Negatively Correlated Gamma Variates Using the Beta-Gamma Transformation, *Proc. 1983 Winter Simulation Conference,* Washington, D.C., pp. 175–176 (1983).

Lewis, P.A.W., A.S. Goodman, and J.M. Miller: A Pseudorandom-Number Generator for the System/360, *IBM Syst. J., 8:* 136–146 (1969).

Lewis, P.A.W., E. McKenzie, and D.K. Hugus: Gamma Processes, *Comm. Statist. Stoch. Models, 5:* 1–30 (1989).

Lewis, P.A.W., and G.S. Shedler: Statistical Analysis of Non-Stationary Series of Events in a Data Base System, *IBM J. Res. Dev., 20:* 465–482 (1976).

Lewis, P.A.W., and G.S. Shedler: Simulation of Nonhomogeneous Poisson Process by Thinning, *Nav. Res. Logist. Quart., 26:* 403–413 (1979).

Lewis, T.G., and W.H. Payne: Generalized Feedback Shift Register Pseudorandom-Number Algorithm, *J. Assoc. Comput. Mach., 20:* 456–468 (1973).

Leydold, J.: Automatic Sampling with the Ratio-of-Uniforms Method, *Assoc. Comput. Mach. Trans. Math. Software, 26:* 78–98 (2000).

Lilliefors, H.W.: On the Kolmogorov-Smirnov Test for Normality with Mean and Variance Unknown, *J. Am. Statist. Assoc., 62:* 399–402 (1967).

Lilliefors, H.W.: On the Kolmogorov-Smirnov Test for the Exponential Distribution with Mean Unknown, *J. Am. Statist. Assoc., 64:* 387–389 (1969).

Littell, R.C., J.T. McClave, and W.W. Offen: Goodness-of-Fit Tests for the Two Parameter Weibull Distribution, *Commun. Statist., B8:* 257–269 (1979).

Livny, M., B. Melamed, and A.K. Tsiolis: The Impact of Autocorrelation on Queueing Systems, *Management Sci, 39:* 322–339 (1993).

Loeppky, J.L., J. Sacks, and W.J. Welch: Choosing the Sample Size of a Computer Experiment: A Practical Guide, *Technometrics, 51:* 366–376 (2009).

Lophaven, S.N., H.B. Nielsen, and J. Sondergaard: DACE: A MATLAB Kriging Toolbox, Version 2.0, IMM Technical University of Denmark, Lyngby, Denmark (2002).

Lotka, A.J.: *Elements of Physical Biology,* Williams and Wilkins, Philadelphia, Pennsylvania (1925).

Macal, C.M.: Agent Based Modeling and Artificial Life, *Encyclopedia of Complexity and Systems Science,* pp. 112–131, Springer, New York (2009).

Macal, C.M., and M.J. North: Agent-Based Modeling and Simulation: ABMS Examples, *Proc. 2008 Winter Simulation Conference,* Miami, Florida, pp. 101–112 (2008).

Macal, C.M., and M.J. North: Tutorial on Agent-Based Modelling and Simulation, *J. of Simulation, 4:*151–162 (2010).

Macal, C.M., and M.J. North: Introductory Tutorial: Agent-Based Modeling and Simulation, *Proc. 2011 Winter Simulation Conference,* Phoenix, Arizona, pp. 1456–1469 (2011).

Macal, C.M., and M.J. North: Personal Communication (2013).

Macal, C.M., M.J. North, and D.A. Samuelson: Agent-Based Simulation, in *Encyclopedia of Operations Research and Management Science,* 3d ed., S.I. Gass and M.C. Fu, eds., Springer, New York (2013).

MacKay, N.: Lancaster Combat Models, *Mathematics Today, 42:* 170–173 (2006).

MacLaren, M.D., and G. Marsaglia: Uniform Random Number Generators, *J. Assoc. Comput. Mach., 12:* 83–89 (1965).

MacLaren, M.D., G. Marsaglia, and T.A. Bray: A Fast Procedure for Generating Exponential Random Variables, *Commun. Assoc. Comput. Mach., 7:* 298–300 (1964).

Margolin, B.H., and W. Maurer: Tests of the Kolmogorov-Smirnov Type for Exponential Data with Unknown Scale, and Related Problems, *Biometrika, 63:* 149–160 (1976).

Marsaglia, G.: Generating Exponential Random Variables, *Ann. Math. Statist., 32:* 899–902 (1961).

Marsaglia, G.: Generating Discrete Random Variables in a Computer, *Commun. Assoc. Comput. Mach., 6*: 37–38 (1963).

Marsaglia, G.: Random Numbers Fall Mainly in the Planes, *Natl. Acad. Sci. Proc., 61:* 25–28 (1968).

Marsaglia, G.: The Exact-Approximation Method for Generating Random Variables in a Computer, *J. Am. Statist. Assoc., 79:* 218–22 (1984).

Marsaglia, G.: The Marsaglia Random Number CD, including the DIEHARD Battery of Tests of Randomness, Department of Statistics, Florida State University, Tallahassee, Florida (1995). See http://stat.fsu.edu/pub/diehard.

Marsaglia, G., and T.A. Bray: A Convenient Method for Generating Normal Variables, *SIAM Rev., 6:* 260–264 (1964).

Marsaglia, G., and T.A. Bray: One-Line Random Number Generators and Their Use in Combinations, *Commun. Assoc. Comput. Mach., 11:* 757–759 (1968).

Marse, K., and S.D. Roberts: Implementing a Portable FORTRAN Uniform (0,1) Generator, *Simulation, 41:* 135–139 (1983).

Marshall, A.W., and I. Olkin: A Multivariate Exponential Distribution, *J. Am. Statist. Assoc., 62:* 30–44 (1967).

MASON: http://cs.gmu.edu/~eclab/projects/mason (2013).

MathWorks: MATLAB software, www.matlab.com (2013).

Matsumoto, M., and Y. Kurita: Twisted GFSR Generators, *Assoc. Comput. Mach. Trans. Modeling and Comput. Simul., 2:* 179–194 (1992).

Matsumoto, M., and Y. Kurita: Twisted GFSR Generators II, *Assoc. Comput. Mach. Trans. Modeling and Comput. Simul., 4:* 254–266 (1994).

Matsumoto, M., and Y. Kurita: Strong Deviations from Randomness in *m*-Sequences Based on Trinomials, *Assoc. Comput. Mach. Trans. Modeling and Comput. Simul., 6:* 99–106 (1996).

Matsumoto, M., and T. Nishimura: A 623-Dimensionally Equidistributed Uniform Pseudo-Random Number Generator, *Assoc. Comput. Mach. Trans. Modeling and Comput. Simul., 8:* 3–30 (1998).

McCormack, W.M., and R.G. Sargent: Analysis of Future Event Set Algorithms for Discrete Event Simulation, *Commun. Assoc. Comput. Mach., 24:* 801–812 (1981).

McIntosh, G.C., D.P. Galligan, M.A. Anderson, and M.K. Lauren, MANA (Map Aware Non-Uniform Automata), Version 4 Users Manual, Defence Technology Agency, New Zealand Defence Force, Auckland, New Zealand (2007).

McLean, C., and F. Riddick: The IMS Mission Architecture for Distributed Manufacturing Simulation, *Proc. 2000 Winter Simulation Conference,* Orlando, pp. 1539–1548 (2000).

McLeod, I.: A Remark on AS 183. An Efficient and Portable Pseudo-random Number Generator, *Appl. Statist., 34:* 198–200 (1985).

Meketon, M.S., and B.W. Schmeiser: Overlapping Batch Means: Something for Nothing?, *Proc. 1984 Winter Simulation Conference,* Dallas, pp. 227–230 (1984).

Menon, M.V.: Estimation of the Shape and Scale Parameters of the Weibull Distribution, *Technometrics, 5:* 175–182 (1963).

Meterelliyoz, M., C. Alexopoulos, and D. Goldsman: Folded Overlapping Variance Estimators for Simulation, *Eur. J. Operational Research, 220:* 135–146 (2012).

Michalewicz, Z.: *Genetic Algorithms + Data Structures = Evolution Programs,* 3d ed., Springer, New York (2013).

Miller, J.O., B.L. Nelson, and C.H. Reilly: Efficient Multinomial Selection in Simulation, *Naval Res. Logist., 45:* 459–482 (1998).

Miller, R.G., Jr.: The Jackknife—A Review, *Biometrika, 61:* 1–15 (1974).

Milton, R.C., and R. Hotchkiss: Computer Evaluation of the Normal and Inverse Normal Distribution Functions, *Technometrics, 11:* 817–822 (1969).

Minar, N., R. Burkhart, C. Langton, and M. Askenazi: The Swarm Simulation System: A Toolkit for Building Multi-Agent Simulations, Working Paper 96-06-042, Santa Fe Institute, Santa Fe, New Mexico (1996).

Minh, D.L.: A Variant of the Conditional Expectation Variance Reduction Technique and Its Application to the Simulation of the *GI/G/*1 Queues, *Management Sci., 35:* 1334–1340 (1989).

Minitab Inc.: Minitab statistical software, www.minitab.com (2013).

Mitchell, B.: Variance Reduction by Antithetic Variates in *GI/G/*1 Queueing Simulations, *Operations Res., 21:* 988–997 (1973).

Mitchell, C.R., and A.S. Paulson: *M/M/*1 Queues with Interdependent Arrival and Service Processes, *Nav. Res. Logist. Quart., 26:* 47–56 (1979).

Mitchell, C.R., A.S. Paulson, and C.A. Beswick: The Effect of Correlated Exponential Service Times on Single Server Tandem Queues, *Nav. Res. Logist. Quart., 24:* 95–112 (1977).

Miyatake, O., M. Ichimura, Y. Yoshizawa, and H. Inoue: Mathematical Analysis of Random-Number Generator Using Gamma Rays I, *Math. Jap., 28:* 399–414 (1983).

Modeling & Simulation Coordination Office: VV&A Recommended Practices Guide, http://vva.msco.mil, Alexandria, Virginia (2011).

Mokashi, A.C., J.J. Tejada, S. Yousefi, T. Xu, J.R. Wilson, A. Tafazzoli, and N.M. Steiger: Performance Comparison of MSER-5 and N-Skart on the Simulation Start-Up Problem, *Proc. 2010 Winter Simulation Conference,* Baltimore, Maryland, pp. 971–982 (2010).

Montgomery, D.C.: *Design and Analysis of Experiments*, 8th ed., John Wiley, New York (2013).

Montgomery, D.C., and G.C. Runger: *Applied Statistics and Probability for Engineers,* 5th ed., John Wiley, New York (2011).

Mood, A.M., F.A. Graybill, and D.C. Boes: *Introduction to the Theory of Statistics,* 3d ed., McGraw-Hill, New York (1974).

Morgan, B.J.T.: *Elements of Simulation,* Chapman & Hall, London (1984).

Moro, B.: The Full Monte, *Risk, 8:* 57–58 (1995).

Morrice, D.J., and I.R. Bardhan: A Weighted Least-Squares Approach to Computer Simulation Factor Screening, *Operations Res., 43:* 792–806 (1995).

Morrice, D.J., and L.W. Schruben: Simulation Factor Screening Using Cross-Spectral Methods, *Operations Res. Letters, 13:* 247–257 (1993a).

Morrice, D.J., and L.W. Schruben: Simulation Factor Screening Using Harmonic Analysis, *Management Sci., 39:* 1459–1476 (1993b).

Murphy, W.S., Jr., and M.A. Flourney: Simulation Crisis Communications, *Proc. 2002 Winter Simulation Conference,* San Diego, pp. 954–959 (2002).

Murray, J.R.: Stochastic Initialization in Steady-State Simulations, Ph.D. Dissertation, Department of Industrial and Operations Engineering, The University of Michigan, Ann Arbor (1988).

Murray, J.R., and W.D. Kelton: The Transient Behavior of the $M/E_k/2$ Queue and Steady-State Simulation, *Computers and Operations Res., 15:* 357–367 (1988).

Myers, R.H., D.C. Montgomery, and C.M. Anderson-Cook: *Response Surface Methodology: Process and Product Optimization Using Designed Experiments,* 3d ed., John Wiley, New York (2009).

Nakayama, M.K.: Fast Simulation Methods for Highly Dependable Systems, *Proc. 1994 Winter Simulation Conference,* Orlando, pp. 221–228 (1994a).

Nakayama, M.K.: A Characterization of the Simple Failure Biasing Method for Simulations of Highly Reliable Markovian Systems, *Assoc. Comput. Mach. Trans. Modeling and Comput. Simul., 4:* 52–88 (1994b).

Nakayama, M.K.: Multiple-Comparison Procedures for Steady-State Simulations, *Ann. Statist., 25:* 2433–2450 (1997).

Nakayama, M.K.: Multiple Comparisons with the Best Using Common Random Numbers, *J. Statist. Plan. Inf., 85:* 37–48 (2000).

Nance, R.E., and C. Overstreet, Jr.: Implementation of Fortran Random-Number Generators on Computers with One's Complement Arithmetic, *J. Statist. Comput. Simul., 4:* 235–243 (1975).

Nance, R.E., and C. Overstreet, Jr.: Some Experimental Observations on the Behavior of Composite Random-Number Generators, *Operations Res., 26:* 915–935 (1978).

Nance, R.E., and R.G. Sargent: Perspectives on the Evolution of Simulation, *Operations Res., 50:* 161–172 (2002).

Naylor, T.H.: *Computer Simulation Experiments with Models of Economic Systems,* John Wiley, New York (1971).

Naylor, T.H., and J.M. Finger: Verification of Computer Simulation Models, *Management Sci., 14:* 92–101 (1967).

Nelson, B.L.: A Decomposition Approach to Variance Reduction, *Proc. 1985 Winter Simulation Conference,* San Francisco, pp. 23–33 (1985).

Nelson, B.L.: Decomposition of Some Well-Known Variance Reduction Techniques, *J. Statist. Comput. Simul., 23:* 183–209 (1986).

Nelson, B.L.: A Perspective on Variance Reduction in Dynamic Simulation Experiments, *Commun. Statist., B16:* 385–426 (1987a).

Nelson, B.L.: Some Properties of Simulation Interval Estimators under Dependence Induction, *Operations Res. Letters, 6:* 169–176 (1987b).

Nelson, B.L.: Variance Reduction for Simulation Practitioners, *Proc. 1987 Winter Simulation Conference,* Atlanta, pp. 43–51 (1987c).

Nelson, B.L.: Batch Size Effects on the Efficiency of Control Variates in Simulation, *Eur. J. Operational Res., 43:* 184–196 (1989).

Nelson, B.L.: Control-Variate Remedies, *Operations Res., 38:* 974–992 (1990a).

Nelson, B.L.: Variance Reduction in the Presence of Initial-Condition Bias, *IIE Trans., 22:* 340–350 (1990b).

Nelson, B.L.: Robust Multiple Comparisons under Common Random Numbers, *Assoc. Comput. Mach. Trans. Modeling and Comput. Simul., 3:* 225–243 (1993).

Nelson, B.L.: The More Plot: Displaying Measures of Risk & Error from Simulation Output, *Proc. 2008 Winter Simulation Conference*, Miami, Florida, pp. 413–416 (2008).

Nelson, B.L., and J.C. Hsu: Control-Variate Models of Common Random Numbers for Multiple Comparisons with the Best, *Management Sci., 39*: 989–1001 (1993).

Nelson, B.L., and F.J. Matejcik: Using Common Random Numbers for Indifference-Zone Selection and Multiple Comparisons in Simulation, *Management Sci., 41:* 1935–1945 (1995).

Nelson, B.L., B.W. Schmeiser, M.R. Taaffe, and J. Wang: Approximation-Assisted Point Estimation, *Operations Res. Letters, 20:* 109–118 (1997).

Nelson, B.L, J. Swann, D. Goldsman, and W.-M.T. Song: Simple Procedures for Selecting the Best System When the Number of Alternatives Is Large, *Operations Res., 49:* 950–963 (2001).

Nelson, B.L., and M. Yamnitsky: Input Modeling Tools for Complex Problems, *Proc. 1998 Winter Simulation Conference,* Washington, D.C., pp. 105–112 (1998).

NetLogo: http://ccl.northwestern.edu/netlogo (2013).

Nicola, V.F., P. Shahabuddin, and M.K. Nakayama: Techniques for Fast Simulation of Models of Highly Dependable Systems, *IEEE Trans. Reliability, 50:* 246–264 (2001).

Niederreiter, H.: Quasi-Monte Carlo Methods and Pseudo-random Numbers, *Bull. Am. Math. Soc., 84:* 957–1041 (1978).

Nilsson, F., and V. Darley: On Complex Adaptive Systems and Agent-Based Modelling for Improved Decision-Making in Manufacturing and Logistics Settings: Experiences from a Packaging Company, *International J. of Operations & Production Management, 26:* 1351–1373 (2006).

North, M.J., N.T. Collier, J. Ozik, E.R. Tatara, C.M. Macal, M. Bragen, and P. Sydelko: Complex Adaptive Systems Modeling with Repast Simphony, *Complex Adaptive Systems Modeling, 1:* 1–26 (2013).

North., M.J., and C.M. Macal: *Managing Business Complexity: Discovering Strategic Solutions with Agent-Based Modeling and Simulation*, Oxford University Press, New York (2007).

Nozari, A., S.F. Arnold, and C.D. Pegden: Statistical Analysis with the Schruben and Margolin Correlation Induction Strategy, *Operations Res., 35:* 127–139 (1987).

Ólaffson, S., and J. Kim: Simulation Optimization, *Proc. 2002 Winter Simulation Conference*, San Diego, pp. 79–84 (2002).

Owen, D.B.: *Handbook of Statistical Tables*, Addison-Wesley, Reading, Massachusetts (1962).

Pace, D.K.: Thoughts about the Conceptual Model, *Proc. of the Simulation Interoperability Workshop,* Orlando, Florida, Paper Number 009 (Spring 2003).

Page, E.S.: On Monte Carlo Methods in Congestion Problems: II. Simulation of Queueing Systems, *Operations Res., 13:* 300–305 (1965).

Panneton, F., P. L'Ecuyer, and M. Matsumoto: Improved Long-Period Generators Based on Linear Recurrences Modulo 2, *Assoc. Comput. Mach. Trans. Math. Software, 32:* 1–16 (2006).

Parker, J., and J.M. Epstein: A Distributed Platform for Global-Scale Agent-Based Models of Disease Propagation, *Assoc. Comput. Mach. Trans. Modeling and Comput. Simul., 22,* No. 1, Article 2 (2011).

Pasupathy, R., and B.W. Schmeiser: The Initial Transient in Steady-State Point Estimation: Contexts, a Bibliography, the MSE Criterion, and the MSER Statistic, *Proc. 2010 Winter Simulation Conference*, Baltimore, Maryland, pp. 184–197 (2010).

Pawlikowski, K.: Steady-State Estimation of Queueing Processes: A Survey of Problems and Solutions, *Assoc. Comput. Mach Computing Surveys, 22:* 123–170 (1990).

Payne, W.H., J.R. Rabung, and T.P. Bogyo: Coding the Lehmer Pseudorandom Number Generator, *Commun. Assoc. Comput. Mach., 12:* 85–86 (1969).

Pearson, K.: On a Criterion That a Given System of Deviations from the Probable in the Case of a Correlated System of Variables Is Such That It Can Be Reasonably Supposed to Have Arisen in Random Sampling, *Phil. Mag.* (5), *50:* 157–175 (1900).

Pegden, C.D.: Personal Communication (2010).

Peng, Y., C.-H. Chen, M.C. Fu, and J.Q. Hu: Efficient Simulation Resource Sharing and Allocation for Selecting the Best, *IEEE Trans. on Auto. Cont., 58:* 1017–1023 (2013).

Peterson, A.V., Jr., and R.A. Kronmal: On Mixture Methods for the Computer Generation of Random Variables, *Am. Statistician, 36:* 184–191 (1982).

Peterson, A.V., Jr., and R.A. Kronmal: Analytic Comparison of Three General-Purpose Methods for the Computer Generation of Discrete Random Variables, *Appl. Statist., 32:* 276–286 (1983).

Pettitt, A.N., and M.A. Stephens: The Kolmogorov-Smirnov Goodness-of-Fit Statistic with Discrete and Grouped Data, *Technometrics, 19:* 205–210 (1977).

Pichitlamken, J., B.L. Nelson, and L.J. Hong: A Sequential Procedure for Neighborhood Selection-of-the-Best in Optimization via Simulation, *Eur. J. Operational Res., 173:* 283–298 (2006).

Porcaro, D.: Simulation Modeling and DOE, *Industrial Engineering Solutions:* 24–30 (September 1996).

Poropudas, J., and K. Virtanen: Simulation Metamodeling with Dynamic Bayesian Networks, *Eur. J. Operational Res., 214:* 644–655 (2011).

Porta Nova, A.M., and J.R. Wilson: Selecting Control Variates to Estimate Multiresponse Simulation Metamodels, *Eur. J. Operational Res., 71:* 80–94 (1993).

Posadas, S., and E.P. Paulo: Stochastic Simulation of a Commander's Decision Cycle, *Military Operations Res., 8:* 21–43 (2003).

Press, W.H., S.A. Teukolsky, W.T. Vetterling, and B.P. Flannery: *Numerical Recipes: The Art of Scientific Computing,* 3d ed., Cambridge University Press, Cambridge, England (2007).

Pritsker, A.A.B.: *Introduction to Simulation and SLAM II,* 4th ed., John Wiley, New York (1995).

ProcessModel, Inc.: ProcessModel simulation software, www.processmodel.com (2013).

ProModel Corporation: MedModel simulation software, www.promodel.com (2013).

ProModel Corporation: Process Simulator simulation software, www.promodel.com (2013).

ProModel Corporation: ProModel simulation software, www.promodel.com (2013).

ProModel Corporation: ServiceModel simulation software, www.promodel.com (2013).

Pujowidianto, N.A., L.H. Lee, C.-H. Chen, and C.M. Yap: Optimal Budget Allocation for Constrained Optimization, *Proc. 2009 Winter Simulation Conference,* Austin, Texas, pp. 584–589 (2009).

Raatikainen, K.E.E.: Sequential Procedure for Simultaneous Estimation of Several Percentiles, *Trans. of the Society for Comp. Simulation, 7:* 21–24 (1990).

Railsback, S.F., and V. Grimm: *Agent-Based and Individual-Based Modeling: A Practical Introduction,* Princeton University Press, Princeton, New Jersey (2012).

Rajasekaran, S., and K.W. Ross: Fast Algorithms for Generating Discrete Random Variates with Changing Distributions, *Assoc. Comput. Mach. Trans. Modeling and Comput. Simul., 3:* 1–19 (1993).

Ramberg, J.S., and P.R. Tadikamalla: On the Generation of Subsets of Order Statistics, *J. Statist. Comput. Simul., 6:* 239–241 (1978).

Rand Corporation: *A Million Random Digits with 100,000 Normal Deviates,* Free Press, Glencoe, Illinois (1955).

Reynolds, C.W.: Flocks, Herds, and Schools: A Distributed Behavior Model, *Proc. of the ACM 14th Annual Conference on Computer Graphics and Interactive Techniques*, Anaheim, California (1987).

Rinott, Y.: On Two-Stage Selection Procedures and Related Probability-Inequalities, *Commun. Statist., A7:* 799–811 (1978).

Ripley, B.D.: *Stochastic Simulation,* John Wiley, New York (1987).

Riverbed Technologies: OPNET Modeler simulation software, www.opnet.com (2013).

Robbins, H., G. Simons, and N. Starr: A Sequential Analogue of the Behrens-Fisher Problem, *Ann. Math. Statist., 38:* 1384–1391 (1967).

Robinson, S.: *Simulation: The Practice of Model Development and Use,* Wiley, Chichester, United Kingdom (2004).

Robinson, S.: Conceptual Modelling for Simulation Part I: Definition and Requirements, *J. Operational Res. Soc., 59:* 291–304 (2008a).

Robinson, S.: Conceptual Modelling for Simulation Part II: A Framework for Conceptual Modeling, *J. Operational Res. Soc., 59:* 278–290 (2008b).

Robinson, S.M.: Analysis of Sample-Path Optimization, *Math. of Operations Res., 21:* 513–528 (1996).

Rockwell Automation: Arena simulation software, www.arenasimulation.com (2013).

Rogue Wave Software: IMSL Numerical Libraries, www.roguewave.com (2013).

Rönngren, R., and R. Ayani: A Comparative Study of Parallel and Sequential Priority Queue Algorithms, *Assoc. Comput. Mach. Trans. Modeling and Comput. Simul., 7:* 157–209 (1997).

Ronning, G.: A Simple Scheme for Generating Multivariate Gamma Distributions with Non-negative Covariance Matrix, *Technometrics, 19:* 179–183 (1977).

Ross, S.M.: *Introduction to Probability Models,* 8th ed., Academic Press, San Diego (2003).

Rubinstein, R.Y.: *Simulation and the Monte Carlo Method,* John Wiley, New York (1981).

Rubinstein, R.Y.: *Monte Carlo Optimization, Simulation and Sensitivity of Queueing Networks,* Krieger Publishing Co., Malabar, Florida (1992).

Rubinstein, R.Y., and D.P. Kroese: *Simulation and the Monte Carlo Method,* 2d ed., John Wiley, New York (2008).

Rubinstein, R.Y., and R. Marcus: Efficiency of Multivariate Control Variates in Monte Carlo Simulation, *Operations Res., 33:* 661–667 (1985).

Rubinstein, R.Y., B. Melamed, and A. Shapiro: *Modern Simulation and Modeling,* John Wiley, New York (1998).

Rubinstein, R.Y., G. Samorodnitsky, and M. Shaked: Antithetic Variates, Multivariate Dependence, and Simulation of Complex Stochastic Systems, *Management Sci., 31:* 66–77 (1985).

Rubinstein, R.Y., and A. Shapiro: *Discrete Event Systems: Sensitivity Analysis and Stochastic Optimization by the Score Method,* John Wiley, New York (1993).

Rudolph, E., and D.M. Hawkins: Random-Number Generators in Cyclic Queuing Applications, *J. Statist. Comput. Simul., 5:* 65–71 (1976).

Rukhin, A., J. Soto, J. Nechvatel, M. Smid, E. Barker, S. Leigh, M. Levenson, M. Vangel, D. Banks, A. Heckert, J. Dray, and S. Vo: A Statistical Test Suite for Random and Pseudorandom Number Generators for Cryptographic Applications, NIST Special Publication 800–22, National Institute for Standards and Technology, Gaithersburg, Maryland (2001). See http://csrs.nist.gov/rng/.

Runciman, N., N. Vagenas, and T. Corkal: Simulation of Haulage Truck Loading Techniques in an Underground Mine Using WITNESS, *Simulation, 68:* 291–299 (1997).

Russell, E.C.: *Simulation and SIMSCRIPT II.5,* CACI, Inc., Los Angeles (1976).

Sacks, J., W.J. Welch, T.J. Mitchell, and H.P. Wynn: Design and Analysis of Computer Simulation Experiments, *Statistical Science, 4:* 409–423 (1989).

Samuelson, D.A: Mass Egress and Post-Disaster, *OR/MS Today:* 20–24 (October 2007a).

Samuelson, D.A.: Panel: Agent Based Modeling of Mass Egress and Evacuations, *Proc. of the 2007 Winter Simulation Conference,* Washington, D.C., pp. 1247–1251 (2007b).

Sanchez, P.J., and S.M. Sanchez: Design of Frequency Domain Experiments for Discrete-Valued Factors, *Appl. Math. and Computation, 42:* 1–21 (1991).

Sanchez, P.J., and L.W. Schruben: Simulation Factor Screening Using Frequency Domain Methods: An Illustrative Example, Working Paper 87–013, Systems and Industrial Engineering Dept., University of Arizona, Tucson (1987).

Sanchez, P.J., and K.P. White: Interval Estimation Using Replication/Deletion and MSER Truncation, *Proc. 2011 Winter Simulation Conference,* Phoenix, Arizona, pp. 488–494 (2011).

Sanchez, S.M., T.W. Lucas, P.J. Sanchez, C.J. Nannini, and H. Wan: Designs for Large-Scale Simulation Experiments, with Applications to Defense and Homeland Security, in *Design and Analysis of Experiments: Special Designs and Experiments,* K. Hinkelmann, ed., John Wiley, New York (2012).

Sanchez, S.M., and P.J. Sanchez: Very Large Fractional Factorial and Central Composite Designs, *Assoc. Comput. Mach. Trans. Modeling and Comput. Simul.,15:* 362–377 (2005).

Sanchez, S.M., and H. Wan: Work Smarter, Not Harder: A Tutorial on Designing and Conducting Simulation Experiments, *Proc. 2012 Winter Simulation Conference,* Berlin, Germany (2012).

Sanchez, S.M., H. Wan, and T.W. Lucas: Two-phase Screening Procedures for Simulation Experiments, *Assoc. Comput. Mach. Trans. Modeling and Comput. Simul., 19,* No. 2, Article 7 (2009).

Santner, T.J.: A Restricted Subset Selection Approach to Ranking and Selection Problems, *Ann. Statist., 3:* 334–349 (1975).

Santner, T.J., B.J. Williams, and W.I. Notz: *The Design and Analysis of Computer Experiments,* Springer, New York (2003).

Sargent, R.G.: Event Graph Modelling for Simulation with an Application to Flexible Manufacturing Systems, *Management Sci., 34:* 1231–1251 (1988).

Sargent, R.G.: Verification and Validation of Simulation Models, *J. of Simulation, 6:* 1–13 (2012).

Sargent, R.G., K. Kang, and D. Goldsman: An Investigation of Finite-Sample Behavior of Confidence Interval Estimators, *Operations Res., 40:* 898–913 (1992).

Sargent, R.G., and T.K. Som: Current Issues in Frequency Domain Experimentation, *Management Sci., 38:* 667–687 (1992).

SAS Institute Inc.: JMP statistical software, www.jmp.com (2013).

SCALABLE Network Technologies, Inc.: QualNet simulation software, www.scalable-networks .com (2013).

Schelling, T.C.: Dynamic Models of Segregation, *J. of Mathematical Sociology:* 143–186 (1971).

Scheuer, E.M., and D.S. Stoller: On the Generation of Normal Random Vectors, *Technometrics, 4:* 278–281 (1962).

Schmeiser, B.W.: Generation of the Maximum (Minimum) Value in Digital Computer Simulation, *J. Statist. Comput. Simul., 8:* 103–115 (1978a).

Schmeiser, B.W.: The Generation of Order Statistics in Digital Computer Simulation: A Survey, *Proc. 1978 Winter Simulation Conference,* Miami, pp. 137–140 (1978b).

Schmeiser, B.W.: Generation of Variates from Distribution Tails, *Operations Res., 28:* 1012–1017 (1980a).

Schmeiser, B.W.: Random Variate Generation: A Survey, *Proc. 1980 Winter Simulation Conference*, Orlando, pp. 79–104 (1980b).

Schmeiser, B.W.: Batch Size Effects in the Analysis of Simulation Output, *Operations Res., 30:* 556–568 (1982).

Schmeiser, B.W., and A.J.G. Babu: Beta Variate Generation via Exponential Majorizing Functions, *Operations Res., 28:* 917–926 (1980).

Schmeiser, B.W., and V. Kachitvichyanukul: Poisson Random Variate Generation, School of Industrial Engineering Research Memorandum 81-4, Purdue Univ., West Lafayette, Indiana (1981).

Schmeiser, B.W., and V. Kachitvichyanukal: Non-Inverse Correlation Induction: Guidelines for Algorithm Development, *J. Comput. and Applied Math., 31:* 173–180 (1990).

Schmeiser, B.W., and R. Lal: Squeeze Methods for Generating Gamma Variates, *J. Am. Statist. Assoc., 75:* 679–382 (1980).

Schmeiser, B.W., and R. Lal: Bivariate Gamma Random Vectors, *Operations Res., 30:* 355–374 (1982).

Schmeiser, B.W., and M.A. Shalaby: Acceptance/Rejection Methods for Beta Variate Generation, *J. Am. Statist. Assoc., 75:* 673–678 (1980).

Schmeiser, B.W., and W.T. Song: Batching Methods in Simulation Output Analysis: What We Know and What We Don't, *Proc. 1996 Winter Simulation Conference,* San Diego, 122–127 (1996).

Schmeiser, B.W., and M.R. Taaffe: Time-Dependent Queueing Network Approximations as Simulation External Control Variates, *Operations Res. Letters, 16:* 1–9 (1994).

Schmidt, J.W., and R.E. Taylor: *Simulation and Analysis of Industrial Systems,* Richard D. Irwin, Homewood, Illinois (1970).

Schrage, L.: A More Portable Random-Number Generator, *Assoc. Comput. Mach. Trans. Math. Software, 5:* 132–138 (1979).

Schriber, T.J.: *Simulation Using GPSS,* John Wiley, New York (1974).

Schriber, T.J., and R.W. Andrews: An ARMA-Based Confidence Interval for the Analysis of Simulation Output, *Am. J. Math. Management Sci., 4:* 345–373 (1984).

Schruben, L.W.: Designing Correlation Induction Strategies for Simulation Experiments, in *Current Issues in Computer Simulation,* N.R. Adam and A. Dogramici, eds., Academic Press, New York (1979).

Schruben, L.W.: Establishing the Credibility of Simulations, *Simulation, 34:* 101–105 (1980).

Schruben, L.W.: Detecting Initialization Bias in Simulation Output, *Operations Res., 30:* 569–590 (1982).

Schruben, L.W.: Confidence Interval Estimation Using Standardized Time Series, *Operations Res., 31:* 1090–1108 (1983a).

Schruben, L.W.: Simulation Modeling with Event Graphs, *Commun. Assoc. Comput. Mach., 26:* 957–963 (1983b).

Schruben, L.W., and V.J. Cogliano: An Experimental Procedure for Simulation Response Surface Model Identification, *Commun. Assoc. Comput. Mach., 30:* 716–730 (1987).

Schruben, L.W., and B.H. Margolin: Pseudorandom Number Assignment in Statistically Designed Simulation and Distribution Sampling Experiments, *J. Am. Statist. Assoc., 73:* 504–520 (1978).

Schruben, L.W., T.M. Roeder, W.K. Chan, P. Hyden, and M. Freimer: Advanced Event Scheduling Methodology, *Proc. 2003 Winter Simulation Conference,* New Orleans, pp. 159–165 (2003).

Schruben, L.W., H. Singh, and L. Tierney: Optimal Tests for Initialization Bias in Simulation Output, *Operations Res., 31:* 1167–1178 (1983).

Schucany, W.R.: Order Statistics in Simulation, *J. Statist. Comput. Simul., 1:* 281–286 (1972).

Schwefel, H.-P.: *Evolution and Optimum Seeking,* John Wiley, New York (1995).

Scott, D.W.: On Optimal and Data-Based Histograms, *Biometrika, 66:* 605–610 (1979).

SEAS: U.S. Air Force Space Command, Space and Missile Systems Center, www.teamseas.com, Los Angeles, California (2013).

Seila, A.F.: Spreadsheet Simulation, *Proc. 2005 Winter Simulation Conference,* Orlando, Florida, pp. 33–40 (2005).

Seila, A.F., V. Ceric, and P. Tadikamalla: *Applied Simulation Modeling,* Brooks-Cole, Belmont, California (2003).

Shahabuddin, P.: Importance Sampling for the Simulation of Highly Reliable Markovian Systems, *Management Sci., 40:* 333–352 (1994).

Shahabuddin, P.: Rare Event Simulation in Stochastic Models, *Proc. 1995 Winter Simulation Conference,* Washington, D.C., pp. 178–185 (1995).

Shannon, R.E.: *Systems Simulation: The Art and Science,* Prentice-Hall, Englewood Cliffs, New Jersey (1975).

Shanthikumar, J.G.: Discrete Random Variate Generation Using Uniformization, *Eur. J. Operational Res., 21:* 387–398 (1985).

Shanthikumar, J.G., and J.A. Buzacott: *Stochastic Models of Manufacturing Systems,* Prentice-Hall, Englewood Cliffs, New Jersey (1993).

Shapiro, S.S., and M.B. Wilk: An Analysis of Variance Test for Normality (Complete Samples), *Biometrika, 52:* 591–611 (1965).

Shedler, G.S.: *Regenerative Stochastic Simulation,* Academic Press, San Diego (1993).

Shen, H., and H. Wan: Controlled Sequential Factorial Design for Simulation Factor Screening, *Eur. J. Operational Res., 198:* 511–519 (2009).

Shen, H., H. Wan, and S.M. Sanchez: A Hybrid Method for Simulation Factor Screening, *Naval Res. Logistics, 57:* 45–57 (2010).

Shi, L., and S. Ólafsson: Nested Partitioned Method for Global Optimization, *Operations Res., 48:* 390–407 (2000).

Siebel, F., and L. Kellam: The Virtual World of Agent-Based Modeling: Procter & Gamble's Dynamic Supply Chain, *Perspectives on Business Innovation, 9:* 22–27 (2003).

Siemens: Plant Simulation simulation software, http://www.plm.automation.siemens.com/en_us/products/tecnomatix/free-trial/plant-simulation.shtml (2013).

Sigal, C.E., A.A.B. Pritsker, and J.J. Solberg: The Use of Cutsets in Monte Carlo Analysis of Stochastic Networks, *Math. Comput. Simul., 21:* 376–384 (1979).

Silverman, B.W.: *Density Estimation for Statistics and Data Analysis*, Chapman & Hall, London (1986).

Simio LLC: Simio simulation software, www.simio.com (2013).

SIMUL8 Corporation: SIMUL8 simulation software, www.simul8.com (2013).

Slifker, J., and S.S. Shapiro: On the Johnson System of Distributions, *Technometrics, 22:* 239–246 (1980).

Smith, R.L.: Efficient Monte Carlo Procedures for Generating Points Uniformly Distributed over Bounded Regions, *Operations Res., 32:* 1296–1308 (1984).

Snell, M., and L.W. Schruben: Weighting Simulation Data to Reduce Initialization Effects, Technical Report 395, School of Industrial Engineering, Cornell University, Ithaca, New York (1979).

Som, T.K., and R.G. Sargent: A Formal Development of Event Graphs as an Aid to Structured and Efficient Simulation Programs, *ORSA J. Comput., 1:* 107–125 (1989).

Song, W.-M.T., and B.W. Schmeiser: Optimal Mean-Squared-Error Batch Sizes, *Management Sci., 41:* 110–123 (1995).

Spall, J.C.: *Introduction to Stochastic Search and Optimization,* John Wiley, New York (2003).

Spieckermann, S., K. Gutenschwager, H. Heinzel, and S. Voss: Simulation-based Optimization in the Automotive Industry—A Case Study on Body Shop Design, *Simulation, 75:* 276–286 (2000).

Srikant, R., and W. Whitt: Variance Reduction in Simulations of Loss Models, *Operations Res., 47:* 509–523 (1999).

Stadlober, E.: The Ratio of Uniforms Approach for Generating Discrete Random Variates, *J. Comput. and Applied Math., 31:* 181–189 (1990).

Stanfield, P.M., J.R. Wilson, G.A. Mirka, N.F. Glasscock, J.P. Psihogios, and J.R. Davis: Multivariate Input Modeling with Johnson Distributions, *Proc. 1996 Winter Simulation Conference,* San Diego, pp. 1457–1464 (1996).

Stat-Ease, Inc.: Design-Expert statistical software, www.stat-ease.com (2013).

Staum, J.: Better Simulation Metamodeling: The Why, What, and How of Stochastic Kriging, *Proc. 2009 Winter Simulation Conference*, Austin, Texas, pp. 119–133 (2009).

Stefánescu, S., and I. Váduva: On Computer Generation of Random Vectors by Transformation of Uniformly Distributed Vectors, *Computing, 39:* 141–153 (1987).

Steiger, N.M., E.K. Lada, J.R. Wilson, J.A. Joines, C. Alexopoulos, and D. Goldsman: ASAP3: A Batch Means Procedure for Steady-State Simulation Analysis, *Assoc. Comput. Mach. Trans. Modeling and Comput. Simul., 15:* 39–73 (2005).

Steiger, N.M., and J.R. Wilson: Convergence Properties of the Batch Means Method for Simulation Output Analysis, *Assoc. Comput. Mach. Trans. Modeling and Comput. Simul., 13:* 277–293 (2001).

Steiger, N.M., and J.R. Wilson: An Improved Batch Means Procedure for Simulation Output Analysis, *Management Sci., 48:* 1569–1586 (2002).

Stephens, M.A.: EDF Statistics for Goodness of Fit and Some Comparisons, *J. Am. Statist. Assoc., 69:* 730–737 (1974).

Stephens, M.A.: Asymptotic Results for Goodness-of-Fit Statistics with Unknown Parameters, *Ann. Statist., 4:* 357–369 (1976).

Stephens, M.A.: Goodness of Fit for the Extreme Value Distribution, *Biometrika, 64:* 583–588 (1977).

Stephens, M.A.: Tests of Fit for the Logistic Distribution Based on the Empirical Distribution Function, *Biometrika, 66:* 591–595 (1979).

Sterman, J.D.: *Business Dynamics: Systems Thinking and Modeling for a Complex World*, McGraw-Hill, New York (2001).

Stidham, S: A Last Word on $L = \lambda w$, *Operations Res., 22:* 417–421 (1974).

Sullivan, D.W., and J.R. Wilson: Restricted Subset Selection Procedures for Simulation, *Operations Res., 37:* 52–71 (1989).

Swain, J.J., S. Venkatraman, and J.R. Wilson: Least-Squares Estimation of Distribution Functions in Johnson's Translation System, *J. Statist. Comput. Simul., 29:* 271–297 (1988).

Swart, W., and L. Donno: Simulation Modeling Improves Operations, Planning, and Productivity for Fast Food Restaurants, *Interfaces, 11:6:* 35–47 (1981).

Swisher, J.R., P.D. Hyden, S.H. Jacobson, and L.W. Schruben: A Survey of Recent Advances in Discrete Input Parameter Discrete-Event Simulation Optimization, *IIE Trans., 36:* 591–600 (2004).

Swisher, J.R., S.H. Jacobson, and E. Yücesan: Discrete-Event Simulation Optimization Using Ranking, Selection, and Multiple Comparison Procedures: A Survey, *Assoc. Comput. Mach. Trans. Modeling and Comput. Simul., 13:* 134–154 (2003).

Tadikamalla, P.R.: Computer Generation of Gamma Random Variables-II, *Commun. Assoc. Comput. Mach., 21:* 925–928 (1978).

Tadikamalla, P.R.: Kolmogorov-Smirnov Type Test-Statistics for the Gamma, Erlang-2, and the Inverse Gaussian Distributions When the Parameters Are Unknown, *Commun. Statist.-Simulation and Computation, 19:* 305–314 (1990).

Tadikamalla, P.R., and M.E. Johnson: A Complete Guide to Gamma Variate Generation, *Am. J. Math. Management Sci., 1:* 78–95 (1981).

Tafazzoli, A., N.M. Steiger, and J.R. Wilson: N-Skart: A Nonsequential Skewness- and Autoregression-Adjusted Batch-Means Procedure for Simulation Analysis, *IEEE Trans. Auto. Cont., 56:* 254–264 (2011).

Tafazzoli, A., and J.R. Wilson: Skart: A Skewness- and Autoregression-Adjusted Batch-Means Procedure for Simulation Analysis, *IIE Trans., 43:* 110–128 (2011).

Tafazzoli, A., J.R. Wilson, E.K. Lada, and N.M. Steiger: Performance of Skart: A Skewness- and Autoregression-Adjusted Batch Means Procedure for Simulation Analysis, *INFORMS J. Comput., 23:* 297–314 (2011).

Tang, W.T., R.S.M. Goh, and I.L.-J. Thng: Ladder Queue: An $O(1)$ Priority Queue Structure for Large-Scale Discrete Event Simulation, *Assoc. Comput. Mach. Trans. Modeling and Comput. Simul., 15:* 175–204 (2005).

Tausworthe, R.C.: Random Numbers Generated by Linear Recurrence Modulo Two, *Math. Comput., 19:* 201–209 (1965).

Taylor, J.G.: *Lanchester Models of Warfare*, INFORMS, Hanover, Maryland (1983).

Tekin, E., and I. Sabuncuoglu: Simulation Optimization: A Comprehensive Review on Theory and Applications, *IIE Trans., 36:* 1067–1081 (2004).

Tew, J.D., and J.R. Wilson: Validation of Simulation Analysis Methods for the Schruben-Margolin Correlation-Induction Strategy, *Operations Res., 40:* 87–103 (1992).

Tezuka, S.: *Uniform Random Numbers: Theory and Practice,* Kluwer Academic Publishers, Norwell, Massachusetts (1995).

Thoman, D.R., L.J. Bain, and C.E. Antle: Inferences on the Parameters of the Weibull Distribution, *Technometrics, 11:* 445–460 (1969).

Thomson, W.E.: ERNIE—A Mathematical and Statistical Analysis, *J. Roy. Statist. Soc., 122A:* 301–324 (1959).

Trocine, L., and L.C. Malone: An Overview of Newer, Advanced Screening Methods for the Initial Phase in an Experimental Design, *Proc. 2001 Winter Simulation Conference,* Washington, D.C., pp. 169–178 (2001).

Tukey, J.W.: *Exploratory Data Analysis,* Addison-Wesley, Reading, Massachusetts (1970).

Turing, A.M.: Computing Machinery and Intelligence, *Mind, 59:* 433–460 (1950).

Van Horn, R.L.: Validation of Simulation Results, *Management Sci., 17:* 247–258 (1971).

Vassilacopoulos, G.: Testing for Initialization Bias in Simulation Output, *Simulation, 52:* 151–153 (1989).

Venkatraman, S., and J.R. Wilson: The Efficiency of Control Variates in Multiresponse Simulation, *Operations Res. Letters, 5:* 37–42 (1986).

Ventana Systems, Inc.: Vensim simulation software, www.vensim.com (2013).

Volterra, V.: Variations and Fluctuations of the Number of Individuals in Animal Species Living Together, in *Animal Ecology*, R.N. Chapman, ed., McGraw-Hill, New York (1931).

von Neumann, J. (Summarized by G.E. Forsythe): Various Techniques Used in Connection with Random Digits, *Natl. Bur. Std. Appl. Math. Ser., 12*: 36–38 (1951).

Wagner, H.M.: *Principles of Operations Research,* Prentice-Hall, Englewood Cliffs, New Jersey (1969).

Wagner, M.A.F., and J.R. Wilson: Graphical Interactive Simulation Input Modeling with Bivariate Bézier Distributions, *Assoc. Comput. Mach. Trans. Modeling and Comput. Simul., 5:* 163–189 (1995).

Wagner, M.A.F., and J.R. Wilson: Recent Developments in Input Modeling with Bézier Distributions, *Proc. 1996 Winter Simulation Conference,* San Diego, pp. 1448–1456 (1996a).

Wagner, M.A.F., and J.R. Wilson: Using Univariate Bézier Distributions to Model Simulation Input Processes, *IIE Trans., 28:* 699–711 (1996b).

Wakefield, J.C., A.E. Gelfand, and A.F.M. Smith: Efficient Generation of Random Variates via the Ratio-of-Uniforms Method, *Statist. Comput., 1:* 129–133 (1991).

Walker, A.J.: An Efficient Method for Generating Discrete Random Variables with General Distributions, *Assoc. Comput. Mach. Trans. Math. Software, 3:* 253–256 (1977).

Wan, H., B.E. Ankenman, and B.L. Nelson: Controlled Sequential Bifurcation: A New Factor-Screening Method for Discrete-Event Simulation, *Operations Res., 54:* 743–755 (2006).

Wan, H., B.E. Ankenman, and B.L. Nelson: Improving the Efficiency and Efficacy of Controlled Sequential Bifurcation for Simulation Factor Screening, *INFORMS J. Comput., 22:* 482–492 (2010).

Wang, C.-L., and R.W. Wolff: Efficient Simulation of Queues in Heavy Traffic, *Assoc. Comput. Mach. Trans. Modeling and Comput. Simul., 11:* 62–81 (2003).

Wang, C.-L., and R.W. Wolff: New Estimators for Efficient *GI*/*G*/1 Simulation, *Probability in the Engineering and Informational Sciences, 19:* 219–239 (2005).

Watson, E.F., P.P. Chawda, B. McCarthy, M.J. Drevna, and R.P. Sadowski: A Simulation Metamodel for Response-Time Planning, *Decision Sci., 29:* 217–241 (1998).

Wegman, E.J.: Density Estimation, in *Encyclopedia of Statistical Sciences,* Vol. 2, N.L. Johnson and S. Kotz, eds., John Wiley, New York (1982).

Weiss, W.E.: Development and Use of the Dynamic Security Model for Airports, *J. of Airport Management, 5:* 245–254 (2011).

Welch, B.L.: The Significance of the Difference between Two Means When the Population Variances Are Unequal, *Biometrika, 25:* 350–362 (1938).

Welch, P.D.: On the Problem of the Initial Transient in Steady-State Simulation, IBM Watson Research Center, Yorktown Heights, New York (1981).

Welch, P.D.: The Statistical Analysis of Simulation Results, in *The Computer Performance Modeling Handbook,* S.S. Lavenberg, ed., Academic Press, New York (1983).

Welch, P.D.: On the Relationship between Batch Means, Overlapping Batch Means, and Spectral Estimation, *Proc. 1987 Winter Simulation Conference,* Atlanta, pp. 320–323 (1987).

White, K.P.: An Effective Truncation Heuristic for Bias Reduction in Simulation Output, *Simulation, 69:* 323–334 (1997).

White, K.P., M. J. Cobb, and S.C. Spratt: A Comparison of Five Steady-State Truncation Heuristics for Simulation, *Proc. of the 2000 Winter Simulation Conference,* Orlando, Florida, pp. 755–760 (2000).

Whitt, W.: Bivariate Distributions with Given Marginals, *Annals Statist., 4:* 1280–1289 (1976).

Wichmann, B.A., and I.D. Hill: An Efficient and Portable Pseudo-random Number Generator, *Appl. Statist., 31:* 188–190 (1982).

Wichmann, B.A., and I.D. Hill: Correction to "An Efficient and Portable Pseudo-random Number Generator," *Appl. Statist., 33:* 123 (1984).

Wieland, F.: Parallel Simulation for Aviation Applications, *Proc. 1998 Winter Simulation Conference,* Washington, D.C., pp. 1191–1198 (1998).

Wikipedia: Agent-based model, http://en.wikipedia.org/wiki/Agent-based_model (2013).

Wilensky, U.: NetLogo Wolf Sheep Predation Model, http://ccl.northwestern.edu/netlogo/models/WolfSheepPredation, Center for Connected Learning and Computer-Based Modeling, Northwestern University, Evanston, Illinois (1997).

Wilensky, U.: NetLogo, http://ccl.northwestern.edu/netlogo, Center for Connected Learning and Computer-Based Modeling, Northwestern University, Evanston, Illinois (1999).

Wilk, M.B., and R. Gnanadesikan: Probability Plotting Methods for the Analysis of Data, *Biometrika, 55:* 1–17 (1968).

Willink, R.: A Confidence Interval and Test for the Mean of an Asymmetric Distribution, *Commun. Statist.—Theory and Methods, 34:* 753–756 (2005).

Wilson, J.R.: Proof of the Antithetic-Variates Theorem for Unbounded Functions, *Math. Proc. Camb. Phil. Soc., 86:* 477–479 (1979).

Wilson, J.R.: Antithetic Sampling with Multivariate Inputs, *Am. J. Math. Management Sci., 3:* 121–144 (1983).

Wilson, J.R.: Variance Reduction Techniques for Digital Simulation, *Am. J. Math. Management Sci., 4:* 277–312 (1984).

Wilson, J.R.: Modeling Dependencies in Stochastic Simulation Inputs, *Proc. 1997 Winter Simulation Conference,* Atlanta, pp. 47–52 (1997).

Wilson, J.R., and A.A.B. Pritsker: Variance Reduction in Queueing Simulation Using Generalized Concomitant Variables, *J. Statist. Comput. Simul., 19*: 129–153 (1984a).

Wilson, J.R., and A.A.B. Pritsker: Experimental Evaluation of Variance Reduction Techniques for Queueing Simulation Using Generalized Concomitant Variables, *Management Sci., 30:* 1459–1472 (1984b).

Winston, W.L., and S.C. Albright: *Practical Management Science,* 4th ed., Cengage Learning, Independence, Kentucky (2011).

Wolff, R.W.: Poisson Arrivals See Time Averages, *Operations Res., 30:* 223–231 (1982).

Wolverine Software Corporation: Proof Animation software, www.wolverinesoftware.com (2013).

Wolverine Software Corporation: SLX simulation software, www.wolverinesoftware.com (2013).

Wright, R.D., and T.E. Ramsay, Jr.: On the Effectiveness of Common Random Numbers, *Management Sci., 25:* 649–656 (1979).

Wu, C.F.J., and M.S. Hamada: *Experiments: Planning, Analysis, and Optimization,* 2d ed., John Wiley, New York (2009).

Xu, J., B.L. Nelson, and L.J. Hong: An Adaptive Hyperbox Algorithm for High-Dimensional Discrete Optimization via Simulation Problems, *INFORMS J. Comput., 25:* 133–146 (2013).

Yang, W.-N., and W.-W. Liou: Combining Antithetic Variates and Control Variates in Simulation Experiments, *Assoc. Comput. Mach. Trans. Modeling and Comput. Simul., 6:* 243–290 (1996).

Yang, W.-N., and B.L. Nelson: Multivariate Batch Means and Control Variates, *Management Sci., 38:* 1415–1431 (1992).

Yarnold, J.K.: The Minimum Expectation in χ^2 Goodness-of-Fit Tests and the Accuracy of Approximations for the Null Distribution, *J. Am. Statist. Assoc., 65:* 864–886 (1970).

Yuan, M., and B.L. Nelson: Multiple Comparisons with the Best for Steady-State Simulation, *Assoc. Comput. Mach. Trans. Modeling and Comput. Simul., 3:* 66–79 (1993).

Yuan, M., and B.L. Nelson: Autoregressive-Output-Analysis Methods Revisited, *Ann. of Operations Res., 53:* 391–418 (1994).

Yücesan, E., and L.W. Schruben: Structural and Behavioral Equivalence of Simulation Models, *Assoc. Comput. Mach. Trans. Modeling and Comput. Simul., 2:* 82–103 (1992).

Yücesan, E., and L.W. Schruben: Complexity of Simulation Models: A Graph Theoretic Approach, *INFORMS J. Comput., 10:* 94–106 (1998).

Zanakis, S.H.: Extended Pattern Search with Transformations for the Three-Parameter Weibull MLE Problem, *Management Sci., 25:* 1149–1161 (1979a).

Zanakis, S.H.: A Simulation Study of Some Simple Estimators for the Three-Parameter Weibull Distribution, *J. Statist. Comput. Simul., 9:* 101–116 (1979b).

Zeimer, M.A., and J.D. Tew: Metamodel Applications Using TERSM, *Proc. 1995 Winter Simulation Conference,* Arlington, Virginia, pp. 1421–1428 (1995).

Zeisel, H.: A Remark on AS 183. An Efficient and Portable Pseudo-random Number Generator, *Appl. Statist., 35:* 89 (1986).

Zouaoui, F., and J.R. Wilson: Accounting for Parameter Uncertainty in Simulation Input Modeling, *IIE Trans., 35:* 781–792 (2003).

Zouaoui, F., and J.R. Wilson: Accounting for Input-Model and Input-Parameter Uncertainties in Simulation, *IIE Trans., 36:* 1135–1151 (2004).

Index

(*a*)

(*b*)

PLATE 1
Examples of Animations: (*a*) FlexSim; (*b*) Simio

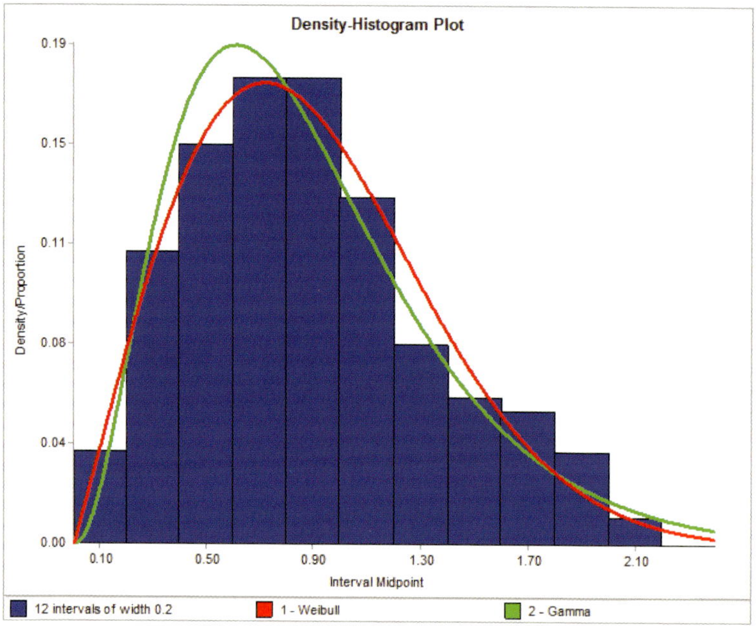

(*c*)

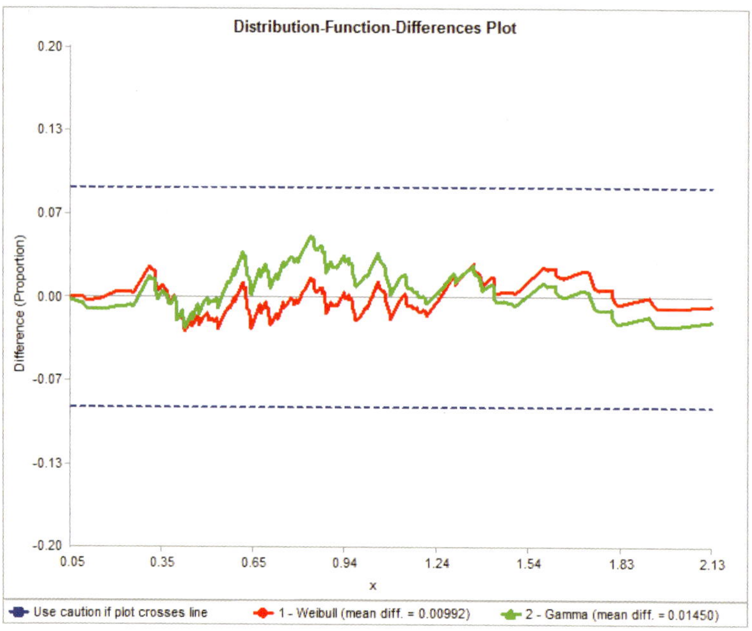

(*d*)

PLATE 1 (*continued*)
Chapter 6: (*c*) Figure 6.51; (*d*) Figure 6.52

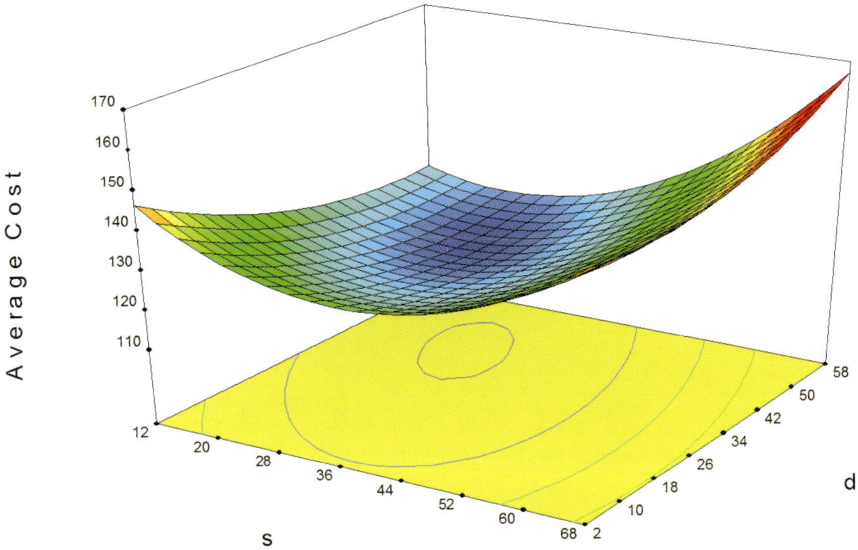

(*a*)

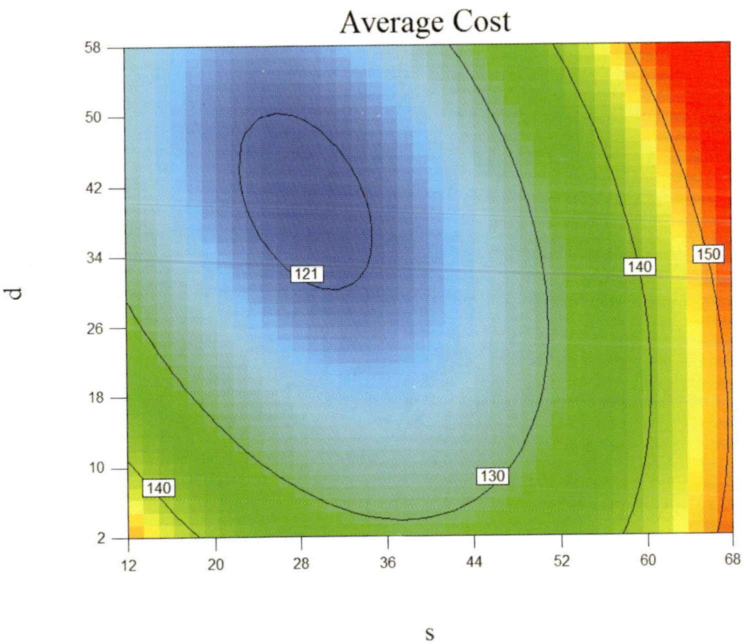

(*b*)

PLATE 2
Chapter 12: (*a*) Figure 12.11*a*; (*b*) Figure 12.11*b*

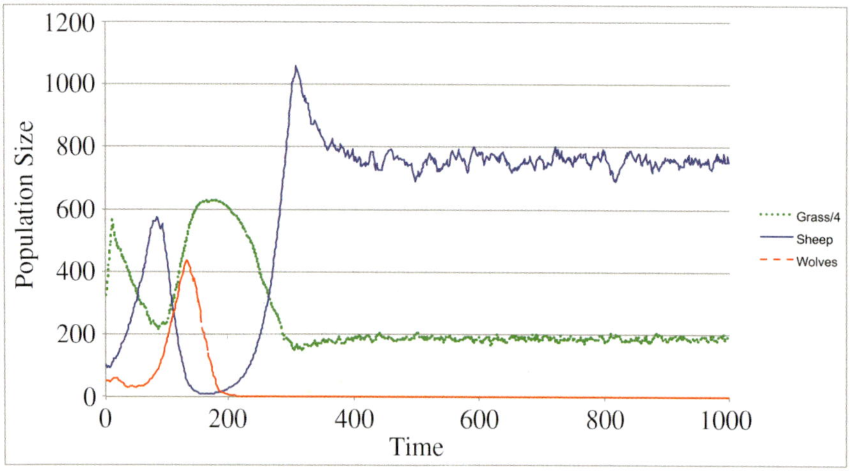

(*c*)

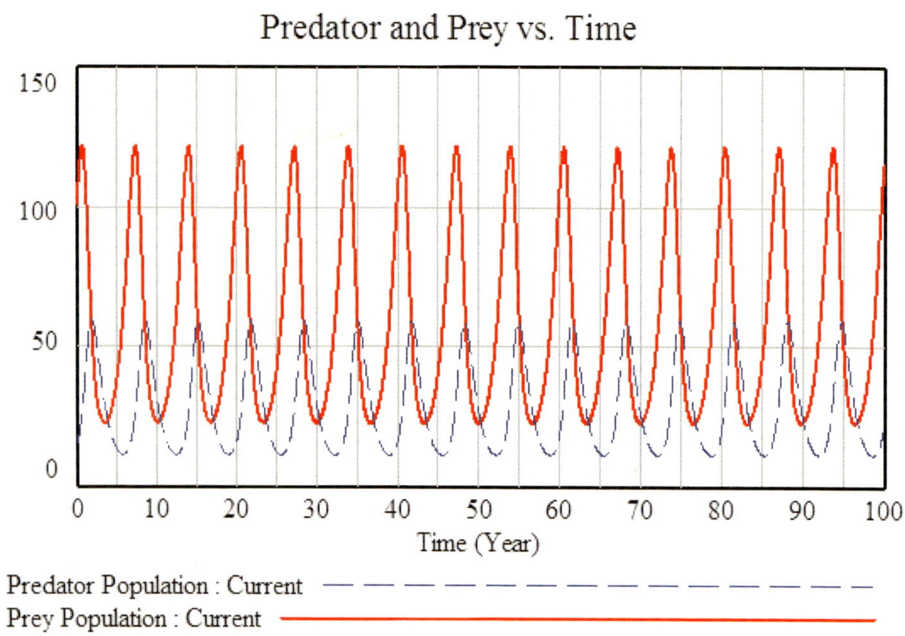

(*d*)

PLATE 2 (*continued*)
Chapter 13: (*c*) Figure 13.4; (*d*) Figure 13.9